WASHINGTON

A Guide to the Evergreen State

✦

Compiled by workers of the Writers' Program of the Work Projects Administration in the State of Washington

✦

AMERICAN GUIDE SERIES

ILLUSTRATED

Sponsored by the Washington State Historical Society

BINFORDS & MORT : *Publishers* : PORTLAND, ORE.

FIRST PUBLISHED IN 1941

FEDERAL WORKS AGENCY

JOHN M. CARMODY, *Administrator*

WORK PROJECTS ADMINISTRATION

HOWARD O. HUNTER, *Commissioner*
FLORENCE KERR, *Assistant Commissioner*
CARL W. SMITH, *State Administrator*

PRINTED IN THE UNITED STATES OF AMERICA BY THE METROPOLITAN PRESS, PORTLAND, OREGON

Foreword

THIS GUIDE, written by the Washington Writers' Project of the Work Projects Administration, has had a succession of sponsors. Next to the last of these, the Washington State Planning Council, withdrew because it lacked trained personnel to handle the manuscript. The Washington State Historical Society, after much urging, finally accepted the sponsorship. The Society, therefore, has not been concerned with planning the work, nor with compiling and writing. There was before the Society only the question of accuracy and inclusiveness. The members of the Project had written well, but errors are inevitable in a work of this magnitude.

The final sponsor, the Washington State Historical Society, has had to do in four or five months what other historical societies serving as sponsors—as Virginia, Nebraska, Iowa, and Nevada—had three or four years to do: namely, to put to rights any faulty passages and, more happily, to verify the large amount of excellent and interesting material. There was the additional chore of bringing some parts up to date; for more than a year—and that a census year—had elapsed between the closing of the Project and the time of the manuscript's going to press.

It is not claimed that the Society has caught all errors; in fact, it would be virtually impossible for any State guide—and we have studied thirty-six—to be wholly free from error. We have done this work for Washington as a labor of love, in addition to our regular job.

Mr. T. C. Elliott of Walla Walla, Mr. Lancaster Pollard of Seattle, and Mr. W. P. Bonney of Tacoma, though frequently called on, have always given most valuable and most enthusiastic help. Mr. W. L. McCormick, newly elected President of the Society, has given constant encouragement. To Miss Charlotte Shackleford, a new and enthusiastic member of the Society, we give credit for the excellent index. She was assisted by Miss Elizabeth Shackleford and Mrs. Bessie S. Matthews.

O. B. Sperlin, *Acting President*
Washington State Historical Society

Preface

WASHINGTON: *a Guide to the Evergreen State* is the result of the collaboration of many minds. Working as a group, the staff of the Washington Writers' Project gathered, checked, re-checked, and assembled a multitude of facts gleaned from many and varied sources. Of inestimable value in the compilation of these data was the assistance received from hundreds of consultants—historians, pioneers, newspaper men, scientists, teachers, business men—who gave generously of their time, and from the many unselfish and friendly persons who assisted the field workers and the tour checkers, as they traveled from town to town along the thousands of miles of highways and byways that were covered. Without exaggeration, this book may be said to represent a community endeavor and a community interest.

Each day, as the staff worked, the mass of interesting material grew, so that when the time came for final selection of what could be included in a book, much had to be omitted; so much, in fact, that this volume, comprehensive as it is, may be looked upon simply as an introduction to other volumes still to be written about the State—its people, its history, its resources, its cities and towns, its industries, its culture, its recreational areas and scenic wonderlands.

As one of the volumes of the American Guide Series, this book is an integral part of a dynamic and vibrant picture of these United States. Basically, it is a guide for the use of tourists, both those from other States and those within the State's borders. For them, in addition to a fund of practical information, there is a mass of interesting material about the State and its people, information which will add to the pleasure and understanding of all those who travel in Washington. The appeal of the book, however, does not end here—nor does its value. Many are destined to be armchair travelers, and for these the book, with its fragments of history, short biographies, thumbnail pictures of people and places, with its many colorful pictures and carefully drawn maps, will afford hours of recreation, less exciting than actual travel but enjoyable, nevertheless, and far less strenuous; it will be sure to bring a feeling of the close bonds that tie the State of Washington to the other States of the Union. Against the panorama of the past, the reader will be able to see the moving picture of the present.

The staff gratefully acknowledges the aid of Federal, State, and local governmental agencies and of civic, commercial, and sports associations. Particular appreciation is due the University of Washington and the Washington State College, to the staffs of the Seattle Public and of the University of Washington Libraries, to the State Planning Council, to the State Progress Commission, to the Federal and State parks departments, to the State Bureau of Fisheries, to the Bureau of Indian Affairs, and to the Forest Service. Appreciation is also due to postmasters, to chambers of commerce, to pioneer societies, and to newspaper editors throughout the State for the assistance given in many phases of the work. In addition, we are indebted to the Oregon Writers' Project for the completion of the maps. The final manuscript was edited by Mary Barrett and Harold Rosenberg, of the Washington, D.C., Office of the Writers' Program.

Among the many to whom the editors wish to express their gratitude for generous aid in special fields are: R. B. Inverarity, State Supervisor, Washington Art Project, who helped with the photo collection and designed the jacket; Professor Melville Jacobs, University of Washington, who read the Indian material; Paul Ashford, who volunteered his services on the tours; Marian R. Jenkins, who worked on the Literature essay; Professor J. B. Harrison; C. Frank Mahon, for assistance on Architecture; Kenneth Callahan; Dr. Garland Ethel; James F. O'Brien; John Guerin, who did much work on the maps; Professor G. E. Goodspeed; C. F. Pautzke; Dr. Viola Garfield; Professor Harry Burns; Dr. Harold Eby; Dr. Elton Guthrie; John Sproule; Robert Camozzi; and, finally, the sponsor, Washington State Historical Society, whose Acting President, O. B. Sperlin, worked through the entire manuscript twice, supplying many vital corrections, and read both galley and page proofs.

ANNE E. WINDHUSEN
State Supervisor

Contents

Part III. Tours

Part IV. Appendices

Illustrations

HISTORY: THE INDIANS—Continued

THE DAMS

AGRICULTURE

IN THE CITIES AND TOWNS *Between pages 312 and 313*

INDUSTRY, COMMERCE AND TRANSPORTATION *Between pages 342 and 343*

LUMBERING

IN THE MOUNTAINS

Maps

General Information

Railroads: Chicago, Milwaukee, St. Paul & Pacific R.R. (Milwaukee), Great Northern R.R. (G.N.), Northern Pacific R. R. (N.P.), Union Pacific R.R. (U.P.). Intrastate: Spokane, Portland and Seattle R.R. (S.P.&S.). Milwaukee, G.N., and N.P. cross the Cascades; U.P. and S.P.&S. parallel the Columbia River between Washington and Oregon.

Highways: 9 Federal highways, 7 with interstate connections; 22 State highways. Highways through the three passes of the Cascade Range: Stevens, Snoqualmie, Chinook; only Snoqualmie open during winter. Satus Pass through the Horse Heaven Hills gives access to the Columbia River Gorge. Inspection only at the Canadian Border. State highways policed by State patrol. Water and gasoline stations somewhat scarce in eastern Washington off main highways. Gasoline tax 6c.

Bus Lines: Interstate: Washington Motor Coach System to the East from the Puget Sound area; Union Pacific Stages to the East and South from southeastern Washington; Priest River Stage Line to Idaho from Spokane; North Coast Lines to Canada and Oregon; Pacific Stages, Ltd., to Canada; Spokane-Butte Motor Stage Co. to Idaho and Montana; Independent Stages, Inc., Consolidated Transportation Co., and Benjamin Franklin Lines along the Coast. Intrastate: Numerous lines connecting cities and towns.

Air Lines: Trans-Canada Air Lines, Ltd., between Vancouver, British Columbia, and Seattle; Northwest Airlines between Chicago and Seattle via Spokane, Wenatchee, Yakima; United Air Lines between New York and Seattle and Vancouver, B. C., and between Spokane and Pendleton Oregon, via Walla Walla; Pan-American Airways between Seattle and Alaska.

Water Transportation: Trans-Pacific from Seattle: Pacific Northwest-Oriental Steamship Co., Inc., and Nippon Yusen Kaisya. Coastwise from

Seattle: Canadian Pacific Steamship, Ltd., boats to British Columbia ports; Alaska Steamship Co., Alaska Transportation Co., and Northland Transportation Co., to Alaska. Puget Sound: Black Ball Ferry Lines, Ballard-Ludlow Ferry Co., and Kitsap Transportation Co. connect important ports. Auto ferries and steamers, operating on the inland waters of the State, serve most shore-side towns.

Motor Vehicle Laws (digest.): Maximum speed, 50 m.p.h.; on curves and intersections and past schoolhouses and crossings between hours of 8 a.m. and 5 p.m., 15 m.p.h. Nonresident license good for 90 days. Minimum age for drivers, 16 years. Speed limit through towns usually 25 m.p.h. Uniform signs mark State highways: diamond indicates *slow*; square, *caution*; Octagonal, *stop*; and round, *railroad crossing*. Hand signals must be used. Spotlights permitted, provided beam is directed to right while on main-traveled routes. Windshield wipers and rear-vision mirrors required. Personal injury or property damage must be reported to local authority within 24 hours. Complete State motor vehicle laws available at all towns and cities.

Prohibited: Coasting in neutral; parking on highway or with less than 16 feet clearance from main-traveled road; use of stickers (except certificates required by law); use of sirens; passing to right on highways; passing loading or unloading streetcars except at safety islands.

Accommodations: Except in urban centers, accommodations are limited to numerous auto camps; facilities generally good. Provisions and supplies available at auto camps on main highways and roads. Accommodations are limited at Mount Rainier from October 15 to June 20, except at Paradise Valley (*open all winter*). Island resorts on Puget Sound usually closed during winter; accommodations scarce on Olympic Peninsula.

Climate and Equipment: In coastal regions, climate is temperate, with heavy seasonal rainfall; in eastern Washington, hot, dry summers and fairly cold winters. Snowfall heavy in mountain areas. Average-weight clothing, including topcoats, is suitable. Special equipment for hunting, fishing, or mountain climbing available locally (*see Tours*). Some mountain passes closed by snow in midwinter; information available from weather reports and State highway bulletins. Most springs and streams in mountain and forest regions are safe for drinking purposes, but care should be taken in settled and farming areas.

Associations: Washington State Sportsmen's Council, 1001 Fourth and Pike Bldg., Seattle, comprising 132 clubs, supplies information on 90 per cent of State associations and recreational clubs. The Mountaineers, 214 Rialto Bldg., Seattle. Olympicans, Henderson Bldg., Bremerton. Ski and yacht clubs at various cities (*see Cities*).

Forest Fire Season: April 15 to October 15. During season, some forest sections entirely closed. Campers in State and National Forest areas, except at designated campgrounds, must be equipped with shovel, bucket, and axe; permits must be obtained for campfires. Fires must be extinguished before camp is abandoned.

Forest Headquarters: Snoqualmie National Forest, Federal Bldg., Seattle; ranger stations, North Bend, Skykomish, Mineral, Parkway, Naches. Wenatchee National Forest, P.O. Bldg., Wenatchee; ranger stations, Entiat and Leavenworth. Chelan National Forest, Okanogan; ranger stations, Winthrop, Conconully, Twisp, Mazama, Chelan, and Stehekin. Columbia National Forest, P.O. Bldg., Vancouver; ranger stations, Carson, Randle, Spirit Lake, Trout Lake, and Packwood. Colville National Forest, P.O. Bldg., Republic; ranger stations, Tonasket, Republic, Kettle Falls. Mount Baker National Forest, P.O. Bldg., Bellingham; ranger stations, Darrington, Glacier, Sauk, Marblemount, Granite Falls, and Concrete. Olympic National Forest, P.O. Bldg., Olympia; ranger stations, Port Angeles, Quilcene, Hoodsport, and Quinault. Kaniksu National Forest, P.O. Bldg., Sand Point, Idaho; ranger stations, Ione, Newport, and Colville, Washington. Umatilla National Forest, P.O. Bldg., Pendleton, Oregon; ranger stations, Walla Walla, Pomeroy, Dayton, and Ukiah, Washington. Information, regulations, and fire permits available at forest headquarters and ranger stations.

Fish and Game Laws: Laws filed by State Fish and Game Commission annually; open season and bag limits vary. (*Pamphlet of laws, obtainable at all sporting goods stores, includes open seasons, bag limits, and exceptions*).

License Fees: Hunting and fishing: resident $3 (State), $1.50 (county); nonresident, $25 (State); alien, $25 (State). Fishing: resident, $5 (State); nonresident, $5 (State), $3 (county); alien, $5 (county). Nonresident must hold permit to carry firearms in order to obtain license. License obtainable at most sporting goods stores and from county auditors.

Liquor Laws: Wines and distilled liquors for sale at State liquor stores, found in most cities and towns, to persons with permits. Permit granted to person 21 years of age; fee 50c per year. Beer and wine are sold by the drink in restaurants and bars; by the bottle, in grocery and drugstores; no permit required. No restrictions on bringing liquor into State for private consumption.

Poisonous Snakes, Plants, Insects: The rattlesnake, only venomous reptile in the State, is restricted almost entirely to arid sections of eastern Washington. Hikers there should be equipped with heavy leather boots or puttees and simple snake-bite kit, obtainable at drugstores. Wood ticks infest some sagebrush areas of eastern Washington during early summer. They may be carriers of the Rocky Mountain spotted fever, but the disease is not common; inoculation unnecessary. Wood ticks should not be pulled off, but saturated with turpentine or kerosene. Numerous species of poisonous mushrooms are common; edible varieties should be positively identified. Black widow spiders infrequent; bites should receive immediate treatment. Poison oak and poison ivy, native to Washington, are found on both sides of the Cascades.

Flowers and Trees: Picking, cutting, or destruction of plants within 300 feet of State or county roads, or on street or highway, or in any State or city park is prohibited by law.

Recreational Areas

LEAVENWORTH (*see Tour 1C*), Wenatchee National Forest. Winter Sports area with numerous forest camps, lakes, and trails. Tumwater Canyon, Drury Falls; Wenatchee River; Icicle River. Abundant wild life; berrying.

SKYKOMISH (*see Tour 1C*), Snoqualmie National Forest. Hundreds of lakes, rivers, and creeks and numerous trails. Certain sections along North Bank of the Skykomish River, Foss River, Beckler River and Index Creek, closed during fire season except under special weather conditions. Popular fishing points at Lake Isabel, North Fork of the Skykomish River, Silver Creek, Silver Lake, Twin Lakes, Troublesome Creek, Trout Creek in North Fork of the Skykomish section; South Fork of the Skykomish and Money Creek in same section; both forks of Miller River and Lake Dorothy, Bear Lake, Deer Lake, Snoqualmie Lake, Beckler River, and Rapid River in Miller River section; Foss River, Trout Lake, Delta Lake, Copper Lake, and Angeline Lake in Foss River section; Tye River and Martin Creek, Deception Creek, Surprise Creek and Lake, Glacier Lake, and Lake Josephine in Tye River section. Winter sports in Stevens Pass; ski development under way.

LAKE WENATCHEE (*see Wenatchee and Tour 1C*), Wenatchee National Forest. Lake Wenatchee and Fish Lake, on highway; swimming, camping, picnicking, fishing, boating. Winter sports in season at Stevens Pass, State 15. Forest roads 18 *m.* up little Wenatchee River from Lake Wenatchee; 14 *m.* up White River; about 35 *m.* up Chiwawa River.

CLE ELUM (*see Tour 2c*), Snoqualmie National Forest. Salmon LaSac Guard Station and Camp, 18 miles from Cle Elum; Salmon LaSac to Cooper Lake, 5 *m.* to Jolly Mountain Lookout, 6 *m.* by trail; to Lake Waptus, 11 *m.*; to Fish Lake, 16 *m.* Trails well developed. Trout fishing; deer and bear hunting. Heavy snows in winter. Tobogganing and skiing area, 21 *m.* W. of Cle Elum near US 10. Highway open all winter.

WHITE RIVER AND NACHES (*see Tour 2c*), Snoqualmie National Forest. Bumping Lake: fishing, outboard racing, skiing, American River; Rattlesnake Camp Preserve; Mather Memorial Parkway; Greenwater River; Naches River; lakes on Cascade Crest Trail. Summer forest homesites; numerous trails; berrying.

TIETON (*see Tour 2c*), Snoqualmie National Forest. Tieton River; Rimrock Lake. Deer, elk, bear, blue grouse hunting; fishing and boating.

WIND RIVER (*see Tour 3a*), Columbia National Forest. Governmental Mineral Springs Camp, one-day hiking trips; Little Soda Springs camp; Trout Creek Camp; Wind River; Wind River Nursery. Huckleberrying, Indian horse racing, deer hunting, steelhead fishing.

TWIN BUTTES (*see Tour 3a*), Columbia National Forest. Race Track Guard Station, 22 *m.* NE. of Carson. Goose Lake, 5 *m.*; fishing, forest camp, lava beds. Peterson Registration Station, 36 *m.* NE. of Carson, forest road fair; starting point to Mount Adams huckleberry fields (*reserved for Indians*) and numerous Indian camp grounds. Guler and Ranger Station, 25 *m.* NW. of White Salmon; starting point for ice cave explorations, 5 *m.* W.; headquarters for fishing at Trout Lake; hotel accommodations.

KETTLE FALLS (see *Tour 5*), Colville National Forest. Game preserve W. of highway between South Fork of Deadman Creek and Boulder Creek. Area sparsely settled, bordered by Kettle River.

CARIBOU TRAIL (*see Tour 7a*). Colville National Forest. Bonaparte Lake, 21 *m.* E. of Tonasket; good fishing, camping; no hunting.

REPUBLIC (*see Tour 7a*), Colville National Forest. Trout fishing at Swan, Fish, and Long lakes, reached by new branch road, 10 *m.* S. of Republic; camp-grounds.

LAKE CHELAN (*see Tour 7a*), Chelan and Wenatchee national forests. Domke Lake and return, 5 *m.,* fine fishing; Rainbow Falls, 3 *m.* up Stehekin River; Lyman Lake Trail via Glacier Trail, 11 *m.* up Stehekin River, L. 19 *m.* along Agnes Creek, to Lyman Lake. Lower Horseshoe and Upper Horseshoe basins near Cascade Pass. Horses, guides, equipment available at Lucerne and Stehekin.

MOUNT ADAMS (*see Tour 7b*), Columbia National Forest. Alpining and mountaineering.

NOOKSACK (*see Tour 8A*), Mount Baker National Forest. Lakes frozen in winter; summer fishing; alpining; skiing; trail trips; public camp accommodations.

HEATHER MEADOWS (*see Tour 8A*), Mount Baker National Forest (area usually called Mount Baker). Road open to Mount Baker Lodge; downhill, slalom, cross-country skiing, escalator, hotel, cabin accommodations; first-aid stations. Winter sports from November to June; meadow flowers, alpining, and hiking in summer.

BAKER RIVER (*see Tour 8B*), Mount Baker National Forest. Forest road through area from Concrete to Baker Lodge, 22 *m.* Eleven trail trips; to Dock Butte, 6.5 *m.;* Mazama Park, 9 *m.*; Wanlick Creek to Elbow Lake, 14 *m.;* Upper Creek Park to Martin Lake, 5 *m.*; Baker Hot Springs, 2.5 *m.,* swimming; Swift Creek Trail, through Austin Pass, about 11 *m.*; Upper Baker Trail to Eagle Creek, 13 *m.,* trout fishing; Baker Lake Lookout, 2.5 *m.*; Shuksan Lake, 11 *m.* (3 miles rough walking), good fishing in late summer; Anderson Butte, 6.5 *m.,* forest lookout station.

RANDLE (*see Tour 8E*), Columbia National Forest. North Fork Forest Camp, 10 *m.* S. of Randle; Chain of Lakes District 30 *m.* Excellent camping, fishing, huckleberrying, hiking. Area between North Fork and Registration Station, 16 *m.,* closed to camping July 1-Sept. 30. Varied views of Mount Adams.

PACKWOOD (*see Tour 8E*), Columbia National Forest. Packwood Lake; Soda Springs; Cowlitz River. Fishing, forest camps and trails; hiking and alpining.

GOAT ROCKS RECREATION AREA (*see Tour 8E*), Columbia National Forest. Accessible only by trail; no developed campgrounds; fishing limited; goat hunting not allowed. Lost Lake Trail; Purcell Creek Trail, Clear Fork Trail. Guides and horses available at Packwood.

SPIRIT LAKE (*see Tour 8e*), Columbia National Forest. Mount St. Helens (9,671 alt.), active volcano as late as November 23, 1842; alpining. Spirit Lake: boating, fishing, swimming, camping, hiking. Smith Creek Butte Lookout, 8 *m.* SE. of Spirit Lake; St. Helens Lake 3 *m.,* fishing; good road.

HOOD CANAL (*see Tour 9a*), Olympic National Forest. Lake Cushman: Skokomish Primitive Area; Olympic National Park; Mount Ellinor; Duckabush River; Mount Olympus; Mount Constance. Elk and deer hunting; salt-water fishing; trout fishing.

SNOW PEAKS (*see Tour 9b*), Olympic National Forest and Olympic National Park. Quilcene River, Elwha River, Dungeness River, Dosewallips River; lake and river fishing. Mount Angeles; Deer Park skiing area; forest camps; horse and foot trail trips. Olympic Hot Springs.

LAKE CRESCENT (*see Tour 9b*), Olympic National Forest. Lake Crescent, Lake Sutherland; Beardslee trout at Crescent. Sol Duc Hot Springs, Bogachiel, Calawah, Soleduck, and Hoh Rivers. Olympic National Park; few trails in western section, several in eastern; logging operations.

QUINAULT LAKE (*see Tour 9c*), Olympic National Forest. Trail riders' trip, 13 days by horseback; start and finish at Graves Creek Inn, near Lake Quinault; guides necessary; fishing, alpining, photographing; hike over Anderson Glacier, climb to summit of Mount Christie, Olympic National Park. Season: mid-June to mid-September.

Calendar of Events

JANUARY

First	from Seattle to Tacoma	Annual Midwinter Yacht Cruise
Tenth to fourteenth	at Spokane	Roller Canary Show
Fourteenth	at Spokane	Intermediate Ski Council Meet
Twenty-second	at Marietta (Lummi Reservation)	Treaty Day Powwow
Twenty-second	at Swinomish Reservation	Treaty Day Powwow
Twenty-second	at Tulalip Reservation	Treaty Day Powwow
Twenty-third	at Spokane	Ski Jumping Competition at Wandemere
Third week	at Seattle	Mining Institute, University of Washington
No fixed date	at Mount Rainier	Winter Sports Carnival
No fixed date	at Seattle	Institute of Washington State Press Association
No fixed date	at Guler (Klickitat County)	Ski and Toboggan Tournament

FEBRUARY

Twenty-ninth	at Spokane	Inland Empire Stock Show
Third week	at Cle Elum	Ski Tournament
Fourth week	at Odessa	Spring Breeding Cattle Sale
Third and fourth weeks	at Leavenworth	Ski Jumping Tournament

MARCH

Third	at Snoqualmie Pass	Mountaineers' Twenty-two-Mile Ski Patrol Race
Thirteenth	at Deer Park	Ski Tournament
Seventeenth	at Snoqualmie Summit	Snoqualmie Pass Four-way Ski Championship
First week	at Tacoma	Philharmonic Season Opens

First week	at Spokane	Inland Empire Shorthorn Breeders' Show
No fixed date	at Seattle	Northwest A.A.U. Basketball Championships
No fixed date	at Seattle	State High School Basketball Championships
Easter Sunday	at Blaine	International Service at Peace Arch
Easter Sunday	State-wide	Easter Sunrise Service

APRIL

First	State-wide	Fishing Season Opens
Twenty-sixth and twenty-seventh	at Port Townsend	Rhododendron Festival and Carnival
First week	at Spokane	Inland Empire Moose Frolic
First week	at Mount Rainier	Spring Ski Carnival
Second week	at Lynden	Daffodil Festival
Third week	at Mount Rainier	Silver Skis Championship
	at Auburn (Muckleshoot)	Indian Festival
No fixed date	at Tacoma, Sumner, and Puyallup	Puyallup Valley Daffodil Festival

MAY

First week	at Seattle	All-City Flower Show
First week	at Spokane	Inland Empire Junior Livestock Show
First week	at Seattle	Northwest Yachting Season Opens
First week	at Spokane	All-Breeds Dog Show
Third week	at Spokane	Sportsmen's Show
Fourth week	at Tacoma	Yacht Club Races
No fixed date	at Wenatchee	Apple Blossom Festival
No fixed date	at Bremerton	Olympican Caravan Tour of Olympic Peninsula
No fixed date	at Pullman	State High School Track Championships
No fixed date	at Republic	Festival and Flag Day

JUNE

Twentieth	at Seattle	Repertory Playhouse Summer Drama Festival Opens
Second week	alternates	State Golf Championships
Third week	alternates	Pacific Northwest Golf Association Championships

No fixed date	at Okanogan	Pet Parade
No fixed date	at Seattle	Annual Meeting Washington State Press Association
No fixed date	at Keller	Indian Salmon Derby
No fixed date	at Bellevue	Strawberry Festival
No fixed date	at Spokane	Junior Chamber of Commerce Stampede Rodeo
No fixed date	at Tacoma	Salmon Fishing Derby Finals

JULY

First to fourth	at La Push	Indian Festival
First to fifth	alternates	Pacific International Yacht Association Regatta
First	at Taholah	Treaty Day Powwow
Second	at Blaine	International Flag Day, Peace Arch
Third	at Seattle	Sixty-day Horse Racing Season Opens at Longacres
Fourth	at Chelan	Lake Chelan Rodeo
Second week	at Toledo	Cheese Day
Third week	at Tacoma	Pacific Northwest Tennis Championships
Third week	at Seattle	Fleet Week
Third week	at Seattle	Navy Crew Regatta
Fourth week	at Ferndale	Old Settlers' Picnic
Fourth week	at Mount Vernon	Hickory Hat Days
Fourth week	at Seattle	State Tennis Tournament
No fixed date	at White Swan	Yakima Indians' Tribal Council
No fixed date	alternates	Senior (over 60) Golf Tournament
No fixed date	at Yakima	Outboard Regatta on Bumping Lake
No fixed date	at Seattle (alternates)	Puget Sound-Nanaimo, B.C., Power Boat Race
No fixed date	at Seattle	Rock Garden Flower Show, Woodland Park
No fixed date	at Centralia	Pioneer Days Celebration

AUGUST

Fourteenth	at Seattle	Air Show at Boeing Field
Twentieth-Twenty-fourth	at Chehalis-Centralia	Southwest Washington Fair
Twenty-sixth	at Neah Bay	Makah Indian Festival
Second week	at Chelan	Lake Chelan Regatta
Third week	at Omak	Omak Stampede
Fourth week	at Shelton	Farmers' Day

Fourth week	at Goldendale	Jamboree
Fourth week	at Walla Walla	Southeastern Washington Fair
No fixed date	at Coupeville	International Indian War Canoe Races
No fixed date	at Seattle	Seward Park Outboard Regatta
No fixed date	at Bellingham	State Gladioli Show

SEPTEMBER

First	at Port Townsend	Clambake and Pioneer Day
Tenth-Thirteenth	at Lyndon	Northwest Washington Fair
Eleventh	at Seattle	Salmon Derby Finals
Labor Day	at Conconully	Pioneer Picnic
Labor Day	at Spokane	Three weeks Horse Racing Meet opens at Playfair
Labor Day	at Ellensburg	Rodeo
Labor Day	at Port Angeles	Salmon Fishing Derby Finals
Second week	at Colfax	Roundup
Fourth week	at Puyallup	Western Washington Fair
Fourth week	at Bellingham	Harvest Festival
No fixed date	at Spokane	Inland Empire Kennel Show
No fixed date	at Yakima	Central Washington District Fair

OCTOBER

First	State-wide	Hunting Season Opens
Twenty-seventh	at Bremerton	Navy Day
Thirty-first	at Spokane	Halloween Festival
No fixed date	at Spokane and Seattle	Ice Hockey Season Opens
No fixed date	at Seattle	Symphony Season Opens

NOVEMBER

Eleventh	State-wide	Armistice Day; Admission Day
No fixed date	at Tacoma	Symphony Season Opens

DECEMBER

Last two weeks	at Toppenish	Indian Christmas Ceremonial
Last Saturday before Christmas	at Okanogan	Christmas Festival
Twenty-fifth	State-wide	Christmas Day Services

(*For dates of county fairs see Cities and Tours.*)

PART I

Washington: Past and Present

From Sagebrush to Seacoast

DESPITE the multiplicity of means of communication today, many people still conceive of the State of Washington as virtually a frontier wilderness, accessible only to the rugged and the adventurous. This impression derives in part no doubt from the State's geographic location, in part from its historical association with an Indian war, and in part also from frontier fiction, which usually offers an exaggerated, romantic account of pioneers, cowboys, lumberjacks, and desperadoes.

One hundred years ago, this region was largely unexplored. The eastern section was a semiarid plateau of rolling hills covered with sagebrush and bunchgrass, the habitat of prairie dogs, coyotes, and rattlesnakes. Here Indians roamed, hunted, and fished. Through these sun-drenched barrens, the majestic Columbia River cut its way to the Pacific Ocean. Forests of lodgepole and ponderosa pine, fir, and tamarack ascended the northern highlands and the eastern slope of the Cascades. On the more humid western side of the range, another dense forest of spruce, Douglas fir, cedar, and hemlock swept down to the coast, unbroken except for Indian trails and occasional prairies and lowland valleys, and somber save when brightened by pink rhododendrons, the shimmering white of dogwood trees in flower, the golden catkins of maple and alder, or in some localities the flame of autumn leaves.

Within these forests, bear, deer, elk, and cougar were plentiful, and the many lakes and rivers, abounding in fish, were frequented by beaver, mink, and otter. Grouse and ptarmigan whirred across the uplands, ducks sought the sheltered waters of inland lakes, and geese honked along the rivers and lowland marshes. Coastal waters and the larger streams teemed with salmon; blackfish and porpoise sported in the Sound and Strait, and whale spouted offshore.

Something of this primitive condition remains today. The visitor to the Evergreen State can still find magnificent virgin forests, vocal with the songs of many birds. He can follow miles of woodland trails and enjoy the beauty of mountain summits, deep gorges, turbulent streams with cascading waterfalls, and clear alpine lakes, mirroring snow-capped peaks and tree-lined shores. He can scale rugged mountains or traverse blue-white glaciers, made dangerous by deep crevasses. He can find many a secluded lake or stream or saltwater channel, where he can test his skill with rod and reel; he can try his luck at bagging a deer, a bear, or a cougar in the pathless wilds. He can drive through deep canyons or along surf-pounded beaches; he can pilot his motorboat through the maze of channels of Puget Sound, or sail before a spanking breeze among hundreds of enchanting islands.

Interesting, too, are the historic relics of the conquest of this wilderness: early mission houses, forts, blockhouses, and other pioneer buildings; the crumbling tombstones in lonely prairie cemeteries; markers on old trails; war canoes, tomahawks, arrowheads, feathered head-dresses, and other mementos of the culture of the Indians, whose descendants now live on reservations. All these are a part of the great epic of the march of the pioneer. To see them is to gain a clearer understanding of the history of the Nation.

In the course of the rapid development of the State, the country has been greatly altered. Forests have been cut, leaving vast scarred and denuded areas; grasslands have been broken and planted to wheat; and the arid range, now the feeding ground of cattle and sheep, has been enclosed with barbed-wire fences. Desert lands have been converted by means of irrigation into productive gardens, orchards, and alfalfa tracts. Trains and automobiles now speed where native trails once ran, steamships and ferries ply waters formerly crossed only by primitive dugouts, and airplanes hum overhead. Factories and mills stand where Indians set their weirs; and on the sites of communal Indian villages, large modern cities, with clean, well-lighted streets and tree-lined boulevards, have been built.

On every side lies tangible evidence of the toll that this general and haphazard development of the country has taken; but works designed for the conservation and reclamation of depleted resources are also to be met with everywhere. Selective logging methods have supplanted to a considerable extent the wasteful methods of former years, and a carefully planned system of reforestation of logged-off and burned-over lands, in conjunction with the establishing of extensive national forests, bears promise of the intelligent utilization of existing stands of timber and the partial replacement of those that have been removed. The mighty Grand Coulee Dam and other major power developments, such as the Bonneville, the Skagit, and the Cushman projects, are near completion or already in service. At Bonneville Dam, ingenious fish ladders have been constructed to facilitate the migration of salmon upstream to spawn. And many national and State parks spread over lands withdrawn from commercial use and dedicated to the enjoyment and inspirational needs of man. All of these measures are expressive of a people with broad vision and with the capacity for significant, long-range planning.

The people of the State came from many sources. Attracted by timber, free lands, minerals, railroad construction, the fish industry, irrigation, and power developments, successive waves of settlers have come to Washington: dissatisfied and restless folk from the older States; Southerners, ruined and uprooted by the Civil War; immigrants from Europe and from the Orient; and discouraged farmers from eroded, worn-out lands of the Middle West. Each group has brought its distinctive folkways, which have modified and enriched the cultural life of its new homeland.

Natural Setting

WASHINGTON, the Evergreen State, occupies the northwest corner of the United States, with the Pacific Ocean on the west, Canada on the north, Idaho on the east, and Oregon on the south. Although its northwest corner is chewed out by the sea, and its southern border is determined by the meanderings of the Columbia River from the point where it swings westward, the State is roughly rectangular, measuring 360 miles east to west and 240 miles north to south. With a water area of 1,721 square miles and a land area of 66,836 square miles, Washington is larger than all New England, but its population is only 1,736,191 or 25.9 persons to the square mile.

The State, consisting of seven distinct physiographic areas—the Olympic Mountains, Willapa Hills, Puget Sound Basin, Cascade Mountains, Okanogan Highlands, Columbia Basin, and Blue Mountains—represents virtually every topographic variation known in the United States.

The Olympic Mountains, a part of the coastal range, lie between Puget Sound, Juan de Fuca Strait, and the Pacific Ocean, and are separated from the Willapa Hills by the valley of the Chehalis River. The region presents a labyrinth of peaks—Mount Olympus (8,150 alt.), Mount Fitzhenry (8,098 alt.), and Mount Constance (7,717 alt.), outstanding—and serrated ridges, broken and eroded. Alpine valleys lakes, and torrential rivers are numerous.

South of the Olympic Mountains are the Willapa Hills, a region of sedimentary and igneous rocks of the Tertiary period. Relatively low, rarely approaching 3,000 feet in elevation, this area receives less rainfall than the northern region, yet vegetation is rank, and there are many streams draining into the Columbia River and Willapa Harbor. Only along the bank of the Columbia River do the hills become abrupt.

The Puget Sound Basin lies between the Olympic and Cascade Mountains in the form of a broad trough, extending from Juan de Fuca Strait, which connects Puget Sound with the Pacific, half way to the Columbia River. It averages 100 feet in elevation in its central portion, while its flanks rise to join the mountains. Based upon rugged folds of sedimentary rocks, rock beds, glaciation, and lava flows, the erosion of innumerable streams has made it relatively uniform. At its southern end are extended plains, reaching almost to the Columbia River. Puget Sound, for which the basin is the trough, is 80 miles long, 8 miles wide at the broadest point, and has depths of 900 feet: a body of water flanked by forested bluffs and low dikelands, with extensive bays, inlets, and passages between the 300 islands that lie within its shores. Of these, the 172 inhabitable islands of the San Juan group (*see Island Tour 3*) and Whidbey Island, second largest in continental United States, are most noteworthy.

Extending across the State from north to south at its approximate middle longitude is the great barrier of the Cascade Mountains—shaped somewhat like an hour-glass—a range, 100 miles wide at the Canadian and Oregon boundaries, and 50 miles at its middle. The numerous peaks average from 6,000 to 8,000 feet in elevation, while the volcanic cones of Mounts Rainier, St. Helens, Baker, Adams, and Glacier Peak rise much higher. Of these peaks, only one, Mount Adams, is on the range axis; the others, St. Helens, Baker, Glacier Peak, and Rainier are on the western flank. Because of their origin, the northern and southern Cascades are quite dissimilar. The rugged southern portion resulted from great igneous activity due to volcanoes, while the northern portion, seemingly a great raised plateau at one time, is more uniform; whatever ruggedness it possesses has resulted from erosion rather than from volcanic action. The streams of the range, as a whole, are strong and deeply bedded. Mountain valleys, once the beds of great glaciers, have been deeply eroded—leaving grand cirques and amphitheaters, such as the water-filled gorge of Lake Chelan, that are among the great attractions of the range. Only the Columbia River crosses the Cascade Mountains. Three tunnels—the Cascade, the Rockdale, and the Stampede—pierce the Cascades for rail transportation; and the Chinook, Stevens, and Snoqualmie passes make them surmountable by highways.

North of the "Big Bend" of the Columbia River and north of the Spokane River, and merging into the Cascades on the west and the Rockies on the east, are the Okanogan Highlands: beautifully rounded, broad, low hills sloping gently from watersheds to the river beds, with divides—often 6,000 feet in elevation—never sharp or abrupt. The Highlands, unlike the heavily wooded Cascades, are largely open and park-like, with a minimum of undergrowth.

South of the Okanogan Highlands almost to the Oregon boundary and extending east of the Cascades almost to the Idaho boundary, is the Columbia Basin, an area of approximately 1,500,000 acres of sage and scabland. From an elevation of 500 feet at the Columbia River, lowest point in the region, the basin rises rapidly westward toward the foothills of the Cascades; eastward, the rise is more gradual to an elevation of approximately 2,000 feet at the Idaho Line. Ridges, extending east and west through the basin and marking the eroded course of past ice sheets, once rose across streams, but the latter in time have cut through them. The area of the Big Bend is scarred by great, ancient, long-dry river courses, of which Moses Coulee and Grand Coulee are excellent examples. Some of the coulees, however, still hold chains of lakes, strongly alkaline. From the region of the deep canyons of the Snake River and its tributaries, rolling plateaus—the Palouse Country—extend north and east, a fertile region of wind-borne soil deposits.

In the southeastern corner of the State are the Blue Mountains, a prominent uplift of some 7,000 feet in the lava plain. The rounded domes, rising 2,000 to 4,000 feet above the surrounding basin lands, receive, in contrast to the contiguous country, enough rainfall to support forest growth. The streams, in deep valleys, have affected general contours very little.

CLIMATE

Washington's topography, together with warm sea currents, strongly affects the climate, which varies greatly in different areas. Rainfall ranges from extremes of 6 inches in the eastern part to 160 inches in the western. East of the Cascades summer temperatures are often above 100° F. Not uncommonly, eastern Washington winters drop to —20° F. and —30° F., and crop seasons in the northern and higher portions are sometimes less than 100 days, increasing to 200 days towards the south. The average annual precipitation of 16½ inches in this section ranges from 60 inches in the mountains to 6 inches on the plains. The westerly prevailing wind's average velocity is low—between 5 and 6 miles per hour—but occasional sand or dust storms visit the arid areas.

In western Washington, the heaviest rainfall in the United States occurs on the southwestern slope of the Olympics, at Wynooche, where the average is 141 inches. On the northern side of the Olympics, Sequim has the lightest rainfall, averaging 17 inches, and requires irrigation. The average in the western section, however, is 36 inches. The rainiest month is likely to be December, and the driest, July. Winter temperatures average 40° F., with a daily average minimum of 35°. Summers average 61° F. with a daily average maximum of 74°. Yearly snowfall varies widely, averaging less than 13 inches at Seattle, while Snoqualmie Pass has had 400.

Puget Sound area crop seasons average 207 days, diminishing to 185 in the valleys south. First frosts usually occur in November, and the last frosts in March. Wind velocities vary from a yearly average of greater than 12½ miles on the coast, with occasional seasonal bursts of hurricane intensity, to 6 miles per hour in the interior.

Washington is a region where nature, on the whole, has been kind, barring it from catastrophic earthquakes, cyclones, drouths, and extensive floods, and endowing it with a climate assumed by scientists to be highly favorable for physical and mental exertion.

GEOLOGY AND PALEONTOLOGY

When western Washington experienced the most severe earthquake in its recent history in November 1939, the relevance of geologic history to present-day life was made dramatically clear. During the period of gigantic mountain building millions of years ago, the ancient peak Mount Si was covered by the Cascades, but never has there been real conformity between the hard primeval rock and the younger volcanic formation. The younger rock slips from time to time, as some earth movement takes place, and the resultant tremendous jar is felt throughout the region. (This explanation may be superseded by another differing in detail, but the general theory is substantially correct, according to authorities.)

In the Proterozoic era, the earliest of the four geologic divisions of time, long before the Cascades had risen, an embayment of the primeval sea covered most of the Pacific Northwest region. The Blue Mountains, in the extreme southeastern corner of the present State, have been described by some geologists as a rocky promontory extending into this arm of the sea. Some 300 or more miles to the west of the old coastline, south from what is now Washington, lay an island, or islands, the existence of which has led to the erroneous belief that another continent lay to the west of this one in prehistoric ages.

After hundreds of millions of years, with alternating periods of submersion and dry land, the region was invaded by the sea from the north, in the Paleozoic era. The depositing of silt from adjacent land areas and other natural processes resulted in the filling up of the original embayment to a maximum depth of 30,000 feet. Present deposits of quartz, slate, marble, and schist represent these ancient ones, but greatly altered in structure and recrystallized. Paleozoic rocks found in various places across northern Washington contain valuable fossil specimens of marine life of that period.

During the Mesozoic era, which probably lasted for more than 100,000,000 years, the essential features marking the existing topography were formed. It was during the latter part of this era (Jurassic period), according to John Hodgdon Bradley, that the original uplift of the Sierra Nevada, the Coast Range, the Cascades, and the Klamath Mountains occurred. Also in this period, another great inundation laid down beds of mud and sand that gradually were transformed into the bedrock of the San Juan Islands. Large deposits of magnesite, especially in Stevens County, probably originated at this time. With the making of mountains, great masses of molten rock pressed upward through the earth's crust, and gold, silver and other metals were fused with the rock while in this liquid state. As the Cascades first, and later the Coast Range, were formed, successively they made new coastlines, low-lying barriers to the ocean. The Mesozoic era, the age of reptiles, gave to the world some of its most curious life forms, including the giant dinosaurs; many of these have been unearthed on the San Juan Islands and in other parts of the State. Many marine specimens have been found in the shales and limestones of Stevens County.

The latest era, the Cenozoic, was marked by some of the most dynamic changes of all, including the greatest lava flow in geologic history and the age of ice; it also gave to the region some of its most productive natural resources—rich soil left by extensive lava flows, the great rivers and bays taking shape during this period, and the rich deposits of coal and other minerals being laid down. Of this era, the last 2,000,000 years constitute the recent epoch, within which came great volcanic eruptions and the period of glaciation. The Tertiary period, enduring for more than 50,000,000 years, was marked by long periods of sedimentation, erosion, and vegetation, alternating with periods of immense volcanic activity.

The western part of the State, except for the highest, or central, part of the Olympic Mountains, was covered with water, and great swampy flats extended along the edge of the present Puget Sound Basin. From these were derived the shales and sandstones, the gold-bearing gravel of Sauk River, the commercial coal deposits. Gradually the sea floor was raised, and the Olympics were united with the mainland. Volcanic action, accompanying the building of the Columbian Plateau, brought forth great streams of lava, covering more than 200,000 square miles (estimates vary) in present Washington, Idaho, and Oregon. The weight of hot plastic rock tended to wear away all but the highest hills and to force streams to seek new outlets, with the changing of the watershed. The Columbia River was forced from its old channel into its present one, cut through granitic slopes at the edge of the lava plain.

With the cessation of volcanic activity, in the long periods of sedimentation and erosion, many forms of animal and reptile life inhabited the region. Immense forests arose; petrified logs remain to indicate something of the size and type of these ancient trees. Gingko Petrified Forest was formed by the flow of lava over fallen gingko trees; ground water creeping through the rock brought quantities of silica which, in the form of quartz, gradually took the place of the wood. Whole stone logs are found, some wonderfully and delicately colored, in the shape of the Asiatic gingko tree.

Toward the close of the Tertiary period, various plateaus and hills were formed—the Badger Mountains and Waterville Plateau, prominent folds of the Frenchman Hills, and the Spokane Divide. Large basins were created, and the Yakima River cut its way through ridge after ridge, as each in turn arose.

The Quaternary (later Cenozoic) period was one of discordant events that completely changed the topography, producing marked climatic differences between eastern and western Washington. From a chain of vents along the line of the Cascade Mountains, volcanoes discharged great quantities of cinders and ash and exuded molten rock. Temporary cessations of the latter allowed incrusting materials, chiefly andesite, to build up great cones to form such peaks as Baker, St. Helens, Adams, and Rainier. The largest of these was the truncated mass of Mount Rainier. Active as late as the early part of this century and still steaming and emitting gases, this mountain once attained a height of more than 16,000 feet, only to lose 2,000 feet of its peak in an explosion. Other unrelated lava flows occurred at this time throughout the Cascade Mountains.

Later, as the climate turned colder, enormous glaciers slid down from the north to cover the upper part of the State. Elevations were greater than now. Puget Sound was dry. On the lofty Cascade Mountains and the major volcanic peaks, constant snows packed into glaciers that plowed down the slopes.

With a reversion to comparative warmth, melting ice sent debris-laden floods roaming over the Columbian plain, seeking or creating new channels as they rushed down the gradients caused by an earlier tilting. The abandoned rock-walled channels are today known as coulees. The Columbia River, much greater in volume than it is today, was blocked by the Okanogan Ice Lobe at the present site of Coulee Dam. The powerful stream, augmented by the run-off from adjacent and distant glaciers and the sudden draining of large lakes as far east as Montana, excavated a new channel. Abandoned when the retreating glacier allowed it to resume its former course, the old channel is now known as the Grand Coulee. A waterfall, one of the greatest in earth's history, thundered over the cliffs in what is today Dry Falls State Park.

A great lake, named by geologists Lewis Lake, and many minor bodies of water covered large areas of central and eastern Washington. The White Bluffs, 600 feet high and 30 miles long, on the Columbia River in Franklin, Grant, and Benton Counties, were created at this time. The force of the streams stripped sediments from the underlying lava, and these, transported southward, fill the fertile farming areas today. The denuded regions are the Channeled Scablands, more than 2,500 square miles of bare lava intricately channeled by ancient streams, now dry.

The shallow edges of the glaciers in the Puget Sound region, reaching as far south as Tenino, melted quickly, forming "mystery mounds" —the hundreds of little hummocks and hills of that "mound prairie" region. Vast clay deposits, characteristic of Puget Sound topography south of Admiralty Inlet and Deception Pass, indicate a damming of the melting waters at these points. With the disappearance of the ice dams, the quick run off carved numerous valleys out of the sea bed. When the sea level rose again these became deep harbors and channels bordered by high cliffs.

Fossils found in central Washington beds tell of lush vegetation and abundant animal life — temperate zone and subtropical flora and fauna — maintained by the rich lava-formed soil. Fossilized leaves of fig, oak, cypress, elm, and gingko (the Sacred Tree of China) have been uncovered. Sequoia trees grew in several parts of the State.

Rocks along the margins of Puget Sound have revealed marine forms of the recent, or Cenozoic, era. Bones of mammals of this period, including the mammoth, the horse, and the bison, may be seen in the Whitman College Museum at Walla Walla. A skeleton of the mastodon (*Elephas Columbi*), built up from remains uncovered in the vicinity of Latah near Spokane in 1878, is a highly valued exhibit in the Field Museum in Chicago.

ANIMAL LIFE

It was the rich animal life of Washington that drew to the territory its first white inhabitants—hunters, trappers, fishermen, and traders. Today, too, the State is renowned for its native fauna, especially for its game fish. The coastal waters contain five famous varieties of salmon: Chinook (king, tyee, or spring), large and game, which predominates in the Columbia River and its tributaries; sockeye (blueback), found in the Sound and the Strait and fresh water lakes; chum (dog), a lower grade fish; pink (humpback), and silver (coho). The quinnat salmon, noted for its delicacy and size, and of leading importance commercially, is a member of the king family.

Besides the salmon, several other migratory fish ascend Washington's rivers from the sea in breeding season; chief among these is the fighting steelhead, a large-sized rainbow trout. Two cutthroat trout are favorites of sportsmen: the coastal variety and the so-called Montana black-spotted trout. The blueback trout (*salmo beardsleei*) is found only in Lake Crescent, on the Olympic Peninsula. Also much sought are the silver trout, a fresh-water variety of sockeye, and the western spotted char, called the Dolly Varden trout. The squawfish, a predatory pike, is frequently found in lakes and streams; and the white sturgeon, of the Columbia, Snake, and Pend Oreille Rivers, largest fresh-water fish in North America, was once such a nuisance that an attempt was made to exterminate it. Species planted in Washington waters include the gamy largemouthed and smallmouthed bass, the eastern brook trout (comparatively rare), and the mackinaw trout found in Spokane, Pend Oreille, and Stevens counties. Other importations now distributed on both sides of the Cascades are the spiny-rayed fish: perch, crappie, catfish, and sunfish.

Native salt-water fish are the halibut, now increasing in numbers; the albacore tuna, which have been taken in great numbers since 1936, when fishermen first went far out off the banks to catch them; the herring and the pilchard, used largely for oil, meal, and bait; the flounder; the red snapper; and the ling, the rock, and the black cod. Two varieties of eulachon are common: the Columbia River smelt, the heavy spring run of which draws hundreds of people to the Cowlitz River near Kelso; and the candlefish of Puget Sound, so called because the Indians used to dry it and burn it for light. The devilfish, or octopus, is also found in coastal waters; and the eel frequents some rivers, especially the Columbia.

These are some of Washington's food and game fish, but the list scarcely suggests the extent and variety of the State's marine fauna. Near the shore in shallow waters, tiny sponges and mussels cling to rocks and pilings, jellyfish pulse their way in search of food, starfish sometimes grow to unusual size, and sea anemones open and close at the slightest prod. Other forms inhabiting these grounds are sea urchins, limpets, chitons, whelks, segmented and flat worms, tube worms, periwinkles, and shell-less bronze and rose sea slugs. Among the shellfish are butter clams, the staple food of Puget Sound Indians, and still abundant today; razor clams of the ocean beaches, sought by tourists; the small Olympia oyster, famous for its flavor, and the rock oyster, both native to Washington waters, and the large Japanese oyster introduced here a few years ago, scallops with exquisitely fluted rose-tinted shells; and the geoduck, elusive and comparatively rare. Crabs of different sizes thrive in the sheltered pools and rocky coves along the many miles of coastal waters; and shrimp, small, firm, and flavorful, occur in considerable numbers in Hood Canal. Not to be overlooked are the common barnacles, which cling tenaciously to rocks, logs, and sea-going vessels.

Among oddities of the sea are the opalescent squid and the sea squirt, the latter a cylindrical, bag-like creature, tapering slightly at both ends, which attaches itself to rocks or shells and squirts water like a clam. The porpoise is not infrequently seen sporting in schools; and the hair seal, sometimes accompanied by the sea lion, also visits Puget Sound. The shark family is represented here by the mud shark, the more common dogfish not being a true shark. Even the whale leaves the deep waters now and then and detours into the blind alley of Puget Sound.

Land animal life is also unusually abundant here. Insects and bugs are relatively few in kind, although the State has its quota of the usual varieties. Outstanding among the invertebrates of eastern Washington are the warrior grasshopper, the coulee cricket, and the locust, and in the coastal regions the various pine-borers. The red ant, with its dome-like hill, is common in dry pinewood areas. Most noteworthy of the butterflies is the swallowtail, largest of the western species, with double "tails" on each hind wing. Among the imported pests are the codling moth and the earwig. The tent caterpillar (larval stage of the moth) is often a destructive nuisance in western Washington. Except for the black widow spider, which is found now and then, and the wood tick, carrier in some instances of Rocky Mountain fever, there are no poisonous or disease-bearing insects. Among amphibians, the most numerous are the tree frog and the western wood frog. There are several varieties of the lizard, the salamander, and the toad; the horned toad, however, is rare. Turtles are represented west of the Cascades by the terrapin, and east of the mountains by the western painted turtle. Snakes of various kinds are fairly numerous, notably the garter snake, the bull snake of the pine woods, and, in some parts of eastern Washington, the poisonous rattlesnake.

In the forests and mountains elk, deer, and bear are plentiful, and are frequently seen from the highways traversing timbered areas. Of especial interest is the Roosevelt elk, named in honor of Theodore Roosevelt, which is found within the State only in the Olympic Mountains and the Tatoosh Range. Largest of all wapiti, it is identified by its light color and massive spread of antlers. The mule deer and the Columbian black-tailed deer — distinguished by its broad flat tail — are familiar to sportsmen. Though more rare, the mountain goat is increasing in number under protective laws.

Larger predatory animals have been almost exterminated by hunters seeking State bounties. The Canadian lynx, red western bobcat, timber wolf, and red fox are seldom seen. The coyote, once widely prevalent, has retreated into the foothills in depleted numbers. Strangely enough, it is the mountain lion or cougar, upon whose head there has long been a price, that remains numerous, though he is encountered only in remote places.

Among lesser native mammals are several species of the shrew, mole, bat, western fisher, and weasel; and racoon, skunk, badger, marten, and mink are plentiful. The beaver, almost exterminated, is now returning. The Washington and Cascade varying hares, the white-tailed rabbit, and that little cave dweller, the cony or rock rabbit, belong to a family of rodents. Strangest of the lesser mammals is the shrew mole, who, combining the features of both shrew and mole but related to neither, has an ancestry going back to some remote Asiatic strain. Other common rodents are the squirrels, chipmunks, woodchucks, porcupine, and gophers. Several are of special interest: the mantled ground squirrel, the Cascade flying squirrel, the strange mountain beaver (not a beaver), who burrows in wet hillsides and is found only in the western part of Washington and Oregon; and the largest of the rodents, the marmot, noted for his whistling.

As might be expected in such an extensively wooded region, perching birds are numerically great, constituting two-fifths of the entire bird life. Members of this order are, in general, small in size, with the exception of the raven. The 18 families represented include the crow, blackbird, and sparrow, as well as many colorful birds and attractive singers: the tanager, warbler, lark, pipit, thrush, kinglet, titmouse, creeper, wren and thrasher, dipper, swallow, waxwing, shrike, vireo, and flycatcher. The crows are the most intelligent of this group; the chattering sparrows, particularly the gambrel sparrow, is the most often seen; and the golden-crowned kinglet is the most numerous. Among curious birds are the chat, the great mimic; and such finely costumed creatures as the lazuli bunting, the western tanager, the rare purple martin, the violet-green swallow and the crested gray-brown waxwing, the dainty water ouzel, and the rough-winged swallow with hooked wingtips. The most tuneful songbirds are the western lark, the black-headed grosbeak, the gold warbler with his silken black cap, and Audubon's warbler. Washington has chosen the willow goldfinch as its State bird.

Most of the perching birds are hardy. The varied thrush particularly loves the rain; the wren, kinglet, bushtit, chickadee, and Sitkan kinglet are evident in flurried throngs throughout the winter.

Weak feet and powerful wings mark the insect eaters, such as the swifts and the humming birds. Gaudy as are all the hummers, the most resplendent is the calliope with its emerald-green back and rose or purple gorget. Though less colorful, the swifts are extraordinarily graceful in flight.

The brilliant red coloration of the climbers and their unmistakable tapping play a vivid part in the chorus of the woods; they vary in size from a species no bigger than a sparrow to one as large as a robin. The Harris's woodpecker, black and white of head, with body of scarlet and gray, is perhaps the most beautiful. The white-headed and the pileated woodpeckers are rare.

The belted kingfisher — blue and gray with white pompadour — is a noisy fellow, usually found beside some stream awaiting the flash of an unsuspecting fingerling. The band-tail pigeon is the most common member of its family.

Strong talons and hooked bills distinguish the birds of prey. The owls, with 16 species, are numerically preponderant, but in spite of their number they are infrequently seen. The western horned owl and that rare winter visitor, the great horned owl, approximate the goose in size. The very common Kennicott screech owl, the hoot owl, and the burrowing owl, found in the arid regions of eastern Washington, are the most prevalent of the family. Both the prairie falcon and the sparrow hawk are extremely predacious. Once a familiar sight above crested peaks and arid wastes, the California condor is now extinct in the area; only the turkey vulture and an occasional bald or golden eagle may be seen today.

With the introduction of the Chinese pheasant in 1880, another brilliant member was added to the already plentiful drummers. A sly bird, colorful in plumage (and delicious in the pan), it is one of the greatest game birds in the State. Although not comparable to it in size or delicacy, the mountain partridge, with its long straight chest, the gray-blue grouse, the white-tailed ptarmigan, and the sage hen are also popular among sportsmen.

With more than 1,700 miles of shoreline and a moderate climate, Washington is a haven for marsh, shore, and water birds. The sandhill crane, eagle-sized, gray and brown in color, and the American coot are the most common of the marsh birds. In mating season, the ungainly crane performs a comical love dance, dipping, sidling, and shuffling. Of the true waders, the great blue heron, with slender bare legs and unwebbed toes, is the most picturesque.

Four orders are found among the shore birds: the *Limicolae* (sandpipers, avocets, turnstones, surfbirds and oystercatchers); the *Longipennes* (gulls, terns, and jaegers, noted as long-winged, strong fliers); the *Anseres* (ducks, geese, and swans); and the *Steganopodes* (cormorants and pelicans, fish eaters, with four toes joined by three webs). The latter are strong fliers, but are usually observed sitting on rocks. The avocet is the rarest of the sandpeeps — an awkwardly poised bird on stilt-like legs, with brilliant red, black, and white plumage. He has an upcurved bill, which he sweeps back and forth through the shallows, scooping up his microscopic food. Of the gulls, the white-headed is the most plentiful, although there are great migrations of the California and new gull. Among the shore birds, the jaeger, a rapacious tyrant, plays a role as villainous as that of the sparrow hawk and the prairie falcon farther inland.

Ducks and geese are abundant. Redhead, canvasback, scaup duck, goldeneye, honker, and black brant are found on river, lake, and bay. Favorite of the naturalist and the hunter is the wood duck, with its crested head — iridescent with black, green, violet, and purple — and white throat, chestnut breast, and purple sides. Although 60 species of this order are found in North America, only the cinnamon teal is peculiar to the Northwest. His chestnut coat and bill, and his peculiar habit of playing leapfrog during mating time, distinguish him from his more resplendent fellows. The rare blue-winged teal is sometimes seen. The tube-nosed birds include the albatross, fulmar, shearwater, and petrel. These, and the grebes, loons, auks, murres and puffins, known as *Pygopodes* — diving birds capable of remaining under water for long periods (as they commonly do when alarmed) — make their homes along the sandy shores and in the waters of Washington.

PLANT LIFE

The narrow fringe of ocean shore, the humid western slopes between the Cascades and the coast, the towering mountain ranges, the Columbia Basin with its extremes of summer and winter temperatures, and the intermontane plateaus — each region has its distinctive flora. And in each, climatic and topographic factors have influenced the number of species and the abundance or rarity of flowers of the various species. More than 3,000 species are found. Among the native plants are some of the rarest specimens: Flett's violet and the exquisite Piper bluebell of the mountain tops, the phantom orchid of the deep woods, the delicate rock pink of the Columbia Basin, and the sea rose of the coastal waters.

Conspicuous among marine plants are numerous algae, varying from blue-green to brown and red. Of this group the most common is the floating kelp with its brown-bulbed whip. The sea rose, rarest and most complex of the red algae, is found in its branched form, native only to the western coast of North America and the northeastern coast of Asia. Two species of eelgrass also grow here; one in exposed tidal waters, the other in protected marshes. Marine lichens and fungi of various kinds abound along the coast.

In season, even the sand dunes are abloom with sturdy plants. To windswept wastes cling the delicately fragrant yellow and pink abroma or sand verbena and the saltbush with pale, scurvied leaves; sand strawberries, beach pea, and blue, yellow, and purple lupine advance upon the rippling dunes, wherever some slight protection is afforded by driftwood or rock or hummock of solid earth. Fennel, spurrey, ruppia, willow, and the yellow-blossomed sneezeweed grow in rank profusion about the salt marshes.

Above the dunes and beaches along the littoral runs a narrow band of Sitka spruce, also called tideland spruce, a tree of great commercial importance. Douglas fir, a species forming the greater part of the stand in the rain belt between salt-water shores and the Cascade Mountains, is tall and stately, of great strength, comparative lightness, and straight grain. First reported by Archibald Menzies at Nootka Sound in 1792, it was known as Oregon pine until named in honor of David Douglas, who introduced it into Europe in 1827. Other conifers are the western hemlock, known for its size, drooping branches, and gracefully tapering trunk; western red, Port Orford, and Alaska cedars; and, in the mountains, the six-leaved pine and the silver, white, and noble firs. Winter and summer, these forests keep their green ranks closed against the winds, their moss-hung boughs blotting out the sun. Today, wilderness roads wind between the green walls made by these ancient forest giants, whose branches, interlacing overhead, sough and murmur in vagrant winds. Seen from an elevated vantage point, seemingly miles of dark-green brushy tips cover the valley floors and sweep up the mountain slopes, staggering as they near the rocky summits. Scattered through the coniferous forests at the lower levels is the madrona, with its red-skinned trunk, classed as an evergreen because its new leaves have formed by midsummer, when the old ones fall.

In most of the forested areas of lower altitudes are several deciduous species. Common among these is the big-leaf maple, usually found as an incidental tree growing in clumps or singly among the conifers. In bright contrast to the evergreens is the vine maple, so called because of the sprawling appearance of its weak and crooked stems. In the spring, its leaves are a gorgeous rose red; in the fall, reddish yellow or bright scarlet. Other hardwoods are the red alder, one of the first species to take possession of burned or cut-over land; the black cottonwood, found only at lower elevations in coastal regions; the Oregon white, or Garry, oak; the western yew, the California myrtle, and the Oregon ash. Most spectacular is the western dogwood, easily recognized in spring by the button-like clusters of small, greenish-yellow flowers, surrounded by four to six snowy white, or slightly pink, saucer-like scales, popularly presumed to be petals of the real flower. Late in summer the foliage turns a brilliant scarlet and orange, and the small seed-like fruit becomes bright red; autumnal flowers are not uncommon. Abundant also are shrub-like hazel trees and Cascara-buckthorn trees, whose bark is used in making cascara sagrada.

Except for open prairie lands, restricted to a few localities, the western forest floors are covered with dense thickets of ferns, mosses, Oregon grape, and salal, discovered by Archibald Menzies and described in the Lewis and Clark journal. Drenched by the rain, one stormy winter day in 1805, Captain Clark had found shelter in a Clatsop Indian hut, and there was presented with a bowl of "syrup pleasant to the taste made from a species of berry common in the country, about the size of a cherry, called by the Indians shelwell. Of these berries a bread is also prepared, which being boiled with roots, forms a soup, which was served in neat wooden trenchers." Later, Douglas found the Indians in Oregon calling the plant salal, the name by which it is usually known today.

Most spectacular of the many ferns is the swordfern, often exceeding four feet in height. Others are the omnipresent brake, the fragrant licorice fern, and the delicate maidenhair and lady ferns, found under overhanging ledges where the earth is always cool and damp. Creeping over the ground are the lycopodium and the mosslike selaginella, much used for Christmas decorations. Common throughout the lower levels of the western part of the State is the fernlike horsetail, which in early spring covers the open uncultivated spaces. In the dense forests, the vivid coloration of shrubs and flowers breaks the green-shadowed monotone; the deerhead orchid growing out of Hypnum moss or rising from the rotting trunks of a fallen tree; the rare phantom orchid, with yellow-throated flowers on a waxen stem; the spotted and striped coralroot; the tall barber's pole, white and scarlet; the drooping wax-white Indian pipe, the starflower, and the wake-robin; the white, purple, and blue anemone, and the green, pink, and red pyrola. Earliest of all, the snowy trillium bears its single flower in dampness and shadow.

Shrubs abounding in the western Washington forest include the early blooming currant, spiraea, ocean spray, and manzanita. Berry pickers search the open woods for the flavorous wild blackberry, which grows in bush formation or trails its thorny vines over burned logs in clearings, as well as for the red mountain huckleberry and the blue varieties, found in coastal and mountainous regions. Other shrubs are the fragrant white syringa, the wild rose, found on both sides of the Cascades, the red-berried elder of coastal regions, and the blue-berried variety of eastern Washington.

But queening it over all others is the delicate rhododendron, fitly chosen as the State flower. A sturdily beautiful shrub, braving ocean blasts and mountain heights, it borders the woods in great massed banks of rose, pink, lavender, and white. Its fluted bell-shaped flowers spring in clusters from shiny evergreen leaves. These are the "bouquets of splendid flowers . . . thousands of them together," which Father De Smet delightedly noted in the 1840's. Every spring the rhododendron inspires festivals and pilgrimages on the Olympic Peninsula. Less celebrated but equally spectacular is the Scotch broom, which has rioted across the western part of the State since its introduction by homesick fur traders from Scotland.

Common in the vicinity of bogs and lakes and meadowlands are the swamp laurel, buttercup, sphagnum mosses, sundew, cranberry, and Labrador tea, splashing the landscape with shimmering white, rose-purple, and yellow. In the wet bottom lands grow the yellow-fruited salmonberry, the gold-sheathed skunk-cabbage, the false nettle, and the prickly devils-club. Forest and meadow yield many species of edible mushrooms as well as other fungi. Most poisonous mushrooms will be identified by the "death-cup" or ring around the bottom of the stalk, though it is a safe rule to take no chances with unfamiliar species.

Strikingly different is the plant life east of the Cascade Mountains. The arid and almost treeless Columbia Basin, cut by coulees and arroyos and spotted with sinks and dunes, has remained since Cretaceous times virtually untouched by geologic upheavals. In this area the omnipresent low-growing sagebrush covers miles of brownish-red hills; it is silvery gray, with small wedge-shaped leaves and yellow bloom in spring, and emits a spicy, pungent odor. Companion plants are the rabbit brush, antelope brush, and hop-sage, and in the more alkaline soils, greasewood. Even in some parts of this arid region, spring brings forth an evanescent loveliness of grassy slopes dotted with yellow bells, grass flowers, sunflowers, and lupine. On rocky ledges, serviceberry bushes for a few days are swaying white towers; tules, cattails, and yellow water lilies appear along edges of sloughs and lakes, and willows of various kinds are brightly green.

In the eastern part of the State, where the rainfall is somewhat heavier, grasses and flowering plants increase. The first warmth of the spring sun ushers in a host of annual plants and herbs, which first carpet the area with green and then quickly burst into bloom. The pearl-white flower of the everlasting; the graceful white, blue, and bicolored lilies; the rose-purple, pink, and white flowers of the wild onion; the buttercup, with its waxy yellow chalice; and the low rose-red bitterroot, often called the rockrose, which springs forth on the driest hillsides or nestles among the rocks.

In the deep shade of woods and in the cool dampness of meadow and sloughs grows the miner's lettuce (famous salad dish among Indians and early settlers), from the center of whose shield-like leaves spring flower clusters, lining only one side of the central stalk; purple-tufted wild peppermint and Solomon's seal; watercress in clear running water of creeks; and in the lowlands and along sloughs the slender spires of the wapato, or arrowhead, tipped with small white blossoms, and the camas, which turns springtime meadows into pools of blue. Altogether 500 plant species occur in this area. Many of them, including the tansy mustard, hairy-stickseed, purple mustard, gilia, and three-veined violet, are indigenous. Other colorful flowers are the wild geranium, the brown-eyed Susan, and the goldenrod. In open places they are short-lived, but on shady north slopes or along more humid lowlands, under the protection of red alder, scaly hackberry, pine, and willow, they linger throughout the summer.

Encircling Columbia Basin and including the Palouse and Big Bend regions, Walla Walla, Douglas, Lincoln, Yakima, and Klickitat Counties, and the Rattlesnake and Horse Heaven Hills, some bunch-grass plains survive, though many have been planted to wheat. Lupines and sunflowers, including the unusual black sunflower, enliven the landscape. Along draws grow the adder's tongue, the flaring white hellebore, and the Indian paintbrush (also found in western Washington). Where this comparatively treeless area merges into the foothills of the Cascade Mountains, the Okanogan Highlands, and the Blue Mountains, the dominant growth is the yellow pine. Where yellow pine grows, there also are found varieties of mistletoe and ginseng. Pine-grass and the shrubs of ninebark, buckbrush, and rose are freely scattered in the lower levels, but more rarely on the higher ground, where the Engelmann spruce, western larch, and red fir appear.

Last of all the blossoming areas the traveler might find are the alpine meadows of wildflowers. Between towering peaks and below hanging glaciers stretch these great ponds of bloom, breaking in waves of color. In unrestrained profusion grow the painted cup, pink valerian, shooting star, crimson penstemon, monkey flower, mountain phlox, and mertensia. The white-green and pinkish-purple of the hellebore and giant helleborine, both touched with yellow and gold, mingle with the delicate white, blue, and purple of mountain anemones; the creamy cat's-ear or mariposa lily, the pure pink dogtooth violet, and the red columbine, create a riot of color. More fragile and aloof are the avalanche lily, alpine beauty, and spiraea, ghost-like in their whiteness. The air of these floral parks is fragrant with perfume.

Among the very glaciers and rocks grow lupine and lace fern; red, white, and yellow heather; kinnikinnick, which the Indians used to smoke; yellow mustard, mountain polypody, white saxifrage, and broad, heavy mats of partridgefoot. Rockbrake and the yellow stonecrop, with its leafy rosettes, are prolific. Plant life survives even in the snow, for underneath it the alga *Protococcus nivalis* thrives, giving the drifts themselves a reddish tinge.

RESOURCES AND THEIR CONSERVATION

Vast timber stands, varied mineral deposits, fertile lands, invaluable fisheries, and many rivers providing power and irrigation have aided the rapid growth and development of Washington, and have made the State an important factor in the economic life of the Nation. Today, revolutionary changes are anticipated in almost every industry through the construction of the two great dams, the Grand Coulee and Bonneville, and numerous smaller reservoirs and hydroelectric plants. Agriculture will feel the effects of vast irrigation programs; mining and metal production, of an almost unlimited quantity of cheap power; lumbering, of conversion processes expedited by electricity; and fishing, of the hatcheries and elevators built in conjunction with water-control structures.

East of the Cascades much of Washington's soil is a surface decomposition of mile-thick lavas, with deposits of volcanic ash rich in phosphates and other plant foods; these elements are characteristic to some extent of virtually all of the State's arable land. Westward, in the Puget Sound Basin and its southerly extension, soils are either volcanic ash and fragmentary lava, or clays, sandy loams, and silts. Many peat bogs and bottom lands have made the wide, shallow river valleys of the coastal plain among the most fertile farming regions in the West.

The open ranges in the eastern part of Washington provided rich grazing for extensive herds of cattle and sheep during the seventies and eighties. But the land soon proved too valuable for cattle raising, and farming encroached upon and finally broke up the enclosed ranges. Large areas still remain, however, which, with their native grasses, are better suited for cattle raising than for agriculture; but it is in the national forests that cattlemen now find the best grazing lands in the State. These forests are under control of the United States Forest Service, and uniform charges are made for grazing privileges.

Wheat was grown early in the rich Palouse country, in the southeastern corner of the State, where the rainfall is moderate. Towards the south central region, however, in the Columbia River Basin, agriculture could not flourish, despite the richness of the soil, because of the low rate of rainfall; the area became a waste of sagebrush and scablands. Irrigation was introduced by the Protestant and Catholic missionaries. Later, several private companies, most of which went bankrupt, attempted to supply water to the farms of the Columbia River region. Since 1905, when the United States Reclamation Service took over the Sunnyside project, irrigation has been the life of eastern Washington's arid sections. The Sunnyside, Kittitas, Wapato, Benton, and Tieton units were built with Federal assistance: Sunnyside irrigates 107,000 acres; Kittitas, 72,000; Wapato, 113,000; Tieton, 32,000. One of the more recent projects is the Roza, contemplated since 1918, which will ultimately bring 72,000 acres under irrigation; it is estimated that 10,000 acres under the latter project will be irrigated by 1941. The irrigation of 40,000 acres in the Rathdrum project near Spokane has been considered since 1932; at present 9,300 acres have been successfully watered.

The major irrigation project in the State, however, is the construction of dam, powerhouse, and reclamation works at Grand Coulee, undertaken by the Federal Government in 1934 (*see Tour 1B*). When completed, the project will carry water by flumes and canals to 1,200,000 acres in the Columbia Basin. An Anti-Speculation act passed by Congress regulates prices of the reclaimed land and lays down the conditions for its distribution to farmers.

Education for soil conservation, sponsored by the Washington State Planning Council, the United States Department of Agriculture, and the Washington Agricultural Experiment Station at Pullman, is leading to crop rotation for the renewal of fertility, the use of forage crops to check erosion, and the construction of earthworks and concrete dams in denuded areas. In eastern Washington, wheat production is being curtailed and the rolling hilltops and blown areas returned to grass. Test farming is conducted on a large scale at the experiment station at Pullman. Other projects at South Palouse, Badger Pocket, Wiley City, Cashmere, and Goldendale, dealing with native grass conditions, hilltop breaks and buffer strips, and gully and grazing control, have been carried on by the Soil Conservation Service of the Department of Agriculture.

Timber is Washington's foremost natural resource, and was once so plentiful as to lead to the belief that it would never be exhausted. The great forest areas today hold 277,000,000,000 board feet of timber of an original stand of an estimated 578,000,000,000. Nineteen per cent of all the soft wood timber in the United States is in Washington.

West of the Cascades are more than 245,000,000,000 board feet, or 88 per cent of the State's standing timber. Douglas fir comprises about 40 per cent of this, and western hemlock is but little less plentiful.

Other important species of Washington trees include western red cedar, Sitka spruce, Shasta fir, mountain hemlock, ponderosa pine, and Port Orford cedar.

The national forests contain 101,000,000,000 board feet of timber, of which 88,000,000,000 are west, 13,000,000,000 east, of the Cascades. The remainder of the total stand is divided almost equally between private and public ownership.

Forests conserve water for irrigation, prevent soil erosion and floods, and maintain the purity of drinking-water sources. Standing timber also serves as a sanctuary for birds and game and furnishes summer range for cattle, horses, and sheep. In the past, these resources suffered from the "cut-up-and-get-out" logging methods employed. Present conservation programs, however, are aimed at safeguarding, through planned use, what is left of the State's forests and, ultimately, in restoring some of the lost woodlands.

Seven national forests lie wholly in Washington, and two others partly in Washington, Idaho, and Oregon. To the west, mainly in the high Cascade region, are the Mount Baker, Snoqualmie, Wenatchee, Chelan, Columbia, and Olympic national forests. In the northeastern section is Colville National Forest and, farther east and extending into Idaho, the Kaniksu National Forest. From the extreme southeastern quarter of the State, Umatilla National Forest extends into Oregon. These forests cover almost 10,000,000 acres, a large area, but of their growth only 37 per cent is marketable timber.

The average annual cut between 1926 and 1929 was above 7,000,000,000 board feet. The demand dropped to 2,250,000,000 by 1932 but rose again thereafter until it had reached almost 5,000,000,000 in 1937. Since only a fraction of the depletion was replaced by new growths, the importance of reforestation and conservation is apparent. Although 29,057 acres had been replanted with approximately 18,900,000 trees in 1938, a staggering task remains, according to a survey made by the Charles Lathrop Pack Forestry Foundation. The United States Forest Service, assisted by Civilian Conservation Corps camps, is striving to increase the scale of present reforestation efforts and to publicize the need for planned conservation. The foregoing agencies, the State Forestry department, and lumbering associations also co-operate to provide fire protection.

The mineral resources of Washington were noted by the Hudson's Bay Company, and mining was begun in the area before the middle of the nineteenth century. Gold and silver were found in eastern Washington Territory (now northern Idaho) in such quantities that $7,000,000 in gold were, it is said, shipped through Walla Walla in 1862. In all, it is estimated that about $750,000,000 have been derived from mineral production in the State since it was settled.

Potential mineral wealth in the State is almost incalculable, but for many years these resources were neglected because most of the metallic ores are low-grade and not concentrated. Recent developments in chemistry and electric power make it possible to work ores on a large scale in regions heretofore unprofitable. The State's mining income was more than $30,000,000 in 1937. In addition to paying deposits of gold, silver, copper, lead, and zinc, Washington has manganese, aluminum, magnesium, chromium, mercury, molybdenum, nickel, and tungsten. Most of the mine products of the State are, however, nonmetallic. These include more than 30 elements and compounds, among which are: coal, sand, gravel, lime, granites, marbles, micas, slates, clays, talc, sandstone, magnesite, and diatomite (used as a fertilizer and in building materials). Magnesite beds in Stevens County, estimated to be the largest in the country, produce 67 per cent of the Nation's total output.

The Federal and State Governments maintain surveys, which conduct exhaustive studies of Washington's mineral resources. Advancement of mining is aided by the State Division of Mines and Mining, which seeks the introduction of modern methods, compilation of data from field surveys, and technical instruction for prospectors. Valuable contributions to mining technique have also been made by the University of Washington and Washington State College, and by the State Electrometallurgical Laboratory at Pullman with the co-operation of the United States Bureau of Mines. The electric power which will be made available by the Coulee Dam, Bonneville, and other plants, promises to revolutionize mining in the State.

Perhaps potentially the most important resource of the State is its waterpower. Washington, possessing one-fifth of the Nation's hydroelectric power, with an aggregate potential of more than 10,000,000 horsepower, leads the country in this respect. According to the United States Corps of Engineers there are 280 possible power sites on Washington's rivers.

The Columbia River, 1,210 miles in length, is the largest stream west of the Rockies and drains an area of 259,000 square miles. At Grand Coulee it has an average volume of about 109,000 cubic feet per second. As a whole, the river is capable of generating more than 8,000,000 horsepower in a possible total of 145 plants along the main stream and tributaries. In its course through the State the Columbia has a total fall of about 1,300 feet. Its tributaries offer immense possibilities, as yet unsurveyed and undeveloped.

It is estimated that the Puget Sound region has 83 sites for power plants, allowing the development of 1,500,000 horsepower. At present one of the largest hydroelectric installations is the Skagit River development of the Seattle municipal system, which has a seasonal capacity of more than 500,000 horsepower and a peak capacity that is much higher. In the Pacific Coast drainage area, embracing the Olympic Peninsula, there are sites for 52 hydroelectric plants with an aggregate potential of 500,000 horsepower. The Lake Cushman development of the City of Tacoma has a present rating of 157,000 horsepower. In addition to those mentioned above, a large number of major dams supply power, irrigation, and navigation facilities.

The relation between hydroelectric development and land conservation has been studied by the Federal and State Governments, and plans for control of soil erosion and floods are being put into practice. River flood control is already being effected by construction of dikes and revetments (stone retaining walls) by the State and the counties, under the direction of the War Department, with the aid of Federal funds.

The Washington State Game Commission operated in 1938 twenty hatcheries and nine bird farms, and maintained divisions of biological research, public education, licensing, and game protection. The United States Forest Service aids in re-stocking impoverished streams and lakes; 36,000,000 fry and fingerlings were planted during 1935, and in the previous year 47,000,000. The closing of various lakes and streams, particularly within national-park boundaries, has been an effective aid in bringing the fish to maturity in re-stocked waters. Laws prohibiting pollution of streams and consequent destruction of fish by industrial plants and mines are strictly enforced.

The reduction of the commercial fish runs has created serious problems, some of which are well on their way towards solution, often as the result of international co-operation. For example, the Washington State Planning Council reported in 1938 that the Fraser River run of sockeye salmon, in which Washington has a joint interest with British Columbia, had declined from a value of $30,000,000 in 1913 to one estimated at $3,000,000 in 1933. On the other hand, the council reports, the halibut fishery of the North Pacific, threatened with extinction, was rescued by regulation based on the scientific study and planning of the International Fisheries Commission set up by a treaty between the United States and Canada. Through the co-operation of Federal and State Government agencies, the University of Washington's School of Fisheries, labor unions, commercial groups, and organized sportsmen, valuable results are being obtained.

With the Columbia and many smaller rivers dammed by power and irrigation projects, fish were prevented from reaching upriver spawning grounds. Here, too, fruitful remedies have been devised. At Bonneville Dam elaborate fish ladders and locks were constructed, and a daily count was taken of the various species passing over them. Refrigerated, air-conditioned tank trucks remove the salmon trapped below Coulee Dam to spawn elsewhere. It is anticipated that fish propagation may be developed in the 150-mile lake that will result from the completion of Coulee Dam. Most species of salmon are at least holding their own, except the Chinook, which still appears to be decreasing. In the Columbia River district alone, however, many millions of Chinook eggs are taken annually for artificial or natural hatching.

Restriction of hunting to brief seasons protects game birds and native elk, bear, and deer. Deer and elk are on the increase over most of the State. Trapping is licensed and rigorously confined. Mountain goats are protected the year round in sanctuaries. Predatory animals, such as the cougar and coyote, are hunted down and bounties are paid for their extinction.

Game conservation is supervised jointly by the State Commission and the United States Forest Service. Typical of the activity of the nine game farms in Washington was the liberation of 60,000 pheasants in 1936. One hundred and sixty protective areas and game preserves have been set aside in the national forests. The Wild Life Conservation Act, passed by Congress in September 1937, has made Federal aid available for carrying on the State conservation program.

The beauty of Washington's mountains, virgin forests, lakes, bays, and waterfalls is unexcelled in the most publicized scenic resorts of the world. Thousands of tourists are drawn annually to its parks and beaches and, in the winter, to its ski courses and skating areas. Municipal, State, and Federal funds have been expended in improving Washington's natural playgrounds and in making them available to a growing public.

Indians

AMERICAN history written in terms of the white man is a story of his triumphant march westward, clearing the land, breaking the sod, draining swamplands, and setting up frontier settlements, which quickly developed into sprawling towns, or sometimes into bustling cities. For the Indian, however, this never-ceasing advance into his lands has meant the end of his way of life. From the moment of the first encroachment upon his preserves and the enforced contacts with white men — at first with trappers and fur traders and later with other occupational groups — the breakdown of Indian culture was inevitable. This included the alteration and disarrangement of his economic and linguistic forms, and adjustment to the life imposed upon him by the unyielding and ruthless intruders. The process of acculturation still goes on, and it is apparent that, when the informed remnant of the old Indian line has departed, the native culture and its unrecorded native lore will be forever lost. In comparatively recent years, however, there has been an awakened interest in the Indian, and scientific ethnological and archeological study has been undertaken to preserve for future generations a true record of the first Americans and their culture.

Archeological research in the State of Washington has merely scratched the surface, only a few studies having been made of the early cultural remains found in the Yakima River Basin and the Puget Sound region. In all probability, prehistoric people made the pictographs and petroglyphs found in eastern Washington and along the Columbia River. The origins, functions, and meanings of these picture writings and rock carvings are still a matter of conjecture, and they are not explained either by the Indians or by anthropologists and archeologists. Studies do indicate, however, that the culture of the early peoples did resemble to some extent that of historic Indians. These researches, moreover, have furnished additional evidence to support the theory of the Asiatic origin of the Indian. Remains of later periods are much more numerous, and considerable progress is being made in collecting and preserving them.

The best collection of Indian archeological and ethnological material in Washington is in the State Museum, University of Washington campus, Seattle. Among the items are baskets, drums, carvings, clothing, tools, and various weapons. In several towns in central and eastern Washington are smaller collections made by individual members of the Columbia River Archeological Society, with headquarters in Wenatchee. The State Historical Society Museum, located in Tacoma, has a fairly large collection. Museums in the East, notably the American Museum of Natural History, in New York City, and the Smithsonian Institution, in Washington, D.C., also display collections of Indian objects from the State.

On the basis of culture traits, the Indians of Washington may be divided into two major groups, one comprising those bands east of the Cascade Range, and the other those west of it. The sharp cultural differences that developed between these groups arose in large measure from the barrier to intercourse formed by these lofty mountains. Contributing also to the formation of distinctive culture patterns was the sharp contrast in the physical character and climatic conditions of the two areas. East of the Cascades, in the semiarid plateaus and grasslands of the Columbia River system, considerable cultural similarity existed. West of the Cascades as well, from British Columbia south to the Umpqua River in Oregon, native cultures were sufficiently homogeneous to permit this region to be regarded as a single culture area. Within this coastal area, sub-areas are discernible, such as the Makah and the Puget Sound groups to the north and the Chinook along the Columbia.

Cultural diffusion did take place, however, as evidenced in the development of the Chinook jargon, a kind of trade language. This language, in its basic content the Chinook tongue, was formed by accretion of corrupted words from native groups who traded together, plus words later added by the whites. It arose from intertribal communication and the demand for a medium of communication in exchange and barter. It finally became the trade language used by the natives throughout the Northwest in their dealings with the whites.

Frequently northern Indians, from the region that is now British Columbia and southeastern Alaska, journeyed south in their war canoes, through the protected Inland Passage, to attack the Puget Sound Indians for the purpose of capturing slaves; and these onslaughts resulted in a transfer of culture. Some interchange also took place between inhabitants of the Columbia River region and those of the Rocky Mountain and Plains areas.

The summer abodes of the coastal Indians were temporary lodges built of rushes or bark, for little shelter was needed; but for the winter, when the weather was cold and rainy for protracted periods, permanent houses were built. Cedar planks, two or three feet wide and from three to six inches thick, were cut with crude wedges made of elk-horn or with chisels of beaver teeth and flint. From these planks and from logs, rectangular houses, 40 to 100 feet or more in length and 14 to 20 feet wide, were built. The only openings were the one left along the ridgepole to permit the escape of smoke, and a single door. These long houses accommodated a number of families, each with its own small fire in the shallow excavation which ran lengthwise down the middle. Bunks lined the walls, and the four or five feet of earthen floor between them and the fire was the living space of each family.

The most important food of the Indians of western Washington was salmon, which they caught in their primitive weirs and traps. Halibut, cod, shellfish, sturgeon, and fresh-water fish were also widely used. Game of many kinds, especially deer, elk, and wild fowl, was obtainable throughout the area. Agriculture was unknown, but wild berries, roots, bulbs, nuts, and various herbs supplemented the basic diet of fish and game.

Clothing was in the main fairly well standardized, though there were differences owing to changes in the weather or indicating social status. In mild seasons men wore either nothing or a robe or blanket thrown over the back and fastened across the chest with a string; they also had buckskin shirts, belts, breechcloths, leggings, moccasins, and basketry hats. The basic dress for women was a sort of petticoat, usually made of twisted strings of cedar bark or grass, fastened to a cord or band around the waist and falling to the knees. Occasionally wool was used. Additional garments were worn in cold and rainy weather. Upper-class women of some bands also wore woven or skin shirts or capes. Tattooing was more common among women than men, but it was usually limited to a few lines or dots on the arms and legs. The face was rarely, if ever, marked. Among some bands, especially those of the lower Columbia, heads were flattened in babyhood.

A high level of technique was achieved in the crafts. The hides of animals, both large and small, were tanned with the hair on, and from these, various articles, such as moccasins, skirts, and drums, were made with considerable skill. Woodworking was in an early stage of development; though the forms were broadly similar to those used by the Indians farther north, they lacked the technical and artistic skill achieved there. Perhaps the best example of the woodwork of the region was the dugout cedar canoe. Weaving was in most instances crude: the hair of dogs, shredded bark, the fur of bears, and the wool of mountain goats were woven on looms made of two uprights connected by rollers at top and bottom. The Indians of Juan de Fuca Strait region were famous for their dog-hair blankets. Some of their articles were skillfully colored with vegetable dyes, reds, yellows, greens, and black, being most prevalent. Mats were woven from shredded cedar bark and dried rushes, and baskets for many uses were twined from fine roots and grasses. Pottery was unknown, although some stone carving existed before white men came.

To a limited extent, the crafts, especially basketry and wood carving, are still practiced, but almost entirely for the tourist trade, the original motive for such work having been largely eliminated by the introduction of machine-made goods. Baskets, rich in color and design, represent the most highly developed phase of Indian art in the coastal regions. Today, as in the past, grasses, cedar and spruce roots, willows, and straw are the materials most commonly used, with thread, string, and animal hair often woven in as decoration. The weaves have great variety — hard and soft coil, turned and open twine, straight and crossed warps, hemstitching, and imbrication. Skill is also displayed in the working out of color patterns and in the many shapes of the baskets. Curios made by the Indians for tourist trade are sometimes authentic in detail, such as the small model canoes; but the miniature totem poles that some carve are mere imitations of the genuine totem art common to the tribes of Alaska and parts of British Columbia.

Well-defined classes existed among the coastal bands, although there was neither a totemic nor a clan system like that developed among the people of the North. Society was divided into a hereditary nobility, a middle class, and a slave class, composed in the main of captives taken in war and their descendants. A certain degree of economic freedom prevailed; individuals, exclusive of the slaves, were allowed to enjoy most of the fruits of their labors. Social lines, however, were more strictly drawn: marriage between commoners and the wealthier and more important classes was frowned upon to such an extent that disgrace was passed on to the offspring. Government was centered in a chief, whose office as a rule was hereditary, and tribal councils, at which men of importance stated their opinions. Women occupied a position of inferiority, much of the drudgery of daily work falling to their lot. This inferiority was also reflected in the practice of determining descent by the paternal line.

A belief in personal guardian spirits was the most marked characteristic of Indian religious life. These spirits were presumed to bring success in war enterprises and in the acquisition of wealth, rank, and recognition in tribal councils. A boy frequently received a spirit that had been in his family before; a person of high rank was likely to have a powerful spirit, and women or persons of lower classes usually acquired only a small and not very effective guardian spirit. Occasionally, an individual, usually a man, became a *shaman* by acquiring one or more spirits effective in curing illness. These *shamans,* although they could never become chiefs, often rose to great power; and since they could exact high pay for their services, became at times exceedingly rich, even richer than the chief himself.

The region east of the Cascade Mountains, approximately two-thirds of the area of the State, is occupied by Indians having a "basin" type of culture. The introduction of the horse, shortly before the arrival of the explorers, led to complications and change in the economic life of the natives and to a rapid spread of material cultural elements associated with the horse and with the new mode of life. The Indians of eastern Washington wandered in bands, the range of their wanderings and the size of the bands depending largely on the nature of their food. Because of their nomadic life, the general dwelling was a mat lodge, which could be transported from place to place. Usually, this lodge, a single large room, was rectangular in shape, 20 to 60 feet in length and about 16 feet in width. Occasionally, the lodges were circular. Two to eight families might live in one lodge. The underground dwelling was probably known throughout the region, but it seems to have been utilized by relatively few bands; the semi-subterranean dwelling consisted of a circular pit from 4 to 6 feet in depth and from 10 to 15 feet in diameter. Surmounting it was a flat or conical roof of sod, supported by cedar planks and matting. The influence of the Plains tribes and of the whites is seen in the increased use of skin and canvas tepees and, in some sections, of log cabins.

As with the coastal Indians, salmon was a major food item. Most bands lived near enough to the rivers to keep supplied with fish. Another important food was roots, especially the root of camas, which grew in the grasslands and lowlands throughout the region. Seeds and roots were, in fact, the staple food for some bands. Near the Cascades and in the northern highlands, berries, especially huckleberries, were widely used, and small game and deer were hunted. Usually the food was boiled in watertight baskets with hot stones, but some of it, especially roots, was baked over heated rocks.

The basin Indians had not developed a high degree of skill in the crafts except in the making of skin clothes and in basketry. Utensils, such as spoons, dishes, and bowls, were made of wood, but because of the scarcity of timber in the greater part of this area, little artistry in woodworking developed. Canoes, used infrequently, were only rude dugouts. Certain tribes, notably the Sanpoil and the Shoshone, manufactured a crude type of clay ware, although they were several hundred miles from the nearest deposits of good pottery clay. In basketry, coiling, twining, and imbricating were skillfully employed. Fine decorative effects were achieved with dyes and with a kind of embroidery. In historic times clothing in this area was of the same general character as that of the more easterly peoples. Tanning processes were well understood, as evidenced in the wide use of dressed buckskin, ornamented with fringe, and of skirts, leggings, and moccasins, decorated with beads and porcupine quills. Skin caps and robes were also common.

Compared to the rigid class divisions of the coastal regions, or to the system of the war-hero of the plains area, early social structures in eastern Washington had little class differentiation and were characterized by a general equality and pacifism. Chieftainship was nominally hereditary, but actually depended upon personal qualifications. Holding advisory rather than dictatorial powers, the chief was easily approachable and rarely possessed great individual wealth. Catches of salmon and meat obtained from hunting were divided equally among all present, foreigners included. Slavery, where it did come into existence, was an incident of war rather than an institution.

Concepts of the supernatural varied throughout eastern Washington. The Sanpoils, who have been carefully studied, divided supernatural beings into five categories: the soul, the soul-spirit, ghosts, spirit-ghosts, and "dangerous beings." During life, they believed, everyone possessed a soul. After death the soul went to the land of the dead at the end of the Milky Way, or stayed on earth and roamed about in the transformed nature of a soul-ghost. Spirits were numerous; plants, animals, and inanimate objects were believed to be endowed with spirits, and it was among them that the youth sought his guardian spirit. Once found, a guardian spirit became an integral part of the self, and could not depart without serious physical consequences. Upon the death of the individual, the guardian spirit became a spirit-ghost and might then become the guardian spirit of a relative or of a *shaman*. "Dangerous beings," that is, ogres, monsters, demons, and evil dwarfs, were described in many interesting tales.

Eastern Washington bands had their *shamans,* too, with healing and other supernatural powers bestowed during their quest for their guardian spirits. The *shaman,* who could here be either a man or a woman, administered to the sick and officiated at ceremonies. Every winter, for a period of several months, dramatic spirit dances were held in the mat longhouses as part of initiation ceremonies for novices obtaining a guardian spirit, or as a special occasion under the sponsorship of a prominent *shaman,* or when the guardian spirit of any individual commanded a spirit dance.

Indian bands on both sides of the Cascades had festivals and celebrations, some of which are still held today. A festival common throughout the coastal regions north of the Columbia, but especially important in the Puget Sound regions, was the potlatch, a ceremonial feast at which valuable gifts were distributed to friends and neighboring tribesmen, each of whom was obligated to respond in a similar manner at a potlatch of his own. These feasts are still observed in a modified form. In the coastal areas, too, secret societies reached moderate development. Among modern festivals are Treaty Days celebrated in some reservations with a period of feasting, water sports, dances, songs, games, and exhibits of native handiwork. One of the most interesting of these celebrations is held annually in August on Whidbey Island, at which Puget Sound bands engage in war canoe races and other water sports (*see Tour 2C*).

Today, about 14,000 Indians, or roughly one twenty-fifth of the total Indian population in the United States, live in the State of Washington, most of them on reservations and public domains. The reservations are administered from four central agencies: the Taholah Indian Agency, with headquarters at Hoquiam, has under its jurisdiction the Quinault, Makah, Squaxin Island, Nisqually, Skokomish, Chehalis, and Ozette reservations, with a total Indian population of about 3,000; the Tulalip Agency at Tulalip has jurisdiction over about 3,500 on 6 reservations—Tulalip, Puyallup, Swinomish, Lummi, Port Madison, and Muckleshoot—and 3 public domains; the Colville Agency at Nespelem has jurisdiction over the Spokane and Colville reservations, with a population of more than 4,000; and the Yakima Agency at Yakima has jurisdiction over the Yakima Reservation, with almost 3,000 Indians.

Especially in western Washington, Indians, as a rule, constitute a racial minority in most villages, both on and off the reservations. Moreover, throughout the State the location of reservations does not coincide with early band distribution. Thus the Indians living on the 7 reservations in the Taholah division represent many dialect groups and include many persons with white blood. Group intermarriage and modern conditions have obscured for all but a few very old people the original dialect or group divisions and affiliations. Descendants of former Upper, Middle, and Lower Spokane now consider themselves members of one Spokane "tribe." The present-day Colville "tribe" is made up of remnants of Lakes, Sanpoil, Nespelem, Nez Percé, Moses, Columbia, Okanogan, Methow, Wenatchee, and Colville bands. The contemporary Yakima "tribe" is the product of a confederation formed in the middle of the last century of the original Yakima with 13 other bands.

Co-operative practices have been readily accepted by the Indian, for group activity was an integral part of his native social and economic pattern. Three coastal groups, the Snohomish, the Muckleshoot, and the Tulalip, incorporated themselves in 1936 in order to acquire and "to secure for members of the tribe an assured economic independence." In the same year the Puyallup, Tulalip, Swinomish, and Makah "tribes" were legally organized, with constitutions and bylaws, for the purpose of mutual welfare. The Swinomish Indians of LaConner have a tribal fishtrap, which has been operated successfully despite the general depression in the area. East of the Cascades, the Indians in the Yakima country have formed a co-operative livestock association.

The Indian of today differs in important respects from the Indian of a century ago. Blood mixtures are common, and most groups to a greater or lesser degree have altered their native cultural patterns. Moccasins, buckskin jackets, and basket hats are giving way to "store clothes"; pinto cayuses to automobiles; and Indian tobacco to factory-made cigarettes. More significant changes are also taking place: about 5,000 children now attend public schools, their tuition being paid by the Federal Government. Vanishing, too, are the tribal councils, and, in their stead, many of the Indians, since receiving full citizenship rights, are assuming the legal and political status of the people around them.

History and Government

THE exploits of Columbus inspired the Old World maritime powers to feverish activity during the sixteenth century. When it had become apparent that two continents lay between Europe and the Orient, a race began for discovery and control of the shortest water route through or around them. Balboa crossed the Isthmus of Panama, and Magellan led the way through the strait that bears his name. Meanwhile, incomplete and inaccurate information obtained by other explorers suggested the existence of a navigable waterway across the upper half of North America. For almost three centuries, European naval powers sought this Northwest Passage, or Strait of Anian.

Imperial Spain was foremost in the quest. In 1542, Bartolome Ferrelo, commanding a Spanish expedition sent northward along the coast of what is now California to look for the passage's western opening, sighted the coast of what is now southern Oregon.

In 1578 Francis Drake sailed to the Northwest coast and named the land New Albion. Apostolos Valerianos, allegedly a Greek pilot, under the name of Juan de Fuca, claimed that in 1592 he entered a broad inlet between the 47th and 48th degrees of north latitude. His story was published in an English book (*Purchas, his Pilgrimes,* 1625), but no facts concerning his Northwest voyage have been verified. Nevertheless, his Spanish name — Juan de Fuca — was later given to the strait between the Olympic Peninsula and Vancouver Island.

During the seventeenth century, no noteworthy additions to geographical knowledge of the Northwest resulted from attempts to find the passage. In 1670, Charles II of England granted a charter to "The Company of Adventurers of England Trading into Hudson's Bay," with instructions to work for "the discovery of a new passage into the South Seas, and for the finding of some trade in furs and other considerable commodities." The company was given a monopoly on trade in regions not ruled by "Christian Princes."

Early in the eighteenth century, Peter the Great of Russia announced his intention of taking over all territory in North America not actually occupied by other powers. Catherine, his successor, sent the Dane, Vitus Bering, on two expeditions in North Pacific waters. Bering discovered the inter-continental strait that now bears his name, explored and charted the Aleutian Archipelago, and coasted along the Alaskan mainland; but, when he died in 1741 on Bering Island, he still believed Alaska to be an island separated from the mainland by the Northwest Passage. Russia's first permanent settlement in Alaska was made in 1784, and important trading interests and other colonies were established between that year and 1863. (In 1867, Russia, having grown tired of its American adventures and probably fearing to lose control to England, sold its interests on this continent to the United States for $7,200,000.)

France, at no time a serious contender for territory in the Northwest, was definitely eliminated by England in the Treaty of Paris, 1763. For 30 years thereafter the struggle was between Spain and England, with Russia holding the region now known as Alaska. Spain strengthened her claims by expeditions first along the coast and later into Juan de Fuca Strait. In 1774, Juan Perez sighted a mountain (Mount Olympus), which he called Santa Rosalia. Bruno Heceta and Juan de la Bodega landed near Point Grenville in 1775, and claimed the land for Spain. It is believed that Heceta saw what is now called the Columbia River, without recognizing it as the "River of the West" so long sought.

Captain James Cook, commanding an English expedition with instructions to search for the Northwest Passage and lay claim for England to any unoccupied lands he might discover, sighted land off the Umpqua on March 7, 1778, and proceeded to Nootka Sound, where he spent a month. He was quite painstaking in charting the coast lines north of Juan de Fuca, but the Strait itself escaped his notice.

The North Pacific voyage of the great French navigator, La Perouse, in 1785, was recorded in his journal, but, by the time the record was published in 1787, his discoveries were common knowledge among seamen. Now came the captains of the great fur-trade era, like the later gold rush to California. In 1787 Captain Charles William Barkley, an Englishman, found and named the passage now known as Juan de Fuca Strait. Barkley gave directions for finding the Strait to John Meares, once a lieutenant in the British Navy, who was preparing for a trading voyage along the Northwest coast. Early in the following year, Meares and another English trader, William Douglas, flying both the Union Jack and the Portuguese flag, joined in the rush for furs that replaced the search for the Northwest Passage.

Meares and Douglas established themselves at Nootka in 1788, claiming to have bought a tract of land from the native chief. Later in 1788, the American flag appeared in Northwest waters with the arrival of the *Washington* and the *Columbia,* captained respectively by Robert Gray and John Kendrick, on an expedition financed by a Boston syndicate interested in the fur trade. Early in 1789, a Spanish naval force under Estevan Jose Martinez appeared at Nootka Sound and claimed the country for Spain. The Americans were not molested, but Martinez seized several English ships. Meares escaped and carried his grievance to London. In 1790, a second Spanish force under Francisco Eliza occupied and fortified Nootka and took possession of the mainland at Neah Bay. Manual Quimper, Eliza's lieutenant, sailed among the San Juan Islands, sighting the present Mount Baker, but turned back at Admiralty Inlet, thus missing discovery of Puget Sound.

The Nootka controversy lost intensity in 1790, when England and Spain signed a convention providing for the appointment of commissioners, one for each nation, who were to go to Nootka and dispose of the points at issue. The commissioners, Captain George Vancouver for England and Juan Francisco de la Bodega y Quadra for Spain, resolved to let the matter be settled through arbitration by their home governments. The outcome was a convention signed February 12, 1793, whereby Spain and Great Britain mutually agreed to abandon Nootka Sound, and Spain agreed to make restitution for the property seized. Before the conference with Bodega y Quadra in 1792, Vancouver discovered and thoroughly explored Puget Sound, giving their present names to many of the region's prominent geographical features. He had met the American Captain Robert Gray in April 1792, but he paid no attention to Gray's suggestion that the opening near Captain Meares' Cape Disappointment might mark the mouth of a river. Gray, on May 11 of the same year, passed through the entrance in the *Columbia Rediviva;* he anchored off the north bank and, after profitable trade with the natives, he named the river Columbia, for his ship.

THE UNITED STATES AND ENGLAND IN THE OREGON COUNTRY, 1793-1849

With the fading of the hope of a Northwest Passage and the elimination of Spain as a contender, England and the United States began a long contest for ownership or what became known as the Oregon country—a vast area bounded on the east by the Rockies, and on the south by California and other Spanish possessions, and on the west by the Pacific, and extending north indefinitely. By 1803, the coast line had been explored, but little or nothing was known of the interior.

England's claims rested on the work of Cook and Vancouver, on the ceded Spanish rights, and on the overland trip of the Canadian, Alexander Mackenzie, who in 1793 reached the British Columbia coast after crossing the Rocky Mountains and Coast Range by canoe and portage. American claims were supported only by Gray's discoveries of the Columbia, Gray's Harbor, and Tillamook Bay.

After Thomas Jefferson negotiated the Louisiana Purchase in 1803, whereby the United States acquired title from the Mississippi River to the Rockies, he followed up with the overland expedition to the Pacific he had already planned, headed by Captain Meriwether Lewis and Captain William Clark. Lewis and Clark left St. Louis on May 14, 1804, and spent the winter of 1804-5 in a camp near the present site of Stanton, North Dakota. With Toussaint Charbonneau, a French-Canadian *voyageur,* as interpreter, and Sacajawea, his young Shoshone wife, they crossed the Rockies in the summer of 1805. Descending the western slope, they discovered the Salmon, Bitter Root, Clearwater, and Snake Rivers and followed the Columbia to its mouth, near which they established Fort Clatsop and spent the winter of 1805-6. On September 23, 1806, they were back in St. Louis.

David Thompson, the great English geographer, in 1796 began surveying the 49th parallel westward from Lake Superior for the North West Company, to determine whether the company posts were in Canada or the United States. By the winter of 1808-9, he was on the headwaters of the Columbia. Between 1807 and 1811, he established for the company some of the first trading posts in the Northwest, notably Spokane House in 1810. In 1808, Simon Fraser, a Canadian, traced the Frazer River to its mouth.

In 1810, John Jacob Astor of New York organized the Pacific Fur Company and sent two parties, one by sea and one by land, to the mouth of the Columbia, where, on April 10, 1811, construction of a trading post, Astoria, was begun. During the time of construction, the post was visited by David Thompson, who, working his way methodically down the Columbia in the interests of the North West Company, was disappointed to find the Americans already established. Thompson turned back and continued his survey, going up the Snake and Palouse Rivers, then across country to Spokane House. Astor's men also established inland posts, including Fort Okanogan, near the confluence of the Okanogan and Columbia Rivers, where the American flag first flew over a settlement within the bounds of the present State.

Within a year after word of the War of 1812 reached Astoria, the Astor representatives sold the Pacific Fur Company interests to the British North West Company. The Treaty of Ghent, in 1814, ended the war but failed to relieve tension over the Oregon question. A joint occupation convention was arranged in 1818, providing that the country "westward of the Stony Mountains" should be free and open for a period of 10 years to the "vessels, subjects and citizens" of both powers. Negotiations dragged on, and in 1827 both countries agreed to extend the treaty indefinitely with the added provision that either might end it on 12 months' notice. Meanwhile, the Hudson's Bay Company had absorbed the North West Company in 1821 and, by 1825, had established Fort Vancouver on the north bank of the Columbia, a few miles east of the mouth of the Willamette; and both England and the United States had signed treaties with Russia, in which the southern boundary of Russia's American realm was fixed at latitude 54° 40′ North.

American exploring expeditions into the Oregon country during the period of joint occupation included a party under Captain B. L. E. Bonneville, with headquarters in the western Wyoming region, who appeared at Fort Walla Walla in 1834; the Wilkes naval expedition, which explored Puget Sound and contiguous territory in 1841; and, in 1843, an expedition under Lieutenant John C. Fremont, who descended the Columbia to Vancouver, returned to the Dalles, and went southward to California. Bonneville, who supposedly had been trading for furs, was regarded as a poacher by Hudson's Bay men, and they refused to sell supplies to him. The company gave the naval and military parties a polite welcome, however, and land parties from the Wilkes expedition made trips to the company's inland posts.

Richard Gill Montgomery, in his *The Whiteheaded Eagle* (1934), describes "the King of the Columbia," Dr. John McLoughlin, chief factor of the Hudson's Bay Company west of the Rockies, as a man of limitless patience, cool and just and kind. The Hudson's Bay Company became so well established in the Oregon country that rival traders, including Americans, were in effect barred from doing business in the area. Nathaniel Wyeth, an American, launched a fur-trading venture in the Columbia Valley in 1834 but, a few years later, was forced to leave. McLoughlin had undersold him, outbid him, built

Fort Boise to compete with Wyeth's Fort Hall in the Shoshone country, and used his greater influence with the Indians to discourage fur sales to Wyeth—yet McLoughlin and Wyeth were friends. McLoughlin had simply carried out his company's established policy toward "poachers." The Hudson's Bay Company ruled in Old Oregon, and John McLoughlin was czar. Had the question of ownership been decided on the respective merits of the rival Nations' claims, no reasonable doubt exists that England would hold the Oregon country today. Fortunately for the United States, other forces were at work.

About 1834, American missionaries began to appear in the Oregon country, and Dr. McLoughlin advised them to make the Willamette Valley the field of their activities. This seemed to indicate a feeling on the part of England that the Oregon country might have to be divided, with the river as the boundary; but Americans had visions of the Stars and Stripes flying along the coast from California to Alaska; and so the bloodless fight for the Oregon country went on.

When Jason Lee, the missionary, and his party arrived at Fort Vancouver in 1834, the factor helped them establish a mission in the Willamette Valley. Two years later, Marcus Whitman and Henry Spalding and their wives crossed the Rockies and, with McLoughlin's help but against his advice, set up a mission at Waiilatpu, near Fort Walla Walla. In 1839, Father Francois Blanchet and Father Modeste Demers established a Roman Catholic mission at Cowlitz. Lee is quoted as saying there were but 151 Americans in the Oregon country in 1839; but, by 1844, American settlers were as numerous as the British French-Canadians in the Willamette Valley, and other settlers were on the way.

Hudson's Bay Company authority, however fairly it may have been wielded, would not do for the American pioneers. Out of their dissatisfaction grew the establishment, at Champoeg (Champooick) on May 2, 1843, of the Provisional Government of Oregon. Nominally international in character, it was actually the first government established by citizens of the United States west of the Rockies, and lasted until the Oregon Territory was created in 1848, although it was never formally recognized. Its first governor was George Abernethy, elected in 1845; it used the laws of Iowa (the only ones available in book form in the Oregon country at the time); it made wheat legal tender, fixing a bushel at 60 pounds. Theoretically, it ruled the entire Oregon country; in practice, it was supported only by part of the settlers in the Willamette Valley and along the lower Columbia. The Hudson's Bay Company apparently was not opposed to the establishment of the government; and the oath of office read, "I do solemnly swear that I will support the organic laws of the Provisional Government of Oregon insofar as said organic laws are consistent with my duties as a citizen of the United States or subject of Great Britain, and faithfully demean myself in office." Following the massacre at Waiilatpu in 1847, in which Whitman, his wife, and 12 others were killed by Indians, the Provisional Government conducted a successful expedition to arrest members of the guilty Cayuse band.

By 1844, the Oregon question loomed so large in national politics that the slogan "Fifty-four-forty or fight!" helped sweep James K. Polk into the Presidency. Britain, engrossed in European troubles, decided to compromise. The Oregon question was settled on June 15, 1846, by a treaty fixing the line at the 49th parallel, with England retaining Vancouver Island.

Final approval of the bill creating Oregon Territory came on August 13, 1848. Abraham Lincoln was offered the governorship but declined; the choice then fell on General Joseph Lane, who took office at Oregon City on March 2, 1849.

THE TERRITORIAL PERIOD, 1849-1889

Most of the early settlers in Old Oregon made their homes south of the Columbia in the Willamette Valley. After the Treaty of 1846, however, the country north of the river developed rapidly, and by 1851 a thriving frontier village, Olympia, stood at the southern end of Puget Sound. Fort Steilacoom, farther north, housed two companies of Regulars, a mile inland from the busy seaport of Steilacoom. There was also a settlement at Alki Point, within the limits of present Seattle. Port Townsend, on the Olympic Peninsula, was the Sound's most promising seaport. These and other settlements were separated from the Territorial capital at Salem by miles of wilderness road and the broad unbridged Columbia. It was always inconvenient, sometimes impossible, for delegates to the legislature to make the trip. There had been an aggravating tendency on the part of the Provisional Government to slight the needs and wishes of the northern settlers, in its preoccupation with problems nearer home, and to a certain extent its Territorial successor had the same failing. These conditions inspired a movement for division of the Territory, which found expression in public meeting and in the columns of the *Columbian,* the Olympia weekly.

On August 29, 1851, a group of pioneers met at Cowlitz Prairie and framed a memorial to Congress favoring the creation of a separate territory north of the Columbia River. The next year, on October 26, a convention assembled at Monticello and voted another memorial to Congress. Before this reached Washington, D.C., Territorial Delegate Lane, on December 6, introduced a resolution asking Congress to investigate the expedience of dividing Oregon. There was some opposition from Whigs and Republicans, but the Democrats, who were in the majority, favored the idea. At the suggestions of Stanton of Kentucky, the name was changed from Columbia to Washington; Stephen A. Douglas proposed, but did not insist upon, adoption of the name "Washingtonia" in order to avoid possible confusion with the name of the National Capital. On March 2, 1853, President Fillmore signed the bill creating Washington Territory, with an area of 193,071 square miles, including the present State, northern Idaho, and western Montana. Isaac Ingalls Stevens was appointed governor, and on November 28, 1853, Olympia was proclaimed the capital. The white population of the Territory was 3,965.

Lumbering then, as now, was Washington's principal industry. Shipments were made by water, and the sawmills stood at the more accessible ports. Demands created by the California gold rush sent the price of lumber at San Francisco to $200, $300, and even $500 per 1,000 board feet, and the Territory's mills prospered accordingly.

During the winter of 1854-5, many Indian tribes of the Northwest organized and prepared to drive the whites out of the country. Governor Stevens, who was also Superintendent of Indian Affairs, signed treaties with the Indians west of the Cascades and called a council at Walla Walla, which convened May 29, 1855. There were present between five and six thousand Indians, headed by Chiefs Lawyer of the Nez Percé, Weyatenatemany of the Cayuse, Wenapsnoot of the Umatilla, Pio-pio-mox-mox (or Peupeumoxmox) of the Walla Walla, and Kamiakin of the Yakima, and about 60 white men headed by Governor Stevens and Joel Palmer, Superintendent of Indian Affairs for Oregon. At first all the tribes except the Nez Percé were opposed to signing the treaty, because they thought the reservations offered them were small and poor, in comparison with the lands they were asked to give up. Chief Looking Glass, war chief of the Nez Percé, arrived at the conference, after a three-years' absence in the Blackfeet country, too late to prevent signing of the treaty; all but the Yakima had already accepted by that time. Only the intervention of Lawyer prevented a massacre of the whites in the course of the conference, which ended on June 11 with the signing of a treaty. However, the Indians, dissatisfied with the reservations and, according to some historians, angered by the methods used in obtaining signatures to the treaty, began a series of bloody massacres of white settlers in western Washington, when Stevens went into western Montana, then part of Washington Territory, to negotiate other treaties.

War followed, in which many of the "Canoe" tribes of the coastal region remained neutral. The Snoqualmie under Patkanim co-operated with the whites. The "Horse" tribes, east of the mountains, were leaders in the war. Events of the 1855 campaign included the defeat of Major Granville O. Haller and 84 soldiers by a band of Indians in the Simcoe Mountains, and the march of General Gabriel J. Rains and 700 men into the Yakima Valley, where they forced Kamiakin to take to the hills. The 1856 campaign began with an attack by Indians on the village of Seattle, in which they were repulsed, the guns of the sloop-of-war *Decatur* in Elliott Bay playing a decisive part in the engagement. Later in the year, a second expedition into the Yakima Valley inflicted a telling defeat on Kamiakin. By military order, eastern Washington was closed to settlement.

Leschi and Quiemuth, two Nisqually chiefs, met tragic deaths. Quiemuth surrendered in 1856 and, while confined in the Governor's office on the night following his arrest, was murdered by a vengeful settler. Leschi, charged with the murder of noncombatants, was betrayed, twice tried, convicted, and, after a series of delays due to the intervention of lawyers, Army officers, influential Hudson's Bay Company friends, was hanged on February 19, 1858. According to reports of Lieutenant A. V. Kautz and Colonel Granville O. Haller, who participated in the Indian Wars, and in the opinion of Ezra Meeker, Leschi, chief of the Nisqually, was a man of intelligence and character, whose course during the wars was marked by greater humanity than that of any of the other chiefs. Haller says Leschi was found guilty "on the testimony of a perjured man," and Meeker refers to him as "a sacrifice to a principle, a martyr to a cause, and a savior of his people." The treaty with the Nisqually was revised later, and the Indians given a larger and better reservation.

The character and policy of Governor Stevens have been—and were, even in his lifetime—a matter of dispute. It seems generally agreed that he was an honest and intelligent man, of humane intentions, but obstinate and somewhat conceited. The proclamation of martial law in the Territory during the course of the Indian Wars was censured by President

Pierce. Later, Governor Stevens was exonerated. He lost his life while serving in the Union Army during the Civil War.

On May 17, 1858, a band of 1,000 Indians attacked and defeated 150 soldiers under Colonel Steptoe near the site of present Rosalia. The troops retreated to the new military post, Fort Walla Walla. In September a punitive expedition under Colonel George Wright encountered and defeated a force representing a confederation of the Yakima, Spokane, Coeur d'Alene, Nez Percé, and Palouse tribes. The horses of the Indians were rounded up and shot.

By 1859, the Indian treaties had been ratified by Congress. The "Canoe" Indians were for the most part domiciled on reservations by 1864; the "Horse" tribes were similarly settled on the Yakima (1865), Colville (1872), Columbia (1879), Spokane (1881), and Kalispel (1914) reservations.

Coincident with, and a contributing cause of, the Indian wars were discoveries of gold in eastern Washington and British Columbia. In 1857 and 1858, a rush of miners came over the old fur-trader trails into the Okanogan and Fraser River districts. For several decades, strikes and rumors of strikes inspired stampedes into various parts of the Territory. Chiefly because of its strategic position in relation to the area of discovery, Walla Walla, near Fort Walla Walla, became the largest city in the Territory and remained so until overtaken by Seattle about 1880.

Next came the troublesome echo of joint occupation known later as "the Pig War" (*see Tour 8*). England and the United States both claimed the San Juan Islands, and both attempted to collect taxes and customs. English and Americans lived there in a state of constant tension. The situation came to a head in 1859, when a pig belonging to Charles J. Griffin, an Englishman, raided a vegetable garden belonging to Lyman A. Cutler, an American. Cutler shot the pig and threatened similar action against British authorities who might venture to disapprove. Troops of both Nations were sent to the island to protect the rights of their people. Captain George Pickett, who later led the famous charge at Gettysburg, commanded the Americans and distinguished himself by his firmness. In time, the quarrel simmered down to an interchange of parties and banquets between the English and the American garrisons. Emperor William I of Germany, selected to arbitrate the dispute, awarded the San Juan Archipelago to the United States in 1872.

Sentiment in Washington Territory during the Civil War was overwhelmingly pro-Union, and peace prevailed except for a few isolated incidents involving sympathizers with the Confederacy. Ten companies of Washington volunteers manned Pacific Coast Army posts, releasing Regulars for active duty. Residents followed with interest the careers of Grant, Sherman, Sheridan, McClellan, and Pickett, who had served in the Territory, as well as that of former Governor Stevens, who lost his life in the Battle of Chantilly.

The outstanding local event of 1861 was the opening at Seattle of the Territorial University, now the University of Washington.

Oregon became a State in 1859, with its present boundaries, and Washington Territory was enlarged to include all of the original Oregon Territory not incorporated in the new State. By 1861, the eastern part of Washington Territory had begun to rival the western in population, and a movement to divide Washington, with the Cascades as the line of separation, found expression in a bill, which was defeated in the Territorial legislature on January 29, 1861, by a vote of 18 to 12. On March 3, 1863, Congress created the Territory of Idaho, leaving Washington with its present boundaries except for the San Juan decision of 1872. Partly as a result of the attempt to divide the Territory, the movement for statehood began in 1861. The legislature of 1867 submitted a memorial to Congress in favor of statehood. In 1876, a vote of the Territory favored a constitutional convention. This was held in 1878, but Congress refused to heed the plea for statehood.

Communications with the East were immeasurably improved by the completion in 1864 of a transcontinental telegraph line. On September 4, Governor William Pickering sent a message of about 100 words to the President. The reply came two days later: "Gov. Pickering, Olympia, W. T. Your patriotic dispatch of yesterday received and published. A. Lincoln."

Early attempts to facilitate transportation in the Territory included the building of military roads, development of river navigation, and the building of two short, narrow-gauge railroads, one around the Cascades of the Columbia and the other from Wallula to Walla Walla.

On September 8, 1883, a gold-plated spike driven at Deer Lodge, Montana, completed the Northern Pacific to its main western terminal —Portland, Oregon. Previously, 1870-3, the Northern Pacific had built a line from Kalama, on the Columbia, to Tacoma, a new city on Puget Sound. The transcontinental, or main line, was now built across the Cascades. On June 6, 1887, direct main-line communication by this route was established by means of switchbacks and the first train from the East pulled into Tacoma. Stampede Tunnel was completed the next year, 1888.

The movement for statehood was augmented by the disgust with which Washington citizens received news of the apportionment of Federal river and harbor funds on the Pacific Coast between 1860 and 1888. Of $2,156,733, California, a State, received $1,492,428; Oregon, a State, $649,305; Idaho Territory, $10,000; Washington Territory, $5,500. On February 22, 1889, the enabling act by which Washington was permitted to organize as a State was approved by Congress and signed by President Cleveland the same day. This last year of the Territory brought a series of disastrous fires in which Seattle, Ellensburg, Spokane, Vancouver, and other cities suffered severe losses.

STATEHOOD, 1889

In May, 1889, an election was held in Washington Territory to choose 75 delegates to a constitutional convention, which assembled at Olympia on July 4 and began the work of drafting a State constitution. On August 22, seventy-one delegates signed the completed document, and it was approved by the voters on October 1 by a count of 40,152 to 11,789. At the same election, the people rejected amendments establishing woman suffrage and prohibition and elected the State's first public officials.

Elisha P. Ferry, former Territorial Governor, became the State's first chief executive; Charles E. Laughton was elected lieutenant-governor; Allen Weir, secretary of State; William C. Jones, attorney general; and John L. Wilson was sent to Congress as Representative. All were Republicans. The same party won control of the State legislature, which met and elected John B. Allen of Walla Walla, former Territorial Delegate, and Watson B. Squire of Seattle, former Territorial Governor, as the State's first United States Senators. President Benjamin Harrison proclaimed Washington a State on November 11, 1889, and a week later Governor Ferry took the oath of office at Olympia.

The population of the new State was 357,232, an increase of 375 per cent since 1880. The rapid growth was traceable to the coming of the railroad. In 1893, the Great Northern was completed, giving the State its second transcontinental railway system. Among the industries, fishing, mining, and shipbuilding had developed swiftly during the Territorial period, while lumbering and agriculture had made steady progress.

Washington State College was opened at Pullman in 1892, and

State normal schools were established, at Cheney and Ellensburg in 1890 and at Bellingham in 1893.

The Republican party retained control of the State in the elections of 1892; John H. McGraw succeeded Ferry as governor. Ferry's administration had been marked by extravagance; McGraw's was distinguished by attempts at retrenchment. The panic of 1893 contributed heavily to unrest among the voters, who laid their grievances at the door of the party in power. In 1896, the Fusionists—Populists, Democrats, "Silver Republicans"—won a sweeping victory. John R. Rogers became Governor; W. C. Jones and James Hamilton Lewis were elected Representatives to Congress; and a Fusionist legislature sent George Turner to the United States Senate.

In 1898, the Republicans regained many seats in the legislature and sent Wesley L. Jones and Francis W. Cushman to Congress. By 1900, the Republicans were able to make a clean sweep of all contested offices save one. Governor Rogers, re-elected, died shortly after taking office and was succeeded by Lieutenant Governor Henry McBride, a Republican.

Economic conditions in Washington were greatly improved by the discovery of gold in Alaska in 1897. Seattle became the port of embarkation for the thousands who rushed to the Yukon and the Klondike; it was their outfitting station, their source of supplies, and, on their return, their port of entry. The result was a boom for the whole State.

The Spanish-American War drew from Washington 1,332 men and 46 officers; 25 men were killed and 703 were wounded. The "First Washington," a volunter regiment, distinguished itself in action and was warmly commended by ranking Army officers.

The decade 1890-1900 witnessed progress in the reclamation of semiarid lands in eastern Washington. The "apple fever" dominated the Wenatchee Valley and near-by districts; thousands of acres of orchards were set out, marking the beginning of what is today one of the State's best-known industries. In 1902, the Federal Government authorized irrigation projects in the Yakima and Okanogan Valleys.

The population in 1900 was 518,103, of whom 76,365 were foreign-born whites; about 97 per cent of the foreign-born were English-speaking peoples, Germans, and Scandinavians. Chinese, barred by Federal Exclusion Acts of 1881 and 1888, were further discouraged by anti-Chinese riots and demonstrations in the middle eighties. A subsequent wave of Japanese immigration was halted by Federal legislation.

The rise of the labor movement led to the creation in 1905 of a State

Bureau of Labor. As the problems incident to expansion of railroad systems became more numerous and complex, the need of a State executive department to cope with them was recognized, and the 1905 legislature created the State Railroad Commission. The same body set up the State Tax Commission, with a board of equalization to hear the controversies in tax disputes.

The Union Pacific and the Chicago, Milwaukee & St. Paul railway systems reached Puget Sound in 1909. The State then had four transcontinental systems; and the ports of Puget Sound were gateways through which passed a tremendous volume of world trade. The Alaska-Yukon-Pacific Exposition, held in Seattle in 1909, brought to national attention the growth of the State.

Progressive legislation marked the opening years of the twentieth century. The State legislature enacted the direct primary law (1907), woman suffrage (1909), and the initiative, referendum, and recall laws (1911). The 1911 legislature also enacted an eight-hour-day law for women workers, a pure food and drug act, which entailed the creation of a State Food Commission, and industrial insurance laws.

The population in 1910 was 1,141,990, an increase of 120 per cent since 1900. Development of the rich farming districts of eastern Washington was reflected in the swift growth of its cities—Spokane, Pasco, Ellensburg, Yakima, Walla Walla, and Wenatchee.

Three Republican governors, all supported by Republican legislatures, followed McBride. Albert E. Mead was elected in 1904. Samuel G. Cosgrove served as Governor for one day, then was granted leave to go to California for his health; there he died. Lieutenant Governor Marion E. Hay, who had performed the duties during the time of Cosgrove's incapacity, became Governor.

Ernest Lister, a Democrat, nominated by the direct primary early in 1912, fought a long legal battle to establish his candidacy and went on to win against divided Republican opposition in the fall elections. Republicans and "Bull Moosers" held control of the legislature and of many State offices. During Lister's first term, a widow's-pension law and minimum-wage laws for women were enacted, and the initiative and referendum laws improved. In 1914, State-wide prohibition was approved by referendum. Lister, re-elected in 1916, died in office in 1919, and Louis F. Hart, Republican Lieutenant Governor, finished Lister's term and, in 1920, was elected Governor.

With the entry of the United States into the World War, the shipyards of Puget Sound, the lumber industry, the wheat belt of eastern

Washington, and the State in general were launched on a period of prosperity unequalled before or since. Camp Lewis (now Fort Lewis), Puget Sound Navy Yard, and other military centers hummed with wartime activity. Washington is closely associated with the famous 91st (Wild West) Division, which, although composed of men from many of the Western States, was trained at Camp Lewis. In all, Washington furnished to the various service branches 67,694 men and 632 women, of whom 1,622 men and 3 women lost their lives.

On March 5, 1923, a State flag was officially adopted. The law requires that the emblem be of "dark green silk or bunting, and shall bear in its center a reproduction of the Seal of the State of Washington, embroidered, printed, painted, or stamped therein." The State flower is the Western variety of rhododendron, which grows abundantly on the Olympic Peninsula. The State song, "Washington Beloved," was adopted by the legislature of 1909.

Problems arising from changing economic and social conditions have been placed under newly created executive departments. Eighteen departments, divisions, and bureaus were set up between 1907 and 1922, chief among them being the Public Service Commission, Department of Public Works, Department of Business Control, State Highway Commission, Department of Conservation and Development, and State Parole Board.

Roland H. Hartley, Republican, elected Governor in 1924, was the first governor of the State to complete two full terms in office. His administrations were marked by improvements in the State highway system, the work being financed by a tax on gasoline.

A law permitting the people of any city or county in the State to establish by ballot a water-power utility district within their community was enacted by initiative on November 4, 1930, and proclaimed on December 3. The districts thus established may buy or sell power within or without their limits. They have the right of eminent domain and may purchase, condemn, or lease property necessary to their purposes. The affairs of each district are conducted by a board of three commissioners elected by the district's voters.

In the 1932 election, there was a Democratic landslide. The only Republican remaining in the State administration was Noah D. Showalter, Superintendent of Public Instruction. Clarence D. Martin became Governor, and Victor A. Meyers, Lieutenant Governor. Democrats were in the majority in both houses of the legislature, and all seats in the Congressional delegation were given to Democrats. Similar results attended the elections of 1936; Martin and Meyers were re-elected, the latter receiving the largest number of votes ever given any candidate for office in the history of the State. Democrats won all offices in 1940, with the exception of the governorship, which went by a small majority to Arthur B. Langlie, Republican.

After repeal of the State prohibition law by initiative in 1932 and the repeal of Federal prohibition laws the year following, a State Liquor Control Board was created to supervise all phases of the traffic in alcoholic beverages in Washington. It operates State-owned stores for the distribution of liquor and controls the licensing and operation of privately owned retail establishments selling beer and wine.

The 1933 legislature passed a law granting pensions, fixed at a minimum of $30 per month, to persons of 65 or more years of age who qualify for assistance. At the same session a tax of 2 per cent was imposed on retail transactions, with dairy products, bread, fresh vegetables, and fruit, and certain other commodities exempted; later, in 1939, the exemptions were removed from all foodstuffs. The consumer pays the tax and the retailer collects it.

Following the lead of the Federal Government in its enactment of the Securities and Exchange Law, the legislature added to the State's "blue sky" laws another statute, concerned with the promotion and development of mineral resources. In the same year, laws were passed providing for the licensing of real estate agencies.

Since 1932, State and Federal Governments have co-operated in the fight against depression and its consequences. Closely following the pattern of national security legislation, the legislature of 1937 created a State Department of Social Security to assume the functions of the old Department of Public Welfare and to co-ordinate the work of all State agencies in relief, rehabilitation, and re-employment. Through this department, the State co-operates with United States agencies and distributes Federal funds along with its own.

In recent years, protection of the public health has been stressed in the enactment of laws requiring health certification of persons handling foodstuffs and those engaged in personal service, such as beauticians and barbers. The workmen's compensation and insurance act, which originated at the beginning of the century, also received legislative attention resulting in many improvements of the original measure.

As might be expected in a period of economic stress, organized labor brought pressure to bear on both employer and legislative groups. In 1933, a mass procession of unemployed converged on the Capitol and urged an immediate appropriation for the relief of unemployment. In 1934, a maritime strike tied up Seattle's water front for more than two months; and, in 1936, a second and more widespread strike involved Washington maritime workers. In 1936, also, the Seattle chapter of the American Newspaper Guild conducted an eventful strike on the *Post Intelligencer* (*see Labor*).

Early in the thirties, the theory of technocracy attracted many followers and locally attained the proportions of an organized movement. After the disintegration of this loosely formed organization, in 1934, there arose a number of groups advocating old-age pensions, production-for-use, social credit, and other social theories; the youth movement also developed. In 1935, several of these groups, joined by labor unions and Democratic clubs, united as the Washington Commonwealth Federation. Outgrowing the several persuasions that gave it birth, the federation became a delegate body pressing for social reform.

The construction of large municipal plants at Seattle and Tacoma, together with the huge blocks of power to be released by Grand Coulee Dam (completed 1941) and Bonneville Dam (completed 1937), on the Columbia River, were, and still are, the subject of State-wide controversy concerning the relative merits of public versus private power control; and the setting up of public utility districts has been quite as vigorously opposed and supported.

The completion of these dams, however, with their reservoirs of cheap electrical power for industry and water for irrigation, is significant of the shift that is taking place in the State's economy. The traditionally dominant lumber industry, faced by receding forests, uncertain markets, and the necessity for conservation, is tending toward a policy of "sustained yield." This new program is based on the possibility of maintaining, through reforestation and conservation measures, a continuous supply of selected woods for special purposes in different fields—wood pulps, plywoods, and other products into which the wood cell may be resolved by chemical and technological processes. The lumber industry looks forward to planned production on a more stable basis than during the booms and slumps of the past.

Wholesale power production and the vast extension of irrigated lands also change the prospects for agriculture. An area of many thousand acres in eastern Washington, potentially one of the most fertile in the West, awaits the life-giving touch of water, which is to be dammed behind the great concrete barrier at Grand Coulee, then pumped and stored in a balancing reservoir in Grand Coulee itself. A plan is being promoted for releasing tremendous flows of electrical energy, from a series of linked generating plants, into a common pool of power. Opinion as to the possible results of such an operation ranges from claims that it would have but little effect on an already saturated market to prophecies that the State will become an electrified wonderland of industrial and domestic felicity. Beyond the certainty that industry generally will be stimulated by ready floods of power at cheaper rates, the most interesting possibilities seem to lie in the proposed development of Washington's mineral resources. Concerning this also there are several schools of thought. It is, however, certain that in these two fields of production—power and agriculture—eastern Washington will experience tremendous development in the future.

Washington celebrated the year 1939 as its Golden Jubilee, the fiftieth anniversary of its statehood, and 30 years after its World's Fair of 1909, the Alaska-Yukon-Pacific Exposition. To the north, a new empire is building in Alaska, and Washington, its nearest home port, will inevitably share in its upbuilding. To the west, although strife in the Orient at present has dislocated transoceanic trade, Washington, as the closest American port, possesses great natural advantages for commerce with the Orient. The effect of this interchange of commerce and of culture has been marked in the past, and probably will be increasingly apparent in the future of the State.

GOVERNMENT

The constitution now in effect in the State of Washington is substantially the same as that adopted by the voters of Washington Territory in 1889.

Elective officers of the executive branch include a governor, lieutenant governor, and seven departmental heads. Executives appointed by the governor number 11. All these officers are elected or appointed for four-year terms. The governor has the powers of veto and pardon and may call extraordinary sessions of the legislature. The lieutenant governor presides over the senate and fills the office of governor in event of the latter's death, disability, or absence from the State.

The State is divided into 46 legislative districts, each of which elects from one to three representatives, depending on population, and one senator. The number of senators must be no more than one-half, nor less than one-third, of the number of representatives. Senatorial terms are staggered in order that there may never be an entirely new body. The legislature may override a gubernatorial veto by a two-thirds vote of both houses.

The judiciary consists of a supreme court of nine members elected for six years from the State at large, the terms being staggered; a superior court of one or more judges elected for four years in each county, having as many departments as the pressure of litigation may warrant; justices of the peace in rural precincts; such other courts as the legislature may provide. Candidates for judicial positions do not declare party affiliations.

Each of the State's 39 counties is governed in local matters by a commission of three members elected for terms of four years and wielding limited executive and legislative powers. The commission is supplemented by the sheriff, an elective officer with police powers, and by minor officers.

The State's 221 municipal corporations are divided according to population into four classes: first class, 20,000 or more; second class, 10,000 to 20,000; third class, 1,500 to 10,000; fourth class, 300 to 1,500.

Cities of the first class are established through a charter drawn up by 15 landholders selected by a vote of the community. If the charter is acceptable to the people and complies with State law, the city government is set up in accordance with its provisions. First-class cities may choose whatever form of government they wish; but municipalities choosing the commission form are subject to the laws governing second-class cities.

Second-class cities may choose between two forms: mayor-council type (mayor and councilmen elected for terms of two years) or commission type (three commissioners, one of whom serves as mayor, elected for terms of three years). Third-class cities of less than 2,500 population are limited to the mayor-council type; those with more than 2,500 are permitted the same choice allowed second-class cities. Towns (fourth-class) are limited to a variation of the mayor-council type, in which mayor and council of five are elected for five-year terms. The city-manager type is permitted first-class cities by State law, but it has never been tried in Washington.

The State has 7 first-class cities, of which 3 use the mayor-council and 4 the commission type; 8 cities of the second class, of which 2 employ the commission type; 50 cities of the third class, 41 of them governed by mayor and council; and 156 cities of the fourth class, usually denominated towns or villages. The division known as the township is not common as a political entity; it is confined to the surveyor's usage.

Transportation

OVER routes, of which some were considered impassable a century ago, four railroads, two transcontinental bus lines, and five national highways connect Washington with the rest of the country and Canada. Planes of three air lines fly to points north, south, and east, while on rivers, lakes, and bays half a hundred ferries serve shoreside towns. From the many ports along the coast and on Puget Sound, 81 steamship lines, with an average of 62 sailings weekly, keep the State in touch with approximately 250 world ports.

Change in transportational methods within the State has been swift. Prior to 1850, water travel was dependent on the canoe and bateau, flatboat, or sailing ships; travel on land was on horseback or by cumbersome oxcart or covered wagon. Between 1850 and 1870, the river steamboat and the stagecoach had their brief colorful day. Following the gold rush in California, steam-driven vessels came to Washington ports to load lumber and piling—which were at a premium in San Francisco—booming settlement and the construction of sawmills along the watercourse. On the Columbia River, the number of steamboats increased to carry the many gold seekers who took that route to the interior.

Along the Columbia were such steamboats as the *Jason P. Flint, Mountain Bird, Wasco,* and *Carrie Ladd,* part of the Oregon Steam Navigation Company's imposing line, now a memory. The mention of the name Johnson's Landing, The Dalles, and Wallula evokes the stirring story of the days when a vast new country was being pioneered and settled.

Co-existent with the river steamboats and the stagecoaches were numerous river ferries, which in the late fifties and early sixties reaped handsome profits at the main crossings of unfordable rivers. Tolls were fixed by the legislature. Typical were those granted to J. T. Hicklin for the operation of a ferry below the mouth of the Wenas River on the Yakima—$2 for a wagon drawn by two animals; $1.50 for a sulky or hack, one horse; 75c for man and horse; 50c for a packed animal;

25c for a man afoot; 25c each for loose horses or cattle; 8c each for goats, sheep, or pigs.

On Puget Sound, sailing vessels were the first means of water transportation. The first American steamer on the Sound was the *Fairy,* a small side-wheeler put in service in 1853. In 1854 the steamboat *Major Tompkins* came north to serve the growing villages and towns along the Sound with weekly mail service. The famous *Elisa Anderson,* built in Portland in 1859, with its steam calliope, was brought north and served the Sound ports for 40 years; in 1871, the old *North Pacific* arrived from San Francisco to ply Puget Sound waters for 30 years.

On the rivers, such as the Duwamish and Snohomish, the tiny sternwheelers *Black Diamond, Comet,* and *Wenat* operated as far as 40 miles upstream, transporting settlers, freight and mail.

Around the Cascades and Celilo Falls, virtually unnavigable waters, portages were necessary. Along the north side of the river, the first tiny railroad in the State was laid in 1851—a wooden-railed affair owned by Bradford & Company, over whose mile and a half of track a flatcar hauled by two mules transported the pioneers and their chattels. At either end of this portage, veterans of Mississippi steamboating and younger men from the Willamette fought for fares and freight. On the banks of the river, fuel cutters brawled and stole each other's wood. Steamboat fares varied with the tide and the weather.

Another tram line was built on the north side of the river around the entire portage and several steamboat landings. Boat captains, failing to beat this new competition, sought a merger in 1860. Overnight the tide of gold seekers swung northward from the California fields; 100,000 persons pushed through the area on their way to the strikes at Boise City, Oro Fino, Clearwater, Powder River, and Coeur d'Alene. In 1863 the Cascades Railroad Company replaced the Bradford tram with a six-mile line of five-foot gauge and put on the first steam locomotive in the State. By 1870 boats above Celilo Falls plied the Columbia and its tributaries as far north as Revelstoke, British Columbia, and as far east as Lewiston, Idaho Territory. Monopolizing transport during 1860-70, when this region produced $140,000,000 in gold, the company reaped a fortune. The little boat *Tenino* is said to have cleared $18,000 on a single trip.

Between the mines and Walla Walla, the principal outfitting center, and Wallula on the Columbia, stage lines began operations—the Ben Holladay lines, Wells-Fargo, and the Northwestern Stage Company, connecting with the Central Pacific Railroad at Kelton, Utah. It was a day of quick fortunes and quick bankruptcy—of road agents, gamblers, and "Lady Lils"; of shoot first and question afterward.

Conditions west of the Cascades were more stable. Although the Oregon Provisional Government had established haphazard mail service in 1845, and had authorized the "viewing" of roads—which meant merely marking routes—travel remained difficult; one almost impassable road led from Warbassport on the Cowlitz to Olympia on Puget Sound. In 1853 a former Indian trail over the Cascades was opened between Walla Walla and Fort Steilacoom; but stage service between Olympia and the Columbia River extended only as far south as Arkansas Creek in 1857. The next year the road was improved to Monticello; the steamer *Cowlitz,* owned by H. D. Huntington, Charles Holman, and Cliff Olsen, operated to Portland, and through stage service began. As many as six horses were required to haul stages through the ooze and mire, over stones, stumps, and logs encountered on this early road. Passengers often found it necessary to put their shoulders to the wheels. Prior to the coming of the railroad this route was the only link, except by sea, between Puget Sound and the Columbia.

Completing the Union-Central Pacific to California in 1863, railroad builders cast a speculative eye toward the Northwest. The small Oregon Steam Navigation Company on the Columbia River and the gold rushes to the Northwest demonstrated to "empire builders" that this new, raw land was well worth railroading into. They knew the first to reach the Pacific Northwest would control a vast wealth.

By 1870 steamboating had expanded to its limit, and though supplemented by the stage lines, it could not handle the traffic of the new frontier. Untouched timber, wheatlands, and minerals lay waiting. The next two decades were a period of waiting for the railroad, which, chartered in 1864, was said to be slowly creeping across the Plains by the northern route. Many towns started lines of their own, hoping to connect with something—anything to get a chance at the markets of the East. In 1873 the Kalama-to-Tacoma line was completed; between 1872-75 Dr. D. S. Baker constructed his narrow-gauge "rawhide line" between Walla Walla and Wallula on the Columbia; Seattle began the Seattle-Walla Walla line, ran it 20 miles, then gave up, lacking funds. Through the late seventies and early eighties, towns and cities fought for railroad connections, offering bonuses of land and gold, using political influence; and when these failed, they moved all but their streets to the nearest junction of the completed end of the railroad.

The Northern Pacific spent two anxious decades in reaching the

Pacific. Started at the Great Lakes in the East, construction by various firms lagged dismally during the uncertain days of the Civil War; the project also suffered from inability to sell stock to foreign nations during the Franco-Prussian War. Finally its financial backer, Jay Cooke's company, failed during the depression of 1873. Despite the financial difficulties and the political machinations of groups trying to gain control of the road, construction slowly proceeded, culminating in the driving of a silver spike at Gold Creek, Montana, on September 8, 1883, completing the line. When the ends of the Northern Pacific were connected, tapping the vast wealth of the Territory, other railroads jerked political strings to gain rights-of-way. By 1900 the tentacles of railroads were creeping up every fertile valley, seeking the farm, mine, and forest lands, bringing immigrants. The Great Northern came in 1893 under the guiding hand of Jim Hill, king of the "empire builders," who visioned a world traffic with the Orient. In 1909 the Chicago, Milwaukee and St. Paul arrived, via Spokane, at Tacoma and Seattle; in 1908 the Spokane, Portland and Seattle built from Spokane to Portland. From these main lines many branch lines extended into every valley, facilitating development of vast wheat areas, timberlands, mineral deposits, and the scenic areas of the Cascades and the Columbia River. The four railroad systems that service the State have 5,438 miles of track.

An outstanding event in recent railroad history was the completion of the Cascade Mountain tunnel of the Great Northern between Scenic and Berne, the longest railway tunnel in the Americas and one of the longest in the world. This project includes the new tunnel, approximately 8 miles long, and 34 miles of high-speed trackage replacing 43 miles of winding and precipitous mountain line. Tracklaying began on Christmas Day in 1925, and the whole project, costing $25,000,000, was completed in January 1929.

With the arrival of the railroads in the eighties, competition between the many independent ship operators and the lines operated by the railroads was keen. Rate wars, constant schedule enlargements, and superior capital finally resulted in the absorption of the independent group. These amalgamations laid the foundation for some of the modern lines.

The first regular steamship service with San Francisco was started in 1867 on a monthly schedule. In 1886 regular service with Alaska was established, and the *Ancon,* first steamer, brought some $35,000 in gold; the Alaska Steamship Company was formed in 1895. The Northern Pacific Railroad placed the *Phra Nang* in service with the Orient from Tacoma in 1891. The *Miike Maru,* first transpacific steamship from the Orient, arrived on Puget Sound from Japan in 1896. From then the ports of the world lay open to steamship service out of Puget Sound. The Klondike gold rush of 1897-8 made Seattle the outfitting point for Alaska and transformed it from a lumber camp to a sizable commercial center. The opening of the Panama Canal in 1914 further stimulated coastwise trade.

Following the covered wagon, the democrat wagon, the buggy, and the hack, the automobile arrived in 1900, confounding the conservative with its 8- and 12-mile an hour speed. As the automobile proved no ephemeral freak, highways became the paramount problem, for improved Indian trails were difficult for the new vehicles to negotiate. Dirt roads were built, then macadam, later, concrete. With Federal aid, beginning in 1916, highways branched out to every county seat, and over these highways the farmers chugged to market. Later they found it more profitable to stay on the farm and ship by motor freight. Motor busses came, connecting the smaller towns with the railroads and the larger cities; then airplanes, connecting the larger cities with the rest of the Nation.

From the year 1889, when Washington became a State, until 1905, when the State Highway Department was formed, only $131,800 was expended for the development of so-called "county roads." Constructed under the direction of appointed commissions, the roads were little better than the old military trails of earlier times. Until 1913 only a few roads —known as "aid roads," because the counties were required to match the State appropriation for this purpose—were constructed. The common idea of a State road in those days was one that led off into the mountains and ended there. Then a plan for interconnecting roads was adopted, and Washington was able to take advantage of the benefits offered by the Federal Aid Road Act of 1916. In the main the system then devised forms the nucleus of the present State highway system. The roads and highways of the State, 43,881 miles in extent, cover many of the old trails, routes, and mountain passes. The State Highway Patrol numbers 250, and a personnel of approximately 1,420 persons are employed in the maintenance of 6,012 miles of primary and secondary highways.

With the coming of the automobile and better roads, the motor bus superseded the stagecoach. A number of lines started operating almost simultaneously, and a dozen men claim to have been the first bus driver in the State. Twenty years ago anyone could purchase a hack and set up in business. Service was commonly erratic and unreliable until the legislature, in 1921, passed laws requiring stages to obtain operating licenses and laid down certain requirements to assure regularity, safety, and a common rate. Companies were formed in nearly every locality to connect feeder-lines with systems of transcontinental service. Independent lines have brought about closely knit intercommunication within the State, ending the isolation of districts inaccessible by railroads. Today (1941) more than 500 common carriers cover routes over 5,000 miles of highway.

A little slower in development was motor-truck freight service; but of approximately 65,000 trucks in Washington in 1939, two-thirds were used in freight hauling. With truck farming, fruit raising, and dairying carried on extensively, truck transport, which offers refrigeration facilities in transit, is of vital importance in maintaining city markets.

The history of air operations is as spectacular as it is brief. A pioneer of the air lanes, Edward Hubbard, opened the first international mail service between the United States and Canada. Starting the service on October 15, 1920, he carried mail from Seattle to Victoria, connecting there with the transpacific mail ships. The first regularly scheduled air-mail service, operated by the Varney Air Lines between Pasco, Washington, and Elko, Nevada, started on April 6, 1926. Another factor that helped to establish air service on a firm basis was the Boeing Aircraft Company, in Seattle, which, since 1916, has been expanding its properties and building an impressive line of commercial and combat ships.

The State now has about 50 air fields, including 22 municipal and commercial, 4 Army and 1 Navy, 12 emergency landing fields, 7 intermediate fields, 6 seaplane bases. The main routes of the air lines, which make regular stops at Seattle, Spokane, Wenatchee, Tacoma, Walla Walla, and Pasco, are well equipped with beacon lights, radio directional beams, and weather reporting service.

Agriculture

PUSHED into the background by the more glamorous fur trade, and then by lumbering and mining booms, agriculture in Washington was negligible until the early sixties. Attempts at farming by the Hudson's Bay Company at Fort Vancouver in 1825 and near Fort Nesqually after 1833 were directed only toward immediate needs. Also significant was Marcus Whitman's first garden planted at Waiilatpu in 1837.

The territory was seemingly unsuitable for large-scale agriculture. Forests lay on the west side of the Cascade Mountains and arroyos and scablands on the east—dissimilar regions that produced two distinct types of farming when agriculture was finally recognized as a stable, profitable activity in itself.

The end of the Indian wars in 1858 and the discovery of gold in the northeastern districts of Washington Territory were followed by the lifting of the military ban on the regions north of the Snake and Walla Walla Rivers. Fort Walla Walla had been established near the site of the present city, guaranteeing a measure of protection. Thousands trekked into the area. Prairie schooners, 3 in tandem and drawn by 20-mule teams, could not bring supplies into the region fast enough: flour sold at times for $1 a pound, and table board ranged from $5 to $10 a day. The premium on food, as well as the bunchgrass lands along the Snake River and in the Columbia Basin, attracted cattlemen, sheep ranchers, and farmers.

Between 1860 and 1880, cattle and sheep raising dominated agriculture east of the Cascades, although 4,782 bushels of wheat, 4,515 bushels of oats, and some corn and barley were produced in 1863. There were 327,811 head of cattle in this Territory in 1860 and sheep were almost as numerous. Despite the freezing weather from December 1866 to March 1867, which littered the plains with starved and frozen cattle, S. M. Wait drove 5,000 head of sheep up from Umatilla in 1869. Others included the so-called "native," California stock bred to Merinos,

Merinos from Vermont, the Southdown, Leicester, and Cotswold breeds. Cattle were largely of longhorn stock.

The great freeze emphasized the need for crops and forage, bringing hundreds of farmers to the "forty-bushel" land. Soon broad wheat farms, supplemented by staple crops of potatoes, corn, and apples, appeared. Yet the increase from 1,330 farms in 1860 to almost three times this number in 1870 was made in the face of many obstacles. The heavy rootage of bunchgrass necessitated ploughing the land a year in advance, in order that the roots might decay and the arid land, lying fallow, might store up moisture for the growing period. Flax aided in breaking up the roots and early became an important crop. For ploughing, the farmer had only his back, his "foot-burner" (as the old-fashioned shallow plough was called), and his mules and oxen. Fence wood was scarce; barbed wire was unknown; most of the land was held by pre-emption, homesteaded, or first occupation rights only. Sheep and cattle ranged the public domain. The enmity between the cattlemen and sheep ranchers was often redirected against the farmer; both resisted the steady influx of ranchers who purchased the land for agriculture. Yet the farmer built dirt or sod fences and doggedly persisted.

In 1867 fifteen barrels of flour went from Walla Walla to Portland. Within a fortnight after this trial venture, 5,000 barrels were shipped, indicating a good market and foreshadowing the growing importance of wheat. The Farmers' Co-operative Company, dedicated to collective irrigation efforts in the Yakima Valley, was organized in 1868. By 1870 wheat production increased to 190,256 bushels; truck crops were valued at $74,462, and orchard crops at $71,863.

The farms gave rise to numerous mills along the streams, industries that became the nuclei of such towns as Waitsburg, Dayton, Pomeroy, Ritzville, and even Spokane Falls. There were 23 gristmills in the Territory in 1872, of which 7, with a capacity of 270 bushels daily, were in Walla Walla.

Vital factors in eastern Washington's agriculture during the seventies were the building of the Walla Walla-Wallula Railroad by Dr. D. S. Baker between 1872-5—a line that opened the wheat lands to export—and the organization of the first local Grange in 1873. In 1878 Dr. Baker chartered the vessel *Alice D. Cooper* and shipped 68,000 bushels of wheat to England at a profit of $68,867.75.

The potential production of the fertile plateaus of the Walla Walla, Snake, and Palouse River valleys attracted the railroads, and during the eighties railroad building and land promotion led to the rise of many towns. These near-by markets brought about expansion and diversification; wheat continued to lead, but other crops, including fruits and vegetables, dairying, and beef cattle and poultry raising, were developed. The success of these, however, was contingent upon irrigation. By 1890, though irrigation was still in the experimental stage (only one farmer out of ten irrigated his lands), 48,799 acres had received water, indicating a new trend.

Changes came rapidly. Towns and sections were boomed by irrigation companies. Some failed. Then, in 1905, the Federal Government took over the Sunnyside Project, the first of several that vitally affected the region in the decades following. With irrigation, horticulture became a specialized field in itself—one that began to compete with wheat.

West of the Cascades, agriculture developed more slowly. Lumber found such a premium at San Francisco and in foreign markets that agriculture was relegated to the background, until the rise of populated commercial towns lent impetus to small farming after 1890. Fruit, berry, and poultry farms gradually occupied the cutover benchlands; dairying established itself in the low moist valleys. The urban centers and the relatively small areas available for cultivation resulted in numerous small, intensively worked truck farms.

The railroads, heavy immigration, and increasing urban development throughout the State had a salutary effect upon agriculture after the turn of the century. From 1900 to 1910 farms increased from 33,202 to 56,192; the years from 1910 to 1920 showed a gain of almost 18 per cent; and from 1920 to 1930, when many farms were abandoned, of 5 per cent. From 1930 and 1935, there was an increase of 13,477 farms, bringing the total to 84,381. During recent years the farm population of Washington has continued to increase, a large proportion of the new farm residents coming from the drought-stricken areas of the Great Plains. Of the State's 42,775,040 acres, more than one-third was given over to farming in 1935.

Washington is noted for its fruit, wheat, dairy and poultry products, berries, nuts, and potatoes. Annually, 2,000,000 acres in the Palouse, Big Bend, Horse Heaven, and Walla Walla regions of eastern Washington produce an average of 40,000,000 bushels of wheat. Washington's white (club) varieties are well known, the State product approximating one-third of the Nation's crop. The average wheat yield is 19.3 bushels per acre. In western Washington, the grains produced are used mainly for feed purposes. Oat production has reached a very high level in the alluvial flats of Snohomish, Skagit, and Whatcom Counties;

there, 50 to 100 bushels to the acre indicate the high average, while Skagit has set a mark of 175 bushels to the acre. Whidbey Island, one of the State's small wheat regions, has a record production as high as 117 bushels to the acre.

Washington produces annually about one-third of the Nation's apple crop, and 75 per cent of this is produced around the junctions of the Wenatchee and the Yakima Rivers with the Columbia. These districts also contribute largely to the total quantity of pears and peaches produced in the State.

Along the base of the Cascade Mountains and in the highlands of the Okanogan, Snake, Yakima, and Spokane valleys, where dry farming is impracticable, there are extensive cattle and sheep ranches. There were 327,000 head of beef cattle, largely within these regions, in 1935, breeds including the Aberdeen-Angus, Galloway, Hereford, and Shorthorn. Other livestock on farms (exclusive of dairy cows) comprised 172,155 horses and colts, 752,000 head of sheep, and 20,000 mules. The Belgian and the Percheron horses are the most favored. The breeding of thoroughbred horses has been stimulated since horse racing became legal in 1932. Until 1935, when 73,301 hogs were marketed, half the hogs used commercially in Washington were imported; local production has since become commercially stabilized.

Large-scale dairying is centered in the western Washington counties, Whatcom, Pierce, King, Clark, Snohomish, Skagit, and Lewis, where the lowlands provide green pasture the year round; the foremost dairy counties of eastern Washington are Yakima, Spokane, and Stevens. The Carnation Farms in King County (*see Tour 1b*), with the largest herd of registered Holsteins in the world, have raised the standard of breeding stock throughout the State. Carnation Ormsby Butter King, a member of this herd, in 1935 produced an average of more than 50 quarts of milk per day, not only bringing back to the United States a world's record that had been held by Canada for 10 years, but also combining with it a record for butterfat—a feat unequalled in 30 years.

Rapid development has occurred in the poultry industry during the last two decades, particularly in western Washington, where mild winters and relatively low feed costs are favorable factors. Since 1917, when 160 carloads of eggs were imported from the East to meet western Washington demands, the industry has increased 300 per cent. Washington produced 780,000,000 eggs in 1935; shipments were valued at $3,944,000. That year there were 7,080,000 chickens on Washington farms.

Certain areas of the State are noted for specialized crops. The berry lands around Puyallup and Sumner, in Pierce County, are among the finest in the world and produce approximately one-fifth of the raspberries and blackberries grown in the United States. The loganberry was developed in this district. Extensive cranberry fields are cultivated in the boglands of Grays Harbor and Pacific Counties. Clark County annually produces from 10 to 15 million pounds of prunes and 25 per cent of the Nation's filbert crop.

Whatcom and Skagit Counties produce sugar beets, and much of the cabbage, turnip, beet, and cauliflower seed used in the United States. The Palouse region of Whitman County is Washington's heaviest producer of dry field peas. Of the 1935 yield approximately 49 per cent of the Nation's output was raised in that area.

Specialized truck farms are found near the urban centers—Seattle, Tacoma, Spokane, Walla Walla, Pasco, Kennewick, and Yakima; the later four, with especially long growing periods, produce some of the earliest fresh vegetables in the State. Lettuce, rhubarb, asparagus, strawberries, cantaloupes, onions, and celery are a few of the products composing the 70,000 carloads of produce grown annually in these vicinities. In conjunction with the truck farms are many of the largest hothouses in Washington, some covering thousands of square feet.

Bulb raising is an important branch of agriculture. Sixty million bulbs are planted annually at Lynden, Orting, Sumner, and Kelso—one of the largest plantings in the United States. It is estimated that Whatcom, Pierce, and Thurston Counties produce one-third of the daffodils grown in the country.

The State's total farm acreage has increased steadily in recent years, yet there has been a decline in the average size of farms—from an average of 275 acres in 1860 to 174 in 1935. The total value of farm products in 1935 was four times that of 1900, but only a little more than half of that of 1920. Leading crops in 1937 were: wheat, 48,725,000 bushels; apples, 30,340,000 bushels; prunes, 28,800,000 pounds; hay, 1,735,000 tons; pears, 5,694,000 bushels; potatoes, 9,400,000 bushels; oats, 8,060,000 bushels; and dry field peas, 1,858,000 hundred-weight. The 1937 fruit crop was valued at $33,981,000; truck crops at $5,678,000; general field crops at $70,871,000; and livestock and livestock products at $64,875,000.

Aiding in the development of agriculture in Washington have been the local bureaus of the United States Department of Agriculture, the Washington State Agricultural College at Pullman, with experimental stations at Lind, Long Beach, Prosser, and Puyallup; the State Department of Agriculture, the Agricultural Advisory Committee of the Washington State Planning Council, and various commercial agencies. The State has a strong 4-H membership. According to recent figures, there are 490 local Granges with a membership of 71,000; the Washington Co-operative Egg and Poultrymen's Association has a membership of 22,000; and approximately 200 co-operative agencies, with a membership of 40,000, offer marketing service and financial aid to their members.

Industry, Commerce, and Labor

THE initiation of commercial and industrial activity in Washington must be credited to the Hudson's Bay Company and its trading posts. At Vancouver, during 1826 and the year following, a sawmill, forge, and gristmills were installed, and Fort Nesqually, after 1833, became for many years the leading port of clearance for domestic and foreign trade on Puget Sound. The company imported supplies and sold them to the settlers, who in turn brought such commodities as they produced to the trading posts for export to distant markets.

The first American gristmill on Puget Sound, operated at Tumwater in 1846 by Colonel Michael T. Simmons and his associates, used stone burrs taken from the stream that furnished power for the mill. Between the years 1852-4, Nicholas De Lin built a barrel factory, brewery, sawmill, and salmon-packing plant at Steilacoom. With goods to sell and in great need of articles of every kind, the settlers soon turned to shipbuilding. Captain Thomas Coupe launched several small schooners from Whidbey Island in 1852.

The major market for the people of Washington Territory was San Francisco, which was ready to buy lumber, fish, and hides and to sell the manufactured goods demanded by the pioneers. For many years, retail prices in Washington were determined largely by this traffic with California. In the early fifties, flour sold at Olympia for $20 a hundred pounds; potatoes at $1.50 a bushel; butter at $1 a pound; eggs at 75c a dozen. Sugar cost a "bit" a pound; coffee, 30c; and tea, 75c or $1. Molasses was 50c to 75c a gallon; hickory shirts, $1 each; sheeting and drilling, 16c a yard; axes, $2 to $8.50, according to design, size, and quality; candles, 62c to 75c a pound; sperm oil, $1.50 a gallon; whiskey, $1.25; brandy a little more, and gin twice as much.

Other imports, advertised in the pioneer press, included Franklin stoves, airtight cookstoves, tinware, tools, plows, cutlery, paints, glass, books, medicines, boots, "super super fine cloth coats," doeskin, satinette and corduroy pants, overcoats, and "new style hats."

During the sixties and seventies, lumber, coal, fish, and—decreasingly

—furs were the principal items of outgoing cargoes. Development of eastern Washington was aided by gold rushes and the opening of new roads, and trade flourished between settlements on opposite sides of the Cascade Range. Coastal commerce caused a rapid growth of marine construction; by 1875 Puget Sound had 14 shipyards, which launched 11 sailing ships and 1 steamer during that year. Exports in the same year were valued at more than $800,000.

Manufacturing had expanded by 1876 to include 25 grain mills, 16 breweries, 13 cooperages, 12 foundries and machine shops, 12 harness-makers' and saddlers' shops, 4 tanneries, and 1 wool factory. River traffic on the Columbia to inland points and increasing settlement in the Walla Walla, Yakima, and Spokane areas aided the growth of the milling industry. The availability of water power encouraged small water-powered mills, even as hydroelectric development later aided in the transition to mass-production plants. By 1879 manufacturing consumed 4,395 horsepower, and, although lumber continued to hold first place among exports, diversified goods comprised 40 per cent of all manufactures in 1880.

The entrance of the Northern Pacific Railroad into Spokane in 1881 and railroad construction in subsequent years on the Coast—opening new markets—caused money to pour into the Territory and precipitated a great commercial upsurge. By 1885 vessels of Puget Sound registry numbered 169, of which 80 were steamers. Sound shipyards built 14 craft during the year, including 8 with steam engines. Factories multiplied so rapidly that by 1889 Washington industry employed 42,579 horsepower, representing an almost tenfold increase during the decade; while the importance of diversified manufactures also gained, until they constituted slightly more than 50 per cent of the $41,768,000 total value produced.

Major influences in the 1890's were the initiation of shipping lines to the Orient and, late in the decade, the gold rush to Alaska. The latter not only stimulated new marine commerce but became the foundation for several new industries, chief products of which were clothing, furniture, camp equipment, heavy machinery, and stoves. Almost 2,000 factories employed in excess of 30,000 persons in 1899, with machinery using 87,425 horsepower; and a heavy influx of population brought the total number of plants to 3,674 in 1909. A trend toward mass production was evident: while the number of employees doubled, machine horsepower increased four and one-half times, totaling 297,759. The 69,120 workers received an average wage of $706 for the year, and production was valued at $220,746,000.

All industry made exceptional advances after the beginning of the World War. Aircraft construction, started at Seattle in 1916, and shipbuilding became leading enterprises within the years that followed. Puget Sound shipyards built one-fourth of all the emergency freighters constructed for the United States Shipping Board. In the eastern part of the State, the flour-milling industry reached its peak during this period. Industrial plants numbered 4,198 by 1919; horsepower and employment had been doubled between 1912 and 1919, and production increased nearly fourfold, to a peak of $800,000,000 for the State.

The cessation of the war boom sounded the death knell of Northwest shipbuilding and caused a general contraction of markets. The stronger companies survived; but the others were caught in the vise of debts and shrinking sales, many being also overcapitalized, and within two years all but 2,908 factories had been eliminated. New developments during the slow revival of commerce were the rise of the food-processing industries and a period of extraordinary prosperity in the building trades.

By 1929 the number of plants in operation had regained the 1919 total, and technological improvements and large-scale manufacturing had brought the installed horsepower of industry to a record of 194,891. Production neared the war-time high, with $795,561,000 worth of commodities, although wages remained somewhat lower, averaging $1,398 for the year.

The general depression forced reductions in all industries. Plants dropped 37 per cent in number by 1933, employment more than 50 per cent, and the average annual wage was lowered 34 per cent; while the value of commodities produced receded to $331,225,000. Once again, a stabilizing factor in the midst of the general downward trend was food processing, which maintained a relatively high level of activity, along with metal working, aircraft construction, and diversified manufacturing. These industries, which accounted for more than 60 per cent of commodity values in the State in 1929, were leading contributors to its wealth in 1937. The pack of canned and frozen vegetables, berries, and fruits in 1937 was valued at $29,566,163.

The most significant changes in commerce during recent years are the advance of maritime shipment and motor freight over rail transport. Particularly marked is the growth of waterborne commerce; the total for 1937 was $132,375,649, of which exports amounted to $92,566,594. Lumber exports rose from 36 per cent of the total produced in 1910 to

91 per cent in 1935, with other commodity shipments following a similar trend to a lesser degree.

LUMBERING

Washington is the leading lumber-producing State in the country. Though distinctly different in composition, the forests on both the east and west sides of the Cascade Range are predominantly softwoods. Eastward lies the "short log" country of white pine, ponderosa pine, cottonwood, and aspen; westward to the Pacific Ocean extends a dense growth of Douglas fir, cedar, hemlock, soft maple, alder, and spruce.

Lumbering, of prime importance in Washington's development, began with the first white men to come ashore in the region — in 1788 Captain John Meares left Puget Sound with a cargo of ship spars, China-bound, though he ran into a storm and had to jettison his load. Four years later Captain George Vancouver replaced a broken spar with one cut from the forest of Puget Sound. With the establishment of fur-trading posts, wood was used in construction, and this soon led to processing of logs. At Fort Vancouver in 1825, millwright William Cannon first whip-sawed logs into boards, and the next year a sawmill was set up with machinery imported from London.

The Hudson's Bay Company regularly accepted shakes and shaved shingles from American settlers in exchange for supplies. The first mill on Puget Sound and the second north of the Columbia River was built at Tumwater in 1847 by Colonel Michael T. Simmons and his associates of the Puget Sound Milling Company; it employed discarded machinery from the Vancouver mill.

When settlers appeared, timber was not only an obstacle to farming but also the readiest source of revenue, and the new arrivals at once set themselves to cutting away the edge of the forests. The Alki settlement at Seattle sent a cargo of piling to San Francisco in 1852, introducing oxen, borrowed from Puyallup Valley, to aid in moving the logs. A mill was started on Whatcom Creek, and Nicholas DeLin set up a mill at Tacoma with a wooden wheel turned by the flow from a 10-foot dam; but DeLin's mill, capable of cutting 2,000 feet daily, incurably sawed boards "on the bias," tapering them from end to end or both ways from the middle.

The *Columbian* of Olympia in 1853 reported: "There are now no less than fourteen sawmills run by water power, and one steam sawmill in process of construction on Puget Sound . . . a large number of our citizens are . . . getting out cargoes of hewed timber, piles, shingles, and cordwood . . . faster . . . than the number of vessels engaged in that business can carry them to market."

Henry Yesler completed the first steam mill on Puget Sound in 1853, and, as lumber was selling from $200 to $500 a thousand feet, more mills soon appeared: J. J. Fell built one on Appletree Cove in 1853; the Puget Mill Company started a steam sawmill and shingle mill at Port Gamble the next year; and in 1855 Peter Goutre and John Gould found water power and a mill site on Tulalip Bay. After the creation of a tribal reserve in 1857, the Tulalip Bay mill reverted to the Indians, who operated it successfully for the next 50 years.

Balked by the tall timber of great girth—trees 200 feet high and 12 feet in diameter were common—early loggers thinned out smaller trees with familiar tools and methods. River drives were impracticable, and logs were skidded over crude roads designed for the purpose. These skidroads, formed of short logs half-imbedded in earth and greased with the oil from dogfish liver, made it possible for 10 or 12 oxen to drag even the largest logs to the waterways.

Cutting ship knees, an early trade, was profitable but wasteful of timber, since only the angle of a big root or limb could be used. A heavy demand for spars and piling in 1860 increased lumber workers to 381. Early settlers at Olympia made barrel hoops of hazel-brush for shipment to San Francisco. In 1866 the Territorial loggers proudly sent to the Paris Exposition a slender flagstaff 150 feet tall, of which Governor William Pickering said: "The glorious flag of our beloved country will float from its top to the admiration of all visitors, far above the emblems and banners of any other Nation."

Sawmills began to tap the pine forests of eastern Washington during the sixties, but the heavier timber stands and more numerous waterways west of the Cascades led to more rapid development in that area. By 1871 the Territory ranked 21st in lumber production, with 56 mills, including 16 with steam engines, producing 128,743,000 feet of lumber.

In 1864 Congress granted to the Northern Pacific Railroad all odd sections of land in a 40-mile strip along its tracks in the Territory. This grant included huge areas of timber, and the railroad incorporated a land company to administer it. Since the agents of the railroad sold even forest areas for as low as $2 an acre, many new sawmills were started. Timberland with a minimum of 25,000 feet per acre cost no more than $120 for 40 acres, and while this condition prevailed many operators pyramided their holdings, and the industry entered a period of rapid growth.

"Fallers" chopped the trees down, while "buckers" cut or "bucked" them into 24, 32, or even 40-foot lengths, using a crosscut saw, or "Swede Fiddle." In the late sixties, some weary axman borrowed a saw and discovered an easier and more efficient method of felling. From that time, fallers worked on springboard scaffolds, set high off the ground to save clearing underbrush and to avoid the pitchiness of the lower tree trunk; this type of cutting not uncommonly left stumps 15 feet in height. A high-wheeled carriage or "big-wheel rig" was chained to a log and rolled away—the whole looking like an underslung siege gun. Logs could thus be moved faster and with fewer oxen or horses than on a skidroad. In the mills, the primitive saw-pit was superseded by the swift but wasteful circular saw, which often cut a kerf one-half inch wide.

In 1880 the lumber industry employed 1,687 persons, contributing 57 per cent of the value of all manufactures in the Territory. The eighties marked the initial use of power equipment in logging. The earliest logging locomotive was built at Marysville in 1883 and ran on a maple-wood track. The donkey engine appeared at Bellingham Bay in 1887, and soon, on Grays Harbor and lower Puget Sound, adaptations followed. First tried was the Dolbeer donkey, an upright steam engine with a capstan. Improvements brought greater power, substituting a windlass, and the engine was mounted on skids for mobility. A "choker" loop of cable encircling a log was fastened to the long line, which the engine coiled, dragging in the log and "yarding" it. To keep pace with these innovations in the woods, circular head saws, gang edgers, power log-turners, and carriages were installed in the sawmills, and the logging railroads, using geared locomotives, were extended.

Helped by new railroad transportation and plentiful capital, production was boosted to 645,000,000 feet in 1887, more than half the total originating on Puget Sound. Machinery began to supersede manual labor, reduce costs, and speed up operations in general.

High-lead logging was begun in 1896 near Port Townsend. Instead of drawing logs with a straight, level pull, the cable from the donkey-engine drum was reeved through a block suspended from a spar tree and thence to the log. An even faster method, using the "skyline," by which a slingload of logs can be lifted and carried bodily on an aerial train, clearing underbrush, gullies, and streams, was introduced later.

New capital, poured into Washington lumbering by Michigan and Wisconsin operators, notably the acquisition of enormous tracts by the Weyerhaeuser interests, was a decisive factor in the organization of the industry. Purchases were quietly negotiated with the Northern Pacific

Land Company, until, in 1900, the title to much of the remaining railroad lands was transferred. Following a survey of marketable timber, prices soared, and in some cases the cost of 1,000 feet of standing timber exceeded the original price per acre. By 1900 Washington had risen to fifth place among lumbering States; and doubled production gave it first position in 1905.

Important in stimulating the use of lumber was the development of a Douglas-fir-plywood fabricating process, supposedly at St. Johns, Oregon, in 1906, shortly after which mills were equipped for this purpose at Tacoma, McCleary, and Sedro-Woolley. Plywood is made by gluing together an odd number of veneer sheets, with the grains alternating at right angles; the result is a panel of great strength, reasonable flexibility, and unusual resistance to warping or shrinkage.

Lumber production exceeded 4,000,000,000 feet in 1910 and, by 1914, embraced 912 plants, employing 37,734. Tractors, introduced into the woods at Gig Harbor in 1912, quickly found favor in handling lighter timber. The use of gas engines and electric motors spread among small mills, and the electrification of a large plant was tried in Seattle. Because electricity permitted greater efficiency in plant design, installations followed at Snoqualmie, Port Angeles, and, later, Longview. The Snoqualmie mill reduced costs with automatic stackers, electric trimmers and dust collectors, and an elaborate conveyor system of transfer cars.

Wages were maintained at an average of $2.50 for a 10-hour day until 1918, when the 8-hour day was made general; around this time wages were doubled, and production increased fivefold. After a temporary slump in 1921, an increasing variety of machine tools appeared, and production rose to a peak of 7,541,229,000 feet in 1926. The lumbering industry's pay roll of 87,000 was 37 per cent of the State's annual total; 61c was the average hourly wage.

Automatic trimmers, improved high-speed planers, and efficient kiln-drying systems were perfected, as was a machine for removing pitch-pockets and gluing on patches in their place. Improved gear and new machines were introduced in the woods; for accelerating yard movements of lumber, electric or gasoline-powered carriers came into use, performing the work of 36 horses and 18 teamsters at a saving of 60 per cent.

In 1929 a total of 901 plants, employing 52,170 persons, turned out lumber valued at $286,084,000, but within two years the plants in operation numbered only 500, with employment and production proportionately decreased. In some sections wages fell to the $2-a-day level; but, as production gained in 1935, organized labor raised wages to the 50c basic rate for the 39,658 persons employed in 574 plants. Production reached 4,572,397,000 feet in 1936, and 4,712,698,000 feet for 1937.

Two major trends are evident in the industry: the increase in numbers of small marginal operators employing 5 to 20 men—known as "gyppo outfits"—which usually offer little more than subsistence; and the growth of mammoth enterprises such as those of the Weyerhaeuser and Long-Bell Companies, often through absorption or elimination of moderate-sized plants. As the consolidation of timber holdings was effected, the advantage fell to the large corporation-owned mills, and, as depletion of timber resources advanced, these contributed the major part of the State's lumber output. About 100 mills, or less than one-fifth of the State's total, can turn out more than 100,000 feet each in an 8-hour shift; a few have 500,000-foot capacities, and one Longview mill is capable of 1,000,000 feet daily. Eastern Washington mills average 50,000 to 100,000 feet daily. Approximately four-fifths of the State's 574 plants operate in the Puget Sound and coastal regions.

From 1905 to 1926 the yearly production of plywood rose to more than 150,000,000 square feet, then soared to 700,000,000 in 1936. Of Washington's 30 or more veneer plants, 20 also manufacture plywood, using white pine, alder, birch, maple, Sitka spruce, hemlock, and imported Philippine mahogany. The uses of plywood range from map, model, and toy making to trailer, streamlined-train, and aircraft construction.

Wood-pulp and paper production have also developed rapidly, principally between 1921-9, when plants increased from 7 to 30, employment from 1,714 to 5,168, and the value of products from $10,233,000 to $47,093,000. A trend toward mechanization of existing plants rather than new construction caused the number of plants to remain stationary; while employment fell to 2,754, and the value of products increased to $53,226,000 in 1936, when pulp manufacture amounted to 859,210 tons.

Socially as well as economically, lumber has exerted important influences in the life of the State. The growth in complexity of lumber manufacture has stabilized plant locations and led to the development of important cities. The mass-production methods of the great mills in these centers are extremely specialized and have required the training of a highly skilled personnel of a different order from the skilled men of the woods. Backwoods camps represent another phase of the industry. Hundreds of little communities remain, though the timber cutting may be 20 miles away; others survive as supply centers, and some have become mere ghost towns. A few towns are literally "mounted on wheels"—and consist of railroad rolling stock in the form of bunk cars, cook shacks and commissary, and tool and shop cars.

Washington retains approximately 280,000,000,000 board feet of its original stand of about 580,000,000,000. The most readily accessible forests have dwindled before axe and saw, or have been ravaged by fire and plant diseases.

The general industrial depression has curtailed the demand for lumber, and this, together with technological improvements, has resulted in widespread unemployment among lumber workers, and in the economic decline of many towns and cities dependent upon timber. Yet the great lumber resources of the State continue to hold out the promise of prosperity, and steps are being taken to conserve and replenish them. Today the industry looks expectantly, not only to the older markets for wood, but to new uses in products, such as rayon, plastics, and cellulose, that are being created through chemical and other scientific processes. Along these lines unlimited possibilities seem to exist.

MINING

Nonmetallic minerals, including coal, cement, clay, building stone, and other commercial materials, today yield Washington a much greater return than its metals. It was, however, the metals, particularly gold, that provided the first incentive to mining as a whole. Early-day prospectors, searching first for placer gold and later turning their attention to lode mining, blazed the way for the discovery and exploitation of the numerous minerals now known to exist within the State.

Gold rushes colored Territorial history and attracted streams of immigrants, some of whom settled down and occupied the new land. One of the first gold excitements in Washington Territory occurred in 1855 in the vicinity of Old Fort Colvile, on the east bank of the Columbia River, which for 30 years previously had been the chief inland post of the Hudson's Bay Company. The metal was discovered on the Columbia near the mouth of Pend Oreille River, and something in the nature of a gold rush followed. But, although considerable gold in the aggregate was removed from the area in subsequent years, the district proved disappointing to individual placer miners. At this time, conflicts with the Indians were frequent and most of the Territory was unsafe for prospectors. In 1858, however, peace was established with the various tribes, and this gave an impetus to prospecting that resulted in gold discoveries at widely separated points. The placers along the Similkameen River in what is now Okanogan County were first worked in 1859, and prospectors searched over a vast area in that locality. The first quartz lode was discovered near Conconully in 1871. Gold mining began near the present city of Wenatchee in 1858, and for a time extravagant claims were made for this district; but here again results fell short of expectations, and the ground was soon worked out or proved to be of a low grade.

Two factors that encouraged early gold seeking were the completion of the Mullan road over Mullan Pass in the Rocky Mountains in 1862, which made access to the Columbia River much easier for miners working their way westward, and the establishment of steam navigation on the Columbia. Working south from British Columbia in the early sixties, prospectors discovered the placer deposits of Ruby Creek in Whatcom County, of the Sultan Basin in Snohomish County, and, across the Cascades, of the Peshastin Creek district, near Blewett, and of the Swauk country, near Mount Stuart. Most of these proved to be important gold-bearing districts.

The early prospectors with few exceptions sought gold mainly along streams and in surface deposits. The chief reasons for this were that placer mining required little preparation or equipment, and that the gold thus obtained was practically in a pure state and readily negotiable as money. Lode deposits of gold-bearing ore were therefore disregarded at first, even when they were known to exist. Gradually, however, as more permanent mining camps were established, miners devised ingenious methods of recovering gold from free-milling ores. The arrastra, a crude ore-grinding apparatus, was usually built almost entirely by hand from material on the ground. It consisted of a stone-lined pit in the center of which stood an upright with crossarms. Attached to the crossarms by a line were huge stones. The upright, powered generally by a hand-constructed water wheel, revolved, dragging the stones around the pit and grinding the ore that had been introduced into the pit with water. Arrastras were used in early days in the Blewett district, where oxidized, free-milling ore was available: remains of them may still be found. Stamp mills were installed around 1880, and hard-rock mining became prevalent. The Culver gold-quartz ledge at Blewett was, according to all available data, the first lode from which ore was taken to be milled by arrastras.

Prospectors in the early eighties, turning their attention to lode mining, made important discoveries, such as the silver-bearing lodes in the Colville district and the iron deposits of Snoqualmie Pass. But little mining development took place until 1887, when the industry throughout the State began a major advance. The important mineral district of Monte Cristo in Snohomish County, discovered in 1889, was considered so promising that a railroad was constructed into the district at great expense. The ore, however, was complex and refractory, carrying gold, silver, copper, lead, and other minerals. Other discoveries in Western Washington were in the Index and the Berlin districts, and for a time there was considerable mining west of the Cascades.

Spokane experienced a gold rush when part of the Colville Indian Reservation was opened in 1896-8. New money poured into the industry in the Cascade area, justifying the *Post-Intelligencer's* statement in 1897 that while the district was "not a poor man's mining country . . . judicious investment of large capital will pay good dividends." Mines installed concentrators and slime tables to supplement the stamp mills of the reduction plants, and the cyanide process was found profitable.

In general, however, operations often proved disappointing and there were many failures. When ores of a complex or "base" nature were encountered, the attempt to recover the gold content through methods successful with free-milling ores usually led to losses. Then, to, in many cases ore bodies did not prove constant; faults and slips in the leads were encountered; heavy rains flooded top workings; and snow hampered operations. These adverse conditions finally brought about a depression in the mining industry in western Washington, which continued to some extent until well past the turn of the century.

Among the important mineral regions in which gold is the principal economic metal is the Republic district, in the Okanogan Highlands, first worked in 1896. The ores here are complex and somewhat refractory, but are found in well-defined bodies and uniform veins. The Mount Baker district in Whatcom County has gold-bearing ores that yield readily to reduction processes, the gold being easily recovered by means of amalgamation or cyanidization; this district once occasioned considerable excitement, but the rush soon subsided. The Swauk placer district in Kittitas County has produced a large gold total, mostly through small, individual operations. Some lode mines have also been worked in the district. The Peshastin district in Chelan County, before mentioned as one of the oldest in the State, has been a heavy gold producer, from both placer and lode operations. Some gold has also been recovered from the beach sands of the Pacific Coast of Washington; the gold there is usually very fine and is associated with heavy minerals, which makes separation difficult. Lastly, some placer workings, mostly individual, have long been carried on intermittently along the Washington side of the Columbia. Traces may still be found here of the diggings of early-day Chinese miners, who often worked ground scorned by white miners as low-grade. In all, there are some 30 mining districts in Washington in which gold is of prime importance among the metals mined.

The latest chapter in the history of the search for gold within the State began in 1933, when the price of gold rose from $20 to $35 an ounce. The new price made possible the resumption of operations in many long-abandoned properties, and also gave great impetus to prospecting. Thousands of men, many of them unemployed, took to the mountains to search for new deposits, or combed over the old mining districts for gold that might have been overlooked. In many cases, owing to lack of experience or some other factor, these latter-day prospectors were unsuccessful, but a few of the more skilled or more fortunate came upon important new sources or rediscovered old ones.

Silver is a by-product in many of the mines of the State, often being found in conjunction with other metals, particularly gold, lead, or copper. In the Swauk district, for example, gold is alloyed with silver to such an extent that it has lost its rich, yellow color and is of a much paler tone. The Ruby silver camps, four miles south of Conconully, were very active for a few years, beginning in 1889. It was estimated that about 1,000 miners were in the camp at one time. The drop in the silver market stopped operations in 1893. That year prospectors discovered the Old Dominion Mine, near Colville, from which rich lead-silver ore was at first packed on horses to Spokane at a cost of $100 per ton. Five years later, the Young America and Bonanza deposits were opened up near what is now the town of Bossburg. More attention was then given to the search for ores of lead, silver, and copper. With the construction of the Spokane and Northern Railway into Stevens County, work was begun on the great ore bodies of the Chewelah district, Deer Trail, and other areas. Ores carrying a high content of silver have been mined in the Colville district, and in recent years about half of the State's silver has come from the mines near Republic. Twice in the history of Washington the annual value of silver produced exceeded that of gold.

Copper ores of various kinds occur in separate bodies, and the metal itself appears in nearly all metalliferous veins throughout the State. Copper ores are found in larger deposits in the Chewelah, Chelan, and Index districts. The Tacoma Copper Smelter, a plant started in 1889 by a Tacoma financier, W. R. Rust, has increased its capacity through the years and is now capable of handling 45,000 tons of ore per month.

In the Metaline district of Pend Oreille County, lead and zinc have been mined for decades. Lead is also commonly found in ores containing other metals. Engineers report large, unexploited bodies of lead ore in certain parts of the Northern Cascades, and there are lead-producing mines in Whatcom, King, and Okanogan Counties. In Seattle is a large lead-processing plant, capable of utilizing much of the State's output of that metal in the manufacture of articles for trade. The commercial use of lead is varied and constantly increasing, and, since Washington has considerable deposits, the outlook for the industry appears promising. Zinc is often found in conjunction with lead, and a high-grade zinc is mined in Washington.

Large bodies of iron ore have long been known to exist in Washington, notably in the Cle Elum district of Kittitas County, around Snoqualmie Pass in King County, the Hamilton district in Skagit County, and the Colville and Valley districts in Stevens County. Some attempts have been made to smelt these native iron deposits—a blast furnace at Irondale, near Port Townsend, produced the first pig iron in the locality—but no permanent iron industry has been established.

Manganese, chromium, tungsten, molybdenum, and silicon are found at various points on the Olympic Peninsula and, in some measure, throughout the Cascade Range. Some of these deposits are of considerable potential value. Large manganese deposits are found principally on the headwaters of the Dungeness, Dosewallips, and Skokomish Rivers, and on Little River, south of Port Angeles; this metal is used in a steel alloy in armament manufacture. It has other important uses.

Platinum occurs with gold along Shishi Beach in Clallam County, along the Similkameen River, in Sultan Basin, and elsewhere. Cinnabar, from which mercury is extracted, has been discovered and mined at various points, particularly near Morton, in Lewis County. Antimony, widely used as an alloy in type metal, is found in Ferry, King, and Okanogan Counties. Deposits of nickel occur in Ferry and Okanogan Counties; recently, this metal has been employed as an alloy of copper in various kinds of sheet-metal products. Tin has long been produced from ores found at Silver Hills, near Spokane; and the ore has also been reported in Kittitas and Stevens Counties. Other metals, most of which are used in alloys, such as bismuth, cadmium, strontium, and cobalt, are found in small quantities throughout the State.

While the metal-mining industry of Washington has been a source of much wealth, the State's ore bodies, except for some iron, copper, and perhaps, magnesium deposits, are not large, in comparison with those of other mineral regions. Yet Washington does have a great deal of known mineral wealth that has remained undeveloped because it is distributed over a wide area. Recent road building and power development, and the rapid technological progress being made in metallurgy, seem to favor progress for the local metal-mining industry.

Nonmetallic mineral resources have become increasingly important in recent years. Among these are cement, coal, clay, sand and stone, and other construction materials. In 1905 the Portland Cement Company established its mill at Concrete, on the Baker River. Today, six plants manufacturing Portland cement, situated at various points within the State and utilizing local limestones and clays, have a reported capacity of about 5,000,000 barrels.

The annual production of stone quarries is valued at nearly $2,000,000. There are granite quarries near Index, in Snohomish County, and sandstone quarries near Wilkeson and at Tenino. Some marble has been produced in Washington, and the new Capitol building at Olympia and other public and private buildings have been faced or partially constructed of local stone. Other building materials are the clays used for brick and tile and the colored mineral aggregates used in stucco, terrazzo, cement stone, and roofing. Magnesite—employed in the manufacture of building board and allied products—is found near Chewelah in deposits said to be the largest in North or South America. A considerable quantity of diatomite, used for insulation, is mined and processed here.

Of commercial value also are clays for stoneware and art pottery; the white kaolins of eastern Washington, suitable for the finest types of chinaware; silica sands, used as abrasives and in foundry work and glass manufacture; soapstone and talc, found in Skagit River Valley; sodium sulphate; and the red and yellow ochers, siennas, umbers, and other mineral pigments of which paints are made. There are also barylites, celestite, fluor spar, marl, shell, and a few gem stones. Asbestos is mined near Pateros, in Okanogan County, and processed in Seattle and Wenatchee.

The discovery and exploitation of coal deposits preceded the earliest gold rush. Dr. William Frazer Tolmie, of the Hudson's Bay Company, recorded coal outcroppings near the junction of the Cowlitz and Toutle Rivers in 1833, and 15 years later the company dug small amounts of lignite in the vicinity. Discoveries were also made on the Stillaguamish River in 1851, and on the Black River, near Renton, where the first mining was attempted in 1852.

The Bellingham Bay mines made the first commercial shipment to San Francisco before 1860, and were the only source of export until

1870. In the early sixties, a man named Van Ogle found extensively distributed coal in Carbon River Canyon but, fearing a single claim would be valueless, filed none. Mining in King County was undertaken after Lyman B. Andrews, in 1863, trudged into Seattle with a flour sack full of coal dug near Issaquah. Other deposits, comprising the Newcastle properties of the later-formed Pacific Coast Coal Company, also east of Lake Washington, were located in 1863. Railroad construction between Seattle and Newcastle during 1874-7 stimulated the industry.

In 1880 the Oregon Improvement Company, organized by Henry Villard of the Northern Pacific, acquired the Newcastle mines and railroad, and coal production in the Territory rose to 145,015 tons for the year. At Chicago's Columbian Exposition in 1893, the Northern Pacific's Roslyn mine displayed a 25-ton block of coal, supposedly the largest ever cut at that time. Coal mining, following the trend in related industries, fell increasingly under the control of a few large companies; mines, railroads, and steamship lines were often combined under the same ownership. Legislation was passed in the attempt to restrain monopolies. In 1918 coal production broke all records with more than 4,000,000 tons, and continued to maintain a relatively high level throughout the twenties, when other mining was curtailed.

Kittitas, King, and Pierce counties, in the order named, have been the principal coal-production areas in the State. Most of the coal mined has been consumed locally, the bulk of it going to railroads, domestic use, coke and gas manufacturing, and the bunker trade for steamships. The coal deposits of Washington include almost every type, from subbituminous to anthracite; and, though coal-mining has declined to some extent in recent years, it is hoped that in the near future the industry will be stimulated by new uses of coal and its by-products.

FISHERIES

The waters of the North Pacific are among the world's great fishing grounds, and the offshore banks of Washington, its salt water inlets and bays, and its coastal rivers are of leading importance in this region. Convenient to the coast of Alaska, the Aleutian chain, and the Bering Sea, Washington ports are outfitting, processing, and shipping headquarters for the whole vast Northern Pacific area.

The Indians had caught salmon long before the coming of the white man. In 1792 Captain George Vancouver described Puget Sound natives as "fishing for salmon with crude nets made of bark and young willows"

—and also saw their racks for drying the fish; while Captain Robert Gray was offered smoked salmon by Columbia River Indians. Salmon was a principal food and an important commodity for barter, especially among the Indians of the Columbia River region.

A device used for salmon fishing by the Puget Sound natives was the weir. Several tripods of alderwood poles were set up in a river or creek where the water was shallow, and, on these, platforms about six feet square were constructed above the level of the water. A fence of willow staves about eight feet long and one to two inches thick, lashed together with string, was built across the stream. The fishermen stood on the tripod platforms with a long dip net and took out the fish, held back by the fence.

Indians along the Columbia used nets woven of flax fibers or of strips of willow bark, with ropes of twisted cedar withes. Reef and seine nets varied in size, and were sometimes as large as 12 feet in depth and 100 feet in length. On the lower Columbia, fishing stations were, according to custom, passed on by inheritance. Fish was preserved by drying, then pulverized and packed securely into baskets lined with straw, dried fish skins, and mats. Each of these baskets weighed about 100 pounds, and, at The Dalles in 1805, Lewis and Clark noted a stock that totaled 10,000 pounds. Fish prepared in this manner, called pemmican by the Indians, kept sound and sweet for several years.

Early explorers and pioneers were amazed to find streams literally choked with fish during the spawning season. Around the first decade of the nineteenth century, the North West Company introduced the salting process; later, the Hudson's Bay Company developed a considerable export trade in quinnat, sockeye salmon, and isinglass (produced from sturgeon), to the Hawaiian Islands, Australia, China, Japan, and eastern United States. David Maynard and Chief Seattle packed salt salmon on Elliott Bay for shipment to San Francisco; the shipment, however, spoiled in transit. Before long, several small traders and fish packers were operating on a minor scale in various parts of the Territory.

The *Olympia Columbian* of September 10, 1853, reported that several men were engaged in salmon fishing at Point Roberts. About 1857, John West, who later invented a canning machine, began salting salmon in barrels on the lower Columbia. Four years later, the Territorial legislature passed an act prohibiting nonresidents from taking fish on the beach of the Columbia between Point Ellis and Cape Hancock. The first floating cannery in the Territory, equipped with a brick furnace and an iron cauldron, was launched in 1867 by an ex-shipwright, S. W. Aldrich, a jack-of-all-trades, who fished alone and made his cans himself.

In 1871 Megler and Jewett, canners at Beachfield on the Columbia, introduced the first can-soldering and lacquering machine and the steam box. V. T. Tull started to pack salmon in 1873 at Mukilteo, and here, four years later, the Jackson-Meyers Company opened the first Puget Sound cannery. Whaling out of Sound ports gained importance early, and oils were obtained from the eulachan, or candlefish, and the dogfish, the latter yielding 60,000 barrels annually. In 1876 F. W. Warren's cannery at Cathlamet installed the first steam pressure cooker, built of three-inch planks. This mechanism so reduced spoilage that it quickly replaced the earlier iron retorts.

In 1881 there were 35 canneries on the Columbia River, with an output of 550,000 cases valued at about $2,475,000. During that year H. Levy exported 100 barrels of smoked salmon to London. The completion of the Northern Pacific Railroad, which made it possible to ship fresh fish to Eastern markets, soon helped expand the local industry.

Capital investment and consolidations in the packing industry multiplied during the nineties, culminating in the incorporation under the laws of New Jersey of the Pacific Packing and Navigation Company in 1901, with an authorized capitalization of $32,000,000. The company gained control of many Puget Sound and Alaska plants but, as the result of stock manipulations, collapsed with great loss to stockholders.

Fishing gear up to this time represented in a large measure a development of the reef nets, basketwork, brush weirs, and traps employed for centuries by the Indians; although a crude fish wheel had been introduced on the Columbia as early as 1879 by the patentees, S. W. Williams and Brother. Gill nets, the oldest type of apparatus used in the fisheries of the region, are either of the "drift" or "set" type—that is, movable or fixed. The gill net, which entangles the fish, is used chiefly in stream or channel fishing. The purse seine, reputedly introduced by the Chinese in 1886, came to be much employed in deep waters, especially after the appearance of the gasoline-powered boat equipped with winches to close and raise the seine when filled. The "beach-haul" type of seine was much used along the bars of the Columbia, horses dragging the laden nets ashore. Traps or pound nets, built of webbing or wire netting supported by piling, were generally placed in estuaries. The fish wheel, which became increasingly popular, was a rotary scoop, mounted on a stationary or floating base and revolved by the stream or tidal flow. Trolling has also been much practiced in northern waters.

Around the turn of the century, drastic changes occurred in fishing and packing. In 1903 E. S. Smith patented the "Iron Chink"—so called because it replaced Chinese labor—a machine that butchered and cleaned 60 to 85 salmon a minute. During the same year, the *Pioneer,* a gasoline-powered purse-seine boat, appeared on Puget Sound and motorboats began to replace scows.

Experiments with by-products, in order to find use for the enormous wastage, were widely undertaken at this time. Oil and fertilizer derived from herring proved a profitable venture from the beginning.

The annual value of fisheries products by 1910 reached $5,559,000, exclusive of oysters, and the industry employed 3,643 workers. In 1913 a record catch of nearly 41,500,000 fish was taken, representing a wholesale value of $5,312,000. That year the value of processed salmon alone reached the sum of $14,073,000, and 15,611 workers engaged in the industry earned a total of $3,065,000. An important innovation was the introduction in 1908 of the Japanese oyster, found to thrive better here than in its native waters.

Several factors, among which unlimited catches were but one, had led to the serious depletion of Washington's fishing resources. Logging operations had caused the drying up of many small streams that had served as spawning beds for the salmon; sewage from waterway cities and villages had been permitted to empty into near-by streams; sawmills, woodworking plants, and pulpmills had crowded river mouths and streams; dams had been built for electric power and irrigation, without provisions being made for the passage of salmon. Natural losses had been caused by the trout, which follows the salmon to the spawning grounds and there devours countless thousands of eggs.

The first regulatory legislation to lower the rate of depletion was enacted in 1890, a year after the State had been admitted to the Union. By provision of this and subsequent laws, only certain types of fishing were allowed in specified waters; seasons and quotas were established, and fishbreeding grounds were rotated. In 1934 an initiative measure abolished the use of fish wheels, traps, all fixed gear, and "beach hauls"; specified areas were set aside for gear fishing, and regular fishing seasons, quotas, and the rotation of fishing fleets were established. Steps were also taken to conserve and replenish the stocks of rivers and streams. (*See Natural Setting*).

In 1939 the total salmon pack for the State was 727,116 cases. Seattle is a leading halibut port of the world, with an average annual load of 22,000,000 pounds. The appearance of albacore (tuna) in commercial quantities, in August 1938, off the shores of Washington, created much excitement; this species continues to be a valuable item in Washington fishing. The importance of by-products is steadily increasing; from parts of halibut, ling cod, and sable fish, once wasted, more than 1,000,000 gallons of oil are extracted annually. The conversion of waste into fish meal and fertilizer has also been found profitable. Improved methods of freezing have made possible the development of new products and different ways of handling the old. In 1937 a total of almost 3,000,000 pounds of clams, scallops, and crabs were taken. More than 2,000,000 pounds of fresh, and 70,000 cases of canned, oysters were shipped in 1935, accounting for more than 90 per cent of the Pacific Coast total; since that time the quantity has steadily increased. A rise in the quantity of devilfish caught has been noted since 1938, when the catch totaled over 40,000 pounds.

The fisheries in 1937 employed 9,300 workers (3,400 in canneries), who received an average of $250 for a season of two and one-half months. Fishermen on 400 or more ships worked on a share basis. For a season of 7 and 8 months, respectively, the purse seiners averaged $460, while the deep sea fishermen averaged $800.

Probably the most effective technological change during recent years has been the shift to the Diesel-powered scow; several of these are in operation on Puget Sound and in the North Pacific. New fishing methods are coming in slowly, however, due chiefly to the pinch in the industry caused by the depression and other factors. Sport fishing is growing in popularity, and the manufacture and sale of gear for this purpose is a prosperous business.

LABOR

Workingmen of Washington have been mainly migrants, laboring in gangs in the woods, mines, and fields, and on the seas and rivers, often living in camps and bunkhouses that any day might be knocked down and transported elsewhere. It was so in the early days of building the Territory, and now that cities have arisen, it is still true, though to a lesser degree. Today, temporary work-towns shelter the men laboring at Washington's great power dams; and transient camps spring up during harvest time in the fruit-growing valleys. Lumber camps burrow deeper into the remaining forests; and, in the spring, fleets of vessels, large and small, spread out along the coastal ways as far as Alaska.

This more or less fluid character of Washington labor, its lack of domestic stability, has had its effects both on the workingmen and on their labor organizations. If the State has at times been called "radical," the cause may be found, not in the existence here of tensions deeper than those prevailing elsewhere, but in a certain directness and ruggedness of manner in which the men and their employers have bargained or fought it out. Perhaps on both sides there has prevailed a kind of impatience, based on a sense of the brevity of time in which problems would have to be solved.

On the other hand, despite its local peculiarities, Washington's labor history follows the general pattern of that of the country as a whole and consistently reflects national influence and events. Washington's growth was part of the westward expansion of the Nation, and of its railroads, industries, and finance, following the Civil War. The beginning of modern development in the Territory was marked by a great influx of settlers from the industrial East and Middle West. Population increased from 23,955 to 357,232 between 1870 and 1890.

During this period, the labor movement nationally was changing in form and growing in strength and stature. The Knights of Labor rose from secrecy to become an open, nation-wide organization. Assemblies of the Knights were soon formed throughout Washington Territory. As part of their social aim "to secure to the workers the full enjoyment of the wealth they created," their platform in the territorial elections of 1886 advocated a bureau of labor statistics, postal savings, industrial compensation laws, graduated income taxes, and weekly payment of wages. They favored compulsory arbitration and "ultimate" prohibition of alcohol—measures no longer favored by labor—as well as abrogation of anti-labor and vagrancy laws and the abolition of imported contract, child, and convict labor.

The Knights played a prominent part in the anti-Chinese riots of 1885-6. The completion of the railroads had stranded many Chinese along the coast; and these had been collected by contractors and hired out in gangs in the hopfields, mines, canneries, and mills. With a depression under way, this cheap labor aroused the hostility of the unions, of small employers unable to compete with hirers of contract labor, of businessmen who disliked the frugality of the Chinese, and of the unemployed who regarded the Chinese as competitors for jobs. The Knights, under the leadership of Otto F. Wagener, took advantage of prevailing feelings and organized widely. Violence was provoked during 1885, and militiamen were used to suppress disorders at Seattle, Tacoma, and other coastal towns.

Seattle and Spokane Falls were burned in 1889, and in the reconstruction, which synchronized with a period of general prosperity, labor was in great demand. Wages rose, and organization increased. But the trend that set in was away from the Knights and towards the newly formed American Federation of Labor. The Western Central Labor Union was created in 1888, and marine organization first showed power in 1889, when inland boatmen on Puget Sound, supported by sympathetic strikes on the Columbia River, prevented wage reductions. In the coal strikes of 1888-9, militia and imported strikebreakers were used against the Knights.

In the first years of the 1890's the American Federation of Labor had almost completely supplanted the Knights. The new organization confined itself strictly to hours, wages, and conditions of labor; abandoned political campaigns for lobbying; and restricted membership mainly to skilled workmen organized by crafts—a policy directly opposed to that of the Knights.

During 1890, the carpenters' brotherhood joined the national strike for an 8-hour day; the Tacoma Trade Council, earliest central body in the State, was formed; smeltermen, printers, shingle weavers, and the railroad brotherhoods gained strength. The State legislature approved Labor Day as a legal holiday in 1891, and by 1893 locals of the Western Central Labor Union had organized a State federation. When the Western Federation of Miners was formed, most remaining miner assemblies of the Knights passed into it intact.

Shop and maintenance labor on the railroads flocked into the American Railway Union, founded by Eugene Debs on the basis of industrial rather than occupational categories. A new depression around the middle of the decade threw many out of work, and Coxey's Army attracted support from Puget Sound cities; 1,600 joined for the march on the National Capital and many crossed the Cascades. The Governor ordered out militia against them, and at Yakima they were waylaid by railroad police and scattered. The Great Northern Railroad strike of the American Railway Union won improved conditions early in 1894, but the later Pullman strike in Washington, felt mostly at Spokane and Tacoma, was defeated.

Organized labor aided the Populist movement so effectively that William Jennings Bryan carried the State in 1896, and John Rankin Rogers was elected governor. As the Populists began to wane, the unions' political activity continued under other influences, conspicuously that of the Social Democratic party after 1900. The *Seattle Union Record* was founded in that year, and the State federation of the American Federation of Labor in 1901.

Legislation to improve industrial conditions reached an impressive total in Washington subsequent to 1903, often preceding such regulation elsewhere. Acts were passed restricting the employment of women, requiring safety devices in factories, establishing the 8-hour day for public employees, and providing for the "permit system" for child workers between the ages of 12 and 14. In 1905, the State Bureau of Labor was created, and laws were enacted providing for wage payment in legal tender, rather than company scrip, and giving labor the power to secure wage liens.

The American Federation of Labor maintained that collaboration must replace strife between capital and labor, but an organization with a different view, the Industrial Workers of the World, emerged in 1905. Soon active in Washington lumber and agricultural centers, the I.W.W. adopted at first the Socialist concept of class struggle, asserting that trade unions, through a general strike, would supersede the capitalist system and establish a free society. It planned unions based on industrial lines and addressed itself also to unorganized, semiskilled, and unskilled migratory labor. The new organization was bitterly attacked by Samuel Gompers, head of the A. F. of L., and by employers and local authorities. Spokane banned street speakers in 1909, and the I.W.W. worked up a "free speech" campaign, during which more than 600 were arrested. The struggle ended in a compromise, when the police granted a permit system for speakers.

In 1907 the State legislature enacted a 16-hour law for railroad crews, but, although it thus limited the workday, it required that the individual worker bring suit before penalties might be invoked. The protection of miners was strengthened at succeeding sessions, and in 1911 a compensation act established the principle of industrial insurance.

The thirty-third national convention of the A. F. of L., held in Seattle in 1913, sanctioned the amalgamation of existing lumber unions and promised to aid a campaign for the long-sought 8-hour day. Since the shingle weavers in 10 years had made but small gains, a membership drive was launched, and a paper, the *Timber Worker,* was founded; but the drive failed. Resisting wage cuts after 1914, teamsters and longshoremen struck in the Puget Sound area, despite widespread efforts to reaffirm the principle of the open shop. The strike was ended by Federal mediation.

A minimum-wage bill for women and the establishment of an industrial welfare commission marked the 1915 session of the State legislature. An initiative fixing a general 8-hour day in industry was lost at the polls in 1914, after being opposed by lumber operators and some farm groups; and a measure prohibiting collection of fees by employment agencies was passed, but proved ineffectual.

A local employers' organization, the Commercial Club, intervened in a shingle weavers' strike at Everett in May 1916; forty men suspected of membership in the I.W.W. were seized and beaten, and street meetings were prohibited. The I.W.W. called for a free-speech demonstration, and on Sunday, November 5, workingmen embarked from Seattle on the vessels *Verona* and *Callista*. As the *Verona* entered Everett at Pier 2, which was crowded with special deputies, gunfire broke out. Men dropped on the decks, and panic swept the ship. Listing heavily, the *Verona* was backed away; and both ships returned to Seattle. Two on the dock and five on board the *Verona* were killed, several were reported drowned, and 50 were wounded. At Seattle, 300 passengers were jailed; 74 were held for murder in the first degree, but were released without trial when the first to be tried was acquitted.

As wartime living costs mounted, the timberworkers' demand for the 8-hour day at a $3 wage, for better sanitary conditions, and for union recognition was reinforced by strike action, which won support in other vital industries. The Lumbermen's Protective Association raised $500,000 to fight the unions and to defend the old hours and wage rates. Lumber strikes in the Northwest increased from 44 in 1916 to 295 in 1917, and so demoralized production that the War Department intervened and appointed Colonel Brice P. Disque to co-ordinate the industry. Under the sponsorship of the Government, the Loyal Legion of Loggers and Lumbermen, often called the "4-L," was created. It united employers and workmen in the same organization, and worked towards patriotism and a maximum output. Strikes were reduced to 74 in 1918, and in the same year the 8-hour day in the lumber industry was decreed by Colonel Disque.

The end of the war brought a cut in production, and the mounting unemployment and a renewed open-shop campaign combined to weaken the unions. In Seattle, a general strike—the "Seattle Revolution"—began in support of thousands of striking shipyard workers. On February 6, 1919, approximately 60,000 walked out. Shops, mills, newspapers, and transportation stopped; the strike committee organized labor guards to keep order, and maintained vital services. Mayor Ole Hanson spent $50,000 for special police and deputized 2,400 businessmen. The strike ended peaceably, leaving a vivid impression. Raids and arrests soon began against Socialist and union groups, as fears were fanned of the "bolshevik" menace. Under the pressure of a powerful campaign, public sentiment was turned against the unions in spite of the well-known conservatism of local labor leaders. The Associated Employers of Washington was formed to combat radicalism in the State.

In the nervous atmosphere thus created, a tragic event occurred at Centralia on Armistice Day, 1919, during an American Legion parade in that city. The I.W.W. had attempted to organize the lumbermen of the Centralia region and, despite several conflicts, had established headquarters there. According to Commons' *History of American Labor,* the Armistic Day parade took the route leading to the I.W.W. hall, and shooting broke out in which four legionnaires were killed. An I.W.W. member, Wesley Everest—also a veteran—was mutilated and lynched; and another I.W.W., a 19-year-old boy, was arrested and became insane while in jail. Almost 1,000 arrests were made of I.W.W. members and persons suspected of radicalism. A feverish attack was begun against all organized labor. A trial was held in Montesano at which nine workingmen were convicted of murder in the second degree, after the testimony of nearly 300 witnesses had revealed an extreme conflict of opinion as to which group had actually begun the assault. After church groups, investigating the trial, recommended clemency, all but one of the defendants were released; the last prisoner was freed in 1930.

Organized labor was subjected to various kinds of attack while the "red scare" prevailed; conservative unions were suspected, the more aggressive were branded "bolshevik," and the legislature passed a criminal-syndicalism act. Spokane conducted a trial costing $250,000 but failed to secure convictions; Tacoma police arrested 50 delegates to the Central Labor Council. Associations of water-front employers, lumber operators, and the Inland Empire Employers pressed a drive for the open shop.

Maritime labor on Puget Sound was disorganized by the defeat of the coastwise strike in 1921, and the coal mine and railroad unions of the A. F. of L. lost ground the next year. The "4-L" dwindled to the point where it maintained a foothold only in smaller camps and mills, although it still claimed 10,000 members in 1921; the A. F. of L. lumber unions in 1922 had only 800 members and listed none in 1923. The last serious strength of the I.W.W. vanished in an abortive lumber strike called in 1923.

Labor banks were started in 1922, the first being the Trade Union Savings Loan of Seattle. The railroad brotherhood banks opened branches in Seattle, Tacoma, and Spokane and purchased buildings in Spokane and Tacoma, but remained solvent only a few years. Various Washington unions joined in the Farmer-Labor campaign of 1922-24, the leading candidate being Homer T. Bone, later United States Senator (1932-). Weakened by protracted struggles and many defeats, organized labor lapsed into quiescence, the number of strikes diminishing from 112 in 1919 to 5 in 1925. As prosperity mounted, the skilled unions improved their position, though without expending further energy on the unorganized majority. Thus, despite the relatively high percentage of craftsmen's unions within the State, the basic industries were, after 40 years, never more than briefly and partially organized. Lumber, fishing, marine transport, and agricultural unions did not develop until after 1929-30.

The early thirties were characterized by widespread organization of the jobless. In the Puget Sound region, two groups, the Union Producers and the Unemployed Citizens' League, organized in 1931, gained members by tens of thousands; in Spokane, the Order of the Forgotten Man, founded in 1932, soon had 11,000 members. Co-operatives, self-help groups, and "production-for-use" associations sprang up throughout the State. With this impetus, labor's political activity revived. A lumber workers' industrial union, formed in 1931 at Seattle, enrolled 3,000 members and won a minor strike. Similar industrial unions appeared on the water front and in agriculture, all affiliated with a union federation called the Trade Union Unity League. During the next few years, these unions dissolved, and their members went into the A. F. of L.

Workers in hopfields and orchards of the Yakima Valley struck in 1933 and were attacked by vigilantes and police. Later organizational attempts among harvest hands in this area were resisted by the Associated Farmers. In central Washington, serious conflict flared in the Roslyn-Cle Elum mines, where the workmen were organized in the National Miners' Union.

Finding encouragement under the N.R.A., labor began rapid organization in 1934. The marine unions, under the stress of a coastwise strike, attained a membership of 35,000 within 6 months. During the strike, the "Committee of 500" was formed to open the port of Seattle; while strikers resisted efforts of police and strikebreakers to move cargo at Smith Cove. Arbitration settled the struggle, and the unions won wage increases, control of hiring halls, and union recognition; also, the longshoremen secured a 6-hour day.

In western Washington, another influence appeared at this time.

The A. F. of L. teamsters' union, under David W. Beck, took jurisdiction over brewery employees in 1934, and later gained control over bakery, laundry, milkwagon, and cab drivers, as well as garage employees and department store clerks.

An organizing drive among lumberworkers of the State culminated in strike action by approximately 40,000 in May 1935, closing mills and camps. The Washington Industrial Council was formed to oppose the strike, and the National Guard intervened with drastic measures, particularly in Aberdeen and Tacoma; charges of Communistic activity were reiterated. A settlement was reached, however, which resulted in improved wages and conditions. Subsequently, a Northwest woodworkers' federation was formed with 100,000 members.

When water-front employers refused to renew existing agreements in October, 1936, the Maritime Federation closed coastal ports for nearly four months. The unions declined to settle separately, and, owing to their unity and their campaign for public support, the struggle was referred to as a "streamlined strike." A greater readiness to take political initiative became apparent among the maritime and woodworkers' federations. These policies paved the way locally for the influence of the Committee for Industrial Organization in the maritime, lumber, and mining industries. Membership in the C.I.O. was also swelled by the cannery workers (predominantly Filipino) and the fishermen, most of whom hire out from Seattle for seasonal work in Alaska waters. The State C.I.O. Council was chartered in September 1938, and held its first convention in the same month.

Trade-union organization was resorted to by professional and "white-collar" workers; unions of teachers, office employees, and newspaper and editorial workers had an unprecedented growth. For the first time in the Nation's journalistic history, a daily newspaper was suspended because of a strike of newsroom workers. In 1936 the *Seattle Post-Intelligencer* closed for three months during a strike, which ended in recognition of the American Newspaper Guild. Later a prolonged strike against the *Seattle Star* ended favorably for the Guild.

Noteworthy in 1936-7 was the return of the labor movement to the electoral field. The Washington Commonwealth Federation, an association of unions and other groups, including Democratic clubs, farmers, pension advocates, and unemployed, sponsored and helped to elect both State and national representatives. The federation also helped to block passage of a compulsory arbitration measure and to repeal criminal-syndicalist legislation.

Today, organized labor seems once more on the defensive, as employer groups seek, through legislation and other means, to restrict its scope and power of action. The division between the A. F. of L. and the C.I.O. has been recognized as a source of danger to both bodies and to the future of labor as a whole. These federations temporarily put aside their differences in 1938 in order to defeat in Washington, with the aid of the State Grange and other groups, measures which they regarded as union-crippling.

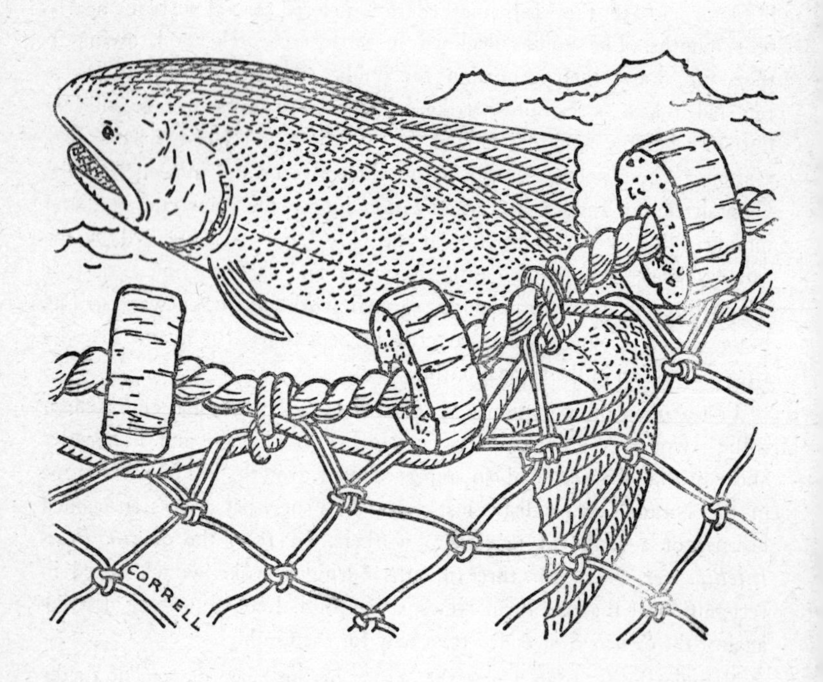

Education

JOHN BALL, Dartmouth graduate, a member of Wyeth's first expedition, having enjoyed the bountiful table and comfortable quarters of Dr. John McLoughlin in old Fort Vancouver, began teaching the sons of the officers and employees of the Hudson's Bay Company. Speedily they learned that only English might be spoken in school, under penalty of being obliged to wear a metal tag around the neck. Classes in the ordinary subjects of a grade school were followed by hours spent in gardening, by special request of Dr. McLoughlin. This school was opened in the third week of November 1832, and continued for five or six years, although Ball stayed only three months.

Contemporaneous with this Vancouver school was another in eastern Washington. Spokane Garry, an Indian educated in the Red River mission, opened a school for his tribe within the boundaries of the present city of Spokane, about 1833. A long building of poles, covered with tule mats woven by Indian women, housed this interesting adventure in education.

The next school was established in 1837 at Waiilatpu by Dr. Marcus Whitman and his wife, Narcissa, a former New York teacher. This school had only Indian pupils for the first few years but later was attended by the children of white settlers and several orphans adopted by the Whitmans. The murder of Dr. and Mrs. Whitman and 11 other members of the mission in 1847 ended any further attempt to open schools for Indians for several years. Fear of Indian outrage closed the schools opened at Tshimakain in 1839 by the Reverend Cushing Eells and Reverend Elkanah Walker.

Education went hand in hand with religion in pre-Territorial days. Missionaries opened schools in their own homes or in the rough log cabins that served also as church, courtroom, and townhall. Textbooks in bewildering variety confronted the pioneer teacher. Relics of father's and mother's schooldays, transported by covered wagon, had to serve the second generation. Sanders' readers and spellers, Thompson's arithmetic. Olyney's geography, Wells' grammar, Youth's botany, and the *Church Psalmist and Choir* were most frequently encountered.

Ushering in the Territorial period was the governorship of Isaac Ingalls Stevens, and popular education was an important plank in Governor Stevens' platform. His first message to the newly constituted legislature envisioned the day when every Washington boy, however humble his environment, should have his chance to enter college. He set in motion the machinery to procure from Congress a land grant in support of a university.

This first Territorial legislature of 1854 passed a law designed to provide public schools for all children between the ages of 4 and 21. Schools were to be financed by direct tax and by fines imposed for infractions of the penal code. Naturally, a thin and scattered population, poor roads, and the meager funds arising from small county and district levies resulted in crude buildings, mostly of logs, scanty equipment, and short terms. For decades, additional schools were built by private subscription in many counties.

But, even during this period of pioneering, higher education was brought within reach of frontier settlements. A private academy offering all high school branches was opened in Olympia in 1855 by Reverend George Whitworth, Presbyterian minister, afterward president of the Territorial university. Tuition might be paid in wood, hay, fruit, or vegetables. Puget Sound Institute, a Methodist school, opened in the same town the following year. A gray December day in 1856 brought five young nuns from House of Providence, Montreal, to start a day and boarding school in Vancouver. Providence Academy, an outgrowth of this earlier school, opened in 1873. One year earlier, the first Protestant school for girls, St. Paul's, opened in Walla Walla. This town had a select school or private academy in 1863, three others by 1865. For many years, Walla Walla was regarded as the educational center of the Territory.

Contesting the field with these private ventures, the university flung open its doors in Seattle on November 4, 1861, to 1 college student and 30 others below high-school grade. The university, which had existed on paper for 5 years, its proposed location shuffled from one town to another, had a grim struggle for existence for many years. Today it is the State's leading educational institution, with a registration of more than 10,000 (*see Seattle*).

Another educational landmark of 1861 was the creation of the office of Territorial superintendent to co-ordinate the work in the counties, issue teachers' certificates, hold conventions, and secure suitable textbooks. The office was abolished the next year and not re-established until 1871. The first report published by this office in 1872 gave the Territory 144 public schools, with 10 or more private ones. Another decade found only 10 graded schools in the Territory. The first teachers' convention was held in 1870, but there was no educational journal until 1884.

The first contract Indian school in the United States was established at Tulalip in 1869, when the Government undertook to pay for the board and tuition of a few Indian pupils in a Catholic school.

Washington's admission to statehood in 1889, with the resultant increased Federal land grants, additional revenues, and a rising tide of immigration, had a marked effect on educational development. Within one year, six high schools had opened. A State normal school opened in Cheney in October 1890; at Ellensburg in 1891; and at Bellingham in 1899. (These normal schools are now designated Eastern, Central, and Western Washington colleges of education).

Washington State College, the State's agricultural institution, opened at Pullman in January 1892 (*see Tour 4b*). This liberally endowed and popular college ranks next in importance to the University of Washington. The third largest institution, College of Puget Sound, opened its doors in 1890 as an academy and advanced to college rank in 1914. It is a Methodist college. Whitman College, Walla Walla, founded as a seminary in 1859 by Reverend Cushing Eells as a memorial to the martyred Whitman, has the distinction of holding the first charter granted by the Territorial legislature to any institution. Its early history held years of incredible hardship and frequent suspension. A new charter was granted in 1883, changing the name to Whitman College. Scholarship is high in Whitman, and the school has an enviable reputation.

Gonzaga University, Spokane, opened as a Jesuit school for boys in 1887, became a college in 1894 and in the amended charter of 1922, adopted the title of university. Whitworth College, also in Spokane, a Presbyterian school, opened at Sumner as an academy in 1883; the school reached college rank in 1890 and adopted its present name, honoring the man who founded the first Presbyterian church in the State. Seattle Pacific College, a Free Methodist institution opened in 1893 as a seminary, has enjoyed college status for more than a quarter-century. In the outskirts of Tacoma, at Parkland, is Pacific Lutheran College, which opened as an academy in 1894. Following a merger with another Lutheran college at Everett in 1920, the Parkland institution added liberal arts and normal departments. Walla Walla College, near the city of Walla Walla, was established by the Seventh Day Adventists in 1892. This school has sent more than 300 of its graduates to the foreign field as missionary doctors, nurses, and teachers.

In 1895, a year of grave economic depression, Washington passed the "barefoot schoolboy law," sponsored by John Rogers, later twice elected Governor of the State. This law provided for State support for schools, originally amounting to $6 per year for each child on the school census rolls. This law, and the subsequent increases in the amount of support to be given, permitted the development of a State-wide public school system.

Washington now has more than 350,000 pupils in public elementary and high schools, with undetermined thousands in private schools. A national survey (Ayres and Phillips, 1910-30), gave Washington fourth place, based upon literacy, per capita expenditures for education, and attendance. There are 8 junior colleges in the State—in Aberdeen, Centralia, Longview, Mount Vernon, Spokane, Yakima, Wenatchee, and Vancouver. There are also two denominational junior colleges and scores of private academies, nonsectarian and denominational, in various parts of the State, offering instruction in liberal arts, music, and the dance, and in commercial subjects. Edison Vocational School, Seattle, opened in 1930, offers industrial training from boat building to commercial art.

The Washington State school system faces one very serious problem: the equalization of financial support for the common schools. Due to haphazard formation of districts, the unequal distribution of taxable wealth, and the existence of both very sparsely and very densely populated areas, the State now has approximately 1,500 districts (June 1938); many of these are very large and irregularly shaped, while many are small and poorly financed. Thus it is difficult to provide equal educational opportunity for all the children in the State. A *Survey of the Common School System of Washington* (1938), made by the Washington State Planning Council, presents a careful study of the situation and makes some valuable recommendations; among these are the reorganization of the State department of education and the organization of a commission for the equalization of educational opportunity, to be appointed by the governor. In 1937 an attempt was made by the legislature to provide for equalization of financial support; this was one of several such attempts to meet the problem. Consolidation of schools and districts has increased, and transportation by bus is provided wherever necessary. Both of these solutions, according to the survey, are costly and, at the same time, not wholly successful.

During 1939, Work Projects Administration education classes had an average enrollment of 34,562 each month. The education program is sponsored by the State superintendent of public instruction, and contributing sponsors include local schools, public libraries, churches, clubs, and civic associations. Courses in general adult education and vocational education cover a wide range of subjects: mathematics, languages, mechanical drawing, creative writing, psychology, drama, first aid, safe driving, Braille for the blind, international affairs, horticulture, typing, bookkeeping, business English, printing, and carpentry. Instruction has been given in band music, orchestra, choral work, voice training, music appreciation, and history of opera. In co-operation with schools, lodges, churches, parent-teacher associations, and the Grange, cantatas, operettas, and orchestra and band concerts have been given. Americanization, naturalization, and literacy education have been outstanding phases of the program. The classes include both aliens seeking citizenship and foreign-born citizens.

There are 13 WPA nursery schools in Washington, all located in public-school buildings. They were developed to help pre-school children from under-privileged homes. During 1940, approximately 500 children were served in the State. The parent and home-making education program includes classes in family relationship, parent problems, child care and guidance, the family and its relation and obligations to the community, home planning and budgeting, sewing and tailoring, food and nutrition, consumer education, and various related subjects. Classes in sewing and homemaking are operating in many Indian reservations, and an especial effort has been made to preserve the arts and crafts of the Indians. In Spokane an outstanding Negro center has been maintained for several years, under the supervision of a graduate of Tuskegee; as a result, the county commissioners reported that there was practically no juvenile delinquency among the Negroes of that city.

Workers' education has been quite successful in the State of Washington, conducting on an average about 200 classes with a registration of 4,400 students. A good example of this activity is found among the employees of the Boeing Airplane Company plant, where classes are sponsored by the Aeronautical Mechanics' Union. This union, which requires all its members to take a short course in trade unionism, maintains a circulating library, and conducts special courses in economics and labor problems for the shop stewards and executive board members.

The WPA recreation program embraces a large number of activities, such as sports and athletics, play-center activities, dancing, crafts and visual arts, recreational music, and recreational drama. Recent reports show a total participation of 235,457 in the entire State for one month. The recreation project is sponsored by the department of physical education of the University of Washington, and various city and county school districts and park departments act as co-sponsors.

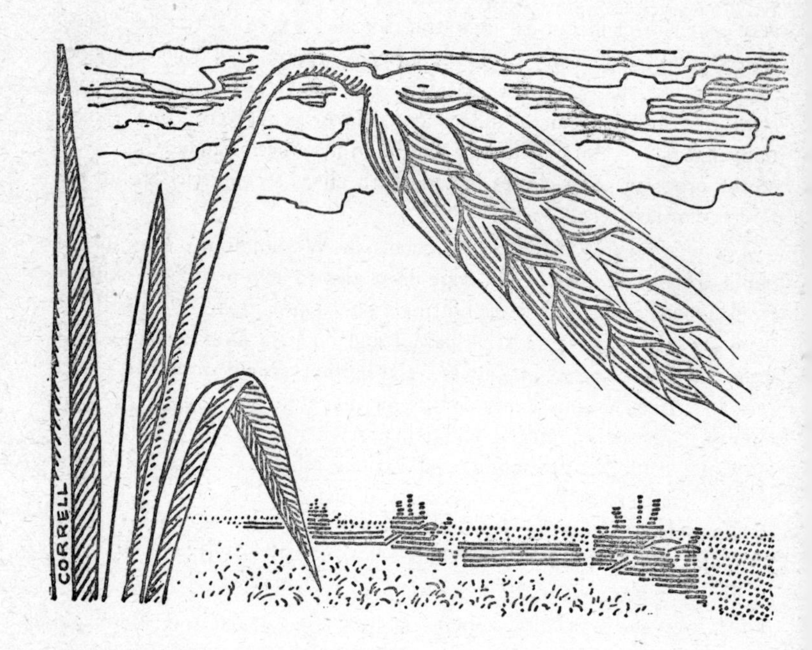

Religion

CHURCHES helped lay the foundations of the State in Washington. Missionaries shared all the hardships of the frontier with trader and trapper, making trails over mountain ranges, navigating the Columbia, threading their way through a wilderness. In building churches and schools, promoting agriculture and encouraging immigration, they did much to consolidate the earliest American settlements and strengthen the claim of the United States to this outpost, in opposition to Great Britain.

A little group of ministers volunteered for service in the unknown Northwest as a result of publication of the story of four Nez Percé Indians, who made the long journey to St. Louis in 1831 to ask General William Clark, Indian Agent, to supply them with the white men's Book. First to arrive were the Reverend Jason Lee and his nephew, Daniel Lee, representatives of the Methodist Episcopal church, who reached Fort Vancouver in September 1834, and continued on to the Willamette Valley. Dr. Marcus Whitman, the Reverend H. H. Spalding, and W. H. Gray, sent by the American Board of Commissioners for Foreign Missions (an agency of the Congregational, Presbyterian, and Dutch Reformed churches), arrived in 1836 and established a mission at Waiilatpu, near the present Walla Walla, and at Lapwai, on the Clearwater. The Reverend Cushing Eells and the Reverend Elkanah Walker, sent by the same agency in 1838, established a mission at Tshimakain, north of Spokane. In 1839 the first printing press landed in the Northwest, a gift from the Sandwich Islands mission to Lapwai, and the first books in the Nez Percé and Spokane languages were printed here.

Roman Catholic priests, Father Francois Norbert Blanchet and Father Modeste Demers, conducted the first Mass in the Northwest in a schoolhouse in Vancouver, November 25, 1838. Blanchet established a mission on Whidbey Island in 1840. In 1844, Father de Smet and Father Ravalli, with laymen and six Sisters of Notre Dame de Namur, arrived. Further reinforcements came from France in 1847. In 1866

Father Cataldo founded the Spokane Mission on Peone Prairie, and Father Ravalli opened a church in Spokane in 1881. Seattle heard its first Catholic service in 1853 and became the administrative center for the Western See in 1907. A bishop of Spokane was appointed in 1914 for the Eastern Washington Diocese.

The Methodist church, pioneering since 1834, established itself in Olympia in 1852, at Steilacoom in 1854, Seattle in 1855, and at Walla Walla in 1860. The Presbyterian church, after destruction of its mission at Waiilatpu, organized no other group until a church was incorporated at Chambers Prairie in 1858. Dr. George Whitworth organized the First Presbyterian Church in Olympia in 1860, another in Seattle in 1869. The Seattle group did not have a building of its own for six years, but in recent years it claims the largest Presbyterian congregation in the United States.

The Episcopal church organized at Olympia in 1865 and in Seattle the same year. The first pipe organ in Washington Territory was installed in Trinity Church, Seattle, in 1882. The Congregational and the Baptist churches both established congregations in Seattle in 1869.

The Lutheran church, highly organized and vigorous, is represented in Washington by many congregations: Norwegian, Swedish, Danish, German, Icelandic, Finnish, and American. Seattle alone has 29 Lutheran congregations. The Christian denomination and Seventh-Day Adventists are organizations numerically small but very active. The latter is particularly zealous in conducting schools all over the State. Russian Orthodox Church, Seattle, has a history of 45 years behind it. A second congregation was organized in 1937. Buddhist temples, one in Tacoma and two in Seattle, serve the Orientals in western Washington.

The first Jewish congregation in Seattle, Ahabath Shalom, was founded in 1889; and its successor, the present Temple de Hirsch congregation, was established in 1899. According to the Religious Census of 1926, there were 11 Jewish congregations in Washington, with a membership of more than 13,000.

According to this same census, the leading denominations in the State, in point of membership, were the Roman Catholic (121,249), the Methodist Episcopal, (48,140), and the Presbyterian U.S.A. (34,425). The Methodist Episcopal led in number of churches. Among the various Lutheran groups, the Norwegian congregations totaled the largest membership. Other relatively large memberships were those of the Protestant Episcopal and Baptist churches. The churches of the Brethren, the First Church of Christ, Scientist, the Congregational church, several smaller bodies of the Methodist and Presbyterian denominations, and numerous other faiths were also represented in Washington.

A growing desire for co-operation among the larger Protestant denominations led to the organization of Washington State Council of Churches in 1933. This union throws its strength behind movements directed towards civic betterment and religious education.

Social Institutions

THE State Department of Social Security superseded the State Department of Public Welfare by act of the legislature in 1937. From its headquarters in Olympia, the department supervises all public assistance programs, which are administered by the counties. There are four divisions: the division of children, division of the blind, division of old age assistance, and division of general public assistance. The Employment Service and Unemployment Compensation in this State operate under a division, separate from the Department of Social Security, known as the Unemployment and Placement Program.

The division of children of the State department, in co-operation with the United States Children's Bureau and the Federal Social Security Board, administers aid to dependent children in their own homes, services for crippled children, and child welfare services, including foster care. Rehabilitation and training of blind persons, programs of prevention of blindness and restoration of vision, and public assistance to the needy blind are provided by the division of the blind. Old-age assistance in Washington is on a budgetary basis; resources that cannot be included are established by law. The citizenship requirement has been abolished, and persons living in private institutions are eligible under certain conditions. The general public assistance division supervises assistance and services to all needy persons other than those in the preceding categories; these services include home assistance, medical and institutional care, Work Projects Administration certification, Civilian Conservation Corps selection, and Federal Security Administration referrals.

Through the WPA Housekeeping Aide Project, in co-operation with local welfare agencies, experienced women are employed to give assistance in housework and child care in needy homes, where the homemaker is temporarily incapacitated. Approximately 400 women employees have made more than 160,000 visits to needy Washington families. Countless instances show that older children, previously forced to miss school, were allowed to return to their studies through this service. These WPA workers also have helped to make livable and attractive more than 500 motherless, nearly or entirely destitute homes. The project is sponsored mainly by women's clubs of the State.

The WPA Hospital Assistance Project began in 1938 in the Pierce County Hospital, sponsored by the Pierce County Commissioners. Here women were employed to supplement the regular staff by performing unskilled tasks, thus allowing the technically trained personnel to spend more time in specialized services.

One of the outstanding institutions in the State is the King County (Harborview) Hospital in Seattle, which was opened on March 9, 1931. Dr. R. G. Broderick, of California, was engaged by county commissioners in 1927 to survey local public hospital facilities and to make recommendations; following the publication of his report—a detailed and shocking revelation of inadequate facilities and inhumane conditions—a bond issue of $2,750,000 was passed for the construction of a modern hospital and health center. The King County Hospital, embodying Dr. Broderick's recommendations, has been considered so successful in planning and arrangement that a model of Unit Number One, exhibited at the Century of Progress in Chicago, was chosen as part of a permanent display of hospital design under the auspices of the Rosenwald Fund in that city.

The medical service is completely supervised and, in the main, provided by the King County Medical Society through a voluntary nonpay hospital organization. Leading practitioners direct the medical services and supervise intern, resident, post-graduate, and clinical training. Scientific advances in methods of treatment initiated at the King County Hospital include the Harborview Burn Treatment, now used extensively in this country and in Europe. The school of nursing, general internship, and post-intern training in residence are all fully accredited.

The Orthopedic Hospital, also in Seattle, originated in 1907, when a group of women planned a hospital for the treatment of crippled children. At first they arranged for space in Seattle General Hospital, then built the Fresh Air House; finally in 1911 construction was begun on the first unit of the present building. A nonprofit organization, supported largely by endowment, the hospital provides care without cost to patients unable to pay; complete facilities for general as well as orthopedic treatment are offered, and a school staff is maintained for student patients by the Seattle School Board. Approximately 3,500 children from the Northwest, Alaska, and Hawaii are cared for annually in this institution, which has behind it the ceaseless activities of many women, bequests from banker and lumberjack, and contributions from persons in all ranks of life.

The United States Marine Hospital was established in Seattle in 1932, under the United States Public Health Service. It is supported by Federal funds. Services are available for Government employees injured in the line of duty, as well as for members of the Merchant Marine, Coast Guard, Army, Navy, and Lighthouse branches of service.

The church has nurtured many powerful social agencies. The Young Men's Christian Association, organized in 1878, has a membership of several thousands in its 22 centers. In addition to athletic training and recreation, it offers vocational training in both day and night classes in the Washington Technical Institute, Seattle. Similar in purpose is the Young Women's Christian Association, which has established attractive homes for business girls in the larger towns, with arts and crafts classes and recreation facilities. Knights of Columbus, Catholic fraternal order of more than 40 years' standing, has 30 councils throughout the State.

Jewish social service is administered by the guilds belonging to the different synagogues. The leading Hebrew cultural organization, Education Center in Seattle, is directed by the Council of Jewish Women and conducts classes in languages, arts, and crafts.

The Salvation Army, organized in Washington since 1887, operates 23 centers. Men's service institutions are maintained in Seattle, Tacoma, and Spokane. Seattle has the Evangeline Hotel for young working women and Red Shield Home for transient girls, while the Maternity Home is located in Spokane. Welfare work, especially directed toward rehabilitation, is carried on by Volunteers of America and Goodwill Industries.

Ruth School for Girls, Seattle, is maintained by women of the Protestant denominations, for the benefit of young girls who are wards of the Juvenile Court, but whose delinquencies are not serious enough to warrant commitment to the State School for Girls.

Since 1921 the Community Fund has provided general support for a network of social welfare groups in the large cities. Representative of character-building agencies are the Boy Scouts and Camp Fire Girls. In Washington, as elsewhere, social organizations and church groups continue to afford substantial help and encouragement to the economically dependent. As an example, a sewing center organized in 1921 by Mrs. Bertha K. Landes, former Mayor of Seattle, and maintained by the help of club women, formed the nucleus of sewing depots that were taken over by the State in 1933.

An important beginning has been made in the migratory labor camp program, under the Farm Security Administration. Each year thousands of farm workers descend into the Yakima Valley to help in harvesting the apple crop, and, after the great droughts of 1934 and 1936, many more families came from the stricken States. An investigation of living conditions showed that the transient workers lived in insanitary and inadequate camps, where sickness was prevalent. The Yakima Chamber of Commerce, in 1935 and again in 1937, appealed to the Farm Security Administration (formerly the Resettlement Administration); various studies were made by the State College of Washington and other agencies; and the proposal was finally approved.

According to the report of the Farm Security Administration, as of January 1, 1940, one standard camp, in Yakima County, and a mobile camp, with headquarters in Walla Walla, have been established; 142 tent platforms, 200 shelters, and 48 labor homes are under construction. When camp construction is completed, facilities for 342 families will be available. While these camps offer only the minimum of decent living facilities, they provide far better shelter and sanitary arrangements than the migrant workers have previously endured. Wherever they have been established, a great improvement in comfort and health has been apparent, and the spread of disease has been decidedly checked.

Sports and Recreation

FAVORED by its size and natural setting, Washington offers almost unlimited opportunities to the sports lover and to those who seek recreation. Mountains, forests, lakes, streams, and ocean coastline, vast primitive areas, in some cases unexplored, appeal to the most hardy seeker of wilderness trails and offer opportunity for every form of outdoor activity.

On the other hand, the sports enthusiast who does not care for untamed country, and the possible attendant discomforts, can find modern recreational facilities in attractive settings. While comparatively new as a State, Washington has golf courses, tennis courts, and athletic clubs, particularly in the larger urban centers, that vie with the finest anywhere. The first golf club in the Pacific Coast States is said to be the one organized at Tacoma in 1894. Now there are 65 well-maintained courses in the State: 15 private, and 50 open to the public.

Those who prefer a spectator's role may witness the unusual sight of Indians paddling war canoes in intertribal competition (*see Tour 2C*), lumberjacks in log-rolling contests, and hard-riding stalwarts "fanning" pitching mounts or roping steers at Old West rodeos. Football, basketball, hockey, soccer, crew, and automobile and motorboat racing are enjoyed in season. Professional boxing and wrestling bouts, frequently of championship caliber, are staged in Seattle and other cities; two of organized baseball's minor leagues—the Pacific Coast and the Western International—offer both day and night games; and there are several city leagues.

Horse racing is perhaps the oldest known sport in the State. Long before the arrival of white pioneers, the Yakima Indians of eastern Washington ran their ponies. In Snowden's *History of Washington* is a reference to early horse racing: "During treaty negotiations (1855) by Governor Isaac Stevens a holiday was suggested by Young Chief, one of the Cayuses' main men and a day was set aside for horse racing . . . in which the Indians delighted and the utmost good feeling prevailed." The typical Indian track was a straightaway, with a post at one end, around which the racers turned and headed back for the starting point. As they neared the finish, the mounts were occasionally "helped in" by frenzied backers, who rode alongside and plied whips. The sport continues today on the Yakima Reservation. Blankets, shawls, clothing, saddles, feed, money, and mounts are staked on the results.

At the present time, three race tracks operate in the State under the supervision of a three-man commission appointed by the governor, with pari-mutuel betting permitted by law. The larger tracks are Longacres, near Seattle, and Playfair, Spokane; brief meets are held at a smaller track at Wilbur. A total of $7,250,000 passed through the pari-mutuel betting machines at the three racing courses during 1938 and 1939, an average of $48,000 for each racing day of the season. The old-age pension fund was enriched to the extent of $360,000 by the 5 per cent allocated for that purpose from the revenue taken in the mutuel gross receipts.

Washington's mountain ranges and high peaks have lured venturesome climbers and explorers since early Territorial days. The first organized group of mountaineers were the Mazamas, of Portland, formed in 1894. Under the sponsorship of the Mazamas, the Mountaineers came into being in 1906. During the initial decade of organization, the Mountaineers climbed the State's principal peaks and constructed two rustic lodges; in 1921, after repeated efforts had failed, they obtained legislation for State parks.

Washington now has a total of 56 State parks, and 26 recreational areas in national forests are supervised by the United States Forest Service. There are more than 700 Forest Service camps, with accommodations for a total of 20,000 persons. The Cascade Crest Trail, beginning at the Canadian Border and extending to the Columbia River without leaving the confines of a national forest, has been well marked by the Forest Service; it follows the hump of the Cascades the entire length of the State. Information on sports and recreation centers is furnished by sportinggoods stores, chambers of commerce, and outdoor associations (*see General Information*). For the visitor to recreation areas, Washington has one admonition: "Remember the fire hazard." Regulations concerning entry to national parks and forests should be observed carefully and fire permits obtained where necessary.

In winter and spring, when the snow is deepest, Washington's mountains are thronged with skiing devotees. It is estimated 60,000 persons spend $3,000,000 annually on this sport. Prior to 1930, skiing was practiced only by a few Scandinavians, private schools, and Mountaineers. Today there are more than 100 miles of well-developed skiing trails, numerous ski jumps, ski lodges, and modernized equipment; and international competitions have been held in the State. While jumping tournaments have been held at intervals since 1914, slalom and downhill races were not introduced until 1930. Yet the sport became so popular that the national ski championships in slalom and downhill racing were decided in Washington in 1934, and the United States team trials for the Olympic Games were held at Paradise, Mount Rainier, in 1935.

To keep pace with the increasing interest in the sport, the National Park and Forest Services have defined a number of skiing areas. Mount Rainier offers 10 courses at Paradise, the shortest 1 mile, and the longest approximately 4 miles, in length. Chinook Pass, just east of Mount Rainier, has 6 courses; Snoqualmie Pass, 9; Mount Baker, 10; Stevens Pass and Leavenworth, 5, and Deer Park (Olympic Peninsula), 2. In addition, there are areas in the Umatilla and Wenatchee national forests, at Blewett Pass, at Mount Spokane, and at Walla Walla. The 16 or more ski clubs in the State are members of the Pacific Northwestern Ski Association, which also covers Oregon and Idaho and is affiliated with the National Ski Association.

Countless lakes, streams, and extensive reaches of salt water have made Washington a mecca for fishermen; rugged heights, sagebrush plains, broad wildernesses, and logged-off territory attract the hunters of big and small game. Before 1932, however, the control and regulation of game by counties resulted in laws so inconsistent and confusing that depletion of game through lack of conservation measures was imminent. In that year the legislature gave the State control of the laws, their regulation and enforcement, and of the propagation of game, under the supervision of a 9-man commission. Uniform game laws and enforcement have given protection to wild life without necessarily curbing the sportsman. Virtually every city and town has its sportsmen's group, affiliated with a State or national organization, which aids the State game commission in determining the opening and closing of seasons so as to give the maximum of protection to game. (*Fishing and hunting seasons vary from year to year; for license fees see General Information.*)

Whether a stream wader, a lake fisher, or a salt-water enthusiast, the angler will find sport to suit his taste in Washington. Cutthroat and rainbow trout flash in the rivers; lake trout include Eastern brook, Dolly Varden, and Mackinaw, and the Beardslee trout of Lake Crescent (*see Tour 3A*), said not to be found elsewhere. Other fish rising to bait in fresh water are bass, perch, chub, catfish, and crappie. Sturgeon are caught in the larger rivers—the Columbia, Snake, and Clark Fork. State hatcheries annually stock streams and lakes.

Salmon fishing, one of the leading outdoor sports, is followed by both the expert and the novice. Spinning and trolling are popular methods in catching the silver, the king, and other varieties. A light rod with drag reel is used in spinning, with a medium-test line and leads, depending upon the tide. Trolling is practiced in a powered or oared boat, with a heavy-test line from 600 to 900 feet in length.

Annual salmon derbies are held in a number of Puget Sound cities. Women as well as men enter these events, which begin in the spring and continue through the summer months. Qualifying preliminaries require contestants to catch a salmon of a certain weight; but, on Derby Day, finalists must fish at a specific time, accompanied by an observer. The size of individual catches determines the prize winner.

The hunter seeking big game will find bear, cougar, and deer in the mountainous country. In deer season, which seldom lasts more than 15 days, the bag is limited to one buck; the law also forbids slaying a doe and the use of dogs. The mule deer, averaging 140 pounds dressed, is found on nearly all the islands of Puget Sound; the larger whitetail, dressing from 250 to 300 pounds, roams the Cascades. Herds of Roosevelt elk (wapiti) range the Olympic National Park, one of the three abodes in the country for this species. Complaints by farmers of elks' raids on crops, coupled with alleged deterioration of the species from overcrowding, have moved the State game commission to permit a short open season. The Olympic area is the haunt also of predatory animals, including the savage mountain lion (cougar).

The uplands of eastern Washington afford grouse, pheasant, and quail, while the best duck hunting is found in the marshes, sloughs, and lowlands west of the Cascades.

Puget Sound is ideal for boating, whether in the "flattie," the sailboat, or the expensive cruiser. Yacht clubs hold cruises and competitions throughout the year, featuring annual races from Seattle or Tacoma to British Columbia ports. Since 1926 outboard racing has built up a large following, more than 100 racers being listed with the Northwest Outboard Association. Regattas are held virtually every week-end from June until Labor Day.

Washington's rivers, lakes, and salt-water beaches provide every type of swimming. Indoor pools are also common; a number have been constructed recently in the arid regions of eastern Washington, with the aid of the Works Progress Administration. Beaches and lakes of the bigger cities are serviced by lifeguards, and park boards hold free instruction classes for youngsters during the summer. The intense interest in swimming has produced an impressive array of aquatic stars, among them two former world's champions, Helene Madison and Jack Medica. Ray E. Daughters, of Seattle, is considered one of the Nation's outstanding swimming coaches.

The triumphs of the University of Washington's crew have been noteworthy. Coached by Alvin Ulbrickson, Washington oarsmen swept the Intercollegiate Regatta at Poughkeepsie in 1936 and 1937, with victories in the varsity, junior varsity, and freshman events. The University crew won at the Olympic Games in 1936. Hiram Conibear, first crew coach at the University, is credited with revolutionizing rowing technique among college crews throughout the country. Oddly enough, Conibear never had coached the sport prior to his arrival at Seattle in 1907, but had been a trainer for the Chicago White Sox Baseball Club. Nevertheless, within a decade, he developed the Conibear System, which has been almost universally adopted by other colleges. Eight of thirteen head rowing coaches in the United States are graduates of the University of Washington and disciples of Conibear. Racing shells made by George Pocock of the University of Washington are used by a majority of colleges.

Three colleges in the State have achieved national prominence in football. The University of Washington at Seattle and the State College of Washington at Pullman are members of the strong Pacific Coast Conference, and each has thrice sent an eleven to the Rose Bowl. Gonzaga University, of Spokane, is recognized as having one of the best independent college teams. The State's three large stadiums are: University of Washington Stadium (40,000); Rogers Field Stadium at Pullman (25,000), and Tacoma Stadium (23,000).

Amateur tennis is one of the oldest competitive sports in Washington, the first Pacific Northwest and Washington State title tournaments having been staged in Tacoma and Seattle, respectively, in 1891. These tournaments remain the major annual net events in Washington, with local entry lists supplemented by players from Oregon, California, British Columbia, and elsewhere.

Famous Washington sports figures include Gil Dobie, James Phelan, "Babe" Hollingbery, Mel Hein, "Turk" Edwards, Bill Smith, George Wilson, Bill Nesbit, Vic Markov, Ed Goddard, Charles Carroll, Max

Krause, and Ed Flaherty, in football; Helene Madison, Jack Medica, and Ray Daughters, in swimming; "Hec" Edmundson, Herman Brix, Ed Genung, Paul Jessup, and Steve Anderson in track events; and Al Unbrickson, Ky Ebright, Ed Leader, Tom Bolles, Russell Callow, George Pocock, in crew.

In hockey, Frank Foyston, Bernie Morris, and Bobby Rowe are well known, while the field of baseball has produced Vean Gregg, Spencer Harris, Fred Hutchinson, Geoffrey Heath, and Earl Averill. Harry Givan, Bud Ward, Jim Barnes, Mortie and Olin Dutra, "Scotty" Campbell, and Jack Westerland have added luster to the roll of golfers, and Wallace Scott and "Hank" Prusoff to that of the tennis court. In equally popular though less-publicized events, Will Thompson, Dr. J. W. Doughty, Ralph Miller, and I. M. Stamps appear for archery, and Hamilton Law, Richard Yeager, T. N. Royce, Mrs. Del Barkhuff, and Zoe Smith for badminton.

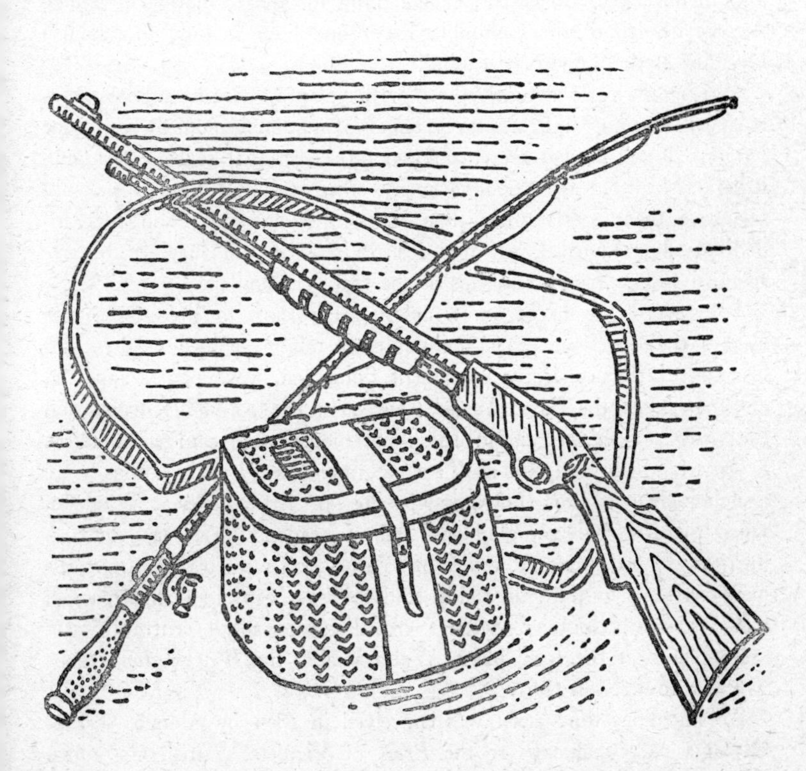

Newspapers and Radio

JOURNALISM'S first effort in the territory now embraced by the State of Washington was the *Columbian,* pulled from the forms of a 70-year-old Ramage press at Olympia on September 11, 1852, and "published every Saturday at $5 a year." The Philadelphia wooden press had made journalistic history in Mexico City, Monterey, San Francisco, and Portland; and the first publication in Washington was also to have a useful career, campaigning for the formation of a new territory north of the Columbia River and later helping to establish Olympia as the Territorial capital.

During the early decades, the Territorial press was acutely sensitive to local opinion, and, whatever issues of national moment might be ignored, bitter clashes were common on a sectional scale. Since publishers risked but meager investments, their columns showed no subservience to interests other than those of subscribers; and the tendentious pioneer press, however absurd its heat and fury, readily responded to current enthusiasms of the frontier populace.

Wherever a boom began, a newspaper sprang to life—there was always the off-chance that the publisher might achieve wealth, and his paper influence, if the settlement flourished. Two papers appeared at Steilacoom: the *Puget Sound Courier* in 1855, a Whig organ, and the *Puget Sound Herald* in 1858, notable because it urged investors to buy land—at the site of Tacoma, miles away! Publications were also launched at Port Townsend in the late fifties, and at Whatcom when the Fraser River gold rush gained headway. After a gold rush into the eastern territory, copies of Washington weeklies, bearing first-hand accounts of the gold fields, sold for $5 a copy in California and what is now Montana. Settlers crowded into south central Washington, and, at the focal point, Walla Walla, the *Washington Statesman* was founded in 1861.

An ingenious innovation was conceived in 1861 by Alonzo A. Poe, Olympia correspondent for the *Press* of Victoria, British Columbia. While waiting for the weekly mail boat at Olympia, Poe printed local news to be inserted as a supplement in the Canadian journal. The supplement quickly won a large Canadian subscription list, and soon afterward Poe printed a briefly successful local edition called the *Overland Press*. Later the paper was renamed the *Pacific Tribune* and, during the legislative sessions of 1867, was issued daily. It is often called the earliest Territorial journal to show such enterprise, but the *Puget Sound Daily,* at Seattle, a year earlier, had lasted for 81 days.

The *Gazette,* first paper north of the Columbia to introduce a wire service (1864), was printed at Seattle by J. R. Watson, who had quarters in the Gem Saloon building. When the local telegrapher received a dispatch, Watson would take up a collection at the bar to pay the toll, hastening then to issue a handbill with the latest news, which also appeared in the next regular edition. In 1867 the *Gazette* was transformed into the *Weekly Intelligencer.*

Other publications arose during the sixties at Vancouver, Kalama, Fairhaven, and Walla Walla, where the *Statesman* (1861) was soon rivaled by the Walla Walla *Union.* Olympia, the nexus of Territorial politics, was the scene of a disordered succession of short-lived weeklies, including the *Temperance Echo* of 1868, which eventually absorbed the *Columbian.* Of such brevity were the lives of most papers that, in the entire Territory, only 12 were active in 1872.

The pioneer press had served to further political partisanship and to attract new settlers to the region; and, through surprisingly unanimous espousal of the Union cause, it had helped to prevent any rift on the frontier during the Civil War and Reconstruction. But the heyday of the editor-owner-printer soon ended, as publishing, increasing in complexity and scope, required more specialized talents and greater resources than the lone printer could muster.

In the seventies, successful daily newspapers made their appearance, mainly representing the expansion of influential weeklies. The *Pacific Tribune* moved from Olympia to Tacoma in 1873, became a daily the following year, crusading against vice and crime, and was taken to Seattle in 1876. That same year the *Weekly Intelligencer* in Seattle also began daily publication and, in 1878, merged with the Seattle *Post,* which had been founded in 1876. The Tacoma *Weekly Ledger* began publication April 21, 1880, and became a daily in 1883. One of the partner-publishers of the *Ledger* sold his interests in 1882 and purchased *Pierce County News,* which as the Tacoma *News* became a daily in 1883.

The Puget Sound press and that of eastern Washington became

clamorous at the approach of the Northern Pacific Railroad; publishers wooed the railroad's favor and issued promotion appeals to attract settlers; journals poured from a score of presses, in many instances subsidized by railroad, land, and timber interests. The *Times,* founded at Spokane Falls in 1879, was soon taken over by the *Chronicle;* other Spokane publications subsequently merged into the *Spokesman-Review,* which continues to be the leading Inland Empire newspaper. On the coast, the Tacoma *Ledger* attracted settlers from other States by its widely circulated special editions. In 1884 a new daily in Seattle, the *Call,* unwisely supported a current anti-Chinese campaign. In opposition, business men subscribed a fund to start the *Times,* which presently absorbed the *Call* and several other papers and, as the *Press-Times,* acquired both Associated Press and United Press franchises and developed into a powerful conservative organ. In July 1896, Colonel Alden J. Blethen came to Seattle, purchased the *Press-Times,* and on August 7, 1896, brought out the first issue of the present Seattle *Times.*

These were years of efflorescence in the newspaper field; there were 109 publications in the State in 1890, but the casualty list was long, too. Changes already in process became marked. The day of modest independent ventures overlapped a period marked by the absorption of many papers, and the bankrupting of others, by publishers with timber, land, or railroad interests at stake. In the years of consolidation that followed, the influence of the smaller publisher was definitely eliminated. Newspaper plants were developing into great enterprises; heavy expenditures were involved.

Some of the larger contemporary papers, strengthened by consolidation during this period, have continued to expand their circulation and to modernize their equipment and methods. The Tacoma *News* and the Tacoma *Tribune,* which began publication in 1908, united in 1918 as the *News-Tribune* of today. The Tacoma *Times* was founded in 1903. In Seattle, the *Post-Intelligencer,* descended from the city's first newspaper, the *Gazette,* founded in 1863, was sold to W. R. Hearst in 1922. It has a continuous-publication record, marred only by a lapse of 97 days during the American Newspaper Guild strike in 1936. Even during the fire of 1889, the *Post-Intelligencer* continued to print as usual. The *Olympian,* founded at Olympia in 1877, was continued under different names and different owners—subject to the stress of political change—and is still the important journal at the State's capital. Aberdeen-Hoquiam, Bellingham, Everett, Yakima, Walla Walla, Wenatchee, Vancouver, and numerous other Washington cities have good daily newspapers, many of them descended from the days of individual and pugnacious journalism.

Of the small independent publications, mostly weeklies, whose influence proved disproportionate to their size, the earliest, the vitriolic *Rebel Battery,* appeared in 1878, attacking a Kitsap County lumber company. The *Model Commonwealth* was subsidized by a Socialist colony at Port Angeles, 1887-8, and the next year *The Workingman,* a weekly supported by the Knights of Labor, appeared in Seattle. The *Union Record,* beginning as a labor weekly after 1900, became a daily during the World War and attained a large circulation before its insolvency in 1926. Nine labor weeklies continue publication in the State. The unemployed movement of the early thirties developed several Seattle weeklies, of which the *Vanguard* and the *Voice of Action* were most widely distributed. The latter, before its suspension in 1936, was influential as a left-wing labor journal.

Since the eighties, Washington has had a varied and culturally influential foreign press. Groups in Seattle, Tacoma, Bellingham, Everett, and South Bend, in particular, have been served by newspapers in their own languages, and most numerous among these are the German and Scandinavian journals. In 1938 Seattle had Italian, Japanese, Negro, Jewish, Swedish, German, and Norwegian-Danish papers; in Spokane only the *Svenska Pressen,* Swedish and English, survives, and in Tacoma, the *Western Viking,* Norwegian and English. In South Bend, the *Willapa Harbor Pilot,* founded in 1890, publishes editions in German, Polish, Swedish, Norwegian, Finnish, and English.

The most significant change in the character of the press generally has been brought about by chain publishing associations, concurrent with the increasing dependence on syndicated material. With the extension of chain ownership and the widespread use of syndicated features, the pattern of the average newspaper's make-up has tended to become standardized, and its principles generally conservative.

Since the World War the State's daily-newspaper map has been undisturbed except by the suspension of a few prominent papers, such as the 57-year-old Tacoma *Ledger* in 1937, of which a Sunday edition is still published. New enterprise has been confined to trade journals and community weeklies—"throwaways" distributed free in urban neighborhoods or small towns. In 1937 Washington had 8 daily and Sunday journals, 23 six-day papers, 7 semiweeklies, and approximately 200 weekly publications.

RADIO

At the Alaska-Yukon-Pacific Exposition, held at Seattle in 1909, a vocalist sang into a mysterious device, and the melody came sputtering through earphones some distance away. After this first crude appearance in Washington, the radio retired to its proper sphere as wireless telegraphy, used solely to safeguard shipping. It did not remain long in seclusion, however, for Lee De Forest and William Dubilier, in Seattle, were experimenting independently of each other. Largely through their work, Washington was able to witness the swift evolution of radio from an early stage. In 1912 Dubilier set up a broadcasting transmitter in Seattle, and visitors to Seattle's summer Potlatch were invited to a curbside booth to listen through earphones to broadcast phonograph music. The Continental Wireless Telegraph Company began to broadcast recordings from a 320-foot wooden tower near the city. The enthusiasm of amateurs was contagious. Rooftops began to sprout antennae, and enthusiastic experimenters filled the air with code signals and weird static shrieks.

In 1919, Vincent I. Kraft, radio instructor at the Seattle YMCA schools, built the first local vacuum-tube station. A station at Everett began experimental broadcasts in November 1920. In 1921 the Seattle *Post-Intelligencer* went on the air from a five-watt station. This and the Kraft station began scheduled broadcasting, on July 2, 1921, with a ringside account of the Dempsey-Carpentier bout.

The public response resulted in immediate expansion, and also in new difficulties. Broadcasters roaming freely over several frequencies caused such confusion that in 1922 the Federal Government established regulations requiring broadcasters to obtain licenses. By that time there were six regular stations in the field, all operating on 360 meters. Among these pioneer stations was KTW, owned by the First Presbyterian Church of Seattle, one of the earliest to broadcast religious services. Allotment of broadcast time was settled by daily argument before the United States Radio Commissioner. Radio broadcasting was still a nonprofit enterprise; advertising was prohibited, and stations were established by various firms chiefly as good-will offerings, in the hope that the publicity might return something on the investment.

In Spokane, a boys' club, under the guidance of a science teacher, set up that city's first station, KFIO, in 1922. By 1924 the number of small stations made broadcasting conditions intolerable, and the Federal Government allotted definite channels for commercial stations, licensing KJR and KFAO in Seattle, KEPY and KHQ in Spokane, and KMO in Tacoma. Radio broadcasting became a business. The arrival of the transcontinental networks, NBC in 1928, CBS in 1929, and MBS in 1937, gave radio a new significance, heralding the time when it would draw the Nation and the world into community.

Education programs were begun in 1921 by Father Sebastian Ruth of St. Martin's College, near Olympia. Leading educational programs at present are sponsored by the University of Washington, Seattle, with lectures on science, home economics, current events, and general topics; and by the State College of Washington, Pullman, which serves eastern Washington with advice on new agricultural methods, farm management, and home economics.

Among nationally known radio artists from Washington are Bing Crosby, Lanny Ross, Mary Livingston, Helen Jepson, and Hugh B. Dobbs ("Captain Dobsie"). "Major" Edward Bowes, famous as a discoverer of amateur talent, was long a resident of Tacoma.

Literature

THE region of Washington, until 1853 merely an undefined part of the vast Oregon Territory, was first presented to the rest of the country by workaday writings not intended as literature but simply as factual depictions of the unknown Northwest. Yet these early ships' logs and explorers' journals are of literary value today, both as authentic first impressions of an untouched wilderness and as source material for modern story tellers.

First to describe the Puget Sound country was the English explorer, Captain George Vancouver, who twice visited it in the early 1790's and recorded his findings in *A Voyage of Discovery to the North Pacific Ocean, and Round the World,* published just after his death in 1798. From 1799-1814, Alexander Henry, a fur trader for the North West Company, kept a journal, which together with much material from the journals and notebooks of David Thompson, surveyor, was printed in 1897 under the editorship of Elliott Coues as *New Light on the Early History of the Greater Northwest.* Lewis and Clark's famous expedition was recorded in the journal of Patrick Gass (1807) and in their own journals (1814). Extensive scientific material on the coastal and Puget Sound region was made available in the five-volume report of Lieutenant Charles Wilkes of the United States Navy, commander of an exploring expedition that visited the Pacific Northwest in 1841. An absorbing account of life in the Oregon country during the late 1830's and early 1840's was given by the Belgian missionary, Father Pierre Jean De Smet, in his *Letters and Sketches* and *Oregon Missions and Travels.*

The Astor expedition to the mouth of the Columbia was chronicled by the Scotch trader, Alexander Ross, and the French-Canadian clerk, Gabriel Franchere, and the Irish clerk, Ross Cox; and upon accounts of Astor's fur-trading venture was based the first literary work dealing with the Northwest, *Astoria, or Anecdotes of an Enterprise beyond the Rocky Mountains,* by Washington Irving. The publication in 1836 of this romantic portrayal greatly stimulated the interest of the East in the western territory. A literary man who was actually among the early western travelers was Theodore Winthrop, a well-born New Englander who, after his graduation from Yale, journeyed across the Cascade Mountains in 1853. His *The Canoe and the Saddle* preserves delightfully the fresh reaction of a young mind to a young country. The book, originally entitled *Klalam and Klickitat: Nature and Natives of the Northwest,* was not published until 1862, soon after Winthrop's death on a Civil War battlefield.

The era of settlement produced a local historical literature, whose aim was to record names and dates and happenings before they faded from memory. Author of the first book to be published by a resident of Washington Territory was James G. Swan, a Massachusetts lawyer, who came West to represent Boston shipping interests, took a donation land claim in 1852 at Shoalwater Bay, and later moved to Port Townsend. His *The Northwest Coast, or Three Years Residence in Washington Territory* was published by Harper's in 1857, and the following year saw the publication by a Philadelphia firm of his *Indians of Cape Flattery.* Swan's friendly relations with the Indians led to his appointment as director of the Makah Indian School at Neah Bay and as Northwest representative of the Smithsonian Institution; his unpublished diaries are now in the University of Washington library. Other early recorders were the Reverend Myron Eells, whose *History of Indian Missions on the Pacific Coast* and *The Hand of God in the History of the Pacific Coast* appeared in 1882 and 1888; Caroline Leighton, whose *Life at Puget Sound* was issued in 1884; and Arthur A. Denny, who wrote of the founding of Seattle in *Pioneer Days on Puget Sound* (1888). In 1889 appeared the first formal *History of the Pacific Northwest,* by Elwood Evans of Tacoma, who later collaborated with Edmond Meany in another history of the young State.

The Indians have provided a recurrent theme in Washington writing, from incidental mention in explorers' chronicles to specialized studies by later authors. Joseph A. Costello's *The Siwash, Their Life, Legends and Tales* was published in 1895. Edward S. Curtis' monumental work, containing firsthand ethnological and cultural data on Indian peoples of the United States and Alaska, was brought out in 20 volumes of text and 20 of photographs by the Harvard University Press, from 1907 to 1930. Katharine Berry Judson's *Myths and Legends of the Pacific Northwest* (1910) was the forerunner of a long series popularizing Indian myths. In 1923, Chief William Shelton of the Tulalip reservation undertook to write a booklet of Indian legends himself.

Interest of writers in local Indian material lapsed, however, until the late 1920's and the 1930's, when the subject was approached scientifically in monographs by Doctors Erna Gunther, Melville Jacobs, and Verne Ray, of the University of Washington, and the independent student Arthur Ballard of Auburn, who contributes to the University's anthropology series.

After the coming of the railroads had broken down Washington's isolation and multiplied its population, a new perspective towards its past became possible. As early as 1903 appeared Colonel William Prosser's two-volume *History of the Puget Sound Country.* In 1909 Edmond Meany and Clinton Snowden set down their account of the colorful process by which fur-traders, homesteaders, military expeditions, shippers, and lumbermen introduced modern civilization among the timeless evergreens; and histories were written in 1916 by Clarence Bagley and in 1917 by Herbert Hunt and Floyd Kaylor. The literature of reminiscence continued to expand during the first two decades of the twentieth century with Albert Atwood's *Glimpses of Pioneer Life on Puget Sound* (1915) and *The Busy Life of Eighty-five Years* (1917). Ezra Meeker also ventured into fiction with *Kate Mulhall: A Romance of the Oregon Trail* (1926). Special historical subjects were taken up in *The American Fur Trade of the Far West* (1902) by General Hiram Chittenden, who later edited the life, letters, and travels of Father De Smet, and *The Columbia River* (1917) by William D. Lyman of Walla Walla. Two early novels based on fact were *General Claxton* (1917) by Cornelius Hanford, who afterward wrote on Seattle and Port Townsend, and *Looking Forward; or, the Story of an American Farm* (1898) by the Populist governor, John R. Rogers, who also published two economic treatises dealing with land and money.

Works with a literary, rather than a purely descriptive, intent began to appear at a time when their authors were, literally and sometimes indignantly, voices in the wilderness. The historian Edmond Meany, who in his later years became the embodiment of the State's history and tradition, spoke for these writers in 1889, the year that Washington became a State. Writing in the new *Washington Magazine,* he plunged thus into his topic—"Has Puget Sound a Literature?"

"No, Puget Sound has no literature but this region has plenty of real estate, timber, coal, iron and fish, and at present the inhabitants are scrambling over each other in their efforts to become rich out of the natural wealths of the land. There is no time to devote to the production or the appreciation of a distinctive literature. . . . They buy and sell too eagerly. Literature will be fostered by and by."

Though Professor Meany died in 1935 without having seen literature exactly fostered in Washington, he did live to see a great deal of it produced in many genres. The State was five years old when Ella Higginson published the earliest of the many volumes of fiction and verse that were to gain her a national reputation. Much of her verse (including the familiar "Four-Leaf Clover") has been set to music and sung by noted singers. Mrs. Higginson also wrote a travel narrative about Alaska, but she expressed the Northwest best in her novel, *Mariella of Out West* (1904)—recently re-issued as a girls' story—a shrewd sketch of personalities and foibles in a new community. Mrs. Higginson, who died in December, 1940, had been chosen State poet laureate by the State Federation of Women's Clubs in 1931.

Mrs. Higginson's early work received the backing of the regional magazine, *The Literary West,* published in San Francisco from 1902 to 1904 under the editorial direction of a Washington writer, Herbert Bashford, author of *Songs from Puget Sea* and other verse and fiction. Between 1908 and 1915 Ada Woodruff Anderson wrote her Columbia River and Puget Sound stories—*Heart of the Red Firs, The Strain of White* (about a half-breed Yakima), and *Rim of the Desert.* About this time, too, Owen Wister lived in the Okanogan country and wrote *The Virginian.* Between 1899 and 1915 Mary Crawford Fraser penned a succession of travel narratives typified by a two-volume work published in 1910, *A Diplomat's Wife in Many Lands.*

The World War and the years immediately following represented a lapse in literary activity. A new mood was discernible in the first notable post-war novel, *The Bitter Country,* written in 1925 by Anita Pettibone of South Bend: it drew upon the somber atmosphere of Swedish and Finnish fishing communities on the Naselle and Chehalis Rivers in southwest Washington, and its "dripping gloom" reminded one critic of Martha Ostenso's themes. This harbor country was also the scene of three later novels which deal with the social problems of the timber area: Robert Cantwell's *Land of Plenty* (1934), Clara Weatherwax's *Marching! Marching!* (1935); and the strike novel *Disillusion* (1939) by a young writer, Ben Cochrane.

Belonging to another strain in American writing was Melvin Levy's *Matrix,* supposed to be based upon actual figures on the university campus, published in 1925; this and *The Wedding* (1927) sounded a note of sophistication, repeated around 1930 by Bertrand Collins in his novels, *Rome Express* and *The Silver Swan.* Levy and Collins afterwards turned to pioneer themes: Collins in *Moon in the West* and Levy in *The Last Pioneers* and in his play, *Gold Eagle Guy.*

A resurgence of folklore also occurred in the middle twenties. Accounts of the feats of Paul Bunyan were collected almost simultaneously by James Stevens and Esther Shephard. Mrs. Shephard, whose *Walt Whitman's Pose* (1938) later presented an interesting critical thesis, repeated the exploits of the mighty logger as she had heard them told; Stevens dealt more freely with the legends, and later traced their sources eastward in *The Saginaw Paul Bunyan.* Stevens' other books, including the semiautobiographical *Brawnyman* (1926), are robust portrayals of the lives of footloose teamsters, loggers, and field-hands in the fluid society of yesterday.

Despite the beginnings made, there was still dissatisfaction with the progress of Washington literature. In 1927 Stevens and H. L. Davis (afterwards author of the Oregon pioneer novel, *Honey in the Horn,*) vented their exasperation in a pamphlet bluntly titled *Status Rerum: A Manifesto, Upon the Present Condition of Northwestern Literature . . . Privately Printed for the Craft.* Sternly they began: "The present condition of literature in the Northwest has been mentioned apologetically too long. Something is wrong with Northwestern literature. . . . It is time people were seeking the cause of this. Is there something about the climate, or the soil, which inspires people to write tripe? Is there some occult influence, which catches them young, and shapes them to be instruments out of which tripe, and nothing but tripe, may issue?" There was, of course, no reply, except the reply of time.

In 1934 appeared Archie Binns' *Lightship,* a story of coast guardsmen on duty south of Cape Flattery. *The Laurels Are Cut Down,* an appealing story of a childhood on Puget Sound and a disillusioning experience with the American interventionist forces in Siberia, followed three years later; and in 1939 his *The Land Is Bright,* which utilized a diary kept by an Oregon Trail emigrant. *Mighty Mountain,* published in 1940, aroused considerable controversy with respect to its presentation of Stevens, first territorial governor. In 1937 the pioneering theme was developed also by the former Seattle newspaperman, Michael Foster, who after a sketchy first novel, *Forgive Adam* (1935), produced the Literary Guild selection *American Dream* (1937). Rooted in Washington soil is the work of Nard Jones, who wrote of eastern Washington in *Wheat Women* (1933) and *All Six Were Lovers* (1934), of young Seattle in *The Petlands* (1931), and of the Columbia

Basin in *Oregon Detour* (1930) and *Swift Flows the River* (1940), a story of steamboat days. Among these writers of genre stories is the State's newest novelist, Elizabeth Marion, whose *The Day Will Come* (1939) is a family chronicle laid in her native Palouse country. Sophus Keith Winther, of the University of Washington, sets his scenes among Danish immigrants in the Middle West in his trilogy, *Take All to Nebraska* (1936), *Mortgage Your Heart* (1937), and *This Passion Never Dies* (1938).

Of the impressive number of publications by faculty members at the University and the State College, the majority are scientific rather than literary. Yet two University professors, Vernon Louis Parrington and his friend and preceptor, J. Allen Smith, have produced works so influential as to establish a new trend in American critical thought. Smith's pioneer work *The Spirit of American Government,* published in 1907, was a realistic political appraisal of the origins of the American Constitution; it offered the general conclusions which Charles A. Beard later documented and reinforced in his *Economic Interpretation of the Constitution.*

As Smith interpreted the Constitution in terms of economic realities, so Parrington applied to American literature the epoch-making method of social and economic analysis. The result of 20 years of labor quietly conducted at the University, Parrington's *Main Currents in American Thought* delivered a mortal blow to the "genteel tradition" in American literary criticism, and brought forward in a coherent pattern the chief lines of America's cultural development. Upon their publication in 1927, the first two volumes of Parrington's monumental work created an immediate effect and won the Pulitzer prize in history. Parrington died suddenly in England before completing the final volume of his study, but the materials for it were arranged for publication by his former student and associate, Harold Eby.

Other University faculty members who have written books of general interest include Edward Wagenknecht, biographer of Charles Dickens, Mark Twain, Geraldine Farrar, and Jenny Lind; and Ottis B. Sperlin, portrayer of Indian life in the novel, *Heart of the Skyloo* (1934). Vernon McKenzie, director of the school of journalism, has utilized his annual trips abroad to compose such commentaries as *Through Turbulent Years* (1938) and *Here Lies Goebbels* (1940), a study of Nazi propaganda. Melvin Rader, of the philosophy department, published in 1939 a searching analysis of the philosophic sources of fascism entitled, after a phrase of Mussolini, *No Compromise.* Glenn Hughes, of the drama division, is the author of *Imagism and the Imagists* (1931), several plays, and *The Story of the Theatre* (see *The Theater*). Contributions by the University faculty to history and literary scholarship include: Frederick Morgan Padelford's studies in Spenser, Allen Rogers Benham's *English Literature from Widsith to the Death of Chaucer,* Herbert Gowen's histories of China, Japan, and Asia, Edmond Meany's standard *History of the State of Washington,* and Russell Blankenship's *American Literature.*

Professor Hughes was also the originator of the pamphlet series, *University of Washington Chapbooks,* which for several years around 1930 presented advanced ideas on a variety of cultural topics. Brochures were contributed by American and European authors; and significant attitudes held abroad were discussed, including the social philosophy of Julien Benda, "Bovaryism," and the aristocratic estheticism of T. E. Hulme. Of special interest is the chapbook on Parrington by Joseph B. Harrison, of the English department, who from 1920 to 1922 headed the editorial board of the *Pacific Review,* a critical quarterly. In the later 1930's, a group of University students issued an experimental magazine, *Perspectives,* later replaced by *Tempo.*

Two fields in which Washington has been rather richly endowed are juvenile and mystery fiction. Writers for children have included Ezra Meeker with his *Uncle Ezra's Pioneer Short Stories for Children, to Point a Moral or Teach a Lesson;* Lurline Mayol, author of *The Big Canoe* (1933); Nora Burglon, whose latest work is *The Cuckoo Calls* (1940); Elizabeth Williams Champney, who wrote more than 40 juveniles and travel books between 1878 and 1917; Walter W. Phillips, whose Indian stories published from 1896 to 1902 were issued under the pseudonym of *El Comancho*; Howard Brier, whose *Skycruiser* (1939) was selected by the Junior Literary Guild; and many others. Among plotters of mysteries who write under their own names are Babette Hughes and Harlan Reed, of Seattle, and Leta Adams, of Spokane. Two former Washingtonians employ pseudonyms: the mathematician Eric Temple Bell became "John Taine" when his pen dripped blood rather than algebraic symbols; and Zenith Jones Brown turns out American mysteries as "Leslie Ford" and English mysteries as "David Frome."

Despite its romantic history and inspiring countryside, Washington has produced little of importance in poetry. Audrey Wurdemann's *Bright Ambush* won the Pulitzer prize in 1936, but her work, as critics have pointed out, bears little relation to the surroundings in which she grew up. A few nationally known poets spent brief periods in Washington: Vachel Lindsay lived in Spokane during the late 1920's; Genevieve Taggard spent her childhood years in Waitsburg; Mary Carolyn Davies was born in Sprague. In light verse, no one here has outdone the rhymes of Stoddard King of the *Spokane Spokesman-Review,* whose regionalism expresses itself thus:

In Western towns 'tis many years since it was last the rage
For men to earn their daily bread by holding up the stage,
Yet story writers still ascribe such wild and woolly bosh
To Saskatoon, Saskatchewan, and Walla Walla, Wash.

Among the best known of recent Washington writers are journalists who have done much of their work outside the State. Most prolific of these is Anna Louise Strong, once feature editor on the *Seattle Union Record,* who has spent years in the Soviet Union as an editor of the Moscow *Daily News.* Among her books are *China's Millions* (1928), *Red Star in Samarkand* (1929), *I Change Worlds* (1935), *This Soviet World* (1936), and *My Native Land* (1940). Oriental topics have also interested Josef Washington Hall, formerly of the University of Washington, who under the pen name of Upton Close wrote *Moonlady* (1927), *The Revolt of Asia* (1927), *Eminent Asians* (1929), and *Challenge: Behind the Face of Japan* (1934). Harvey O'Connor worked on a Seattle labor paper before writing *Mellon's Millions* (1933), *Steel: Dictator* (1935), and *The Guggenheims* (1937). The late Ellery Walter's *The World on One Leg* (1928) and Dwight Long's *Seven Seas on a Shoestring* (1938) record the adventures abroad of two Seattle youths. Norman Archibald sketched his career as a World War pilot in *Heaven High, Hell Deep* (1935). Victor Hurley, now on the staff of a Seattle radio station, painted tropical life in several books. Harder to classify is the work of Max Miller, who writes of his experiences, sometimes faintly glossing them with fiction, as in *I Cover the Waterfront* (1932), and *For the Sake of Shadows* (1936), an impression of Hollywood. His latest books are *Harbor of the Sun* (1940), a history of San Diego Harbor, and *Reno* (1941).

One of the most interesting developments of the 1930's is the return to pioneer themes, in formal history and informal memoirs as well as in fiction. Within this decade have appeared a *History of the Pacific Northwest* by George W. Fuller, Spokane librarian and author of *The Inland Empire; A History of the State of Washington,* by Lancaster Pollard; Arthur H. Hutchinson's *Little Saints Annoy the Lord,* which sweeps away some myths about Marcus Whitman; Roberta Frye Watt's *Four Wagons West* and Sophie Frye Bass' *Pigtail Days in Old Seattle;* James McCurdy's *By Juan de Fuca's Strait;* Dorothy Fay Gould's *Beyond the Shining Mountains;* Robert Walkinshaw's *On Puget Sound;* Guy Waring's *My Pioneer Past;* Glenn Chesney Quiett's *Pay Dirt* and *They Built the West: An Epic of Rails and Cities.* Apparently, the time has come when Washington writers in all fields feel moved to take stock of the past of their State and to examine it in the perspective of the present.

Arts and Crafts

THE first artists among the white men in Washington Territory were the draughtsmen who accompanied the expeditions sent out by the British and United States governments. Lieutenant Zachary Mudge, T. Heddington, and J. Sykes, members of the Vancouver expedition of 1792, recorded scenes and events of the Puget Sound exploration. Titian Ramsay Peale, son of the outstanding Philadelphia artist and naturalist, Charles Willson Peale, was among the scientists and draughtsmen who accompanied the Wilkes Expedition, which reached the Pacific Northwest in the early 1840's. Peale and Lieutenant Wilkes himself made drawings of the local landscape, and Alfred A. Agate and Joseph Drayton, draughtsmen, sketched native tools, canoes, costumes, and portraits of Indians, as well as many geographical subjects; engravings of these drawings were published in the official report of the expedition.

Gustave Sohon, German soldier-artist of the 4th U. S. Infantry, accompanied Governor Isaac I. Stevens on his treaty-making expeditions of the 1850's, sketching scenes along the route and portraits of the great Indian leaders. Unlike most early painters of Indians, Sohon made no attempt to dress his subjects in the conventional war paint and feathers. His drawings are often the only existing portraits of the prominent Columbia River chiefs. Sohon and an artist named Stanley also executed sketches of the countryside, which were made into lithographs and included in Governor Stevens' general report of the United States railroad surveys.

Traveling artists not connected with official expeditions likewise found Washington scenery attractive. Henry J. Warre, a British artist, published in 1846 lithographs of Columbia River and Puget Sound views. Paul Kane, noted Canadian artist, sketched along the Cowlitz River country during his travels, recounted in *Wanderings of An Artist,* London, 1859. "Porte-Crayon," an artist for *Harper's,* drew Washington scenes which appeared in the magazine in 1873. Edmund T. Coleman, a British landscapist living at Victoria, worked in the Territory about

1868; some of his drawings are now in the possession of the Washington State Historical Society, Tacoma.

Apart from these travelers, however, there were few in Washington who gave much thought to art during the nineteenth century. Indian craftsmen made baskets or dugout canoes that in design and execution often achieved the qualities of art. The pioneers and their descendants, in providing themselves with the simple necessities of shelter, clothing, and furniture, revealed imagination and a sense of beauty and form. But the strenuous life of the newly settled territory was scarcely favorable to professional painters, patronage, museums, or art study.

Records of the Indian and pioneer arts of Washington are fairly numerous. In the State Museum, University Campus, Seattle, are two especially important collections: an exhibition of Indian material grouped ethnologically, and one of pioneer relics. Spokane has a valuable collection of Indian objects and wares in the Eastern Washington State Historical Society; and there are similar exhibits at the Conner Museum in Pullman and at the Washington State Historical Society in Tacoma. The Whitman College Museum, in Walla Walla, displays Indian objects and a historical collection drawn from the period of white settlement.

Although commonly associated with the remote past and with musty relics, the handicrafts are far from dead today; they survive as important activities both among the Indian and white populations. Tribesmen are still engaged in basket weaving, miniature totem carving, and the hewing of dugout canoes. While they have, apparently, no special interest in blankets or rugs, the Washington tribes produce baskets that rank in quality with any found outside of Alaska; their rich coloring, skillful imbrication, and design based on geometric forms, on the whale and other animals, bespeak a high level of skill and imagination. Whidbey Island dugouts are still hewed and carved with the ritual ceremony of a century ago; and the Makahs on the Strait still fashion by hand their spear heads and harpoons for salmon fishing.

While modern production has replaced the handicrafts among the majority of the native-born citizens, immigrants have brought to the State many of their homeland crafts. Among the Dutch at Lynden, wooden shoes, worn in the garden, are carved with a skill and artistry maintained for generations. Scandinavian and Dalmatian fishermen may be seen making nets according to the traditions of their ancestors. Finnish women hold annually a summer exhibit at Seattle to display their delicate and richly patterned needlework. In obscure Scandinavian settlements along the Columbia River cloth is spun at home, and tools and farm implements are forged by hand. Even in the cities, within the very gates of industrialism, craftsmanship is honored; and handwrought precious metals and gems, hand-woven tweeds, handmade shoes, and objects of bone, wood, ivory, and wrought iron give proof that handiwork there is not dead.

The fine arts evolved more slowly. The early development of Washington spanned an era in which America experienced a rising financial control of its social life and the most violent impact of materialism upon its culture. After 1850 the daguerreotype became widely popular throughout the country, taking the place of much portrait painting. Of interest today is the following advertisement in the *Washington Pioneer* of May 13, 1854: "Samuel Holmes, DAGUERREOTYPIST, Olympia, W. T. will attend to all orders for the taking of Daguerreotype likenesses, and all other matters connected with the art. Rooms over the cabinet shop of D. C. Beatty." Several painters, most of them unknown to later generations, drifted westward and obtained commissions to immortalize the well-to-do. Time-darkened portraits in commercial houses and public buildings and sentimental landscapes, anecdotal subjects, and occasional copies of famous masterpieces adorning homes, provide a key to the taste of the times. What the captains of the age may have lacked in gentleness, the painters were, apparently, expected to provide in gentility.

Washington became a State in 1889. Eighteen years later citizens of Seattle organized the Society of Seattle Artists; and soon the people of Seattle attended the first annual exhibition of Northwest art. In less than 100 years, local society had progressed from a struggle for existence in an actual wilderness to an artistic appreciation of it as portrayed in landscape paintings. If people had acquired more leisure during this process, they seemed to have lost no energy for organizing and creating—sometimes for the sake of richer living, often in a spirit of promotional competition between cities. Out of the Society of Seattle Artists evolved the Seattle Art Museum with its extensive collection of American, European, and Oriental art, and its many-sided educational program. The Seattle Music and Art Foundation has been a patron of the arts since 1923, and its annual exhibitions have been effective in broadening art appreciation. Outstanding, however, is the work done by this organization's Creative Art Class, which gives instruction without charge to children of four or more years, placing emphasis upon freedom of expression; it is one of the few schools of its kind in the world. In 1926 the H. G. Henry Art Gallery of the University of Washington was founded, and has since presented many exhibitions of European paintings. The Puget Sound Group of Northwest Painters was organized in 1928 and had 40 members at the end of its tenth year. Tacoma, with the Ferry Museum, established while Washington was still a territory, has felt no inclination to acknowledge Seattle as a cultural superior.

To the south, San Francisco with its metropolitan bigness and power and its cosmopolitan manners claimed leadership in every enterprise. On familiar terms with artists and dealers, San Franciscans frequented downtown galleries during noon hours; and the people of Washington were advised to cultivate this habit. In 1931 a local critic instructed the public that: "Seattle, as the metropolis of the Pacific Northwest, must lead in developing a distinctive regional art, which is as important to us in holding our place in the national scheme of things as our libraries, symphony orchestras, and big factories."

If regionalism has so far fallen short of developing a style peculiar to the Northwest, an important group of artists is now striving to express the special character of the Washington scene. In his *Art in America* Holger Cahill mentions Kenneth Callahan, Peter Marinus Camfferman, and Ambrose Patterson as Seattle representatives of the new regional movement in American art. Regional exhibitions have served to support and encourage artists, and, by prompting discussion in the press, have tended to improve the quality of public taste. Recent activity, centering in Seattle, includes the annual exhibitions of Northwest artists, the monthly one-man exhibitions arranged by the Seattle Art Museum, and the shows of the Group of Twelve and of the Women Painters of Washington. Tacoma is also on the rise as an art center, with its organization of artists, the exhibitions arranged by the Tacoma Art Association.

Several Washington artists have achieved considerable reputations. Paul Morgan Gusten of Seattle, born in Vancouver, Washington, in 1886, attracted attention with his mountain landscapes and Northwestern subjects, and has contributed murals to the University of Washington library, Roosevelt High School, in Seattle, and to Washington State College. Roi Partridge was born in Centralia in 1888. Widely known for his etchings and illustrations, he has received numerous prizes and awards, and has work on display at many of the country's most prominent institutions. He is now professor of art at Mills College, California. Thomas Schofield Handforth, born in Tacoma in 1897, is also the winner of many distinctions, including a Guggenheim Fellowship for study in the Far East. At present (1941) a resident of California, he is perhaps best known in America and abroad for his etchings and book illustrations. The murals of Eustace P. Ziegler (1881-), of Seattle, adorn several buildings in that city and the Capitol at Olympia, as well as buildings in the East.

Since 1932 the shrinking of private support for art which accompanied the depression has been met by the sponsorship of the United States Treasury Department, and by the WPA Washington Art Project, headed by R. B. Inverarity. Themes pertinent to the Northwest appear in murals commissioned for post offices of the region: *Local Pursuits,* by Ambrose Patterson, at Mount Vernon; *Mail Train in the 80's,* by Ernest Norling, at Prosser; and *Incidents in the Lives of Lewis and Clark at Mount Kelso,* at Kelso, are among the works sponsored by the Section of Fine Arts of the Federal Treasury. An all-over mural decoration devoted to marine scenes of Seattle, by Kenneth Callahan, was also commissioned by the Section of Fine Arts for the United States Marine Hospital, in Seattle; and Jacob Elshin has executed murals for the same agency in Renton and Seattle. Peggy Strong, of Tacoma, whose easel paintings have been widely exhibited on the Pacific Coast, was recently awarded a mural commission for the post office at Wenatchee. Exhibitions by artists employed on the Art Project have brought to light much new, vigorous talent; and the Index of Design division of the project has unearthed and reproduced many valuable examples of early American design. The Spokane Art Center, sponsored by the Art Project, includes an art school and an exhibition program, both of which have been eagerly received.

In the principal cities of Washington are sculptural works by some of America's leading craftsmen. Seattle displays *George Washington,* by Lorado Taft; *William H. Seward,* by Richard H. Brooks; *Thomas Burke,* by H. A. MacNeil; and *Chief Seattle,* by James Wehn, founder of the department of sculpture at the University of Washington. The *Beloved Pioneer,* a memorial to Ezra Meeker, by Victor Alonzo Lewis, stands in Puyallup; the same sculptor's *Abraham Lincoln* is in Spokane. In Fort Lewis is the Ninety-first Division war memorial, by Avard Fairbanks; in Hoquiam, *Civic Government,* by Dudley Pratt; and in Tacoma, the *Cushman Memorial,* also by V. A. Lewis.

Among the works by local sculptors at the Seattle Art Museum are *Air Spirit,* by Dudley Pratt, assistant professor in sculpture at the University of Washington, who has contributed several notable decorations and portraits to Seattle's public buildings; the wood sculpture *Revelry of the Winds,* by Dudley Carter, a pupil of Pratt; and wood sculpture by Halford Lembke. James Wehn, of Seattle and Crescent Beach, has executed many monuments, reliefs, and medallions for institutions in various parts of the State, and designed the corporate seal of the City of Seattle. Other local sculptors of note are Drusilla Albert and V. Claflin Pratt, both of whom have won prizes at the Northwest Annual Exhibition. A. Phimister Proctor, celebrated modeler of animals and one of America's leading sculptors, is now a resident of Seattle.

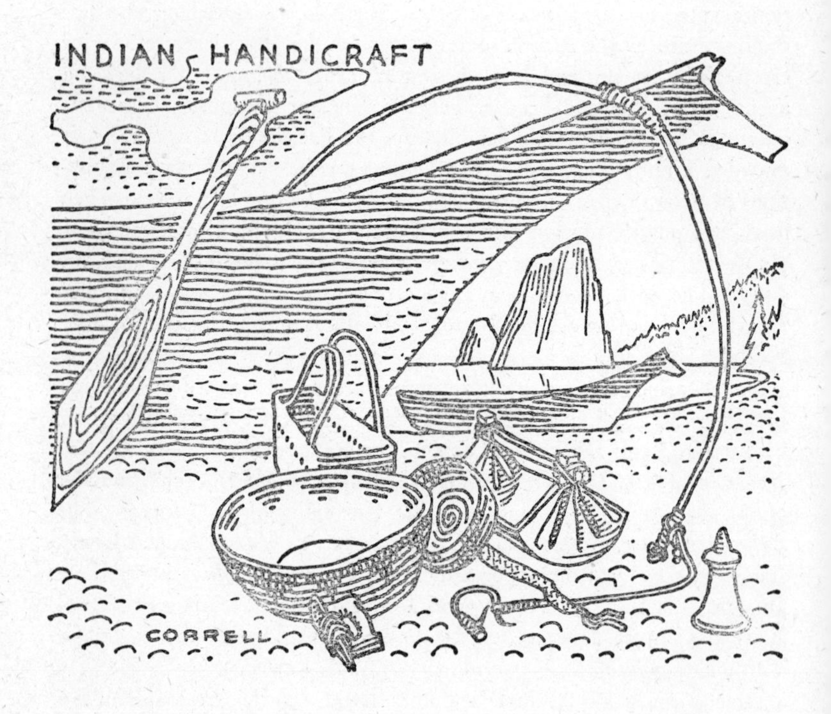

Music

"A SONG too shrill for melody," a wild and piercing "oh-ah we-ah!" was the Indian "Song of the Catch," as they drove their canoes over the Columbia for the salmon run. Indian songs were magic songs, continuing monotonously to the steady drumbeat and the rhythm of the rattles in an effort to gain the assistance of superhuman powers.

Then came the boat songs of the French-Canadian *voyageurs* of the fur brigades—work songs to strengthen the rhythm of their labor as they paddled their canoes and barges along the Columbia and other rivers of the Northwest. Their boat songs and the songs they sang to cheer themselves around the campfire were centuries-old French songs, such as "Dans Mon Chemin A Saint Malo," and "En Roulant Ma Boule," popular in France at the time their forefathers left for the New World. In every brigade there were fiddlers, and sometimes a Scot with his bagpipes went along to rouse the men in a black hour with "The Cock of the North." Around the fire a Scot might dance a Highland fling, and an Indian a native step, while the French and half-breeds danced French folk dances to the old tunes. In the morning a bugle call roused the men for the day's travel.

Dr. John McLoughlin, chief factor of the Hudson's Bay Company at Fort Vancouver, always stationed a Highland piper behind his chair at the head of the banquet table; and bagpipes were prominent on all state and ceremonial occasions. Religious instruction of the Indians was part of the duties of the factors, and McLoughlin began teaching them hymns and chants. Outside the forts on Sundays the Indians danced their old worship-dances in honor of the new God they had learned about.

The Whitmans came in 1836. Narcissa Whitman had a clear soprano voice, "as sweet and musical as the chime of bells." While her husband was making Waiilatpu ready for her, she stayed at Fort Vancouver, teaching the children "Rock of Ages" and other hymns. She had already taught her husband to sing on the long journey over the mountains. The Indians at Waiilatpu loved to hear Mrs. Whitman sing, and it was song more than anything else that won them, before they were crazed by the famine and pestilence of that last bitter winter. The Indians learned quickly the songs the missionaries taught; Indian choirs were the first in Washington.

The American immigrants brought the songs of the times, particularly those that had been made popular by black-face minstrel troupes—the songs of Stephen Foster and others. For instruments they had Jew's harps, mouth organs, banjos, accordions, and occasionally a melodeon, a small reed organ. But most popular of all were the fiddles, and a fiddler who could play a dance tune, such as "Old Dan Tucker" or "Turkey in the Straw," was always in demand.

Richard Covington brought the first piano to Vancouver in 1846, quickly transforming his home into a social center. In 1851 George A. Barnes of Olympia imported a piano. Three brothers named Cornell were gaining popularity there as dance fiddlers, and Oliver Shead, "a splendid ballroom performer" who "had the advantage of being able to 'call' the quadrille changes," was also "in very general request." Vocal concerts soon followed. The *Pioneer and Democrat* reported one in 1855: "The vocal concert given by Mrs. M. A. Ham . . . Monday evening last, was well attended by the ladies and gentlemen of this place. Mrs. Ham labored under several embarrassments, much, no doubt, to her mortification . . . and we understand she was seconded several times by the instrumental accompanist she had engaged for the occasion."

The first Protestant church north of the Columbia River was built at Steilacoom in 1853. With the growth of the churches, choirs gained favor and from these came the first singing societies. In 1870 at Yesler's Pavilion, 30 women and girls "filled the hall with the sweet airs and pretty harmony" in a cantata, *The Flower Queen,* for the benefit of the Episcopal Church. In the same year, St. Paul's Episcopal Church acquired the first pipe organ.

The first theatrical musicians to arrive were black-face minstrels in the 1860's. In 1864, the Taylor Brothers, singers and dancers, and Tom Lafont, the great "American Mocking Bird," noted whistler, appeared at Yesler's Hall. The same year Bob Ridley gave a banjo recital. Barney, the violinist, appeared first with Herman, the magician, in 1860 and returned frequently. In 1872 came David W. Nesfield, baritone, and Mlle. Marie Gaugain, danseuse, with Vivian, an impersonator. Miss Fanny Marston, with a powerful and well-trained voice, gave a concert in 1875, and Louise Irving, the "mocking-bird vocalist," gave a musical soirée with her husband, W. H. Nielson, violinist.

In 1877 appeared the first foreign artist, Ilma de Mirska, the Hungarian nightingale, said to have "the most flexible voice in the lyric profession." Maggie Webb, the "colored nightingale," who sang with the Kentucky Jubilee Singers in 1881, was immensely popular. The first opera troupe arrived in 1876, returning again the next year. The next opera came in 1881, and in 1884 three professional grand opera troupes and two local talent groups played the Standard Theater in Seattle. From then on the Northwest heard all the leading opera companies and all the leading concert stars.

Mrs. M. A. Snyder's Music Class gave their first juvenile opera, *Little Red Riding Hood,* with 20 fairy attendants in dances and tableaux, at Yesler's Hall in 1878 and continued annually for several years. The Arion Singing Club gave *Pirates of Penzance* in 1884, and in 1885 the Club was remodeling Yesler's Hall for its own use.

All special occasions and celebrations required music. Oftentimes it was impromptu, as in 1865 when a crowd at the Olympia wharf greeted the arrival of a new fire engine with the nonsense song:

> 'Tis half-past twelve o'clock and daylight's advancing,
> Johnny am a lingo-lay;
> O hoova-hava, hoova-hava, hoova-hava, hoova,
> Johnny am a lingo-lay.

Bands were organized early, and often the pieces played for celebrations were of local composition. One of the early Seattle organizations was the Pacific Silver Cornet Band, which played for the opening of Squire's Opera House in 1899.

Music became less spontaneous and more refined under the polishing efforts of music masters; it became something to listen to with your hat off. However, there was one place where the fiddle was still a fiddle, and men still sang for fun—the old saloon and dance hall. Saloons usually employed two, and sometimes three, musicians: one to pound out a tune on the piano, the other to play the fiddle. Although the songs were sometimes bawdy, they were just as often maudlin and sentimental ditties; and those who were adept in the playing of tear-squeezing melodies were well repaid. The vocalist was usually an itinerant laborer with more voice than caution, who could remember the words of songs or improvise his own; the tune was not so important.

Yet even here refinement began to creep in. Variety theaters took the musicians, vocalists, and specialty dancers out of the hall and set them on the stage. Then they began to train their acts, seeking ever more polished performers. Soon vaudeville was polite enough for anyone, though not yet rating a dress suit on opening nights. Orchestras were increasingly employed in the theaters during the eighties.

The prosperity of the Alaska gold rush period brought an acceleration of cultural development. Churches began to employ paid soloists and directors; one of these, at least, Theo Karle of Olympia and Seattle, became a star of the concert and operatic stage. Pipe organs were installed in all the larger churches. Operatic associations, singing societies, and choruses increased in number. German singing societies had been organized early in Washington; Turner Hall in Seattle was the home of one of these. Now several more were formed, and Norwegian, Swedish, and Welsh groups had their own singing societies. Thirty choral organizations were flourishing in the early 1900's. The Ralston Male Glee Club, organized by Bowman Ralston (who came to Seattle in 1907), a chorus of 55 voices, won second prize at the Alaska-Yukon-Pacific Exposition; the chorus was accompanied by the Seattle Symphony Orchestra. The club sang repeatedly at Meany Hall to audiences of 10,000 or more. Changing the name to the Seattle Male Glee Club, Ralston continued the organization until his death in 1914; the Amphion Society was an outgrowth of the Ralston Glee Club.

In 1916, eleven American, German, and Scandinavian singing societies, two bands, the Seattle Philharmonic Orchestra, and two other orchestras, co-operated in a five-day summer music festival in Seattle. The last day, a Sunday, opened with a Grand Trombone Reveille, at six o'clock, from the Smith Tower and closed with Handel's *Messiah,* sung by the combined choruses.

The Seattle Symphony Orchestra, the first and leading symphony orchestra in the State, was organized in 1903, with Harry West as conductor. Henry Hadley directed the organization for two years following the exposition. Then as the Seattle Philharmonic Orchestra, with John M. Sparger as conductor until 1921, it continued to expand and to gain wider recognition. It was reorganized in 1926 as the Seattle Symphony Orchestra, Karl Kruger directing, and came under the brilliant English conductor, Dr. Basil Cameron, in 1932. Beethoven's *Ninth Symphony* was given its Northwest *premiere* in 1935; two years later the orchestra, with the co-operation of symphony musicians and choristers from Portland, Oregon, gave a very successful festival performance. Frequent broadcast concerts under Dr. Cameron won a large Pacific Coast audience. From 1938 through 1940 Dr. Nikolai Sokoloff, formerly director of the Federal Music Project of the Works Progress Administration, was conductor. Since then Sir Thomas Beecham has headed the orchestra.

Following the gold rush period, and simultaneously with the organization of formal music groups, there were interesting developments in theater music. Early in the century, all the legitimate theaters had orchestras, but the first motion picture houses employed pianists. One of the first theater organs in the country was an Estey installed in Klemmer's Dream Theater in Seattle. The pianist in that theater, Oliver W. Wallace, of London, England, was interested in organ music but found that, as played in churches, it was not suited to the theater. A skillful musician with a keen sense of theater, Wallace probably did more than any other man to adapt the organ to silent pictures. He became known as one of the country's leading organists and also as a popular composer. By the 1920's, organs had been installed in all the movie theaters in the State. Bernard Barnes, composer of "Dainty Miss," for the piano, wrote a textbook for theater organists, *From Piano to Theater Pipe Organ* (1928).

Then a few small orchestras began to appear in the movie theaters. The first theater concert orchestra in the State was introduced in the Klemmer Theater; this was the Russian Concert Orchestra, a symphonic group without piano. Arthur Kay organized the Coliseum Theater Orchestra; and Liborius Haupman, who had come to Seattle with the Russian Concert Orchestra, organized the Klemmer Theater, later the Columbia, Orchestra. George Lipschultz, violinist, conducted the Liberty Theater Orchestra. Classical numbers at first were played by the movie theater orchestras, but late in the 1920's they were replaced by jazz.

Ragtime developed, during the early 1900's, in and about the saloons and dance halls, largely the product of untrained musicians, with such instruments as they could get their hands on. Saloon pianists playing by ear had a part in its development; Negroes, with the elemental sense of rhythm, had a larger part. Gradually the quality of the instruments improved, saxophones were added; and jazz arrived. Theater orchestras were the first to play jazz, and most of them had gone over completely to it by the end of the 1920's, when the theaters began to be mechanized for sound.

Musical unions vainly fought this technological development. Organists and orchestras were laid off in theaters throughout the State. For a time, jazz orchestras and bands were used on the stage between shows. Oliver Wallace, who is now writing music for Walt Disney pictures, conducted one of these groups in Seattle and Tacoma. However, no mechanical invention has yet proved satisfactory in the dance hall, and dance orchestras, playing mostly jazz or swing, provide employment today for a large number of musicians.

In the field of chamber music, the Spargur String Quartet, founded in 1914 and still retaining its original personnel, has a national reputation. The Peter Merenblum String Quartet, organized at the Cornish School, was also well known.

Each year opera is brought to Washington by touring companies; and the Seattle Civic Opera Company, directed by Paul Engberg, gives a series of operas annually. Besides the Seattle Symphony Orchestra, there are good orchestras in several Washington cities: the Spokane Civic Symphony, directed by George Poinar; the Spokane Symphony Orchestra, directed by Gottfried Hearst; the Tacoma Philharmonic Orchestra, established in 1934 and directed by Eugene Linden; the Walla Walla Symphony, established in 1907; the Everett Symphony Orchestra; and the Lewis County Symphony Orchestra at Chehalis, shared by the neighboring city of Centralia.

In addition to the many glee clubs and choruses of the various schools in the State, there are 30 singing societies. Twenty-one music clubs sponsor concerts and encourage local musicians. The Ladies' Musical Club in Seattle, a leader in this work, also sponsors lectures on musical subjects. Washington has numerous fraternal bands, drum and bugle corps, and, in Bellingham, a Scotch bagpipe band.

David Sheetz Craig in 1915 founded *Music and Musicians,* a monthly journal published in Seattle to report musical activities on the Coast; Mr. Craig continued as editor until 1937. Oscar Thompson, formerly editor of a Tacoma newspaper, is now editor of *Musical America.*

The Whitman Conservatory of Music of Whitman College, in Walla Walla, is the oldest school of music in the Northwest. Its activities include glee club, chapel choir, opera, band, and orchestra. The College of Puget Sound in Tacoma maintains the Conservatory of Music; and Seattle College, Seattle Pacific College, Pacific Lutheran College at Parkland, Washington State College at Pullman, and Gonzaga University at Spokane, each has a department of music. Bing Crosby, radio and screen star, is a graduate of Gonzaga. At the Washington State College, the Associated Students co-operate with the students of the University of Idaho to bring famous concert musicians to the State.

Cornish School in Seattle, which has become one of the leading centers of musical instruction in the West, was founded as a private school of music in 1914 by Miss Nellie C. Cornish. The establishment of the Cornish School Foundation made it a civic institution, privately operated on a nonprofit basis, and it was enlarged to include drama, dance, and art. Many of the musicians in the Seattle Symphony Orchestra were trained at Cornish, and a number of Cornish students have danced in New York, London, and Paris. The school sponsors a children's orchestra, open to all children in Seattle.

The University of Washington School of Music, with an enrollment of 200, has a symphony orchestra of 70 pieces, concert band with 64 members, a chorus, and other singing groups. The annual High School Music Festival is sponsored by the University, and each year the Summer High School Music Institute offers instruction in band, orchestra, and choral work to students from Washington and neighboring States.

Earl Robinson, a native of Washington and educated at the University, recently won praise and national recognition for his *Ballad for Americans.* Howard Biggs, Negro composer, a graduate of the University school of music, composed the songs, incidental music, and orchestral overtures for the Federal Theater productions of *Br'er Rabbit and the Tar Baby, An Evening with Dunbar,* and *The Dragon's Wishbone;* he also composed the organ music for the theater's *Spirochete.*

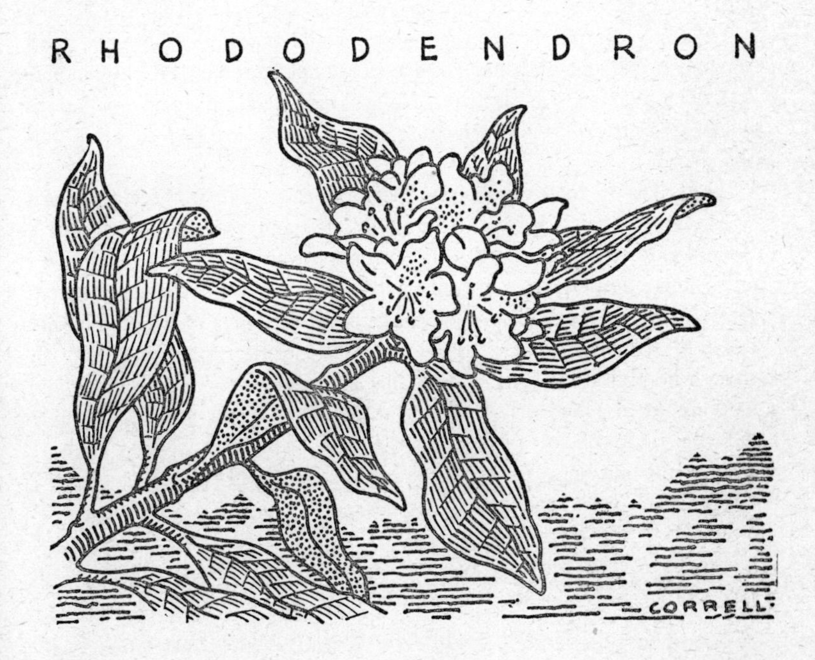

The Theater

THE first entertainments in Washington Territory took place outdoors around the campfires of the immigrant trains: spontaneous affairs depending upon whatever talent was available in singing, dancing, fiddle playing, reciting, and storytelling. As the people settled down and built houses, entertainment moved indoors into the buildings with the largest seating capacity. In the earliest period, these were the cookhouses of sawmills and mining camps. The first entertainments in Seattle were given in the cookhouse of Yesler's sawmill. As the towns grew, halls, and then theaters, were provided for the people's entertainment. The first entertainments were amateur, but as soon as the population grew large enough to support them, professional entertainers appeared; they came singly at first, when the country could not support even a small company. Instrumental and vocal concerts, elocutionary recitals, impersonations and readings, lectures, magical and sleight-of-hand exhibitions made up their repertoire; selections from Shakespeare formed a substantial part of it.

The first of these wandering performers of whom there is record was "General Jack Rag," "celebrated actor and vocalist," who gave a "grand entertainment," in the dining room of Olympia House, Olympia's only hotel, March 19, 1853. Tickets were 25c, children and Negroes free. Although Rag's repertoire consisted mainly of a series of tableaux called "Grecian Statutes," accompanied by explanatory song, and although he played without support, his shows were a marked success and were repeated frequently. Also in those "days when larger companies did not condescend to notice Puget Sound," Professor C. B. (Yankee) Plummer came to give "parlor entertainment" consisting of poetic and dramatic readings and comic recitations. He appeared frequently at Yesler Hall in Seattle and at Walla Walla and other Northwest cities, where he toured for several years. Said to have perfect command of face and voice, he was the universal favorite until about the time Charles Vivian arrived, and then he disappeared from Washington for several years.

Vivian made his first Northwest appearance in Olympia in 1872, supported by a variety troupe. Not only was he acclaimed a greater actor than Yankee Plummer, but Vivian was also a very handsome man. In the days when dress for men consisted almost entirely of jumper and overalls, he created a sensation when he "strolled out of the hotel in patent leather shoes, lavender trousers, black velvet sack coat, white vest and grey crush hat and exceptional linen and underwear." Small wonder Yankee Plummer disappeared! Dry-goods stores owed much to Vivian, who made the men of the old Northwest clothes-conscious. From then on, customs in dress changed so rapidly that in the early 90's in Spokane a dress suit was required for first performances.

Small troupes of black-face minstrels were among the earliest and most popular traveling companies, making their first appearances in the early 60's and holding their popularity until the turn of the century. In 1877 the Tennessee Jubilee Singers, the first Negro troupers, appeared. Callender's Colored Minstrels appeared in 1883 and crowded the seats and aisles of Yesler Hall, and when the Kentucky Jubilee Singers came in the same year, more than 200 people were turned away.

Circuses made an early appearance and were invariably well attended. Bartholomew's Great Western Circus showed at Walla Walla in 1867, and the Royal European Circus visited Port Townsend and Seattle in 1869. In 1871 Mlle. Lucy Jeal brought her circus featuring "lady gymnasts who threw somersaults with masculine ease." Sells Brothers and Barrettes played to 8,000 the first night in Spokane in 1889, just after the great fire.

Washington pioneers welcomed all types of theatrical entertainment: Barker's Great Panorama (1871); Dr. C. Pinkham's lectures on Phrenology closing with the examination of two heads, "admission gentlemen 25c, ladies 10c" (1871); Japanese acrobatic performers (1872), burlesque throughout the 70's, Haskell's Royal Marionettes (1874), McDonald's Band of Trained Indians (1875); Pedestrian Tournament, a pioneer version of the walkathon (1882); Polar Bear Sam's Alaska Indians in native songs and dances (1887). Trained cats were a town sensation at Yesler's Hall in 1875. In 1877 appeared the "Great Egyptian Mystery, or the London Sensation," a "full dramatic company of first-class artists, featuring living persons dissolved into air, tableaux, transformations, and the legendary tragedy of *Faust*."

The first dramatic presentations also were given by amateurs. Later, professional companies appeared, barnstorming up the Coast from San Francisco. One of the first of these, the Pacific Theatrical Troupe, appeared at Columbia Hall in Olympia in 1862. *Uncle Tom's Cabin* arrived in 1871. In 1875 the Fanny Morgan Phelps Company brought Shakespeare.

In 1866 the Pixley Sisters first appeared at Yesler Hall in a program including songs, dances, and a farce. Annie, the oldest of the three, was 14 at the time. They lived in Olympia and appeared frequently in the Northwest cities. Annie joined various of the traveling stock companies, and for 10 years she was Washington's favorite actress. Then she went to San Francisco and the East. When she played Spokane in a return engagement in 1888, she was considered one of the leading actresses of the country.

The first transcontinental railroad to serve Washington was completed in 1883, and "Everybody's Favorite, the little sunbeam, Charming Katie Putnam, supported by an excellent company," was "one of the first to cross the plains to entertain the pioneers of the Northwestern country." For 12 years, until her farewell tour in 1896, she brought a large repertoire of popular plays, such as *The Old Homestead, Lena the Madcap, East Lynne,* and *Old Curiosity Shop.* She was a special favorite of the mining camps. Other Eastern companies followed in increasing numbers, and soon Washington was seeing all the leading American players in their latest hits.

The Von Sou Foong Company brought the first Chinese Theater to Seattle in 1883 for a very successful run. Although intended primarily for the Chinese residents, the performances, lasting from 7:30 to 12:30, drew many Americans, who found enjoyment in the clever pantomime, the weird music, and the strange theater technique. Chinese theaters have continued to appear from time to time.

Grand opera made its Washington debut in 1876 when a company of five, but "a host in talent and execution," performed *The Grand Duchess, Maritana,* and *The Bohemian Girl.* Deakin's Lilliputian Comic Opera Company, a small troupe of tiny people with a seven-foot giant, scored a hit with *Jack the Giant-Killer* in Washington cities in 1877.

Emma Abbott was a pioneer operatic favorite. When Harry C. Hayward brought her to Spokane in 1883 in *The Bohemian Girl* there was no suitable theater, "so he engaged a warehouse that stood on the northeast corner of Riverside and Post streets. The audience paid two dollars each for reserved seats on gang plows and farm implements. Nail kegs in the rear were a trifle cheaper. It was a fifteen-hundred-dollar house altogether." In 1887 Haywood received a wire from Portland, "How much will you pay for one night of Emma Abbott?" He wired back, "$1,000 for Abbott." By nightfall he had raised the whole sum by popular subscription in a town of 4,000. When the train arrived with the singer and her company, a great crowd was there to give them greeting.

In 1895 *Pinafore* was played on a scow on Lake Washington, with the audience seated in a grandstand on the beach. Little Buttercup arrived in a small boat, and the Admiral and his relatives in a steam launch; the villain was thrown bodily into the lake at each performance.

Besides this entertainment for "nice people," the early West demanded another kind. In the earliest days, a large portion of the population were single men of the Wild West type—adventurers and prospectors and seamen of the coast cities. For entertainment they demanded "wine, women and song," a need which the saloon-dancehall supplied. The first women of the dance halls were squaws and half-breeds, but in the late 50's enterprising managers brought in the "Frisco Lillies" from California. While a measure of theatrical ability in music, song, and dance was welcomed, their first qualification was a talent for stimulating liquor sales. From the saloon-dance hall grew the variety theater, and from variety developed vaudeville, which, as the pioneer period passed, became polite family entertainment.

Washington's first theater, the Theater Comique in Seattle, was opened as a variety house in the basement of a saloon on Washington Street in 1876. It was of the "box" type: that is, it had a small stage and auditorium and, most important, a row of boxes around the sides, connected with a bar in the rear. The women did their song and dance on the stage and then, in costumes that for that period were considered the extreme of indecency, mingled with the customers in the boxes, encouraging the sale of liquors. The women became known as box-rustlers, and box-rustling theaters sprang up all over the West. In the 80's, under the stress of competition, managers began to improve their shows. One manager, opening the New Bijou, proposed to run a clean show in an effort to induce women to visit his theater. He was before his time; it was not till the turn of the century that variety became family entertainment, or vaudeville. In 1886, in order to secure better acts and to provide steadier employment for them, John Cort organized the first variety circuit in the world, extending from Butte, Montana, to San Francisco and including in it Seattle, Olympia, Spokane, Tacoma, and smaller Washington towns.

Spokane's first variety theater made its appearance in 1886. While it was recognized that a variety theater might not add to the moral tone of the city, it was accepted as an indication that Spokane was keeping pace with the other cities. After the great fire of 1889, variety theaters flourished like tropical plants, the most notorious of all being the Coeur d'Alene. In 1895 the Ministerial Association unsuccessfully attempted to close the variety theaters, but by 1897 the proprietors had become so emboldened that they adopted the advertising plan of parading the streets on pleasant afternoons. Behind their bands came performers and a host of box-rustlers in carriages. The spectacle aroused much indignation. Under threat of closing, the theaters promised to abandon box-rustling. But promises are easily forgotten. Not till 1908, after an intermittent warfare of nearly 20 years, did an aroused public sentiment force the closing of the last pioneer box-rustling variety theaters.

The season of 1883-4 marked a high point in theatrical entertainment. Katie Putnam, Emma Abbott, Fanny Janauschek, Callender's Colored Minstrels, and the Kentucky Jubilee Singers all played to packed houses as they toured the State. Henry Ward Beecher was second, and Katie Putnam third. Public performances in Seattle (with a population of 10,000) averaged at least 20 a week, with the Chinese Theater and the Bijou going every night, the Maison Doré two-thirds of the time and Yesler Hall more than half.

The growing cities of Washington were known as good show towns. Not all troupes were successful, however. An unfavorable review could kill a show, and many an inferior company was forced to disband. One company advertised a week's engagement at the Root Hog or Die Hall in Spokane; but, after playing to empty benches for two nights, they slid out of town, because the *Morning Review* had advised giving them a cold shoulder. Said the review: "Let this be a warning to other theatrical companies. No free tickets were left at the office in this case. . . . It will be wise for all others to come and see us at once. We want at least six deadhead tickets to a front seat." However, the press as a rule was very fair and a powerful influence in improving the artistic quality of the show and improving theater manners. It condemned the rowdyism of certain elements of the pioneer audiences, the earliest instance of which was noted at Jack Rag's first performance, when he was "dampened by a discharge of cold water from the pit." In 1884 the *Post-Intelligencer* deplored the "custom of many men to keep their hats on during the performance and to indulge in other like eccentricities." When Cordray's Theater was opened in 1890, intoxicating liquor, the eating of peanuts, cat-calls, whistling, stamping of feet, and profane and boisterous language were forbidden. "We regard our patrons as ladies and gentlemen and expect all to conduct themselves as such," said the management. As late as 1904, Seattle and Olympia papers were indignant because some of the tenderest scenes of a Florence Roberts performance were spoiled by hoodlums in the gallery.

The first legitimate theater buildings erected in Washington were Squire's Opera House in Seattle and the Gaiety Theater in Walla Walla, both opened in 1879. The Alpha Opera House in Tacoma was built in 1882. The theaters of Seattle and Spokane were destroyed in the great fires of 1889, but they were quickly replaced. The five-story Auditorium constructed in Spokane at an estimated cost of $250,000, was for many years the largest and finest theater west of the Mississippi. The opening was one of the great society events of Spokane. Box-office receipts for the first two nights (Carleton Opera Company in *Manon*) totaled $5,000.

John Cort was first to rebuild in Seattle with his New Standard, a variety theater. This old brick building still stands (1941) at Occidental Avenue and Main Street, now serving other purposes. Turner Hall and Armory Hall were remodeled as legitimate theaters. A store on Third Avenue and Madison Street was remodeled as the Madison Street Theater; but it was not a success, as the mice scurrying across the floor frightened the women, who all wore long skirts. After a few months, it was remodeled and modernized as Cordray's Theater. Seattle was not satisfied, however, and the magnificent Seattle Theater was built as a civic enterprise. Advance sales of 199 seats and 8 boxes for the first night totaled $3,771, and the theater opened out of debt.

In Tacoma in 1890, the Tacoma Theater (still standing, 1941), designed by Stanford White, was opened with the Duff Opera Company. Olympia's first legitimate theater, the Olympia, was built the same year. All these theaters boasted electric lights.

In the early 90's, Richard Mansfield, Ellen Terry, Henry Irving, E. H. Sothern, Robert Mantell, Maurice Barrymore, John Drew, Maude Adams, W. C. Fields, and everybody else of any importance in the American theater, toured the Northwest. In 1891 Sara Bernhardt demanded and received a guarantee of $3,000 for one night, in both Seattle and Spokane. This period, the golden age for road shows, saw the beginning of resident stock in Seattle; the Cordray-Wass Company, with R. E. French as the popular leading man, opened in Cordray's Theater in 1890. They advertised clean shows and Saturday matinees for children.

Then came hard times. Road shows disbanded, and many theaters were closed. John Cort went broke and left the city. Cordray's Theater went into the hands of the bankers. Seattle, once the most generous patron of showmen, was now considered the worst show town in the West.

The Alaska gold rush, beginning in 1897, put an end to hard times in Washington. Business boomed, and theaters reopened. John Cort returned to Seattle and in 1898 began building his Grand Opera House, which, at the time he opened in 1900, was considered the finest show house on the Coast. The building still stands at 217 Cherry Street, used as a garage.

At that time the Klaw-Erlanger interests were organizing their gigantic theater circuit, including in it all the leading legitimate theaters in the country. But when they came to the Northwest, they found that John Cort had already secured control of the key theaters from St. Paul to San Francisco; so they were forced to make him the Northwest manager. Klaw and Erlanger controlled the road show business of the country until 1910, when Cort organized 1,200 independent theaters in the National Theatrical Owners' Association, of which he was president until 1917. For this he was known as the "trust-buster." The purpose was to give the owners a chance to book a better class of shows, and under the leadership of Cort the legitimate stage reached the peak of its popularity in the years 1910-15. Cort was said to own more theaters than any other man in the world. He was a popular figure in Seattle and was one of the organizers of the Fraternal Order of Eagles.

Not only did all the larger cities of Washington support resident stock companies (dramatic presentations and musical comedy), but touring stock companies were sent out from Seattle. The first of these was the R. E. French Theatrical Company, organized during hard times in 1895. By 1901 it operated three companies out of Seattle, playing a circuit of every city west of Chicago.

In 1906 Laurette Taylor was playing leads in stock in Seattle. In 1912 John Cort took her to Cort's Theater in New York, to star in *Peg O' My Heart* through more than 500 performances. Other Seattle actors of the period to become stars in New York were Guy Bates Post and Sarah Truax (Albert), at that time Mrs. Post.

During the 90's variety had undergone a metamorphosis, and about 1900 vaudeville appeared, completely separated from liquor selling, and began to move uptown. Usually occupying vacant storerooms and featuring variety acts and short pictures, it became known as "store vaude."

During the vaudeville craze in 1901-2, new shows opened by the dozen in Washington, and in 1902 John Considine, of Seattle, organized the Sullivan-Considine Circuit. It was operated out of Seattle and was the first popular-priced (10c) "polite" vaudeville circuit. By 1906 it had grown so popular that an act booked in Seattle, or in certain Eastern cities, was assured a year's engagement.

Alexander Pantages, a Greek immigrant, learned the show business in the saloon-dance halls of the Alaska gold rush period, where he had arrived penniless. In 1902 he came to Seattle and invested his savings in the Crystal Theater, in which he was everything from manager to janitor. He operated it as a popular vaudeville house. Then he organized a western vaudeville circuit, competing with his friend, Considine. In 1904 he moved into the Pantages Theater, and in 1905 he branched out into stock with the Lois Theater, named for his wife. In 1915 he extended his circuit from coast to coast, showing American and European acts. He always played a lone hand, never combining with other theater men. In 1929, just before the crash came, he sold out.

The forerunner of moving pictures, the Great Stereopticon, featuring dissolving views of England, France, and the Holy Land, showed in Yesler Hall in 1871. In 1894 Edison released the first commercial (kinetoscope) motion pictures, and they were shown on December 12 of the same year in Seattle. The first theater showing of motion pictures was an Edison bioscope exhibition at the Auditorium Theater, Spokane, in 1896. The next year veroscope pictures of the Corbett-Fitzsimmons fight, the first series of pictures about a single subject, were shown in all the cities of Washington. On a film two and one-third miles long were 143,000 distinct pictures. Pictures were shown with increasing frequency in variety theaters and were a factor in the vaudeville boom. In 1902 Edison's Unique Theater, a picture house, was built in Seattle; by 1903 all the cities of Washington could boast of motion picture theaters, showing such subjects as *The Life of a Fireman, The Tramp and the Bulldog, Freight Train Passing Through Royal Gorge,* and May Irwin and John Rice in their great kissing scene.

Then came improved picture technique and Mary Pickford, Mack Sennett, and Charlie Chaplin. Picture theaters were built in all the small towns. Pipe organs were installed to accompany the silent pictures, then orchestras. Slowly but relentlessly, pictures began to crowd out the living professional performer. The movies took the smaller cities and towns first; one-night stands disappeared, and split-week houses became one-night stands.

The first talking pictures in Washington were shown unsuccessfully at the Synchrodrome Theater in Seattle in 1908. Silent pictures continued and reached their zenith in the 1920's. Then came the vitaphone with Al Jolson in *The Jazz Singer,* and in a short time all movies were talkies. Competition became more relentless, until there were only three stock companies left in the State, two in Seattle and one playing intermittently in Spokane and Tacoma. Yet even during the decline, Katherine Cornell, delayed by a railway accident, found her Seattle audience still waiting for her in the theater at eleven o'clock. The scenery was rushed to the theater, the audience watched it as it was set up, and the show went on at two in the morning.

The depression administered the knockout blow to the commercial stage in Washington. The Henry Duffy Players in Seattle, featuring expensive guest stars, were forced to close; Tobey Leitch's Comedians, playing popular-priced stock and vaudeville circuits, in partnership with the movies and as "presentations" before the movies, continued for a time and then closed down. Vaudeville shows have been reopened from time to time in picture houses. Burlesque and "girl shows," however, continued throughout the depression in certain theaters that catered largely to men. Floor shows in clubs and roadhouses still offer a limited field for vaudeville acts.

With the decline of the commercial theater, the college and community theaters inherited the responsibility of maintaining the legitimate drama. *Bread upon the Waters,* a melodrama, was the first University of Washington theatrical production. In 1920 the department of dramatic art (superseded by the division of drama of the English department in 1930) was created, and the University was on its way toward developing an excellent theatrical school. In 1926 it inaugurated a series of famous films, one of the first to be established in any American educational institution, enabling students to follow the evolution of screen art. In 1934 the division of drama, whose plays had been given in Meany Hall, opened the small Studio Theater (seating capacity of 60) under the direction of Glenn Hughes, in order that the actors might have the experience and discipline of a long run.

The long-run record for an American college production was established at the Studio Theater during the 1934-5 season with Sidney Howard's *Alien Corn,* which ran for 50 performances. In the principal role was Frances Farmer, who shortly afterwards was discovered by Hollywood and is now a star. In 1935, after two seasons of experimentation, the unique Penthouse Theater was opened. It was designed for the performance of drawing-room plays in a central acting space, surrounded on the four sides by elevated seats for an audience of 120 persons. Both these very successful theaters were located off the campus in the University business district. The Showboat Theater, set on piling on the campus water front on Union Bay, constructed as a joint enterprise of the Works Progress Administration and the University's division of drama, was opened in September 1938. The equipment is modern throughout, with a revolving stage. It is one of the few college theaters that run six nights a week throughout the year. The new Penthouse Theater has been opened recently on the campus, near the Showboat.

Under the management of the executive director, Glenn Hughes, playwright and authority on theaters and theater history, all operation expenses are met by box-office receipts, and surpluses are used to augment the equipment and to purchase books for the division of drama library. This library, now numbering more than 12,000 volumes and increasing at the rate of 100 a month, includes a circulating library of 2,000 plays for loan by mail throughout the State. The division of drama also has a puppet theater.

Cornish School, which operates a professional school of the theater, opened the Cornish Theater in 1920 with a group of one-act plays, directed by Maurice Browne and Ellen Van Volkenburg. From this start developed the Moroni Olsen Players, who annually toured the country. The theater maintains three groups of players, offering classic and modern dramas.

The development of community theaters began in the period following the First World War. Some of the more successful ventures are the Tacoma Drama League (organized in 1919), the Bellingham Theater Guild, and the Spokane Little Theater, each of which presents a series of outstanding plays each year. Sarah Truax Albert has become a favorite of little-theater groups and ladies' clubs in readings of Broadway successes.

Seattle's civic theater, the Repertory Playhouse, was founded in 1928 by Florence and Burton James, who see the theater as a social force and a force for education. A series of six or more high-quality plays each season, with an annual summer drama festival that attracts visitors from many different States and foreign countries, have made the Playhouse one of the leading institutions of its kind in the country. Some of the notable successes have been Ibsen's *Peer Gynt,* Goethe's *Faust, No More Frontier* by Talbot Jennings, and Thornton Wilder's *Our Town.* In its fourth season, in collaboration with the school authorities, the Playhouse inaugurated a series of weekly matinees for high-school students, which proved so successful that in 1936 the Playhouse, the State Department of Education, and the Rockefeller Foundation co-operated to found the Washington State Theater, the first State theater in the country. It was a professional touring company playing throughout the State—Shakespeare's plays and classic and romantic productions—with matinees for high-school students and evening performances for adults. Audiences totaling seventy thousand the first year justified the experiment. Other activities of the Playhouse include public readings of worthwhile plays, which they cannot give production, and a complete theater school.

From pioneer times, Washington authors have shown an interest in the theater. Joaquin Miller's *Forty-niners* was included in the repertory of one of the early traveling companies. In 1895 in the Auditorium in Spokane, a light opera, the *White Faun,* by Professor Franz Mueller with libretto by Reginald F. Mead, was performed. It was described as a "romance of the wide, wild west with Indians, cowboys and refined young ladies disporting on the stage." The Moore Theater in Seattle was opened in 1907 with a comic opera, *The Alaskan,* by Joseph Blethen, libretto by Harry Girard, both Seattle men. When taken to Broadway, a New York reviewer noted particularly the song "The Totem Pole is My Family Tree."

The Wayfarer, a play "symbolic of doubting, wondering humanity," with scenes showing rivers of ancient Babylon, the plains of Judea, the streets of Jerusalem, and a war-torn village of Flanders, was written by a Seattle man, James E. Crowther, and produced by another Seattle man, Montgomery Lynch; it had its introductory performance at Columbus, Ohio, in 1919, running 24 days, with tremendous crowds in attendance. Later it ran at Madison Square Garden in New York for five weeks. July 24-29, 1922, it was produced out of doors at the University of Washington Stadium and was repeated the following year on popular demand. *Gold Eagle Guy,* by Melvin Levy, a former Washingtonian, was presented on Broadway; and *Wings,* by John Monk Saunders, educated at the University of Washington, was an excellent screen presentation.

More recently University of Washington courses in playwriting under Glenn Hughes have given impetus to young authors, and Washington's community and little-theater groups have given encouragement to local playwrights. Seattle Repertory Playhouse has produced plays by Garland Ethel, Albert M. Ottenheimer, Marianne

King, William Kimball, and Glenn Hughes. The prize play *See How They Run,* by George M. Savage, Jr., was produced by the Federal Theater. The Tacoma Drama League authors include Marietta Hunter Kennard, Elsa Nessensen, and Douglas Wight.

Federal Theater activities in Washington included an art project to build models of historic theaters (the completed models may be seen at Denny Hall on the University campus); a historical research project collecting and classifying material on Washington theaters, 1852-1910, from newspaper and program files; and three acting companies. Notable among the Federal Theater's productions were the *Living Newspaper's Power, One Third of a Nation,* and *Spirochete* and the Negro company's *Stevedore* (written by Theodore Browne, a member of the company), and *Br'er Rabbit and The Tar Baby.*

Washington has contributed many famous names to stage and screen. Besides those already mentioned, the roll includes Robert Armstrong, Bing Crosby, Josephine Hutchinson, Constance Cummings, Elena Miramora, Mary Livingstone, Guthrie McClintic, and the dancers, Caird Leslie and Marcel LePlat.

Washington has the equipment, theaters, actors, artists, technicians, musicians, and playwrights needed to create a great theater. It has a history of achievement, and certain groups again show an intense interest in the art of the theater. Its cities may become once more leading theatrical centers of the Pacific Coast.

Architecture

THE first explorers in the region east of the Cascades found the dwelling of the horse Indians was, quite naturally, the tepee. Light in construction, its simplicity and mobility well suited the nomadic tribes who inhabited the Plains and were constantly changing their camps. But west of the Cascades an entirely different type of dwelling was common—the long house, with walls of crudely split wood and gabled or shed roofs, which were covered with cedar slabs or bark held together with wood pins or, sometimes, thongs. Floors, usually of dirt, had pits in the center for fires. Pins on the walls held dried fish, blankets, and trinkets. When numerous persons occupied the house, tiers of crudely fashioned bunks lined the walls, much in the manner of the early logging-camp bunkhouses.

As fish was the main sustenance of these Indians, many of their dwellings extended over the water on piling. Deep mounds of shells—the accumulated refuse from clams and mussels—mark the sites today. Examples of the long house are located at LaConner and Toppenish.

With the entry of the white men, the era of the log cabin began. The log cabins built around 1825 by the Hudson's Bay Company at Fort Vancouver, the oldest continuous settlement in the State, had a distinct style derived from Canadian and Great Lakes types.

To meet the constant threat of the Indians, the cabins in the various early posts were surrounded by bastions and palisades. The palisades, usually rectangular in plan, were formed of perpendicular rows of logs, driven close together in the ground, with the tips sharpened to prevent scaling. The corners were surmounted by blockhouses: square, peak-roofed forts that projected beyond the face of the palisade, the overhang enabling the defenders to fire upon attackers through loop holes in the blockhouse walls.

These first cabins were most primitive, having one room with a crude loft. Then followed cabins having two rooms separated by an open corridor or "dogtrot," which served as entrance and washroom. A steep stairway or ladder led from this passage to the loft. Job Carr's

Cabin, the first house built by white settlers in the Tacoma region, has been reconstructed and is now in Point Defiance Park.

Unpeeled logs were used for the early types, although some were not only peeled but squared as well. The bottom log was placed directly on the ground, notched at each end to fit the next log. Cracks were caulked with mud, chips, and moss. This form of construction caused drift and pull, in spite of the wooden pins, and resulted in many lopsided cabins. A good existent example is the two-room Sawyer cabin near Yakima, which, although built in the eighties, represents one of the earliest types. To overcome drift, the end of the log was cut on the upper side in the shape of an inverted V, upon which the end of the next log, cut to match on the lower side, was fitted to form a tighter joint. A good example is the Jackson Prairie Courthouse, south of Mary's Corner. At the time of its building in the 1840's, the house was on a branch of the Oregon Trail.

Roofs were covered with hand-split shingles or shakes, although clay was sometimes used, as for example in the Wayfarer's Cabin at Omak (*see Tour 7a*). The most common method of supporting the clay was to allow the top log of the end walls to project beyond the side walls sufficiently to support a pole along the eaves, which took the thrust of the close-fitted, clay-covered rafters and rose far enough above them to retain the clay. Along the gable ends the clay was held in place by boards that followed the slope of the roof.

The Whitman Mission, built in 1836 at Waiilatpu (about six miles from Walla Walla), was a rare example of adobe construction in the State. Crudely built by unskilled workmen, the little mission was also roughly, but ingeniously, furnished. Edmond S. Meany, historian, quotes Mrs. Whitman's description: "We had neither straw, bedstead nor table, nor anything to make them of except green cottonwood. All our boards are sawed by hand." The Jesuit Ahtanum Mission, near Yakima, which was built in 1847 and rebuilt in 1872, is a good example of pioneer architecture.

With the advent of sawmills and skilled workmen, about 1837, lumber squared by ax and saw began to replace the rough log; the shifting log-and-pin construction gave way to mortise and tenon, dovetail, and tongue and groove work. The latter system was much used by the Hudson's Bay Company in its forts. An excellent example of the tongue and groove joining is preserved in the restored Fort Nesqually at Point Defiance Park in Tacoma, and a typical example of dovetail work may be seen at Fort Simcoe. The Covington House in

Vancouver, the oldest in the State (1845), was reassembled from the original materials in 1931; it shows the dovetail work, clapboarding, and gabled roof.

The interior of the early cabin was as roughhewn as the exterior; the floors were of tamped earth or of puncheons (split logs) covered with planks; windows were unglazed but often covered with hides or canvass; one end of the cabin, marked by a stick and mud or stone fireplace, was used for cooking. Later, the outer wall surfaces, as well as interior walls and ceilings, were finished with vertical boards and battens. Furniture was not only expensive but difficult to obtain. Crude box cupboards, stools, drop-leaf tables secured to the wall, and handmade bedsteads constituted the furnishings of the pioneer house.

Following the boom in California (1849-50), sawmills multiplied rapidly in Washington. To these mill settlements came disappointed prospectors from the gold fields and others attracted by the Donation Land Law of 1850; forests were cut to feed the saws, and there arose, not log cabins, but mill houses. Clapboards, shingles, boards, and battens were used for the walls. Usually a story and a half or two stories high, with gabled roofs, the houses stood in uniform ugliness along the muddy streets. Wings, bay windows, hipped roofs, and porches were seen occasionally, but almost invariably the lean-to and the string of outbuildings—woodsheds, stables, milkhouses, and smokehouses—necessary in a period when fall slaughtering, soapmaking, and milking were important home processes.

The settlers, for the most part, were poorer people of New England, the Middle West, and the South, who sought the freedom, opportunity, and equality of the frontier. They followed the rules and conceptions of building known to their fathers. Predominant among the types brought to the West was the New England Colonial. Such houses as Major Granville O. Haller's and Captain Thomas Coupe's sprang up at Coupeville, Whidbey Island. One of the first brick buildings in the Territory was erected during this period (1855-60): the old Whatcom Courthouse at Bellingham, built of bricks from Philadelphia. The Barracks at Vancouver are typical of the period, having log walls sheeted with siding, narrow windows, and severe lines.

The church of the time was typically Georgian Colonial. The simple tower, usually above the portal, was of siding or shingles, broken here and there by small windows or louvers. The tower was frequently surmounted by a belfry, and a round or many-sided steeple. In some cases, such as the Claquato Church (west of Chehalis), the towers showed excellent mortise and tenon work. In most churches some attempt towards finish was made; woodwork and pews were painted, often a soft yellow, and the walls were papered. The floors, however, were roughly finished.

During the Territorial period, while structures reminiscent of Colonial days were being built in Washington, a new architectural style—the Greek Revival—had developed in the East. It spread westward in the wake of the covered wagon and the oxcart, bringing the Greek style to schools, hotels, jails, and other public buildings, and Greek names to streets and towns—Ionia, Sparta, Athens, Corinth.

The people of early Seattle were determined to have a Territorial university and the building was erected in 1861, on the site now occupied by the Metropolitan Center buildings. Influenced by the Greek Revival, it had a two-story portico with four Ionic columns and classic entablature. Above the cornice ran a balustrade, over which rose the roof crowned by a square drum, in turn balustraded and topped with a belfry. It was the first and last example of classic architecture until almost 1900.

The influence of the Victorian Gothic was not appreciable in Washington until the railroads arrived in the late seventies and eighties. Then, in the "Parvenue Period," it was gratefully received by a people tired of the barrenness of pioneer life and more than eager to portray their social equality with the rest of the Nation. From extreme simplicity, architecture veered to extreme ornamentation; jigsaws and lathes were speeded up in an orgy of production. Houses of the period, such as the two-story Samuel Benn home in Aberdeen (1887), were high and narrow. A high, shallow porch with chamfered posts was often topped by another equally slim and ornamented; towers and roofs were edged with scalloped shingles; chimneys were numerous; bay windows with small diamond panes of colored glass sprang from corners embellished with scrolls, brackets, patterned wood panels, and jigsaw fretwork. The Stacy home in Seattle, built in 1883, shows an adaptation of the French style of the Third Empire, with mansard roof, dormers, and cupola. (It is now used as a restaurant.)

In 1889 disastrous fires swept the wooden business sections of the State's four largest cities. In rebuilding these, wood was replaced by brick, stone, and the new-fangled cast-iron fronts. Columns of one order were piled upon those of another; pilasters ran from base to cornice or, in some cases, embellished every other story. There were cornice-high tiers of bays, crenelated parapets, and fantastic brick and stone tracery. A mixture of any and all styles commonly appeared: Gothic, Renaissance, Byzantine, Romanesque, and Georgian. The Spokane County Courthouse (1895), an example of modified French Renaissance, the Colfax and Dayton courthouses, and commercial buildings in the older business sections of the larger cities are excellent examples of architecture at the turn of the century. Among the good adaptations of the Gothic are the Saint James Church in Vancouver (1884-5) and the First Presbyterian Church in Tacoma, designed by Ralph Adams Cram.

Just before the twentieth century opened, however, the Romanesque style of architecture as adapted by H. H. Richardson brought a more restrained note. Washington has several good examples, notably the Pierce County Courthouse (1890-3) in Tacoma, built by Proctor and Dennis; the Old Capitol Building at Olympia, built in 1893 after the design of Willis A. Richie; and St. Aloysius Church in Spokane, built in the nineties by Preusse and Zittel. During this same period Stanford White, of McKim, Mead and White, designed the Tacoma Theater and the Tacoma Hotel, which was destroyed by fire in 1935. The theater building is in the style of the Norman chateau. The buildings of the Western Washington College at Bellingham, opened in 1899, are good adaptations of the Romanesque. While the Richardsonian style was not adapted to frame structures, it did influence residential architecture in the State, as elsewhere; the tendency toward the high and narrow gave way to broader and lower lines.

The Romanesque influence persisted into the early 1900's; one of the well-designed later buildings is Our Lady of Lourdes Cathedral in Spokane, built in 1908. The Renaissance and Classic styles were still popular for public buildings and churches. Among the outstanding adaptations of the Roman Classic is the Federal Building in Spokane, erected in 1909. The Stadium High School in Tacoma was originally designed by Frederick Heath as a hotel for the Northern Pacific (1906), but was remodeled for use as a school building after the interior had been destroyed by fire; it is a fine example of early French Renaissance style. The Stadium beside it on the water front was constructed in a natural gulch in the form of a classical amphitheater. Tacoma's Public Library (1903) was designed by Jardine, Kent, and Jardine in the French Renaissance style. The Italian Renaissance is well represented by St. James Cathedral in Seattle, built in 1907.

With the growing industrialization of the country, land prices rose higher and higher. Then with the introduction of steel-frame construction in the later eighties, the skyscraper type of architecture began to evolve. The struggle between old styles and new forms and materials continued; and the early skyscraper represented a compromise solution of the problem based upon the old formula of a classic column: base, shaft, and cap. The first three or four stories constituted the base with columns and classic voids; upon this rose the main shaft which, in turn, was topped with a classic frieze and projecting cornice, often out of all proportion to the building itself. A good example of the early skyscraper is the ten-story County-City Building (1916) in Seattle. Two years before the construction of this building, the 42-story Smith Tower had arisen in the same city. Designed by Gaggin and Gaggin, the Smith Tower is one of the tallest buildings on the Pacific Coast.

One of the important building programs in the State was begun during the second decade of the twentieth century—the construction of the Tudor Gothic buildings of the University of Washington in Seattle. Several architects who had come to the State to help in the planning of the Alaska-Yukon-Pacific Exposition (1909) buildings remained to work on the University campus. Other State architects contributed their designs, as the buildings continued to arise between 1913 and 1940. The firm of Bebb and Gould, with Carl F. Gould, one of the leading Northwest architects, and Charles Herbert Bebb, of Mortlake, England, as partners, were responsible for the general plan and for the designs of many individual buildings. Among other architects having a share in the University program were Abraham Horace Albertson, Charles Henry Alden, John Graham, George Willis Lawton (Denny Hall), David J. Myers (Women's Dormitory), and P. D. Richardson. Three buildings of the Alaska-Yukon-Pacific Exposition, designed by John Galen Howard, now stand on the campus at Seattle: Meany Hall, Physiology Hall, and Engineering Hall.

Another large-scale program was begun in 1906 in Seattle: the construction of the Metropolitan Center, a planned business district, said to be the first in the country. John Mead Howells, the late Robert C. Reamer, Isaac N. P. Stokes, and other State architects have helped to design the eight modern structures in Renaissance style, including the Olympic Hotel, which now stand on the site of the old University campus.

In 1916 New York City passed an ordinance against the old skyscraper type building, at least in cases of excessive height; other cities were not slow to follow. This indirectly produced the "set-back" type of architecture. The Northern Life Tower (1929) in Seattle, designed by P. D. Richardson, is one of the best examples in the State. The Larson Building in Yakima, built in 1931 after a design by the local architect, John W. Maloney, the King County Hospital (1931), and the United States Marine Hospital (1932) by Bebb and Gould, both in Seattle, are also in the set-back style.

With the gradual development of modern functional design, numerous buildings have been erected in Washington approaching this ideal. One of the most admirable examples is the Hotel Edmond Meany in Seattle, built in 1931 after the plans of R. C. Reamer. Structural symmetry and free treatment of planes in this building show the influence of post-war German architecture. The city of Everett possesses two unusually good modern structures: the brownstone Public Library (1934), designed by Bebb and Gould with perfect relation to its function; and the City Hall (1930), designed by A. H. Albertson. The Thurston County Courthouse in Olympia, planned by a local architect, Joseph Wohleb, is simple and forthright in design. Seattle's Art Museum (1933), by Bebb and Gould, is another good example.

The modern style, with its stress on function, has been used frequently in industrial and public buildings. The City Light Building in Seattle (1935), designed by Earl W. Morrison, is exceptionally pleasing and suited to its purpose. An interesting application of modernist design may be seen in the remodeled Colman Street Ferry Terminal (completed in 1937), Loveless and Fay, architects. The Water Department Shop in Tacoma (1939) succeeds in being both attractive and functionally admirable. The big United States Courthouse Building, recently completed in Seattle, is distinctly modern.

Interesting architecturally and reflecting the dominant industries of the State are the numerous lumber mills, paper and plywood plants, canneries, oyster-packing plants, dehydrating plants, piers, grain elevators and docks, found especially in the port cities. Prominent among these are the Weyerhaeuser Sulphite-Pulp Plant at Everett, the Terminal Grain Elevator in Vancouver, the Aberdeen Plywood Plant, Olympia's Oyster-Packing Plant, Fisher Flouring Mills Company and Boeing Aircraft Company plants in Seattle, the Tacoma Smelter, the dehydrating plants in Yakima, and the piers of Seattle, Vancouver, Everett, Grays' Harbor, and Tacoma.

As in other States, the traditional styles have been used for special purposes. Thus, the neo-Classic style is still popular for such buildings as post offices, libraries, banks, and public buildings. Examples may be seen in the Seattle Public Library and, most imposing of all, in the

State Capitol Buildings at Olympia. The Legislative Building, with its dome modeled after that of the Capitol at Washington, D. C., would have warmed the hearts of classicists a century ago. The group, designed in Roman-Doric style by Wilder and White, of New York City, was begun in 1911, and the latest building was finished in 1935. The Governor's Mansion, strictly and beautifully Georgian in style, in contrast to the other buildings, was designed by Bebb and Gould, of Seattle, consulting architects for the whole group.

The Gothic has been generally adapted for churches and schools. The University of Washington buildings at Seattle and those of the College of Puget Sound (1924) in Tacoma, designed by the local firm of Sutton, Whitney and Dugan, are excellent treatments of collegiate Gothic. The Community Church at Longview, the unfinished Cathedral of St. John the Evangelist in Spokane, designed by Whitehouse and Price, and St. Mark's Cathedral in Seattle (1928-31) finely illustrate the ecclesiastical Gothic. The Trinity Episcopal Church (1921) in Everett, designed by E. T. Osborne of Seattle, is a noteworthy example of the perpendicular, or late English, Gothic style. Holy Rosary Church in Tacoma, designed by C. Frank Mahon of Seattle, is an admirable adaptation of the Gothic; its tower was voted by architects of the region as the finest example of Gothic architecture in the Northwest.

Holy Rosary Church in Seattle (1938), also designed by Mr. Mahon, is an outstanding example of Lombard Romanesque, a style born in Italy and, in the opinion of the architect, eminently suited to the Northwest. Its campanile, as in the Italian churches, is the dominant feature. Another good adaptation of the Romanesque is the Church of Our Lady of Perpetual Help (1926) in Everett.

Washington offers unusual examples of modern engineering and structural design in its huge dams and many notable bridges. Largest among the dams are the Grand Coulee, Cushman, Long Lake, Cle Elum, Bonneville (partly in Oregon), Lake Chelan, Diablo at Skagit River, and the Ariel on the Lewis River. Interesting also are the Lake Washington Ship Canal Locks at Seattle (completed in 1916 under the direction of Carl F. Gould), with a capacity second only on this continent to the Panama Canal.

The Longview Bridge (1930) over the Columbia, connecting Washington and Oregon, is the longest cantilever span in the country and also the highest over a navigable stream. The Tacoma Narrows Bridge, which recently collapsed, was one of the longest of the suspension type ever constructed; and the Lake Washington Floating Bridge, completed in 1940 at Seattle, is the largest concrete pontoon bridge in the world. The George Washington Memorial Bridge in Seattle (1932) is a noteworthy example of the deck-cantilever type. The Monroe Street Bridge in Spokane (1911) is one of the most graceful structures in the State.

Washington's contemporary architecture, as a whole, displays an honest use of materials and a sense of the relation between form and function. School buildings, such as those constructed with the aid of the Federal Housing Commission in Bellingham and Mount Vernon, reflect this modern point of view. Several new banks in Seattle, designed by C. A. Merriam and the firm of McClelland and Jones, show the same trend.

In domestic architecture, forms that are more appropriate to the local setting are gradually developing.

tograph courtesy Washington State Progress Commission

VIEW OF THE OLYMPIC MOUNTAINS FROM SEATTL

UNT BAKER FROM MOUNT CONSTITUTION IN SAN JUAN ISLANDS

Photograph courtesy Washington State Progress Commissio

NORTH HEAD LIGHTHOUSE AT ENTRANCE TO COLUMBIA RIVER

(White water in background marks confluence of the river with the Pacific Ocean)

tograph courtesy of the Milwaukee Road
SUNSET OVER THE PACIFIC AS SEEN FROM THE OLYMPIC PENINSULA

RVIEW, DECEPTION PASS BRIDGE

Photograph courtesy of Seattle Post-Intellige

HALIBUT FLEET IN SEATTLE HARBOR

FISHERMEN REPAIRING NETS ON OPEN DOCKS AT SALMON BAY TERMI

(This work is now done in a net shed constructed by the W

Photograph courtesy of Seattle Post-Intelligencer

graph courtesy Washington State Progress Commission

PURSE SEINING, PUGET SOUND

Photograph courtesy Washington State Progress Commission

Photograph by R. B. Inver

SURF FISHING

DIGGING FOR CLA

Photograph courtesy Washington State Progress Commission

graph by Otto M. Jones

INDIAN CREWS BRING THEIR CRAFT NEAR THE FINISH LINE
IN THE INTERNATIONAL WAR CANOE SWEEPSTAKES

BOATS RACING ON PUGET SOUND

Photograph by A. N. Nickols

Photograph courtesy of Harry A. Kirwin

BACHELOR'S HALL TAKES TO THE AIR

An old houseboat is being lifted onto a new raft

A CATCH OF SALMON FROM PUGET SOUND WATERS

PART II

Cities

Aberdeen and Hoquiam

Railroad Stations: *Aberdeen*—Foot of K St. for Northern Pacific Ry., Union Pacific R. R., and Chicago, Milwaukee, St. Paul and Pacific R. R.
Hoquiam—Foot of 8th St. for Northern Pacific R. R., Union Pacific R. R., and Chicago, Milwaukee, St. Paul and Pacific R. R.
Bus Stations: *Aberdeen*—111 W. Wishkah St. for Grays Harbor Lines.
Hoquiam—422 8th St. for Grays Harbor Lines.
Piers: *Aberdeen-Hoquiam*—Grays Harbor Port Development Project, foot of Myrtle St.
Taxis: 25c a mile; 50c to any point within city limits.
City Busses: To residential sections of both cities and to Cosmopolis; fare 10c.

Accommodations: *Aberdeen*—Six hotels; cabin camps. *Hoquiam*—Two hotels; cabin camps.

Information Service: *Aberdeen*—Chamber of Commerce, Morck Hotel, Heron and K Streets; AAA, 114 So. K St. *Hoquiam*—Chamber of Commerce, Emerson Hotel, Simpson Ave. and 7th St.

Motion Picture Houses: *Aberdeen*—Five. *Hoquiam*—Two.
Radio Station: *Aberdeen*—KXRO (1340 kc.).
Golf: Highland course at Cosmopolis, SE. of Aberdeen on US 101; 18 holes; greens fee, 50c.
Tennis: Public courts at North Pioneer Park, E. Cushing St., South Aberdeen.
Swimming: On the harbor, W. on Grass Creek Road, swimming at half or full tide only. *Aberdeen*—Miller Natatorium, B St. near Stewart Field, 10c and 25c; Lake Aberdeen, 3 m. E. of city, off US 410; fee 10c.
Riding: Club near Cosmopolis.
Hunting and Fishing: Deer and duck in season in near-by regions; salt water fishing; clam digging on ocean beaches.
Baseball: Hoquiam—Olympic Stadium, 28th and Cherry Sts.

Annual Events: *Hoquiam*—Farm-Merchant Dinner, Jan. or Feb.; *Aberdeen-Hoquiam*—Fourth of July Splash, with log rolling and Indian Water Carnival; High School Football Game, Thanksgiving Day.

ABERDEEN (365 alt., 18,846 pop.) and HOQUIAM (300 alt., 10,835 pop.), originally settlements four miles apart, have grown into a single population center, divided only by Myrtle Street. In an atmosphere hazy with smoke from mill stacks and burners, these twin cities spread along Grays Harbor and the tidal waters of the three rivers flowing into it: Aberdeen lies at the confluence of the Chehalis and the Wishkah Rivers; Hoquiam borders the banks of the Hoquiam River.

Both cities face Grays Harbor, whose entrance, 12 miles westward, is often blanketed by the fog or rainfall characteristic of the region. The industrial area of both cities stretches along the water front. Here are numerous sawmills, with their sheds, yards, and loading docks. Stacks of freshly cut lumber diffuse through the streets the pungent odor of fir cedar, and hemlock. Straddle-legged lumber carriers, motor driven, roll swiftly about the yards. Large cranes swing arms laden with lumber from the yard to the deck of a ship berthed against the wharf. From the mill comes the shrill whine of high-speed saws and the muffled thunder of a huge log as it is hurled about on a rushing saw-carriage by the iron kick of the mechanical "nigger." Over the acres of roofs covering mills and woodworking plants, jets of live steam escape in white plumes, and here and there a tall stack pencils a drifting pattern of smoke against the sky.

Together, Aberdeen and Hoquiam were born of lumber, and through it chiefly have they lived. Aberdeen, the larger of the cities, with compact blocks of substantial office buildings, stores, hotels, garages, and theaters along Wishkah Street, the main thoroughfare, has the appearance of a small metropolis. North of the business section, the terrain rises to the higher ground of the residential area until it reaches the heights of Bel-Aire, which, with its fine homes, is the social as well as the topographic apex of the city. Here a panoramic view of the city and Grays Harbor may be had, with Chehalis Point Lighthouse at the entrance, and a glimpse of the rolling Pacific to the west.

On the border of the planked streets fringing the mills and factories, are "crackerbox" buildings whose shoddy rooming houses, pool halls, beer parlors, and shops cater to workingmen. In East and South Aberdeen, where most of the mill workers live, national origins are reflected in the Swedish cottages and in the octagonal-shaped Finnish houses with their many windows. Here, too, still stand a few old farmhouses, with soot-encrusted shingles and weather-beaten sides.

Hoquiam, reached through Aberdeen, is situated on deep water at the mouth of the Hoquiam River, 12 miles from the Pacific Ocean. Pioneer settlement of the Grays Harbor region, it is the elder of the two cities. In economy, industrial development, and general character, it is much like its sister city. West of the river the streets, starting at the water front, run diagonally through the business area until they join with the east-west avenues. To the north is a residential area, dominated by Hoquiam Heights. East of the river, streets run from the flats of the water front up to the heights of Campbell Hill.

The two cities have separate municipal governments, but, since they act jointly in many administrative matters, and are so largely interdependent industrially and socially, it has become difficult to speak of one without mentioning the other. Together, they represent the culture and industry of the Grays Harbor district, a territory which, walled in by one of the heaviest stands of timber in the Pacific Northwest, by mountains and hills on three sides, and by the Pacific Ocean on its entire western length, was once almost unapproachable except by water.

The earliest recorded visit of an American to this part of the coast occurred in 1792, when Captain Robert Gray sailed his ship, the *Columbia,* over the bar and into the harbor which today bears his name. No attempt was made to establish a permanent settlement, however, until 1859. In that year James Karr and his family arrived and settled on the banks of one of the rivers flowing into the harbor. Shortly thereafter he was joined by four brothers named Campbell. To the little settlement thus formed, and to the river on whose banks it stood, the name Hoquiam (Ind. hungry for wood), was given. Within the decade a number of other pioneers arrived, drawn by the promise of wealth in the virgin forests which stretched in an almost unbroken expanse from the Pacific Ocean to the Cascades. By 1869 a post office had become necessary, and in 1873 a school was opened.

In the meantime, some four miles to the east, a young Irishman, Samuel Benn, had staked a claim in 1867, at the juncture of the Chehalis and the Wishkah Rivers. Here he built a cabin, in which he lived alone until he was joined in 1875 by Alexander Young and James W. Stewart.

Three years later, George R. Hume, of Scotland, established a small fish cannery on Sam Benn's Point. The cannery was named the Aberdeen Packing Plant, for Aberdeen, Scotland, home of some of the stockholders. This new venture and the rich natural resources of the region soon attracted a number of settlers, and the community they formed was named Aberdeen.

From the beginning, lumbering was the key to the growth and development of the Grays Harbor region. The greatest stand of Douglas fir ever found in the Pacific Northwest was located here. Famous timber tracts, such as the "21-9" (meaning Township 21, N., Range 9 W.), lay adjacent to the harbor; this one prodigious tract, 6 miles square, was logged for over 30 years. The towering trees of the region grew so compactly that they were invariably felled in one direction only, and at times the fallen trees were so crowded together that it was difficult to saw them into log lengths. Besides these splendid stands of fir, Sitka spruce and hemlock rose in great abundance, and some cedar was also to be found.

As soon as the means were developed to transfer this timber to market, lumbering in the region could go ahead at top speed. A trading connection between Grays Harbor and the Columbia River settlements was established in 1879 when the schooner, *Kate and Ann,* began to offer service between the two points. This was followed in quick succession by the beginning of logging operations on the lower Chehalis in 1881; the unloading of the first sawmill equipment on consignment to George H. Simpson in 1882; the construction of a mill and the platting of the townsite of Aberdeen in 1884; and of Hoquiam in 1885.

By the middle of the eighties, business and industry in the Grays Harbor settlements were sufficiently active and the population large enough to invite the publication of a newspaper. The *Grays Harbor News* was started in Hoquiam in 1885, followed in 1886 by the Aberdeen *Herald,* and in 1889 by the Aberdeen *Weekly Bulletin* (later the *World*) and the *Washingtonian,* another weekly, in Hoquiam. The completion of telegraph lines to the Harbor in 1890 gave the newspapers wire service. School facilities were provided, a hotel was built in

Hoquiam in 1884, and a church in 1885. In 1890 a planked road was laid between the towns, presaging their united development.

Improvement in logging methods and in sawmill equipment speeded lumber production, making transportation an increasingly pressing problem. The Northern Pacific Railway had completed its line from Kalama to Puget Sound. Yet, despite their need for rail connections with broader markets, Hoquiam and Aberdeen failed to become the terminal of the Northern Pacific when Karr, founder of Hoquiam, proved unable to come to terms with the railroad for the sale of his holdings.

The Northern Pacific then built Ocosta, a few miles away on the south side of the harbor, as its terminal. To meet this situation, the citizens of Aberdeen, in 1895, bought and laid down the rails linking their mills with the Northern Pacific, thus gaining supremacy not only over Ocosta, whose development ceased, but over Hoquiam as well. In 1898, Hoquiam, after long negotiations, secured an extension of the railroad. In 1899 the first hull was launched from an Aberdeen shipyard.

In the early decades of the twentieth century, the national requirements for building materials increased; and, the Eastern forests having been in a large measure depleted, a growing demand arose for Western timber. Operators, needing more man power, started an advertising campaign to bring additional workers to the region. In response, loggers and mill hands came in large numbers, many from the woods of Wisconsin and Minnesota, others, Scandinavians and Finns, directly from their homelands. They were a hardy crew, these men who bore the hardships of the lumbering industry, and they brought new life to Aberdeen and Hoquiam. The days of ox-team logging were over; and the introduction of the powerful donkey engine and the "high-lead," or spar tree, to which great logs were jerked with taut steel cables, had brought logging to a high level of efficiency. With vast profits to be made, work was speeded ahead with little heed to accident prevention, timber breakage, or destruction of young growth. Men who worked in the woods needed rare courage and toughness. Straining back against his safety belt, the "high rigger" walked casually up the side of a tall tree with an axe in his hand, stopped somewhere between 100 and 200 feet above the ground, braced himself at a sickening angle against the swaying trunk, and, with a flow of cheerful profanity, severed with deft strokes of his razor-edged axe the green plume that rose above him; the shock of the falling crest sent the trunk and the logger on it gyrating dizzily through the air. Men saw their companions mutilated or killed from time to time by snapping steel cables, falling timber, rolling logs, or whirling saws; and this unremitting danger was reflected in their speech and tales and in their Saturday night blowoffs in Hoquiam and Aberdeen.

Usually, the men who worked in the forests remained wage earners, but sometimes one rose from the ranks of the loggers to become an operator. Alex Polson, who started as a member of a logging crew, emerged in time as one of the leading timber barons of the region. It was his crew that logged off the "21-9" forest of the Olympic peninsula. Polson personified the history of Pacific Coast lumbering, in every phase of which he participated. Today (1941) his mantle has descended upon his son, who is preparing to cut Washington's last great stand of cedar and spruce, in the Ozette region of the Olympic Peninsula.

For Grays Harbor, the early years of the century were busy and exciting, despite recurrent depressions of the lumber market. Sawmills and woodworking plants of various kinds were constructed; jerry-built houses were hastily erected to accommodate the flood of loggers. The shipyards, too, were active. In 1903 Aberdeen suffered a devastating fire. Reconstruction started immediately, and a fever of real estate speculation swept the town. In 1906 the harbor was dredged and improved, and an area of salt marshes drained and filled in to allow for the extension of the crowded business area.

Following the 1907 depression, the lumber market slackened, and for about five years lumbering was seriously curtailed. Labor, dissatisfied with wages and working conditions, struck in 1912 for an 8-hour day and a daily wage of $2.50. The operators refused these demands, and a citizens' committee, who attacked the strikers as members of the I.W.W., armed itself with pick handles to defeat the strike. The employees' hall was ordered closed as a nuisance by the civil authorities, but attorney Homer T. Bone, of Tacoma, now (1941) senior United States Senator from Washington, acting as counsel for the workers, secured its reopening. Finally, however, the loggers were forced to accept the old scale and hours and return to work.

This strike proved to be but one of a series that disturbed the industrial routine of Grays Harbor. During the First World War, loggers and sawmill workers again went out on strike with substantially the same objectives, this time winning the support of the numerically strong shipyard workers of Grays Harbor. Federal intervention resulted in a settlement granting the workers a considerable measure of their demands.

Declining prices, decreased demand for lumber and an influx of ex-servicemen and those released from war-geared industry brought falling wages, lengthened hours, and general dissatisfaction. The problem was temporarily solved, however, by the building and industrial boom of the twenties. Plywood and pulp and paper plants were built; an accredited junior college was established; and radio station KXRO, the first on Grays Harbor, began its broadcasting career.

The 1929 depression hit the Grays Harbor district hard. Mills closed or ran part time; wages fell, unemployment increased, and, as in the rest of the Nation, a general uneasiness prevailed. In 1933-4 a revival of labor organization, encouraged by favorable Federal legislation, led to improved working conditions and a recognition of the principle of collective bargaining. A strike of loggers and lumber mill operatives in 1935 was settled, after the calling out of five companies of the National Guard, to protect the operation of the mills, had been protested by a demonstration and a parade of several thousand citizens. With a strongly unified employer group and equally determined workingmen's organizations clinging fast to their aims, labor relations in Grays Harbor have been periodically turbulent. Today, both the American Federation of Labor and the Congress for Industrial Organization maintain labor councils in the Grays Harbor cities.

Lumber and wood products remain the key industry of Aberdeen and Hoquiam. The Grays Harbor district is now the largest plywood-producing area in the world. Hoquiam people send their friends a veneer postcard shaped like a human foot, which they call the "Board Foot"; Aberdeen enthusiasts identify themselves by means of the "Glad Hand," also made of local plywood. There are more than 30 woodworking plants of various types near the water front, and their output includes furniture, sounding boards for pianos, and numberless items of woodenware.

The lumber industry finds itself today at the beginning of a new era, in which chemistry and scientific technological processes will permit a fuller exploitation of the economic possibilities of the wood cell. Illustrating this development is the comparatively recent rise of wood pulp, rayon, and paper manufacture. In the new fields of production in which the lumber industry is now conducting research, timber of but 20 to 30 years growth may be used; and the industry looks forward to stabilizing its operations on a year-round basis, and to becoming less dependent upon the alternate booms and slumps of the construction industries.

In Grays Harbor, fishing, canning, and the production of sea foods are also growing in importance. About 200 fishing vessels go out into the Pacific and divide their catch—chiefly salmon, halibut, tuna, cod, and pilchard—between iced shipments to market and local fish canneries. Two oyster canneries and an oyster-smoking plant are supplied by commercial oyster beds on the harbor tide flats.

POINTS OF INTEREST

(Hoquiam)

1. The PUBLIC LIBRARY (*open 12-9 weekdays*), corner of 7th and K Sts., is housed in a two-story, red-brick, tile-roofed building. Its collection of 23,373 volumes includes 50 volumes in the Swedish language.

2. OLYMPIC STADIUM AND RECREATIONAL FIELD, entrance 28th and Cherry Sts., opened Thanksgiving Day 1939, is the leading athletic field in Grays Harbor district. The city purchased the site in 1929, but no improvements were made until 1938, when construction began under the WPA, with the Hoquiam Park Board furnishing the materials.

The grandstand has a seating capacity of 10,000, and the grounds are lighted for night games. There are fields for baseball, football, and softball, and two tennis courts. Plans call for the completion of an archery range, horseshoe courts, a bowling green, children's playfield, and picnic grounds.

3. The GRAYS HARBOR PULP & PAPER COMPANY PLANT

(*open by arrangement with the Chamber of Commerce*), Railroad Ave. and 22nd St., is an interesting example of industrial architecture, with a concrete stack and two water towers rising above the terraced, two-, four-, and six-story buildings. The plant has its own powerhouse, a chipping mill where the hemlock logs are chewed up before going to the "digesters," a pulp mill with rows of digesters of black painted steel and innumerable tubes, and an eight-story paper mill with metal-glass windows. An overhead two-story conveyor from the adjacent Polson Mill supplies hogged fuel and chips. The plant, the Grays Harbor Division of Rayonier, Inc., is equipped to produce fine bond paper; the bulk of its pulp is shipped to Japan for rayon manufacturing.

4. The POSEY MANUFACTURING PLANT (*open by arrangement with the Chamber of Commerce*), Railroad Ave. and Ontario St., converts Sitka spruce into such diverse products as piano sounding boards, dogsleds, bungs, and breakfast tables. Material for the wings of Colonel Lindberg's *Spirit of St. Louis* was furnished by this plant.

5. At the POLSON LUMBER AND SHINGLE MILLS (*open weekdays by appointment*), E. of Hoquiam Waterway No. 1, foot of Ontario St., cedar blocks, or "shingle bolts," are sawed into shingles, while speedy "shingle weavers" stack them in groups of 250 each in machines that bind them into bundles.

(Aberdeen—Hoquiam)

6. PORT OF GRAYS HARBOR, foot of Myrtle St., midway between the cities, is the center of a complicated system of railroad tracks, highways, and waterways. A pier 2,000 feet long, with a gray warehouse at its 400-foot outer end, extends diagonally from the shore. On the east and west sides are slips for freighters and for the storage of logs and pulp wood. Two five-ton hammer-head cranes and one steam locomotive operate along the pier. The cranes sling logs from trains aboard waiting boats. The swinging booms of the freighters transfer incoming cargo into cars. Of the 538,861 tons of cargo handled in 1938, 221,330 tons were of forest products, including 134,000,000 board feet of lumber. The Port Development Project is operated by the county and is administered by a board of three elected commissioners, who appoint a port manager.

The Port of Grays Harbor also maintains No. 10 dock at Westport, at the entrance to the harbor. This is a 200-foot pier, used by the 250 or 300 fishermen and trollers of the vicinity. In 1938, 667 tons of tuna were loaded here: of the 1,721 tons taken in the State, approximately 1,000 passed through Grays Harbor. Also at Westport are moorage and other facilities for crab fishermen, who reported a catch of 13,630 dozen crabs in 1938. These are brought in by the boatload and stored in "live boxes" until orders from city food markets are received.

(Aberdeen)

7. The HARBOR PLYWOOD PLANT (*open by arrangement with the Chamber of Commerce*), E. of the Port Terminal, is per-

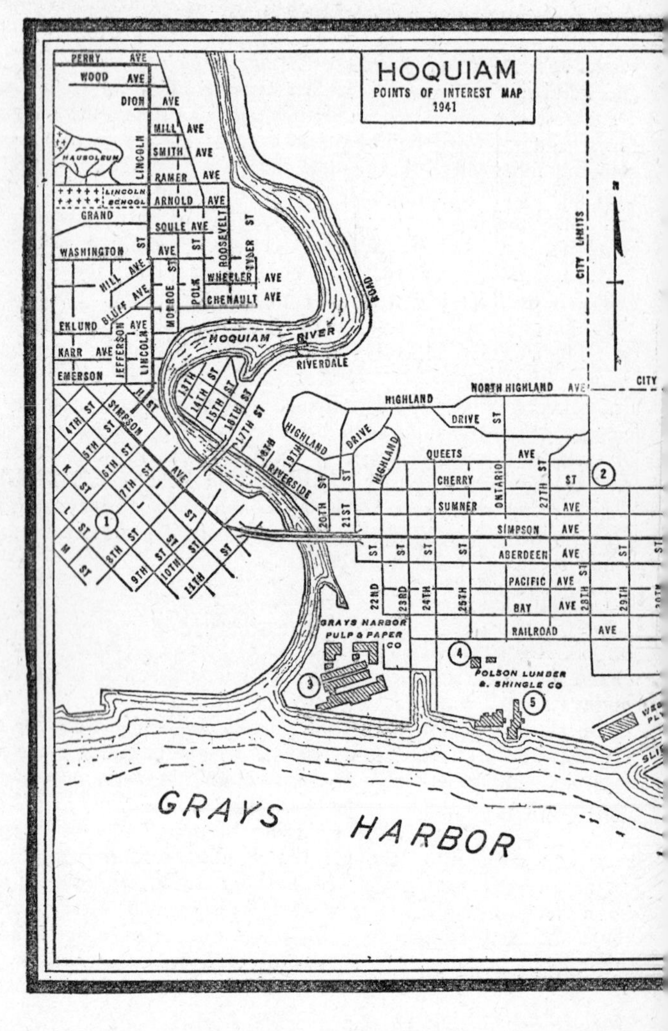

ABERDEEN AND HOQUIAM—POINTS OF INTERES

1. Public Library (Hoquiam)
2. Olympic Stadium and Recreational Field
3. Grays Harbor Pulp and Pa Company Plant
4. Posey Manufacturing Plan

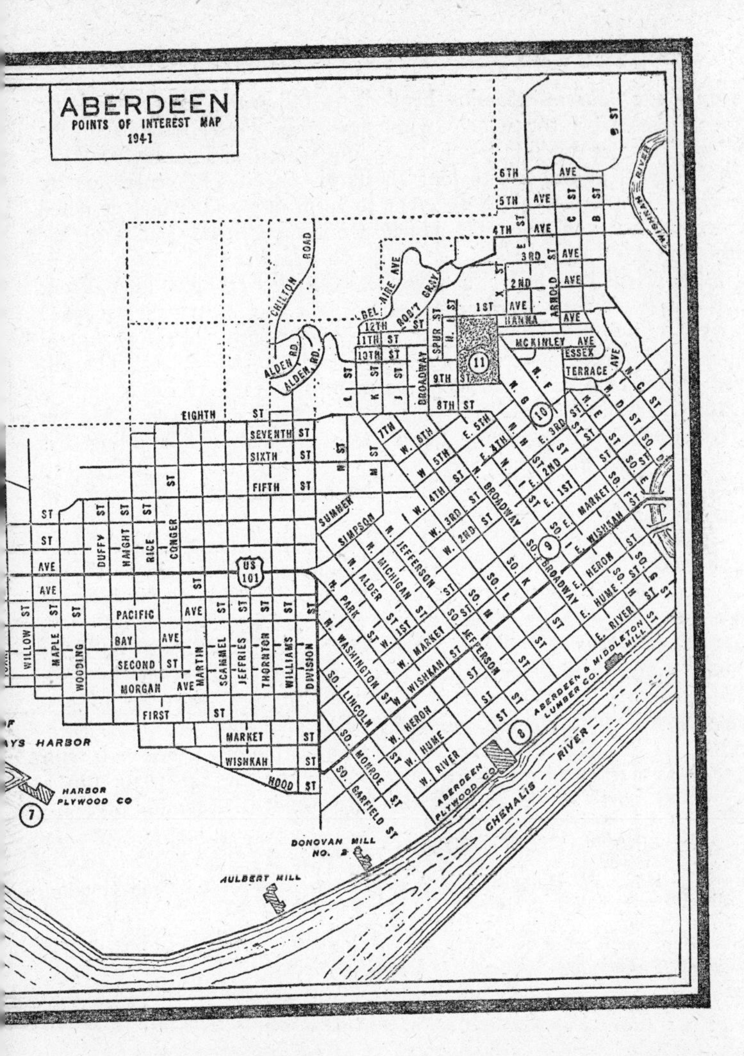

5. Polson Lbr. and Shingle Mill
6. Port of Grays Harbor
7. Harbor Plywood Plant
8. Strand Fisheries Incorporated
9. Public Library (Aberdeen)
10. Samuel Benn Home
11. Samuel Benn Park

vaded by the odor of steaming hemlock; a tall water tower stands on latticed legs above the widely windowed mill. Here, sections of big logs are softened by immersion in boiling water, and peeled, or "unwound," by giant lathes into long sheets of veneer. The veneer, cut to size and kiln-dried, is glued together to form plywood, which is noted for its rigidity and strength, gained from the crossed grains of the alternating sheets of veneer.

8. STRAND FISHERIES INCORPORATED, 400 East Front St., the first pilchard (sardine) packing plant in the State, was opened in 1936. This is the largest of the seven local plants, including several floating canneries, engaged in preparing sardines for market. The pilchard season lasts only two or three months of each year.

9. The PUBLIC LIBRARY (*open* 10-9 *weekdays;* 3-9 *Sun.*), Market St. between Broadway and I St., a one-story, red-brick building, has 22,451 volumes, a collection of Northwest Americana numbering 150 volumes, and 64 works in the Finnish language. A section is devoted to books on the pulp and paper industry.

10. The SAMUEL BENN HOME (*private*), 4th St., between G and F Sts., a two-story clapboard-sided building, painted in battleship gray, was built in 1887 by the pioneer, Samuel Benn. It displays the filigree and scroll-work characteristic of the period.

11. SAMUEL BENN PARK, N. I St., between 8th St. and 1st Ave., occupies a four-acre slope north of the city center. It is cut by deep gullies, through which tumble small streams spanned by rustic bridges. The park, which has tennis courts, a wading pool, and picnic furniture, is noted for its shrubs and trees. The site, a section of the original Benn estate, was purchased for park purposes by the city in 1929. On a promontory north of the park is Bel-Aire, residential community.

POINTS OF INTEREST IN ENVIRONS

State Fish Hatchery, Humptulips, 17 *m.*; Ocean Beaches and Crab Hunting, Copalis, 23 *m.*; Taholah, Quinault Indian Reservation, 32 *m.*; Lake Quinault 41 *m.* (*see Tour 9c*). Lake Aberdeen, 3 *m.*; Cosmopolis, Indian Treaty Ground, 3 *m.*; Deep Sea Fishing, Westport, 19 *m.*; Cranberry Bogs, 20 *m.*; Tokeland, 39.5 *m.* (*see Tour 9e*).

Bellingham

Railroad Stations: Foot of E St. for Great Northern Ry.; Magnolia St. and Railroad Ave. for Northern Pacific Ry.; 1100 Railroad Ave. for Chicago, Milwaukee, St. Paul & Pacific R.R.
Bus Stations: 1329 State St. for North Coast Lines; 2119 Otter St. for Bay Shore and Lummi Island Stage Co. (Orcas and Lummi Island service).
Airport: Graham Field, 1.5 m. NW. via Eldridge Ave. and Patton St.; charter only.
Piers: Quackenbush Dock on Central Ave., foot of Chestnut St.; two small boats daily for island points.
Taxis: 48c one mile or less, 25c each additional mile.
City Busses: Fare 7c, or five tokens for 25c; free transfers.

Accommodations: Nine hotels; tourist cabins and trailer facilities.

Information Service: Bellingham Chamber of Commerce, Herald Bldg., State and Chestnut Sts.; Automobile Club of Washington (AAA), Hotel Henry, Holly and State Sts.; Headquarters, Mount Baker National Forest, Post Office Bldg.

Theaters and Motion Picture Houses: Mount Baker Theater, 106 N. Commercial St., American Theater, 308 Cornwall Ave., Grand Theater, 135 W. Holly St.; occasional road shows. Five motion picture houses.
Radio Stations: KVOS (1230 kc.).
Athletics: Battersby Field, F and Girard Sts.; Downer's Field, Lakeway Drive and Moor St.; Waldo Field, Western Washington College of Education.
Golf: Lakeway Golf Course, near James St., 9 holes, 35c weekdays, 50c Sun.; Riverside Golf Course, 8 m. N. on Pacific Highway, 9 holes, 35c weekdays, 50c Sat. and Sun.
Tennis: Fairhaven Park and Rose Gardens, on US 99-Alt. between Ulia and Connelly Aves.; Cornwall Park on Cornwall Ave.; Whatcom Falls Park on Lakeway Drive; Elizabeth Park, Broadway and Elizabeth St.
Swimming: Perfection Beach on Chuckanut Bay and Chuckanut Drive; Whatcom Falls Park; Lake Samish, 5 m. SE. on State 1.
Bowling: Broadway Park, Cornwall Ave. and Park Drive.
Riding: Silver Beach, Lakeway Drive.
Winter Sports: Mount Baker National Forest, 36 m. (*see Tour 8A*).
Hunting and Fishing: Hunting in foothills; fishing in Puget Sound and lakes and streams.

Annual Events: Baseball season opens, Apr.; State Gladioli Show, Aug.; Salmon Derby Finals, mid-Aug.; Whatcom County Dahlia Growers' Flower Show, Sept.; Harvest Festival, sponsored by Whatcom County farmers and merchants, first week in Oct.

BELLINGHAM (sea level to 640 alt., 29,314 pop.), port of call 18 miles south of the Canadian Border, industrial and educational center, and distribution point for northwestern Washington, borders the broad curve of Bellingham Bay, sweeps back over the level valleys of Whatcom, Squalicum, and Padden creeks, and climbs the slopes of Sehome Hill, which rises practically in the middle of the city. Industrial life is concentrated along the water front, where squarely massed warehouses, coal bunkers, and piers are punctuated with the black smokestacks of mills and factories, harsh against the green hills. Moored at the docks are large, ocean-going freighters, sturdy cannery tenders, numerous small fishing boats, and trim pleasure craft. From the bayside, streets radiate into the business and residential areas, which mingle in a casual manner as a result of the merging of four separate boom towns in the formation of Bellingham.

To the west are the San Juan Islands and the interlaced ribbons of sounds and straits; more distant are the white-tipped Olympics, remote and austere, and the dark bulk of Vancouver Island, visible only on clear days. Stretching eastward from the city for 40 miles are broad fertile valleys, once unbroken evergreen forest but now largely logged off and converted into dairy farms, truck gardens, pastures, berry fields, and poultry ranches. Higher areas between the lowlands are covered with second-growth timber, interspersed with charred or bleaching stumps and fallen logs. Gradually the foothills become more rugged as they ascend toward the serrated line of the Cascades, from which rise the snow-capped peaks of Mount Baker and the Three Sisters.

From this extensive area of land and water, Bellingham has drawn sustenance: salmon for canneries, cedar and fir and hemlock logs to supply the lumber mills, and coal to feed furnaces and fill the holds of freighters. The pace of exploitation of these natural resources has been rapid; a brief half-century has seen them in a large measure depleted, so that today the prosperity of the city is becoming increasingly dependent upon the agrarian pursuits of the back country and upon the canning and processing of farm produce.

The mild climate of the region is favorable to the development of agriculture. Autumn months are temperate, with alternate rain and fog and bright, sunshiny days. In winter, freezing weather is not unknown; but, according to the records of the United States Weather Bureau, not once in 75 years has the temperature fallen to zero. Occasionally a cold, raw gale howls down from the mountains, and the city awakens in the morning heavily blanketed with snow. Now and then a sudden shift of the wind to the north converts the melting snow to a silver sheath of ice. Blustery winds sometimes sweep moisture-laden clouds up the Strait and dash them against the mainland. Then streams swirl in fury at their banks, lowlands are flooded, and the unsupported earth of steep hillsides, undermined by water, begins to slide on the clay hardpan.

Spring comes early. By March, meadows and pasture lands have lost the sallow tinge of winter, and soon the grass becomes lush and green. Throughout the mild summer, when temperatures seldom reach 90° Fahrenheit, and late into the fall, dairymen find ample pasturage for their herds, no inconsiderable factor in the growth of the dairying industry.

The earliest exploration of this part of the northwest coast was by Francisco Eliza, who in 1791 sent a small ship into the bay and, according to Spanish charts, named it Seno de Gaston. In 1792, Captain George Vancouver, who was exploring the Straits of Georgia, sent a small party under Joseph Whidbey to chart the southern shoreline. Upon receiving the report of the surveying party, Vancouver named the large protected body of water Bellingham Bay, in honor of Sir William Bellingham.

More than 50 years passed before white men again turned their attention to this immediate area, for during the first half of the nineteenth century the United States and Great Britain centered the struggle for possession along the Columbia River, and largely in the diplomatic field. The settlement of the boundary question in 1846, fixing the line at 49° North latitude, served to release colonizing energies. On December 15, 1852, Captain Henry Roeder, son of a German immigrant and formerly a captain on a Great Lakes schooner, and Russell V. Peabody left California and made their way northward, planning to start a salmon cannery or a sawmill. Finding that Henry Yesler's mill adequately supplied the little settlement on the Duwamish, Roeder and Peabody continued to Port Townsend, where they embarked in an Indian canoe for Bellingham Bay.

Circumstances were propitious; the market was booming, the San Francisco fire having skyrocketed lumber prices to $1,000 a thousand board feet. All that was needed was a mill. Roeder and Peabody looked upon the virgin wilderness and pronounced it good—at least for lumbermen. Sweeping back from the sheer bluffs at tide line was an unbroken forest, with scarcely a foot of open ground. Along the creek were giant cedars, while on higher ground were Douglas fir and hemlock. Here, below the falls of Whatcom Creek, (creek with the rumbling noise, as the Indians called it), they built a crude, temporary shelter. At once they established friendly relations with the Indians and obtained permission from Cha-wit-zit, chief of the Lummi, to appropriate a place near the falls as a site for the mill.

At once they started to build, laboriously hewing the logs and cedar shakes with their far from adequate tools. Not being able to get sufficient help or supplies from Budd Inlet or Victoria, Roeder sailed for San Francisco early in 1853, returning in a few months with a small party including Captain Edward Eldridge, his wife and baby daughter, William Brown, Henry Hewitt, and William Utter, a millwright. He also brought back necessary supplies and equipment, although the high prices and his small finances severely limited the quantity he could buy. By the summer of 1853, the little mill on Whatcom Creek was whining and snorting away, while the friendly Nooksack and Lummi watched with mingled awe and pleasure.

This was the first industrial development on Bellingham Bay; and although the dreams of quickly accumulating profits faded when the bottom dropped out of the lumber market and the price fell to $20 a thousand, this little water-power mill pointed the way to what was to be one of the area's major industries.

In the meantime, while Roeder was in California, the second industry in the region had been started by William R. Pattle, who discovered outcroppings of coal on his donation claim. Roeder and his associates were not at once distracted from the sawmill; later in the same year, however, when Hewitt and Brown stumbled upon a richer vein at the base of an uprooted cedar tree, the vision of a new industry glowed so brightly that Brown was sent to San Francisco with power to dispose of the claims in order to finance development of the mine. San Francisco was ripe for any kind of promotion, and Brown succeeded in selling the claim for $17,000, but, unable to resist the pull of Colorado and the new mining developments there, he went to Denver and, with the nest egg from the sale of the claim, started a career which included the building of the famous Brown's Palace Hotel.

During the next few years, the little settlement met a succession of reverses and disappointments with a faith and dogged perseverance that would not give way. The sawmill proving to be unprofitable, Captain Roeder in 1854 built a small schooner, the *H. C. Page,* named for one of the settlers, and with this small boat established regular communication with the outside world. The mine began to operate on a small scale, and some coal was shipped to Puget Sound points and to San Francisco. Also in 1854 Whatcom County was organized, and Whatcom, as the settlement was called, was made the county seat. Within two years, regular governmental procedures had been instituted, and the little town of 30 persons had come to look upon itself as permanently established.

Indian unrest, widespread throughout the Territory in 1855-6, alarmed the settlers in the Whatcom area, especially so because of the feud between the Indians of the north (British Columbia and Alaska) and the Bellingham Bay Indians. The settlers built a small blockhouse and manned it as well as they could, but this slight protection did not allay their fears, and they sent an urgent appeal for aid to the Federal Government. In response to their request, re-enforcements were sent under the command of Captain George E. Pickett, who eight years later was to lead the famous Confederate charge at Gettysburg. Fort Bellingham was built, Whatcom Creek was bridged, and a road was cleared between the fort and the village. Life in Whatcom soon resumed its monotonous if none too easy pace. In addition to the infrequent trips of Roeder's little steamer, connection with the outside world was maintained by a mail service furnished at irregular intervals by "Blanket Bill" Jarman, in a canoe paddled by nine Indians. (Jarman had received his nickname after being ransomed for 52 blankets by Governor Douglas of Vancouver Island).

In 1857 the magic cry "Gold!" drifted down from the Fraser River, gathering volume as it traveled; by April 20, 1858, the San Francisco *Examiner* could report a rush comparable to that of forty-nine. Early in the summer, fewer than 100 men were going about their tasks along Bellingham Bay. A few log cabins fringed the shore, and the only sounds of industry were the drone of the little sawmill and the echoes of pick and shovel at the Sehome mine. Then a small boat, its deck black with passengers, moved slowly into the bay. The rush was on, and within a few days a tent city had sprung up and blazed with the lights of campfires. The editor of the first newspaper, the *Northern Light,* reported that the boat on which he arrived carried a load of 1,000 to 1,300 passengers. For a few short weeks there was feverish activity: buildings were hastily erected, a new wharf was built, pilings were driven. It is reported that some lots sold for $500. More persons thronged into Whatcom to make their way to Canada by trail, boat, or canoe than were to be found in all the rest of the Territory. Then, an order came that all those going to the gold fields must get licenses at Victoria. This order, coupled with the failure to find rich strikes, led to an almost instantaneous collapse of the boom, and by the end of the year 1858 population had dropped from some 15,000 to a few hundred.

Among the goldseekers who settled on Bellingham Bay was John Bennett, who came in 1858, bringing with him a chest filled with roots and bulbs and seed of flowers and grasses that he had gathered in his wanderings. He worked in the mine at Sehome, until in 1860 he had saved sufficient money to buy a piece of land where he could cultivate his many choice varieties of fruit. In the course of years, his claim became the show place of the county. Credited to his endeavors are the Bennett pear, Bennett's Champion plum, and several varieties of apples and flowers.

The dreams of fortune faded with the decline of real-estate values and the exodus of miners and adventurers, but some optimism survived. The Sehome mine, which had imported experienced English miners from Nanaimo, continued to ship some coal, and the little sawmill still whined and sputtered beside the creek. A telegraph line was strung, and boats continued to call occasionally. Hope rose with land values again in 1870, when the Northern Pacific bought land for a proposed water-front terminal. The town of Sehome was platted and filed in 1871, and mining operations were accelerated again.

Then came 1873 and the Nation-wide panic. Jay Cooke's empire tottered and fell, and the force of its crash put an end to the short-lived boom along Bellingham Bay. Then the mill burned, and a few more settlers drifted away in search of work. The final blow was the closing and dismantling of the Sehome mine in 1878 as a result of slow markets, diminishing deposits, water seepage into the tunnels, and financial difficulties. Gloom settled over the two little towns; the few remaining settlers—some 20 in all—doggedly stuck to their land and waited for a change of fortune.

This change began with the arrival in 1880 of 600 Kansans. Meeting what they felt to be an inhospitable reception from the local land-owners, the newcomers founded New Whatcom, across the creek from the older town. Three years later Dan Harris, who had succeeded to the claim of John Thomas, recorded "Fair Haven on Harris Bay." Four small towns now fringed the bay: Whatcom, New Whatcom, Sehome, and Fairhaven.

The Bellingham Bay settlements, having tried two industries, now ventured upon a third—the canning of fish. For years salmon and herring had been shipped, slightly cured, in barrels and boxes to San Francisco and even to the east coast. It was not until 1881, however, that a cannery was built and put into operation. For a few years the plant struggled along, but the evidence of failure was so obvious that the plant was closed; the fish-canning industry had to wait for development in technology and science.

The nineties marked the beginning of growth and prosperity for the Bellingham Bay area. A number of salmon canneries began successful operation. As transportation facilities were improved and the demand for lumber increased, new sawmills and shingle mills were built, and the dense forests that had separated the four small towns disappeared. Whatcom and New Whatcom consolidated.

Tulip cultivation spread to the mainland from Orcas Island, dairy cattle were introduced, and general agriculture began to develop. In September 1899, the normal school awarded to the Bellingham Bay area was opened with 6 instructors and an enrollment of some 200 students.

In 1900, Fairhaven merged with New Whatcom, and, in 1903, the addition of Sehome brought the population of the united city of New Whatcom to 13,236. At the first city election the name was changed to Bellingham.

Expansion continued throughout the early years of the twentieth century. New railroad connections were secured, sawmills and shingle mills increased in number and size and improved their technique; canneries sent hundreds of thousands of cases of salmon by steamship and rail to eastern United States and Europe. Docks and piers were constructed, coal mines were extended, streets were paved, and scores of small industries were established. An experimental bulb farm was established in the vicinity in 1907, and diversified farming, dairying, and poultry raising became increasingly important as logged-off land was cleared, at a cost of hundreds of dollars an acre, and put into cultivation. Cultural interests began to assume greater importance, new churches and schools were built, and the normal school rapidly increased its enrollment. The 1910 census gave to Bellingham over 24,000 population, an increase of almost 100 per cent.

Succeeding years were marked by less spectacular changes. Sawmills and shingle mills continued to hum as the lumberjacks cut their way deeper into the forests to get the necessary supply of logs. Canneries increased their output, but whispers were already being heard of the day when steadily decreasing runs would force the curtailment of the industry. The Port of Bellingham Commission (which directs the affairs of the port district, co-extensive with Whatcom County) was organized in 1911. Shipments of canned salmon and other fish were for a long time an important part of port traffic, but lumber was (and remains) the leading commodity.

The city continued to grow slowly, its growth being reflected in new homes and business buildings, paved streets, new docks and piers, and better schools. The Normal also was becoming increasingly popular as an education center, partly because of the mild, salubrious climate and delightful natural setting. Adjacent rural areas were also being developed. Stumps were uprooted and burned, and land drained, fertilized, and planted. Bulb culture expanded, truck farming was beginning to be profitable, and the herds of dairy cattle increased in size and number.

With the World War, the clamor for lumber and for canned salmon to feed the men in the trenches brought increased production in mills and canneries and speeded up the shipping industry. The brief post-war depression was followed by a decade of expansion in building and considerable speculation. Mining and prospecting for mines in the Deming and Mount Baker regions were resumed, and thousands of acres were put under farm cultivation. Dairying was by this time a well-established source of income, and poultry raising for the market and for egg production had proved itself. Concurrently the fears about the diminishing salmon runs became an actuality, and canneries began to limit production or to close altogether. Lumber mills, too, were being affected more and more by both the depletion of their sources of supply and the slackening of the market as the decade of the twenties moved to its close. Under the fever of speculation and unrestrained optimism, which in Bellingham as elsewhere marked the Coolidge era, was a slackening of industrial pace.

Then came the crash. The burners of mills were cold and black, canneries closed, fishing boats were tied up at the docks, mining operations were curtailed; men began to walk the streets in search of work. The history of the thirties in Bellingham is different from that of the Nation only in details. To assist local enterprise, several Federal agencies provided work on various projects: improvements in docks and warehouses; the construction of a new sea wall and of a fishing harbor for small boats; the modernizing of school and other public buildings; the building of an airport; and the repair of streets and sewers. Today local industry has recovered to some degree. The huge mills of the Bloedel-Donovan and the Puget Sound Pulp and Paper Company are in operation; seining boats are again busy; a cement plant is at work; and business as a whole has improved. More and more the effect upon the economy of the city of agricultural expansion in the surrounding country is being recognized; this is evident in the strength of such organizations as the Grange, the Whatcom County Agricultural Association, the Dairymen's Association, and the Washington Co-operative Egg and Poultrymen's Association, and in the increasing importance of creameries, cheese factories, and powdered and malted milk plants.

Culturally, the city has learned to depend largely upon itself. Churches are numerous and well attended and fraternal organizations are varied. The city supports a little theater and several music and art clubs. The Western Washington College of Education, formerly the Bellingham Normal School, offers lectures, concerts, and amateur theatricals. Recreational opportunities are almost limitless: fresh and salt-water fishing,

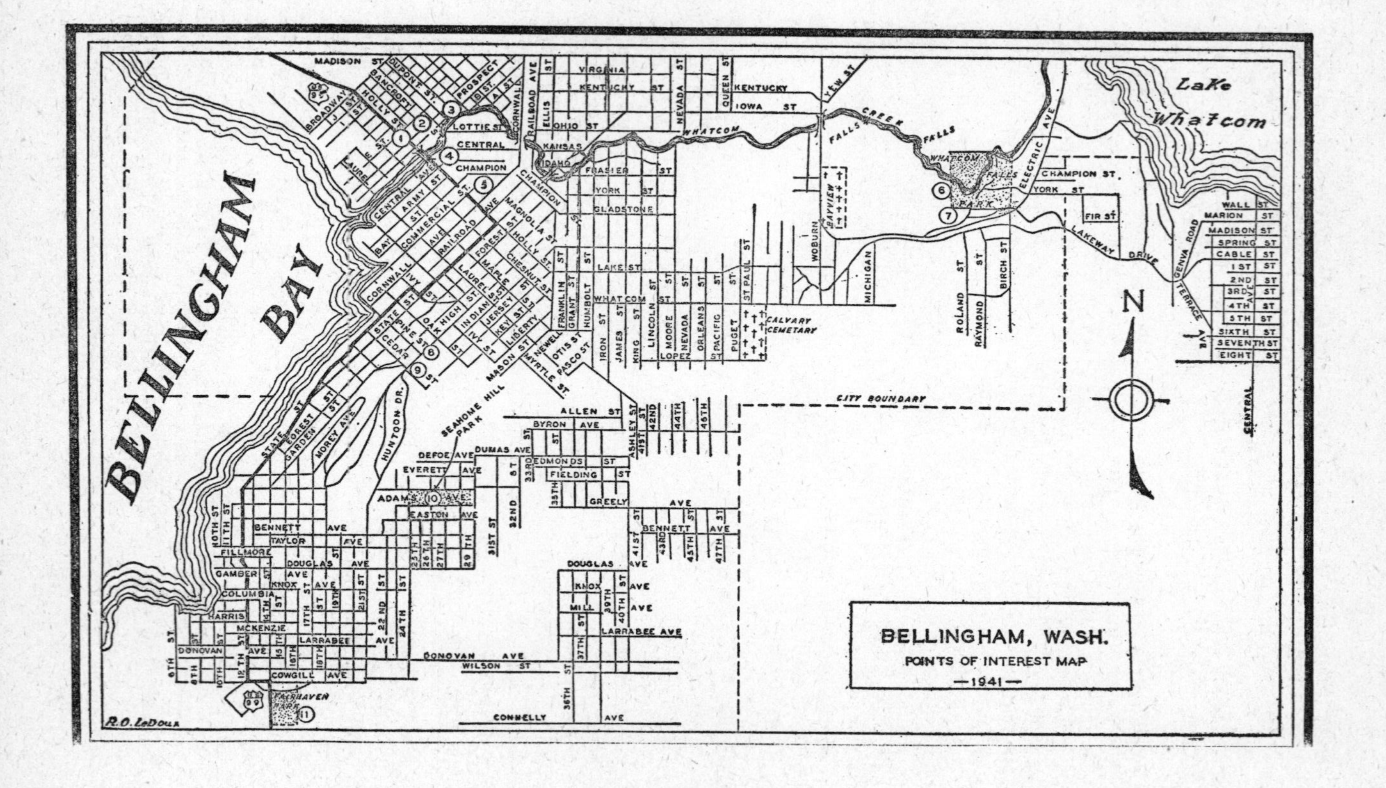
BELLINGHAM BAY
Lake Whatcom
WHATCOM FALLS PARK
WHATCOM CREEK
SEAHOME HILL PARK
CALVARY CEMETARY
BAYVIEW
FAIRHAVEN PARK
CITY BOUNDARY
N
R.O. LeDoux
BELLINGHAM, WASH.
POINTS OF INTEREST MAP
—1941—

hiking along mountain trails, skiing and climbing, sailing and yachting.

Bellingham looks toward the past to plan its future. Coal mining can become important again if new veins are uncovered; lumber manufacturing will thrive with conservation and selective logging; fishing and canning will very likely regain their importance; and shipping will be commensurate with the healthy growth of other industries. Boom times are ended, but with planning and foresight a steady, solid expansion is within reach.

POINTS OF INTEREST

1. The OLD WHATCOM COUNTY COURTHOUSE (*open by appointment*), corner W. Holly and E Sts., was built in 1858 of bricks shipped from Philadelphia. It was purchased by the county in 1885 for use as a courthouse. In turn thereafter it was a jail and a newspaper plant, and now is used by the Junior Order of United Mechanics for lodge rooms.

2. The CAPTAIN GEORGE PICKETT HOUSE (*open* 2-4, *last Thurs. each month*), 910 Bancroft St., was built between 1856 and 1860. It is maintained by the Washington State Historical Society and contains many relics of historic interest.

3. The PICKETT MEMORIAL BRIDGE, Dupont St. at Prospect Ave., a concrete structure across Whatcom Creek, bears at the north end a tablet commemorating Captain George E. Pickett, who in 1856 built the town's first bridge.

4. CITY HALL, Lottie St. between Grand Ave. and Commercial Sts., formally dedicated on January 5, 1940, is a long, low, two-story building of white sandstone. Two broad wings extend from a slightly higher center section. Across the front of the building the recessed entrance and a series of tall, closely placed windows give a columnar effect. The base course is of Minnesota granite, and the marble used in the lobby and first-floor corridors is Montana travertine. Wood panels of the main staircase and council chambers are of quarter-sawed white oak and gumwood.

5. The WASHINGTON CO-OPERATIVE CHICK ASSOCIATION PLANT (*open* 7:30-4:30 *workdays:* 7:30-1:00 *Sat.*), 1220 Central Ave., organized in 1924 to promote the co-operative hatching and marketing of baby chicks, has a membership of approximately 1,500 and operates 9 branch stations. Experiments made here in 1935 in the

---

BELLINGHAM—POINTS OF INTEREST

1. Old Whatcom County Courthouse
2. Captain George Pickett House
3. Pickett Memorial Bridge
4. City Hall
5. Washington Co-operative Chick Association Plant
6. Public Library
7. Whatcom Falls Park
8. Ella Higginson Home
9. Western Washington College of Education
10. Sehome Hill Park
11. Fairhaven Park

Japanese method of determining sex in chickens proved so successful that many other commercial hatcheries have adopted it. The output for the Bellingham plant during 1936 was 1,600,000 baby chicks, thousands of which were shipped in cardboard boxes to all parts of the country.

6. The BELLINGHAM PUBLIC LIBRARY (*open* 11-9 *weekdays*), on a huge rock at the corner of Champion and Commercial Sts., is a vine-clad, concrete building constructed in 1906 with Carnegie aid. The library has 45,000 volumes. One of the most interesting collections is the Northwest Americana section, numbering 350 books and including a file of the *Bellingham Bay Mail* for the years 1875 and 1878.

7. The WHATCOM FALLS PARK, on Lakeway Drive, is a 41-acre forested area, through which Whatcom Creek flows in a series of falls and cascades. At the falls, known to the Indians as Whuks-qua-koos-tsa-qua (creek with the rumbling noise), Captain Henry Roeder filed his original homestead claim and built a small lumber mill. Wild flowers, bridle paths, and trails make this natural park a most attractive recreational spot. The WHATCOM FALLS PARK STATE TROUT HATCHERY (*open* 8-5 *daily*), a 5-acre tract donated to the State by the city, has 48 trout hatcheries and 10 rearing ponds. Millions of rainbow, silver, cutthroat, and Eastern brook trout are hatched and reared here annually as a part of the program of restocking the Washington streams.

8. The ELLA HIGGINSON HOME (*private*), 605 High St., was the residence of the Washington novelist, short story writer, historian, and poet, who died in 1940. Some of Ella Higginson's lyrics have been set to music by noted composers and have been sung by famous singers, including Calvé, McCormack, and Caruso. The quaint, ivy-covered house, erected in 1892, is the center of terraced gardens. The living room, called the Rose Heart Room, has woodwork cut from the heart of a native tree of British Guiana, the *Copaifera publiflora.* Rose-colored lights in a cut glass chandelier serve to bring out the natural glow of the wood. A small reception room has a frieze of nearly 300 rosaries. Multi-colored Government soil maps are arranged in a mosaic on the walls of the library. Other interesting items are pieces of antique furniture, including a Dutch marquetry desk with inlaid floral design, and a collection of Alaskan Indian baskets.

9. The WESTERN WASHINGTON COLLEGE OF EDUCATION (*open* 9-9:30 *school days*), High St. between Huntoon Drive and Sehome Hill, overlooks the city and the bay. The buildings, in the Romanesque style of architecture, are surrounded by extensive lawns, landscaped with native shrubs and flowers. The college offers the full four years of college work. The LIBRARY (*open* 8-8:30 *school days,* 2-4 *Sat.*) contains John M. Edson's collection of shore birds gathered in the region over a 40-year period, a complete herbarium of 2,000 specimens, and an exhibit of cultural objects from the various Indian tribes.

10. SEHOME HILL PARK, Adams St. between 25th and 29th Sts., includes 69 acres of hillside terrain, but the center of interest is the flat summit of the hill, possibly an acre in extent. Reached by a winding

road, the hilltop offers an exceptional view over the city and the harbor, with Lummi Island and some of the San Juan group lying in the bay and the mountain ranges rising superbly in the distance. The campus of the Western Washington College of Education is adjacent on the north. The hill, named for Sehome, a subchief of the Clallam Indians, probably made an excellent lookout.

11. FAIRHAVEN PARK AND ROSE GARDEN (*swimming, tennis*), US 99-Alt., between Julia and Connelly Aves. in South Bellingham along Padden Creek, contains 16 acres of flower beds and rock gardens. The roses, some 100 varieties, constitute an important collection. In 1915, the park was enlarged, from the original small tract given to the city in 1909 by C. X. Larrabee and Cyrus Gates, to its present size. The famous Chuckanut Drive forms the western boundary.

POINTS OF INTEREST IN ENVIRONS

United States Department of Agriculture Nursery, 2.5 *m.*; Chuckanut Drive, scenic, 3.5 *m.*; Perfection Beach (Camp Perfection), 5 *m.*; Lake Samish, recreation, 7 *m.*; Lummi Indian Reservation, 8 *m.;* Wiser Lake, recreation, 10.5 *m.;* Wildwood Park, Lake Whatcom, 11 *m.*; Lummi Island Ferry, 16 *m.;* (*see Tour 8a*). Mount Baker National Forest, entrance at Glacier, 36 *m.*; Mount Baker Lodge and heart of recreational area, 56.8 *m.* (*see Tour 8A*). San Juan Islands (*see Island Tours*).

Everett

Railroad Stations: Bond St. between Hewitt Ave. and Wall St. for Great Northern Ry.; 3201 McDougall Ave. for Chicago, Milwaukee, St. Paul and Pacific R.R.; corner Pacific Ave. and Chestnut St. for Northern Pacific Ry.
Bus Station: Corner Colby and Pacific Aves., for North Coast Lines, Pacific Stages, Independent Stages, Inc., and Mukilteo and Whidbey Island Stages.
Taxis: 35c one mile or less, one person; 50c one mile or less, two to four persons; 15c for each additional half-mile. Special rates for parties.
Ferry: Everett-Whidbey Island ferry from Mukilteo, 5 m. SW.
City Busses: Fare 10c; four tokens for 25c.

Accommodations: Four hotels; cabin camps.

Information Service: Chamber of Commerce and Automobile Club of Washington (AAA), Monte Cristo Hotel, corner Wall St. and Hoyt Ave.

Motion Picture Houses: Four; occasional road shows and concerts.
Radio Station: KRKO (1400 kc.).
Athletics: Forest Park, Federal St. between 40th and 45th Sts.; Legion Memorial Park, 8th St. between US 99 and Rockefeller Ave.; Lincoln Playfield, 25th St. and Rockefeller Ave.

Golf: Everett Golf and Country Club, 2 m. SW. on US 99, 18 holes, greens fee $1; Cedar Crest Golf Club, N. on US 99 to Marysville, R. on Arlington road, 18 holes, greens fee 50c; Legion Memorial Park, 8th St. between US 99 and Rockefeller Ave., 18 holes, greens fee 50c.
Tennis: Lincoln Playfield, 25th St. and Rockefeller Ave.; Clark Park, 24th St. and Oakes Ave.; Legion Memorial Park, 8th St. between US 99 and Rockefeller Ave.
Swimming: Municipal bathing beach, south bay front; Silver Lake, 5 m. S. of city limits on old Pacific Highway; Lake Stevens, 8 m. E., branch road from State 15.
Hunting and Fishing: Pheasant and grouse hunting on adjacent upland areas; duck hunting on east lowlands and north tideflats. Fishing in the harbor and near-by streams.

Annual Events: Civic Symphony Concerts, third week in Apr.; Snohomish County Music Festival, late in May; Sailboat Races, third week in June; Everett Yacht Club Regatta, July 4; Gladioli Show, third week in Aug.; Intercity Fair, Tyee Roundup (Salmon Derby), last week in Aug.; Flower Show, second week in Sept.

EVERETT (30 alt., 30,224 pop.), county seat of Snohomish County, lumbering center, seaport, and distributing point for a fertile agricultural and dairying area, lies on a promontory between the sluggish Snohomish River, with its muddy delta, on the east and north, and Port Gardner Bay, an arm of Puget Sound, on the west.

In the business district, near the center of the city, substantial middle-aged buildings border broad avenues that run east-west across a ridge extending southward from the river to the high bluffs of Rucker Hill.

Noticeable among the older structures are a few newer, more modern buildings. On the hill and along the bayside to the north are attractive residences, surrounded by broad, close-clipped lawns, brightened in season by daffodils, rows of irises, blossoming shrubs, roses in profusion, beds of flaming gladioli, and golden autumn leaves; even the sombreness of winter is broken by the sheen of laurel leaves and the orange and red berries of thorn and holly. Between these residential districts and the business and industrial areas are scattered sections where the mass of the population lives.

The industrial life of the city centers in the area along the bayside and the river front. Here, fringing the city, are factories and mills with their stacks and burners, smoking volcanoes by day and glowing infernos by night. Except when a holiday or curtailed production brings a temporary lull, the air reverberates with the whine of saws, the strident blasts of whistles, the hiss of steam, and the clank of wheels as engines shunt cars of freight on the sidings.

Moored along the docks are freighters, their strong booms swinging incoming cargo to the docks and outgoing cargo, mostly lumber and lumber products, to the decks and into the holds. Quickly the gangs of longshoremen load and unload the slings, expertly using their claw-like hooks, and alert to the hazards of snapping cables and shifting cargo. Trucks rumble over the docks, which vibrate on supporting pilings. Dotting the bay are numerous pleasure craft, trawlers, sturdy tugs with rafts of logs in tow, and rowboats, in which fishermen drift for hours with the tide or row, face forward, with the peculiar skill and ease acquired only through years of practice.

The prevailing westerly winds are usually brisk and occasionally become gales that whip the slate-gray waters of the bay into whitecaps. Sometimes a pall of fog settles over the area, and then foghorns moan their warnings to shipping. The salt air is charged with the pungent odor of seaweed from the brine-soaked tidelands, the resinous tang of newly cut lumber and of smoke from the burning slabs and sawdust, the clean odor of tar from nets and creosoted pilings, and the musty smell of rotting logs, heavy with barnacles. At night the low, musical throb of Diesel engines and the impatient chugging of gasoline motors float across the water, or the whistle of a train, clear and resonant, echoes through the moisture-laden air.

Here is registered the heartbeat of Everett. When mills and factories are running and wages are steady, customers crowd the local stores, bills are paid, houses are painted or re-shingled, and old cars are exchanged for new ones. But when the pulse is weakened by curtailed production and consequent unemployment, not only does local business diminish, but the neighboring farming area, which finds a market for its produce in the city, also suffers.

The first white man to leave a record of discovery of the bay along which rise today the smokestacks of Everett was Captain George Vancouver, whose ship furled its sails at Possession Sound on June 4, 1792; he took possession for Britain, changing the name of the entire region from New Albion to New Georgia, in honor of King George III. Two other place names commemorate Vancouver's visit: Port Gardner Bay and Port Susan.

Not until 1862 did the area around Port Gardner Bay become of interest to white men. In that year, for reasons not ascertainable from the records, Dennis Brigham, who had been listed in the census of 1860 as living in House No. 67, Whidbey Island, age 50, left the comparative comfort of his island home for Port Gardner Peninsula, cleared a bit of land along the bay near the point which today marks the foot of California Avenue, built a small shack, and planted a few apple trees.

In 1860 a trading post had been established at Elliott Point at Mukilteo, as the Indians called it, to the south of Port Gardner Bay, and to the east the small settlement of Snohomish had become the seat of the newly created county. By this time, too, the Indians in the environs of Port Gardner Bay had sealed their fate by signing the treaty of 1855, under the provisions of which they retired to the Tulalip Reservation. But until Brigham cleared his little patch of land, the promontory of Port Gardner Bay had remained a dead center in the eddies of settlement that swirled around it.

In the seventies and eighties, a few settlers trickled into the area; a telegraph station was set up on the top of the bluff, and a combination hotel, store, and saloon was opened. But conditions that were to lead to the establishment of a new town on Port Gardner Bay were developing. News of the wealth of timber in the Northwest had been carried down the coast to San Francisco and had even sounded in the ears of more astute and farseeing promoters in the East. The industrial expansion following the Civil War had ushered in a period of railroad building; it was only a matter of time before the existence of a market for lumber and of necessary transportation facilities led to the development of lumbering in the Snohomish Valley.

In 1889, Bethel J. Rucker and his brother, Wyatt J., made a reconnaissance of the area and apparently appreciated its industrial and commercial possibilities. Here was a vast forest reached by means of the Snohomish River and its many tributaries, down which logs could be floated for miles to sawmills accessible to ocean-going vessels. Further, rumors were afloat that the western terminus of the Great Northern might be located on Port Gardner Bay. Soon the Rucker brothers and other men, who also perceived the speculative possibilities of holdings in this area, acquired large tracts of land.

The Ruckers, prompted to action by rumors that different interests were eager to acquire control, filed in 1890 the 50-acre townsite plat of Port Gardner, only to withdraw it in the same year in order to re-file, under the name of the Everett Land Company, with Henry Hewitt, Jr., and eastern capital represented by Colby, Hoyt, C. W. Wetmore of the American Steel and Barge Company, Rockefeller, and others. The town was replatted and named Everett in honor of the son of Charles L. Colby.

This announcement was followed by a rush for the choice locations; the pot of gold was seen in real estate, trade, timber, and commerce. Extra steamers brought in promoters, laborers, land agents, bartenders, merchants, cooks, and engineers by the hundreds. Some of the newcomers hastily constructed shacks and log cabins, but many were forced to live in makeshift shelters or in tents. So much in demand were places to sleep that, according to accounts, John T. Rogers found his coffins more in demand for bunks than for funerals. Bars were constructed from a few planks and a bit of canvas. With as much dispatch as possible, patches of land were cleared of trees and underbrush; the nights were bright with the glow of burning stumps, and smoke hung heavy and pungent over the new settlement. A few rutty roads and trails served as streets, along which settlers cautiously picked their way by day or stumbled through mud holes by night. Rain fell steadily, but it could not drown the high hopes and visions of wealth born of rumors that a projected factory, a barge plant, a pulp mill, and other industrial ventures would soon make the jumble of tents and shacks into a thriving and populous city.

The town grew rapidly. By 1891 it had a population of 3,000, a fire department, a schoolhouse, a bank, and three newspapers. In 1892 the city's first department store was erected by John Hudson Clark, of Wisconsin; it stood in a "stump patch" so far from town that a free bus was used to attract customers. The Puget Sound Wire Company had opened and was furnishing light and power to a number of business establishments and homes; the Puget Sound Pulp and Paper Company (now known as the Everett Pulp and Paper Company), the first such mill in the State, had begun to operate with a daily capacity of 15 tons; the Sumner Iron Works, a smelter and reduction plant, a tannery, a few small shingle mills, six banks, numerous real-estate offices, several stores, and telephone service had been established. By this time, too, development of the Monte Cristo silver holdings by the Rockefeller interests was well along, and many saw Everett as a mining center as well as an industrial city. Regular government not yet having been organized, a self-constituted law enforcement agency, the Committee of Twenty-One, was formed to combat lawlessness, which ran from rowdiness and drunkenness to robbery and murder. On April 27, 1893, the town was incorporated.

But the dreams of becoming an industrial center could come true only if ready access to markets were provided by means of transcontinental railroad connections. Even before the town was platted, Hewitt and the Ruckers had envisioned the coming of the Great Northern Railway; Hill's announcement that he would make the town the terminal was the stimulus to further expansion. The last spike was driven early in 1893, and on June 15, 1893, the first through train left Minneapolis for the West. Now, with rich natural resources and land and water transportation, the future of Everett seemed assured.

Scarcely was the boom well under way before the new town was hit by the nation-wide depression and panic of 1893. Hundreds were thrown out of work. Everett was not hit so hard as were many other towns; nevertheless, conditions were bad. Through the winter of 1893-4, the jobless filled the streets by day, and at night slept in hovels or flophouses or kept warm in saloons. The slight upturn in the summer of 1894 was not maintained, even though the first whaleback barge was launched with much fanfare on October 24, 1894. The only bright spot in 1895 was the construction of the Bell-Nelson Sawmill, and the same year saw the first bank failure, with attendant hardships. The depression continued through 1896. By this time the barge works and the nail factory were admitted failures, and the Rockefeller mining venture at Monte Cristo was bogging down. Then came the disastrous floods of 1897, when the river, swollen with unusually heavy rains, inundated hundreds of acres, swept bridges away, and washed out a section of the tracks to the Monte Cristo mines. Within a short time this venture shut down permanently.

Before the turn of the century, the rough edges of town life were beginning to be worn off. Women had arrived in increasing numbers, and their coming meant the stabilizing of community life through the establishment of family groups. This change in social structure was accompanied by an increasing emphasis on schools and churches, and by agitation for better living conditions, and against saloons and drinking, gambling, prostitution, and other forms of vice. The coming of women also meant an increase in social life. Theatricals, tableaux, and dances became frequent occurrences, the Firemen's Ball being one of the leading social events of the year. For quieter evenings at home, charades and the stereoscope offered diversion. The talking machine had made its appearance in 1897, when a local drugstore offered with every 10c purchase the privilege of listening to a record. Excursions up the river on the little stern-wheelers, bicycling up the road toward Snohomish to the Bicycle Tree, berrying, fishing, and hunting were popular forms of amusement in summer. Holidays were great events, with canoe, sack, and egg races. Theaters had been established, the naughtiest and liveliest being the Casino. These were the days of the hack and the surrey, of leg-of-mutton sleeves, of cuspidors, blacksmith shops and rock candy and rye whisky for colds. Social affairs began to be more elaborate for those whose incomes were sufficiently large, but simple and inexpensive amusements, picnics for the family or a bucket of beer from the corner saloon for the men, were about all that a mill worker's family could afford. For the floater, who came to town on Saturday night to enjoy a few riotous days after the hazards of daily work and the brutal life in vermin-infested camps, there were numerous saloons and brothels, where his wages were extracted from him in short order.

During the first ten years of the town's existence, considerable building had been done. In 1896 the main thoroughfare was Hewitt Street, the bayside area and Rucker Hill still being largely undeveloped. Along the river were the low sprawling buildings of the "old" town, while upon the ridge the newer business blocks were being erected. Some of these buildings are still standing, dark and gloomy, with narrow windows

History: The Indians

Photograph courtesy of Olympia Chamber of Commerce
CROWD ASSEMBLED AT THE CAPITOL FOR INAUGURATION OF ELISHA P. FERRY AS GOVERNOR IN 1889, THE FIRST YEAR OF STATEHOOI

STATE CAPITOL, OLYMPIA
tograph courtesy of Olympia Chamber of Commerce

ORT WALLA WALLA

Reproduction of old print by courtesy of U. S. Army Signal Co

CHEMAKANE MISSI(

eproduction of an old Lithograph by courtesy of U. S. Army Signal Corps

Photograph by Stuart B. Hertz

ALEXANDER'S BLOCKHOUSE, COUPEVILL

"OFFICERS' CLUB," VANCOUVER BARRACKS

Photograph courtesy of Camera Shop, Vancouv

REEPORT, A TYPICAL WESTERN TOWN

RIVERSIDE AVENUE, SPOKANE, AFTER THE FIRE OF 1

Photograph courtesy Hudson's Bay Company

S.S. BEAVER, FIRST STEAMSHIP ON THE PACIFIC COAST

This picture was taken in 1888 after this historic vessel, launched in 1835, came to its end on the rocks at Prospect Point.

SEATTLE WHARVES (1878)

PETROGLYPH, NEAR ROCK ISLAND

COAST INDIANS WEAVING BAS

ograph by R. B. Inverarity

MAKAH INDIAN

NEZ PERCE WAR PARADE (July 4, 1901)

Braves and their families from all parts of the Colville Reservation attended this celebr

Photograph courtesy of R. B. Inverarity

INDIAN VILLAGE—NESPE

set in deep recesses. By 1900 the population had reached 7,838, the main thoroughfare had been planked, and board sidewalks were laid along many of the streets. During the hot, dry months the streets were dusty and the boards of the walks warped in the sun, while wet weather turned many streets into seas of mud. Residences of relatively affluent families were ornate, with cornices and scrollwork; those of the workers were still largely makeshifts. The open country was within walking distance, and cows were occasionally pastured within the limits of the city.

Here as elsewhere in the United States, the expansion of industry was accompanied by considerable unrest. The hard times of the nineties, with consequent unemployment or sometimes inadequate pay and long hours, led to a growing movement for labor organization. In 1900, the Everett Central Labor Council was formed. Within 6 months, 27 trade unions were organized, and for the first time Everett celebrated Labor Day. Wages at this time averaged from $1 to $2 a day for a 10-hour day; the monthly wage was seldom much more than $60. Layoffs were frequent, and, particularly in the sawmills, hazards were many. The shingle weavers demanded a 10c-an-hour increase; other unions demanded a 9-hour day. No concrete gains seem to have been made, but labor was beginning to feel the need for united action. Moreover, the increasing size of plants and the increasing influence of eastern capital made a definite cleavage between th employers and workers.

Various social issues were also assuming importance. As early as 1900, the conflict betwen the wide-open-town advocates and the anti-vice and anti-alcohol forces had begun. By 1901, at least 29 saloons were doing a lively business. The new Washington Brewing Company, established in 1900, was finding a good local market for its output. By 1904 the number of saloons had risen to 34, one of the most elaborate being Feeney's. Opposing the open-town forces were most of the church groups and the International Order of Good Templars and the Women's Christian Temperance Union, two organizations that were finding considerable support among the more sedate and steady elements in the population, particularly the Scandinavians.

In the early 1900's, the glamorous vision of Everett as an industrial center was beginning to fade. The barge works, after the single abortive venture that revealed the unseaworthiness of the whaleback craft, was out of the picture. The brave venture in the manufacture of nails also proved to have overlooked certain practical features, such as the distance from the source of supplies and the limited demand for this product. The smelter remained, but its days, too, were numbered. New enterprises, however, had been launched, stimulated partly by the growing local demands and partly by the demands from outside markets. A tile works, brickyards, machine shops, and a flour mill were all in operation; and the Sumner Iron Works was active, having launched with great pride in 1900 the *Telegraph,* generally considered the fastest sternwheeler afloat at the time.

At the opening of the twentieth century, the role that lumber was to play in the growth of the city was clearly seen by some promoters.

Already the waterways were bordered by 10 shingle mills and 8 sawmills, and the pulp mill was operating. The city's destiny, at least as long as timber could be cut in the hinterlands or towed in, was certain —Everett was to be a sawmill town. The dominance of lumber was indisputably established by the advent of the Weyerhaeuser lumber interests; actually as early as 1893 they had been reaching into the region in preliminary surveys, but not until 1902, when they purchased the Bell-Nelson Mill, did they enter into active operation.

The groundwork for the Weyerhaeuser expansion in the area was laid by the provisions of the Forestry Reservation Act of 1897, by which a system of forest reservations was established, with the provision that owners of land taken into the reserve should be allowed to select a like amount of acreage elsewhere. This provision led in 1899 to the acquisition by the Northern Pacific Railway of big stands of timber, which were sold to the Weyerhaeuser interests for $6,000,000, the company thus acquiring a vast domain of 40,000,000,000 feet of timber.

During the first decade of the twentieth century, the mills of the city were operating full blast; tugs with rafts in tow were working 24 hours a day; the whine of saws often sounded day and night. Over 250,000,000 feet of lumber were cut in 1902. Mills continued to expand their plants and to increase in number. By 1904 two more lumber mills and two more shingle mills had been built. Farther and farther inland the lumber camps went, with their ox teams to snake the logs out on skidroads and float them down the river. By night the sky along the river glowed from the light of the burners, and smoke hung heavy over the lowlands or swept inland with the brisk winds from Puget Sound. Some 3,000 workers answered the whistles.

Timber had indeed become the recognized first resource of Everett and the adjacent valley regions, and only a few prophetic individuals shook their heads in apprehension as they saw the big trees, source of so much local pride, crashing by thousands under the impact of the logger's ax. Still to be seen in Clark Pit is a relic of this decade, the "Tree-House," constructed from the base of an enormous tree, which was exhibited at the World's Fair at St. Louis in 1904-5.

In 1906-7 another big enterprise, the Canyon Lumber Company, built a huge mill on a 52-acre tract on the Snohomish River at the foot of Everett Avenue. These were years of considerable prosperity for the owners of the mills: lumber prices had advanced and demands had increased. Wages averaged $1.75 to $2 a day, and employment was steadier, thus insuring a higher annual wage.

The early years of the twentieth century saw an influx of immigrants to the West; about 50,000 came to Washington, and many settled in Everett, attracted there by the publicity of the Great Northern Railway and by the opportunities for employment in sawmills, fisheries, factories, logging camps, and railroad shops. Most of these newcomers were unskilled laborers. Many were Scandinavians from their homeland or the Middle West, thrifty, hard-working, serious-minded people, who were seeking a better life for themselves and for their children and who contributed a stabilizing element to Everett.

As in most cities, some of the more interesting spots were known in Everett only to a few. Such a place was Adam Hill's Bookstore, where, amid a jumble of books, an assortment of people gathered to talk about politics, pioneer days, and philosophy, as well as about homelier bread-and-butter affairs; and to swap tall tales and loggers' yarns. Here were books of all kinds: romances, adventure stories, and yellow-backed thrillers; dull-covered scholarly tomes; and volumes by Jack London, Robert Ingersoll, Tom Paine, Morris Hillquit, Upton Sinclair, Gustavus Myers, and Voltaire. The browser was as welcome as the customer, and, whatever were his tastes or preferences, he usually could find what pleased him.

A premonition of the panic of 1907 was seen in the tremors of the financial market, which were felt early in the spring as far as the Pacific Northwest. But activity continued throughout the summer. Then in the fall the panic broke with dramatic suddenness. A week before the crash, burners were glowing and all the town was busy. Industries were booming, and not enough workers could be found to fill the demand. Wages, too, were at record high levels. Two weeks later, however, the bottom had fallen out of everything. Industry had simply stopped, and while the market gamblers rubbed their bruised financial heads and considered methods of recouping their fortunes, armies of unemployed, appearing as if by magic, marched the streets in broken ranks, looking for jobs that did not exist and eating and sleeping where their few dollars would stretch the farthest or where charity handed out its rations. No banks closed in Everett, but the city was hard hit and did not entirely recover for years.

By 1910 Everett had reached the 10,000 mark in population. The Ballinger scandal had broken. River steamers were disappearing, although a few stern-wheelers and an occasional four-master were still to be seen. Livery stables and four-in-hands were giving way to garages and automobiles; the interurban to Seattle was running on an hourly schedule. Men were taking to golf, although fishing and hunting were still the most popular forms of recreation. Moving pictures were in, and an attempt had been made to stop the showing of the Johnson-Jeffries fight pictures. At this time most of the streets of the residential districts were unpaved, and hazel bushes and blackberry vines still grew prolifically in the suburbs.

Local agitation for temperance and prohibition came to a head in 1910, when the local "dries" won a victory at the polls. For a number of years the battle had been waged with moral, economic, and political arguments. Militant reformers, many of them women, had noted with anxiety the number of saloons and their flourishing business; they had visualized the primrose path that stretched before the small boys who were to be seen, occasionally, carrying home a pail of "suds." More and more frequently temperance groups made themselves audible. Their victory was forecast in the Sunday-closing blue law passed by the State legislature in 1909. A final campaign led to triumph at the polls the next year, a triumph, however, of brief duration; the local-option law was repealed by a narrow margin in 1912.

Although labor unions had existed in Everett since 1892, and agitation for shorter hours, job security, higher wages, and better working conditions had been growing stronger, there was little organization until the closing years of the first decade of the twentieth century. Workers in logging camps were coming to be largely migratory laborers, who traveled by brake rods, blind baggage, or boxcar, carrying their rolls of bedding from camp to camp, often a dirty, vermin-infested, and disease-ridden place. Partially because of their migratory tendencies, the loggers found in the I.W.W. the type of organization best-suited to their needs. Formed in 1905, the I.W.W. had become very active in the second decade of the century. During these years, increasing pressure from the workers and resistance to their demands on the part of employers and operators led to intermittent clashes, accompanies sometimes by violence. However, the increased demand for lumber at higher prices, as a result of the World War, brought steadier employment, higher wages, and general improvement in working conditions. At the same time, the I.W.W. ceased to be a factor of importance.

Everett prospered throughout the war years and in the period that followed. In 1918 the municipally owned Port of Everett was established to serve the commercial and industrial growth of the city, now nearing the 30,000 population mark. In 1921, however, when the lumber market cracked and prices dropped from $31 a thousand board feet to $13.50, Everett, like other cities dependent primarily upon the lumber industry, fell upon dull times. Wages declined, employment dropped off along with the decline in production, and stores and service trades, supported mainly by the pay rolls of industry, felt the pinch; some trouble between employers and employees resulted, with violence flaring spasmodically. By 1923, increased efficiency in industry permitted greater individual output, the nation-wide building boom had started, and wages began to rise. Locally, a period of construction followed, comparable to that of the nineties; fireproof business and hotel structures, two schools, two hospitals, a new labor temple, many churches, and a modernistic city hall were constructed. This period terminated in 1929 with Black Friday and the depression.

Everett is at present in transition, as the factors that led to its growth diminish in importance and new ones appear. Railroad pay rolls are no longer significant, and the partial depletion of timber resources in the surrounding area has brought considerable unemployment. Snohomish County has an estimated pulpwood stand of 10,000,000,000 feet, and Everett, with two of its mills adapted to the handling of pulpwood, hopefully looks to pulp production for the solution of some of its more pressing industrial problems. An iron works, a shipyard, a brick and tile kiln, plywood factories, and wood-processing plants add to the volume of local industry and commerce. Fishing still is an important industry, and the surrounding agricultural area is contributing more and more to the stability of the city.

Today a brisk industrial city, Everett has a fine school system (including a high school and two junior high schools), many churches, various cultural and social organizations, a daily newspaper, several entertainment centers, and, what is perhaps most significant for its future, an energetic and progressive citizenry. An interesting development is the new Army airport, now (1941) under construction at a cost of several million dollars. It is to be the base for the Fifty-fourth Pursuit Group and the Thirty-fourth Air Base Group—180 officers and 1,800 men. It was begun by the county in 1936, on elevated land exceptionally free from fog, about seven and one-half miles southwest of Everett. The Civic Auditorium, on Colby Avenue, completed early in 1940, is an expression of strong community interests and cultural development. Here the Everett Civic Symphony gives its concerts, and audiences of 3,000 or more gather for the Snohomish County May Music Festival.

POINTS OF INTEREST

1. The SNOHOMISH COUNTY COURTHOUSE, Rockefeller Ave. between Wall St. and Pacific Ave., completed in 1910, replaces the old courthouse, which burned in 1909. The building, an adaptation of Spanish mission architecture, is of white stucco, with a red-tile roof and an attractive clock tower and cupola. A. F. Heide of Seattle was the architect. The interior is finished in dark oak. The Annex (1908) was saved when the original courthouse (1897) was destroyed by fire.

2. The CITY HALL, corner Wetmore Ave. and Wall St., erected in 1930 after a design by A. H. Albertson of Seattle, is trimly modern in appearance. Ivory-tinted pilasters, ornamented with guilloches of cast stone, soften the severity of the concrete and cream-colored brick walls. Over the main entrance, through which prisoners pass to the third-floor jail, there was originally a bronze plaque inscribed "Eternal Vigilance Is the Price of Liberty," but public ridicule caused city officials to remove the plaque, with its ironic pronouncement.

3. The EVERETT PUBLIC LIBRARY (*open* 11-9 *weekdays*), SW. corner Hoyt and Everett Aves., admirably expresses its function in the fine simplicity of architectural treatment, both exterior and interior. It is entirely modern, not only in style of architecture, but also in structural materials and equipment. The building, of brown smooth stone with terra cotta trim of the same color, was designed by Bebb and Gould, Seattle architects, and was completed in 1934. The main entrance doors and the portico over the main entrance are faced with aluminum. The interior walls of the main lobby and the counter, shelves, and other equipment are paneled in oak. Plastered panels above the doors to the reading rooms and above the balcony are decorated with murals depicting the city's history, by John T. Jacobsen of Seattle. Sculptural detail in britannia metal fill other similar panels. In the main reading room, four plaques of the same metal, sculptured in bas-relief by Dudley Pratt, illustrate the history of book-making. In this room the

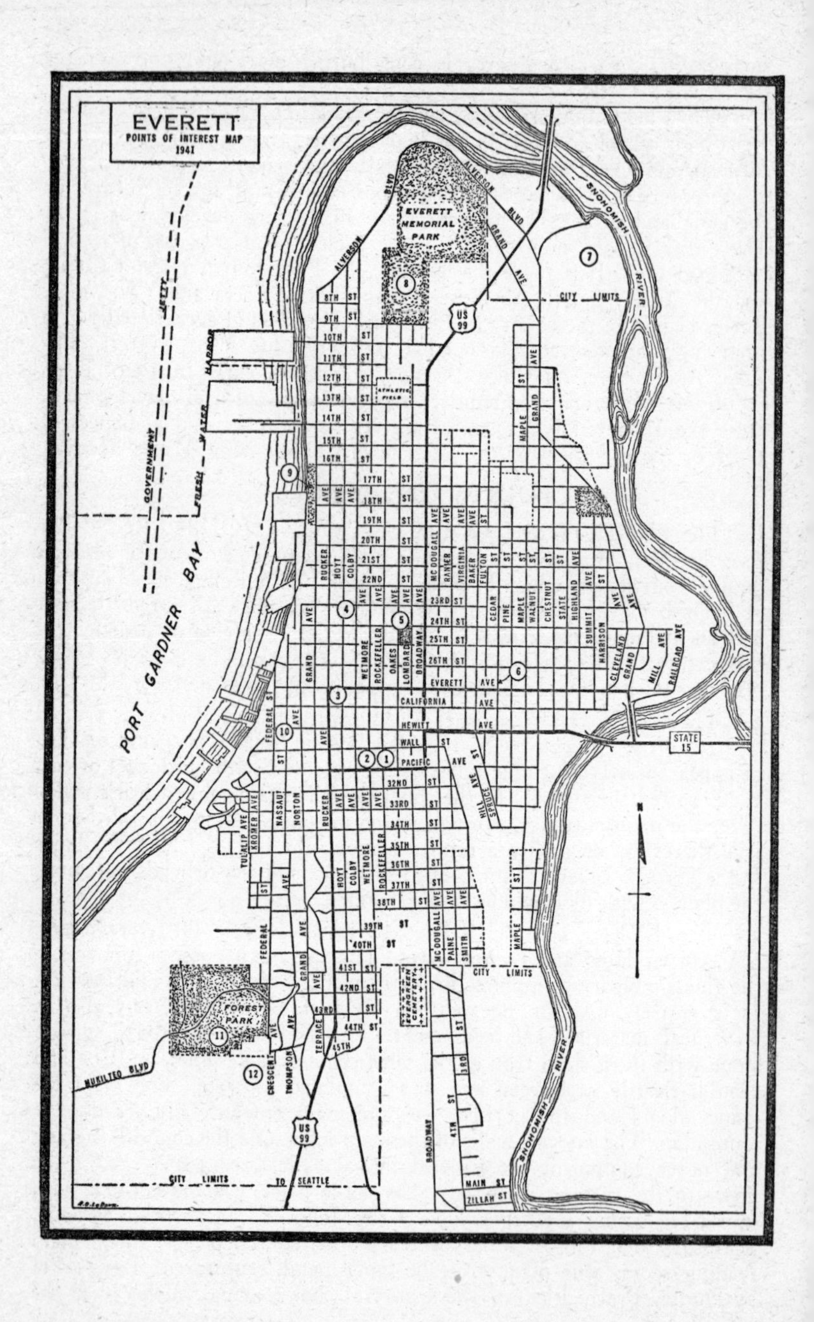
EVERETT
POINTS OF INTEREST MAP
1941
EVERETT MEMORIAL PARK
ALVERSON BLVD
GRAND AVE
CITY LIMITS
SNOHOMISH RIVER
GOVERNMENT JETTY
FRESH WATER HARBOR
PORT GARDNER BAY
ATHLETIC FIELD
US 99
STATE 15
FOREST PARK
MUKILTEO BLVD
EVERGREEN CEMETERY
CITY LIMITS TO SEATTLE
BROADWAY
MAIN ST
ZILLAH ST
N

ceiling is beamed with fir, and here, as in the lobby, the lighting is indirect. The floors in all sections open to the public are of cork tile. The library's 38,000 volumes include a genealogical section, special collections on lumbering and drama, and a file of early newspapers.

4. TRINITY EPISCOPAL CHURCH (*persons desiring to view interior call at rectory,* 2309 *Hoyt Ave., weekdays* 10-4, *Sun.* 1-4). SE. corner Hoyt Ave. and 23rd St., was dedicated by Bishop Frederick W. Keator on Trinity Sunday, 1921. A bronze tablet on the wall opposite the entrance is inscribed: To the glory of God and in commemoration of the victory of Christianity and civilization in the World War this church is built by a grateful people 'Lest we forget.'

The War Memorial Church was designed by E. T. Osborn, Seattle architect, and is a fine example of perpendicular, or English Gothic, architecture. The exterior walls are of buff-colored tapestry brick, with trim and ornamental work of cast stone in a somewhat deeper buff. The moderately gabled, slate-roofed nave rises some 20 feet above the lean-to roofs of the aisles; surmounting the points of either gable are small Celtic crosses of buff-colored stone. The facade, at the west end of the building, is chiefly notable for its expanse of mullioned, transomed windows of stained glass in geometrical design; the three-centered arch is richly decorated with stone tracery. Dominating the facade and immediately north of the nave is a 70-foot octagonal tower, flat-roofed with decorated belfry. In the northwest corner of the structure is an austere and low-arched doorway, the main entrance to the church auditorium.

In this spacious rectangle, a grand sweep of Gothic arches, soaring up from the low-roofed aisles, terminates in a maze of slender ribs supporting the roof of the nave. Overlooking the chancel is the large east window with its Biblical figures and texts—a poem of iridescent color. The artist, Charles Jay Connick, is known for his windows in St. Martin's Chapel, Cathedral of St. John the Divine and in the Princeton University Chapel. To the left and right of the altar are narrow panels in oil by Mary G. Allen—figures of St. Francis and St. John. On the east wall of the auditorium, to the right of the chancel rail, hangs a carved crucifix given by Anton Lang of Oberammergau; and near by stand a pair of tall wooden candlesticks from the first Episcopal church established in the State of Washington.

5. CLARK PARK, 25th St. between Oakes and Lombard Aves. and extending to 24th St., contains the GIANT CEDAR STUMP that was

---

EVERETT—POINTS OF INTEREST

1. County Courthouse
2. City Hall
3. Public Library
4. Trinity Episcopal Church
5. Clark Park
6. Our Lady of Perpetual Help Church
7. Weyerhaeuser Sulphite Plant
8. Memorial Park
9. Site of Vancouver's Landing
10. S.S. *Black Prince*
11. Forest Park
12. Children's Home

exhibited at the St. Louis Exposition in 1904. The "Tree House" in the interior of the stump is not open. The park was named in honor of John Judson Clark, who established a store in the bayside section in 1891, dealing extensively with the Indians.

6. OUR LADY OF PERPETUAL HELP CHURCH, Cedar St. between 26th St. and Everett Ave., built in 1926, is an impressive example of Romanesque architecture, with the traditional cruciform ground plan. Corinthian columns, supporting the low arches of its facade, soften the effect of sombre massiveness characteristic of this style of architecture.

7. The gigantic WEYERHAEUSER SULPHITE-PULP PLANT (*open by permission*) blocks off Everett's southwest water front. The plant can be identified by its six digesters—steel-sheathed tanks like great inverted bottles—in which chips are cooked preparatory to making wood pulp.

The EVERETT WATER FRONT, extending W. of Vernon and Grand Aves. and inland from Puget Sound along the Snohomish River, is thronged with industrial activity; a score of mills and factories may be seen close up, although visitors are warned of the mechanical hazards. Northward are numerous piers and canneries, headquarters for the fisheries industry; another pulp plant and several lumber and shingle mills, including the Clough-Hartley properties; casket factories and an establishment for creosoting poles and piling. Eastward along the river, below the northern extension of Grand Avenue, are Weyerhaeuser mills B and C, the latter noted for its operation with electric and compressed air equipment. On the southeast river front are other lumber mills, a foundry and iron works, and the Everett Pulp and Paper Company mill.

8. EVERETT MEMORIAL PARK, at 9th St. between US 99 and Grand Ave. along Port Gardner Bay, embraces 187 acres on the site of the ancient Snohomish Indian village Hay-bohl-ub, or Hebolb, where in 1863 a combined store, hotel, and saloon marked the local advent of civilization. Overlooking the bay, Snohomish River, and Whidbey, Camano, and Hat Islands, the site served as a lookout for the Indians.

The park was established in 1932 by the Earl Faulkner Post of the American Legion, with the double purpose of creating a memorial to soldiers of the World War and, at the same time, providing work for the unemployed. The park has an 18-hole golf course planned by the late Chandler Egan (*greens fee* 50c), six paved tennis courts, a baseball diamond, and a free campground equipped with kitchen.

9. The SITE OF VANCOUVER'S LANDING is included in Grand Avenue Park, between 16th and 19th Sts., a landscaped strip extending for a quarter of a mile along a steep bluff overlooking Port Gardner Bay. A small granite marker, erected in 1915 by the Marcus Whitman Chapter of the Daughters of the American Revolution, commemorates the arrival of the explorer, Captain George Vancouver. The inscription reads: On the beach near this spot Vancouver landed June 4, 1792.

10. The S.S. BLACK PRINCE (*open weekdays by permission*), Pier 2, foot of Hewitt Ave., an old stern-wheeler built in 1901 at Everett, is used by yachtsmen as a club. The vessel has been preserved on piling, and the hull and exterior are intact, even to the big paddle wheel. Alterations in the interior and additions have been made by the Yacht Club.

11. FOREST PARK, Federal St. between 40th and 45th Sts., an area of 112 acres in woodland setting, is bisected by Mukilteo Highway. The south section, covering a low hill, contains playfields, wading pool, picnic grounds, and a small zoo and aviary, with a collection of game birds of the Northwest. The north, and lower, section of the park remains mostly in its natural state, although trails have been cut along either side of the ravine that traverse it from north to south. A camping ground with kitchen has been established near the highway, and an arboretum to contain native shrubs is being planned.

The nucleus of Forest Park was a 40-acre tract given to the city in 1900 by William G. Swalwell, an Everett pioneer. During the last few years the area has been improved and beautified by Works Progress Administration workers; in the zoo, the animal houses have been renovated, and pastures made for deer, elk, and bison; the hillsides have been terraced and planted, and bridle paths and trails laid out. Seventeen dams within half a mile provide beautiful cascades, as well as prevent erosion and check the flow of Pigeon Creek. Flowering crab apple trees will cover acres of hillside.

12. The PARKLAND LUTHERAN CHILDREN'S HOME (*open* 8:30-5 *weekdays,* 1-4 *Sun.*) 45th St. and Federal Ave., a three-story concrete building, whose dome, overlaid with rust-resistant metal, shines like burnished silver, has been a conspicuous landmark for years. The Norwegian Lutheran College was opened here in 1908; after reorganization as the Columbia Lutheran College, the institution was finally closed because of lack of funds. In 1925 the building was converted into an orphanage.

The 80-foot TOTEM POLE, 44th St. and Rucker Ave., was carved by Chief William Shelton of the Tulalip Indian Reservation to commemorate Chief Patkanim of the Salish Indians. In 1855, Chief Patkanim, with three other chiefs, signed the Mukilteo Treaty (*see Tour 8b*), which ceded to the United States the lands from Elliott Bay to the Canadian boundary. Patkanim died in 1858 and is buried in the Tulalip cemetery.

On a bronze tablet set into the west base of the pole, the work of J. A. Wehn of Seattle, is a relief bust of the Indian warrior, who fought for the white people, and a commemorative inscription. Chief Shelton, the carver of the 16 groups of figures on the pole, has given an interpretation of the legends represented, in his *Story of the Totem Pole, or Indian Legends* (1935).

POINTS OF INTEREST IN ENVIRONS

Snohomish River Mills, 3 *m.*; Mukilteo Treaty Monument, 4.8 *m.*; Tulalip Indian Reservation, Indian Village, 11.6 *m.* (*see Tour 8b*). Whidbey Island and site of Port Ebey, 7.5 m., including 5 m. to ferry at Mukilteo and 2.5 *m.* across Puget Sound, (*see Tour 8C*). Lake Stevens, 8 *m.* (*see Tour 1C*). Paine Field 7.5 *m.*, SW. on Mukilteo Highway off US 99.

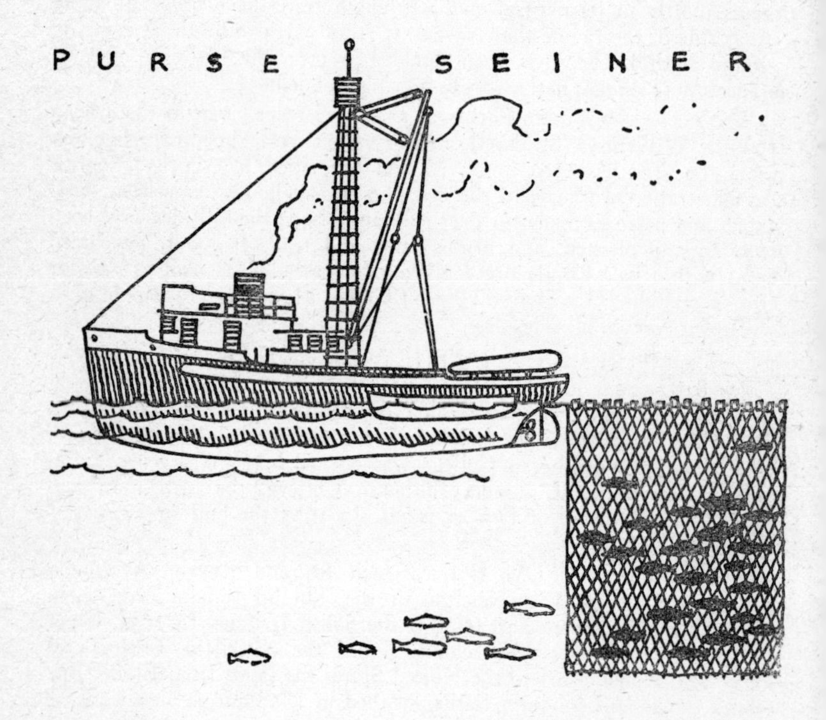

Olympia

Railroad Stations: Fourth and Adams Sts. for Union Pacific R.R.; Columbia St. between 7th and 9th Sts. for Northern Pacific R.R.
Bus Station: 107 7th Ave. E. for North Coast and Greyhound Lines, Union Pacific Stages, and Washington Motor Coach Lines.
Taxis: 20 blocks 35c; 3.5 miles 50c.
City Busses: Fare 10c.
Traffic Regulations: No one-way streets; main arterial streets: Capitol Way and 4th St. All streets adequately marked for parking limitations in business section.
Street Order and Numbering: E. and W. from Capitol Way; N. and S. from 4th St.

Accommodations: Five hotels; several cabin camps.

Information Service: Olympia Chamber of Commerce, Automobile Club of Washington (AAA), Olympian Hotel, Legion Way and Washington St.

Motion Picture Houses: Three.
Radio Station: KGY (1240 kc.).
Athletics: Stevens Field, 22nd and Washington Sts.; YMCA, 510 Franklin St.
Golf: Mountain View Golf and Country Club, 3.5 *m.* E. on Pacific Highway, 9 holes, greens fee 50c; Glengary Golf Course, 4 *m.* W. on Shelton and Aberdeen Highway, 9 holes, greens fee 50c; Olympia Golf and Country Club, 3 *m.* N. on W. side of bay, 9 holes, greens fee 50c.
Riding: East Bay Drive near Priest Point Park, 50c per hour.
Parks: Sylvester Park, Capitol Way, between Legion Way and 7th St.; Priest Point Park, East Bay Drive, 2 *m.* N. of Olympia, recreational facilities; Woodruff Park, West Olympia.
Yacht Club: Foot of Franklin St.

Annual Events: Thurston County Festival, last two weeks of Aug.; Olympia Flower Show, near the 15th of Aug.

OLYMPIA (71 alt., 13,254 pop.), State capital and seat of Thurston County, spreads fan-like from its harbor on Puget Sound over gently sloping hills, with Mount Rainier on the east and the more distant Olympics visible to the north. Here, near the place where the Nisqually once met in solemn council to devise means of protection against the *soleeks itsweet* (angry brown bear), today legislators convene to represent the citizens of the State named in honor of the Great White Father.

From a broad knoll near the center of the town rise the massive white sandstone buildings of the Capitol Group, with the tall white dome of the Legislative Building conspicuous for miles around. In general Olympia has an atmosphere of conservatism and moderate prosperity. Modern buildings predominate in the small compact business district, while residential areas represent an older architectural mode, quiet and attractive, with substantial homes, smooth lawns, and long colonnades of shade trees. The Pacific Highway bisects the city, giving a glimpse of practically every phase of activity and a panoramic view of the surrounding mountains and the harbor. Southernmost port on Puget Sound, Olympia is the center of an industrial area concentrated along the water front, where the Deschutes River flows into Budd Inlet. Sawmills and woodworking plants, knitting mills, and oyster-packing houses cover the area between the east and west bays. About two miles south of the city center is Tumwater, home of the locally famous brewery. Adjacent to the mitten-shaped tideflat is anchorage deep enough for ocean-going freighters; and in the shallow waters near by are the beds of the delicious Olympia oyster—a bivalve so small that 1,600 to the gallon makes an average pack.

Governmental employees of city, county, and State constitute a substantial part of the residents. The days of such citizens are for the most part well-ordered in the long-established routine of their work, and the city reflects in some measure this placidity and economic stability. But, being a capital city, Olympia is greatly influenced by shifting political winds and registers recurrent changes in tempo in the life of its population, as the legislature convenes or disperses or State administrations change. With the convening of the legislature, an air of hurry and bustle pervades the city. Legislators, their families, friends, and attendant lobbyists come and go; the hotels fill, and restaurants and shops do a thriving business; groups of people, generally engaged in political discussion, gather in lobbies, in capitol corridors, on the street; visitors throng the galleries as lawmakers deliberate; traffic is thick on Capitol Way.

The history of Olympia goes back to 1848, when Edmund Sylvester, a Gloucester fisherman, and Levi Lathrop Smith, a Presbyterian divinity student, came to the region, called by the Nisqually tribe *stechchass* (place of the bear). These strangely assorted partners each secured a 320-acre land grant from the Oregon Provisional Government. The former chose Chamber's Prairie; the latter, the south shore of Budd Inlet. They agreed that, upon either's death, the survivor would become heir. They adopted for their lands a composite name, Smithter—later modified by usage to Smithfield.

In 1845 a group of five settlers under the direction of Michael T. Simmons had arrived at near-by Tumwater. Eight of the new arrivals planned and built the first sawmill of the region near the northwestern part of lower Tumwater Falls. With the arrival of Father Pascal Ricard and nine Oblate fathers in June 1848, St. Joseph's Mission was established on Budd Inlet. The site, today called Priest's Point, a beautiful wooded park overlooking the bay, is the city's principal playground.

Accident decided which one of the two founders should succeed to control of the site; Smith, while traveling by canoe to the sessions of the Oregon Provisional Government, suffered an epileptic attack and was drowned when his craft capsized. Under the Oregon Provisional Land Laws, Sylvester became the owner of Smith's claim—the present site of Olympia.

The village was practically depopulated during the California gold rush of 1849. Even Sylvester succumbed to the hope of striking it rich, but it was not long before this hope grew dim. Disappointed and homesick, he joined with several others in the purchase of the brig *Orbit* and set sail for Budd Inlet, arriving there on New Year's Day, 1850. Later, the *Orbit* sailed to San Francisco with a cargo of piling and returned with a supply of clothing, sugar, and miscellaneous supplies for the shelves of a small general store, the first in the region.

Congress authorized the establishment of a custom-house in the growing village on February 1851, thus creating the first port of entry on Puget Sound. S. P. Moses was appointed collector, and five months later the first mail contract was let to A. B. Robbeson for service by horseback and canoe between Smithfield and the Columbia River settlement.

Inspired by the magnificent panorama of the Olympics, Colonel Isaac N. Ebey, who succeeded Moses as collector of customs, persuaded Sylvester and the townfolk to rechristen the village Olympia. A townsite was platted and the lots were put up for sale.

In close succession a series of memorable events occurred. In 1852 George A. Barnes opened a general merchandise store at the west end of First Street, the first sessions of a district court were convened in the custom-house; the *Columbian* was established with T. F. McElroy and J. W. Wiley as publishers; stage service to the Columbia River region began; and in December, the Reverend Benjamin Close delivered a sermon to the first Methodist congregation. Two years later, Presbyterian services were conducted in a cooper's shop by the Reverend George P. Whitworth, and the first church edifice in the region was erected by Roman Catholics in 1854.

In 1852 agitation for the separation of the territory north of the Columbia got under way, and the *Columbian* was a powerful factor in developing public sentiment. The campaign was successful, and the new territory was created and named Washington in March 1853. So slowly, however, did dispatches travel from Washington, D. C., that the *Columbian* continued its urgent editorials for some weeks after the new Territory had been created. Major Isaac I. Stevens, appointed Territorial Governor, arrived November 25, 1853, and on November 28 proclaimed Olympia the Territorial capital. Then he launched vigorously into the problems of the new commonwealth. The first Territorial legislature was convened in 1854.

Indian unrest hastened completion of a 15-foot stockade around Olympia. The revenue cutter *Joe Lane* was stationed in the harbor so that if need be her cannon might aid in the defense of the town. After a year of war, United States troops restored tranquillity, and the citizens dismantled their stockade and planked the streets with its timbers. Soon activity was stimulated by the arrival of new settlers, and when Olympia was incorporated on September 4, 1859, the town's population was 1,489.

The next decade saw the extension of transcontinental telegraph lines into the Territory, service being initiated by Governor William Pickering, who exchanged greetings with President Lincoln in 1864. Six years later, a brick building was constructed at a cost of $20,000 to provide for the first bank. The number of steamships increased and the scope of their service was extended, until communication with other Puget Sound ports became regular. Despite bad roads, frequent stage service was maintained with Columbia River cities. Finally, in the 1880's a branch of the Northern Pacific entered the city. In 1889 another attempt was made to move the capital, but Olympia won 37,413 ballots out of a total of 41,416.

Since 1900, development of Olympia, as a city, has followed a steady and uneventful course, which remains fundamentally unaltered even by the shifting pattern of Olympia, the capital. The bulk of the population consists to an appreciable extent of those who have steady employment in civil service and other governmental agencies, but new industries, such as that of oyster culture, and the expansion of old industries, particularly in the field of lumber products, have contributed materially toward the general stability. Another fact of real economic importance is that the city serves as a distributing center for freight shipped by inland waterways from down-Sound points to all southwest Washington.

The Port of Olympia, an area of more than 700 square miles, coextensive with Thurston County, serves a region highly productive in agricultural, mineral, and lumber resources. The Port, established at Olympia in 1926, receives annually more than 200 vessels; the trade is largely in lumber or finished products, such as furniture and plywood. Besides the county port, with its wharf, transit shed, and modern coldstorage plant, there are several oil docks and the wharf of the Olympia Oyster Company. In addition to fruit growing, the surrounding region has developed a stone quarry, logging and lumbering enterprises, diversified agriculture, and dairying as important industries. Thus, Olympia a center of government has become also an interesting modern city.

POINTS OF INTEREST

1. The SITE OF THE FIRST LEGISLATIVE HALL, Capitol Way between State and Olympia Aves., is marked by a bronze tablet set in the sidewalk. Here, on the second floor of a two-story frame store building, the first Territorial legislature met on February 27, 1854. The second and succeeding sessions were held in the Masonic Hall until 1863, when the legislators were convened in a frame building that was intended for temporary use but served until 1903. Thereafter the legislature met in a building that had served as the county courthouse. In addition to the purchase price of $350,000, a sum of $475,000 was spent for alterations and enlargements. The building housed all State departments until the present building was ready for occupancy.

2. The J. J. BRENNER OYSTER PACKING PLANT (*open 8-5 workdays*), 502 4th Ave., is one of the oldest and largest of the numerous oyster-packing plants in the city. Workmen, wearing "mud-shoes" with webbed metal soles, pick the oysters by hand from the beds at low tide. The oysters are sorted at a grading depot, the smaller ones are returned, and those of marketable size are taken by the boatload to the packing plant. From refrigerated storage the oysters pass to the opening room, where skillful workmen open the shells with a putty-knife, scoop out the meats, and toss the shells into a chute. The meats are conveyed to the skimmer, washed, drained, packed, and sealed by machine in rustless metal cans, and put on ice until marketed. The shells are conveyed back to the oyster beds, where they are used as a cultch for seedling oysters that attach themselves to the shells during the growing period.

3. SYLVESTER PARK, Capitol Way between Legion Way and 7th Ave., named for its donor, Edmund Sylvester, is a one-block plot, attractively landscaped with shade trees, shrubs, and a pool. In the park is the STATUE OF JOHN RANKIN ROGERS, twice Governor and author of the "barefoot schoolboy law," designed to give "every poor son of this commonwealth a fair education."

4. The OLD STATE CAPITOL BUILDING (*open 9-5 Mon.-Fri., 9-12 Sat.*), 7th Ave. between Washington and Franklin Sts., of gray stone in the Richardsonian Romanesque style, has pointed towers and high arched windows like those of a feudal castle. It was built in 1893, and is one of the best examples of Romanesque style in the State; Willis A. Ritchie was the architect. It still houses many State offices.

5. The SYLVESTER HOUSE (*open by permission*), 114 8th Ave., was built in 1856 by the pioneer, Edmund Sylvester, who hoped to have the house recognized as the finest in the Territory. He had a guard tower erected on the roof and shutters added to doors and windows. At that time, house paint was considered an extravagance, but he had his house painted white and, in spite of the contemporary belief that plumbing was a folly, had a running-water system installed. The high-ceilinged rooms are ornamented with copper moulding. The fireplaces in the house were added several years after the house was built.

Here in the Sylvester House, the Olympia Women's Club was organized March 10, 1883, with the stipulation that applicants for membership "must be honest, intelligent, and have good moral character."

6. The MASONIC TEMPLE (*open 9-12, 1-4 daily; Masons only*), 804 Capitol Way, was built in 1911. It bears little resemblance to the original homely structure, built in 1852 at the edge of the forest; around this early temple were charred stumplands, and leading to it was a trail, muddy or dusty according to the prevailing weather. Old timers recall zigzagging lanterns slowly converging at the temple as the members picked their way through the stumps and over logs on winter nights. Two early sessions of the legislature were held here.

In 1930 the original temple door, which had been lost for almost 20 years, was found in a barn. Upon the 8 panels of the door appro-

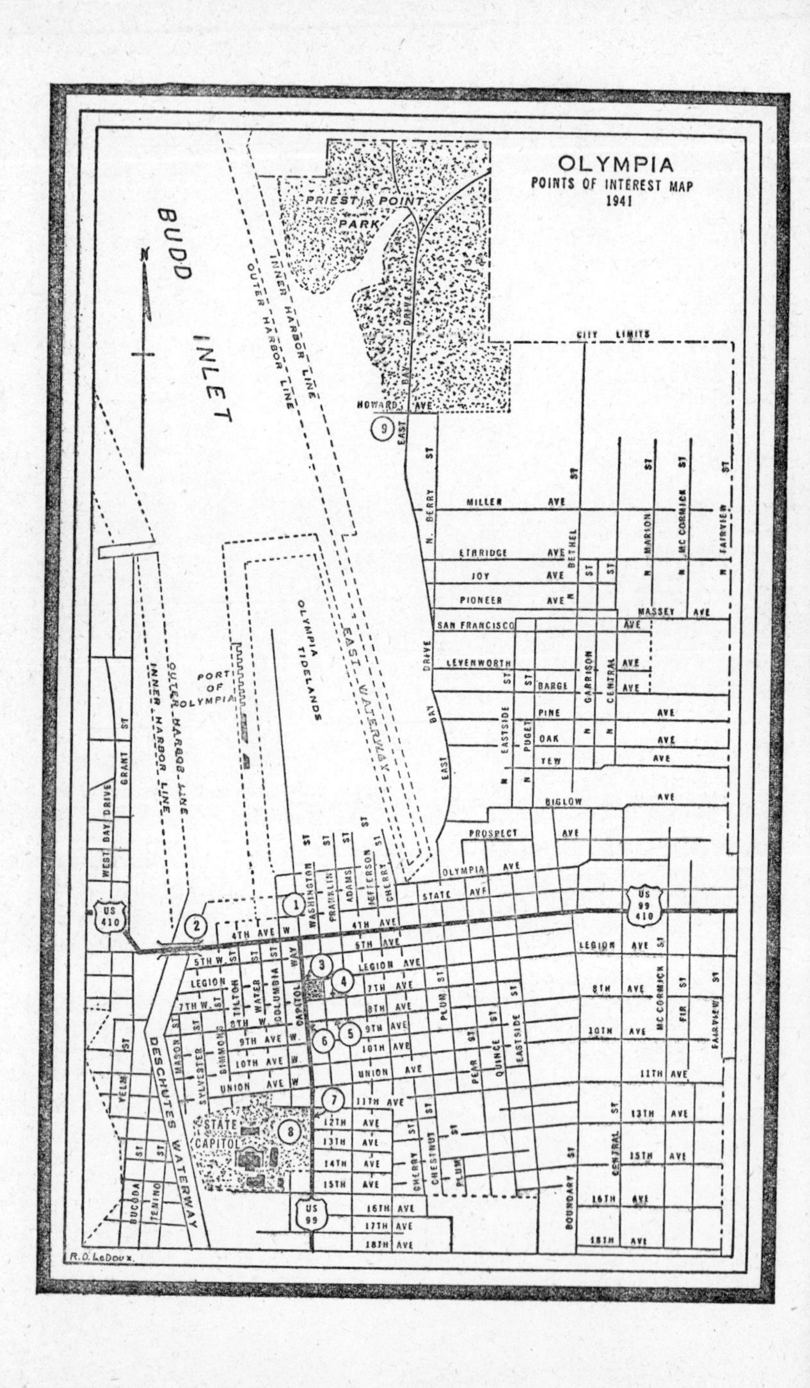

OLYMPIA
POINTS OF INTEREST MAP
1941
BUDD INLET
N
PRIEST POINT PARK
INNER HARBOR LINE
OUTER HARBOR LINE
CITY LIMITS
HOWARD AVE
EAST BAY DRIVE
N. BERRY ST
MILLER AVE
ETTRIDGE AVE
JOY AVE
PIONEER AVE
SAN FRANCISCO AVE
LEVENWORTH AVE
BARGE AVE
PINE AVE
OAK AVE
YEW AVE
BIGLOW AVE
PROSPECT AVE
OLYMPIA AVE
STATE AVE
MASSEY AVE
N. BETHEL ST
N. MARION ST
N. MC CORMICK ST
N. FAIRVIEW ST
N. EASTSIDE ST
N. PUGET ST
N. GARRISON ST
N. CENTRAL ST
OLYMPIA TIDELANDS
EAST WATERWAY
PORT OF OLYMPIA
WEST BAY DRIVE
GRANT ST
US 410
US 99 410
US 99
4TH AVE W
4TH AVE
5TH W. ST
5TH AVE
LEGION
LEGION AVE
7TH W. ST
7TH AVE
8TH W
8TH AVE
9TH AVE W.
9TH AVE
10TH AVE W
10TH AVE
UNION AVE W
UNION AVE
11TH AVE
12TH AVE
13TH AVE
14TH AVE
15TH AVE
16TH AVE
17TH AVE
18TH AVE
WASHINGTON ST
FRANKLIN ST
ADAMS ST
JEFFERSON ST
CHERRY ST
CAPITOL WAY
COLUMBIA ST
WATER ST
TILTON ST
SIMMONS ST
SYLVESTER ST
MASON ST
YELM ST
BUCODA ST
TENINO ST
DESCHUTES WATERWAY
STATE CAPITOL
PLUM ST
PEAR ST
QUINCE ST
EASTSIDE ST
CHESTNUT ST
BOUNDARY ST
CENTRAL ST
MC CORMICK ST
FIR ST
FAIRVIEW ST
1
2
3
4
5
6
7
8
9
R. D. LeDoux.

priate historical inscriptions were made, and the door itself hangs on one of the temple walls.

7. The THURSTON COUNTY COURTHOUSE, (*open 9-5 weekdays*), 1110 Capitol Way, an unpretentious four-story structure faced with gray Tenino sandstone, was finished in 1930. Joseph Wohleb, Olympia, was the architect. Simple and forthright in design, with little surface ornament, it is a good example of modern architectural design.

8. The CAPITOL GROUP, Capitol Way (US 99) between 11th and 14th Aves., is modified Roman-Doric architecture, evidenced in the severity of line and in the sparsely ornamented columns, cornices, and pediments. The massive white sandstone buildings are set in a 35-acre tract overlooking the bay. Lawns, cut by curving driveways and walks, surround the buildings.

The buildings were designed by the firm of Wilder and White of New York City, which submitted the winning design in a nation-wide architectural competition. Construction started in 1911. The first building, the Temple of Justice, was completed in 1921, and the latest, the Public Lands and Social Security Building, in 1935. The group, including the Legislative Building, Insurance Building, Highway Building, and Transportation Building, represents an expenditure of $14,-000,000.

The LEGISLATIVE BUILDING (*open 8-6 weekdays*), Capitol Way between 13th and 14th Aves., the sixth home of the legislature, is the central structure in the group. With its massive white dome, its monumental design, and its placement in relation to the other buildings, it has the general effect of "a broad base from which an adequate dome rises."

The 287-foot dome is the fourth highest in the world and one of the two domes of solid-stone construction in the United States. It is supported by four piers, each 80 feet high and 19 feet square, which in turn rest on huge monolithic concrete mats. Stone setters required 15 months to complete the masonry, the pieces of which ranged from a few pounds to 18 tons in weight. Above the capstone of the dome and accessible from within, a slender stone lantern, which rises 47 feet, affords an unexcelled viewpoint.

The two-tone bronze doors at the main entrance are ornamented with a series of bas-relief panels depicting pioneer life. The interior is marked by the use of several tints and kinds of imported marbles. Throughout the structure lavish detail has been used. The high cost,

---

OLYMPIA—POINTS OF INTEREST

1. Site of First Legislative Hall
2. Brenner Oyster Packing Plant
3. Sylvester Park
4. Old Capitol Building
5. Sylvester House
6. Masonic Temple
7. Thurston County Courthouse
8. Capitol Group
9. Scientific Oyster Laboratory

more than $7,000,000, inclusive of furnishings, was severely criticized by legislators and by their constituents as well.

The TEMPLE OF JUSTICE (*open 9-5 weekdays, 2-4 Sun.*), Capitol Way between 11th and 12th Aves., is a severe rectangular structure with formal windows and ponderous walls. It contains the chambers of the State Supreme Court and the attorney general's office. In the basement is the STATE LIBRARY (*open 9-5 Monday-Friday, 9-12 Saturday*), with rare books, pioneer relics, and varied historical material. The State's first library, brought around the Horn in 1854, consisted of scientific, legal, and medical texts and fiction, which Governor Stevens, with a $5,000 grant from Congress, had selected. The present library comprises 100,000 volumes and extensive newspaper files. The STATE LAW LIBRARY of 85,000 volumes is also in this building.

The WAR MEMORIAL MONUMENT, on the Capitol grounds at the head of the driveway, the work of Victor Alonzo Lewis, was unveiled in 1938. Funds for the monument were provided from the sale of State lands and from a Federal grant.

The GOVERNOR'S MANSION (*private*), of Georgian design, occupies a wooded knoll at the rear of the capitol group. Simple and charming, with bright red-brick walls, trimmed with marble keystones above the windows and stone at the portals, it offers a pleasing contrast to the other buildings of the group.

9. The SCIENTIFIC OYSTER LABORATORY (*open 9-5 workdays*), foot of Howard St. off East Bay Drive, is an experimental station conducted by the State Department of Fisheries for the study of shellfish culture. The staff at present (1941) seeks a method of propagating Japanese oysters in Puget Sound to obviate the necessity for importing seed. Water from various localities is sampled weekly and kept at various temperatures while development of the seed is tested. Preceding these experiments, there was several years' study of the native Olympia oyster. Salinity, acidity, and nutriments in the water are continually changed and the effects recorded.

In addition to the experiments with the oyster, several varieties of native clams are being studied. Young specimens are brought in and their shells marked with an emery wheel; then they are returned to the clam beds. Diggers who find these branded clams send them to the laboratory, and thus records of their growth can be charted; for, just as tree-rings indicate the age of a forest giant, so is the age of a clam shown by the rings on the shell. The clam may reach a ripe old age of 18 years if it is unmolested, but its chances of surviving more than 5 are negligible in regions where clam digging is carried on commercially.

POINTS OF INTEREST IN ENVIRONS

Oyster Beds, 5 *m.* (*see Tour 2d*). Priest Point Park on East Bay Drive, 1 *m.;* site of old Fort Nesqually, 14.6 *m.;* Nisqually Indian Reservation, 16 *m.* (*see Tour 8c*). Tumwater, 1 *m.;* Millersylvania State Park, on Deep Lake Road, 10 *m.* (*see Tour 8d*).

Seattle

Railroad Stations: King Street Station, 3rd Ave. S. and Jackson St. for Great Northern Ry. and Northern Pacific Ry.; Union Station, 4th Ave. S. and Jackson St. for Union Pacific R.R.; Southern Pacific R.R., and Chicago, Milwaukee, St. Paul & Pacific R.R.

Bus Stations: Central Terminal, 8th Ave. and Stewart St. for North Coast Lines (Greyhound), Washington Motor Coach System, Union Pacific Stages, California Bus Lines, Renton-Bothell-Seattle Stage Lines Inc., and Suburban Transportation System; 3rd Ave. and Virginia St. Stage Terminal, for Diamond Stage Company, North Bend Stage Lines Inc., and Puyallup-Sumner Stages; 113 1st Ave. S. for Independent Stages Inc.

Piers: (Alaska service): Alaska Steamship Co., foot of Cherry St.; Northland Transportation Co., foot of University St.; Alaska Transportation Co., foot of Union St. (Trans-Pacific Service): Smith Cove, Nippon Yusen Kaisya. (British Columbia service); Canadian Pacific R.R. dock, foot of Lenora St. Ferries to Puget Sound points, Colman Dock, foot of Marion St.; Lake Washington ferries, foot of E. Madison St. (Coastwise service): McCormick Steamship Co., foot of Main St.; Luckenback Steamship Co., foot of Jackson St.

Airport: Boeing Field (county), Airport Way at S. city limits for United Air Lines, Northwest Airlines, Pan-American Airways to Alaska, and Canadian Airways, Ltd., charter service; taxi fare $1.55, 15 min.

Taxis: 25c first quarter-mile; 10c each half-mile thereafter; extra passengers 10c.

Rapid Transit: Trackless trolleys and motor busses. Fare 10c or three tokens for 25c.

Traffic Regulations: Speed limit 25 m.p.h. except on designated arterials where 35 m.p.h. is allowed. Turns in either direction permitted at intersections except where signs prohibit; "stop" signs denote arterials. Watch street signs for parking limitations.

Street Order and Numbering: Avenues run N. and S., streets E. and W.; even numbers on right side of thoroughfares going N. and E.; 100 numbers to the block; symbols such as NW., SE., etc., denote directions of outlying addresses.

Accommodations: 83 hotels; auto and cabin camps and trailer facilities on adjacent highways; inns and hotels at near-by resorts charge higher prices during spring and summer; large conventions increase local rates.

Information Service: Chamber of Commerce, 215 Columbia St.; Washington Automobile Club (AAA), 1109 Pine St.; Rainier Nat'l. Park Bureau, 416 University St.

Theaters and Motion Picture Houses: Repertory Playhouse, 4045 University Way; Moore Theater, 1928 2nd Ave.; Metropolitan Theater, 415 University St.; Cornish Theater, 710 E. Roy St.; Music Hall, 7th Ave. and Olive Way; Showboat, foot of 15th Ave. NE. Occasional concerts, Meany Hall, University Campus, and Civic Auditorium, 3rd Ave. and Mercer St.; 46 motion picture houses.

Radio Stations: KEVR (1400 kc.); KIRO (710 kc.); KJR (1000 kc.); KOL (1300 kc.); KOMO (950 kc.); KRSC (1150 kc.); KXA (770 kc.).

Athletic Fields: 43 parks, 46 playfields.

Golf: Jefferson Park (municipal), 4100 Beacon Ave., 27 holes, 25c for 9; West Seattle Golf Links (municipal), 35th Ave., SW. and W. Genesee St., 18 holes, 25c for 9; Jackson Park (municipal), E. 137th and 10th NE., 18 holes, 25c

for 9; Queen Anne, 6th Ave. N. and Galer St., 9 holes, 25c; University (semi-public), on campus, 9 holes, 40c, 75c, and $1; and 10 others in environs.
Tennis: Municipal courts at all playfields and the following parks: Volunteer, Woodland, Leschi, Mt. Baker, Lincoln, Madrona, Cowen; free.
Swimming: 10 municipal beaches, three saltwater and seven freshwater; Moore Hotel, 1928 2nd Ave., 27c; Crystal Pool, 2035 2nd Ave., adults 37c, children 27c; YMCA, 4th Ave. and Madison St., adults 25c, children 10c; Alki Natatorium, 2617 Alki Ave., adults 37c, children 27c; YWCA, 5th Ave. and Seneca St., adults 25c, children 20c.
Yachting: Queen City Yacht Club, 2715 Fairview Ave. N.; Seattle Yacht Club, 1807 E. Hamlin St.
Riding: Boulevard Riding and Boarding Stables, E. 92nd and Victory Way; Gaylands Riding Academy, 7028 24th Ave. NE.; Overland Riding Academy, 13751-17th Ave. NE.; Don Emerick Clearbrook Riding Academy, E. 140th and 17th NE.—average rate first hour $1, varies thereafter. Mountain View Riding and Boarding Stables, S. 126th and 4th Ave. SW., 50c per hour weekdays, 75c Sun.
Hunting and Fishing: Hunting in near-by hills, marshes, and on Olympic Peninsula; fishing in Puget Sound and adjacent lakes and streams; boats, guides, and complete equipment for hire in many parts of the city; information and licenses at fishing tackle stores.
Baseball: Civic Stadium and playfields, 3rd Ave. and Harrison St., amateur only; Sick's Seattle Stadium, Rainier Ave. and Bayview St., Seattle Rainiers, Pacific Coast League.

Annual Events: Seattle-Tacoma Yacht Cruise, Jan. 1; Annual Mining Institute, University Campus, 3rd week in Jan.; Salmon Fishing Derby Opening, Washington State High School Basketball Championship tournament, Northwest A.A.U. Basketball Championship, Mar.; Washington-California Crew Regatta, Apr. (alternate years); All-City Flower Show, Woodland Park, 1st week in May; Boating Season Opens, Lake Washington, 1st Sat. in May; Summer Drama Festival Opens Repertory Playhouse, June 15; Rose Show, Woodland Park, June; Fleet Week, Potlatch, July or Aug.; Air Show, Bon Odori, Japanese Harvest Festival, Aug.; Salmon Derby Finals, 1st Sun. in Sept.; Labor Day Parade, Labor Day; Dahlia Show, Woodland Park, Sept.; Intercollegiate football season opens, University of Washington, 1st week in Oct.; Northwest Artists' Annual Exhibition, Seattle Art Museum, Oct.; Armistice Day Parade, Nov. 11; Founder's Day, Nov. 13.

SEATTLE (12 to 514 alt., 368,302 pop.), largest city of the Pacific Northwest, lies along Elliott Bay, on the east shore of Puget Sound, 128 miles from the Pacific Ocean. Built on seven hills, with intervening lowlands, it extends between Puget Sound and Lake Washington, which are joined by two canals and Lake Union. It is a city of steep descents and sudden turns, with streets that fall away inevitably to the waterside, lined with docks and moored ships of every description. Many bridges, ranging from the imposing concrete George Washington Memorial Bridge to small spans straddling the ravines, pass between the different parts of this city broken by water routes.

Today, Seattle is one of the most important import-export cities of the United States. Its rapid growth is due in a large measure to its commercially strategic location and to its terminal improvements. Four large railroad systems connect Seattle with the East and with the Southwest; and its position in relation to the short "great circle" route to the Orient gives it a substantial advantage in shipping over other west coast cities. Also, Alaskan shipping centers in Puget Sound ports because of the greater degree of safety provided by the protected Inland Passage, favored water route to Alaska from Seattle.

Local industry has depended largely upon lumber and fish, with the processing of agricultural products next in importance. Already substantially developed, manufacturing will probably expand and become more diversified as full use is made of the extensive electrical power projects now under construction in the State.

Approaching Seattle from the east, the route passes through the semi-wilderness of the Cascade Mountains, with their bare peaks, virgin forests, and logged-off lands; then through the foothills region, characterized by stump ranches and small dairy and poultry farms; and finally, as the land levels out into rolling cut-over lands, runs through a region of small tracts, orchards, roadhouses, camping grounds, and suburban homes—until it enters the city limits, some seven miles from the central metropolitan area.

If the approach is by water, the city is hidden from view by the projecting headlands or is only partly visible until the boat enters Elliott Bay. Once within Alki and West Points, the striking panorama of the whole city emerges, its many hills rolling upwards from the crescent-shaped shoreline of the bay. From Smith Cove at the left, north of the metropolitan area, to Alki Point at the right, runs a saw-toothed rim of piers, docks, and wharves, broken only on the south by tide flats and the Duwamish River, which forks around the man-made Harbor Island. Beyond the water front and Alaskan Way, a broad commercial avenue, are the warehouses and the factories, and behind them the ragged skyline of the business area, marked by some eight or ten modern skyscrapers, which tower above the smaller business blocks. Past these are hills covered with residences and apartment houses, with here and there a wooded area where the precipitousness of the slope has so far prevented building.

The city is impressively beautiful on a clear day, when the Olympics, with their serrated, snow-covered ridges can be seen to the west, and the Cascades, blue-green in the distance, are visible in the east and southeast, with the snowy cone of Mount Rainier looming above the other peaks of the range. At night, too, the city is beautiful, with its myriads of lights reflected in the waters; and even in the sombreness of rainy weather, when the slate-grey waters of the bay are broken by whitecaps and low clouds scud across the sky, the city does not lose its charm.

The water front preserves the past of Seattle. In its cafés, quaint murals, the work of sign painters of an earlier day, still adorn the walls. Mirrors behind bars are encased in heavily carved wooden frames, and the shop signs of employment agencies and outfitters recall the heroic epoch of lumbering and the gold rush. The harbor was the embryo of Seattle, and to this day the city derives its character from the wharves and its people.

Broad Alaskan Way is a long sweep of activity, which subsides but does not entirely cease during the early rush of the morning. Locomotives noisily shunt their cars, and trucks rumble along the wide dock-lined street. Stevedores expertly load and unload slings swung by booms and squeaking winches. Tug boats whistle petulantly, and ferries push their way in and out of the slips. Occasionally, an airplane drones overhead and swoops down to a landing on the waters of the bay. From unostentatious docks and from piers longer than any in the country, vessels depart for Alaska and the Orient. And the seagulls drift out over the entire city, coming to rest everywhere, even on cornices and the spires of churches.

Seattle seems to alter its nature with each change of perspective. Physically, its vistas seem constantly shifting, as its streets move swiftly from one plane to another. Here, one sees automobiles parked on roofs of houses built on the avenue below. Board sidewalks climb the older sections of the town, where fragile frame dwellings cling to the steeps above Lake Union and gaze down upon the towers of tall apartment hotels. And socially, too, Seattle is many-angled. For some it is a city of fashionable shops, theaters, motion picture shows, art gallaries, and modern hotels and restaurants. To others it is a market and manufacturing center—and the educational and cultural capital of the State of Washington. For the mass of its employed population, it is a place where living standards are comparatively high, the environment pleasing, and the climate agreeably mild. For the itinerant and seasonal worker of logging camps, mills, canneries, and steamships, it is a city where he can hope to stretch his savings over the winter months until he lands a job when work picks up in the spring.

Seattle is a town of many races and nationalities. The early settlers were largely of native stock, but as the city grew, Scandinavians and Finns were attracted by lumbering and fishing; Irish, Italians, and peoples from the Balkan Peninsula found employment in construction and railroads, and Germans, French, and English in the various service trades, the food industry, and the professions. Among the early arrivals were also Chinese, Japanese, Filipinos, Hawaiians, and Negroes.

Among cities of the Nation with a population of 300,000 or more, Seattle ranks third in the percentage of home ownership. As in other large communities, residence districts are distinctly differentiated here according to income groups. With the growth of the community the better homes have steadily shifted towards the outskirts of the city, particularly to the highlands along Puget Sound and to the shores of Lake Washington. Yet those areas formerly favored by the well-to-do—First and Capitol Hills to the east of the metropolitan area, and Queen Anne Hill, the highest in the city, which looms north of Smith Cove—have not been entirely abandoned; and within a few minutes drive from the civic center many fine houses with lovely gardens and spacious lawns are still to be seen.

Scattered throughout the city are many pleasant districts inhabited by families of middle income. Free from congestion, five- to seven-room dwellings cover an unusual proportion of the city's space, and, owing to the moist and mild climate their tenants have been able to surround themselves with flowers, shrubs, trees, and grassy lawns. Cheap electricity has helped to make these homes comfortable and up-to-date. Moderately priced apartment houses and hotels loom here and there among the low roofs of the cottages.

Seattle also has its poorer districts and its slums and near-slums. In the industrial area of South Seattle, along the flats and the railroad tracks, in the sawmill district along the shore of the Lake Washington Ship Canal, and in the streets bordering on the metropolitan district are the habitations of the poor and underprivileged of Seattle. Many of these are slums, different in detail but not in character from those of the eastern cities and of Europe, crowded with unsanitary firetraps, some hastily constructed in the days immediately following the fire of 1889, others during the World War boom days. The rookeries and shacks immediately south of the business district house most of the city's Orientals; in the same area, rooming houses and cheap hotels provide lodging for large numbers of itinerant and seasonal laborers.

Thousands of houseboats lie along the shores of Seattle's lakes, canals, and bays. Some, principally in the Lake Washington area, are commodious floating villas, with hardwood floors, electric lights, frigidaires, and oil burners. Others are fairly comfortable dwellings. The great majority of the water abodes are, however, substandard shacks, without equipment for sanitation, shakily constructed on the flats or on old pilings, where some float with the rising tide, then sink back to the muddy shallows. Today, low-cost housing units are being built to replace some of Seattle's slums, especially those of the Yesler Hill district, which has already been cleared for new construction.

Only 90 years have passed since the time when the first small band of settlers dug clams along the beach and built their cabins on Alki Point. These pioneers came to Seattle from Illinois in a covered wagon train led by Arthur A. Denny. While the main group rested in Portland, David Denny and John N. Low proceeded northward by land to Olympia, where they embarked on Puget Sound with Leander Terry and Captain Robert C. Fay on the latter's boat. On September 28, 1851, they sailed into Elliott Bay. Upon landing, they learned from Indians that a settler had taken a donation land claim a year before, near the mouth of the Duwamish River. Captain Fay and Low soon left, but Terry and Denny set to work building a cabin on the south headland of the bay. Soon Denny wrote to his brother: "Come as soon as you can. We have found a valley that will support a thousand families."

Within two months, on November 13, the other members of the party, 5 families, consisting of 12 adults and an equal number of children, arrived from Portland on the schooner *Exact*. The group named the point on which they settled New York, probably in the hope that some day the settlement would become the metropolis of the West. Later, with a touch of humor, they added the word *Alki,* Chinook jargon for "by and by," and it is this latter name which today clings to the point where the pioneers first settled.

Scarcely were the cabins finished and the families established in their new homes when the little settlement made its initial venture into what was destined to become its major industry—lumbering. Early in 1852 the brig *Leonesa,* seeking a cargo of piling for the San Francisco market, anchored offshore. The load she picked up, 35,000 board feet of logs cut by the settlers from their claims, was the first shipment to leave Elliott Bay.

The difficulty of getting this shipment aboard in open water convinced the settlers that better facilities for water transport were needed, and that the shallow, sandy beach where they had established themselves was not suitable for the loading and unloading of ships. Accordingly, they set out to find some place where the shore sloped more steeply; and after sounding the water at various places (with Mary Denny's clothesline weighted with horseshoes), the Bells, the Borens, and the Dennys in February 1852, staked claims to the present site of the city, and named the new settlement Seattle after the friendly chief of the Duwamish Indians.

Other settlers soon arrived. One of these, Dr. David S. Maynard, opened the first general store, and also made a trial shipment of salmon to San Francisco. This first venture in the fish business was a dismal failure, the salmon spoiling en route, and the commercial exploitation of this great natural resource had to await the development of better methods of preserving and speedier transportation to market. In 1852 Dr. Henry A. Smith took land near the north end of the bay on a cove which now bears his name, and where large piers for the Port of Seattle are located. In December of the same year, Thomas Mercer arrived from Illinois with the settlement's first horse, Old Tib, and a wagon; with these he provided the first express and milk delivery service.

In the following year, on May 23, a plat of the "Town of Seattle" was filed with the Territorial government of Olympia by Boren, Denny, and Maynard. The lumbering industry in the community also took its next forward step, when Henry Yesler, from Portland, was given a tract of land along the south side of the new town, and, with the assistance of volunteer labor, built there the first steam sawmill on Puget Sound. Social life as well as work centered around the cookhouse of the mill, which was used as an all-purpose meeting house, a jail, or a church, as the occasion demanded. Another store was started by Denny, and his clerk, Dexter Horton, began to accept money for safekeeping from trappers, loggers, and sailors; his banking consisted of placing the cash in individual sacks, each tagged with the owner's name, and burying them in his "safety deposit," a coffee barrel. In 1853 the *Louisiana* took a cargo of ship spars for China, the first shipment from Puget Sound destined for a foreign port. When in October 1853, the Reverend David E. Blaine organized the first church, the town comprised 8 houses, grouped around the mill, and the total population of the county was 170. The first school was opened in 1854, the minister's wife, Catherine E. Blaine, being employed as teacher; the school term was three months, and the salary was $65 a month.

The settlers had from the first received friendly treatment from Chief Seattle, and when Isaac I. Stevens, first Territorial Governor, called the local bands together to a powwow at "The Point" (now Pioneer Square) and laid reservation plans before them, Chief Seattle, of the Duwamish and allied bands, proved agreeable to the proposals. Other bands, however, resented the imposition of reservations upon territory they regarded as their own, and in which they had always wandered at will. Rumors soon followed of Indian trouble among the Puyallup bands to the south, and outlying settlers were frightened into Seattle, where in 1855 two blockhouses were erected and preparations made for defense. In December, a few settlers on White River, and Lieutenant W. A. Slaughter were killed by the Indians. Then, on January 26, 1856, word came that Klickitats were on the warpath and had crossed the mountains to the shores of Lake Washington. At this news, the settlers flocked to the blockhouse at the foot of Cherry Street, where, with the aid of the guns of the United States sloop-of-war *Decatur,* they repulsed the attackers with the loss of but two men. This was the first and last Indian trouble in the immediate neighborhood of Seattle.

The discovery of gold on the Fraser River in Canada, in 1858, started a stampede during which 20,000 men hurried northward through Seattle. The rush resulted in a slight gain in permanent population, and in the building of a blacksmith shop, a foundry, a saloon, a hardware store, and a dance hall.

At the beginning of the sixties, Seattle was little more than a mill, a few stores, and some scattered houses. Its citizens were nevertheless determined that the town should be designated as the site of the University then proposed for the Territory. In addition to its educational benefits, the University would stimulate real estate development, and increase the political prestige of the town. Through persistent lobbying in the Territorial legislature, Seattle succeeded in having itself chosen as the University city, and on a tract donated to the Territorial government and cleared by the townsfolk a modest wooden structure was built. In accordance with the classical tradition observed in schoolhouse architecture, the entrance had four Ionic columns. Around the building ran a white fence, designed, according to a contemporary wag, "to keep the stumps from getting out of the yard." Asa Mercer, the new University's only instructor, canvassed the Puget Sound country in quest of students, offering young men $1.50 a cord for split wood, as a credit against tuition charges. The response was gratifying in point of numbers, but the pioneer University's study courses had to be adjusted to meet various educational levels, since only one student was discovered who qualified above high school grade.

The first number of the Seattle *Gazette* (now the *Post-Intelligencer*), a four-page weekly, was issued by J. R. Watson in 1863 from a room in the Gem Saloon. In the same year Dr. Maynard opened the first local hospital. In the following year transcontinental telegraph connections were completed, and coal mines were opened at Coal Creek (later Newcastle), this development offsetting to some extent a slump in the lumber business. John W. Pennell started a squaw dance hall, the Illahee, in the outskirts of the town, where it flourished for a number of years, despite the condemnation showered upon it by the moralists of the community.

As is usual in a frontier community, there was a scarcity of unmarried women. Of the 182 persons in the village at the beginning of the decade, 96 were bachelors. In 1864 Asa Mercer decided to intervene in this unhappy situation and went east to induce unmarried women to seek husbands in the frontier settlement. He succeeded in persuading 11 women of good family to return with him. Upon the arrival of the "Mercer Girls" on May 16, the single men of the town turned out "looking like grizzlies in store clothes and their hair slicked down like sea otters." A second venture, 2 years later, brought 46 additional women, 10 of them widows. Mercer himself married one of the group.

A court order having dissolved the first incorporation of the city, Seattle was re-incorporated in 1869. In 1870 a census showed a population of 1,107 persons. That year the town elected its first Mayor, Henry A. Atkins; and Dexter Horton's coffee-barrel evolved into the town's first formal bank, occupying its first brick building, erected on the site where the Dexter Horton Building stands today. In 1870, also, the Central School was opened on Third and Marion, with two teachers and more than 100 pupils. This school soon became so crowded that the younger pupils had to be sent home to await the building of a second room. The new schools were constructed in time to accommodate the enrollment of 480 in the next year.

The Northern Pacific Railway, then under construction, was well on its way across the continent; and townfolk were hopeful that its terminus might be established at Seattle. With this expectation business doubled, population increased rapidly, valuable land, water-front trackage, $50,000 cash, and $200,000 in bonds were pledged in support of the venture. After months of negotiations and tense anticipation Seattle learned, however, that Tacoma had been selected as the terminal.

Undaunted, the citizens of the town organized the Seattle & Walla Walla Railroad and Construction Company in 1873 and projected a line over Snoqualmie Pass. In 4 years the road had been extended to Newcastle, 12 miles away. Coal shipments quickly made the short line profitable. The inauguration, in 1875, of regular steamship service between Seattle and San Francisco also compensated to some extent for the inadequacy of rail transport.

The seventies brought improved living conditions and more social diversions. Gas street lights were installed in 1874. The streets were still unpaved, except for occasional short sections of cobblestones; board walks, however, had been laid along most of the main streets. A contemporary article on Seattle states: "It is a model pioneer city in its architecture—substantial comfort, rather than ostentatious display, being the object sought." School attendance, including that of the University, was increasing, the total enrollment at the end of the decade being nearly 800. In 1877 an opera company from San Francisco received such enthusiastic welcome that two opera houses were constructed: the Watson C. Squire, in 1879, and the Frye, in 1880. The performance of Emma Abbott at the opening of the Frye was a highlight in the cultural life of the town.

At the time of the census of 1880, population had risen to 3,533. This decade saw considerable industrial development. A shingle mill was built with a daily output of 200 bundles, and the machine shop of Robert Moran, several forges, and a brewery were established. In 1882 a group of businessmen organized themselves into a body similar to a Chamber of Commerce. Suffragist groups worked vigorously and won a temporary victory in 1883. In the same year Seattle was finally linked with the Puyallup Valley by the Columbia and Puget Sound Railroad, and the event was celebrated with barbecues and salmon bakes. Speech makers toasted "Seattle—the largest town for its age in the world." Frank Osgood, a newcomer, imported four horsecars from Boston and laid tracks for the first city railway in the Territory. Frequently, one horse failed to make the pull on steep hills, and passengers had to get out and push; later, an extra "helper" horse was added on steep grades.

Courts had been established, but lynchings were still carried out, occasionally, by men who had been too long without the discipline of legal institutions. Violence also broke out in the neighborhood of Seattle against Chinese laborers who had been imported to work on the railroads and in mining camps, and who were left stranded when the lines were completed. These people worked for low wages, and during hard times other workingmen in the area saw in them a threat to their own scales of pay. Two years of agitation came to a head when mobs made an effort to deport the Chinese forcibly. Martial law was declared, and the Seattle Rifles, a forerunner of the National Guard, controlled the town for ten days. Eventually the antagonism subsided, as the Chinese were absorbed into industry and the service trades or moved on to other towns.

Cultural and social activities continued to expand. In 1888 the Ladies' Library Association was instrumental in establishing a permanent public library. In the same year the Rainier Club was formed, the first club organized in the town for the sole purpose of recreation and social activity for men. The steady growth in population led to the establishment of new newspapers and to the expansion through mergers of some of the older ones. The *Times* and the *Press* absorbed several of the smaller papers and strengthened their influence. Eventually, the *Press* itself merged with the *Times,* which already at that date was the spokesman for conservative and industrial interests. The *Gazette* continued to be the leading morning newspaper. Labor, too, set up its first press in the city in 1889, the local section of the Knights of Labor sponsoring the publication of a weekly newspaper, *The Workingman.*

Towards the end of the 1880's, horse-drawn streetcars no longer satisfied the needs of the community, and in 1888 cable cars were introduced. During that year electric lighting was begun on a commercial scale, and streetcars, too, were electrified.

The decade closed with the great fire of 1889. About 2:30 p.m., on June 6, a fire broke out in a cabinet shop at First Avenue and Madison Street. The blaze spread rapidly, and before midnight the entire business section of 50 blocks was consumed, despite the fact that aid was rushed not only from near-by Tacoma but from Olympia, and from Portland, Oregon, and Victoria, British Columbia, as well. The loss was estimated at $15,000,000. Approximately $100,000 was donated by other cities for relief work in the devastated community. Almost at once, the rebuilding of the city in brick and iron was begun, and during the next year more than $10,000,000 was spent in reconstruction. The new city that rose upon the ashes included 465 commercial buildings, 60 wharves and warehouses, an improved sewage system, and paved streets. Wooden structures were barred in the business zones. In 1890 the population of Seattle had risen to 42,800.

The nineteenth century ended in a vast boom which overrode a number of temporary setbacks. Along the water front extensive shipyards were built, while from the lumber camps in the forests money came rolling into Seattle for food and supplies, and a wide traffic in raw materials, timber, fish, and minerals, left the city for distant markets. Robert Moran, who had made his start with a small machine shop and had risen to the position of mayor of the city, now took into his hands the control of one of the largest shipyards in the port. The Great Northern Railway entered Seattle from Everett in 1893, providing a new link with the East. The city made its initial venture into municipal ownership of public utilities by purchasing the Spring Hill water supply system. The metropolitan commercial area expanded northwards, and businessmen clamored for the removal of the University from its downtown location; a site was selected on the shores of Lake Washington, and the cornerstone of the first of the new buildings, Denny Hall, was laid in 1894.

The depression that struck the industrial East in 1893 caused a slump in the lumber and shipping industries of the Puget Sound region. Many of those thrown out of work joined Coxey's march on Washington in 1894, but were stopped at Wenatchee by local law enforcement agencies. In 1896, the State was carried by Bryan and free silver; a Populist, John Rogers, was elected Governor. This same year saw the establishing of the Great Northern steamship line, which was operated until suspended because of monopoly charged by the Federal Government.

Just before the turn of the century, an unexpected stroke of luck quickened vigorously the growth of the city. In 1897 the steamship *Portland* hove into port with some $800,000 worth of gold from the Yukon River district in Alaska. The news of "a ton of gold" brought a feverish stampede of gold seekers, and Seattle was advertised throughout the Nation as the outfitting center and point of departure for the North Country. Seventy-four ships were launched between January and July. Old industries expanded and new ones sprang up to meet the demand for machinery, tools, camp equipment, clothing, and foodstuffs. By 1905 Seattle interests had control of 95 per cent of the total amount of Alaskan shipping. Saloons, dance halls, and gambling joints gathered in the coins of the departing and the gold dust of those who struck it rich.

The census of 1900 gave the city a population of 80,671, nearly double the figure of 1890. In the same year the first horseless carriage, an electric runabout, with a top speed of 20 miles an hour, appeared on the streets. Seattle, confident of its future, now took steps to extend its business district, cramped by the surrounding hills. The method of sluicing employed in Alaskan mining to remove hills caught the imagination of engineers and real estate promoters, and workmen began to wash away the Jackson Street and Dearborn Street hills and part of Denny Hill. The loosened earth was used to fill in 1,400 acres of tideflats, making it available for factory sites. The venture was so successful that within the next 30 years 41,500,000 cubic yards of dirt were shifted.

City traffic had become a problem with the increase of population and industry. Streets were widened and improved, and Stone and Webster, visualizing the future of the bustling city, consolidated the various street railways. Eager to establish Seattle as a shipbuilding center, businessmen and industrialists subscribed $100,000 to enable the Moran shipyards to submit the lowest bid for the construction of the U.S.S. *Nebraska*.

The desire for municipal ownership of utilities grew in popularity, with the result that in 1901 the city added the Cedar River watershed to its water system, and in the ensuing year installed a small generating plant which laid the basis for the City Light Department. With this modest beginning, Seattle embarked on a municipal water and electric program which grew to proud proportions during the succeeding decades.

The cultural life of Seattle also reached a new level during the early years of the twentieth century. With the aid of Carnegie funds, a large library was constructed of greystone (completed in 1905) to replace the small building burned in 1901. The first local symphony orchestra, later re-established under the direction of Henry Hadley, gave a concert in 1903 under the leadership of Harry West; and a string quartet of exceptional merit was organized by John Spargur. University enrollment grew rapidly, and new schools, notable among them the Cornish school of fine arts, were started. More than 100 churches and religious societies of many different denominations, including some Buddhist groups, made their appearance. The Children's Orthopedic Hospital began to operate in January 1907.

The Alaska-Yukon-Pacific Exposition in 1909 drew 3,750,000 persons to Seattle, and many of them stayed at least long enough to be counted in the census of 1910, which set the city's population at

237,194. The city limits had been extended into the outlying districts and had come to include (in 1907) West Seattle, Ballard, and Columbia City and (in 1910) Georgetown—thus practically completing the present boundaries of the city.

Another transcontinental railroad, the Chicago, Milwaukee & St. Paul, arrived in 1909, and in 1910 a branch line of the Union Pacific came in from Portland, both lines operating out of the newly-constructed Union Station. The Duwamish River channel was dredged to accommodate ocean-going vessels, and water transport was further aided by the organization of the Port District by the county in 1911, and by the increase of terminals, wharves, and docks, and the digging of the Sound-to-Lake-Washington canal, 1911-16, which allowed boats to enter fresh water and be cleared of barnacles without lying at drydock.

Seattle, with a population in excess of 200,000, was now a ranking city of the Pacific Coast. As in other modern cities, civic corruption and bitter political strife flowed through the seams of the growing structure. Labor was eager and restive, and numerous clashes occurred between employers and wage earners. The hall of the I.W.W. was raided in 1913 but the organization remained active, and labor unions increased in number and membership. The workingmen of Seattle helped to build sentiment resulting in the enactment of an 8-hour day law, but this was declared unconstitutional by the State Supreme Court.

The World War carried Seattle's industrial boom to its peak. Twenty shipyards employed more than 40,000 men; commerce increased, as shipping was diverted from eastern ports because of the hazards of submarine attack; Government orders stimulated airplane construction; lumber prices soared, and sawmills ran at top capacity; wages rose and unemployment all but disappeared. The sudden influx of workers into Seattle swamped its hotels and lodging houses, and led to the construction of thousands of makeshift buildings.

In 1918, the city acquired control of the upper waters of the Skagit River and took steps to develop the hydroelectric potentialities of the Skagit. Another venture into municipal ownership was made at about the same time, when, apparently under the prodding of the War Industries Board, the city purchased the privately-owned street railway system at a war time price of $15,000,000.

The end of the war was followed by a collapse in the lumber market, a drop in agricultural prices, the falling off or diversion of trade, and the closing down of the war industries. Unemployment and wage cuts led to labor unrest, which culminated in a five-day general strike, the first in the United States. More than 60,000 union members were involved in the walkout, which started on February 6, 1919. The authority of the strike committee and the self-discipline of the strikers prevented disorder, and there was little disruption of essential services. Negotiations led to the return of the workers to their jobs.

The financial collapse of 1929 struck Seattle a hard blow, as it did all other cities of the country. The decline of the lumber industry cut off the trade coming from the small environing towns. Unemployment became a persistent burden, of which the city was forced to carry a large share. Several major strikes occurred, including water-front strikes in 1934 and 1936, the timberworkers' strike of 1935, and the Newspaper Guild strike of 1936. The labor movement gained in membership, and both the American Federation of Labor and the Congress of Industrial Organizations set up central labor councils. The unemployed formed leagues, and the old people turned to group action to obtain Government pensions. As usual, the impact of social and economic issues upon local politics led to spirited contests, frequently misunderstood by outsiders.

Though production and commerce still lag behind their capacities, Seattle shows considerable recovery and progress, despite the depression. In 1936 water-borne commerce attained a tonnage of 6,307,265 tons, valued at $909,562,467. The city has one of the finest municipal power systems in the United States. Whatever the future may have in store for it, Seattle gives ample evidence that it will meet its destiny vigorously and with the assurance of triumph, *alki,* by and by.

POINTS OF INTEREST

1. The SITE OF THE TERRITORIAL UNIVERSITY, Seneca St. between 4th and 5th Aves., is marked by a plaque at the Seneca St. entrance to the Olympic Hotel. The METROPOLITAN CENTER, which replaced the University building and campus, comprises four city blocks (nine acres), including all buildings on both sides of 4th and 5th Aves., between Seneca and Union; it is said to be the first planned business district in the United States. The center was started in 1907, with the formation of the Metropolitan Building Company. Theaters, motion picture houses, the huge Olympic Hotel, office buildings, and the higher priced shops and salons are located in this area. Under an existing contract, the center with all improvements will revert to the University of Washington in 1954.

2. The CHILDREN'S FREE CREATIVE ART SCHOOL (*open 9-12 Sat., Sept. to June*), located on the third floor (3308) of the White Building, corner of 4th Ave. and University St., is one of the few free schools of art for children in the West. It was organized in 1928 by a group of women interested in the artistic education of children, under the auspices of the Music and Art Foundation, which also sponsors activities in music, literature, and drama. No formal instruction is given, and the children are encouraged to express themselves freely. Exhibitions of pupils' work reflect the wide variety in the artistic insights of children. Scholarships to more advanced institutions are awarded to those who show exceptional talent.

3. The NORTHERN LIFE TOWER BUILDING (*open 8:30-6 weekdays, 9-11 Sun., 25c*), University St. and 3rd Ave., was completed in 1929 and is built in setback style. Marble used in the construction of the building came from many sections of the world: France, Spain, Italy, Alaska, as well as Vermont, California, New York, and Tennessee; Texas supplied polished pink granite. The cavernous foyer

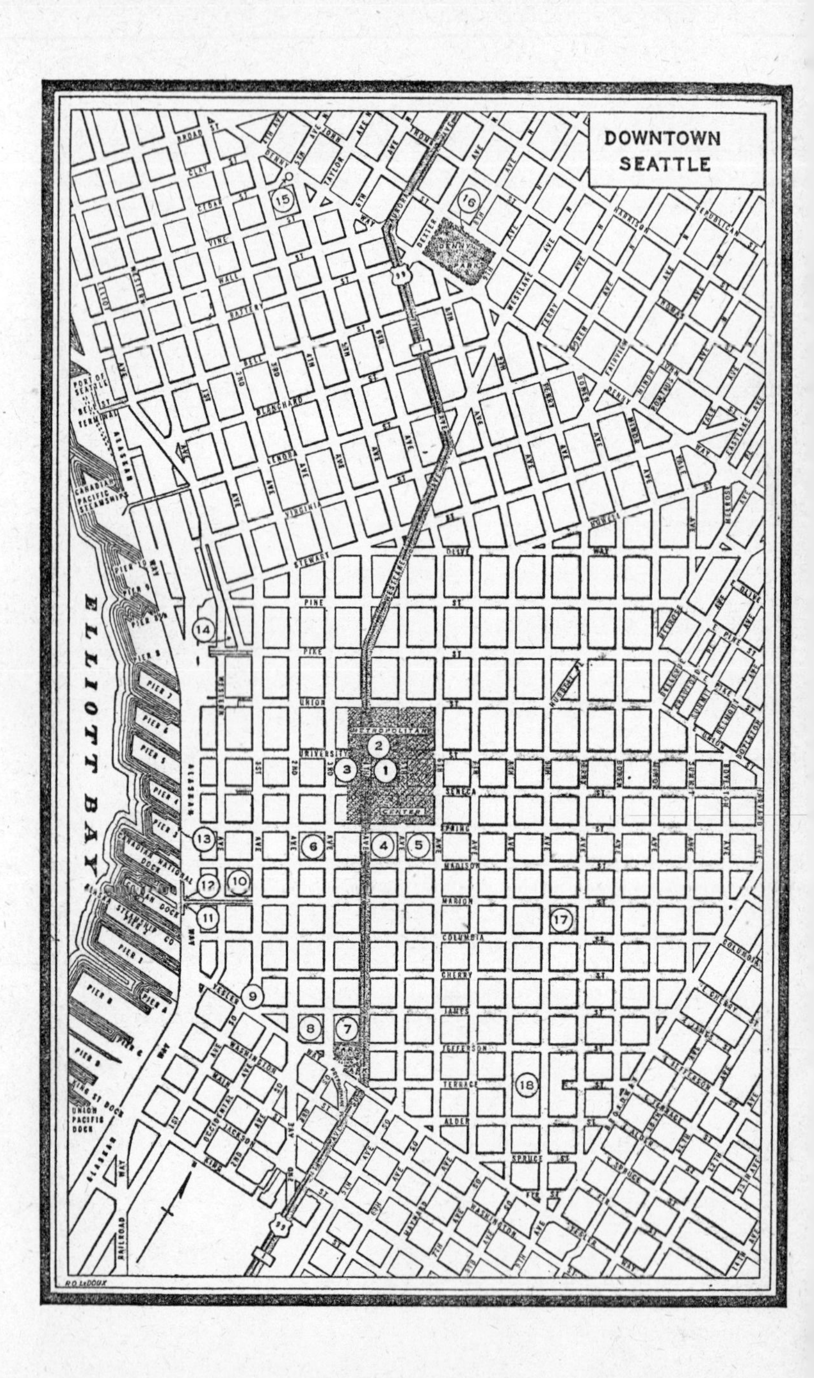

DOWNTOWN
SEATTLE
ELLIOTT BAY
DENNY PARK
METROPOLITAN
CENTER
CANADIAN PACIFIC STEAMSHIPS
PORT OF SEATTLE
PIER 9
PIER 8
PIER 7
PIER 6
PIER 5
PIER 4
PIER 3
CANADIAN NATIONAL DOCK
ALASKA STEAMSHIP CO
PIER 2
PIER 1
PIER A
PIER B
PIER C
PIER D
KING ST DOCK
UNION PACIFIC DOCK
ALASKAN WAY
WESTERN
1ST
2ND
3RD
4TH
5TH
6TH
7TH
8TH
9TH
STEWART
VIRGINIA
LENORA
BLANCHARD
BELL
BATTERY
WALL
VINE
CEDAR
CLAY
BROAD ST
DENNY
PINE
PIKE
UNION
UNIVERSITY
SENECA
SPRING
MADISON
MARION
COLUMBIA
CHERRY
JAMES
JEFFERSON
TERRACE
ALDER
SPRUCE
YESLER
WASHINGTON
MAIN
JACKSON
KING
OCCIDENTAL
WESTLAKE
DEXTER
AURORA
TERRY
BOREN
FAIRVIEW
MINOR
HARRISON
REPUBLICAN
OLIVE
BROADWAY
EASTLAKE
MELROSE
BELMONT
SUMMIT
BOYLSTON
HARVARD
RAILROAD
MAYNARD
1
2
3
4
5
6
7
8
9
10
11
12
13
14
15
16
17
18
R.O. LEDOUX

is finished in golden tones. The tower on the twenty-seventh floor provides a good view of the city.

4. The SEATTLE PUBLIC LIBRARY (*open 9-9 weekdays; 2-9 Sun. and holidays*), was founded in 1891. The central building, 4th Ave. between Madison and Spring Sts., was opened in 1906 with a grant of $220,000 from Andrew Carnegie. Under its roof are more than 500,000 volumes, with special divisions devoted to technology, art, and reference, and a periodical room with nearly 2,000 publications, 33 of which are in foreign languages. More than 6,000 volumes in Braille are made available to the blind. Eight thousand books in French, German, Scandinavian, Russian, Italian, Jewish, and Oriental languages are on the shelves; and works on Alaska number in excess of 500. The library provides an information service, art exhibits, adult education assistance, and a children's department. Ten branch libraries are conveniently located throughout the city to serve the residential districts.

5. The UNITED STATES COURTHOUSE BUILDING occupies the entire block bounded by 5th and 6th Aves., and Madison and Spring Sts. It consists of ten floors, supplemented by two penthouses used as machine rooms for the elevators and air-conditioning systems. The building is constructed of concrete, reinforced with seismic steel, making it impervious even to violent earthquake disturbances. A granite base and ceramic terra cotta encircle the building from the ground to a height of ten feet.

In this new structure are housed the Federal Courts; the Circuit Court of Appeals; the United States Marshal's office and detention cells; the United States District Attorney and assistants, and a spacious circuit court library. A rifle range will be set up in the basement, sharing space with operating machinery and storage vaults.

The 80-foot main entrance, encompassed by a terrace, enlivened by shrubbery and flowers, is on Fifth Avenue. Another entrance on Sixth Avenue leads directly to the second-floor offices. Smaller supplementary entrances are provided on Spring and Madison Streets.

DOWNTOWN SEATTLE—POINTS OF INTEREST

1. Site of the Territorial University
2. Children's Free Creative Art School
3. Northern Life Tower Building
4. Seattle Public Library
5. United States Courthouse Building
6. City Light Building
7. County-City Building
8. Smith Tower Building
9. Pioneer Square
10. Site of the Seattle Fire of 1889
11. Colman Street Ferry Terminal
12. Ye Old Curiosity Shop
13. Aquarium
14. Pike Place Public Market
15. Chief Seattle Monument
16. Denny Park
17. St. James Cathedral
18. King County (Harborview) Hospital

The Federal Works Agency and the Public Building Administration of the Treasury department were entrusted with the planning, designing, and erecting of this structure.

6. The CITY LIGHT BUILDING (*open 8-6 weekdays*), 3rd Ave. between Madison and Spring Sts., was designed by Earl W. Morrison and completed in 1935. It is the property of the city and contains the offices and departments of City Light. The building is modern in architecture and interior decoration; in the foyer a frieze in chrome by Albert G. Booth and John W. Elliott depicts the history of artificial lighting. On exhibition in the sales room is a diorama by artists of the WPA art project depicting Diablo Dam (*see Tour 8b*), to which City Light sponsors tours, tickets for which may be purchased in this building.

7. The COUNTY-CITY BUILDING (*open 8-5:30 weekdays*), at NE. corner of 3rd Ave. and Jefferson St. (Prefontaine Place), was built in 1916 and enlarged in 1930. The conventional ten-story concrete structure, with medallioned frieze and projecting cornice, is but a few feet from the site of King County's first courthouse built in 1860. It houses both city and county offices, 15 superior courtrooms, and a county jail.

At the southwest corner of the building is a drinking fountain in a huge rock, upon which is a plaque commemorating the defeat of the Klickitat Indians in 1856 and the participation of Seattle men in the Spanish-American War.

8. The SMITH TOWER BUILDING, NE. corner 2nd Ave. and Yesler Way, 42 stories, is the tallest building in Seattle. It was erected in 1914 and designed by Gaggin and Gaggin, New York City architects.

On the 35th floor is the CHINESE ROOM (*open 8-10; adm. 25c; guide*), a reproduction of a Chinese temple. The room is decorated with Cantonese furniture, bronze temple lanterns, and ornamental panels of porcelain and hand-carved teak. The Wishing Seat, bearing the inscription in Chinese: "Long life and good luck," is supposed to bring marriage to anyone who sits in it. Surrounding the Chinese Room is the OBSERVATION BALCONY, which offers a splendid view of the city. Above are seven additional stories, which may be reached by stairs.

9. PIONEER SQUARE, 1st Ave. and Yesler Way, is the site of Yesler's mill, where the life of Seattle centered in the early days. Around the mill were the cookhouses, Dr. Maynard's store, the first in the settlement, and the Conklin House, better known as Mother Damnable's, after its shrewish proprietor who drew her crowds with good cooking and frontier entertainment. In this neighborhood three men were lynched by a mob in 1872, and it was here that the Seattle Rifles subdued a mob attempt to deport 100 Chinese in 1886.

The "square" is a small triangular plot, graced with a green pavilion above the entrance to a men's lavatory, and surrounded by flophouses, pawnships, beer parlors, loggers' employment agencies, offices of quack doctors, and outfitters for Alaska and the lumber camps. Still known as the Skidroad, the district is thronged with men of all races and occupations—lumberjacks in town for a few weeks, fishermen back from Alaska, sailors on leave or in search of a ship, wandering farm laborers, boys far from home, drifters, cripples, beggars. Indians from out of the city make a habit of meeting at the square. Knots of men form around arguments concerning politics, religion, economics; and street speakers and the Salvation Army carry on their work.

Until 1939, a 140-year-old totem pole, brought to Seattle in 1889, stood in the square. Fire and the inner deterioration of the wood necessitated its removal. It served as a model for a new pole carved by Indians of Alaska from a log furnished by the Forestry Department, and set up on the site of the old one.

10. The SITE OF THE SEATTLE FIRE OF 1889, on 1st Ave. between Madison and Marion Sts., which started in the cabinet shop of Clairmont and Company, is now occupied by the Federal Office Building, nine stories high and designed by Federal engineers. The 13th Naval District headquarters, the weather bureau, and various other governmental agencies are housed here.

11. The COLMAN STREET FERRY TERMINAL, Alaskan Way and Marion St., from which boats leave for Puget Sound points, is a ferry slip remodeled by Loveless and Fay, architects, in modern style, with horizontal lines accentuating the length of the structure and an interior finished in pressed wood paneling with boxwood trim. Completed in 1937 the 550-foot building is supported by pilings and painted in aluminum. The terminal lies in the midst of a typical stretch of Seattle water front. To the south is Pier 2, regular point of arrival and departure for boats of the Alaska Steamship Company; Alaskan sourdoughs and *cheechakos* (tenderfeet of the North) like to frequent this place. To the north are piers of the Northern Pacific, at which a freighter is usually to be seen, and the fireboat station, with its two modern firefighters.

12. YE OLD CURIOSITY SHOP (*open 9-5 weekdays*), at the Colman Ferry Dock, exhibits for sale a rich collection of curios from all parts of the world. Opened in 1899, the shop has the character of a museum, and visitors may linger as long as they please without being pressed to buy. The proprietor, J. E. Standley, though more than 80 years old, still (1941) plays an active part in the shop and personally welcomes visitors. Among the many oddities in the exhibition are shrunken heads of Ecuador Indian warriors, a rare duckbill platypus, tiny carved elephants one-thirty-second of an inch in size, a giant 13-foot crab from the Yellow Sea, a Chinese dog of blue vitreous porcelain estimated to be 800 years old, the Lord's Prayer engraved on the head of a pin, and a snail weighing 67 pounds. The jaw bones of a whale are mounted outside the shop, and fossil ivory tusks and Indian relics are prominent items of the display.

13. The AQUARIUM (*open 10-10 daily, adults, 10c; children, 5c*), Pier 3, Alaskan Way, foot of Spring St., displays native sea plants and animal life in glass tanks containing continuously flowing sea water.

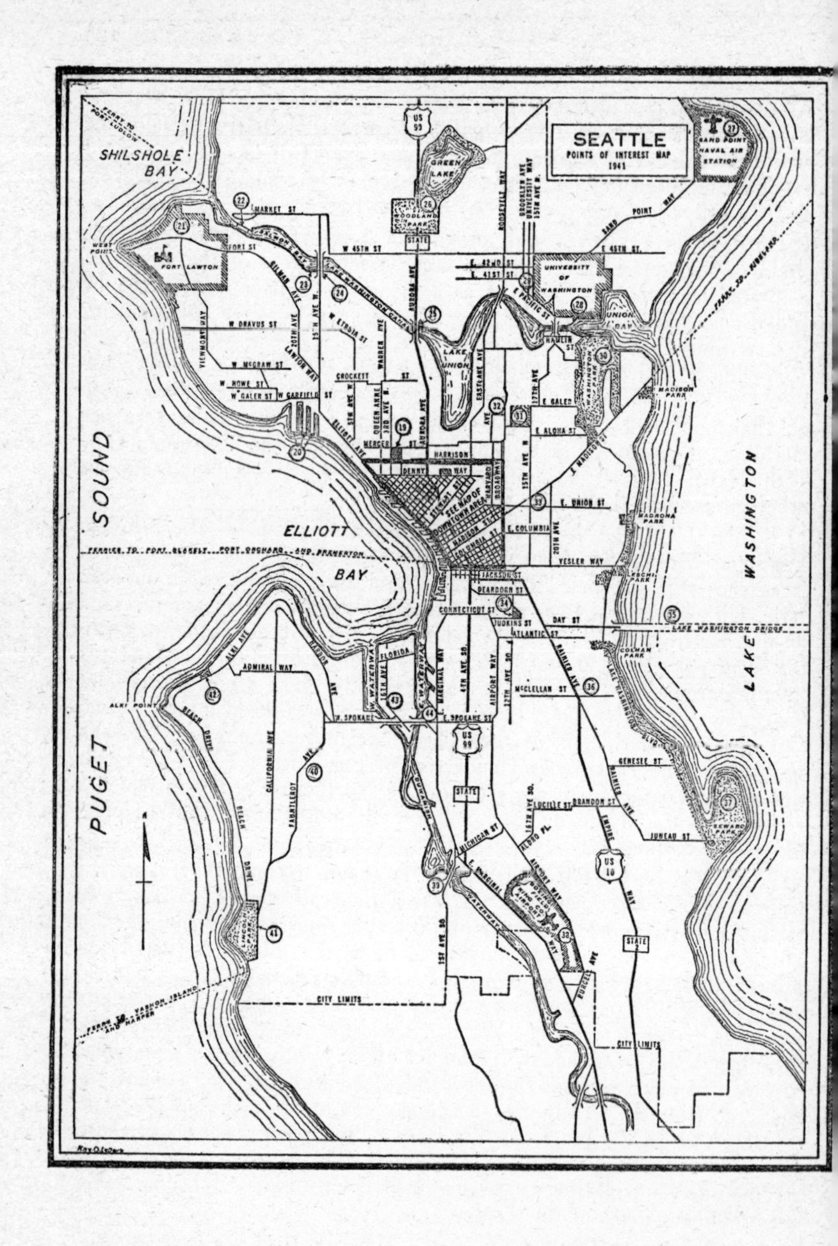
SEATTLE
POINTS OF INTEREST MAP
1941
SHILSHOLE BAY
SOUND
ELLIOTT
BAY
PUGET
LAKE WASHINGTON
FERRY TO PORT LUDLOW
FERRIES TO PORT BLAKELY, PORT ORCHARD, AND BREMERTON
FERRY TO VASHON ISLAND AND HARPER
FERRY TO KIRKLAND
SAND POINT NAVAL AIR STATION
GREEN LAKE
WOODLAND PARK
FORT LAWTON
WEST POINT
UNIVERSITY OF WASHINGTON
UNION BAY
LAKE UNION
WASHINGTON PARK
MADISON PARK
MADRONA PARK
LESCHI PARK
COLMAN PARK
SEWARD PARK
LINCOLN PARK
ALKI POINT
BOEING FIELD KING CO. AIRPORT
SEE MAP OF DOWNTOWN AREA
LAKE WASHINGTON BRIDGE
LAKE WASHINGTON CANAL
CITY LIMITS
MARKET ST
W 45TH ST
E 45TH ST
SAND POINT WAY
ROOSEVELT WAY
BROOKLYN AVE
UNIVERSITY WAY
15TH AVE N.E.
E. 42ND ST
E. 41ST ST
E PACIFIC ST
FORT ST
GILMAN AVE
20TH AVE
15TH AVE W.
W ETRURIA ST
W DRAVUS ST
VIEWMONT WAY
W McGRAW ST
W HOWE ST
W GALER ST
W GARFIELD ST
LAWTON WAY
CROCKETT ST
5TH AVE W
QUEEN ANNE
3RD AVE N.
WARREN AVE
AURORA AVE
EASTLAKE AVE
ELLIOTT AVE
MERCER ST
HARRISON
DENNY WAY
STEWART ST
MADISON ST
COLUMBIA ST
HARVARD
BROADWAY
HAMLIN ST
12TH AVE
E GALER
E ALOHA ST
E MADISON ST
15TH AVE N
E. UNION ST
E. COLUMBIA
20TH AVE
YESLER WAY
JACKSON ST
DEARBORN ST
CONNECTICUT ST
JUDKINS ST
DAY ST
ATLANTIC ST
RAINIER AVE
McCLELLAN ST
LAKE WASHINGTON BLVD
GENESEE ST
BRANDON ST
LUCILLE ST
JUNEAU ST
EMPIRE WAY
16TH AVE SO.
ALBRO PL.
AIRPORT WAY
12TH AVE SO.
4TH AVE SO.
E MARGINAL WAY
1ST AVE SO
MICHIGAN ST
E. SPOKANE ST
W. SPOKANE
W. WATERWAY
E. WATERWAY
16TH AVE
FLORIDA
HARBOR AVE
ADMIRAL WAY
ALKI AVE
BEACH DRIVE
CALIFORNIA AVE
FAUNTLEROY AVE
DUWAMISH WATERWAY
BURDETT AVE
US 99
US 10
STATE
STATE 2
21
22
23
24
25
26
27
28
29
30
31
32
33
34
35
36
37
39
40
41
42
43
44
19
20
Ray O. Jeffers

Octopuses, tube worms, starfish, flying clams, and a hundred other varieties of marine and plant life are in the exhibition.

14. The PIKE PLACE PUBLIC MARKET, at 1st Ave. and Pike St., extending three blocks to the north and two blocks to the west, is operated jointly by the city and the Pike Place Public Market Company, Inc. It was organized in 1907 to enable the small truck farmer to sell his goods directly to the public. Originally housed in a single building, the market has been expanded and improved so that today it is one of the leading markets in the country, both in size and in modernity of equipment. The stalls are assigned by drawing lots daily, thus preventing any stallkeeper from obtaining a permanent advantage over the rest. Part of the market is leased to sellers of meat and staple commodities. Japanese, Italians, and Slavs predominate among the truck gardeners. The bright array and fresh odors of the foods, the hawkers' cries, the variety of racial and national types, and the bustle and excitement under the electric lights, have made the market famous for its color as well as for the food it offers.

15. The CHIEF SEATTLE MONUMENT, center of Denny Place, at the intersection of Denny Way, Cedar St., and 5th Ave., is a bronze statute by James A. Wehn, representing the Indian Chief with hand outstretched in a gesture of peace and friendship. The memorial, sponsored by two local organizations, the Tillicums (meaning "friends") and the Founders Committee of Seattle Pioneers, was begun in 1908 and unveiled in 1912.

16. DENNY PARK, at the intersection of Battery St., Denny Way and Dexter Ave., is on the site of the city's first park, donated in

---

SEATTLE—POINTS OF INTEREST

19. Civic Auditorium Group
20. Port of Seattle, Smith Cove Piers
21. Fort Lawton
22. Lake Washington Ship Canal Locks
23. Fishing Fleet Harbor
24. Ballard Bridge
25. George Washington Memorial Bridge
26. Woodland Park
27. Sand Point U. S. Naval Air Station
28. University
29. Repertory Playhouse
30. University of Washington Arboretum
31. Volunteer Park
32. St. Marks Cathedral
33. Temple De Hirsch
34. United States Marine Hospital
35. Lake Washington Bridge
36. Sick's Seattle Stadium
37. Seward Park
38. Boeing Field
39. Boeing Aircraft Plant
40. West Seattle Municipal Golf Links and Recreational Centers
41. Lincoln Park
42. Alki Point
43. Fisher Flouring Mills Company Plant
44. Frozen Fish Museum

1884 by David Denny. The original tract of five acres also included a cemetery, until the final leveling of Denny Hill was begun in 1928. Remains of the pioneers buried there were removed to Lakeview cemetery, adjoining Volunteer Park. A cupola from the old grade school built on the hill near the park, is preserved as a historical memento in the present park.

17. The ST. JAMES CATHEDRAL, 9th Ave. at Columbia St., was built in 1907. The twin, green-domed towers rise 150 feet above the street. Cruciform in shape, the Cathedral is in Italian Renaissance style, with rich stained glass windows and a delicately carved reredos. The four-manual pipe organ has more than 80 sets of pipes. The surrounding Church properties house the Chancery and private school.

18. The KING COUNTY (HARBORVIEW) HOSPITAL, 9th Ave. and Jefferson St., opened in 1931, is a 12-story setback structure, designed by Thomas, Grainger, and Thomas. Clinics, dispensary, and X-ray facilities are provided free of charge to those unable to pay. This unit of the hospital contains 394 beds and a nurses' training school, affiliated with the University of Washington; it serves from 500-to-700 out-patients daily. All but the resident physicians serve without remuneration.

19. The CIVIC AUDITORIUM GROUP, Mercer St. at 3rd Ave. N., was built in 1928 and includes the Ice Arena, Auditorium, American Legion Hall, recreation field, and grandstand. The Ice Arena features skating and hockey; and the Auditorium, boxing and wrestling matches, conventions, concerts, and public meetings. The recreational field is used by high school athletic teams and by other community organizations sponsoring athletic tournaments.

20. PORT OF SEATTLE, SMITH COVE PIERS, on W. Garfield St., between 15th Ave., W. and 22nd Ave., W., include four piers, two of which (piers 40 and 41 of the Port of Seattle) are among the largest pier-type terminals in the world. Twelve vessels the size of the *Queen Mary* could berth at the terminal and still leave room for three or four smaller vessels. On Pier 40, which is 2,530 feet long, are 7 transit sheds, a derrick, and a fumigating plant; the pier was built in 1913 at a cost of $1,717,000. Pier 41, built in 1920 at a cost of $2,811,000, is 2,544 feet long and 367 feet wide with 2 transit sheds and 8 tracks of the Great Northern Railway; it is used for Oriental ships and cargoes. A great warehouse for storage of Alaska canned salmon, with a capacity of more than 2,000,000 cases, and a municipally-owned grain elevator are located at the terminal.

21. FORT LAWTON, the 640-acre Army reservation on Magnolia Bluff overlooking Puget Sound, was established in 1897 and a year later named for Major General Henry W. Lawton, an American officer killed in the Philippines. A half million dollars have been spent on improving the reservation, which now includes rifle, pistol, and long distance firing ranges, powder magazines, a cemetery, warehouse, and nine-hole golf course. The fort grounds have room for troop maneuvers,

eight barracks, accommodations for 600 men and officers, a post hospital and headquarters.

Fine views of Puget Sound, Mount Rainier, and the Olympic Mountains are offered from drives encircling the parade grounds. A road winds down to the beach below and to West Point Lighthouse, built in 1881. Once a crude wooden structure with a lighting system consisting of fish- or whale-oil-burning lamps, the lighthouse is today (1941) of the most modern type, with a flashing, or occulting, electric light, showing alternate red and white as it rotates, and with a combined candlepower of 17,000.

22. LAKE WASHINGTON SHIP CANAL LOCKS, 32nd Ave. NW. and W. 54th St., are located one and one-quarter miles from the western end of the eight-mile Lake Washington Canal which connects Lake Washington, Lake Union, and Puget Sound. The canal and locks were completed in 1916. Their capacity is exceeded on this continent only by the Panama Canal locks. One lock is 80 feet wide, the other 30 feet. Vessels are raised and lowered from 6 to 26 feet, requiring 8 minutes in the larger lock and 4 in the smaller. The locks are operated 24 hours daily, and have served as a passage for more than 3,000,000 tons of freight and 1,000,000 passengers in a single year.

Clipper Ship St. Paul (*open 9-6 daily; adm. 10c*), berthed at the Government Locks, the last of a great fleet of trading clipper ships which came around Cape Horn, was built in 1874 at Bath, Maine. The *St. Paul* was notorious as a "hell ship," whose sailors were usually shanghaied. Today, it houses a marine museum containing ships' models and an aquarium.

23. FISHING FLEET HARBOR, at 15th Ave. W. and W. Thurman St., on Salmon Bay below Ballard Bridge, is the winter port for Coast and Alaska fishing boats. Over 200 ships are repaired here and their gear put in order each fishing season. Among these are two codfish schooners, *Wawama* and *Azalea,* which are more than half-a-century old.

24. BALLARD BRIDGE, on 15th Ave. W. and 15th Ave. NW., extending from Emerson Street to Ballard Way, spans the Lake Washington Ship Canal. It has a concrete deck on steel-girder spans with a 42-foot roadway sufficient to accommodate two-way traffic. Walks for pedestrians on each side are two feet wide. A steel bar railing with cement posts protects the walks along the entire 3,081 feet of the bridge. The bascule span in the center of the bridge is capable of rising sufficiently to permit the passage of the largest steamer afloat. The bridge stands 50 feet above water level, permitting ordinary boats to pass underneath without resorting to the bascule.

25. The GEORGE WASHINGTON MEMORIAL BRIDGE, Aurora Ave., between N. 36th St. and Hillside Place, generally known as the Aurora Avenue Bridge, was built by the State of Washington, and dedicated in 1932. Of deck cantilever type, it is 2,103 feet in length and 135 feet above high water. More than 25,000 vehicles cross it daily.

26. WOODLAND PARK, between Phinney Ave., N. 50th St., N. 59th St. and Greenlake Way, is one of Seattle's largest parks. In its 188 acres are baseball diamonds, tennis courts, playgrounds, and picnic and tourist accommodations. The WAR GARDEN, in the southwest section of park, is dedicated to Spanish-American War veterans; east of the War Garden are the ROSE GARDENS, laid out around a lily pond. In the center of the park is the HARDING MEMORIAL, erected in 1923. The ZOOLOGICAL GARDENS, (*open 8-7 daily*), contain 200 buildings, cages, and dens, housing 1,407 animals and 277 species of birds. GREEN LAKE, northeast of the park, is 250 acres in area; on its borders are two municipal bathing beaches, with bathhouses, a fieldhouse, tennis court, and playgrounds.

27. SAND POINT U.S. NAVAL AIR STATION (*open daily*), at the city limits, E. 65th St. and Sand Point Way, covers the sand spit near the northern end of Lake Washington, and forms part of the defenses of the 13th Naval District. At various intervals during the year, air shows are put on at the field. At the entrance gate, Sand Point Way north of E. 70th St., is the 20-foot granite ROUND-THE-WORLD FLIGHT MEMORIAL to the flyers who left Sand Point Aviation Field on March 17, 1924, to make the first successful flight around the world.

UNIVERSITY OF WASHINGTON

28. Largest University in the Pacific Northwest, the University of Washington is situated in northern Seattle on 582 acres lying between 15th Avenue Northeast and Lake Washington, and East 45th Street and Lake Union. Wide rolling lawns, formal beds of flowers and shrubs, and a variety of native trees afford an unusually beautiful setting for the 66 college buildings. The blue waters on the rim of the campus have given activities there an amphibious character—along the shore are a canoe house, crew quarters, oceanographic laboratories, and a showboat theater. In the distance the Cascades are visible and far-off Mount Rainier.

A movement for the establishment of a University in this region began just before Washington Territory was created by separation from Oregon Territory. The first recorded proposal was made in 1852 by the *Columbian,* Olympia's pioneer newspaper: "The people north of the Columbia expect soon to have a territory of their own, we want a university here." In response to the urging of Governor Stevens, the first legislature, in 1854, memorialized Congress for the necessary land grants, and two townships were allotted. Despite considerable division of opinion as to the best site, the final choice was Seattle, where ground was secured in 1860.

To meet the cost of clearing the land, still heavily wooded, the Congressional grant was sold for $3,000. With this money, construction was begun at once. The single white building, with four classical pillars at the entrance, was still unfinished when instruction began on November 4, 1861, with a curriculum "offering everything from A B C's to the classics."

Lack of funds, however, caused several suspensions between 1867-77; and difficulties arose again in 1882, when the legislature failed to provide the necessary financial aid—the school was sustained for two years by a $4,000 gift from Henry Villard, promoter of the Northern Pacific Railway. Subsequent legislatures, however, regularly voted funds for the institution, which expanded rapidly.

In the meantime Seattle's business area was steadily closing in on the University, and agitation began for its removal to a new site. One hundred and sixty acres were acquired west of Lake Washington, and this tract was later enlarged to its present size. In 1894, construction of Denny Hall was begun and was completed the following year.

The teaching staff, however, as in later years, lagged behind the needs of the institution. It is reported that President Charles W. Eliot, of Harvard, on visiting the University asked a faculty member what chair he held. "I teach astronomy, botany, physics, zoology, and . . ." the professor began, at which point Eliot interrupted, "Oh, I see! You don't occupy a chair; you occupy a settee!"

Expansion and enrollment increased steadily as the population and the wealth of the State grew. In 1909 the buildings of the Alaska-Yukon-Pacific Exposition reverted to the University. During the presidency of Dr. Henry Suzzalo (1915-26), an extensive building program was initiated. It began with the erection of the Home Economics building in 1913, in the Tudor-Gothic style popular in the first decades of the twentieth century; and during the succeeding years numerous structures were added, designed under the same influence. The Chemistry Building, constructed in 1938-9, marked a shift to a more modern, functional style of architecture.

Today (1941) the University has an enrollment during the regular term of more than 11,000; and a faculty of about 450 professors and instructors, as well as about 250 fellows who combine teaching with graduate study. The summer term, always popular because of the climate of the Puget Sound region, attracts over 3,000 students. Dr. Lee Paul Sieg, formerly of the University of Pittsburg, is the present (1941) President of the University, which is governed by a board of seven regents appointed by the Governor.

An exceptionally wide range of study is offered. Twenty-six departments in liberal arts and science offer degrees. There are also schools in architecture, the fine arts, the social sciences, home economics, journalism, music, and nursing. The College of Fisheries, the only one of its kind in the United States, is one of the two in the world to award a degree in this field. Undergraduate and graduate work is offered in mining, pharmacy, law, engineering, forestry, economics, and business administration. A 1938 innovation is the air-training course for men and women, introduced at Washington and other colleges through the Civil Aeronautics Authority. Eighty hours of ground training are combined with 35 of dual and solo flying in sea and land craft.

The University has made many valuable contributions to the cultural, scientific, and industrial life of the State. Excellent creative work has come from the Colleges of Liberal Arts and Fine Arts. Orchestra, band, and vocal concerts, frequently presented without charge, dance drama, and popular stage productions have enriched the cultural life of the community. The social science departments have done notable work in such fields as investigating income levels and juvenile delinquency, analysing housing needs, and studying Indian cultures and languages. The University has also provided special public services: psychological testing and guidance are made available to children of the State without charge at the Institute for Child Development, administered under the Bailey and Babette Gatzert Foundation for Child Welfare; the speech division of the Department of English conducts clinics throughout the State for the correction of speech defects; the Law School, in conjunction with the Seattle bar, conducts a free Legal Aid Bureau; and a Bureau of Governmental Research furnishes consultation to cities and counties on their administrative problems.

In industrial research and conservation, the College of Mines and the Schools of Fisheries, Forestry, and Engineering have made significant contributions. Experimental work in forestry, conducted at the 2,000-acre Pack Demonstration Forest, includes the improvement of methods of fire prevention and of soil and timber conservation. The College of Mines devised a waste-elimination process in coal washing, and discovered new uses for local sand and fire clay. An improved gas-making machine and a paper-preserving process were developed by the Department of Chemistry. The School of Fisheries and the Department of Biology have introduced new varieties of oysters and new methods of oyster culture and are doing valuable work in the conservation and propagation of fish.

A number of co-operative and self-help ventures have been organized by University students, about 50 per cent of whom work for their schooling. The Students' Co-operative Association, started in 1933, controls 9 houses, grouped in 5 units, with a yearly membership averaging 300. The University Bookstore is owned and operated by the Associated Students of the University of Washington.

CAMPUS TOUR

The main entrance to the campus is at 15th Ave. NE. and East 40th Street. Auto roads also enter the grounds through 17th Ave. NE. or 22nd Ave. NE.; from the east through Montlake Boulevard and Stadium Way; or from the southwest through East Pacific Street; there are many footpaths on every side.

At the main entrance, a large map of the campus stands between uprights. (Maps are also provided in the University catalogues and bulletins.) Straight ahead, the HENRY SUZZALO MEMORIAL LIBRARY, (*open 7:45 a. m. to 10 p. m. Mon. to Fri.*), set at a diagonal, dominates the campus. The building, named for a former president of the University, represents the most consistent application of Gothic style on the University grounds. As indicated by the miniature model displayed in the lobby, the library is still to be completed by the addition of a tower and another wing. Its broad steps are a focus of campus life for students from the scattered buildings of upper campus and lower campus. Inside are almost 450,000 volumes, including 5,000 items of Alaska, among which are many rare Russian manuscripts; 80 volumes of Italian plays published before the fifteenth century; 6,000 works on pedagogy; extensive material on fisheries. The NORTHWEST ROOM is now being used for the preparation of the Union Catalog of the Pacific Northwest Bibliographic Center. Stacks, directly connected with this room, hold the library's outstanding collection of Pacific Northwest Americana. In the room, map murals by Paul M. Gustin and John T. Jacobsen depict highlights of Northwest history and North American exploration. James M. Wehn of Seattle designed the window medallions, which represent seals of the Hudson's Bay Company, the Provisional Government, and Washington Territory.

The library lies midway between the upper campus, home of the liberal arts, and the lower campus with its scientific and technical schools. On the upper campus, the main concentration of buildings is the QUADRANGLE, begun in 1913 and not yet complete. Its southern corner is formed by CONDON HALL, just across from the library, and named for a former dean of the law school, which it houses together with an excellent law library. Adjoining Condon at right angles is the SOCIAL SCIENCE BUILDING, newest unit of the quadrangle. It is a duplicate in appearance of COMMERCE HALL, which, with adjoining PHILOSOPHY HALL, forms the western corner of the quadrangle. The other angles are occupied by HOME ECONOMICS HALL and EDUCATION HALL; the latter contains the administrative offices as well as the school of education and the art department. Along the corridors of Home Economics Hall, glass cases present changing displays of fine and applied arts, including porcelains and textiles. In the textile laboratory on the third floor is a Fade-ometer, a delicate machine designed to test the durability of textile dyes. In the basement of this building is the university commons, cafeteria serving students and public (*open weekdays*).

Southeast of the quadrangle is the MUSIC HALL, a large white frame building, home of University presidents until 1932, when the late Edwin Ames turned over his mansion in the Madison Park district for that purpose. Mr. Ames also bequeathed a trust fund to bring visiting scholars to the University.

Most conspicuous in the eastern periphery of campus buildings is the new brick HEALTH CENTER overlooking Lake Washington. Here students receive medical care for a small annual fee. Next to it on the south is the long low FACULTY CLUB of dark stained wood.

North of the Music Hall lie LEWIS HALL and CLARK HALL. Clark Hall now serves as a student union building, housing the Associated Students, Associated Women Students, Dean of Women, University employment service, and fraternity councils. In the basement is a coffee shop operated by the University commons. Lewis Hall is occupied by the University publications and the extension service.

Before Lewis Hall stands the WASHINGTON ELM, grown from a slip of the Washington Elm, Cambridge, Massachusetts, under which Washington took command of the Continental Army. When the Cambridge elm fell, a slip was sent to Harvard University and planted near the original site in 1931. Two other slips were set on the capitol grounds at Washington, D.C. and at Olympia, and another has been planted in the arboretum.

Carrying out the Tudor Gothic architecture of the quadrangle buildings are two recently built structures to the north: the WOMEN'S GYMNASIUM and the WOMEN'S RESIDENCE HALLS, with accommodations for 300.

West of the women's dormitory stands the square wooden CHIMES TOWER, gift of Alden J. Blethen, early editor of the Seattle *Times*. The bells are rung by George Bailey, a blind musician, who for many years since his graduation from the University has given daily recitals.

A path from the chimes tower leads to the mushroom-like OBSERVATORY (*usually open clear nights during the school year*); built in 1895 of Tenino stone in Romanesque revival style, it contains a six-inch telescope, a transit for measuring sun time, and a master clock controlling all others on the campus. The path then enters MEMORIAL WAY, which, flanked by two pillars commemorating University students lost in the World War, bisects a wooded area at the northern edge of the campus.

Along the southern end of Memorial Way, three buildings, older and more individual in style than the others, still hold their own. Historic DENNY HALL, oldest building on the campus, presides in mellowed dignity over its sweep of green lawn, carrying out in slate-roofed gray stone the pattern of a Francis I chateau. The only inconsistent detail is the cupola which roofs the original DENNY BELL, brought around the Horn in 1862 for the first University building. This bell called out the Seattle Rifles at the time of the anti-Chinese riots in 1886 and sounded the alarm for the fire of 1889. It is rung now but once a year, on Homecoming Day. On the top floor is an extensive DRAMA LIBRARY financed by college plays.

Southwest of Denny, across a maze of formal shrubbery, rises the oval bulk of PARRINGTON HALL, suggesting a pink-iced cake. It is screened from the street by a picturesque grove of madrona trees, whose glossy green leaves and roan-colored trunks border the campus at its western edge. Formerly Science Hall, the structure some ten years ago was turned over to the English Department and renamed for the department's most illustrious figure, the late Vernon L. Parrington, whose sudden death in England in 1929 followed closely on his winning the Pulitzer prize for his critical history of American letters (*see Literature*). On the top floor is the WALKER-AMES ROOM, lined with the books of Edwin Ames, and given over to upper class students for study and lounging. It contains a BUST OF SHAKESPEARE, executed by an artist of the Federal Art Project.

Imbued with associations is the ivy-covered tan-brick building with its apron of steps which flanks the main campus entrance to the left—MEANY HALL. Serving as an assembly and concert hall, it was named for the late Edmond S. Meany, history professor who came to represent the pioneering traditions of the University. Oil paintings of Professor Meany and others, by Morgan Padelford, alumnus, hang in the lobby. The basement contains the University broadcasting studio, connected by direct wire with all Seattle stations, which carries a variety of programs throughout the college year.

In the stone court to the rear of Meany Hall stands the GEORGE WASHINGTON STATUE, a bronze by Lorado Taft, unveiled at the Alaska-Yukon-Pacific Exposition. Services are held here annually on February 22. Just south of Meany Hall the bronze EDWARD GRIEG BUST, by Finn H. Frolich of Seattle, presented to the University by the Association of Norwegians of the Pacific Northwest and Alaska, is mounted on a granite shaft.

The small windowless brick building beyond the Washington monument is the HORACE C. HENRY ART GALLERY (*open 12:30-5 weekdays; 2-5 Sun.*). Mr. Henry presented the building, together with his collection of nineteenth- and early-twentieth-century paintings in oils and water colors. Other rooms house a succession of traveling exhibits, varied by student work. Friezes, niches, and stone figures symbolizing Egyptian, Chinese, Greek, and European culture, were carved by Dudley Pratt of the University art faculty.

Outpost of the lower campus, the old library building, now the WASHINGTON STATE MUSEUM, (*open 8 a.m.-6 p.m. weekdays; 2-6 p.m. Sun.*), stands to the east of the present library. Another survival of the A-Y-P Exposition, commemorated by a plaque on a boulder near by, it is a pillared building in baroque classic. The MAIN WING holds a comprehensive collection of Northwest Indian material, including models of primitive Indian villages done by the Federal Art Project. Long war canoes are mounted in the center of the room, and one especially large one takes the weather on the grounds outside. To the left of the room are cases of geology specimens; to the right are collections of North American animals and birds. The ALASKA ROOM, at the rear of the stairway, features totems and house posts, as well as clothing and implements used by northern tribes. On the stairway landing is an Egyptian mummy.

The second floor contains Australian, Melanesian, Malayan, and Polynesian exhibits. In a separate wing is the ORIENTAL ROOM, lined with exquisite examples of Chinese porcelain, jewels, and household furnishings. Japanese art is represented by the Shoinzukuri, a set of rooms in the eighteenth-century style of the Tokugawa period, presented by the International Society for Cultural Relations of Japan. The innermost room, or *tokonoma,* has walls of translucent ricepaper traced with a gold and silver design of clouds and mist. In an alcove stands the RAMAGE PRESS, on which our first newspaper, the *Columbian,* was printed at Olympia.

At the head of RAINIER VISTA, which divides the lower campus on a direct line with distant Mount Rainier, are the twin science buildings, PHYSICS HALL and JOHNSON HALL. The latter contains the SEISMOGRAPH (*visitors apply at Room 104*). Below lies GEYSER BASIN, a circular pool which has recently acquired a stone basin, having been known to generations of students as reed-grown, wooden-walled Frosh Pond. Southward the vista leads past the SYLVAN THEATER, a terraced glade containing the four white columns from the original University building. Here are two bronze plaques, one of Edmond Meany presented by the class of 1885, the other of Lafayette, a gift of the State's French colony.

Facing Geyser Basin is BAGLEY HALL, the new Chemistry and Pharmacy Building, simpler in manner than the prevailing Tudor Gothic. Its name was taken from an old building flanking the campus entrance to the right, and now renamed PHYSIOLOGY HALL. The lobby of the present Bagley Hall contains an exhibit of chemicals in industry.

Directly across the water from Bagley is another red-brick structure, GUGGENHEIM HALL, built with a grant from the Guggenheim Foundation, home of the schools of civil, mechanical, and aeronautical engineering. Electrical engineering is still housed in the old building to the south, ENGINEERING HALL. Immediately behind Guggenheim Hall is a small box-like brick WIND TUNNEL. Built partly with Works Progress Administration funds, it is the largest tunnel in any American educational institution. Two 15-foot, 7-blade propellers, driven by powerful motors, force cooled air through the two rings of the tunnel at a velocity of 250 miles per hour to test airfoils for aircraft design.

At the south end of the campus, on either side of Rainier Vista, are MINES HALL, containing a United States Bureau of Mines, and ANDERSON HALL, the forestry building, named for its donor, Mrs. Alfred H. Anderson, and her late husband, a pioneer lumberman. Forestry students spend one-quarter of each year in the PACK FOREST DEMONSTRATION, a 2,000-acre tract set aside in Snoqualmie National Forest (*see Tour 8E*) by the Lathrop-Pack Foundation for the study of forest conditions. Across the boulevard, in a triangle which forms the tip of the campus proper, cluster the shed-like buildings of the COLLEGE OF FISHERIES.

Athletic headquarters lie to the east: the tennis courts, where many champion squads have practiced; the huge brick ATHLETIC PAVILION; and the football STADIUM, its rim surmounted by a huge totem designed by C. Ken Weidner to symbolize the spirit of the husky, Washington's mascot. Here, track coach Hec Edmundson, former Olympic half-miler, has been training world-record holders like Steve Anderson, hurdler, Herm Brix, shot-put, and Paul Jessup, discus. Washington has supplied coaches to many prominent universities. The frail shells, launched from the CREW HOUSE at the east end of the Lake Washington Canal, may be seen on any spring or fall day streaking the water of Lake Union or Lake Washington. George Pocock's "one-man shipyard," at the Crew House, has built shells for most of the Universities, using Western red cedar.

Bordering Lake Washington Canal, the GOLF COURSE rounds off the campus to the south. Its southwestern limits are marked by the R.O.T.C. HEADQUARTERS and DRILL FIELD (*two years military training is compulsory*). Facing Lake Union is the brick building of the OCEANOGRAPHIC LABORATORY, built jointly in 1931 by the State and the Rockefeller Foundation. It has a circulating system of 45,000 gallons of sea-water, kept at nine degrees Centigrade, the average temperature of Puget Sound. The adjoining wharf is the mooring of the motorship *Catalyst* between her research cruises.

Just north of the oceanography building is an outdoor scale model of the lower Puyallup River, built by the University and the Works Progress Administration for experimentation in flood control.

Near the foot of 15th Avenue NE. is mounted the most surprising of all the University units, the SHOWBOAT, theater of the Drama Division. Designed like a river boat, under the direction of James Hicken, it rests on piling above the water and measures 140 feet long by 40 feet abeam. It was built by the WPA and completed in 1939. Also constructed by WPA is a second theater, evolved by Glenn Hughes, director of the Drama Division of the Department of English. The new building, behind Physiology Hall, carries on the work of a stageless theater that was begun in the penthouse of the Meany Hotel. It has a novel, circular seating arrangement around a central arena.

29. The REPERTORY PLAYHOUSE (*open three nights a week and Sat. matinee, Oct.-July*), corner University Way and N. 41st St., is a rambling structure in English style, built in 1930. The theater company, organized in 1928 by Mr. and Mrs. Burton W. James, has presented many types of plays with professional performers drawn from all sections of the country. The playhouse is a non-profit civic organization (*see the Theater*).

30. The UNIVERSITY OF WASHINGTON ARBORETUM, a tract of more than 260 acres, extends from the Lake Washington Canal opposite the University campus to E. Madison St., and from Broadmoor on the east to Montlake District on the west. It is designed to make use of every type of plant and shrub that the climate will support; and the moderate climate of the Puget Sound district makes it possible to grow most of the temperate-zone plants. Featured areas are a nine-acre planting of rhododendrons in beautiful RHODODENDRON GLEN; a three-quarter-mile path planted on both sides with azaleas, flowering cherries, and dogwoods—about 8,000 azalea plants are required; and on a hilltop,

the magnolia group comprising 50 of the finest varieties. These, and many thousands of other plants, will make this one of Seattle's most picturesque areas. The Works Progress Administration and the Arboretum Foundation are active in these developments.

31. VOLUNTEER PARK (*open 9-5 daily*), E. Prospect to E. Galer Sts., between 11th and 15th Aves. N., is laid out in formal design with flower beds, sunken gardens, a bandstand, and a CONSERVATORY (*open 9-5 daily*). Near the conservatory is the SEWARD STATUE, commemorating the Alaska purchase by William Henry Seward, Secretary of State, in 1867.

A spiral stairway leads to top of OBSERVATION TOWER where a splendid view is obtained of the city. Sighting devices donated by the Mountaineers Club identify distant mountain peaks.

The grave of Princess Angeline, daughter of Chief Seattle, is located in Lakeview cemetery at the north end of the park.

The SEATTLE ART MUSEUM (*open 10-5 weekdays; 2-6 Sun.; Wed., and Fri., adm. 25c: Public lecture and gallery tour second Thursday of each month; children's story hour Sat. 10 a.m. Oct.-May*), is a rectangular structure of modern design, faced with stone and with niches and fountains at the ends of the facade. Two marble rams and two camels guard the entrance; these are from the approach to the tomb of a Chinese Ming Prince of the Fifteenth Century A.D. The museum was presented to the city in 1933 by Mrs. Eugene Fuller and her son, Dr. Richard Fuller. The architects were Bebb and Gould.

The Museum has an outstanding Oriental collection, covering the development of Chinese art from the Shang Dynasty (Eighteenth-Twelfth Century B. C.) to the Nineteenth Century, and many other phases of Chinese art. The Japanese collection ranges from the Eighth Century A.D. to the Nineteenth Century. There are also interesting pieces of Siamese, Indian, Korean, Cambodian, and Persian craftsmanship.

The Museum's permanent collection of European and American art includes paintings, sculpture, textiles, and an extensive collection of graphic arts from the Fourteenth Century to the present day; 500 facsimile prints of European masterpieces; and a group of paintings and sculptures by artists of the Northwest. The Northwest Artists' Annual Exhibition is shown here in October.

32. The ST. MARKS CATHEDRAL, 1245 10th Ave. N., is the seat of the Episcopalian diocese of the Bishopric of Olympia. Designed by Robert Brown, the structure was started in 1928 and services were first held on Easter Sunday, 1931. The edifice, which overlooks Lake Union, is still unfinished.

33. The TEMPLE DE HIRSCH (*open 9-5:30, Mon. to Fri.*), 15th Ave. and E. Union St., a white brick building in Italian Renaissance style, was dedicated in 1908. Seattle's first Jewish congregation was formed in 1889 under the name of Ahabath Shalom, and after a lapse in the years of 1895-9, the present congregation organized with a membership of 65. A religious school with some 400 students is operated in

conjunction with the synagogue, meeting on Sunday mornings, 10-12 a.m.

The TEMPLE CENTER, adjoining the synagogue, is used for social and cultural activities by the Jewish and general population. The SAMUEL ROSENBERG MEMORIAL LIBRARY, on the main floor of the Temple Center, has a circulating collection of 5,300 volumes dealing with Jewish subjects; it is the most extensive library of Jewish literature in the Northwest.

34. The UNITED STATES MARINE HOSPITAL (*visiting hours 1-3:45, Sun., Tues. and Thurs.*), 14th Ave. S. and Judkins St., was built in 1932, under the supervision of the United States Health Service; the site was given by the city of Seattle. Rising to 16 stories, the hospital commands one of the finest views of the city and is visible for many miles. The building was designed by Bebb and Gould, and John Graham associate architect, and cost $1,608,000. Ten murals by Kenneth Callahan adorn the lobby. Four hundred and fifty patients can be accommodated comfortably, and all modern equipment is provided.

35. LAKE WASHINGTON BRIDGE, constructed by the Washington Toll Bridge Authority and PWA, at a cost of nearly $9,000,000, is a new development in the history of engineering and the largest pontoon bridge of its type in the world. Starting at a point on Rainier Ave., between Day and Atlantic Sts., it passes to Mercer Island over a series of 25 floating sections of reinforced concrete, and thence across the East Channel and Mercer Slough to connect with US 10. The entire project is 6½ miles in length, with a 45-foot, 4-lane, freeway highway, over-crossings and under-crossings, sidewalks, entrances, and exit ramps. The floating bridge structure is the most interesting feature of the bridge. Each standard floating unit is securely anchored and weighs 4,558 tons. At each end of the floating bridge, provision is made for the passage of small watercraft requiring a vertical clearance up to 35 feet. Near the center of the floating structure is a 200-foot opening for larger boats and vessels formed by a retractile floating drawspan. The length of this combined floating section is over 1¼ miles.

36. SICK'S SEATTLE STADIUM, Rainier Ave. at Bayview St., named for Emil Sick, financier and businessman, is the home field of the Seattle baseball club, a member of the Pacific Coast League and holder of the Coast Championship for 1939 and 1940. The new field, bleachers, and grandstand were opened in April 1939 on a site which for more than 20 years has been dedicated to the national sport. Costing $350,000, the ball park and buildings can accommodate 15,000 persons.

37. SEWARD PARK, Lake Washington Boulevard at Orcas St., was once an island, but the lowering of the water level of the lake by the opening of Lake Washington Canal in 1916 exposed a connecting stem of land. A *torii,* copy of the famous *torii* at Miajima and presented by local Japanese, forms the "Gateway of Welcome." A reproduction of an ancient granite LANTERN, weighing six tons, presented by citizens of Yokohama in gratitude for relief given during the earthquake of 1923, stands in the center of a circular garden.

Adjoining the park on the east, the 14 pools and rustic buildings of the SEWARD PARK REARING PONDS occupy a wooded hilltop. On the lake front bordering the boulevard is the WILD DUCK SANCTUARY, where mallards and other species find a refuge.

38. BOEING FIELD (King County Airport), 6.5 miles from the city center, is bordered by East Marginal Way (which is US 99 and State 1) on the west and Airport Way on the east. Only a small portion of its 550 acres is outside of the city limits, and the field is often erroneously referred to as the municipal airport, though it is entirely under the supervision of the King County Commissioners. Nearly every bit of the field is suitable for plane landing. Four concrete runways, ranging from 2,600 to 7,300 feet in length, and illuminated by a modern lighting system, are in use. Four hangars, each 100 by 200 feet, are available for storage purposes; one is reserved for rental to owners of private planes. Several schools for instruction in aviation are located at the field.

An average of 62 take-offs and an equal number of landings occur daily. Twelve transport flights and arrivals, carrying both passengers and mail, and about 8 Government planes are scheduled for each 24-hour period.

39. The BOEING AIRCRAFT PLANT (*admission by pass only*), where some of the largest planes in the world are built, specializes in large four-engine machines. One of the West's pioneer aircraft establishments, the Boeing Company grew out of the experiments of H. A. Munter in 1912. Plant Number One, at 200 W. Washington St., houses the general offices, main shop, and assembly buildings for flying boats; the giant Pan-American Airways Clippers are assembled here. Plant Number Two, 7901 Marginal Way, covers a 20-acre tract, and is used mainly for the final assembling of land planes; Plant Number Three to the south is used mainly for out-assembly work.

40. WEST SEATTLE MUNICIPAL GOLF LINKS AND RECREATIONAL CENTERS, begun in December 1935 under WPA grants, has 161 acres of landscaped area, with an 18-hole golf course of 208 acres. A rustic head-house, a stadium, an outdoor checkerboard, a tennis court, and other recreational features are included. A clubhouse for boy scouts is also planned. The Seattle Park Board was co-sponsor of the project.

41. LINCOLN PARK, on Puget Sound, bounded on the east and north by W. Fontanelle St. and Fauntleroy Ave., is a wooded 107-acre salt-water recreational area, the best-equipped in the city for family picnics, and generously supplied with fire grates, tables, and sheltered retreats. There is profusion of wild flowers of many species, and sloping green lawns afford a restful retreat. The park is maintained by the Seattle Park Board and all accommodations are free of charge.

42. ALKI POINT, on the beach front, at Alki Ave. and 59th Ave. SW., is the SITE OF THE FIRST SEATTLE SETTLEMENT, on September 28, 1851. It was at this point that David T. Denny, John N. Low, Lee Terry, and Captain Robert C. Fay established the first permanent

settlement. Most of the timber had been burned away, making it a suitable place to put up the shelters that were immediately needed. It has an unobstructed view of the Olympic Mountains and of Puget Sound northward and southward. Here, the first city salt-water bathing beach, which now occupies a mile-long stretch, was provided by the City of Seattle. At Alki Ave. and 63rd Ave. SW. is the shaft commemorating the arrival of the Denny family. At the extreme end of the point is ALKI POINT LIGHTHOUSE (*open 12:30-5 Tues., Wed., Fri.*), erected in 1916.

43. The FISHER FLOURING MILLS COMPANY PLANT (*open to visitors by appointment only*), West Waterway, Harbor Island, the largest flour mill west of the Mississippi, has a daily capacity of 6,000 barrels of flour and 4 tons of feed. Established in 1910, the company now employs approximately 700 persons and, with affiliated companies, owns and operates more than 100 grain warehouses throughout the Northwest. The huge storage tanks have a capacity of 2,500,000 bushels of grain, approximately 2,000 carloads. The mills' products are sold in the United States, Alaska, Hawaii, Central and South America, Europe, Asia, and the Philippines.

44. The FROZEN FISH MUSEUM (*Open* 8-5 *weekdays*), Spokane St. and E. Marginal Way, at the PORT OF SEATTLE'S SPOKANE STREET TERMINAL, contains a nationally known collection of more than 200 frozen specimens of rare fish, retaining their natural color and appearance. Included in the exhibit are several sharks, a whale, an enormous octopus, and a 536-pound swordfish. In addition to wharf and warehouse, the terminal has a cold storage warehouse of more than 2,000,000 cubic feet capacity.

POINTS OF INTEREST IN ENVIRONS

Bainbridge Island, 45 min. by ferry, 9.5 *m.* (*see Island Tour* 1). Vashon Island, 20 min. by ferry, 3 *m.* (*see Island Tour* 2). Bremerton, 1 hr. by ferry, 15 *m.* (*see Cross-Sound Tour* 3). Snoqualmie Falls, 33 *m.* (*see Tour 1b*). Lake Washington Drive, 52 *m.* (*see Tours 1b and 8c*). Lake Lucerne, 26 *m.*; Green River Gorge, 29 *m.* (*see Tour 1D*).

Spokane

Railroad Stations: 416 W. Trent Ave. for Union Pacific R.R., Oregon-Washington R.R. & Navigation Co., Spokane International Ry. (Canadian Pacific Ry.), and Chicago, Milwaukee, St. Paul & Pacific R.R.; 221 W. 1st Ave. for Northern Pacific Ry.; Stevens St. and Havermale Island for Great Northern Ry.; Spokane, Portland, and Seattle Ry. uses both Northern Pacific and Great Northern Stations.
Bus Station: Motor Bus Terminal, 229 N. Howard St. for Union Pacific Stages, Washington Motor Coach System (Greyhound Lines), Priest River and Priest Lake Intrastate & Interstate Motor Coach Line, and Auto Interurban Company lines to Inland Empire points. Desert Hotel, 725 W. First Ave., for Burns Auto Stages (interstate only, Washington-Idaho).
Airport: Felts Field (municipal), 4 m. E. from city center via Trent Road and Fancher Way, for United Air Lines and Northwest Airlines. Taxi fare $1.15, time 15 min.; bus fare, 10c, hourly service from Riverside Ave. between Monroe and Division Sts., time 20 min.
Taxis: 25c first mile, 10c each additional half-mile or fraction; $2 per hour.
City busses: Fare 10c, or four tokens for 30c.
Traffic Regulations: Maximum speed limit 25 m.p.h.; one-hour parking limit on weekdays in retail zone 8-6; three-hour parking limit in area bounded by Division and Adams Sts. and Trent and Third Aves.; two-hour parking 2-6 p.m.; five-hour maximum in other parts of city.
Street Order and Numbering: Blocks numbered E and W. from Division St.; N. and S. from Sprague Ave.

Accommodations: 34 hotels; 9 tourist camps; Highbridge Tourist Camp (municipal) near US 10 on Latah Creek, has trailer facilities.

Information Service: Davenport Hotel, 807 Sprague Ave.; Chamber of Commerce and Inland Automobile Association (AAA), Civic Bldg., 1020 W. Riverside Ave.

Theater and Motion Picture Houses: Spokane Little Theater, 1019 W. 1st Ave., frequent local productions and road shows; 13 motion picture houses.
Radio Stations: KFIO (1150 kc.); KFPY (920 kc.); KGA (1510 kc.); KHQ (590 kc.).
Baseball: Ferris Field, Main Ave., and Altamont St.
Horse Racing: Playfair, Main Ave., and Altamont St.
Golf: Two municipal courses: Downriver, on Downriver Drive at NW. city limits, 18 holes, greens fee 50c; Indian Canyon, on Indian Canyon Drive and West Drive near US 10, 18 holes, greens fee 50c.
Tennis: 15 municipal courts in parks and playgrounds.
Swimming: Five municipal pools; Liberty Pool, E. 5th Ave. and Perry St.; Sinto Pool, E. Mission Ave. and Perry St.; Hillyard Pool, Columbia Ave. and Market St.; Cannon Pool, W. Maxwell Ave. and Cannon St.; Comstock Pool, W. 29th Ave. and Howard St. Natatorium Park Pool (open 11-11 daily), W. end of Boone Ave., adults 52c (including suit rental); children 27c.
Riding: Ajax Riding Stables, E. Hartson Ave.; Brown's Mountain Riding Academy, 29th Ave., and Havana St.; Cooper's Riding Club Stables, Indian Canyon Road; Mac's Riding Stables, Riverside State Park, at Seven Mile: 50c

an hour, average charge weekdays; usually 75c first hour, Sat., Sun., and holidays.

Ice Skating: Spokane Ice Arena (open 1-11 daily, winter), 1407 N. Elm St.; adults 25c daytime, 40c evenings; children 15c daytime, 30c evenings; admission subject to change. Municipal tennis courts flooded for winter skating; free.

Hunting and Fishing: Grouse, pheasant, duck, and deer hunting in environs. Good fishing in lakes and rivers.

Annual Events: Spokane Ski Club and Inland Empire Ski Tournament at Mount Spokane, Jan., or Feb.; Automobile Show, Mar.; Easter Sunrise Service on Mount Spokane; Sportsmen's Show, May; Polo Tournaments, June; Spokane Rodeo, July; City Amateur Swimming Championships, Aug.; Inland Empire Amateur Golf Tournament, Aug. or Sept.; Flower Show, Sept.; Halloween Parade and Harvest Home Festival, Oct. 31; Shrine Football Game, last week in Nov.; Spokane Civic Symphony and Spokane Symphony concerts, Nov. to May.

SPOKANE (1,981 alt., 122,001 pop.), second-largest city in Washington and largest inland city west of Omaha and north of Denver, is the metropolis of an extensive farming, lumbering, and mining area known as the Inland Empire. This uneven plateau, south of British Columbia, extends beyond the Coeur d'Alene Mountains on the east, spreads southward beyond the rolling Palouse and Walla Walla districts into Oregon, and circles through the Big Bend country to the Columbia River on the west. Geographically, this region embraces a variety of terrain—fertile wheatlands, bunchgrass ranges, sagebrush deserts studded with scab-rock, wooded foothills, and rugged mountain ranges. A spiderweb of railroads, highways, and airlines radiates from the city in all directions.

Concentrated around the falls of the Spokane River, the city spreads outward toward the east over the level valley floor and stretches upward on the north and south beyond the rocky rim of steep, pine-covered hills. The river, which practically bisects the 41 square miles included within the corporate limits, courses in a westerly direction through a shallow channel until it reaches Havermale Island, a huge rock just above the falls. Here the stream divides. Beyond the island it swirls through a narrow basaltic channel and tumbles 150 feet in a series of plunges over rocky ledges to the channel below. In summer, when the level of Lake Couer d'Alene, source of the stream, is low, a bare trickle of water is to be seen, but at high water in early spring the falls are a fury of green-white water, foam, and iridescent spray.

Below the falls the stream sweeps in a broad curve between a high, dirt railroad embankment on the right (with a squatters' settlement at its base) and the narrow flat of Peaceful Valley on the left, where unpretentious houses huddle at the base of the precipitous wall of the canyon. Then turning northward, it flows past tree-lined avenues, parks and playgrounds, Fort George Wright, and the Downriver Golf Course, until it passes beyond the northwestern limits of the city. Most impressive of the many bridges crossing the river is the graceful, arched span at Monroe Street.

Running approximately north-south, at the west end of town, is Latah Creek, known locally as Hangman Creek. Here the expansion of the city faltered but did not entirely stop. In the narrow valley are small suburban homes and truck gardens and Highbridge Park; beyond is an area of residences interspersed with grocery stores, garages, and vacant lots. Latah Creek Bridge, an arched concrete structure, spans the canyon.

South of the river is the metropolitan area, an elongated strip centering along Riverside Avenue and bounded by Trent and First Avenues on the north and south respectively, and Division and Monroe Streets on the east and west. In this compact area are the leading hotels, motion picture houses, restaurants, and civic buildings. A few of the more modern office buildings tower above the other business blocks. Along Trent, once the center of the city, are hotels, chop houses, secondhand stores, pawnshops, beer parlors, and pool halls, rescue missions, and employment brokerage offices frequented by men seeking work in mines, fields, and woods, for whom the cryptic messages chalked on the boards often mean the difference between a job with regular meals or a handout in the breadline. Bordering the river is the main industrial district—flour mills, factories, machine shops, bakeries, sawmills, foundries, breweries, hydroelectric plants, and the tracks of the Great Northern and Union Pacific lines. A smaller industrial area lies south of First Avenue; here are the elevated tracks of the Northern Pacific Railway, warehouses, print shops, small factories, and wholesale houses.

Beyond the Northern Pacific tracks, the streets begin to climb gradually. As the grade becomes more pronounced, occasional switchbacks are used to effect the ascent of Cannon Hill, an area of attractive residences set amid spacious grounds, where huge basaltic rocks and towering pines give individuality to the landscaping. Other fine residential districts center around Manitou Park, Cliff Drive, Rockwood Boulevard, Coeur d'Alene Park, and North Hill. Scattered throughout the city are pleasant, middle-class residential districts, where neat lawns and well-painted houses give evidence of the extensiveness of home ownership; more than 57 per cent of the 35,000 homes are the property of those who live in them. Spokane has no well-defined tenement district, but fringing the industrial and commercial areas are nondescript working-class houses, frequently drab and unsightly.

The greater part of the population of Spokane is native born, less than 20 per cent claiming foreign birth. Second-generation national groups are, however, well-represented — Irish, Germans, and Scandinavians in particular, and Italians, Greeks, Scots, and French to a lesser extent. Among racial minorities are 1,000 Negroes, most of whom are engaged in service trades; a few score Chinese in restaurants, laundries, and truck farming; a number of Indians, who wander in and out of the city; and some Japanese. The population on the whole is relatively stable, partly perhaps because the city has drawn to it from surrounding agricultural areas farmers who have disposed of their property or who have turned it over to the management of children or renters. Drifting through the city, however, are thousands of migratory workers, mostly single men, who find seasonal employment in mines and in lumber camps and on the farms.

In the early decades of the nineteenth century, this region, the Inland Empire, was the domain of the Spokane and other Indian bands, whose control was as yet not openly challenged. A few explorers had passed through it, and fur traders of Great Britain and the United States were trickling in, the advance guard of the army of settlers to follow. But these men had no desire to stimulate settlement, for their source of income—fur-bearing animals—depended upon the preservation of the wilderness.

Earliest among the traders and trappers in the country of the Spokane were Finan McDonald and Joco Finlay, who, in 1810, acting under the authority of David Thompson of the North West Fur Company, built Spokane House, about ten miles below the falls, at the junction of the Spokane and Little Spokane Rivers. Two years later, John Clarke, a chief trader of the Pacific Fur Company (John Jacob Astor's corporation), built Fort Spokane not far from Spokane House. A grand opening, to which neighboring Indians as well as trappers and traders were invited, was given to celebrate the completion of the fort. Friendly speeches, the displaying of merchandise, and dancing to the squeaky music of the fiddle marked the first big social event of the Spokane country. For a brief period the Astorians and the Nor' Westers traded side by side.

After the purchase in 1813 of the Pacific Fur Company by the North West Company, the post continued to be a popular meeting place for trading parties, Indians, and company employees. Alexander Ross, describing the social attractions, says, "At Spokane House there were attractive buildings, a ball-room even; and no females in the land so fair to look upon as the nymphs of Spokane; no damsels could dance so gracefully as they; none were so attractive." In 1821 the Hudson's Bay Company absorbed the North West Company, and five years later dismantled Spokane House, removing all equipment to Fort Colvile, which had been established at a point more in line with the usual route of the fur traders.

Again the Spokane country became the undisputed home of the Indian, although fur traders continued to drift through and some marks of the white men's culture remained. Chief Garry, of the Middle and Upper Spokane, who had been sent to the Red River Mission school, returned in 1830 a zealous convert to Presbyterianism. He set about teaching his people how to live according to the precepts of the new religion; and, on the more practical side, how to practice the arts of agriculture. He also built a school, a special lodge of poles covered with mats. Here during the winter months he strove to teach English and religion to his people, although his work was suspended frequently, for attendance was irregular whenever the food supply ran low.

The 1830's saw the coming of the first missionaries to the valley of the Spokane River. In 1835 the Reverend Samuel Parker had surveyed the field for the American Board, representing the Congregational, Presbyterian, and Dutch Reformed churches; three years later Reverend Cushing Eells and Reverend Elkanah Walker established a mission on

Walker's Prairie, about 25 miles northwest of the falls, but no permanent settlers followed them.

The boundary between the United States and Canada having been established in 1846 at the 49th parallel of latitude, the way was cleared for settling the Northwest, or the Oregon Country as the expanse of wilderness was called. The trickle of immigrants rose to hundreds in 1843 and to thousands in 1845. The Indians began to look with suspicion upon the white settlers, their fears, aggravated by other causes, culminating in the Whitman Massacre. One result of this tragedy was the virtual closing to settlement of the country east of the Cascade Mountains and the abandonment of Protestant missionary work in this area; Eells and Walker moved on into the Willamette Valley.

The creation of Washington Territory in 1853 stimulated a renewal of settlement. In 1851, Antoine Plante had established a ferry a few miles above the falls, and in 1853 a man named Pelletier, with the permission of Chief Garry, settled on the Walker-Eells mission site. In the same year, Governor Stevens passed through the country on his way to Olympia and was apparently impressed by the grazing lands and by the agricultural pursuits of Chief Garry and his people. Also in 1853, Francis B. Owens, a cattleman driven out of Montana by the Blackfeet Indians, brought some 600 head of cattle and 500 head of horses to feed in the valley. More settlers continued to come, so that by 1855, when the newly discovered Colville mines brought many adventurers into the region, it was already clear that the days of Indian control were numbered.

Settlement in the immediate vicinity of the falls began in 1871, when J. J. Downing, with his wife and stepdaughter, and S. R. Scranton, two cattlemen from Montana, located claims on the banks of the river. In the next year, Richard M. Benjamin joined them with his family, bought a third interest in the claim for $500, and built a small, water-powered sawmill. A post office was established, with Scranton as the first postmaster, on July 5, 1872. In the fall of the same year, James Nettle Glover and J. N. Matheny arrived from Salem, Oregon, bought Benjamin's share for a few hundred dollars, took an option on the remainder, and then went back to Oregon to seek financial assistance. In 1873 they returned with Cyrus F. Yeaton, bought out Scranton and Downing, and improved the mill and built a small store. Of this store, Glover, years later, wrote: "My store was just across the street and directly west of the city hall. It stood about the center of the block and was a frame building. My first stock was made up of Indian supplies—cheap blankets, calicoes, beads and paints (I did a big business in paints), tobacco, sugar, tea, and coffee, cutlery and all sorts of groceries. I lived in my store building—Mr. Yeaton lived in the rear of the store and Mr. Matheny in a log house on the present site of the Coeur d'Alene hotel. At that time the present business district from the river to the present line of the Northern Pacific tracks was a beautiful prairie of bunch grass and sunflowers." In exchange for the assurance that a flour mill would be built, Glover gave Frederick Post 40 acres of his land.

Quickly the little settlement began to take root. A school district was organized, and in 1875 the Reverend H. T. Cowley, appointed to be the teacher, began holding classes for six pupils in his home. In the same year the Reverend S. G. Havermale preached the first sermon to a white congregation in Glover's store, Mrs. Yeaton playing a small organ she had brought with her. This year also saw the introduction of baseball at a grand centennial celebration of the Fourth of July, settlers from as far north as Canada and as far south as the Snake River joining in the festivities.

In 1877, news that the Nez Percé Indians were on the warpath sent the settlers into a panic. Those within a radius of some 25 miles flocked to the settlement by the falls and sought refuge on Havermale Island. Late in the autumn two companies of soldiers arrived and stayed until the following spring.

On February 13, 1878, the town was officially born, when Glover filed the plat of Spokane Falls in Colville. In the same year J. J. Browne and A. M. Cannon bought half-interest in the townsite from Glover, and soon the first boom was under way. A schoolhouse was built in 1878; the first paper, the *Spokane Times,* was started in 1879 by Francis H. Cook, and the First Congregational and First Methodist churches were organized. By 1879 population had jumped to 75, and by 1880 a village of some 50 houses (mostly one-story board shacks) had grown up on the south bank of the river, centering at Howard Street and Trent Avenue. A tiny rope ferry and two canoes were still the only means of crossing the stream.

Baseball was by this time an established institution. The *Spokane Times,* of July 10, 1879, describes one of the games: "The crowd picked from the survey party and the Spokane Falls club. The surveyers had their choice, and took the field. The Spokans made thirteen runs and then took the field, the surveyors making eight runs before getting out. At the conclusion of this inning the rain began to fall, and the game was called by the umpire, Captain Pease, the score standing, Spokane 13, Surveyors 8. This ended the afternoon's sports."

By this time the town had achieved some degree of permanency and stability, and the townsfolk, now that the problems of food, clothing and shelter were less pressing, could give more time and attention to the cultural aspects of community life. Enrollment in public schools was increasing; in 1881 the foundation for what was to become Gonzaga University was laid. Father J. M. Cataldo, a Jesuit, who had established St. Michael's Mission east of Spokane Falls in 1877, acquired purchase rights for half a section of land from the Northern Pacific Railroad for $2.60. Final title having been acquired, building of the university started in 1884 and was completed in 1886. The school opened in 1887 with an enrollment of eight students.

The first theater, the Globe, opened in 1881, and Joy's Opera House the next year. In 1883 a large rink was erected and, within a short time, was converted into a general community auditorium. This same year was marked by the first outstanding theatrical attraction—the appearance of Emma Abbott in *The Bohemian Girl.* No hall of sufficient size being available, a warehouse was pressed into service. A local paper writing of the performance said: "The audience paid two dollars each for reserved seats on gang plows and farm implements." Nail kegs in the rear were a trifle cheaper. Before the close of the decade two other theaters, the Falls City and the Concordia, had opened.

The optimistic spirit that prevailed sprang to a considerable extent from the approach of the Northern Pacific Railroad. There was much talk of the improvements that would follow the establishment of rail connections and of profits to be made. A. M. Cannon, who had opened a store, became active in real estate and started the first bank. "The N.P. is coming this way," he observed, "and there will be all sorts of checks to cash and I might as well be ready to take care of them." The completion of the western extension of the line from Gold Creek, Montana, to Spokane Falls was accomplished in June 1881. Great was the excitement when the first train puffed in. When the town was incorporated as Spokane Falls, by an act of the territorial legislature on November 29, 1881, it had a population of 1,000. Enclosed within the boundaries of the city limits was an area of approximately one and one-half square miles.

In 1883 the Northern Pacific Railroad was completed through Montana, thus establishing transcontinental mail service. Extravagantly worded notices were circulated widely in the East, publicizing "the luxuries of limitless wealth" that "the manufacturing center of the Great Northwest" offered. So rapidly did the settlement grow that its boundaries were extended in 1883 to enclose four square miles. The *Spokane Falls Review,* May 19, 1883, under the heading "Fresh Industry" said: "New dwellings, new stores, and new manufacturing establishments are springing up like magic, and the end is not yet." The town was definitely emerging from the shack and cabin stage. Four two-story brick "blocks," as these new buildings were called, were the pride of local citizens. The big stampede to the placer camps on the North Fork of the Coeur d'Alene River was on, and every train brought hundreds of men whose imaginations had been fired by stories which in retelling had converted mere prospects into fabulously rich mines. Over all the country was the glamor of gold, and Spokane Falls was the supply point and promotion center. By 1884 at least 1,000 new settlers had arrived; the dusty streets were crowded with rattling stagecoaches and lumbering prairie schooners. Heavily laden freight wagons and strings of pack horses and burros set out almost daily for outlying settlements and mining camps. Miners, lumberjacks, construction workers, and Indians jostled each other on the wooden sidewalks, in stores, and on the dance floors of the local amusement halls. Brawls were a daily occurrence, and not infrequently guns were drawn, occasionally with fatal results.

Less spectacular was the steady progress of agriculture. Every year thousands of additional acres were broken and planted to wheat, and throughout the region small towns sprang up like mushrooms. As farming became profitable, more and more closely did the white settlers press for possession. Sometimes the Indians were merely dispossessed; at other times they received token payments, a second-hand saddle or a few dollars. At the last conference, held in 1887 in a livery stable on Riverside Avenue, a final indignant but unsuccessful protest was made by Chief Garry in behalf of his people.

Population growth was reflected in cultural developments. Newspapers sprang up overnight. Among those that survived for a considerable length of time were the *Spokane Review*, the *News-Democrat*, the *Spokane News*, and the *Spokane Weekly Times*. Three mining journals appeared. The foundation for the library was laid in 1885 by a self-constituted committee of women, who canvassed the town for donations of books. By 1890 seventeen religious denominations had formed congregations and nearly as many churches had been built. Manners and modes of frontier life were passing, and social activity was assuming a more important part in the life of the city. A favorite place for elaborate social functions and for theatrical attractions was Concordia Hall, on Second Avenue west of Monroe Street, a building owned by the Concordia Singing Society, a German organization. Here in 1886, the Bachelor's Ball, social event of that winter's season, was held.

The liveliest, and apparently the most popular and most profitable, form of entertainment was the variety theater. The first of these, the Coeur d'Alene, opened in December 1886, in a tent on the corner of Main Avenue and Howard Street. The entertainers supplemented their stage acts by mingling with customers on the dance floor and at the bars. The *Review* balanced the weights of morality thus: "A variety theater may not add to the moral tone of a city, but it indicates that the place has grown to a size where a regular place of amusement is in demand. Other cities support theaters of this class and Spokane Falls will not stay in the rear of the procession."

On a sultry Sunday evening, August 4, 1889, a fire broke out in an eating house on Railroad Avenue. Fanned by a brisk wind, the flames spread rapidly until the entire section of the city from the Northern Pacific Railway tracks to the river, and from Lincoln to Washington streets, was devastated. The newly installed Holley system of water works was useless, for the only man who knew how to operate it properly had left town on an outing; efforts of voluntary bucket brigades proved futile. The business district, an area comprising 32 blocks, was destroyed, with an estimated loss of $6,000,000. Only one building was standing on Riverside Avenue next morning. No lives were lost, but the city was a mass of blackened ruins. Not missing an issue, the *Chronicle* appeared, printed on borrowed paper as a small sheet; it sold for as much as 75c a copy.

A tent city sprang up, and business was carried on as well as it could be in flimsy shacks. Reconstruction began at once. In rebuilding, the business district was shifted from Front (Trent) Avenue, along the river, to Riverside, two blocks south. Prices of real estate soared, sums up to $1,000 a front foot being paid for lots at the intersection of Howard Street and Riverside Avenue, the new center of the metropolitan area. Within a year more than $4,000,000 were invested in new construction. Nearly 100 business buildings were erected at an average cost of $150,000 each. Railroad and manufacturing interests expanded, new stores opened, and rolling and flour mills more than doubled their output; the assessed value of real and personal property rose to $15,000,000, and population was augmented 50 per cent. Expansion continued at a somewhat slower rate in 1892-3.

Spokane Falls, now well on the way towards city status with a population of almost 30,000, was reincorporated in 1890 under the provisions of the new State constitution, by which home rule was given to cities. In this year the matter of the proper spelling of the name of the town —that is, to spell it with or without the final "e"—was decided, when the council adopted Spokane as the official name instead of Spokane Falls, and further decreed that henceforth Spokane should be spelled with the final "e." The charter, which was adopted by popular vote on March 24, 1891, extended the city limits by adding 16 square miles to the previously designated 4 square miles.

Civic improvements accompanied this expansion. Sewers were laid, street lighting was improved, and bridges were built at Howard and at Division Streets. A crude cable-car line was started in the Fort Wright district. Horsecars gave way to small electric streetcars, which clanked and rocked along on their four wheels. Streets, however, remained unpaved, and perilous was the crossing for ladies during rainy weather. Horse racing continued to be one of the most popular sports, professional baseball was organized in 1890, and tennis, which was introduced in 1892, was rapidly gaining favor. Another newspaper, the *Spokesman,* was established, only to merge with the *Review* in 1893 to form the *Spokesman-Review*. Bicycles were common, although the youth of the city still preferred to ride their mustangs and cayuses. The first automobile appeared in 1900; wise people, who smiled and shook their heads as the flimsy contraption made its faltering way up Cannon Hill, continued to get around in horse-drawn vehicles.

The show business was prosperous throughout the 1890's. In the spring of 1890 a grand opera company presented Emma Jack and Company in *Carmen* and *Faust,* and the *Review* reported: "Never before have the wealth, beauty, and fashion of this fair city turned out in such numbers." Late in the same year a $300,000, five-story auditorium opened with a performance of *Manon*. In 1891 Sarah Bernhardt was paid $3,000 for a single performance. Less respectable were the variety theaters that flourished like weeds after a spring rain. The most notorious was the Coeur d'Alene, with the Comique a runner-up. Local disapproval of this type of entertainment mounted, and, led by local ministers, an aggressive campaign was directed against the variety theaters. An ordinance prohibiting them was passed in 1895, only to be vetoed by the mayor. Soon the town was more wide open than ever; proprietors of shows paraded the streets with bands, followed by their box-rustling ladies in carriages. In 1897 Mayor Olmstead called for the enforcement of regulatory laws. "While I am not a puritan," said the mayor, "I am convinced that vice and immorality have put on too brazen a front . . ." As a result all dance halls and variety shows were closed, but the Coeur d'Alene and the Comique reopened within a few weeks.

One of the best-known and most popular characters of this lusty period was Jimmy Durkin, whose bars, as even his critics conceded, were as unobjectionable as bars can be. Everyone knew and liked this genial, kindly saloon keeper, who boasted that he would cash any check offered to him. He had advertisements to that effect painted on roadside rocks, until a miner brought in a rock one day and asked: "See anything peculiar about that rock, Jimmy?"—"No. I can't say I do," answered Durkin.—"Well," said the miner, "I found that rock 4,000 feet below the surface and it's the only one in this part of the country without your name on it." When denounced by a crusading minister, Durkin promptly offered window space for an antisaloon display. The display only served to attract larger crowds, and the minister admitted defeat in a comment which Durkin had inscribed on his tombstone (ordered some 30 years before his death in 1934): "The minister said, a man of his word."

In 1892, Chief Garry, who had seen his people lose their lands, at first slowly and then at an accelerated pace, died in poverty in his tepee near the mouth of Indian Creek. For years he had been a familiar figure, impressive in spite of his small stature and even when age and drink had altered his proud bearing. Since the loss of his farm, he had led a precarious life. Astride his white horse, he had gone about the streets of the city seeking enough food and clothing to keep his aged, blind wife and himself alive. The funeral services at the Presbyterian Church were attended by many, and the old chief was buried with proper ceremony in an obscure corner of Greenwood Cemetery—and forgotten until 1925. Then his remains were moved to a place of honor near the main entrance, and a tall granite shaft was erected to commemorate this "friend of the white people."

Ever since the advent of the railroad in 1881 a storm had been brewing over exorbitant freight rates. Spokane, although 300 miles nearer the East than coastal cities, was forced to pay a much higher tariff. The Northern Pacific contended that this differential was unavoidable, for the competition of water transportation forced reductions for the long haul. Protests being ineffective, the case was carried to the courts, where the legality of the railroad's action was upheld and relief was denied. In 1892, however, James J. Hill, the Great Northern Railroad magnate, challenging the Northern Pacific monopoly, sought a right-of-way worth $1,000,000. He promised an adjustment of rates and asked in return free passage through the city. A refusal, he implied, would probably necessitate choosing a cheaper route 10 miles to the north, and in such an event, Spokane freight rates would go unchanged. The right-of-way was granted on the terms Hill offered, and for a brief time it seemed that the battle for equitable rates had been won. Then came the panic of 1893; the Northern Pacific passed into the control of Hill, and the promised reduction of tariffs was forgotten. The city had spent nearly $1,000,000 and had gained new railroad connections, but the long-and-short-haul battle was not to be settled for a quarter of a century.

Alternate slumps and booms marked the economic history of the period. The older mining districts were producing fairly steadily by this time, and new mines were opening up in the Coeur d'Alenes and in the Kootenai district in British Columbia. Farms were increasing in number, size, and productivity; villages were becoming small towns, where farmers disposed of produce and purchased supplies. The volume of trade and traffic through Spokane steadily increased. The 1893 depression swept over the city, and business remained in the doldrums until 1895, the completion of the county courthouse marking the beginning of the upswing and the end of widespread unemployment. The strength of the Populist Party, whose banner had been carried locally by *Ryan's Progressive Weekly,* was waning, and in spite of the popularity of William Jennings Bryan and free silver, McKinley's full-dinner-pail slogan was soon to triumph. The century ended with Spokane entering upon a period of unprecedented expansion.

For ten years Spokane prospered and grew, with only short periods of dull business. New silver and lead mines were opened in the Coeur d'Alenes and in lesser mining districts. The rapid development of industries was reflected in extensive building; construction in 1904 alone included three schoolhouses, several churches, a theater, a hospital, the Masonic Temple, a Carnegie library, 10 apartment houses, and numerous smaller buildings and residences. A "city beautiful" campaign resulted in the planting of 80,000 shade trees. Streetcar service was improved, and paving was extended into the residence districts. Downtown streets were crowded with the wagons of farmers, beer trucks drawn by sleek powerful horses, heavy drays, and shiny carriages; interurban lines were being laid to outlying towns, and automobiles were becoming an accepted if not trusted means of travel. Irrigated orchard tracts in the Spokane Valley were producing, and the price of wheat was relatively high. Annually at the Interstate Fair and Livestock Show, the agricultural wealth of the area was displayed to thousands, who flocked to the city from all parts of the Inland Empire. In 1910 building permits totaled an all-time high of $8,766,226, the largest single building being the 15-story Old National Bank, Spokane's first skyscraper.

Throughout these years population was increasing with extraordinary rapidity. Land-hungry emigrants, particularly from Germany, Poland, Russia, and the Scandinavian countries, came in a steady stream. This influx reached its peak in 1909, when the Spokane, Flathead, and Coeur d'Alene Indian reservations were thrown open. More than 250,000 applications were filed within a few weeks. Newcomers were forced to put up tents in outlying districts and on vacant lots, for construction could not keep pace with the demand for housing. From a population of 36,848 in 1900 the city reached 104,402 in 1910.

The Dams

ograph courtesy of The Pioneer *and the Department of Interior*

NIGHT VIEW OF COULEE DAM UNDER CONSTRUCTION

RIGGERS RIDING A HOISTING CABLE HIGH ABOVE WATERS DURING DAM CONSTRUCTION

Photograph courtesy of Department of Interior

WORKMEN ON THE DOWNSTREAM FACE OF DAM IN THE SPILLWAY SECTION

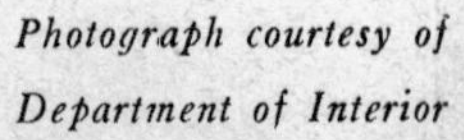

Photograph courtesy of Department of Interior

Photograph courtesy of Department of Interior

GENERAL VIEW OF COULEE DAM, SHOWING CONTRACTOR'S TOW
IN FOREGROUND AND ENGINEER'S TOWN IN BACKGROUN

GRAND COULEE COUNTRY

UPSTREAM FACE AND RESERVOIR, COULEE D.

Photograph courtesy of Department of Interior

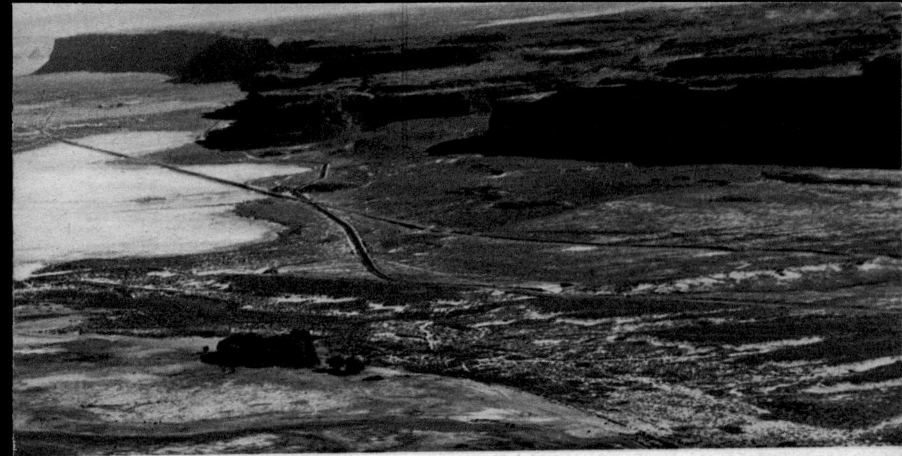

Photograph courtesy of Department of Interior

DWNSTREAM FACE AND POWER HOUSE UNDER
NSTRUCTION, COULEE DAM

Photograph courtesy of Department of Interior

Photograph courtesy Washington State Progress Commissi

BONNEVILLE DAM

otograph courtesy of Puget Sound Power and Light Company

ROCK ISLAND DAM NEAR WENATCHE

ABLO DAM

Credit: Seattle City Light Compan

Photograph courtesy of Department of Inter

ALMON ENTERING ELEVATOR AT ROCK ISLAND DAM

Following this (lift) the salmon are taken to streams below Grand Coulee Dam for spawning

VIEW OF FISHWAY AND CONTROL GATE SPILLWAY F
MIGRATION OF SALMON BY SIDE OF ROCK ISLAND DA

hotograph courtesy of Department of Interior

These years saw the passing of the last surviving element of the convivial frontier mining town. In 1900 the variety theater was still an accepted institution, and proprietors could safely dismiss with little concern the onslaughts of reformers. Thus, in November 1901, during one of the periodic reform waves, "Dutch Jake" Goetz offered the large barroom of the Coeur d'Alene for religious services. Some 400 men gathered there, drawn by curiosity and the lure of the three bars, the gambling house, the variety theater, the café, and the Turkish bath. The account in the morning paper said: "Mingling with the hymns of salvation and the message of religion were the clink of glasses, the maudlin utterances of tipsy men, the noise of shuffling feet, the hurrying to and fro of waiters with calls of 'one stein,' 'one egg sherry,' 'one gin fizz and four cocktails,' 'ham and eggs,' and a score of other phrases of the barroom. During the brief wait for the services to begin, the crowd was entertained with selections on the big mechanical pipe organ, while the electric fountain winked its myriad of electric lights."

Before the end of the decade, the Coeur d'Alene and other "infamous" and "iniquitous" theaters were to darken their doors forever. Early in January 1908, Mayor Moore warned saloonkeepers that the Sunday closing law would be enforced. His warning was ignored. Wholesale arrests followed. When quiet was restored the chastened saloonkeepers had agreed to conform to the law, but on January 11 the Coeur d'Alene, the K.K., and the Comique variety theaters closed. Soon they were merely the subject of reminiscences by aging men, who regretfully wove their way homeward on Saturday nights, lamenting the passing of the good old days.

Prewar years were comparatively quiet, although extension of interurban lines continued, and, as the number of automobiles increased, enthusiasm for good roads mounted. Twinkling lights before moving picture shows flashed the names of Louise Fazenda and Charlie Chaplin in *Tillie's Punctured Romance* and of Lewis Stone and Theda Bara in *The Vampire.* Crowds still flocked to the circuses, the Interstate Fair continued to attract thousands for a week of harvest celebration, and Billy Sunday periodically held forth in a huge canvas tent. In 1913 the State went dry, and Jimmy Durkin and other saloonkeepers closed their doors. A huge electric sign, a bottle from which beer flowed in a stream of twinkling lights, flashed off for the last time—to the regret of every youngster who reveled in the bright surprise of its intermittent flashes.

Much of the activity of Spokane has been bound up with the construction of railroads. In 1908 the third transcontinental line had come into the picture when Robert Edmund Strahorn, acting secretly for E. H. Harriman of the Union Pacific, acquired valuable downtown property and organized the Spokane Union Terminal Project. By 1914 Strahorn effected a junction of the Canadian Pacific, the Union Pacific, and the Chicago, Milwaukee, and St. Paul railroads at the Union Station. In addition to the station, 4,000 feet of bridges costing $7,000,000 were built. Thus Spokane came to have five transcontinental lines. Grade separation of the Northern Pacific Railroad had been under way for some time, and in 1916 the *Spokesman-Review* was able to announce that "regular passenger and freight trains passed over the new elevated railway yesterday for the first time." Two years later the fight over the long-and-short-haul interpretation of railroad tariffs ended, when the United States Supreme Court reversed its earlier decisions favorable to the railroads and supported the rulings of the Interstate Commerce Commission, thus giving Spokane more equitable rates.

The war slump followed the war boom. In 1918 new building dropped to $422,956, the low point of the century. Production of mills and mines was sharply curtailed, and prices of wheat and other farm produce dropped lower and lower. During the twenties, construction revived, the annual investment fluctuating between two and four millions between 1921 and 1929, with a top figure of $5,002,024 in 1928. Thousands of cars were now whizzing along the spiderweb of highways centering in Spokane. Slowly the interurban electric railroads gave way; before the decade closed, almost all lines had been abandoned and tracks had been torn up.

Agricultural prices, however, continued generally low. Farmers found it increasingly difficult to pay interest on mortgages, to buy new cars or farm equipment, or to build new houses and barns. The irrigated tracts in the valley suffered from an inadequate supply of water, low prices, and high freight rates. Thoughtful persons, who looked beneath the surface prosperity of the city and saw the repercussions that inevitably would follow continued depression of agriculture, already were studying the feasibility of a huge dam across the Columbia to furnish power and water for the fertile but arid lands of the Big Bend country.

Black Friday and the gloomy months that followed hit Spokane hard. Already dizzy from the effects of the depression of agriculture, business and industry reeled as banks closed their doors, stores closed or went into voluntary bankruptcy, sawmills ceased to operate, and mines curtailed production when silver and lead prices hit new lows. Bread lines formed, and panhandling on city streets increased. Men stood in front of employment offices hopelessly looking for jobs that did not exist. Hard-pressed businessmen, too, appealed to State and Federal governments for assistance, joining their voices with those of workers and farmers.

In the thirties, conditions slowly began to improve as various relief measures alleviated the most pressing needs. Urban workers found jobs on various Works Progress Administration projects—street and sewer replacements, park and playground improvements, and building and construction work of various kinds. Agriculture, too, improved measurably under the Federal farm program; slowly the price of wheat, which remains the principal farm crop, rose; the prices of eggs, chickens, beef, hogs, and fruit followed. The most important single factor in recovery for Spokane and the Inland Empire has been the construction of Grand Coulee Dam, which has given employment to many thousands.

Spokane today looks forward with some assurance to the next decade. Between 300 and 400 factories employ about 15,000 persons. Included among the city's diversified industries are 3 flour mills, 5 meat packing plants, 23 creameries, 17 bakeries, and 6 poultry plants. Since the repeal of prohibition Spokane has become again a center of the State's brewing industry. In the city and its environs are some of the largest sash and door factories in the United States; 12 plants turn out 1,000,000 units annually, nearly 50 per cent of the Nation's output. The city is also the center of the white-pine match-block industry, about 90 per cent of match blocks being produced in Spokane and its environs. Among other industrial plants are machine shops, railroad shops, small iron and steel works, an oil refinery, and hydroelectric plants.

The whole Inland Empire draws upon Spokane's educational and cultural institutions. In addition to 36 elementary schools, it has 3 public and 2 parochial high schools, 2 junior colleges, 2 denominational colleges, and 1 university. There are more than 100 churches and a number of denominational schools. The townspeople show a strong spontaneous interest in music, literature, and the other arts. The first symphony society was formed in 1920, a second orchestra was organized in 1928, and a little symphony orchestra in 1936. Two singing societies, a little theater, a repertory players group, and the WPA art center are active organizations that show this impulse toward the world of art.

A great recreation area is easily accessible from Spokane, and the long, sunshiny summers are an invitation to vacationing. Scores of lakes are within easy driving distance, and every June sees an exodus of thousands to resort hotels, cabins, and tent cities. The many lakes, open pine forests, and mountain wilderness offer a variety of forms of recreation—swimming, hiking, motorboating, and mountain climbing in summer; hunting for deer, bear, and game birds in fall and spring; and skiing, tobogganing, and skating in winter. The city is also a gateway to Jasper Park and Banff Park, in Canada, and Yellowstone, Glacier, and Rainier national parks.

POINTS OF INTEREST

1. The FEDERAL BUILDING and POST OFFICE, NW. corner Riverside Ave., and Lincoln St., a three-story, gray-stone building of Roman Classic design, was built in 1909 at a cost of $600,000. It houses the Federal Land Office, the offices of several other Government departments, and the United States District and Circuit courts. Wide granite steps, with granite buttresses surmounted by ornamental lamps, lead up to the principal entrance on Riverside Avenue. The main entablature is supported by huge Ionic columns; and above the cornice is a decorative parapet. The main corridor merits special attention, with its marble floors, golden oak panels, and Gothic arches.

2. The CIVIC BUILDING, 1021 Riverside Ave., headquarters of the Spokane Chamber of Commerce and the Inland Automobile Association, is an Italian Renaissance structure with open loggia, designed by Whitehouse and Price, Spokane. In the frieze and decorative panels of the entrance and lobby are symbolized the industries and products of the Inland Empire. It was opened April 17, 1921.

3. The SPOKANE ART CENTER, 106 N. Monroe St., (*open*

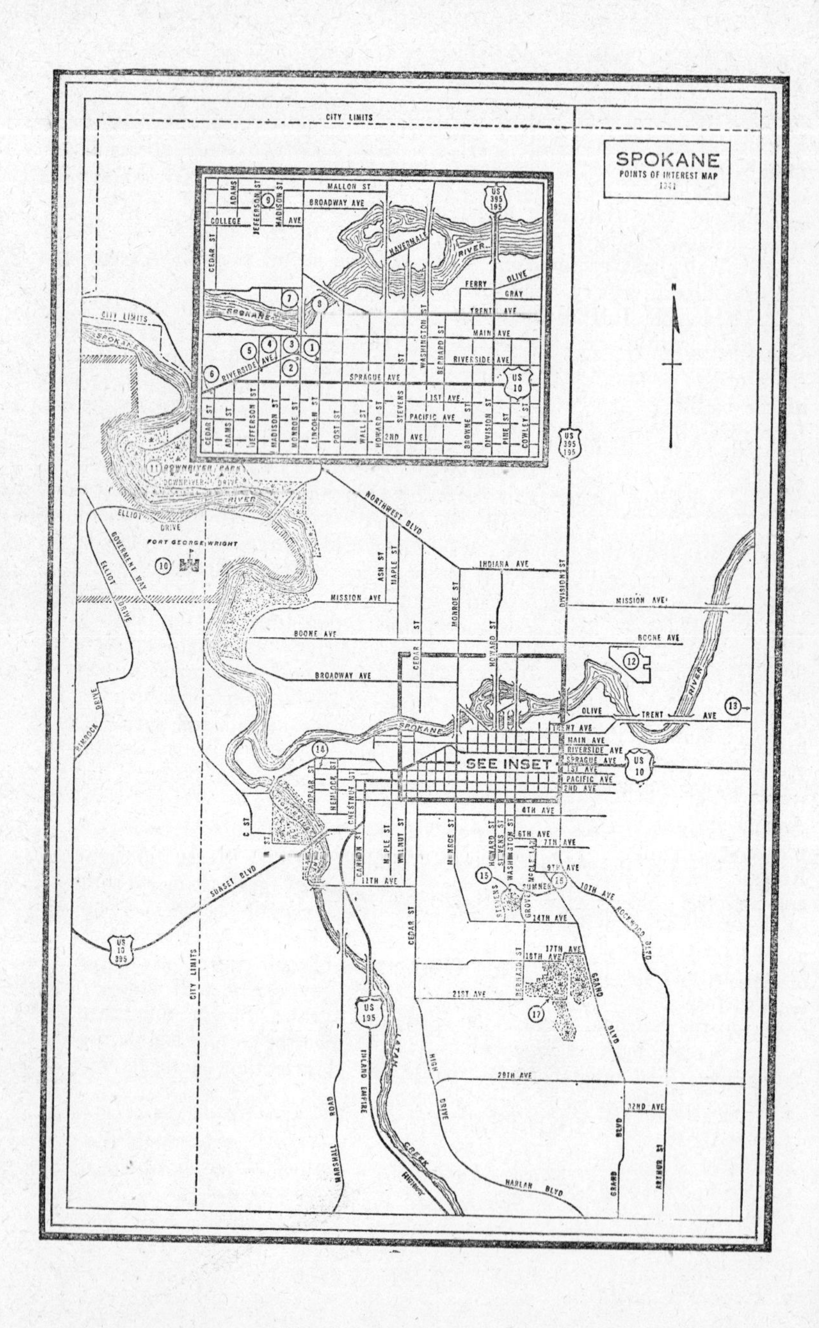
SPOKANE
POINTS OF INTEREST MAP
CITY LIMITS
SEE INSET
MALLON ST
BROADWAY AVE
COLLEGE
AVE
CEDAR ST
ADAMS
JEFFERSON ST
MADISON ST
HAVERMALE
RIVER
SPOKANE
FERRY
OLIVE
GRAY
TRENT AVE
MAIN AVE
RIVERSIDE AVE
SPRAGUE AVE
1ST AVE
PACIFIC AVE
2ND AVE
MONROE ST
LINCOLN ST
POST ST
WALL ST
HOWARD ST
STEVENS
WASHINGTON ST
BERNARD ST
BROWNE ST
DIVISION ST
PINE ST
COWLEY ST
DOWNRIVER PARK
DOWNRIVER DRIVE
ELLIOT DRIVE
FORT GEORGE WRIGHT
GOVERMENT WAY
NORTHWEST BLVD
INDIANA AVE
ASH ST
MAPLE ST
MISSION AVE
BOONE AVE
CEDAR ST
HOWARD ST
DIVISION ST
RIMROCK DRIVE
OLIVE
TRENT
AVE
POPLAR ST
HEMLOCK ST
CHESTNUT ST
C ST
A ST
SUNSET BLVD
4TH AVE
6TH AVE
7TH AVE
9TH AVE
10TH AVE
11TH AVE
14TH AVE
17TH AVE
18TH AVE
21ST AVE
29TH AVE
32ND AVE
CANNON ST
WALNUT ST
SUMNER
GROVE
STEVENS
ROCKWOOD BLVD
GRAND BLVD
HIGH DRIVE
INLAND EMPIRE
MARSHALL ROAD
LATAH CREEK
HARLAN BLVD
ARTHUR ST
US 195
US 10
US 395
N

weekdays except Mon. 10-4; *Sun.* 1-5; *Tues. and Thurs. evening 7 P.M.; free*), first of its kind in the State of Washington and third on the Pacific Coast, was opened in September 1938, by the Federal Art Projects of the Works Progress Administration, acting jointly with community sponsorship. The gallery provides traveling exhibits through a circuit covering the entire country, including more than 50 such galleries established through WPA. The exhibits, usually changed every three weeks, bring to Spokane art from all parts of the Nation.

4. The MASONIC BUILDING (*open 9-5 weekdays, evenings by appointment*), 1108 Riverside Ave., follows the curve of the street, thus giving prominence to its colonnaded facade. Designed by Rigg and Cantyne in the Classical style, it has 18 columns of the Roman-Corinthian order, supporting a stone-railed promenade that extends the length of the building. At both ends of the promenade are stone tripods, and from these, on ceremonial occasions, vapors rise, tinted by colored lights. Busts of Senmut, an Egyptian builder of temples, flank the entrances.

5. OUR LADY OF LOURDES CATHEDRAL, 1115 W. Riverside Ave., opened on Thanksgiving Day, 1908, is the oldest existing Roman Catholic church in the Inland Empire. It is built of granite and brick in Romanesque style, with two square towers at the corners, 164 feet in height, dominating the main facade.

The altars, communion rail, pulpit, and episcopal throne are of Italian marble and Mexican onyx. The woodwork throughout is of quartersawed oak, and the windows of Munich stained glass. The firm of Julian and Williams, architects, designed the cathedral.

6. The SPOKANE PUBLIC LIBRARY (*open 9-9 weekdays*), 18 S. Cedar St., is a four-story brick structure of neoclassic design, built in 1904 through a grant of the Carnegie Foundation. Preusse and Zittel were the architects. The library contains more than 150,000 volumes. Among the exhibits are a page from the Gutenberg Bible, several rare editions of the Bible, and examples of early printing. The NORTHWEST ROOM, a section devoted to regional Americana, contains 5,000 volumes and includes original letters and manuscripts in addition to the journals of early explorers and settlers.

7. The MONROE STREET BRIDGE, completed in 1911 at a cost of $500,000, has one of the largest monolithic concrete arches in the world. The single center span measures 281 feet in length, 71 feet in

---

SPOKANE—POINTS OF INTEREST

1. Federal Bldg. and Post Office
2. Civic Building
3. Art Center
4. Masonic Building
5. Our Lady of Loudres Cathedral
6. Public Library
7. Monroe Street Bridge
8. Spokane Falls
9. County Courthouse
10. Fort George Wright
11. Down River Park
12. Conzaga University
13. Centennial Flouring Mill
14. Public Museum
15. Cliff Park
16. Cathedral of St. John the Evangelist
17. Manito Park & Flower Garden

width, 136 feet in height, and weighs 13,430 tons. Small arches above the main piers carry out the graceful design of the bridge; concrete buffalo skulls are affixed to the sides of the roadway. The structure, designed by city engineers with the firm of Cutter and Malgram as consulting architect, has been cited for its beauty; drawings and plans of the bridge are on exhibit at the Sorbonne, Paris.

8. Near SPOKANE FALLS, between Monroe and Division Sts., where the Spokane River plunges over the rocks in a series of roaring cataracts, the Indians used to pitch their tepees. In flood times the falls seen from Monroe Street are a shimmering, rainbow-tinted tumult of mist and spray, framed by the arch of the Post Street Bridge; here the river cascades over the first drop near the bridge—a fall of some 70 feet—boils over the power company's dam, and swirls down between the abutments of the Monroe Street Bridge.

9. The SPOKANE COUNTY COURTHOUSE, Broadway between Madison and Jefferson Sts., was built in 1895 in modified French Renaissance style; Willis A. Ritchie, the designer of several Washington courthouses, was the architect. A massive square tower with a conical roof surmounts the round-arched main entrance; sharply tapering pinnacles rise above the edge of the tower, the peak of which is 200 feet high. Flanking the central building are two large wings, with minarets at the corners. The fortress-like county jail, surmounted by a parapet, stands at the rear.

10. FORT GEORGE WRIGHT, on Government Way, with the Spokane River on the north, east, and south, established in 1894, was named in honor of Colonel George Wright, whose command camped here after defeating the Indians at the battle of Spokane Plains (*see Tour 1a*). The fort stands on a 1,500-acre plateau overlooking the river, its red and gray buildings surrounded by a wide parade ground and green lawns.

In 1892 Congress was petitioned to approve establishment of the fort, but difficulties in securing land grants and in raising the required $15,000 donation, prevented approval for 2 years. Eleven buildings, to house 5 officers and 70 men, were completed and placed under the command of Captain C. C. Cassieus.

The area has been increased to include 9 miles of river frontage and 8 square miles of reservation. Twenty-four buildings house a hospital, barracks and officers' quarters, radio training schools, stables, post exchange, and guardhouse. The Fourth Infantry, with a total of 29 officers and 580 enlisted men, occupies the fort. The CCC maintains administrative offices here for 20 camps and 2,800 men, and the fort also serves as headquarters for the summer encampment of the C.M.T.C. and as training grounds for the R.O.T.C.

11. DOWN RIVER PARK, Summit Blvd. and Mission Avenue, northward along Spokane River to Euclid Ave., contains more than 93 acres, including the Municipal Golf Course. It is a very popular spot, not only because of the excellent greens, but also because of the picturesque setting. To the west the river swings in a wide arc at the

bottom of a canyon; beyond the river rise pine-covered hills and the ridges along Rimrock Drive.

12. GONZAGA UNIVERSITY, 502 E. Boone Ave., was opened by the Jesuit Fathers in the fall of 1887 with an enrollment of 18 students. The present physical plant of the university includes the main administration building, built in 1889; De Smet Hall, the men's dormitory, named for Father Pierre Jean De Smet, the earliest Jesuit missionary to the Northwest Indians; a football stadium, and gymnasium. The five-story administration building is of buff brick, with granite trim. Of eclectic design, it is adorned with Tudor-Gothic detail and has a towering mansard roof in French Renaissance style.

The GONZAGA MUSEUM (*open by permission of librarian*), fourth floor of the administration building, has sections devoted to numismatics, minerals, ethnological specimens, and a special collection of relics of the early mission days. The most treasured exhibits in the collection are a tree stump used by Father Cataldo at his first outdoor Communion service, the baptismal font of scrap tin used at St. Michael's Mission, founded near Spokane by the Jesuits, and a Bible that once belonged to Father De Smet.

ST. ALOYSIUS CHURCH, designed in the nineties by the firm of Preusse and Zittel, architects, adjoins the administration building on the west. The colonnaded portico, Corinthian columns, and the rose windows in the east and west transepts harmonize with the richly Romanesque style of architecture. The spires on the two corner turrets are 180 feet high and are surmounted by 9-foot crosses, electrically illuminated when special services are held at night.

13. The CENTENNIAL FLOURING MILL (*open daily except Sat. and Sun.* 8-5). between Crestline and Lacey Sts., on E. Trent Road and Broadway Ave., one of the most modern flour-producing mills in the country, occupies an area of 13 acres. The newly erected 10-story plant, constructed of reinforced concrete, is of unusual design, with pilasters ornamenting the spaces between jutted walls. A penthouse extends 80 feet above the uppermost story. Modern machinery capable of producing 3,000 barrels of flour a day has been installed. All types of manufactured feed are produced here, as well as other by-products of grain harvested in the surrounding region.

14. SPOKANE PUBLIC MUSEUM (*open* 1-5 *weekdays,* 2-5 *Sun.; free*), 2316 W. 1st Ave., is maintained by the Eastern Washington State Historical Society in the Grace Campbell Memorial Building, a three-story house in the English half-timbered style, designed by Kirtland K. Cutter. Formerly the house of Mrs. W. W. Powell, the building was dedicated to the memory of Mrs. Powell's mother, a pioneer.

Since its beginning in 1916, the museum has grown from a single six-foot-counter exhibit to an institution of importance, with an average of more than 2,000 visitors a month. Many of the relics on display are of great value. Of special interest to the Northwest are the exhibits in mineralogy, geology, paleontology, conchology, entomology, ornithology, and forestry.

The collections housed on the ground floor include many paintings and etchings, Indian implements, and a variety of mounted fish. Several valuable exhibits are sponsored by the Spokane Art Association. Book collections, relics of pioneer days in the Northwest, Indian pottery and basketry may be seen in other rooms in the museum. An old stagecoach, for 30 years in the passenger and mail service of the Northwest, is an interesting item.

15. CLIFF PARK, 13th Ave., between Stevens and Grove Sts., four and a half acres in area, is located on a rocky bluff overlooking the city. REVIEW ROCK, a huge basaltic mound surrounded by a miniature forest of pine and rare shrubs, is the park's most prominent feature. The rock, a half-acre in extent at its base, is the highest point in the city, and its summit, reached by means of steps cut into the rock on the south side, affords an excellent view.

16. The CATHEDRAL OF ST. JOHN THE EVANGELIST (*Episcopal*), 1125 S. Grand Blvd., was designed in the Gothic style by Whitehouse and Price, architects. Only the main body of the building has been completed. Two towers, terminating in lofty pinnacles, dominate the sandstone structure. On either side above the elaborately carved main entrance arch are triangular spandrels, ornamented with the rose as a symbol of love and the pomegranate for unity; interwoven are the heraldic arms of the missionary district and of the bishop of the diocese. The rose window on the facade is 23 feet in diameter. Other windows, not all of which are yet in place, are fine examples of stained-glass work by Charles J. Connick, Boston.

Oaken doors form the entrance to the narthex. The interior, designed to give full advantage to the curves and proportions of the aisle arches and the clerestory windows, has a lofty blue ceiling ornamented with gold and aluminum. Medallions in the aisle windows illustrate the development of Christianity from apostolic times to the present.

17. MANITO PARK AND FLOWER GARDENS, bounded by Bernard St., Grand Blvd., and 17th and 25th Aves., is the largest and most frequented of the city parks. Oiled and graveled drives circle through the park's 90 acres, leading to playgrounds, tennis courts, a bowling green, and spacious tree-shaded lawns. Lily ponds and small mirror-like lakes dot the natural woodland; in summer wild ducks swim on their surface, and in winter the ponds become small skating rinks.

The CITY NURSERY, which supplies plants for all 49 city parks, is an important feature, and the sunken gardens are much admired. All shrubs and trees common in the locality are to be found here. For the benefit of visitors, many of the flowers are listed by the month when they may be seen in bloom.

POINTS OF INTEREST IN ENVIRONS

Liberty Lake, 17 *m.;* Coulee Dam, 90 *m.* (*see Tour 1a*). Bowl and Pitcher, geologic formation, 2.5 *m.* via Government Way; Deep Creek Canyon, scenic drive, 7 *m.;* and Long Lake, 7 *m.* via Nine Mile Road; Mount Spokane State Park, 37 *m.* (*see Tour 4a*); Geiger Field, United States Army air base, 4.5 *m.*

Tacoma

Railroad Stations: Union Station, 1713 Pacific Ave. for Northern Pacific Ry., Great Northern Ry., and Union Pacific R.R.; Milwaukee Station, 102 E. 25th St., for Chicago, Milwaukee, St. Paul & Pacific R.R.
Bus Stations: Central Terminal, 14th St. and Pacific Ave., for North Coast Line (Greyhound), Grays Harbor Stages, Bremerton Stages, and connections with points N., S., and E.; Croft Hotel, 1519 Pacific Ave., for Ace Stage Co. for points S.; Tacoma Auto Stage Terminal, 8th St. and Pacific Ave., for Independent Dollar Line, Blue Line, Puyallup-Tacoma Transit Co. and Lake Shore Lines; Lewis Hotel, 1522 Pacific Ave., for Benjamin Franklin Lines; Rainier National Park Bureau, 776 Commerce St., for National Park Stages.
Airports: Mueller-Harkins Airport, 8 m., US 99 (charter service).
Piers: Municipal Dock, foot of S. 11th St.; McCormick Terminal, Dock St., for Alaska Transportation Co.
Ferries: Point Defiance Park for Gig Harbor and Vashon Island; west end of 6th Ave. for Fox Island and Point Fosdick; Steilacoom for Anderson Island and Long Branch; 1105 Dock St. for Black Ball Line.
Taxis: One to five passengers 35c first mile, 20c each additional mile.
City Busses: Fare 10c, three tokens for 25c; hour transfers.

Accommodations: 14 hotels; cabin camps available.

Information Service: Chamber of Commerce, S. 11th and A Sts.; Automobile Club of Washington (AAA), 772 Commerce St.; Rainier National Park Bureau, 776 Commerce St.; Winthrop Hotel, S. 9th St. and Broadway.

Theaters and Motion Picture Houses: Little Theater, 210 N. I St., stage productions: Temple Theater, 2nd St. and St. Helens Ave., occasional stage productions; 15 motion picture houses.
Radio Stations: KMO (1360 kc.); KVI (570 kc.).
Athletics: Stadium, N. 2nd and E Sts., Lincoln Bowl, S. 34th and G Sts.
Golf: Allenmore Golf Course, S. 24th and Cedar Sts., 18 holes, 60c and $1; Highland Golf Course, 1302 N. Vassault, 18 holes, 35c; others on the outskirts of the city.
Tennis: Municipal courts at all playfields and at Point Defiance and Lincoln Parks; free.
Swimming: YMCA, 714 Market St., 25c; YWCA, 401 Broadway, adults 25c, children 15c; Titlow Beach, municipal salt water lagoon, west end of 6th Ave.; free.
Yachting: Tacoma Yacht Club, Point Defiance Park.
Riding: Seven riding stables and academies with average rates of 75c first hour, 50c each additional hour.
Hunting and Fishing: Hunting in Cascade foothills and on Olympic Peninsula; good fishing in Puget Sound and near-by lakes and streams.
Baseball and Football: Athletic Park, 15th and Sprague Sts.; Lincoln Bowl, S. 34th and G Sts.

Annual Events: Seattle-Tacoma Yacht Cruise, Jan. 1; Woodbrook Hunt Club's New Year's Hunt; Salmon Fishing Derby Opens, 1st week in Mar.; Salmon Fishing Derby Finals, Point Defiance, 2nd Sun. in June; Rose Show, Scottish Rite Cathedral, June; Pacific Northwest Tennis Tournament, 3rd week in July;

Fleet week, July or Aug.; **Pacific Northwest Power Boat Races, 3rd week in Aug.**; Dahlia Show, 2nd week in Sept.; Northwest Army-Navy Football Game, Stadium, Armistice Day.

TACOMA (21 alt., 109,408 pop.), lying along the protected waters of Puget Sound and Commencement Bay, into which the Puyallup River drains, is about midway between Seattle to the north and Olympia to the southwest. Commencement Bay, a fine natural harbor on the Sound, is recognized as one of the country's leading ports. Few cities may boast a more beautiful setting. To the west is the sweep of Puget Sound with wooded bluffs rising from the water's edge, and far to the northwest are the Olympic Mountains, visible in clear weather, a soft line in the haze of summer, a clear-cut jagged ridge in winter. On the landward side are the flats of the Puyallup River, the semi-wooded farming area stretching eastward to the foothills, and prairies with patches of woodland. Marking the eastern horizon are the Cascade Mountains, and looming majestically to the southeast is the snow-capped, truncated cone of Mount Rainier—serenely beautiful in midsummer, mysterious when half-shrouded in the gray mists of autumn, and unforgettable if seen at sunset of a clear midwinter day, suffused with an alpine glow that slowly gives way to blue shadows, which creep up the long snowy sides with the sinking of the sun.

Along the bay and on the flats are sawmills, factories for lumber products, railroad shops and other industrial establishments, including two important electrochemical plants. Railroad tracks are lined with freight cars and noisy switch engines. The acrid odor of coal smoke and the penetrating smell of tideflats mingle with the resinous fragrance from piles of newly cut lumber. Beyond the sluggish river, smoke rises from burning piles of refuse. Sometimes the air is heavy with the biting, choking smell of sulphur from the pulp mills. To the northwest is the towering smokestack of the Tacoma Smelter, one of the two highest stacks in the world and visible for miles, with its drifting trail of light, lemon-colored smoke. The smelter is operated by the American Smelting and Refining Company in the little town of Ruston, at the edge of Point Defiance Park. Steamships from all parts of the world are busily loading and unloading cargo; puffing tugs with tows of logs, slow freighters, and small pleasure craft and fishing smacks, manned by European fishermen, dot the bay. Gulls wheel on flashing white wings or perch on floating logs, old pilings, or dock roofs, on the alert for refuse dumped from the galleys of passing steamers. Always the tang of salt water is in the air, redolent of seaweed on hot summer days, or sharp and fresh when a brisk wind sweeps inland from Puget Sound. It is not easy for the pedestrian to get an impression of the Tacoma water front as a whole; but Bayside Drive, following along the edge of Commencement Bay, permits a good over-all view of the harbor itself, the numerous docks, with an occasional freighter moored alongside, the fishermen's docks and small fishing craft; and across, almost at a right angle with the drive, may be seen the Port of Tacoma piers and the terminals and piers owned by the various railroads and industrial concerns.

Rising above the industrial area of the water front is the business district, with modern department stores, hotels, apartment houses, and lofty office buildings alternating with middle-aged structures and dingy shops, second-class hotels, second-hand stores, and chop houses. North, west, and south from the city center, wide boulevards and streets ascend steep hills to a broad plateau, given over to residence districts and community retail centers. Quite justifiably Tacomans are proud of the fine residential sections, notably the north end of the city, on and beyond Prospect Hill, with beautiful modern estates and occasional old-fashioned mansions, dated by hitching posts and mounting blocks. Other attractive residence districts, with clean streets, neat lawns and comfortable houses, are scattered throughout the city. Beautiful, too, are the broad tree-lined streets and the parks, some comprising many acres of shaded lawns and gorgeous flower beds. But Tacoma, like all modern cities, has its slums—dingy old buildings converted into rooming houses, squalid unsanitary shacks, and crowded, cheap hotels.

The people of Tacoma are on the whole a stable population; more than 50 per cent own their own homes, and local pride and interest are strong. About one-fifth of the townspeople are foreign born, and many more are the children of foreign born, representing a variety of ethnic groups. Scandinavians, Germans, and Irish are numerically and culturally important, contributing to the industrial and intellectual life of the entire city. The Swiss and American-born Swiss, a small but active group, have their own societies, wrestling and other clubs, and social hall. The Croatians form a large group, especially in the section now known as Old Town; they work in the smelter and fisheries and are commonly seen in their small fishing smacks. The Poles are another important element in the population; St. Peter's Roman Catholic Church has an entirely Polish congregation, and parts of the services are read in that language. About 700 or 800 Negroes live in Tacoma; many work in the smelter and as employees of the city, and a fair proportion have entered the professions. Indians from Muckleshoot Reservation are often seen in the streets of Tacoma, but the majority live outside the town. Many Filipinos, Chinese, and Japanese are found in the service trades. Truck gardening is a favorite occupation also with the Oriental people, and they peddle their fresh and brightly colored produce about the streets.

The city has approximately 50 churches, representing virtually all the great religions, and among them are many of architectural interest. The oldest is St. Peter's Episcopal Church, a simple frame structure built in 1873; at that time a bell was contributed by St. Peter's in Philadelphia, brought around Cape Horn, and placed in a bell tower made by topping a small fir tree; the improvised tower served for many years, and the bell is still in use. Holy Communion Church, on South I Street, is one of the larger Episcopal congregations today. Roman Catholic churches include the beautiful Holy Rosary Church on Tacoma Avenue and Saint Patrick's Church. The Church of the Immaculate Conception, built near Fort Steilacoom in the early 1850's, was moved to Steilacoom in 1867 and is still in regular use. Old Saint Leo's Catholic Church, which burned in 1921, was built, so it is said, as an auditorium for William Jennings Bryan in 1896. The small Presbyterian Church on 14th Street, built of Tenino sandstone, is one of the finest architecturally in the city. The other Protestant denominations are well represented; among the larger edifices are the First Congregational Church, a Gothic building of smooth-cut sandstone, Central Lutheran Church, First Baptist Church, Immanuel Presbyterian Church, and Unity Temple. The Talmud Torah Synagogue, built in 1925, is an impressive brick and stucco structure. One of the more unusual churches is the Hong Wanji Buddhist Temple, a simple red-brick building, with a lavishly decorated, pagoda-shaped altar within; here Sunya Pratt, said to be the first white Buddhist priestess in the United States, was ordained.

Tacoma is about 70 years old. The earliest recorded exploration of the area was made by Captain George Vancouver, who in 1792 sailed his ship up the Sound and named the magnificent mountain peak Rainier, in honor of Peter Rainier, later an admiral in the British Navy. Another early explorer was Lieutenant Cadwalader Ringgold of the Wilkes Expedition, who on May 15, 1841, at the beginning of his surveys, charted and named Commencement Bay.

During the nineteenth century the westward march of pioneers, hungry for land, for independence, and for freedom from heavy taxes and high interest rates, had moved steadily forward, halted neither by the Indians nor by forests, swamps, mountains, or deserts. Some of the newcomers, after following the Oregon Trail to its western terminus in the Willamette Valley, crossed the Columbia and pushed northward through trackless forests. Others made their way by a more northerly route through the Cascade Mountains, and still others made the perilous trip around the Horn. In 1853 the first ox-train, consisting of 29 wagons, struggled through the Naches Pass by a route so difficult that, at one point, the emigrants were forced to kill steers and cut strips of hides to use as ropes to lower the wagons down a precipice. Some of these hardy adventurers, both family groups and single men, settled about Parkland.

One of the early settlers was Nicholas De Lin, a Swede, who arrived on April 1, 1852, and who shortly thereafter started the first industrial development of the new settlement. With the assistance of a few friends, he cleared land near the end of Gallagher's Gulch, at the junction of two creeks, and built a small sawmill. Soon he was cutting lumber with a water-driven saw, the mill being capable of cutting 2,000 board feet a day, if conditions were favorable for maximum production. It is reported that curious Indians had to be pushed away so that the men could work. Within a year De Lin shipped a cargo of 550,000 board feet of lumber to San Francisco on the brig *George Emory,* which had waited several months for this first cargo.

The Indian uprising in the White River Valley and other areas in 1855 checked the growth of the small community for a short time. Local Indians had been friendly and peaceful, but when one day a small boy of the community came scurrying to report strange goings on in the longhouse—Indians from across the mountains, excited speeches, a war dance, and a whispered warning from an Indian lad, *"Klat-a-wa'"* ("Go hence!")—the little band of settlers hurriedly loaded a scow and, under cover of darkness, made their way to Fort Steilacoom. It was not long, however, before the Indian hostilities were terminated, and the Commencement Bay band was persuaded, as were other groups, to retire to a reservation and to leave the shores of the bay to the white settlers.

Immediately thereafter, De Lin with his family returned and worked his little mill until 1861, when he sold it and moved to Portland. Job Carr, in 1864, homesteaded land on a site called by the Indians Chebaulip, now Old Town. An interesting man was Job Carr, and a most unusual pioneer, who neither smoked, chewed, nor drank, and who insisted on wearing a wig even in this wilderness. If we can believe accounts, his most emphatic exclamation was, "Well, I'll be consarned." Upon his claim he built a fine cabin for himself and his children; this has been moved to Point Defiance Park, a memento of log-cabin days.

But much of the credit for promoting the settlement should go to General Morton Matthew McCarver, one of those who followed the pioneers westward and made a business of staking out tracts in the wilderness, giving names to nonexistent streets and selling "cities" to land-hungry people. Having heard of Chebaulip from De Lin in Portland, and seeing the advantage of holding title to lands that would be needed as terminus for the Northern Pacific Railway, McCarver traveled to Commencement Bay, looked the site over, bought Job Carr's homestead, and with partners acquired additional land. Then having renamed the settlement Tacoma, he proceeded to boost it as a town with a future. Almost at once the settlers responded to the enthusiastic promotion of McCarver and his associates.

A factor of considerable importance was the revival of the lumbering interest. In 1869 a group of San Francisco businessmen had sent a scout north to look for a mill site; and as a result of his report on the Tacoma location, "the best I've seen," the Hanson and Ackerman Mill was constructed. This started Tacoma toward its future as the lumber capital of the world. Moreover, the advent of the mill started a small-scale boom. Construction workers were followed by mill hands, loggers, shopkeepers, mechanics, bartenders, many bringing their wives and families with them. The village now became a regular port of call for the mail steamer, which heretofore had passed it by; telegraph connections were obtained; and the first electric lights on Puget Sound flickered at the mill. Other building was stimulated by the advent of the mill and the influx of settlers in search of jobs. So sudden and so great was the increase in business that a distinct shortage of currency occurred, and to meet this emergency the Hanson and Ackerman Company issued hammered-metal discs and rectangles to be used locally as a medium of exchange. These circulated briskly and served as a usable means of exchanging goods and services.

During the seventies Tacoma began to develop its community activities. In 1870 the name of the town appeared for the first time on a map of the State issued by Hazard Stevens. At about the same time the post office was moved from its inadequate quarters in Job Carr's cabin to the mill office, and the jail, which had been housed in a livery stable, was transferred to a building constructed of two-by-four scantlings for the special purpose of detention of lawbreakers. St. Peter's Church, which claimed to have the oldest bell tower in the United States—a 500-year-old tree trunk—was built in 1873. A hotel and a saloon were opened; it is said the "swearing Deacon," regularly on Sunday nights, put his head over the swinging doors and shouted, "I want every damn one of you to come to church tonight; and you'll each put fifty cents in the collection plate."

The year 1873 was a red-letter one in Tacoma history. On July 14, McCarver, who had clung to his idea that the Northern Pacific Railway would select the town for its terminus, and who had therefore continued to buy up land as a speculation venture until he held some 2,000 acres, received a telegram announcing the selection of Tacoma for the terminus. Great was the excitement of the town's 200 inhabitants, even though it was soon revealed that the railroad had decided to locate about a mile and a half south of the town. Thus was New Tacoma started among stumps and logs; but within a short time, before the rails were laid into town, a Steilacoom paper could write: "Three new stores, one blacksmith shop, and legions of whiskey mills have sprung into existence in Tacoma since the location of the terminus, and are in full blast. The Johnson Bros., of Seattle, have moved their extensive stock up here; and in a few days the firm of Hoffman and Frost, of Olympia, will move hitherward their tin and hardware establishment." The Pierce County Commissioners authorized the formation of a city government; Thomas Prosch brought the *Pacific Tribune* from Olympia to Old Tacoma; a doctor came to town, a drugstore was started, more and bigger ships came into the bay, and the first postmaster of New Tacoma, W. H. Fife, was appointed.

But 1873 was the year of a panic, whose waves swept westward as far as the village on Commencement Bay. Construction of the Northern Pacific Railway stopped 20 miles south of Tacoma, when the crash swept away most of the investment funds held by Jay Cooke and fellow promoters. The company's contract with the Government called for completion of the line before the end of the year 1873, and to fulfill the contract the 250 white workers and 750 Chinese were called upon to continue work in spite of the fact that a sum of some $10,000 in back wages was due them. They refused to work. When threatened they threw up barricades and said, "Nobody moves this train until we get paid." The men were paid, and on December 16, 1873, the western end of the line from Kalama to Tacoma was completed. The event was celebrated with much speech making, and in the evening, when the train pulled out with its first load of passengers, furs, and fish, Indians stood in awe of the *hiu chick chick.*

Tacoma now began to draw upon the rich resources of the area. Industrial development was stimulated by the advent of the railway, and increased profits made new financing comparatively simple. Coal mines were opened up at Wilkeson in 1875, and after the completion of a spur railroad line in 1878, between 100 and 150 tons of coal were mined daily. Giant coal bunkers were built along the bayside, Tacoma becoming the most important coaling station on the Pacific Coast. Logging operations moved farther into the woods, and the drone of sawmills became a familiar sound. A flour mill, a salmon cannery, and machine shops were established. Population grew, and soon the little cluster of scattered houses became a compact settlement, with a seminary, several churches, more than a score of saloons, a chamber of commerce, and a combine of workers under the banner of the Knights of Labor. Cultural activities also flourished; the first literary society was organized with R. A. Chilberg as president, additional newspapers appeared, and a branch of the YMCA was established. Finally, in 1884, Old Tacoma and New Tacoma were consolidated with a total population of about 4,400, and late in the same year New Tacoma was officially recognized as Tacoma.

The early eighties were marked by unemployment; the completion of construction work on the railroad had thrown many out of work, and here as elsewhere there was at times a surplus of workers, who were coming in increasing numbers to the new country. The rising dissatisfaction among the workers was sharpened by the preference of some employers for cheap Chinese labor. White workers objected and turned upon the Chinese, mistakenly holding them responsible for the situation. The widespread feeling crystallized in the organization of the Law and Order League, which on November 5, 1885, forcibly deported the Chinese "without disorder." Later 27 citizens, including some city officials, were brought to trial on charges of participating in the incident, but were acquitted.

The next few years were marked by considerable expansion. Speedier and less costly connections with Eastern and Middle Western buyers were sought by leading townsmen. Served only by a spur from the Northern Pacific Railway's new terminus at Portland, the city set out to get direct transcontinental connections. In 1886 work was started on the Stampede Pass Tunnel, over which it was planned to project tracks for a connection with the eastern section of the Nation. Meanwhile, a switchback had been built over the summit of the Cascade Range, and the first train to travel this temporary route reached Tacoma on June 6, 1887. Inauguration of direct transcontinental service on July 3 fulfilled hopes born 20 years before; Tacomans celebrated with three days of revelry.

The new rail tie-up resulted in a phenomenal growth of Tacoma enterprise. The lumber industry was advancing in seven-league boots, production figures soaring to 87,000,000 board feet for the year 1887. Technological improvements swelled the output, the railroads not only furnishing access to new markets but also using thousands of ties. The

St. Paul and Tacoma Company was organized; it purchased some 80,000 acres of timberland and started to turn out lumber on a large scale. Eastern Washington wheat, which previously had been shipped through Portland, was brought to Tacoma for milling and shipment to Pacific Coast ports; flour mills, warehouses, and grain elevators appeared as if by magic upon the reclaimed tideflats; a smelter was built, new docks were constructed, and steamships and sailing vessels in increasing numbers made Tacoma a regular port of call. The mines shipped more than 212,000 tons of coal during the autumn of 1887. Rail transportation was further improved the following year by the completion of the Stampede Pass Tunnel and the Northern Pacific's establishment of general offices in Tacoma.

People flocked into what they envisaged as the coming metropolis. Between 1885 and 1890, the population increased from less than 7,000 to 36,000, and the city found it necessary to improvise shelter for the newcomers. Real-estate prices soared, and speculation was rife. During the fall of 1887, some 1,200 children crowded the schools. The Annie Wright Seminary, a private preparatory school for girls, was founded in 1884. (Present building was erected in 1925). Stores and offices multiplied on the slopes; 1,016 buildings were constructed in 1888, and the cornerstone was laid for the College of Puget Sound. Most pretentious of the new buildings was the Tacoma Hotel, designed by Stanford White, which was completed at a cost of $267,000.

As in other towns marked by rapid growth and easy money, Tacoma had its dives and its honky-tonks. One of the most famous was Harry Morgan's Gambling House and Comique Theater, with bar, dance hall, and variety of methods for separating a drink-befuddled customer from his money. An underground passage to the water front was reputedly used for smuggling narcotics and shanghaiing sailors, or for quick getaways when trouble threatened. Morgan, shrewd and ruthless, controlled local politics for several years.

Tacoma politics were lively during these days, with much concern over vice and gambling and much personal rivalry. Other issues were also debated with considerable heat. The Union Labor Party appeared and split upon the question of whether its platform should advocate anarchism or socialism. Conservative Democrats and Republicans joined forces to defeat the Union Labor Party, whose platform included among other proposals a demand for public ownership of street railways, water works, power, and ferries and the right to recall public officials. The labor party was defeated in 1888, after a violent campaign, but today many of the measures it stood for are in operation.

Tacoma was on the way toward outshining all other Puget Sound ports, when the crash came in 1893. Of 28 banks only 7 survived. "The commercial universe seemed to be but a house of cards," wrote a local historian. Townspeople "picked blackberries, sawed wood, and dug clams for a livelihood," and building owners became janitors. The Tacoma Trades Council held unemployed demonstrations, a detachment of 600 men marched out of town to join Coxey's Army on its march on Washington, and a Pierce County Farmers' Alliance sent delegates to the Populist Party Convention at Ellensburg. Although panic had a sobering effect on the expansion of industry, factories of various kinds, foundries, machine shops, and many small enterprises were established during the nineties, and the town still looked hopefully towards the future. Observing the Northern Pacific's profitable tie-up with Tacoma, the Great Northern and the Union Pacific extended competing lines to the city. The Northern Pacific established repair shops at Edison, now South Tacoma.

The discovery of gold in Alaska put an end to the crisis, and for a short time the future again was rosy. Then Tacoma slowly began to lose ground. The Great Northern Railway acquired control of the Northern Pacific, the Oriental Line was given up, the grain export market was shifted to Seattle; oil replaced coal as fuel for ships, and the coal bunkers were idle. Except for an occasional boat coming to the smelter, the Alaska trade had vanished. Small logging camps and sawmills slowly gave way to large timber interests, backed by Eastern capital.

The citizens of Tacoma were dumbfounded but not ready to admit that their plans for the future had been mere dreams. Agitation for a port commission with provision for modern, municipally owned docks properly equipped and open to shipments at reasonable charges, finally was successful; and the establishment of the Port of Tacoma piers brought some revival of trade. Neighborhood improvement clubs and civic-minded individuals successfully worked for city water works and city power system. These and other measures regained for Tacoma some of the lost ground. The First World War boom in shipbuilding and trade, and the activity resulting from the proximity of Fort Lewis, brought considerable increase in business and industrial development.

With this upswing in business came a tremendous rise in the cost of living. This condition stimulated widespread unionization among the workers, which was climaxed in the first year of the war by the general Northwest lumber strike. The agreement that ended the strike in Tacoma granted the eight-hour day and other improved conditions. Again in January 1919, during the Puget Sound shipyard strike involving 40,000 men, 14,000 struck in Tacoma. Some concessions were granted, the strike was called off, and the men went back to work.

The years following the war were marked by general disillusionment; the number of unemployed grew, and times were hard. The Farmer-Labor Party was organized in Tacoma and the State in 1921, and during this period the feeling for industrial unionism grew. So militant did Tacoma labor become that Samuel Gompers, national president of the American Federation of Labor, threatened to withdraw the charter of the Tacoma Central Labor Council. This threat and the fact that the Coolidge boom was under way brought a decline in the labor movement; the wood-working unions all but ceased to exist.

During these years Tacoma once more stirred with intense activity. The blackboard room in the Rust Building was crowded with speculators, $4,000,000 in new industry located in the city, ships lined the

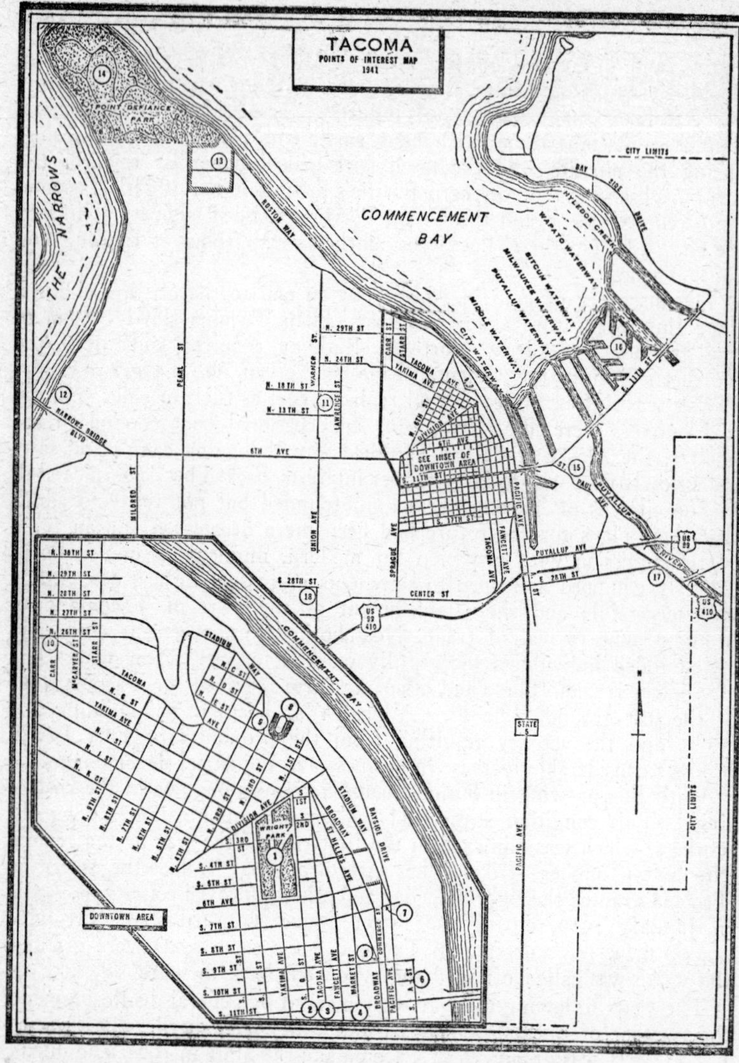

TACOMA—POINTS OF INTEREST

1. Wright Park
2. Pierce County Courthouse
3. Public Library 4. Pub. Mkt.
5. Tacoma Theatre Building
6. Totem Pole 7. City Hall
8. Stadium High School
9. State Hist. Society Museum
10. Chinese Museum
11. College of Puget Sound
12. Narrows Bridge
13. Tacoma Smelter
14. Point Defiance Park
15. St. P. and Tacoma Lbr. Plant
16. Port of Tacoma
17. Indian Sanatorium
18. Water Department Shops

wharves, and the stores were doing a rushing business. Bobbed hair, short skirts, prohibition, bootleg liquor, marathons, flagpole sitters, the Charleston, the new Ford, the talkies, installment buying—a dizzy succession of changes blinded most people to the day of reckoning which was coming, a day forecast in growing unemployment and a nervous, speculative market.

Then came 1929 and Black Friday, followed by the years of steadily deepening depression. Tacoma was hard hit. Both lumbering and shipping went into a slump, and, unlike previous depressions when the construction of a railroad, the Alaska gold rush, and the World War had pulled the city out, this depression persisted. "Help Wanted" signs disappeared, and armies of unemployed began a desperate search for jobs. Self-help movements—communal gardening, woodcutting, collective begging—were instituted. Then the city slowly began to revive as the national deflationary trend was halted. The demand for lumber increased and prices rose. Some of the unemployed went back to work, and others received a measure of subsistence from direct relief or from jobs created by the Works Progress Administration.

Tacoma achieved a measure of recovery. Today it is a regular port of call for several steamship lines; it has a water front with 67 piers and wharves (according to 1938 report of War Department), the largest of which is owned by the Port of Tacoma; it has a municipally owned power plant, which distributes electricity at one of the lowest rates in the United States; it has a fine school system, many churches of various denominations, excellent hospital facilities, and many social and cultural clubs; it has beautiful parks and golf courses, and lies within easy distance of a great outdoor playground. The hopes of the booming nineties have faded; but the "City of Destiny" has re-adjusted itself to the slower pace, as it sees more clearly how its future is bound up with the State and the Nation.

According to the 1938 report prepared by the Board of Engineers of the War Department and the United States Maritime Commission, the volume of water-borne commerce during the period 1925-36 averaged 3,876,491 short tons a year; of the port's total traffic, nearly 78 per cent was accounted for by coastwise shipments and receipts and local traffic (26 per cent), with the lumber industry comprising by far the greater part. The report concludes as follows:

"It seems only reasonable to expect that with the greatly improved terminals and the steadily increasing traffic, the port will become a more important gateway not only to the port area and its immediate hinterland but also to the entire country served by the northern railroad systems.

"With its present and proposed equipment, its railroad facilities, and its increasing commerce, it is believed that the port will become a more important factor in the development of the commerce of the country."

POINTS OF INTEREST

1. WRIGHT PARK, bounded by S. G and S. I Sts. and 6th and Division Aves., is a 27-acre tract of pastoral calm and beauty near the

center of the city. No automobiles are allowed in the park, but parking is permitted on all adjoining streets. A rustic bridge across twin lagoons, where swans float serenely, and winding and shady paths lead from the lagoons to all parts of the park. The arboretum, one of the largest in the State and one of the oldest in the country, contains about 1,200 trees, including more than 300 varieties of native and foreign trees, shrubs, and subtropical plants. A marker gives the history and habitat of each specimen. Near the Yakima entrance to the park are playgrounds, horseshoe courts, and a wading pool. A CONSERVATORY (*open 8-4:30; adm. free*), fronting S. G St., the gift of W. W. Seymour, former Mayor of Tacoma, houses a large variety of palms, orchids, and other rare and exotic plants.

2. The PIERCE COUNTY COURTHOUSE, corner 11th and S. G Sts., a five-story structure of gray Wilkeson and Tenino sandstone, was begun in 1890 and completed in 1893. Architecturally it is an adaptation of the Richardsonian Romanesque style, following a design by Proctor and Dennis, of Tacoma. The main tower, 30 feet square and rising 230 feet to the top of its finials, is faced with an illuminated four-dial clock.

3. The TACOMA PUBLIC LIBRARY (*open 9-9 weekdays*), 1120 Tacoma Ave., organized in 1886, is housed in a brick building in the French Renaissance style, erected in 1903 with the aid of Carnegie funds; Jardine, Kent and Jardine, of New York, were the architects. The library has approximately 145,000 volumes, including a special collection on forest products, lumber, and wood pulp and another on the history of Tacoma and the Northwest. A loan collection of 55,000 mounted pictures is maintained.

4. The PUBLIC MARKETS, Market St. between 11th and 13th Sts., unlike the public market maintained in Seattle, are under private ownership entirely. On both sides of the street lessees operate well-kept, sanitary stalls, booths, and stores; and here, as in other coastal cities, may be heard the cries of Oriental and European hucksters and salesmen. Berries from Vashon Island, fruit from the orchards of Puyallup Valley, poultry products from the Brookdale district, fish from Gig Harbor and other points on the sound and from the deep sea, all are to be found in the market place. Fresh green vegetables are brought in every day from the many truck farms in the surrounding agricultural area.

5. The TACOMA THEATER BUILDING, corner 9th St. and Broadway Ave., was designed by Stanford White in the manner of a Norman chateau. Of red brick with white trim and slate roof, it was completed in 1890. It is used now as an office building and motion picture theater, but in its early days many famous artists and lecturers were presented here: Sarah Bernhardt, Henry Irving, Joseph Jefferson, Richard Mansfield, E. H. Sothern, and Maude Adams; Bill Nye, George Francis Train, and Mark Twain.

6. The TOTEM POLE, at 10th and A Sts., is 76 feet high and was carved in Tacoma by Indian sculptors brought from Alaska, since the removal of genuine Alaskan totem poles from the jurisdiction of the

tribe is not permitted. The pole was presented to the city in 1903 by Chester Thorne and W. T. Sheard. According to the plaque at the base of the pole, the figures, from top to bottom, form an impressive record of the tribal succession, glorifying the Eagle Clan of the North.

7. The CITY HALL, S. 7th St. between Pacific Ave. and Commerce St., designed by Heatherton and McIntosh, local architects, is an adaptation of the Italian town hall. The attached campanile, instead of tower bells, has a chiming clock with four dials.

8. The STADIUM HIGH SCHOOL, 111 N. E St., occupies a high bluff overlooking Commencement Bay. First built as a hotel by the Northern Pacific Railroad, the building was converted into a school in 1906, after the interior had been burned out. The structure, designed by Frederick Heath, is a fine example of early French Renaissance architecture, somewhat reminiscent of the Castle of Blois in France. The front step, a slab 20 feet long, 6 feet wide, and 16 inches deep, was cut from a granite boulder found near Fern Hill.

Immediately adjoining the high school on the NW. is the STADIUM. Once a wooded gulch, now a great classical amphitheater, it is a beauty spot on the Tacoma shoreline. The bowl, with the grassy slopes above, accommodates 40,000 spectators. General Morton Matthew McCarver, who came to Tacoma from Oregon in 1868, built his first home, a log cabin, on the site now occupied by the Stadium, nearest the present State Historical Society Building.

9. The WASHINGTON STATE HISTORICAL SOCIETY MUSEUM (*open 9-5 weekdays; 2-5 Sun. and holidays*), N. Stadium Way between N. 3rd and 4th Sts., houses the collections of C. P. Ferry and those of the society. The building, of pressed-brick trimmed in sandstone, was designed by George W. Bullard in the Classic style with Corinthian portico; subsequent alterations were planned by Mock and Morrison.

Before the main entrance is an old iron cannon from the Russian gunboat *Politkofski,* a souvenir of the purchase of Alaska in 1867. The main floor is devoted to the historical exhibits of the society. Indian pottery, baskets, weapons, hunting, and fishing gear vie for attention with nineteenth-century pewter, spinning wheels, and cradles that reached pioneer Washington via Cape Horn in territorial days. Paintings and photographs of pioneers and Indians prominently associated with the early history of the Northwest adorn the walls.

Exhibits include the mummy of Ankh Unnefir, the oxen and covered wagon used by Ezra Meeker in retracing the Oregon Trail in 1906 and 1911 (when he was an old man); the billiard table upon which George E. Pickett, William Slaughter, and George B. McClellan played in the days before the Civil War, when all served at Fort Steilacoom as young officers; the pipe belonging to Chief Seattle; the first stove and first piano in Washington Territory; and a large collection of personal belongings of Isaac I. Stevens, first Governor of Washington Territory. In the grounds at the rear of the building are the boiler, wheel shaft, and some of the bearings from the *Beaver,* built at Blackwell, England, in 1834-5, the first steamboat on the Pacific The vessel was wrecked inside the harbor of Vancouver, B.C., July 26, 1888.

10. The CHINESE MUSEUM (*open 2-4 Sun., adm. 27c; evenings by appointment, adm. 58c*), N. 26th and Carr Sts., housed in the home of Walter Sutter, contains an extensive collection of Oriental art, brought from Peking in 1937 and said to be from the Dragon Throne room. Seventeen carved teakwood panels overlaid with beaten gold, two of silver worked with kingfisher feathers, ivory carvings, pottery, and an exhibition of 2,000 Chinese dolls are on exhibit. The fireplace is inset with fluorescent rocks that glow softly by means of concealed neon lighting.

SUTTER'S FRIENDSHIP GARDEN (*adm. "just one stone"*), adjacent to the museum, begun as a hobby when friends laughingly volunteered to furnish the boulders, is now a collection of neatly labeled rocks, from all the counties of Washington, every State in the Union, and 22 foreign nations representing all the continents.

11. The COLLEGE OF PUGET SOUND (*visited by arrangement*), Warner St. between 13th and 18th Sts., founded in 1903, was moved to its present site in 1924. Formerly a university, it was reorganized as a co-educational college of liberal arts in 1914. The largest privately endowed institution in Washington, it is governed by the Puget Sound Conference of the Methodist Episcopal church, under the presidency of Edward Howard Todd since 1913. The red-brick collegiate Gothic building, designed by Sutton, Whitney & Dugan, Tacoma architects, forms an open square on the new 40-acre campus. The college has 22 departments, with an enrollment of 665 students. A permanent EXHIBIT OF PRE-INCA POTTERY AND TEXTILES, more than 3,000 years old and one of the few collections of Peruvian relics extant, is housed in the C. H. Jones Hall.

12. The TACOMA NARROWS BRIDGE, its deck now fallen but soon to be rebuilt, is reached by way of 6th Avenue and a new highway intersecting the avenue at a point 500 feet west of Mildred Street. The rebuilt bridge will afford a direct highway to the Kitsap Peninsula lying to the north. From the western approach to the bridge is the new section of the Navy Yard Highway, making a greatly shortened route between the Puget Sound Navy Yard at Bremerton and Fort Lewis, 17 miles south of Tacoma. It also will constitute an important link in an attractive route between the mainland and the Olympic Peninsula and Hood Canal country, shortening the distance by more than 100 miles and eliminating the necessity for ferry service in many instances.

The bridge, of the suspension type, will be supported from pier towers built of steel and securely anchored in cement submerged in 120 feet of water. Each of these towers stands 425 feet above the water, and each is equipped to carry the strain of the huge suspension cables, which in themselves will weigh in excess of 11,000 tons. It is the third longest center-suspension span in the world, being 2,800 feet in length between the towers. A vertical clearance above the water will permit the convenient passage of the largest ocean-going vessels. Other details of the reconstruction of the famous bridge are being worked out.

Financed through Federal grants, and loans, and by State appropriations, the bridge is under the Washington State Toll Bridge Authority; toll will be exacted on all traffic until the bridge is paid for. Construction on the original bridge was started November 25, 1938, and was completed in July, 1940.

13. The TACOMA SMELTER (*open by appointment*), N. 51st St. and Ruston Way, is operated by the American Smelting and Refining Company in the little town of Ruston. The smelter refines one-twelfth of the world's copper; and during normal times smelts 60,000 ounces of gold and 450 ounces of silver. The stack, erected in 1917, is the second highest in the world, rising 572 feet, 10 inches above its base. Ruston is surrounded by the city of Tacoma, excepting along its water front, but it retains its political identity; near by is Old Town Dock, owned by the city of Tacoma.

14. POINT DEFIANCE PARK, entrance at 45th and Pearl Sts., on the northern tip of Tacoma Peninsula, comprises 640 acres of natural forest, with an artificial lake and landscaped gardens; it contains reconstructed Fort Nesqually and other points of historic interest. Permission to use the area for park purposes was granted by Congress in 1905. The landscaping was done by Hare and Hare, of Kansas City, Missouri. The artificial lake, surrounded by large weeping willows, the rose gardens, and the zoo are outstanding attractions; picnic grounds and the pavilion offer recreational facilities for thousands.

The AQUARIUM (*open 10-7 daily; adm. 5c and 10c; student groups free on Wed.*), in the pavilion, is under the supervision of Wilhelm Jordan. In a darkened room, 48 illuminated tanks display representative marine life from local waters; specimens range from dogfish and many varieties of crab to geoducks and other shellfish, sea anemones, sea cucumbers, sea urchins, polyps, jellyfish, and an octopus family.

JOB CARR'S CABIN (*open 8-10 daily*), opposite the athletic field on Five Mile Drive, is a reconstruction of the first house built by white men in Tacoma. This unpretentious log cabin was the post office and social center of the early settlement.

FORT NESQUALLY (*open 8-10 daily*) was moved to its present site and restored in 1934. In 1833 Archibald McDonald of the Hudson's Bay Company established the post in a 15-by-20-foot house of hand-hewn logs, on the beach near what is now Dupont, about 17 miles south of Tacoma. Moved to higher ground soon afterward, it became the center of trade with the Indians and, ultimately, between American settlers and the British. After the arrival of the *Beaver* in 1836, the fort's commercial importance grew swiftly. Dr. William Frazier Tolmie, surgeon and scientist, became factor in 1843 and moved the trading post still farther inland. A stockade, 250 feet square, was built in 1847 as protection against Indian attack. Trouble came suddenly in 1849, when the Indians, seeing their way of life threatened, made a vigorous but futile attack under the leadership of Chief Patkanim. Troops dispatched by Governor Joseph Lane from Fort Vancouver remained at adjacent Fort Steilacoom. Controversy over ownership centered around Fort Nesqually until the Hudson's Bay Company was awarded $650,000 for its holdings on September 10, 1869. The original door hinges and latches, hammered from scrap iron, are used in the restored building.

15. The ST. PAUL AND TACOMA LUMBER PLANT (*admission by groups only; permission obtained at general office*), 1220 St. Paul Ave., dates back to 1888. The plant and lumber yards, which cover 200 acres, are supplied with logs by a private railroad to the logging camps in the company's approximately 90 thousand acres of timberland. The mill has its own electric powerhouse, 23 miles of railroad tracks in the yards, and a millpond with a capacity of 10,000,000 board feet of logs.

Boom men float the logs to the log haul, which draws them up a slide to the log deck, where they are fed into a large band saw by means of a moving carriage. The boards fall off like flitches of bacon and are carried by power-driven rollers to the edger to be squared and to the gang saw to be cut into standard sizes. An endless belt runs over a long table, from which the planks are sorted for the dry kilns or for yard storage. In the planing mill, revolving knives smooth the dried rough lumber at a speed of more than 400 lineal feet a minute. The waste slabs cut from the outside of the logs are made into fuel wood or "hogged" into chipped fuel; fine sawdust goes to the burner.

Adjuncts of the main mill are the lath and shingle mills, machine shops, a creosoting plant, and a general store and hotel for employees. Shipping facilities include two large docks, served by three hammerhead cranes and loading sheds with a capacity of forty cars daily.

16. The PORT OF TACOMA owns and operates Pier Number One on the Wapato Waterway, a public pier for the handling of lumber and general cargo, Pier Number Two, with a concrete and steel transit shed, and the grain elevator pier, from which grain is transferred by mechanical devices to the holds of ships. The port's cold-storage plant is equipped with modern mechanical devices and has a capacity of one million cubic feet.

17. The TACOMA (INDIAN) SANATORIUM (*open 9-12, 3-8 daily*), 2002 E. 28th St., formerly the Cushman School, is a Federal institution for the care and education of Indian wards of the Pacific Northwest and Alaska. The 32 buildings occupy 31 acres.

The INDIAN CEMETERY, adjoining the hospital grounds and overlooking the Puyallup River, is the cemetery of the Puyallup Indians. Among those buried here are Leschi, of the Nesqually; Charlie Satiacum, of the Duwamish; Chief Squatahan, of the Puyallup; Richard Sinnaywah (Tyee Dick), chief of three tribes—the Cowlitz, the Squally, and the Puyallup; and John Hoate, a wealthy Indian noted for his potlatches, who died penniless.

18. The TACOMA WATER DEPARTMENT SHOP (*open during business hours*), 28th St. and Union Ave., reached by way of Center

Street, a handsome modern plant completed in 1939, houses the city water department warehouse and workshops. Of concrete and steel construction the building is architecturally pleasing and equipped with huge cranes, for handling pipes and valves, and other modern mechanical devices.

POINTS OF INTEREST IN ENVIRONS

Puyallup Valley, 5 *m.* (*see Tour 2c*). McChord Field Army Air Base, 10.2 *m.*, one-fourth mile off US 99, east; U.S. Veterans' Hospital, 11.1 *m.*; Steilacoom, historic sites, 13*m.*; Fort Lewis, 16.4 *m.* (*see Tour 8c*). Rainier National Park, Nisqually Entrance, 54.9 *m.* (*see Tour 8 D*). Gig Harbor, by ferry, 2 *m.* (*see Tour 9 A*).

Vancouver

Railroad Station: Union Station, W. end of 11th St. for Great Northern Ry., Northern Pacific Ry., Union Pacific R.R., and Spokane, Portland & Seattle Ry.
Bus Station: 5th and Main Sts. for North Bank Highway, North Coast Transportation Co., Yacolt, and Yakima (Washington) Motor Coach Lines.
Taxis: 25c first mile; 20c each additional mile.
Traffic Regulations: Parking in business district, daytime, two-hour limit; on Main St., one-half hour. No U-turns.

Accommodations: Two hotels; two cabin camps.

Information Service: Chamber of Commerce and Automobile Club of Washington (AAA), Evergreen Hotel, 604 Main St.

Motion Picture Houses: Three; occasional road shows.
Athletics: Stadium, 40th and Main Sts.
Golf: Evergreen Golf Course, 3 m. E. on US 830, 18 holes; greens fee 50c.
Swimming: Memorial Hall, corner 13th St. and Broadway; fee 15c and 20c; monthly rates.
Tennis: Municipal court, corner 14th St. and Broadway.
Hunting and Fishing: Good hunting in season in near-by foothills; fishing in Columbia River.

Annual Events: Columbia River Regatta, July 4, speedboat, fish boat, sailing, and rowing races.

VANCOUVER (115 alt., 18,788 pop.), seat of Clark County and oldest settlement in the State, is strategically located on the navigable lower Columbia River, north of Portland, Oregon, in an important agricultural region, within 40 miles of Bonneville Dam. Lumber and paper mills, docks, grain elevators, and canneries are concentrated on the riverside; a little farther back are breweries and other industrial concerns. The streets leading from the banks of the Columbia through the business section are flanked by modern brick and terra-cotta structures, intermingled with buildings reminiscent of the late nineteenth century or of the jerry-building of boom days. In the residential districts are old but substantially constructed houses. One of the more interesting old buildings is the Courthouse, made of red brick and gray stone and designed in the style of the seventies.

Traversing the city is the Pacific Highway (US 99), east of which is the military reservation, Vancouver Barracks. North and east of the city, streets meander through prune orchards, which spread over the surrounding hills and valleys and extend to the fir and hemlock forests. To the south, across the broad river, rise the green hills of Oregon; to the southeast, the white cone of Mount Hood; and to the north, the smaller but equally beautiful Mount St. Helens. Lewis and Clark, who camped near the mouth of the Lewis River below Sauvies Island in November 1805, describe in their *Journal* their view of the peak some 70 miles upstream: "Three miles below the Image Canoe Island ... we had a full view of the mountain ... [Mount St. Helens]; it rises in the form of a sugar loaf to a great height, and is covered with snow."

Inevitably, the westward expansion of Great Britain and of the United States in the early decades of the nineteenth century eventuated in bitter rivalry; and, despite the Treaty of Ghent, signed in 1818, which conceded to both parties equal rights to the Oregon territory, dissension continued.

A decade after John Jacob Astor had established Astoria (1811), the Hudson's Bay Company acquired possession of the post and, in 1824, moved headquarters to the site of the present military reservation; Dr. John McLoughlin was named factor, and plans were made for a great depot to serve the area west of the Rocky Mountains. Sir George Simpson, governor of the company, who had helped select the site, visited the fort in May, 1825, and named it Vancouver for Point Vancouver near by, the upper limit of Lieutenant Broughton's explorations in 1792. The fort eventually covered a rectangular area 750 by 500 feet, enclosed by a stout palisade of 20-foot fir posts, and consisted of 40 wooden buildings—workshops, storehouses, and dwellings—and a stone powder magazine. Opposite the double-ribbed, riveted gates of the main entrance stood the factor's mansion, two 18-pound guns mounted before it. A schoolhouse and a library were provided. Social life centered in the dining hall and in the Bachelors' Hall, a room modeled on a baronial hall of feudal days, its walls covered with weapons, trophies, and all the accouterments of pioneer and savage life.

The dominant force in this trading post, 2,000 miles overland from the well-settled communities of the East, was Dr. McLoughlin. This man, who is credited with being an aggressive and efficient administrator, was described by his contemporaries as a towering figure, usually dressed in black; his strong, solemn face was framed by a mass of flowing snow-white hair. To the Indians, he was known as the "White-Headed Eagle." A second appellation, "the despot west of the Rockies," was bestowed upon him because of his ruthlessness in shutting out any competition arising in conflict with such industries as he fostered and developed, and because of his dictatorship over the natives. Apparently, however, his justice was tempered with mercy, and he was always willing to give valuable assistance to new settlers, American as well as British.

In 1826 McLoughlin imported sawmill equipment, installed a forge, and planted the first fruit trees along the Columbia River. In 1829 the fort was rebuilt at a more convenient spot, now the site of Pearson Army Airport. Commerce with Hawaii began after the construction of a sailing vessel, the *Vancouver*. About 300 islanders were imported by the company as laborers and established near the post, at a point where Eighth and Main Streets intersect today; the district was called Kanaka Town. The Islanders kept to themselves in the main, but some intermarried with whites, and their descendants are said to be numbered among the residents of present-day Vancouver.

Distant as this territory was from the centers of civilization, it was nevertheless within the orbit of scientific investigation. The enthusiastic search of botanists for new specimens led to the Royal Horticultural Society's sending David Douglas to Fort Vancouver in 1825, to study the vegetation of the region. One of the most characteristic trees of the Pacific Northwest, the Douglas fir (which is a "false" hemlock and not a fir at all) was named for Douglas. For the Fort Vancouver library, a stock of books and papers, including copies of the London *Times,* was secured from England at considerable cost. Modest though the library was, it represented a genuine achievement for the time and place.

One of the first Americans to visit the fort was Nathaniel J. Wyeth, of Massachusetts, who arrived in October 1832. With him came John Ball, who opened a school to six pupils in the following year. In 1838 Fathers Francois Norbert Blanchet and Modeste Demers, from Montreal, established a Catholic mission. Shocked by the contract marriages made by the fur traders, "a hideous assemblage of persons of both sexes . . . stripped of all moral principles," Blanchet collected a congregation of 40 persons, married 13 couples, and brought about the separation of several couples who were living together without benefit of law or of clergy. On Wyeth's second trip in 1834, he brought with him Jason and Daniel Lee, Methodist missionaries, and Solomon H. Smith, who succeeded Ball as schoolmaster.

The panic of 1837 and the subsequent period of depression in the East sent hundreds of families trekking westward to start life anew. Among those who settled in the vicinity of Fort Vancouver were Richard Covington and his wife, who built a cabin a few miles from the fort in the early forties. In November 1843, a party under the direction of Lieutenant John C. Frémont arrived from the East, coming down the Columbia River from The Dalles on rafts. Although Fort Vancouver was not, strictly speaking, on the Oregon Trail, it was considered the water terminus; many of the early settlers stopped for supplies and crossed the Columbia here to gain the mouth of the Willamette River, from which point they worked their way upstream to the Willamette Valley.

Aside from company employees, the earliest settlers at the townsite was Henry Williamson, of Indiana, who made a clearing in 1845. On March 20, McLoughlin wrote to his superior: "We found a shack built four legs high in the forest west of the fort. I ordered the men to pull the place down and destroy the fence surrounding it." Williamson rebuilt his cabin and filed a claim at Oregon City. On Christmas Day, 1845, Amos and Esther Short arrived with their eight children, and shortly thereafter became embroiled in trouble with Williamson, who averred that they had "jumped his claim." The company, acting as arbiter of the dispute, decided against the Short family and refused them supplies.

In the meantime the rivalry for these western lands between Great Britain and the United States had assumed such proportions that the cry, "Fifty-four Forty, or Fight," meant more than a mere political slogan. The domination of the Oregon Country by England was, however, abruptly ended when the Treaty of 1846 definitely established the international boundary at the forty-ninth parallel of latitude. Many company agents, nevertheless, continued to treat the American settlers as squatters. McLoughlin, accused of overt friendliness to Americans, was removed by his superiors. He took land at Willamette Falls (Oregon City) but, being an alien (he did not become a citizen until 1851), he was deprived of the holding and died in impoverished obscurity. Thus ended the life of the man who, by his sympathy with, and aid to, American settlers, helped the United States in its struggle for the Oregon country.

Fort Vancouver was officially made a part of the United States defense system in 1848, when the Secretary of War formally recognized it as a military post. In the same year Williamson and others platted a townsite, which they named Vancouver City. The departure of Williamson for California in 1849, in response to the lure for gold, opened the door for controversy over rights to the townsite. Dr. David Gardner laid claim to the site, but was removed from the controversy by the gunshot of Amos Short, who was acquitted of the charge of murder after establishing his assertion that he had acted in defense of his home. The following year Short acquired the townsite through the process of resurveying it. Further honor was bestowed upon him when he was elected a judge of the probate court and given a commission by Governor Joseph Lane.

The 1850 census listed 95 houses in the newly organized Clark County, of which Vancouver City was the county seat. Two schools were opened, a ferry franchise was granted for river service, and construction began on the Army reservation. R. H. Lansdale, appointed county agent, replatted the townsite, ignoring the lines used in earlier surveys, which started from the "Witness Tree," a giant cottonwood on the river bank. This new survey not only kindled private boundary disputes, but also infringed on the military reserve. One group of local patriots wished to change the name of the town to Columbia City, but the Washington Territorial Legislature ruled, in 1855, that the legal name was, and should remain, Vancouver. Colonel B. L. E. Bonneville arrived at the military reservation, called Columbia Barracks, in 1852, and began intensive development of the Fort. Much later, in 1879, the fort was renamed Vancouver Barracks.

The town by this time was settling into the routine of ordinary daily life, with now and then a dramatic interlude. "Judge" Amos Short was drowned in a shipwreck off the Columbia Bar in 1853, while returning with store goods from San Francisco. The first commercial building, Peter Fulkerson's saloon and bowling alley, was opened on July 4, 1854; the Pacific House, started by Esther Short, and the Alta House, located near the boat landing, were also finished that year. In September, the sheriff rented the courthouse for school use at $3 a month, stipulating, however, that "school was not to interfere with court proceedings." Joseph Brant, the next year, built the two-story Metropolis Hall, the upper story to serve as a dance hall and theater, and the ground floor as a livery stable.

Incorporation papers were granted to the town in 1857, at the fourth session of the Territorial legislature, and in 1859 a campaign to name Vancouver as the Territorial capital was inaugurated. A bill actually passed the legislature the next year authorizing the removal of the capital to Vancouver, but no date was stipulated, and at the subsequent election this authorization was rescinded; 1,239 votes were cast for Olympia, and 639 for Vancouver. L. E. V. Coons and John Murphy established the *Chronicle* in 1860.

Gold rushes to eastern Washington and to Idaho during the sixties augmented river traffic and stimulated the town's growth. With the increase in wealth and population came also a greater emphasis on social life, and several public entertainments were staged during the middle sixties. For the Saint Patrick's Day ball at the Alta House in 1866, tickets were sold at $5 each. An amateur dramatic society presented *Robert Macaire,* a melodrama, and, later, in 1867, *Toodles,* a comedy. In 1869 a traveling troupe played *Man: the Good for Nothing* and *A Kiss in the Dark.*

At the same time that the gold-rush boom abated, construction started on the Northern Pacific line from Kalama to Tacoma (1870-3). The extension of the railroad southward from Kalama later increased Vancouver's importance as a shipping center, and railroad ferry service across the Columbia began in the eighties. Following a series of allegedly incendiary fires that razed the business district in June 1889, considerable rebuilding was necessary. Construction of the Cascade Locks in 1896 opened navigation to The Dalles and again increased river traffic.

McLoughlin had demonstrated the region's suitability for growing fruit, especially prunes. This product was given much publicity during the Spanish-American War when Company G, recruited from this area, was named the "Prune Picked Platoon."

Lumbering developed rapidly between 1890 and 1910. Completion of the first railroad bridge across the Columbia below the mouth of the Snake River, in 1902, eliminated the use of ferries for trains connecting with the south. The Port Commission was organized in 1912. In 1915 construction of the Interstate Highway Bridge was begun jointly by Washington and Oregon, and two years later this final link in the Pacific Highway was completed. During the First World War, Vancouver became the headquarters of the Spruce Division, numbering 30,000 men, and the construction of lumber plants underwent hurried expansion during this period.

The construction of the huge and well-equipped Port of Vancouver Terminal Number Two in 1936 gave a great impetus to commerce and trade; and the erection of a large grain elevator on port properties in 1934 reflects the increasing importance of Vancouver as a shipping

Agriculture

tograph courtesy Washington State Progress Commission

THE OLD AND THE NEW

"Caterpillar" tractors, such as pictured below, are gradually replacing mule and horse power in large scale farming operations

Photograph courtesy of Caterpillar Tractor Compan

Photograph by Asahel Cur

CATTLE ROUNDUP

otograph courtesy of Department of Interior

SHEEP ON THE RANG

AIRY FARM SCENE ON YAKIMA PROJECT

Photograph courtesy of Department of Interic

Photograph courtesy of Department of Interior
FRUIT PICKER

TO GATHER THE HARVEST

MIGRATORY FARM WORKERS PICKING HOPS
Photograph courtesy of Department of Interior

Photograph by Lange; courtesy Farm Security Adm.
WIFE OF FARM MIGRANT

CHINESE LABORER IN POTATO FIELD
Photograph by Rothstein; courtesy of Farm Security Adm.

Photograph by Lange; courtesy of Farm Security A

CLEARING THE LAND

In areas where the forests have been cleared, one of the first tasks of the prospective farm families who move in is to clear the land of stumps uprooted by the "bulldozer."

STACKING ALFALFA

Photograph by Rothstein; courtesy Farm Security Adm.

A FARMSTEAD IN THE YAKIMA VALLEY (Hops in Foreground)

Photograph by Lange; courtesy Farm Security Adm.

Photograph courtesy of Department of Int

RECLAMATION

Endless stretches of arid land covered with greasewood and sage-brush, as pictured above, are being brought into use through the great irrigation projects of the Northwest. Below, a section of a canal on the Yakima Project is shown.

center. Excellent highway and rail connections and the port's situation at the head of deep-water navigation, 83 nautical miles from the Pacific Ocean, make it a logical point for transshipment of ocean-going cargo. Approximately 20 steamship lines make Vancouver a port of call, and it is estimated that more than 200 ocean-going vessels dock annually at the port.

Flax and wool products are produced in factories along the water front, where two of the largest mills in the Northwest are located. Other important local plants are the breweries and those engaged in the processing of fruits, nuts, and dairy products.

A factor in the future development of Vancouver, the importance of which cannot yet be judged, is the completion of Bonneville Dam, 39 miles east of the city. This makes possible the shipment of raw materials from a rich inland area to tidewater, and it furnishes cheap power for industrial development. The Aluminum Company of America, with headquarters in Pittsburgh, Pennsylvania, has been the first to make large-scale industrial use of the Bonneville power; the company has built an enormous aluminum plant at Vancouver, the first of its plants to be located west of the Mississippi. In the short time since its establishment, the capacity of the plant has been doubled.

POINTS OF INTEREST

1. The TOLL-FREE INTERSTATE BRIDGE, foot of Washington St., crossing the eastern tip of Hayden Island, spans the Columbia and connects the two northwestern States. From here the white-coned peaks of Mount St. Helens and Mount Rainier may be seen to the north, Mount Adams to the east, and Mount Hood to the southeast. In the foreground are intermingled the old and new buildings of Vancouver, with the docks along the water front; directly across the river, in Oregon, is Jantzen Beach, a popular bathing beach and amusement park. This steel bridge, completed in 1917, was built under the direction of John Lyle Harrison, Kansas City, Missouri. The OREGON TRAIL MARKER, at the Washington end of the bridge, was placed in 1916.

2. The ESTHER SHORT PARK, bounded by 6th and 8th Aves. and Columbia and Esther Sts., four acres near the heart of downtown Vancouver, part of the claim taken by Amos and Esther Short in 1845, was deeded by them to the town of Vancouver in 1855. Diagonal walks divide the wooded square, with its many beautiful Douglas firs. A wading pool and playground are popular attractions.

The PIONEER MOTHER STATUE, in the northern section of the park, designed by Avard Fairbanks and donated by Mr. and Mrs. E. G. Crawford, is a monumental figure in bronze of a pioneer woman, flintlock in hand, her three children clinging to her skirts. In memory of Esther Short, it also typifies all the brave mothers of the frontier. A plaque on the monument shows a man plodding along, with his oxen drawing a covered wagon, from which his wife looks out anxiously.

The FLOUR MILL WHEELS, two at either end of the diagonal walks, are made of solid stone, with iron rims. They were brought around the

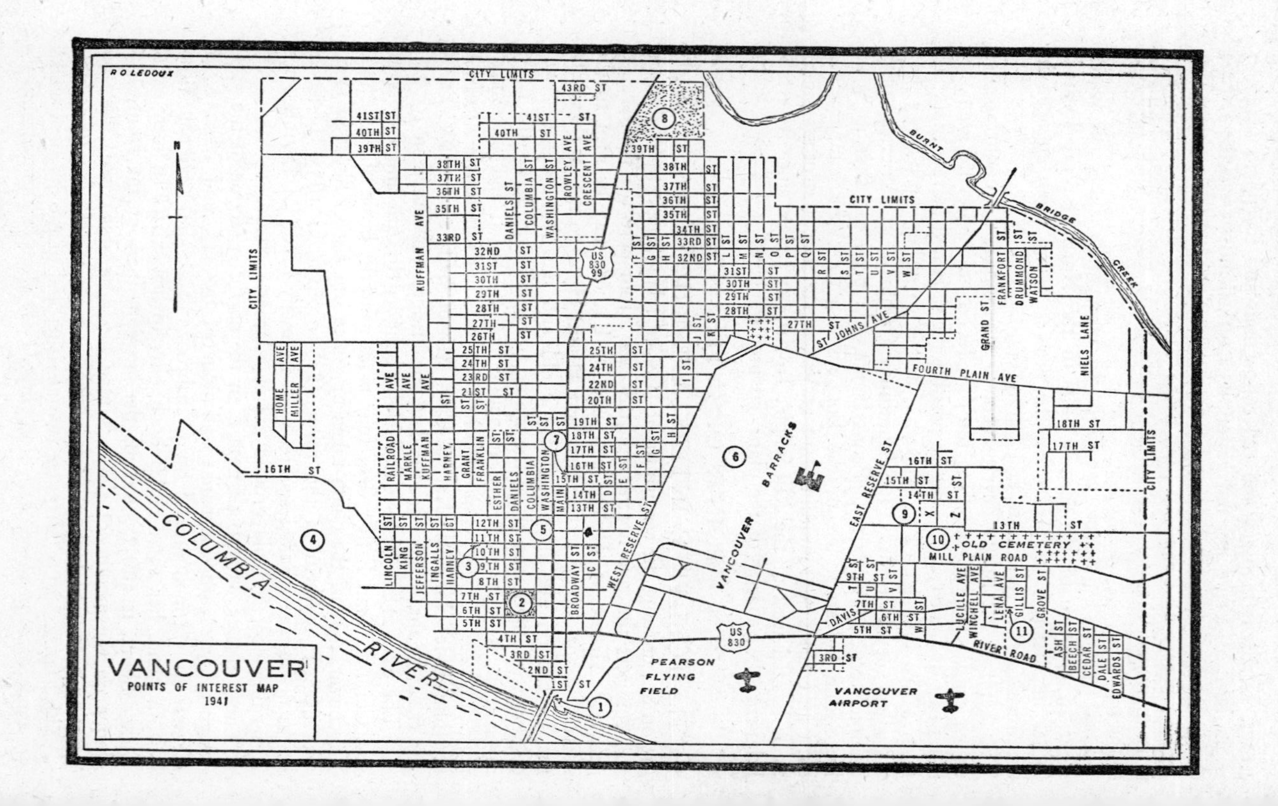

VANCOUVER
POINTS OF INTEREST MAP
1941
R O LEDOUX
CITY LIMITS
BURNT BRIDGE CREEK
COLUMBIA RIVER
VANCOUVER BARRACKS
PEARSON FLYING FIELD
VANCOUVER AIRPORT
OLD CEMETERY
MILL PLAIN ROAD
RIVER ROAD
FOURTH PLAIN AVE
ST JOHNS AVE
EAST RESERVE ST
WEST RESERVE ST
NIELS LANE
GRAND ST
FRANKFORT ST
DRUMMOND ST
WATSON
KUFFMAN AVE
CRESCENT AVE
ROWLEY AVE
WASHINGTON ST
COLUMBIA ST
DANIELS ST
MAIN
BROADWAY ST
ESTHER
FRANKLIN
GRANT
HARNEY
INGALLS
JEFFERSON
KING
LINCOLN
MARKLE AVE
RAILROAD AVE
HOME AVE
MILLER AVE
LUCILLE AVE
WINCHELL AVE
LENA AVE
GILLIS ST
GROVE ST
ASH ST
BEECH ST
CEDAR ST
DALE ST
EDWARDS ST
DAVIS
US 830
US 830 99

Horn from Massachusetts in 1877, to be used in the gristmill of Moore and Stevens.

3. The CLARK COUNTY COURTHOUSE, W. 11th St., between Franklin and Grant Sts., completed in 1892, replaced the former one, which burned in 1890. It was designed by W. A. Ritchie, architect. A brick building of four floors, the courthouse contains the various wards of the county jail on its basement floor; the other three floors are devoted to the offices of county government. A new and much larger courthouse is under construction on the north.

4. PORT OF VANCOUVER TERMINAL NUMBER TWO, water front west of bridge, at city limits, was completed in 1936 and is modern in construction and equipment, with berthage for two large ocean-going vessels. The dock stands in deep water, the passage to the sea entirely unobstructed; close to main railroad lines, it is well situated to handle the increasing traffic.

The Port of Vancouver was established in 1912, and TERMINAL NUMBER ONE was built at the foot of Columbia Street, just below the present Interstate Bridge. Since then the port has expanded to its present value of nearly $2,000,000 in properties and facilities. Along the water front are many of the city's important industrial plants and mills, including the Pacific Coast Linen Mill, the Columbia River Paper Mill and Sawmill, the plants of the Vancouver Plywood and Veneer Company and the Union Bag and Paper Company, and the DuBois Lumber Company Mill, one of the oldest sawmills in Vancouver; back from the water front a short distance is the Interstate Brewery (formerly the Star Brewery).

The TERMINAL GRAIN ELEVATOR, at the foot of W. 13th St., operated by the Archer-Daniels-Midland Company on land leased from the Port of Vancouver, is one of the largest west of the Mississippi Valley. Built of reinforced concrete and steel, it has a total capacity of more than 2,000,000 bushels. The cost of erection was $1,250,000.

5. SAINT JAMES CHURCH (ROMAN CATHOLIC), 12th St. between Washington and Columbia Sts., a massive brick structure in the Gothic style, was built in 1885. Hedges enclose the carefully tended lawns. The middle, or bell, tower rises more than 150 feet above the 12th Street entrance and is adorned by a cross of white metal. On either side is a lower tower, some 80 feet above street level. The main altar of Saint James is a beautifully executed piece of carved oak,

---

VANCOUVER—POINTS OF INTEREST

1. Interstate Bridge
2. Esther Short Park
3. Clark County Courthouse
4. Port of Vancouver
5. Saint James Church
6. Vancouver Barracks
7. Public Library
8. Leverich Park
9. State School for the Blind
10. Old City Cemetery
11. State School for the Deaf

imported from Belgium. In a crypt beneath the platform before the altar lie the remains of the first two bishops of the Nesqually Diocese: A. M. A. Blanchet, V. G., and Aegidius Junger, V. G.

Fort Vancouver became the seat of the first diocese north of the Columbia River in 1850. Old Saint James Church, built in Vancouver Barracks in that year, was destroyed by fire in 1889. North of the barracks, at the northeast corner and close to the military cemetery are SAINT JAMES ACRES, where are buried several of the devoted nuns who taught and worked with the pioneers in the Vancouver region. Most of this ground was purchased by Bishop Blanchet; a small additional plot was added by Bishop Junger.

6. The VANCOUVER BARRACKS, bounded by 5th St. (Evergreen Highway), 4th Plain Road, and E. and W. Reserve Sts., was established in 1848 on a plot four miles square. In the reservation, now reduced to one square mile, are the Pearson Airport, the reservation monument, and the first apple tree planted in the region.

NUMBER TWO BARRACKS, in Officers' Row, was one of the earliest of the 300 buildings on the reserve. Its log walls have been sheathed with siding, but the narrow windows, angular outlines, and peaked roof with brick chimneys at each end are characteristic of domestic buildings of the period. When young Ulysses S. Grant was stationed here in 1852-3, he planted a crop of potatoes in the near-by lowlands to augment his meager income, but spring floods washed his crop away. At the time, potatoes cost $45 per hundred pounds.

The GRANT MEMORIAL, at 5th St., southeast of the barracks, was erected in 1927 by the Hill Military Academy, Portland, Oregon, in honor of the Civil War general and his potato patch.

PEARSON ARMY AIRPORT, corner 5th Ave. and E. Reserve St., base of the U.S. Army Reserve Air Corps, measures 2,100 by 5,200 feet. The hangars, shops, and administration buildings are at the east end of the field. Here ended the 63-hour North Pole flight of the three Russians who hopped off from Moscow on June 18, 1937, to test the feasibility of air transportation in the Arctic.

The RESERVATION MONUMENT, E. 7th Ave. and T St., erected by the Washington State Historical Society, commemorates important events in Washington's early history and the establishment of the reserve.

The FIRST APPLE TREE, also at E 7th Ave. and T St., was planted in 1826 by Dr. John McLoughlin. According to accounts Captain Aemilius Simpson, a dinner guest of Dr. McLoughlin, presented the factor with several appleseeds given him by a woman friend in London and suggested that they might blossom in the wilderness. McLoughlin carefully nurtured the seeds into shoots, which he planted inside the stockade.

7. The PUBLIC LIBRARY (*open 1-9 weekdays; 2-5 Sun.*), Main St. between 15th and 16th Sts., a small red-brick building with ivy-festooned walls, was built in 1910 with the aid of Carnegie funds. It has 18,000 volumes, including a sizable collection of books on early Northwest history.

On the front lawn stands a large COTTONWOOD, a cutting from the witness tree, which marked the spot where Lewis and Clark landed in 1805. From this spot, survey lines started when the first town plat, covering ten square miles, was made. The famous Witness Tree was washed away by a freshet in 1912.

8. LEVERICH PARK, N. of 39th St., E. of Pacific Highway, an L-shaped area of about 33½ acres, lying partly within and just north of the city limits, was deeded to the city for park purposes by Mrs. Anna Leverich. It was established as a municipal park in 1931; and in the same year an obelisk was erected and a Douglas fir planted by the Columbia District Federation of Women's Clubs, in anticipation of the bicentennial celebration of George Washington's birth. In accordance with the terms of the deed, the natural beauty of the area has been preserved as much as possible. Burnt Bridge Creek, branching out among low hills and small groves of native firs, deciduous trees, and occasional cedars, gives the park a truly sylvan charm. About three acres in the southwest section have been developed into an athletic field around the grandstand, which is known as Kiggins Bowl in honor of John P. Kiggins, pioneer citizen and mayor of Vancouver for a number of years. Within the last few years a large Works Progress Administration project has constructed recreational facilities.

COVINGTON HOUSE (*open 11-4, 2nd and 4th Tues. each month*), 39th and Main Sts., at the SW. corner of the park, the oldest house in the State, was built by Richard Covington between 1840 and 1845 on his homestead about a mile north of what is now Orchards. In 1931 the house was taken down, each piece numbered, and the whole rebuilt on its present site. The house, of roughly squared logs dovetailed at the corners, is covered with clapboard siding and has a sharply gabled roof. The Covingtons kept a kind of boarding school, and their home, containing the first piano in the region, was a social center for young Army officers and trading company officials in the early days.

9. The STATE SCHOOL FOR THE BLIND (*open 9-12; 2-5 daily*), 2214 E. 13th St., houses most of its school activities in the four-story, red-brick administration building. The two dormitories and the primary school, erected in 1938, are also of brick, trimmed with Tenino sandstone. The school enrolls about 100 students and has a faculty of 16; vocational, musical, and mechanical training supplement academic instruction. The institution was established in 1905 by the State legislature and, until 1913, cared for both the deaf and the blind.

10. The OLD CITY CEMETERY, east of the reservation, between 10th and 13th Sts., accessible by Winchell Ave. lies on a gentle slope originally part of the Vancouver Barracks. Its moss-covered tombstones commemorate many pioneer settlers, including members of the Short family.

11. The STATE SCHOOL FOR THE DEAF (*open 8-12; 1-3:30 daily*), 2901 E. 7th St., directly east of the military reserve on a slight rise overlooking the Columbia River, was founded in 1886. The seven

modern buildings, dominated by the three-story, buff-brick administration building, are surrounded by well-kept lawns bordered with trees and shrubs. The Reverend W. D. McFarland of Tacoma is in charge of the school, in which both oral and manual methods of education are used. A literary society, athletic clubs, social clubs, and motion pictures provide activities and entertainment for the students.

POINTS OF INTEREST IN ENVIRONS

Jantzen Beach, Oregon, 1 *m.*; Portland, Orgeon, 8 *m.* Crown-Willamette Paper Mills, Camas, 14.2 *m.*; Beacon Rock, 36 *m.*; Bonneville Dam, 39.6 *m.*; Bridge of the Gods, 41.8 *m.* (*see Tour 3a*).

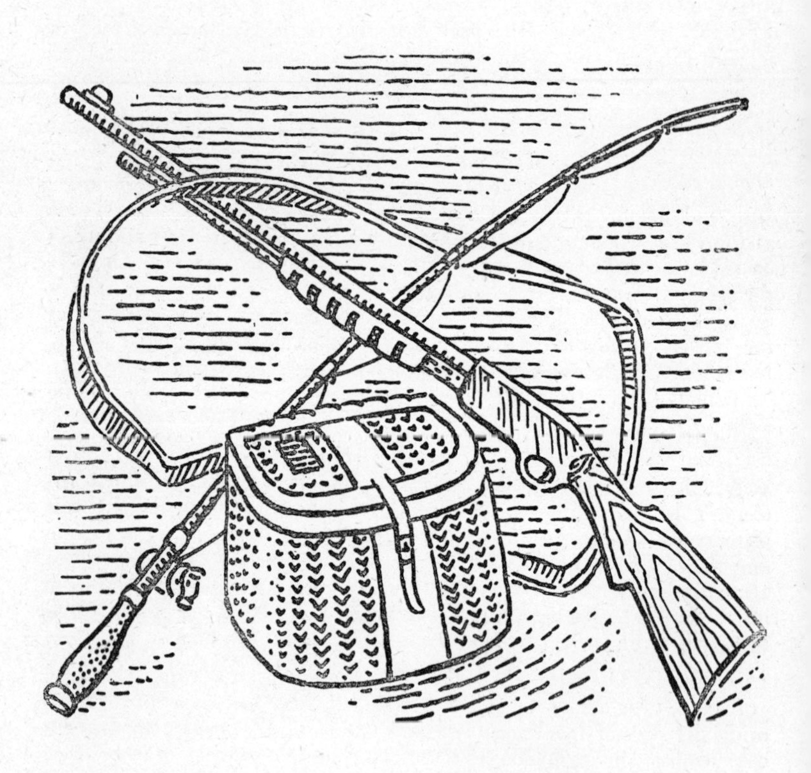

Walla Walla

Railroad Stations: West end of Main St. for Union Pacific R.R.; 2nd Ave. N. and Oak St. for Northern Pacific Ry.; 15th Ave. N. and Cherry St. for Walla Walla R.R.
Bus Station: 1st Ave. S. and Poplar St. for Union Pacific Stages and Washington Motor Coach System.
Airport: 2.5 m. NE. for United Air Lines; taxi fare $1; 15 min.
Taxis: 15c first mile; 10c each additional mile.
City Busses and College Place Bus: Fare 10c; loading zones on Main St. at 1st, 2nd, and 6th Aves.
Traffic Regulations: Double or all-night parking prohibited; no U-turns.

Accommodations: Five hotels; tourist cabins; trailer facilities.

Information Service: Automobile Club of Washington (AAA), Marcus Whitman Hotel, 2nd Ave. N. and Rose St.; Chamber of Commerce, City Hall, 3rd Ave., S.

Motion Picture Houses: Three, local productions and occasional road shows.
Radio Station: KUJ (1420 kc.).
Athletics: Stadium, foot of N. Idaho St.
Golf: Walla Walla Country Club, 9th Ave. S., 9 holes, greens fee $1 weekdays, $1.50 Sun. and holidays.
Tennis: Pioneer Park, Alder and McKinley Sts.; Jefferson Park, 9th Ave. S. and Malcolm St.; Green Park, Alvarado Terrace and Division St.
Swimming and Wading: Municipal pools at Pioneer Park, Alder and McKinley Sts.; Jefferson Park, 9th Ave. S. and Malcolm St.; Washington Park, 9th Ave. N. and Cherry St.; and Green Park, Division St. and Alvarado Terrace. Natatorium, Wilbur and Granville Sts., 10c and 25c; summer months.

Annual Events: Walla Walla Civic Symphony Concerts, winter-spring; Southeastern Washington fair, Sept.; Christmas Show at State Penitentiary.

WALLA WALLA (954 alt., 18,109 pop.), seat of Walla Walla County, lies in the center of the rich farm lands of the Walla Walla Valley. To the southeast rise the hazy peaks of the Blue Mountains; northward, gently rolling hills fade into the distance. Many streams water the valley, Mill Creek meandering through the very heart of the city. The pioneers retained the Indian name for the site, Walla Walla, which means the "place of many waters," a name eminently suited to the region.

From its beginning as a trading and distributing point, the city has grown as circumstances dictated, not according to plan. Today commercial and industrial buildings mingle freely with residences. Here and there among the newer, more pretentious structures, are a few old stores and office buildings, relics of the boom days of the sixties and seventies. The residential streets, quiet and peaceful, are bordered by many trees, which change kaleidoscopically with the seasons; from brilliant green of spring through the heavy fragrance of locust trees in bloom, to the dark lacing of autumn with its cascades of yellow leaves, and, finally, winter, with snow and the bare-brown sheen of branches. In settings of neat green lawns, brightened by seasonal flowers and shrubbery, are homes representing various adaptations—Colonial, English, and American farm houses. Several church spires rise above the tops of the trees.

The Walla Walla region has been intimately bound up with the history of the Northwest. Before the coming of the white men, an Indian trail ran through the valley, its course approximating the location of Main Street today. The valley on Mill Creek was a favored council ground of the Indians. Six miles west, in the "valley of the rye grass," Marcus Whitman and his wife, Narcissa, set up a mission in 1836, and for a decade carried on their efforts to convert the Indians to the belief and the ways of the white man. This first period of settlement, however, ended in 1847, when Indians massacred the Whitmans.

The town of Walla Walla was founded at the end of the Indian wars of 1855-8. On the spot where the city now stands, Governor Isaac I. Stevens, as superintendent of Indian Affairs, and Joel Palmer, superintendent of Indian Affairs for Oregon, held a great council, to which were invited Kamiakin and Ow-hi of the Yakima, Peu-peu-mox-mox of the Walla Walla, a young chief of the Cayuse, and Lawyer, Looking Glass, Joseph, and Timothy of the Nez Percé, and many others.

For days, supplies and gifts that had been brought upriver from Portland to the Hudson's Bay fort, now Wallula, came overland by pack-train and wagons to the council grounds. Roasting sticks for barbecues were driven. Only about 100 white men attended, including 50 soldiers who camped across the creek. Of the Indians present, the Nez Percé, with more than 2,000 tribesmen, were numerically the strongest. Almost 3,000 horses were pastured on the surrounding grasslands.

The council opened impressively on May 29, 1855, with Governor Stevens outlining the benefits of schools, stores, mills, and supervised husbandry for the tribes accepting the reservations in the Yakima Country and in the Nez Percé country. The Indians, however, pleaded for time, stalled, and became resentful, and more than a week passed without any agreement.

According to accounts, Stevens had almost persuaded them to accept the plan of reservations, when the Nez Percé chief, Looking Glass, rode in, after a long absence in the country of the Blackfeet. Not deigning to dismount, the chief listened until he learned what had taken place, and then cried out in anger and disappointment: "My people, what have you done? While I was gone you have sold my country. I have come home, and there is not left for me a place on which to pitch my lodge. Go home to your lodges, I will talk with you." In spite of the opposition of Looking Glass, Stevens won partial acceptance of the three treaties, which were signed in June 1855.

Many of the Indians north of the Snake River persisted in their hostility to the settlers. Pioneers who had planned to establish homes farther north remained under protection of the fort that had been constructed at Mill Creek as a defense against possible Indian attacks. A settlement sprang up as the immigrants took homesteads, tilled the fertile soil, and marketed their products at the garrison. The village for a short time was called Steptoeville after Colonel Steptoe, who had made his winter quarters at the fort in 1856. Two years later, the name of the settlement was established as Walla Walla. In 1862 the town was laid out and incorporated.

In the meantime various factors had contributed to the growth of the settlement. The beginning of construction on the Mullan Military Road between Wallula and Fort Benton, Montana, in 1858, and the lifting of the ban on immigration into the territory north of the Snake River shortly thereafter, brought several new families to the rich plateau lands.

Discovery of gold in Idaho, a few days' travel from Walla Walla, brought transients through the valley during the sixties and transformed the thriving little settlement into a boom town. When in 1861 news of the gold strike at Orofino, in present Idaho, reached other parts of the Nation, gold seekers bought their supplies at Walla Walla. Then the precious metal was found in other Idaho areas: Boise Basin, Powder River, Salmon, Owyhee, Kootenai, and Blackfoot. Thousands of men surged into Walla Walla en route to the gold fields, and those who struck it rich returned to Walla Walla, which became the miners' winter resort. Hotels, stores, livery stables, saloons, and dance halls, hurriedly constructed, flourished as the lucky prospectors freely spent the valuable dust from their pouches. At the Pioneer Race Track, three miles away, there was frenzied betting for big stakes. Neither the excessive prices demanded for supplies and services, nor a period of meat shortage, due to the death of cattle on near-by ranges during the severe winter of 1861, appeared to check the rush. By October 1862, fifty new buildings had been erected on the main streets, and 30 more were under construction. Stages were operated between the town and The Dalles, Wallula, and Lewiston; Wells-Fargo inaugurated stage service to the mines. The Mullan military road was completed, and mail service started to Elk City, Pierce City, and Hell Gate.

The courts proved a feeble defense of law and order in these pioneer days of riches and recklessness. Sheepherders and cattlemen squabbled over range and water rights; well-organized gangs of rustlers drove stolen cattle over the Canadian border. Dance halls and saloons prospered, for the cowboys from the range and miners from the creeks were easy spenders.

The ineffectiveness of the courts and officers of the law resulted in the organization of vigilante groups in 1865. They took the law into their hands, and soon the neighboring trees bore gruesome fruits; in one month several men were hanged. The law could no longer be broken with impunity in Walla Walla. The reform wave even forced saloon-keepers to close their bars on Sundays. In 1865 the troops stationed at the fort were removed, for Indian attacks no longer threatened.

Many of the new arrivals, who were by this time coming in a steady stream, turned to agriculture for means of livelihood. At first, farms were located only alongside deep or wide streams, and orchards were planted only in the valleys. But when settlers discovered, in the late seventies, that the uplands were arable without irrigation, golden waves of wheat began to cover the hills. Cattle raising for beef began to be supplemented by dairying. Improved transportation facilities gave the region access to wider markets for its agricultural products. Walla Walla was well on its way toward becoming a regional center.

Throughout the sixties forward-looking citizens began working for a better order and balance in the life of the community. Classes were held in a rented room until a regular school building was constructed. A post office was established, a packing plant and a flour mill were built in 1859, and additional mills were opened within the next three years. In 1861 one of the earliest journals between the Missouri and Cascades, the *Washington Statesman* (combined with the Walla Walla *Union* in 1914), started publication. A fire razed the older portions of the city in 1865, and more substantial structures were constructed to replace those destroyed. The first courthouse was erected in 1867. Two years later the Baker-Boyer Bank, earliest in the Territory, was established. By this time several churches had been organized.

Walla Walla secured its first telegraphic service in the seventies. A far more sensational event, and one which foreshadowed significant changes, was the completion, in 1875, of Dr. D. S. Baker's steam railway, which linked the city to Wallula on the Columbia River. An engine was brought around Cape Horn by boat from Pittsburgh to push the "hearse," as the passenger car was called. Foreseeing bitter competition from this crude-looking monster, teamsters promptly reduced their exorbitant freight rates. Cheaper and speedier transportation facilities gave the region access to new markets for its farm produce. As a consequence, additional acreage was broken to the plow, and planted to crops, especially to wheat. In 1878, Dr. Baker was able to ship, via the railroad, river barge, and the schooner, *Alice D. Cooper,* 66,000 bushels of wheat to England.

Arrival of transcontinental railroad lines ushered in an era of great prosperity. The history of succeeding decades was largely written in terms of expansion of agriculture and related industries. Granaries and mills were built to handle the wheat produced in ever-increasing quantities in the region; new canneries and factories, required for the marketing of fruit, produce, poultry, and dairy products, were opened. Streetcar tracks were laid and telephone lines were installed; an opera house was constructed and opened with considerable display. Today, organizations like the Grange, Chamber of Commerce, and Co-operative and privately owned stores have replaced the prospector, trader, and dance hall proprietor. Modern schools, including a college which has achieved considerable distinction, a city library, and numerous motion picture theaters afford social and cultural outlets for the community. Several congregations established in Walla Walla during the nineteenth century have built new edifices during the past few decades; these include St. Paul's Episcopal Church, the Congregational Church, First Presbyterian, Central Christian, St. Patrick's, Pioneer Methodist, and the White Temple Baptist Church.

A popular event in Walla Walla is the Christmas Show at the State Penitentiary. As a rule the entertainment takes the form of a vaudeville performance, with inmates playing all the parts.

In August 1936, Walla Walla celebrated the Whitman Centennial, honoring the establishment of Dr. Marcus Whitman's mission beside the Walla Walla River. The festival included Mother Whitman's Day, in honor of Narcissa Whitman; a colorful parade depicting "Wagons West"; and a Doctor's Day, in memory of the first American physician to practice in the Northwest. Old settlers and their descendants thronged from afar to join in the celebration.

POINTS OF INTEREST

The SITE OF THE SECOND FORT WALLA WALLA, corner of Main and Colville Sts., is marked by a plaque on the A. M. Jensen Building. The fort was established in 1856, but was removed in 1858 to the present site of the United States Veterans Hospital.

The BAKER-BOYER NATIONAL BANK, corner of 2nd Ave. and Main St., established in November 1869, is the oldest bank in the State, and still operates under its original charter.

WHITMAN COLLEGE, between Isaacs and Boyer Aves. and College and Stanton Sts. was chartered by the Washington Territorial legislature in 1859 and is the oldest institution of higher learning in the State. Originally a seminary, it was founded by Cushing Eells, Congregational missionary, in honor of his friend and fellow missionary, Dr. Marcus Whitman, and his wife, Narcissa Prentiss Whitman.

The college, co-educational and non-sectarian, is privately endowed and receives no aid from church or State. The average enrollment is betwen 500 and 600 students, chosen by a selective admission system. The campus covers an area of about 50 acres, shaded by locust, elm, and birch trees and bisected by College Creek. Nine buildings house the college. WHITMAN MEMORIAL BUILDING, corner Boyer Ave. and College St., contains classrooms and the offices of administration. It was built in 1899, a gift of Dr. D. K. Pearsons of Chicago. BILLINGS HALL, Boyer Ave. between College and Stanton Sts., is devoted to the use of the department of physics, biology, and chemistry. CONSERVATORY OF MUSIC, corner Boyer Ave. and Park St., a large, ivy-covered, brick building, was constructed in 1910. Instruction is given in theory of music and in vocal and instrumental music, including band and orchestra.

Other campus buildings are REYNOLDS HALL, the college library, LYMAN HOUSE, first-year men's dormitory, PRENTISS HALL, dormitory for all out-of-town women students, and the GYMNASIUM. The president's house and the home of Dr. S. B. L. Penrose, president emeritus of the college, are also on the campus.

The WHITMAN MUSEUM (*open by permission*) gives special attention to representative material of the Pacific Northwest. Exhibits include letters, photographs, tools, and documents of the Whitmans, Mrs. Whitman's diary, an 1835 map of the Nation, a map of the Oregon Trail, and the *Journal* of Lieutenant John Mullan, builder of the Mullan Military Road. Also included are collections in geology and paleontology, zoology and botany, anthropology and ethnology. The collections are housed in Billings Hall, Memorial Building, and the Conservatory of Music.

CHIEF LAWYER MONUMENT, on the campus near Lyman House, a 17-ton rock with a bronze tablet, commemorates the Indian chieftain who befriended Governor Stevens and gave him the protection of the Nez Percé tribe in 1855.

The PUBLIC LIBRARY (*open 10-9 weekdays*), Palouse St. between Alder and Poplar Sts., occupies a red-brick building in a triangular lawn. It is a continuation of the third oldest library in the State. The building was opened in 1905 with the aid of a Carnegie grant. It contains 29,000 volumes and special collections on art and Northwest history.

ST. PAUL'S EPISCOPAL CHURCH, Birch and Catherine Sts., is a simple wood and stone building, with two fine stained glass windows brought from Boston for the original church building. It was constructed in 1902, replacing the church built in 1870 after the Reverend Lemuel H. Wells had organized a congregation. Aided by the architects, Cutter and Malmgren, Wells, who was made Bishop of Spokane in 1893, planned the present structure, and then joined in the manual labor of construction.

The PIONEER METHODIST CHURCH, Colville and Poplar Sts., was founded on October 11, 1859, and grew so rapidly that four removals to larger quarters were necessary in as many decades. The present building was completed in 1925 at a cost of $50,000; it has a large electric pipe organ.

ST. PATRICK'S ROMAN CATHOLIC CHURCH, W. Alder St. and 6th Ave. S., was constructed in 1870. The interior was destroyed by fire in 1916 and has been completely renewed. Above the white marble altar is a large stained-glass window, costing $2,500, which was imported from Munich together with the two companion windows on either side of the altar.

POINTS OF INTEREST IN ENVIRONS

U. S. Veterans Hospital, formerly U. S. Fort Walla Walla, 0.5 *m.*; State Penitentiary, 0.5 *m.*; Ransom Clark Cabin, pioneer structure, 3 *m.*; site of Whitman massacre, 6 *m.*; Blue Mountains (Umatilla National Forest), 15 *m.*; Palouse Falls, 65 *m.*; Skyline Drive, 75 *m.*; Snake River Canyon, 85 *m.* (*see Tour 2 A*).

Wenatchee

Railroad Station: Columbia St., at foot of Kittitas St., for Great Northern Ry.
Bus Station: 132 South Mission St., for the Washington Motor Coach System.
Taxis: Business section to any part of town 35c, two passengers or more 50c across town 50c.
City Busses: In Wenatchee and to Apple City, 2 m., fare 10c; three tokens for 25c.
Traffic Regulations: Right and left turns permitted at all intersections except off Wenatchee Ave., at Orondo, Palouse, and First Sts. Parking in business district limited to one hour.
Accommodations: Five hotels; tourist camps with cabins and trailer facilities.
Information Service: Wenatchee Chamber of Commerce, 2nd floor Chamber of Commerce Bldg.; Automobile Club of Washington and AAA, 106 Wenatchee Ave., N. Headquarters of Wenatchee National Forest, Post Office Bldg.
Motion Picture Houses and Concert Halls: Wenatchee Auditorium, Wenatchee Ave., and Second St.; four motion picture houses; occasional road shows and stock companies.
Radio Station: KPQ (1490 kc.).
Athletics: Baseball park, S. Orondo at city limits.
Swimming: Muncipal bathing pool, at the foot of 5th St.; 9c, children; 15c, adults; children free, mornings.
Golf: Wenatchee Golf and Country Club, East Wenatchee, RD 3.
Tennis: Municipal courts, at foot of 5th St.
Annual Event: Apple Blossom Festival, usually in May.

WENATCHEE (639 alt., 11,620 pop.), seat of Chelan County, center of a great fruit-growing region and point of entrance to a beautiful recreation area, is in almost the exact center of the State, just below the confluence of the Wenatchee and Columbia Rivers. Mountain ranges tower all around, protecting the Wenatchee Valley with its seemingly endless orchards. Rising west of the city, practically from its edges, are high, treeless, yellow-brown hills—cut by deep, wide erosion gullies, where purple shadows lie. Beyond the treeless hills begin the wooded foothills, and beyond these the snow-crested Cascades, with their evergreen forests.

The city merges into the orchard areas; houses become more scattered, but there is no definite break. Apples made Wenatchee, and apples maintain it; it is surrounded by a sea of orchards, covered in spring with a pink foam of blossoms, mile upon mile, filling the valleys and covering the slopes; the air of the town is sweet with the fragrance. In summer and fall the spicy odor of apples is everywhere. In the Wenatchee Valley proper and the four fertile valleys for which Wenatchee is a distributing point—the Entiat, Lake Chelan, Methow, and Okanogan valleys—about 50,000 acres are under intensive cultivation, aided by huge pump and gravity irrigation systems. The yield per acre in the apple orchards is probably higher than anywhere else in the world, and the quality of the product is famous; the Delicious, the Winesap, the Jonathan, the Stayman, and other excellent varieties are grown in the Wenatchee district.

The town itself, though small, is compact and, partly because of this, somewhat cosmopolitan in appearance; there is continuous activity on Wenatchee Avenue, the broad main street running north and south with the river. East of the main business district, toward the Columbia, are immense warehouses, fruit-packing and cold-storage plants, and many railroad tracks lined with yellow refrigeration cars, all plainly showing the importance of the fruit-growing industry in the life of the city. The Great Northern changes from steam to electric at Wenatchee, and it is no uncommon sight to see a hundred freight cars climbing the steep grade.

To the west is the main residential area, with slightly sloping paved streets, shaded by many trees; enormous weeping willows appear here and there. The homes all have neat lawns with flower gardens and, usually, small vegetable gardens at the back. Across the river is the section known as East Wenatchee, (268 pop.), an integral part of the town. The whole of Wenatchee gives the impression of being very clean.

In May the town turns out for the Apple Blossom Festival; visitors come in crowds to see the parade of flower-trimmed floats and to live for a while in a city bright and sweet with blossoms. With the opening of the harvest season, migratory workers begin to arrive and continue through September into October; they are mostly American stock, with some Croatians, Germans, Armenians, and Scandinavians. "Cider for Sale" signs show up in the town, and fruits, particularly apples, are everywhere. Wenatchee is a busy place; the town is crowded; business houses do a rushing business; the fruit workers throng the streets. Finally the harvest ends, the champion in the apple-packing contest is declared, and the exodus begins. Many of the migratory workers leave the valley, but a large number remain from season to season, finding a livelihood as best they can during the winter months.

As early as 1811, fur traders from the North West Fur Company entered the Wenatchee Valley to trap and trade with the Indians. In 1863, Father Respari, a Catholic priest, began his missionary work with the Indians and was followed some 20 years later by Father De Grassi, who built a log cabin on the Wenatchee River, near the present town of Cashmere. The first irrigation was carried on in the Wenatchee Valley by Father De Grassi, who taught the Indians to farm and to use water on their gardens.

Miners returning from the Fraser River gold rush came to the neighborhood of what is now Wenatchee in 1860 and discovered some gold; here Chinese placer miners in early days worked the sand and gravel banks along the Columbia. Many Indian trails, used by stockmen, the Government supply trains, and the surveying parties for the railroads, centered in the Wenatchee Valley, the old council ground of the Indians. Gradually the valley became the trading center for miners and early settlers from Walla Walla and the Puget Sound country and, during the 1880's, for wagon trains from the East.

Don Carlos Corbett founded the town of Wenatchee in 1888, and shortly afterward a sawmill, a hotel, and post office were established. In 1892 the town moved from its original site to the banks of the Columbia River, in order to be near the Great Northern Railroad, which reached that point on October 17, 1892—an event occasioning a great celebration.

Prior to the coming of the railroad, few settlers located in the valley. Water was needed to make the fertile but arid land bear crops. Several irrigation projects of limited capacity were built by the early settlers, and these demonstrated the possibilities of the rich volcanic soil around Wenatchee. But the greater part of the valley remained a desert until the construction of the Highline Canal in 1903 by irrigation men from the Yakima country. This canal, winding about hillsides and tunneling through mountains, distributes water for a distance of 25 miles, irrigating approximately 20,000 acres. The building of the Columbia River Bridge in 1908 was another major event. Nature had provided the Wenatchee country with the soil, the sunshine and the long growing season perfectly adapted to fruit growing; now, with water, orcharding began to develop into a highly specialized industry.

A few years later the valley was covered with row upon row of young fruit trees. Apples were shipped to all parts of the world, and more and more people, learning of "the valley of the apples," came here to stay. Within 25 years, Wenatchee became the center of the greatest apple-producing region in the world. At present, this fruit industry employs more than 10,000 persons in the work of caring for the orchards or harvesting the crop. An average of 23,000 carloads of apples are shipped from the city annually. In addition, each year about 5,000,000 boxes are put in cold storage for seasonal shipments. About 3,200 cars of soft fruits, including apricots, peaches and cherries are also shipped each year.

Cultural development has proceeded side by side with the industrial, and the town today has a good educational system, two small but adequate libraries, two good daily newspapers, and more than 20 churches. Besides the fruit-growing industry, various other enterprises are of considerable importance in the Wenatche region—diversified manufacturing and farming, lumber, irrigation projects, and some mineral development. The Grand Coulee Dam, less than 100 miles away, undoubtedly will be a strong influence toward industrial growth.

Fishing, hunting, hiking, mountain climbing, and virtually every kind of outdoor recreation may be found in the lake and mountain country around Wenatchee. Mountain resorts and many beautiful lakes, including Chelan, Wenatchee, and Lyman, are within easy driving distance. The Wenatchee National Forest, extending over nearly 1,000,000 acres from the summits of the Cascades down to the Columbia, has many well-developed recreational areas; and the Chelan National Forest, an even larger area reaching down from the Canadian border, includes most of the Lake Chelan country, known for its recreational possibilities, and many beautiful mountainous sections. The Caribou Trail area, in Colville National Forest, and lovely Blewett Pass, in the Wenatchee Mountains, are easily accessible.

POINTS OF INTEREST

Points of interest in Wenatchee include MEMORIAL PARK, COLUMBIA RIVER VALLEY ARCHEOLOGICAL SOCIETY COLLECTION, the MUIRHEAD RESIDENCE, and COLUMBIA STREET WAREHOUSES.

Yakima

Railroad Stations: N. Front and A Sts. for Northern Pacific Ry.; S. 2nd Ave. and Chestnut St. for Union Pacific R.R.
Bus Station: 106 S. 3rd Ave. for Washington Motor Coach System.
Airport: Yakima County Airport, 4.5 miles SW. off US 410 for Northwest Airlines; taxi fare $1; time 10 min.
Taxis: 15c in downtown district; 25c to residential district; extra passengers 10c each.
Streetcars: Fare 10c.
Accommodations: Eight hotels; two auto camps; trailer facilities.
Information Service: Automobile Club of Washington (AAA), Hotel Commercial, 310 E. Yakima Ave.; Chamber of Commerce, N. 3rd and A Sts.
Motion Picture Houses: Six; occasional local productions and road shows.
Radio Station: KIT (1280 kc.).
Athletics: Yakima Senior High School Park, S. 6th Ave. and Pine St.
Golf: Yakima Country Club, via E. Yakima Ave. to Terrace Heights; 9 holes, greens fee (for 18 holes) $1.50, $2 Sun. and holidays. Riverside Golf Club, N. from Yakima on US 97, L. across second bridge; 9 holes, greens fee (for 18 holes) $1; $1.50 Sun. and holidays.
Tennis: Lions' Park, S. 6th Ave. and Pine St.
Swimming: Lions' Park, S. 6th Ave. and Spruce St.; adults 15c and 20c; children 10c; City Park, N. 4th and F Sts.; adults 15c and 20c; children 5c.
Baseball: Parker Field, Western International League, S. 16th and Lenox Ave.
Annual Events: Conservation League Sportsmen's Show, last week in June; Pioneer Days, July 2-4; 4-H Clubs' State Fair, Sept.

YAKIMA (1,075 alt., 27,221 pop.), county seat of Yakima County in south-central Washington, is on the Yakima River at the geographic center of the great Yakima Valley. The town owes its growth to the development of the surrounding region, where approximately 500,000 acres of irrigated land, formerly a sagebrush desert, now produce bountiful crops of fruits, vegetables, hops, hay, and alfalfa.

Almost ringed by sage-covered hills, the city lies upon level ground except for elevations in some of the suburban areas. Along broad Yakima Avenue, the chief east-west thoroughfare, is the main business district, its modern buildings interspersed here and there with surviving nineteenth-century structures. At the west end of Yakima Avenue are the better residential areas. North to south on Front Street, the tracks of the Northern Pacific Railroad bisect the city into Yakima, the commercial and metropolitan center, and East Yakima, a residential and suburban section which rises from the end of East Yakima Avenue to Terrace Heights; from here may be seen the huge cleft of the Columbia River Gap and long vistas of irrigated lands and orchards spreading fanlike into the distance.

Along the railroad tracks, a swarm of fruit- and vegetable-processing and packing plants, refrigerated warehouses, and related enterprises crowd upon the pulsing artery of Produce Row, center of Yakima's prosperity, which extends for more than a mile and a half along First Avenue. Here, from midsummer to late fall, thousands of persons are engaged in the handling and processing of cherries, peaches, pears, apples, and other small fruits. Packing houses sort, pack, and store the fruits and vegetables that have made Yakima's name familiar the world over. Vinegar factories and fruit dehydrating plants convert cannery by-products and cull-apples into salable merchandise. In addition to the more familiar products are such unusual items as a breakfast food made from apples, an apple flour, and an apple powder, recommended for infants' diets. Hay, grain, melons, potatoes, asparagus, tomatoes, and other fresh vegetables are distributed by truck to coast city markets, or by "iced freezer" railway cars to more remote populations.

With the beginning of the cherry harvest, toward midsummer, Produce Row, always busy, becomes more hectic, and the narrow paved street is a shifting mass of trucks and shunting freight cars. Day and night the Row is a river of flowing traffic; gasoline fumes mingle with heavy odors of ripened fruit and the clank of hurried machinery. Above the roar of trucks and motors, the sounding of horns, and the shouts of drivers, rise the hoarse whistles of railroad locomotives and warning switch engine bells. In a mounting crescendo of industrial activity, peaches, pears, and apples follow each other in season. Overalled women clad in dull blue or grey uniforms, heads covered with close-fitting bonnets, crowd in increasing numbers into the various plants to care for the freshly gathered fruits hauled from thousands of acres of orchards in numberless trucks, horse-drawn wagons, family automobiles, freight cars. Transient fruit workers, "apple knockers" (packers), wives and daughters of near-by farmers, and townspeople are drawn into service and labor at terrific speed.

During the annual harvest, the routine of the city is interrupted by an influx of migratory workers and their families. At the height of the season in September, approximately 35,000 agricultural workers are required full-time in the fields and orchards, in contrast to late fall and spring, when only about 500 are needed. The migratory family solves the problem of seasonal labor for Yakima Valley agriculture; but it raises another problem, for its annual income is seldom sufficient to sustain it during periods of unemployment between harvests.

Wearing straw or old felt hats, blue denim shirts, jeans, cotton dresses, or slacks, these migratory workers arrive just before the active season begins. Shortly, lodging houses and camps are filled; tent camps are set up along irrigation ditches and at the edges of orchards; streets are crowded with job seekers. During free time they seek recreation in movies or beer parlors, or throng the sidewalks, window-shopping along the streets where many stores keep open to catch late business.

When the harvest is over, the throng of fruit workers dwindles to a comparative handful of girls and women, who pack the orders withdrawn from cold storage for shipment to England, France, Germany, Canada — to all parts of the world and to every State in the Union.

The Yakima Valley was not settled until 1858, primarily because of Indian troubles, which crystalized in the Indian War of 1855-7. In 1858, however, the Yakimas accepted a reservation provided for them by the Government, and cattlemen drove their herds into the valley. Three years later, Fielding M. Thorpe and his wife, Margaret, became the first permanent settlers in the region. They settled in the Moxee district, four miles southeast of the site of the present city. A few other families followed and a school was opened. Until irrigation became prevalent, however, settlement lagged, for despite the extreme fertility of the volcanic ash soil the 8.15 inches of rainfall was insufficient for farming.

Irrigation began early. In 1852-3, the Roman Catholic fathers at St. Joseph's mission, and Kamiakin, a chief of the Yakimas, irrigated by primitive methods a small area of the desert and demonstrated its productiveness. In 1870 John W. Beck planted the first orchard: 50 peach and 50 apple trees. The first irrigation system was established in 1872 when Sebastian Lauber and Joseph and Charles Schanno constructed a canal from the river to the town. Before long, throughout the Yakima Valley, where cattlemen had fought over range and water rights, irrigation became the major interest. These early water systems marked the end of cattle-raising in the valley and the beginning of its prosperity as a diversified farming and fruit-growing area.

During the last quarter of the nineteenth century, an increasing number of families moved into the new community. In 1879 the first newspaper, the Yakima *Record,* was established, and in 1883, a second, the Yakima *City Signal.* The town was incorporated in 1883 as Yakima City, with a population of 400. Shortly thereafter, the Northern Pacific Railway selected a site for a station four miles northwest of the town, naming the site North Yakima. After much controversy, in which the newspaper joined loudly, it was decided to move Yakima City to the railroad station. In the winter of 1884 the entire town of some 100 buildings was trundled on rollers and skids to the new location, the hotel and some of the stores continuing to do business as they rolled along. On December 24, 1884, the first train reached the new settlement. The new city retained the name North Yakima until 1918, when the "North" was dropped, and the former Yakima became Union Gap.

The boom that followed the coming of the railroad temporarily gave the town a character typical of the storied West. Horse-thieves, gamblers, and outlaws moved into the region and soon found themselves opposed by citizens' committees and vigilante groups. Colonel H. D. Cox, an Indian fighter, was appointed town marshal, and shortly succeeded in introducing legal procedures. On January 27, 1886, the day it received its city charter, the town was named as county seat. By 1892 it had a population of 5,000, and the business district boasted 62 stores and office buildings. Despite the panic of 1893, the town put on the first State Fair that year. Business recovery was rapid, and, with improved transportation facilities and extended irrigation, the community continued to grow and prosper.

The Federal Government became interested in irrigation at the turn of the century; with the beginning of the Sunnyside Project in 1905, the entire valley was affected. In 1912 the Rimrock (Tieton) Project was completed. Since 1918 enormous sums have been invested to create reservoirs at Bumping Lake, Lakes Keechelus, Kachess, Meadows, McAlister, Cle Elum, and at Toppenish, Simcoe, and Ahtanum. The completion of each project was marked by an influx of new settlers; and an expanding rim of green orchards and cultivated fields followed the long, interlaced fingers of irrigation ditches, steadily pushing back the desert with the magical touch of water. In the city each development of the hinterland gave impetus to commercial and industrial growth; new buildings displaced some of the old structures along Yakima Avenue; warehouses, fruit processing and canning plants sprang up along Produce Row; production was speeded by the introduction of traveling belts and machines; a somewhat exclusive residence section on the west side reflected the profits made from increasing harvests; and population mounted from 14,082 in 1910 to 27,221 in 1940.

In 1938 Yakima had five public markets, one of the most modern streetcar systems in the State, transcontinental rail, bus, and air service, a junior college, and 52 churches of many denominations. Two daily newspapers, the morning *Herald* and the evening *Republic,* had succeeded the early *Signal* and *Record;* they were owned for over a quarter of a century by the late Colonel W. W. Robertson, one of the most picturesque figures in Washington journalism, and renowned for his vigorous, and sometimes vitriolic, editorials.

As in other Washington towns, Indians from the near-by reservation are frequently seen along the streets of Yakima, as are also Japanese, who operate truck farms in the vicinity. Along South Front and part of Chestnut Street is a small Chinatown, and a few Negroes also make their home in the city. At harvest time many Filipinos come to work in the fields and factories.

As the center of the Yakima Valley apple region, the city gives much publicity to the local apple. Hotels make lobby displays of the fruit, and guests are urged to send boxes of apples to friends. Gallon jars of apple juice adorn restaurant shelves, and apple juice cocktails are featured on dinner menus.

All of Yakima's industry is not, however, dominated by agriculture; a lumber and box shook manufacturing plant is its largest single factory, and a wide variety of other manufactures, including such items as clay products, furniture, and clothing, play their part in the industrial life of the city.

POINTS OF INTEREST

The JANECK HOUSE MUSEUM (*open by permission*), 415 N. 2nd St., the home of L. O. Janeck, contains more than 8,000 Indian arrowheads and stone relics, numerous paintings and wood carvings, and some exquisite needlework by Mrs. Janeck. It includes also a large collection of dolls from many foreign countries. A ROCK GARDEN, adjoining the house, contains many varieties of rare cactus and rock plants from all parts of the United States, South and Central America, and many other lands.

ST. MICHAEL'S EPISCOPAL CHURCH, Naches and E. Yakima Aves., is built of native lava rock. It was designed by Edward T. Potter, son of Bishop Alonzo Potter of Pennsylvania. First services were held here on January 6, 1889, by the Reverend John Adams Paddocke. A portico, added in 1923-4, was copied from the English church described by the poet Gray in his "Elegy Written in a Country Churchyard."

The LARSON BUILDING, corner of S. 2nd St. and Yakima Ave., designed by John M. Maloney, of Yakima, is the city's outstanding business edifice, an 11-story reinforced-concrete structure of modern setback type, faced with brick. It was built in 1931 at a cost of $600,000, and named for the late A. E. Larson, wealthy pioneer. Larson's will provided that, after the death of his widow, the family home at 1011 W. Yakima Ave. be turned over to the city for use as a public museum and art gallery, for which a private collection of Indian relics and several fine paintings are to serve as a nucleus. Larson also left a $50,000 bequest to the city library.

LIONS PARK, S. 6th Ave. and Pine St., was established in 1927 as a recreational center by the local Lions Club. A swimming pool, wading pool for children, and tennis court are provided.

The McWHORTER HOUSE MUSEUM (*telephone for appointment*), 1408 W. Yakima Ave., contains a large collection of Indian weapons and a manuscript library of Indian and historical material gathered by L. V. McWhorter. McWhorter is the author of *The Crime Against the Yakimas* and *Yellow Wolf, His Own Story,* which present, from a point of view sympathetic to the natives, the story of early conflicts between Indians and whites.

The WASHINGTON DEHYDRATED FOOD COMPANY PLANT (*visitors permitted on application to office*), 709-11 1st Ave. N., constructed in 1917, the first of its kind in the State, contains 21 drying units, and is said to be the largest fruit dryer in the United States. Its output of evaporated apples is among the largest in the country. The Yakima plant is one of six operated by the same company, principally in the State of Washington.

YAKIMA FRUIT GROWERS ASSOCIATION PLANT (*apply at office; visitors permitted subject to operating convenience*), 1320 S. 1st Ave., is one of the leading packing and canning plants in the city, and is known as the "Big 'Y'." Here, boxes of apples are carried by an endless belt from trucks at the receiving platform to the cold storage rooms, where they are cooled. Washers then remove spray residue, and the fruit is graded and packed. Lidding machines automatically press the apples tightly into a box and nail on the lid.

CALIFORNIA PACKING COMPANY PLANT (*apply at office; visitors permitted subject to operating convenience*), 215 1st Ave. S., occupies two blocks and cans a variety of fruits and vegetables. Pears, which are one of the most important products, go through coring, peeling, and slicing processes in an almost continuous operation; cans come from the lidding machine in an apparently endless stream.

POINTS OF INTEREST IN ENVIRONS

Union Gap, historic site, 4 *m.*; Site of the Battle of Two Buttes, 5 *m.*; Yakima Indian Reservation, 5 *m.*; Painted Rocks, geologic formation, 5 *m.*; Ahtanum Mission, historic mission, 8.4 *m.*; Sawyer Cabin, pioneer cabin, 14 *m.*; Rimrock (Tieton) Dam, 38 *m.*; Yakima Park Entrance to Mount Rainier National Park, 72 *m.* (*see Tour 2b*). Moxee, hop fields and flowing wells, 8.6 *m.*; Lookout Point, scenic view, near Selah, 6 *m.*; Roza Irrigation Project, 7 *m.* (*see Tour 7b*).

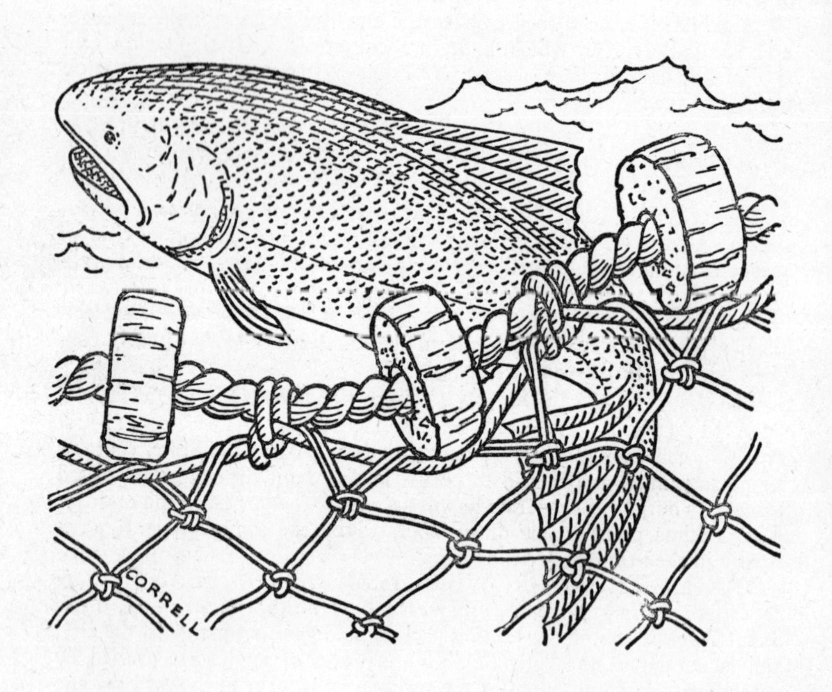

PART III

Tours

Tour 1

(Coeur d'Alene, Idaho)—Spokane—Davenport—Wenatchee—Teanaway—Seattle, US 10. Idaho Line to Seattle, 347 m.

Concrete-paved and bituminous-surfaced roadbed. Steep grades are encountered along the Columbia River and in the Cascade Mountains. Heavy snow in mountains during winter months; chains advisable from December to March. Caution advisable at railroad crossings. Great Northern Ry. parallels route between Harrington and Odessa and touches it at Wenatchee, Cashmere, and Dryden; Northern Pacific Ry. parallels route between Reardan and Almira, Cle Elum and Easton, and Edgewick and Seattle; Chicago, Milwaukee, St. Paul and Pacific R.R. parallels route between Cle Elum and Falls City and between Renton and Seattle.
Good accommodations in larger towns; tourist camps, some with trailer accommodations, in and near most towns; forest camps at many points through the mountains.

Section a. IDAHO LINE *to* TEANAWAY JUNCTION, *246.8 m. US 10-97*

A constantly varying panorama is unfolded on the cross-State route between the Idaho Line and Seattle. Wheat and orchard lands, outcroppings of ancient lava flows exposed by erosion, a great dry falls, rock-walled coulees through which a mighty river once plunged, immense hydroelectric projects, the Columbia River with its deep-cut canyon, the apple-growing district of Wenatchee, mountain passes, towering rugged peaks, mining towns, cutover lands, and fertile valleys.

US 10 crosses the IDAHO LINE, 0 *m.,* fifteen miles west of Coeur d'Alene, Idaho.

EAST FARMS, 0.5 *m.* (2,010 alt., 88 pop.), is one of many prosperous communities in the Spokane Valley. Here Louis Lee maintained his Half-way House for travelers during the mining boom in the Coeur d'Alene district in 1884-5.

Right from East Farms 7 *m.* on a bituminous-surfaced road that crosses the Spokane River to NEWMAN LAKE (boating, fishing, camps).

SPOKANE BRIDGE, 1 *m.* (2,114 alt., 48 pop.), a boom town in the early sixties, has now only a store, a railway station, and a few scattered houses. In 1862 A. C. Kendall built a cabin and established a trading post here; two years later a bridge was constructed, and in 1867 a post office was established. Mail carriers on horseback followed the Mullan Road through the settlement on their way to the mines of the Coeur d'Alenes and the Bitterroot Mountains. The murder of Kendall in 1875 by one Joe Leonard is still gossiped about by old timers. Leonard escaped, only to be slain in 1877, while serving as a scout for the United States Army during the Nez Percé Indian War.

On the SITE OF HORSE SLAUGHTER CAMP, 1.4 *m.,* Colonel George Wright's troops in September 1858, shot 700 horses belonging to a band of Indian herders, in order to prevent the continuation of the war. For years farmers used the "bone pile" for fertilizer, and even today bones of the slain ponies are occasionally found.

At 4.2 *m.* is a junction with a graveled road.

Left on this road to LIBERTY LAKE, 2 *m.*, a summer resort (fishing, boating). The lake was named for Stephen Liberty (or Liberte), a native of Quebec and one of the earliest settlers. Liberty chose the career of guide and mail carrier, after having been educated for the priesthood. He married an Indian woman and finally settled on the Coeur d'Alene Reservation. Liberty Creek, 4 *m.,* is the starting point for a trail trip to MICA PEAK, 10 *m.* (5,225 alt.).

West of the junction US 10 follows the course of the Spokane River.

GREENACRES, 6.8 *m.* (2,039 alt., 1,000 pop.), is a community of garden tracts. Once this area was the center of extensive irrigation, but shortage of water has led to retrenchment. CENTRAL VALLEY HIGH SCHOOL, at the western edge of the village, was completed in 1928, and is an important institution in the valley, with its spreading grounds and five-acre playfield.

VERADALE, 8.6 *m.* (1,995 alt., 35 pop.), is the trading center for prosperous truck-farmers, who grow and ship great quantities of cantaloupes and tomatoes. A larger community in this truck-farming region is OPPORTUNITY, at 10.6 *m.* (1,975 alt., 1,500 pop.).

DISHMAN, 12.6 *m.* (1,950 alt., 300 pop.), marked by numerous fruit stands and small produce markets, was founded in 1889 by A. T. Dishman, who shot the granite cliffs just south of town to open a quarry. Modern business buildings line the highway, and during the growing season the town is a busy shopping center. Brick and lime plants and a factory for the fabrication of aluminum truck and bus bodies employ more than 200 people. Stone is still being cut in the quarry.

Right from Dishman on Argonne Road is MILLWOOD, 2 *m.* (1,953 alt., 242 pop.), with a paper mill surrounded by mill workers' cottages. On the brink of Riblet Point, a brown cliff rising 450 feet above the Spokane River, is WHITE MISSION (private), once reached by a specially constructed electrical aerial tramway.

West of Dishman, 13.8 *m.,* US 10 crosses the old Mullan Road, once a military wagon road connecting Walla Walla with Fort Benton, at the head of navigation on the Missouri River. It was surveyed and constructed by Captain John Mullan between 1859-62. US 10 is locally known as the Apple Way.

At the OHIO MATCH COMPANY PLANT, 14 *m.,* wood blocks for matches are made from white pine for shipment to the company's factories in the East. Lava in pillared formations and weathered piles, with clusters of lupine, Juneberry, serviceberry, and rockroses in the crevices, give character to the landscape.

SPOKANE, 19 *m.* (2,039 alt., 122,001 pop.). (*See Spokane*).

Left from center of Spokane on Riverside Ave. to Monroe St.; R. on Monroe St. to Northwest Blvd.; L. on Northwest Blvd. to the junction of Seven-Mile Road, 7 *m.* Left on Seven-Mile Road across a bridge to DEEP CREEK CANYON, 9.2 *m.,* a deep gash cut by the force of glacial water. Egg-shaped boulders balance on end, and needles of basaltic stone, left by the rushing waters, rise above the level of the canyon floor. The little creek at the bottom is almost lost at times among the rock formations; finally it emerges, eddying swiftly over smooth, round boulders and tumbling in a series of cataracts over the jagged rocks below.

NINE-MILE DAM, 10.7 *m.,* is one of the power developments of Spokane River. Across the bridge, at 11.2 *m.,* the road swings left to the SITE OF SPOKANE HOUSE, 13.2 *m.,* the earliest post of the North West Fur Company in Washington. Spokane House, established in 1810 under orders from David Thompson, the surveyor, for nearly 16 years bartered for the furs of the wilderness. In 1821 the North West Company united with the Hudson's Bay Company, and in 1826 the business of the post was transferred to Fort Colvile (*see Tour* 5). A journal of March 21, 1826, states: "The blacksmith and cook, the only two men we have now here, employed collecting all the iron about the place, stripping the hinges off the doors . . . ."

At 26.2 *m.* on US 10 is the western junction with US 395 (*see Tour 6b*). West of the junction, the highway climbs gradually but steadily. The southern extremities of the Pend Oreille Highlands and Mount Spokane (R) appear darkly purple. Scabrock vestiges of the lava plain that survived the eroding glacial waters of prehistoric times are visible. The buttes (L) form the eastern end of the Spokane Divide, a small distinct fold in the earth's crust originating in the Badger Mountains. The highway runs through a barren plain sprinkled with dry grass; snow fences appear at intervals on both sides of the road; scrubby trees dot the landscape. Fairly large farmhouses, red barns, and windmills are seen at infrequent intervals.

SPOKANE PLAINS MONUMENT, 30.5 *m.,* a rustic stone pyramid, nine feet high, commemorates the SITE OF THE BATTLE OF SPOKANE PLAINS, fought on September 5, 1858. Rumors that the Mullan Road would bring a flood of whites into the region had caused an uprising of allied Coeur d'Alene, Palouse, and Spokane Indians. Colonel George Wright, with 700 men, decisively defeated the Indians at this point after a running battle from Four Lakes (*see Tour 6b*).

A cluster of neat houses and buildings marks DEEP CREEK, 33.6 *m.* (2,309 alt., 35 pop.). Founded in 1878, it was a milling point during the eighties. Deep fishing holes are formed by Deep Creek Falls, and there is a trout farm near by.

At 36.8 *m.* is a junction with Coulee Hite Road, graveled.

Right on this road 7 *m.* to Coulee-Hite Road Extension: Right here 1.8 *m.* to CAMP WASHINGTON MONUMENT. The stone, now marking the historic Colville-Walla Walla Road, was erected in 1908, at Four Mound School, approximately five miles to the northeast. After a storm of protests by historians, it was moved to the present site in 1928.

Three-fourths of a mile southwest at the Forks of Coulee Creek is the site of Camp Washington, where Isaac I. Stevens, first Territorial governor, made his first camp in the Territory.

REARDAN, 46.2 *m.* (2,498 alt., 422 pop.), came into existence after enterprising settlers dug a well here and proved to railroad engineers that water was available. It once was called Capp's Place, but the name was changed to honor a civil engineer of the Central Washington Railway after the line was extended through the site in 1889. Mule shows, at which especially fine animals of the Northwest were exhibited, were held annually until 1915; by then tractors had superseded draft animals in wheat farming. Reardan is mostly dependent upon the farmers of the surrounding territory. Facing the highway are several modern buildings and a flour and feed mill. In a two-story brick building at city center is the Reardan branch of the Old National Bank of Spokane, and to the right is the large steel grain elevator of the Washington Grain and Milling Company.

West of Reardan the highway, paralleling the railroad, cuts through rolling, treeless lands and a few isolated farms. Occasionally a band of sheep may be glimpsed, browsing on the yellow grass or around stacks of straw. Snow fences made of wired wooden pickets lie rolled up along the highway, awaiting winter use. At 53.3 *m.* is a junction with a gravel road to MONDOVI, 1 *m.* Farther along the main highway several gas tanks, with small buildings grouped about them, come into view. The railroad crosses the highway at 56.7 *m.,* and continues parallel with it. At 59.2 *m.,* is a cluster of Standard Oil Company tanks.

DAVENPORT, 59.9 *m.* (2,409 alt., 1,337 pop.), situated in the Big Bend wheat country, is the largest town on the Columbia plateau and the seat of Lincoln County. The highway enters on Morgan Street, which is lined with prosperous-appearing buildings, mostly of yellow and red brick. The red-brick Presbyterian Church looms prominently.

For 12 years, citizens of Davenport and Sprague contended for the county seat. An election held in 1884 resulted in more votes being cast than there were people in the two towns. It was charged that children and passengers on through trains voted, and that names were taken from the tombstones in cemeteries. Sprague won the election chiefly because it could import voters by railroad, while Davenport was forced to transport them by horseback. Davenport citizens threw breastworks around the courthouse and posted guards to prevent removal of county records, but Sprague forces obtained the ledgers when the local guards tired. In 1896, however, Davenport was made the county seat by legislative action. Near by was Cottonwood Springs, a favorite campsite of Indians and traders as late as 1878, when C. B. Sparks took a claim one mile north of the present town. Davenport, named for J. C. Davenport, who established a store here shortly after 1880, is now a trade and shopping center for the Cedar Canyon mining district and has several huge grain elevators, mills, and a soda water factory.

At Davenport are junctions with State 22 (*see Tour 5*), and with State 7 (*see Tour 1A*).

CRESTON, 81 *m.* (2,462 alt., 281 pop.), was named about 1889 by engineers for the Northern Pacific Railway, because Brown's Butte, overlooking the town on the south, is the crest of land in the Big Bend Country. The town made headlines August 5, 1902, when Harry Tracy, notorious outlaw, committed suicide here. Tracy had roamed the country as a desperate criminal until finally confined in the Oregon State Penitentiary. On July 9, 1902, he escaped with a convict named Merrill, after killing one guard and wounding another. Identified by a rancher near Creston, he was trailed by a posse and shot himself rather than surrender. Creston pioneers remember the keen competition and occasional warfare between cattlemen and early settlers. Survey stakes were pulled up so that homesteaders could not establish claims, and local surveyors thrived on homeseekers' fees. The town has a farm-implement factory and two grain elevators. Scattered across the valley west of town are low-lying ranch houses.

WILBUR, 89.9 *m.* (2,166 alt., 1,011 pop.), depends largely on the Columbia River Flour Milling plant, where flour, bran, shorts, and middlings are produced. It is also a shipping point for the San Poil mining district in the Okanogan country (*see Tour 7a*). Completion of the Grand Coulee Dam will increase Wilbur's importance as a trading center.

The few scattered maple and poplar trees lining the business streets are noticeable in a country where trees are rare. The E. R. HESSELTINE LIBRARY (*open* 7-9 *Wed.;* 1-5 *Sat.*), named for the man who donated the first books to the collection, is housed in the City Hall. In the tiny CITY PARK is a municipal swimming pool, 125 feet long, a popular spot in the hot summer months when it offers the only facilities for swimming within many miles. To the left of the park is Wilbur Creek, locally called Goose Creek.

At 85.7 *m.* is the junction with a bituminous-surfaced road.

Right on this road to the CONDIT CABIN (private), 0.3 *m.*, the first homestead of Samuel Wilbur Condit, who founded Wilbur in 1887. Condit, who traded with the miners and Indians, was known as "Wild Goose Bill" because, while freighting supplies to the Okanogan, he shot into what he thought was a flock of wild geese, only to discover later he had brought down a tame gander belonging to a pioneer settler. Prior to the platting and incorporation of Wilbur in 1889, the little community was nicknamed "Goose-town."

West of the junction is a municipally operated recreational area and RACE TRACK, with a half-mile oval and grandstand. The track is one of four in the State where pari-mutuel betting is carried on under the jurisdiction of the Washington State Racing Commission. The racing events, lasting three days, are usually held in late September, following the close of the season at Playfair in Spokane.

Beyond the junction with State 4 (*see Tour 7a*), at 90.8 *m.*, US 10 traverses mile after mile of wheatlands. ALMIRA, 101.5 *m.* (1,917 alt., 446 pop.), named in honor of Mrs. Almira Davis, wife of the town's first merchant, has grown rapidly since construction on the Coulee Dam began. It is a shipping point for wheat; nearly 750,000 bushels are handled each year through its warehouses. At Almira is a junction with State 2, which runs to Coulee Dam (*see Tour 1B*).

HARTLINE, 110.7 *m.* (1,911 alt., 168 pop.), with its row of towering wheat elevators along the railroad tracks, owes its economic existence to the fertile wheatlands surrounding it. The townsite was part of the holdings of John Hartline.

West of Hartline are evidences of a large lake that once flooded the area. According to geologists, this silty depression among the scablands, known locally as Dry Alkali Lake, is a part of the Hartline Basin. Glacial deposits of silt, sand, and gravel are several hundred feet deep. As US 10 continues across the ancient lake bed, the scablands appear again, and plant and animal life are limited. The scaly hackberry, rabbit and antelope brush, peppergrass, and occasional lupine harbor jack rabbits, sage hens, and rattlesnakes. In the summer tumbleweeds roll aimlessly down the highway.

At 119.4 *m.* is the junction with State 2-F, a bituminous-surfaced road (*see Tour 1B*).

At 122.3 *m.* is a junction with a bituminous-surfaced road.

Left on this road is COULEE CITY, 0.5 *m.* (1,584 alt., 744 pop.), the only point between the site of Coulee Dam and Soap Lake, (*see Tour 1A*) where the Grand Coulee can be crossed. In the early days of the region, Coulee City was the junction point of the railroad and stage lines running to points along the Columbia River and to the Okanogan country. Guy Waring, in *My Pioneer Past,* comments: "At Coulee City the branch train arrived too late for the stage which took you to Bridgeport on the Columbia River. Train and stage were scheduled to miss each other, and were invariably faithful to schedule. Had they connected the hotel would have died . . . ."

At 122.8 *m.* is the junction with a branch of State 7, a bituminous-surfaced road.

Left on this road to DRY FALLS STATE PARK, 1.5 *m.* (*hunting, discharge of firearms, removal of shrubs, flowers or rocks prohibited*). A rustic stone VISTA HOUSE (*visitors register*) overlooks the scarred walls of the extinct falls, where a cataract many times greater than Niagara once plunged, a gigantic waterfall with a sheer drop of 417 feet and a width of nearly 3 miles. The dry falls were caused by the erosive glacial waters, the ice cap having changed the course of the Columbia River. Various geologic periods are illustrated in the strata of the walls, and leaves and trees are fossilized in the strata. A trail winds from Vista House down the face of the cliff to the bottom of the falls. At the base of the cliff are Perch and Deep lakes.

As the road winds south from the vista house down many horseshoe curves, the canyon ahead may be seen at various angles. At 4.3 *m.* on the main side road is a junction with a dirt road to FALL LAKE, 2 *m.* and DEEP LAKE, 3 *m.*

The main side road runs between cliff walls resembling cordwood stacked end on end, each piece of different color because of the moss and lichen. At PARK LAKE, 4.7 *m.,* the canyon walls are reflected in dark, still water.

DRY COULEE, 6.6 *m.,* extends east and south into the Hartline basin. The erosion of this lower half of the Grand Coulee is even more interesting than that of the upper coulee. Because of the presence of a narrow outlet into Hartline Basin, glacial waters coursed through interlacing channels. At times spread out over a width of 13 miles, they rushed down the southern slope of a fold, forming a series of rapids and waterfalls that carved out the wildest and most spectacular of the abandoned channels of the scablands. Monads, grim relics of rocks not eroded by the sand-laden water, rise from the canyon floor.

In the Cities and Towns

Photograph courtesy Washington State Progress Commission

TACOMA (MOUNT RAINIER IN BACKGROUN

Photograph by Frank Jacobs

SINESS DISTRICT, SEATTLE

Photograph courtesy of Seattle Post-Intelligencer

JAPANESE GIRLS DANCE IN A FOURTH OF JULY
CELEBRATION IN SEATTLE

YOUNGSTERS TAKING A RIDE IN A WPA NURSERY SCHOOL

Photograph courtesy of Work Projects Administration

THE FIRST HOME OF THE UNIVERSITY OF WASHINGTON

Built in the early 1860's. The columns are now in the Sylvan Theatre on the University Campus

COVINGTON HOUSE,
VANCOUVER

Photograph courtesy of Vancouver Chamber of Commerce

otograph by Bert Huntoon

BELLINGHAM

RVIEW, SPOKANE

Photograph courtesy of Spokane Chamber of Commer

Photograph courtesy of Camera Shop, Vanco[cut off]

THE PIONEER MOTHER

Statue by Avard Fairbanks, Vancouver

ograph courtesy of Hutchison Photo Service

CAMPUS, WASHINGTON STATE COLLEGE, PULLMAN

TRANCE TO FORT LEWIS, TACOMA

Photograph by Lange; courtesy of Farm Security

MAIN STREET OF A TYPICAL BOOM CONSTRUCTION TOWN

MILL WORKERS' COTTA

Photograph by Lange; courtesy of Farm Security Adm.

AT BLUE LAKE, 9.7 *m.,* at the southern end of Park Lake, are bathing beaches and camp grounds. The stained sections of the rock walls record the history of many lava flows and of intervening periods when soil accumulated. After the seventh flow from the top cooled, trees grew up, but the next flow covered them. Only fossilized stumps remain.

At SOAP LAKE, 21.0 *m.* (1,206 alt., 622 pop.), the branch of State 7 reaches its junction with State 7 (*see Tour 1A*).

West of the junction with branch State 7, US 10 winds up from the coulee floor, allowing a comprehensive view, especially of the lower coulee. Wheat fields again appear as the summit of the plateau is reached. The Cascade Mountains come into view.

MOSES COULEE, 135.5 *m.,* named for Chief Moses (*see Tour 1A*), was also formed by glacial floods. The highway at first descends gently along the coulee's eroded upper walls, serpentines along a man-made shelf blasted from solid cliffs, then levels off across the coulee floor. Nearly every color in the spectrum appears with the change in seasons and the play of light.

Leaving the coulee, the highway dips up and down through waving fields of wheat to the Waterville plateau.

In the bottom of a small coulee, at 159.1 *m.,* is DOUGLAS (2,509 alt., 60 pop.). In 1883, four days after Lincoln County was created, the Territorial legislators cut out of it another county, and named it for Stephen A. Douglas. The town adopted the name.

At 163.6 *m.* the highway curves through the shaded streets of WATERVILLE (2,617 alt., 939 pop.). Clay pits and limestone quarries add to the town's revenue. Waterville has had three names: it was Okanogan City in 1884, when it was the main stopping point on the road to the Okanogan country toward the north; later it was called Jumper's Flats because of claim-jumping activity prior to the construction of the railroad; it was finally platted as Waterville, when water was secured from a 30-foot well. Horse racing is an annual fall event, with a pari-mutuel track operating under the Washington State Racing Commission.

US 10 descends into picturesque PINE CANYON, 166.6 *m.,* (2,800 alt.), where yellow pines grow on steep rocky slopes. Many hairpin turns, cut from rocky walls, permit brief glimpses of the road far below in the canyon. As the bottom of the canyon is reached, after a 2,000-foot descent, the road winds among willows and cottonwoods.

Right at 173.4 *m.* is a junction (R) to Orondo Ferry.

ORONDO, 175.1 *m.,* (704 alt., 325 pop.), was founded by J. B. Smith in 1886 and named for the Indian Orondo, whose people worked in the ancient Lake Superior copper mines. The village is at the mouth of Pine Canyon, on the Columbia River. A ferry (50c *daytime,* 75c *at night*) connects with Entiat (*see Tour 4A*).

Right from Orondo on a graveled road along the Columbia River to what is locally known as an ABORIGINAL CAVE DWELLING, 6 *m.* When the cave was cleared by a rancher to make room for apple storage, a flint knife with a wooden handle, an ornate pipe in a cedar case, and various other articles were found in it. Circular underground dwellings, similar to this cave, were often used as shelters by Okanogan Indians before the white man came.

US 10 turns south at Orondo and follows the eastern bank of the Columbia. At 180.5 *m.* a roadside marker calls attention to LINCOLN ROCK, across the river.

At 189.4 *m.* EAST WENATCHEE (268 pop.) lies at the east end of the long, high steel bridge spanning the Columbia River (*see Wenatchee*). In east Wenatchee is a junction with State 10.

Southeast on State 10 along the eastern bank of the river to ROCK ISLAND, at 8.4 *m.*, (615 alt., 130 pop.). At 11 *m.* is the Picture Rock Service Station. Opposite the latter, between the highway and the small red railroad station, is a rock with thousand-year-old petroglyphs and crude aboriginal carvings, now barely visible. Before the Rock Island dam was built, numerous rocks with petroglyphs could be seen on islands in the river.

ROCK ISLAND DAM, 11.5 *m.*, on the Columbia River, owned by the Puget Sound Power and Light Company, was completed in 1931. Its abutments, spillway, power house, flood gates, and fish ways are easily accessible from the highway.

South of the dam, tourists are warned against falling rocks, for the bluffs (L) consist of cracked stone. At 16.4 *m.* a bridge crosses Moses Coulee Creek. Only during the early springtime is there any water in the creek, and then it becomes a turbulent stream.

East of TRINIDAD, 24 *m.* (900 alt., 210 pop.), State 10 winds up-grade from the Columbia River. The quality of the land improves, scattered orchards and farms appear. At 29 *m.* is a sweeping view of the Columbia River from the Columbia Plateau. In QUINCY, 31.2 *m.* (1,302 alt., 318 pop.), (*see Tour 1A*), is a junction with State 7 (*see Tour 1A*).

West of the junction with State 10, US 10 crosses the Columbia River to reach WENATCHEE, 190.9 *m.* (639 alt., 11,627 pop.), (*see Wenatchee*).

US 10 crosses the winding Wenatchee River, turns north at 194.3 *m.*, and unites with US 97 (*see Tour 7a*) until it reaches Teanaway.

Outside of Wenatchee, the highway becomes a narrow lane between apple orchards, a foam of bloom in the spring. At the opening of the harvest season, which begins early with peaches, pears, and soft fruits, the valley is the mecca for thousands who seek work in the orchards. Men, women, and children in all sorts of vehicles invade the city, crowd the auto camps, and fill the camps established on the fruit ranches by the owners. Far and wide amid the immense, heavily laden trees the workers move, with picking bags and long stepladders. While the soft fruit is being gathered, the long sprays of the apple trees sag with reddening fruit. Even though thinning has been done, props must be placed under the heavy limbs to prevent them from being torn off by the weight. Finally the main business of the year, the apple harvest, begins. Trucks rumble to the warehouses; pickers and packers, boxmakers and nailers work with flying hands; mountainous piles of new boxes vanish into the orchards and emerge filled with luscious fruit; there is labor, bustle, and the all-pervading scent of apples.

MONITOR, 198.8 *m.* (697 alt., 165 pop.), is a typical apple-country town. Its warehouses and attractive school plant are conspicuous.

CASHMERE (E. Ind. valley city), 203.1 *m.* (797 alt., 1,465 pop.), shaded by locust and maple trees, is known as the home of "Aplets, the confection of the fairies," a sweetmeat flavored with apple juice and enriched by walnuts and spices. Mills manufacture boxes for the shipment of apples, pears, and cherries. In the early spring, hundreds of sportsmen throughout the State and British Columbia are attracted by the Clam Bake sponsored by the Eastern Washington Sportsmen's Association.

West of Cashmere, US 10-97 follows the banks of the winding Wenatchee River, above which rise foothills dotted with clumps of pines. Orchards claim every available foot of valley land. DRYDEN, 208.2 *m.* (938 alt., 250 pop.), a fruit-packing and shipping center, was named by the Great Northern Railroad in honor of a noted Canadian horticulturist. At 211.2 *m.* is a junction with State 15 (*see Tour 1C*); US 10-97 turns left here.

At INGALLS CREEK LODGE, 214 *m.* (1,955 alt.), is a foaming fall of considerable volume. A store and other facilities are to be found at Ingalls Creek Forest Camp, near the border of the Wenatchee National Forest.

Right from the forest camp on a trail along the creek to INGALLS LAKE, 15.5 *m.,* at the base of Stuart's Pass.

South of the Guard Station the route is marked by many sharp curves. (*Cars with trailers should halt at turnouts; falling rocks are hazards*).

There is a legend that NIGGER CREEK, 215.5 *m.,* was so named because a Negro took a fortune in gold from its bed. Along slopes bordering the creek, soldiers under Captain George B. McClellan discovered quartz veins in 1853.

BLEWETT, 216.5 *m.* (2,325 alt., 54 pop.), now only a handful of cabins, once had a population of more than 250 miners. Prospectors returning from the Cariboo and Fraser districts in 1860 wandered into the foothills of the Cascade Mountains and began placer mining on the creeks. Prior to 1879, Blewett was reached only by trail; in that year a wagon road was built from Cle Elum over the Wenatchee divide. Instead of wagons, saddle horses, and pack mules, today shiny new cars and rattling older models are parked under the pines. Numerous perforations visible in the mountain sides around Blewett are test holes sunk by early prospectors to tap quartz veins. Despite the large-scale development of gold mining, few prospectors continue their lone search for the scarce yellow metal.

SHASER, 220 *m.,* below Sheep Mountain (L), is a Forest Service Guard Station (*camping facilities*).

BLEWETT PASS SUMMIT, at 225.2 *m.* (4,071 alt.), is reached after a twisting climb. A rustic lodge overlooks the upper reaches of the Yakima Valley (*winding descent; drive carefully*). The next few miles southwest are dense forest. The highway passes through the canyon of Swauk Creek, where tunnels and tailing dumps of old mines are still in evidence along the steep sides. This Swauk formation occupies an area of 1,000 square miles, extending from Lake Wenatchee across the Wenatchee River and over the Wenatchee Mountains to the Yakima Valley. Many people come here for winter sports because of deep snows and clear, cold weather.

At 226 *m.* is a junction with a forest road.

Left into the Swauk Recreation Area, 1 *m.* Camping sites are on the bank of a quiet stream, amid a beautiful stand of ponderosa pine.

MINERAL SPRINGS FOREST CAMP, 228 *m.* (2,700 alt.), on Baker Creek, is a sulphur spring around which a forest camp has been built.

LIBERTY, 235 *m.* (2,412 alt., 78 pop.), is a placer settlement. Along Williams Creek, which winds past the settlement, nuggets valued as high as $65 have been found. According to old-timers, a single pan once ran as high as $1,365. The LIBERTY RANGER STATION is headquarters for the Liberty District of the Wenatchee National Forest.

SWAUK PRAIRIE, 238 *m.* (2,250 alt., 100 pop.), another placer-mining community, is at a point where the highway gradually emerges from the shade of the ravine to the brightness of the open prairie. South of Swauk Prairie, meadows and occasional swampy lands stretch on both sides. The carpet of green is welcome after so many miles of sand, rocks, and sagebrush eastward along the route.

TEANAWAY, 246.8 *m.* (1,936 alt., 100 pop.), came into existence as a stopping point at the foot of two mountain passes, when four-horse vehicles caromed through the canyons and along the dusty roads. An old, weather-beaten, T-shaped building (R) is a remnant of the past.

At Teanaway US 10 and US 97 divide; US 10 turns westward (*see Tour 1b*); US 97 continues southward (*see Tour 7b*).

Section b. TEANAWAY *to* SEATTLE, *100.9 m.* *US 10*

West of TEANAWAY, 0 *m.,* US 10 follows the northern bank of the Yakima River. Scrubby pines, with a scattering of willows along the river's edge, mark the semi-arid country. The highway runs through the flat area marking the western side of the Kittitas Valley and crosses the Cascade Range over Snoqualmie Pass, artery of the heaviest travel between eastern and western Washington. Traversing a vast recreational area of national forests, with many lakes, streams, and rugged mountains, US 10 reaches the summit at 3,004 feet elevation and drops down to the populous region along the eastern shores of Puget Sound.

CLE ELUM (Ind. swift water), 4 *m.* (1,907 alt., 2,230 pop.), on a flat between the mountains at the junction of the Cle Elum and Yakima Rivers, was named for the river that tumbles down from Lake Cle Elum, eight miles to the northeast. Although the first settler, Thomas L. Gambel, a prospector, came in 1870, the town did not begin to develop until after the discovery of coal in 1884, when Northern Pacific Railway Company geologists surveyed the area for fuel deposits to supply locomotives on the long haul over the mountains. In 1886 the railroad tracks reached the settlement. Despite a disastrous forest fire and the removal of the town's sawmill, the discovery of new coal veins and pockets in 1889 kept the town alive. Completion of the railroad connected Cle Elum with the Puget Sound region. Four years later, a fire left the 1,900 inhabitants homeless, but the town was quickly rebuilt. The market for coal has been reduced, partly because of the development of water power, but mining is still important to the town. Cle Elum also ships lumber and farm and dairy products. HOTHOUSES (*visitors welcome*), at the end of 4th St. E., grow and ship 100,000 blooms of roses and carnations a year.

In Cle Elum at 5 *m.* is a junction with State 2-E, a paved highway.

Right here 0.5 *m.* to the CLE ELUM RANGER STATION, headquarters of the Cle Elum Ranger District of the Wenatchee National Forest. This district embraces the headwaters of the Yakima, Cle Elum, and Teanaway Rivers and, because of its high mountains and dense forests, conserves an important part of the water supply for irrigation projects in the Kittitas and Yakima valleys.

North of the Ranger Station is ROSYLN, 3.2 *m.* (2,218 alt., 1,743 pop.), a coal-mining town. After the Northern Pacific began mining here in 1886, with approximately 500 laborers, life in the little settlement was disturbed periodically by industrial strife and tragic disasters. Forty-five men were killed in a mine explosion in May 1892; in a second explosion in October 1909, ten miners were killed. Today modern mining methods are in operation, greatly lessening the danger of explosion, and the town has achieved a peaceful solution of its industrial troubles. Descendants of Negroes, who were imported in 1888 to break a strike led by the Knights of Labor, now join with the miners in celebrating Seven Hour Day on the first of April each year; and Roslyn fittingly observes Emancipation Day on August 4. Machine methods, introduced in the mines in 1929, have cut down the time required for digging out the coal "workrooms," and explosions are prevented by spraying mine walls with lime, which keeps combustible dust from collecting.

Many quaint Old-World traditions survive among the citizens, who are mostly of European stock—Slav, Italian, and Austrian. A courtship custom among the Croats and Slavs decrees that, when a man wishes to propose, he must take a crowd of men friends to the girl's house and there, on bended knees, make his proposal. If he is rejected, he buys a keg of beer in which the common grief may be drowned; if he is accepted, his friends pay the wedding fees.

The NORTHWESTERN IMPROVEMENT COMPANY MINE (*visitors welcome*), east end of Pennsylvania Avenue, is the largest mine in operation. The company took over the Roslyn claims in 1898, when legislation denied railroads the right to work mines.

The JOHNSON HOUSE, corner N. 2nd and Utah Sts., the only log cabin remaining in Roslyn, was built in 1880 by "Cayuse" Johnson. CASTLE ROCK, on Pennsylvania Ave., three blocks E. of the city limits, is a picturesquely turreted formation. A cave under the rock is used for picnics.

RONALD, 5.2 *m.* (2,346 alt., 496 pop.), is a mining camp on the site of the old Number Three stope of the Roslyn field, which furnished coal for trains crossing the Cascades when it was owned by the Northern Pacific. It was taken over later by the Northwestern Improvement Company.

A graveled road leads straight ahead to CLE ELUM LAKE. At 8 *m.*, the southern end of the lake, is a dam (L) which aids in water conservation control for the Kittitas Valley irrigation projects. It was completed in 1933. The water storage capacity created by the 140-foot dam is 450,000 acre feet. Here, according to Indian legend, was the habitat of Wishpoosh, an enormous beaver, who roamed over the earth destroying lesser creatures. At that time only the animal people inhabited the earth. Speelyia, the Coyote-god, challenged Wishpoosh to combat, and during the struggle that followed, Wishpoosh tore out the banks of the Keechelus, sending most of the water rushing down the canyon, creating many lakes in the Yakima Valley. The greatest lake of all, backed up by the Umatilla Highlands and the Cascades, finally broke through the mountains and created the Columbia River. Wishpoosh was washed into the ocean, where he devoured whales and fish, until Speelyia, transforming himself into a floating branch, drifted down the river and into Wishpoosh's mouth. Once inside, Speelyia resumed his former shape and size and with his knife-edged teeth slew the belligerent beaver. He then divided the carcass of Wishpoosh and from it formed Indian tribes.

The forest road skirts the lake to SALMON LA SAC GUARD STATION, 18 *m.* (2,395 alt.), headquarters for trail trips. North of Salmon La Sac the forest road is through beautiful mountain meadows. The FISH LAKE GUARD STATION, 34 *m.* (3,325 alt.), is on Fish Lake, which affords excellent fishing (*eastern brook trout*) during July and August. Huckleberries are plentiful in the region during September. Near by is a granite formation, some of whose serrated spires rise more than 8,000 feet. The area is characterized by swift mountain streams that rise in perpetual snows and glaciers, numerous lakes with abundant trout, and a variety of large and small game. Many crumbling cabins and prospect holes remain from early attempts to find precious metals in the vicinity.

West of the junction at Cle Elum, rugged, forested mountains, scarred by rock slides, rise on either side of US 10. Stands of second-growth timber grow above the charred skeletons of burned-over forest areas; beyond are growths of green spruce and fir. After crossing the Cle Elum River, at 6.5 *m.,* the highway roughly parallels the Yakima River, which it crosses at 8.5 *m.* At 10.8 *m.* Little Creek is crossed, and Big Creek at 12.2 *m.*

EASTON, 16.1 *m.,* (2,168 alt., 251 pop.), serves as a junction point for both the Northern Pacific and the Chicago, Milwaukee, St. Paul and Pacific railroads. Most of the buildings are new, having been erected since 1934, when the town was virtually destroyed by fire.

At 17.7 *m.* is a junction with a dirt side road.

Right here 1 *m.* to KACHESS (Ind. many fish) LAKE, (2,231 alt.). Trappers' trails are clearly marked in the neighborhood woods. During the road surveys of 1853, George B. McClellan's men camped here. The young officer had been asked by Governor Isaac I. Stevens to explore the Cascades and find a pass over which a railroad could be built. Spending three months with his well-equipped party in the mountain wilderness. McClellan reached the Canadian Line but failed to discover a pass to Puget Sound.

West of the Junction, US 10 ascends through green forest to a junction with a dirt road at 25 *m.*

Left here 5.5 *m.* to the eastern entrance of the STAMPEDE TUNNEL of the Northern Pacific Railway. The tunnel, completed May 3, 1888, after two years of work on the two-mile cut, cost $1,000,000 and at least 13 lives. Its name was derived from a "stampede" of trail-cutters, driven so hard by their foreman that they abandoned their tools, rolled their blankets, and stampeded down the trail.

The highway skirts the timbered mountain slopes. Vegetation is much thicker; canyons and steep hills alternate along the winding road. At 26.1 *m.* is the NOBEL CREEK FOREST CAMP.

KEECHELUS (Ind. few fish) LAKE, 27 *m.* (2,475 alt.), is in a basin, whose timbered sides rise abruptly 1,000 feet. LAKE KEECHELUS DAM, 500 feet long, extending across the lake's southern end, regulates the flow of the Yakima River for irrigation and conservation purposes. Pyramidal peaks, bristling with greenish-black forest and flecked with snow, are mirrored in the lake. Skeleton trees, part of the forest inundated by the construction of the dam, stand in the shallower shore waters.

SUNSET LODGE (*hotel accommodations*), 28.5 *m.* (2,490 alt., 20 pop.), has a stage depot and telegraph station. ROCKY RUN FOREST CAMP (*stoves and tables*), 30.8 *m.,* (2,500 alt.), is operated by the Forest Service on Rocky Run Creek, where numerous falls have been sculptured out of bedrock. The toll road used by early travelers over Snoqualmie Pass is plainly marked through the camp. Westward the highway cuts through solid rock, high above the water that laps against the precipitous cliff.

HYAK (Ind. hurry), 32.9 *m.* (2,499 alt., 60 pop.), a commercial resort, overhangs the lake bank, at the eastern end of the Chicago, Milwaukee, St. Paul and Pacific Railroad tunnel through the Cascades. At this point the highway swings away from Lake Keechelus.

Left from Hyak 2 *m.* by trail to SNOQUALMIE SKI BOWL (*limited hotel accommodations*), operated during the winter (*December through March*) by the Chicago, Milwaukee, St. Paul and Pacific Railway. The 250 acres of the bowl contain five slides, ranging in length from 1,200 to 1,600 feet. A lift conveys skiers to the top of the hill.

The route turns from the northern shore of the lake and enters the forest. SUMMIT, 35.4 *m.* (3,004 alt., 80 pop.), is the highest point on US 10. Snoqualmie has the lowest altitude of the three main passes across the Cascades; and, in the days when travel was slower, it was the first night's stop east of Puget Sound. Rainfall in this area is frequent in early and late summer; mists obscure the heights. Markers here indicate the boundary between the Wenatchee and Snoqualmie National forests.

At 35.5 *m.* is the junction with a narrow trail.

Left on the trail 200 feet to the log chalet of the SEATTLE SKI CLUB. At 1.2 *m.* are the two jumping hills, one with a 30-foot, and the other a 60-foot, takeoff.

At 35.6 *m.* is the junction with another trail.

Left here 0.2 *m.* to the warming house of the MUNICIPAL SKI LODGE of the City of Seattle. Behind the house are three hills cleared and marked for skiers. One slide is approximately 300 feet long, the second, 500 feet, and the third, a slalom course with turns, 600 feet long. A privately owned ski lift takes skiers to the top of the hill (*$1 daily; 2 rides 25c*).

US 10 begins the descent of the western slope of the Cascades, where differences in climate, vegetation, and the flow of creeks and streams are apparent. Thick tangles of salal and Oregon grape grow beneath tall Douglas fir and hemlock, and huckleberry bushes jut from decaying stumps and windfalls. At 35.9 *m.* is COMMONWEALTH CREEK (*camping space, stoves, tables; good water*) (2,000 alt.).

DENNY CREEK FOREST CAMP (*picturesque cabins and camping facilities*), 36.5 *m.,* is operated by the Forest Service. Many tracts of land within this section of the Snoqualmie National Forest, isolated from the highway, have been set aside for summer homes. The tracts may be leased from the Government for as little as $15 a year, with privileges of renewal. (*Information is obtainable from District Ranger at North Bend, or from Forest Supervisor, Federal Bldg., Seattle*).

The Snoqualmie River was named for a tribe of Indians who dwelt on this slope. Edmond S. Meany, historian, in giving the origin of the word, said: "The Whites have softened the native word *sdob-dwahlb-bluh* (Ind. moon) which refers to the legend that their people came from the moon." Indian legend asserts that Si'Beow, the beaver, climbed to the sky, brought the trees and fire to earth, set the sun for daylight, and created the Snoqualmie.

At 40.1 *m.* the highway crosses the South Fork Snoqualmie River, traverses a flat plateau covered with meadows where herds of cattle graze. Rustic shake fences of interlocking split-cedar rails line the roadside, and lonely farm-houses occasionally appear.

At 56.9 *m.* is the NORTH BEND RANGER STATION of the Snoqualmie National Forest, and at 57 *m.* is a junction with a dirt road.

Right on this road 1 *m.* to the foot of a trail leading to the summit of MOUNT SI (4,190 alt.), a towering and lone sentinel. It is a day's trip from the base to the summit and return. A small creek, about one-fifth of the distance up, offers the last water.

NORTH BEND, 57.7 *m.* (456 alt., 646 pop.), where the South Fork of the Snoqualmie swings northward, is the trade center and shipping point of a farming and dairying district. When platted by William T. Taylor and his wife, Mary, in February 1889, the townsite was called Snoqualmie; later it was called Mountain View and South Fork. Loggers and sawmill hands from near-by camps and mills make it their headquarters. Paved streets, a city-owned water system, and trim houses testify to the town's progressiveness. The shingle mill, opened here in 1890 by William C. Weeks, made most of the wooden pipe used in Seattle's Cedar River pipe line.

SNOQUALMIE, 60.7 *m.* (434 alt., 775 pop.), became a town during the boom days of lumbering and milling. The first white settlers were the Kellogg brothers, who settled on the prairie above the falls in 1858. Lumbering in the district still employs about 1,800 men, but, since the surrounding country has been logged over, the town has begun to ship more cattle than lumber. Ranches in the hills provide both hogs and steers for Puget Sound packing houses. The local Hop Growers' Association was incorporated in 1882.

SNOQUALMIE FALLS, 62 *m.*, is a 270-foot cataract, whose energy is utilized by a private power plant. The falls have cut their way through solid rock, and wind-swept spray forms miniature falls that issue from rock faults at the sides.

STATE TROUT HATCHERY NO. 1, 63.3 *m.*, formerly the Tokul Creek Fish Hatchery, is operated by the State Game Commission. From the surrounding creeks more than 3,000,000 trout eggs are gathered annually, in addition to great quantities of eggs of other species.

US 10 follows a steep and winding, but safe, grade. During the fishing season anglers line the banks of the Snoqualmie River, which flows close to the highway for a distance, then winds far below it.

At 65.8 *m.* is the junction with State 15-B, a bituminous-paved road.

Right on this road to CARNATION, 5.2 *m.* (90 alt., 754 pop.), largely a settlement of Scandinavians engaged in farming and dairying. Founded in 1865, it was called Tolt for the Indian band living near by. In 1917 the State leigslature renamed the town Carnation for the neighboring dairy farm.

At 6.8 *m.* is a junction with a dirt side road. Left here 1.7 *m.* to the CARNATION MILK PRODUCTS COMPANY FARMS (*visitors welcome on week days*), established by E. A. Stuart in 1909, to breed sires to improve the dairy herds of the Pacific Northwest. Here are registered Holstein-Friesians. In 1936 Carnation Ormsby Butter King produced 38,606 pounds of milk, an average of 50 quarts a day. A statue of a former world-champion cow, also produced at Carnation, is at the entrance.

At 16 *m.* on the main side road is DUVALL (50 alt., 234 pop.), a trading center for the lower Snoqualmie Valley. Large stands of timber supply the near-by mills. During the fall the town is a base point for upland bird hunting. Left from Duvall on State 2-C, a concrete paved road, to WOODINVILLE, 26 *m.* (50 alt., 425 pop.), in the fertile agricultural district of the Sammamish Valley. At BOTHELL, 28 *m.* (54 alt., 794 pop.) (*see Tour 8b*), is a junction with State 2 (*see Tour 8b*).

West of the junction with State 15-B, the Snoqualmie River is crossed by US 10 over a concrete bridge. As late as 1934 men panned the sands below the bridge for gold.

Many of the buildings in FALL CITY, 66.1 *m.* (389 alt., 400 pop.), once known as The Landing, reflect the architectural taste of the eighties. Poultry raising, dairying, and truck farming are the basic activities.

In Fall City is a junction with the concrete-paved northern branch of State 2 (State 2-Alt.), an alternate route to Seattle.

R. on State 2-Alt. to REDMOND, 13 *m.* (53 alt., 530 pop.), on the Sammamish River. The town was named for its first postmaster and founder, Luke Redmond, who settled here in 1861. Redmond derives its income from sawmills in the district and from dairying, stock raising, and some fruit growing. Excitement ran high in 1935, when a black bear strayed into town, was treed, and, despite efforts of townspeople and police, sheriff and deputies, remained in the tree three days.

North of Redmond State 2-Alt. parallels roughly the Sammamish River, along the western edge of Sammamish Valley. At BOTHELL, 19.1 *m.* (54 alt., 794 pop.), it swings southwest, along the western shore of Lake Washington, into Seattle, 31.1 *m.* (*see Tour 8b*).

South of Fall City, US 10 follows Raging River, which, though not raging in late summer, is boulder-strewn and moves swiftly. Grassy banks, beneath stands of maple and willow, and shady pools provide recreation for campers and fishermen. The highway, after a steady climb, runs between a border of tall evergreens, then descends rapidly into the Sammamish Valley. PRESTON, 69.6 *m.* (508 alt., 405 pop.), is a settlement bordering the millpond of the Preston Mill Company, whose plant quite overshadows the village.

ISSAQUAH, 75.8 *m.* (97 alt., 812 pop.), settled in 1862, is a trade center for the valley. During the World War, the German Count von Alvenslaben organized the Issaquah and Superior Coal Mining Company, purchasing land and coal rights of a 2,000-acre tract. After more than $1,000,000 had been spent in improvements, the project was abandoned. At the western end of town is a newly constructed FISH HATCHERY, with 20 rearing ponds, 4 of them natural; each pond has a capacity of 50,000 fish. Silver and sockeye salmon are reared here and planted in the Issaquah Creek watershed.

At 77.6 *m.* is a junction with State 2-D, a concrete paved road.

Right on this road to LAKE SAMMAMISH, 2 *m.,* whose shores are lined with summer homes and resorts (*camping, picnic grounds, fishing*). The lake is nine miles long and from one to three miles wide.

At 87.8 *m.* is the junction with a branch of State 5, a concrete-paved road (*see Tour 1D*).

RENTON, 88.8 *m.* (40 alt., 4,488 pop.), the largest and most active trading center in the vicinity of Seattle, covers the flats formed by the Cedar River and the former Black River. The main street is flanked by one- and two-story frame and brick buildings, some with false fronts reminiscent of early twentieth-century architecture. Many Italian and Austrian names appear above stores and on the windows of taverns, shoe shops, and greengrocer establishments. The Star of Italy and the Italian-American Council are active associations within the town.

Dr. R. H. Bigelow discovered coal in the hills at the end of what is now Williams Street in 1853. William Renton, for whom the town was named, was one of the organizers of the coal company which began large-scale operations in 1873. Today, coal mines, clay-products plants, foundries, mills, truck farms on the fertile surrounding flats, greenhouses, and poultry ranches furnish employment for much of the town's population. The Chicago, Milwaukee, St. Paul and Pacific Railroad curves through the southern edge of town.

LIBERTY PARK, Park Avenue and Bronson Way, contains two acres of lawn, with playground facilities, tennis courts, wading pools, and picnic grounds. At the edge of the park is the CARNEGIE LIBRARY (*open* 2-5; 6:30-9 *weekdays*), a two-story burned-brick structure built in 1914.

The HORSE TROUGH, Wells St. between 2nd and 3rd Aves., near the City Hall, was presented to Renton in 1910 by the local fire department. It is a combination trough and drinking fountain, presided over by a bust of Chief Seattle.

The PACIFIC FOUNDRY COMPANY PLANT (*admission by pass only*), at the foot of Factory St., extends over approximately 40 acres, two-thirds of which are under cover. Glazed and rough tile and heat-resistant clay products are made at the GLADDING MCBEAN COMPANY PLANT (*open* 7:30-4 *workdays*), E. end of Walla Walla Ave., along the tracks of the Chicago, Milwaukee, St. Paul and Pacific Railroad.

1. Left from Renton on Main St. (State 5-C) 0.5 *m.* to the SITE OF THE OLD STRAIN MINE, now marked only by a collection of sway-backed, weather-worn bunkers, the remains of a slag heap, and a ramshackle coal washer.

Seepage and slides have nearly obliterated the former entrance. The mine was worked until 1933, when water seepage and thinning of the seams made operations unprofitable. For years the slag heap of waste continued to burn slowly, and the city was overhung by a gray pall. The heap, 500 feet long, 300 feet wide, and 150 feet high, finally was excavated; the slag was taken for the Boeing Airport fill in Seattle and the fill of the Renton Junction cutoff.

2. Right from Renton on Park Ave. (State 2-A), 0.7 *m.* to the north, the highway crosses the lowlands of the Cedar River Valley, marked by meadows, thickets of willow, and alder, and sparse patches of truck gardens. At 1.3 *m.* is the SHUFFLETON STEAM POWER PLANT. Here and there reminders of other days contrast oddly with compact modern structures: the remains of an old mill or a dignified old country house of three stories, with columned porch or circular veranda.

KENNYDALE, 2.8 *m.* (223 alt., 400 pop.), overlooking Lake Washington, is the center of a small farming and poultry-raising district. Offshore to the west is Mercer Island, mantled with woodland, orchards, and gardens. A huddle of black sheds and creosote tanks between the lake and tracks of the Northern Pacific Railway, which parallels the route, is the REPUBLIC CREOSOTING PLANT, 3.7 *m.*

A blue sign beside State 2-A, at 4.2 *m.,* indicates the steep, graveled road to the home of J. B. Migg, Swiss cheese maker. Born near Ragatz Hot Springs in the Swiss mountains along the upper Rhine, Migg arrived here at the beginning of the century and started a small dairy, which grew into a one-man cheese factory. Curded, pressed, and moulded in the Swiss fashion, Migg's product has earned more than a local reputation.

At HAZELWOOD, 4.8 *m.,* is a junction with a graveled side road known locally as the Kenyon Road. At 1.7 *m.* on Kenyon Road is a junction with a bituminous-surfaced road: Left here 1.3 *m.* to the SITE OF NEWCASTLE, marked by an old tipple, slag heaps, and a few bunkers. A winding ditch along the road indicates the former bed of the Seattle-Walla Walla Railroad, built by Seattle citizens in the seventies. Here was once a booming coal-mining town. Now cattle graze in the yard of the abandoned schoolhouse, and a cluster of shabby little dwellings clings to the side of a bare hill.

On the gulch of COAL CREEK, 3.6 *m.,* is the STRAIN COMPANY STRIP MINE, where a seam of lignite coal 16 feet thick has been uncovered on the hillside. The seam lies a few feet below the surface, embedded in solid rock. The coal is taken out by power shovels and delivered by trucks to the washer at Renton.

North of Hazelwood, the main side road winds above Lake Washington. NEWPORT, 6.7 *m.,* on the lake shore, is at the edge of fertile lowlands, where truck farms make an attractive geometric pattern. During the spring, Japanese gardeners, in broad-brimmed straw hats, work in the fields. Roadside stands, laden in season with fruit, berries, vegetables, and jars of honey, are tended by alert youngsters. Bordering the truck farms are the FACTORIA NURSERY GARDENS, 7.4 *m.,* where the road swings through the underpass of a bridge reaching out over the lake to Mercer Island; here it connects with the Lake Washington Pontoon Bridge to Seattle.

At 7.9 *m.* is a junction with a bituminous-surfaced road: Left here 0.5 *m.* to BEAUX ARTS VILLAGE, a settlement patterned after the garden villages of England. Sidney Lawrence, known for his paintings of Alaskan landscapes and marine subjects, was one of the organizers of the Beaux Arts Society that founded the village in 1908; it was intended to become a center of arts and crafts but is known today principally as a lakeside residential area. North of the junction the route bears away from the lake shore through truck gardens and nurseries in a lowland between gently sloping hills; the green of alder, willow, fir, and hemlock along the way is broken in early summer by the brilliant yellow of Scotch broom in flower.

At 10.1 *m.* is a junction with a concrete-paved crossroad: Left here 0.2 *m.* to BELLEVUE (200 alt., 1,114 pop.), a trading center for the berry farmers and vineyardists in the rich lowlands. The Annual Strawberry Festival, usually held in June at the Community Hall, is attended by from 2,000 to 3,000 people, and hundreds of pounds of shortcake are served to visitors.

The AMERICAN-PACIFIC WHALING COMPANY FLEET, one of the fleets of whalers in the north Pacific, is operated from Bellevue. The six stubby steam-whalers, the *Tanginak, Moran, Paterson, Kodiak, Unimak,* and *Aberdeen,* are all oil burners, with speeds of from 10 to 12 knots and crews averaging 12 men each. During the season from June to October a good catch averages about 60 whales per boat. The boats work out of Port Hobron and Akutan in the Aleutian Islands, hunting blue, humpback, sperm, and right whales off the banks in the Gulf of Alaska and the Bering Sea. During the winters the whalers lie idle, their engines silenced and their harpoon guns covered. Twice a year the Bellevue wharfs are crowded with members of families, watching the departure and return of the seamen for the five-month season in the North. A favorite song of these North Pacific and Bering Sea whalemen is:

> Bad luck to the day,
> I wandered away
> And to the man who said I'd make a sailor.
> He wrote my name out
> To be tumbled about
> Aboard an old-fashioned whaler.

North of the junction with the Bellevue road, State 2-A returns to the shore of Lake Washington, across which appear the residential districts of Laurelhurst and Madison Park in Seattle.

HOUGHTON, 13.4 *m.* (26 alt., 260 pop.), a quiet community on the hillside overlooking the lake, is devoted almost entirely to shipbuilding. The LAKE WASHINGTON SHIPYARDS and drydock is a center for construction and repair of both Puget Sound and lake boats, and, during early spring, whaling vessels are prepared for the summer's work. Here the ferryboat *Kalakala* was remade with an all-weld superstructure. This plant pioneered all-weld ship construction with the *Paramount* in 1937, and the first of the kind constructed on the Pacific Coast, the *Northland,* was built here in 1929.

The busy little town of KIRKLAND, 14.2 *m.* (177 alt., 2,084 pop.), is by Moss Bay on the east side of Lake Washington. (*Ferry service with Seattle from pier just off Main Street*). The town, founded in 1886, was named in honor of Peter Kirk, an English millionaire, who visioned a huge steel plant here, because of the iron ore discovered in the Snoqualmie River headwaters 60 miles away. Lots were platted and new buildings were constructed. The industrial bubble burst, however, when mining the ore proved too expensive to be practicable. The town is now the stable center of a prosperous agricultural district.

North of Kirkland at 15.7 *m.* is the JUANITA BEACH GOLF CLUB, which spreads down the slope toward the lakeshore, a popular center for social activities. JUANITA (*picnic facilities*), 16.3 *m.* (64 alt., 1000 pop.), lakeside recreation center, is situated on a cove with a fine sandy beach. It was known as Hubbard, when the vicinity was first settled in 1870. North of Juanita, State 2-A leaves the lake and climbs a hill to a benchland, then drops down through a narrow valley to the Sammamish River Bridge, 19.6 *m.,* where old barns and snake fences make a curious border to the road. At 19.9 *m.* is a junction with State 2 (*see Tour 8b*).

West of Renton, US 10 curves north, winding upward to a level where vistas of the White and Duwamish River valleys, spotted with many farms, are seen far below in checkerboard array.

SEATTLE, 100.9 *m.* (16 to 514 alt., 368,302 pop.), (*see Seattle*). In Seattle is a junction with US 99 (*see Tour 8b*).

Tour 1A

Davenport—Harrington—Odessa—Wilson Creek—Soap Lake—Quincy—Vantage—Gingko Petrified Forest—Ellensburg; 167 m. State 7.

Great Northern parallels route between Harrington and Quincy. Bituminous-surfaced roadbed.
Hotels at larger towns.

State 7 runs in a westerly direction at an altitude of about 2,400 feet through the fertile wheatlands and the sagebrush barrens of the Big Bend Country, so called because of the sweeping curve made by the Columbia River in the central part of the State. Gradually, the highway loses elevation until it crosses the Columbia at 450 feet; then it climbs by a long but fairly easy grade. Throughout the region large, well-cultivated farms alternate with stretches of uninhabited range; at widely-spaced intervals small towns, ganglia of settlement, are strung along the highway.

The Big Bend Country, a rugged plateau cut by deep coulees and scarred with patches of scab rock, is treeless except for a few willows, quaking aspens, and cottonwoods, which grow beside the shallow lakes and streams. It is a desolate-looking country in midsummer, when heat waves shimmer over the roads and scorching dry winds blow across the sage lands; and is even more desolate in winter, when storms sweep down from the Canadian plains and drive the snow into smudgy, hard-packed drifts, across the roads. The main highway, a ribbon of gray asphalt bordered by barbed-wire fences, against which winds have piled the skeletons of last year's tumbleweeds, Russian thistles, and Jim Hill mustard, winds toward the horizon. Telephone poles, their green insulators catching the sunlight, race dizzily toward the speeding motorist; by him flashes the endless procession of signboards advertising shaving marvels, chewing tobacco, and patent medicines.

Yet, desolate as the region is, it has moments of distinctive beauty. Spring transforms the barrenness for a brief season: wild flowers and grass almost overnight cover the hillsides; serviceberry bushes, rooted precariously in rocky promontories, become swaying towers of white blossoms; lupine and sunflowers make a tapestry of blue and gold. Even the dun-colored sage takes on a livelier hue. In summer, purple shadows of late afternoon lie on the bare brown hills; seas of ripening grain are rippled by vagrant breezes; and the multi-colored walls of rocky canyons glow in sharp contrast to the green water of the river below. Autumn brings goldenrod by the wayside, flocks of whistling blackbirds in stubble fields dotted with pyramids of yellow straw, and wild geese, flying wedges in the cloudless evening sky, honking their way southward. Even in winter there is magnificence in the seemingly limitless expanse of snow-covered hills, and in the flaming sunrises that transform the sky with rippling colors.

Branching south from DAVENPORT, 0 *m.* (*see Tour 1a*), at a junction with US 10 (*see Tour 1a*) and State 22 (*see Tour 5*), State 7 runs through large wheat farms. Precipitation is light, averaging less than 15 inches annually; nevertheless bountiful crops are the rule, for the moisture, most of which falls between October and April, is retained by the deep, rich soil. Soft wheat is best adapted to the soil and the climate; one variety, bluestem, is so popular that a small settlement in this region has been named for it.

The larger farms have become almost completely mechanized, but on the smaller farms horses and mules are still used. Gangplows, often with harrows attached, break the stubble fields with speed and efficiency. Sometimes the furrows swirl toward the center; more frequently they run from north to south to check the "blowing" of the land, a form of erosion likely to result from the strong prevailing westerly winds. After the ground is broken it is seeded by a drill—tractor-drawn on the more properous farms—or left to summer fallow in order to insure a cleaner, heavier yield of grain the following year.

The history of this region since the grasslands were broken by the plow has been written largely in terms of wheat. The early settler came in response to the inducement of cheap land and the promise of bountiful crops. During the early years, in spite of the low prices of wheat, he was able to make a comfortable living. The First World War skyrocketed the price to $2 a bushel and for a brief period brought big profits and consequent dizzy land speculation. The deflation of the post-war period resulted in heavy losses and hard times for this area as well as for other wheat-producing areas throughout the country. The index of prosperity for the wheat farmer is in truth the price per bushel: dollar wheat means that bills will be paid in the fall, a gasoline motor will replace the windmill or the handpump, the barn will be given a coat of paint, or the son be sent to college.

HARRINGTON, 14.2 *m.* (2,167 alt., 545 pop.), is a shipping point for wheat and cattle and a source of supplies for a considerable area. Like most towns in the Big Bend Country, it dates from the coming of the railroads. The first settler, Adam Luby, homesteaded on Coal Creek in 1879, and in 1883 Mrs. Emily H. Cutter platted the town on a land grant from the Northern Pacific Railroad. The name of the town commemorates a California banker and land speculator, W. P. Harrington, who with Jacob Furth, a banker of Seattle, saw the investment possibilities attending the development of the fertile wheat lands of this region.

Harrington is a solidly matter-of-fact town, with long lines of boxcars on the sidings, storage tanks for gasoline, grain elevators, and several flour and feed mills. Its busy Main Street is lined with small, well-constructed buildings, among which is an "opera block" of red brick, ornamented with scroll work and a mansard roof, reminiscent of late Victorian architecture. The population of Harrington has fluctuated little in the last quarter of a century, its 500 people representing the number which the surrounding farms can support in service trades and professions. The nearest large city, Spokane, is too far away to compete to any degree for local trade.

West from Harrington, State 7 continues through large wheat farms. Life in the wheat country is a cycle of plowing, planting, and harvesting. Once the grain is in, there is nothing the farmer can do but watch the weather anxiously and hope that none of the many hazards will wipe out his single crop: prolonged winter cold may freeze the tender shoots of fall-sown grain unless a protective covering of snow has fallen; strong winds may blow the seed from the soil if the ground is dry; drought and heat may shatter the ripened grain, or fire destroy the crop. The final hazard is faced after the wheat has been harvested, for, if he is to survive, the farmer must receive a price sufficiently high to return to him at least the cost of production.

MOHLER, 21.1 *m.* (1,985 alt., 100 pop.), consists of a number of grain elevators and a few stores and widely scattered frame dwellings. Characteristic of the small towns of the region is the prominence of the schoolhouse, with old-fashioned cupola and bell. The town was named for Morgan Mohler, a stagecoach driver who served this area in the days before the coming of the railroad.

LAMONA, 29.4 *m.* (1,790 alt., 75 pop.), a shipping point, is a nondescript collection of scattered buildings, grain elevators, a water tank for locomotives, and freight cars on the siding. During the harvest season it is the scene of intense activity, as grain, piled high on trucks, is brought in for shipment or storage.

State 7 runs almost due west from Lamona through a region with stock ranches and wheat farms. The farmhouses, miles apart, are gaunt frame structures, with bare, dust-blown yards in which occasionally a few flowers grow, or scrawny gnarled trees, bent by the steady force of the prevailing winds. As a rule, the barns and other outbuildings are behind the houses, a windmill, also, which turns intermittently with gusts of wind or whirls during a gale. Around the watering trough there are usually horses and cattle and, not infrequently, a huddle of sheep.

Regardless of the size of the farm, near the gate securely fastened to a post is almost invariably a galvanized mail box, which receives letters from relatives back East, tax notices, farm journals, announcements of meetings of the Grange, and not least important, the comprehensive mail-order catalog, salesman at the service of the isolated farm. Some of this isolation, to be sure, is passing: a network of telephone lines links farms to each other, electricity is rapidly replacing kerosene and gas lamps, and the radio is bringing the outside world to the farm kitchen.

ODESSA, 39.5 *m.* (1,539 alt., 816 pop.), is another wheat town, that ships some 2,000,000 bushels annually. It is also the trade and social center of a stock raising area. When prices were high, the town prospered; and even now it thrives in spite of the current low prices, in part because of brisk local trade in consumers' goods and farm equipment. Today automobiles and trucks line the curb on a Saturday afternoon where a generation ago the farmers tied their teams to the hitching rack. Imperceptibly, the business blocks give way to neat yards around simple houses, each protected by picket or wire fences and shaded by trees. In the section near the railroad tracks are several large grain elevators and flour and feed mills.

The town, which dates back to 1886, was settled by German immigrants chiefly from southern Russia, where they had settled during the time of Catherine the Great, who hoped their industry would set an example for her peasants. The Great Northern Railroad officials selected the name of the Black Sea port as suitable for a place in the highly productive wheat country. The inhabitants of the town have markedly swarthy skins and dark eyes, and German is a secondary language.

West of Odessa, State 7 follows a slightly winding course through sagebrush barrens broken occasionally by orchards or surprising vistas. This section of the highway is an invitation to night driving, especially during the hot weather of midsummer. As a rule, traffic is not heavy after dark, and the traveler can speed with comparative safety, for only occasionally is the straightaway broken by a sharp curve, a dip, an incline, or a winding stretch of road around the base of some cliff or coulee wall. Now and then the eyes of an approaching car appear in the distance, grow brighter and brighter, give a brief close glow, disappear. Occasionally, a truck with heavily laden trailers thunders past, or a jack rabbit, phantom-like, leaps across the road. In the spring the scent of apple blossoms reveals an orchard hidden by the darkness. Again, the headlight of a locomotive creeps across the plateau, the light growing larger as the train approaches with seemingly accelerating speed; then with a flash the engine thunders by, and is gone, leaving only the throb of the automobile motor and the whistle of the wind.

MARLIN (KRUPP) 68.6 *m.* (1,315 alt., 94 pop.), on the south bank of Crab Creek, is little more than a whistle stop, with a siding, a warehouse, a grain elevator, and a few stores and houses. Before the First World War, the settlement was called Krupp, but feelings arising from the conflict caused it to be renamed in honor of the first settler, John Marlin, who arrived in 1871.

West of Marlin is CRAB LAKE (R), one of the many connected by Crab Creek, which drains into Moses Lake toward the south. These small lakes, by serving as reservoirs, prevent Crab Creek from going dry in the summer as do other creeks in this region, though it does disappear underground several times.

At 66.6 *m.* is a junction with a gravel road.

Right here 0.5 *m.* to WILSON CREEK (1,267 alt., 210 pop.), another trade center of stock raisers and dairymen. The lowlands and creek bottoms furnish excellent pasturage. Natural corrals are formed by the high, precipitous cliffs surrounding some of the meadows. Crab Creek is a good trout stream, with rapids and natural caves.

STRATFORD, 74.5 *m.* (1,277 alt., 19 pop.), consists of a gasoline station, a power substation, and a handful of houses on the flats at the base of high rocky bluffs.

ADRIAN, 81.1 *m.* (1,206 alt., 75 pop.), is a junction point of the Great Northern Railroad and the Central Washington, branch of the Northern Pacific.

West of Adrian, the road after a slight jog to the south runs directly west for miles through sagebrush hills. Today this region is a semi-arid waste, but when the water from the Coulee project is available, the rich volcanic soil is expected to yield abundant crops.

At 85.9 *m.* is a junction with a graded road.

Left here 6 *m.* to the CRAB CREEK FISH HATCHERY, a privately owned fish farm just north of Moses Lake. During the glacial period, Crab Creek was partly dammed at its narrow outlet, with the result that a lake covering 250 square miles was formed in flood time. Gravel and silt were deposited to a depth of 500 feet.

SOAP LAKE, 86.9 *m.* (1,189 alt., 622 pop.), is a health resort on the shores of Soap Lake, southernmost in a string of lakes in the Grand Coulee. The lake clearly shows its volcanic origin in the cliffs of black basalt along the shore and in the accumulated minerals and salts. This mineralization gives the water its therapeutic value, and also accounts for the suds-like froth that is frequently piled up along the shores by the wind. The town is dependent on the lake for existence. Hotels and sanitariums along both the main and the side streets advertise hot and cold salt-water baths, blanket treatments, and mud baths. Facilities for outdoor bathing are available along the lake shore. During the summer months most of the inhabitants, residents and visitors alike, lounge about in scanty attire, and are so bronzed by the intense sunlight that they resemble the aborigines, who years ago recognized the health-giving properties of the water, which they called the Witch Doctor.

West of Soap Lake the highway climbs gradually.

EPHRATA, 94.4 *m.* (1,265 alt., 516 pop.), at the extreme southern end of the Grand Coulee, is in the heart of the fruit belt, where irrigation is carried on by means of wells, water being obtainable at a depth of 100 feet. The excellent crops produced near by demonstrate the fertility of this soil of decomposed lava rock, and indicate the reason for the high hopes raised by the building of the Grand Coulee Dam and irrigation districts. The parallel rows of tall poplars bordering the main street shade the otherwise sun-baked highway. The town is today the center of increased activity because of the work on Grand Coulee Dam, and the brick courthouse, with its somewhat incongruous Corinthian pillars, is a focal point of that activity.

The settlement dates back to 1882, when the Egbert brothers found here a splendid range and ample spring water for raising horses. Ten years later the present name was adopted, presumably because the method of irrigation from wells recalled the Palestine village mentioned in the Old Testament. The town was platted in 1901 by J. Cyrus.

The last great round-up of wild horses in the State occurred in this part of the Big Bend Country on April 23, 1906, when about 300 cowboys rounded up and drove approximately 2,400 head of horses south to the mouth of Crab Creek. Here they were corralled and shipped to the Bad Lands of the Dakotas. It is told that a few of these deported horses, under the leadership of a white-maned stallion, escaped and came back to the isolated coulees and rocky valleys.

Left from Ephrata 11.2 *m.* on a bituminous-surfaced road to MOSES LAKE. This shallow lake, named for Chief Moses (*see Tour 7a*), warrior, diplomat, and friend of the early settlers, is 16 miles long and a quarter of a mile wide, with a maximum depth of 30 feet. Its shape is that of a pipe with a long curved stem. Artesian wells as well as the lake furnish water for orchards and truck farms. MOSES LAKE (NEPPEL), 20 *m.* (1,055 alt., 622 pop.), on the eastern shore is an agricultural trading center.

West of Ephrata, State 7 runs in a southerly direction for a number of miles, and then swings west, continuing through sagebrush flats.

Winchester, 105.6 *m.* (1,277 alt., 39 pop.), is a farming hamlet on the Great Northern Railway.

QUINCY, 112.4 *m.* (1,302 alt., 318 pop.), has a nucleus of gasoline stations, stores, and lunchrooms amid small frame houses. The summer sun beats down on the shadeless dusty streets, and choking winds, pungent with the odor of sage, sweep up from the canyon and coulee. Periodically, the monotony is broken by the arrival of loaded busses, which stop only long enough to allow passengers to gulp a cup of coffee, or to stretch their cramped limbs before beginning the next lap of their journeys.

This part of the Columbia Basin is both a land of promise and a graveyard of hope. Despite the lightness of the precipitation, which is seldom more than six inches annually, there are productive farms and flourishing stock ranches on the deep soil, rich in nitrates, lime, and magnesium. Scattered along the highway are ghost farms with their deserted houses, weather-beaten barns, and uprooted skeletons of fruit trees, a tragic residue left by settlers, who, at the turn of the century, hopefully broke the land and waited for the promised irrigation to materialize. The dream which they dreamed too soon is now about to become a reality.

Quincy is at a junction with State 10 (*see Tour 1a*).

State 7 bears (L) directly south toward the rugged hummocks of Frenchman Hills, scene of recent unsuccessful attempts to strike oil, across a treeless rugged plateau. Westward lies the long line of the Wenatchee Range, blue in the haze. The highway veers to the southwest, descends a curving grade, and follows the course of the Columbia southward for about ten miles.

At 135.2 *m.* is a junction with an improved road.

Left here along the river. The route affords sweeping views of the Columbia. For miles the river has cut deep into the plateau, and the rocky walls glow in the sunlight or fade into opalescent shadows as twilight falls. At the foot of the canyon the green waters swirl in slow eddies or flow, smooth and turgid, in the deeper parts of the channel. BEVERLY, 10 *m.*, (564 alt., 40 pop.), has one short street where in summer the dust, swept in by small-scale simoons, is ankle deep. Here the Columbia River has chiseled a passage through the

Saddle Mountains (2,455 alt.), whose bold bluffs guard both shores. In the heyday of river navigation, this was a busy shipping point; today it is a distribution point for dairy and poultry ranches.

West of the junction, at 135.6 *m.,* State 7 crosses the Columbia on the high steel Vantage Bridge.

VANTAGE, 136.2 *m.* (450 alt., 6 pop.), is a gasoline station, a small store, and a lone frame house. State 7 twists up the right bank of a rocky coulee, at the bottom of which patches of vivid green indicate the bushes growing along the trickle of water, and furnish the only contrast to the dun-colored sage and red-brown rocks.

The GINKGO PETRIFIED FOREST STATE PARK (R), 140.1 *m.,* is an area of fossils, discovered in 1932 by George F. Beck, a geologist of Ellensburg. The fossils of the ginkgo tree were a find of much interest, since they provided the last examples of the fossilized wood of this prehistoric gymnospermous tree. Descendants of the ginkgo still flourish in the Orient, where they are known as temple trees and sometimes reach a height of 80 to 100 feet. Since the first discoveries, fossils of many other kinds of trees have been found here over a wide area; they include elms, oaks 6 feet in diameter, maples, walnuts, and sequoias 10 feet in diameter, a spruce 100 feet in length, and a maple of 50 feet. About 75 prehistoric species have been found; further explorations will probably add several more to the list. Though this forest perished millions of years ago, descendants of about 80 per cent of the 75 species are still alive.

Within the boundaries of the park are about 7,000 acres, but the Ginkgo Forest itself actually covers about 3,000 square miles, roughly centered around the park. Although the youngest of all the known petrified forests of the Miocene Age of the Tertiary Period, it is, nevertheless, at least 10,000,000 years old. Most pertified forests are found buried in mud or volcanic ash, but this one is embedded in basalt. To explain the fact that the trees were not charred and consumed, a theory is advanced that at the time of the flow they were probably submerged in the waters of some prehistoric lake. The petrified trees are embedded in from 6 to 15 layers of soil and rock; some lie separately, some in close rows. Occasional specimens lie on the surface, in whole or half sections; others occur in peat bogs, amid tangles of roots, stumps, empty tree molds, and now and then an erect trunk. It is estimated that there are between 5,000 and 10,000 logs in the bed. The fossils are of an opal formation and in many instances are clearly and beautifully grained and reflect the color of the original wood. This opal formation represents a distinct point of difference from the agate formation of fossils of Arizona and the calcite formations of Scotland.

Fossilized remains of prehistoric mammals have also been discovered in clay pits of the vicinity, among them camels of various sizes and kinds, mastodon, deer, antelope, rhinoceros, three-toed horses, cougar-sized cats, wild pigs, and rodents of various types.

The ADMINISTRATION BUILDING (R) contains polished specimens, microphotographs of the grains of petrified wood, samples of crystal, and shells and pieces of rock specimens from many parts of the world. Trails lead (R) from the building to spots where fossils of fir and cedar have been unearthed. (*Chipping and appropriation of specimens, and removal of shrubs, flowers, or rocks prohibited*).

West of the Petrified Forest, State 7 winds up the side of the coulee, and then traverses miles of practically level sagebrush lands, utterly devoid of habitation, to reach the flat Kittitas Valley, with its network of irrigation canals, prosperous-looking farms, neat houses and capacious barns, fields of hay and alfalfa, herds of sleek cattle, and flocks of sheep. Long rows of Lombardy poplars break the force of the prevailing winds.

ELLENSBURG, 167 *m.* (1,518 alt., 5,944 pop.), (*see Tour 7b*) is at a junction with US 97 (*see Tour 7b*).

Tour 1B

(Junction US 10)—Almira—Grand Coulee—Coulee Dam—Mason City, 23.5 m. State 2.

Washington Motor Coach System operates direct service to Coulee Dam in summer months; passengers transferred at Almira and Coulee Junction in winter.
Government-built railroad to Grand Coulee Dam, operated by contracting companies; does not carry passengers.
Cabin, trailer, and hotel accommodations at Grand Coulee. Hotels at Mason City. Vista shelters at damsite.
Hard-surfaced road, occasional rough stretches.

The route north to Coulee Dam from its junction with US 10 at Almira (*see Tour 1a*) is upgrade through dry wheatlands and occasional patches of scab rock and sagebrush. Rising slowly, with curves and dips, the highway reaches the Columbia River, then descends dizzily by a winding three-mile grade into the canyon carved by the river to Coulee Dam, now in process of construction.

When completed, Coulee Dam will be one of the wonders of the world. It will bring nearer to realization a plan to irrigate a semi-desert area almost as large as the State of Connecticut; and, as a secondary function, it will generate electric current to the extent of 2,520,000 horsepower. The dam is designed to halt the full flood of the mighty Columbia, which drains most of the northwest, back it up into a vast artificial lake 151 miles long, and regulate its flow for 450 miles to the Pacific. Over the giant spillway will plunge a roaring cataract, three times the height of Niagara Falls and several times its volume. By means of the mightiest pumping system yet devised, enough water will be elevated in a vertical lift of 280 feet to fill and keep filled a great natural chasm, Grand Coulee, which will become a balancing reservoir some 30 miles long and several miles wide. From this second man-made lake, canals as long as 100 miles will carry water to the rich volcanic soil of three counties.

This prodigious project, begun in 1933 and expected to be finished in 1940, employed at its peak-figure in 1937 about 6,500 persons. It is estimated that between four and five hundred thousand visitors have come annually to watch the construction of the dam; 7,000, it is said, visited the spectacle in a single day.

North of ALMIRA, 0 *m.,* is an area adapted to dry wheat farming and sheep and cattle grazing. This terrain will not benefit directly from the Coulee Dam, since the level to be irrigated begins 30 miles to the southwest. Sufficient water is supplied here by deep wells, manned by tall windmills which are turned by the prevaling westerly winds. The dry climate and sandy soil are most favorable to the raising of hard Bluestem wheat—a crop which brings a high price in western markets.

At 12 *m.* is a junction with an alternate road, route from Wilbur (*see Tour 1a*) to Coulee Dam. The route twists through areas of sagebrush and wheatlands, crossing the Grant County line at 14 *m.*

Carcasses of ground squirrels and gophers are often strewn along the roadside during spring and early summer; a major enemy of crops, they multiply rapidly in early spring, making their first appearance in late February. Gophers feed on the young shoots of grain and later attack the budding stalks, sometimes causing considerable destruction in the grainfields. Farmers try to exterminate them through poison and shooting, and they are hunted for sport by men and boys from the city; yet, so far, no way has been found to get rid of them. In July, their winter food supply safely stored away, they return to their burrows, while farmers plan the next season's campaign against them. A tale, often repeated among farmers, shows the gopher continuing his war against the farmer even during the winter: "An old man from west of Davenport . . . planted a lot of fruit trees. When winter came he was surprised to note that the snow in his orchard kept getting deeper all the time, while it remained about the same everywhere else. Finally, it got up to the limbs of the trees. When a thaw set in, the mystery was solved. The gophers, working underground, had first devoured the roots of the trees and then eaten the trunks, little by little, the tops settling down as fast as the trunks were cut off below."

At 17 *m.* (*drive slowly*) the road breaks suddenly over a rise, giving a breath-taking view of the State's greatest power and reclamation project. Somewhat comparable to Grand Canyon, with the purple and rust of its towering walls, the Columbia canyon is here made especially awesome by grotesque lava formations and rounded pinnacles in the rock strata cut through by the river centuries ago. A descent of three miles by a series of dizzying switchbacks to the canyon floor 400 feet below is so rapid that many experience a sensation in the ear drums.

State 2 forms a junction with State 2-F, a hard-surfaced road, at the entrance to Grand Coulee.

West from the junction, State 2-F, the alternate route used by visitors from the western part of the State to Coulee Dam, swings southward into the Grand Coulee, a dry canyon 50 miles long, from 400 to 1,200 feet deep, and from 2 to 6 miles wide. Part of this area is to be flooded by water pumped from the backwater of Coulee Dam and retained in storage by two dams in the upper coulee. This will be the balancing reservoir of the vast irrigation project.

Bordering the highway are several mushroom communities, with rude frame buildings, cabin camps, and even an occasional "card-board" shack.

At 0.7 *m.* is DELANO (est. pop. 500), at 1.8 *m.* ELECTRIC CITY (est. pop. 1,500), and at 2.6 *m.* OSBORNE (est. pop. 900).

At 8 *m.* is a junction with a dirt side road. R. here 0.5 *m.* to STEAMBOAT ROCK. Visible along the route before the junction is reached, this mesa was an island in the prehistoric Columbia River which carved the coulee. The ancient stream, swollen by glacial floods, is believed to have rushed through the valley at tremendous speed. Steamboat Rock once lay between twin falls two miles wide and with an 800-foot drop, 633 feet greater than that of Niagara. Today, the rock, its upper stratified lava resembling the decks of an ocean liner, gives the effect of a derelict adrift on a sea of sage. On a low granite outcropping, near the rock's northern end, are Indian ROCK PAINTINGS of indeterminate age.

To the east (L) is the mouth of deep, shadowy NORTHRUP CANYON, a rocky passage cut by a tributary glacial drainage. In the wet season numerous trickles of muddy water, falling hundreds of feet, cascade down the canyon walls.

The highway continues south, skirting dark purple walls and passing through arid sagebrush areas to a junction with US 10 at COULEE JUNCTION 27.8 *m.* (*see Tour 1a*).

GRAND COULEE, 19.8 *m.* (1,584 alt., 3,659 pop.), is entered by way of a steep grade. Still new and raw, this lusty little city clings to the rocky slopes above the Columbia River, a hot, dusty, and often windswept "boom" metropolis cherishing hopes of permanence. In Grand Coulee three former towns are merged: Coulee Heights, Coulee Center, and Grand Coulee.

The short, steep business blocks are faced with stores, cafés, hotels, beer taverns, and motion picture theaters. One of the latter offers occasional stage shows. The *News* and the *Times,* established as weeklies in November 1933, were combined as the *News-Times* in 1937.

Grade and high school buildings have been erected, but a library is still lacking. The CITY HALL (L) has the appearance of a low, white shed. Somewhat more imposing, on a hill above, is a white-painted, black-trimmed LABOR TEMPLE.

Since 1933, many sensational stories have been told of Grand Coulee's frontier abandon and rough pleasures, but little of these are apparent to the visitor. When the laboring hordes first poured in, life in the burgeoning town was undoubtedly vigorous and untrammeled. Today, however, leading citizens deny that wide-open gambling exists or that alcohol is sold outside the state liquor store. It is recalled that Grand Coulee has had no major robberies and but one killing in a five-year period. Grand Coulee offers three hotels, two trailer camps, and some cabin camp accommodations.

At 21.5 *m.* is the UNITED STATES GOVERNMENT WEST CONSERVATION POINT, supervised by the United States Bureau of Reclamation. The roofed vista house (R) seats 275 persons, and affords a splendid view of the slowly rising dam. Additional benches are scattered through the commodious parking area. Modern rest rooms equipped with hot and cold water and a first aid room are provided in the vista house, open the year round, and a public address system carries short lectures on the purposes and scope of the dam. A small vista house, open only in the summer months, is across the river on the east side.

In one of the lower rooms of the west side vista house is displayed a model of the dam, constructed on a scale of 1 to 600, showing three stages of the project: First, the Grand Coulee before the work started; next, the site after the completion of the excavation; and finally, the completed dam, with powerhouses and pump station.

The dam will be 550 feet in height, but seems lower because of its length of 4,300 feet and a thickness at its base of 500 feet, which tapers to a crest of 30 feet. Its sides are thrust deep into scarred rock and its base is anchored in bedrock far below the river's bottom. It will be capable of holding a flood of 1,000,000 cubic feet of water per second, although the greatest recorded flow of the Columbia is less than half that volume. The river pours through channels arranged in the center of the dam; on the down side are twin powerhouses.

One may say that the site of Grand Coulee Dam was determined centuries ago. Lava, hissing and boiling, fought with angry waters, cooled, and bore plant life; then lava came again, repeating the same cycle in successive periods, until seven flows had been recorded in the dark porous rock, streaked with reds and greens, of the high coulee walls. Centuries passed, and then a great ice sheet, which scientists say was 4,000 feet thick, descended from the North. Tearing the earth's surface, pushing huge quantities of boulders and gravel before it, the ice sheet moved southward, melting, and forming a mighty flood. The flood boiled over the river's channels, grinding out great gorges and forming new channels. Temporarily, at the present site of Coulee Dam, the river was diverted from its regular course and roared south across the gently sloping tableland, forming what is now known as the Grand Coulee, a chasm over 50 miles long, 800 feet deep and from 2 to 5 miles wide. It then plunged over the great cataract now known as DRY FALLS (*see Tour 1a*) and rejoined the old channel further to the south. When the great ice mass finally melted away, the river resumed its age-old course, leaving the Grand Coulee high and dry. The dam is being built where the river was once diverted, and by great pumping machines is causing the water to flow down the ancient waterway, this time to irrigate 1,300,000 acres which have long been desert land.

There were other important factors that determined the site. The junction of the river with the coulee has a natural dam foundation of hard, white granite, over 800 feet deep. Nature also left a measureless quantity of gravel on the bank of the valley. Most important of all was the fact that here, bordering a river whose discharge is more regular throughout the entire year than any other river of the land, and whose runoff is five times as great as that of the Colorado River at Boulder Dam, is a vast stretch of arid land which needs to be irrigated—an authority on reclamation called it "one of the most fertile bodies of irrigable land in this or any other country."

Despite the natural advantages of the site, construction involved many problems never before confronted by engineers. It was necessary to build a massive structure larger than any ever built before, which would withstand the pressure of water 355 feet deep across a width of 4,300 feet. The Columbia, flowing as fast as 14 miles an hour, had to be diverted from its ancient channel and made to flow through a man-made passage while the foundations were being laid. By means of a tremendous belt conveyor 15,000,000 cubic yards of earth and rock were transported more than a mile to a level 600 feet higher and then dumped into Rattlesnake canyon. A million tons of wet earth had to be frozen by means of great icing tubes to prevent the mass slipping into the excavation area.

Work on Coulee Dam site began with core-drilling in the late summer of 1933. Prior to that time numerous engineers, among them General G. W. Goethals, of Panama Canal fame, had gone into the wild and almost uninhabited Upper Coulee country to inspect the undertaking. The starting of work on the dam project was hastened by the depression, when funds were allotted for public works to relieve unemployment. The Mason-Walsh-Atkinson-Kerr Company, holding the first contract, began work in October 1934; the first unit was finished early in 1938. The foundation, or so-called "lower dam," was then in place. The MWAK company joined with other bidders in a new contract to continue construction, forming the Consolidated Builders, Incorporated.

The most spectacular features of construction are now over. On May 21, 1939, a bucket of concrete was poured which marked the completion of 60 per cent of the 10,500,000 cubic yards necessary to complete the dam proper. The dam had already surpassed in size any other man-made construction on the face of the earth. On March 22, 1941, the first generators began to produce Grand Coulee power.

The problem of lifting the water from the river to the bed of the coulee was complicated by the fact that the new level of the lake behind the dam will be 280 feet below the point necessary to deliver water on the floor of the Grand Coulee. Twelve mighty units of the pumping plant, each driven by a 65,000 horsepower motor and capable of handling 1,600 feet of water per second, will force water upward through pipes 13 feet in diameter and deliver it into the coulee at a point 1.7 miles distance. Engineers state that probably at no other place would such a pumping system be practicable.

The secondary reservoir into which the water will be pumped will be 30 miles long, in the northern half of the Grand Coulee. Through construction of earth-filled dikes across it, one near the dam site and the other near Coulee City 27 miles away, a reservoir will be made. Man-made canals will conduct the water from the south dam into the irrigation area by gravity flow; by use of the fall of the water in the main canals, supplemental and seasonal power can be generated to lift part of the water an average height of 70 feet, making additional acreage available for irrigation.

Although the Columbia Basin project is primarily an irrigation development, it will also provide the world's greatest power plant with a capacity more than one-fourth greater than that of Boulder Dam. Power is to be distributed over a wide area, and it is predicted that the proceeds from its sale will not only pay for the project, but will eventually bring the Nation a profit on its investment. This investment is, like everything connected with the undertaking, huge: an estimated $174,000,000 in the dam and power plant and approximately $394,000,000 by the time (25 to 50 years) all contemplated reclamation and conservation features are added.

The dam is intended to make possible new homes in the farmlands for from 25,000 to 40,000 families, and for an urban population of equal size; and to make available to the people of two States and perhaps more an abundant supply of cheap power. One of the interesting by-products will be a lake 151 miles long, extending from the dam site to the Canadian Border, which may be developed for recreational and industrial purposes. This lake will cover an area of 82,000 acres at an elevation of 1,290 feet, and the backwater will eliminate many falls and rapids which formerly existed there. Many towns and villages along the Columbia valley will have to be removed before the backwater reaches its final height. Steamers, pleasure yachts, and speed boats will ply on it. The Federal Government has established strict supervision over the future irrigated section. The Anti-Speculation Act, passed by Congress on May 27, 1937, provides heavy penalties if the lands are sold at speculative prices to prospective irrigation settlers. No water may be obtained from the canals of the project until these penalties are paid.

Farmers who locate in the reclaimed area will buy at prices ranging from $5 to $15 per acre land estimated to be two and one-half times as productive as the average soil. They will be required to pay, over a period of 40 years, without interest, the sum of $88 per acre for water rights, plus $3.19 per acre maintenance charges. Their houses will be lighted and heated by cheap electricity, which they may use to do much of their work.

Leaving the observation point, the route winds down to enter COULEE CITY (1,085 alt., 744 pop.), at 22.5 *m.* Usually termed "Engineers' Town," Coulee City presents a pleasing picture of neatly arranged, inviting residences with lawns and flower beds laid out on a gentle slope to the left of the highway. The gleaming white ADMIN-

ISTRATION BUILDING (L), headquarters for Government construction engineers, is in the background.

The highway bears sharply right beyond Coulee Dam to span a suspension bridge across the Columbia. When the dam is completed, another highway will cross its top, 30 feet wide, giving an awe-inspiring view of the plunging waters, roaring through man-made channels.

MASON CITY, 23.5 *m.* (1,510 alt., 2,500 pop.), is called an "all-electric" community. The result of a planned housing program by the MWAK Company, it was named after the senior partner of the firm. Buildings were shipped piecemeal to the site and assembled; all are painted white. The town has schools, stores, several tennis courts, a motion picture theater and a well-equipped hospital.

Tour 1 C

Junction with US 10—Leavenworth—Scenic—Snohomish—Everett; 113.3 *m.,* State 15.

Bituminous-surfaced roadbed except for graveled stretch between Gold Bar and Chiwaukum: route closed between Scenic and Chiwaukum from November to May.

Fire permits required on trail trips in Snoqualmie and Wenatchee national forests. Great Northern roughly parallels route. Hotels in larger towns; resorts and trailer accommodations; free Forest Service camps on trails.

One of the four routes across the Cascade Mountains, State 15, known as the Stevens Pass Road, traverses rugged, sparsely settled territory almost from its eastern point of departure near Leavenworth. Ascending the watershed of the Wenatchee River toward the summits of the Cascade Range, the highway passes through portions of the Wenatchee and Snoqualmie national forests, where recreational areas may be reached by numerous side roads and trails. Downward from the summit, the route lies between mile-high peaks along the valley of the Tye, Skykomish, and Snohomish Rivers, streams that are never placid and, during floodtime, are torrential. West of the mountains are dairy lands, with large herds of grazing milch cows and groups of trim farmhouses, large red barns, and silos. Near the highway, the Snohomish flows sluggishly towards Puget Sound. The soil and the humid atmosphere of the valley favor intensive farming and dairying; often three crops of garden produce are raised in one year on this alluvial bottom land.

From its junction with US 10-97, 0 *m.,* State 15 passes numerous fruit-packing plants, warehouses, and piles of box shooks, necessary adjuncts of the immense apple orchards in the Wenatchee Valley. At 1.3 *m.* is a junction with a side road.

Right here across a bridge over the Wenatchee River to PESHASTIN (Ind. broad-bottom canyon), 0.3 *m.* (1,047 alt., 1,058 pop.). Fruit warehouses and a box factory dominate the business section of the small town. Beginning in 1892 with the arrival of the Great Northern Railroad, Peshastin developed with the introduction of irrigation. Pine forests in the adjacent country supply box-making mills.

West of the junction, State 15 looks down on the orchards—500,000 mature trees in a two-mile radius. In the cool springtime the whole countryside is faintly pink with the blossoms. Hundreds of migratory fruit pickers swarm through the region seeking work during the harvest season.

Near LEAVENWORTH, 5.3 *m.* (1,166 alt., 1,608 pop.), where Tumwater Canyon opens from Tumwater Mountain and Icicle Ridge into river flats, the broadening valley is flanked by sand hills, sparsely overgrown with pine. Leavenworth originated as a Great Northern construction camp, and when an enterprising proprietor moved to track-side from the Icicle settlement miles away, the camp secured a store and a post office. In 1892 the Leavenworth Townsite Company platted and named the town. The railroad made it a division point in 1898, where shops and roundhouses were maintained until completion of the new Cascade Tunnel in 1929. Fruit-packing and storage plants serve the orchardists of the vicinity. More than 170 carloads of apples were shipped in 1936.

Irrigation was practiced even by early agriculturalists in this region. Wooden casks mounted on wagons were used to haul water from the river, truckers charging 25c for a tankfull. Now, extensive irrigation systems developed by the Bureau of Reclamation draw water from the Icicle, Chumstick, and Chiwawa Rivers to supply a wide area of valley orchards.

At the eastern end of the town is the LEAVENWORTH RANGER STATION, where fire permits are issued and information is available concerning trails, camps, and fishing conditions. Leavenworth is the entrance to the LEAVENWORTH RECREATION AREA, nearly 300,000 acres of mountainous country extending up to the headwaters of Peshastin, Ingalls, Icicle, and Chiwaukum creeks. Two miles (R) from the ranger station is the WINTER SPORTS AREA (*ski huts*). ROOSEVELT HILL is ideal for first-class jumpers; the record of 270 feet was made in February 1941. The Leavenworth Winter Sports Club conducts a ski tournament annually in February.

At 5.8 *m.* is the junction with a dirt road.

Left from the junction, traversing orchard lands, 5 *m.* to BROWN'S RESORT, a dude ranch. Through a V-shaped gorge the road enters a cradle-like basin to EIGHTMILE CAMP, 8 *m.,* adjacent to the well-stocked fishing lakes and to streams at the base of Mount Stuart. At 10 *m.* is BRIDGE CREEK CAMP.

Near CHATTER CREEK GUARD STATION, 17 *m.,* the road ends at a junction with two trails: R. here 4 *m.* along the Icicle River to FRENCH CREEK and FROSTY CREEK 5.5 *m.*; at 6.1 *m.,* is a junction with a side trail: R. here 4 *m.* to the three DOELLE LAKES. The main trail passes LELAND CREEK 2 *m.,* and ends amid CHAIN OF LAKES, 12.7 *m.* Left on the other trail from Chatter Creek Guard Station along Jack Creek; at Meadow Creek, 5 *m.,* is a side trail: L. here 4 *m.* are the old VAN EPPS MINES beside VAN EPPS CREEK. Retrace to main trail from junction on Meadow Creek; at 5.5 *m.* is PADDY GO EASY PASS (5,500 alt.), and at 9.5 *m.* the trail ends at a junction with the CLE ELUM RIVER ROAD (*see Tour 1b*).

State 15 passes POWER CREEK, 7.8 *m.,* and the hydroelectric plant that supplies the Great Northern's electrified division across the Cascade Range. DRURY, 10.9 *m.,* is a tourist camp with a view of DRURY FALLS. The highway crosses the boundary of the TUMWATER RECREATION AREA, 15.6 *m.* At 15.8 *m.* is a junction with a side road.

Left on this road 0.3 *m.* is the State Fish hatchery, which stocks the alpine lakes and streams, principally with trout.

The CHIWAUKUM FOREST CAMP (*tourist facilities*), lying between Chiwaukum Creek and the Wenatchee River, is reached at 15.9 *m.* From here the highway descends into TUMWATER CANYON, a cliff-shadowed chasm carved into the mountains by the rushing Wenatchee River, swollen by numerous creeks and cascades that join it in its descent from the summit. Spring brings to bloom great clusters of rock lily in crevices and sets dozens of small waterfalls to polishing the rock walls of the canyon. Streamlets from the higher snowfields survive into midsummer.

West of WINTON, 19.1 *m.* (2,085 alt., 26 pop.), a lumber camp and post office with a few stores and service stations, State 15 ascends the eastern slope in a series of curves. At 20.4 *m.* is the junction with State 15-C, an improved road.

Right on this road through hilly country of sparse vegetation and small trees to LAKE WENATCHEE, 4.7 *m.* (1,870 alt.), a body of deep-blue water, five miles long, filling an indentation in the slope of the Cascades.

At the eastern end of Lake Wenatchee is a junction with State 15-D, a dirt road: L. here 4 *m.* to LAKE WENATCHEE RANGER STATION and TELMA, 9 *m.,* a resort and campground at the other end of the lake. At 11 *m.* is a junction with a forest road: L. here to SODA SPRINGS, 9 *m.,* a forest camp, popular since 1895 because of the supposed medicinal value of the waters. Here the forest road ends. From the junction at 11 *m.,* the main dirt road leads to WHITE RIVER FALLS, 21 *m.*; at 25 *m.* is INDIAN CREEK and the end of the road, from which trails lead into the Glacier Peak Recreation Area.

At 6.6 *m.* on State 15-C is FISH LAKE, where the fishermen for perch and bass are well rewarded. The route leaves State 15-C at 11 *m.,* and bears left to ascend the Chiwawa River basin.

At 32.9 *m.* is a tiny settlement. Here the road ends at a junction with a trail. Straight ahead 12 *m.* on the trail is BUCK CREEK PASS (5,796 alt.) at the head of Buck Creek, within the Glacier Peak Recreation Area. Connecting trails lead to many points in the area.

DARDANELLES, 24.9 *m.* on State 15 (2,162 alt., 28 pop.), is a railroad siding at the confluence of Coulter and Butcher creeks with Macon Creek. At MERRITT, 26.9 *m.* (2,186 alt., 40 pop.), a railroad way point, is a Forest Service camp. Adjacent to FIRE ROCK AUTO CAMP (*privately operated*), 28.2 *m.,* is a small silica mine. The deposit is 97 per cent pure mineral; a small fountain at the camp, playing into a silica basin, glows with strange light after nightfall.

BERNE, 33 *m.* (2,918 alt., 55 pop.), a small huddle of frame dwellings, is at the east portal of the Cascade Tunnel, adjacent to the railroad station. The tunnel, approximately eight miles long and one of the largest projects of its kind in the country, was completed in 1929. Only four or five Alpine railway tunnels are longer than the new Cascade.

During construction in 1897 of the original Cascade bore, now abandoned, a camp town grew up in the vicinity of Berne and was called Tunnel City, or simply Tunnel. Its existence was one prolonged spree, according to tales of the times; the dance halls and kindred institutions had no doors—and needed none, since they never closed. Early in 1900 a correspondent of the New York *World* described Tunnel City as "the wickedest place in the world." A fire swept Tunnel City out of existence in June 1900, and forest growth has obliterated every remaining trace.

Rising toward the summit, State 15 follows the narrow valley of Nason Creek, flanked by extremely mountainous country, abounding in large and small game and many varieties of upland trees and wildflowers. STEVENS PASS (4,061 alt.), named for John F. Stevens, the Great Northern Railroad construction engineer, is reached at 41.9 *m.* The summit marks the boundary between the Snoqualmie and Wenatchee national forests. Here are forest camp and guard station. The Forest Service maintains a warming shed at the base of a 1,500-foot ski course. Each winter, the western section of State 15 is cleared of snow to Scenic (*see below*); visitors from eastern Washington, seeking hotel accommodations at Scenic, can cover intervening snowdrifts on skis. In the summer, good fishing is found at 20 small lakes within a 10-mile radius, and huckleberries are plentiful in August and September. At the summit is a junction with the Cascade Crest, or Skyline Trail.

1. Right from Stevens Pass on the trail to STARLIGHT LAKE, 1.5 *m.,* and LIGHTENBERG MOUNTAIN, 6 *m.* (5,920 alt.).
2. Left from Stevens Pass on the trail to LAKE JOSEPHINE, 5 *m.,* and MILL CREEK RUN, 12.5 *m.*

The SITE OF WELLINGTON, 46.6 *m.,* a station that existed at the western portal of the abandoned Cascade Tunnel, is marked by a hillside snowshed (R). A passenger train and a fast mail stalled here in deep snow on February 22, 1910. Small snowslides started crashing down upon the track at the end of the week, and about two o'clock in the morning, March 2, a great avalanche swept down from 2,000 feet above, brushing both trains and station to the bottom of a 400-foot canyon. One hundred eighteen persons were killed, and only a few escaped from the most serious railroad wreck in the State's history. Residence in the station itself was never attempted again.

West of Wellington, State 15 strikes downward on a steeply winding route (*cautious driving is imperative*) and reaches the course of the Tye River. SCENIC, 48.8 *m.* (2,106 alt., 50 pop.), is the highest town on the west Cascade slope and, though accessible only by railroad during the months of heavy snowfall, attracts many winter sport enthusiasts. Following the completion of the railroad, a health resort called the Scenic Hot Springs was opened here by J. V. Prosser. The well-advertised curative power of the hot mineral waters made the spa popular for many years, although rumor whispered that the water was artificially heated and piped to the resort through conduits insulated with cedar logs. A Forest Service camp (*complete facilities*) stands west of the resort site.

State 15 continues through upland country, crossing the Snoqualmie National Forest boundary line at 52.8 *m.* Near a junction with a dirt road, 56 *m.*, is a tourist camp (*camping and cabin accommodations*).

Left from the junction to the end of the road 4 *m.*, where parking space has been cleared. From here a trail leads past an abandoned CABIN at the edge of the forest and, leaving the railroad at 0.5 *m.*, enters a timbered gorge. After crossing the WEST FORK of Foss River at 2 *m.*, the trail continues to TROUT LAKE, 2.6 *m.* (2,500 alt.), which is stocked with Montana black-spotted trout. Clambering up the canyon wall (R) of the lake, the trail follows a small creek and emerges from a clump of Douglas fir on a higher level at 3 *m.* Here is a view of BALD PEAK (6,200 alt.) and the FALLS that descend 600 feet from the outlet of Copper Lake.

At 4.1 *m.* is a shallow ford across an unnamed creek. A distinct change in the flora becomes marked at this point. Douglas fir, hemlock, and cedar give way to Alpine fir and mountain hemlock, and the luxuriant growth of forest ferns and mosses is replaced by short grass and scattered patches of avalanche lilies. At 4.5 *m.* is COPPER LAKE (4,300 alt.), a small snow-fed pond, where a lean-to shelter is provided. Snow clings to the barren slopes above the lake throughout the summer. (*Nights are chilly and a heavy blanket roll is a necessity*).

At 5.2 *m.* the trail reaches a high benchland, revealing a widespread view of LITTLE HEART LAKE (4,700 alt.) and (L) OTTER LAKE (4,500 alt.); between them the outlet of LAKE ANGELINE (5,100 alt.) clothes the rocky bluff in spray, as it drops 1,000 feet toward the tranquil DELTA LAKE (3,800 alt.). Above the group of lakes rise the ragged peaks at the summit of the Cascade Range; MOUNT HINMAN (7,454 alt.) appears to the southeast.

At BIG BEAR LAKE (5,200 alt.) is a Forest Service shelter camp (*rowboats*). The lake shore is scalloped by glacial troughs. Hikers are advised not to leave the Forest Service trails, for ridges and dense forests make it impossible to reach one lake from another except by roundabout trails. In the event of becoming lost, small streams should be followed down to the main rivers. After completing this trip, hikers must report to the Skykomish Ranger Station, and fishermen should report catches.

SKYKOMISH, at 59 *m.* on State 15 (930 alt., 479 pop.), a railroad division point and sawmill town, lies on the bank of the South Fork of the Skykomish River, here known as the Tye. Settled during the building of the Great Northern, the town remains dependent on the railroad, which maintains a roundhouse for "helper" engines and a substation for the electrified section eastward to Appleyard. The

Industry, Commerce and Transportation

otograph courtesy Washington State Progress Commission

LUMBER MILLS, EVERETT

Photograph by Lange; courtesy of Farm Security Adm.

COLUMBIA RIVER

LAKE UNION - PUGET SOUND SHIP CANAL

Photograph copyrighted by Charles R. Laidlaw
AIRVIEW, SEATTLE WATERFRONT (MOUNT BAKER IN BACKGROUNI

PORT OF LONGVIEW

Photograph courtesy of Longview Chamber of Commer

IOLDEN MINE

Lake Chelan, from which comes half the gold and half the copper mined in the State.

tograph courtesy of Longview Chamber of Commerce

INTERSTATE BRIDGE, LONGVIEV

KE WASHINGTON FLOATING BRIDGE, SEATTLE

Photograph by Howard J. Burnham

AMPERE"—BONNEVILLE DAM TRANSFORMER

POWER HOUSE, DIABLO DAM

Photograph courtesy of Seattle City Light Company

A FORTY-TWO TON CLIPPER
Made in Boeing Plant for Pan-American Airways takes off at Seattle

WIND TUNNEL, UNIVERSITY OF WASHINGTON

Photograph courtesy of Camera Shop, Vancouver

VANCOUVER WATERFRONT, SHOWING PORT TERMINAL AND GRAIN ELEVATOR

WRAPPING AND PACKING APPLES IN A YAKIMA PLANT

Photograph courtesy of Jerry Dwyer

town was platted in 1899, by John Maloney and his wife, and incorporated in 1909. Its name means inland people.

At 61.5 *m.* is a junction with a forest road.

Left on this road to MILLER RIVER LODGE, 2 *m.*, where the Forest Service maintains a public campsite and picnic grounds. From the end of the road, 4 *m.*, a trail leads along the east fork of the Miller River to FLORENCE FALLS and DOROTHY LAKE (*shelter camp*), 8 *m.* (3,150 alt.), where fishing for eastern brook trout is good.

A Forest Service camp (*tourist facilities*) is maintained at MONEY CREEK PARK, at 62.8 *m.* on State 15. GROTTO, 64.8 *m.* (821 alt., 65 pop.), a settlement around a cement plant, was named by fanciful visitors, seeing for the first time the deep gorges and ravines of GROTTO MOUNTAIN (5,333 alt.), which overhangs the town. Grotto was a railroad construction camp for a short time in the nineties.

BARING, 68.7 *m.* (759 alt., 95 pop.), a lumber town, was named for its proximity to Mount Baring (6,125 alt.). At 71.2 *m.* in EAGLE FALLS, the Skykomish plunges in a tumult of white water.

At 74.1 *m.* a trail leads L. to SUNSET FALLS, 0.3 *m.*, and Sunset Falls Inn (*tourist facilities*). Down the rocky face of the canyon, BRIDAL VEIL FALLS drapes a ribbon of lacy spray. Towering above is MOUNT INDEX (5,639 alt.), named for the peculiar leaning rock needles that make up its sharp-crested bulk, pointing toward the northern sky. West of the falls, State 15 follows the South Fork of the Skykomish River.

At 74.5 *m.* is the junction with a graveled road.

Right here to INDEX, 0.9 *m.* (532 alt., 217 pop.), a quaint little town, cowering beneath jagged peaks, on the North Fork of the Skykomish River. Wooden sidewalks and paintless frame buildings line the short main street. In a region of rich mineral resources, it was a brisk mining center 30 years ago; the SUNSET MINE, largest of the old mines and famed as a man-killer, continues operation. Amos D. Gunn opened a tavern here in 1890, secured a post office the next year, and platted the town in 1893, naming it after Mount Index. Gunn's name was given to adjacent GUNN PEAK (6,245 alt.). Besides bornite (a high grade copper ore), gold, silver, antimony, molybdenum, and several arsenates are found in the vicinity.

North of Index the road narrows, running parallel to a logging railroad and the North Fork of the Skykomish River, which is fed by numerous small creeks that cross the route. At 3.9 *m.* the road crosses the boundary of the SNOQUALMIE NATIONAL FOREST. At 8.9 *m.* is GALENA GUARD STATION, where visitors to up-river points are requested to register before entering the forest. Near the site of the old Galena mining camp, at 9.5 *m.*, is the junction with a forest road; L. here 4 *m.* through the steep-walled canyon of Silver Creek, past abandoned mine shafts to MINERAL CITY, virtually a ghost town since its miners departed; here the forest road ends, and a trail leads to MONTE CRISTO, 8.7 *m.* (*see Tour 8b*).

At 11.7 *m.* on the main side road is TROUBLESOME CREEK, where the Forest Service maintains a camp, with the usual facilities, and has set aside an area for private summer homes. Crossing a bridge the road sweeps past BEAR FALLS, 12 *m.*, where the steelhead fishing is good, and climbs SAN JUAN CREEK, 13 *m.*, overlooking the North Fork River. Here is another Forest Service camp with picnic grounds. The road ends at GARLAND HOT SPRINGS, 14 *m.*, a private resort (*hotel, store, cabin, camp, and restaurant facilities; swimming pool*).

From here a trail leads to GOBLIN CREEK, 2 *m.*, near its confluence with the North Fork River. At 3 *m.* the trail passes a double falls that cascades into the North Fork River. The ascent sharpens rapidly. At 4 *m.* is a RANGER CABIN (*campgrounds and pasturage for horses*) with barn and corral beside it. QUARTZ CREEK flows through the camp site; L. from the ranger cabin a side trail climbs 2 *m.* to the divide separating the valley of the North Fork of the Skykomish from the drainage basin of SLOAN CREEK.

At 4.3 *m.* on the main trail is a junction with Benchmark Trail: R. here across the river and up the backbone ridge overlooking West Cady Creek to BENCHMARK LOOKOUT, 6 *m.* (5,815 alt.). From the junction, the main trail continues through forests where the tops of the trees are so close together that sunshine scarcely penetrates. At 7.5 *m.* is a junction with Pass Creek trail: R. here through CADY PASS, 3.3 *m.*, to the mountain terminus of the WENATCHEE RIVER ROAD, 10.5 *m.*

At 8 *m.* on the main trail is TWO-JACKS CABIN. Stands of white fir and hemlock are scattered across open meadowland. Passing a well-constructed CABIN, 12.8 *m.*, which marks the site of a silver mine, and making a steep ascent, the trail reaches DISHPAN GAP, 14.8 *m.* Here the route becomes a part of the incomplete Cascade Crest Trail, which, as planned, will extend south through Oregon into the Sierra Nevada Range. At 15.8 *m.* is MEANDER MEADOWS, where the trail levels off for a short distance, before skirting KODAK PEAK, 17 *m.* (6,105 alt.), and descending INDIAN PASS, 18.5 *m.*

From WHITE PASS, at 23 *m.*, overshadowed by WHITE MOUNTAIN, (6,986 alt.) the trail swings northeast over broken terrain. At 25 *m.* is WHITE RIVER GLACIER, source of an eastward flowing stream, and at 27 *m.*, WHITE CHUCK GLACIER, a great spread of pure ice flanked by rocky cliffs. (*Inexperienced mountaineers should not attempt to go farther, and guides are required by the most hardened and experienced.* Here a view is clear of GLACIER PEAK (10,436 alt.), its rounded dome sloping away into enormous snowfields, and a series of other glaciers, including Chocolate, Suiattle, and White Chuck. The Glacier Peak Recreation Area, except for Forest Service trails and lean-to shelters, is undeveloped and unimproved. Hiking and climbing parties will find the region comparatively easy of access, but must depend entirely on their own equipment and resources on the trail.

GOLD BAR, at 82.4 *m.* on State 15 (206 alt., 307 pop.), is a logging headquarters and center of an area of small farms. A prospectors' camp in 1889, it was named by an enthusiast who found traces of wealth on a river bar. After Gold Bar became a construction camp for the Great Northern, anti-Chinese sentiment was inflamed by a shooting fray started by disreputable camp followers. To save the lives of the threatened Chinese, Edward Bauer, a construction engineer, shipped them out of camp in rude, hastily contrived coffins.

Right from Gold Bar a dirt road leads along the Wallace River and, at 4.5 *m.*, connects with a trail to Wallace Falls and Wallace Lake, 7 *m.*, at the base of Mount Stickney (5,312 alt.) Both river and lake provide good fishing.

STARTUP (*tourist accommodations at inn*), 84.2 *m.* (158 alt., 450 pop.), where the Wallace River flows into the Skykomish, is not so called, strangely enough, because it is the place from which begins the real ascent of the Cascade slope. The town at first was named Wallace, but its mail was frequently misdirected to Wallace, Idaho; so it was renamed for George S. Startup, manager of a sawmill. Startup is a logging town, but diversified farming is gaining a foothold in its environs. Like other lonely pioneers, F. M. Sparling, the first settler, advertised for a wife in the *Heart and Hand*

Magazine and happily married Eva Helmic, of Ohio, in 1889

SULTAN, 88.3 *m.* (114 alt., 961 pop.), at the confluence of the Sultan and Skykomish Rivers, was formerly a lumber-manufacturing center. It was named for Tseul-tud, a chief of the Snohomish tribe. Ranchers of the vicinity divide their time between the land and near-by logging camps. On week-ends the town is often crowded with lumberjacks, mainly single men, who keep the beer taps running on paydays. Reckless, hardy, and high-spirited, for all their periodic spells of joblessness, the loggers are colorful in their woods garb: mackinaws and waist overalls, "stagged" at the boot tops; oilskins and tarpaulin trousers, or "tin pants"; red felt hats—worn because they are easily seen in the woods; calked boots that leave a myriad tiny punctures on a wood floor.

In 1870 placer miners found "color" along the Sultan River, and further discoveries in 1876 attracted more fortune hunters. The first settlers were several Chinese, who remained to pan for meager returns in the yellow flakes. In 1880 John Nailor and his Indian wife occupied a claim at the present townsite, their home becoming a stopping place for "mavericks" and "hornspooners" who combed the region. Mining companies hauled in machinery, regulated the industry, and created a boom in 1887. Light-draft river steamers soon pushed up the river, the *Mama* being the first to reach Sultan, in 1888. Forests surrounded the settlement, so dense—some have claimed—that lamps were lighted at three o'clock each afternoon. Prosperity lasted through the construction period of the Great Northern Railroad, which in 1891 made Sultan a base for tracklayers west of the Cascades. But shanty towns fringing the settlement, where gambling, drinking, and immorality flourished, demoralized the work and were the scene of several violent deaths.

West of Sultan, State 15 traverses logged-off land, some acres masked by second-growth timber, others partially cleared of stumps and given over to farming. At 95.9 *m.* is the junction with a graveled road.

Right on this road is LAKE ROESIGER, 12 *m.,* where the angler finds good catches of trout, crappie, perch, and bass.

MONROE, 96.2 *m.* (68 alt., 1,590 pop.), is entered from the east on the main street, which is lined with well-painted frame buildings. It lies in gently rolling country adjacent to the Skykomish River. Monroe is exceptional among Washington towns in that no speculative frenzies or booms have stimulated its gradual transition from a logging center to a rich farming community. Nurseries and greenhouses are maintained by the Great Northern; other industries include a large cannery and a milk condensery.

In 1873 Salem Wood began a settlement one mile from the site of Monroe, naming the region Park Place. John Vanasdlen, who opened a store and post office here in 1889, renamed it Monroe at the request of postal authorities. Another town, plotted when the Great Northern arrived, was called Tye, although the station was designated Wales. Vanasdlen moved to the new site, and railroad officials changed the station name to that of the post office. Sawmill construction moved into the region. During the chaotic period in the early thirties, a study group of farmers and unemployed emerged, which finally became the Self-Help Co-operative of Monroe, now operating a cannery, woodyard, and distributing agency.

Entrance to the WASHINGTON STATE REFORMATORY (*open 9-4 daily*) is at 100.8*m*. The 700 inmates cultivate the 600-acre farm and sell produce to other State institutions. Athletics are an important activity, and a minstrel show is held annually in November. The Snohomish County Hospital and Poor Farm are to the left.

The SNOHOMISH LETTUCE FARM, 101.3 *m.*, 1,500 acres in extent, is one of the largest farms of its kind in the State. During the growing season the pale green plants extend in rows across the black loam; in midsummer the farm is thronged with field hands, mostly migratory families. In recent years some opposition to labor organization developed among growers in the vicinity, and State police were called in to disperse strikers during this period. A narrow-gauge railway collects the produce from tractor-drawn wagons and transports it to the central loading depot, where the lettuce is sorted, crated, and packed in refrigerator cars for shipment. The annual production averages 800 carloads.

SNOHOMISH, 104.5 *m.* (92 alt., 2,794 pop.), at the confluence of the Snohomish and Pilchuck Rivers, is the market center of outlying truck and dairy farms; small shingle mills operate part of the time. Snohomish, for long the seat of Snohomish County, was founded after Congress, in 1853, approved the building of a military road from Steilacoom to Fort Bellingham. The next year five Steilacoom settlers formed an impromptu syndicate to acquire land claims beside the proposed ferry crossing on the Snohomish River. One of these five, E. C. Ferguson, framed a house at Steilacoom in 1860, and shipped it by steamer to be set up in the new settlement.

After the legislature separated the mainland district from Island County and made Mukilteo the county seat in 1861, the seat was moved by the voters to the newer town, Snohomish City, whose population numbered 25 males. County business was conducted over the bar of the Blue Eagle Saloon. The town's first family, that of John Palmer, arrived in 1863, logging began in 1864 with a yoke or two of oxen, and a community sawmill was incorporated in 1866. At the head of navigable waters, the village prospered; a shipyard launched the steamer *Ruby* in 1867.

A school was opened in 1869; the townsite was platted in 1871; and by 1873 cultural forces were strong enough to support an Atheneum Society and a public library. The population reached 200 by 1876, with 20 logging camps in the vicinity. The first church and a newspaper—Eldridge Morse's *Northern Star*—were started. The population increased to 400 by 1882 and nearly doubled in the next two years. During the middle eighties the *Snohomish Eye* succeeded the defunct *Star;* the first shingle mill in the county began operating; a minor wave of the anti-Chinese riots elsewhere culminated in the dynamiting of a laundry. In 1888 rail connections with the Seattle, Lake Shore & Eastern Railroad were finished. Next year an electric power plant was built. With a population of 2,469 in 1890, Snohomish was incorporated as a third-class city.

A vast expenditure of corporate funds to develop the industries of Everett soon aroused civic rivalry; the crisis came after 1894, when a second change of the county seat was proposed. After the hotly contested election, a court order was necessary to remove the records to Everett. Snohomish, however, showed a steady growth until about 1910, having nine mills and other plants in that year. A fire destroyed the largest mill and, after several others were dismantled, the city became primarily an agricultural center.

The PUBLIC LIBRARY (*open 2-8 weekdays*), Cedar St. between 1st and Pearl Aves., with 4,300 volumes, has supplanted its early predecessor of 1873. The building differs considerably from the majority of Carnegie libraries; it is of frame and buff-colored concrete, designed in modified mission style, with a tile roof. Among valuable donations made by Snohomish citizens are three volumes of Shakespeare, more than 100 years old, given by P. W. Fobes, an old settler. The Snohomish High School now stands on the SITE OF THE OLD COURTHOUSE, 5th St. and Ave. D.

Crossing the tree-shaded Pilchuck River at the eastern edge of town, State 15 leaves the city on Avenue D and continues along the edge of the Snohomish Valley, until it descends sharply to Ebey Slough, 110.3 *m.* Westward from this point it runs through bottom lands, cut by swamps and bogs, and crosses the Snohomish River at 112.2 *m.*

At 110.5 *m.* is a junction with State 15-A, a concrete-paved road (*see Tour 8b*).

State 15 enters EVERETT, 113.3 *m.* (30 alt., 30,224 pop.) (*see Everett*), at the junction with US 99 (*see Tour 8b*).

Tour 1D

Renton—Enumclaw—Buckley—Mowich Entrance to Mount Rainier National Park; 53.9 *m.*, State 5.

Road concrete-paved from Renton to south of Wilkeson; elsewhere gravel-surfaced.
Chicago, Milwaukee, St. Paul and Pacific R.R. roughly parallels route

between Renton and Enumclaw; Northern Pacific Ry. parallels route between Enumclaw and Fairfax.
Limited accommodations in larger towns. Occasional tourist and forest camps.

This branch of State 5 runs southeast from Renton through Maple Valley and Black Diamond to Enumclaw, then drops south until it approaches Mount Rainier National Park. The road crosses many rivers and gorges, often picturesque, and terminates within sight of the peaks of the Cascades. The major interest of the route, however, is the old mining country it traverses. Once the richest coal area of the State, these sections of King and Pierce counties are today spotted with ghost towns, some completely shut down, others still feebly carrying on their traditional occupations.

East in RENTON (*see Tour 1b*) 0 *m.*, (40 alt., 4,488 pop.), at the junction of US 10 and a branch of State 5.

South of Renton, State 5, a concrete-paved road, follows the course of the Cedar River, traveling through an aisle of large softwood trees. COTTONWOOD PARK (R), 0.8 *m.*, which lies under the shade of branches on the bank of the river, is a popular picnic ground during summer and spring months.

After running along the side of a high cliff (L), the highway passes a group of summer homes (R) beside the river. To the north the expansive lawns of the MAPLEWOOD GOLF CLUB COURSE (*week-days 50c; Sat., Sun., holidays 75c*), 1.9 *m.* (L), enhance the charm of the languid woodland setting.

State 5 crosses the Cedar River over a bridge at 2.2 *m.*, and penetrates a valley dotted with truck gardens, dairy farms, and dwellings. The river and the tracks of the Chicago, Milwaukee, St. Paul and Pacific Railroad run alongside the road.

At the PACIFIC COAST COAL COMPANY POWERHOUSE, 5.5 *m.* (R), a few feet from the highway, is a towering wooden frame skeleton and immense slag heaps.

At 6.2 *m.* is a junction with crossroads leading to a number of lake resorts. The region within a radius of several miles from the highway is dotted with lakes which attract large week-end and vacation crowds during spring and summer months.

Across the railroad (L), 6.6 *m.*, the old CEDAR MOUNTAIN COAL MINE is still in operation. Modern homes with flower gardens mingle with wayside shops, near the river bank where great alders and maples rise. Farther south are several small chicken ranches, fields of berries, and farms. On a hillside near the railroad tracks is MAPLE VALLEY, 10.3 *m.* (343 alt., 250 pop.), with a school, a tavern, a water tank, and an old depot.

South of Maple Valley State 5 crosses the Cedar River over a bridge, 10.4 *m.*, and enters a valley where dairy cattle graze in lush pasture lands. Then the road passes a stretch of stumps and second growth trees and swings westerly through an aisle formed by dogwood, tall firs, and maples.

At 14.3 *m.* is a junction with State 5-A, a concrete-paved road.

Right on this road 1.2 *m.* to a junction with a concrete-paved ro on the latter road to LAKE WILDERNESS, 2.9 *m.,* a heavily f summer bathing, boating, picnicking, and camping resort. Near by is LUCERNE, another popular resort.

State 5-A, west of the junction, continues to KENT, 10 *m.,* (42 alt., 2,588 pop.), (*see Tour 2c*), where it joins another branch of State 5.

Left from the junction of State 5 and State 5-A on a gravel-surfaced road to SELLECK, 6.5 *m.* (1,070 alt., 415 pop.), a lumber town which in recent years was the scene of protracted labor strife.

South of the junction State 5 passes through an area of second-growth fir to enter stump lands. The Cascade Mountains rise on the east.

At 17.5 *m.* is a junction with a graveled road.

Left on this road through leafy woods to the STRAIN MINE (R), 0.2 *m.* A coal-laden bunker overhangs the road. Northwest of the mine the road is cut through stump fields to the edge of a hill covered with great smoking slag heaps and the black, dusty sheet iron structure of the CONTINENTAL COAL MINES (R), 2.5 *m.* Ahead are the silhouettes of snow-capped mountains, and square little dwellings, all in need of paint, scattered on both sides of the road.

RAVENSDALE, 3.2 *m.* (619 alt., 109 pop.), built along a fluffy green hill which hovers above a gullied flat, is a cluster of modest houses about a red two-story depot. A red-brick schoolhouse stands on the main street. The town is on the main line of the Northern Pacific Railroad and depends largely on the operation of near-by coal mines for its livelihood. In 1915 a great explosion in a Ravensdale mine killed 31 persons—one of the worst tragedies in local mining history. There is some logging in the vicinity for pulpwood, alder, and maple, and a few small tie mills that utilize the second growth in the hills. Truck gardening, dairy farming and poultry ranching are on the increase.

BLACK DIAMOND, 18.1 *m.* (610 alt., 1,400 pop.), is readily identifiable as a mining town by the great coal-loading bunkers which are spread over lines of freight cars. It has a shabby, ancient depot and a few uniform ramshackle frame houses, which perch on the brow of a hill, and at certain times of the year cows may be seen grazing in the streets. The town derives its name from the Black Diamond Coal Company of California. Profitable coal veins were found in the vicinity in 1890 and the Black Diamond mines were soon opened; by 1895 they had taken first place in King County production and held this position for many years.

At 20 *m.* is a junction with a gravel-surfaced road which leads (R) 2 *m.* to FLAMING GEYSER PARK, (*see Tour 2c*) and becomes part of State 5-B as it continues to AUBURN, 13 *m.* (90 alt., 4,213 pop.), (*see Tour 2c*).

Penetrating an area of dairy farms, where wide green pastures alternate with fields of bleached and charred stumps, State 5 passes the Krain Ball Room (L), 23.9 *m.,* a large frame structure in which miners hold dances. The rolling hills (L) are tinted with shades of green which range from the bright emerald of maple and alder growth to the greenish black of Douglas fir. Behind the hills rises the giant silver bulk of Mount Rainier.

At 25.6 *m.* is a junction with a gravel-surfaced road.

Left on this winding thoroughfare to GREEN RIVER GORGE, 4 *m.* Here,

Green River cuts through sandstone and shale to form a deep, rugged canyon with numerous "kettles" and other grotesque formations carved by the water. Small falls gush down the rocky walls. A bridge from which an excellent view of the Gorge is to be had spans the river, but vehicles are not permitted to stop on it. Catwalks are provided at lower levels. Heavy forest growths creep to the brink of the five-mile canyon. Tourist resorts have commercialized the gorge to some extent, and motorists are usually charged a parking fee of 25c, which permits the inspection of the canyon at close range. Cabins, provisions, and meals are also available.

South of the junction State 5 winds through pastures, berry farms, and fields of stumps and second growth.

ENUMCLAW, 26.2 *m.* (742 alt., 2,627 pop.) (*see Tour 2c*), is at the junction of State 5 with US 410, which is another branch of State 5 (*see Tour 2c*).

South of Enumclaw, State 5, offering a clear view of Mount Rainier and the serrated peaks of the Cascades, runs through an area of prosperous dairy farms. Crossing the White River over a bridge, 29.6 *m.*, the highway ascends to BUCKLEY, 30.4 *m.* (723 alt., 1,170 pop.), on the south side of the White River. Buckley is sometimes called "The City of Good Water," because of the cool, clear water with which the community is supplied.

First known as "Perkins' Landing," it became White River Siding when the Northern Pacific Railroad built through the settlement. It retained this name until 1888, when Alexander Wickersham platted the townsite and called it Buckley in honor of the division superintendent of the Northern Pacific. The White River Shingle Mill was built in 1886, and in 1888 the Whitten brothers started the *Banner,* one of the first county newspapers. Drawing from the largest untouched timber belts east of the Olympic Mountains, the town was made by lumbering. Today, Buckley is no longer a lumber center, but the back country is still being logged and many carloads of logs are shipped annually through the town. Mining has also played a part in the local economy. The rich soil of the surrounding plateau lands, known as "Buckley loam," has made several types of agriculture profitable. Fruit growing and diversified farming are increasing and the community boasts of the quality of its peaches, annually celebrated at its "Peacherino Festival."

In the town proper, old, comfortable houses are widely spaced on the sleepy streets. Railroad tracks divide the town, where a large portion of the business district is located near the depot. The nearness of the mountains, where game is abundant, has made the place an outfitting center for hunting parties.

In BUCKLEY PARK, a triangular plot of grass at Main Street and River Avenue, is a tree stump 12½ feet in diameter and 38 feet in circumference. From this tree 56,000 board feet of timber were cut. Its estimated age is 2,000 years.

Right from Main Street on Cottage Street, which becomes a gravel-surfaced road, 0.5 *m.* to Ryan Road. Left on Ryan Road, 1.8 *m.* to the WASHINGTON STATE CUSTODIAL SCHOOL, a group of seven low white buildings completed in 1939 with the aid of the Work Projects Administration at a cost of $550,000.

It is a model custodial school, among the first in the country, and makes use of the most modern developments in medicine and psychiatry.

Right from the Buckley City center on Main Street which becomes another branch of State 5. At 2.2 *m.*, the road bridges a flume, beginning of the Puget Sound Power and Light Company's power canal to near-by Lake Tapps. Water from the White River, which flows north of the road, forms an artificial lake here. In the canal, set in the concrete dam, are eight ROTARY FISH SCREENS, reputedly the largest in the world, which prevent fish from entering the flume, saving from death thousands each year. Each of the fish screens is 12 feet long and is rotated by electric power. They were constructed in 1938 and 1939 by the WPA under the sponsorship of the State Department of Fisheries.

West of the canal, this branch of State 5 winds drunkenly along the edge of Dingle Basin (R) and ascends through a lane of large trees to wide fields.

West of the orchard the highway, when it is not bordered with groves of trees, presents a vista of rambling old farmhouses in wide fields touched with the gold of yellow mustard and buttercups. The highway crosses a planked POWER FLUME, 4.5 *m.*, through which the water from White River is conveyed to Tapps and thence to the Puget Sound Power and Light Company's power houses at Dieringer (*see Tour 2c*).

After passing chicken houses, long and barrack-like, the highway reaches CONNELL PRAIRIE BLOCK HOUSE (L) 5.1 *m.*, on the brow of a small terrace-like bench overlooking Connell Prairie. The old blockhouse is made of cedar logs, split so that the inner wall is comparatively flat, and chinked with moss. Such nails as were used in its construction are of the old square cut type. Rocks piled around the base of the structure when it was built have been scattered. In the upper part are apertures for rifles. There is a junction here with a dirt road. Left on this road, 0.6 *m.*, is a MONUMENT with inscriptions telling of the death of several army officers and men in two Indian ambushes in 1855. The monument also notes that the old Fort Steilacoom military road ran 50 feet away from this spot.

West of the junction this branch of State 5, after pushing through the heart of a good farming area, ends in SUMNER, 13 *m.* (69 alt., 2,140 pop.), at a junction with US 410 (*see Tour 2d*).

South of Buckley the railroad tracks, lined with log-laden flat cars, parallel the highway. The mountains (L) rise abruptly in the distance. At 33.4 *m.*, near a bridge which crosses South Prairie Creek, is a large slag pile, still burning, the remains of an abandoned mine.

Once a bustling mining town, BURNETT, 33.6 *m.* (517 alt., 75 pop.), has lapsed into somnolence since the Pacific Coast Coal Company closed its mines near by in 1927. Burnett residents sustain themselves from "gyppo" mines—small coal operations conducted usually by family groups—back in the foothills. A few drab houses, many of them abandoned, constitute the town, which was named for Charles H. Burnett, a pioneer Northwestern mine operator.

Ascending through a thick growth of small timber, State 5 crosses bridges over Gale and Wilkeson Creeks.

In the heart of what was once a rich coal-producing region, WILKESON, 36.5 *m.* (851 alt., 369 pop.), has been transformed into a ghost community by the depletion of its coal deposits and forests. Sandstone quarries were also worked here. The town was named for Samuel Wilkeson, secretary of the board of the Northern Pacific Railway, which built a line to the town in 1876 and began cutting coal in 1879. The Oregon Improvement Company, a branch of the Union Pacific, acquired control of the mines in 1883 and operated them until 1885. The Wilkeson Coal and Coke Company took over the operations in the early nineties. Today, a few small mines are still being worked, but the town has been largely abandoned and many of the houses are empty and decayed. The present population, a remnant from the earlier days of prosperity, is for the main part dependent upon relief.

South of Wilkeson, the highway crosses a bridge over Wilkeson Creek and sweeps upward, rounding the contour of a hill between a grove of tall trees.

At 37.8 *m.* is a junction with a concrete-paved road.

Right on this road 0.5 *m.* to CARBONADO (1,146 alt., 75 pop.), a "model" mining community, which passed into virtual oblivion when the Pacific Coast Coal Company abandoned its operations here in the late twenties. The company, which owned the town, paved the streets, installed a sewerage and drainage system, and on occasion repainted the houses, which were rented at an average of $14 monthly. At one time 300 were employed in the mines; the town maintained soccer and baseball teams, and there were several fraternal organizations and societies. A large community hall, a store, a school building, and long rows of chocolate-painted picket fences with houses behind them, constitute the present settlement.

Downhill from First Street is the old Carbonado mine, which once kept the town busy. When the company closed the mine, it removed the pumps, and five miles of collieries were so heavily flooded as to make their reclamation impossible.

South of the junction, State 5 passes a coal-loading chute (R) built on the edge of a pasture. The railroad parallels the highway. Climbing along a deep valley (R), the road winds along a cut in the hillside and reaches a wild canyon with stone cliffs among the young second-growth trees. A bridge, 41.2 *m.*, swings high over a deep gorge through which rushes the waters of the Carbon River.

At 41.7 *m.* is a junction with a gravel-surfaced road.

Left on this road, which swings through the Carbon River valley past a coal-loading, bunker, is an old mine. From the bunker the road drops rapidly to the bottom of the river canyon where FAIRFAX, 3.0 *m.* (1,350 alt., 200 pop.), at one time a flourishing mining and lumbering town, is marked by an abandoned depot. A few houses scattered under large trees are occupied; but across the river the deserted structures built by the Eatonville Lumber Company during an earlier logging boom are mournful reminders of feverishly active days. Near the depot and mine bunkers are an old school and a rambling structure which once housed a large lumber mill. A few logging locomotives lie rusting along the tracks.

In Fairfax is a junction with a forest road. Left on this road, which crosses the Carbon River over a bridge to CAMP ELECTRON, a CCC camp, 0.6 *m.* East of Fairfax the main side road crosses the boundary of the Snoqualmie National Forest at 4 *m.* Here towering trees shade Tolmie Creek, a crystal stream which plunges over great boulders on its way down the abrupt mountainside into the Carbon River.

Under the supervision of the United States Forestry Department, logging by private companies is carried on in this forest, and occasionally the road provides views of logging operations on the timbered hillsides.

The CARBON RIVER ENTRANCE TO MOUNT RAINIER NATIONAL PARK (*open weekdays, 6 a.m. to 9:30 p.m.; Sat., Sun., holidays, 5 a.m. to 11 p.m.*) 7.5 *m.*, is marked by a building on the bottom of the canyon floor on the brink of the river. The building and the small rustic structures of the ranger station are dwarfed by huge trees. Directly north are the grizzled sides of Burnt Mountain and Carbon Ridge, where the spired peak of Old Baldy Mountain rises 5,790 feet. Once a great fire burned over the slopes of these mountains, leaving only a scattering of white dead trunks. Through a thin covering of second growth, the cliffs and rock slides are grey scars sometimes crossed by the thread of a falling stream. To the south is Tolmie Peak, Castle Rock, and Mother Mountain, whose altitude of 6,540 feet is almost hidden by the heavy growth of timber all about it. From here the road extends almost to the foot of Carbon Glacier, and in the summer time motorists may drive six miles farther east and south almost to the snowline.

Southeast of the junction, State 5, now a narrow gravel-surfaced road, winds back and forth in ascending an abrupt mountain slope, clinging to the crest of a high plateau. Straight ahead Mount Rainier lifts itself high above clumps of peaks, while far below (R) is the Carbon River.

At 48.6 *m.* the highway descends through giant timber; from below (R), in the valley of the Mowich River, come sounds of logging operations.

At 53.4 *m.* a deep basin (R) is walled with sheer cliffs. Along the forested floor is the river, its roar reaching through the stillness of the forest.

The road ends 53.9 *m.*, 0.2 *m.* from the MOWICH ENTRANCE TO MOUNT RAINIER NATIONAL PARK, which is announced by a wooden sign. The TOLMIE MONUMENT near by commemorates the arrival here in 1833 of Dr. William Fraser Tolmie, the first white man to explore this area. The monument was dedicated September 2, 1933, in the presence of Tolmie's son, Simon Fraser Tolmie, then Prime Minister of British Columbia.

Tour 2

(Lewiston, Idaho) — Clarkston — Dodge — Walla Walla — Pasco—Buena Junction—Yakima—Tacoma—Olympia—Aberdeen; US 410, US 410-97, US 410-99.

Idaho Line to Aberdeen, 461.1 *m.*

Concrete-paved or bituminous-surfaced roadbed throughout; Chinook Pass over Cascade Mountains usually closed during midwinter; chains advisable over mountains from November to March.

Camas Prairie R.R. roughly parallels route between Clarkston and Silcott; Oregon-Washington R.R. and Navigation Company between Pomeroy and

Yakima; Northern Pacific Ry. between Pasco and Yakima and between Auburn and Aberdeen.

Hotel accommodations in cities and in larger towns; tourist camps, some with trailer facilities, in or near most cities; forest camps in mountains.

This longest trans-State route presents a cross section of the diversified and contrasting terrain, climate, and economy of Washington. West of the Idaho Line, US 410 climbs upward from the irrigated orchards of the Snake River Valley through rugged, treeless hills, cut by narrow valleys and steep-walled canyons; traverses the fertile, undulating benchlands of the Walla Walla country and the sandy wastes along the Columbia River; crosses the river and then runs for miles through alfalfa and hop fields, orchards, vineyards, and truck farms, hemmed in by hills covered with sagebrush, dun-gray in the glare of noon, or softly purple as the sun sinks behind the Cascades.

Continuing in a northwesterly direction, the highway climbs perceptibly, sweeping in broad curves through sparsely settled foothills, marked by scattered evergreens and clumps of aspen and poplar. By degrees the relatively open stands of pine and fir on the eastern slope of the Cascades merge into the heavy forests of cedar, hemlock, and Douglas fir on the windward side. Along the highway as it descends are wooded areas, stump lands, dairy farms, poultry ranches, truck gardens, berry fields, and occasional towns. Then it swings southward through Tacoma and Olympia at the head of Puget Sound and cuts almost due west through rolling hills, once densely forested. Ever more noticeable is the smell of salt in the moist air. At length, in a final broad curve, the route reaches its western terminus at Aberdeen on Grays Harbor.

Section a. IDAHO LINE *to* PASCO; *148 m. US 410, US 410-395*

This section of US 410 follows the route of an old Indian trail from the confluence of the turbulent Clearwater River and the silt-laden Snake to the junction of the latter with the Columbia, about 100 miles west of the Idaho Line. Captain Meriwether Lewis and Captain William Clark followed this trail on their return journey in 1806, and Captain Benjamin Bonneville approximated it in 1834-5.

Most of the region is sparsely populated. Strung along the highway at widely spaced intervals are several small cities and numerous towns, often little more than a cluster of dwellings around a service station, a grain elevator or two, and a general store and post office combined. Some of these are ghosts of settlements that 60 years ago echoed with the crack of stagecoach whips and the creak of wheels, as heavily loaded wagon trains moved at a turtle's pace toward the mines. From these towns, too, rattled the Conestoga wagons of settlers headed for the lands north of the Snake River. Today weather-worn frame structures, bold-faced frauds with two-story fronts, are reminders of the men and women who with high hopes founded these towns. But discouraged by low prices and droughts and the failure of mining prospects, they moved on when fears of Indian raids diminished and railroads made hitherto remote areas accessible. The settlements that survived now serve as distributing points or railroad junctions and supply the tourist with hamburgers, beer, and cigarettes, or with gasoline and oil for his car.

On this rolling plateau between the Snake River and the Blue Mountains, the colonizing efforts of two Nations met: the one old and experienced in the art of conquest and settlement; the other aggressive in its youth, convinced of its manifest destiny. Down the Snake to the Columbia River, fur traders of the Hudson's Bay and North West companies guided their canoes to old Fort Walla Walla, at Wallula, whose site is today marked by a few foundation stones. Following the traders came missionaries, whose first attempt to establish a permanent settlement ended in the tragedy of Waiilatpu. Still traceable along stream beds and mountain slopes are old trails, first trod by Indians and later worn deep by the feet of thousands of prospectors who rushed from one area to another, as rumors spread of Eldorados on lonesome creeks and rivers.

Geologic formations here are unusually interesting. Violent upheavals of the earth's crust spread successive layers of lava over this region, and when these movements ceased, water began to sculpture deep canyons, and wind to shape the rough terrain into rolling hills and narrow valleys. US 410 skirts the south bank of the Snake River, with its precipitous walls, for a short distance and then climbs steadily around the steep hillsides, whose rocky slopes, exposed along the narrow shelf of the roadbed, change from bright vermillion to brownish-black as the highway winds upward. Cattle and sheep forage on the hillsides, parched brown except for a brief interlude in early spring, when the warm winds sweep up the Columbia River and, almost simultaneously with the melting of the snow, bring forth a carpet of grass and flowers.

Beyond the summit of the grade, the route zigzags through arable benchlands, where small farms and orchard tracts alternate with extensive wheat acreages and fields of peas, beans, tomatoes, corn, and asparagus. To the south rise the Blue Mountains, shrouded in smoky haze in summer or sharply outlined on clear midwinter days.

West of Walla Walla fertile fields give way to nearly level sagebrush barrens. Bordering the highway are shifting hummocks of sand, corrugated by the brisk, steady wind that whips dry tumbleweeds across the waste and piles them in gullies and abandoned irrigation ditches or against deserted farmhouses. In midsummer the heat waves shimmer over the sand dunes and the oily surface of the road. Little wild life is seen: now and then a hawk soars far overhead, or a raven — black scavenger of the wastelands—sits red-eyed on a rocky promontory. Occasionally a coyote, a gray shadow, slips over the horizon, or a jackrabbit springs from beneath the brush like a coil released, and races across the hills. For 15 miles the highway runs northwest, parallel to the Columbia, and then at the confluence of this river and the Snake swings over a long steel bridge into Pasco.

US 410 crosses the IDAHO LINE, 0 *m.,* which here is fixed at midchannel of the Snake River, over a steel suspension bridge that straddles the stream and links the twin cities — Lewiston on the flats east of the river and Clarkston on the west.

CLARKSTON, 0.5 *m.* (825 alt., 3,116 pop.), spreads north-south over the sandy flats of the Snake River. Hemming it in on both the east and the west are steep, treeless bluffs, beyond which stretches a rolling plateau. Most of the valley is now under irrigation. Early in the spring the bare branches of the trees and vines glow red-brown with the renewed flow of the sap. In April the orchards are a riot of delicately pink and white blossoms, and gardens and vineyards make geometric patterns of green against the well-cultivated earth. Harvest season is equally beautiful; then red, yellow, and purple grapes load the vines, apples and pears bend the branches of the trees, and melons ripen in the fields. All this produce, as well as the grain and stock of the plateau regions, finds a natural outlet through Clarkston, which serves as the shipping and processing center. Among its industrial units are included meat-packing plants, canneries, box factories, and flour and feed plants.

Clarkston is a pleasant town. Its business section is compact, clean, and modern; its residential areas pleasant and uncongested. Shade trees line the streets, and throughout the hot, dry summer the murmur of sprinklers is heard day and night. It has a fine school system, at least a dozen churches, and a weekly paper, the Clarkston *Herald.*

The early settlers found nothing to attract them to Jawbone Flats, as they called the barren basin now the site of Clarkston. In 1863 William Craig, trader and trapper among the Nez Percé, and colonel in the forces that fought the Indians in 1855, established a small ferry at this point and for a number of years furnished transportation to the thousands of prospectors rushing to the gold fields of the Salmon River and the Clearwater districts. Lewiston sprang up on the east side of the stream, but Jawbone Flats remained a range for the horses of John Greenfield.

The beginning of Clarkston dates from 1896, when the Lewiston Water and Power Company, with the backing of eastern capital, platted a town and called it Vineland. The next year a bridge was constructed across the river at this point, and soon traffic, which had been handled by the small ferries at various river points, was focused at Vineland, renamed Concord. The town boomed and land sold for as much as $1,000 an acre. By popular petition in 1900, the town officially became Clarkston.

West of Clarkston, US 410 for several miles traverses orchards and vineyards spread along the river flats. High hills, barren and eroded by wind and rain, rise on the west, and on the east flows the Snake River, visible through the trees. Beyond it looms a steep bank dominated by pyramidal bluffs, scarred by deep gulleys. At the foot of the bank the sunlight catches the gleam of rails, and now and then a train slips by, its whistle echoing against the hills and its smoke a trailing ribbon that diffuses slowly into the robin's-egg blue sky.

In Clarkston is a junction with State 3.

Left on this road, the route of an old Nez Percé Indian trail, downhill along the west bank of the Snake River. Sand spits extend from the shore to form natural jetties. On the right, hills tower to the sky and end in a high plateau that rolls gradually upward to the mountains breaking the southern skyline.

SWALLOWS NEST ROCK, 3 *m.,* a rocky cowl, shoots at a sharp angle from the road. Years ago thousands of swallows nested on this cliff, but blasting for an irrigation tunnel killed many and frightened the rest away. Beyond the cliff is the river; a jetty serves to deepen the channel for navigation by diverting the main stream from behind an island. The route runs through an almost continuous succession of orchards and vineyards, down a steep grade, and through a rocky cut. Far below the Snake River swirls around the base of basaltic canyon walls and shifting sand bars.

At 5.9 *m.* is a junction with an improved road; L. here is the ASOTIN FLOUR MILL (*visitors by permission*), 0.1 *m.* This mill has in succession been operated by water, steam, and electric power. JERRY, 3 *m.* (1,200 alt., 25 pop.), a cluster of nondescript buildings, was named for Jerry McGuire, a burley Irishman who settled here with his Indian wife in the early seventies. Horses were then in great demand for pack trains and stagecoaches. Soon the hills were filled with half-wild mustangs and cayuses, the band at one time numbering more than 1,000, all marked with McGuire's brand, the head of a horse.

South of Jerry the road after winding up a steep grade traverses miles and miles of wheat farms. CLOVERLAND, 12.5 *m.* (1,400 alt., 25 pop.), surrounded by irrigated orchards, wheat farms, and stock ranches, is the center of activity for a population of about 300 people. South of Cloverland the rolling plateau gives way to the wooded foothills of the Blue Mountains. As the grade becomes steeper the road twists and turns, following the contours of the slopes, into wild country where upland birds, deer, and elk are plentiful. This dirt road is rough and narrow (*caution is advised*).

UMATILLA NATIONAL FOREST, 24.5 *m.,* extends westward into Garfield County and southward into Oregon. At 30 *m.* is the WENATCHEE GUARD STATION and a junction with a forest road that loops back to POMEROY, 40 *m.* (*see below*).

On State 3, the main side road, is ASOTIN, 6.1 *m.* (760 alt., 686 pop.), at the confluence of the Snake River, which bends sharply west at this point, and ASOTIN (Ind. eel) CREEK, a bold mountain stream walled in by bluffs several hundred feet in height. The protected triangular flats were for generations a favorite camping ground of Indian bands. Few settlers came to the fertile land along Asotin Creek until the close of the Nez Percé war in the late seventies stimulated rapid homesteading. Two settlements, Asotin and Asotin City, were started within half a mile of each other. In 1881 J. J. Kanawyer built the first ferry on the upper Snake River and began operating it from Asotin at the mouth of the creek, and in the same year Frank Curtis erected a sawmill here. Except for a few rough mountain trails, the only means of transportation was the river. Heavy democrat wagons rolled in from the back country with cargo, chiefly wheat and lumber, for Lewiston. The bitter rivalry between the two settlements ended with the removal of the business houses to the younger settlement at the mouth of the creek; and in 1886, by an act of the Territorial legislature, the name Asotin was adopted for the combined settlement. Reminiscent of these early boom days is the Fryxell Opera House, an old-fashioned frame structure, once the center of community social life.

Today Asotin is the center of vineyards and orchards and wheat farms and the threshold to one of the few remaining primitive areas—the Grande Ronde Valley. The town is still a river freighting point, although most of the traffic is now handled by motor truck. The *Asotin County Sentinel,* started in 1883, is published weekly; its editor, David Grew, is the author of several novels.

Right from Asotin, State 3 leads southwest across an undulating plateau.

Once the range of horses and cattle, this area is now largely under cultivation. ANATONE, 25 *m.* (2,800 alt., 300 pop.), a score of old frame buildings clustering along narrow streets, nestles at the foot of the Blue Mountains. One of the oldest trading posts of the region, it was the center of considerable activity in the sixties, when it was a regular stopping point on the Asotin route to the gold-fields of Florence and Elk City in the Salmon River country of Idaho Territory. In the late seventies rumors of impending trouble with the Indians sent the settlers of the region scurrying to the John Carter place, a half-mile from Anatone, where they built a stockade 100 feet square and stocked it with provisions and arms. No hostilities occurred, but the fort served to hold settlers in the region until they recovered from their fright. At about this time William Farish built a small sawmill near Anatone; within a few years he was running at least eight mills and was hauling the cut lumber by ox team to the Snake River to be rafted downstream. This activity slowly died, and today Anatone sleeps, dreaming of its past, while it supplies the needs of the wheat farmers and stockmen of the surrounding area. South of Anatone State 3 winds through sparsely settled foothills to FIELD'S SPRINGS STATE PARK (*camping facilities*). The large evergreens, grassy open spaces, low summer temperature, and excellent spring water of this 100-acre park make it a favorite refuge from the summer heat of the Snake River Valley. Old settlers still cling to the original name, Puffer Springs.

The GRANDE RONDE (Fr. great round) RIVER, 37.9 *m.,* marks the end of this branch of State 3. Here the river cuts its tumultuous course through a winding canyon eastward to the Snake. The region is wild and beautiful with its rugged mountains and rocky draws, its broad peaceful valleys and forests abounding in elk and deer, and its sparkling streams filled with salmon and trout. This was the home of the Nez Percé Indians, whose last great chief, Hallshallakeen (Eagle Wing), or Chief Joseph as he was called by the white settlers, was born at the mouth of Joseph Creek, a tributary of the Grande Ronde. A continuation of State 3 across the Grande Ronde to the Oregon Line, 42.8 *m.,* and thence to Paradise, Oregon, 48.8 *m.,* has been recently opened.

Left from Asotin a dirt road leads along the west bank of the Snake River. High, rugged cliffs, yellow, brown, and vermilion, rise in precipitous terraces from both sides of the stream. Long sand bars glint dull yellow in the bright sunlight. The cloudless blue sky fades to dull saffron at the horizon line.

BUFFALO ROCK (L), 16.7 *m.,* projects from the scarred cliffs of the eastern canyon wall. On the Washington side are a number of pictographs on the low rocks near the river's side. Most of the drawings represent men, with huge, square shoulders, short legs, and horned headdresses; others resemble mountain goats, deer, and elk. According to an explanation advanced by the Smithsonian Institution, these pictographs were made by the Basket Maker Indians some 3,000 years ago.

South of Buffalo Rock the road continues along the winding course of the Snake River through rugged and picturesque terrain. Time-scarred peaks, sometimes 2,000 feet in height, rise above the tortuous course of the stream. In some places the canyon walls are said to be as steep as those of the Grand Canyon of Colorado. Fantastically contoured rocks present a variety of rich colorings under varying conditions of light and shade. The road ends at the ROGERSBURG FERRY, 22 *m.*

ROGERSBURG, 22.5 *m.* (810 alt., 42 pop.), at the junction of the Snake River and the Grande Ronde, is set among rocky bluffs of remarkable grandeur and beauty. Here Captain Benjamin Bonneville and his men camped after enjoying a generous reception in the Indian village at the mouth of the Joseph Creek. Bonneville's notes about the valley inspired Washington Irving's description of the country.

Rogersburg was born of mining booms and nourished during its vigorous youth by the optimism characteristic of booms. The lower Grande Ronde region has experienced a number of mining stampedes. One of these rushes occurred in 1865 as a result of a story of a fabulous gold strike made five years earlier.

In 1860, according to the story, three men beached their canoes on the bar of Shovel Creek, an insignificant stream emptying into the Snake River. In the morning they discovered pay dirt so rich that a pailful of nuggets was secured in a short time. Finding themselves short of supplies, the men hid the nuggets and went to Walla Walla to outfit themselves. There one of them was killed, a second died of natural causes, and the third disappeared.

But the report of the find on Shovel Creek lingered, and with each retelling the nuggets grew larger and more numerous. Prospectors, stimulated by the story, year after year made their way to the creek to search for the cached gold and the rich sands where it was found. In 1865 there was a regular stampede, and for a brief time this small creek in the wilds echoed with the sounds of men at work. Soon, however, the men drifted away as hopes faded; but the story persisted. Succeeding years saw other booms come and go, and with them activity in Rogersburg expanded and contracted. Abandonment of river service in the early twentieth century, however, left the town without any ready means of communication with the outside world until the completion of the Asotin-Rogersburg road in 1938.

At 7.1 *m.* is a junction with a dirt road. About a mile down this road is a rock where Indian pictographs are still visible, although decades of weathering have dimmed their sharp outlines. Some of the drawings are easily decipherable. One, a petroglyph, is a carving of two men with flint knives engaged in mortal combat. Others show men, horses, and mountain goats.

SILCOTT, 8.7 *m.* (1,724 alt., 50 pop.), once a bustling pioneer river village, is now only the center of the orchard lands at the junction of Alpowa (Ind. place of rest) Creek and the Snake River. Here Lewis and Clark camped in 1805 and made peace with the Nez Percé bands, and here along the banks of the creek Chief Red Wolf, who had been given some seeds by the Reverend H. H. Spalding, planted, in 1837, the first orchard in the Snake River Valley. In 1861 Sam Smith established a trading post in this part of the country and for years the post was an important crossing point on the river and a stage stop on the Lewiston-Pomeroy route.

The name commemorates one of the early sheriffs, John Silcott, who was known for many miles as a man quick on the draw and worthy of respectful attention from would-be law breakers. Silcott with his wife, the daughter of Chief Timothy, ran a little ferry across the river, and the village that took root was known familiarly as Silcott, or Silcott's Landing, until 1882, when it was platted and named Alpowa. For a brief time the settlement flourished around a flour mill and warehouses, but in 1885 the miniature boom collapsed and the original name was restored. A few years later most of the buildings were destroyed by fire.

Just north of Silcott the Snake River (R) plunges into the SNAKE RIVER CANYON, 2,000 feet deep, its contorted and convoluted walls revealing the lava flow that once covered the region. Here the highway leaves the river and begins to climb, winding between steep rocky slopes, running along man-made ledges, or skirting creek beds, dry except during spring freshets. Instead of orchards are cattle ranches and well-built, substantial farmhouses with corrals and barns. An occasional band of sheep stands motionless in a corral or on a hillside, or moves along the highway, a gray undulating mass, heads bobbing with regular irregularity, while a sheep dog nips at the heels of the laggards.

TIMOTHY MEMORIAL BRIDGE, 9.6 *m.*, an arched concrete span over Alpowa Creek, commemorates Chief Timothy, who led Colonel E. J. Steptoe to safety by guiding him safely across the river at night. Basaltic cliffs and promontories tower above the narrow, arid valley. The stream, clear except at spring freshets, sparkles through gravelly barrens, interspersed with bright islands of watercress and little groves of cottonwoods and willows. In early days this stream was a trout fisherman's paradise.

West of the SUMMIT OF THE GRADE, 21.6 *m.* (2,785 alt.), US 410 winds through a rocky gorge, above which scraggly brush and timber stagger up the slope. Emerging from the draw the highway runs across a rough, semiarid plateau dotted with willows and scrub trees. This is cattle country, fenced with barbed wire, affording practically year-around grazing.

PATAHA (Ind. brush), 29.1 *m.* (1,850 alt., 25 pop.), is a scattering of buildings far removed from the town's flour mill, which rises tower-like from a clump of trees. The first settler of the site was James Bowers, who arrived in 1861. In 1867 the land was acquired by "Vine" Favor, who for years had driven a stage on the Lewiston route. Favor platted the town in 1882, and for a brief time it was successively known as Waterstown and Favorsburg. Finally it took the Indian name Pataha. When Garfield County was formed in the eighties, Pataha, or Pataha City, was the county seat, but it soon lost out to the rapidly expanding neighboring settlement, Pomeroy.

West of Pataha US 410 follows Pataha Creek Canyon. To the south the terrain mounts gradually toward the Blue Mountains. The highway traverses mile after mile of rolling hills, which 75 years ago were covered by thick bunchgrass and today are a checkerboard of wheat and barley fields.

POMEROY, 32.1 *m.* (1,849 alt., 1,720 pop.), seat of Garfield County and terminus of a branch line of the Union Pacific, is the center of the surrounding wheat, barley, and cattle country and for the irrigated acreage to the north, where quantities of beans, alfalfa, fruits, and vegetables are produced.

In 1864 Joseph M. Pomeroy came to this region from Ashtabula, Ohio, and started a blooded-stock farm on Pataha Creek, to supply the demand of stagecoach operators. In the late seventies a flour mill was erected, rail connections were constructed, a bank established, a fire department formed, and the townsite platted. The town was then on the stage route to Lewiston, and old timers still talk of the St. George Hotel, where travelers swapped tall tales and stood each other up for drinks. Several times daily during these boom days six-horse coaches clattered into town, the animals in a lather, and dust clouds flying. In 1882 the town was named seat of the newly formed Garfield County.

During these frontier days Pomeroy was beset with gamblers, road agents, miners, and cattle rustlers. In an effort to maintain order and to control traffic in liquor and drunkenness, the town adopted a local-option measure but this was soon declared unconstitutional. Recalling these boom days an old-timer said, "Main Street had twenty saloons and things were poppin'. The town ain't bigger now an' nothin' is poppin'."

Pomeroy, nevertheless, is a prosperous town with a compact business section, neat, shaded, residential districts, and a city park. Its newspaper, the *East Washington,* is in its sixty-first year (1941). Annually old settlers and their descendants come from miles around to celebrate at a pioneer picnic.

In Pomeroy is a junction with State 3-K, a graveled road.

Left from Main and E. 1st streets, on State 3-K through an agricultural area, largely devoted to wheat and barley. Occasionally bands of sheep and herds of cattle range the more precipitous slopes. Imperceptibly the rolling hills become sharper, and scrubby stands of timber begin to appear as the road penetrates the foothills of the Blue Mountains.

At 7.5 *m.* is a junction with an improved road: R. here through increasingly rugged country, mostly forested, to the northern boundary of the UMATILLA (Ind. water rippling over sand) NATIONAL FOREST, 15.2 *m.* A fairly heavy stand of ponderosa pine, Douglas fir, western tamarack, Engelmann spruce, and white fir, still mostly virgin timber, make up this forest. The eastern boundary of the TUCANNON GAME PRESERVE (R), an area of 54,560 acres, begins here and extends nine miles southward. At 18 *m.* is a junction with a dirt road: L. here 0.3 *m.* to ROSE SPRINGS, a popular mountain resort.

CLEARWATER LOOKOUT TOWER, 100 feet high, on the improved road, is a vantage point affording unobstructed views of the rugged upper Pataha Creek and Charley Creek country to the east and of the Tucannon River region to the west. The ASOTIN DISTRICT RANGER STATION here furnishes information and issues fire permits. This lookout station is practically on the divide of the Blue Mountains, a low range that derives its name from the soft, distinctly blue haze that hangs over it during summer and winter months.

The first recorded use of the name Blue Mountains occurs in David Thompson's journal under the date of August 8, 1811. Nearly half a century later the Reverend Gustavus Hines, recounting his travels in *Exploring Expedition to Oregon* (1851), describes the mountains as rising "with indescribable beauty and grandeur" and adds that this range "from its azure-like appearance, has been called the 'Blue Mountains'."

At 24 *m.* is a junction with another dirt road; L. here 1.2 *m.* to TEAL CAMP GROUND (*spring water, storm shelters, and camp stoves*), pleasantly situated in a grassy clearing surrounded by towering pines, their yellow-brown trunks bright through the dark green needles.

SPRUCE SPRING CAMP (*camping facilities, spring water*), 27.5 *m.,* on the improved road, offers a woodland wilderness with paths leading into the forests. SUNSET POINT, 30 *m.,* affords an excellent view, especially to the west, across country as primitive as it was when only Indians and wild animals inhabited it. From ravines, rugged and beautiful, the Tucannon flows through deep canyons toward the undulating plateau that merges into the treeless Snake River country. In SMOOTHING IRON GAME PRESERVE, 31 *m.,* an area of 30,720 acres, elk and deer are plentiful.

At 33 *m.* is a junction with crossroad: L. here 5 *m.* to the foot of DIAMOND PEAK; R. 7 *m.* to WENATCHEE GUARD STATION, where the road loops back to Asotin and Clarkston (*see above*). The OREGON LINE is crossed at 43 *m.* (7 miles from Troy, Oregon).

West of Pomeroy US 410 dips and climbs through mile after mile of farmland, largely planted to winter wheat. The fields, left fallow in alternate summers, are seeded in late August or early September. Then come the rains, and within a few days the tender leaves of the wheat appear. By the time the first flurries of snow fill the air, the shoots, toughened and multiplied into bunches, have set their roots firmly in the earth. Serious damage occurs only when intense cold turns the earth to flint before snow has fallen, or when a cold snap follows upon a midwinter chinook that has swept the snow from the fields.

These chinook winds may be expected every winter throughout the Inland Empire. For days the country will be held in the iron grip of cold; snow crackles underfoot; and at night the aurora borealis flashes overhead. Then, almost without warning, comes the chinook, usually at night. There is a low moaning sound, as of a prolonged sigh; the air seems alive. Water drips from the eaves of houses, and icicles shatter on the walk below. When morning comes the snow, which a few short hours before had glittered with blinding light, is sodden, turning to rivulets before the eyes. Sometimes as suddenly as the temperature rose, it drops again, as the wind veers from the west to northeast. Then the melting of the snow is halted, and streets and sidewalks are covered with treacherously corrugated ice.

At 35 *m.* is a junction with State 3-L, an improved road.

Left here to MARENGO, 4 *m.* (1,631 alt., 35 pop.), a score of buildings centered around a gas station, a schoolhouse, and a general store. In 1877 the Grange erected a flour mill here, and a post office was established the following year. In Marengo is a junction with a dirt side road; L. on this road through picturesque Tucannon Canyon. High, rocky walls hem in the narrow valley, broken here and there by scattered brush or an occasional clump of cottonwoods. Fishing is good and Chinese pheasants, quail, and partridge are plentiful. (*This road is impassable or dangerous in winter.*)

The RANGER STATION (R), 17 *m.* on the dirt road, marks the entrance to the Umatilla National Forest (*visitors must report for permits to enter the forest and for fire permits*). LITTLE TUCANNON CAMP (*picnic facilities*), 19.5 *m.*, lies in an open glade at the fork of the Tucannon and the Little Tucannon Rivers.

At 23.5 *m.* is a junction with Skyline Drive; L. on the drive 31.2 *m.* to IDAHO LINE; R. 14 *m.* to Dayton (*see below*).

West of the junction with State 3-L, the highway runs between hills which, except for the most precipitous slopes, are planted to wheat and barley. Furrows at right angles to the slope, strip farming, and gully-control measures are evidence of the growing interest in soil conservation. A few of the steeper slopes are used for cattle range. For several miles the railroad tracks parallel the highway and during harvest season, freight trains labor by in a succession of red box cars and yellow refrigerator cars.

DODGE (*service station, with rest rooms and luncheon*), 44.9 *m.* (1,400 alt., 10 pop.), at the junction of US 410 and US 295 (*see Tour 4b*), is a stage junction for Idaho and other eastern points. Originally this hamlet was named for Charles Buckley, who owned most of the land in the district, but when it was discovered that a western

Washington town was also called Buckley, the name was changed to Dodge, commemorating another early settler.

West of Dodge US 410 traverses a sparsely settled area. Extending to the horizon line on either side of the road are wheat and barley fields. Paralleling the highway, Pataha Creek (R) flows through a narrow channel. In DELANEY, 53.6 *m.* (910 alt., 15 pop.), is a junction with a graveled road.

Right on this road along the north bank of TUCANNON (Ind. abundance of bread root) CREEK, which sweeps in broad curves through the rolling hills. The sweep of the hills is unbroken except for an occasional gully, rocky cliff, or stretch of old-fashioned wooden fence. Cattle and sheep graze on the grass-covered hills, so steep in places that it is hard to believe that animals can maintain a foothold.

STARBUCK, 8.3 *m.* (644 alt., 251 pop.), in its heydey was a bustling town of 1,500 people, most of whom were employed in the shops of the O.-W.R.&N. railroad; the monthly pay roll in 1905 amounted to $20,000. The bell, given to the Presbyterian Church by General Starbuck, still sounds from the tower of the town hall. One of the factors in the decline of the town was the introduction of the Mallet locomotive, which generated enough power to negotiate the runs on this section of the line without helpers. In 1932 the shops were closed. Today (1941) the natural process of disintegration is being accelerated by wreckers, who are moving the town piecemeal to Walla Walla. A number of wheat farmers and sheep ranchers continue to make the town their headquarters.

Boats of the Oregon Steam Navigation Company in early days plied between the Columbia and GRANGE CITY, 12.3 *m.* (520 alt., 2 pop.), at the confluence of the Snake and Tucannon Rivers, today marked by only two houses. In 1873 the merchants and grain shippers of Dayton established a freight and shipping point here. In 1876 a number of farmers identified with the Grange movement, which had spread westward after the panic of 1873, formed the Grange Warehouse Company and named the place Grange City. The completion of a rail line to Dayton in 1881 ended the importance of the water route.

LYONS FERRY, 16.3 *m.*, is the point of departure for the ferry (*fee $1, car and passengers*) to the north bank of the Snake River. The road continues northward along the west side of the Palouse River.

At 20.8 *m.* is a junction with a dirt road: R. here 1 *m.* to a junction with a trail: 0.1 *m.* on this trail to PALOUSE FALLS, which plunges over a sheer rocky precipice 198 feet to a great rimrock basin and seethes onward down a gorge to the Columbia. The picturesque falls are described in David Thompson's journals and are mentioned by virtually every later explorer.

South of Delaney US 410 swings across the Tucannon River through hilly country. As a conservation measure most farmers in this district seed only half of their land each year. Frequently as an additional safeguard against erosion, the farm is cultivated in strips, following the contours of slope and gully. Here the route follows the old Walla Walla-Colville wagon trail, over which thousands of settlers and miners traveled when land north of the Snake River was opened to settlement in 1858. The highway winds downhill through mile after mile of carefully cultivated fields.

The BLUE MOUNTAIN CANNERY, 68.9 *m.* (*open by permission*), is one of several large pea canneries in the Walla Walla district. Modern technology has so revolutionized this canning industry that now the entire process consumes only a few hours. Huge viners, operating in the fields, strip the peas from the vines, remove them from the pods, and load them in small boxes. These are rushed to a cannery, where the peas are weighed, graded, washed, sorted, blanched, inspected, put into cans, sealed, and finally cooked by steam and pressure.

DAYTON, 69.3 *m.* (1,615 alt., 3,026 pop.), a pleasant, bustling city, spreads over the V-shaped valley formed by the conjunction of Patit Creek, which courses through the northern section, and the Touchet River, which cuts through the southern section of the city. Main Street, a broad thoroughfare bordered with substantial frame and brick structures, is flanked on the south by an attractive residential district and on the north by the older residences of the original town.

Early history of Dayton centered around the point where Pioneer Bridge now crosses the Touchet River. Here an Indian trail crossed the stream, and the grassy flats were a favorite camping ground for Indian bands. Here, too, Lewis and Clark rested on their return journey in May, 1806, and 30 years later Captain Benjamin de Bonneville also camped here. In 1855 H. M. Chase, the first settler, took up lands at the bend of the Touchet, and other settlers soon followed. Among these was Henry C. Rickey, who erected a hotel and, in 1862, started a stage line between Walla Walla and Lewiston by way of the Touchet Valley. Newcomers continued to arrive in increasing numbers, particularly after the Civil War, but little thought was given to the establishment of a town until 1871, when the townsite was platted and filed. Five years later the town was incorporated under the name of Dayton.

The town flourished. Situated at the intersection of stage routes, it profited from the transient trade of hundreds of men stampeding to the various mining districts. Additional impetus came from the discovery that the upper benchlands as well as the valleys were eminently suited to growing wheat. In 1875 it became the seat of Columbia County. By 1880 Dayton had a population of 6,300. Then the wave began to recede: a series of fires, the coming of rail lines and the end of stage routes, the deflation of mining booms all contributed to the recession. Only agriculture continued to increase in importance.

The Dayton of 1940 is the hub of a highly productive farming area; the major crops are wheat, barley, hay, apples, and peas. Cattle also are raised for beef, the Wheatland Shorthorns, owned by C. J. Broughton, being one of the famous herds of beef cattle in the United States. An average of 20,000 sheep are raised annually in the county. The industrial plants include a pea cannery, with a capacity of 500,000 cases a season, apple-packing plants, sawmills, a box factory, a creamery, and several grain warehouses.

Dayton Days, an annual three-day event, features horse racing, bucking contests, stunt riding, and steer bulldogging. This event and the picnic of the Columbia County Pioneer Association are both held in June at the Dayton Fairgrounds.

In Dayton is a junction with a graveled road leading east, the Eckler Mountain Road.

Left on this road along a draw between rolling fields of alfalfa and wheat to a plateau, which rises gently toward the south. Spreading left of the road is

Patit Creek Valley, and the valley of the North Fork of the Touchet River on the right.

A boundary of the UMATILLA NATIONAL FOREST, 18 *m.*, marks the beginning of the Mountain Skyline, or Skyview, Road (*open June to September*). The road ascends steadily with many undulations and curves through woods of pine, fir, and tamarack to the backbone of the Blue Mountains. Far below, to the left, the little Tucannon River ripples and tumbles over gravelly shallows and rocky ledges.

At 14.8 *m.* is a junction with a dirt road.

Right from the junction the road swings due south and runs along the crest of the divide to GODMAN SPRINGS and the GODMAN SPRINGS RANGER STATION, 28 *m.* (5,740 alt.). Copious springs issuing from the side of the mountains near the camp form the headwaters of Punjab Creek.

At Godman Springs is a junction with a forest road.

(1) L. here 3.5 *m.* to TEEPEE CAMP (*picnic facilities; spring water*) at the foot of the Oregon Buttes.

(2) R. here 0.3 *m.* on another forest road to a vantage point for a magnificent view. Southwest are the Wallowa Mountains and toward the east the Seven Devils' Peaks in Idaho, some 40 miles away. In the foreground lies the rugged Butte Creek and Crooked Fork country as it was when Indians tracked deer and bear through its forests or caught mink and beaver along its water courses.

As it ascends toward the divide the Skyline Road skirts the heads of deep canyons and runs along shelves on the precipitous hillsides sprinkled with yellow pine, Engelmann spruce, and Douglas fir. In some places the divide is so sharp that the road seems to lie precariously on the very top. Here are the headwaters of streams flowing both north and south but all eventually tributary to the Snake River.

At 31.3 *m.* is a junction with another forest road: R. here 5 *m.* to the Twin Buttes region and the end of the road.

STAYAWHILE SPRINGS, 31.5 *m.*, lies in a pleasant dell at the base of Buck Ridge, in the heart of the Blue Mountains. Deer, elk, and upland birds are plentiful, and some of the land has been set aside as protected areas. From Stayawhile Springs the road cuts back across the main ridge of the Blue Mountains, circling the base of TABLE ROCK, and then climbs to TABLE ROCK FOREST CAMP (6,310 alt.), 43 *m.* So narrow is the summit of the mountain ridge that at certain points the rolling wheatlands can be seen stretching northwestward toward the Cascades 200 miles away, while on the south, seemingly at the very foot of Table Rock, lie the wilderness gorges of the Grande Ronde and Wallowa valleys between the snow-topped peaks of the Wallowa Mountains.

At 46 *m.* the Mountain Skyline Road crosses the OREGON LINE, 27 *m.* north of Tollgate.

Once the hilly terrain south of Dayton was covered with bunchgrass, but with the discovery that heavy yields of wheat and barley could be grown on these benchlands, all but the steepest hillsides were put under cultivation. Soon both wind and water erosion began to take their toll. Deep gullies began to appear, and during the spring freshets every little rivulet carried away part of the fine top soil. Today most farmers, aided by the various State and Federal conservation agencies, have adopted farming techniques that are reducing the amount of soil loss due to erosion. Discing, which mixes stubble with the soil, is supplementing plowing; strip farming reduces wind erosion; contour cultivation slows up drainage and conserves both soil and water. Gully erosion has been checked by planting grass, alfalfa, and clover on vulnerable slopes; these crops either are used for forage or plowed under to add humus to the soil. Steep slopes and possible water courses are not cultivated.

LEWIS AND CLARK TRAIL STATE PARK (*camping facilities*), 74.7 *m.*, is a 50-acre, partially improved tract adjacent to the highway and the Touchet River. It is marked by a grove of stately pines, the only grove of its kind in the valley. Here Lewis and Clark's expedition camped in 1806 on its return trip.

HUNTSVILLE, 76.4 *m.* (1,350 alt., 150 pop.), founded by the United Brethren Society in 1878-9, once had dreams of becoming an important center of industry and education. A flour mill, the second in the valley, was erected, and when the town was platted, a college, the Washington Institute, was projected. An ephemeral boom, marked by considerable expansion and the opening of the college, collapsed before the close of the century. At present Huntsville is a wheat-shipping point.

WAITSBURG, 79.3 *m.* (1,272 alt., 936 pop.), a pleasant old town with shaded streets, lies on the miniature delta formed by the Touchet River and Copper Creek. In 1859 Robert Kennedy settled here; a few miles away on Copper Creek, a settlement was started, and in 1861 a tiny sawmill was built there. In 1865 a few small buildings were erected on the site of Waitsburg, then called Delta. Sylvester M. Wait, recognizing the power possibilities of the Touchet River, and noting that flour was selling for $44 a barrel, decided to build a flour mill. Farmers donated land for the mill and agreed to hold their grain until spring, at which time Wait was to pay $1.50 a bushel. They were pleased with this arrangement, which eliminated the cost of wheat shipments to Walla Walla. The enterprise was successful, and the town, platted in 1869 and named Waitsburg, prospered in spite of occasional setbacks.

In 1881 the Oregon Railroad and Navigation Company extended its lines into Waitsburg, and in the same year the first municipal government was organized. Churches and a school were organized, streets were improved, new stores were started, and a bank was opened. The milling industry steadily expanded as population figures rose and wheat acreage increased. Among those who settled in the environs during these years were a number of Southerners. Names such as Sorghum Hollow, Whiskey, Whetstone, Hogeye, Misery, and Whoopemup still cling to roads and creeks and mountain peaks.

Situated in one of the most fertile farming regions in Washington, Waitsburg today as in earlier years depends upon wheat for its income. Annually more than 1,000,000 bushels are shipped from the town. Three flour mills are in operation, including the one established by Wait, which has been in continuous service since 1865. Hundreds of carloads of apples are also exported each year.

The Days of Real Sport, sponsored by the Waitsburg Racing Association, is a popular celebration held annually in late spring. The local track, one of the best east of the Cascades, is used as a proving ground for race horses, some being brought from as far away as California.

South of Waitsburg US 410 continues through rolling wheat lands, where crop failures are seldom known. A deep rich soil, a sufficiency of moisture during the growing months, and the absence of rain during the harvest season practically guarantee an average of from 25 to 40 bushels an acre.

Many kinds of birds are found in this region south of the Snake River. Early in spring the chickadee and the grosbeak awaken the woods with their excited chatter, the robin's whistle is heard in budding orchards, the mountain bluebird appears on fence posts and ridge poles, and the lark trills from the meadows. Every day the bird population grows, as swallows, blackbirds, sparrows, orioles, goldfinches, thrushes, mourning doves, and kingbirds arrive. Magpies shriek from clumps of trees, crows fly noisily by, woodpeckers begin to beat their tattoos, and hawks soar overhead. Game birds, too, are plentiful, especially ring-necked pheasants, quail, and grouse. Only during the severest winter weather are the fields and woods practically deserted.

DIXIE, 89.4 *m.* (1.606 alt., 200 pop.), began in the sixties when the three Kershaw brothers, who danced and played and sang their way across the Plains to the tune of Dixie, settled here at the confluence of Mud and Dry Creeks. The crossing at this point soon came to be known as Dixie Crossing. Today it is an attractive little town.

Southwest of Dixie the slopes become less steep; and wide, far-flung valleys hemmed in by gently rolling hills alternate with expanses of level fields, as US 410 descends into the Walla Walla Valley. Here the Walla Walla (Ind. little river people) fished in the many streams, pastured their ponies on the bunchgrass and wild rye, and hunted in the foothills of the Blue Mountains to the south. At first, settlers farmed the lowlands only, but after the discovery that the benchlands would produce good crops of grain, cultivation was rapidly extended.

WALLA WALLA AIRPORT, 97.3 *m.,* borders on the highway.

WALLA WALLA, 100.6 *m.* (975 alt., 18,709 pop.). (*see Walla Walla*).

West of Walla Walla US 410 traverses a broad flat crisscrossed by the Walla Walla River and its tributaries. This area is a veritable garden producing many crops; asparagus, peas, onions, potatoes, and other vegetables; apples, peaches, pears, and Italian prunes; alfalfa hay, and wool.

The vegetation of the Walla Walla country is varied and colorful. Drier sections are covered with rabbit bush and sagebrush. Along the watercourses are clumps of willows and cottonwoods, interspersed with chokecherry, serviceberry, and elderberry bushes. In the late spring the arid dunes are brightened by the rose-colored sand dock, and the low uncultivated hills are covered with grama grass, or bunch grass, and lupine; the stream banks are yellow and purple with buttercups, yellow bells, honeysuckle, shooting stars, and purple grasswidows.

At 106.7 *m.* is a junction with a graveled road.

Left here, 0.5 *m.* to a junction with a dirt road: R. on the dirt road 0.4 *m.* to the entrance of WHITMAN MEMORIAL PARK, site of the Waiilatpu (Ind.

place of the rye grass) Mission. A group of graves and a large crypt sealed, with a massive block of stone mark the burial place of the pioneer missionaries. A flight of steps and a winding road lead to the crest of the hill, where a tall shaft has been erected.

In 1836 Marcus Whitman constructed a crude cabin of cottonwood logs on the right bank of the Walla Walla River, at Waiilatpu, near the mouth of Mill Creek. The larger buildings of the mission soon rose alongside. Myron F. Eells, a missionary from Massachusetts who visited the mission in 1838, described it thus: "It was built of adobe, mud dried in the form of bricks, only larger—there are doors and windows of the roughest material, the boards being sawed by hand and put together by no carpenter, but by one who knows nothing about the work. There are a number of wheat, corn and potato fields about the house, besides a garden of melons and all kinds of vegetables common to a garden. There are no fences, there being no timber with which to make them. The furniture is very primitive; the bedsteads are boards nailed to the sides of the house, sink fashion; then some blankets and husks make the bed." The mission buildings and grounds are in process of restoration as an historic site, under the auspices of Whitman Centennial, Inc., a Walla Walla organization.

At 109.6 *m.* is a junction with a dirt road.

Right here 0.6 *m.* to a path: L. here 0.2 *m.* through fields to an Indian cemetery and the neglected grave of Chief Peu-Peu-Mox-Mox, who was killed here in a fight between the Oregon Volunteers and the Walla Walla. The wooden cross that once marked his grave has fallen to the ground.

LOWDEN, 113.5 *m.* (490 alt., 250 pop.), was one of the first farm sites in the valley of the Walla Walla. A general store and a large grain warehouse stand by the highway. To the south the Umatilla Highlands loom in the distance.

Left from Lowden, 1.5 *m.* to a geologically interesting ARTIFICIAL CANYON. In the spring of 1926, when the water of the Burlingame Irrigation Ditch was diverted for one week into a diversion channel, a miniature grand canyon, in places 100 feet wide and 100 feet deep, was created; thousands of tons of silt were carried to the Columbia. In the walls of this gully, the stratified deposits of an ancient lake bed may be advantageously studied. Deep-well drilling in artesian basins has revealed that this region was occupied in succession by four lakes. That the earliest antedated the uplift of the Cascades is shown by the blue clay deposits characteristic of the pre-Cascadian period, and characteristic granite boulders indicate that the last lake existed in the Glacial period.

At 117.9 *m.* is a junction with a dirt road.

Left on this road, which crosses the railroad track, is the lively little town of TOUCHET, 0.3 *m.* (441 alt., 500 pop.), at the confluence of the Touchet River and the Walla Walla. Lewis and Clark named the main Touchet River "White Stallion," but by the time the town was platted April 12, 1884, the name Touchet was generally accepted. In the period of prairie schooners, road agents, and Indians, numerous stage lines carrying mail followed this route. One line operated between The Dalles and Walla Walla; the Thomas line ran from Wallula to Boise by way of the Woodward toll road and Walla Walla. In 1864 the great transcontinental stage lines of Ben Holladay, who later became one of the West's foremost railroad builders, were extended into this territory.

West of Touchet the walls of the valley seem to close in upon the highway. Here the trees and bushes, so familiar along the upper Walla Walla, gradually disappear; rolling, sage-covered hills are crisscrossed by jack-rabbit trails on both sides of the road, and the wind whips tumbleweeds into roadside ditches.

The Walla Walla & Columbia, one of the earliest railroads in the Territory, once ran along this route. Begun in 1872, the old road was a monument to the perseverance of Dr. D. S. Baker, its builder, who, in spite of general ridicule, laid the tracks that were later purchased by a transcontinental line. Part of its train crew was a collie dog that ran ahead of the train to drive cattle from the right-of-way.

At 130.5 *m.* US 410 forms a junction with US 395-730.

Left from the junction, following along the east bank of Columbia River, US 395-730 enters Columbia Gap. Bold escarpments of rock, with palisades higher than those of the Hudson River, attest the force of the current. Beyond, a vast plain extends southeast to the line of the Blue Mountains. The highway crosses the OREGON LINE, 6.5 *m.,* about ten miles north of Cold Springs, Oregon, and continues over a scenic route along the Columbia River to Portland.

US 410, identical for a short distance with US 395, swings northward across the MADAME DORION BRIDGE over the Walla Walla River, named in honor of Marie Dorion, a member of the Overland Astorians of 1811-12.

At 130.7 *m.* is a junction with a graveled road.

Left on this road to WALLULA (Ind. abundance of water) 0.4 *m.* (324 alt., 160 pop.), a hamlet surrounded by sagebrush and sand, about one-half mile from the confluence of the Columbia and the Walla Walla Rivers. Little remains to suggest the importance of this spot in the early days. As a junction point for Dr. D. S. Baker's railroad, numerous stage lines, and river boats operating up and down the Columbia and the Snake Rivers, Wallula was a rough-and-ready town. Teamsters, miners, crews cutting wood for the boilers of river boats, and cattlemen, all made it a stopping place. The town was platted by J. M. Vansycle and S. W. Tatem in 1882, and for two decades (until the coming of the Oregon-Washington and Union Pacific railroads in 1882) the town pursued a wild career.

Today Wallula is a railroad junction point. Eight railroad tracks run through the town, and lines of cars stand on sidings, many of them ice refrigerator cars, or "reefers." A railroad ice house, with long platforms above the tracks, is equipped to ice 40 cars simultaneously.

Left 0.4 *m.* from Wallula on a bituminous-surfaced road to a junction with a similar road: L. here to a junction with a graveled road: L. (straight ahead) at 0.9 *m.,* the embankment of Baker's "Rawhide Railroad" may still be seen. At 1 *m.* is all that remains of OLD FORT WALLA WALLA, huge foundation stones tracing the lines of the old structure. First called Fort Nez Percé and later Fort Walla Walla, it was built in 1817-18 by Alexander Ross and Donald McKenzie of the North West Fur Company. In 1817 a brigade of 86 men left Oregon for the "upper country" with orders to build a fort and trading post at some point near the confluence of the Snake and Columbia Rivers. It was to be a convenient stopping place between Fort Vancouver and points north and east of the Columbia River.

One hundred feet square, the fort was surrounded by an outer wall of whipsawed planks 30 inches wide, 6 inches thick, and 20 feet long. A balustrade, 4 feet high, was provided with loopholes and slide doors. A gallery inside enabled a guard to pace the wall and keep an eye on the surrounding territory. The houses, one of stone, the others of driftwood, were inside this wall. At the corners were water tanks to be used in case of fire. Indians were compelled to transact their trading from the outside at a small window. When rebuilt in 1843 after a fire, adobe took the place of timber.

US 410 traverses desolate sand heaps on a flat stretching between the Columbia River and the basin lands to the east.

At 133.4 *m.* is a junction with a graveled road.

Left on this road is ATTALIA, 0.4 *m.* (356 alt., 50 pop.), a junction of the Northern Pacific Railway and the Oregon-Washington Railway and Navigation Company line. Of a once prosperous community, only a few buildings remain among scattered dying trees. The town was named for a little hamlet in Italy.

TWO RIVERS, 136.4 *m.* (600 alt., 50 pop.), lies amid sand dunes partially overgrown with sagebrush and bunch grass. Fifteen years ago this area was dotted with orchards and gardens, irrigated by water pumped from the Snake River through ditches. The expense proved too great, farmers could not pay their water bills, and the company went bankrupt. All that remains are a few weed-filled gullies, once irrigation ditches.

US 410 cuts through BURBANK, 141 *m.* (354 alt., 160 pop.), formerly a center of the irrigated area, and crosses the SNAKE RIVER BRIDGE, 144 *m.* The broad, shallow mouth does not suggest the river's deeply eroded upper reaches. The greenish-gray water blends into the bleak wastes of sand, the sagebrush, and the white-streaked alkali plains. The confluence of the Snake and the Columbia Rivers, a half-mile away, can be seen from the bridge. Along the Snake River on the east and the Columbia on the west are tracts irrigated by means of pumping plants. High-grade fruits, berries, and vegetables are raised on these small farms.

At 144.5 *m.* is a junction with an improved road.

Left here to SACAJAWEA STATE PARK, 1.8 *m.,* a ten-acre tract at the confluence of the Snake and Columbia Rivers, established in 1926. The land was donated to the State by the city of Pasco. The name of the park commemorates Sacajawea, the Indian woman who guided the Lewis and Clark expedition through the Rocky Mountains to the lower Snake River country.

In PASCO, 148 *m.* (378 alt., 3,913 pop.), (*see Tour 6*), is a junction with US 395 (*see Tour 6*).

Section b. PASCO *to* YAKIMA, *87.4 m. US 410*

This section of the tour crosses an arid district with numerous towns, born of the coming of the railroads in the eighties and, by the introduction of irrigation at the turn of the century, developed into rich agricultural centers. The highway curves northward through grain, hop, and alfalfa fields, broad fruit orchards, truck gardens, and dairy ranches, some of the earliest specialized farms in the State.

West of PASCO, 0 *m.,* US 410 crosses the COLUMBIA RIVER, 0.8 *m.,* on the Inter-county Bridge connecting the two cities which, like two children of some western tribe, have grown up in the desert together. Kennewick and Pasco lie in a depression, created during the geologic period when the Cascades and the Okanogan Highlands were elevated and the entire plateau of eastern Washington altered.

KENNEWICK (Ind. winter paradise), 2 *m.* (355 alt., 1,918 pop.), a compact little city in the middle of fertile lands and orchards, was a bunchgrass waste until platted by the Northern Pacific Irrigation Company in 1892. The Yakima Irrigation and Improvement Company later boomed the town by importing settlers from the Middle West and the Mississippi Valley. The business district is fronted by brick stores that date back to 1907, the time of the town's first boom. Large grain elevators sprawl along the railroad track. The Twin Cities Creamery is an important concern.

The region around Kennewick, with its brief winter season, is the best grape-growing area in the State. The Church Grape Juice Company maintains here its main office, a factory and bottling works, and probably the largest private Concord vineyard in the United States. Cherries, also, are an important crop; 25 per cent of all the cherries shipped in the State are shipped from here. A rodeo is held annually during Fourth of July week in conjunction with the three-day Pioneer Reunion.

West of Kennewick, US 410 traverses an area of sagebrush, berry fields, alfalfa farms, and orchards, between networks of irrigation flumes and ditches. The wide reaches of the Columbia River are visible.

At 6.6 *m.* is a junction with an oil-surfaced road.

Right on this road, which crosses a flat farming country alongside the Columbia, is RICHLAND, 3.8 *m.* (390 alt., 247 pop.), one of the irrigation boom towns that has settled into a farming community. An important annual event is the Old Time Picnic, held the last part of July.

A haze appearing at certain times over this section is, according to Indian tradition, smoke from the camp of departed warriors and chiefs, who have come back to earth for a short sojourn. Old tribesmen say they have seen their shadowy forms performing ceremonial dances around campfires and corn-shock tepees. Many Indian relics have been found on a near-by island and along the shores of the Columbia. Indians in the vicinity still, according to custom, bury personal belongings with the dead; for tobacco users, a small supply of tobacco is provided so that the departed may smoke in the hereafter.

West of the junction US 410 continues along the south bank of the Yakima River. In this area of sagebrush and coulee, geese and ducks remain all winter, offering excellent sport for hunters. Cottontails, jack rabbits, Chinese pheasants, and the sage hen are elusive targets. The young sage hen is delicious when cooked, but a venerable member of the species tastes like the sagebrush on which it feeds.

A high railroad embankment divides KIONA (Ind. brown hills), 19.9 *m.* (514 alt., 50 pop.), into two strikingly contrasting sections. Scattered on the hillside above the tracks between the station house and a large group of sheep pens, old weatherbeaten structures are framed against a background of desolate, sage-covered desert. Below the hill the buildings are sprucely painted, the houses are neat, and a few trees are growing. Originally the town was named Horseshoe Bend, for the bend in the Yakima River at this point.

In Kiona is a junction with a dirt road.

Right on this road to BENTON CITY, 2 *m.* (490 alt., 150 pop.), settled in 1909. The town was named for Benton S. Grosscup, who was active in securing separation of Benton County from Yakima County.

West of Kiona, US 410, following the Yakima River, climbs along the northern slope of the Horse Heaven Hills (*see Tour 7b*), where sheep and cattle find good grazing grounds. At night will-o-the-wisps are frequent along this bleak and lonely road. Flame-colored, and about three feet above the ground, they are often mistaken by motorists for a single vehicular light. Sternly realistic farmers, their hands still smarting from the handle of a plow, have reported "balls of fire" coming down the road at the speed of an automobile. During dust storms, which are frequent in this area, tumbleweeds roll over rounded hills and dance across the highway.

At 34.2 *m.* is the VALLEY EVAPORATING COMPANY PLANT, where fruit is dehydrated.

Passing through a viaduct of the Northern Pacific, the highway reaches PROSSER, 35 *m.* (661 alt., 1,719 pop.), largest city and seat of Benton County, and a shipping point for cattle and sheep. On the bank of the Yakima River, with the Horse Heaven Hills rising behind it toward the south, Prosser is a solidly built little town, with a busy flour mill and dehydrating plant. An annual event is States' Day, held early in December, originally an occasion for assembling of emigrants from eastern parts of the United States.

In years before white men came, the Indians camped here at Tap-Tap Falls during the salmon runs, and near here James Kinney made the first permanent settlement in 1880, filing for a homestead at "Tap-Tap Falls." The site was also known as Yakima Falls. Two years later Kinney was joined by Colonel William Prosser, who opened a trading store for the scattered ranchmen and crews of the railroad building through at that time. The settlement was renamed Prosser Falls in 1883, and later "Falls" was dropped from the name. The advent of the Northern Pacific, and subsequent development of the power site at Tap-Tap Falls between 1890-4, lent impetus to the town's growth. A new county courthouse was built in 1926 at a cost of $100,000.

In PROSSER CITY PARK, between 7th and 9th Sts. and Prosser and Yakima Aves., is a petrified sequoia taken from a hillside south of the city in 1925. Some million years ago, this species of tree, which is found now only in California, also grew over a part of the Northwest. There is a public SWIMMING POOL (*open May* 30-*Sept* 10) in the park.

The PROSSER FLOURING MILL (*open by arrangement* 8-4 *weekdays*), 10th St. and Grand Ave., beside the Yakima River, is one of the few remaining flour mills in the State operated by waterpower. Started in 1887, the mill was improved in 1890 and has operated continuously ever since. A low dam and a break in the river bed combine to make a small falls, which creates a nine-foot head of water.

In CARNEGIE PUBLIC LIBRARY (*open* 2-5; 7-9 *weekdays*), Sherman Ave. between 6th and 7th Sts., is the city's most cherished possession: a first edition of the three-volume biography of Abraham Lincoln, by William H. Herndon (his law partner for 20 years) and J. W. Weik. The book, published by Clarke and Company, Chicago, in 1889, was suppressed and is now a valuable item.

In Prosser is a junction of US 410 and State 3-A, which follows the

Lumbering

UNDERCUTTING A FI

Photograph by Kinsey; courtesy Simpson Logging Company

)GGING OPERATIONS AT A LOADING STATION
N THE OLYMPIC PENINSULA

TRACTORS ARE USED FOR HAULING LOGS THROUGH THE FOREST
otograph courtesy of Western Tractor and Equipment Company

Photograph by Rothstein; courtesy of Farm Security Adm.
WASHINGTON LOGS BEFORE SAWING IN A LONGVIEW MILL

SAWMILL IN THE FOREST
Photograph courtesy of Caterpillar Tractor Company

IN A SEATTLE
LUMBERYARD

otograph courtesy of Longview Chamber of Commerce

AIRVIEW, LUMBER MILL AT LONGVIEV

RVIEW OF LUMBER PLANT ALONG
AKE WASHINGTON SHIP CANAL, SEATTLE

Photograph by Frank Jacot

The old photographs on these pages are reproduced through courtesy of the U. S. Forest Service
OXEN DRAGGING LOG OVER SKID ROAD THROUGH FOREST

YARDING DONKEY

raph courtesy of U. S. Forest Service
REST HOMESTEAD (1910)

Photograph by Gifford Pinchot
MAIN STREET, MONTE CRISTO (1897)

NLOAD OF LOGS ON WOODEN TRESTLE
Photograph by Gifford and Prentiss, Portland, Oregon

CUTOVER LAND

Photograph courtesy of Caterpillar Tractor Compan

CCC BOYS WEEDING A FOREST NURSERY

Photograph courtesy of Civilian Conservation Corps

Yakima River through a productive farming area in an alternate route to UNION GAP, where it again forms a junction with US 410.

US 410 leaves Prosser on 6th St. and swings across a concrete bridge spanning the Yakima toward the northwest. Along the river, extending in both directions from the bridge, are the Yakima River Game Preserves, for the protection of quail, duck, and pheasant. This is a flat country, where farmers' hay derricks tilt over neatly piled haystacks. The highway passes the Prosser Airport, 35.9 *m.,* and crosses an irrigation ditch.

GRANDVIEW, 43.2 *m.* (811 alt., 1,449 pop.), a city with wide, well-lighted and paved streets, was founded in 1906, during the wholesale town-building and real-estate promotion era. Division Street, the main business thoroughfare, is bounded on either side by substantial, two-story business buildings. There are few frame structures. The snow-capped volcanic peaks of Mount Adams and Mount Rainier are signal points in the view for which the town was named. Benefited by the Yakima Irrigation Project, Grandview is the second most important shipping point in the Yakima Valley for fruit, alfalfa, sugar beets, garden truck, and dairy products.

The GRANDVIEW CITY PARKS, on E. C and 3rd Sts., in the east side of town and on W. 2nd and W. G Sts. in the west, are provided with wading pools and recreational equipment. The west side park has, in addition, an open gas stove and picnic facilities. The ATHLETIC FIELD has a seating capacity of 500 and lighting facilities that make possible night athletic contests.

The PUBLIC LIBRARY (*open* 2-5, 7-9; *Tues., Thurs., Sat.*), in Town Hall, corner W. A and 2nd Sts., has a collection of 4,000 volumes, of which 27 volumes on *The Union and Confederate Navies in the War of the Rebellion,* official records, are of special interest.

On E. 4th St. along the railroad tracks is the WASHINGTON DEHYDRATING FOODS, INC. plant (*visitors by appointment*), where interesting processes in the drying of fruits and vegetables may be observed. Two other important plants are the GRANDVIEW COLD STORAGE PLANT, W. B St. and S. 4th St., and the BIG Y. STORAGE PLANT outside the city limits.

The Grandview Harvest Festival, held early each September, features farm and orchard exhibits, a flower show, a parade, a horse show, 4-H Club contests, and handicraft exhibits. In 1938 more than 12,000 persons watched the parade.

SUNNYSIDE, (*cabin camps*), 51 *m.* (747 alt., 2,368 pop.), is walled by the Horse Heaven Hills and surrounded by valleys checkered with farms and orchards. This arid region attracted the attention of land promoters in 1893. Walter N. Granger, president of the newly formed Sunnyside Canal Company, named the town in 1893 and opened the first store in January 1894. By the middle of that year the town was given a post office, and a stage connected it with Mabton.

Aiding in the development of the town was the Christian Co-operative Movement, sponsored by a branch of the Dunkard Church, and organized under the leadership of S. J. Harrison, Christian Rowland, and H. M. Lichty in 1898. The co-operatives made a large settlement and, in 1901, established their own telephone system; the next year a bank was formed, and an election for incorporation was held.

Several years earlier, the Sunnyside Canal Company, headed by Walter N. Granger, had purchased much of the land in the region and had begun its reclamation by irrigation. The Sunnyside Land and Investment Company (still operating) was founded in the early 1900's. The town was chartered in 1904, the same year the Northern Pacific Railway extended its lines into the town. In 1905 the United States Reclamation Service took over the Sunnyside Irrigation Project, one of the first in the State.

Most of the early inhabitants were farmers who were attracted by the religious basis of the new community, as well as by the agricultural possibilities of the irrigated region. Recently a number of families fled the Middlewestern drought and came to Sunnyside. These new settlers are learning the technique of irrigation farming. Seventy-five other families have come to Sunnyside from the same district in South Dakota as did the original co-operative colony. With the influx of drought victims a difficult housing situation was created; in some cases two families are crowded into one small cabin, barely large enough for two persons.

Asparagus and tomatoes are the most important products grown on the rich soil of the irrigated farm plots that surround Sunnyside. There are also vineyards, orchards, and dairy farms in the vicinity. Two wineries, a warehouse for sugar beets, a vegetable-packing plant, and a storage plant are among the major economic assets of the town. The Roza Irrigation Development is giving added impetus to agricultural enterprise in the valley.

Among impressive buildings in the wide business district are the new American Legion Hall and the new Federal Post Office Building. In Sunnyside CITY PARK, 3rd St. and Grant Ave., a 40-piece high school band gives a concert each Friday night during the summer months.

For a time known as the "Holy City," Sunnyside has 22 churches. The major religious denomination is the Zionist. The city's charter provides that no saloon is to be maintained and no hard liquor is to be sold within the city limits, and the State Liquor Store is located beyond the boundary line. Paradoxically, Sunnyside taverns sell some of the largest 10c glasses of beer in the State.

The MILK PRODUCTS COMPANY PLANT (*open* 8-5 *workdays*), W. Edison Ave. and 6th St., housed in a concrete building, employs modern methods to produce butter, milk powder, and casein. In manufacturing milk powder, the milk is separated from the cream, which is used for butter, and is heated in vacuum pans to 126° F., when it boils. Under pressure of 3,000 pounds to the square inch, the milk passes through spray disks into a chamber, where it is heated to 300° F.; the solids instantly dry and fall in the form of powder, which is then sifted and bolted in much the same way as is flour. The coarser type of powder produced is sold as animal food; the finer quality is used by bakeries and ice cream manufacturers.

An annual event is the Sunnyside Fete Day, which was held for the nineteenth consecutive year in June 1940. High points of the fete were the flower show, soap-box derby, gas-model airplane contest, night pageant, and street dance carnival.

North from Sunnyside US 410 makes an abrupt turn westward, penetrating flat country with rounded hills in the background. Farther east, irrigation canals line both sides of the road.

GRANGER, 60.1 *m.* (731 alt., 752 pop.), founded in 1902, was also named by Walter N. Granger, of the Sunnyside Canal Company. The town, situated in a flat valley, is the center of a dairying and livestock area. Three or four crops of alfalfa are shipped from here annually. Granger achieved notoriety in 1936, when an enterprising justice of the peace announced a price of only 39c for performing weddings. The justice, who lives in a junction gas station, still maintains the reduced marriage rate.

The YAKIMA VALLEY ACADEMY, on the southern edge of town, a boarding school maintained by the Seventh-Day Adventist Church, is housed in a three-story brick building.

The HISLOP SHEEP PENS, Alfalfa Ave., and N. 1st St., in a compact, intricate, but orderly arrangement, are surrounded by a sweeping circle of towering haystacks, topped by roofs but open at the sides. Here lambs purchased in the spring are housed and fed until the following spring, when the sheep are ready to be clipped for wool and sold for mutton.

Northwest of Granger US 410 passes sheep ranches and productive orchards. The road parallels the Yakima, and a few miles from town a steep canyon looms, where the river has cut deep into the rocks.

ZILLAH, 66.4 *m.* (821 alt., 802 pop.), is another town developed by irrigation and promoted and named by Granger. Rows of warehouses and packing sheds are strung along the railroad tracks paralleling the highway. Apples, cherries, and peaches are packed here, and the Mount Arbor Nursery maintains its Yakima Valley branch in Zillah. The Zillah Community Picnic is held annually in mid-June.

The Vix Air Circulation Company's plant, near the town, manufactures a large fan, which is used as a frost expeller in the orchards, as a cherry-tree drier, and as an air circulator for refrigerator cars when they are loading.

North of Zillah, US 410 climbs up a steep grade and into the central valley of the Yakima.

At BUENA, 70.6 *m.* (785 alt., 400 pop.), another Yakima Valley fruit-shipping base, is a junction with US 97 (*see Tour 7b*).

At 73.0 *m.* is a junction with a dirt road.

Left here 0.2 *m.* across railroad tracks to the MATTOON SAWYER CABIN, one of the earliest types of cabin. The little two-room house is built of peeled cottonwood logs, chinked with white clay. In 1884, the year he was appointed farm instructor for the Indians at Fort Simcoe, J. P. Mattoon built the cabin, one of the first in the valley.

In SAWYER, 73.4 *m.* (827 alt., 50 pop.), is a large red-tile warehouse of the Yakima Fruit Growers' Association.

At 75.6 *m.* is a junction with a concrete-surfaced road.

Left on this road across a bridge to DONALD, 0.2 *m.* (875 alt., 101 pop.), a small fruit-packing center; and across a second bridge to WAPATO, 2.2 *m.* (875 alt., 1,483 pop.), a potato-shipping base.

North of the junction US 410 follows the curve of the river, lined with balsam and cottonwood trees. Sagebrush struggles for existence above the irrigation ditches. Beyond are farms, orchards, and prairies hedged about by blue-brown hills.

Irrigation in the Yakima Valley is entirely independent of the rainfall. Water is controlled by a simple gate and delivered by canal to the highest points on farms, whence it flows to the furrowed fields.

Four crops of alfalfa mature annually in this region, and the cutover fields afford successive pasture areas. Another abundant crop is the pear. The trees are almost hidden by supporting poles, necessary to prevent the boughs from breaking under the heavy burden of fruit. Strawberries, asparagus, potatoes, rhubarb, tomatoes, and other fruits and vegetables thrive under irrigation. A profitable adjunct to the larger alfalfa fields is the dairying industry, and the blooms of the orchards and alfalfa fields supply hundreds of apiaries.

An irrigation canal intake, 78.5 *m.,* a dam across the Yakima River, is part of the Sunnyside Canal, which runs nearly 80 miles south to Prosser. It is filled with water from March to September.

At 82.3 *m.* is the junction with State 3-A, bituminous-surfaced road.

Left on this road 0.3 *m.* to a huge boulder of basalt weighing seven tons, placed by the D.A.R. to commemorate the victory won by the United States troops over the Yakima tribe on November 9, 1855. Another monument a short distance away was erected in 1917 by the Yakima Indians and their friends, to commemorate a Yakima noncombatant, who was killed by a Government scout, an Indian, in the war of 1855-6. In 1855 troops under Major Rains entered the Yakima Valley to quell an uprising led by Kamiakin, chief of the Yakima. When the troops opened fire with howitzers, the natives retreated across Ahtanum Creek to the present site of Yakima and into Naches Canyon. Kamiakin fled to the Columbia River and disappeared.

The highway, curving eastward, crosses the Yakima River and reaches the narrow gap between Rattlesnake and Ahtanum ridges where the Battle of Two Buttes ended. This was an important engagement in the Yakima War, 1855-6.

UNION GAP, 82.4 *m.* (930 alt., 976 pop.), once fought a losing battle with a great railroad. When, after many delays the Northern Pacific Railroad built through the valley in 1884, Union Gap (then known as Yakima City) refused to make concessions for terminals. The railroad deliberately created a new town four miles to the north, which was called North Yakima; most of the old town moved to the new settlement.

North of Union Gap the road skirts brown hills, which overlook the valley of Ahtanum Creek. Irrigation ditches line both sides of the road. Entering Yakima, US 410 continues straight ahead on S. 1st to Yakima Ave., the city center.

YAKIMA, 87.4 *m.* (1,067 alt., 27,221 pop.), (*see Yakima*).

Left from 1st St. on W. Yakima Ave. to 10th Ave., L. here to Nob Hill Blvd.; R. on Nob Hill Blvd., which becomes Ahtanum Blvd., a concrete highway.

AHTANUM (1,250 alt., 165 pop.) is at 8.4 *m.* on this road, on the edge of the Yakima Indian Reservation and the Ahtanum Creek. The hills of Ahtanum Ridge on the south justify the Indian meaning of the name, "creek by the long mountain."

In striking contrast to the new brick buildings of Ahtanum is a ramshackle old blacksmith shop. On the sign in large bold letters is the word "Blacksmithing"; in somewhat smaller letters, "Horseshoeing"; and at the bottom in tiny letters, "Auto Repairing." The varying emphasis seems to express the owner's grudging concession to modern industrial civilization. Across the road from the blacksmith shop are the remains of weatherbeaten OLD WOODCOCK ACADEMY, a three-story structure erected in 1892.

WILEY CITY, 10.2 *m.* (1,325 alt., 851 pop.), a junction point, was named by Wallace Wiley in 1910 for his father, Hugh Wiley, pioneer, upon whose homestead the town was built.

At 16.5 *m.* is ST. JOSEPH'S MISSION, established in 1847 by the Jesuit fathers. During the Indian Wars of 1855-6, soldiers under Major G. J. Rains, finding the mission deserted and a keg of powder buried in the mission garden, burned the building to the ground, believing that the missionaries were in sympathy with the Indians. The mission was rebuilt in 1872 and stands today in a fair state of preservation, an interesting example of mortise and tenon work of the period. The mission served as a center for settlers coming into the country, and today the Reclamation Service is carrying on soil conservation projects in the vicinity.

Section c. YAKIMA *to* OLYMPIA, *177.4 m.* *US 410*

In YAKIMA, 0 *m.,* US 410 follows N. 1st to N. Walnut Ave., the junction with US 97 (*see Tour 7b*), bears L. from the junction to N. 5th Ave., and R. on N. 5th.

West of Yakima, the highway follows a slight incline through the orchards of the Naches River Valley. Brown, rock-cleft hills rise gradually toward the Cascade Mountains.

At 5 *m.* is a junction with a bituminous-surfaced road, known locally as the South Naches River Road.

Left on this road along the south side of the Naches River, splashing noisily beneath a canopy of cottonwoods and aspens, to a junction with a trail, 0.1 *m.;* R. on trail by foot for 50 feet to the base of a basalt cliff. The INDIAN PAINTINGS on the rock wall are very old; legends of the Yakima say they were there before the tribes came to live in this land. West from the trail junction is ESCHBACK PARK (*adm.* 25c; *boating, swimming, and picnicking facilities*), 2.5 *m.* The South Naches River Road continues into Naches to the junction with US 410 at 12 *m.*

US 410 continues its westward climb, flanked by sienna-colored hills with a mottled nap of gray-green sagebrush and glistening bunchgrass. Isolated masses of black lava scar the gentle slopes. A HYDROELECTRIC PLANT, 11.1 m., stands R. from the highway, its spillway emptying into the river.

At 13.8 *m.* is a junction with a concrete-paved road.

Right on this road to NACHES, 0.1 *m.* (1,817 alt., 536 pop.), a bustling town with a small, compact business district. Naches began to grow in 1908 when valley farmers, aided by the Federal Government, started the irrigation system. Two apple-packing plants and a small sawmill, which cuts box shooks from yellow pine, are the economic backbone of the town. One of the packing establishments, a million-dollar concern employing 250 men and women seasonally, is owned and operated by Horticultural Union Local 21.

West of the junction, US 410 leaves the bronzed, grass-tufted hills and runs close along the Naches River, almost hidden by the timbered mountains. The Naches Valley narrows to a canyon between towering cliffs of somewhat porous stone, folded and faulted into spire-like forms and palisades. Time-etched rocks project like gargoyles from the canyon walls; porous layers of lava, broken up by moisture and frost, present many color variations.

At 18.4 *m.* is a junction with State 5, a bituminous-surfaced road, which is the eastern part of the projected highway over White Pass.

Left on this road, which follows the Tieton River through Tieton Canyon with its bizarre formations, massive rocks, and rocky columns, to TIETON DAM, 20 *m.*, known also as Rimrock Dam. This earth-filled irrigation dam is 220 feet high. Water, flowing eastward from the many lakes and streams just east of the Cascade crest, is dammed at Rimrock for irrigation storage and forms a lake six miles wide in the center of the recreation area.

The TIETON RECREATION AREA (*see Recreation Area Map*) in the southeastern part of the Snoqualmie National Forest, is bounded by the Yakima Indian Reservation and State forest on the south, the summit of the Cascades on the west, and the upper Naches drainage on the north; on the east are the sage-covered hills and fertile orchard lands in the bottoms of the Tieton and Naches valleys.

Scenic interest centers around Rimrock Lake and is climaxed in the Goat Rocks Primitive Area, at the head of the north and south forks of the Tieton River. This rugged area of 72,440 acres includes a group of peaks approaching 8,000 feet in elevation, with living glaciers and mountain meadows carpeted with rare alpine flowers. It is the natural habitat of the mountain goat.

Wildcat Mountain on Bethel Ridge, Cowiche Mountain, Goose Egg Mountain (4,500 alt.), and Kloochman Peak, all foothills of the Cascades, have legendary significance. Goose Egg Mountain was once the chaste bachelor chief Me-ow-wah, whose people lived in the Yakima Valley. Chiefs far and near sent their fairest daughters to dance before Chief Me-ow-wah, believing that he would succumb to their charms. Me-ow-wah consulted with Speel-yia, the crafty, who counseled him to sacrifice the maidens and himself in order to preserve the chastity of the tribe. Seeing the maidens coming up the valley, Me-ow-wah shouted in a voice of thunder, "Mit-whit" (stop). The astounded maidens were turned to stone. Kloochman, on the south, is the Spokane maiden; Wildcat Mountain on the north, the Okanogan; and Bethel Ridge to the west, the Cowlitz.

The NACHES RANGER STATION, 35.5 *m.* (R), a group of neat white frame structures, is just within the entrance of the Snoqualmie National Forest. Here also is the Naches CCC camp, with spacious, well-kept buildings. The station marks the beginning of the MATHER MEMORIAL PARKWAY, 50 miles of the most scenic section of the Chinook Pass Highway, set aside by Congress March 24, 1931. The highway passes the COTTONWOOD FOREST CAMP (L) at 36.1 *m.*

North of the junction with the Gold Creek Trail, at 37.6 *m.*, is EDGAR ROCK.

At 38.8 *m.* is a junction with a dirt road.

Left on this road to MOUNTAIN AIR INSTITUTE, 2 *m.*, a summer camp maintained by Yakima churches. From the institute a foot trail leads to BOULDER CREEK CAVE, 0.5 *m.*, formed by the collapse of the hillside over the stream bed; the water eventually washed out the rubble, leaving a rock-vaulted passage 400 feet long and 15 feet high. In summer, tiny streams trickle through the passage. In spring, freshets roar through the tunnel. The stream above the cave is called DEVIL CREEK, and from it a 75-foot waterfall leaps far beyond the edge of the cliff, forming an aquatic arch over the trail.

CLIFFDELL, 39.2 *m.* (40 pop.), is an exclusive resort town owned by Yakima Valley residents. Fishing is usually good in the Naches River. SAWMILL FLATS, 42.7 *m.* (2,500 alt.) (L), has camping facilities furnished by the Forest Service.

At 44 *m.* is a junction with a forest trail.

Right on this trail to the LITTLE NACHES FOREST CAMP, 0.2 *m.* North of the camp the trail leads to the CROW CREEK GUARD STATION, 2.8 *m.*, where the first Forest Service cabin in Rainier National Forest was built in 1907. At that time the forest included the area that has since been designated as Snoqualmie National Forest. The trail continues to RAVENS ROOST, 16.5 *m.*

West of the junction US 410 crosses the Naches River over a bridge, 44.1 *m.*, from which the precipitous Fife's Ridge, known locally as Deadhorse Hill, is visible.

At 44.6 *m.* is a junction with a dirt road.

Left on this road are HALFWAY FLAT, 2 *m.*, and BOULDER CAVE, 3 *m.* (*Travel over this road at certain times of the year is perilous*).

North of the junction with Crow Creek Trail, 45.5 *m.*, US 410 passes the INDIAN FLAT FOREST STATION, 46.6 *m.*

At 47.8 *m.* is a junction with a dirt road.

Left on this road through the AMERICAN RIVER RECREATION AREA, popular with game hunters; elk are plentiful. The AMERICAN RIVER LODGE, 0.2 *m.*, handles sports supplies and offers accommodations. The AMERICAN RIDGE SKI BOWL, 0.9 *m.* is a 50-acre snowfield set aside by the Forest Service. Here is a lodge building and shelter for skiers. A 220-foot slide and a slalom course are being developed. Ski meets are often held here, and the bowl is becoming a ski center of eastern Washington.

The road follows the gorge of the Bumping River to GOOSE PRAIRIE, 10 *m.* (3,265 alt., 12 pop.), a small resort center in the glen at the base of GOAT PEAK (6,444 alt.). BUMPING LAKE, 11.5 *m.* (3,265 alt., 6 pop.), is a tiny settlement on the shore of BUMPING LAKE, in the heart of the Cascade Mountains. The lake serves as a reservoir for irrigation purposes in the lower Yakima Valley. Numerous mountain trails lead from here.

A copper concentrator and a sawmill at COPPER CITY, 23 *m.*, operate during a 9-month season, and approximately 25 persons live there during that period.

West of the Bumping Lake Road the grade becomes more pronounced, as US 410 enters a defile between towering peaks, some bare and rugged, others heavily forested. Here are the last of the heavy lava flows to be seen throughout eastern Washington. Looming north of the road is FIFE'S PEAK (6,954 alt.), the highest point of Fife's Ridge. Geologists believe it to be a remnant of an old volcano, which was probably the source of some of the lava flows of Yakima County.

A concrete bridge, at 61.2 *m.,* crosses MORSE CREEK, (2,700 alt.), which flows into American River, a roaring mountain stream. The creek runs through a dell carpeted with wild flowers and ferns. Wild life is abundant.

From the heights at the head of American River the Cascade Range appears as waves in a turbulent sea. The ramifications of the river canyons and watersheds fade off into the gray plain east of the Columbia River.

In 1790, the Spanish explorer, Manuel Quimper, roughly mapped the Cascades as *Sierra Madras de San Antonio.* About 1825 David Douglas, the botanist, used the name "Cascade." An attempt was once made to call the peaks after former Presidents and to christen the range "Presidents' Range."

Mounting a long easy grade with many curves, US 410 climbs high above a forest (L), which is covered with snow in winter. The green of alpine fir and mountain hemlock is brightened by yellow splashes, where clumps of larch trees stand with bleached needles. The larch is the only tree in western United States that loses its needles in winter. On the hillside are thickets of mountain ash, from which dangle clusters of bright red berries. Mats of huckleberry bushes partially cover the rocks.

The highway pierces the main divide by way of CHINOOK PASS some 20 miles south of the old immigrant crossing through Naches. The pass offers the first good opportunity to see glacier-ribbed MOUNT RAINIER (*see Rainier National Park*). From the summit of the pass, 66.6 *m.,* (5,440 alt.), a tumbled rampart of mountain peaks is visible to the west. To the east is the deep valley of the American River; northward is an orderly staircase of cliff-sided peaks, dropping away from the summit; and to the south are jagged hills, their snowy slopes stubbled with sparse green forests.

The pass is named for the warm wind that comes from the southwest, melting depths of snow in a few hours. The Indians had so named the wind because it came from the direction of the Chinook tribe, who lived near the mouth of Columbia River (*see Tour 7b*).

The sharp broken peaks around the pass, vestiges of old lava flows, were tilted to an acute angle by intrusions from below. Only rock pyramids resting on a solid foundation escaped the abrasion of glaciers. Red rock, andesite, and gray granite occur in patches along the roadside.

The forest becomes more dense, as the highway follows the western slope down from the summit. Douglas fir and western hemlock, the dominant species in this humid area, attain a thickness of from 4 to 8 feet at the base and tower to more than 200 feet in height. At higher levels the lodgepole pine and species of fir mingle with the Douglas fir and hemlock. Lower down are found many red cedar and white fir.

The historic old trail over Naches Pass, to the north, was used by the Puget Sound and Plains Indians. The inland Klickitat, riding this narrow trail on their hardy ponies, would visit their cousins on Puget Sound and feast on first-run salmon and clams. In early fall the Puyallup, Nisqually, and other Sound tribes, mostly afoot, would come to the higher altitudes to gather huckleberries, seeds, and nuts. Later, this same trail was used by horse brigades of Hudson's Bay Company, carrying supplies to interior posts.

The Longmires, Ezra Meeker, and other pioneers left the Oregon Trail at The Dalles and turned northward through the Yakima Valley to Puget Sound. Vestiges remain of the narrow road cut by these pioneers up the eastern slope of the divide.

TIPSOO LAKE (R), 66.9 *m.* (5,400 alt.), shaped like the ace of clubs, drains a chain of ponds in the center of a skiing area. A small picnic area in the green bowl surrounding the lake, a natural basin, has tables, stoves, and running water. (*Overnight camping is not allowed*). Trails radiate to great spires of rock affording excellent viewpoints. A BRONZE PLAQUE, set in a large boulder, has a bas-relief bust of the late Stephen T. Mather, who laid the foundation of the National Park Service.

At 70.2 *m.* is a junction with State 5, which leads away to the south in a long downward curve to Ohanapecosh Hot Springs and the Ohanapecosh entrance to Mount Rainier National Park. (*See Tour 8E and Mount Rainier National Park*).

An OREGON TRAIL MEMORIAL, 74.4 *m.,* depicting a covered wagon drawn by oxen, commemorates the memory of George Howland Parsons, a pioneer from Colorado who crossed through Naches Pass. At this point an excellent vista of Mount Rainier, its valleys, glaciers, lakes, and meadows, spreads out to the west. A macadam road that winds up the slope seems to terminate in the clouds. Below is a forested canyon, toothed with great snags of granite and lined with dark giants of trees.

At 74.1 *m.* is a junction with a macadam-surfaced road.

Left on this road to the YAKIMA PARK ENTRANCE TO RAINIER NATIONAL PARK, 16 *m.* (3,470 alt.). (*see Mount Rainier National Park*).

At 78.1 *m.* US 410 enters Mount Rainier National Park.

SILVER CREEK RANGER STATION, 78.2 *m.,* is the headquarters of the Forest Service in charge of the White River District of the Snoqualmie National Forest, one mile within the forest boundary. Important fire prevention and recreational improvements, including 112 modern summer home cabins, have been made adjacent to the station. Special lot leases are available at a low yearly cost through the Forest Service.

Near by, at the confluence of the White River and Silver Creek, is a FISH HATCHERY, maintained by the Bureau of Fisheries for the planting of fish in lakes and streams in the forest and in Rainier National Park. More than a million fish annually, including brook, rainbow, and black spotted trout, are hatched and nursed to planting age. The

PARKWAY POST OFFICE, 73.7 *m.,* stands by a lodge (*cabins*) where supplies are sold. Here is a junction with a dirt road.

Left on this road 0.3 *m.* to THE SILVER SPRINGS FOREST CAMP (*community kitchen, tables, picnic and trailer accommodations*), adjoining the hatchery on White River. The road passes summer cabins nearly concealed by trees.

The DALLES FOREST CAMP (*tables, stoves, and running water*), 85 *m.,* stands between the road and the river in an open wooded area. Among the tall trees, protected under the Mather Memorial Parkway development, is a large, roofed kitchen with several smaller log buildings adjacent. Adjoining the picnic area is the JOHN MUIR SCHOOL GROVE, a bit of natural forest preserved under the auspices of the student body of the John Muir School, in Seattle, in memory of the naturalist, John Muir.

North of the camp, US 410 starts down the western side of the Cascades. Mount Rainier, its snow and ice glittering in bright sunlight, appears close enough to touch. Light-colored granite has replaced the brown lava cliffs and the glacial drift. To the right the foaming White River appears through openings in the woods. At the BOUNDARY GUARD STATION, 87.6 *m.,* a peeled-log marker indicates the western end of the Mather Memorial Highway. At 87.7 *m.* is a boundary of the Snoqualmie National Forest.

In GREENWATER, 92.7 *m.,* at the confluence of the Greenwater and White rivers, are camp grounds and rustic Greenwater Lodge.

Right from Greenwater Lodge by trail to HUCKLEBERRY MOUNTAIN, 2.5 *m.* The trail steeply ascends a difficult ridge and drops down into a cup-like depression, its floor covered by huckleberry bushes. During July the Indians erect their picturesque tepees in the hollow and prepare to can their winter's supply of jam.

West of Greenwater US 410 follows the north bank of the White River. The action of glaciers on the comparatively soft material of Rainier's cone results in rapid disintegration of the rock; and the river is milky with rock flour.

At 96.4 *m.* is the WHITE RIVER RANGER STATION, a group of rustic buildings. The road crosses TWIN CREEK over a concrete bridge, near the point where the creek flows into the White River.

Evergreens more than 150 feet in height form a colonnade along both sides of the road. In this virgin timber area, loggers are busy felling the forest giants for shipment to the near-by White River Mills and other lumber plants in western Washington. A short distance west are the tracks of a logging railroad, its locomotive sheds, and repair shops. Paralleling the railroad, the highway enters a logged-off and burned-over area.

At 107.7 *m.* is a junction with a graveled road.

Left here 2 *m.* to Mud Mountain, where a five-million-dollar earthen dam, the PUYALLUP AND WHITE RIVER CONTROL PROJECT, is under construction. This dam will be four hundred twenty feet high—the highest earthen dam in the world. Salmon will be transported over the dam by means of a special railway to be operated by the State department of fisheries.

An enormous waste burner and concrete stack tower
buildings of WHITE RIVER MILL, 108.8 *m.*, a large lumb
and planing mill. The buildings are strategically clustered in a
circle around a storage pond where logs are dumped.

West of the mill is an auto camp beside a grove of trees near the White River. On the camp grounds is a large pool from the center of which spurts a geyser. Leaving the bank of the river US 410 swings north and west, passing the GOOD HOPE DAIRY (R) at 111.8 *m.*, and a Forest Service Station (L).

ENUMCLAW, 113.2 *m.* (742 alt., 2,627 pop.), on a plateau between the White and Green Rivers in the Cascade foothills, is the gateway to Chinook and Naches passes and to the skiing and recreation areas of Mount Rainier and the Snoqualmie National Forest. Lumbering, dairy and poultry farming, and trade connected with recreation provide the bulk of Enumclaw's business. Many residents find employment in the lumber mill and in the logging operations east of the town, and a few still work in the coal mines at Black Diamond, Carbonado, and Durham.

The natural timber resources of the area first drew settlers to the site, which was platted on October 3, 1885, and named by Frank Stevenson and his wife for the mountain about six miles to the north. According to a legend, a band of Indians encamped one night at the base of the mountain ridge; they were caught in a terrific thunder storm and became so frightened that they fled, calling the mountain "Enumclaw" (place of the evil spirits).

The settlement was relatively isolated at first. For a while a small rowboat was used as a ferry to cross the torrential White River; a cow's horn, hidden in a stump known to all the settlers, was blown to summon the boat whenever a passenger desired to cross. In 1884-5 the main line of the Northern Pacific Railroad, building through from Cascade Junction, connected the settlement with Tacoma and lent impetus to logging, commerce, and other enterprises. The store of Arthur Griffin and John Blake prospered; and skins and hides, often used as tender in trade at the store, gave way to real money. The first school was opened in 1887; the first church services were held in Union Sunday School by David Jones; and by the nineties, a weekly—*The Enumclaw Evergreen*—was started by A. C. Rogers, son of Governor John Rogers. Improved marketing facilities drew many lumbering concerns to the White River, where Nelson Bennett (later to build the Cascade Tunnel) had established the first mill.

Among the factors that have contributed most to Enumclaw's growth are its co-operative organizations. The settlers, mostly Norwegians and Danes, brought the principles of the co-operative with them from their homelands and quickly put them into effect here. The ENUMCLAW CO-OPERATIVE CREAMERY PLANT, 2nd and Myrtle Sts., is a major income-producer for the town, employing 48 men and doing an annual business of $1,000,000. The butter, which is shipped all over the State, has won national awards. The plant also has a powdered milk department. The Enumclaw branch of the Washington Co-op Egg and Poultry Association and other dealers handle the output of the surrounding region.

The Enumclaw Rochdale Co-operative, which maintains a Co-operative Department Store, 1453 Cole St., was founded by Scandinavians in 1905. The co-operative enjoyed its greatest success between the years 1915 and 1925, when it maintained a store with grocery, hardware, furniture, and clothing departments and a hay, seed, and grain warehouse, which sold its products directly to the countryside farmers. The building now occupied by the department store was erected in 1924. However, the Co-operative abandoned its grain, hay, and seed department when a private milling company began selling to farmers at lower prices. Because of competition from national and regional chain stores, the Rochdale group reorganized in 1929 into a "co-op group of retailers."

Foreign-born residents of Enumclaw are gathered in several lodges and fraternities. The Danish Hall, Myrtle and Porter Sts., is a center for the social life of the town, both Norwegian and Danish groups making their headquarters here.

The Old Enumclaw Hotel, the first building erected in the town, still stands at 1704 Railroad Avenue.

West of Enumclaw US 410 swings downgrade. Rolling hills form a background on both sides of the highway for the scattered houses and occasional poultry farms.

At 122.9 *m.* is a junction with a gravel road.

Right on this road 0.2 *m.* to a junction with a crossroad; R. here 0.8 *m.* to a junction with a narrow gravel road; R. here 0.1 *m.* to an old Indian Graveyard, a part of the MUCKLESHOOT INDIAN RESERVATION. Fifty or more families of the tribe, whose territory once extended as far east as the Columbia, live on the reservation. They have been taught by Government agencies to sew, can foodstuffs, and develop their native arts. Small totem poles are carved by the Indian children. To celebrate a successful harvest, the Muckleshoot (Ind. river junction) hold a festival in the tribal Community Hall, 0.5 *m.*

Following the defeat of the Indians at the Battle of Seattle (*see Seattle*), in January 1856, the tribesmen retreated to Muckleshoot Prairie. In the spring of 1857 a force of 250 men under Colonel Casey left Steilacoom to take the field against them. Warriors led by Chief Leschi, ill-fed and discouraged, made slight resistance, and after one attack at White River, they were repulsed. This engagement ended one phase of the Indian War.

At 125.6 *m.* is a junction with a dirt road.

Right on this road to Auburn Academy, 0.4 *m.*, maintained by the Seventh-Day Adventist Church. The long, low, white wooden buildings of the academy are closely grouped and surrounded by green fields. The academy has an enrollment of about 250.

AUBURN, 129.4 *m.* (90 alt., 4,211 pop.), division point of the Northern Pacific Railway, is dominated physically and economically by the huge red buildings of the expansive railroad yard. The fact that Auburn is situated almost equidistant from Seattle and Tacoma, in the fertile White River Valley between the Cascades and Puget Sound, made it one of the earliest important railroad centers.

In this pleasant valley, in 1887, Dr. Levi W. Ballard, one of the first settlers, platted the town of Slaughter, to honor Lieutenant W. A. Slaughter, who was killed near the townsite during the Indian wars. It became a settlement, with one or two stores, a shingle mill, and scattered hop farms. With the coming of the Northern Pacific Railway, the town boomed, and Slaughter's citizens became name-conscious. It was embarrassing to have the hotel runner board the trains and cry: "This way to the Slaughter House." By special act of the legislature in 1893, the name was changed to Auburn, from Oliver Goldsmith's opening line in "The Deserted Village": "Sweet Auburn, loveliest village of the plain."

With hop culture definitely unprofitable, the countryside was given over to berry and dairy farms, to which the land was well suited. The town was made the terminal of the Northern Pacific line in 1913, and the breaking-down of freight trains for north and south "drags" resulted in the installation of 50 miles of trackage and an impressive pay roll.

In the railroad yards is a large 24-stall ROUNDHOUSE (*visitors permitted*), or locomotive repair shop, and several other railroad service buildings. On entering the roundhouse the visitor is greeted with a deafening roar, which may dampen his desire to view the processes of locomotive repair. Freight trains from eastern points are broken-down here, and the cars hauled on branch lines to Seattle, Tacoma, and other cities in the region. In turn the cities pack their products in boxcars, which are sent to Auburn on the branch lines to be made up into trains for eastern points.

Left from the railroad yards is the LANGE POTTERY COMPANY FACTORY (*open to visitors*), a low one-story frame building where all types of pottery are made. All the work is done by members of the same family, and the beauty and sturdiness of the ware has made it possible for the factory, without advertising, to market all it can produce. In the rear of the building, with its pottery wheels and drying racks, is the kiln. The owner will demonstrate to visitors on a crude mechanism how pottery was made in Europe before the advent of modern methods.

A NOVELTY TOY DISPLAY (L), in the backyard shop of Otto Lieske, a terra-cotta worker, features toy windmills, brightly painted, animated toys, and animals propelled by vanes. Around a large goldfish pool is a toy city peopled with gaily outlandish figures.

In 1938, twenty thousand people participated in the celebration of Auburn Day, an annual event.

In Auburn is a junction of US 410 and State 5-B, a concrete-paved road.

At 2.8 *m.* on State 5-B is a junction with a graveled road; R. here 1.6 *m.* to GREEN RIVER GORGE. The road twists and turns along the picturesque gorge to FLAMING GEYSER PARK, 11 *m.*, operated commercially (adm. 25c). In the **Flaming Geyser**, which is not active now, natural gas forced its way through salt water at irregular intervals and would burn brightly, when ignited, for a few minutes or for hours. The Baby Geyser, several hundred yards from the larger spout, burns almost continuously through cold sulphur water. The Flaming Geyser was discovered when prospectors were drilling holes in search of the McKay coal bed. After they had bored to considerable depth, gas began flowing. Failing to locate the coal vein, the investigators pulled out their drill, leaving the sheet iron casing in the hole. Subsequent rusting of the casing allowed water to enter, and under the water, gas accumulated until pressure grew sufficient to make it bubble to the surface.

In Auburn is a junction of US 410 and a branch of State 5.

Right (straight ahead) on the concrete-paved branch road through the extensively cultivated White River Valley, where great fields of lettuce or celery and smaller acreages in cauliflower, peas, beans, and beets adjoin poultry ranches. The packing season generally starts in May with the shipment of rhubarb. Much of the produce is expressed to New York.

The SITE OF THE WHITE RIVER MASSACRE, 1.7 *m.*, marked by a granite monument enclosed by an iron railing, commemorates the victims of the massacre of October 28, 1855. The scattered settlers of the White River Valley were in constant fear of Indian attack, and when Allen Porter fled down the river valley one night late in October, 1855, spreading the alarm, they retreated to Seattle with their families. Soldiers, sent through the valley to investigate, were received by the Indians with such disarming friendliness that they returned to report there was no danger and that the settlers had been scared by their own shadows. On a Sunday morning about three weeks later the Indians, under the leadership of Chief Nelson, attacked three homes. Nine members of the three pioneer families—Brannon, King, and Jones—were killed, and their houses were burned.

KENT, 5.4 *m.* (42 alt., 2,586 pop.), on a flat bisected by railroad tracks, is a town of attractive residences and a substantial business district. First known as Titusville, then Yesler, honoring Henry L. Yesler of Seattle, the town was platted as Kent by Ezra Meeker on July 3, 1888. The area, like that of the Kentish region in England, was noted for its hop culture. A crop of 859,436 pounds in 1888 spurred the town onward; prior to that time it had been simply a point for scow and boat traffic on the White River.

The fertility of the surrounding black-loam valley lands made Kent an important berry, dairy, and truck-garden center. As shipping point of the valley's agricultural produce, it has two railroad lines and a busy motor freight terminal with a fleet of 80 trucks. The town became the home of the first Carnation Condensed Milk plant on September 6, 1889. The Carnation Company was soon followed by the Pacific Coast Condensed Milk Company and canneries of Libby, McNeill and Libby, a cheese factory, and large commercial incubating plants.

Although hop culture has declined throughout the area, Kent remains noted for the quality and quantity of its crops. The production of lettuce, however, has outstripped that of hops. On Kent's annual Lettuce Day in early summer, a group of girls in bathing costume, standing in a huge bowl, pitchforks in hand, prepare a gigantic lettuce salad. The town's fairest Titian dumps the bucket of mayonnaise over the shredded lettuce. The WASHINGTON FROSTED FOODS, INC. PLANT (*open by permission*), N. 6th and W. Shinn Sts., produces a wide variety of frozen vegetables in its nine-month operating season. The plant purchases all of the vegetables it uses from tillers of the fertile valley soil. Asparagus is the only vegetable not grown heavily enough in the valley to satisfy the demand.

The plant is crowded with modern machinery. The south building, which has outdoor boilers, shelters three production lines, where rubber-gloved men and women remove undesirable parts of the raw vegetables that pass on metal-webbed conveyor belts through great rotary washers; from the washers the vegetables are carried on the conveyor to steam boxes, where they are precooked and sterilized at a temperature of as high as 210° F. As they leave the boxes, they are sorted by girls and sent up an incline conveyor, which moves them overhead to an icing department. Here they are subjected to a quick-freeze process, under a temperature as low as 30° F., and then packed in containers.

At 12.4 *m.* State 5 forms a junction with US 10 (*see Tour 1b*).

South of Auburn US 410 passes long rows of freight cars in the railroad yards (R). At 134.4 *m.* is DIERINGER (75 alt., 143 pop.). To the left of the highway is the big PUGET SOUND POWER AND LIGHT COMPANY PLANT (*visitors welcome*), where turbines generate electrical energy from the falling waters of near-by Lake Tapps. The artificial lake, though large, is not especially adapted to recreational pursuits.

Sprawled among the trees on the banks of the Stuck River, which links the White and Puyallup Rivers, is SUMNER (72 alt., 2,140 pop.), 137.4 *m.*, an industrial and trading center for the Puyallup Valley. A clean and bustling community, it is noted for its berries, vegetables, rhubarb, and flower bulbs. Some of the streets leading from the business district terminate in berry fields and produce gardens. A number of warehouses and canneries line the bank of the river, and there are two large floral supply houses and two dairy plants. Sumner is headquarters of the Washington Berry Growers, The Puget Sound Vegetable Growers, the Sumner Rhubarb Growers, Washington Packers, the Puget Sound Bulb Exchange, the Rhubarb Growers' Association, and other such associations. From the district 150 carloads of rhubarb are shipped annually. The United States Department of Agriculture maintains an Entomological Research Laboratory here.

The Fleischmann Yeast Plant is neatly laid out along the river bank. It maintains a recreational field for workers. Among other industrial plants serving the region are the Standard Brand Plant; the Fibre Boards Products, Inc.; Speas Vinegar; Sumner Sash and Door; Pacific Lumber Agency, which ships spruce to all parts of the country for airplanes and refrigerators; the Sumner Packing House; and the Sumner Grain and Milling Company.

Half-hidden by a giant butternut and a luxurious holly tree, the PUBLIC LIBRARY (*open weekdays* 2-5; 7-9), at 1204 Main St., containing 7,000 volumes, occupies the former residence of Mrs. Lucy V. Ryan, pioneer. A frame structure built in 1870, with a balustraded front porch and narrow entrance hallway, the house has been only slightly altered. A few museum pieces are on display, including a section of the first wooden water pipe used in Sumner, a heavy ox yoke, samples of petrified wood, and a collection of Civil War relics.

In Sumner is a junction of US 410 with an alternate branch of State 5, the road to Enumclaw (*see Tour 1D*).

West of Sumner US 410—State 5 continues to a junction with State 5-E 3 *m.*

Left from the junction on State 5-E, a concrete-paved road penetrating the farm-dotted valley lowlands between the Carbon and Puyallup Rivers, to ORTING (Ind. prairie in the town), 9.2 *m.* (198 alt., 1,211 pop.) This sleepy-looking but prosperous village, supported by the farming and dairying activities of the valley, is built, like an early fort, around a large square. On Calistoga Ave. is the WASHINGTON STATE SOLDIERS' HOME (*open 9 a.m.-4 p.m.*), dedicated in May, 1891, as a home for Civil War veterans. At that time only one three-story building occupied an eight-acre tract; now the grounds cover more than 180 acres, with buildings to accommodate 160 persons. Since 1899 the colony plan has been used, whereby veterans with families are given allowances and permitted to live outside the home.

Near the eastern limits of Orting is the VOIGHT FISH HATCHERY, where steelhead trout are reared for planting in the surrounding streams.

The Von Zonneveld BULB FARM, a 120-acre tract, one mile northwest of Orting, is the largest bulb-producing land unit in the valley. Of the 54,000,000 daffodil bulbs produced annually in Washington on approximately 830 acres, this valley yields 25,000,000 bulbs from 500 acres. Growers never use the same piece of ground two years in succession for bulbs; every other year the ground is planted to green vegetation, and commercial fertilizer is added. Bulb planting starts in August and ends in September, and the new bulbs are harvested during the following July. On bigger farms the bulbs are dug by power cultivators. Most of the bulbs produced in the State are marketed in the East and in European countries.

South of Orting State 5-E, becomes a gravel-surfaced road and continues to ELECTRON, 7.5 *m.* (125 alt.) inhabited exclusively by families of Puget Sound Power and Light Company employees. The company operates a POWER PLANT, (*visitors welcome*) on the Puyallup River, a mile and a half east of the settlement. The town came into existence in the fall of 1904.

On November 23, 1936, a terrific slide, caused by the slow infiltration of water beneath the plant, carried away nearly one-half of the structure and damaged thousands of dollars worth of eqsipment. Luckily none of the inhabitants were injured. Twenty-two families now reside here.

In Electron, State 5-E forms a junction with another gravel-surfaced road (R), which rims the northern shore of Lake Kapowsin and ends at KAPOWSIN, 9 *m.* (630 alt., 582 pop.), (*see Tour 8D*).

South of Sumner, US 410 winds among trellised berry fields and hop lands, where, during the picking season, single persons and families crowd the highway in nondescript cars, seeking farms where they may eke out a meager living. During the berry season, as many as 3,000 transient workers are employed for picking. Indians come equipped to camp for the entire hop season. Hops were formerly a big crop in the valley, but farmers have largely abandoned them for the more profitable berry growing. The cost of harvesting and cultivating the hops was made greater by the necessity of fighting pests that infested the hop fields.

PUYALLUP, 140.6 *m.* (49 alt., 7,889 pop.), is on the rich valley floor along the dyked banks of the Puyallup River, lying 300 feet below the surrounding plateau.

Formerly a dense wooded expanse, now a busy modern city, Puyallup is the center of broad berry fields, orchards, and green pasture lands. Here, as in Sumner, its sister city, berry fields encroach as far as the main streets; many of the dwellings, some modern and some dating back to the 1880's, are surrounded by orchards and berry rows.

The immense yields of the district have attracted canneries, preserving plants, sawmills, woodworking plants, and box factories. The largest bee-hive factory west of the Mississippi is in Puyallup. In 1933 the canneries handled nearly 15,000,000 pounds of berries and small fruits.

Like Sumner, Puyallup has many associations co-operating in the marketing of lettuce, eggs, poultry, berries, rhubarb, bulbs, and hops.

The oldest city in the valley, Puyallup as a settlement was known as Franklin. In February 1877, Ezra Meeker, (1830-1928), platted the first townsite and named it Puyallup (Ind. generous people), so that the town would have a name unlike any other in the world. The town was incorporated in 1890.

Meeker first crossed the Plains by covered wagon in 1852. Later, in order to mark definitely the old Oregon Trail and to obtain funds from Congress for the survey and location of a national highway over its route, Meeker retraced the route by oxcart and covered wagon in 1906, when more than 70 years old. He later made approximately the same trip by automobile and, in 1924, by airplane at the age of 94.

In PIONEER PARK, Meridian St. between 3rd and 4th Aves. SE., is a lifesize statue of Ezra Meeker, by Victor Alonzo Lewis. Behind the monument, ivy vines planted by Meeker drape over a shelter and fountain. Pioneer Square was donated to the city by Meeker, and the public library building occupies the site of his original home. Another residence, the OLD EZRA MEEKER HOME, 321 E. Pioneer, is used as a clubhouse by the G.A.R.

On East Meridian, across the Puyallup River Bridge, a cobblestone monument with four marble plaques marks the SITE OF OLD FORT MALONE. Here in 1856 soldiers erected a fort to protect the John Carson ferry from Indian attackers. The WESTERN WASHINGTON FAIR GROUNDS, on Meridian St. S., spread over 35 acres, with exhibition and amusement buildings covering 8 acres. When "Dad" Chamberlin started a livestock show in the nineties with a bull and a goose, the town laughed. Now, annually, the third week in September a fair is held for western Washington, something of an apology to Chamberlin. A nonprofit affair sponsored by a private corporation on land owned by the State, it draws an unusually large attendance. Horse racing, rodeo, and carnival features vie with agricultural, cattle, and poultry exhibits.

The WESTERN WASHINGTON EXPERIMENT STATION, W. Pioneer Way, under the supervision of the State College at Pullman (*see Tour 4b*) makes a study of crop production, farm management, marketing, soil analysis, diseases, and other problems associated with the agriculture of the region. The station has helped to develop new varieties of berries adapted to local soil conditions. Poultry research has included studies of improved rations and diets and in the prevention and cure of poultry diseases. Dairying methods have also been studied; better hay, grazing grasses, and feeds have been developed. Exploration of frozen-pack methods and search for plants best suited to this treatment have been undertaken with considerable success.

During April each year, when the bulb farms are aflame with color, Puyallup and the neighboring communities hold their Daffodil Festival, with thousands of blooms decorating floats and displays.

The HUNT BROTHERS PACKING COMPANY PLANT (*open by per-*

mission), 203 5th St. NW., largest plant of its kind in Puyallup, processes beans, peas, and other vegetables. It is busiest during August and September.

West of Puyallup US 410 hugs the south side of the Puyallup River, which has its source in Puyallup Glacier on Mount Rainier and is fed by the North Mowich and South Mowich glaciers (*see Mount Rainier National Park*). The Carbon River and the White River via the Stuck River also flow into the Puyallup. The highway cuts across thousands of acres of daffodil, berry, and truck farms. On distant hillsides may be seen occasional silver-fox farms, enclosed with close-meshed wire fences.

US 410 bears L. across the Puyallup River and unites with Bay St. (Tacoma). At Puyallup Ave., at the south end of a long bridge spanning the Puyallup, is a junction with US 99 (*see Tour 8c*). Left on Puyallup Ave., where there is a junction with State 5, the Mount Rainier Highway (*see Tour 8d*); continue on Pacific Ave. to Tacoma City Center.

TACOMA, **147.4** *m.* (sea level to 110 alt., 109,408 pop.) (*see Tacoma*).

Retrace Pacific Ave. to junction with US 410-US 99; straight ahead on this road to Olympia (*see Tour 8c*).

OLYMPIA, **177.4** *m.* (71 alt., 13,254 pop.) (*see Olympia*).

Section d. OLYMPIA *to* ABERDEEN; *48.3 m. US 410*

West of OLYMPIA, **0** *m.,* US 410 swings around the southern tip of Budd Inlet into a suburban district formerly known as Marshfield.

In 1936 the State Canal Commission was appointed to further plans for a canal from this inlet to the Columbia River, through McCleary and by way of Grays and Willapa harbors. Efforts had been made in behalf of this canal since the fifties when Jefferson Davis, Secretary of War under President Franklin Pierce and later President of the Southern Confederacy, had engineers of the United States Army make a survey of the route. The report of 1854-5 declared the project not only feasible, but vital to the development of the Northwest. In 1933 the State legislature, thoroughly in accord with the old report, made an appropriation of $50,000 for further survey and appraisal. The cost of the canal, which would include locks with a lift of 90 feet, is estimated at between thirty-five and forty-five million dollars. The canal is considered an important commercial and naval-defense project.

MUD BAY (R), **4** *m.,* at the end of Eld Inlet, supports broad oyster beds where the famous Olympia oysters, of exceptional delicacy and small size, are grown. These are Washington's only native oysters.

At **5** *m.* is a junction with US 101, the Olympic Peninsula Loop Highway (*see Tour 9a*). West of the junction the highway leaves the southern fringes of Puget Sound and climbs a low pass through the rugged Black Hills.

McCLEARY, **19.2** *m.* (287 alt., 1,200 pop.), on a grassy flat in an area of logged-off land, is cut by a creek that washes under the highway and across the town through a straight ditch, marked by numerous footbridges. Around the town are several ranches of millworkers. An extension of the main street runs into the millyard of the town's only industrial plant, a sash-and-door factory owned by the McCleary Mill Company, which was named for Henry McCleary, mill operator, in 1910. The business district is made up mostly of frame buildings with false fronts—all recalling lusty days and nights when the logger, in his boots and "tin pants," was king of the bars and gambling rooms.

McCleary millworkers took part in the lumber strikes general throughout the State in 1935, and in 1936, when 17 men were discharged, allegedly for labor organization activities, another strike was called. An anti-picketing injunction had been secured in a Mason County court to restrain picketing of a mill in Shelton owned by the McCleary operators; this injunction was applied to the McCleary mill in Grays Harbor County, which had reopened under armed guards. The plant was picketed, however, until several carloads of State police arrived and dispersed the strikers. Since the incident, there has been little union activity in the town.

Three hundred workers are now employed in the operation of the sash-and-door factory, at one time one of the largest in the country. The company's lumber mill has been shut down. The employees are buying little acreages, improvising small impermanent homes, and, after clearing their land, attempting to supplement their factory wages by gardening, berry growing, poultry raising, and dairying; thus they are helping transform a dismal logged-off region into an agricultural community. When the remaining stands of timber disappear from near-by forests, McCleary will lose its importance as a lumber center, but the development of farms will give the town a chance to survive.

In McCleary is a junction of US 410 and State 9-D, a bituminous-surfaced road, which leads northeast to a junction with US 101 (*see Tour 9a*).

West of McCleary is a junction with State 9-K, which passes through an area of stump land and scrubby second-growth trees. At intervals newly cleared plots, with little shacks, make their appearance. Tiers of pulpwood and ricks of fuel wood are piled along the highway awaiting shipment.

WHITES, 22.8 *m.* (200 alt., 100 pop.), is the location of a logging camp, which has been in operation for more than 30 years. In the community are also two lumber mills.

West of Whites, US 410 enters a wide valley dotted by farms. Small attractive houses line the road. West of a bridge across the Cloquallum River the valley widens, and here the tracks of the Northern Pacific parallel the highway. Adjacent to the ELMA FAIR GROUNDS, 25.7 *m.*, with a race track and grandstand, are the buildings of a CCC camp. Wide fields and luxuriant pastures are on both sides of the highway.

ELMA, 27.3 *m.* (69 alt., 1,376 pop.), in the Chehalis River Valley, is a pleasant agricultural town with wide, quiet, tree-arched streets. D. F. Byles and his family, Elma's first citizens, who took a land donation claim in 1853, were members of the first party of immigrants to come over Naches Pass. A short time later J. M. Anderson erected a store building, and other settlers from the Mississippi Valley arrived. It was suggested that the town be called Elmer, for Elmer E. Ellsworth, first Union soldier killed in the Civil War, but the postal authorities rejected the name and substituted Elma. Municipal government was established in 1886, and J. J. Carney (later postmaster at Aberdeen) was elected first mayor. The *Chronicle,* Elma's first newspaper, was begun by Carney on May 25, 1889, and is still published.

Residents of Elma and the surrounding community rely on dairying, poultry raising, truck gardening, and bulb growing for their livelihood. The town is also a trading center for woodworkers and loggers in McCleary, Whites, and logging operations in the region.

West of Elma the monotony of green pasture land is broken by clumps of large Douglas firs and by the giant evergreens and smaller maples that surround each farm.

At 29.9 *m.* the OAKS GOLF COURSE (*fees 50c weekdays, 75c Sun. and holidays*) stretches its clipped lawns away from the highway.

SATSOP, 31.3 *m.* (58 alt., 300 pop.), a cluster of buildings about a store and a church, is the center of a populous area of dairy farms, poultry ranches, berry fields, and bulb farms. The village and the Satsop River by which it stands are named for an Indian tribe.

Right from Satsop 8.6 *m.* to SCHAEFER STATE PARK (stoves, rest rooms, dance floor, and recreation facilities), on the upper course of the Satsop River. The small park has a fine stand of big-leaf maple and giant firs. There are excellent fishing spots along the river. A State fish hatchery is near by.

Across the sluggish Satsop River, 32.8 *m.,* is BRADY, a small group of old buildings hugging the highway on either side. A logging-donkey yard, at 33.1 *m.,* filled with donkey engines, steam shovels, and other heavy equipment, seems to be waiting for a period of activity that may never return. In a logging railroad yard farther west, 34.3 *m.,* dinkeys rust in idleness in the roundhouse.

Continuing west, the highway penetrates fertile fields, then hurries across a wide valley bottom, where small houses stand among tangled thickets and underbrush. Stretching along the road is a small, well-kept park, 36.8 *m.* A monument in the park, dedicated to World War heroes by the American Legion, represents a stack of muskets and helmets on a concrete base. To the left is an athletic field.

MONTESANO, 37.3 *m.* (65 alt., 2,241 pop.), seat of Grays Harbor County and one of the oldest cities in the region, lies at the confluence of the sluggish Wynooche (Ind. shifting sands) and the Chehalis Rivers. First settlement, however, was made on the south bank of the Chehalis, almost opposite the mouth of the Wynooche, by Isaiah Scammon, who had come from Maine. His journey to this corner of the country is illustrative of the difficulties that beset travelers in his day. He came around the Horn to San Francisco and thence to

Astoria by boat; crossed the Columbia River to Ilwaco near Fort Canby, then went by stage to what was known as Peterson's Point (now Westport); from there he crossed Grays Harbor and went upstream to the present site of Montesano. The settlement was known for a long time as Scammon's; later, as Wynooche. Chehalis County was created April 14, 1854, and the home of D. K. Welden named county seat. Virtually at the head of navigation on the Chehalis River even at that time, the settlement made up a popular subscription and built the steamer *Enterprise* in 1859, to run between Satsop and Grays Harbor. On February 9, 1860, the *Enterprise,* loaded with troops of Company A, Fourth Infantry, under the command of Captain M. Maloney, stopped at the harbor mouth to establish a fort at Point Chehalis (Westport).

In 1860 the county seat was removed to the J. L. Scammon place. The name Montesano, which by then had been given to the settlement, derived from *monte* (Sp. mountain) and *sano* (Sp. health), was probably suggested by the large hill back of the town (now usually known as Boy Scout Knob).

Settlers came in increasing numbers, but many of the newcomers crossed to the north side of the Chehalis and began a second settlement. The new site was bought up in 1870 by C. N. Byles, of Elma (*see above*). A town was platted and given the name of the old settlement, which then became known as South Montesano. The new Montesano prospered during the seventies and eighties. The first store was established by John Esmond in 1872. The Arland brothers set up a hand shingle mill in 1881 and received as high as $200 per thousand feet for products shipped to San Francisco. In 1881 Squire Zenor put up the first hotel.

Joseph E. Calder and James W. Walsh founded the present *Chehalis Valley Chronicle* in February, 1883. When the two young men heard that the Government was going to require filers on timber claims to advertise notice of application and notice of final proof, they hastily moved to Montesano, with a $400 roller press and eight fonts of type. Although the *Chronicle* was only a four-page affair, with the front and back printed in Portland from stock forms, nevertheless the two editor-printers experienced many difficulties.

When Calder retired after ten months, his profits had reached 2,400 per cent. More than anything else, this indicated the number of timber claims being taken in the region, particularly up the Wynooche River. Mills were springing up all along the Chehalis River also; and in the early eighties a mill was built on Lake Sylvia, just back of the townsite. Montesano turned on its first electric lights in October 1889, approximately a month before the Northern Pacific Railroad stopped its first train at the boxcar station.

Montesano industries now are in a state of transition, seeking to develop on the basis of expanding agriculture in the vicinity. Schaefer Brothers operate a shingle mill employing 90 men; their sawmill here burned in 1931, cutting off the largest industrial pay roll in this community. Of growing importance is the Blue Mountain Pea Cannery, started in 1936. Growing and shipping of seed is becoming a local industry; and a dairy plant of some size is in operation. Last year the town took over the 4-H fair previously held in Elma.

The residential districts are notable for the number of large and elaborate dwellings. Numerous timber operators, who had grown up with the county and acquired wealth in the process, settled here and built lavish homes. Most striking reminder of these days is the ALBERT-SCHAEFFER ESTATE, covering a city block east of the courthouse.

The MONTESANO CITY HALL, at the city center, houses a fire station, library and executive offices of the city government.

The GRAYS HARBOR COUNTY COURTHOUSE, at First and Broad Sts., a sandstone-faced building with coppered dome, dominates the town and the wide valley to the south. When the lumbering industry was rich and location of timber property netted heavy tax returns for Grays Harbor County, the citizens built the courthouse, one of the outstanding county structures in the State. It was designed by the late Watson Vernon, Aberdeen architect. Among the murals decorating the interior is one by F. Rohrbeck, a Milwaukee artist, depicting the discovery of Grays Harbor by Captain Gray on May 7, 1792. Flanking it are panels of timber and mill scenes by F. Biderstein. Another Rohrbeck mural *Governor Stevens Treaty with the Indians, February* 25, 1855, is also flanked by panels done by Biderstein.

The courthouse was the scene of the trials in the "Centralia Massacre" case between January 26 and March 12, 1930 (*see Labor*).

The MCKENZIE-ELMER PLAQUE in the courthouse memorializes the late county deputy sheriffs, Collin McKenzie and A. V. Elmer, who were slain by John Turnow (or Tornow), known variously as the "Beast Man," "The Wild Man of the Olympics" and the "Human Gorilla." Between 1910 and 1913 Turnow was a half-legendary figure of terror in the Grays Harbor and Olympic Wilderness country, a muscular giant, 6 feet 5 inches in height and weighing 250 pounds. He is said to have known the woods and its creatures intimately, to have clothed himself in skin and bark, and to have been a dead shot. Turnow escaped in 1909 from an institution for the insane in Salem, Oregon, and a year later killed two young hunters in Grays Harbor County. Not until March, 1912, was he reported seen near Oxbow, on the Satsop River. Sheriff Colin McKenzie and A. C. Elmer, a deputy, went after him and were found shot to death 13 days later. With a reward of $5,000 offered, and at times a thousand men combing the wilderness, Turnow baffled his pursuers for many months. On April 16, 1913, his hideout was stumbled upon by Giles Quimby, deputy sheriff, Louis Blair, and Charles Lathrop. In the rifle battle that followed, Blair and Lathrop were killed, but a bullet from Quimby ended the life of the bearded giant.

North from the Montesano city center is the SCHAEFFER BONEYARD, where donkey engines and other logging equipment are retired. All ages, sizes, and types of steam donkeys are rusting away in this boneyard, offering a picture of the development of steam-power engines as used in northwestern logging from the nineties until recent years.

Right on 3rd Street 1.5 *m.* to MONTESANO STATE PARK (*picnicking facilities*) at Sylvia Lake, a 247-acre wooded area.

Left from the city center on State 9 to the ruins of the SCHAEFER BROTHERS MILL, a few feet north of the Chehalis River Bridge.

West of Montesano the highway cuts through the Wynooche Valley, its broad fields golden with flowering mustard or emerald with new clover and luxuriant pasturage. Sleek dairy cattle graze near large barns and comfortable rural houses. In the stump lands a few miles further west, however, a less happy spectacle is presented; scattered farms standing in the midst of stumps, infant second-growth fir, cedar, alder, and maple, and thick underbrush. Signs tacked to some of the fence posts tell the story of failure in two concise words—For Sale. Conversion of the marginal stumplands into productive farms is a long, tedious, and expensive process, and many who undertake it are forced because of financial difficulties to abandon the enterprise, after months of toil, and sell their land.

The GRAYS HARBOR GOLF AND COUNTRY CLUB COURSE (*private*) 43.5 *m.* borders the highway. Near by are fine suburban homes with well-kept gardens.

The highway passes an abandoned lumber mill at 45.6 *m.*; forested hills rise to the right. Along the edge of the river is the rusted mass of another old mill, 47.6 *m.* Great log rafts in the waters are moved by groaning tugs or lie anchored near the shore. Here is a junction of US 410 and US 101 (*see Tour 9c and Tour 9d*).

Left here on US 101 (State 9) across the Chehalis River. At the south end of the bridge is a junction with a gravel-surfaced road; Right on this road 0.3 *m.* to the SCANNON HOUSE. Built in 1856, this was the first home, church, store, post office, and courthouse in what was later to be Grays Harbor County.

ABERDEEN, 48.3 *m.*, (sea level to 10 alt., 18,846 pop.)—HOQUIAM (sea level to 300 alt., 10,835 pop.) (*see Aberdeen-Hoquiam.*)

Tour 3

Maryhill Junction—Vancouver—Longview Junction—Longview—Cathlamet—Johnson's Landing; 216.5 *m.;* US 830.

Spokane, Portland and Seattle R.R. parallels route between Maryhill and Van-

couver; Northern Pacific, Great Northern, and Union Pacific R.Rs. parallel route between Vancouver and Longview.
Hotel accommodations at Camas, Vancouver, Longview, and Cathlamet; numerous tourist camps, some with trailer accommodations. Forest Service camps in Columbia National Forest.
Bituminous-surfaced road between Maryhill Junction and Washougal; concrete-paved road between Washougal and Longview; bituminous-surfaced road between Longview and Johnson's Landing.

Section a. MARYHILL JUNCTION *to* VANCOUVER, *104.5 m. US 830*

Beginning among brown, treeless hillsides, US 830, the North Bank Highway, threads downstream along the Columbia River through a deep and spectacular gorge which, laying open a cross section of the otherwise unbroken 2,000-mile Cascade-Sierra mountain chain, separates the States of Washington and Oregon. Below thundering cataracts, the river plunges into swirling pools. Bleak rocky islands break the river channel. Canyon walls reflect the heat of noon and the varied colors of sunrise and sunset. Wispy waterfalls leap from high "hanging valleys." A large Indian population once occupied villages along the river banks and lived and fought within the gorge's frowning walls and among the green islands of the lower river, until decimated by the white man's whisky and the ravages of smallpox. At least five nations disputed possession of the region north of the stream, a territory delimited by treaty with Great Britain in 1846 (*see History*) and awarded by virtue of discovery and colonization to the United States.

West of the junction of US 97 and US 830 at MARYHILL JUNCTION, 0 *m.,* (*see Tour 7b*), US 830 leads along the rocky north side of the Columbia Gorge. The banks of the river on the Oregon side rise steeply, forming terrace on terrace as they mount hundreds of feet to a flat-domed top. Farther west, cultivated lands and orchards are visible.

At 3.9 *m.* is a junction with a dirt road.

Left here 0.2 *m.* to MARYHILL CASTLE, an isolated mansion which resembles a palace and blends strangely with the setting of the wild gorge. It was completed in 1926 by the late multimillionaire, Samuel Hill, pioneer good roads advocate, international peace promoter, royalty's friend, and the son-in-law of "Empire Builder" James J. Hill. It was originally selected as the site for a Quaker colony, but Samuel Hill discovered that many of the colonists he imported from Belgium were reluctant to settle on the parched slopes of the gorge. Although colonizing ideas were abandoned, Maryhill Castle rose in desolate grandeur. The mansion, planned by New York architects, includes large garages, spacious driveways, and electric and gas equipment. The castle is approached through lanes of white poplars, which provide an impressive setting for the gray stone structure overlooking the gorge. Hill decided to convert the building into a museum, and invited Queen Marie of Rumania to dedicate it in 1926.

West of the junction, the gorge drops sharply toward the river below, where sand dunes form a large island. A stone farmhouse, built sturdily to resist the unrelenting winds, stands on a sheep ranch. Rocks are strewn in profusion on both sides of the road, and steep hills (R) rise from the highway. Farther west the gorge widens. Visible across the Columbia is the rolling plateau of north central Oregon.

At 8.2 *m.* is a junction with an asphalt-paved road.

Left on this road down a precipitous grade to WISHRAM, 1 *m.* (166 alt., 300 pop.), nestling in a little dell and overlooking the curving rocky cascades of the river. The town is the division point of the Spokane, Portland, and Seattle Railroad, which maintains a yard and a roundhouse here. Small, well-kept houses, roofed in red, blue, and green, give a tidy appearance. A cosmopolitan touch is provided by a two-story stucco bungalow court apartment and a large hotel. Railroad employees reside in yellow-painted houses near the hotel. Numerous poplar trees border winding graveled streets. Since this is a stopover point for trains, itinerants who "ride the rods" assemble at a "jungle" near the town. A PIONEER MEMORIAL stands 100 feet east of the railroad station along the mainline track. It consists of several basalt columns bound together with an iron cable; on it is a bronze plaque bearing the name of pathfinders and pioneers, beginning with Meriwether Lewis and ending with John C. Fremont. The monument was erected in 1926 by the Great Northern Railroad, with which the S. P. & S. is closely affiliated. Wishram once was called Fallbridge, but the name was changed in 1926.

One-half mile west from Wishram by trail to CELILO FALLS, where the Columbia River plunges 20 feet over a knife-edged precipice extending across the river. The falls mark the entrance to a narrow channel, bordering precipitous cliffs of basalt.

The ancient village of Wishram was a "food emporium" and trading mart of the Indians. Here Indians gathered from east and west to barter with the Klickitats, who fished below Celilo Falls for the salmon struggling up the river to their spawning grounds, and dried and packed the fish in bundles and bales of varied sizes for trading purposes. Washington Irving, in *Astoria,* explains that tribes from the Pacific Coast brought sea foods, *wapato* (Ind. wild potato), and other roots and berries. From the interior, along the lane of the Snake and Columbia Rivers, natives drove in with horses, or rowed downstream in canoes laden with bear grass roots and other edibles. Today, during the salmon run, Indians stand on frail scaffoldings, fastened precariously on the rocky sides of the channel above the falls, with ropes fastened to their waists and long-pointed javelins in hand, awaiting the leap of the salmon. In the split second when the fish are arrested in midair, the spears are driven home. Treaty rights allow the Indians the exclusive privilege of taking salmon by this primitive method.

Near the Oregon side is the upper end of the locks which furnish portage for river steamers through the narrow gorge and around the falls. The locks were completed by the Federal Government in 1892; though little used by navigation, the $5,000,000 investment effected a reduction in freight rates that paid for its construction.

West of the junction US 830 affords a sweeping view of the river, a railroad bridge, and Wishram. A short distance west are farmhouses (R) surrounded by yellow poplars. Then, as the gorge widens, pasture lands come into view at various points alongside the road. Adjacent to a steeply-terraced, brown, rocky cliff are velvety hills speckled with green trees.

At 17.6 *m.* is a junction with a trail.

Left on this trail 1.5 *m.* across rocky open land to CALDWASH BOTTOM, where red and white Indian pictographs on rocks are found. Here also are a few scattered graves.

At 18.5 *m.* is a junction with a concrete-paved road.

Left on this road, that descends to the level of the river channel, is NORTH DALLES, 8 *m.* (123 alt., 14 pop.), consisting of a few bleached buildings clinging to the river bank. The NORTH DALLES FERRY (*day and night service; 50c for auto and driver*) connects with The Dalles, Oregon.

North Dalles was the first seat of Klickitat County and in Territorial days was known as Rockland. In 1891 this flat was the scene of a projected boom town, promoted by the Reverend Orson D. Taylor, who came as a Baptist missionary in 1880. Elaborate illustrations of the "city" showed fine boulevards, streetcars, and three railroads. On Taylor's maps, the Klickitat River emptied into the Columbia at this point, instead of at its actual location nine miles westward. Holding companies were organized; offices were opened in many eastern cities. Arrested in 1895, Taylor carried his case to the Supreme Court which released him on a technicality. The site marks the down-river end of the locks through The Dalles. The name was given the narrow, rocky stretch by the French-Canadian *voyageurs.* The channel is between 280 and 400 feet deep, and only 165 feet wide as the great river pours through the narrow gap. Several stone images, including the heads of monkeys carved in basalt, have been found in the vicinity. Along the railroad tracks E. of North Dalles at a point known as SPEARFISH, 2 *m.,* are extensive Indian pictographs and petroglyphs.

Some distance west of the junction, the backwash of Bonneville Dam widens the Columbia River. Paralleling the highway, the PAHA CLIFFS (R), perpendicular walls of lava rock, are not remarkable for height, but are of such regularity and symmetry as to seem fashioned by human hands. Indian legends state that Speelyia, the coyote god, created the many pillars of stone by turning mortals and beasts into rock. Geologists explain that seismic and volcanic action raised the mountain area, and river erosion left the odd-shaped formations.

LYLE, 26.2 *m.* (101 alt., 250 pop.), marked by a few houses along the highway, is a railroad shipping point for a farm and orchard district. Below the road, on a sloping hill, is the business section of the town, near which is a boxwood mill. Lyle has a hotel, a schoolhouse, a church, and a community clubhouse.

At 27.1 *m.* is a junction with a gravel-surfaced road.

Right on this road along the eastern bank of the Klickitat River, which flows between canyon walls a thousand feet high, to KLICKITAT FALLS, 3 *m.,* an Indian fishing ground. KLICKITAT, 14 *m.* (440 alt., 620 pop.), on the north bank of the river, is the site of the Gas Ice Corporation's plant which manufactures "dry ice" from natural carbon dioxide wells at Klickitat Mineral Springs. Three tons of the product, used for refrigeration in long-distance hauling, are shipped daily. The town, however, is dominated by a large sawmill which employs 500 men.

West of the junction, US 830 crosses the Klickitat River, which has its source in Klickitat Glacier on Mount Adams. Through a high plateau, the winding river has cut a deep gorge to its mouth at Lyle. Near the mouth of the river, along the western bluffs, are strange round depressions surrounded by stones that seemingly form a wall.

Continuing westward, the highway enters the pass cut by the Columbia through the Cascade Mountains. Mount Hood (11,225 alt.), in Oregon, rears (L) its snowy cone above the countryside.

With a boat, which can sometimes be secured from farmers along the river, it is possible to reach MEMALOOSE (Ind. place of the dead) ISLAND, a desolate basalt isle a few hundred feet out in the river. For centuries the Indians built platforms here and placed the dead and their possessions upon them. On the island, facing the south, the large white TREVITT MONUMENT commemorates Vic Trevitt, a pioneer of The Dalles, who chose to be buried on the island sacred to his Indian friends.

Many years ago three pioneers, John Martin, Amos Underwood, and Vic Trevitt, while drinking in a Dalles saloon, began a discussion of death; they formed a compact to be buried together on the island, Trevitt asserting that he wanted to sleep among honest people. He was the only one of the three whose friends or relatives would honor the agreement; after his death in San Francisco his remains were shipped to the island.

A FRUIT PACKING PLANT, 37.4 *m.,* stands (L) of the road.

BINGEN, 37.6 *m.* (101 alt., 600 pop.), named for "Bingen-on-the-Rhine" by early German settlers, lies between bluffs and the river on a narrow strip of rich sandy loam. On the fringes of the town are luxuriant meadows dotted with dairy cattle. Irrigation from the river permits extensive truck farming. According to "Believe-It-Or-Not" Ripley, the railroad depot of White Salmon-Bingen is the only one in the Nation with the names of two separate towns on it. Controversy between the towns over which was the location of the station caused the dual name. Bingen today has two sawmills, a fruit company, a hotel, taverns, and restaurants.

In Bingen is a junction with a dirt road.

Right on this road, which is steep and winding, to WHITE SALMON, 1.5 *m.* (586 alt., 985 pop.), located in step-like formation on a hillside. Like Bingen it is in the center of a ranching and farming district. The town is sheltered from the east wind that sweeps down the gorge by Burdoin Mountain (2,200 alt.). Jewett Creek emerges from a canyon at the base of the mountain and flows through a small valley. While the terrain of the townsite is rocky, there is fertile alluvial soil in adjacent areas. White Salmon also is a logging and dairy products shipping point. It is a brisk little town with modern stores in brick buildings.

North of White Salmon on Jewett Street to NORTHWESTERN LAKE, 3.5 *m.,* formed by the backwater of a power dam. Numerous camp sites and picnic grounds are on the grassy shores. The lake is stocked with trout and has boating and swimming facilities.

West of Bingen rocky hillsides merge with verdant growths and lush meadows along the banks of streams and creeks. The odor of sweet-smelling pine and cedar permeates the cool air. Snow-white syringa grows profusely. The road skirts lofty tree-covered cliffs (R), while (L) the Columbia River gradually widens as it approaches Bonneville Dam.

The WHITE SALMON-HOOD RIVER TOLL BRIDGE, 75c; pedestrians 10c), 39.3 *m.,* across the Columbia River, links Washington and Oregon.

At 39.5 *m.* is a junction with a gravel-surfaced road.

Right on this road, which is paralleled throughout most of its length by the west bank of the White Salmon River, where steelhead trout challenge fish-

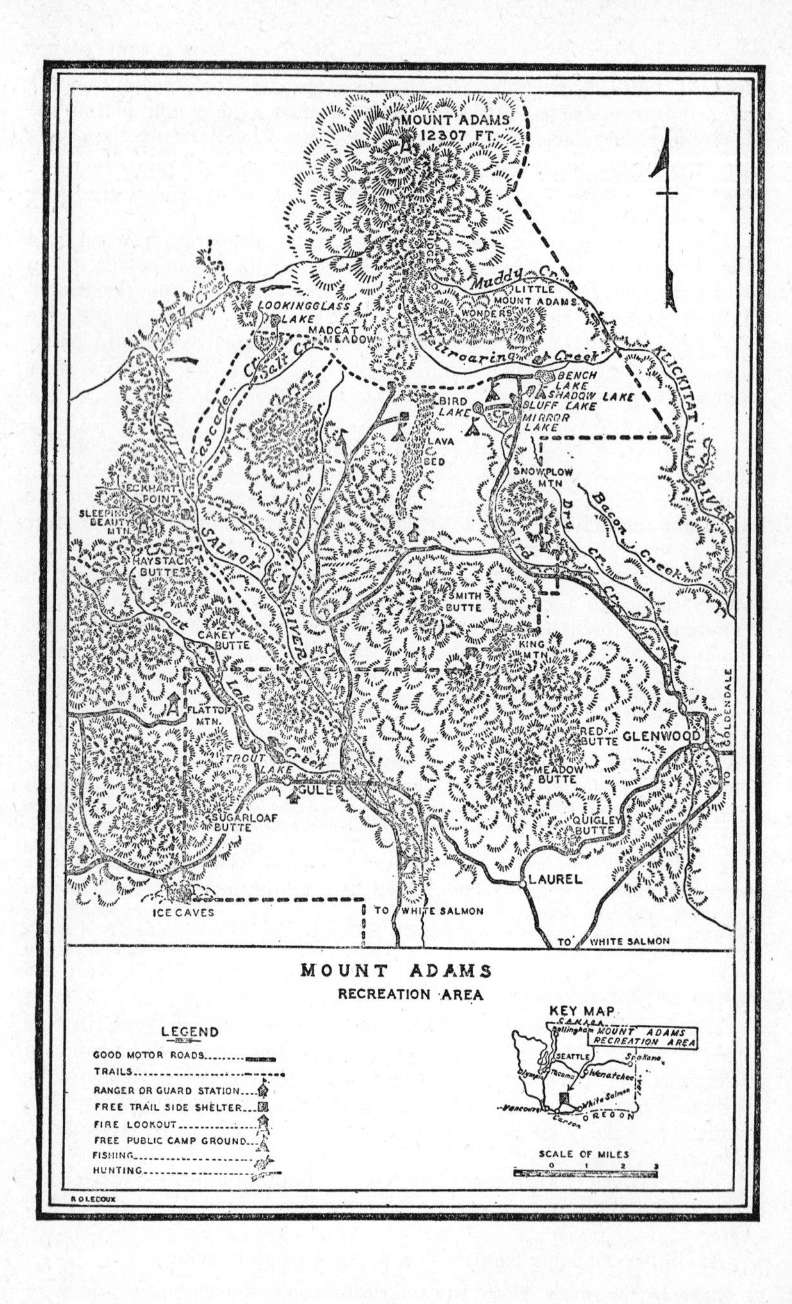
MOUNT ADAMS
12307 FT.
RIDGE
Muddy Cr.
LITTLE
MOUNT ADAMS
WONDERS
KLICKITAT
RIVER
LOOKINGGLASS
LAKE
MADCAT
MEADOW
Hellroaring Creek
Salt Cr.
Cascade Cr.
BENCH
LAKE
SHADOW LAKE
BLUFF LAKE
MIRROR
LAKE
BIRD
LAKE
LAVA
BED
Morrison
SNOWPLOW
MTN
Bacon Creek
Dry Cr.
Bird Cr.
ECKHART
POINT
SLEEPING
BEAUTY
MTN.
SALMON
RIVER
HAYSTACK
BUTTE
Trout
SMITH
BUTTE
CAKEY
BUTTE
KING
MTN
Lake Creek
FLATTOP
MTN.
TROUT
LAKE
GULER
RED
BUTTE
GLENWOOD
TO GOLDENDALE
MEADOW
BUTTE
SUGARLOAF
BUTTE
QUIGLEY
BUTTE
LAUREL
ICE CAVES
TO WHITE SALMON
TO WHITE SALMON
MOUNT ADAMS
RECREATION AREA
LEGEND
GOOD MOTOR ROADS
TRAILS
RANGER OR GUARD STATION
FREE TRAIL SIDE SHELTER
FIRE LOOKOUT
FREE PUBLIC CAMP GROUND
FISHING
HUNTING
KEY MAP
CANADA
Bellingham
MOUNT ADAMS
RECREATION AREA
SEATTLE
Spokane
Olympia
Tacoma
Wenatchee
White Salmon
Vancouver
Carson
OREGON
SCALE OF MILES
0 1 2 3
R O LEDOUX

ermen from November until April. Early in spring, slopes are carpeted with blue grasswidows, yellow bell, large patches of blue lupine, and wild sunflowers. The California lilac blossoms late in May in a riot of blue tones.

TROUT LAKE, 22 *m.*, is a post office and store near the confluence of the White Salmon River and Trout Lake Creek. Two roads branch from Trout Lake.

1. Left from Trout Lake post office is GULER, 1 *m.* (*see Mount Adams Recreational Area Map*), a ranger station and post office at the foot of Trout Lake. Across the street from the ranger station is a hotel. One-half mile long, Trout Lake has grassy shores enclosed by forest growth. West of Guler the forest road continues around the base of Sugarbowl Butte (3,000 alt.) to the ICE CAVE, 8 *m.* Through an aperture fringed with wild flowers icy draughts issue from the 400-foot cave. Visitors descend a tree ladder by torchlight to the crystal floor of ice; within are thousands of stalactites and stalagmites like organ pipes. Geologists explain the formation of the cave as a bubble in the plastic rock. The entire region south of Mount Adams is full of these caves, most of them without openings but known to exist by the hollow sound made when horses clatter over them.

2. Right from Trout Lake post office, by forest road across the White Salmon River to GOTCHEN CREEK GUARD STATION, 10 *m.*, at the foot of a long lava flow on the slopes of Mount Adams. At 13 *m.* the road crosses Bird Creek where it turns N. paralleling the stream through an area of meadows and lakes to BIRD CREEK MEADOWS CAMP, 19 *m.* Innumerable small streams with their waterfalls and cascades add to the charm of a setting of green meadow, multicolored wildflowers, and scrubby green trees.

Trails radiate from Bird Creek Meadows Camp along ridges and through valleys to MOUNT ADAMS (12,307 alt.), whose four distinct summits and central dome form a symmetrical and majestic picture of white against a blue sky. Lesser peaks, mostly sharp crags along the slopes, protrude from the mountain. The snowline belt is splashed with yellow and vermilion crags across the dark purple cliffs. Seven distinct glaciers, defined by the black lines of ridges, clutch the cone, like talons of a great bird.

UNDERWOOD, 40.6 *m.* (101 alt., 200 pop.), a collection of small homes and fruit warehouses along the river and the railroad tracks, is a junction point of rivers, railroads, and highways. The White Salmon River, joining the Columbia at Underwood after a tumultuous career in a narrow, rocky canyon, is so named because salmon swimming up the stream to spawn change from a deep red color to a pinkish white.

The town consists of a railroad station, a few houses along the banks of the Columbia, a service station, and a large three-story hotel. It offers a view of snow-covered hills (R), and of the expansive Columbia (L), where the wind stirs up white caps against the blue-white water. On the Oregon side of the river, towering behind the buildings of Hood River and wooded hills, is majestic Mount Hood. Near the western boundary of the town, warehouses line the highway next to the railroad tracks.

In Underwood is a junction with a dirt road.

Right on this road 1 *m.* to the UNDERWOOD CEMETERY, on a knoll, where the remains of Amos Underwood and other pioneers have been buried.

US 830 extends beneath the now extinct volcanic cone (R) of MOUNT UNDERWOOD (2,725 alt.), along a seven-mile section of highway opened in May 1937. Construction here lent itself to the most modern highway engineering, including heavy rock work, riprap, tunnels, grade separation structure, drainage culverts, and a major bridge. The first construction is an overhead crossing above the railroad tracks, 42.7 *m.* Right of the highway is a combination sawmill and shingle mill unit, which provides employment for many residents of Underwood and the surrounding area. Drano Lake (R) collects the waters of the Little White Salmon River, spanned by a bridge at this point, and discharges them into the Columbia River.

COOK, 47.6 *m.* (99 alt., 150 pop.), once a busy boat landing, is composed of a schoolhouse, a general store, and a few other buildings, all sitting on a steep hill. The town looks down on the Columbia, flowing in blue peacefulness after its turbulent course through The Dalles.

WIND MOUNTAIN, 53.2 *m.* (R), (1,910 alt.), a solitary rounded hill, looms in bold relief. Wooded slopes cover the east side of the mountain; on its west side are jagged peaks. The mountain has a peculiar slant, caused by the river that sawed through the rising mountain barrier. Climatic differences between the arid and desolate region east of the Cascades and the green lushness of the western slope become increasingly evident in this area.

The highway enters HOME VALLEY, 54.1 *m.,* a modern farming community, with a post office, cabins, a schoolhouse, and a few dwellings. In the forested hills near by are logging operations.

At 55.5 *m.* is a junction with a dirt road.

Right on this road, which offers a vista of hills and the winding river far below, to SAINT MARTINS' HOT SPRINGS, 0.4 *m.* on the west bank of Wind River, opposite the mouth of Little Wind River and the dark, green-forested pyramid of Buck Mountain. It is set in an attractive glen overlooked by rows of white and green cottages. Hot mineralized baths are offered in an adjunct to Hotel St. Martins, a three-story white frame building. Sixty years ago the resort was opened by the St. Martins, an Indian family, descendants of whom operate it today.

At 56.6 *m.* is a junction with State 8C, a gravel-surfaced road.

Right on this road is CARSON, 1 *m.* (98 alt., 276 pop.), a few scattered buildings at the mouth of Wind River Valley. North from Carson, State 8-C crosses a crook in Wind River and follows its east bank. The two peaks of Mount St. Helens (L) and Mount Adams (R) rise above the surrounding elevations of the Cascade Range. Wind River dashes violently within confining canyon walls. At 8 *m.* is TROUT CREEK FOREST CAMP (1,100 alt.), in the Columbia National Forest, at a junction with a dirt side road. Left on this road 1.8 *m.* to WIND RIVER NURSERY AND FOREST EXPERIMENT STATION. The DeMolay organization of Portland, Oregon, contributes funds to the maintenance of the station, which develops seedlings for reforesting lands denuded by fire and logging operations.

North of the junction at 10 *m.* on the main side road is a junction with another dirt side road: Right on the dirt side road 13 *m.,* rounding the slopes of South Butte (2,825 alt.) and Red Mountain (4,100 alt.), on the north, and BIG LAVA BED, on the east and south, to the RACE TRACK GUARD STATION. The dirt road skirts the lava bed to GOOSE LAKE, 18 *m.* On the shore of Goose Lake are curious imprints in the lava rock which appear to have been made by human hands and feet. Their origin is not known and, together with Lemei Rock (5,927 alt.) (R), they are the subjects of Indian legends.

On the main side road, 19 *m.,* is LITTLE SODA SPRINGS FOREST CAMP, in a

In the Mountains

Photograph by T. W. Norcross; courtesy of U. S. Forest Service

MOUNT BAKER

Photograph courtesy of Orville Borgersen

SKIERS RESTING ON SLOPES OF MOUNT RAINIER

SKAGIT BASIN

Photograph courtesy of Seattle City Light Company

CREVASSE ON MOUNT BAKER

Photograph by Stuart B. Hertz

MOUNTAIN CLIMBERS SCALING ICE WALLS NEAR SUMMIT OF MOUNT RAINIER

Photograph courtesy of Rainier National Park Company

Photograph by Frank Jacobs

TROUT REARING PONDS AT SEWARD PARK HATCHERY

TROUT FISHING

Photograph courtesy of Washington State Progress Commission

Photograph courtesy of Seattle City Light Company

ON DIABLO LAKE (Excursion

MOUNT ST. HELENS

Photograph courtesy of Washington State Progress Commission

Photograph by Bert Huntoo

ALONG THE HIGHWAY TO MOUNT BAKER SKI FIELD

hotograph by Oliver T. Edwards

MOUNTAIN GOATS, CHELAN NATIONAL FOREST

LOWERS BLOOM AT THE EDGE OF RECEDING
NOW DRIFTS ON MOUNT RAINIER

Photograph courtesy of Rainier National Park Company

MOTHER BEAR AND CUBS, IN RAINIER NATIONAL PARK

region of mineral springs. A recreational area, with tables, stoves, water, and sanitary facilities, is located here.

West of the junction, US 830 continues along the curving north bank of the Columbia River, on which stand beautiful summer homes. Steep cone-shaped rocks flank the road (R).

STEVENSON, 59.8 *m.* (98 alt., 563 pop.), seat of Skamania County, on low bluffs above the river, spreads back against rolling hills. A beautiful town square slants up a hill, on top of which is a three-story hotel with a glassed-in porch. The SKAMANIA COUNTY COURTHOUSE (R), on top of the hill, in the center of an expansive lawn, is a two-story, green-roofed, wooden structure erected in 1903. It has a tall, green belfry tower above the jail, and houses administrative offices and a courtroom. Next to the courthouse is the STEVENSON COMMUNITY HALL, a two-story building. On the courthouse lawn is a section, ten feet high and six feet in diameter, of a PETRIFIED SEQUOIA TREE. Behind the courthouse is a grade school and a two-story brick high school. A SPHERICAL ROCK at the entrance to the high school grounds (R) bears in rough characters the inscription: "H. B. Co. 1811." It is believed to have been a corner marker for an early Hudson's Bay Company boundary, but the Hudson's Bay Company did not enter this region till 1821. To the left, down the slanting hill, are the buildings of the business district; a number of warehouses stand alongside the railroad tracks.

The town was founded by the Stevenson family who came from Missouri in 1880 to settle in the old town of Cascades near by. Driven from there by a flood in 1894, they platted Stevenson.

West of Stevenson, the modern BRIDGE OF THE GODS (L) (*toll*: 50c *driver and auto; 10c pedestrian*), 63.3 *m.*, spans the Columbia River to Oregon.

FORT RAINS BLOCKHOUSE (R), 64.4 *m.*, was rebuilt by the Skamania County Historical Society in 1927 partly from old timbers that formed the structure erected by Major Gabriel Rains after the Indian Wars of 1856 and the Cascades Massacre. A band of Yakima, Klickitat, and Cascade made raids on two white settlements near Bradford Island, March 26, 1856. The besieged settlers withstood attacks for two days, until two forces from The Dalles, Oregon, commanded by Colonel Edward J. Steptoe and Lieutenant Phil Sheridan (later General Sheridan of Civil War fame) came to the rescue.

West of the bridge, US 830 crawls at the base of the great crumbling cliffs (R) of TABLE MOUNTAIN (3,420 alt.). Through ridges and deep pits, numerous hot springs flow out of the near-by hills.

NORTH BONNEVILLE, 65.0 *m.* (74 alt., 643 pop.), was named for Captain Benjamin Louis Eulalie Bonneville, who experienced amazing adventures in the Rocky Mountains, California, and the Northwest as early as the year 1832. His journal, amplified by Washington Irving, was published under the title, *Adventures of Captain Bonneville, U.S.A., in the Rocky Mountains and the Far West.* The town marks the Washington side of Bonneville Dam and was born of an influx of workers on the project. It grew from a wild, sparsely settled community into a boom town typical of those which have sprung up near construction camps. Short side streets, filled with mud during the rainy season and choked with dust during the summer, branch sharply from either side of the highway. Temporarily constructed cabin camps line the highway.

The town relies entirely upon the pay roll of the dam for its livelihood; when construction work lags, it is affected at once. Business men, however, are optimistic about its future. The largest building is a large barn-like structure used as a dance hall. The town also has a small community church, a post office, a railroad station and several hotels, restaurants, and taverns.

The BONNEVILLE OBSERVATION TOWER, a square wooden structure built on stilts, offers a view of the dam, a large concrete masonry structure. From the tower, big MEMALOOSE ISLAND, once an Indian burial ground, is visible. A few years ago, when it became apparent that the backwater from the dam would submerge most of the island, the graves were removed.

Left from the highway 200 feet to the ENTRANCE TO BONNEVILLE DAM, (*visitors* 10-12, 1-4; *guides furnished; Federal Police Service*). The ADMINISTRATION OFFICE is on the left. Authorized September 30, 1933, under the National Recovery Act, construction was begun immediately on Bonneville Dam by the Army Engineer Corps. It was opened by President Franklin D. Roosevelt on September 28, 1937. Smaller than the Grand Coulee Dam farther up the river (*see Tour 1B*), the project provides flood control for the lower Columbia River, creates electric power for northern Oregon and southern Washington, and, by its locks, aids water transportation through the Cascade rapids to the upper Columbia.

Of the concrete gravity type, the dam has 18 vertical-lift, steel gates, 30 feet square, giving a spillway crest of 900 feet. The spillway is on the north side of Bradford Island, which divides the river into two channels at this point. On the south side are the powerhouse and navigation locks, connected to the spillway by a levee across the island itself. The dam backs the river upstream, creating a lake extending 40 miles to The Dalles, with a minimum depth of more than 30 feet. The navigation locks consist of a single chamber, 76 feet wide and 500 feet long, with a minimum depth of 27 feet at low water. The water above the dam, being 72 feet above the river level, necessitates a lift of 59 feet—the highest in the world at present (1941).

Fish ladders and elevators allow salmon to ascend the river through the dam, and it is claimed the annual $10,000,000 income derived from the industry will not be endangered. One hundred fish pools, 40 feet long, 15 feet wide, and 6 feet deep, and each a little higher than the other, spiral to the top of the dam. Water cascades down this 5,900-foot watery stairway. The fish elevators work on a principle similar to canal locks; as chambers are filled with water and salmon they are lifted automatically to upper-dam level and dumped. To prevent fingerlings from being crushed in the giant turbine and generators as they make their way to the sea, the engineers have left openings large enough for the baby fish to pass through.

West of North Bonneville along the north bank of the river, the shorelines reveal the slight rise and fall of the river, first effect of tidewater from the Pacific Ocean, 150 miles westward. The highway enters the broad valley that begins with the western slopes of the Cascade Mountains.

GREENWOOD CEMETERY, 65.9 *m.* (L), enclosed by a wooden fence, contains many graves of early settlers, Indian fighters, and Indians. Ancient iron fences surround individual plots, some the graves of soldiers stationed at Old Cascades. The cemetery was moved from a former site on the railroad right-of-way.

Along this section of the route ran the old Portage Railroad; and Lower Cascades, original seat of Skamania County, was located in this vicinity. No trace of either remains.

West of the junction, US 830 traverses a peninsula formed by the backwater of the Columbia.

BEACON ROCK (L), 68.8 *m.,* with fluted, almost perpendicular sides of columnar lava that rise about 900 feet from the edge of the river, is the second largest monolith in the world. Its summit is strewn with great blocks of red cinder and cloaked with stunted, deformed trees. From the entrance, a trail winds upward in zigzag fashion, leading over precarious-looking wooden bridges to the top of the conical-shaped rock. A defiant challenge to climbers, its "inaccessible" heights were conquered in 1901, when the banner of a Columbia River steamship company was raised as an advertising stunt.

LITTLE BEACON ROCK (L) rears its scrubby head against the corrugated face of its big brother. The two monoliths are vestiges of material harder than the loose columnar lava plucked away by the rapacious early floods of the river. The Lewis and Clark Expedition camped at the base of the rock November 2, 1805, and again on the return trip April 8, 1806.

West of Beacon Rock US 830 again affords scenic glimpses of the Oregon side of the river. The green-painted buildings of a CCC camp are arranged in orderly rows a short distance from the highway, 69.7 *m.*

SKAMANIA, 71.3 *m.* (51 alt., 75 pop.), consists of a gas station, a general store, and a post office. Up the hill (R) a short distance from the highway are the three gray buildings of an attractive grade school with a large playground. In the hills in the background logging is carried on.

West of Skamania the highway skirts the great frowning cliffs (R) of ARCHER MOUNTAIN. Of the many legends and folk tales that have grown up around these conspicuous cliffs, the leading ones deal with the "Hermit of Archer Mountain," who lived on top of a 2,000-foot cliff in a house built of materials salvaged from a wrecked river boat. The highway overlooks LOWER POND (L), 72.9 *m.,* fed by the backwaters of the Columbia River. Fishermen have told of an enormous sturgeon here, weighing perhaps 1,000 pounds, which has eluded the juiciest baits and the most ingenious nets. The road winds up and down through beautiful green country and wooded hills, and affords a view of silvery Multnomah Falls, on the Oregon side.

PRINDLE, 76.4 *m.* (51 alt., 125 pop.), is a roadside stopping place composed of a store and a few scattered houses. The town was named for its first settler, a German sailor who planted an orchard and garden to supply the soldiers at Cascades in 1851. Many persons of Polish origin remained after construction of the Union Pacific R. R. in the seventies to form a community of small farms. Older residents still converse in Polish. Robert Prindle, son of the founder, is postmaster here.

West of Prindle, the route is on a slight grade overlooking the river. Towering tree-covered hills slope down to the swiftly moving Columbia on the Oregon side. FIR POINT (L) is a small, rocky peninsula projecting into the river. Here, years ago, Indian mothers brought their babies in the springtime for the ceremony of uncradling, which included hiding the cradles to keep away evil spirits. Bindings, used by the Indians on the heads of their infants to make the skull slope back from the forehead, were also hidden in a cave as a part of the ceremony.

US 830 follows a bench covered with a checkerboard of cultivated fields, in the shadow of MOUNT ZION (R).

CAPE HORN, 79.4 *m.,* is a steep jagged promontory from which sufficient rock and dirt have been blasted to permit passage of the highway. Perpendicular cliffs have been left. A snow shed protects the highway from snowslides and rockslides. Rock blasted from the road during construction covered a good portion of a farm in the valley. The highway widens at each end of the snow shed, providing parking space. The sheer drop of the cliff hundreds of feet below to the little valley nestling on the banks of the Columbia, is an awe-inspiring view, with a background of steeply wooded hills on the Oregon bank.

MOUNT PLEASANT, 81.5 *m.* (48 alt., 15 pop.), beneath a mountain of the same name, is composed of a service station and a few houses along the railroad track.

A few miles west of Mount Pleasant the highway penetrates an area of fruit orchards.

WASHOUGAL (Ind. rushing water), 87.8 *m.* (48 alt., 1,267 pop.), is at the mouth of Washougal River. Shady trees line the road into town, the main street of which is bordered by frame buildings. Houses are scattered over a wide area on both sides of the river. The town was settled on part of the donation claim of Betsy Ough, wife of Richard Ough, a Hudson's Bay Company employee. Mrs. Ough, an Indian of the Waunaisses tribe, was a trusted friend of the early white settlers on the Columbia River.

Washougal's major industrial plant (L) is the WASHOUGAL WOOLEN MILLS, 1st and Main Streets (*visitors Mon. to Fri.* 8-4). The plant is housed in a large gray frame building, in the rear of which is a powerhouse. Fabrics of this mill are shipped to manufacturers throughout the United States. Many woolen novelties also are manufactured. Entire families, each member an expert weaver, are often employed; some come from New England mills, others from Europe.

West of Washougal US 830 crosses the Washougal River and spans the outlet of Lackamas Lake (R), formed by a powerdam backing up the waters of Lackamas Creek. Houses line both sides of the highway. The CROWN WILLAMETTE INN, 89.9 *m.*, is a hotel housing some of the employees of the paper mill in Camas.

CAMAS, 90.3 *m.* (48 alt., 4,433 pop.), in a semicircle of evergreen hills dropping to cultivated prairie land bordering the Columbia River on the south, is a "City of Paper." Wide, concrete-paved streets and modern brick business and residential buildings give a pleasant, lively appearance to the town. The mill buildings and the ever-present odor of sulphite suggest the industrial background of the city.

Construction of a sawmill by Jacob Hunsacker in 1846 on Lake Lackamas brought the first industrial activity to the district. First settlement was in 1860 near a sand bar where the camas, a blue-flowered, sweet-flavored bulb, grew prolifically; the village retained the name of this favorite food of the Indians.

The growth of Camas was the direct result of paper manufacture. The uncertainty of paper delivery from eastern mills, because of slow sailing around Cape Horn and oxteam transportation across the country, long handicapped the newspapers of the Northwest. In 1884 construction of a paper mill began on Lake Lackamas; after 18 months of operation, it was completely destroyed by a $150,000 fire. The mill was rebuilt the following year, with provision for new methods of pulp production and additional machinery. With its unlimited pulpwood resources, Camas grew as the factory expanded.

The CROWN-WILLAMETTE PAPER COMPANY PLANT, division of Crown-Zellerbach Paper Company (*visitors 12-3 p.m. Mon., Tues., 9 a.m.-3 p.m. Wed., Fri.; 9-12 Sat. Guides required; available for small fee. Children under 15 not allowed*), NE. 4th St. and NE. Adams St., has 12 gigantic paper-making machines capable of producing more than 300 tons of paper, 5,000,000 paper bags, and 2,000 cases of tissue and towels daily. This industrial town is highly unionized, more than half its population holding union cards.

Docks on the river front handle shipments of materials and products for the paper mill. Fruit from near-by prune orchards is packed and prepared for shipment by water and rail. Smelt fishing during the spring and salmon fishing during the summer also contribute to Camas' revenue. Pails, basins, and washboilers are used during the smelt run to scoop the tiny, oily fish from the streams (*no license required for smelt fishing*).

The CAMAS PUBLIC LIBRARY (*open 1-9 weekdays*), 417 NE. Cedar St., contains a collection of volumes dealing with the early history of the Lower Columbia region.

The PULP AND INDUSTRIAL SCHOOL, 3rd and Clark Sts., is conducted by the Crown-Zellerbach paper mills from October to March. It offers technical schooling to employees and awards visits to Pacific Coast paper plants as scholarships.

The collection in a HOUSE MUSEUM (*open by permission*), 1600 Division St., maintained by James T. Self, an early settler, includes an Indian "fishkiller" of highly polished basalt, a stone moccasin last, not unlike a cobbler's, and an old cutlass once used at Fort Vancouver by the Hudson's Bay Company.

LAKE LACKAMAS, in the northern section of the city, is a popular resort.

The CAMAS CHRISTIAN CHURCH, NE. 6th Ave. and NE. Cedar St., is octagonal in shape and painted yellow.

The western city limits of Camas overlook the dilated river channel, here dotted with sandy islands and bordered by silty banks. With loaded bateaux, voyageurs of the fur-trading days passed this point on their way to old Fort Vancouver. INDIAN ROCK CARVINGS are to be found on the banks of the Columbia (L) at 95.2 *m.;* and the Gentry Store (L) has a collection of arrowheads, stone bowls, and other utensils.

FISHER, 96.3 *m.* (48 alt., 35 pop.), is a railroad center among orchard lands. A large camping ground near by has picnic facilities.

West of Fisher is a junction, 98.4 *m.*, with a dirt road.

Right on this road to the BIDDLE FISH HATCHERY, 1.3 *m.*, owned by Stephen Biddle, a student of Indian lore. The hatchery is surrounded by timber and enclosed by a wire fence hidden from the road.

ELLSWORTH, 98.4 *m.* (48 alt., 60 pop.), is a small settlement around the Ellingsworth Company, which operates during the salmon run on the Columbia.

West of Ellsworth prune orchards are abundant. In the spring their pink blossoms soften the landscape and their heavy, fragrant odor scents the air. Large drying bins for the ripe, picked fruit stand in each orchard.

The STATE GAME BUILDINGS, maintained by the Department of Game, a fine group of white and green structures, were constructed with the aid of the Work Projects Administration. Twelve fish-breeding tanks are set in a green carpet of grass in front of the buildings. The main building, situated on a knoll immediately behind the outdoor tank, also contains breeding pools. Right of the main building are a residence and a service building.

At 5th and Main Sts. is a junction with US 99 (*see Tour 8e*).

VANCOUVER, 104.5 *m.* (75 alt., 18,788 pop.), (*see Vancouver*).

Section b. VANCOUVER *to* JOHNSON'S LANDING, *112 m.* US 830

North of VANCOUVER, 0 *m.*, on wide Main Street, US 830 coincides with US 99 (*see Tour 8e*).

At LONGVIEW JUNCTION, 41.6 *m.*, 830 bears L. from US 99, spans the Cowlitz River, and follows California Way to a junction with Commerce Street; R. on Commerce to city center.

LONGVIEW, 45.2 *m.* (13 alt., 12,385 pop.), the first planned city in the Pacific Northwest, is one of the great lumber centers of the world. It occupies the tip of a 14,000-acre delta formed by the Cowlitz River on the east and the Columbia River on the south. To the west are wooded hills; northeast, contiguous to Longview, is Kelso.

Seventy per cent of the population is employed in lumber mills. Little industrial activity is evident in the city proper; trim commercial buildings border wide, tree-lined parkways, and the residential district is set among lawns and flowers. Along the banks of the Columbia are mammoth mills, switch engines, boxcars, and freighters loaded with lumber. Connecting the Washington and the Oregon shores of the mile-wide Columbia is Longview Bridge, a steel structure completed in 1930.

Before modern drainage methods were developed, the delta on which Longview stands was subject to seasonal floods from the rain-swollen Cowlitz River. Yet, because of its key position on the river, the Hudson's Bay Company chose it as a site on which to build two warehouses in 1846-7 for the storage of hides, wool, furs, and the wheat raised on near-by clearings. In 1849 two American settlers, Jonathan Durbee and H. D. Huntington, took up claims near the present location of the city. Soon, other settlers joined them, some clearing land and starting farms, others turning to lumbering. By 1852 logging camps had sprung up, and their cuts were moved by sailing ships, which found no difficulty in making their way up the Columbia.

On November 25, 1852, the memorable Monticello Convention was held here. Partly as the result of this and the preceding Cowlitz Convention Congress created the Territory of Washington, and in 1854 the Washington Territorial legislature formed Cowlitz County and made Monticello its seat.

Though the town got off to a good start and made gains during the next ten years, the settlement was virtually washed away in 1866-7 by high water, and thereafter the fear of floods kept settlers away. The county seat was moved elsewhere, and most of the farms around Monticello reverted to swamps and brambles.

A turn came in 1920, when R. A. Long, capitalist and lumber baron, having acquired a large tract of timber in the adjoining hills, decided to locate a model city on the site of old Monticello. The land was diked and an elaborate drainage system was installed. Sloughs and swamps were converted into sunken gardens and a chain of lakes was created in the heart of the city. A central square, streets and boulevards, residential and commercial districts, public buildings, schools, and a park were laid out, and the city was dedicated in 1923 and named Longview for its founder.

By 1933 the city had 18 manufacturing establishments with an annual production valued at $3,824,550 and paying nearly $500,000 in wages. A difficult housing problem arose, since working people could not afford to buy property and build the elaborate homes required by the building restrictions.

In general, Longview is a fairly prosperous city. In addition to its lumber industry it is a market and shipping center and does some processing of farm products. It has an excellent school system, including a junior college, and a library, public parks, churches, hotels, railroad and bus stations, motion picture houses, and athletic facilities.

JEFFERSON SQUARE, west end of Broadway, a six-acre civic center, is an admirably landscaped park with broad drives and rhododendrons. Many of the vines and fruit trees in the park were planted in the fifties, when the tract was a part of the Seth Catlin donation land claim.

The COMMUNITY CHURCH, 2327 Washington Way, was designed by R. L. Copeland, and completed in January 1926. It is constructed of yellow brick trimmed with granite, and has tall, arched windows of amber-toned glass. In the tower is one of the largest sets of chimes in the State, the gift of R. A. Long.

SACAJAWEA LAKE PARK, between Kessler and Nichols Boulevard, surrounds crescent-shaped Lake Sacajawea. In its 70 acres, the park has more than 2,000 perennials, thousands of bulbs, 58 varieties of trees, and 4,000 shrubs. Small islands dotting the lake are connected by rustic bridges. It is a refuge for game birds, swans, and pelicans.

The SUBSISTENCE HOMESTEADS, 34th to 38th Aves., between Pennsylvania and Oak Sts., were established by the Federal Government in 1934 for 60 families of low-income workers. A model community of four-room and six-room houses was planned, with tracts as large as three acres for each house.

The WEYERHAEUSER TIMBER COMPANY PLANT (*open by appointment*), foot of Washington Way, is one of the largest sawmills in the world. There are four units which turn out products of fir and hemlock: a planing mill, a red-cedar shingle mill, a pulp and sulphite plant, and a woodworking factory. One of the most interesting processes at the plant is the manufacture of a wood pulp from which paper, rayon, and cellophane are made.

The LONGVIEW BRIDGE, foot of Oregon Way, connects Washington and Oregon. With a clearance of 195 feet and a central span of 1,200 feet, it is the longest-spanned cantilever bridge in the country, as well as the highest bridge over a navigable stream. It was opened to traffic March 29, 1930.

The LONG-BELL LUMBER COMPANY PLANT (*open by appointment*), foot of Columbia Way, has a sawmill with a productive capacity of 1,800,000 board feet per eight-hour day. The buildings of the plant—sawmill, shingle mill, and woodworking units—occupy 78 acres; the total area, 643 acres, includes a 125-acre log pond. A dock 1,400 feet in length lines the water front. The mill smokestacks, 21 feet in diameter and 300 feet high, are visible for miles.

The M & M PLYWOOD PLANT (*open by appointment*), near the Long-Bell mill pond, is devoted to another phase of lumber processing —the making of veneer from Douglas fir. The daily output of plywood is 160,000 square feet.

The LONGVIEW FIBRE PLANT, (*open by appointment*), SE. of

Long-Bell mill site, employing about 800 men and women, daily manufactures 4,000,000 square feet of fibre board and 30 tons of Kraft wrapping paper, besides paper bags and corrugated boxes.

US 830 continues on Commerce St. to Maple St.; L. on Maple to Washington Way, where Olympia Way intersects it.

Right on Washington Way to Main St.; R. on Maine St. across Cowlitz River Bridge to 2nd Ave. is KELSO, 1.5 *m.* (26 alt., 6,749 pop.) (*see Tour 8e*), at the junction with US 99.

Left on Olympia Way to Ocean Beach Highway, US 830, which bears L. across flat country with numerous sloughs and inlets in dense growths of willows. During prohibition days this sparsely settled region, with its many creeks and heavy underbrush, was a haven for bootleggers.

STELLA, 54.2 *m.* (12 alt., 298 pop.), a dairying and lumbering village, received its name from the daughter of Richard Packard, who in 1880 established a store and post office here. During August, salmon from the Columbia abound near the mouth of Germany Creek. Black clusters of scavenger birds feed on the fish that die after spawning.

Several brightly painted buildings (L) constitute OAK POINT, 59.2 *m.* (94 alt., 177 pop.), where Mill Creek flows into the eddies of the Columbia River.

EAGLE CLIFF, 60.2 *m.* (110 alt., 16 pop.), represented on the highway by only a shed, is a village lying L. beneath a cliff on the river bank. Here the world's first commercial salmon cannery was built in 1865. In the early days all the work was done by hand, and great losses were caused by the slowness of the process. Chinese were employed for the most part.

COFFIN ROCK (L), 63.6 *m.,* is a small promontory crowned with cedar and coniferous trees projecting into the river; here the Indians buried their dead in canoes. The canoes were placed high in the cottonwood trees, their sharp prows pointed to the west with every paddle in place. The deceased were wrapped in their robes and furs and their wealth in beads and trinkets was placed at their feet. They lay in the war canoes awaiting the flood of life which prophecy said would come in some day with the tide. The last of the canoes was seen about 1850.

CATHLAMET (Ind. stone), 69.4 *m.* (340 alt., 621 pop.), a bustling river town and seat of Wahkiakum (Ind. tall timber) County, was thus named because of the rocky course of the river. Lewis and Clark in 1805-6 spelled it "Cathlamah" in their reports. Hotels, stores, and cafés border the crooked main street which follows the base of a steep hill overlooking the island-choked Columbia. Fishing, lumbering, canning, and trading are the major occupations. A short distance west of Cathlamet are a cheese factory, which produces some 600 pounds of fine cheese daily, and the International Wood Products Company Plant, which makes wooden containers for cheese products. Each day some 60,000 cheese boxes (made of spruce lumber, cut in blocks, kiln dried, edged, and cut to lengths) are shipped.

The Wahkiakum and Cathlamet Indians built their Indian cedar houses on the present site of Cathlamet. Panic-stricken by epidemics about the year 1825, the natives wandered homelessly about for several years. Some returned to old Cathlamet. John Wallaka (Ind. lizard) was one of the last to die. He asked to be buried in "a black diagonal suit, a blue shirt with pearl buttons, a red necktie and blue socks with white toes and heels."

Left from Cathlamet, a ferry (*infrequent*) connects with PUGET ISLAND, 1 *m.* (800 pop.), a green rectangle five miles long and two miles wide, bisecting the channel of the Columbia. A network of roads covers the island, much of which has been diked with the aid of Federal funds. Dairying is the principal industry. A few of the Puget Island folk, a large percentage of whom are Scandinavians, work the Columbia and the adjacent waters of the Pacific for salmon and other seasonal fish. The island was named by Lieutenant W. R. Broughton, October 1792, in honor of Lieutenant Peter Puget, officer aboard one of Captain Vancouver's ships. It was referred to by Lewis and Clark as Sturgeon Island.

Peppermint culture is profitable, with approximately 150 acres cultivated. The fragrant mint's dark green leaves, contrasting with their purple, pink, white, and violet flowers, are trucked to a central point and distilled into an aromatic essential oil. An acre of ground will often yield more than 50 pounds of oil, worth nearly $2 a pound.

Among the festivals celebrated by the Puget Islanders are Norwegian Independence Day, May 17; St. John's Feast, June 24; and the anniversary of the landing of Leif Ericson in America early in October 1,000 A.D. Scandinavian delicacies such as *lutefisk, pastejar,* goat cheese, and sugar-sprinkled *kaffebrod,* are included in generous *smorgasbords* (a kind of buffet lunch). Most of the festivities are livened with *schottische* and other folk dances, often executed to the raucous tone of the *hardengerfiddle,* an instrument with a resined wheel, motivated by a hand crank, which rasps against catgut strings producing melodies similar to a hurdy-gurdy. Several days of feasting mark the Christmas season. Jul Otta is a special candlelight service on Christmas Day.

At 71.2 *m.* is a junction with State 12-D, a gravel-surfaced road which penetrates the valley of the ELOKOMIN RIVER.

Picturesque SKAMOKAWA (Ind. smoke on the water), 77.7 *m.* (10 alt., 750 pop.), once called "Little Venice," is scattered about the mouth of winding, muddy Skamokawa Creek, which threads its way through a rocky gap to empty into the Columbia River. Ghost buildings cling to one bank of the creek, which during early settlement was the only means of transportation. A number of warped structures covered with circus posters, in the older part of town, are built on floats that rise and fall with the tide. The first co-operative creamery in the State is said to have been organized in Skamokawa in 1898. A shingle mill and rock quarry are active today. A county fair is usually held here in mid-September.

The highway rubs against rock cliffs and meanders through back yards to emerge finally by way of a cut through a stony ridge.

West of Skamokawa, US 830 enters the upper Grays River Valley. Dairy farms with unpainted, warped buildings, and a careless array of rail fences enclosing mud-splashed stumps, spread across the green meadow. After passing farms in the mountain valleys, US 830 climbs a steep winding stretch past a logged-off region, then into an area of virgin timber, where logging operation may be seen occasionally.

Over a bridge, 89.6 *m.,* US 830 crosses the Grays River, named in honor of Captain Robert Gray (*see History*). West of the bridge it parallels the river, which rolls along the floor of the valley. Rich dairy pastures alternate with groves of alder, maple, and other leafy trees.

GRAYS RIVER, 91.8 *m.* (112 alt., 40 pop.), trading and marketing center for the adjoining dairy region, is a cluster of buildings beside old maples. High hills contact the town. A co-operative dairy, a church, a store, and a few other enterprises are housed in neatly painted, well-kept buildings. The income of the town is supplemented by nearby logging.

The first forge brought into Grays River Valley is said to have produced everything from ox yokes to dental forceps. The smith, H. P. Anderson, made the forceps for Thomas A. Holden and pulled his tooth. Holden purchased the forceps and became the chief "tooth-puller" of the settlement.

West of the junction, the route descends into Deep River Valley with its thousands of acres of diked land tilled by Finnish fishermen and dairy farmers.

At 98.9 *m.* is a junction with a dirt road.

Right on this road which runs on top of a dike. A narrow area of sloughs and swamps stretch L. to heavily wooded hills. Deep River, a silent, slow-moving stream, where logs from near-by camps are rafted, separates the road from stretches of wet pasture land.

DEEP RIVER, 1.7 *m.* (113 alt., 301 pop.), center of a region of logging camps, is a cluster of impermanent-looking buildings edged between the river and the near-by hillside. There is a log dump in the town, and the great tires of heavy trucks have torn ruts in the dirt street.

At 104.7 *m.* is a junction with State 12-B, a gravel-surfaced road.

Left on this road is NASELLE, 0.9 *m.* (130 alt., 100 pop.), a dairying center in a sparsely settled district at the confluence of the Naselle and Deep Rivers. The town is named for a tribe of Chinook Indians who lived on the river banks. A State-operated salmon hatchery is here.

South of Naselle on State 12-B is KNAPPTON, 7.9 *m.* (133 alt., 39 pop.), a cluster of ancient buildings around a ferry slip. The KNAPPTON-ASTORIA FERRY (*car and driver,* $1*; passengers,* 25c*;* 4 *times daily*) crosses the Columbia River to Oregon.

State 12-B proceeds southwesterly, ending in MEGLER, 10 *m.* (88 alt., 10 pop.), (*see Tour 9d*), where it forms a junction with US 101. (see *Tour 9d*).

At 112 *m.* is JOHNSON'S LANDING, a crossroads point believed named in honor of Captain James Johnson, the first Columbia River bar pilot, who was drowned in 1854 when his sloop capsized during a storm.

Johnson's Landing marks the junction of the western terminus of US 830 with US 101 (*see Tour 9d*), 16 miles E. of the Pacific Ocean.

Tour 4

(Priest River, Idaho)—Newport—Spokane—Colfax—Pullman—(Lewiston, Idaho); US 195.

Idaho Line to Idaho Line, 151.8 *m.*

Great Northern Ry. parallels route between Newport and Spokane; Northern Pacific Ry. between Spokane and Pullman.
Concrete-paved or bituminous-surfaced roadbed throughout.
Hotel accommodations in cities and larger towns; auto camps, some with trailer facilities, in and near cities and towns.

This route, known locally as the Pend Oreille-Palouse Highway, roughly parallels the Idaho-Washington Line. US 195 cuts across the southwest corner of Pend Oreille County and runs almost due south through Spokane and Whitman Counties, swinging slightly to the east near the end of the route at the Idaho Line. It continues to Lewiston, Idaho, where it forms a junction with US 410 (*see Tour 2a*). The route traverses two distinctly contrasting regions, different in topography, vegetation, climate, economy, and cultural development, but held together by a common dependence upon Spokane, the hub city of the Inland Empire.

Section a. IDAHO LINE *to* SPOKANE, *49.1 m. US 185*

The northern section of the route winds through sparsely settled foothill country cut by small streams, dotted with lakes, and interspersed with prairies and shallow valleys. A hundred years ago these hills were covered with open forests of lodgepole and ponderosa pine, tamarack, and fir; the prairies were unbroken expanses of bunch grass; and the watercourses ran full and clear. Fur traders and trappers, who early in the nineteenth century began to trickle into this region, could find an abundance of beaver and muskrat along the lakes and streams and plenty of deer and bear in the woods. The few thousand Indians who hunted, fished, gathered roots and berries, and grazed their ponies on the bunch grass prairies had not disturbed the balance of nature. But these first nomadic white men were the vanguard of the army of settlers to follow. Before the century had closed, fur traders and trappers had become history, the Indians, much diminished in numbers, had accepted the confining life of the reservation, and the lumberman, the railroad builder, and the farmer were well on their way toward transforming the countryside. Today, most of the virgin timber has been cut, and the settlements which sprang up and flourished briefly around sawmills and logging camps are little more than crossroads villages, except where the cutover land has been cleared and successfully converted to agriculture.

Even the most casual visitor will be able to catch some hint of the geological story of this region. Along the greater part of the route, the land is marked by outcroppings of granite rock, formed under pressure, and then forced upward by successive convulsions of the earth. Occasional lava cliffs and patches of scab rock appear toward the end of the route. One of the latest chapters was written by the glaciers, which about 20,000 to 30,000 years ago retreated, after grinding their way southward, scouring out valleys, piling up hills, and leaving behind new lakes, dammed-up streams, and other evidences of glacial action.

US 195 crosses the IDAHO LINE, 0 *m.,* and the Pend Oreille River, or Clark Fork, five miles west of Priest River, Idaho. Not until 1906 was a bridge constructed across the river at this point. The new Interstate Bridge was built in 1926.

NEWPORT, 0.5 *m.* (2,124 alt., 1,174 pop.), seat of Pend Oreille County, is laid out on the gentle curve of a hill that slopes northeast down to the sweeping arc of the Pend Oreille River. Rising in the rugged Bitter Root and Rocky Mountains, this stream drains westward into Washington, and then, bending abruptly northward, flows into British Columbia, only to loop back to join the Columbia River almost directly upon the Canadian Boundary Line. In spring the river, fed by the rapidly melting snows of the mountains, rises rapidly, and the swollen waters creep dangerously near the top of the banks, sometimes overflowing them in places and flooding lowland areas. The danger of floods has been greatly increased by careless methods of logging and by the destructive fires that have swept over the logged-off areas and killed the protective covering of humus and vegetation of the watershed.

Newport began in the eighties as a village on the Idaho side of the river. The few settlers obtained their supplies in Sand Point, on Lake Pend Oreille, and transported them either by overland trail or down the river by raft or canoe. In 1890 a boat was put into this service from Lake Pend Oreille, and landings were constructed on the Washington side of the river. Stimulated by the mining boom in the Idaho mountains and by the extension of logging operations, both Old Town and New Port, as the Washington settlement was called, began to grow. Stores and saloons were opened, and Cottage House became a favorite stopping place for miners and prospectors. By 1892 the Great Northern Railway had laid its rails into New Port, and within a year the town was linked with the rapidly growing city of Spokane some 50 miles to the south. Expansion followed quickly; in a few years a substantial business district had been built along the river front and the residential area was beginning to creep up the hillside. Putting an end to the rivalry that existed between the towns on both sides of the river, the United States Government officially wiped Newport, Idaho, off the map, retaining only Newport, Washington. The report reads: "Newport, Idaho, moved 3,175 feet to Newport, Washington."

Although farming and mining contribute to its economic life, Newport today depends primarily, as did its growth in the past, upon logging and the manufacture of lumber products. The mills of the Diamond

Match Company, across the river in Idaho, draw their employees largely from Newport. The town is also the shopping and distributing center for the surrounding territory on both sides of the Washington-Idaho Line.

West of Newport US 195 winds through sparsely settled countryside along the rim of a narrow valley and down an easy grade. Bordering the road are green meadows which merge into a marsh visible a short distance to the right. There, amid the willows, cattails, and tules, blackbirds chatter in the summer and mud hens and grebes build their floating nests. Mallard ducks are plentiful, and occasionally a pintail or a butterball may be seen. Bordering the road as it continues down the valley are hay and grain fields, potato patches, and pastures where cattle and sheep feed. Leaving the valley, the highway traverses barren, burned-over uplands, where a few pine and fir trees still stand.

DIAMOND LAKE (R) (*camps and campsites; fishing; boats*), 9.2 *m.,* in a shallow depression on a high plateau, spreads over nearly 1,000 acres. Fed by large underground springs, its waters are always fresh and cool. The lake is well stocked with fish of many kinds—cutthroat, Eastern brook, and silver trout; bass, perch, crappie and whitefish. Surrounding it are small stock and dairy farms, chicken ranches, and patches of scrub timber.

Skirting the south shore of the lake, US 195 continues in a southwesterly direction. Scattered along the route are farms, usually small; green meadows alternate with dry bunch-grass pastures, fields of grain, and clumps of pines. Low hills partially covered with small second-growth pine and fir still give evidence of the destructive fires that have swept over them, leaving dead snags, blackened stumps and logs, dried-up streams, and eroded hillsides.

This region is marked by the frequent occurrence of granite cliffs and boulders formed during the Mesozoic era, when quantities of liquid granite were forced up and through the earth's crust. The lava flows of a later date apparently did not extend this far to the northeast. During the glacial ages, the ice sheet ground its way over this region, diverting the river now known as Clark Fork southward along practically the same course as that of the Little Spokane today. Not until the ice cap had retreated far to the north did the river resume its course. The lakes that dot southern Pend Oreille County are products of this glacial action.

PEND OREILLE STATE PARK (R), 17.6 *m.,* a 100-acre tract of virgin forest, was set aside from school lands in 1927. Except for considerable work in clearing out the underbrush and old logs, the forest has been left in its natural state. Spring Creek, only a few feet wide, flows clear and cold through the park; along its grassy banks are a number of choice camping grounds.

At 21.9 *m.* is a junction with a graveled road.

Right here 1 *m.* is ELOIKA LAKE (*fishing; boats*), seven miles in length and one mile wide. In former years this lake was surrounded by heavy forests, but logging operations followed by destructive fires have left little except patches of scrub pine and ugly, blackened scars.

Crossing the West Branch of the Little Spokane River, US 195 continues southward through Spokane County. In 1929 a disastrous fire swept over this area and left it a wasteland. Of late years, however, thousands of small fir and pine trees have sprung up and are rapidly hiding the fire-swept earth. Mingled with the evergreens are serviceberry, elderberry, and chokecherry shrubs. In the spring they brighten the landscape with their swaying, white-tipped branches, and in late summer, when their fruit is mature and ripe, they are alive with chattering sparrows and nervous bulfinches in search of food. In the lowlands toward the Little Spokane River (L) are groves of willow and alder and quaking aspen, whose leaves quiver and whisper with the slightest breeze. A striking feature of the landscape is the large number of huge granite boulders. Here and there along the highway are well-cultivated farms and stump ranches.

At 25.3 *m.* is a junction with a dirt crossroad.

Right here is MILAN, 1 *m.* (1,780 alt., 115 pop.), a village on the west bank of the Little Spokane River. Not many years ago, it was a prosperous sawmill town; today, it is little more than a few stores and small dwellings clustered around the dismantled sawmill.

CHATTAROY, 31.2 *m.* (1,800 alt., 65 pop.), a crossroads village, lies in a beautiful little valley. Out from the northeast the Little Spokane meanders, joining with Deer Creek at the village to form a stream 30 feet wide and 3 to 4 feet deep. Both the creek and the river are well-stocked with trout of several species. Mink, weasel, and a few raccoon are still found along these streams, and numerous beaver make dams and even raid the farmers' orchards, fields, and gardens.

The site of Chattaroy was a familiar spot for most of the early fur traders. Near the place where Deer Creek empties into the Little Spokane, the Colville-Coeur d'Alene and the Spokane House-Clark Fork trails crossed, and the Hudson's Bay Company utilized this protected valley as a camping ground and trading post. Before the coming of the fur traders, the Indians had from time to time established temporary villages here while they fished and hunted.

Permanent settlement dates from the early eighties, when Robert P. Cowgill settled here, opened a general store, and contracted to carry mail from Spokane Falls to Kidd, as the embryo settlement was named by the Post Office Department. In 1889, the Indian name, Chattaroy, was restored, largely because of the persistent agitation of Mrs. Cowgill.

At 36.2 *m.* is a junction with a graveled road.

Left here is COLBERT, 0.2 *m.* (1,823 alt., 40 pop.), a scattering of warped frame buildings. Thirty years ago Colbert was a booming lumber town with five sawmills, two saloons, three livery stables, two blacksmith shops, and several stores. Within a few years, however, the available supply of merchantable timber had been logged. One by one, the mills closed down and were dismantled, and most of the inhabitants who did not turn to agriculture moved away.

At 37.7 *m.* is a junction with a graveled road.

Left here across a rolling prairie dotted with bull pine and up a long, winding grade to the summit of MOUNT SPOKANE (5,208 alt.) and MOUNT SPOKANE STATE PARK, 21 *m.* Many years ago Francis H. Cook, pioneer Spokane newspaper editor, acquired land on the summit of the mountain, built a cabin there, and began a campaign to have the area set aside as a recreational center. For a long time the only way to reach the summit was by trail; then a poor road was built; in recent years the construction of a good road with an easy grade brings the park within an hour's drive from Spokane. From the lower pine-covered slopes the road winds upward, skirting the great ledges of weather-stained granite that jut out from the mountain side. Many species of wildflowers grow profusely on the forest floor, and in the open spaces are clumps of mountain ash, heavily loaded with scarlet berries in summer and early fall. The slopes are often carpeted with Indian bear grass, its great white tufts like ice cream cones on two-foot stalks. The bare summit on the mountain is a mass of light gray granite flecked with mica. On bright, clear days the granite appears almost white and the mica flashes in the sunlight. It is not surprising that the local Indians came to associate the mountain with the supernatural; and the Spokane (Ind. *Spehkunne,* sun people) apparently felt that they had a peculiarly close spiritual association with the sun.

On the summit of the mountain a lookout point offers a sweeping view of the Inland Empire. Here is a burnished-copper sun ball, four feet in diameter, mounted on a pedestal of native stone and concrete; on a clear day, it reflects the sun like a beacon. The ball was the gift of Spokane club women.

In recent years Mount Spokane has become a popular skiing center. Easily accessible from Spokane and other population centers in eastern Washington, the snow-covered slopes attract hundreds of skiers every week-end during the winter months. Ski tournaments are held here by the Spokane Ski Club.

South of the junction, US 195 swings slightly southwest across a windswept prairie broken occasionally by shallow draws and low knolls. During the dry summer months the land is an expanse of yellow grass except where the prairie has been put under cultivation. But in the spring the tufted, blue-green bunchgrass is sprinkled with golden sunflowers and deep blue lupine. Clusters of low-growing sand verbena, which flowers in lovely variegated colors, and clumps of gracefully swaying and fragrant serviceberry and wild cherry.

At 43.3 *m.* US 195 joins with US 395 (*see Tour 6a*), from this point the two highways coincide to Spokane.

The Lane of Remembrance (*see Tour 6a*), as this stretch of US 195-395 is known locally, runs through an open forest of bull pine. Here and there are basaltic rocks, evidence that the Columbia lava flow extended this far eastward.

SPOKANE, 49.1 *m.* (2,039 alt., 122,001 pop.), (*see Spokane*).

Section b. SPOKANE *to* THE IDAHO LINE, *102.8 m. US 195*

This section of US 195, known as the Inland Empire, or Palouse, Highway, traverses one of the most fertile farming areas in the United States. Practically the entire route runs through rolling hills, treeless except for clumps of willow and brush along the creeks and in the swampy lowlands. When the first settlers arrived, they found the entire region covered with lush bunchgrass, waist high in places. Here

Indian bands hunted, dug roots, and pastured their ponies. Quick to recognize the productivity of the soil, the newcomers staked claims, strung miles of barbed-wire fences, and set to work breaking the sod, in the meantime turning their cattle out on the range to fatten. Within a few years, thousands of acres had been planted to wheat and were producing exceptional yields.

Wheat continues to be the chief crop of the region. In the spring the entire countryside, seen from an eminence, is a checkerboard of green fields and dark brown squares of fallow land. Vagrant winds sweep over the hills toward the horizon, billowing the maturing grain like the waves of a heavy sea. By midsummer the wheat has ripened. Then the combines come, most of them tractor-operated, but a few still drawn by many teams of horses. Cutting wide swathes as they swing around the fields, they leave in their wake small piles of golden straw and dun-colored sacks of wheat. Seldom is a crop failure known, for the rainfall, although rarely more than 20 inches, comes in the fall and winter months when it is most needed, while the harvest months are almost always rainless.

The basis, however, for the productivity of this region is the soil. The top layer, averaging 10 to 12 inches, is rich brown silt, often exceedingly dark because of its humus content. Next is a lighter brown layer 30 to 40 inches deep. A third layer, from 50 to 75 feet in depth, is hardened light-yellow silt, or loess, which was deposited many thousands of years ago in lake bottoms. Apparently, all three are of the same material, differing only in hardness and in humus content. These layers rest upon a fourth layer of granite or basalt with no intervening material. For a long time geologists have puzzled over the mystery of how this Palouse soil was formed. One explanation was that the soil was decayed basalt. Today, opinion leans toward the theory that it was formed in the Pleistocene age by the depositing of wind-borne dust blown from arid to more humid regions, where it stuck. Whatever the origin of the famous Palouse, there can be no question as to the part it has played in the development of this section, nor about the urgency of checking the disastrous erosion which has already wrought great damage.

West of SPOKANE, 0 *m.,* US 195 turns sharply left down a steep grade and runs southward along the east bank of Latah Creek, a small stream that flows northward through a deep narrow valley to a confluence with the Spokane River. Clustered along the creek are several pleasantly shaded frame houses; surrounding them are small orchards, pasture lots, and truck gardens, many of them owned by Chinese and Japanese. Although it is within the corporate limits of Spokane (*see Spokane*), this district is distinctly suburban in character and seems isolated from the residences of the city proper which cling to the rim of the canyon, their terraced lawns creeping timidly a short distance down the precipitous sides. To the north, straddling the valley, is the gracefully arched, concrete LATAH CREEK BRIDGE, and beyond it two high steel railroad bridges. Below these bridges is HIGH BRIDGE PARK, an open pine woods cut by roads and bridle trails.

For years, LATAH CREEK was known as Hangman Creek, the name deriving from the hanging of Qualchan, a Yakima chief, by Colonel George Wright in 1858. In 1855, after the Walla Walla council (*see Walla Walla*), Kamiakin and other Yakima chiefs warned the intruding white men to stay out of the Yakima country or be killed. Shortly thereafter, Qualchan, a nephew of Kamiakin, with five other Indians encountered and killed a number of white men on the Yakima River. For this act Qualchan became a marked man.

In the guerilla warfare of the next three years, both Qualchan and his father, Owhi, took leading parts. Shortly after the Horse Slaughter Camp incident (*see Tour 1a*), Colonel Wright encamped on Latah Creek and summoned those Indian chiefs who had not yet made satisfactory treaties to a council. In response Owhi rode alone into the camp to discuss the possibility of peace. Having been led to disclose where Qualchan was camping, Owhi was promptly seized and put in irons. Then Wright sent a message to Qualchan that unless the son surrendered within four days the father would be hanged. What happened after this cannot be exactly determined. In his report for September 24 Wright stated briefly: "Qualchan came to see me at 9 o'clock, and at 9:15 he was hung." It seems possible, however, that when Qualchan came to the camp he was unaware that his father was a prisoner; perhaps he had been sent there by Kamiakin to discover the kind of treatment Wright intended to mete out to the recalcitrant Yakimas. Numerous objections were raised to the name Hangman Creek and, as a consequence, the legislature changed the name to Latah Creek.

The highway swings across Latah Creek and, continuing to parallel it, winds up an easy grade. Bull pine, with a scattering of fir and cedar, cover the lower slopes, becoming sparser near the top of the grade.

The Latah formation has had an interesting geologic history. Floods of lava advancing over the Columbia Plateau were checked by a line of hills near the present site of Spokane. Unable to enter the valleys to the east, the lava flowed south, thus damming their drainage. In time layers of clay and shale to a depth of some 1,500 feet accumulated on the bedrock of the lakes formed in the valleys behind these lava dams. In these Miocene lake beds are preserved fossil remains. Glaciers, however, advanced as far as this region, diverting many of the streams, including Latah Creek, southward; and, except where dams held back the rush of water, most of the soft clay and shale were washed away.

After reaching the top af the grade, US 195 cuts across a rolling plateau. Scattered farmhouses surrounded by small fields of wheat, patches of scrub pine, and stretches of scabland border the highway. As the route leads southward the soil becomes perceptibly darker and the patches of lava rock appear with less frequency. Here the Palouse country begins.

SPANGLE, **19.1** *m.* (2,432 alt., 203 pop.), a village of weather-stained houses clustered about a few brick buildings, is one of the oldest settlements in the Inland Empire. The first house built in the vicinity was erected in 1862 and for years served as a stopping place on the Mullan Road. In 1872, William Spangle, a Civil War veteran, and his family arrived from Walla Walla. Before the end of the summer Spangle, a skilled craftsman, with the aid of his two sons, had erected a house of hewn logs, finished with carefully made sills, frames, and doors, and roofed with pine shakes. Everything in the house but the square, hand-wrought nails brought from Walla Walla, and the flooring obtained from Scranton and Downing's little sawmill on the Spokane River (*see Spokane*), was the work of the Spangle family.

During the summer of 1872, settlers continued to arrive in such numbers that Spangle decided to start a school. With true communal frontier spirit, all set to work building a schoolhouse. Within a day, the walls and roof were finished, and before long the structure was completed and furnished with handmade desks and benches. This occasion called for a special celebration consisting of a day of feasting, horse racing, and story telling, topped off in the evening with a dance, for which music was furnished by an orchestra consisting of an organ, three violins, and a harmonica.

South of Spangle, US 195 begins to twist through the hills of the Palouse country. On either side of the road, an almost unbroken expanse of wheat fields and fallow land stretches toward the horizon. Until recent years, the usual method of cultivation was to plow the stubble under completely, a practice tending to result in great damage by erosion. In the spring, when the snows were melting rapidly, muddy torrents cut deep gashes in the hillsides and converted unprotected draws into hideous gullies. Equally destructive when the fields were dry were the strong westerly winds which swept tons of powdery soil away. Various State and Federal agencies have aided in making farmers aware of the waste involved in allowing erosion to proceed unchecked; and they now engage in such conservation practices as disking, contour farming, and seeding gullies to erosion-resistant crops.

PLAZA, 27.5 *m.* (2,353 alt., 250 pop.), a score of frame buildings, straggles along the highway and railroad track. Dominating the village are several wheat warehouses and a large grain elevator. In late summer trucks piled high with sacks of grain roll into town, and the farmer, his annual crop safely harvested, begins to study the quotations of the grain market and to figure his profits or, as frequently happened in recent years, his losses.

The route continues southward, skirting a rocky, pine-covered ridge that marks a divide from which some streams flow northward and others in a southwesterly direction. Here the terrain is marginal in character, resembling in some respects the lava formations of the Columbia Basin to the west and in others the Palouse country.

ROSALIA, 34.7 *m.* (2,237 alt., 598 pop.), in the narrow valley of Pine Creek, a self-sufficient modern town, is the marketing and servicing center for a prosperous farming area. Numerous stores, cafés, garages, and other business structures flank the main street from which side streets, bordered with locust, maple, and poplar trees, lead eastward to the residential part of town.

South of Rosalia US 195 crosses PINE CREEK, 35.5 *m.,* over a concrete-and-steel bridge. A short distance east of the highway is the hill where Lieutenant-Colonel Edward J. Steptoe and his troops made a stand against the Palouse Indians and their allies on May 17, 1858. Early in May the expedition, consisting of part of a company of infantry with two howitzers and three companies of dragoons, set out from Walla Walla to march through the Palouse country, in search of the Indians who had raided the Walla Walla Valley in April, and to investigate conditions in the Spokane and Colville areas. Finding that the northern tribes were hostile and united, and feeling that his troops were inadequately armed, Colonel Steptoe decided to withdraw. Before this withdrawal could be accomplished, however, the Indians attacked. After a fight-and-retreat running battle in which both sides suffered casualties, the troops escaped under cover of darkness from the hill where they had made their final stand, crossed Ingossomen Creek, now called Pine Creek, and dashed southward across the Snake River to safety.

To commemorate the Battle of Te-Hots-Nim-Me, or the Battle of Rosalia as this skirmish is usually called, a five-acre tract has been set aside on the hill to form STEPTOE MEMORIAL PARK. In the center of the park is a 26-foot monument of blue-gray granite, polished to the smoothness of glass. Some of the old settlers say that the battle was actually fought a mile southwest of the monument and that the fortified army camp was a mile north of it.

At 36.2 *m.* is a junction with a concrete-paved road, State 3, which bears the name Inland Empire Highway from this point. This road offers an alternate route to Pullman.

Swinging southeast, State 3 winds around the slopes of low hills that are cultivated to their very summits. On every hand is evidence of the stability of agriculture in this region: except for an occasional splash of yellow-blooming mustard, the fields are almost free of weeds; houses, barns, and outbuildings are neat and substantial; fence posts are erect and securely set and the strands of barbed wire are taut; new automobiles and trucks are seen very frequently.

OAKESDALE, 10 *m.* (2,300 alt., 590 pop.), spreads over a shallow valley. A small, compact business district centers in a few blocks along the highway, and along the railroad tracks are grain elevators, warehouses, and feed stores. Shading the quiet residential streets are large trees, many of them planted by the early settlers. On Saturday and during the planting and harvesting seasons the streets are lined with cars and all the stores are busy.

GARFIELD, 22 *m.* (2,485 alt., 674 pop.), like most of the towns of Whitman County, has an air of permanency. The men and women who first settled here came to find homes. Some came directly from the south and east; others hesitated for a short time in the Walla Walla country, crossing the Snake River after the danger of attack by Indian bands had passed. Many of the present-day farmers are the children or grandchildren of the original homesteaders. Garfield, served by good roads and three branch rail lines, is an important shipping and marketing town.

South of Garfield, the highway winds down an easy grade into the fertile Palouse River valley. For many years wheat was the most important crop of this area, but recently considerable acreage has been planted to peas, which are harvested green for canning or for the market, allowed to ripen for seed, or processed to produce split peas, green and dried.

PALOUSE, 31 *m.* (2,433 alt., 1,028 pop.), third largest city in Whitman County, is the commercial hub of the North Palouse River valley. The stream, which runs through the center of the town, is bordered by several blocks of one-story and two-story business buildings, and warehouses, industrial plants, and the railroad tracks. Wide paved streets lead to pleasant residential districts on the slopes of the hills that crowd down upon the town.

In the course of its existence Palouse has had a varied history. When Modoc Smith settled here in 1875 he found a well-defined trail running from the fertile valley, called Our Home by the Palouse Indians, eastward to the forested mountains of Idaho, where the natives went on hunting, fishing, and berry-picking expeditions. Among the early settlers were some of the Quantrell bands, outlaws who were active in Missouri and other border states during the Civil War. Later, when settlers began to come into the country in increasing numbers, and mining in Idaho began to boom, Palouse became a stage stop and outfitting point. In the eighties a flour mill and several sawmills were operating, and logs were floated down the river from the heavily forested Idaho mountains a few miles to the east. Today Palouse has several pea-processing and canning plants.

South of Palouse State 3 bends slightly toward the west through fields of peas, wheat, and forage crops. All the land is under cultivation except the narrow strips along the roadway, where dandelions, grasswidows, wild iris, roses, larkspur, thistles, goldenrod, and other flowers bloom in season.

KAMIAK BUTTE PARK (R) 34.8 *m.,* an undeveloped area of several hundred acres, centers around a rocky butte upon which is found the only standing timber in the region. Trails lead to the summit; which affords a fine panoramic view.

At PULLMAN, (see below) 46 *m.,* State 3 joins US 195.

South of the junction with State 3, US 195 climbs a slight grade and then descends with a sweeping curve to the valley of Thorn Creek, a tributary of Pine Creek, to THORNTON, 43.6 *m.,* a few small stores, a score of houses, and wheat warehouses strung along the railroad tracks.

With hardly a break in the wheat fields the highway crosses Thorn Creek and continues toward the Snake River. Within the experience of the present generation of farmers a major transition has taken place in the methods of cultivating, seeding, and harvesting. Headers, binders, and threshing machines which puffed and snorted as they expelled the chaff from blowers into golden pyramids, marked a definite technological advance. Large crews continued to be necessary, however, and unless a cook wagon accompanied the threshing outfit, the farmer's wife, with the aid of extra help, still had to prepare during harvest time enormous quantities of meat and gravy, home-baked bread, potatoes, peas, and corn on the cob, apple pie, and coffee for the hungry harvest hands. Then came the horse-drawn combine, which made its way along the slopes to the sound of cracking whips. Today, on the larger ranches, the one-operation, tractor-drawn thresher cuts its wide swath around the field, threshing as it goes, and pouring the grain into sacks, which are automatically discharged on the ground in piles of five or more. A few men perform the work that formerly required the strenuous labor of a crew of a score or more, and the migratory harvesters, once known as "bundle stiffs," now seek other employment.

CASHUP, 48.7 *m.* (2,328 alt., 50 pop.), an important wayside stop in pioneer days, was named for its first settler and storekeeper, James H. Davis, widely known as "Cash-up" Davis because he extended credit to no one. Now the town is marked by a small store, a grain elevator, and a few nondescript houses.

In Cashup is a junction with a dirt road.

Left here is STEPTOE BUTTE (3,613 alt.), 4 *m.*, the highest point between Mica Peak, southeast of Spokane, and the Blue Mountains. This pyramid-shaped mass, topped by an almost solid expanse of granite and basaltic rock, is without trees or shrubs, except for a few wild cherry and serviceberry bushes on its northern slope. The lower slopes are grass-covered and sprinkled with flowers in spring and early summer. Near the summit the grass is stunted and only a few sunflowers find sufficient moisture to survive.

A wagon road, not much more than a trail, winds up to the summit. From here on clear days the entire Palouse country can be seen—fields of grain, corn, and peas; patches of yellow stubble and dark-brown summer fallow; farm buildings flanked by clumps of evergreens and small orchards; and the canyon of the Palouse River, easily traceable by the dark line of trees along its course.

In 1888, Davis conceived the idea of building a resort on the bit of level land at the summit of the butte. He erected a two-story hotel there, with an auditorium and an observatory on the roof equipped with a telescope. After the death of Davis in 1895, the hotel fell into decay and finally burned to the ground. The whole butte was sold by the sheriff in 1902 for approximately $2,000.

STEPTOE, 52.7 *m.* (2,300 alt., 172 pop.), a trading center for farmers, lies on the floor of a wide valley. During harvest season trucks and wagons, piled high with sacks of grain, lumber into town to unload at the warehouses and elevator along the tracks, where box-cars stand on the sidings.

In Steptoe is a junction with State 11-c, an improved road.

Right here in a northwesterly direction about 12 *m.* is ST. JOHN (1,800 alt., 526 pop.), a prosperous shipping and marketing town on the Union Pacific Railroad.

EWAN, 20 *m.* (1,200 alt., 50 pop.) sprawls along the track of the Chicago, Milwaukee, St. Paul and Pacific Railroad.

In Ewan is a junction with a dirt road: Right here is ROCK LAKE, 1.7 *m.*, ten miles long and two miles wide, the southernmost and largest of a chain of three lakes. Except for the marshy lower end, where tules and cattails grow, it is hemmed in by steep rocky cliffs of volcanic origin. Numerous caves are found at the northern end and along the western side.

For a number of years Kamiakin, the Yakima chief who in the fifties took a leading part in the resistance to the white settlers, lived here. In 1861, urged by his homesick wife, he returned to Washington from voluntary exile among the Crow Indians. Eventually, Kamiakin was crowded off his farm, and about 1880 he died in his camp near the Palouse River.

The route continues southward, now skirting the base of a hill, now dipping through a shallow valley. After traversing several miles of wheat, corn, and pea fields, the highway descends gradually into a canyon, crosses the Palouse River, and then ascends an easy grade.

At 62.8 *m.* is a junction with US 295, a bituminous-surfaced road.

Right here on US 295 in a south-southwesterly direction through an area of large farms, usually planted to wheat. At widely spaced intervals are farmhouses, flanked by huge barns. Long steep grades, sweeping curves, and stretches of level road mark the route.

DUSTY, 18.5 *m.* (1,400 alt., 40 pop.), midway between Colfax and the Snake River, is a cluster of service stations and a garage and café fringed by a score of frame houses.

South of Dusty the country begins to level out between diminishing and receding hills. For several miles the highway follows Alkali Creek, dry except during spring freshets. Then hills begin again, low-lying and planted to wheat or left fallow. Since this section of Whitman County is swept by strong southwesterly winds, strip farming is widely practiced. The hills grow steeper, and the highway twists and turns as it descends a steep grade. Some of the slopes are too steep to cultivate; here cattle and sheep graze. Sagebrush begins to appear, and here and there are rocky cliffs and ledges.

The SNAKE RIVER BRIDGE, 36.1 *m.*, a steel span, straddles the river, which is very wide at this point. For many years prior to the completion of the bridge, a ferry operated by Robert L. Young, connected Whitman and Garfield Counties.

Leaving the river, US 295 winds up a steep, rocky grade, crosses Deadman Creek, again climbs until it reaches the summit of the grade, about 1,000 feet above the level of the river, and then winds downhill through wheat fields and range, where cattle and sheep graze.

DODGE, 47 *m.* (700 alt., 40 pop.), (*see Tour 2a*).

COLFAX, 63.6 *m.* (1,966 alt., 2,853 pop.), seat of Whitman County, spreads along both sides of the Palouse River. Hemming in the town are rounded hills, formerly covered with bunchgrass but now largely given over to wheat growing. Main Street, nearly a mile in length, parallels the river, which occasionally goes on a rampage, when the spring runoff is exceptionally rapid, and floods the lower levels of the town.

The business district, centered along Main Street, is a conglomeration of modern brick and concrete structures and dingy, old buildings, some of them dating back at least to the nineties. The residential districts also reflect contrast of yesterday and today—dilapidated frame houses, show places of early years, adjoin substantial, well-built, modern residences.

Colfax is, in fact, an old town, but it has not lost its vigor. When the ban against settlement in this region was lifted in 1858, settlers swarmed in over the trails which trappers, traders, missionaries, and soldiers had worn through the Palouse hills; but it was not until 1870 that the first settler, J. A. Perkins, took up land in the part of the Palouse River valley where Colfax is located. Perkins was soon joined by H. S. Hollingsworth, Captain James Ewart, and others. The settlement, at first called Belleville, was renamed in honor of Schuyler Colfax, Vice President of the United States during Ulysses S. Grant's first term. For a few years it was almost exclusively a cattle center, and during this period gun fights were everyday events and sometimes there were lynchings. By the end of the eighties, however, Colfax was deriving its main income from wheat, and had left behind its turbulent youth. Its history has since been marked by expansion rather than change, for, although other crops are grown in considerable quantities, wheat continues to be the main resource of the Palouse country;

and Colfax, like other Whitman County towns, is prosperous or hard-pressed depending on the wheat harvest and market prices.

South of Colfax US 195 veers slightly to the east and winds around low, rounded hills. Here are some of the finest farms in the county.

PULLMAN, 79.6 *m.* (2,345 alt., 4,417 pop.), home of the State College of Washington, and a commercial, grain storage, and shipping center, lies on the eastern edge of the wheat belt, only six miles west of the Idaho Line. On three sides of the town are the fertile, treeless hills of the Palouse, and on the east, beyond a rolling plain, are the forested foothills of the Moscow Mountains. Flowing through the town in a northwesterly direction is South Fork, a branch of the Palouse River.

The business district of Pullman centers at the intersection of Grand Street, identical with US 195, and Main Street, once the route of an Indian trail, and spreads over a hollow formed by three valleys. Modern stone, brick, and concrete buildings line the paved streets, with a few older structures standing here and there. Adjacent to the business area on the northwest is the industrial section, where numerous grain elevators, produce houses, and warehouses border the many railroad sidings. Streets, often winding and steep, run from the business center to attractive residential districts which spread over seven small hills.

Pullman began in the late seventies when Bolin Farr, a young cattleman, and two others filed homestead claims here. In rapid succession two stores, a tavern, a sawmill, a land agency, a school, and a church were established as settlers came to Three Forks, the name given the townsite when it was platted in 1882. Two years later the town was renamed for George Pullman, the sleeping-car magnate. In 1885 the Oregon Railway and Navigation Company's railroad was completed as far as the town, and in 1888 the Northern Pacific's branch was extended from Spokane. Succeeding years were marked by the rapid expansion of farming in the surrounding area and a corresponding growth of Pullman. Newspapers started and failed; twice the town was nearly destroyed by fire; artesian wells were developed. Depressions came, with the accompanying low price for wheat, failure of business houses, and closing of banks; but recovery followed, and slowly the town grew into the modern city of today.

Pullman is the commercial and cultural nerve center for the agricultural area around it. Its stores supply the local farmers with machinery, tools, automobiles, seed, house furniture, clothing, food, equipment, and services. But besides being a prosperous trading town, Pullman has another life which it derives from the State College of Washington. The thousands of students who flow into the town during the school year build a world of their own there, and the influence of the institution flows out into the surrounding countryside.

Shortly after Washington became a State, a commission was appointed to select a place for an agricultural, land-grant college. When the citizens of Pullman learned that the commissioners were due to visit their town, word was sent out for everyone to appear in the streets on the day set, in order to create an impression of great bustle and enterprise. The strategy proved successful. The commissioners found Pullman with the air of a boom town—cattlemen on horseback, farmers in their buckboards, pedestrians crowding the sidewalks and stores, two artesian wells spouting. The city offered 150 acres of land and $12,000 in cash, and on January 13, 1892, the Washington Agricultural College opened its doors as a co-educational institution to 46 students. Twenty-five years later the name was officially changed to the State College of Washington.

The STATE COLLEGE OF WASHINGTON is situated between Campus Ave., College Ave., Oak St., and College Farm. The main entrance is at Thatuna St. and Campus Ave.

Since the college opened in 1892, it has grown from one building and a registration of less than 100 students to the second largest educational institution in the State, with about 4,000 students. The college is housed today in several large, modern red-brick buildings, grouped in harmony with a landscape of park-like woods, flower-bordered walks, and spacious lawns. Although started as an agricultural college, it has expanded its curriculum to include arts and sciences other than those related to agriculture: engineering and mechanical arts; mining and geology; home economics; veterinary medicine; pharmacy; education; music, literature, and fine arts; physical education and military science and tactics. Supplementing the usual classroom and laboratory work, a practice farm and an experiment station provide the opportunity to put theory into practice.

The E. A. BRYAN HALL, a three-story, red-brick structure, with a square tower rising two stories above the main facade, is the center of extracurricular activities other than athletics. The south wing contains the COLLEGE AUDITORIUM, which has a seating capacity of 1,175, a serviceable stage, and a pipe organ. The entire north wing is occupied by the COLLEGE LIBRARY (*open 8-10 weekdays, 2-6 Sun., special hours in summer*), second largest land-grant college library in the Nation not supported by endowment. There are more than 330,000 bound volumes and approximately 1,500,000 pieces of unbound material. The building was named for President Emeritus E. A. Bryan, who served as active head from 1893 to 1916.

COLLEGE HALL, a four-story building, houses the departments of English, Business Administration, Pharmacy, and Education. The print shop and offices of *The Evergreen,* student publication issued thrice weekly, are in the basement of College Hall.

The ADMINISTRATION BUILDING, a four-story structure, is the central structure of the group. In it are the principal administrative offices and the Extension and Placement bureaus.

ROGERS FIELD AND ATHLETIC PLANT includes the men's and women's gymnasiums and the field house; here, too, is a regulation-size football field. Rogers Field is an eight-acre area with a quarter-mile cinder track, a horseshoe-shaped stadium capable of seating nearly 25,000, a baseball diamond, tennis courts, and a golf course.

Other buildings are VAN DOREN HALL, occupied by the departments of Music and Speech, HOME ECONOMICS BUILDING, SCIENCE AND ARTS BUILDING and SCIENCE HALL, the MUSEUM, WILSON HALL, the MECHANIC ARTS BUILDING, and FINCH MEMORIAL HOSPITAL.

The STATE FARM includes six soil-conservation plots located on the campus. Among the chief activities carried on here are experiments in plant breeding—the farm has had much success in developing new varieties of wheat suited to the soil and climate of the Palouse country. Many different crops are analyzed, and experimentation is conducted in tillage and crop rotation. Branch stations are maintained at Lind, Long Beach, Prosser, and Puyallup. The STATE COLLEGE EXPERIMENTAL STATION, a 200-acre farm, located three miles northwest of Pullman on the Pullman-Palouse Highway, has developed new methods of farming. A soil-conservation NURSERY is two miles southeast of Pullman on the highway to Moscow, Idaho.

South of Pullman, US 195 swings southeast toward the Idaho Line. Wheat fields continue to line both sides of the highway. In the distance are the blue-green Moscow Mountains.

COLTON, 93.9 *m.* (2,564 alt., 269 pop.), is a village of well-kept lawns, shaded streets, and substantial buildings, neatly arranged on a large flat bordering the main street, identical with the highway.

UNIONTOWN, 96.7 *m.* (2,575 alt., 332 pop.), so nearly resembles Colton that the two have been called sister towns.

The OLD COLLINS ROADHOUSE (R), 96.8 *m.,* stands at a fork in the road. The barn and some of the outbuildings are still occupied, but there is little to remind one of the days when this was a stopping point for stages and express riders.

The route continues southeast, winding down a grade to the IDAHO LINE, 102.8 *m.,* ten miles north of Lewiston, Idaho, the junction of US 195, US 95, and US 410 (*see Tour 2a*).

Tour 4A

Newport—Cusick—Ione—Metaline Falls—(Nelson, B. C.); State 6.
Newport to the Canadian Line, 76.4 m.

Bituminous-surfaced or graveled roadbed throughout.
Chicago, Milwaukee, St. Paul and Pacific freight line parallels route.
Limited hotel accommodations and few camps.

Throughout practically the entire route, State 6, often called the Pend Oreille Highway, parallels the Clark Fork River, which bisects Pend Oreille County, one of the most sparsely populated in the State. Swinging in a westerly direction from Newport, the highway climbs for a few miles and then, turning to the north, winds along the west side of the river as far as Metaline Falls. Here it crosses to the east bank and continues northward to the Canadian Line.

The route is marked by a succession of logged-off and forested hills, stump ranches, valley farms, and small mill and mining towns. Ages ago this region was covered by glaciers, which ground their way southward, forcing the river to reverse its direction. When the glaciers retreated, the river resumed the northward course.

North of NEWPORT, 0 *m.* (*see Tour 4a*), State 6 leads through heavy forests of pine, tamarack, and fir. Rising from the deep cleft of the river's channel are benchlands, a series of ascending terraces, which break into steep, rugged mountain slopes. East of the river the Kaniksu National Forest extends into Idaho. After climbing for a few miles the highway dips sharply down to the benchlands. This is a region of cutover lands, with stumps, snags, and small second-growth trees.

At the beginning of the century, a vast forest spread over these foothills and up the mountain slopes. In the spring, when the heavy blanket of snow melted, the water level of the river, and of the numerous small streams draining into it, rose; but serious floods were rare, the dense woods and the underbrush holding back part of the water. Within a generation, however, logging operations have denuded much of the region, and fires have destroyed what remained of the protective covering. Today most of the small streams are silt-laden torrents in the spring, but turn to dry channels as summer advances.

DALKENA, 11.4 *m.* (2,000 alt., 25 pop.), an almost deserted village, stands slightly above the river. On both sides of the tracks of a branch line of the Chicago, Milwaukee, and St. Paul Railway are the remains of a big lumber mill that burned in 1935—the planer, the dry kiln, and the burner, all stripped of machinery, and the charred remains of the mill itself. A few dilapidated houses and a little schoolhouse are scattered up the hill. In 1902 the Dalton and Kennedy Sawmill was built, and for a number of years the town prospered. Even before the destruction of the mill, however, the supply of timber was nearing exhaustion. Still visible in the river are jam breakers, resembling lean-to huts on pilings; and below is a quiet lagoon where a few years ago thousands of logs floated.

Along the route at frequent intervals are stretches of blackened hillside, sprinkled with charred snags and logs, residue of the destructive forest fires. By midsummer the trees are dry as tinder and require only a chance spark from a donkey engine, a burning match carelessly dropped, or a bolt of lightning to burst into flame. A tiny blaze fanned by dry winds will become a roaring, moving wall of reddish flame and black smoke. An army of firefighters, with shovels, axes, and dynamite, do what they can to check the fire, but before a blaze is brought under control, it usually has destroyed many square miles of timber and brush, homes, and even small towns. Even many miles away the air is heavy with smoke, through which the sun is seen as a smoldering red disc.

At 16.6 *m.* is a junction with a dirt road.

Right here is USK, 0.2 *m.* (2,051 alt., 100 pop.), with stores, a post office, and a service station, along the flats west of the river. Some logging is still being done in the vicinity, but the merchantable timber is almost exhausted.

The history of the district around Usk is in a measure typical of the county. Isolated from population centers and off most rail lines, this region was not opened to logging operations until about the beginning of the century. Exploitation was rapid, boom times and depressions alternating with the fluctuation in the prices and the demand for lumber. Rapidly logging operations ate into the forests, leaving behind large areas of stump lands, which were then offered at about ten or twelve dollars an acre. Land-hungry men and women, seeing a possibility of realizing the American dream, bought, cleared, and attempted to farm this land, little realizing that it costs from one to three hundred dollars to clear a single acre. Even when cleared the land was often unproductive, because of its gravel or clay composition.

Many families moved elsewhere; those who remained, disheartened and disillusioned, struggled on, trying to make a living by growing potatoes and forage crops, selling milk and butter, and, if any trees remained, by cutting cordwood, frequently the farmer's best crop. Much of the land around Usk is now cleared of farmers and will be returned to the status of timber land.

The side road continues eastward over a bridge to the site of St. Ignatius Mission and the KALISPEL INDIAN RESERVATION, 2 *m.* Here on 5,000 acres live about 100 Indians, most of them very poor. About the middle of the nineteenth century Father de Smet and Father Hoecken built a mission near the bank of the river. One spring, high water destroyed the buildings and washed away most of the soil. The mission was not rebuilt.

At 18.5 *m.* is a junction with a dirt road.

Right here to CUSICK, 0.5 *m.* (404 pop.), surrounding the tall, aluminum-painted water tower and the black stacks of the Diamond Match Company's plant. The streets of Cusick jog to conform to the line of the fence around the mill yard. The town, named for Joe Cusick, a homesteader of the early nineties, was started in 1902.

North of the junction, the highway passes a succession of lumber-yards, traverses a wide level valley rimmed by hills, where forested areas alternate with fenced pastures, and descends by a circuitous course to a lower benchland. Here are a few small orchards, fields of timothy and redtop, and a few dairy farms.

JARED, 28.6 *m.* (2,060 alt., 20 pop.), with a post office, a tavern, and a general store, clings to the side of the road. Here the mountains close in on the valley, and the river flows quietly for a short distance between its rocky walls.

The highway, continuing in a generally northerly direction, swings slightly eastward, crowded to the very edge of the river by the encroaching mountains. Pine and tamarack grow along the steep hillsides and, rooted in narrow ledges, lean over the brink of the canyon. Most of the merchantable timber has been logged in the immediate vicinity, but in the river log booms can be seen occasionally.

BLUESLIDE, 37.5 *m.* (2,067 alt., 80 pop.), a few neatly painted houses surrounded by gardens and small orchards, is a center of valley farms and dairy ranches.

North of Blueslide, the highway alternately climbs steep slopes, curving sharply around jutting rocks, and descends sharp grades. Along the route are evidences of abandoned logging operations—dismantled mills, empty houses, the bed of a railroad spur line where the track has been torn up.

IONE, 51.5 *m.* (2,095 alt., 594 pop.), the second largest town in the county, is largely dependent on the sawmill of the Panhandle Lumber Company, which employs about 150 workers. About a mile northeast of town is some good skiing terrain, and the winter festival of the Ione Ski Club is a popular local event.

In 1906 an English engineer built a Portland cement plant about one and one-half miles north of Ione. This venture, one of the first attempts to make cement in this State, failed, and in 1934 the abandoned plant was destroyed by fire.

The narrowing channel of the river is visible at 53.9 *m.;* here is the approach to BOX CANYON, the purple-gray portals of which stand out sharply. The canyon is 1,200 feet long, and the rocky walls range from 20 to 100 feet in height. The white water flows with extraordinary rapidity through the narrow gorge. Logs, which are still sent down Box Canyon, whirl in the narrow corridor before they go booming over Metaline Falls (*see below*).

At 58.5 *m.* is SWEET CREEK BRIDGE. Dark forests of pine and fir are spotted with the golden-brown of tamarack. On a high embankment, State 6 crosses the 5,000-foot tunnel of the American Lead and Zinc Smelting Company development, 59.5 *m.* The Pend Oreille Mine and Metal Company's plant is the chief industrial development at METALINE, 60.5 *m.,* on the west bank of the Clark Fork River.

State 6 ascends a slow grade north of Metaline. At 65.1 *m.* is a junction with a dirt road.

Left here 10 *m.* to the west bank of Z Canyon, 18 feet wide and 400 feet deep; at 11 *m.* is Gardiner Cave, which may be explored for 600 feet. In the cave are stalactites and stalagmites and other beautiful formations. Two large fluted pillars, dividing the main passageway, display all the colors of the spectrum, with violet and pink predominating. Numerous nacreous pillows rise from a few inches to several feet. In another section a curious formation resembles a frozen waterfall; over it hangs a canopy of glistening icicles of lime. Crystal formations hang like chandeliers from many points on the ceiling.

State 6 crosses the Clark Fork River on a high narrow bridge, 66.1 *m.* to METALINE FALLS, a cascade with a 19-foot descent. At the foot of the falls is Dudenay Trail, one of the most often used of the fur-traders' trails. David Thompson, who twice made the trip to the falls, recorded the name of the Indians of the region, the Kalispelus.

METALINE FALLS, 66.4 *m.* (1,925 alt., 316 pop.), occupies a rocky, sloping bench on the east bank of the Clark Fork River. The town was founded in 1910, and the promotion of the Mammoth and Morning mines brought the first settlers to the site. Silver, lead, cement materials, fire clay, and lime are found in this region. Mining activities, as elsewhere in the State, have known periods of boom and decline.

The Grange and the Nonpartisan League have considerable strength in the Metaline Falls vicinity. It is said that, in its time, the I.W.W. had great influence in this region, even among the farmers.

Important plants are those of the Lehigh Cement Company, the Pend Oreille Mines and Metal Company, American Lead and Zinc Company, and the Metaline Mining and Smelting Company. Two hydroelectric plants supply power for municipal and industrial use.

At 63.9 *m.* is a junction with two side roads.

Right here on a bituminous-surfaced road to SULLIVAN LAKE (*camp grounds; resort; fishing and boating facilities*).

Left on a graveled road to the GRANDVIEW MILL, the concentrator of the American Lead and Zinc plant.

At 72.4 *m.* is a junction with a trail.

Left here 1.5 *m.* to the east bank approach to Z CANYON (*see above*).

The Customs and Immigration station at the Canadian Line is reached at 76.4 *m.*

Tour 5

Davenport—Hunters—Kettle Falls—Marcus—Northport—Velvet—(Paterson, B. C.); State 22.

Davenport to the Canadian Line, 121.8 *m.*

Graveled or bituminous-surfaced roadbed; dangerous curves; narrow roadway. Accommodations limited except in one or two larger towns; service stations at widely spaced intervals.

This route traverses one of the most sparsely settled and most isolated parts of the State. Leading directly northward, it runs through hilly wheat lands, marked here and there by patches of scrub pine, sagebrush, and scablands, until it winds down a steep grade and across the Spokane River at a point about two miles east of its confluence with the Columbia. North of the crossing, the route continues upward through rugged hills to practically treeless benchlands. Along the east bank of the Columbia is a broken fringe of peach and apple orchards; the arable benches are largely planted to wheat, and the steeper slopes are given over to grazing. Some lumbering is still being carried on in the pine- and tamarack-covered foothills. Scattered throughout the region are small mines, and also abandoned mines that were worked in the seventies, eighties, and nineties, when on nearly every lonely creek some miner patiently washed the gravelly sands for gold. Today most of the mining is in hardrock, although some small-scale placer operations are being carried on.

Cutting across US 395, State 22 continues northeast along the east bank of the Columbia, which here cuts a tortuous channel through granite and other hard rocks to Northport and the Canadian Line. Ages ago volcanic eruptions and glacial action left their marks deep upon this region, which includes the northern limit of the lava flows and the southern limit of the glaciers.

Some of the most thrilling pages of Northwestern history were written about this area; and again history is being made in the construction of the Grand Coulee Dam (*see Tour 1B*) and the creation of one of the largest man-made lakes in the world. As a result, a mass migration is taking place, for the sites of ten towns, the homes of some 3,000 persons, will be entirely flooded by the rising waters.

In 1934 surveyors began their work in the reservoir area above Coulee Dam, running lines along the Columbia and tributary canyons to determine the water level of the huge artificial lake. Although the normal level of the lake-to-be will be approximately 1290 feet above sea level, the actual height of the dam, 1310 feet above sea level, determines the lake shore. When the work of surveyors was completed, the immensity and intricacy of the problems ahead became clear.

Almost 100,000 acres of land had to be acquired by the Government and made ready for a lake bed. More than 5,000 buildings were to be demolished or moved. Ten towns with postoffices—Keller, Lincoln, Peach, Gerome, Inchelium, Figgord, Daisy, Kettle Falls, Boyds, and Marcus—were doomed. Railroad lines, factories, and nearly 7,000 town lots had to be bought. More than 200 miles of highway, 26 miles of Great Northern trackage and roadbed, and 14 new bridges had to be built. It will cost the Government approximately $10,000,000 to acquire all property in the area and another $10,000,000 for clearing and reconstruction work. These problems are all in the hands of the United States Bureau of Reclamation. Much of the work has already been done, but much more is still to do. Where old landmarks have been destroyed, it is hoped that gardens and orchards, beautiful homes, and new cities will rise in the reclaimed areas, for an estimated population of 1,200,000.

North of DAVENPORT, 0 *m.* (*see Tour 1a*), State 22 traverses an uneven plateau, broken here and there by small hills. The greater part of this area is planted to wheat. Most of the farms are large, and, although the houses and barns are usually weatherworn and dilapidated, the land is well cultivated. Gradually the terrain becomes more rugged, and the hills, partially covered by scraggly bull pine, crowd closer to the highway. Alarmed by passing automobiles, plump ground squirrels, numerous in this section, tumble into their burrows with shrill cries.

At 13.2 *m.* is a junction with a dirt road.

Left here in a northwesterly direction, up a steep grade through second-growth scrub pine to slightly rolling terrain. On either side of the road are wheat lands broken by patches of range and grass-covered hills. Neat farmhouses are flanked by large barns, windmills, numerous outbuildings, small orchard and garden tracts. A white schoolhouse nestles at the foot of a hill. Near by are an old log cabin, relic of pioneer days, a steepled, white church, and another schoolhouse.

LINCOLN, 10.5 *m.* (1,800 alt., 200 pop.), a short distance from the confluence of the Spokane and Columbia Rivers, will be moved to higher ground when the waters rise behind Grand Coulee Dam. The peach orchards along the river below Lincoln are already being uprooted and burned.

Right from Lincoln on a dirt road is the SITE OF THE UNITED STATES ARMY POST, FORT SPOKANE, erected in 1881. For a time it was occupied by a small detachment of infantry, but as the Nez Percés on the Colville Reservation (they were military prisoners after the Chief Joseph War of 1877) were giving no trouble, the fort was abandoned in the early years of the twentieth century. Here the Spokane River cuts its way towards the Columbia.

North of the junction, State 22 begins to wind down a steep grade on the west side of the narrow, deep Spokane River Canyon. Sharp curves (*caution; dangerous when wet*), rocky cuts, precipitous cliffs, and patches of timber on high hills mark the route. For several miles it skirts the western rim of the river; now and then a crudely made road leads off to some ranch house hidden in a deep draw between the hills. Drab farmhouses, in windswept yards, cling to the steep hillsides or cower behind protecting bluffs. Dead and dying orchards, old log cabins, the staring windows of deserted houses, all point backward to pioneer days.

Seen from the vantage point of DE TILLIAN BRIDGE, 23.1 *m.*, a steel structure at the bottom of the steep grade, the country is wild, rough, and beautiful. Hemming in the narrow rocky canyon are jagged hills, green in early spring and sprinkled with wildflowers. At their base is a narrow rugged valley, through which flow the angry blue waters of the Spokane River.

Now the highway begins to climb, twisting and turning through the draws between the hills. A backward glance from some safe point at the top of the grade is well worth the few minutes consumed; below, the river makes its tortuous way through the deep canyon, and beyond it are quiet valleys and rolling yellow-brown hills.

Northward the highway winds and climbs, with short intervening stretches of level road. Familiar things take on added significance in this sparsely settled expanse—a line of white birch trees, a man on horseback seen against the horizon, a small Catholic church of wood and stone cemented with red mortar, a gas station, cattle feeding by a haystack, a stand of timber. Gradually the valley begins to open, as the route nears the Columbia River.

FRUITLAND, 36.8 *m.* (1,831 alt., 35 pop.), was founded in 1886. At one time, this district, once called Spring Valley, was also called Robbers' Roost; and it is said to have been one of the toughest hell holes in the State in early days, a rendezvous for desperadoes and cattle thieves.

Fruitland will not be affected by the dammed-up waters of the Columbia, while Gerome, a few miles southwest, will be wiped out. The Old Queen mine here still employs a dozen men.

HUNTERS, 41.2 *m.* (1,610 alt., 200 pop.), at the end of a dangerous grade, is a bustling little town above the boulder-strewn east bank of the Columbia. A small, compact business center is fringed by frame houses, a neat white church, and a dance hall. Across the river the high bluffs rise, chalky-white in brilliant sunshine.

Roughly paralleling the river, State 22 threads its way northward. On the east, the Huckleberry Mountains are a blue-green line; on the west, beyond the Columbia, which can be seen through the trees, is the Kettle River Range about 20 miles distant.

North of CEDONIA, 44.8 *m.* (1,500 alt., 26 pop.), the route runs through a draw and up a grade. Hills of greatly varying height and contour border the highway. Most of this area has been logged off, but much is again forested with young pine, fir, and tamarack. At BISSELL, 50.9 *m.* (1,800 alt.), are three temporary buildings of a reforestation project.

When the river is at flood level, DRIFTWOOD ISLAND, at 56.7 *m.,* serves as a harbor for drifting logs and uprooted trees. GIFFORD, 57.1 *m.* (1,250 alt., 39 pop.), was the trading point for several poultry breeders and orchardists of this district, until dust storms, cloudbursts, low prices, and unseasonable weather drove them away. The village, named for James O. Gifford, a pioneer of 1890, will soon lie under ninety feet of water.

Left from Gifford across the river (*ferry: day rate, 50c; night rate, $1*) is INCHELIUM, first called Buffalo and later Troy. Since the site will be under 135 feet of water when Coulee Dam Lake reaches its final level, the inhabitants are beginning to move to the benchland, where the town, which is an Indian agency, will take new roots. Timber and brush and old buildings are already being removed or burned.

DAISY, 60.8 *m.* (1,235 alt., 80 pop.), a scattering of old business buildings and houses on a hillside, will also be abandoned when the water rises. In early days, placer mining attracted many to the upper Columbia and tributary streams.

Near Daisy are two small silver-lead mines, the Tempest and the Daisy. Some dragline placer operations are still yielding meager returns. Considerable farming and cattle ranching are carried on in the surrounding country.

State 22 winds northward along the benchland above the river, which is deep and placid at this point. The west bank is marked by a series of benchlands, gargantuan steps leading to the irregular hills beyond. To the northeast rise the saw-toothed Huckleberry Mountains. Orchards, farms, and stands of tamarack, pine, and fir border the highway.

This route along the east bank of the Columbia was followed by John McLeod, superintendent of the Hudson's Bay Thompson River

District, when in 1826 he drove the first herd of cattle to be brought into this Northwest region through hundreds of miles of Indian country to Fort Colvile.

At 71.6 *m.* is a junction with a dirt road.

Left here 0.5 *m.* to the point where the Columbia flows into narrow Rickey Canyon.

At 73.3 *m.* is a junction with another dirt road.

Right here is the SILVER QUEEN MINE, 2.5 *m.*, a small mine that has been worked for about 40 years. The concentrates are shipped by truck to Kellogg, Idaho, for smelting. The owner of the mine, J. S. Budd, a Seventh-Day Adventist, refuses to sell unless the prospective buyer promises to observe Saturday as a day of rest.

North of the junction the highway traverses rugged terrain, partially a semidesert waste, relieved by patches of second-growth evergreens and a fringe of irrigated apple orchards, their pipelines arching down to the river.

KETTLE FALLS, 75.6 *m.* (1,300 alt., 560 pop.), a thriving town with broad main street, modern hotels and business buildings, and an airfield near by, stands on a flat above the river. It is another of the doomed towns, for the backwaters of Coulee Dam will cover it to a depth of 30 to 35 feet. The settlers here planned to move, but in doing so, to retain the town's identity. They have accomplished this object through an amazing bit of strategy.

About four miles north of Kettle Falls is Meyers Falls, a village of approximately 100 population. When citizens of Kettle Falls knew their town was doomed to be flooded, they asked Meyers Falls to vote for consolidation, and a majority of the populations of the two towns voted accordingly. Kettle Falls then annexed a 60-foot strip of land that paralleled the highway between the two towns, and later a second strip completely surrounding the town of Meyers Falls; and then it started to move its citizens. When the vote of consolidation came, a majority vote retained the name of Kettle Falls. The two post offices still exist, but probably this problem will be solved when the floodwaters cover the site of the original Kettle Falls.

North of Kettle Falls the route swings eastward for a short distance, State 22 coinciding with US 395 (*see Tour 6a*). At 78 *m.* State 22 and US 395 separate again. State 22, the main route, turns left across the Colville River meadows.

At 81.7 *m.* is a junction with a graveled road.

Left here to the SITE OF OLD FORT COLVILE, 0.5 *m.* Erected in 1826, this fort, named for Lord Colvile, served the Hudson's Bay Company for many years (1826-71). With its history is interwoven the lives of John Work, Archibald and Angus McDonald, and other factors of the post. Around the fort, stock raising, farming, milling, and trading began. In 1853 Angus McDonald entertained Governor Isaac Stevens and Captain George B. McClellan at the fort. "I had fifty imperial gallons . . . to entertain the gentlemen," wrote McDonald. "The governor was rather fond of it. 'Mac' he said, 'this is powerful wine.' The captain put his arm around my neck and whispered in my ear:

'Mac, my proud father, too, was at Culloden,' and . . . slipped from the sofa to the floor."

MARCUS, 83.0 *m.* (1,260 alt., 393 pop.), six miles above Kettle Falls, will disappear beneath 50 or 60 feet of water. The town will be moved to a higher bench about a mile and a half farther north, near the big plants of the Spokane-Portland Cement Company and the United States Gypsum Company. A new schoolhouse has already been built at a cost of $135,000.

The town, the oldest in Stevens County, was named for Marcus Oppenheimer, first settler and pioneer merchant. In 1859 the British Boundary Commission built comfortable barracks here. Oppenheimer used these barracks until 1881, when, after the withdrawal of American troops, the buildings were removed.

Around Marcus is a farming and dairying region. There is some mining and considerable prospecting along the river and in the near-by hills.

North of Marcus, State 22 leads through brush-covered hills above the Columbia River Valley. Until recently the route led, twisting and turning, along a narrow ledge at the top of sheer cliffs, hemmed in on the right by steep mountain walls. This twisting road, known as the Seven Devils, with seven switchbacks, was abandoned when the new highway was cut through at a higher level. Along this part of the river, Chinese miners worked so diligently in the sixties and seventies that every trace of soil was sluiced away; nothing remains on the fantastically gullied slope except huge boulders and barren rock.

The SPOKANE-PORTLAND CEMENT PLANT (R), 88.3 *m.*, a large concrete structure, manufactures and ships considerable quantities of cement. A mine back in the hills furnishes the rock for the mill.

In EVANS, 89 *m.*, is a plant (L) operated by the American Gypsum Company. From the quarry on the hill opposite the plant, an elevated cable carries raw material to the mill. A screen hangs across the road to protect traffic from falling boulders.

North of Evans the highway, following the river, winds between narrow benches, rising to rugged hills, dotted with pine and tamarack, or western larch—a graceful deciduous tree with long, slender branches thickly covered with soft short needles. In the autumn, these needles turn a rich golden brown. Another tree occurring in the upper valley is the western yew; its tough-fibered wood was esteemed by the Indians for making paddles and other smaller articles. Much of the rock in this region is granite, which was forced upward under great pressure during the Pleistocene age.

Vegetation between Kettle Falls and the Canadian Boundary has been stunted, or in some cases destroyed, by fumes from a large smelter at Trail, British Columbia. These fumes tend to follow down the valley of the Columbia, settling to the ground along the way, especially when humidity is high. Farmers are seeking compensation from the owners of the smelter for damaged orchards and ruined fields.

Seldom out of view for any considerable length of time, the green-blue river flows between sloping banks. When the water is low in late summer, these sandy banks and jutting gravelly bars resemble ocean beaches.

NORTHPORT, 112.3 *m.* (1,333 alt., 391 pop.), spreads along a valley below Silver Crown Mountain. On the right rises the white-brick chimney of the smelter, now closed, which in former years employed 500 men. Now many of the houses are vacant and falling to pieces. The United States Customs and Immigration is housed in a building near the Great Northern Railway track.

Today there is a little activity in the lumber industry. A sawmill, approximately 13 miles out of town, employs about 50 men during the summer months. A few piles of lumber and logs line the railroad track. Here the Long Lake Lumber Company has cut thousands of pine and tamarack trees, which are excellent for ties and poles. When the Columbia River has backed up behind Grand Coulee Dam, the waters will lap at the edge of Northport.

North of Northport the highway crosses the Columbia River and runs through a narrowing valley into hilly terrain. VELVET, 121.3 *m.* (1,600 alt., 50 pop.), is a border town.

State 22 ends at the CANADIAN LINE, 121.8 *m.,* about two miles south of Paterson, British Columbia.

Tour 6

(Cascade, B. C.)—Laurier—Colville—Spokane—Pasco, US 395.
International Boundary to Pasco, 275.5 *m.*

Great Northern R.R. parallels route between Laurier and Spokane; Northern Pacific between Spokane and Pasco. Route is used by the Spokane Auto Interurban Line.
Highway paved or hard-surfaced entire route.
Accommodations in larger towns; cabin-camps at intervals.

This tour traverses a region of mountains, rolling prairies, and sagebrush wastes. From the Canadian Border to Deer Park, the highway curves through mountain-flanked highland valleys. South of Deer Park, it dips down to Spokane, crosses a palisaded metropolitan area, and winds southwesterly through a country of lakes, parks, escarpments and wooded hills, until it sweeps down into the "Big Bend" wheatlands. Continuing southwesterly, US 395 descends through a succession of lava-walled coulees and breaks into an open, semidesert country, where the Snake River joins the Columbia, southeast of Pasco.

A part of the area traversed by this route, adjacent to the Columbia River, on either side of Kettle Falls, will be drastically affected by the backwater from Coulee Dam (*see Tour 1B*). This dam across the Columbia River will, when completed, create a vast artificial lake. The depth of this lake, directly behind the dam, will be 377 feet, lessening gradually up the river as the ground rises. The flooding waters will creep up not only the Columbia itself but also tributary streams such as the Kettle, San Poil, and Spokane rivers; forming a shore line estimated at 5,000 miles, extending irregularly far up many valleys, canyons, and gullies.

Section a. LAURIER *to* SPOKANE, *121.4 m. US 395*

South of the Canadian Line is LAURIER, 0 *m.* (1,644 alt., 35 pop.), a group of white-painted houses, dominated by the customhouse, a large structure in Colonial style. Here are the personnel of the United States Customs and Immigration Service, a port of entry to the United States. A stopping point for wagon and pack trains in early days of mining excitement, Laurier, it is said, had at that time a population of 2,000. The surrounding region is mountainous and forested, with some tamarack and other timber.

Over ORIENT, 10.4 *m.* (1,441 alt., 175 pop.), looms (L) First Thought Mountain. The town originated as a mining camp in 1902 and was at first called "Morgan," but was renamed for a near-by mine. The rise in the price of gold in 1935 brought about renewed activities in mines near Orient.

1. Right from Orient a forest road winds over the Kettle River Range through the Colville Indian Reservation.

2. Left from Orient along a forest road that ascends the south slope of First Thought Mountain to FIRST THOUGHT LOOKOUT STATION, 2 *m.* Here, from a high tower, are seen lakes and mountain peaks, some of which are far beyond the Canadian border.

South of Orient US 395 borders the Kettle River, flowing swiftly between rocky banks. At 22.5 *m.* is BOYDS, a small village. When the waters of the man-made lake created by Coulee Dam rise to this point the community will have moved to a higher ridge, together with the highway and railroad.

The highway winds uphill; cliffs tower on the right and Kettle River flows swiftly (L) toward the falls below.

At 30 *m.* is KETTLE FALLS (*see Tour 5*) and the Kettle Falls Bridge. Here is the confluence of the Kettle River and the Columbia River, US 395 crosses a half-mile-long steel and concrete bridge over the Columbia. From the bridge (L) are visible the boiling waters of the Columbia, forming the falls called *Les Chaudieres,* "The Kettles," by early-day French-Canadian trappers when they saw the water churning in holes ground in solid rock by action of the plunging water at flood time. The holes are 15 to 20 feet deep and 8 to 10 feet in diameter. Above the main fall the Columbia, augmented by the Kettle River, widens to a steady stream of blue-white water which foams and boils in a series of falls, surging furiously around rocky islands and half-submerged rocks. Some of these rocky islands immediately below the main falls are wholly or partly submerged in high water season but jut as high as 15 feet above water when spring floods have subsided. The pools and holes among the islands are at certain seasons rife with salmon, and are a favorite fishing place for Indian families who have fishing rights granted by the federal government.

For many years the Indians of the vicinity were known as *Les Chaudieres*. Here, under treaty rights, they took their season's supply of fish during the various salmon runs. Kettle Falls will be entirely submerged by the rising backwater from Coulee Dam, and the water will even submerge the site of the present bridge. This will necessitate the tearing down of the bridge and its reconstruction at a point where the lake is narrow in order to connect with the re-aligned highway on both sides of the river, just above the "1310" level, where the waterline of the lake will be. The depth of the lake at the falls will be 80 feet. Below the falls (R) are slanting slabs of rock where Indians once sharpened their spears and shaped their arrowheads. Long grooves may be seen in these rocks—marks made by generations of Indians whetting their spears there.

Left from the east end of the bridge on a dirt sideroad to the ruins of the OLD JESUIT MISSION, 0.2 *m.*, built by Father Anthony Ravalli, S.J., in 1846. Father Ravalli came to the Colville district in response to a request made by a chief of the Colville Indians, Martin Vlemuxsolix. Formerly known as St. Paul's Chapel, the weather-bleached, crumbling structure was rebuilt in 1858, and its original wooden pegs were replaced with iron nails.

At 32.2 *m.* is a junction with State 22 (*see Tour 5*).

East of the junction, US 395 bears away from the Columbia River. At 32.8 *m.* is a junction with another branch of State 22 (*see Tour 5*). Here the country is more open, with scattered growths of pine.

MEYERS FALLS, 36.6 *m.* (1,631 alt., 200 pop.), is a picturesque town, with towering trees lining its main thoroughfare. The Hudson's Bay Company maintained gristmills in this neighborhood; in 1872 a mill was built by American interests. Meyers Falls will be above the Coulee Dam backwater.

At 38.3 *m.* is the St. Regis Mission (R), a small settlement consisting of several large wooden buildings. The highway runs roughly parallel with the Colville River through rolling meadows.

COLVILLE, 45.8 *m.* (1,512 alt., 2,408 pop.), the seat of Stevens County, is enclosed by peaks of the Okanogan Highlands and the Calispell Mountain Range on the northeast and south. On the west the city slopes down to the floor of the Colville Valley. The business center of tidy brick and stone buildings rises from a 60-foot plateau in the shadow of MOUNT COLVILLE (L). Towering grain elevators and church steeples give the city an aspect of compactness. In a fringe of hills at the base of Church Flat plateau are the clustered dwellings of the residential district. The main street is paved and 12 acres have been set aside for a public park.

During the gold rush days, Colville saw much brawling and gunfighting. In 1861 soldiers from Fort Colville, an early military post, raided the town's laundry, ran off the Chinese proprietor, and took all the clothing. The next year a lieutenant killed a civilian in cold blood, but was acquitted because no one dared to testify against him. To check pilfering and murder, Major Curtis, commanding officer of the post, dismantled the town's distillery, confiscating all of the whisky. To the depredations of the soldiers were added those of roving desperadoes who occasionally visited the town.

Left from Colville about 3 *m.* on an improved road to (L) the SITE OF "AMERICAN" FORT COLVILLE. First known as Harney's Depot, in honor of General Henry S. Harney, who in 1858 opened the district north of the Snake River to white settlers, the fort was built in 1859 on a flat skirted by Mill Creek Adjacent to the fort was Pinkney City, the first seat of Stevens County, named after Major Pinkney Louganbeel, commander of a battalion of the Ninth Infantry, which first occupied the fort.

South of Colville, the highway follows the Colville River upstream. The low range of the Huckleberry Mountains, on the right, and the Pend Oreille Range, on the left, enclose the valley. Some geologists believe that the Columbia River once flowed southward along this channel in a direction opposite that of the present Colville River.

A few villages are passed, including ADDY, 53.8 *m.* (1,633 alt., 150 pop.), a scattered hamlet supported by trade with Swiss dairy farmers in the vicinity.

At 56.7 *m.* is a junction with an improved road:

Right here 0.2 *m.* to BLUECREEK (1,637 alt., 76 pop.), once a logging and mining center, and still a shipping point for farm products and some copper and dolomite from neighboring mines.

At 57.6 *m.,* just off the highway (L), is the REGENERY CABIN, built by Charles Regenery, one of the first settlers of the region. Today part of a farm dwelling, the original structure was made of squared tamarack logs, ten high, chinked with white plaster.

The TRADING POST AND STAGECOACH HOUSE, 59 *m.* (L), is now used as a barn. Originally twelve logs high, it was of peg-and-mortise-joint construction, and so solidly put together that crowbars and dynamite had to be used to break the joints when it was moved to its present site a few years ago. As the owner of the farm on which it stands commented: "Those joints were made by a man who didn't count the cost of his time."

CHEWELAH (Ind. garter snake), 63.1 *m.* (1,669 alt., 1,565 pop.), was a military post in the sixties. Today, it is the largest industrial town in the region, and home of the Northwest Magnesite Company, which manufactures Thermax board, a mineral composition material used in building. The first newspaper in Stevens County, the *Stevens County Sun,* was published here. The town now maintains *The Chewelah Independent,* and has six churches, two banks, and a library.

The MCPHERSON CABIN, two and a half blocks east of the city hall, was built in 1860. It is a one-story log cabin, T-shaped, with three rooms and a peaked roof. It once served as an Indian agency; papers stored in the attic were recently removed to the Historical Museum at Washington State College, Pullman (*see Tour 4b*).

In front of the Congregational Church in Chewalah is a plaque, dedicated in 1938, commemorating the first Protestant religious service held in the Colville Valley, September 8, 1838, by the Reverends Cushing Eells and Elkanah Walker.

Left from Chewelah to the QUARRIES OF THE QUARTZITE MOUNTAIN, 1 *m.*, rising 1,500 feet above the town. Rocks suitable for terrazzo, cement, stone, and stucco building materials are quarried here.

The road descends due south from Chewelah along the floor of the river valley enclosed by hills. VALLEY, 71 *m.*, is important as a recreational center.

Right from Valley on a graveled road, 3.2 *m.*, is WAITS LAKE (*cabin accommodations; supplies*), popular fishing and hunting area.

SPRINGDALE, 81.3 *m.* (2,087 alt., 227 pop.), has never fully recovered from the devastating effects of a fire in 1908 which practically destroyed the town. The graveled main street stretches up a steep grade; the brick and frame buildings stand flush with the sidewalks. The Farmers and Merchants Bank, a white, square, brick structure adjoining the post office and the Camas Valley Grange Hall, on the same street, are the most prominent buildings in the town. On the hill (L) are 20 or more residences, shaded by pines.

At Springdale is a junction with Tshimakain Mission Road.

Right from the junction on an improved road, 11.5 *m.*, to SITE OF TSHIMAKAIN MISSION (pronounced Shim-ik-in), marked by a monument to the missionaries, Cushing Eells and Elkanah Walker, who came to Tshimakain, now Walker's Prairie, in 1838 upon the advice of Archibald McDonald, in charge of the Hudson's Bay Post at Fort Colvile. The mission was situated on Chamokane Creek. ("Chamokane" is another form of the Indian word meaning "plain of springs"), applied to this terrain because of the large number of subterranean streams. The mission was not a success. The Indians would not abandon dancing and gambling. One Indian confessed to Walker that he and his fellow tribesmen were not the least concerned about their souls—suggesting the missionaries would attract more recruits by keeping a good supply of tobacco on hand. Mr. Eells complained in a letter to a friend: "We have been here almost nine years and have not yet been permitted to hear the cry of one penitent, or the song of one redeemed soul."

LOON LAKE, 87.5 *m.* is a roadside village. For about two miles, the highway skirts Loon Lake (R), warm and clear and shallow along its sandy shores; it is about a mile long and one-half mile wide, with wooded hills on the west down to the water's edge.

At 90.2 *m.* is a junction with a dirt road:

Right 2 *m.* on the west bank of Loon Lake is a LOG HUT; it was once occupied by Harry Tracy, better known as "Tracy, the Bandit," probably the most notorious outlaw of the State since the turn of the century (*see Tour 1a*).

At 93.3 *m.* is a junction with a dirt road:

Left here to DEER LAKE, 6 *m.*, four miles long and one and one-half miles wide (*boats and cabins for rent*). The shores of the lake are a runway for the deer from Telescope and Jump-off Joe mountains to Deer Lake Mountain.

The name of CLAYTON, 93.5 *m.* (2,266 alt., 200 pop.), established in 1889, refers to the deposits of clay found near the village. The tall chimney and squat flues of the dry kilns rising at the left belong to the WASHINGTON BRICK AND LIME COMPANY PLANT, which manufactures ceramics, as well as brick, terra cotta, fire brick, and flower pots.

DEER PARK, 98.8 *m.* (2,118 alt., 1,070 pop.), is divided by the highway which traverses its main street. It has a weekly newspaper called the *Deer Park Union,* a three-story high school building costing $45,000, six churches, and a ball park. A large sawmill (L) is the chief industrial plant.

In the eighties, the broad valley surrounding Deer Park was a virgin forest of pine, fir, and tamarack. The construction of a Great Northern R.R. branch from Spokane to Deer Park in 1884 stimulated exploitation of the rich resources of the region. Since then, lumber companies and farmers have steadily cut the timber line back to the mountains. Large deposits of fire clay, kaolin, and mineral pigment are found within a short distance of the town. It is an important shipping point for lumber, grain, and fruit.

Outstanding annual events are the 4-H Community Fair, held during the first part of September, and the Settlers' Picnic held on the third Thursday in June.

DENISON, 102.2 *m.* (1,951 alt., 40 pop.), is a crossroads settlement that was first named Buckeye, after the Buckeye Lumber Company, at Hawkspur downriver.

South of Denison, US 395 winds through a series of rolling hills. Well-tilled farm lands, unfenced, extend to the rim of the highway, which is bordered occasionally by pine trees. At 111.8 *m.* the highway spans Little Spokane Creek and enters DARTFORD (1,840 alt., 27 pop.); here stands Dart's Mill, built in 1883, for which the hamlet was named.

At 115.6 *m.,* US 395 merges with US 195 (*see Tour 4a*). Along this northern entrance to Spokane (known as the North Division Highway) the "Lane of Remembrance," a series of trees planted on both sides of the highway, has been established by the Spokane Parkways and Roadside Protective Association. When the trees reach maturity, the long lane will be one of the most beautiful boulevards in the State.

South (straight ahead) on Division Street to Sprague Avenue, the junction with US 10 (*see Tour 1a*); R. on Sprague Avenue to Howard Street; R. on Howard to Riverside, the city center.

SPOKANE, 121.4 *m.* (2,039 alt., 122,001 pop.), (*see Spokane*).

Section b. SPOKANE *to* PASCO, *154.1 m. US 395*

West of SPOKANE CITY CENTER, 0 *m.,* the route (US 395-US 10) reaches a junction with US 195 (*see Tour 4b*); R. on Sunset Blvd. across Latah Creek Bridge.

At TWO-WAY JUNCTION, 7.2 *m.*, US 395 turns L. from US 10 (*see Tour 1a*), cutting through wheatfields to enter a wooded area where dark green pines spring from rocky crevices. Small thickets of aspen, willow, and cottonwood denote underlying water; cattails dip into inky ponds by the roadside.

FOUR LAKES, 13.4 *m.* (2,340 alt., 125 pop.), a hamlet strung along the highway, contains a grange hall, post office, and service station. Here, an arrow-shaped, stone pyramid marks the SITE OF THE BATTLE OF FOUR LAKES. On August 7, 1858, Colonel George Wright of the United States Army led a force of 700 soldiers against 5,000 allied Indians, following the defeat of Colonel Steptoe at Rosalia (*see Tour 4b*). The battle was fought on the morning of September 1, 1858. The Indians employed their customary tactics, charging up, firing, and riding quickly away; but on this occasion they were met by a hail of shot before they could complete the maneuver. To their surprise, the troops kept advancing, as if on parade. Observing that the foe was becoming panic-stricken, mounted dragoons went forward through platoons of infantry at a gallop, cutting down the Indians with their sabres to clear the plain.

At Four Lakes is a junction with a paved road:

Right from the junction the road zigzags through a bunch-grass and farming area, occasionally spotted with clumps of bull pine. Orchards here, once fairly productive, are now far from prosperous-looking. Slightly to the left of the road is SILVER LAKE BUTTE, partly wooded at its base, nearly bald at the summit.

SILVER LAKE, 3.4 *m.*, once offered excellent bass, perch, and crappie fishing. A scheme to use the water for irrigation, promoted by former Governor M. E. Hay and others, resulted in the draining away of half the lake, until the granite rocks that lined the bottom were left high and dry and the cattails and tules at the north end of the lake had marched forward half a mile. Today, the level of the water is slowly rising.

At 3.5 *m.* is a GRANITE QUARRY, operated by the Washington Monumental Stone Company's plant, which yields good quality gray granite.

The road ascends a slight grade between scattered pine trees to a junction with an improved road. Here (R) is an ornate, three-story, red-brick house, built by Stanley Hallett, who served as a State senator. The senator built his house in what he considered to be the style of an English manor. Right from the junction to US 10 and Spokane.

MEDICAL LAKE, 4.9 *m.* (2,114 pop.), sprawls north and south along the shore of a mile-long lake bearing the same name. Scattered along the main street are a few stores, garages, a post office, beer parlors, and an undertaking establishment. Once the town was a lively trading and summer resort center. Interurban electric trains carried crowds of people from Spokane to the two dance halls, the salt waters of the lake, and the camps along its shores. On the Fourth of July, thousands flocked to the town, the trains running on 15-minute schedules. With the coming of the automobile, however, and the opening of other recreational centers, the crowds began to dwindle. One dance hall burned to the water's edge; the other closed up; the camp grounds were sold to the State Hospital for the Insane; shoppers began to buy in Spokane. Andrew Lefévre, gold prospector, named the town and lake in 1859. The waters of the lake, extremely salty, were once thought to possess medicinal properties. Only a few kinds of marine life can survive in it: there are mud turtles and frogs and a species of salamander called axolotye.

Right from Medical Lake city center, the road runs along the northwest shore, then climbs a pine-covered hill overlooking the lake to the entrance of the EASTERN WASHINGTON STATE HOSPITAL FOR THE INSANE. A small white guard house (R) is at the entrance. The road winds past a large greenhouse (L) to the top of the hill, where the main buildings are located. There are gardens, lawns, a baseball diamond, and aviaries. The first building of the hospital was started in 1889; the institution now has approximately 1,800 patients.

In the town of Medical Lake is a junction with an improved road; L. here 2.1 *m.,* to the STATE CUSTODIAL SCHOOL for the feeble-minded, established in 1907, which comprises several large brick structures centered around the administration building. The grounds are pleasingly landscaped, with gardens in the rear.

South of Four Lakes, paralleling the main line of the Northern Pacific Railway, US 395 crosses a rock-strewn plain, dotted with pine trees.

CHENEY, 19.1 *m.* (2,336 alt., 1,551 pop.), is platted in a triangle, with its base on the Northern Pacific Railway. It is a pleasant busy town. Several railroad lines run through it, and it is the home of the Eastern Washington College of Education, one of three such schools in the State.

At one time Cheney was connected with Spokane by an electric interurban line, and for a decade or so, until the automobile cut into its traffic, the line and the town prospered. For a few years Cheney was the county seat, only to lose out in a bitter fight with Spokane Falls. Today, Cheney is a servicing and distribution center.

Slightly north of the railway station (R) is the F. M. MARTIN MILL, a large flour mill owned by ex-Governor Clarence Martin. Another important factory in the town is the CHENEY WEEDER COMPANY'S PLANT, which manufacturers farm implements.

Cheney has a weekly newspaper, the *Cheney Free Press,* now in its forty-second year, a bank, several churches, stores, a hotel, and a theater. Its chief annual event is the Four-H Community Fair, usually held late in September or early in October. There is a city park, located between Fourth and Fifth and D and E Streets.

South of Cheney, the highway descends imperceptibly in broad, sweeping curves through an uneven grazing region. Scab and lava rock ledges, brownish-black in color and very jagged, are frequently seen near clumps of bull pine. Gradually, the terrain alters; evergreens become scarcer; suddenly, at 38.7 *m.,* the timber line ends, and soon the rolling hills are gray with sagebrush. Herds of beef cattle graze on both sides of the road. During the spring months the landscape is gayly colorful with sunflowers and lupine.

SPRAGUE, 44.9 *m.* (1,889 alt., 641 pop.), was named for General John W. Sprague, director of the Northern Pacific Railway. The town is laid out at a 45-degree angle to the highway, as are most of the towns on this route, with the business section comprising a few blocks along First Street. On a gentle slope (L) are a residence district, the high school, and grade school. In and around Sprague is a considerable settlement of Irish Catholics, as indicated by names like Brislawn, Balfe, Gaffney, and Moylan. Dominating the town from the top of the hill (R) are the Roman Catholic Church and St.

Joseph's Academy, a parochial school. The building of the academy, erected in 1886, was formerly used as a county courthouse, the first in the county, when Sprague was the county seat.

Stage routes once ran from Sprague to the north and west. Later, it became the shop headquarters of the Northern Pacific, rivaling Cheney and surpassing Spokane. The coming of good roads and fast cars diverted trade away from the town, and this, together with hard times for farmers and stock men, has contributed to its slow decline.

At 45.9 *m.* is a junction with a dirt road.

Right from the junction, 1 *m.*, to the HERCULES RANCH, a 54,000-acre stock ranch. Modern in equipment and one of the largest ranches of its kind in the State, it has long been a show place and point of interest.

SPRAGUE LAKE, also called Colville Lake (R), is a favorite recreation spot for the residents of Sprague and Ritzville. About six miles in length, partially obscured by growths of willow and cottonwood, it offers good fishing for bass, perch, and crappie and, when winters are sufficiently cold, provides excellent skating.

Southward, the highway runs through level land where well-tilled grain fields stretch for miles. There are few signs of wild life: occasionally a hawk soars overhead, or an owl stares, silently motionless, from the top of a fence post, or a covey of Hungarian partridge whirs swiftly to safety.

RITZVILLE, 69.5 *m.* (1,814 alt., 1,748 pop.), seat of Adams County, is an important milling and shipping center of the dry and dusty wheat country. The RITZVILLE FLOUR MILLS and a farmer-operated, wheat-shipping warehouse contribute to the city's income. The town has modern hotel accommodations, a Carnegie library, a weekly newspaper, eight churches (two of them German-speaking), and a school system serving an area of 250 square miles through a fleet of busses. A city park on an eminence in the eastern part of town has a large swimming pool.

Philip Ritz located a homestead here in 1878 and gave his name to the site. Between 1891-1900, a large group of German-Russians settled in Ritzville, and many of their old-country customs still survive. With the arrival of the Northern Pacific Railway, the town grew from a drab village into the busy community it is today.

South of Ritzville US 395 runs through high plateau lands, where arable soil has been planted to wheat. The rougher areas of scabrock and sagebrush are used for grazing. Occasionally, a waterhole or slough is bordered by willows and aspen; serviceberry bushes, for a brief time in spring, form swaying towers of white, and sunflowers and lupines brighten the dun-colored sagelands. In the fall, blackbirds chatter in the yellow stubble fields, and swallows gather on the telegraph wires, or a flying wedge of geese, lined against the saffron evening sky, honk their way south above the quiet land.

LIND, 86.8 *m.* (1,365 alt., 679 pop.), is spread out in a hollow on both sides of Nielsen Coulee, which protects it slightly from the winds which blow steadily from the west. The town is an important shipping point, and will be the southeast gateway to the Grand Coulee irrigation districts. It has seven churches.

Two Nielsen brothers settled here in 1888 and platted the town in such a manner that the initial letters of its street-names spell out their surname. The *Lind Leader* claims to be the oldest paper in the county; in 1935-6 it was given the award of excellence in its class by the Washington Press Association.

At the corner of 1st and 2nd streets in Lind is a junction with the Cunningham-Othello Road, an improved road.

Right from the junction, 8 *m.*, to the PHILLIPS FARM, the largest wheat farm in the State, containing 22,000 acres. Here, scientific dry farming and machine agriculture have been highly developed. The farm is planted on a fifty-fifty basis: each year 11,000 acres are sown, the remaining acreage lying fallow. In the harvest season five outfits work day and night shifts, with crews consisting of four men—a cat skinner (caterpillar tractor driver), a separator tender, a jigger, and a sack sewer. The tractor-drawn combine reaps, threshes, and sacks the grain and spreads the straw as it moves through the field. In this manner, the entire crop is harvested in less than two weeks.

South of Lind the highway traverses a succession of parched slopes and sterile hillsides studded with igneous rocks.

CONNELL, 116 *m.* (838 alt., 365 pop.), has three blocks of main street starting at the railroad tracks in the bottom of a coulee and ending (L) on a small knoll. Vacant lots overgrown with weeds lie between the buildings. Connell is a farm community, its trade depending on the farmers in the vicinity.

South of Connell, US 395 descends through a desolate region of gray sand, gray-green sagebrush, dried water courses, slabs of rock jutting from old fissures, and sandy mounds which seem to have been piled by a steam shovel. Cuts on the road reveal the columnar structure of the igneous rock underlying the region. Tumbleweeds drift and roll across the harrowed earth. Isolated houses and withered farms, now deserted, give evidence of the hopeless struggle waged here in years past by drought victims. Water supplied from the Grand Coulee reclamation project (*see Tour 1B*) will soon give new life to this area.

At 123.5 *m.* is a junction with State 11-B, a graveled road.

Left from the junction to KAHLOTUS (Ind. hole-in-the-ground), 18 *m.* (612 alt., 163 pop.), a sleepy village on the west shore of Washtucna Lake that vies with Connell for the farm trade. The town was at first called Hardersburg but the post office department objected to the length of the name and the Indian one was chosen. Near Kahlotus is the DEVIL'S MONUMENT, an immense dome of lava in Devil's Canyon, a branch of the coulee.

The road parallels WASHTUCNA LAKE, two miles long and one-half mile wide, which is fed by several large springs in the near-by hills. The lake is motionless and white, like molten silver. At 29 *m.* is WASHTUCNA, (995 alt., 261 pop.), a scattered, two-street village squeezed into a bend of the coulee. A rodeo, held here annually each fall, is attended by farmers from as far away as the Yakima Valley. WASHTUCNA VALLEY cuts across the southeastern corner of Adams County.

ELTOPIA, 134.9 *m.* (591 alt., 85 pop.), is a drab, forlorn settlement hugging the railroad tracks. The following story is told in connection with the town's name: during grading of the Northern Pacific line in 1889, a freshet resulting from heavy rains washed out the grade, undoing weeks of labor. A disgusted Cockney worker commented that there would be "'el to pay!" The construction crew nicknamed the camp "Hell to Pay." Railroad headquarters accepted the name, but when the finished map of the surveyed district was returned, the "H" had been dropped and the word written "Eltopay." Later, the name was converted into the more soothing Eltopia.

Dust storms here are frequent and severe. A dark, wall-like cloud appears on the horizon and moves leisurely nearer until its gritty substance can be clearly detected, rolling inward and down; then suddenly everything is enveloped in a black suffocating blizzard of dust that filters through the most cautiously tightened window-frame.

At 149.8 *m.* is the PASCO-FRANKLIN COUNTY AIRPORT, a 66-acre field with two runways and a modern four-plane hangar.

PASCO, 154.1 *m.* (381 alt., 3,913 pop.), the seat of Franklin County, spreads its attractive public buildings, landscaped grounds, and business blocks over a level desert plain. The city is an important division point on the Northern Pacific Railway, and the majority of its skilled workers are employed in the roundhouse and machine shops. Pasco also is the hub of the social, political, and commercial activity of the large farming population in the vicinity.

Although the Pasco district was traversed by early explorers, adventurers, and fur traders following the near-by Snake and Columbia Rivers, the history of the present city dates from 1880, when the rails of the Northern Pacific reached the site. The name Pasco is said to have been bestowed by Virgil Bogue, a railroad surveyor, when extreme heat, rust, and sand storms reminded him of the disagreeable conditions in the Peruvian mining city, Cerro de Pasco. Prior to the development of Pasco, the county seat was at Ainsworth, a lusty railroad center a few miles away, with a population of 5,000; Ainsworth deteriorated as Pasco flourished, until not a stick now remains of it.

Incorporated in 1891, Pasco has grown steadily.

Most of the city's industrial activity is centered in plants which border the railroad tracks in the eastern part of the town. These include the Pasco Union stockyards, the Miller Addison Icing Plant, and freight terminals, grain elevators, and sheds. The city is served by the Washington Motor Coach and Union Pacific stages, and several good hotels and restaurants cater to visitors.

On 4th Street (R), set in a neatly landscaped plot, is the FRANKLIN COUNTY COURTHOUSE, a structure of buff brick and limestone with Corinthian columns and a gilded metal dome visible for miles. Near the courthouse is OUR LADY OF LOURDES HOSPITAL (R), conducted by a Roman Catholic sisterhood, which is housed in a five-story brick building. The CITY PARK (L) has been artistically landscaped. At the edge of the business district is the mission-style CARNEGIE LIBRARY (L), with a collection of 6,000 volumes. The Pasco *Herald,* a weekly newspaper, was voted the second best weekly in the State a few years ago.

An unusual nine-hole golf course is about two miles southeast of the city on US 410; the fairways are rough and sand greens are utilized. The land was donated by the city and the course is maintained through assessments. The links are free to the public.

At Lewis and 4th Streets, US 395 forms a junction with US 410 (*see Tour 2a*).

Tour 7

(Osoyoos, B. C.)—Oroville—Teanaway—Maryhill. US 97.
Canadian Boundary to Oregon Boundary, 333 m.

Route paralleled by Great Northern Ry. between Oroville and Dryden, and by Northern Pacific between Teanaway and Toppenish; Washington Motor Coach stages entire route. Canadian Boundary—Wenatchee River, bituminous-surfaced road; Wenatchee River-Dryden, concrete-paved; Blewett Pass, subject to closing by winter snows; Dryden-Thorp, bituminous surfaced; Thorp-Toppenish, concrete-paved; Toppenish-Maryhill, bituminous-surfaced. Hotels and cabin camps at convenient intervals.

US 97, also known as the Cascade International highway, and sometimes referred to as the Okanogan-Cariboo Trail, follows the route over which, before 1847, the fur brigades of the Hudson's Bay Company carried pelts from Canada to Fort Vancouver on the Columbia River. The year 1858 brought the first of a long series of stampedes by gold-seekers over the Cariboo Trail to rich diggings along the Fraser River and in the Similkameen district. Since then, the trail has borne much traffic, and the proposed highway to Alaska destines it to bear more. The days of the fur brigades and the gold rushes are now at an end, and the country has settled down to the long task of developing the resources ignored by the early trappers and miners. The region is an extremely varied one: rugged badlands are set beside level plains, sawtoothed ridges rear above gently rolling foot-hills, riotous mountain streams tumble into smooth lakes, rivers cut their way across drab deserts; mantles of timber spread over many hills, while others are bare and rocky. As for the settlers who peopled this region, they represent today both the old and the new West. Pioneer living and modern enterprise may often be found side by side, taking each other's measure.

Section a. CANADIAN BOUNDARY *to* TEANAWAY, *193.9 m. US 97*

The CUSTOMHOUSE (R), 0 *m.,* at the International Line, is the central building of an attractive group surrounded by artfully landscaped grounds. The contrast between the green lawns and shrubbery and the barren, lifeless aspect of the surrounding hills is sharp and impressive.

South of the Customhouse the highway follows the flat, sandy shoreline, bare of habitation, of long, narrow OSOYOOS LAKE. The Kalispel Indian word for "narrow" is *soyoos,* and it was by that word that this lake was originally designated; among the region's early settlers, however, was an Irishman who insisted that the word be civilized by the addition of the Irish "O".

OROVILLE, 4.5 *m.* (921 alt., 1,206 pop.), port of entry and customs and immigration station, north of the confluence of the Similkameen and Okanogan Rivers, is noted for mining, lumbering, and fruit canning. The development that came with the railroad is visible in the substantial modern structures of the compact little business section beyond the depot.

Originally named Oro (Sp. gold), the "ville" was added by the Post Office Department to avoid confusion with Oso, another town in the State. A rush of placer miners into the district began just prior to the Civil War. Although Oroville's site was included in land claimed by Chief Moses in 1873, Alexander McCauley, an early settler and friend of the chief, was allowed to hold a tract adjacent to the present town. When Chief Moses' district was thrown open to settlement in 1886, development of the near-by mineral resources assured the town's future.

Oroville's first store, established in 1891, was soon followed by other enterprises, including more than 20 saloons. Wheat is now being reintroduced after a decline caused by several years of drought. Today, fruits and vegetables raised on irrigated land are processed and prepared for shipment in the town's half-dozen canneries and dehydrating plants. Sheep and other livestock grazing, under the supervision of the Department of Agriculture, are assuming greater proportions in the surrounding hills. Pure epsom salts (magnesium sulphate), as well as a lower grade, are mined near Oroville from two deposits. Ore deposits with fair yields of gold, silver, lead, and arsenic are mined. Limestone and terra-cotta clay are found in commercial quantities.

During the first two days of September each year, the Oroville Fair entertains visitors from neighboring towns and counties with horse-racing, ball games, dancing, and carnival features.

From Oroville a number of roads lead to lakes, mountain gorges, ghost towns, and busy hamlets. The roads branching off the main highway are of earth and gravel, and, although open to travel most of the year, are often damaged by heavy rains. Cautious travelers carry chains, shovel, and axe. Two mountain roads leave Oroville:

1. Left from Oroville on an improved road is a junction with a dirt road: L. here 2 *m.* to OKANOGAN SMITH'S ORCHARD AND HOME, on the eastern shore of Osoyoos Lake. The ancient and dilapidated log cabin encircled by trees, was erected by Hiram F. (Okanogan) Smith in 1860. The nickname was bestowed on Smith by the Indians because his place was a rendezvous for the early inhabitants of the region. A colorful character, he played an important part in the Okanogan country's history. Elected to the legislature in 1865, he had to trek north through British Columbia and proceed by steamer down the Fraser River and across Puget Sound in order to reach the Territorial capital. Returning, he brought with him a number of small apple trees and peach seeds, which he planted on his claim. Today, some of the apple trees are 40 feet high, have a spread of 50 feet, and measure 3 feet or more in diameter.

At 3 *m.* the main side road crosses Tonasket Creek, a mountain stream following a rocky canyon.

At 11.4 *m.* on the main side road is a junction with a dirt road: R. here through Eden Valley to HAVILLAH, 6 *m.* (16 pop.). Here are a number of German families of the Lutheran faith, most of whom arrived in 1910. The main side road continues up Tonasket Creek Canyon and crosses MUD LAKE VALLEY.

CHESAW, 21.5 *m.* (2,910 alt., 202 pop.), a small mining settlement, was named in honor of a Chinese who, with his Indian wife, lived here in the early days. Their hospitable "bungaloo" housed the few white and Indian travelers on trips through the north country. Five miles north of Chesaw is the Customhouse. Agriculture supports the scattered population.

2. Right from Oroville on a graveled road along the Similkameen River through beautiful SIMILKAMEEN GORGE. NIGHTHAWK, 14 *m.* (50 pop.), on the Similkameen River just south of the Canadian boundary, once a boom town, has maintained a semblance of life throughout lean years. MOUNT ELLEMEHAM (4,770 alt.) looms austerely to the east; PALMER MOUNTAIN and PALMER LAKE, 17 *m.,* were once the scene of great mining activity. "Similkameen," a name of vague meaning and origin—old timers say it is Indian for "treacherous waters"—appeared in the reports of the Wilkes Expedition of 1841 as "Similameigh."

LOOMIS, 24 *m.* (1,306 alt., 180 pop.), named after the first merchant in the locality, is the site of the late Guy Waring's ranch. In his book *My Pioneer Past,* Waring gives a vivid picture of Oroville and Loomis. A friend of Theodore Roosevelt and Owen Wister at Harvard, Waring, after an unsatisfactory trial as an architect in his father's office at Newport, Rhode Island, looked for new horizons. With his wife and three children, he reached Portland in 1885, worked there for a short while on a railroad, then set out for the Okanogan country. Here he became a cowman, storekeeper, barber, cook, farmer, shoemaker, "washwoman," fur trader, carpenter, and justice of the peace. Waring was a confidant of "Okanogan" Smith, staunch and saintly little Father de Rouge, and other characters of the border country. He died in Milton, Massachusetts, in 1936.

In the "old town," the southern edge of Oroville, US 97 crosses a bridge spanning the Similkameen River and turns southward along the curve of the stream. The Okanogan Valley, which the highway follows for 75 miles, once contained what is known as the Okanogan Lobe of the Cordilleran Ice Sheet. Rocks, sandy patches, and gravelly areas indicate thousands of years of glacial action.

Broad-leafed cottonwood, thicketed birches, willows, alders, and aspen (quaking asp), with their smooth, greenish-white bark and easily agitated leaves, line the river banks. Many of these are of commercial value. The willow, flexible and easily cut, is used by Indians in weaving baskets; cottonwood, a soft wood, is especially suitable for paper pulp; aspen wood, because it is odorless, is much used for cheese boxes and butter boxes.

One of Frederic Remington's paintings of a generation ago pictured a group of Indians, sitting languidly astride "cayuses" that were drinking at the willowed riverside of the Okanogan. Other natives appear in the background on the bench above the river, stolidly facing the noonday sun and gazing at the fences of the white settlers, the desolate range, the silent mountains and desert. Owen Wister immortalized these men of the Okanogan in a description beneath Remington's picture.

> Of old, when Okanogan ran
> Good medicine for horse and man,
> The winged shaft was wont to fly
> In peace or war, beneath the sky.
> Gone is the arrow, and instead
> The message of the white man's lead,
> The poison of the white man's drink—
> These lessons by the river-brink
> Are learned, where Okanogan ran
> Good medicine for horse and man.

At 9.2 *m.* is the junction with a graveled road.

Right on this road to a junction at 0.5 *m.* with another graveled road: L. here to WANNACUT LAKE, 3.5 *m.* At the south end of the lake is an undeveloped State park; no recreational or camping facilities are available. Scattered along a low ridge (R) are buildings belonging to the American Rand Mining Company, which operates in this district. In this vicinity the town of GOLDEN, 4.5 *m.,* once existed, with a reputed population of 500. Today not a trace of it remains.

South of the junction US 97 skirts the low hills of WHISKEY RANGE (R). Flumes clinging to the hillside high above the river are the arteries of the Oroville-Tonasket Federal Irrigation Project, which furnishes water for 12,000 acres extending from the Canadian Boundary to five miles south of Tonasket. About one-third of the area is in orchards.

About 30 families of Dunkards, who came during the World War, live on their small orchard farms in the immediate vicinity of ELLISFORD, across the river, 16.9 *m.* The brethren allow their beards to grow, but not mustaches.

At 23.4 *m.* is the junction with State 4, a graveled road.

Left on State 4 across a span over the Okanogan River to TONASKET, 0.4 *m.* (900 alt., 643 pop.), sprawled along the east bank of the Okanogan River on a narrow flat beneath rising hills. It was named for an Okanogan chief and the site was an Indian camping ground. The United States Forest Service maintains a ranger station here. Many sheep graze on the surrounding hills; fields of alfalfa scent the air; apple orchards cover the flats above the town. Some gold, silver, and lead ores are taken from near-by mines.

East of Tonasket on State 4 are vistas of the Okanogan Valley. The road follows the path of Bonaparte Creek and traverses the Colville National Forest.

At 12.9 *m.* is a junction with a side road: R. here into AENEAS VALLEY, named after Chief Aeneas (Indian pronunciation of the French word Ignace), onetime Government guide, who, it is said, lived to be more than 100 years old. His land allotment is now the home of one of his heirs, Joe Aeneas. On a hill within its limits is an old Indian cemetery. In Aeneas Valley are many persons of Austrian descent.

On a rock ledge adjacent to the JOE HILL RANCH, 13.3 *m.*, are ancient INDIAN CARVINGS, which have withstood the weathering of centuries. Occasional dairy ranches and alfalfa fields break the timbered wilderness. Slender-trunked lodgepole pines stand close together, merging their dark-green upper branches. The lodgepole pine was so named because it was commonly used by the Indians in building their lodge and tepee frames. The small trees form dense thickets on burned-over areas. The phenomenal re-seeding power of this tree in the wake of forest fires is due to the fact that the closed cones can endure extreme heat, which would kill the tree itself. The uniform size of the lodgepole pine has made it especially adaptable for use as telegraph poles, railroad ties, and mine timbers. The road follows the west fork of the Sanpoil River downstream. Along its banks are many camping and fishing spots. Campfires may be built only in the designated camping spots, unless a permit is obtained from a forest ranger. The unimproved road reaches another junction with State 4 at West Fork.

The main side road continues northwest along Bonaparte Creek. At 20.6 *m.* is a junction with a dirt road: L. here 5 *m.* to BONAPARTE LAKE (*trout fishing*).

State 4 leaves Bonaparte Creek to enter OLD WAUCONDA, 24 *m.* (4,170 alt., 15 pop.), hidden in the center of an extensive mining and diversified farming district. At 40.8 *m.* is REPUBLIC (2,503 alt., 710 pop.), seat of Ferry County, hidden in the folds of the Okanogan Highlands and the Kettle River Range. Despite a few modern structures, the town retains a flavor of the Old West along its main street, with an ancient "opry house," now a motion picture theater, balconied and false-fronted buildings, and old-time bars untouched by the fire of 1938, which razed a section of the street.

Discovery of gold on Granite Creek by John Welty on February 20, 1896, opened the northern section of the Colville Indian Reservation and brought an influx of prospectors. In its issue of May 14, 1896, the *Republic Pioneer* proclaimed that here was a little city that was moving right along. "Large quantities of whiskey, flour, and other necessities arrived during the week." Gold seekers continued to flock to the frontier town throughout the summer of 1898. By 1900 Republic ranked sixth in population among eastern Washington cities. This was an exciting period of its life, when 28 saloons and two dance halls assisted miners, prospectors, and miscellaneous fortune hunters to while away their evenings. The "Hot Air Line," so called because its completion was deemed improbable, was finished between Republic and Grand Forks, B. C., in April, 1902, but proved unprofitable and was replaced by the Great Northern the same year.

Several gold mines operate more or less sporadically along a mile and a half of gulch leading northward from the end of the main street. Visitors are admitted at the discretion of the foreman in charge but must sign a liability waiver. A recent addition to Republic's industries is a lime kiln four miles west of town.

Left from Republic on State 4-A, a graveled side road: LAKE CURLEW (Ind. karanips, for the snipe-like bird once prevalent in the locality), 6.0 *m.*, five miles long and about half a mile wide, lies among sparsely timbered hills. North of MALO, 16.2 *m.* (2,120 alt., 90 pop.), and CURLEW, 22.4 *m.* (1,791 alt., 100 pop.), weathered villages among mountain peaks, the road passes through mining country along the Kettle River, which flows north into Canada. DANVILLE, 32.2 *m.* (1,739 alt., 75 pop.), port of entry from Canada, was named for a storekeeper who, it is related, built a store on the boundary line and evaded duties by taking Canadian goods in one door, shoving them across the floor, and selling them to customers at the south entrance. Custom officials compelled the removal of the store to a spot south of the line. At the Canadian Boundary, 32.7 *m.* is the Customhouse, two miles south of Grand Forks, B. C.

Right from Republic on State 4, the main side road, which runs due south along the Sanpoil River. At 47.7 *m.* is a junction with a forest road: R. here to SWAN LAKE, 8 *m.,* (*trout fishing, camping*), where there is a Forest Service Guard Station.

At SCATTER CREEK, 47.8 *m.,* flocks of sheep graze on pasture land rented from the Forest Service. TEN MILE CREEK FOREST SERVICE CAMP, 50.1 *m.* (2,200 alt.), is at the confluence of the creek and the Sanpoil River. WEST FORK, 52.6 *m.,* at the confluence of the West Fork of the Sanpoil and the main stream, is a camping ground and supply station. The road follows a valley, which narrows and becomes more rugged, and crosses a number of creeks, dry except in late spring and early summer, when they carry away the melting snows from the adjacent hills.

When Republic was a booming mining center, these creeks were named according to their distance from the town—Nine Mile Creek, Thirteen Mile Creek, and so on—to facilitate the locating of mining claims along them. New names have been bestowed within the past few years. Countless piles of stone and rock recall the bold placer mining of older days; in some sections prospect holes honeycomb the hillsides. The somber hills extend into the Kettle River Range of the rolling Okanogan Highlands.

KELLER, 88.6 *m.* (1,140 alt., 100 pop.), named for J. C. Keller, a storekeeper who began business here in a tent in 1898, retains its frontier aspect. Keller was founded in 1898, when the southern half of the Colville Indian Reservation was opened for mining. The present site of Keller will be under approximately 80 feet of water upon completion of Grand Coulee Dam.

South of Keller, State 4 follows closely the east bank of the Sanpoil River. Approximately 80 miles long, the Sanpoil is not safely navigable by any type of boat. Good catches of trout are made here. Deer, rabbit, and Chinese pheasant and Hungarian partridge abound in the surrounding uplands. CLARK, 95.8 *m.* (1,027 alt., 20 pop.), is a ferry landing on the Columbia River, near its confluence with the Sanpoil. Here an open barge winds on a cable across the Columbia, transporting cars and passengers free. From the south bank of the Columbia, State 4 ascends to the Columbia Plateau in a dizzying series of sharp turns and switchbacks. At 106.0 *m.* is the junction with US 10 (*see Tour 1a*).

South of the Tonasket junction, US 97 climbs along the slopes of the west bank of the Okanogan River. Along the river cottonwoods rustle in the wind and willow and aspen quiver in rhythm with the stream's current. Narrow side roads struggle through canyons to valleys supporting small farms, surrounded by split-rail fences, their houses mottled by the weather and warped from their cornerstones. The frontier spirit, quaint humor, and slow speech of the inhabitants of these interior settlements recall the mountain regions of the southern United States.

At 40 *m.* the highway swings back to the river and the sleepy little village of RIVERSIDE (862 alt., 192 pop.). Confined to a hollow on the west bank of the lazy Okanogan River, it has an air of rustic serenity, emphasized by yellow roses and hollyhocks and vine-covered houses. Nevertheless, Riverside was once a bustling little metropolis and a point of great strategic value in the flow of Okanogan Valley commerce. A short distance north of town McLoughlin Rapids transform a section of the river into a roaring welter of white foam, which once marked the head of navigation on the Okanogan. Riverside was in its heyday in the period when steamboats carried the freight and a glamorous "steamboat-round-the-bend" spirit dominated the life of the town. Beginning with the opening of a general store near its present site by F. J. ("Pard") Cummings in 1898, Riverside quickly became a supply point for the northern part of Okanogan County and the Colville Indian Reservation, the trading center of a region greater in area than some eastern States. To the west lay Conconully, the county seat, and the way to it led through Riverside, which profited accordingly.

In 1915 the railroad came in and the steamboats vanished. Conconully, missed by the railroad, collapsed, and the county seat was moved to Okanogan, below Riverside; while Riverside, chastened and subdued, found its present place in the scheme of things.

The bulk of Riverside's inhabitants are sons and daughters of pioneers from the Cumberland region. As a rule they prefer the quiet life. There are long summer afternoons when the only movement in Riverside is the cloud of dust drifting above some cow nonchalantly marching down the main street. On week-ends, however, inhabitants of the outlying districts invade Riverside and pre-empt the floor of the town hall, where they stage night-long successions of square dances and modern steps to the strains of "good old mountain music."

South of Riverside US 97 leaves the riverbanks and passes irrigated farms, green in spring and dry during the hot summer months, and the apple orchards of ROBINSON FLAT, 43.2 *m.* OMAK, 47.6 *m.* (858 alt., 2,547 pop.), cut by the curve of the Okanogan River, is the largest town in the north-central part of the State. The compact and solidly built business district fronts on the main highway. Across the river are warehouse-lined railroad tracks, old straggling streets, and the stacks of lumber and huge smokestack of the Biles-Coleman Lumber Company mill. Employing normally 500 persons, with the largest single pay roll in the county, the mill has been, during the past few years, the scene of bitter labor disputes. Although built for box manufacture, the mill also ships special interior trim and standard-dimension lumber made from the yellow, beautifully grained ponderosa pine. The name "Omak" is derived from the Indian *omache,* meaning "good medicine." The Omak Stampede, a two-day festival and rodeo, is held in August.

Left from Omak, a dirt road climbs a long grade. At 3 *m.* on the main side road is a junction with a dirt road: L. here 2 *m.* to ST. MARY'S MISSION, a group of buildings including a white-painted Roman Catholic Church, a convent, a boys' school, and a hospital. The original mission building was destroyed by fire on September 30, 1938, and is being replaced by a modern structure. The mission was founded in 1889 by Father Etienne de Rouge, who devoted his personal fortune, and what he was able to solicit from contributors throughout the world, to these sons and daughters of the wilderness. The kindly old French Jesuit held tremendous sway over the tribesmen and Christians of the vicinity. Rebellious Chief Joseph and Chief Moses attended his services, though they seemed to doubt their fitness for the heavenly destiny painted by the priest. Many deeds of violence were prevented by Father de Rouge's intervention. In celebrating the Mass he is said to have mixed Chinook jargon with the traditional Latin. He insisted that the Indians wear hats; and with flapping headgear askew on their braided heads, they sat and listened to him.

Near the mission ground is WAYFARER'S CABIN, made of hewed and dovetailed logs with a sod roof; it once served as a shelter for travelers.

South of Omak US 97 heads through a wide level area along the river.

At 49.3 *m.* is SHELLROCK POINT (L), a huge grayish-white rock, with towering granite intrusions from the period when the Okanogan Highlands rose from the ocean bed.

OKANOGAN, 51.8 *m.* (829 alt., 1,735 pop.), the center of government in Okanogan County since 1915, is also headquarters for the Chelan National Forest. Though less populous than Omak, it has a larger and more impressive business district. The six blocks of brick and frame buildings occupy a narrow valley on a delta bar, at the mouth of Salmon Creek. The Okanogan River winds slowly and quietly a few hundred feet left of Second Avenue, the main thoroughfare. Across a steel bridge spanning the stream are rows of warehouses, packing plants, and the railroad tracks.

On a knoll west of the commercial center is the OKANOGAN COUNTY COURTHOUSE, a semimission type of structure in gray concrete, with a jail above the two floors of offices. An ornate cupola rises above the entrance, and expansive green lawns surround the buildings. On Queen Street, one block right of the highway, is the FIRST METHODIST CHURCH, a building of unusual design, faced with stones of varying shapes and sizes. The FIRE STATION, on Pine St. (R), is an old fashioned wooden building with square tower, erected in 1910. Many fine houses with landscaped grounds, shaded by weeping willows and poplars, occupy a sloping bench on one side of the town. Okanogan's leading hotel offers the "howdy-stranger-hitch-and-come-in" hospitality of the earlier West.

Situated approximately 20 miles from the site of the first American settlement in Washington Territory, Old Fort Okanogan, the town embraces the two prior settlements of Pogue and Alma. Okanogan began with the old trading post of "Pard" Cummings, established in 1886. At that time, river transportation was limited: only during May and June, when the water was high, could steamboats reach Okanogan. Consisting of little but a river landing and a general store for more than a decade, the settlement finally attracted other enterprises. Orchards blossomed near streams on the near-by flats. When irrigation from a reservoir at Conconully was obtained in 1906, it became a thriving town. The name Okanogan was adopted in November 1906. The Great Northern ran a branch line from Wenatchee in 1915, and the county seat was acquired, stimulating future growth.

From the river bank at Tyee Street, a curiously elevated "high bridge" once arched across the Okanogan River to its east bank. Lack of a bridge had troubled Okanogan citizens: Oroville and Riverside had spanned the Okanogan prior to 1907, but Okanogan still depended on a ferry. The building of the "high bridge," now replaced by a steel structure, encouraged trade from the mines and farms and from the Indian reservation across the river. The steeply inclined bridge, widely ridiculed, permitted even the tallest steamer stacks to pass beneath it, with more than 11 feet to spare.

1. Right from Okanogan on a bituminous-surfaced road that climbs westward from the city center to POGUE FLAT, 1 *m.*, 5,000 acres of productive apple orchards. These fruitful orchards, in what was once barren desert, are the direct result of one of the first irrigation projects undertaken by the United States Reclamation Service, in 1906. Feeding of the life-giving water began in 1910.

In April and early May the valley is a fairyland; apple blossoms, with their beautiful tints and sweet aroma, contrast with drab hillsides and the pungent odor of sagebrush. During June and July the trees are thinned; crowded clusters and crossed branches are removed, insuring a larger and more nearly perfect fruit. In the hot summer the apples develop rapidly; their cheeks are reddened by the cool nights of September and the light frosts of early October. The pickers, on high step-ladders, fill their great canvas bags. The fruit is then transported to the packing warehouse, sorted, wrapped, boxed, labeled, and stored in large cold-storage plants for shipment.

The road continues from Pogue Flat through a narrow irrigated valley crowded with small farms and orchards.

At 16 *m.* the road crosses a small creek linking CONCONULLY LAKE (R) and CONCONULLY RESERVOIR (L). The reservoir was formed by the damming of Salmon Creek in connection with a Federal irrigation project. The crescent-shaped lake is a natural body of water, fed by fresh mountain streams and shadowed by pine-fringed ridges. CONCONULLY (Ind. cloudy), 17 *m.* (2,358 alt., 187 pop.), is a cluster of old buildings in a mountain cup. The town came into existence in 1886 with a rush of prospectors to the rich Salmon Creek district. Arriving in the spring, the gold-seekers pitched tents; with the coming of colder weather, cabins replaced canvas; timber operations supplemented, and eventually supplanted, mining as the town's main industry. In 1888 Conconully became the county seat. In 1892 it suffered a disastrous fire; the depression of 1893 caught it off balance; and after 1915 Conconully became a ghost town.

a. Right from Conconully a road winds through a heavily timbered section, the air odorous with pine, to SALMON MEADOWS FOREST CAMP, 10 *m.* (4,500 alt.), from which trails radiate to good hunting and fishing spots. A ski run and lodge have been recently constructed here by the forest service. Lakes are revealed from the tops of knolls and peaks. At 18 m. is SINLAHEKIN CREEK. Along the rocky walls of this turbulent mountain stream are numerous Indian sign writings and paintings. To the right is TIFFANY MOUNTAIN (8,275 alt), named for Will Tiffany, who maintained a camp in a meadow at the foot of its walls. Tiffany, of the same family as the New York jewelers, was one of Theodore Roosevelt's Rough Riders and lost his life in Cuba during the Spanish-American War.

b. Left from Conconully on a dirt road that winds through the forest are the remains of the once thriving town of RUBY, 4 *m.* Vandals, fire, weather, and neglect have reduced it to ruins which convey no hint of the fact that here stood, in the early eighties, the liveliest little town in a lively county, the Babylon of Washington Territory, and Okanogan's first official county seat. Whatever may have been lost when Ruby declined, the peace and dignity of the commonwealth enjoyed a decided gain. Its citizens were miners and the adventurers who commonly follow mining stampedes; quick trigger-fingers and bad whisky were predominant in its civic life. One of its leading citizens combined cattle-rustling with running a butcher shop, until cattlemen of the district descended on Ruby in a body, bringing a rope. The miners rallied to the defense of the butcher, who was esteemed for his generosity in "setting 'em up" at the bar. Civil war threatened and Guy Waring, appointed prosecutor, proposed that the butcher be sent to Colville for trial. Though the miners insisted that the trial be held at Ruby, the accused was eventually started toward Colville under guard. His guards got drunk and let him escape; whereupon Waring issued warrants for the guards as well as for their erstwhile prisoner. All were freed after a trial held at Ruby.

At 8 *m.* on this road is another ghost town, LOOP LOOP (Fr. loup, meaning wolf), which began with a boom but collapsed in a hurry. Fifty years ago a piece of ore, an assay certificate, and a ten-foot shaft in a hillside might at once bring $100,000 in promotion. Falling prices of metals and rocketing living costs combined to halt mining activities. Loop Loop's residents departed, taking with them everything of value that could be moved. All that remains now is one old building and an abandoned brickyard. Recent rises in the price of precious metals have resulted in renewed mining activity in the vicinity, but Loop Loop has not yet revived.

The Indians named the Conconully Valley *Sklow Outiman* (money hole), because here a trapper could catch a beaver any time and use its pelt as money at Fort Okanogan.

2. L. from Okanogan a gravel road crosses the river and at 3 *m.* forms a junction with another gravel road: R. here through rolling semidesert country to OMAK LAKE, 8 *m.*, where the road clings to the heights hundreds of feet above the lake's western shore. Across the waters rise rocky, almost perpendicular walls, with scrubby pines rooted in their many fissures. At the water level a strikingly white band, formed by alkaline deposits, completely encircles the lake. Because of its alkaline content Omak Lake has no fish.

South of Okanogan US 97 clings to the west bank of the Okanogan River.

At 53.5 *m.* is the junction with an unpaved road.

Right on this road along the LOOP LOOP TRAIL, old route to the Methow Valley. In spring or fall this area offers delightful trail trips. The timber and the rich foliage lend fascination to the rapidly changing landscape. Buttercups fringe the meadows bordering moist creek banks. The flaming red heads of the Indian paintbrush glow among the chaparral, from whose roots they derive subsistence. The pure white flowers of the syringa, numerous and fragrant, flash against the blue-gray hillsides. The gay heads, rose-pink, yellow, and white, of the creeping verbena peek from behind the scattered rocks. Goldenrod, bane of hay fever victims, gilds the somber hillsides. Sagebrush, greasewood, and clumps of bunch grass obscure these wild blooms in the distance, while tamarack, ponderosa pine and fir bristle from the rocky foothills.

MALOTT, 60.6 *m.* (815 alt., 381 pop.), virtually wiped out on April 19, 1938, by a flood resulting from the bursting of a dam on Loop Loop Creek, has been rebuilt into an attractive modern town. Its former dingy structures were carried away when the water swept through the main street. No lives were lost, and normal shipments of fruit and livestock were not interrupted. Sand drifts and other scattered evidences of the flood are still visible throughout the vicinity.

At 62.3 *m.* is the junction with a dirt road.

Right, this road follows the old CHILLOWIST TRAIL, an early route to the Methow Valley. Since the carving of a road in the steep rocky sides of the Methow River, farther south, this trail has been little traveled. It winds up through the Chiliwist Canyon, thence over trails that climb the 30-to-50-degree mountain slopes to the summit, then leads down into the beautiful and bounteous Methow Valley. The trail was named after Indian Charley Chiliwist, who formerly lived at the mouth of the creek.

South of Malott, US 97 leaves the Okanogan River and passes through Brewster Flats. A high plateau rises across Okanogan River (L), and the highway is bordered by occasional wheat farms and unpainted houses and out-buildings. Here the mile-wide Okanogan Valley, extending from British Columbia, joins the Columbia River Valley.

At 75.1 *m.* is the junction with a gravel road.

Left here 3.2 *m.* to a point above the west bank of the Okanogan River, near its confluence with the Columbia. On a broad flat across the Okanogan (R) stands a stone tower marking the SITE OF OLD FORT OKANOGAN; no road leads to the site. There, above a crude trading post built of driftwood caught in the bend of the river, the Astor interests in 1811 raised the first American flag to float over a permanent settlement in the Pacific Northwest. As a sequel to the War of 1812, Fort Okanogan passed to the North West Company, then to Hudson's Bay Company. The original buildings of the Okanogan post were replaced in September 1815, by a new dwelling house with large dining hall, two good houses for the men, and a trading post. This establishment lay across the triangular flat and on the Columbia River. It was surrounded by palisades. Brass four-pounders, located at strategic points, discouraged attack. The Okanogan post declined when the Hudson's Bay Company broke a new trail for its brigade along the Similkameen and Coquilla Rivers to Fort Hope on the Fraser River. It was abandoned by them after the Treaty of 1846, which defined the present boundary between Canada and the United States. In the early sixties, some of the buildings at Fort Okanogan were still standing, but now there are only the depressions in the ground where the cellars were dug. Clearer traces of original buildings remain in a spot a mile or more distant—the second Fort Okanogan. A flood in 1894 swept away the timbers left from the first fort, and a stony beach now covers most of the site.

BREWSTER, 77 *m.* (812 alt., 447 pop.), at the confluence of the Okanogan and Columbia Rivers, a village of a few new brick and many old frame buildings, surrounded by lawn-bordered houses scattered among the sagebrush, is an oasis in this desert country. Originally, it was a junction point for navigation on the Okanogan and Columbia Rivers. The first attempt to build here was in 1892, but the depression of 1893 delayed development. In 1896 a steamboat company, which had been mooring across the river at Fort Columbia and was desirous of establishing a new landing, purchased the present site of Brewster from one John Bruster, whose name has been altered in naming the town.

Left from Brewster on State 10, unpaved, across a bridge spanning the Columbia River, is BRIDGEPORT, 12 *m.* (817 alt., 320 pop.). Once an important landing point for boats of the Columbia, it is today a surprisingly modern little settlement, 15 miles from the nearest railroad.

After its liberation from Coulee Dam about 30 miles upstream, the Columbia River behaves weirdly. In Nespelem Canyon the currents leap and dive over basaltic boulders, spewing wrathfully on the confining walls. This turbulence continues for several miles to the mouth of Foster Creek, where wild rapids foam and rage. The current then slackens for a short distance, then rocky points converge and force the Columbia's conflicting currents between them. For 25 miles, the river is a long succession of rapids and whirlpools, surrounded by cliffs, coulees, and headlands.

PATEROS, 82.6 *m.* (780 alt., 484 pop.), with shady streets, is an inviting spot in this customarily hot and dry area. Formerly called Ives Landing, the town was named Pateros by Lieutenant Nosler, an Army officer who had campaigned near a town of the same name in the Philippines during the Spanish-American War. Situated at the mouth of the Methow River, Pateros is the gateway to the mining and farming region of the Methow Valley. The Methow River, draining the larger part of the western half of Okanogan County, is crossed by a concrete bridge at Pateros.

During excavations on the present site of the Pateros Hotel (L), a number of well-preserved skeletons of Indians were unearthed. From time to time similar relics, as well as arrowheads and other artifacts, are found in the vicinity, indicating that in times past an important Indian settlement existed at this point.

South of the bridge at 83.2 *m.* is a junction with State 16, a bituminous surfaced road.

Right on this road into the METHOW VALLEY, which conforms to the windings and twistings of the river from which it takes its name. The valley is extremely narrow, but wherever the hills draw back to form more gentle slopes, or leave level meadows beside the stream, there are orchards, houses, cultivated fields, and grazing animals. Along the road, or above or below it, runs the valley's lifeline, the main irrigation ditch. Without the water it brings them, at the low cost of $3 yearly per acre, farmers could coax but a scant yield from this valley's rich floor. The Methow Valley has no large towns. The people live on their farms, or engage in bounty-hunting, trapping, herding, prospecting, and logging. They regard towns as places in which to trade, vote, and spend holidays—the traditional attitude of the old West. On weekdays and special occasions, these trading centers take on the appearance of pioneer towns, with hitching rails, haphazard sidewalks, and crude plumbing; riders on horseback, buckboards, and buggies; and men with tanned faces and alert eyes in chaps and spurs, or blue jeans and stetsons.

It was mining that, in the nineties, brought the valley its first and only boom; and mines, gold, silver, lead, tungsten, and copper, are being worked in the surrounding hills today. Cattle and sheep are also raised here, and some logging is also carried on; but fruit raising, farming, and dairying are the chief sources of wealth. Apple orchards of the Methow Valley produce mainly four varieties of apple: Delicious, Winesap, Jonathan, and Rome Beauties. The annual apple harvest is a gala event of some six weeks duration, beginning in mid-September and continuing, unless cut short by sharp freezes, until early November. Outsiders flock into the valley by the hundreds, and there are many dances and other forms of entertainment. Some years ago Owen Wister lived for a while in the valley and described several local episodes and characters in his novel, *The Virginian.* The valley has changed but little since Wister's visit.

At 11 *m.* is METHOW (1,158 alt., 54 pop.), its one short street bordered by twin rows of lofty shade trees.

North of Methow the highway twines along the river, skirting sheer banks without railings, and shrinking at times to a width that scarcely allows for passing; its surface, too, is inferior to that of the Pateros-Methow stretch.

Near the mouth of GOLD CREEK, 18.4 *m.,* an improved country road leads westward into the hills, through a farming district to a CCC Camp.

CARLTON, 23.5 *m.* (1,220 alt., 100 pop.), has a store, garage, restaurant, and radio shop. Here the valley widens abruptly. To the west, the river still wets the base of the hills, but eastward from the road and river lies a gently-rolling land of hayfields and orchards.

Left from Carlton to the site of OLD CARLTON, 0.5 *m.* The town stood at this site until 1927, when a change in the highway route left it a half mile off the main road. Residents shifted the town buildings to the present location, with the exception of an old hotel which could not be moved; ancient and dilapidated, it is now occupied as a residence.

At 3 *m.* is a junction with a dirt side road: L. off the Loop Loop into fertile Beaver Creek Canyon. On the side road is TWISP, 34.1 *m.* (1,619 alt., 447 pop.), with a high school, creamery, sawmill, and numerous business establishments. Here the Twisp River, fresh from the Cascades, joins the Methow River.

Left from Twisp, State 17 leads into the Twisp River Valley, at the west end of which an extension, through Twisp Pass (6,066 alt.) and Cascade Pass, will give the Methow Valley a direct link with Puget Sound and western Washington points. Unimproved or indifferently improved roads ascend the grades of most of the Methow River's tributaries above Twisp, penetrating regions similar to Twisp River Valley.

WINTHROP, 43.4 *m.* (1,765 alt., 365 pop.), marks the end of hard surfacing in the Methow Valley. North of Winthrop the Methow Valley is a virtual wilderness, highly favored by sportsmen for hunting and fishing; its roads are usually passable only in summer, and most of the terrain is attainable only by pack-trails.

Northwest of Winthrop State 16, now a dirt road, follows Methow River to the little outpost village of MAZAMA, 55.4 *m.* (21 pop.), a jumping-off place for miners who spend their winters "snowed in" in the mines of the high Cascades. At the summit of HARTS PASS, 68.4 *m.* (6,197 alt), the northwest of Mazama, State 16 ends.

South of Pateros, US 97 follows the west bank of the Columbia River through a region of rocks, sand, and sagebrush. Square boulders of all sizes seem like dice which were thrown against the ridge and tumbled down the sloping terrain toward the river.

In this locality, camels were sometimes encountered about 35 years ago. Introduced into Washington as pack animals during the early mining days, they were found unsuitable to travel on rocky or marshy ground and were turned loose in the Okanogan country.

A species of small cactus that blooms in the spring and resembles the prickly pear of southwestern United States is native to this district. Scorpions, familiar denizens of the desert, are found hereabouts, and black widow spiders are not uncommon.

South of AZWELL, 90.6 *m.* US 97 leaves the Columbia River and bears southwest up a consistent grade.

At 103.7 *m.* is the junction with State 10-D, a bituminous-surfaced road.

Left on this road, the route descends with numerous switchbacks into the Columbia River Canyon. At 2 *m.* is the jagged CHELAN RIVER GORGE which walls in the curving sides of the Chelan River, only four miles in length. This stream, which before hydroelectric and irrigation development was a river of considerable volume, is now little more than the spillway over the great natural moraine dam and the concrete dam constructed to raise the waters of Lake Chelan. There is no trace of vegetation in this rocky canyon except for a gnarled pine looking down from its perch on a high point.

At 3.6 *m.* is a junction with a bituminous-surfaced road; L. here 0.7 *m.* to CHELAN STATION (737 alt., 71 pop.), a shipping point on the west bank of the Columbia River, where fruit packing sheds and cold storage plants stand near the depot. From this point a TOLL BRIDGE (60c) crosses the Columbia River.

At 3.8 *m.* on the main side road is the generating plant (L) of the Washington Water Power Company. On the slope (R) above the road a row of modern brick dwellings house some of the company's employees.

CHELAN FALLS, 4.0 *m.* (737 alt., 100 pop.), is a post office and several weathered old houses. Orchards crowd the space between the road and the river.

At 4.7 *m.* the road ends on the west shore of the Columbia.

West of the Junction US 97 traverses a flat. The highway is lined with orchards.

CHELAN, 104.9 *m.* (1,208 alt., 1,738 pop.), is the trading center and outlet for the Lake Chelan mining and fruit-growing region. Modern brick structures contrast with buildings on the wide main street. Water power, water transportation, fruit raising, lumbering, and mining are Chelan's main industries, and the town also carries on a brisk tourist trade. Launches operate to Stehekin and Lucerne on Lake Chelan (*see Lake Chelan Recreation Area Map*).

SAINT ANDREW'S EPISCOPAL CHURCH (L), one of the oldest institutions in the region, is an old brown log building with a modern frame and stucco annex.

Chelan received wide attention from the press in 1936 when a pension plan was tested by Townsendites. One thousand dollars in dollar bills were circulated, with the provision that a two-cent stamp should be attached each time a bill changed hands. The plan was abandoned after a period of trial.

At LAKESIDE, 106.7 *m.* (1,091 alt., 238 pop.), many boat landings lie below sloping green lawns bordering comfortable cottages.

West of Lakeside US 97 follows the southwestern shore of Lake Chelan and passes many orchards. Leaving the lake, the highway turns southward, winding its way through coulees down to the Columbia River. Large boulders and odd stratifications are numerous.

At 114.3 *m.* a highway tunnel, 600 feet long, 26 feet wide, and 21 feet high, through a portion of Knapp's Hill, eliminates the dangerous cutbacks and steep grades of the old road that winds above.

WINESAP, 117.6 *m.* (699 alt., 30 pop.), is the center of an orchard. RIBBON CLIFF, 119.5 *m.,* is a hamlet named for the lofty crags which rise above it. Two totem poles, unusual sights in this interior country, stand beside the highway (R).

ENTIAT (Ind. rapid water), 124.6 *m.* (689 alt., 290 pop.), a village scattered about the mouth of the Entiat River, guards the entrance to a fertile valley and sportsmen's paradise.

Right from Entiat by an oiled road into the ENTIAL VALLEY, less than a half-mile in width, a flat bottom land with numerous low terraces walled in by steep mountains broken by narrow gorges. STELIKO RANGER STATION, 11 *m.,* is at the mouth of Mad River and at a junction with a dirt side road; L. here along the north bank of the Mad River.

At 4 *m.* on the side road is a junction with a trail. Continuing on the trail up the Mad River to MAD RIVER DUDE RANCH, 23 *m.,* in a setting of small lakes on the eastern slope of the Cascade Mountains. Trails lead in many directions into scenic country and great glacier fields. Numberless varieties of flowers cover the meadows.

South of Entiat, the highway follows the Columbia River; the shallow bar (L), just below the mouth of the Entiat River, was caused by the dumping of thousands of boulders into the Columbia by Entiat's rushing waters.

At 128.3 *m.* a ferry (*24-hour service on signal only; car and passenger* 50c: *night* 75c). connects with Orondo on US 10 and the east bank of the Columbia River (*see Tour 1a*).

Many roads, some of them paved, wind among modern bungalows and farm homes. Fruit ranches in this district average only seven acres, the size preferred for intensive orchard cultivation. The network of roads permits rapid transit to and from near-by WENATCHEE (*see Tour 1a*).

Continuing southward, US 97 hugs the Columbia's west bank. Shallow at this point, the river is pitted with many rocks; small islands snuggle against the shores. White, yellow, and brown cliffs become lower; sunburned hills loom left, green and rocky foothills right. After rounding a high point, the highway enters the Wenatchee Valley. Orchards are everywhere as the lava and sagebrush give way to cultivated lands.

At **141.5** *m.* is the junction of US 97 and the cross-State highway, US 10. From the junction to TEANAWAY, **193.9** *m.* (1,936 alt., 100 pop.), (*see Tour 1a*), US 97 and US 10 coincide.

Section b. TEANAWAY *to* MARYHILL, *139.1 m. US 97*

The Yakima Valley, through which US 97 runs, includes the whole rich territory tributary to the Yakima River, reaching from Lake Keechelus and Kachess to the Columbia River. It includes the valleys of the Kittitas, Naches, Ahtanum, Cowiche, Salash, Wenas, Satus, and the Toppenish. The Kittitas, or Upper Yakima Valley, fan-shaped, with an almost imperceptible slope toward the Yakima River, drains three mountain lakes, Keechelus, Kachess, and Cle Elum.

Southeast of TEANAWAY, **0** *m.* (*see Tour 1a*), US 97 separates from US 10 and continues along the Yakima River. Ice-capped Mount Rainier (R) towers in the western sky (*see Mount Rainier National Park*).

An Indian band under the leadership of William Wilson, a renegade white, roamed the Kittitas district during the 1860's. The only means of access to and from the Swauk mining area was through this valley, and due to their strategic position, the Indians and their white leader exacted a heavy toll from gold-seekers, cattlemen, and farmers. Wilson was drowned in the Snake River in 1869 while trying to escape with stolen horses.

At **0.7** *m.,* US 97 enters a narrow gorge. Massive rock formations rise to form the opposite canyon walls (L), while the river foams and dashes in its rough bed several hundred feet below. Impressive views present themselves from time to time as the highway winds past natural vantage points.

Emerging from the gorge at **7.7** *m.,* the highway swings away from the river and cuts through a wide valley given over to farming. Trees here lean heavily eastward, indicating the force and frequency of the west winds which roar through the gorge. At **16.2** *m.* US 97 crosses REESER CREEK, a small stream pursuing a twisted course across the rich meadows which flank the highway.

Entering the western city limits of Ellensburg on 8th St., US 97 turns L. on A St., hemmed by dark old brick buildings, to the city center.

ELLENSBURG, 20.3 *m.* (1,518 alt., 5,944 pop.), neatly laid out on the flat floor of Kittitas Valley approximately in the geographic center of the State, has preserved much of its early Western atmosphere. Stooped prospectors, squaws in screaming calicos, and leather-jacketed students mingle with sedate professional men. Several Chinese families live in Ellensburg, descendants of a band that followed the eastern Washington gold rush and worked over mine dumps left by white men.

An annual rodeo, staged for a three-day period ending on Labor Day, is second in the Pacific Northwest only to Pendleton's famous "Roundup." The event brings to the city leading professionals in riding and roping and spectators from all portions of the State.

Originally called "Ellen's Burgh," after Ellen Shoudy, wife of John A. Shoudy, one of the original settlers, the town dropped its "h" by order of the Post Office Department. It is the seat of Kittitas County.

The first settlement here was picturesquely styled "Robber's Roost"; this name appeared on the sign of a log trading post, the only structure in the valley at that time. The building was erected in 1867 near a spring, now within the city limits, by Wilson, the renegade. Wilson sold out to A. J. Splawn, a young and adventurous cowboy who called it Robber's Roost after his outlaw predecessor. In 1872 the town consisted of a general store, saloon, post office, blacksmith shop, and a few residences.

Growth was more rapid after 1883. With the coming of the long-awaited Northern Pacific Railway in 1886, the town was incorporated; when the Milwaukee arrived in 1907, Ellensburg boomed.

Gold from the Swauk Creek district continues to pass through. Farming and dairying, stabilized by irrigation, are supplemented by coal mining in near-by mountain communities.

The CENTRAL WASHINGTON COLLEGE OF EDUCATION, E. 8th, D, and Walnut Sts., has a group of ten buildings and several school residences in a setting of green lawns and old shade trees. The administration building, a chateau-type four-story structure, with mansard roofs and a domed central tower over an arched entrance, is the oldest on the campus. Other buildings are rectangular brick structures with pseudo-classic porticos, the pediments supported by fluted columns. Formerly known as the Washington State Normal School, the college is one of the three institutions in the State specializing in training teachers for elementary and junior high schools. It is supported by legislative appropriation, and no tuition is charged; students pay only their living expenses. Established in 1890 by the first State legislature, the school opened in September of the following year.

The departments of the college today include language and literature, mathematics, education and psychology, fine and applied arts, social science and history, training school, health education, and music. About 800 students attend the college.

At Ellensburg, US 97 forms a junction with State 7 (*see Tour 1A*). Left on 8th Street to city limits.

US 97 nears the Yakima River between alfalfa fields and orchards.

At 26.3 *m.* the highway enters the confines of the YAKIMA CANYON. The high varicolored walls glisten in the sunlight; lower crevices are veiled in shadow. Splashing along the canyon floor is the Yakima River. Prior to construction of the present highway, the only route through the canyon was by railroad. Rugged natural obstacles delayed for years the completion of both the Northern Pacific Railway and the highway.

US 97 winds along a shelf carved from solid rock, sometimes by the side of the river, sometimes high above it. From many points along this road, the contour of overhanging cliffs makes the Yakima River appear to run uphill; the river existed before the rocky ridges were heaved up, and it kept pace with the upward movement of the earth in wearing out its channel.

At 32 *m.* an almost perpendicular hill (L) looms along the highway. Pillars of variegated columnar rock crowd on both sides of the road as it cuts through the solid basalt.

ROZA, 37.3 *m.* (1,250 alt., 40 pop.), visible across the river (R), was named after the daughter of a railroad official. Once no more than a railroad stop, it is important today as the site of the diversion dam of the ROZA IRRIGATION PROJECT, from which waters flow southwest through 90 miles of ditches, canals, flumes, and three tunnels cut in solid rock. The Roza irrigation division, beginning here, is a narrow strip, containing 72,000 acres of fertile land extending to Benton City, 56 miles to the southeast. Irrigated at an estimated cost of $195 per acre, the soil on the benchland ranges in altitude from 700 to 1,200 feet. The storage basin is north of the city of Cle Elum in the lakes and streams feeding the Yakima River and its tributaries (*see Tour 1b*).

The history of the Roza Project goes back to 1918, when a board of engineers made extensive investigations. In 1935, President Franklin D. Roosevelt approved an allocation of $5,000,000 of FERA funds for the inauguration of the Roza project. Work was started early in 1936.

At 42.8 *m.* a tunnel takes the highway through a rock point and down into a flat along the river at the mouth of arid Squaw Creek Canyon. The rolling hills slope back from the river. In places they are covered with sagebrush and in others dotted with orchards and farms. Green cottonwood and aspen mark the river's course. White deposits of magnesite gleam in the sunlight.

POMONA, 50.0 *m.* (1,157 alt., 37 pop.), has its railroad station on the opposite side of the river. The name, honoring the Roman goddess of fruit, is justified by an occasional orchard. The valley widens out from the river's banks.

At 56.4 *m.* is the junction with a paved road.

Right on this road to a modern steel bridge that spans the Yakima River at 1 *m.* This spot on the river was used as a ford by pioneers. Here in 1853 the party of Henry Longmire, seeking to traverse the valley to Olympia, lost a portion of its wagons and many personal belongings in the turbulent stream.

A charter was granted to J. T. Hicklin in 1863 to "operate a ferry across the Yakima at a location somewhere between the mouth of the Wenas River and a point three miles below the debouchment of the Naches." Hicklin, who in some manner acquired the nickname of "Jumping Tadpole," operated his little ferry profitably until the spring of 1867, when the river, rising to heights never before known, swept the craft upon the rocks below.

SELAH (Ind. still water), 1.5 *m.* (1,108 alt., 767 pop.), is almost a suburb of Yakima (*see Yakima*). Fruit-packing and cold-storage plants, bordering the railroad tracks, and a modern business district constitute the town. Mountains of boxes, great mounds of apples, piles of peelings, and the smell of fermented fruit are eloquent signs of the region's activities during harvest and packing season. Selah was the name applied to a section of the Yakima River about a mile and a half in length, lying between the present site of Pomona and a point a little south of Selah. Between Ellensburg and Pomona the river is very swift and rough, but on emerging from the Kittitas Canyon into a level valley it flows smoothly for a short distance, then passes over rapids again. The Indians apparently applied no proper name to the entire stream but used words describing peculiar characteristics of different sections. The name Selah was extended to Selah Creek and other parts of the valley by settlers.

Left from Selah on an oiled road that climbs to the top of a high hill; junction at 4.2 *m.* with a gravel road: L. here to LOOKOUT POINT, overlooking the Naches, Cowiche, and Yakima Valleys.

South of the junction, the route crosses the Yakima and Naches Rivers just before they merge. US 97 enters Yakima on N. 1st St.; straight ahead on N. 1st St. to Yakima Ave., the junction with US 410 (*see Tour 2b*). L. on E. Yakima Ave. to city center.

YAKIMA, 57 *m.* (1,067 alt., 27,221 pop.), (*see Yakima*).

Left from Yakima on State 11-A, 6 *m.,* is MOXEE (1,000 alt., 325 pop.). This village might be taken for the suburb of a French city because of the names on street signs or over the shops. The inhabitants of French descent, many of them pioneer settlers, came from Canada. French is still used extensively by the old people of the city. The Moxee rural district is dotted with large prosperous homes. A small colony of Dutch live in harmony with their Gallic neighbors.

Hops in this section, developed by generations of growers, are of high quality, rivaling the best of imported stock. When ripe, the hops become crisp, and their color changes from a light silvery green to a deep yellow, indicating that the lupulin content is at its best. The value of a hop is contained in the lupulin, a yellow substance that possesses a pungently bitter, but agreeable flavor. The brewmaster's ideal hop is said to be not too large, and tender and thin-leaved.

The Hop Dance, held in Moxee the last week in September, marks the end of the harvest.

The route continues S. on S. 1st St. South of Yakima, US 97 and 410 coincide to Buena (*see Tour 2b*).

At BUENA, 72.9 *m.* (785 alt., 400 pop.), at a junction with US 410 (*see Tour 2b*), US 97 bears R. and crosses the Yakima River.

TOPPENISH (Ind. people from the foot of the hills), 76 *m.* (756 alt., 2,774 pop.), like Yakima, is divided by railroad tracks. Old frame structures, relics of the early days, stand beside staunch modern brick buildings. Hotels and stores with long, wide, creaky verandas line sections of the main streets. On Saturday nights during the harvest season, the streets are crowded with hop and fruit pickers; whole families exchange their meager wages for high-priced groceries and cheap entertainment. Indians from the near-by Yakima Indian Reservation are often seen along the streets—the younger generation attired in the slacks and sweaters usually worn by youngsters; the older people in bright shirts, shawls, and bandanas, still inclining towards high-pitched colors.

Potatoes of a high quality are raised around Toppenish. In 1909 the Northern Pacific Railway began featuring a giant baked potato in its advertising, and the large symmetrical tubers grown here played no small part in popularizing the slogan: "Route of the Big Baked Potato." Other important agricultural products are sugar beets, alfalfa, wheat, corn, watermelons, canteloupes, and fruit.

OLNEY PARK, corner Adams and Jefferson Aves., is a small, but beautifully landscaped park, with a large open-air fireplace.

MARY L. GOODRICH LIBRARY, 119 E. Toppenish Ave., has 8,000 volumes, including a small historical collection, and a collection of Indian artifacts.

At the LONG HOUSE (*open to public*), an Indian ceremonial building in the southeastern part of the city, the Yakima Indians of the reservation gather each year shortly before Christmas to celebrate the holiday in their own way. The ceremony lasts for about three weeks. This community hall is constructed after the manner of the ancient long house. It is a long, narrow, windowless frame structure, with a wide opening the full length of the ridge pole; it accommodates 300 persons. The Shakers conduct religious services here; outside spectators are not welcome but are not excluded. Indian handicraft objects may be purchased, including colorful, finely woven, imbricated basketry.

Brady Leyman's HOME MUSEUM (*open by arrangement at store*), at 201 S. Chestnut St., has a display of Indian saddles, painted buffalo hides, basketry, war bonnets, scalp poles, ornamented buckskin dresses, and beadwork.

The social event of the year at Toppenish is the Pioneer Dinner, held May 13.

Near Toppenish, the UTAH-IDAHO SUGAR BEET COMPANY PLANT (*open afternoons, workdays*) is a group of large concrete buildings centered by a towering smokestack. The plant has its own wells which are from 75 to 140 feet deep and which deliver 3,000 gallons a minute. A 2,100-horsepower steam turbo-generator supplies electric power for factory lights and for the 210 motors in the plant.

In the rear are railroad tracks and enormous storage piles of beets. The beets are fed by automatic conveyors into washers, hoisted to the shredders, and passed into a hot water bath to extract the juice, which goes into a battery of cookers. The juice, reduced under heat and vacuum pressure to syrup, is strained, clarified with lime and sulphur gas, and returned to the cookers. When the syrup is of the proper consistency and "grain," it passes to spinners which, like cream separators, divide the molasses from the white sugar. The latter is dried, crystalized, screened, and passed on to the sackers.

The factory, a noteworthy example of advanced engineering methods and industrial design, employs a gravity system for handling materials. The materials are brought to the top floor and descend half a dozen times through various processes, then pass through elevator conveyors or pumps and pipelines to the top to start down into further refining processes.

The factory runs 24 hours daily and has not been closed in two years. Two hundred and sixty pounds of sugar are extracted from a ton of beets, and the daily run is from 1,600 to 2,000 tons of the raw beets. The company maintains another plant in Bellingham.

At S. Elm St. (US 97) and W. 1st Ave., is the junction with a bituminous-surfaced road, State 3-B.

Right on State 3-B, through the YAKIMA INDIAN RESERVATION, the boundary of which is on the western outskirts of Toppenish. Inhabitants of the Yakima Reservation are descendants of a coalition formed in the middle of the last century by the original Yakima and 13 other bands. In 1938 the population of the Yakima Indian tribe, the largest in the State, was 2,933, most of whom live on small farms and ranches. The principal occupations of the Indians are basketweaving, farming, and buckskin clothing manufacture, also some hunting, fishing, berry gathering, and rounding up of wild horses. (*see Indians*).

Indian children attend the regular public schools, to which the United States Indian Service contributes a stipulated amount. Some attend special regional Indian schools, and a few the State institutions of higher learning. The native Shaker church has many adherents. Roman Catholic and Protestant services are also held on the reservation. Just before root-digging time in the spring, and later, about the time of the first salmon run, there are thanksgiving ceremonies.

WHITE SWAN, 20 *m.* (200 pop.), is an Indian village, named for a famous Yakima Chief. Here, the first church in the district, rebuilt by the Indians for the Oblate Roman Catholic Fathers in 1872, still stands. The original mission structure had been destroyed during the War of 1855-6. During July, in the "long house" within this village, future policies and activities are planned. The meetings are open to the public. The TRUESDALE HOUSE MUSEUM (*private*), holds a collection of Indian basketry, clothing, and ornaments. A gravel road continues L. from White Swan over a spur of the Cascade Mountains.

FORT SIMCOE, 28 *m.,* established in August 1856, the year after a defeat of United States troops under Major G. O. Holler by Yakima Indians, is on a small flat known to tribesmen for centuries as MOOL MOOL (Ind. bubbling springs). According to General George B. McClellan, who as a young lieutenant visited the site in 1853, the Yakima had a fort here as early as 1849 to ward off the Cayuse. The buildings of the Army post were constructed by the soldiers of the garrison, two companies under command of Major Robert Selden Garnett. According to W. D. Lyman, historian, four buildings built in Maine, knocked down, shipped around Cape Horn, up the Columbia River and over the hills to Simcoe by pack-train, cost the Government nearly $250,000. The main building, the only one of the original group to escape razing or alteration, was once the commander's residence, and later the Indian Agency headquarters. It is a large, white-painted, two-story structure. Spreading branches of great oaks overhang the main gables of the steep-pitched roof. Little diamond-shaped panes gleam from beneath the eaves. The sides are of vertical batten boards. Windows in the front of the house are tall, usually in groups of three. Within the trellised portico is the large front entrance lighted at top and sides with a score of square panes. The inside walls and ceilings are of random-width boards, some plastered. Chimneys are brick; the several fireplaces of brick and stone. A stair, handrail, and newel post are of white mahogany. The foundation is of rough-cut native stone.

The first Indian agent, R. H. Lonsdale, appointed in 1860, was relieved several months later when serious charges were brought against him. A. A. Bancroft was appointed in 1861 by President Lincoln. His mishandling of the Indians aroused them and brought remonstrances from James H. Wilbur, Superintendent of Schools. Bancroft had Wilbur removed, with the result that Wilbur, with abundant evidence and data, appeared before President Lincoln. The President recalled Bancroft, appointing Wilbur in his place in 1864. His tenure lasted 16 years. Known to the Indians as Father Wilbur, he was honest yet severe; it is said an oak tree, near the buildings, served as a whipping post.

A BLOCKHOUSE (*open*) is in a good state of repair. It has only one story, and is well-fitted, square-adzed logs, with corners dovetailed with two-way pitch. The site of the old parade ground (opposite the building) is covered by the remnants of an old orchard.

South of Toppenish, US 97 heads straight across the flat valley floor, crosses Toppenish Creek, and winds through Toppenish Ridge and upstream on Satus (Ind. people of the rye prairie) Creek. Because US 97 is still within the reservation, hunting or fishing is strictly forbidden.

At 80.6 *m.* is a junction with a dirt road.

Left on this road to CIRCLE JS DUDE RANCH, 1 *m.,* a summer resort.

Known as the HORSE HEAVEN HILLS, the country abutting the highway is a great natural grazing area where roving bands of wild horses feed on the abundant grass. A fat, sleek bay occasionally gallops over broken terrain, without halter, saddle, or shoes, his luxurious mane and tail flowing in the breeze. Smaller pintos, more nervous and less majestic, are easily agitated by an approaching automobile. Perky colts worry their mothers by wandering toward the road to investigate the queer, shiny vehicles that raise so much roar and dirt.

As US 97 winds into the Horse Heaven Hills, minor streams are crossed. Vegetation becomes greener and thicker. Long-needled, large-coned pines bristle from the mountain slopes, occasionally rising almost from the shoulders of the highway. Here in ages past, the sequoia, extant only in the redwood region of northern California, throve in a great forest; petrified logs of this tree are found among volcanic ash and lava in the area.

At 112.5 *m.* SATUS PASS (3,149 alt.), is crossed. Beyond the reach of trampling feet, wild flowers bloom among tufts of wild grass.

South of Satus Pass, the highway crosses Klickitat Creek, flowing between palisaded rock walls. This tempestuous mountain stream, originating in the Satus Pass region, bends westward as the highway spans it and flows through Goldendale and a diversified farming area to empty into the Columbia River at Lyle. It is shaded by great, spreading pines.

GOLDENDALE, 126.6 *m.* (1,610 alt., 1,584 pop.), is the seat of Klickitat County. Brick buildings, new and ancient, front on the well-paved main street. Loggers, farmers, mill-men in pitch-spotted "tin" pants, and cattlemen, some with chaps, spurs, and ten-gallon hats, stride the streets. Lumber and flour mills, box, sash, and door factories, dairying and diversified farming are the principal industries. The town was named after John J. Golden, who homesteaded here in 1863.

Goldendale lies at the southeastern edge of the Mount Adams Recreational Area, a region of lakes, streams, and forests, where game birds and a wide variety of trout and bass abound (*see Mount Adams Recrea-*

tion Area Map). The town is also on the old trail between The Dalles, Oregon, and Fort Simcoe.

In the City Park is a BLOCKHOUSE, a rectangular log cabin that was moved into town from its original site seven miles away. It was built by Major Gabriel Rains during the Indian campaigns of the fifties. Recently, the structure has been used for Boy Scout activities and other purposes.

The Goldendale Jamboree takes place annually early in September. The countrywide Grange picnic is held the last week of each August.

South of Goldendale, where moisture-laden air blows up from the Columbia, US 97 descends in a series of horseshoe bends through hills that rise from the river's deep-cleft course. The curious markings seen everywhere on the steep slopes are sheep trails.

The SAMUEL HILL MARKER (L), 134 *m.,* was erected in 1921 to a pioneer booster of better roads by his Klickitat County neighbors.

MARYHILL JUNCTION, 136.8 *m.,* is the junction with US 830 (*see Tour 3a*).

At 137.4 *m.,* on a windswept promontory (L) at the brink of the Columbia River, is STONEHENGE, modelled after the celebrated ruins in Wiltshire, England. It consists of a circular group of concrete slabs supported on pillars, which enclose five immense arches and a single horizontal slab. A blonze plaque, inlaid in this slab, dedicates the monument to the "Memory of the soldiers and sailors of Klickitat County who gave their lives in defense of their country."

South of Stonehenge, US 97 descends rapidly by a series of loops to the northern bank of the Columbia River.

MARYHILL STATION, 139.1 *m.,* is the depot for the Spokane, Portland & Seattle Railroad. A FERRY (*$1 per car, passengers included*) operates from Maryhill to Biggs, Oregon, on the opposite shore of the Columbia, where US 97 continues southward.

Tour 8

(Vancouver, B. C.)—Blaine—Bellingham—Mount Vernon—Everett—Seattle—Tacoma—Olympia—Chehalis—Marys Corner—Kelso—Vancouver, Wash.—(Portland, Ore.); US 99.
Canadian Border to Oregon Line, 296.2 *m.*

Concrete-paved thoroughfare; four lanes wide between Everett and Olympia. Great Northern Ry. roughly parallels route between Blaine and Seattle; Northern

Pacific Ry., Great Northern Ry., and Union Pacific R.R. (common track) between Seattle and Vancouver, Wash.
All types of accommodations; hotels chiefly in cities.

US 99, the Pacific Highway, main highway in western Washington and most heavily traveled in the State, roughly follows the route of Territorial military roads that linked the settlements of the Puget Sound and of the Columbia River regions. In the southern section, it approximates also the route of a branch of the Oregon Trail, blazed northward around the middle of the nineteenth century.

The northern section of the highway passes through the most popular part of the State. From many points, it affords sweeping views of the island-dotted Puget Sound and the jagged Olympic Mountains to the west, and of the Cascade Mountains, a blue-green ridge tipped here and there with white, in the east. At intervals the route crosses sluggish rivers flowing through fertile bottom lands, or skirts the edges of high, wooded bluffs. Large well-cultivated farms, truck gardens, orchards and berry fields, dairy farms, and poultry ranches alternate with patches of second-growth timber and stump lands. Between the small towns strung out along the highway are the usual roadside inns, gasoline stations, tourist camps, and crossroads general stores.

South of the Puget Sound Basin, US 99 crosses gently rolling prairies, broken by small areas of evergreen, maple, and alder. Dominating the eastern horizon is Mount Rainier, while southward Mount Adams and Mount St. Helens seem less majestic, though only by comparison. The farms, gardens, and poultry ranches of lowlands give way to forested hills, barren cutover lands, and occasional marginal farms. Logging operations have largely retreated into the foothills, but trucks loaded with sections of huge logs thunder along the highway, and cut lumber is stacked in sawmill yards and along railroad sidings of the scattered towns and villages. For miles, US 99 follows the Cowlitz and Columbia Rivers and, finally, crosses the Columbia into Oregon.

Section a. CANADIAN BORDER *to* MOUNT VERNON; *49.1 m. US 99*

Beginning at the Canadian Line, US 99 runs almost due south through a green and pleasant region of truck gardens, orchards, woodland patches, and meadowlands, and neat, attractive houses and well-built barns. Most of this land was once covered by magnificent stands of Douglas fir, hemlock, and Western red cedar, but today much of it has been cleared and brought under cultivation.

This region is favored by an equable climate, tempered by the mild moisture-laden winds from the Pacific Ocean in summer and protected from cold winter winds by the mountain barriers to the east. Seldom are summer days more than comfortably warm, with cool ocean breezes springing up in the evening and frequent showers. Autumn brings fogs and cloudy skies and low-lying mists that settle over the mountains and trail along valleys and lowlands. In winter, cold waves move down occasionally from the north, and, congealing the moisture of warmer ocean air, bring a heavy fall of snow that transforms the land into a white, shimmering paradise, marred only by the hazards of driving on slippery or icy roads.

US 99 crosses the CANADIAN LINE, 0 *m.,* 32.4 miles south of Vancouver, British Columbia, at a point marked by the imposing concrete PEACE ARCH (L). Across the crest of the arch, on the Canadian side are the words: "Brothers Dwelling Together in Unity"; on the Washington side, "Children of a Common Mother." Three annual celebrations are held here: International Easter Services; International Flag Day on July 2; and International Armistice Day on November 11.

The SAMUEL HILL MEMORIAL PARK (L), a wooded seven-acre tract planted with many kinds of shrubs and flowers, was named for Samuel Hill, good-roads enthusiast, and commemorates Canadian-American peace and good will. At the southern end of the park (L) is the UNITED STATES CUSTOM AND IMMIGRATION STATION (*open 8 a.m.-12 midnight*).

At 0.2 *m.* is a junction with a concrete-surfaced road.

Left here is a branch UNITED STATES CUSTOMS AND IMMIGRATION STATION, 1.4 *m.* (*open* 24 *hours a day, June* 1-*Sept.* 30; 7 *a.m.*-1 *a.m., Oct.* 1-*May* 30).

BLAINE, 0.6 *m.* (41 alt., 1,642 pop.), on Drayton Harbor, derives its income chiefly from tourists' trade and from the surrounding farming area. A small co-operative shingle mill operates intermittently. During the Fraser River gold rush in 1858 a tent colony sprang up on the shores of the harbor, only to dwindle away within the year. The town, platted in 1884, was originally named Concord, but was renamed to honor James G. Blaine, presidential candidate.

For a number of years fishing was a profitable industry of the area, and a salmon cannery, now closed, operated at Blaine. Smugglers and fish pirates, working out from the safety of Point Roberts, the American-owned tip of the Canadian peninsula 14 miles west of the town, levied tribute upon legitimate enterprise. Smuggling was brought to a close, however, in 1910, when the Federal Government installed the Point Roberts Light, the northernmost light along the coast of the United States.

In the ANDREW DANIELSON LIBRARY (*open*) is a collection of 1,000 volumes in Icelandic.

South of Blaine at 2.1 *m.* is the junction with State 1-A, a concrete-paved road.

Left here through one of the richest agricultural regions in the State. Logged-off lands, cleared of stumps by a laborious and expensive process of blasting, pulling, and burning, now produce excellent crops of vegetables, berries, fruits, daffodils, and tulips in commercial quantities. Years of intensive cultivation are required to make farming such land profitable. The climate and soil of this part of the State are well suited to the growing of sugar beets, most of the beets coming from five- to ten-acre tracts or from diversified farms. The large fields, comparatively few in number, are planted, cultivated, and harvested by machinery. Much of the work, however, such as the back-breaking thinning and weeding, must be done by hand.

Dairying is another important source of income. The dairy industry has profited from the long season of green pasturage and the mild winters. Today, the area ships large quantities of fresh milk, butter, cheese, and other milk products, in addition to supplying local needs. Poultry raising is also important, especially on logged-off lands not yet sufficiently cultivated to insure good crops. White leghorns are favored because of their high egg yield. Products are processed, packed, and marketed by the Washington Co-operative Egg and Poultry Association. Eggs are shipped by the carload to the East, although in recent years this outlet has been partially lost to poultry ranches nearer the market. Another branch of the industry is the hatching of chicks for sale, hundreds of thousands being sold annually.

LYNDEN, 15.2 *m.* (95 alt., 1,696 pop.), a substantial, thriving distribution and market center of northern Whatcom County, was settled in 1869. Among its industrial plants are an egg warehouse, from which carloads of eggs are shipped to New York City; a barreling plant for packing strawberries and other fruits; a creamery, operated by the Whatcom County Dairymen's Association; and a plant for converting surplus, skim, and sour milk into stock food.

Since 1900, when the first Hollanders arrived, Lynden has been predominantly Dutch. Older Hollanders speak Dutch in their homes and still preserve old-country customs in cookery and decoration. In the town are four Dutch-language churches. The Hollanders introduced their native methods of bulb culture with remarkable success, and for years Lynden has shipped carloads of bulbs to all parts of the world. In the spring acres of golden daffodils and tulips of variegated hues stretch for miles away from the highways. In recent years some of the acreage formerly devoted to bulb cultivation is being planted to crops which meet with less competition. Berries and garden truck are also important agricultural products. The Whatcom County Agricultural Fair is held here annually in the fall.

North of Lynden, State 1-A runs in a general northeasterly direction through orderly fields of daffodils, tulips, truck gardens, berry fields, poultry runs, pasture lands, and trim houses with well-painted barns, interspersed with stretches of forest and patches of stump land. To the right, snow-capped Mount Baker and Mount Shuksan glitter above the line of the Cascade Mountains.

In Sumas Creek Valley is SUMAS, 27.2 *m.* (48 alt., 647 pop.), a boundary town of frame and old brick buildings. In 1858, during the first of the periodic gold rushes, a number of prospectors with great difficulty made their way overland along an Indian trail through Sumas Valley to the wilderness of the upper Fraser River country. Today, the town derives its income largely from the dairy and cattle ranches of the surrounding farming area, supplementing this income by border trade. The two-story brick building housing the UNITED STATES CUSTOMS AND IMMIGRATION STATION (*open* 8 *a.m.*-12 *midnight*) is (L) at the north end of Cherry Street.

South of Blaine US 99 cuts through an area of small farms, with orderly houses set in neat patches of lawn, and woods of vigorous, second-growth fir and alder.

At 2.5 *m.* is a junction with a concrete-paved road.

Right here to BIRCH BAY, 5 *m.* (sea level, 12 pop.) (*tennis, golf, swimming*). Captain George Vancouver named the bay in 1792 for the numerous black birches along its shore. Clam digging along the fine sandy beach and salt-water fishing are popular recreations.

South of the junction, US 99 runs for miles through second-growth forests, logged-off wastelands, and small farms and poultry ranches. In clear weather the highway offers splendid panoramic views of the dark-forested foothills to the east. CUSTER, 8.2 *m.* (32 alt., 250 pop.), is a community trading village.

At 13.5 *m.* is a junction with a concrete-paved road.

Right here to FERNDALE, 0.8 *m.* (26 alt., 717 pop.), a thriving town on the Nooksack River. The surrounding countryside, largely dairy farms and pasture lands, supplies the raw milk for a condensery and powdered-milk plant in the town.

US 99 crosses the NOOKSACK RIVER, 13.7 *m.,* a slow-flowing, turgid stream in summer, a debris-laden torrent when swollen by a heavy downpour or rapidly melting snow. The RIVERSIDE GOLF CLUB (R), 14.2 *m.* (*greens fee 35c weekdays; 50c Sat., Sun., and holidays*), maintains a nine-hole course with a number of interesting hazards. Suburban homes, charming in a setting of shrubbery, lawns, and flower beds, give way to dairy farms and pasture lands.

BELLINGHAM, 22.7 *m.* (sea level, 29,314 pop.) (*see Bellingham*).

Bellingham is at the junction with State 1 (*see Tour 8A*).

Right from Bellingham on Marietta Road, concrete-paved, through a semi-rural area over a section of which the fine, gray dust from the Olympic Portland Cement Plant has settled like a ghostly gray mask.

At 4.2 *m.* is a junction with a dirt road: L. here 0.4 *m.* to the SITE OF OLD FORT BELLINGHAM, where during the Indian war scare of 1856 Captain George Pickett built two blockhouses, which aided considerably in alleviating the fears of the few settlers, by warding off raiders from Alaska and British Columbia.

On the main side road is MARIETTA, 5.6 *m.* (10 alt., 200 pop.), a cluster of weather-beaten houses occupied by families employed in the Bellingham mills or in fishing. Perched above the piles of driftwood on the beach are a number of shacks, where squatters lead a hermit-like life. Gulls drift and soar, white wings flashing against the grey of stormy skies as they wheel and tack and soar with the gale, or swoop down, feet dangling like the landing gear of an airplane, to pick up some bit of floating debris. Straight ahead from Marietta on a graveled road is the LUMMI INDIAN RESERVATION, 6.9 *m.,* on a peninsula between Bellingham and Lummi Bays. Today, most of the Indians eke out a meager existence by fishing, clam digging, and small-scale farming. Tribal historians relate that at GOOSEBERRY POINT, 15.3 *m.,* the end of the road, a great battle was fought with invading tribes from the north. A ferry (*car and driver, 25c; passengers, 10c; 7 a.m.-midnight*) runs westward to slipper-shaped LUMMI ISLAND, a resort center about one mile offshore.

From Bellingham US 99-Alt. (Chuckanut Drive) provides an alternate route to Burlington, above which it joins US 99.

Right from Bellingham on State Street for US 99-Alt., a scenic route along the Sound. State Street runs to 12th Street; L. on 12th to Cowgill Ave., where it becomes Chuckanut Drive. US 99-Alt. winds gradually upward along a shelf cut in the rocky face of CHUCKANUT MOUNTAIN (Alt. 1,629). Far below the cobalt-blue reaches of the Sound shimmer in the sun, or matching the grey of stormy skies, surge in a dizzy race of whitecaps toward the shore.

At 6.2 *m.* is a junction with a graveled road: R. here to CHUCKANUT, 0.2 *m.* (sea level, 60 pop.), where an auto ferry connects with ORCAS ISLAND (*see Island Tour* c). LARRABEE STATE PARK (R), 7.9 *m.,* is a 1,220-acre forest with a good beach and picnic facilities. From turnouts along the road the tree-crowned, rocky slopes of the San Juan Islands are visible—dark green against the quiet glittering water in clear weather, dim masses of land when rain or mist forms a half-translucent curtain. US 99-Alt. skirts the shore of Samish Bay, upon whose expansive tideflats are large oyster beds. Roadside taverns serve oysters—stewed, fried, roasted, or on the half-shell.

At 22.8 *m.* US 99-Alt. forms a junction with US 99.

Southeast of Bellingham US 99 swings inland through a region of slight scenic interest. This route is recommended for fast, through travel and for safety during winter months when slides occasionally interrupt traffic on Chuckanut Drive or ice and snow make it hazardous. The highway runs southward through second-growth timberlands and skirts the edge of LAKE SAMISH (*fishing; cabins*), 32.2 *m.*, glimpsed occasionally through the trees. South of the lake, US 99 passes through rolling terrain, which levels out into the flat Skagit Valley. At the SAMISH STATE SALMON HATCHERY (L), 37.7 *m.*, an average of 18,000,000 salmon fry annually are reared in the nine ponds. All phases of salmon culture may be observed here.

At 44.5 *m.* is the junction with US 99-Alt.

At 45.2 *m.* is a junction with a concrete-paved road.

Left here 0.5 *m.* to BURLINGTON (36 alt., 1,632 pop.), a shipping center and local supply point for the fertile Skagit Valley. First settled in 1882 by John P. Millett and William McKay, it was named for Burlington, Vermont, by T. W. Soules. Logging operations in the surrounding forests became so extensive that in 1890 a sawmill was built and the Seattle and Northern extended its rail lines to the town. For a number of years it boomed, until the depletion of timber stands in the environs forced a change from logging and lumbering to dairying and farming. The mild climate and light, sandy soil of the area have proved well suited to growing strawberries on a commercial scale, one acre not infrequently yielding as much as seven tons. Annually, the town celebrates the Burlington Strawberry Festival near the end of June.

Burlington is a junction with an unnumbered bituminous-surfaced road which runs to Sedro Wooley (*see Tour 8B*).

MOUNT VERNON, 49.1 *m.* (24 alt., 4,278 pop.), seat of Skagit County, was named for Washington's Potomac home. The Skagit River has played an important part in the development of the town; in 1870 fur traders, finding it navigable, established a post here. Prospects of gold along Ruby Creek stimulated the activity of the settlement, and when hopes of striking pay dirt faded many of the prospectors began logging and farming in the Skagit Valley. Today, the bulk of Mount Vernon's pay roll is provided by two pea canneries, two milk condenseries, an egg-storage and poultry plant, and a chicken and turkey hatchery. A shingle mill and a brick and tile plant add to the income of the city.

During the last week-end in July, Mount Vernon has an annual celebration, whose official insignia is a work hat worn with a hickory shirt. Gay booths line the streets; considerable hilarity is added by the ladies of the American Legion Auxiliary, who in gala attire police the town, "arresting" and trying "offenders" who fail to wear the official Hickory Shirt and Hat.

The ALLEN R. MOORE HOUSE MUSEUM (*open by arrangement*), 9th and Section Sts., has a collection of arrowheads, tomahawks, and artifacts in native jade, some of which have been shown at the Smithsonian Institution. The square, three-story brick MOUNT VERNON UNION HIGH SCHOOL, 9th and Fulton Sts., a model high school for the typical American agricultural community, gives special emphasis to manual training and agricultural courses. Housed in a remodeled school building near by is the Mount Vernon Junior College.

Left from Mount Vernon on Kincaid Street W., which becomes a graveled road, to LITTLE MOUNTAIN PARK, 5 *m.* (835 alt.), where a thirty-five-foot observation tower affords a sweeping view of the surrounding area.

Mount Vernon is at the junction with State 1 (*see Tour 8C*).

Section b. MOUNT VERNON *to* SEATTLE; *60.9 m. US 99*

The Pacific Highway continues south across the flats and deltas of the Skagit, the Stillaguamish, and the Snohomish Rivers, which with their tributaries reach back through many miles of rolling land and wooded foothills to the Cascade Mountains. Turbulent at their headwaters, these streams become broad, sluggish, silt-laden rivers, which have built up broad deltas, cut by sloughs rank with cattails and tules. Occasionally a salt marsh is seen, where sea and silt battle for possession.

The region produces some of the most abundant crops in western Washington. The black soil, rich in humus, frequently bears in a single season a succession of spinach, lettuce, onions, peas, and carrots without depleting the soil. Cabbage, beets, and turnips, and their seed, are important local yields. The flatness of the land, in conjunction with the heavy rainfall and the melting mountain snows, often brought floods in early spring. Even before the forests were cut away the rivers frequently overflowed their banks, spreading desolation and destruction over the lowlands; and with the conversion of more and more land to agriculture, the threat of floods proportionately increased, so that the farmer came to look with apprehension at lowering clouds and the steady fall of the rain. He watched the swirling water rising, and not infrequently saw it spread its load of silt, debris, and uprooted trees over his pastures, maroon his stock, and at times even sweep away his house and barns. Today, much of the menace of these floods has been eliminated by the diking of river banks and the draining of sloughs.

The highway heads straight southward for several miles through an area of large farms, dotted with prosperous-looking houses and big, red barns.

At 5.3 *m.* is a junction with State 1-E, concrete-paved, an alternate route to US 99.

Right here to CONWAY, 0.4 *m.* (5 alt., 776 pop.), hub of the surrounding farming area. The road parallels the Sound, which is, however, hidden from view by the embankment of the Great Northern Railway. Like a sluggish stream, a wide drainage ditch winds along the west side of the road. Then the route swings up a grade and affords a splendid view of the valley floor overlooking a checker-board of tilled fields, farm homes, and scattered groves of fruit trees. Across the strips of Skagit Bay and Port Susan rise the tall headlands of Whidbey and Camano Islands.

EAST STANWOOD, 7.2 m. (10 alt., 359 pop.), has a pea cannery supplied by the commercial pea farms, which spread for miles over the diked and drained valley of the Stillaguamish. Bush peas are mowed when sufficiently matured for canning, and the pods are then stripped from the vines by machine; pole peas, frequently yielding as much as seven tons an acre, are picked several times by hand during the season that extends over a period of weeks. The salt air and the long, cool growing season give the peas an unusually fine flavor and succulence.

Right from East Stanwood on a concrete-paved road to STANWOOD, 0.9 *m.* (5 alt., 600 pop.), near the mouth of the Stillaguamish River. Once the land around the town was a desolate marsh where skunk cabbage spread their broad green leaves and massive yellow flowers and cattails throve. In 1866, a settler named Robert Fulton opened a small trading post there; gradually in the course of years the marsh has been reclaimed by the stubborn persistence of the inhabitants. Bit by bit the pools where frogs croaked were drained and the swaying willows were cleared. An important factor in the reclamation was the perseverance and industry of the Norwegians, who brought with them the experience of hard fighting against adverse climatic and topographic conditions. Stanwood has a large oyster cannery and two fruit and vegetable packing plants. Thousands of bushels of oats, destined to be "Quaker Rolled Oats," annually pass through the local warehouse on their way to Iowa. Peas are harvested by the ton. The town is also the distribution center for the dairy farms of the surrounding country.

For 30 years Stanwood had "the world's shortest railroad," an independent line running seven-eighths of a mile to East Stanwood. Trains were drawn by "the dinky," a decrepit old Climax locomotive, which wheezed noisily through the streets. Lack of patronage compelled its discontinuance in 1938.

West of Stanwood a bituminous-surfaced road crosses Davis Slough to CAMANO ISLAND, on which are many summer homes, resorts, and small farms. The waters around the island are noted for excellent salmon fishing. At 5.1 *m.* is a junction with a graveled road: R. here to UTSALADDY 0.8 *m.* (sea level, 196 pop.) (*beach cabins, boats, supplies*). In the sixties, Utsaladdy was a sizable city, manufacturing and shipping lumber; shipbuilders here produced many boats for Puget Sound shipping, including the *J. B. Libby,* a side-wheeler, and the *Cascades,* a large stern-wheeler.

South of the junction, the main side road off 1-E, graveled, bears inland across the island, passing nearly a dozen beach resorts accessible by stub roads, to MABANA, 23 *m.* (sea level, 35 pop.).

Left from East Stanwood, State 1-E swings in a southeasterly direction. In the Stanwood PIONEER CEMETERY (R), 7.9 *m.* are the graves of Zakarias Martin Toftezen, who settled at Oak Harbor on Whidbey Island in 1849, his mother Emmerenze, who came here in 1865, and other early settlers. Honoring them is the NORWEGIAN PIONEER MONUMENT, a rough-hewn, gray-granite slab dedicated by Crown Prince Olav of Norway during his visit to the Northwest in 1939.

SILVANA, 14.3 *m.* (30 alt., 656 pop.), is a Norwegian trading center on the delta of the Stillaguamish River. Slowly, in the course of many years, the river has deposited its load of silt, inching its way toward the Sound. The town still experiences flood conditions during the spring runoff. To gain a measure of safety, houses formerly were built on foundations several feet high and sidewalks were raised a number of feet above the ground. Flood control measures have reduced the periodic threat. The route continues eastward through farmland and small, second-growth fir.

At 16.9 *m.* State 1-E forms a junction with US 99.

South of the junction US 99 veers slightly eastward through rolling, sparsely settled country, logged-off years ago and not sufficiently attractive to induce cultivation. This route is recommended for travel if time is an essential factor.

At 17.9 *m.* is the southern junction with State 1-E, US 99-Alt.

Left here on the eastern branch of State 1-E to a junction with a concrete-paved road, 3.5 *m.* R. here 0.3 to the PIONEER LOG HOUSE, formerly a museum, where the Stillaguamish Valley Association of Washington Pioneers holds an annual reunion, usually in late August.

ARLINGTON, 4 *m.* (103 alt., 1,460 pop.), is at the junction of the north and south forks of the Stillaguamish River. In 1864 the first pioneer, Captain Daniel Marvin, anchored a scow on the north fork of the river to serve as his temporary home. Although it once ranked with the largest shingle manufacturing centers, Arlington now has only one mill and, like many other western Washington towns, has turned to dairying, poultry-raising, truck-gardening, and fruit growing.

Northeast of Arlington on a bituminous-surfaced road are TRAFTON, 8.6 *m.*, a station on the Northern Pacific Ry.; OSO, 15.9 *m.* (207 alt., 65 pop.), in an area of stump ranches; and HAZEL, 22.5 *m.* (313 alt., 34 pop.), a row of old moss-covered houses, badly in need of paint, around the remains of a shingle mill. East of Hazel the country is more rugged and stands of timber are heavier, as the highway gradually ascends.

Beneath snow-capped Jumbo Peak and the Whitehorse Mountains is DARRINGTON, 29.2 *m.* (527 alt., 400 pop.), a lumber town huddled along the banks of the Sauk River. A few modern, well-kept houses contrast with many drab, unpainted, jerry-built structures. In King Tut Hall (L) husky loggers and their women folk view movies, dance to mountain music, and hold their social affairs. "Tarheels," North Carolinians and their families who came here in 1914-16, constitute a large part of the population.

Tourist trade brings revenue to Darrington, the last outpost in the picturesque region of the Sauk and Suiattle Rivers, the Whitechuck Valley, and the Squire Creek country.

Five major trails lead into the wilderness surrounding GLACIER PEAK (alt. 10,436); the Suiattle River trail; the trails up the North and South Forks of the Sauk River; one up the Whitechuck Valley; and another up the rugged Squire Creek Valley to the Jumbo and Squire Creek Pass skiing areas, five to seven miles south of Darrington.

The highway continues southward through sparsely settled country, where stretches of small, second-growth forests alternate with pasture land and occasional farms. The Silvana Cedar Stump (L), 18.5 *m.*, is a section of a red cedar tree about 12 feet in diameter estimated to have reached an age of 1,250 years.

At 20.6 *m.* is a junction with a bituminous-surfaced road.

Right here 5.4 *m.* to LAKE GOODWIN (*cabins, fishing facilities*), which offers good fishing for perch, bass, and crappie. Southeast is SHOECRAFT LAKE (*cabins*), connected by a channel with Lake Goodwin. WARM BEACH, 9 *m.* (sea level, 314 pop.), a summer colony on the Sound, has a long sandy beach, the tide running out over one mile. It is noted for its warm salt water.

South of the junction the highway descends into fertile lowlands which little more than 50 years ago were covered by a dense forest. MARYSVILLE, 27.8 *m.* (15 alt., 1,748 pop.), dates back to 1877, when James P. Comeford established a trading post on Ebey Slough. Today, the city is sustained by mills, woodworking plants, and a boat factory, and is the center of supplies for the several Sound fishing resorts in the vicinity.

Marysville is also the distribution point for a rich farming and dairying district, part of which was reclaimed by draining the swamps and sloughs and by diking the Snohomish River. Farmers still utilize controlled flooding to replenish the soil by catching the river silt. Strawberries are a leading crop, the soil and climate practically insuring a good yield and excellent quality. Annually, the Marysville Strawberry

Festival attracts a crowd from the surrounding countryside and nearby towns.

1. Right from Marysville on 8th Ave., which becomes an improved road, into the TULALIP INDIAN RESERVATION. At 3.1 *m.* is a junction with a graveled road: Left here 1 *m.* to PRIEST POINT, named for the Roman Catholic mission established in 1858 by Father E. C. Chirouse. A scattering of summer homes now occupies the site.

At 5 *m.* on the main sideroad is a junction with a dirt road: L. here 0.4 *m.* to MISSION BEACH CEMETERY, where headstones mark the burial plots of several Indian chiefs, including Chief Patkanim, who signed the Mukilteo Treaty in 1855 which ceded lands to the whites. On Patkanim's tombstone, a large granite monument, is a bronze plaque with an engraved head of the chief and an inscription commemorating the treaty. MISSION BEACH, 0.8 *m.*, is a fishing resort.

On the main side road is TULALIP, 6.3 *m.* (22 alt., 100 pop.), Indian Agency headquarters for the Tulalip Indian Reservation, established in 1859. The old mission bell now hangs in the belfry of St. Anne's Church, and the old potlatch house, once the center of tribal festivities, is now the meeting place for Boy Scouts. Alongside the potlatch house is the Community Hall, a neat white building used for dances and community meetings.

2. Left from Marysville on 3rd Avenue, which becomes a concrete-paved road, 5.7 *m.* along the east side of the Snohomish River flats to a junction with State 15-A: Left on State 15-A to LAKE STEVENS (*cabins, fishing*), 7.9 *m.*, bordered by summer resorts. Attractive cottages, with lawns and flower gardens, alternate with unimproved shoreline where wild blackberry vines cascade to the water's edge. State 15-A skirts the north shore of the lake to the town of LAKE STEVENS, 10.3 *m.* (215 alt., 375 pop.). Northeast from HARTFORD, 11 *m.* (239 alt., 54 pop.), the road continues through pleasantly wooded country roughly paralleling the Pilchuck River, which is visible at times through the trees.

GRANITE FALLS, 16 *m.* (396 alt., 683 pop.), lies between the South Fork of the Stillaguamish River and the Pilchuck River, whose narrow but fertile valleys are being converted to agricultural uses—dairying, poultry raising, berry growing, and truck farming. Two mills in the town manufacture cedar shakes and shingles; and some logs are still obtained from the surrounding forests, although much of the best timber has been cut. Granite Falls, first settled in 1885, was named for the falls about one and one-half miles east of town where the Stillaguamish River cascades over granite ledges and swirls around huge boulders. Deep quiet pools and sandy riffles are excellent fishing spots for trout. For a time the town flourished on the hopes that some of the many copper, silver, and gold prospects would become major mining developments. Today, a few exploratory mines are being worked and a small stamp mill is operating.

East of Granite Falls State 15-A becomes an unnumbered bituminous-surfaced road. The CANYON CREEK LODGE (*camping*), 20 *m.*, on the banks of Canyon Creek, is a favorite recreation spot. Near by is a nine-hole golf course.

ROBE, 23 *m.* (896 alt., 125 pop.), is a trail center above which tower the peaks of the Green Mountains and Mount Pilchuck. East of Robe the country becomes increasingly rough and wild, while far below the road the Stillaguamish River dashes between walls of green-black basalt. Trees cling to the precipitous mountain flanks.

Rustic VERLOT CAMP, 29 *m.*, is a popular headquarters for picnicking, fishing, and hunting. The VERLOT FOREST RANGER STATION should be visited to obtain information on forest regulations. East of Verlot Camp, the road follows the right-of-way of the old Everett and Monte Cristo Railroad, which in the nineties transported the ores from the district to a smelter at Everett.

At the ghost town of GOLD BASIN, 31.1 *m.*, once the center of a mining area, is a camp which furnishes limited accommodations. SILVERTON, 40 *m.*

(1,100 alt., 15 pop.), a ghost mining town, once produced considerable copper.

At the base of BIG 4 MOUNTAIN is the Big 4 Inn (*golf, tennis; saddle and pack horses; guides*), 44.2 *m.* in an area of rugged mountains; crystal streams and alpine lakes afford good fishing. A good trail leads eastward to MONTE CRISTO, 17 *m.*, a wide-open mining town in the nineties, when it had seven saloons, a number of gambling and dance halls, and dreams of Eldorado. Today, mouldering remains of a few buildings, a few gaping holes, once the entrance to mine tunnels, and a few prospectors, still hopefully working with pick and shovel, are all that remain of the town that Rockefeller built.

South of Marysville US 99 crosses Ebey, Steamboat, and Union Sloughs and the Snohomish River by means of large steel and concrete bridges, constructed at a cost of approximately $1,000,000.

EVERETT, 33.1 *m.* (sea level—200 alt., 30,224 pop.), (*see Everett*).

Everett is at the junction with State 15, the Stevens Pass Highway (*see Tour 1C*).

1. Right from Everett on 41st St., which becomes State 1-I, along the shore of Possession Sound. MUKILTEO, 5 *m.* (sea level- 150 alt., 450 pop.), sprawls along the Sound and a salt-water lagoon. Once an active sawmill town, today, since the gutting of the Crown Mill Company plant by fire, little more than the remnants of lumber yards remains as a reminder of the past. Ferries (*passengers 30c one way; car and driver 65c*) run to Columbia Beach on Whidbey Island, whose bluffs are visible to the west across Possession Sound (*see Tour 8C*). A granite shaft at the southeast end of the town on the schoolhouse lawn (R) marks the MUKILTEO TREATY GROUNDS, where on January 22, 1855, Governor Isaac I. Stevens and a number of Indian chiefs signed an agreement ceding all the lands from Point Pully northward to the whites. At 11 *m.* is the southern junction of State 1-I with US 99.

2. Left (straight ahead) from Everett on S. Rucker Ave. on State 2-A, a US 99-Alt. to Seattle. SILVER LAKE, 6.5 *m.* (*swimming, boating*), is a popular lake resort. The route winds southward through fertile valleys between cutover lands. Occasional skidroads and many stumps and snags remain from the years, around the turn of the century, when the area was logged.

BOTHELL, 17 *m.* (54 alt., 794 pop.), on the Sammamish River near the northern end of Lake Washington, was named for the Bothell family, which started a sawmill here in 1886 and platted the town two years later. Early-day transportation was by steamer down the narrow stream and across the lake to Seattle. Today, the town draws its income largely from dairying and farming.

At Bothell is the junction with State 2.

Right from Bothell, State 2 winds southward through the valley of the Sammamish Slough and then runs southwestward paralleling LAKE WASHINGTON. KENMORE, 19.1 *m.* (75 alt., 400 pop.), and LAKE FOREST PARK, 21 *m.* (30 alt., 900 pop.), are suburban-home districts of Seattle.

The ACACIA PARK CEMETERY, 22.4 *m.* (R), with a masonry entrance, centers around an imposing mausoleum set in a sweeping lawn. State 2 becomes Roosevelt Way, which in turn becomes Eastlake Blvd.; R. on Fairview Ave. N.; R. on Virginia St. to Westlake Ave., 31.7 *m.*, where State 2 forms a junction with US 99 in Seattle.

South of Everett US 99 bears in a slightly westerly direction along a high ridge.

At 49.2 *m.* on US 99 is a junction with State 1W, a concrete-paved road.

Right here to EDMONDS, 4 *m.* (9 alt., 1,288 pop.), a quiet town midway between Seattle and Everett on Puget Sound. In 1868 Pleasant H. Elwell built a cabin here; four years later George Brackett, who subsequently became the town's first mayor, seeking refuge from a storm, saw the possibilities of the heavily forested area near water transportation and shortly thereafter, purchased the Elwell Claim. Soon the settlement became a logging and sawmill center. Edmonds is probably the only town in the United States that included the names of animals on its petition for incorporation. It is said that, in 1890, when the petition was drawn up, it was discovered that it fell short by two names of the required number, and those of two oxen, Bill and Bolivar, were added. The income of the town is today drawn chiefly from poultry raising, a large co-operative shingle mill, and commercial flower gardens.

Edmonds offers unusually fine views of the Sound. Westward, across a stretch of water, is the jagged line of the Olympic Mountains. Edmonds is the only port of Puget Sound from which the Juan de Fuca Strait can be seen between the maze of islands. Ferries run to Port Ludlow and Port Townsend on the Olympic Peninsula and to Kingston on Kitsap Peninsula.

ECHO LAKE (L), 49.7 *m.*, is a bathing resort. Here is a junction with a concrete-paved road.

Right here 0.5 *m.* to the FIRLANDS SANATORIUM, the Northwest's largest tuberculosis isolation hospital, surrounded by green lawns and shade trees.

At 50.2 *m.* is a junction with a concrete-paved road.

Right here to RICHMOND BEACH, 3 *m.* (sea level, 780 pop.), a suburban town within easy commuting distance of Seattle. Once industrially active, with a cooperage plant and a brickyard, Richmond Beach today is a quiet suburb deriving its support largely from Seattle. On the shore is a crematory for obsolete ships, where old hulls are beached and burned and their metal salvaged for scrap iron. Richmond Beach is also the location of many large oil storage tanks, which squat like huge mushrooms along the water front.

South of the junction US 99 runs between fruit and vegetable stands, scattered houses, and suburban beer parlors, roadhouses, and skating rinks catering to those seeking out-of-town amusements. Tawdry during the day, the establishments at night are brilliant with the blaze of red, white, green, and blue neon signs. On Saturday night, especially, business flourishes. From the dance floors come the throb of drums, the wail of saxophone, and the blare of trumpet and clarinet. In the early morning hours the music ceases, the lights are extinguished, and the traffic flows back to the city.

EVERGREEN (R) and WASHELLI (L) CEMETERIES 53.8 *m.*, terraced stretches of velvet lawn, flowering shrubs, and scattered trees, border the highway. Houses and small community trading centers increase in number until the suburban area merges with the city and US 99 becomes Aurora Avenue.

SEATTLE, 60.9 *m.* (sea level—514 alt., 368,302 pop.), (*see Seattle*).

Section c. SEATTLE *to* OLYMPIA, *61.6 m. US 99*

This section of the Pacific Highway lies through Washington's State Capital and some of its largest cities. Skirting the bays of lower Puget Sound, US 99 passes through the State's most densely populated and most highly industrialized area, yet woodland stretches and thinly settled farming districts are met with just outside these centers. Towns off the main route are, for the most part, rather widely separated. Rolling hills enclose the numerous river valleys of the northern portion, while, southward, the land levels off into a prairie. Tangles of Scotch broom, masses of yellow bloom in spring and summer, cover miles of the open forest, and in season the prairie is blue with camas flowers.

Around the seaport cities of Seattle, Tacoma, and Olympia are concentrated most of the shipping and the manufacturing of western Washington. Although lumber and fish account for much of the maritime commerce, the Sound ports are also an outlet for the agricultural produce of the entire State, from Wenatchee apples to Puyallup bulbs and berries.

Proceeding south (straight ahead) on 4th Ave. to Airport Way, 0.9 *m.,* a junction with US 10 (*see Tour 1b*), US 99 continues to E. Marginal Way; then L. on E. Marginal Way, skirting the extensive grounds of the KING COUNTY AIRPORT, Boeing Field (L), named in honor of William E. Boeing, founder of the Boeing Airplane Company. Seattle's aviation field ranks with the most modern in the nation (*see Seattle*).

The SITE OF THE MEADOWS RACE TRACK (L), which flourished at the turn of the century, is at the south end of the airport. The KING COUNTY TUBERCULOSIS HOSPITAL, with landscaped grounds, now occupies part of the old track. The sluggish DUWAMISH RIVER (R), winding to Elliott Bay, is visible at intervals; on its banks was the old Duwamish settlement, first in the Seattle area, in 1850.

Along the low, flat, river valley, cut by US 99, are hundreds of acres of truck gardens, most of them farmed by Japanese and Italians. The fertile black loam, painstakingly cultivated, yields vegetables and berries for Seattle markets.

At 8.3 *m.* is a junction with State 5-M, a concrete road.

Left on this road, on the west bank of the Duwamish, to ROCKY HILL, 0.8 *m.* the "stone mountain" of Indian legends. The village of RIVERTON, 1.8 *m.* (alt. 325, 677 pop.), appears to doze within the shadow of the rumbling city to the north, undisturbed by the early-morning rattle of farmers' trucks, laden with garden stuff, on their way to market.

The FOSTER GOLF LINKS, 2.6 *m.* (18 holes, fee 50c), stretch along the banks of the winding Duwamish (L) in the shade of venerable maples.

At TUKWILA (Ind. land of hazelnuts), 3.5 *m.* (521 pop.), there is only a store, and a small frame public library along the road to suggest the presence of a town. The residence section rests on the hill that slopes steeply up from the road.

LONGACRES RACE TRACK (*open July-Sept.; adm. grandstand, 40c; clubhouse,* 80c), 4 *m.,* is the gathering place for turf fans. The pari-mutuel system of betting used here is supervised by the State Racing Commission. A totalizator board, first in the State, was installed in 1938. The track is operated by the Washington Jockey Club.

South of the junction, US 99 bears R., crosses the Duwamish River on a steel span, and climbs on an easy grade out of the valley. A checkerboard of the green fields and dark loams of truck farms, operated mainly by Japanese, spreads to the south on the fertile floor of the Duwamish Valley. At 16.2 *m.* is a junction with State I-K, a concrete paved road.

Right here 2 *m.* to DES MOINES, (50 alt., 800 pop.), facing on a long sweep of crescent beach, its shores lined with summer homes, and suburban residences. Poultry raising, dairying, and berry cultivation are the leading industries.

At 2.7 *m.*, an imposing MASONIC HOME, built at a cost of $800,000, overlooks Puget Sound. The main structure and several small frame buildings stand on formally landscaped grounds within a semicircle of second-growth forest. The road continues to SALT WATER STATE PARK, 3 *m.*, which has an 80-acre tract of old-growth forest, where woodland trails, a salt-water beach, and picnic facilities attract many visitors during the summer.

At 17.7 *m.* is a junction with State 1-V, a concrete road.

Right on this road is REDONDO, 1.3 *m.* (100 alt., 116 pop.), a beach resort. In the old days Redondo achieved notoriety for its illegal prizefights; a barge, loaded to the gunwales with fighters and fans, was towed far enough from shore to escape local constables, but not far enough to appease objecting residents, who finally succeeded in having the bouts stopped.

South of the junction US 99 intersects many short roads leading through wooded areas, to numerous lakes that offer cabin camp accommodations, swimming, boating, and fishing. The main highway leaves the high bench lands and descends to the low delta of the Puyallup River.

FIFE, 27.3 *m.* (30 alt., 135 pop.), at a valley crossroads in the midst of a thickly settled berry growing and truck-gardening district is represented by a string of markets, taverns, shops, and a large, balloon-roofed dance hall along the highway.

Beyond Fife the highway is illuminated at night by a special type of sodium-vapor lights that produce a strong amber glow which penetrates the frequent fogs that drift across the low section in the fall.

At 29.5 *m.* the highway rises on a ramp to cross the Puyallup River over a steel-trussed bridge. Below, sweep the gray, silty waters of the glacial stream born in the ice-clad slopes of Mount Rainier, some 40 miles to the southeast.

TACOMA, 31.8 *m.* (21 to 110 alt., 109,408 pop.), (*see Tacoma*).

At Pacific Ave. and 26th St. is a junction with State 5, the main highway to Mount Rainier National Park (*see Tour 8D*).

In Tacoma US 99 and US 410 coincide (*see Tour 2c*).

At 38.8 *m.*, is a junction with a concrete road.

R. here, around the edge of a commercial landing field, to a junction 0.9 *m.*; L. here to LAKEVIEW (100 pop.), 0.7 *m.*, a growing community of well-kept modern homes scattered over a flat, grassy parkland, covered with scrub oak and pine. Lakeview's COMMUNITY CENTER, the first of its kind in the State, is housed in an adaptation of Georgian architecture in red brick. Under one roof all sorts of community services are provided: apartments, public and private dining rooms, shops, doctors' and dentists' offices, a Christian Science reading room, recreation hall, and a theater, all decorated in a colorful modern manner. The center serves the surrounding residential area, known as the LAKES DISTRICT.

On the main side road is LAKE STEILACOOM, 0.8 *m.*, on whose shores are many beautiful homes.

The WESTERN STATE HOSPITAL FOR THE INSANE (R), 4 *m.*, with attractive grounds and buildings, occupies the site of old Fort Steilacoom, established by the United States Army to protect settlers from Indian attack, the first United States Army post on Puget Sound.

On the hospital grounds are four residences constructed for the officers of

Fort Steilacoom between 1855 and 1858. One was occupied by General Philip E. Sheridan, Civil War hero. Still in good condition, the buildings are used as dwellings by the State hospital doctors. The hospital grounds lie on both sides of the road and occupy 700 acres. Left of the entrance, with its rustic keeper's lodge and bus waiting room, the drive sweeps to the imposing new buildings which have been added to the old structure. Around the latter are ancient honey locusts. There are over 150 buildings connected with the institution, some housing equipment for the poultry, dairy, farm, garden, and swinery. More than 20 miles of roadway, much of it surfaced with concrete, link the divisions of the hospital. The main building, with new additions nearing completion, houses 2,408 patients. There are 40 wards with more than three and one-half miles of main corridors. Three hundred persons are employed by the hospital.

STEILACOOM (*pronounced "Stillakum"*), 6.4 *m.* (50 alt., 832 pop.), the oldest incorporated town in the State of Washington, was chartered in 1853; its name derives from that of an Indian chief. Set amid old orchards and flower gardens, its quaint houses drowse on a hillside above the shore of Puget Sound. McNeil and Anderson Islands and Tacoma's smelter stack and house-covered hills are visible from the village streets. The pastoral picture of comfortable old homes along the quiet avenues is broken here and there by the sharp lines and bright colors of a jaunty modern house. In 1849, Thomas M. Chambers, an American who had taken a donation claim near by, was ordered to leave by Doctor William F. Tolmie of the Puget Sound Agricultural Company, a subsidiary of the Hudson's Bay Company. Chambers not only refused to vacate but urged other Americans to settle here, and colonization of the district began. The Hudson's Bay Company claimed grazing and other land rights under the treaty of 1846, and early American settlers lived in a state of unrest until the controversy was finally settled in their favor. LaFayette Balch founded the town in 1851 by erecting a store and trading center.

The FIRST JAIL in the Washington Territory was housed in the empty, faded old brick building which still stands at Main Avenue and Starlung Street. It was erected in 1858, but when the seat of Pierce County was moved from Steilacoom to Tacoma in 1881, the jail was abandoned. Opposite the jail on Starlung Street is the PETER JUDSON HOUSE, erected in 1855; a few hundred feet away stands the oldest CATHOLIC CHURCH north of the Columbia River. During the fifties the church was built just outside the parade grounds of old Fort Steilacoom for soldiers of the Roman Catholic faith. When the fort was abandoned as a military post in 1867, the church was taken down and moved, in three sections, to its present location, where it has since been in continuous use; it is still in good repair. A monument marks the SITE OF THE FIRST PROTESTANT CHURCH erected north of the Columbia.

A DEEP SEA AQUARIUM (*adm.* 25*c*) was established at Steilacoom early in the century by a retired sea captain. Marine specimens, submerged in glass globes or suspended from rafters, range from the humble sea cucumber to sections of whales. A tour of the rows of glass globes is conducted by a caretaker who, with pointer in hand, describes each specimen. Also on exhibition are Indian artifacts and other historical relics.

South of the junction, US 99 follows the boundary fence of the UNITED STATES MILITARY RESERVATION.

At 40.8 *m.* is a junction with State 5-G.

Left on State 5-G to a junction at 0.1 *m.* with a bituminous-surfaced road.

R. here 0.2 *m.* to McCHORD AIR FIELD, a 1,310-acre field acquired by the War Department in 1938, the first of eight provided by the Wilcox Bill, signed by the President in 1935. Expanding an earlier municipal field, improvements under way or proposed, costing $12,000,000, will equip the military base for 2,000 men and hundreds of planes. The field is named for Colonel William C. McChord of the Army Air Corps, killed in flight during 1937.

In 1924 the ill-fated Shenandoah moored here at a specially constructed steel mast, her only landing-place on this trip to the Northwest. Here are new brick buildings with tiled roofs and a great spreading hangar. Other hangars are proposed and a large construction program is under way. With the completion of this program, McChord Field will be one of the finest air fields under Government jurisdiction.

CAMP MURRAY, 44.9 *m.,* bordering on American Lake, flanks the highway (R). It is a National Guard Military Reserve, and the guard and the Citizens Military Training Camp are located here every summer, when intensive maneuvers are held in co-operation with units of the regular Army.

South of Camp Murray, US 99 traverses a broad prairie dotted with scattered clumps of scrub oak and fir trees. The dwarfed fir trees with heavy foliage growing close to the ground, and the small, thickly branched oak are characteristic in this area, where light, gravelly soil is prevalent.

The entrance to FORT LEWIS (*visitors permitted, subject to military regulations*), 47.9 *m.,* is formed of cobblestone pillars, topped by blockhouse-like structures (L) fronting the highway. Facing the parade grounds, flanked by camouflaged field guns, stands a WORLD WAR MEMORIAL to the 91st (Wild West) and 13th divisions, which were trained at this cantonment. The monument is a stone shaft, at the foot of which stands a group of soldiers in bronze; the sculpture is by Avard Fairbanks; the architecture by John Graham. Behind the high steel-wire enclosure are the red-brick quarters of the officers, with the barracks of the enlisted men in the background. During recent years, many new buildings have been erected to house the garrison.

Some time before the United States entered the World War in 1917, Pierce County voted bonds to purchase 62,000 acres of land midway between Tacoma and Olympia and present this tract for a military cantonment. On that rolling, flat, prairie land rose Camp Lewis, named in honor of Captain Meriwether Lewis. Barracks were quickly constructed, tents pitched, and sewage, water, and lighting systems installed. The accommodations and training facilities necessary for the 30,650 men who were later to be stationed here were hastily improvised. Most of the war-time wooden barracks and other buildings have been replaced by brick and steel structures. Recently the defense program has led to the doubling of Fort Lewis, at a cost of $16,000,000, for training the Forty-First Division on the ground north of US 99, between American Lake and the Sound.

At 48.3 *m.* is a junction with a concrete road.

Right on this road is DUPONT, 0.4 *m.,* (253 alt., 400 pop.), a company-built settlement where approximately 225 employees of the DUPONT POWDER COMPANY PLANT (*no visitors permitted*) have their homes. Winding down a pleasant forested lane, the road is lined with ornamental lamp standards and bordered by tree-shaded houses. The town has an area of 3,600 acres, more than one-half of which are within the enclosed district where high explosives are manufactured.

The settlement stands upon grounds once occupied by old Fort Nesqually, a Hudson's Bay Company trading post established in 1833. The original fort was built close to the beach but was later removed to a site on the hill, within a few hundred feet of what is now the main gate to the restricted area. Indians and traders gathered here to barter. Sea-battered craft lay at anchor off shore, while their crews exchanged news and swapped yarns. The ruins of Fort Nesqually have been removed to Tacoma, and the post has been reconstructed in Point Defiance Park (*see Tacoma*).

Right from Dupont on the Dupont-Steilacoom road to LAKE SEQUALICHEW, 0.7 *m.*, where a granite monument marks the site of the FIRST FOURTH OF JULY CELEBRATION WEST OF THE MISSOURI RIVER, by Lieutenant Charles Wilkes and the men of his exploring expedition in 1841. A MONUMENT left of the junction marks the Fort Nesqually-Muck Creek Road, built in 1833.

South of the junction, US 99 is bordered by the forested area of the military reservation.

At 50.5 *m.* is a junction with a concrete road, which was formerly the main highway.

Left on this road to Olympia, by an alternate route three miles longer than by the main one. It rambles across the Nisqually River and through a park-like forest that fringes the brow of a bluff overlooking Puget Sound and the channels of Nisqually Flats. NISQUALLY, 28 *m.* (86 alt., 150 pop.), is on the delta of the river. Little of the scattered settlement, except a tiny railroad station (L), can be seen from the highway.

At 5.3 *m.* is a junction with a graveled road: L. here 2.9 *m.*, to another junction with a crossroad, which passes the farms of Indians who live on the NISQUALLY INDIAN RESERVATION under the jurisdiction of the Taholah Agency, which has headquarters at Hoquiam. Fishing is the principal pursuit of the fifty inhabitants.

On the main side road is LACEY, 10.8 *m.* (184 alt., 600 pop.). Lacey has not always been as quiet as it is today; there was once a large lumber mill here, and the town was the horse-racing center of the Northwest. Atop a low hill (R) is ST MARTIN'S (Roman Catholic) COLLEGE, (*open to visitors daily, 8 a.m. to 8 p.m.*), constructed in Tudor Gothic style. A scientist on the college faculty pioneered in the field of radio in the Northwest, broadcasting as early as 1921. Here, laity of the Seattle Diocese meet annually for what is known as the Laymen's Retreat, a two-day period of prayer, spiritual meditation, and fasting. The college is under the direction of the Benedictine Fathers.

At 11.2 *m.* is a junction with a road: L. here 0.5 *m.* to LAKE CHAMBERS and the DAVID CHAMBERS HOUSE, a two-story structure built by David J. Chambers on a donation claim where he took up residence in 1845. A stockade and blockhouse which protected the family for a period of three months during Indian wars have been destroyed, but the house, preserved by frequent repairs, survives. It is now nearly surrounded by other structures, and is used as a club house for the MOUNTAIN VIEW GOLF CLUB (*fee 35c*), which operates an 18-hole course bordering the lake.

South of the junction US 99 traverses the delta of the Nisqually River and spans the gray glacial waters of the stream by a steel bridge, 52.2 *m.*

At 53.4 *m.* is a junction with a dirt road.

Right on this road to MEDICINE CREEK PARK (*unimproved*), 0.3 *m.* A large sign marks the place where once stood the TREATY TREES, under which, after a three-day council at Christmas time, 1854, Governor Stevens and the Nisqually, Puyallup, and Squaxon Indian tribes signed the Medicine Creek Treaty. This was the first important Indian treaty concluded by Stevens.

At 55.4 *m.* is the STATE FOREST DEPARTMENT HEADQUARTERS (R).

In Olympia, on 4th Avenue to Capitol Way, US 410 bears R. from US 99 (*see Tour 2d*).

OLYMPIA, 61.6 *m.* (17 alt., 13,254 pop.), (*see Olympia*).

Section d. OLYMPIA *to* MARYS CORNER, *47.9 m.*, US *99*

South of Olympia the highway, lined with service stations, taverns, lunch counters, tourist camps, and billboards, cuts through a prairie. Thickets of alder and willow grow in the low spots; on higher ground are evergreen firs, standing singly or in clumps. The country gradually alters into the broad, fertile valleys of the Chehalis River walled about by hills. Oak and hazel appear, and the highway acquires sweeping curves as it climbs through virgin and second-growth forests, then descends again into river valleys. This section, less thickly populated than the northern country, not only contributes to Puget Sound commerce, but is also a tributary to Grays Harbor on the ocean coast. Grain, truck farming, and dairy products flow both northeast and southwest; mines of lignite and coal and deposits of clay diversify the valley's economy.

TUMWATER (Chinook, waterfalls), 2.7 *m.* (87 alt., 955 pop.), was the Puget Sound terminus of the northern extension of the Oregon Trail. Here, in 1845, the first American Settlement north of the Columbia River was established. During the following year, the presence of settlers provided American treaty makers with an effective claim for a larger portion of the Pacific Northwestern territory than the British had wished to concede (*see History*).

Near the center of the town, US 99 spans the Deschutes River. Near the west end of the Deschutes bridge (R), on the west bank of the river, is the TUMWATER FOUNDERS MONUMENT, a huge, roughhewn granite block marking the spot where Colonel Michael T. Simmons and his travel-worn company ended their journey in 1845. A bronze plate on the monument bears the names of the 32 founders of the town. Although the settlers hopefully named the settlement Newmarket, the local Indians insisted on calling it "Tumwater," for the drumming sound of the waterfalls on the Deschutes River.

Simmons and his associates went to work quickly; with the Deschutes River supplying water power, a rude gristmill was built in 1846 which ground coarse flour. An ancient upright iron saw was purchased for 20c a pound from the Hudson's Bay Company, and the first cutting of lumber soon brought Indians from near and far to observe the magic of the white man.

Today, Tumwater has little industry except for the OLYMPIA BREWING COMPANY PLANT (*open to visitors, guide service*).

South of Tumwater US 99 enters a region of small ranches, reclaimed from stumplands. At 4.8 *m.* is a junction with a bituminous road.

Right here 4 *m.* to MILLERSYLVANIA STATE PARK (*picnic tables, stove, shelter, rest rooms*), where DEEP LAKE, in a setting of 720 acres of old forest, contains largemouthed bass, perch, and crappie. Rowboats, bathhouses, and a diving float are available to the public.

South of the junction, stone monuments set at intervals mark the route of the northern extension of the Oregon Trail. The highway enters an area of farming and grasslands known as BUSH PRAIRIE, after George W. Bush, a Negro, one of the founders of Tumwater. Having moved from Pennsylvania to Missouri, where he acquired a modest fortune in farming and cattle trading, Bush gave up his Missouri home when it became illegal for free Negroes to live in that State. Believing that the Oregon country north of the Columbia River might become British territory, where slavery would not be permitted, Bush and his family joined Colonel Simmons' westbound caravan. During the long journey and after settlement near Tumwater, Bush gave generously to other settlers from his stores of food and supplies and kept open house for travelers between the Columbia River and Puget Sound points. These deeds stood him in good stead some years later: after developing a large farm on the prairie now bearing his name, Bush discovered that the laws of the Oregon Territory denied residence to Negroes. Some years after the creation of Washington Territory, however, his friends secured the passage of a Congressional resolution granting him title to the land.

The highway passes a section of prairie dotted with small mounds of earth covered with prairie grass. The elevations are known as the TENINO MOUNDS, taking their name from a near-by town. The origin of these bumps, scattered over the surface of a half-dozen prairies just south of Puget Sound, has been the subject of speculation for nearly a century. Symmetrical in form, the mounds round out from slightly flattened tops to circular bases; a few of them are surmounted by young trees. They are composed chiefly of gravel with a layer of black soil and rise as high as eight feet. Captain Wilkes, during his expedition of 1841, dug into a number of them, thinking they might be burial mounds, but no traces of human remains were found. Two renowned naturalists, Louis Agassiz and Joseph LeConte, made a study of them and arrived at different conclusions. One believed they had been built by fish for spawning nests during an early inundation; the other was sure they had been caused by erosion following the recession of the ice sheets. Many other explanations have been advanced, ranging from one that they were Indian-built buffalo decoys to another which held that they had been forced up by gas and oil pressure. The most generally accepted is that of J. Harlan Bretz; in his *Glaciation of the Puget Sound Regions* he concludes that the silt blowing across the surface of the ice sheet covering the Puget Sound area had collected in depressions, and that, as the ice melted, this accumulation fell through to the gravel beneath, forming the mounds.

TENINO, 15.5 *m.* (200 alt., 952 pop.), came into existence in the early seventies, when a railroad under construction from Kalama to Tacoma located a camp on the site of the present town. Some local historians relate that the name of the city was taken from the number of the engine that ran on the line—No. 1090, ten-nine-o. Others insist that the Indians called the town "Tenino" (Ind., junction, or fork), when the railroad came through and connected with the Olympia mail stage.

In 1890 an event occurred which almost split the town in two. The depot was moved to a rail junction outside the town center, and a settlement was vigorously promoted at the new site. A hotel was hastily placed on rollers and hustled along after the depot. Several buildings were constructed; business began to spring up, and about 500 people were drawn there. The Tenino fathers, in a desperate effort to keep the original town intact, offered free real estate to anyone who would settle in it and the tide of emigration was stemmed. The truant hotel and other buildings were soon trundled back to the original site.

Tenino was front page news in the Nation's newspapers in 1932, when it issued wooden money following failure of the local bank. The experiment seemed to work; and later, what started as a desperate emergency effort turned out to be very profitable: about $11,000 of the "lumber jack" was sold to collectors throughout the Nation. An echo of the Tenino adventure in "wooden money" was heard in the State when, following enactment of the State sales tax, veneer tax tokens were used during a temporary shortage of metal tokens.

Tenino sandstone, from near-by quarries, has been used in the Seattle Public Library, the Old Capitol Building at Olympia, and Science Hall at Pullman. On February 17, 1912, a blast in which two carloads of powder were exploded was shot at the No. 2 quarry of the Hercules Sandstone Company to supply the first Grays Harbor jetty with 375,000 cubic yards of rock.

A small shingle mill and neighboring farms support the town. Dairy farms and berry fields are seen along the country roads in the vicinity, where one strawberry farm, two thousand acres in extent, is situated.

The CITY PARK, Custer and 1st Streets, has playground equipment, rest rooms, and stoves and tables for picnickers.

At the south city limits of Tenino is a junction with a concrete-paved road.

Left here 3.7 *m.* to BUCODA, (254 alt., 541 pop.), on the Skookumchuck River. In 1854 Aaron Webster settled the site and built a sawmill on the river. The Indians called the community that grew up around the mill *seatco,* a name which clung to the town for over 35 years. The discovery of coal across the river brought John D. David, Portland capitalist, and John M. Buckley, of the Northern Pacific Railway, to the scene, where, with Samuel Coulter, they developed a mine. The village was the site of the first Territorial penitentiary. The use of convict labor in the coal mine and near-by logging camps created a scandal that caused the removal of the institution to Walla Walla in 1887. The name Bucoda, adopted in 1890, was a combination of the first syllables of the names of Messrs. Buckley, Coulter, and David.

South of the junction is the wide Grand Mound Prairie, where again the odd-shaped humps appear.

GRAND MOUND, 25.2 *m.* (102 alt., 200 pop.), is a scattered community of frame buildings, a combined store and post office, and a service station. It was named for a hillock near by, which, highest of the curious mounds in this section, rises from the prairie to a height of 125 feet, and resembles a tree-covered butte.

Just south of Grand Mound is a junction with State 9.

Right 1.1 *m.* on State 9 from Grand Mound are the yellow-brick buildings of the WASHINGTON STATE SCHOOL FOR DELINQUENT GIRLS, on an attractively landscaped 70-acre tract. Offenders are required to remain until they reach the age of 21, unless they previously earn their release through credits gained under an honor system. Elementary and high school courses, with instruction in home economics and office practice, are combined with garden work about the grounds. The long, low administration building, surrounded by gardens and landscaped grounds, faces the highway.

ROCHESTER, 5.1 *m.* (149 alt., 300 pop.), is at a junction of the Northern Pacific and the Chicago, Milwaukee, St. Paul and Pacific railroads. It functions as a trading center for the surrounding district and has several small churches and a modern high school.

OAKVILLE, 12.6 *m.* (72 alt., 418 pop.), once a campsite of the Chehalis Indians, is now a small, quiet farming center divided by the highway. There are a bank, a weekly paper, a creamery, and two tie-cutting mills. Cascara bark, gathered in the adjoining forests, is shipped in considerable quantities every year.

Left from the east edge of Oakville on a concrete-paved road to a junction at 0.5 *m.* with a gravel road: R. here across the Chehalis River to the SHAKER CHURCH, 4.5 *m.,* a tall wooden structure with arched windows and a steepled tower.

At 13.1 *m.* on State 9 is a junction with a bituminous-surfaced road: L. here 3 *m.* to CEDARVILLE (80 alt., 25 pop.), one of the earliest settlements in the Washington Territory. It was homesteaded by James L. (Blockhouse) Smith, so-called because the government built a blockhouse on his land in 1855 as a protection against Indian attacks. The foundation stones of the blockhouse, which burned down in recent years, still remain. Another rugged pioneer, John Armstrong, erected on Cedar Creek one of the first waterpower mills in the district; it was equipped with an upright saw and was said to have had a production capacity of 1,000 feet of lumber a day. The Sam Williams home, a rambling frame structure, was built of lumber from Armstrong's mill.

PORTER, on the main side road at 19.8 *m.* (75 alt., 387 pop.), a scattered roadside settlement, was named in honor of Fairchild Porter, a pioneer settler of 1860.

MALONE, 21.3 *m.* (50 alt., 300 pop.), is a former logging center on Moxie Creek. The remains of a large abandoned mill still stand. Company houses are mainly vacant, and the company-built store, theater, and offices are boarded up.

At 26.1 *m.* is a junction with US 410 (*see Tour 2d*).

CENTRALIA, 30.8 *m.* (184 alt., 7,414 pop.), near the junction of the Chehalis and Skookumchuck Rivers, is often referred to as the "Hub City" of southwestern Washington. With its sister city, Chehalis, it occupies a strategic position halfway between the cities of Puget Sound and Portland, Oregon, in a region rich in timber, mineral, and agricultural resources. Lumber manufacture is Centralia's leading industry, and farm trade is an important commercial asset. Once, coal mining was active near by, but it is no longer carried on today. The town, an early railroad center, is now served by four railroads.

In pioneer days the town was the halfway stopover point for stagecoaches operating between the Columbia River and Seattle. In 1850, J. G. Cochran, coming from Missouri with a young Negro slave named George Washington, filed a donation land claim on the townsite. Later, Cochran freed his slave, adopted him as a son, and in 1852 sold him his claim for $6,000. The new owner built a home and filed a plat for the town of Centerville, offering lots for $10 each, with one lot free to buyers who built houses.

In 1891, the population—over 1,000—found its mail confused with that of another Centerville in the State, and the name of the town was changed to Centralia.

In early August, Centralia celebrates Pioneer Days, an annual event centering around the old Borst Blockhouse. Ox-teams, covered wagons, and Indian costumes are featured in a big parade. The celebration lasts three days. The men of the town have a beard-growing contest, and the longest whiskers are awarded cash prizes. Indian wampum is made legal tender. A rodeo terminates this civic holiday period.

Facing Harrison Avenue at the west city limits is RIVERSIDE PARK (R), with shady picnic grounds along the river. Right, is the entrance to BORST PARK, home of the BORST BLOCKHOUSE (*open*), built in 1855 for defense against Indian uprisings. Flood waters converging on its original site, at the confluence of the Skookumchuck and Chehalis Rivers, necessitated removal of the structure to the present location near the south end of the park. The old blockhouse, still in good condition, is the park's chief attraction. The foundation walls of hewn and dovetailed fir logs rise ten feet to support the overhanging upper fortification. The floor in the extension of this second story is perforated with holes for firing down upon attackers. Floors and doors are of cedar puncheons, heavy enough to resist an arrow or check a musket ball. The usual loopholes for rifles were cut around the sides.

GEORGE WASHINGTON PARK (R), named for the freed slave who gave it to the city, corner of Main and Pearl Sts., occupies a square block in the downtown business center. In the center of the park are the buildings and grounds of the CARNEGIE PUBLIC LIBRARY (*open weekdays, except Fri., 1-5:45 and 7-9; Fri. 10-11:30*), housing 12,028 volumes.

A tall sculptured figure of a sentinel stands in the park, a monument erected by the American Legion to four Legionnaires killed during a riot on Armistice Day, after which a member of the I.W.W. was lynched (*see Labor*).

The CENTRALIA JUNIOR COLLEGE, W. Pearl St. between S. Iron and S. Rock St., in the Centralia High School Building, was established in 1925. It is accredited by the University of Washington and the State College at Pullman.

The DEGGELER MUSEUM (*open*), 712 S. Gold St., operated by W. A. and Mrs. Deggeler, taxidermists, holds an interesting display of taxidermy, Indian relics, mounted horns, fauna, flora, and shells.

South of Centralia US 99 follows Tower Avenue to Chestnut Street, L. on Cestnut to Gold Street, R. on Gold to city limits.

The building and race tracks on the LEWIS COUNTY FAIR GROUNDS, 85.5 *m.*, border the highway (R). Here, each autumn, the local population flocks to view huge vegetables and prize cattle, to cheer on the jockeys and horses, and consume quantities of soda pop and peanuts.

Near the confluence of the Newaukum and Chehalis Rivers is CHEHALIS (Ind. shifting sands), 36.2 *m.* (188 alt., 4,857 pop.), the seat of Lewis County. The business district, compact with modern structures and trim shops, has an air of prosperity and leisure. The city began as a settlement around a warehouse beside a railroad track in 1873, when the Northern Pacific built northward from Kalama to Tacoma, and ignored Claquato, then the county seat, three miles to the west. Some settlers in the vicinity decided that, if the railroad would not go to the county seat, the seat must go to the railroad. By 1874, a store was added to the warehouse, several houses were constructed, and the county seat was moved to the new settlement, leaving Claquato little more than a historic landmark. The new town was first named Saundersville, for S. S. Saunders, on whose donation land claim it was founded. In 1879 the name was changed to Chehalis.

Logging soon began in the near-by forests. Lumber workers of Scandinavian, Anglo-Saxon, and Scotch-Irish descent arrived, and remained to settle in the neighboring valleys. Today dairying, poultry raising, and fruit growing are carried on here. Besides lumbering, local industries include milk condensing, fruit and vegetable packing, brick and tile manufacturing, coal mining, portable house manufacturing, and fern shipping.

In the CIVIC CENTER, an elevated triangular park, intersection of Cascade, Park, and Market Streets, are (L), the CITY HALL, a simple red-brick building, and (R) the CHEHALIS PUBLIC LIBRARY (*open weekdays 1-6, 7-9; Sun. 2-5*), of similar design.

The O. B. MCFADDEN HOUSE (*private*), 1630 Chehalis Ave., is a historic landmark. This two-story, eight-room dwelling was built in 1859 by S. S. Saunders for O. B. McFadden, who was later (1881) appointed Chief Justice of Washington Territory. It served for a time as the Saundersville Post Office. The house, preserved by frequent repair, has been occupied continuously since 1859.

At Division and St. Helens Ave. is the CHURCH OF THE EPIPHANY, perhaps the most interesting building in the city. Left unchanged since it was built in 1884, it resembles the early Episcopalian churches of New England, with its trussed ceiling and ornamented spire. Through stained-glass windows the light sifts in on handmade furniture of native red cedar.

Right from Market St. on 11th Ave. to the WASHINGTON STATE TRAINING SCHOOL FOR BOYS, 1 *m.* The education of delinquent youths proceeds along four major lines: academic, vocational, domestic, and social. Special attention is given to athletics, sports, and music. A large rectangular playfield is bordered on two sides by the school buildings.

Right from Market Street, State 12, a branch of the Ocean Beach Highway, follows Main Street to Riverside Road; L. here 2 *m.* on Riverside Road to ALEXANDER PARK (L), on the Chehalis River. Equipped for camping, picnicking and bathing, the park is the city's leading recreational center. In July an annual celebration, the Farmers' and Merchants' Picnic, is held here. The main event, the frying of a huge omelet in a mammoth frying pan, has been pictured in newsreels and newspapers.

At 3.3 *m.* is all that is left of Claquato, founded by Louis H. Davis in 1852, one of the earliest settlements in Lewis County, and the first county seat. The OLD CLAQUATO CHURCH, among the oldest in Washington, stands on a hill (L) beside an old cemetery. It was built as a Protestant Episcopal Church in 1856. The entire tower framing is mortise and tenon work of high quality; even the lookouts supporting the roof projection on the gables are mortised and wedged into the end rafters. The church, standing upon its original site, is still in use.

RAINBOW FALLS STATE PARK, 16 *m.,* is a 120-acre recreational area of old-growth timber on the Chehalis River. Five miles of shady trails wind through the park. A 200-foot cable footbridge, suspended over the river, leads into a forest wilderness. Twenty acres have been cleared and sown to grass to serve as a playfield.

At 18 *m.* is a junction with a graveled road: R. here 1 *m.* to DRYAD (50 pop.), a group of mill company houses near the site of a dismantled sawmill. The adjacent hills are a scarred wasteland of silver-gray snags and forest wreckage—the residue left by high-speed logging methods.

PE ELL, 23.8 *m.* (412 alt., 825 pop.), is a lumber town that was intended to be called Pierre, but became known as Pe Ell through the inability of the Indians to pronounce the "r's" in the French name. The town was platted in 1891 by Omar Maurmann, first white settler; later many Polish families, attracted by the growing lumber industry, settled here. A large many-windowed Catholic church, a school, and a three-story rectory are among the outstanding buildings.

At 26 *m.,* is the site of McCORMICK, the ghost of a formerly thriving sawmill center. The collapsed ruins of the large mill building (R) are overgrown by alders and other second-growth timber.

At 28 *m.,* the site of WALVILLE, the weathered but once pretentious offices and residences (L) of the mill staff contrast with the shabby shacks occupied by Japanese and other laborers, long since gone, like the mill that was dismantled when the forested hills were denuded.

PLUVIUS, 30.3 *m.* (746 alt., 10 pop.), is at the crest of the divide. Heavy rains in the region are said to have been responsible for the name.

LEBAM, 38.0 *m.* (189 alt., 400 pop.), a former logging town encircled by low, heavily timbered foothills, was named by J. W. Goodell, its founder, for his daughter, Mabel, spelling her name backwards.

MENLO, 46.5 *m.* (87 alt., 400 pop.), dairying center and home of a large creamery and cheese factory, began as a flag station on the property of Lindley Preston, when the railroad built through this area in the late eighties. John Brophy, a pioneer settler, named the town for Menlo Park, his former home in California.

At 50.3 *m.* is a junction with a dirt road. R. here 1 *m.* to WILLAPA (42 alt., 320 pop.), settled in 1852. Several mills were built in the ensuing decade, and the town flourished as the supply point for all of the Willapa Valley beyond until 1893, when the railroad established direct connections with Willapa Harbor. Lumbering, long on the decline here, is being replaced by farming. A small new business center has sprung up adjoining the rail lines. A dusty road continues north through a residence section that reaches down to the bank of the Willapa River, site of the old town.

At 52.7 *m.* on the main side road is RAYMOND (11 alt., 4,045 pop.), at a junction with US 101 (*see Tour 9d*).

South of Chehalis US 99 bears southeasterly over a rolling country, soft in outline, with cultivated valleys and gracefully molded hills. In the distance are oak and evergreen uplands.

At 41.5 *m.* is a junction with a graveled road.

Right on this road to a junction with another graveled road, 1 *m.*

R. 3.1 *m.* on this road to NAPAVINE (Ind. small prairie), (443 alt., 220 pop.), trading and rail center of a dairy, poultry, and fruit district.

FOREST 43.6 *m.* (200 alt., 388 pop.), slumbers quietly along the highway. Pioneers in the middle forties settled here on the banks of the Newaukum. Several modern homes stand in the settlement today.

At 47.7 *m.* is MATILDA JACKSON STATE PARK, a small timber reserve along the highway (R).

At MARYS CORNER 47.9 *m.,* is a junction with State 5 (*see Tour 8E*).

Section e. MARYS CORNER *to the* OREGON LINE; *76.7 m. US 99 and US 99-830*

South of Marys Corner, US 99 follows an old stage route connecting Vancouver, on the Columbia River, with Puget Sound. In the fifties the new country, rich in timber, fishing, mining, and agricultural resources, was tramped by eager homeseekers, prospectors, and fortune hunters. Today, the easily reached timber has been cut, and logging operations have moved back into the foothills and the less accessible regions. In the hidden hinterland, abandoned sawmills and logging operations have left ghost towns in their wake. Of the inhabitants who remain, a few maintain themselves by small-scale farming, poultry raising, and dairying. Bordering the road are alternating stretches of small timber, stump lands, and prosperous farms.

The JACKSON PRAIRIE COURTHOUSE (*see caretaker near by*), in MARY'S CORNER, 0 *m.* (L), is an ancient building that housed the first Federal court north of the Columbia River. John R. Jackson selected this spot for a home in 1844, and it became noted as a stopping place for travelers. The building was converted into a courthouse in 1850. A small one and one-half story structure of peeled logs, with hand-split cedar boards above the first floor, and a long old-fashioned porch, it is one of the State's cherished landmarks. The building is separated from the highway by a cobblestone wall. Screened from the road by a jungle of old trees, its presence is indicated by an arched gateway.

The lofty firs of LEWIS AND CLARK STATE PARK, 0.9 *m.* (R), an improved forest area of 518 acres, shade the highway on warm summer days, and the park's rich vegetation exudes a sweet, refreshing dampness. Woodland trails leading off through heavily timbered sections provide short hikes.

At 6 *m.* is a junction with a dirt road.

Left on this road to ST. FRANCIS MISSION, 0.2 *m.,* the oldest active mission in the Northwest and the site of the first Roman Catholic church in Washington. In 1838 missionaries from Canada, under Father Francois Norbert Blanchet, founded the mission here, converted the neighboring Indian bands to the Christian faith, and ministered to the spiritual needs of Hudson's Bay Company traders and settlers. For many years, St. Francis Mission, also known as the Cowlitz Mission, was the only Catholic establishment in the wilds north of Vancouver. The original structure was destroyed by fire in the late nineties. Adjoining the mission is ST. MARY'S ACADEMY, established 1911 and conducted by the Sisters of St. Francis.

At 7 *m.* is a junction with State 12-E, a concrete road.

Right on this road is WINLOCK, 5.3 *m.* (308 alt., 861 pop.), named for General Winlock W. Miller, one of the first Federal officers sent to the Territory for service during the Indian uprising. Displayed prominently near the highway crossing and the depot, a large white-painted egg advertises the fact that Winlock is the shipping point and center of one of the most productive egg- and poultry-producing districts in western Washington. A cluster of stores along the main street bids for the trade of rich Olequa Valley.

At 7.8 *m.* is a junction with State 1-P, a graveled road.

Right on State 1-P, which sweeps through rolling fields of pioneer-type farms. Near the forested hills are large stump areas, and the countryside becomes wilder and more desolate there. Growths of vine and brush line the road and stretch away toward the scarred hills.

VADER, 8.3 *m.* (139 alt., 479 pop.), is a farming community and rail point on Olequa Creek.

RYDERWOOD, 14.7 *m.* (270 alt., 400 pop.), is headquarters for the Long-Bell Lumber Company's logging operations in the district. The town, built in 1923, was once a booming logging center. The dwindling of near-by timber resources and the effects of the depression are evidenced by weatherbeaten and boarded-up cottages. A nursery is maintained here by the lumber company for reforestation. Roundhouses and machine shops for its railroads are points of activity.

TOLEDO, 7.9 *m.* (142 alt., 523 pop.), situated on the Cowlitz River and named for the *Toledo,* a side-wheel steamer which plied the river in pioneer days, was formerly called Cowlitz Landing, then Warbassport. Here early settlers disembarked, swapped stories, and continued northward by stage, horse, or foot. Today, it is a compact aging village, pushed against the bank of the river, its tranquillity undisturbed by the rush of mainline traffic.

From Toledo, US 99 swings south across a bridge and runs roughly parallel to the Cowlitz River. At 14.5 *m.* are the giant evergreens of BARNES STATE PARK (*no accommodations*), an unimproved 1,000-acre forest reserve on the Cowlitz River.

South of the park, US 99 traverses lush grazing land and crosses the swirling Toutle River. Truck gardens on the valley bottomlands are divided from the forest only by the roadway, along which rumble heavy log trucks loaded with forest giants.

The highway rises to a terrace above the valley floor; below is a panorama of river country. The broad willow-bordered Cowlitz, widening at every tributary, flows with graceful bends and curves, breaking into rapids, then slowing into a smooth mirror. Sandbars occasionally thrust above the surface.

At 22.4 *m.* is a junction with State 1-R, a graveled road.

Left on this road, which a large roadway sign announces as the "Gateway to Mount St. Helens," to SILVER LAKE, 9 *m.,* noted for its fine fishing. Six miles long by one and one-half miles wide, Silver Lake is extremely shallow, with a maximum depth of ten feet. Along the shore the air is heavy with the fragrance of water lilies, whose yellow and white blossoms float in great clusters among cool green pads. Several small islands dot the surface, the largest comprising 55 acres. On the borders of the lake (R) is Cowlitz Chapter of the Isaak Walton League, housed in a large rustic lodge, built of peeled logs, and equipped with a huge stone fireplace.

East of Silver Lake the graveled road climbs gradually from low stump land, in which here and there are small farms and patches of second growth, to higher ground, where heavy forests crowd the highway. The route follows the course of the Toutle River, crossing this turbulent stream, at 14.1 *m.,* over a rough puncheon bridge supported by two huge logs. The big timber along the Toutle River was the scene of a motion picture made in 1936. The route ascends more steeply, winding about mountain faces high above the river, revealing panoramas of mountain and valley wilderness. In the valley between these high points, giant firs raise a dark canopy against the sky. Caution should be exercised at turns and in occasional narrow places in the road, for heavy logging trucks sometimes speed along the highway.

At 24.7 *m.* the road ends near SPIRIT LAKE FOREST CAMP, on the south shore of SPIRIT LAKE (3,199 alt.), the western entrance to Columbia National Forest. Here a free public campground is maintained by the Forest Service. Close by, on either side of the camp, are two cabin camp resorts where motor fuel and supplies may be obtained. Boats are available here, and rainbow, Montana black, and Eastern brook trout are caught in the clear, cold waters of the lake, the bottom of which is of white pumice. Depths of 1,300 feet are common, and in places the bottom has not yet been found. Shaped somewhat like a bent pin, with one shimmering angle reaching about four miles to the east and another slanting off two miles to the north, Spirit Lake, known as a sportsman's paradise, lies in a primitive region of mountains and small lakes, nearly 30 of which may be reached in one day's travel on a score of trail trips that radiate from the forest camp. On the opposite shore is HARMONY FALLS PARK, reached by boat.

During the last eruption of Mount St. Helens, believed to have occurred about 1840, pumice cinders were thrown from the crater, covering the ground to a depth of 10 to 20 feet. Tree trunks, rotting away in this cemented substance, left what is known as "tree wells," of which there are thousands on the south side of the lake. Spirit Lake may have been formed at that time; the eruption burying a whole forest at this point, damming up a stream, and creating the lake. One of the "tree wells" may be seen at the edge of the forest camp. Many of the pebbles along the beach are of light pumice filled with air chambers. Some of them will float for five or more minutes before becoming saturated.

Spirit Lake was so named because Indians of the region, believers in ghosts, interpreted many weird natural sounds of the place as the haunting voices of departed spirits. One legend relates that an Indian brave, seeking food for his starving tribe, trailed a giant bull elk to the lake, only to be led by the phantom to his death in the water; the Indians are said to have believed that each year both of them appeared over the lake on a certain night. According to another legend, the region was the home of fabulous *Siatcoes,* outcasts from other tribes, to whom were attributed ventriloqual and supernatural powers.

At the forest service camp is a junction with a dirt road; R. here 1.5 *m.* to the timber line of MOUNT ST. HELENS (9,671 alt.), which is as far as a car can go. A trail leads off at this point. The climbing time from here to the summit is seven hours. It is said that the steep north side of the mountain, with its yawning glaciers, is one of the most difficult ascents in the Cascades.

CASTLE ROCK, 22.7 *m.* (52 alt., 1,182 pop.), a rural trading center for the fine farms in the valley, is set on low flat ground along the east bank of the Cowlitz River. Founded in 1883, it took its name from the huge rocky upthrust south of town long known as Castle Rock. Several times river floods menaced the town, until it inaugurated a successful dike system. Dairying, truck farming, and lumber manufacture support the bulk of the population today. Swordferns, which grow prolifically in the region, and which can be processed for medicinal uses, are picked by several hundred men, women, and children every fall. In the spring, the countryside is searched for cascara bark, large quantities of which are dried and shipped.

South of Castle Rock, US 99 ascends high above the Cowlitz. It follows a course marked by sweeping curves, passes along a series of terraces, formed by ancient floods, and affords glimpses (R) of the broad and deceitfully peaceful Cowlitz, winding slowly southward. The terraces rise from 300 to 400 feet above the flood plains of the river, along which are fertile farmlands, protected by a dike system. Logging trucks are frequently seen at log dumps tipping their loads into the stream to make up a boom. Bordering the highway at a few points are prosperous-looking modern homes, in strange contrast to the near wilderness at their back doors; precipitous hills (L) lying rank on rank, are freshly scarred by recent logging. Left, on the slopes descending to the Cowlitz Valley, are large second-growth trees.

OSTRANDER, 29.3 *m.* (41 alt., 275 pop.), on the right of the highway, is hidden from view by a jutting hill crowned with trees. It was named for Dr. Nathaniel Ostrander, one of Cowlitz County's first settlers, who took his donation land claim here in 1852. This village, set in the midst of a few farms, is but a gray shadow of the busy little settlement of the late nineties and the early nineteen hundreds, when the Ostrander Timber Company rivaled other Washington logging operators in manufacturing the longest squares and spars produced in the world; some single specimens of these required three flat cars for transportation. Forty miles of railway were extended into the forest; but when the company had logged off all the land at its disposal, it dismantled the mill and transported it to another site, leaving the town to dream of its days of past prosperity.

Ostrander Creek, which runs through the town, has been the scene of recurrent excitement over gold since the pioneer period. The reported finding of a rich piece of gold quartz by one of the early settlers, whose identity is not recorded, fostered the belief that a large deposit lay somewhere in the vicinity. Thereafter the community was periodically stirred by reports that gold had been found along the creek, rumors that gained credence when, on one occasion, a housewife discovered two gold nuggets in the craw of a chicken she was preparing for dinner. No fortunes, however, have been founded on the gold of this area.

KELSO, 33 *m.* (22 alt., 6,749 pop.), has the brisk air of a small metropolis, compact with stores and business blocks. The industries of the town are assembled along the highway (R), paralleling the Cowlitz River. In 1847 the founder, Peter Crawford, a Scotch surveyor, took up a land claim in what is now the northeast section of the town. It was on the main artery of travel between Vancouver and the Puget Sound country; many pioneers on their way north stopped here, and, attracted by the rich bottomland along the river and the timbered hills, decided to go no farther. Gradually, a settlement took form, and in 1884 Crawford platted a townsite, naming it Kelso for his home town in Scotland. Logging on the forested slopes made

Kelso an important lumber center, and the town spread west across the river and absorbed the villages of Freeport and Catlin, which now constitute West Kelso.

From the COWLITZ RIVER BRIDGE on Main St., the river presents a busy scene between January and March, the smelt season; for Kelso is one of the world's principal smelt centers. At this time the river is crowded with small boats, from which nets are lowered and pulled to the surface laden with the tiny fish.

Under the bridge, from time to time, great log rafts drift slowly on their way to the mills. Houseboats line both sides of the river within the area of the town.

Kelso is at a junction of US 99 and US 830, the Ocean Highway (*see Tour 8b*).

R. from West Kelso on 8th Ave., along the Columbia Heights Road, 4.9 *m.*, a concrete highway that curves over the hills through a countryside of well-kept gardens and homes. From the heights, the gleaming Cowlitz and Columbia rivers are visible on the south, a patchwork of farms and forests on the north, and the cities of Kelso and Longview (*see Tour 3b*) below; and on clear days, the white peaks of Mount St. Helens, Mount Adams, and Mount Rainier.

In the early eighties, a colony of Finnish homeseekers settled in this region. Isolated from Kelso and other communities, they retained their language and customs until good roads and the city industries drew them into contact with American culture. By this time, public school training and association with their neighbors have removed almost every trace of their native speech and habits.

Leaving Kelso, the highway passes the velvety course (L) of the COWEEMAN PUBLIC GOLF CLUB (*18 holes; fees: 50c weekdays; Sat., Sun., and holidays, 35c for 9 holes, 50c for 18*), which stretches back along the Coweeman River as it passes under the highway.

At 36.3 *m.*, is another junction with US 830, the Ocean Beach Highway. (*see Tour 3b*). South of the junction US 99 and US 830 coincide.

The highway traverses the base of a wooded promontory and ascends gradually, offering a panorama of the Columbia as it swings westward to join the Pacific. A large island stems the current in the center of this great sweep of water. Ocean-going cargo carriers move ponderously upon its broad bosom and small fishing boats scuttle to and fro. At nights the lights of tiny settlements on the Oregon shore appear.

At 42.5 *m.* is a junction with a graveled road.

Left on this road, which follows the shelf of the Kalama River through a gorge of sheer rock walls rising precipitously above the roadbed.

At 8 *m.* is the KALAMA RIVER SALMON HATCHERY. Here, salmon are on view in several stages of development—from the eggs to lengths of about nine inches, when they are released. During spring occurs the strange phenomenon, the return of the salmon, after years of wandering among the currents of the Pacific, to its birthplace. Ascending the Columbia in great silver hordes, the salmon swarm inland to tributaries remote from the ocean, recklessly leaping forward in upstream plunges, tearing their sides against sharp rocks, wriggling through stony shallows, fighting through rapids, many dying on the way, until they reach the headwaters of their native stream.

The eggs of the salmon are laid in light gravel, frequently high in the mountains and sometimes 1,000 miles from salt water. In from 30 to 120 days the eggs hatch. The young fish remain in fresh water for a period varying from a few months to as long as two years, depending upon the species and to some extent upon variations within the species. Having attained the length of a few inches, the fingerling begins the trek to the sea, where it reaches full growth.

The highway swings against the base of a rocky headland (L).

KALAMA (Ind. pretty maiden), 44.1 *m.* (21 alt., 940 pop.), is on a narrow flat at the confluence of the Columbia and Kalama Rivers. It began in 1853 when Ezra Meeker, noted pioneer, arrived and built a cabin near the present townsite. Leaving his wife and son here for a time, he continued north with his brother to locate land claims in the Puget Sound country.

Although numerous claims were settled along the Columbia and Kalama Rivers in the succeeding decades, the town did not come into being until 1870, when the Northern Pacific Railway selected a point within the district from which to begin construction northward to Puget Sound. On February 15, 1870, the Northern Pacific broke ground for the line, and soon 750 Chinese and 500 other laborers were employed. The town boomed. A ferry across the Columbia River to Goble transported trains to Oregon. General J. W. Sprague of the Northern Pacific in 1871 named the town for the Kalama River. From 1872 it was the seat of Cowlitz County, until the election of 1932 transferred the seat to Kelso. Kalama's strategic importance as a rail and water terminal was ended in 1887 when the Northern Pacific completed its main line across the Cascades to Puget Sound; the branch line was then built south from Kalama to Portland, Oregon. The misfortune of the town was crowned soon after by a fire, which destroyed 25 buildings. However, the long deepwater harbor adjoining the railroad aided in keeping it a shipping point, and Kalama proclaims itself the city "Where Rail Meets Water." Within the radius of one block there are a port dock, the deepest on the Columbia River, three transcontinental railroads, and a US highway. A sawmill and a shingle mill draw raw materials from heavy stands of timber in the hills to the eastward.

Kalama is a typical river town; its main thoroughfare, First Street, follows the river bank, from which the residential section rises steeply. Sawmills and the KALAMA PORT DOCK (R) account for most of its income. Strawberries are an important crop on surrounding farms, and the Cloverdale-Lewis Co-operative Berry Association packs and ships annually 3,000 barrels of berries at their plant at the Kalama Port Dock. The sub-irrigated soil of the district is particularly suited to commercial mint raising.

There is much salmon fishing in the Columbia River at this point, and a fish company ships annually 600,000 pounds of frozen fish to Europe. Caviar, packed in glass jars, is also exported. The fish business here was started by C. A. Doty, a Northern Pacific branch agent with diversified interests. Ordered by the railroad company to choose between his job and his other enterprises, he resigned from the Northern Pacific and devoted his time to the fishing industry.

South of Kalama US 99 traverses a park-like area of wooded country with stands of tall Douglas fir. Descending to a rich bottom land, diked against floods, the highway runs past truck gardens and lush meadows with grazing cattle.

At 52.5 *m.* is a junction with 1-S, concrete-paved for about three miles, then graveled.

Left on this road, which follows the Lewis River, through a farming and grazing area and past logging camps to the LEWIS RIVER FISH HATCHERY 8 *m.*, a $200,000 plant for stocking the lakes and streams of the district with game fish.

East of the hatchery the road traverses a scenic mountainous country thickly wooded with tall virgin timber. The Cascade Range rises to the east, surmounted by the peaks of Mount St. Helens and Mount Adams.

At 10.4 *m.* the ARIEL DAM (R), 1,342 feet in length and 313 deep, stretches across the western end of LAKE MERWIN, an artificial body of water created by the Northwest Electric Company as the first unit of a huge power-development program. Within the dam is a fish-preservation apparatus designed and operated by the State Department of Fisheries. A ten-ton steel tank containing water imprisons the fish as they come up the river. When the tank becomes filled with steel-head, salmon and other game fish, it is elevated by means of a derrick and its contents emptied into the lake above. In season, salmon are transported in specially constructed trucks to the fish hatchery three miles west. The crescent-shaped lake, which is eleven and one-half miles long and one-fourth of a mile wide, is in a basin where towering firs once stood. It offers excellent fishing, boating, and swimming. Surrounding it are 1,000 acres of evergreen forests, maintained for public recreation. Although the company does not permit the shooting of game in the recreational area, the adjoining territory abounds with duck, pheasant, bear, and deer, which may be hunted during the open season.

First-growth timber still crowns the hillsides along the river, and logging camps are busy felling and sawing the huge trees. Long trailer trucks rumble along the road en route to Martin's Slough, on the Columbia River near Woodland; the logs are dropped into the slough and floated in booms to mills in both Washington and Oregon.

East, along the north shore of the lake, the road continues on a gradual ascent to OLE PETERSON'S CAMP on the Lewis River, starting point for trips eastward into the Lewis River area. There are no improved camp grounds hereabout, and permits to build fires must be secured at the LEWIS RIVER GUARD STATION, adjoining the Peterson camp on the east.

At the Lewis River Station is a junction with a trail: L. here up the mountain side to the LAVA CAVES, created by the volcanic forces that once rent that section. The largest of the caves extend about one mile under the mountain to an opening on another face. The caves contain no stalactites or stalagmites, as the formation is lava, not limestone. Flashlights or lanterns should be used when entering them, and tourists should be accompanied by someone familiar with the caves. Sturdy, thick-soled shoes and other suitable clothing should be worn.

The fertile lowlands of the Lewis River form one of the most productive farming areas in the State. In this vicinity, strawberries, raspberries, youngberries, and cranberries grow in generous quantities. The fields yield heavy crops of peas, garden vegetables, and alfalfa. Dairy farms and poultry ranches where many turkey are raised, also thrive on the countryside.

At 53.4 *m.* is a junction with a concrete road.

Right on this road to WOODLAND, 0.5 *m.* (33 alt., 980 pop.), two miles from the confluence of the Columbia and Lewis Rivers. The town, situated on a low, wide plain, is a bustling center of the surrounding farming, dairying, and poultry community, and has a vegetable cannery and a receiving, shipping, and feed station of the Washington Co-op Egg and Poultry Association. A large bulb farm near the town cultivates and harvests daffodil, tulip, narcissus, and iris bulbs for shipment to eastern and foreign markets.

A large percentage of the local population is of Finnish descent, and traces of the old-world culture and speech are discernible. The first Finnish settlers came here in 1901.

US 99 spans the Lewis River, overhung with alders, willows and an occasional birch. In the seventies, LA CENTER, 58.9 *m.* (250 alt., 192 pop.), was an animated business center and head of navigation on the East Fork of the Lewis River. In late summer, the regular schedules of the river steamers *Mascot* and *Walker,* paddle-wheeling to Portland, were often interrupted by low water. Passengers and freight were transferred to scows, which were poled up the river or towed by horses along the bank. The picturesque transportation of the pioneer age vanished with the arrival of railroads and highways; La Center lost importance and lapsed into a small village which functions today as a retail market for a scattered farming district.

South of La Center, US 99 passes through green grazing lands along the base of a long slope extending from the foothills of the Cascade Mountains.

At 62.9 *m.* is a junction with State 1-T, a concrete road.

Right from the junction the road is lined by cultivated wheatlands and orchards. RIDGEFIELD, 5 *m.* (60 alt., 643 pop.), near the Columbia River, is a neat town whose industry is represented by a sawmill.

At 69.3 *m.* is a junction with State 1-S.

Left from the junction on State 1-S, a graveled road, are stands of fir; farther along are stump lands and occasional old farm houses. BATTLE GROUND, 6.2 *m.* (227 alt., 540 pop.), is a brisk little trading center, with a grain elevator and one of the largest cheese factories in the State. About 1888 August H. Richter built a store here and founded the town. The surrounding plains were used by the Hudson's Bay Company and, later, by the United States Army for pasture lands.

Left from Battle Ground to BATTLE GROUND LAKE, 1.8 *m.,* a popular resort, on the crest of a small mountain.

The highway runs straight through an area of orchards and farms. On the outskirts of Vancouver US 99 coincides with Main Street.

Left from Main Street on E. 22nd Street, which becomes State 8-A, the Fourth Plain Road, to Orchards, 6.0 *m.* (100 alt., 100 pop.), site of several of the earliest structures north of the Columbia River. Charles Coulder built here in 1846. Shortly afterward Richard Covington built the noted Covington House. Here he was host to many prominent persons, including Lieutenant Ulysses S. Grant of Fort Vancouver. The house has been removed to Leverich Park in Vancouver (*see Vancouver*).

VANCOUVER 76.7 *m.* (40 alt., 18,788 pop.), (*see Vancouver*).

At 5th and Main Sts. is a junction with US 830 (*see Tour 3a*).

South on Main St., at 76.7 *m.,* US 99 crosses the Columbia River on the OREGON WASHINGTON INTERSTATE BRIDGE, 3.1 miles north of Portland, Oregon.

Tour 8A

Bellingham—Deming—Glacier—Shuksan—Mount Baker Lodge—Austin Pass Guard Station—Kulshan Ridge; 59.6 *m.* State 1.

Forest trails lead eastward into Cascade Mountains from end of highway.
Busses from Leopold Hotel, Bellingham, to Mount Baker Lodge.
Chicago, Milwaukee, St. Paul and Pacific R.R. logging spur roughly parallels route to Glacier.
Concrete-paved roadbed to Deming; oiled surface to Glacier; graveled to Austin Pass Guard Station.
Snow encountered at higher altitudes during winter and early spring, but highway kept open at all seasons.
Accommodations at small hotels and inns and at tourist camps in season; good accommodations at Mount Baker Lodge throughout the year, moderate rates.

State 1 winds up the valley of the Nooksack River through rolling hills dotted with brightly colored farmhouses and big red barns. Cattle graze in the lush meadows of the river flats; higher ground is given over to orchard tracts, poultry ranches, and truck gardens interspersed with small stands of second-growth evergreens. Gradually at first, and then more noticeably, the highway climbs upward, and farms become less and less frequent in the timbered foothills. Small settlements, forest camps, and an occasional mine or quarry are strung along the highway. Dominating the eastern horizon are the snow-crowned dome of Mount Baker and the rugged peaks and ridges surrounding it. Finally the highway winds into the heart of the Nooksack Recreation Area, a flowered alpine meadowland in summer, dotted with glaciers on the higher levels, and a vast snowfield in winter. The road ends about 60 miles east of Bellingham at Kulshan Ridge, from which trails lead into the heart of the Cascade Mountains.

State 1 branches east from US 99 (*see Tour 8a*) at East Holly Street and Cornwall Avenue in BELLINGHAM, 0 *m.*, and follows Sunset Drive, which becomes the Mount Baker Road. Continuing through country marked by sloping green hills and small timber stands, it passes a STATE WEIGHING STATION at 5.6 *m.* Ahead are forested hills, and around lie closely neighboring farms and tracts of orchard. At 8.1 *m.* it is possible to see the entire valley, dotted with alder and fir, stretching away to the distant snow-covered mountains. A green-girdered bridge, 11.6 *m.*, spans the swirling Nooksack River. About three miles beyond may be had the first clear view of Mount Baker.

Scattered clumps of trees give a woodland charm to the business district of DEMING, 15.6 *m.* (203 alt., 250 pop.), trading and market center of the agricultural district. Implements and feed are received at the large warehouse on the railroad siding, center of the community's industrial activity, and dairy and poultry products are shipped from here. On the outskirts of Deming is the attractive two-story Union High School. E. W. Owen, the first postmaster, gave the town its name in honor of the Deming Land Company, which had large holdings in the area. A Roman Catholic Mission was founded by Father J. B. Boulet in 1886, and in 1889 the settlers organized a school, which was held for four years in a renovated hen house.

In 1887 F. B. Hardman founded KENDALL, 24.9 *m.* (447 alt., 289 pop.), now a scattering of houses around a two-story white schoolhouse. Named for Carthage Kendall, a pioneer, it was for many years a logging town, but with the cutting of the timber the settlers turned to farming on a limited scale. The quarry near by brings additional revenue to the settlement.

Left from Kendall on a graveled road to the INTERNATIONAL LIMESTONE QUARRY, 3.3 *m.*, on a high hill overlooking the valley. Its products are shipped to pulp and cement concerns in Bellingham. The road, popular with Canadian visitors to the recreation area around Mount Baker, continues to SUMAS, 8.5 *m.* (48 alt., 650 pop.) (*see Tour 8a*), at a junction with State 1-A (*see Tour 8a*).

State 1 continues through pasture lands dotted with black stumps. Church Mountain, shaped like a saddle with two sharp points, appears ahead, and a little beyond it the snow-covered dome of Bald Mountain.

MAPLE FALLS, 27.9 *m.* (665 alt., 150 pop.), is a multicolored cluster of buildings in a hollow on the North Fork of the Nooksack in a wild and rugged region. The settlement, on a branch line of the C.M.ST.P. & P.R.R., does some logging, truck farming, and quarrying on Boulder Creek. The town received its name in 1901, when G. A. King built a log cabin and a small waterpower sawmill on Maple Creek. The falls, a broken series of cascades, is near the railroad bridge.

Left from Maple Falls on a dirt road to SILVER LAKE (*cabins, boats, fishing and bathing*), 1.5 *m.*, at the base of the timbered slopes of Black Mountain.

East of Maple Falls the highway ascends into a rough, broken country of cedar and hemlock forests, fern-strewn draws, and heather-covered rocks, following the twists of narrow canyons at the base of mountainous foothills and rising above the tortuous course of the Nooksack. In a clump of trees are the orderly rows of cabins of the GLACIER CIVILIAN CONSERVATION CORPS CAMP (L), 30.9 *m.*

East of the camp the winding Nooksack River appears (L), a glistening thread far below in the valley. At the east end of the bridge spanning the river is WARNICK, 33.3 *m.* (800 alt., 12 pop.), with a small lumber mill, around which are gathered a few houses. Yellow piles of lumber rise above the roadside. The highway enters an open valley from which is visible the cone of Mount Baker, surrounded by snow-capped peaks.

GLACIER, 35.4 *m.* (881 alt., 87 pop.), is situated on Glacier Creek, from which it received its name. It is the eastern terminus of the local branch line of the C.M.ST.P.&P. R.R. and an outfitting center for the surrounding region.

At the boundary to the Mount Baker National Forest, which extends

60 miles south of the Canadian Line and comprises more than 1,800,000 acres of wild and rugged mountains and forests, are the attractive buildings of the GLACIER RANGER STATION (R), 35.9 *m.* Maps, fire permits, and general information about the forest are available here. At 37.7 *m.* is a junction with a dirt road.

Left here 0.3 *m.* to DOUGLAS FIR FOREST CAMP (*community kitchens, tables, piped water*), on the bank of the North Fork of the Nooksack River within the shadow of Bear Paw and Church mountains. Tall firs, hemlocks, and cedars soar above the camp; the air is filled with the chatter of the river and the spicy scent of the evergreens. Tables and chairs have been cut from solid logs, and water pipes are encased in bark to achieve a rustic effect. The road ends at 6 *m.;* here a trail follows Canyon Creek, where the fishing is splendid, to CANYON LAKE, 12 *m.*

At 40.4 *m.* is a junction with another dirt road.

Right here 0.2 *m.* to NOOKSACK FOREST CAMP (*community kitchens, tables, piped water*), in a heavy stand of forest on the bank of the Nooksack.

East of the junction the highway frequently traverses low sections, where centuries of leaf mold and seeping snow water have brought forth forest growths of almost tropical rankness. Trailing beards of moss hang from ancient fir, cedar, and maple trees. A steel and wood bridge crosses the Nooksack River at 41.3 *m.*

Right here 0.1 *m.* across the bridge to BRIDGE FOREST CAMP (*stoves, tables*).

At 42.4 *m.* is a junction with a dirt road.

Right on this road to a dirt crossroad, 0.1 *m.*; R. here to EXCELSIOR FOREST CAMP, 0.1 *m.*, on the bank of the river. There are some rustic improvements but few facilities. The road to the left leads to the Nooksack Falls Power Plant (*see below*).

At 43.1 *m.* is a junction with a graveled road.

Right here 0.3 *m.* to NOOKSACK FALLS, where the river plunges more than 100 feet. At the base of the falls are the gray buildings of the Puget Sound Power and Light Company power plant. The road ends at WELLS CREEK, 1.4 *m.*; here a trail continues to CHAIN LAKES, 9 *m.* (*see below*).

East of NINE MILE FOREST CAMP, 44.5 *m.*, the highway skirts a deep narrow gorge faced with walls of tawny red rock, then abruptly emerges in a level-floored canyon through which the river winds. A grove of delicate birch trees beside the river relieves the monotonous green of larger timber. In the winter, huge mounds of snow rise above the roadway.

The road runs high above the river canyon through ridges and slopes shaded by towering western red cedars—one of the few fine stands remaining in the State—and Douglas firs and hemlocks. Some of these trees are more than 250 feet high. The green is animated by an occasional yew, banks of bright red elderberries, elk-horn mosses, and creeping berry vines. Bordering the highway at SHUKSAN CAMP, 48.6 *m.*, are ten attractive log cabins, built of silver spruce, beneath towering red cedars whose balsam scents the air. Operated by the Mount Baker Development Company as an adjunct to Mount Baker Lodge, the camp serves as a base for hiking trips to near-by peaks and up the North

Fork of the Nooksack. To the right of the camp is the Shuksan Inn on the site of a pioneer homestead.

At 48.9 *m.* is a junction with a graveled road.

Left here along the banks of SWAMP CREEK to a junction of forest trails, 4 *m.*; L. here 4 *m.*, on Gold Run Trail to YELLOW ASTER BUTTE and to TOMHOI LAKE (*fishing*); R. (*straight ahead*) on a trail leading to TWIN LAKES (*fishing*), 2.2 *m.*; from here a steep trail leads, 1 *m.*, west to WINCHESTER MOUNTAIN LOOKOUT.

At 49.1 *m.* is a junction with a dirt road.

Left here along the banks of RUTH CREEK (*fishing*) to GOAT MOUNTAIN, 3 *m.*, with a lookout station on its summit. From the end of the road, 6 *m.*, a trail leads right (*straight ahead*) to GRANITE MOUNTAIN (L), 1 *m.*, and to beautiful HANNEGAN PASS, 4 *m.*, at the head of Chilliwak Creek.

The SILVER FIR FOREST CAMP AND GUARD STATION (*camping, picnic facilities*), 49.2 *m.*, is in the shadow of firs and hemlocks.

Crossing the North Fork of the Nooksack River, State 1 negotiates a series of hairpin turns and winds above the canyon to BAGLEY CREEK FOREST CAMP (*no facilities*), 51.8 *m.* On its ascent the highway offers a panoramic view of snow-crowned peaks and ridges. Far below, deep rocky gorges and green fir-clad slopes stretch into the distance. HIGHWOOD FOREST CAMP (*tables, stoves, piped water*), 54.9 *m.* (L), overlooks Razorhone Creek.

Left from the camp by trail over a timbered slope to SALMON CREEK MEADOW, 0.3 *m.*, where the forest dwindles away, exposing benches and slopes that furnish fine skiing ground in season.

At GALENA FOREST CAMP (*tables, stoves, piped water*), 55.6 *m.*, sometimes buried by snow in winter, opens a full view of MOUNT SHUKSAN (9,038 alt.), thrusting a great knife-edged rock 1,000 feet above its main body. Its Indian name means "steep, rocky, precipitous"—and the peak successfully defied mountaineers until 1906. The HANGING GLACIER, a palisade of ice from which huge sections occasionally tumble in clouds of white, is splashed with rainbow colors by the sun.

The MOUNT BAKER SKI CLUB HUT, 55.7 *m.*, is a high-gabled, unpainted, shake building about 200 feet from the highway. The HIGHWOOD LAKE and PICTURE LAKE (L), each in a setting of meadow grass, reflect the distant mountain summits and the surrounding forests of pine, balsam, fir, and hemlock.

MOUNT BAKER LODGE (*restaurant service; hotel, cabin accommodations; skiing equipment*), 56.8 (L), is a chalet-type inn, two stories high, with a sharply gabled roof. A large granite fireplace adds cheer to the lounge. The main floor opens on a porch, from which a view may be obtained of the sheer crags and parapets of Mount Shuksan towering high above. A branch of the Otto Lang Ski School teaches the noted Hannes Schneider controlled skiing method. A few spaces from the lodge is the two-story ANNEX.

A SKI LIFT (2 *trips for 25c*, 10 *for $1*), 57.3 *m.*, operates on the

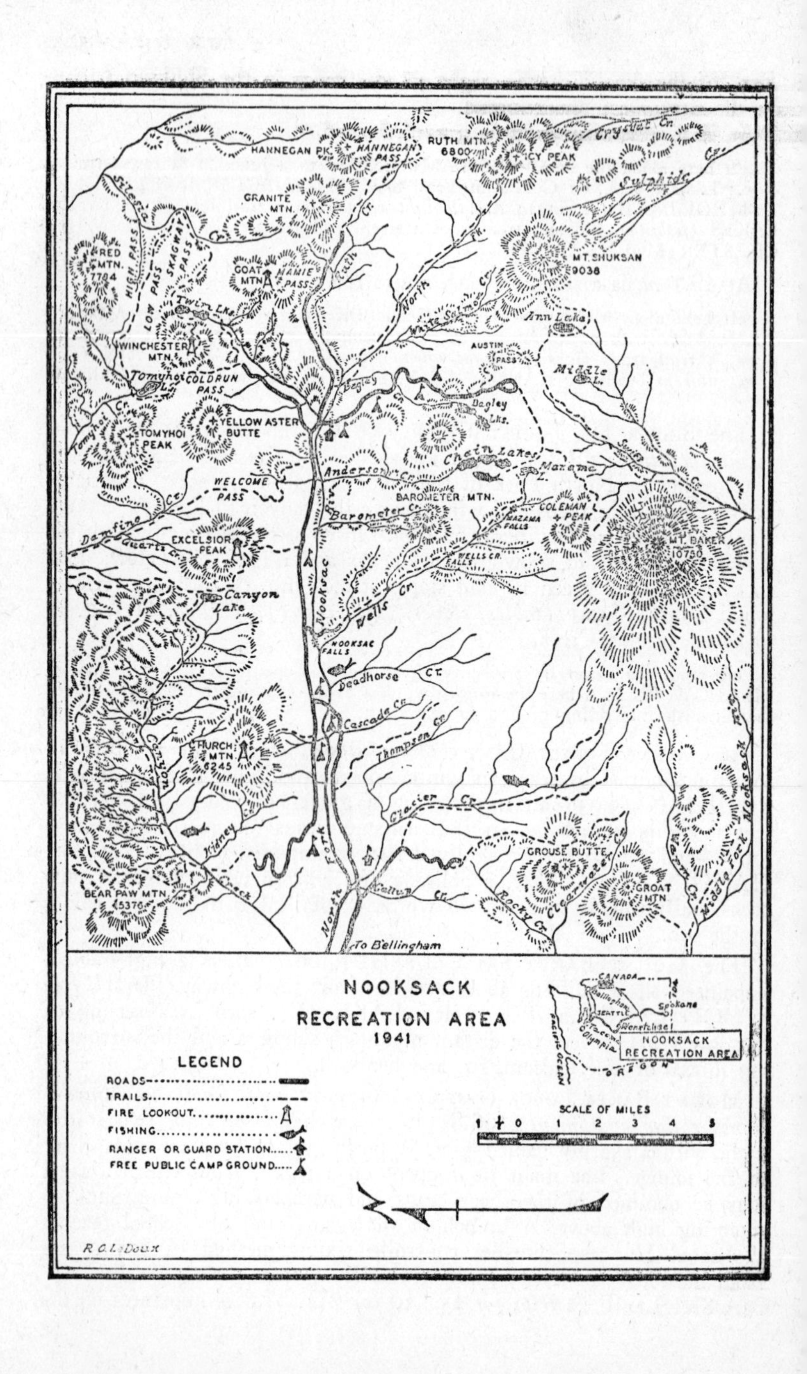
HANNEGAN PK
HANNEGAN PASS
RUTH MTN. 6800
ICY PEAK
Crystal Cr.
Sulphide
GRANITE MTN.
MT. SHUKSAN 9038
RED MTN. 7784
HIGH PASS
LOW PASS
SKAGWAY PASS
GOAT MTN
MAMIE PASS
Twin Lks.
North Fk.
White Salmon Cr.
Ann Lake
AUSTIN PASS
WINCHESTER MTN.
Tomyhoi L.
COLDRUN PASS
Bagley Cr.
Bagley Lks.
Middle L.
Tomyhoi Cr.
TOMYHOI PEAK
YELLOW ASTER BUTTE
Chain Lakes
Anderson Cr.
Mazama L.
WELCOME PASS
BAROMETER MTN.
Barometer Cr.
COLEMAN PEAK
MAZAMA FALLS
Damfino
Quartz Cr.
EXCELSIOR PEAK
WELLS CR. FALLS
MT. BAKER 10750
Canyon Lake
Nooksac
Wells Cr.
NOOKSAC FALLS
Deadhorse Cr.
Cascade Cr.
Thompson Cr.
CHURCH MTN. 6245
Canyon
Glacier Cr.
Kidney
GROUSE BUTTE
Clearwater Cr.
GROAT MTN
Middle Fork Nooksack
BEAR PAW MTN. 5376
Creek
Galbup Cr.
Rocky Cr.
North Fork
To Bellingham
NOOKSACK
RECREATION AREA
1941
LEGEND
ROADS
TRAILS
FIRE LOOKOUT
FISHING
RANGER OR GUARD STATION
FREE PUBLIC CAMP GROUND
CANADA
Bellingham
SEATTLE
Spokane
Tacoma
Olympia
Wenatchee
PACIFIC OCEAN
OREGON
NOOKSACK RECREATION AREA
SCALE OF MILES
1 ½ 0 1 2 3 4 5
R. C. LeDoux

steep slope above LOWER BAGLEY LAKE, by means of an endless cable running about 700 feet. MOUNT HERMAN (6,100 alt.), frowns above the lake.

The AUSTIN PASS GUARD STATION (*parking, picnic facilities*), 59.3 *m.* (4,300 alt.), is at the entrance of the HEATHER MEADOWS WINTER SPORTS AREA (*see Nooksack Recreation Area map*), which lies between the base of Mount Baker and that of Mount Shuksan. In summer it is green with heather and native plants between clumps of mountain hemlock; in autumn it is a riot of alpine flowers. Dozens of small streams, eddying in pools or dashing down the rocks, hold Dolly Varden, cutthroat, rainbow, and blackspotted trout. Ruffed and blue grouse and white-tailed ptarmigan take cover in the tall grasses. There are also marmot, beaver, otter, wildcat, deer, black bear, and mountain goat. Heather Meadows was the "shooting site" of the motion pictures *The Call of the Wild* and *The Barrier,* because its scenery so much resembles that of Alaska.

From the top of PANORAMA DOME, skiers may swing down the steep north face, or along the northeast shoulder to the Galena benches and back to the highway near Galena Cabin, or across country to Mount Baker Lodge. The experienced can follow the more hazardous route across the north face of Shuksan Arm and across the head of Razorhone Creek to White Salmon Meadows; or drop down to Austin Pass, then east to Swift Creek Meadows and through a narrow strip of timber, where a stiff climb leads over a saddle into Lake Ann Basin and on to Curtis Glacier.

At 58.6 *m.,* in Austin Pass, is a junction with a trail.

Left here 0.5 *m.* to SWIFT CREEK at a junction with a side trail: L. again here 3 *m.* through rich meadows and timber land to LAKE ANN, a scenic spot with a commanding view of the Hanging Glacier and Mount Shuksan.

The main trail continues through Swift Creek Canyon, down spirals and switchbacks into sub-alpine meadows knee-deep in summer with daisies, anemones, columbine, and red and white heather. As the forest closes in, its shade encourages the growth of ghost plants, Canadian dogwood, the fragrant twinflower, the white, one-flowered clintonia, and a profusion of ferns and mosses. SHUKSAN CREEK, 4 *m.,* spills into Swift Creek (L) from Lake Ann. At the BAKER HOT SPRINGS, 5 *m.,* (R), a popular but unimproved camp, springs fill a small outdoor pool screened with a split-cedar fence. The temperature of the water averages 110° F. From Baker Hot Springs the trail turns southwest to MOROVITZ GUARD STATION, 6.5 *m.* At 10.5 *m.* is the trail's end and a junction with the Baker Lake Highway (*see Tour 8B*).

Rugged KULSHAN RIDGE (5,000 alt.), 59.6 *m.,* which extends from the west flank of Mount Shuksan to the base of Mount Baker, forming the southern wall of Heather Meadows, is at the road's end.

To the southwest (R) rises MOUNT BAKER, (10,750 alt.), the shadowed canyons in the foreground accentuating the cone's white symmetry. Komo Kulshan (Ind. white, shining mountain), the name given the mountain by the Nooksack Indians, was superseded by El Montana Del Carmelo—the choice of the Spanish explorer Francisco Eliza, who saw in the mountain a likeness to the flowing robes of the Carmelite monks. For a time the mountain was called the White Friar and the Great White Watcher. In 1792, however, Captain George Vancouver named the peak after his lieutenant, Joseph Baker. Abutted by lesser peaks, Mount Baker seems none the less lofty for its broad base, for such is its conformation that each snowy slope upward adds grace and stature. Frequently, swirling winds toss the dry snow into flowing white veils. Such scenes have given rise to rumors of renascent volcanic action, yet no report has been authenticated in the past 20 years. The mountain has 12 glaciers and more than 44 square miles of ice fields. On the northeast slope PUMICE STONE PINNACLE lifts, darkly solitary, against the sheen of RAINBOW GLACIER. A twin pinnacle was shaken from its pedestal in 1906, shattering into the gap between Table Mountain and Mount Baker. Easier of access than Mount Shuksan, Mount Baker was first scaled in 1868 by Edmund T. Coleman, who described his ascent in *Harper's New Monthly Magazine* for November, 1869.

Right from Kulshan Ridge by trail to TABLE MOUNTAIN, 1 *m.* (5,300 alt.), whose broad surface holds a living glacier. (*Hikers are cautioned not to dislodge rocks since it imperils climbers on lower levels.*) At the summit is a view of many lakes and river valleys wedged in among the mountains. At 2 *m.* is a junction with a side trail: R. here 2 *m.* to the three CHAIN LAKES (*trout fishing*), one of which is a miniature polar sea, seldom free of floating ice even in summer. At 7 *m.* the main trail reaches CAMP KIZER, at the timberline. Here is an overnight camp for parties undertaking the two- or three-day ascent of the mountain. Spectacular but not hazardous, the trail crosses MAZAMA GLACIER and SHOLES GLACIER, where there is a near view of RAINBOW GLACIER, as well as of the snow fields and cliffs that mountaineers traverse on the route to the summit. Inexperienced climbers should not attempt to go farther, and those with experience must be in excellent physical condition. (*Guides are required for the ascent.*)

Tour 8B

Burlington—Sedro Woolley—Lyman—Concrete—Rockport—Newhalem—Diablo Dam—Ross Dam; 74.5 *m.* County road to Sedro Woolley; State 17-A to Rockport; Seattle Municipal R. R. from Rockport to Diablo Dam; motorboat to Ross Dam.

Bituminous-surfaced roadbed to Rockport.
Accommodations for excursion from Rockport to end of tour must be reserved at City Light Building, Third Ave. and Madison St., Seattle; excursions twice weekly, Sat., Sun. and Wed. and Thur. (3:30 p.m. one day to 3:45 p.m. the next) from May 15 to October 15.
Great Northern Ry., branch line, roughly parallels route between Burlington and Rockport.

The soil of the lower Skagit River Valley, enriched by alluvial deposits from periodic floods, has been scientifically tilled; and fertile acres that are being intensively farmed may be seen from the road. State 17-A follows the winding river through bottom land, checkerboarded with commercial vegetable gardens, poultry ranches, and dairy farms. In the upper valley are vast stretches of logged-off land, where occasionally an effort is being made to carve out a farmstead. Some distancc from the highway are substantial stands of timber in which logging is in progress. The forests, the immense cement plant at Concrete, and the traffic to the Skagit Power Development are the chief sources of income in this sparsely settled region. Rolling foothills become increasingly rugged and wooded as the highway approaches the Cascade Mountains. From Rockport the narrow-gauge railroad winds upward through the rocky canyon of the Skagit River to Diablo Dam. Here the great Skagit River Power developments of Seattle City Light may be seen in a setting of natural grandeur. Across Ross Lake is Ross Dam, still under construction, the largest unit in the Skagit River development.

From the junction of Fairhaven Avenue and Cherry Street, an unnumbered county road runs northeast from Burlington up the broad valley of the Skagit River.

SEDRO WOOLLEY, 5.6 *m.* (50 alt., 2,954 pop.), is the center of a region that has accomplished successfully the transition from large-scale logging and lumbering to farming. Once covered with heavy stands of western red cedar, the land, lying in the valley of the Skagit River, required only clearing and cultivation to be made productive. The area, gardened in symmetrical lines, yields large crops of strawberries, peas, cabbage, kale, and other vegetables; some sections are given over to dairy farms and poultry ranches. Most of the residents of the valley are home folks, and outwardly the routine of their lives is changed only by the introduction of new methods of crop culture.

David Batey was the first settler on the land where Sedro Woolley now stands. "Bug" was first suggested as a name for the town started in 1884 by Mortimer Cook, but the women of the settlement objected and countered with "Sedro" (Spanish: cedar), for the neighboring Cedar Mountain. Sedro was adopted and hurriedly painted on the rough boards of a store front. The cedar forests attracted logging interests, and a shingle mill was erected in 1886. Because of its strategic location the town became the head of navigation on the Skagit River, and it grew prosperous with the traffic of prospectors headed for the Mount Baker region during the gold rush.

When, in 1889, the Great Northern and Northern Pacific railroads established a junction north of Sedro, P. A. Woolley, an enterprising individual, platted a town site at the crossing. Jealousy arose between the towns, but a reconciliation soon followed, and in 1890 the two cities combined their names and incorporated as one.

At 6.2 *m.* is a junction with a dirt road.

Left here 0.5 *m.* to the NORTHERN HOSPITAL FOR THE INSANE. Its square-face buildings sit amid well-kept gardens and spacious lawns. The institution is partially self-sustaining, the physically strong inmates cultivating the gardens and caring for the stock and poultry.

East of the junction, State 17-A follows the bank of the Skagit River and penetrates the farming area in the valley. Neat homes and barns appear alongside the road.

Once a busy railroad town, LYMAN, **13.6** *m.* (95 alt., 376 pop.), is supported today by a lumber mill, which operates periodically, and the seasonal activities of produce shippers.

Ascending along the river valley, the highway separates sharply contrasting country; on one side are stump lands amid stands of alder and second-growth fir, and on the other the light green of vegetable gardens, extending in precisely harrowed rows.

HAMILTON, **16.8** *m.* (95 alt., 229 pop.), is a settlement of South Carolinians, who gain their livelihood from seasonal work in logging camps and in truck gardens. It is whispered that the hills lifting from the river valley conceal many a copper pot in which "white mule" is condensed. The town was named for William Hamilton, on whose homestead the village was started.

East of BIRDSVIEW, **23** *m.* (192 alt., 200 pop.), the center of a truck gardening community and shipping point for the local limestone quarry, the road is bordered at points by heavy stands of maple and alder; these woods are shipped to city factories for use in the manufacture of furniture.

CONCRETE, **29** *m.* (216 alt., 859 pop.), is the site of the huge PORTLAND CEMENT COMPANY PLANT, the products of which are used in all major construction work in the State. Dominating the town is the skeleton of the overhead conveyor system from the CONCRETE LIMESTONE QUARRY (L), more than a mile west of the city limits; along an endless cable, suspended 100 feet above the highway, large buckets of limestone are sent to the plant, where they automatically empty their contents; the buckets are then returned to the quarry. The three stacks of the plant rise against billowing clouds of cement dust and smoke, and in the dry season the powder-gray dust covers houses, trees, and shrubbery for miles around.

Concrete was founded by Magnus Miller, who settled here in 1890 and named the settlement Baker, for the river which enters the Skagit at this point. Miller's home served as hotel, store, and community center, and in 1892 became the Baker post office. In 1901 the Baker River Lumber Company erected a shingle mill, company store, and other buildings, and the place began to boom. Later, when the lime quarry and cement plant were established, the town was renamed Cement City and later Concrete. Cascade Days, held here the second week in August, is a carnival celebration to publicize the projected Cascade Cross-State Highway.

In Concrete is a junction with a graveled road.

Left on this twisting road into the BAKER RIVER RECREATION AREA, a part of MOUNT BAKER NATIONAL FOREST (*see Tour 8A*). Many of the peaks and gorges of this area challenge the hiker and mountain climber with their very names: Mount Despair, Bald Eagle Creek, Pioneer Ridge, Mount Fury, Lonesome Creek, Damnation Peak, Phantom Pass, and Mount Terror. A long grade spiraling the heights overlooks the narrow reaches of LAKE SHANNON (R), 6.5 *m.* The road claws its way upward, offering frequent glimpses of GOAT MOUNTAIN, WASHINGTON MOUNTAIN, (4,600 alt.), and RED ROCK. It crosses BEAR CREEK, 9 *m.,* just above the BEAR CREEK POWERHOUSE (R), and enters MOUNT BAKER NATIONAL FOREST, 11 *m.* Although the road is fairly wide from this point northward, occasional fills are narrow, and drivers should exercise care in passing. At 11.3 *m.* is a junction with a trail.

Left here to BLUE LAKE (*good fishing*), 5 *m.,* and to DOCK BUTTE LOOKOUT STATION, 6.5 *m.* At 12.3 *m.* is a junction with another trail. Right here on this steeply descending path to the head of LAKE SHANNON, 1 *m.*

The main side road continues to KOMO KULSHAN RANGER STATION, 13.1 *m.,* where campfire permits and detailed information concerning trails are obtainable. At 14.2 *m.* is a junction with a trail. Left here to MAZAMA PARK, 9 *m.,* a meadow bordering the western face of Mount Baker. A switchback climbs to reach PARK LOOKOUT STATION, 10 *m.* Along the road the BIG SANDY CREEK, 15 *m.,* and LITTLE SANDY CREEK, 16.5 *m.,* burr beneath the highway bridges in swift descent to join the Baker River. Two side trails join the main road at the BOULDER CREEK FOREST CAMP, 17.4 *m.*

Right here to BAKER RIVER, 2 *m.*; L, through flower-strewn glades and alpine meadows to the cold gray surfaces of BOULDER GLACIER, 6.5 *m.* On the main side road is LITTLE PARK CREEK FOREST CAMP, 18.8 *m.* At 19.4 *m.,* two trails form a junction with the road. Right here to Baker River, 1.5 *m.*; L. to AUSTIN PASS, 10.5 *m.* (*see Tour 8A*).

At 20.8 *m.* on the main side road is a junction with a dirt road: Left on this road to BAGNELL'S CAMP, 0.5 *m.,* and to BAKER LAKE LOOKOUT STATION, 1.5 *m.,* perched on a tower of round timbers anchored on a slope at the side of Baker Lake.

After passing the BAKER FISH HATCHERY, 22.1 *m.,* the road ends at BAKER LAKE FOREST CAMP (*camping facilities*), 22.3 *m.,* on the south shore of BAKER LAKE (670 alt.).

East of Concrete, State 17-A continues along the Skagit River. Caution should be exercised when rounding the sharp curves at both approaches to the bridge across Baker River, the outlet of Lake Shannon (L).

L. the SKAGIT RIVER FERRY, 1.3 *m.,* crosses the Skagit to a junction with State 1-A (*see Tour 8b*), which leads to Darrington. The ferry, designed like a barge with a trolley running along an aerial cable, is equipped with rudders that point the craft into the current, the stream flow thus providing motive power.

SAUK, 36 *m.* (224 alt., 10 pop.), a railroad junction, is at the confluence of the gray-green Sauk and Skagit Rivers. Glacier-fed and silt-laden, the Sauk has its headwaters in the Glacier Peak Area (*see Recreation Area map*) far southward. SAUK MOUNTAIN (5,510 alt.), rises on the left. The highway crosses the Great Northern Railway tracks, 37.9 *m.,* and ends at a parking lot between the station and the river.

ROCKPORT, 38 *m.* (225 alt., 200 pop.), a cluster of neat buildings and immaculate flower gardens between the highway and railroad, close beside the river, is the starting point for tours managed by the Seattle City Light Company to the power plants and dams on the Upper Skagit. Automobiles are left in the parking lot at the ADMINISTRATIVE

BUILDING under the care of a watchman, and tourists board the bright yellow coaches of the train at the CITY LIGHT RAILROAD DEPOT.

An air of holiday excitement and good fellowship marks the tour from Rockport to Diablo and Ross dams. Reservations for the trip are made in Seattle, and large groups often travel together. (*Because of the danger of fire, smoking is permitted only at designated stops; liquor is prohibited*). The route of the train roughly parallels the river. Herds of dairy stock browse in the level pastures of the broad valley. Visible from the car is State 17-A, tracing a zigzag course along the slopes. A quarter of a mile away is the town of MARBLEMOUNT (313 alt., 55 pop.), the oldest settlement in the region. This hamlet was founded during Civil War days and was once used as a supply base by prospectors who panned the gold-flecked streams of the vicinity. Later a marble quarry was briefly operated at the base of the rock slope to the west (R), and so the settlement received its name.

The foothills of the Cascade Range begin to close in on the railroad line, and the tracks and the river are soon boxed in between the shattered cliffs and the lichen-covered canyon walls. Through a fringe of trees, the stream may be glimpsed, its foam-streaked waters clear blue or chill green as the channel deepens. Approaching THORNTON CREEK, 56 *m.,* the valley widens slightly, and clumps of gnarled cedars appear among tangles of spiny devil's-club. In the glades along the many brooks are deer fern sprays and the handsome blades of the sword fern. East of Thornton Creek, in clearings overgrown with brush, stand a few log dwellings, moss covered and primitive, built by miners for temporary shelter 40 or 50 years ago. Occasionally the road is seen, winding through bottomland groves or crowding in between the railroad track and overhanging cliffs (L); at GOODELL CREEK, 60 *m.,* it becomes little better than a trail. Far up the creek valley (L) stands snowy MOUNT TERROR (8,360 alt.); and southward from it is MOUNT TRIUMPH (7,150 alt.).

NEWHALEM, 61 *m.* (500 alt., 100 pop.), headquarters of Seattle City Light construction projects on the Skagit River, came into existence when the city of Seattle began development of the power site.

Seattle entered the business of hydroelectric power generation in 1902, and a power station was completed at Cedar Falls, 30 miles east of Seattle, in 1905. In the course of the next few years, the plant was expanded on several occasions. With the demand for current during the pre-war period of industrial expansion, the city began to seek a new power site. The late James Delmage Ross, who had become superintendent of the City Light Department in 1911, tried, with his associates, to acquire some satisfactory spot, only to find their efforts blocked by interests who held rights over most of the valuable sites.

In 1917 Ross took steps that led to the acquisition of the Skagit site, long regarded as the best power location in the Pacific Northwest. Lying within the Mount Baker National Forest, it had been held by a private company on a temporary permit from the Federal Government. When the permit expired, Ross filed personally on the Skagit site in the name of the city. (Previously he had requested a permit for the city in a communication to the Federal offices in Portland.) He based his claim on the fact that the company had bought up other sites, while holding the Skagit with no intention of developing it. Later, Ross went to Washington, D.C., to press the claim with David F. Houston, Secretary of Agriculture, and on January 18, 1918, the city was given permission to call for bids on a plant to be built on the Skagit River. After several attempts by the company to re-acquire the Skagit rights had failed, the city was given a permit for the site by the Government, the decision being announced in a telegram received in Seattle on Christmas Day, 1918.

The Skagit site has undergone rapid development, and Seattle City Light is today regarded as one of the country's outstanding municipal power projects, a pioneer in municipally owned and operated hydroelectric developments. When President Roosevelt took office in 1932, he summoned Ross to the White House to discuss proposed Federal power development. Later, Ross was appointed to a position on the Securities and Exchange Commission. He resigned this office to become administrator of Bonneville Project, a position which he held, as well as the City Light superintendency, at the time of his death in 1939.

At Newhalem, shops, barracks, homes, and other buildings stand beyond a meadow between railroad and river. Music from a loudspeaker, concealed on the slopes of MOUNT ROSS (7,300 alt.), greets the train on its arrival at five in the afternoon. Visitors are allowed one-half hour to locate their quarters (accommodations for 600) and to prepare for dinner. After an ample meal served in the huge community dining hall, the visitors are led by guides over the narrow suspension bridge and along the pleasant woodland trail beside the Skagit to the NEWHALEM POWER HOUSE on NEWHALEM CREEK.

Later, a brief moving picture of the several projects is shown at the camp, after which visitors proceed to the GORGE POWER PLANT, where they are shown the giant turbines. This unit is linked to the Newhalem Power House by means of a transformer bank. The Gorge Plant has an installed capacity of 102,413 horsepower and will ultimately produce 320,000 horsepower. Completed in 1924 at a cost of more than $14,000,000, it had yielded revenues amounting to more than $41,000,000 by the end of 1937. This is the first, and lowest, unit of the $86,000,000 "staircase" hydroelectric power development on the river.

Behind and above the power house are tropical gardens, planted under the personal direction of Mr. Ross. With the co-operation of friends of the project, he brought plants, animals, and birds from all parts of the world. In the rock gardens are ferns and mosses, flowers, shrubs and trees, many of which are not indigenous, such as tea, lemon, and grapefruit. An illuminated path leads upward 400 feet past lily ponds, glowing with submarine light, to LADDER CREEK FALLS, transfused at night with lights in ever-shifting colors. Muffled by the rushing sound of the water, inspirational music flows from loudspeakers concealed in the surrounding gardens.

Following an early breakfast, visitors, who are advised to dress warmly, climb into open-air cars, which are pulled by electric locomotive up the gorge. On either side, the mountain peaks loom both nearer and higher than those seen the previous day. At a considerable height above the river, which flows over white gravel beds, the railroad bed is chiseled out of sheer cliffs, or skirts slopes stubbled with old cedar trees and massive granite boulders. Farther along the route, a mountain meadow contrasts strangely with the desolate grandeur of the uppermost rock faces and the numerous glaciers and snow fields on the nameless peak to the left.

The low dam and intake, through which the river is diverted into a two-mile tunnel leading to the Gorge Plant, appear (L). DAVIS PEAK (7,150 alt.) may be seen snow-crested in the distance, above the lesser hills overhanging the river. Along the opposite side of the canyon occasional remnants of old bridges cling precariously to the cliffs. These frail scaffolds of whipsawn lumber are the last vestiges of an old pack trail to northern mines. Eventually the Gorge Dam will be constructed here, after Ross Dam provides complete river storage; it will be the last step of Skagit development, with a capacity of 320,000 horsepower.

Crossing Stetattle Creek, just above its confluence with the Skagit River, the train comes to REFLECTOR BAR, 68.5 *m.,* where a sweeping horseshoe bend of the stream rounds the gravel bar, on which construction camp buildings are neatly grouped. Here was the "spirit boundary" to the upper reaches of the Skagit, according to the Indians, who ominously forecast a dire fate for early hunters and miners venturing into the "country of the ghosts." As if to bear out their prediction, a great forest fire flared from the north, denuded the hills, and destroyed many cabin settlements. Subsequently, disastrous freshets swept down the swollen river. These floods have occurred on an average of once in every five years, and will be controllable only when Seattle's proposed hydroelectric development and water storage system is complete.

DIABLO POWER HOUSE, a substantial concrete building inset in the sloping cliff, is topped by great intake tubes, thrusting down from the hill, and fronted by a giant array of silvery transformers in the midst of a network of copper cables. With a present installed capacity of 190,000 horsepower, this plant, the second step in the Skagit development, will produce ultimately 320,000 horsepower. The powerhouse was begun in 1931, and the turbines started revolving in 1936.

Transported on an inclined railroad up the 68 per cent gradient of the hillside, visitors may view the town and river far below, which are backed by glacier-covered PYRAMID PEAK (7,800 alt.) They may then walk a short distance to see the widespread panorama of DIABLO DAM and the lake, fringed by timbered slopes pushing up toward snow-dappled crags. The dam, screened at each end by torrents of white water rushing from spillways, is obscured by a cloud of spray. Built between 1927-30, the dam, of the constant-angle-arch type, is 389 feet high; and the roadway across its crest is nearly a quarter of a mile long—1,180 feet from end to end. Imported trees, creepers, ivies, and shrubs set off to advantage the natural beauty of the area. Plans are in progress to add Japanese flowering cherries, pink dogwood, lilacs, clematis, wistaria, rhododendrons, and azaleas to the landscaping on the cliffs.

In company with the smaller native squirrel, the orange and gray variable squirrel and the large jet black squirrel of Mexico rollic on the limbs of the fir trees fringing the lake. These semitropical animals have adapted themselves to the thin, icy mountain air with no apparent discomfort. Black-tailed deer and black and brown bears are often seen, but hunting is forbidden in this area, as it lies within the Whatcom County Game Preserve.

Boarding the motor boat and leaving the lake shore, visitors are again greeted by music from loudspeakers concealed on the hillside. In the distance and adjacent to beautiful PYRAMID PEAK, is the equally lofty COLONIAL PEAK, and standing aloof to the left is SOURDOUGH MOUNTAIN (5,977 alt.). Between them spreads COLONIAL GLACIER. Two low islands, sparsely wooded, lie at the entrance to the deeply flooded channel of the Skagit River. Stands of stunted alpine fir and cedar, casting purple shadows on the gray and silver rocks, gradually supplant the tall timber that rises from the margin of the water. Gliding up the tortuous ravine between the quiet hills, the boat enters little basins, seemingly surrounded by sheer slabs of stone. A series of cascades (R) tumbling down from far heights may be seen through the open woods.

Reaching the narrowed extremity of the navigable lake, the boat turns slowly, giving an excellent view of ROSS DAM (formerly called Ruby Dam), 74.5 *m.* The ultimate elevation—1,728 feet—is marked by a white line on the granite cliff above the clearing. The first step in the construction, to an elevation of 1,380 feet, has been completed. Ross Dam will form the largest unit of the Skagit hydroelectric development. Besides generating 480,000 horsepower itself, it will permit capacity operation of the lower plants, thus making possible a total production for the project of 1,120,000 horsepower, at an invested cost of $76 per horsepower, the lowest yet projected. The dam will be 635 feet high and nearly twice as long, second in size to Boulder Dam; and it will create a lake 3 miles wide and 34 miles long, extending through the primitive area of Mount Baker National Forest northward across the Canadian Boundary.

Tour 8C

Mount Vernon—Deception Pass State Park—Oak Harbor—Coupeville—Columbia Beach; 66.1 *m.* State 1 and 1-D.

Great Northern Railway parallels State 1 to Anacortes.
Public campgrounds at Deception Pass State Park; resorts and campsites at beaches; hotel accommodations in small towns.
Concrete-paved road to Deception Pass; oiled gravel-surfaced road to Columbia Beach.

From the fertile lowlands of the rich farming country on the Skagit River Delta, this route leads to the shores of Fidalgo and Whidbey Islands, indented by many inlets. Fantastic carvings of the rocky banks, through the long assault of sea and weather, give these coves an air of austere mystery, and rumor in times past has dubbed them smugglers' retreats. Back from the shores, the gently rolling slopes of Whidbey Island are marked by patches of woodland, fields of waving grain, and fruitful orchards. A favorable combination of soil and climate has given Whidbey, second largest island in the United States, the reputation of being the garden spot among the islands of Puget Sound. The rich soil, known to agronomists as Ebey Sandy Loam, is said to be unique among soils. In 1894 a wheat yield of 117.5 bushels per acre established a world's record that still stands. Along the route tall silos and barns, hangar-like in their proportions, attest to the productivity of Whidbey's agriculture. Bulb raising, seed growing, and berry culture are important branches of farming; but poultry raising and dairying supply more than half of the island's economic structure.

West (R) of the junction with US 99, at 2nd St. and Gates Ave., in MOUNT VERNON, 0 *m.* (*see Tour 8a*), State 1 proceeds to the city limits and crosses the Skagit Flats, an area which produces a large share of the country's supply of cabbage seed. Substantial farmhouses and neat barns and poultry houses suggest agricultural prosperity.

At 6.9 *m.* is a junction with a bituminous road.

Left here across LA CONNER FLATS, where sloughs and marshes attract great numbers of waterfowl and bring many hunters during the shooting season. At 3.9 *m.* is a PIONEER MONUMENT (L), a granite shaft with pictorial reliefs of early scenes around its base. Among the business blocks along the main street of LA CONNER, 4.4 *m.* (10 alt., 624 pop.), the concrete CO-OP FISHERMEN'S BUILDING is conspicuous. Built on the site of the first trading post (1867) on Swinomish Slough, the town was first called Swinomish, but was later renamed by John S. Conner, the first permanent settler, for his wife, Louisa A. Conner. The oldest weekly newspaper in the State, the *Puget Sound Mail,* founded in 1873, is still published in La Conner. A LOOKOUT POINT OBSERVATION TOWER, on a hill above the business section, affords a view of the broad expanse of La Conner Flats, which stretch away to the east.

Crossing the slough, a road leads to the SWINOMISH INDIAN RESERVATION, 0.2 *m.* A scattering of small boats lie at the water's edge, with an occasional dugout canoe of traditional native design. Two rows of small white houses range along gradually rising ground that ascends from the shore to the brow of a hill; where a white-spired church contrasts with a large totem pole that bears aloft the carved symbols of the Thunder Bird, the Bear, Fish, and other figures of Indian mythology.

Right from Swinomish, 2 *m.*, on a graveled road to the tribal LONG HOUSE. Here, late in January, a three-day festival celebrates Treaty Day of January 22, 1855, when the chiefs of the Snohomish, Snoqualmie, Duwamish, and allied tribes, met with Governor Isaac I. Stevens and ceded to the white men all the land from Point Pully to the Canadian Border. Accompanied by the mesmeric beating of tom-toms and wailing chants, solo dancers work themselves into a frenzy, darting about in a flying crouch, eagle fashion with arms outspread, feet padding swiftly over the bare earth. At intervals they come to rigid stops —tense dramatic pauses heightened by complete silence—from which they again leap forward, feathers flying, bone and wood ornaments jangling. During the dances great log fires are kept burning on the dirt floor of the Long House. In the Squad Dance the women shuffle and hop from side to side in slow monotonous rhythm, pausing occasionally to emphasize some word in a tuneless chant, reminiscent of the efforts of the Shakers and Holy Rollers to "get the power."

West of the junction, State 1 crosses TELEGRAPH SLOUGH, 7.3 *m.*, and SWINOMISH SLOUGH, 9.1 *m.*, linking the mainland with FIDALGO ISLAND, where the route continues. The island, separated from the mainland only by shallow sloughs, was named for Salvador Fidalgo, an explorer in one of the Spanish expeditions of 1790-1. A town called Fidalgo flourished briefly in this vicinity until the collapse of a railroad boom in 1892.

At 12.4 *m.* is a junction with State 1-D.

Right (straight ahead) State 1 continues to ANACORTES (*see Island Tour* 3).

The main route swings south on State 1-D, bordered at intervals by heavy growths of fir and hemlock.

LAKE CAMPBELL (*fishing, swimming, camping*), 14.3 *m.* (R), largest of several small lakes on the island, lies at the base of a rounded knoll in a farming area. In the center of the lake is a small wooded island.

At 15.5 *m.* is a junction with a graveled road.

Left here 1 *m.* to DEWEY, ghost of a former town at the east end of Deception Pass. First called Deception, then Fidalgo City, two adjacent townsites were platted in 1889, Gibraltar and Fidalgo. To secure land grants offered as a bonus for a railroad construction, trackage of the Anacortes and Fidalgo City Electric Railway was completed in 1891. Two train trips were made—enough to ensure title to the grants—and the tracks torn up. Local real estate values promptly faded. After the Spanish-American War the settlements united under the present name.

South of the junction the highway passes through luxuriant growths of fir, cedar, and alder, affording glimpses of PASS LAKE (R). Farther south it follows the shoreline of the lake. At 17.2 *m.* the road enters DECEPTION PASS STATE PARK (*swimming, camping and picnicking*). The park is notable for the variety of its land and seascapes; along its borders are wave-tossed, and placid, bays. Rugged, fjord-like shores of rock shelve up to deep forests; across Rosario Strait, to the northwest, lie the tumbled forms of the San Juan Islands; to the southwest, across Juan de Fuca Strait, where ocean sunsets flame in the summer sky, are the rugged contours of the Olympic Range. Eastward are the peaks of the Cascades. The park has six recreational areas with five swimming pools, three of which are salt water.

At 17.6 *m.* is a junction with a graveled road.

Right here 0.5 *m.* through shady groves to the beach at RESERVATION BAY (*large parking area, tables, stone shelter house, and bath houses*).

The DECEPTION PASS BRIDGE, 18.2 *m.* (182 alt.), was completed in 1935, after many years of agitation by the residents of Whidbey Island for such a link with the mainland. The bridge has a total length of 1,350 feet, its 22-foot roadway bordered by railed pedestrian walks. Constructed by the Public Works Administration, the span links Fidalgo and Whidbey islands, and connects Island and Skagit Counties, thus increasing the islanders' market range. Pass Island, a natural support for the bridge at its center, is a cone-shaped rock pier dividing the channel into Canoe Pass and the wider Deception Pass.

Beneath the bridge the narrow, high-walled gorge of DECEPTION PASS spills 2,500,000,000 gallons of water hourly at ebb tide into Rosario Strait; surface shadows and reflections offer a changing study in blues and greens as the foam-streaked tide boils through the rocky aperture. The lull that accompanies slack tide is soon broken by the returning flood, stirring to flight the wayfaring gulls. A sign at the bridge warns that the hunting of rabbits, a profitable part-time occupation on the island, is unlawful after 10 o'clock at night. The ruling was made to prevent hunters in galloping jalopies from racing through farm plots in pursuit of rabbits, easy prey under glaring headlights.

The narrow channel was named Boca de Flon by Quimper for a Mexican governor, and so recorded on Eliza's chart of 1791; it was renamed Deception Pass in 1792, when Captain George Vancouver's expedition learned it was not a closed harbor. Near the center of the bridge, on Pass Island, a memorial commemorates the naming of the pass by Vancouver, and notes that the channel has a tidal velocity of from 5 to 8 knots an hour, and a depth which varies from 4 to 37 fathoms.

The south end of the bridge, 18.6 *m.*, is the entrance to that section of Deception Pass State Park which lies on Whidbey Island. Here is a panoramic view of Juan de Fuca Strait.

At 19.1 *m.* is a junction with a graveled road.

Right here to a junction, 0.1 *m.*, with a graveled crossroads. Left from the junction 0.4 *m.* to forest-fringed CRANBERRY LAKE (*camping facilities, swimming; overnight parking, 50c a car*). Right from the junction 0.7 *m.* is NORTH BEACH, on Deception Pass. From the parking area a rustic trail winds down to the beach.

South of the junction State 1-D leaves the southern entrance of Deception Pass Park, 19.2 *m.*, marked by a large log house occupied by a resident park officer. At 19.7 *m.* is a junction with a dirt road.

Left on a down-grade, bordered by stands of second-growth alder, to CORNET BAY (*boating*) 1 *m.*, a sheltered cove

The main highway continues southward along the center of the island, named for Master Joseph Whidbey who, on June 2, 1792, discovered the pass that proved it an island. Four days before finding the passage, Whidbey, a member of Vancouver's expedition, landed here to make observations. He was met by some 200 Indians who apparently had never seen a white man before; to satisfy them that he was white all over, and not merely smeared with ashes, he opened his waistcoat and displayed his skin. Since Vancouver charted "Whidbey's Island," usage has often dropped the "e" from the name, though the original spelling is officially retained.

According to history, the Indians saw no more white visitors for nearly 50 years; but from other tribes they heard of the "black gowns" who were bringing a new religion into the region, and when Father Blanchet reached the Cowlitz River in 1839, Chief Tslalakum of the island tribe made the arduous trip up-sound to ask for teaching. Unable to return with him, the priest devised a textbook in the form of a Catholic "ladder," or vertical series of scenes representing church and Biblical history from the Creation, which the chief took back to his tribe. When Father Blanchet landed on Whidbey the following year, he received two surprises: first, the Indians had just fought off the Clallam and attributed their victory to their knowing God; second, they had mastered the hymns and rituals the priest had taught their chief. As a climax they presented him with a huge wooden cross. When Lieutenant Charles Wilkes, leading the United States Exploring Expedition, sailed the brig *Porpoise* into Penn's Cove in 1841, he found the Indians building a log church beside this large cross.

Along the main road are occasional views of the broad Juan de Fuca Strait to the west. Bordering Whidbey on the east is Saratoga Passage, separating it from Camano Island, which parallels it for part of its length. Gently rolling hills, checkered by farms and wooded pastures, sweep back from the highway on either hand. Dairy herds graze along the way, and here and there a haystack, chewed cow-high around the periphery, leans tipsily.

OAK HARBOR, 26.4 *m.* (65 alt., 376 pop.), largest of the island's three small towns, is a brisk trading center. Barrington Avenue, the main business street, borders the bay shore, and reveals in the orderly appearance of its substantial buildings the Holland Dutch influence that predominates in the community. Many of the names on stores, and on mail boxes along rural routes, such as Fakkema, Koetje, and Van Wieringer, reflect the land of dikes. The Dutch language is commonly used by the older generation and is often heard along the street.

Oak Harbor got its name from the oak trees on the surrounding prairie. The first settler, Zakarias Toftezen, a Norwegian, came here in 1849. Others soon followed, and John M. Izett, who arrived in 1854 from Scotland, built a shipyard and gave the island its first industry. The schooner *Growler,* named for its complaining builders, was launched here in 1859 and became one of the best-known boats on Puget Sound in pioneer days. Hollanders began to arrive towards the close of the century, and the extremely fertile countryside was developed with characteristic thoroughness by the Dutch farmers who were attracted here. Today the outstanding annual event is the Holland Days Festival; Dutch costumes are worn, old-country games are played; there are prize contests and a livestock show.

South of Oak Harbor the route parallels the curving shore of the bay, through acres of pea fields and cultivated farm lands.

SAN DE FUCA, **32.1** *m.* (30 alt., 150 pop.), is a little village on a hill overlooking Penn Cove, a pea cannery, and a small sawmill. The farm of R. B. Holbrook, who settled here early in the 1850's, was purchased for a townsite, and San De Fuca (a contraction of San Juan and Juan de Fuca) was boomed in the nineties as the east end of a proposed canal to bisect the island.

At **32.8** *m.* is a junction with a graveled road.

Right here **0.6** *m.* to DARST FARM, a filbert orchard of several thousand young trees. In the favorable climatic belt of Whidbey Island, mature trees reach a height of some 30 feet and annually yield about 100 pounds of nuts each.

Bordered by red-trunked madronas, State 1-D reaches the head of Penn's Cove and bears southeasterly. Cranes, standing motionless in the shallows of the sand flats or flapping overhead in ungainly flight, are a common sight.

The OLD COURTHOUSE, **33.1** *m.* (R), built in 1855 as a store, is a well-preserved though weather-beaten frame structure. The many-windowed front facing the road has two entrances, and the gabled roof bears two brick chimneys. A stately maple at one corner reputedly was planted by Captain Henry Roeder (*see Bellingham*).

SITE OF A PIONEER TRADING POST AND FLOUR MILL AT KENNEDY'S LAGOON (R), **33.2** *m.,* is marked only by splintered piling, where once a millwheel ground the settlers' grain. State 1-D rounds the head of Penn's Cove and swings east.

COUPEVILLE, **36.2** *m.* (86 alt., 325 pop.), spreads along the south shore of the cove. Once called the Port of Sea Captains for the number of retired mariners who settled here, the town was officially named for the first of them, Captain Thomas Coupe, who took a donation claim here in 1852. Along the water front a small business section, composed mainly of independent, one-story, frame structures, parallels the tidal shore. A scattering of houses follows the rising terrain up a moderate slope from the shore to the level prairie back of the town. The two-story frame courthouse reflects the period in which it was built (1891).

CITY PARK (*camp ground*), on the edge of town in a setting of tall firs, overlooks Penn Cove. A large section of a Douglas fir stands beside the entrance, with a plaque giving its age as 660 years.

At Alexander and Coveland streets is the ALEXANDER BLOCKHOUSE in a three-sided stockade. Recently restored by the American Legion, it was brought here from the John Alexander claim, where it was built in

1855. Inside are a few relics of early days; outside is an open shelter in which are exhibited Indian craft that have raced in the annual International Water Festival held each August. Hundreds of visitors come to the festival to see the bronzed crews stroke their narrow boats along the course. In these races Washington tribes, including Lummi, Queets, Suquamish, Puyallup, and even Yakimas from east of the mountains, compete with the Haidas, their ancient enemies from British Columbia. It is said that, when the races were initiated, the Indians had to be taught by tribal craftsmen how to fashion the slim Chinook canoe, which old-time sailors declare to be the best native seagoing craft in the world. The method of manufacture was the same from southeastern Alaska to the Columbia River. Expert canoe makers chose a cedar tree as nearly flawless as possible, felled it with obsidian axes called *pe-yah-cuds,* and dragged it to a convenient place. The head canoe maker or *tyee,* scored the bark; his helpers trimmed the branches and peeled the trunks. Slowly, carefully, the hull was shaped; red-hot rocks were employed to burn out the interior. The hull roughly formed, the *tyee* went over it inch by inch, chipping and smoothing until the finished craft would trim properly in the water.

Many hulls were preserved against warping and checking by charring every surface, but the favored practice was to apply several coats of dogfish-liver oil, hand-rubbing the surface after each application until a glossy polish was secured. However malodorous, the process insured long preservation, for canoes more than 100 years old are still staunch and seaworthy. Extreme nicety was needed in placing the thwarts, or seats: these were inserted before the hull had become thoroughly seasoned, producing a slight flare along the rail. Too little spread reduced seaworthiness, but too much might split the wood. Both canoes and paddles were ornamented with various pigments. Iron stain was brown or yellow, copper stain was green, pounded ragweed pods yielded a bright red; soot mixed in oil gave black, and talc from lime-rock deposits made an acceptable white.

Even the 50- to 60-foot war canoe was carved from a single cedar. The earliest canoes were not shapely, but after acquaintance with Bedford whalers, the canoe makers quickly imitated the pudgy prows of the Gloucester vessels. Practically all canoes built within the last 75 years show the influence of the clipper with its curving bow and low bowsprit. Racing canoes, built for a steersman and 10 paddlers, were of narrower beam than war canoes and of somewhat lower freeboard.

The THOMAS J. DOW HOUSE on Front St., past the end of the business section (R), is an old whitewashed building known locally as the Waterworth House. Built in 1855, it has a small porch, bevel siding, and wood walls. The CAPTAIN THOMAS COUPE HOUSE, also on Front St., and its large walnut tree planted by the Captain's wife, date from 1853. The well-preserved two-story house of California redwood, painted gray, shows Dutch Colonial as well as New England farmhouse influence. The front is faced with siding, the ends with perpendicular boards and battens; above the small porch a flat-roofed dormer runs back to the roof peak, and rearward the mossy roof sweeps to a break and extends over the lean-to. The present (1941) occupant is Edward Bruce, a grandson of John Gould, who came here in 1849. The FIRST METHODIST CHURCH, erected in 1933, displays a bronze plaque on a foundation stone from the original church built in 1860. The congregation was organized in 1853.

Straight ahead, Front Street becomes a graveled road. Past the city limits, this road follows the shoreline of PENN COVE, believed to have been touched by Vancouver and named by him for a grandson of William Penn. In deserted Indian villages on both points of the little bay, Vancouver found small sepulchres, standing upright like sentry boxes, containing skeletal remains of both children and adults.

At 2.9 *m.* is a junction with a dirt road: Left here 0.3 *m.* to the JOHN KINETH HOUSE, built in 1855 by itinerant carpenters working for Kineth, pioneer road builder and civil engineer. The rambling two-story building on a slight knoll sloping toward the beach has been remodeled and is now a summer home. Large windows give a panoramic view of Saratoga Passage. So sturdily built was the original structure that very little of the lumber brought around the Horn to build it had to be removed. Walls were of hand-dressed fir and doors of yellow pine. The lime used for the fireplace came from burnt clamshells taken from the beach. WATSAK POINT, 0.7 *m.,* so named by the Wilkes Expedition, is also known as Snakelum Point. The latter name derives from that of Long Charlie or Snakelum, an Indian who once lived there. Summer homes now occupy parts of the area.

Adjacent to the OLD POTLATCH GROUND (R) is a high bluff scarred by an INDIAN TRENCH, 60 feet wide and 400 feet long, which was once covered by a potlatch house.

South of Coupeville on State 1-D is PRAIRIE CENTER, 37.5 *m.,* a wayside trading point dominated by two large white two-story school buildings. Whidbey Island's first car, built in 1902 in Chicago, is exhibited in an automobile agency here; a side-winder, with hard rubber tires, no reverse, and two speeds ahead, it was owned by Judge Lester Still, who lives on the island.

At Prairie Center is a junction with a graveled road.

Right 0.4 *m.* on this road to a junction with another graveled road. Left here 0.8 *m.* to a junction with a dirt road. Right on this road to SUNNYSIDE CEMETERY, 1.3 *m.,* located on a sloping hill. Here many early settlers are interred, their family plots guarded by iron fences or low walls of marble. Within the boundary of the cemetery is the DAVID BLOCKHOUSE, built in 1855, with rifle loopholes staring darkly from the walls of the second story. Its interior is distinguished by a stone fireplace, with a chimney of sticks and dried mud. The house was restored in 1930 by the Ladies of the Round Table.

The road continues (L) from the cemetery to the farm of Frank J. Pratt, Jr., where the JACOB EBEY MONUMENT (*visitors permitted by special permission of owner*), 1.5 *m.,* commemorates the memory of the famous pioneer. Here also the JACOB EBEY BLOCKUOUSE, restored by Mr. Pratt, was built in 1855 by the father of Colonel Isaac Ebey (*see Olympia*).

The main side road, north of the Prairie Center Junction, leads to EBEY'S LANDING, 2 *m.,* on the west shore of the island, where Colonel Isaac N. Ebey settled in 1850 and filed a claim to a section of Ebey's Prairie. Seeking revenge for their defeat and humiliation at Port Gamble (*see Tour 9A*), the Haida Indians from British Columbia raided the island in 1857. Colonel Ebey was called to his door late one night. Others in the house heard shots and groans; panic-stricken, they fled into the forest. The Indians decapitated their victim and escaped with the ghastly prize. The attackers were never apprehended, but years later the head was surrendered to Captain Charles Dodd, of the Hudson's Bay Company, for burial. A marble monument on the bluff above the beach marks the scene of the killing.

Southeast of Prairie Center, 37.9 *m.,* is a junction with a concrete road.

Right on the concrete road through a wooded area, broken by farm clearings. At 2.3 *m.* is a junction with a graveled road. Right (*straight ahead*) on this road to the CROCKETT BLOCKHOUSE, 0.3 *m.,* one of two built on the site in 1855; it was restored by the Work Projects Administration in 1938. The other Crockett blockhouse was sold to Ezra Meeker, for the entrance to his restaurant at the Alaska-Yukon-Pacific Exposition at Seattle in 1909, and was later moved to Point Defiance Park, Tacoma. At 0.9 *m.* on this graveled road, the yellow barracks and residences of FORT CASEY line a ridge overlooking CROCKETT LAKE, a long narrow body of water separated from Admiralty Bay by a sandspit. Lieutenant Colonel Silas Casey here took command of the Puget Sound district in 1856; later he led a detachment to reinforce Captain George E. Pickett at the time of the San Juan boundary dispute.

Left from the junction a graveled road winds over flat country bordering CROCKETT LAKE (R) to KEYSTONE, 2 *m.,* a few houses grouped around a ferry landing. A ferry here connects with Port Townsend (*see Tour 9a*) across Admiralty Inlet.

South of the junction, State 1-D keeps to the middle of the island, a level area devoted to dairying and wheat farming.

At 43.1 *m.* is a junction with a graveled road leading to Keystone and Fort Casey. A view of Admiralty Inlet appears at 44 *m.,* dark islands dotting the water in the distance.

At 47.9 *m.* is a junction with a dirt road.

Left here 0.2 *m.* past Green Bank Farm, a large dairying establishment. The road continues to JIM PRATT'S PLACE, 0.4 *m.,* a summer resort with 20 cabins, located on Holmes Harbor. It has excellent clam beds, and fishing in near-by waters is good.

State 1-D climbs a slight grade to GREENBANK, 48.3 *m.* (50 alt., 100 pop.). The single store, marking the entrance to Holmes Harbor, was named by a settler for his boyhood home of Green Bank, Delaware. To the east, across Saratoga Passage, is CAMANO ISLAND, midway between Whidbey Island and the mainland (*see Tour 8b*). Tiny Hackney Island also is in sight (L).

At 48.8 *m.* is a junction with a trail.

Left here 0.5 *m.* to an AMERICAN YOUTH HOSTEL, one of two on the island.

South of Greenbank the highway follows the central ridge of the island overlooking HOLMES HARBOR (L), named for Silas Holmes, assistant surgeon of the Wilkes Expedition. Noted for its salmon, the harbor is a favorite trolling ground for saltwater fishermen. (*Numerous resorts and cabin camps offer good accommodations*).

At 54.7 *m.* is a junction with a graveled road.

Right here 3 *m.* to BUSH POINT, where a light warns ships in Admiralty Inlet off the point. Pirates' Lair, a huge rustic inn, is constructed of driftwood and planking from wrecked ships, with ship fittings decorating the interior. A great stone fireplace blazes with beach logs that, salt-soaked, burn with colored flames. A ship's bell sounds the call to meals.

South of the junction the highway winds through a heavy stand of fir trees. At 55 *m.* is a junction with a graveled road.

Left here 0.2 *m.* to FREELAND (sea level, 300 pop.), near popular salmon-fishing grounds. The settlement was first named Equality by its Socialist founders, who started a co-operative sawmill but dispersed in 1904, after litigation had been started by creditors. Orchards and dairy farms surround the town, which consists of a modern store, a half-dozen residences, and a small sawmill. (*Resorts, cabins, camp sites, boats and motors are available along the shore*).

Fir prop timbers, cut in the hills, are hauled to Freeland, where they are loaded on the Spanish ship *Providencia* and taken to Mexico for the copper mines there. The *Providencia* returns to Puget Sound about once every six weeks, transporting the ore from Mexican mines to the smelter at Tacoma and stopping at Freeland on its way home to pick up the props. Indians of the district also use Freeland as a trading center.

BAYVIEW, 59.1 *m.,* is a small trading center near a number of small lakes attractive to freshwater fishermen. Alongside the store is the Whidbey Community Hall. This is an outfitting point for a number of Whidbey Island resorts, most of which are accessible from the town.

At 62 *m.* is a junction with a graveled road.

Left on this road, is LANGLEY, 3 *m.* (50 alt., 338 pop.), facing Saratoga Passage. Built on an inviting stretch of sandy beach, it is a trading point for a large part of south Whidbey Island. A high school, library, and movie theater contribute to the cultural needs of the neighborhood, while mercantile establishments in great variety supply ordinary consumer needs. Many beautiful summer homes and resort centers are situated near by. Dairying, poultry, ranching, berry growing, and filbert raising are activities of the countryside. Regular ferry service in the summer makes the beaches and resorts easily accessible from the mainland. Many homes in the vicinity are open to summer boarders.

The big annual event in Langley is the Island County Fair, said to be the oldest continuously celebrated event of its kind in the State. North (L) from Langley on a graveled road is SARATOGA, 4 *m.* (50 alt., 71 pop.), on the shore of Saratoga Passage, named by the Wilkes Expedition of 1841 in honor of the U.S.S. *Saratoga,* which was commanded by Captain Thomas McDonough, of Lake Champlain fame. Saratoga is popular in hunting season; deer, quail, and pheasants are plentiful in the area.

At 63.5 *m.* is a junction with a graveled road.

Right here 5 *m.* to MAXWELTON (sea level, 16 pop.), a sleepy village near the southern extremity of the island, named by the McKee brothers in memory of the "bonnie braes of Scotland." GLENDALE (sea level, 50 pop.), 8 *m.,* nestles on the beach in a narrow declivity between sheer bluffs. On the plain above it, strawberries are raised commercially, maturing several weeks earlier than berries grown on the mainland.

CLINTON, 65.8 *m.* (50 alt., 36 pop.), formerly known as Phinney, looks across Possession Sound toward the city of Everett on the mainland. A number of summer houses line Clinton Beach east of the trading center. From here, hat-shaped Gedney Island is visible.

Facing COLUMBIA BEACH, 66.1 *m.* (sea level, 40 pop.), are a number of substantial beach homes. An attractive yellow two-story structure houses a ferry waiting room, and summer cottages cluster about the wharf. Captain Boyd's Columbia Beach Resort is marked by a red, barn-like building; adjoining it is a group of white cottages with red roofs. The ferry landing extends over the water from the long straight beach. (*Forty-minute ferry service is maintained during the summer to MUKILTEO, 5 miles S. of Everett. See Tour 8b*).

Tour 8D

Tacoma—Parkland—La Grande—Elbe—Ashford—Nisqually Entrance, Mount Rainier National Park; 54.9 *m.* State 5.

Chicago, Milwaukee, St. Paul & Pacific R.R. parallels route between Tacoma and Ashford.
Concrete-paved roadbed, except for bituminous-surfaced stretch between La Grande and Alder.

The main route to Mount Rainier National Park, the State's greatest mountain recreational area, State 5 leads from prairie lowlands upward through rugged, thickly wooded foothills to the southwest entrance of the park. It offers, in rapid succession, views of intense urban activity, of farming on fertile valleys and stump lands, and of logging and lumbering in the shadow of the imposing mountain. Particularly on weekends, automobiles laden with skis, wool clothing, and other winter-sports equipment whiz along the highway, transporting parties from Tacoma, Seattle, and other Puget Sound cities to the alpine playland.

South (R) of the junction with US 99, at 26th St. and Pacific Ave. in TACOMA, 0 *m.,* State 5—usually called the Mountain Highway—follows Pacific Avenue. Beyond the city limits it passes through a thickly settled area of small berry farms and truck gardens.

At 5 *m.* is a junction with a concrete road.

Left on this road is MIDLAND, 1.4 *m.* (460 alt., 200 pop.), on the Tacoma Eastern branch of the Chicago, Milwaukee, St. Paul & Pacific Railroad. A claim was filed here in 1855 by Ezra Meeker, who later planted what is believed to have been the first hopyard in the vicinity. The picked hops were transported over an old military trail between Puyallup and Steilacoom. Meeker sold his claim to Judge W. H. Snell, who platted a town site and named it Midland. Today, the modest homes of the town stand on open prairie beside a small mill.

Beyond Midland the side road, curving sharply, passes stump fields, dairy farms, and poultry ranches. Passing SUMMIT, at 4.6 *m.* (400 alt., 27 pop.), it descends into the rich fruitlands of the Puyallup Valley.

At 5.7 *m.* on State 5 is a junction with State 5-G.

Left here 10.1 *m.* to PUYALLUP (*see Tour 2c*), at a junction with US 410 (*see Tour 2c*).

State 5 descends into park-like terrain as it approaches PARKLAND, 6.2 *m.* (301 alt., 750 pop.), a trading center for farmers and for students from Pacific Lutheran Academy. Many families here are of Scandinavian descent. At Parkland is a junction with an oiled road.

Right on this road to PACIFIC LUTHERAN COLLEGE AND ACADEMY, 0.2 *m.*, maintained by the Lutheran churches of the Pacific Northwest. On the campus are the five-story building, completed in 1894, which houses classrooms and administrative and faculty offices, a two-story frame chapel building, a library, and a gymnasium, equipped with a stage.

Opened by the Synod of the Norwegian Evangelical Lutheran Church of America in 1894, the academy was merged in 1919 with the Columbia Lutheran College, which had been established by the United Norwegian Lutheran Church in 1909; the union of the schools followed the amalgamation of the two churches in 1917.

The three-year liberal arts and normal school departments of the college are accredited by the University of Washington and the State Department of Public Instruction. Enrollment in the school is over 500.

Adjoining the grounds of the college is the 18-hole PARKLAND GOLF CLUB COURSE (*fees 35c; all day, 50c*).

At 7.2 *m.* on State 5 is a junction with a bituminous-surfaced road.

Left on this road to the BROOKDALE GOLF COURSE, 1.5 *m.* (*fees 50c*), also 18 holes. The clubhouse, of varicolored stones and brown shakes, resembles a Swiss chalet. The OREGON TRAIL MEMORIAL here commemorates the spot where the Naches Pass Immigrant Train last camped as a complete unit in October, 1853. Some of the party went south to Oregon from this spot, some north into King County, and others southwest into Thurston County. Large numbers settled near Parkland in Pierce County.

Across the gold course is the MATTHEW MAHON HOME, beside Clover Creek. Christopher Mahon, a veteran of the Mexican War, took up a donation land claim and settled here with his family in 1852. He built a log cabin, planted seven fruit trees, and began clearing land for a farm. In 1862 Mahon built a two-story house with lumber hauled overland from Tumwater. This house was used as a dwelling by Mahon's son Matthew until 1931, when it was replaced by the present structure. Near the thirteenth green of the golf course is the Mahon family cemetery.

A roadside group of dwellings and small stores at 7.4 *m.* is BROOKDALE (400 alt., 500 pop.), sometimes regarded as an extension of Parkland, but really an independent village. The flat prairie country around it is thinly forested with scrub oak and Douglas fir.

At 8.4 *m.* is an intersection with the FIRST MILITARY ROAD built in the State of Washington, marked by a large cobblestone pyramid erected by the Washington State Historical Society. This road was built from Steilacoom to Walla Walla across Naches Pass by the "people of the northern Oregon," after they had become exasperated by the slow progress made by the Federal Government. The first wagon train to cross the northern Cascades traveled on this road, which was completed in 1855.

At 8.7 *m.* is SPANAWAY PARK (*swimming, boating, camping*), a 339-acre tract, popular as a picnic ground. The park lies along the east shore of SPANAWAY LAKE, one and one-half miles long and a half-mile wide.

At 9.2 *m.* is a junction with a bituminous road.

Right on this road to SPANAWAY, 0.2 *m.* (329 alt., 400 pop.), which was one of the earliest settlements in Pierce County. The Hudson's Bay Company's *Nisqually Journal of Occurrences* for April 26, 1849, records the entry, "Two plows sent to Spannuch and one to Muck." When or why the name was modified is unknown. The town has a post office, stores, taverns, and a creamery. Most of the business structures are false-fronted with high windows. A few modern structures mingle with the gray and weather-beaten older buildings.

At 10.6 *m.* is a junction with State 5-H, a concrete-paved road.

Right here through pastures and prosperous farmlands, the fields bright in spring and summer with camas flowers and lupine, to ROY, 7.9 *m.* (315 alt., 261 pop.), a bustling market center near the convergence of the Muck and Nisqually valleys. Three nurseries ship quantities of pine, spruce, and fir seed; a large bulb farm and a dairy farm, with herds of prize-winning cattle, lie adjacent to the town. Mink are bred successfully at two fur farms, and a hop ranch, located three miles east of the town, is noted for its long rows of hops. Another asset for the community is a lumber mill. Comfortable homes cluster around a large red-brick school. A branch line of the Northern Pacific bisects the business district, and the buildings are built about an open area surrounding the depot. Roy was named for the son of James McNaught, who platted the town site in 1884.

South of Roy, State 5-H passes stump lands converted into farms and pastures. On the banks of the Nisqually River is McKENNA, 12.6 *m.* (285 alt., 200 pop.), started as a lumber company town about 1908. An irrigation project on the adjacent prairie was started by the company, and preference was given to laborers who purchased land. A school, a church, and a pool hall were the only institutions not controlled directly by the company. When the timber supply thinned out, and the lumber market sagged, the mill was dismantled, and even the land office was moved away. Only a quiet little village remains today where once a busy industrial town flourished.

Passing a small co-operative creamery, the road swings through irrigated orchard lands. The name of YELM, 14.7 *m.* (350 alt., 378 pop.), in the midst of the prairie, preserves in modified form the Indian word for heat waves such as rise from sun-baked earth; the Indians reverenced *Chelm,* as they called the waves, believing that the Unseen Power radiated them to render the earth fruitful.

Among the earliest settlers on Yelm Prairie was the family of James Longmire, who crossed the Naches Pass with the first immigrant train in October 1853. Longmire, who took up cattle raising, was one of the earliest explorers of the Mount Rainier region. Until the recent introduction of irrigation, the prairies served as grazing land for beef cattle and sheep; and in early days the Hudson's Bay Company, which maintained a herdsmen's station and a farm here, established Yelm Ferry across the Nisqually River on the road to Fort Vancouver. Today young cowhands in sombreros and high-heeled boots drive to McKenna in modern automobiles, and truckloads of stock pass through the streets on their way to Puget Sound cattle markets. Irrigation has made possible the cherry orchards, prosperous farms, filbert groves, and berry patches that sprinkle the prairies near the town.

The highway passes an abandoned sawmill and, paralleling the railroad, sweeps past prairies covered in summer with a mass of bloom. Camas flowers, ranging in color from white to a brilliant sky-blue, blend with yellow buttercups. RAINIER, 20.7 *m.* (430 alt., 500 pop.), served by the Northern Pacific and the Chicago, Milwaukee, St. Paul & Pacific railroads, is the social center for farmers and loggers of the vicinity, although its closed mills and vacant houses mark it as a ghost lumber town.

Southwest of Rainier, the road runs through TENALQUOT PRAIRIE, a district of park-like openings about groves of fir and other softwood timber. According to an Indian legend, Coyote told his favored tribes, a poor and oppressed people living in California, to prepare for a great migration to a new land he would seek out for them. Traveling northward, Coyote reached a beautiful prairie, rich in game, well-watered, and pleasantly wooded. Exclaiming "Ten-al-quelth!" (the best yet!) he sent a messenger to guide his people to their new home. The bands which came, the legend says, were ancestors of the Indians who now live in the neighboring region. The road crosses a bridge, 23.5 *m.*, over the DESCHUTES RIVER, veers westerly, traversing an area of stumps and second-growth timber, then passes Clear Lake, a long winding body of water filled with snags and bordered by large trees.

TENINO, 29.7 *m.* (280 alt., 952 pop.), is at a junction with US 99 (*see Tour 8d*).

State 5, the main route, follows a southeasterly course from the junction with State 5-H and passes a little community set among new cherry orchards. Left of the highway small homes are scattered amid forested areas and stump lands; along the right the Fort Lewis Military Reservation is covered with virgin trees and rich vegetation. Crossing a branch of MUCK CREEK, 18.2 *m.*, the highway winds through a dreary area of stumps. Amid the black chaos of old logging waste and the scrubby brush of new growth are magnificent stands of Scotch broom. The highway, winding in great loops, then drops into a shallow valley. At 19.1 *m.* is JOHNSON'S CORNER, a junction with a bituminous road.

Left on this road through an area of wild cutover land and stump farms. The bituminous paving ends at 2.2 *m.*, and from there on to KAPOWSIN, 6 *m.* (630 alt., 582 pop.), the surface is graveled. Once important as a lumber-producing center, Kapowsin depends upon recreation trade for its major source of income. Small logging operations employ a few of the inhabitants. The town overlooks KAPOWSIN LAKE (*fishing, swimming, boating, camping*), northernmost lake in the fishing and recreation area known as the Blue Water Lakes District, which includes Tanway, Ohop, Clear, and several smaller lakes where resorts, campgrounds, and swimming and boating facilities are available. Beavers have constructed a whole series of dams around the outlet of the lake.

Beginning a descent into OHOP VALLEY, the road passes OHOP BOB'S INN, 28.1 *m.*, which perches on the precipitous slope of an abrupt hill and overlooks the fertile valley far below. Mount Rainier towers above the landscape. Crossing the Ohop Creek Bridge, the highway winds upward through a mass of heavy firs, then descends rapidly to the floor of the valley.

At 30.2 *m.* is a junction with a bituminous-surfaced road.

Left on this road is EATONVILLE, 2.2 *m.* (800 alt., 996 pop.), named after T. C. Van Eaton, who platted its townsite in 1888. Surrounded by dense virgin forests and situated on the lines of the Tacoma Eastern Railroad, it became one of Washington's most important lumber-producing and log-shipping centers. The largest portion of the merchantable timber has been cut, and today but a few scattered logging operations can be found, and the mill in the town operates only at intervals. The development of farming in the valley to the west has provided Eatonville with an income, which compensates a little for the loss in revenue from timber.

During the annual Community Day dance held in the spring, the streets are crowded with loggers and mountaineers recalling the lusty boom days of Eatonville's past.

Tax returns from assessments on the Weyerhaeuser Timber Company's profitable forest holdings enabled Eatonville to establish splendid school buildings and an educational system of high quality. The expansive landscaped grounds, with a group of buildings housing high school, grade school, and gymnasium, resemble a small college campus. School busses transport children over miles of mountain roads. The school plant stands conspicuously at the head of the main business street.

South of the junction State 5 climbs steadily upward, over small rolling hills through virgin cedar forests. The PACK DEMONSTRATION FOREST (L) (*open 9-5 weekdays; guides furnished*) was established in 1926 on 2,000 acres of land donated by Charles Lathrop Pack to the University of Washington. The Forestry School of the University, with accommodations and facilities for 42 students, is in session here during spring and summer quarters. The curriculum includes surveying, erosion control, forestry and conservation, laboratory work in entomology, and a field trip to the Wind River Nursery.

On exhibition at the gatehouse and entrance is a section of a large Douglas fir log with 727 rings. Adjacent are a model of the forest and an erosion model, contrasting wooded with denuded hills. LATHROP DRIVE, a seven-mile loop of graveled road, encircles the major part of the demonstration area. The camp, located on the road up a hill from the entrance, includes a laboratory, a cookhouse, a recreation hall, and a classroom. A sawmill stands about 600 feet from the camp.

LA GRANDE, 32.2 *m.* (942 alt., 105 pop.), perches on a sheer cliff more than 400 feet above the Nisqually River, which tumbles and froths through a 20-foot channel below. A lodge, a village store, and a gas station cling tenaciously to the slope beside the highway, trees hiding the canyon from view. Here is the city of Tacoma's hydroelectric plant below the reservoir, from which four penstocks carry water to the battery of huge turbines in the powerhouse 425 feet below. Completed in 1912, the plant was one of the earliest municipally owned projects in the State. It has a capacity of 25,600 kilowatts.

Southeast of La Grande the highway climbs rapidly into rugged country, skirting the canyon rim and often scratching into great rocky cliffs. So precipitous are the walls that in places solid rock had to be blasted away for the entire width of the roadbed. These abrupt and rocky cliffs are tinged brown and orange. Turnouts are provided at points of unusual scenic beauty; far below, the railroad winds in a serpentine course along the canyon floor, where giant firs strive to reach the level of the roadway. Mountain farms with tiny orchards appear along the road, and cattle graze in the fields among clumps of young alder.

Built on a sloping bench amid logged-off lands, ALDER, 36.4 *m.* (2,247 alt., 265 pop.), serves as a trading center for a community of mountaineers. Dressed in mackinaws, high "tin pants," and red hats, the men group about trucks, loaded with firewood and heavy logs, and chat in drawling tones. Red-cheeked women gather about the town's lone store and exchange bits of gossip. Living on mountain ranches, these people, descended from emigrants who came here from Tennessee, Kentucky, and the Carolinas, supplement a livelihood gained from their own logging efforts with a few vegetables grown on none too productive soil. A three-story frame school building sits on a little hill in the village.

Near the tracks (R) of the Chicago, Milwaukee, St. Paul, and Pacific Railroad is the SITE OF THE STRATOLINER CRASH, 37.5 *m.* The giant Boeing ship was on a test flight in March, 1939, when it fell apart; the ten occupants were killed instantly.

Logging operations are in progress in the forest along the road. ELBE, 41.4 *m.* (1,210 alt., 175 pop.), on a bank of the Nisqually River, is another gathering place for the mountain folk. Settled by German homesteaders in the early eighties, it was named for the German river. The town with its tiny church, log tavern, a store, a service station, and a brilliant-hued railroad depot, peers up at the denuded mountain range and forested peaks. Trucks laden with fuel wood stop at Elbe on their way to Puget Sound cities; and here is a junction with another branch of State 5 (*see Tour 8E*).

Passing a Civilian Conservation Corps camp, 42.3 *m.,* State 5 continues across a broad benchland, bordered on either side by the BALD HILLS, favorite haunt of moonshiners before the repeal of the Volstead Law. Occasionally the Nisqually River is seen curling along the base of logged-off and burned foothills. Lonely farms, dropped in small cleared areas among blackened stumps, struggle for existence.

At 48.7 *m.* is a junction with a bituminous road.

Right on this road to NATIONAL, 0.2 *m.* (1,990 alt., 300 pop.), site of a large lumber mill. The great red buildings of the mill, its rusted stacks belching black smoke and white steam, dominate the town. Crowded close together and fronting crooked, planked streets are tiny box-like cottages, painted in the same dingy red as the mill. The lumber company dominates every phase of the town's activity, and no one who does not gain his living through the business of the mill lives in National. Citizens arise in the morning, eat their meals, and go to bed by the mill whistle.

ASHFORD, 49.7 *m.* (1,771 alt., 290 pop.), the terminal of the Tacoma Eastern Railroad, has a fine school, hotel, stores, cabins, and service station. Built along both sides of the highway on the side of a mountain, it overlooks a valley and the roofs of National's mill and close-grouped cottages. Some of the employees of the mill live in Ashford, and other mill hands frequently drive the short distance to find relaxation in the Ashford tavern.

Ashford has lost much of its importance as a log-shipping center, and relies for the bulk of its livelihood on the trade of recreation seekers. Bear, deer, and other game animals are common in the adjoining region, and parties make it a point of departure for hunting expeditions. One resident keeps a string of "varmint" dogs to track cougar, lynx, and other animals on which bounty is paid.

The SNOQUALMIE FOREST RESERVE is reached at 51.7 *m.* In the highway cuts and in the lower levels are remnants of small glacial formations, while the higher elevations disclose evidences of the Tertiary period. Few places afford a better opportunity to study the slow processes of nature over tens of thousands of years. In the dim past, Mount Rainier grew from successive volcanic eruptions, andesite and basalt in fragmentary condition forming the bulk of the deposits. Erosion through the centuries released much of the rich deposits to blanket the base of the mountain and to nourish wind-borne seed, watered by underground seepage and plentiful rain, until a mammoth forest arose. In the Snoqualmie Forest Reserve and the Mount Rainier National Park are preserved the best of these unspoiled forests.

NISQUALLY ENTRANCE TO MOUNT RAINIER NATIONAL PARK, 54.9 *m.* (2,003 alt.), is marked by a huge arch of logs spanning the highway. Two campgrounds provide full accommodations, campsites, and tent cabins. Visitors register and obtain permits at the booth (L) which is connected by a common roof to the caretaker's cottage of peeled logs (*see Mount Rainier National Park*).

Tour 8E

Marys Corner—Kosmos—Randle—Packwood—Ohanapecosh Entrance to Mount Rainier National Park; 74.8 *m.* State 5.

Concrete-paved roadbed between Marys Corner and Silver Creek; rest graveled. Resort accommodations and forest camps.

This section of State 5, called the White Pass Highway, crosses the fertile flats of the Chehalis and Newaukum Rivers and then roughly parallels the winding Cowlitz River, which, although seldom visible, is never more than a few miles from the highway. The flats and the lower Cowlitz Valley, settlement of which dates back to 1850, is a checkerboard of small orchards, grain fields, and pastures dotted with Jersey and Holstein cattle. Farther eastward, the road runs through logged-off lands, partially overgrown by alder and willow and interspersed with stump farms. In the foothills the valley narrows between slopes covered with virgin forests of Douglas fir and hemlock, broken with patches of cutover and occasional black forest burns. Few settlers penetrated the foothills until the nineties, and even today most of the isolated villages have retained an almost rustic simplicity.

State 5 branches east from US 99 at MARYS CORNER, 0 *m.* (*see Tour 8d*).

At 5 *m.* is a junction with a graveled road.

Left here through logged-off land to ONALASKA, 4 *m.* (500 alt., 1,200 pop.), location of the Carlisle Lumber Plant, largest lumber mill in Lewis County, with an output at full capacity of 150,000 board feet a day. Rows of uniform, drab houses, owned by the company, are separated from the mill by a high board fence topped by barbed wire. As usual in such one-industry towns, the activities of the inhabitants are circumscribed by, and bound up with, "the mill." Recently, the town was the scene of a long and bitter labor dispute. During the general northwest lumber strike of 1935, the company replaced the striking mill hands with non-union crews, who were formed into an employees' association, or company union. The controversy resulted in several clashes between strikers on the one hand and the railroad police and the Washington State Patrol on the other. The strike continued until 1938, when the company began reinstatement of the strikers in accordance with a decision of the United States Supreme Court upholding the major portions of the findings of the National Labor Relations Board. Dissolution of the company union and recognition of collective bargaining rights were also ordered. A later decision, in 1938, ordering the payment of $158,000 in lieu of wages lost by the strikers, was also upheld in 1939 by the Supreme Court.

State 5 continues through a farming area, with neat houses and well-constructed barns, surrounded by rolling fields of grain and pasture land.

SALKUM, 10.0 *m.* (551 alt., 299 pop.), is a cluster of dilapidated, nondescript houses and two mills, the latter closed down as a result of the depletion of timber supply in the vicinity. Today (1941) only a few people remain in what was a flourishing sawmill town a decade ago. The adjacent countryside is largely wasteland, where willows, alders, and vine maple almost conceal the bleaching stumps, tombstones of forests that have passed away.

SILVER CREEK, 11.1 *m.* (678 alt., 92 pop.), a lively settlement consisting of scattered houses and a few stores, stands on the crest of a hill from which State 5 winds down to the banks of the Cowlitz River.

The MAYFIELD BRIDGE, 12.8 *m.,* affords a vantage point from which to see the green, swirling waters splashing between walls of varicolored rock. MAYFIELD, 12.9 *m.* (374 alt., 114 pop.), a few old stores, an ancient hotel, and a service station, is built along a narrow shelf above the deep canyon through which flows the Cowlitz River. This area produces considerable honey; beehives are scattered throughout the fields and logged-off areas. The yield is high, running from 50 to 150 pounds a hive, and the honey has a delicious flavor because much of the nectar is gathered from the bloom of fireweed.

This plant springs up, almost as if by magic, in the cutover or burnedoff lands. For a season the land is an ugly scar; the next it is a purple splash of blossoming fireweed. The long maturing period of the plant is an important factor in its honey yield; for the pod-like buds, extending two or three feet down the tall stalk, first begin to open in May, and as the summer advances, the flowering descends lower and lower on the stalk until in late August the ripened seed pods burst into silken gray tufts. So regular is the progression from the first flower to the final phase of full seeding that the saying is current, "If you don't know the month, look at the fireweed."

MOSSYROCK, 15.3 *m.* (533 alt., 100 pop.), was named by the early settlers in 1852 for the crag which rises 200 feet above Klickitat Prairie. In 1855-6 when the war-like Klickitats made their way through the mountain passes to the east, the few settlers temporarily abandoned their homes. Today the town is a supply point and distribution center for the area.

State 5 continues through farming and dairying country. Most of the land in this area has been under cultivation for more than a quarter of a century, and the farms give evidence of considerable prosperity in the well-painted barns, large silos, and sleek cattle.

RIFFE, 24.2 *m.* (533 alt., 100 pop.), above the Cowlitz River, supplies the needs of the adjacent farming and logging area. Here Thomas L. Blankenship fashioned crude ferry boats for early river passage. Today, the local blacksmith shop is prepared to repair a car or shoe a horse with complete impartiality. Farming is the chief occupation of the region. Also important is small-scale logging, the logs being felled in the back country and transported to the mills by privately owned trucks.

Southern Baptists here have an old-fashioned church building. The Primitive Baptist Church, founded in 1894 by F. L. Riffe, was the forerunner of the present church. No minister leads their meetings.

East of Riffe Valley, farms alternate with patches of second-growth timber and cutover lands, brilliant with flaming maple, fox glove, and fireweed. Some of the denuded hills already show the deep gullies of erosion. Here and there are unpainted shacks of clapboard, where live the families of loggers employed in the near-by logging camps and mills. In the more fertile parts of the bottoms are well-cultivated farms, dating back to pioneer days, with broad fields of grain and clover, meadow lands of timothy and redtop, and occasional orchards.

Farther eastward, the highway again crosses the Cowlitz River and then parallels it for several miles. The hills, encroaching once more upon the narrowing valley, are still covered with forests of cedar, maple, and fir, logging operations having been extended this far inland only within recent years.

KOSMOS, 35.2 *m.* (751 alt., 18 pop.), is a cluster of buildings at a Y-fork in the road through Rainey Valley, near the confluence of Rainey Creek and the Cowlitz River. The recent extension of the branch line of the Chicago, Milwaukee logging railroad to this point has led to a small-scale boom, and has changed a somnolent hamlet, whose life formerly centered around the store and post office, into an aggressive village.

The Y is the junction of two branches of State 5, the left of which is a bituminous-surfaced road.

Left from Kosmos a branch of State 5 winds through timbered hills, into which run several logging roads. The road is bordered by clusters of white and purple fox glove, patches of daisies, milkweed, and scattered beds of California poppies. Cutover areas and heavy stands of maple, fir, and cedar alternate, as the road winds over the ridges, then down toward the valley bottoms. On a hillside (R) at 4 *m.* is the entrance to the MORTON CINNABAR MINE, which formerly produced a considerable quantity of mercury. The thriving mining town of the twenties is today only a few shacks, mostly vacant, the reduction plant, stripped except for the framework and the retorts, and some old vats and ovens.

MORTON, 7.2 *m.* (945 alt., 778 pop.), at the foot of Cutler Mountain, a high, forested, loaf-shaped bluff, sprawls along the highway and the tracks of the Chicago, Milwaukee, St. Paul and Pacific Railroad at the edge of the Tilton River Valley. It is an enterprising town, deriving most of its income from logging operations in the adjacent forests and the milling of the logs; nearly 100 carloads of logs and ties are sent daily to Tacoma and Seattle. Farming and dairying are also carried on. The first person to settle in the vicinity was

Uncle Jimmy Fletcher, who came from Missouri in 1871. Other families took up homesteads, but not until 1891 was the town of Morton settled.

LINDBERG, 9.9 *m.* (20 pop.), one-time logging and mining town, consists today of a row of brick cottages, a row of abandoned company shacks on either side of the highway, a store, and the ruins of a mill (L), nearly obscured by willow and alders. Cascara bark is seen drying on the porches of the cottages.

State 5 descends northward near a section of Snoqualmie National Forest into a valley, where stands of big trees alternate with marginal-land farms.

CARLSON, 18.3 *m.* (1,561 alt., 35 pop.), once a busy sawmill town, exists today only because of the Interstate Power and Light Company plant here. Some of the few houses are occupied by company employees; others are falling into decay along with the abandoned mill (R).

At 20 *m.* is a junction with a graveled road: R. here 2.7 *m.* to MINERAL (1,439 alt., 500 pop.), headquarters of the West Fork Logging Company's operations, carried on over an area of 23,000 acres. On the shores of Mineral Lake stand a large sawmill and a shingle mill. Selective logging technique, employing scientific methods to determine "ripe" timber and to fell trees in such a way as to result in a minimum of destruction of immature trees, has been substituted for the older methods of logging. Over 100 foresters, including graduates of forestry schools, direct conservation measures to insure the continued supply of logs. Stability of future production is reflected in the attractive brick and tile buildings maintained by the company, in contrast with the flimsy impermanence of most lumber towns.

For a number of years mining played an important part in the life of the town. Most important were the deposits of red realgar, from which arsenic is extracted. A surface vein of rich ore discovered in 1900 was worked until 1922, when the perfecting of a smelting process which recovers arsenic as an inexpensive by-product made the operation of the mine unprofitable.

This section of State 5 ends at ELBE, 23.7 *m.* (*see Tour 8D*), forming a junction with another branch of State 5 (*see Tour 8D*).

East of Kosmos the highway runs through a sparsely settled lowland, hemmed in by steep hills, serrated, and in spots heavily forested. In the grassy valley are old homesteads. Rickety snake fences border the road, and here and there are battened or tar-papered shacks. Cattle graze in tree-studded pastures, lush with clover, whose fragrance permeates the air in the spring. In early summer, occasional patches of blossoming mustard, brilliantly yellow, are to be seen.

GLENOMA, 38.5 *m.* (775 alt., 450 pop.), consists of a cluster of houses, brick and frame, gray school buildings, and a State Highway Department depot. The community depends for its existence upon marginal land farming, from which most of the inhabitants of the region gain their subsistence, and upon small-scale logging operations.

East of Glenoma, State 5 leaves the open bottom lands and passes through thin forests that have been cut over, bordering the road. Just off the road small tie-cutting outfits, operated by crews of two or three, find it possible to compete with large-scale production. At the base of the foothills or on their slopes, pyramids of yellow sawdust or piles of freshly cut ties mark the locations of the small saws; huge sawdust piles, turned the color of copper with age, indicate locations that have been worked out and abandoned.

The foothills are still virgin wilderness, well-nigh inaccessible. Deer and bear are plentiful, and cougar not infrequently invade the barnyards of isolated farms. A well-known oldtimer, Cougar Bill, who lives on KIONA CREEK, 43 *m.,* keeps a pack of hounds to track down cougar, an occupation which is both recreation and profit for him, the bounty and the pelts yielding a modest income. When possible he takes his quarry alive. The captive animals are kept in a crude pit, where they are tended carefully. The largest captive to date was a beautiful specimen about nine feet in length. Bill took special care of this animal, hoping to cross-breed it with one of his dogs; but the experiment was terminated when the local game warden declared the animal a public danger and ordered it shot. To this day Cougar Bill laments the lack of biological curiosity among game wardens.

East of Kiona Creek, heavy forests extending down the hills overshadow the highway. In the surrounding hills backwoods people from Virginia, Kentucky, and Tennessee have settled. Their nasal drawl and old-fashioned Anglicisms, their primtive shacks, and packs of hounds, their wild abandon at Saturday night dances in the valley, and fervent evangelistic sermons on Sundays, give the region a strong frontier flavor.

Money never being too plentiful, the members of the community church pay their tithes by working "a spell" on the pastor's farm. "Gatherin's" are held about the valley at regular intervals, where gossip and commodities are traded with God's blessings.

RANDLE, 47.5 *m.* (1,045 alt., 100 pop.), was founded in 1902 by the Randle Logging Company, and today the mill, with a daily capacity of 35,000 feet, is still the center of the town's activity. As land has been cleared, agriculture and dairying have become increasingly important occupations of the surrounding country. A cheese plant gives employment to some of the town's inhabitants and affords a market for surplus milk.

When the sap begins to rise in the early spring, the lone storekeeper in Randle repaints a sign, "We Buy Cascara Bark," and the cascara gatherers, gunny sacks over their shoulders, plunge into the surrounding hills and valleys, where cascara thickets are plentiful. The cascara expert selects only the oldest trees, not only because the bark is thicker, but also to conserve the supply, for he knows that barking kills the tree. With a heavy knife he first girds the trunk from the butt upward at convenient intervals, then makes perpendicular cuts, and finally works the bark off slowly. It is carried home to dry in a loft or in sacks hung behind the kitchen stove. When cured, it is taken to the village store and either sold or applied on personal accounts. Prices range from 3c to 10c a pound, and a modest income can be made by those experienced in the trade, for 40 or 50 pounds can be gathered in an hour from a good stand.

Randle is also the outfitting center for the Randle Recreation Area.

Right from Randle on a dirt road to the CISPUS RIVER, 9.2 *m.,* and then eastward along the course of the stream. At 14 *m.* is NORTH FORK FOREST CAMP (*camping facilities*), in a grove of firs and cedars.

At 14.1 *m.*, on the east side of the North Fork, is a REGISTRATION STATION of the Forest Service. Certain areas are closed from July 1 to September 30 because of fire hazard, and it is essential to visit the station in order to ascertain the regulations.

The road continues along the course of the Cispus River—except for brief intervals, when the stream winds away into the forest, only to reappear again as it pours over some rocky barrier in clouds of spray, or swirls in quiet eddies. A ridge of precipitous hills (R), scarred and weathered, rises above the valley to an elevation of nearly 6,000 feet.

At 19 *m.* is a junction with a forest trail: L. to BLUE LAKE, 3 *m.* (*camping and fishing*).

At 30 *m.* the road swings around a broad bend in the Cispus River beside BLUE RIDGE (L). ADAMS CREEK, which flows into the river at this point, carries such a load of silt in the spring from its glacial source that it discolors the waters of the larger stream before their confluence. Here is a REGISTRATION STATION (L), and a junction with a forest road; L. here to BERRY PATCH GUARD STATION and CHAMBER LAKE, 20.5 *m.* (*camping and fishing*).

The main side road crosses the Cispus River and winds up the valley of Adams Creek to TAKLAHK POND, 35 *m.*, a forest camp surrounded by flower-strewn alpine meadows and forests of fir and hemlock. At Taklahk Pond is a junction with a forest road: L. here to CHAIN OF LAKES, 1 *m.*, a delightful group of small lakes (*camping and rafts*).

The road continues from Taklahk Pond to KILLEN CREEK FOREST CAMP, 39 *m.*, amid extensive huckleberry patches, which ripen in late summer. At frequent intervals, forest trails lead off into the wilderness. The main side road ends at MIDWAY GUARD STATION, 45 *m.*, although it will eventually be extended to Yakima.

East of Randle, State 5 runs parallel with the general course of the twisting Cowlitz River, traverses a meadowland draining into SILVER CREEK, crosses the COWLITZ, 57 *m.*, over a steel span, then runs along the base of precipitous rocky slopes recording the geologic convulsions of this area.

At 63.3 *m.* is a junction with a forest road.

Right on this road along Johnson Creek to JENNINGS FALLS, 3.5 *m.*, (L), and to GLACIER CREEK, 5 *m.*, beyond which the road ends at a junction with a trail. The trail continues to ANGRY MOUNTAIN (alt. 5,520), 1.5 *m.*, center of a wild, uninhabited area, a paradise for sportsmen.

PACKWOOD, 65.5 *m.* (1,054 alt., 150 pop.), was named for William Packwood, who came from Virginia to the Pacific Coast in 1844 and took a donation land claim in Thurston County in the fifties. He gained considerable reputation as an explorer, and as late as 1889 was a familiar figure along the trails with his string of pack horses. It is said that he would guide a party anywhere in the region for $2.50.

The town of Packwood, lying between the Snoqualmie and the Columbia National Forests, is the outfitting center for the Randle and Goat Rocks Recreation Areas. An important social event is the annual spring dance given in the big hall as a farewell celebration for the fire lookouts, the foresters, and the game wardens, just prior to their departure for the forests. People come from the far end of the valley for the occasion. To the music of a four-piece orchestra of piano, fiddle, bass viol, and drum, punctured with laughter, yells, "stomping" of feet, and an occasional shot from the pistol of an over-exuberant hillman, the crowd dances until dawn.

1. Left from Packwood, a dirt road crosses the Cowlitz River to SKATE CREEK GUARD STATION, 5 *m.*, on Butter Creek (*good fishing*), and ends on MUDDY SLOUGH, 11 *m.*, at a junction with a trail. The trail continues along the MUDDY FORK RIVER, crosses BOX CANYON, 3 *m.*, a gash in the rocks through which the waters seethe 100 feet below, and after traversing a region of deep canyons and sheer cliffs, ends at TATOOSH RIDGE LOOKOUT, 10 *m.* From here a superlative view of the Cascade Range is obtainable.

2. Right from Packwood on a trail through woodland to PACKWOOD LAKE, 6 *m.*, named for the guide, Packwood, who was reputedly the first white man to see it. The trail skirts the lake to the edge of GOAT ROCKS PRIMITIVE AREA, 7.7 *m.*, a wilderness region 5 miles in width and 12 in length lying on both sides of the crest of the Cascades. Snow fields, sheer gray cliffs, pools of inky blue rimmed with lush grass and flowers, and sub-alpine streams characterize the area. Mountain goats, black bear, and deer roam the wooded patches, and mink, raccoon, otter, and marten are seen along the watercourses.

Traversing increasingly rugged country, the trail fords UPPER LAKE CREEK at 12 *m.* and again at 13 *m.* At CHIMNEY ROCK, 17 *m.* (L), the trail enters PACKWOOD SADDLE and ascends the steep slopes to the junction with the CASCADE CREST TRAIL, which when completed will extend from the Canadian border to Mexico. The trail swings around EGG BUTTE, and through heather-covered slopes to SNOW GRAND FLATS, 33 *m.*, a camp site (6,400 alt.), reputed to be the highest in the State. It ends at GOAT ROCKS, 35 *m.* (8,201 alt.), jagged pinnacles surmounting walls of granite.

Northeast of Packwood, State 5 runs through a dense forest of cedar, pine, and fir. Many of the trees tower 200 feet or more in the air, and the branches interlace so closely that only random shafts of sunlight can penetrate to the ground.

CLEAR FORK GUARD STATION, 71.6 *m.* (L), is at the confluence of the Clear Fork and Ohanapecosh (Ind. deep blue pool) Rivers. The latter stream widens into a sapphire basin before uniting with the Clear Fork.

Here is a junction with a forest road.

Left on this road 1.5 *m.* to a STATE FISH HATCHERY, which in 1936 planted 2,490,487 salmon fry.

At 74.5 *m.* is a junction with an improved forest road.

Right on this road is SODA SPRINGS FOREST CAMP, 3 *m.*, named for the adjacent springs of bubbling mineral water. The road ends at the junction with the COWLITZ PASS TRAIL to the SUMMIT LAKES, 4 *m.*, 100 small lakes surrounded by meadows on a plateau 4,500 feet or more in elevation. Good campsites and fishing spots are available on Jug, Deerhead, Dumbell, and Frying Pan Lakes.

North of the junction, State 5 continues on a roadbed cut from the face of towering granite cliffs.

At 75.4 *m.* is the park boundary and the OHANAPECOSH ENTRANCE to Mount Rainier National Park (*see Mount Rainier National Park*).

Tour 9

Junction with US 410—Shelton—Sequim—Port Angeles—Forks—Hoquiam—Aberdeen—Raymond—Megler—(Astoria, Ore.); US 101. Junction to Oregon Line, 370.7 *m.*

No railroad passenger service on the peninsula or to Willapa Bay; ferry service between several points on the east shore of Puget Sound and the peninsula. Graveled and oiled roadbeds, with short stretches of concrete-paved and bituminous-surfaced roadbeds.
Hotel accommodations in larger towns and resorts; inns, cabins, and camping spots at frequent intervals; several ocean beach resorts. Summer months best for touring, but winter-sports areas are being developed.

US 101, the Olympic Peninsula and Pacific Ocean Highway, begins about five miles west of Olympia, at the point where it leads northward from US 410, skirts the many-fingered upper reaches of Puget Sound, and then cuts across to Hood Canal, which it follows to Quimper Peninsula. Swinging in a westerly direction, the route roughly parallels Juan de Fuca Strait for nearly 100 miles and then turns to the south and zigzags to Grays Harbor, Willapa Bay and the lower Columbia River country. Practically encircled by the route is the wilderness of the Olympic National Forest and the Olympic National Park (*see Olympic National Park*), a region of rugged, white-tipped peaks and alpine valleys, steep wooded foothills, glaciers and crystal lakes, and turbulent, icy streams fed by the melting snows of the high mountains. A profusion of wild flowers, fostered by the heavy precipitation of fall and winter months, adds to the charm and beauty of this nearly primitive area. Thousands of deer and large herds of Roosevelt elk feed in the high meadows and browse in wooded glades, fish abound in the lakes and streams, ptarmigan and grouse whir across the roads and trails, and bears feed on the tender shrubs and berries. Access to this wilderness is possible from various points along US 101, by means of stub roads that run for short distances into the forests; here, some are met by rigorous mountain trails that lead to high plateaus and mountain meadows, through somber forest aisles, along precipitous slopes, and up the narrow valleys of cascading streams. Several of these trails can be followed on horseback. Resorts, camps, and forest shelters occur at fairly frequent intervals.

But the mountains are only a part of this wilderness wonderland. Salt water is never far distant. Side roads dart down to idyllic beach camps, where time is marked only by the changing shadows of towering fir and cedar upon the mirror of some protected bay or inlet; or they lead to picturesque fishing towns, Indian villages, white-walled lighthouses, seaports, sawmill towns, and isolated trading hamlets. Occasionally branch roads, and even the main highway, swing down to the precipitous, surf-thrashed coast, or to points from which can be seen the sweep of rolling green breakers, as they crash white-tipped upon hard-packed sands or thunder against jagged cliffs.

South of Aberdeen, the main route winds through high hills, some covered with heavy stands of maturing second- and third-growth forests, others bare except for bleaching stumps and charred logs. At Raymond the highway again reaches salt water and, swinging southward, skirts the east shore of Willapa Bay. Branch roads lead across marshlands and cranberry bogs down to the Pacific Ocean. Scattered along this section of the route are tidewater hamlets and beach resorts, Indian reservations, lighthouses on lonely promontories, and miles of sandy beaches, broken by jutting rocks over which the breakers tumble in a swirl of green water and white spume.

The route ends at Megler on the Columbia, where a ferry connects with Astoria, Oregon, and the southward extension of US 101.

Section a. JUNCTION WITH US 410 (*5 m. west of Olympia*) to SEQUIM; *100.2 m. US 101*

This section of US 101, leaving the well-settled industrial and agricultural region at the head of Puget Sound, heads northward through sparsely populated prairies and logged-off hills to Hood Canal, and then pursues a quiet way along the wooded western shore to Quimper Peninsula and Discovery Bay. Cutting across the highway are many rivers and small streams. Dominating the horizon on the left, forested foothills rise in an ascending series to the saw-toothed Olympics, clear-cut and dazzling in bright sunlight, at other times veiled in mist or shrouded in storm clouds, which creep down the canyons and spread out over the lowlands. At infrequent intervals forest roads wind into the deep fragrant woods, bright with wild currants and rhododendron in bloom, splashes of red elderberry, and cascades of creamy-white spiraea and ocean spray.

On the right, seldom entirely out of range of vision, is Hood Canal, sleeping in the summer sun, its oily calm broken only by chance ripples or the forked wake of motor boat or fishing craft; or lying black and still at midnight, except when a leaping salmon or the oar of a passing boatman strikes balls of phosphorescent fire from its surface. At widely separated intervals, small settlements appear along the highway or perched above the water's edge, where tiny docks on barnacle-encrusted pilings afford anchorage to fishing smacks, pleasure craft, and rowboats; and here and there the forests are broken by clearings, small ranches, and dairy farms.

Leading slightly inland, the route cuts across the neck of Quimper Peninsula, down which a branch road turns to Port Townsend; skirts the tip of Discovery Bay, and then turns left along the Juan de Fuca Strait to Sequim.

North of the junction with US 410 (*see Tour 2d*), 0 *m.,* US 101 winds through low hills, where small farms and chicken ranches alternate with patches of immature evergreen and clumps of alder, and skirts the tip of Eld Inlet, known locally as Mud Bay, and of Oyster Bay. Glimpsed through the trees are the stakes of oyster beds and, when the tide is out, the muddy flats dotted with shallow pools left by the ebbing water. Suddenly the highway lifts itself away from salt water and traverses a stretch where sturdy second-growth trees, stump lands, and small areas of virgin timber are intermingled. In the valleys of this rolling country are scattered farmhouses surrounded by gnarled old fruit trees, berry fields, pastures, and truck gardens.

NEW KAMILCHE (Ind. valley), 9.2 *m.* (sea level, 5 pop.), in the valley of Skookum Creek, once a logging town, is today a wayside village where service stations, auto camps, a garage, and a store or two bustle with activity during the summer months. The shallow, protected waters of the adjacent inlet are suitable for oyster culture.

Edging away from the water, US 101 winds up an easy undulating grade. Much of this region, logged off about 40 years ago, is covered by half-mature fir and cedar; small sections, however, are still denuded wastes, where blackened stumps and bleaching snags are half-hidden by clumps of alder and hazel and brightened by the purplish-red of fireweed in bloom. Scattered along the route are farm homes surrounded by old orchards, meadows of timothy and sweet clover, gardens, and neat squares of oats and wheat. Abruptly the highway descends as it nears Oakland Bay, on Hammersley Inlet from Puget Sound.

SHELTON, 15.6 *m.* (22 alt., 3,707 pop.), seat of Mason County, spreads in neat squares over the flats bordering the bay. From here highways radiate to all parts of the peninsula. In 1853 David Shelton settled on a donation claim; then other settlers began to arrive, at first slowly and then more rapidly as the demand for logs and cut timber grew. In 1884 the town was platted and named for its first settler. For a number of years it grew and prospered as a sawmill town and center for logging operations, which ate their way steadily inland, consuming in less than a generation forests that it had taken hundreds of years to produce.

Unlike many sawmill and logging towns, Shelton is finding industries to take up the slack left by the depletion of the supply of timber suitable for milling. Most important of these is the manufacture of wood pulp, for which smaller trees are suitable.

The RAYONIER, INC. PULP PLANT (*visitors by permission*), a number of buildings clustering around a huge smokestack, spreads over nearly 160 acres along the water front. When the plant is operating, sometimes on a 24-hour basis, sulphurous smoke trails across the sky, and the citizens of Shelton welcome the acrid odor, for it signifies jobs for workers and jingling cash registers in business establishments. At present (1941) the plant turns out pulp only, the finished paper or rayon products being manufactured elsewhere. An experimental laboratory (*visitors not admitted*) carries on research directed toward the utilization of factory wastes. One by-product already developed, Purite, a fluid used in batteries, utilizes about one-half of the fluid wastes; the remainder is pumped to a gravelly flat several miles north of town, where it filters slowly into the ground.

In the early thirties the pulp-making industry clashed with another new industry—the culture of oysters on the flats of Oakland Bay. Oyster interests, charging that the dumping of sulphite waste into the bay was ruining the oyster beds, filed damage suits. Attempts to settle the bitter controversy failed, and the mill was closed. Alarmed over the possibility of losing the plant, the citizens of Shelton raised $166,000 by popular subscription to recompense the oyster growers for any losses sustained, and the company in turn agreed to reopen the plant and to work out a suitable method of disposing of the sulphite wastes. Recently, the company acquired the oyster beds that had been injured by pollution and is now experimenting with oyster culture. This work is handled by a separate division of the parent organization.

In Shelton is a junction with State 14-A, an alternate route to Belfair and other points on Kitsap Peninsula (*see Tour 9-A*).

Northwest of Shelton US 101 again climbs gradually away from Puget Sound to gravelly uplands. Spur roads give access to the fishing and hunting areas to the westward.

At 18.7 *m.* is a junction with a dirt road.

Left here 1.6 *m. to the* SHELTON GOLF COURSE (*greens fee 35c, 9 holes; 50c, 18 holes*), an interesting nine-hole course, which employs effectively the park-like prairie and natural hazards.

SCOTT'S PRAIRIE, 20.7 *m.,* a stretch of open grassland with scattered clumps of trees, was named for John Tucker Scott, who settled here in 1854. Two of his children won prominence as journalists; Harvey W. Scott, veteran editor of the Oregonian, a Portland daily, and Mrs. Abigail Scott Duniway, editor, writer, and pioneer advocate of woman suffrage.

At 30.2 *m.* is a junction with State 14, a bituminous-surfaced road (*see Tour 9A*).

North of the junction US 101 runs through the SKOKOMISH INDIAN RESERVATION. Only a few families remain on the reservation, the population, according to the Bureau of Indian Affairs, being about 200. Most of these Indians supplement meager incomes from small farms by fishing; some also work seasonally in berry fields, on truck farms, and in sawmills.

HOOD CANAL, 30.7 *m.,* is really not a canal but an 80-mile-long, tide-washed channel from Admiralty Inlet. Gravelly beaches, stretches of sedge-covered lowlands, and gold-brown tide flats frame the placid waters. Rafts of logs sleep in protected inlets, and fishing craft rock safely at anchor or cut their way across the placid surface of the water. For miles the highway hugs the western shore of the canal, into which flow numerous creeks making stop-and-go, staircase descent. On warm spring days the beaches are dotted with clam diggers, shovels and buckets in hand, trousers rolled above their knees.

The canal was discovered and named by Captain George Vancouver on May 13, 1792. In his journal he records: "Early on Sunday morning, the 13th, we embarked directing our route down the inlet, which after the Rt. Honorable Lord Hood, I called Hood's Channel." For some reason the name appeared in Vancouver's *Voyage of Discovery* as Hood's Canal. The United States Geographical Board dropped the possessive form.

POTLATCH (Ind. to give), 29 *m.* (sea level, 60 pop.), the commercial headquarters of the Skokomish Indian Reservation, was named for the Indian custom of exchanging gifts—blankets, canoes, baskets, guns, and other articles—at a community feast. Here stood the Potlatch House, center of activities during the festivals of former days.

Many of the Skokomish Indians have embraced the Shaker religion, which John Slocum, an Indian, is credited with founding. Services, conducted in the native tongue, begin with a solemn exhortative sermon by the leader. Then he calls for prayers; in turn each worshipper calls out his petition, and the assemblage echoes it in a deep-toned, thrilling chant. After the prayers a deacon, a bell in either hand, leads a ceremonial dance around the room to the accompaniment of rhythmic chanting and the jingle of bells. Each dancer in turn revolves before the altar and passes his hand through flaming candles for purification.

HOODSPORT, 31.1 *m.* (sea level, 500 pop.), spreads westward toward abruptly rising hills and eastward down to the water's edge. Once Hoodsport was a bustling logging town, but today its income comes largely from vacationists, transient trade, and small-scale fishing operations. Native to the waters adjacent to Hoodsport is a small species of shrimp; the firm texture and delicate flavor brought so great a demand that over-fishing resulted. Now only strict adherence to conservation measures can guarantee the survival of the shrimp in Hood Canal.

In Hoodsport is a junction with a graveled road.

Left here up a winding grade through cutover land, where small fir, hemlock, and alder nearly obscure the stumps of the magnificent trees that covered these slopes less than 50 years ago. Logging is still carried on farther west in the foothills of the Olympics. Heavy trucks, their trailers loaded with sections of immense trees, have replaced the oxen, which once snaked the logs from the woods; roaring around the curves of the road, these trucks thunder down the grade.

LAKE CUSHMAN (*good trout fishing; boats*), 5 *m.*, a man-made lake some ten miles in length, furnishes a controlled and dependable supply of water for the Tacoma hydroelectric plant. Early in the twenties the citizens of Tacoma, led by Homer T. Bone and other champions of public ownership of power, took the legal steps necessary as a preliminary to the construction of this municipally owned project. Two dams, 275 and 240 feet in height respectively, were built across the North Fork of the Skokomish River, thus creating Lake Cushman; a large power plant was erected at the lower end of the lake and another near Hood Canal. Today Tacoma claims a lower average electricity rate than any other city in the United States.

The road runs in a westerly direction along the north shore of the lake. Wooded slopes roll upward from the narrow valley to rugged peaks. At 10.5 *m.* is a junction with a forest trail, to MOUNT ELLINOR (4,400 alt.), 7 *m.*

The main side road continues to the head of the lake, 17 *m.*, and then leads along the bank of a turbulent stream to STAIRCASE CAMPGROUND (L), 18.5 *m.*, to LINCOLN GUARD STATION (R), 19 *m.*, and the end of the road, 21 *m.*, where it makes a junction with a forest trail. At BIG LOG (*trail-side shelter*), 2 *m.*, the trail forks; the right branch leads to CAMP NINE STREAM, 4 *m.*, and the left branch to GRAVES CREEK CAMP, 20.5 *m.* (*see Tour 9c*).

North of Hoodsport US 101 runs like a quiet, shaded lane between Hood Canal, visible through the interstices of the trees, and forested foothills that march upward to rocky, snow-capped peaks. Occasionally an old logging road or trail leads into the somber woods, where dense undergrowth of huckleberry and salmonberry bushes, salal, Oregon grape, and ferns forms an unbroken carpet. Here and there water from hidden springs trickles down exposed embankments to form shallow roadside pools. The air is heavy with the mingled odor of green leaves, damp mosses, fungi, decaying vegetation, and rotting logs.

LILLIWAUP (Ind. inlet), 35.4 *m.* (15 alt., 75 pop.), straggles along the highway and the shores of Lilliwaup Bay. Years ago the town was a center of logging activity and an outfitting point for prospectors working in the upper Skokomish River country.

In Lilliwaup is a junction with a forest trail.

Left on this trail, 0.6 *m.*, is LILLIWAUP FALLS. Lilliwaup Creek, an amber-colored stream born in swampy forest pools, pours between bare walls, 150 feet above the valley floor; then plunges into a natural basin, where for a moment it hesitates before falling in a column of mist and spray into the dark pool at the foot of the cliff. From the pool the creek flows quietly seaward between gravelly banks and over sandy shallows. During spawning season salmon, on their upstream migration, struggle futilely in the waters at the foot of the falls. Fir trees bend over the walls of the canyon and rise from the narrow floor; deep shadows lie perpetually against the metallic blue-black of the rocky cliffs.

ELDON, 44 *m.* (sea level, 100 pop.), on Hamma Hamma Bay, was a brisk town in the early 1900's, when logging operations on the upper Hamma Hamma River were extensive. Weathered buildings along the bay and an abandoned railroad fill are reminders of this vanished activity.

North of Eldon US 101 swings across the Hamma Hamma River and again plunges into dense forests broken occasionally by small clearings and open spaces, which afford panoramic views of Hood Canal and the wooded shores beyond.

At 45.8 *m.* is a junction with a forest road.

Left here along the north bank of the Hamma Hamma River. At 1.8 *m.* is a junction with a trail: R. on the trail is the HAMMA HAMMA GUARD STATION, 6 *m.*, just within the Olympic National Forest. At 7 *m.* is the WEBB LOOKOUT STATION, a fine point for a view of Hood Canal and the Olympics. The end of the road, 15 *m.*, is deep in the rugged country near the source of the river.

At 54 *m.* is a junction with a dirt road.

Left here 0.5 *m.* is DUCKABUSH (50 alt., 90 pop.), where the tide flats meet the foothills at the apex of a narrow valley, lying between two ridges that run to the water's edge. Duckabush is the provisioning point for hikers tramping the Duckabush Trail and for a few small-scale ranches in the foothills.

At 55 *m.,* at a point just north of the Duckabush River, is a junction with a forest road.

Left here up a slightly winding grade to INTERROREM CAMP AND GUARD STATION, 4 *m.* As the road leads deeper into the Olympic National Forest, the country becomes increasingly wild and rugged. Continuing up the Duckabush Valley, the road ends at 7 *m.,* at a junction with a trail, which climbs steadily into the wilderness. BIG HUMP CAMP, 1.4 *m.,* on the trail, lies practically at the foot of MOUNT JUPITER (5,650 alt.). To the southwest, across the Duckabush River, rise THE BROTHERS (6,855 alt.), DUCKABUSH CAMP, 22 *m.,* is at the head of the Duckabush River (*open to fishing; steelhead and several species of trout*).

BRINNON, 58 *m.,* lies at the mouth of the Dosewallips River. Much of this fertile delta has been drained and converted into fine farm land. A ferry (*$1 car and driver; 25c passenger*) connects with Seabeck on the Kitsap Peninsula (*see Tour 9A*).

This part of the Hood Canal is a regular camping ground for the Clallam Indians, who have permanent homes along Juan de Fuca Strait. As a rule they arrive in August to catch and dry the dog salmon running at that time; then they pick and dry huckleberries, which grow prolifically in the woods around Brinnon. Occasionally a few families remain all winter, but most return home in time for the winter dances.

At 59.6 *m.,* about a mile north of the Dosewallips River, is a junction with a dirt road.

Left here through a wooded wilderness. Fir, cedar, and occasionally hemlock border the road, their spreading branches at times meeting overhead. Noisy streams sparkle through the thickets of ferns and trailing vines, swirl around fallen logs, and chatter between banks of shale. Here and there miniature niagaras plunge to join the Dosewallips, which dashes headlong down the precipitous slopes.

The entrance to the Olympic National Forest by means of this road is marked by the CORRIGENDA GUARD STATION (*fire permits issued here*), 5.5 *m.* West of the station the road winds and climbs, roughly paralleling the course of the river.

ELKHORN CAMP (*camping facilities*), 11 *m.,* at the end of the road, is the junction point for several interesting trails leading into the primitive area of the Olympic Mountains.

(1) Right from the end of the road a trail ascends steep, wooded slopes, broken now and then by ravines and rocky patches, to LAKE CONSTANCE, 4 *m.,* whose clear blue water mirrors the surrounding woods and peaks. Encircling the lake are mountain meadows, bright in season with a profusion of wild flowers. North of the lake, rising above heavily forested foothills, is MOUNT CONSTANCE (7,777 alt.).

(2) Left (straight ahead) a second trail leads along the north bank of the Dosewallips River. HAPPY CAMP, 4 *m.,* in a pleasant opening in the timber, and MUSCOTT CABIN, 7.5 *m.,* both maintained by the Forest Service, may be used by visitors, although built primarily for the use of forest workers.

At 9 *m.,* the main trail forks: L. across the Dosewallips River is SODA SPRINGS, 3 *m.,* on the branch trail, which continues to DIAMOND MEADOWS CAMP and ANDERSON PASS in the Olympic National Park (*see Olympic National Park*): R. along the north fork of the river a trail leads to DOSE MEADOWS and the HAYES RIVER GUARD STATION (*see Olympic National Park*).

US 101 continues northward along the west side of Dabop Bay, an arm of Hood Canal, and then swings inland through a corner of the Olympic National Forest to round the base of Mount Walker.

The highway climbs perceptibly, as the mountains crowd in upon it for a short distance; ravines lead off into the deep forests. RAINBOW CAMP AND GUARD STATION (L), 67.2 *m.,* in a setting of trees and shrubs beside the Big Quilcene River, lies at the top of the grade. Forest trails lead up the river and Tunnel Creek.

At 67.2 *m.,* on the opposite side of the road from the camp, is a junction with an improved road.

Right here at the end of a road that spirals up the side of MOUNT WALKER (3,018 alt.), is MOUNT WALKER LOOKOUT STATION, 1.2 *m.* This vantage point offers a splendid view of Dabop Bay, Hood Canal, and Juan de Fuca Strait, and of the long line of the Cascades on the east and the Olympics on the west.

North of Rainbow Camp the highway curves downward through a narrow valley. Crossing the Big Quilcene, US 101 turns eastward toward Dabop Bay.

QUILCENE (Ind. salt water people), 69 *m.* (30 alt., 250 pop.), centers along the river flats and straggles down to the water's edge. The lowlands where the town now stands were settled in the late sixties, when Samuel H. Cottle took up land there. Others soon joined him, putting up log cabins and starting small logging operations and farming. In the nineties, the Port Townsend and Southern line was laid to Quilcene, and the hope that the town would become an important link led to a short-lived boom, which collapsed with the abandonment of plans for the rail line. Recently the rails from Port Discovery Bay to Quilcene were pulled up. Today, farming and dairying are the major sources of income for the community. Quilcene is an outing center and is also the district headquarters for the Forest Service.

Quilcene Bay, an arm of Dabop Bay, is known for its oyster culture. Frequently in the propagation of oysters considerable difficulty is encountered in controlling the cultch, or spat, as the young oysters are called. The cultch at first floats in the water for ten days or more; then it attaches itself to some piece of gravel or shell. In many places the force of tidal currents, or the lack of protection from winds, results in the loss of the cultch before it secures an anchor; but the waters of Quilcene Bay recede without greatly endangering the cultch during its floating, unanchored period.

North of Quilcene US 101 turns from the water and runs through a scattering of small farms, dairy and chicken ranches, patches of stump lands, and stands of timber. Numerous small streams make their way down the wooded slopes and through open glades.

At 81.2 *m.* is a junction with State 9, a bituminous-surfaced road.

Right here around the tip of Discovery Bay, skirting its eastern shore. It was in this bay that Vancouver anchored his vessels in 1792, when he set out in his cutter, pinnace, and long boat, on the foggy morning of May 7, to explore the shoreline to the eastward. The area lying between the bay and Port Townsend Bay to the east was named Quimper Peninsula in honor of the Spanish seaman who explored these shores in 1790. Francisco de Eliza, another Spaniard, also used the bay as a temporary base of exploration in 1791, a year before Vancouver.

At 1.8 *m.* is a junction with State 9-E, an improved road.

Right here through level land broken by occasional low hills, partially covered with small trees. At 11 *m.* is a junction with a graveled road: R. on the graveled road is SHINE, 6 *m.* (sea level, 60 pop.). A ferry ($1 *car and driver; 25c passenger*) connects with Port Gamble, (*see Tour 9-A*).

PORT LUDLOW, 12 *m., on State 9-E* (sea level, 400 pop.), in former years was a center of shipping for lumber from Quimper Peninsula. The first sawmill in Jefferson County was erected here in 1852, a makeshift affair that, according to reports, ran one day and then closed down a week for repairs. Improved machinery increased the output sufficiently to enable the mill to supply many of the small settlements that were springing up along the Sound and occasionally to send a cargo to San Francisco. Today, Port Ludlow is a shipping and supply point for the surrounding region, which is becoming an increasingly important agricultural and dairying area. Ferries connect with Edmonds, adjacent to Seattle ($2.50 *car and driver; 50c passenger*).

State 9, the main side road, continues in a northeasterly direction through partially wooded countryside. The Quimper Peninsula in early summer is literally ablaze with the gorgeous pink and rose of rhododendron. These shrubs sometimes reach a height of 15 to 20 feet in the cool depths of the forest. Along the road are berry fields, truck gardens, lush meadows, fields of timothy and clover, and modern poultry and dairy farms.

PORT TOWNSEND, 15.1 *m.* (80 alt., 4,683 pop.), lies on Port Townsend Bay at the extreme northeastern point of Quimper Peninsula. The business section spreads along the water front, the main streets being lined with substantial old buildings dating back to the boom days, when the town was measuring its future in terms of a major city. The residential section is centered on the level top of a bluff that rises above the water front. Eastward across Admiralty Inlet rises the dark bulk of Whidbey Island, and dominating the horizon on the southwest are the Olympic Mountains, some 30 miles distant.

Port Townsend is one of the most interesting historical points in the Northwest. In May 1792, Captain George Vancouver and a party of his men, while anchored in Discovery Bay, started out in small boats to explore the coast line. The fog was heavy when he pushed around a sandy promontory, which he named Point Wilson, and hence he was not aware of the nature of the body of water he had entered until the sun broke through the fog, just as he reached what is Point Hudson. Vancouver was much impressed with the beauty of the setting and the extent and character of the bay, which he called Port Townsend for the English marquis of that name.

Pioneer settlers were Alfred A. Plummer, a young harness maker from Maine, and Charles Bacheller. While in San Francisco they heard of Puget Sound—its forests, its fish, and its fertile soil—from Captain Lafayette Balch; as a consequence they took passage with Balch on the brig *George Emery* to Steilacoom. From there they went by canoe to Port Discovery Bay, which the captain had described to them as they sailed around the point into Puget Sound. On April 24, 1851, they landed on the beach below the high bluffs and were met by a number of Indians who lived on the bay. Soon the two men were joined by Loren B. Hastings and Francis W. Pettygrove (who had recently founded Portland, Oregon) and their families. By May 1852, the settlement consisted of 3 families and 15 bachelors.

Among the early settlers in the area was one Albert Briggs. In 1852 he decided to leave Portland; sending his family by boat, he started overland with a herd of 30 head of cattle. At Tumwater, near Olympia, he loaded his cattle on a scow and, floating with the tide by day and beaching it at night, he reached a shallow harbor opposite Port Townsend. The trip took 15 days. To commemorate his voyage, Briggs named the harbor where he landed Scow Bay.

In the summer of 1852, it was decided to call the settlement Port Townsend, dropping the letter "h", as Commander Wilkes had done for the bay in 1841. Thus the name appeared when the first post office was established, and thus it was spelled in the official record of the plat of the town. Land was cleared, stores opened, and homes were built. Trees were felled and rolled down to the beach, by hand power or with the help of oxen, and then rafted out to ships and loaded for California. During the gold rush to the Fraser River country, Port Townsend received its share of the outfitting business, for most vessels dropped anchor in the bay to clear at the customs house. After the collapse of the boom many of the miners returned to make their homes in the town.

In *Steep Trails* John Muir gives an interesting picture of the town in the eighties: "This being the port of entry, all vessels stop here, and they make a lively show about the wharves and in the bay. The winds stir the flags of every civilized nation, while the Indians, in their long-beaked canoes, glide about from ship to ship, satisfying their curiosity or trading with the crews. Keen traders these Indians are, and few indeed of the sailors or merchants from any country ever get the better of them in bargains. Curious groups of people may often be seen, English, French, Spanish, Portuguese, Scandinavians, Germans, Greeks, Moors, Japanese, and Chinese of every rank and station and style of dress and behavior; settlers from many a nook and bay and island up and down the coast; hunters from the wilderness; tourists on their way home by the Sound and the Columbia River or to Alaska or California."

During the days of sailing vessels and of the early stern- and side-wheelers, Port Townsend was the "Key City," with boat lines radiating to many ports. The coming of the railroad to Tacoma alarmed the citizens of the town, at the same time that it raised visions of a "western New York" in the minds of the more optimistic. Early plans for a Northern Pacific connection with the Columbia River failed to materialize. Port Townsend citizens, convinced that they must take the initiative, incorporated their own company, the Port Townsend and Southern, in 1887, and began to acquire property for a right of way along Hood Canal and to solicit funds to finance construction. Stimulated by the speculative fever, property values soared, population increased to 7,000, six banks did a rushing business, large office buildings were erected, and scores of homes went up almost overnight. The transfer of the franchise to the Oregon Improvement Company, a subsidiary of the Union Pacific, merely served to accelerate the boom. By September 1, 1890, trains were running from Port Townsend to Lake Hooker, but work on the line was beginning to drag; officials seemed more interested in speculating in real estate than in building a rail line. Disquieting whispers of impending failure of the company were confirmed in November, when it was learned that the company had gone into receivership. Real-estate values fell, thousands of people deserted the town, and everyone knew that the dream was over. A city with the facilities for a population of 20,000 soon had fewer than 2,000.

Attempts in the nineties to establish industries also met with indifferent success. A huge drydock was constructed but was towed elsewhere when it was nearly completed; a nail works opened in 1892 and failed soon thereafter; and several other enterprises opened only to close after a short time. The panic of 1893 filled Port Townsend Bay with ships of all kinds and tonnage; there they lay idly at anchor, until the improvement of business conditions in 1897 called them again into the channels of trade.

Since the beginning of the twentieth century Port Townsend has achieved a degree of stability, in spite of serious setbacks from time to time. Strategically situated, it has been the headquartrs for various Government operations for more than 50 years. Fort Worden, adjoining the city, provides a steady pay roll.

One of the most important industrial developments was the building of a $7,000,000 plant here, in 1927, by the Crown Zellerbach Corporation (paper and pulp). The extension of agriculture near Port Townsend and in the Chimacum Valley and the steady increase in tourist and recreation trade are other factors of importance in the economic life of Port Townsend today.

North of the junction with State 9 the highway, US 101, parallels the west shore of Discovery Bay. MOUNT CHATHAM (2,000 alt.) was named by Captain George Vancouver.

PORT DISCOVERY, 84.2 *m.* (sea level, 166 pop.), huddles

along the edge of the bay. It is a minor shipping point for lumber and logs and home port for a few small fishing craft. Near the town was the camp of Captain George Vancouver.

BLYN, 93.2 *m.* (sea level, 300 pop.), lies at the tip of picturesque Sequim Bay. Old buildings nestle at the base of a cliff.

At 95.2 *m.* is a junction with an improved road.

Left here 2.7 *m.* is SEQUIM BAY STATE PARK, an 84-acre natural park, with towering trees and native shrubbery. Roads wind through the forest to secluded retreats for camping and picnicking.

SEQUIM (Ind. quiet waters; pronounced "Skwim"), 100.2 *m.* (209 alt., 534 pop.), with neat stores, a hotel and other business buildings bordering the wide main street, is the commercial center for the surrounding fertile agricultural area. A quirk of nature leaves Sequim one of the driest towns, as well as one of the sunniest, in western Washington, the annual precipitation averaging only 17 inches, much lighter than that of near-by areas. About 35,000 acres near Sequim are under irrigation.

In Sequim is a junction with State 9-F, an improved road.

Right here through irrigated farm lands to DUNGENESS, 5.5 *m.* This picturesque fishing village spreads over a point jutting into Juan de Fuca Strait, a short distance east of a long sandy spit. Clumsy-looking power boats, their sterns piled high with traps, ply the coastal waters for crabs. These famed Dungeness crabs, exceptionally fine-flavored and firm in texture, are shipped in cold storage to Midwestern and Eastern cities. The visitor may experience the thrill of catching crabs in a long-handled net, with which he can rake the ocean bottom when the tide is out. Many octopuses, which are canned in commercial quantities, are also caught in these waters.

The inhabitants of Dungeness are a hardy folk, who have learned to respect the swirling eddies and strong tides of the Strait. In the days of wooden ships and sails many a ship piled up along these shores, and the settlers customarily kept beach fires burning brightly on stormy nights to warn navigators. They also formed a volunteer life-saving corps and pulled their stout boats through the heavy seas to rescue the crews of shipwrecked vessels. Today there is a lighthouse on Dungeness Spit.

Section b. SEQUIM *to* FORKS, *69 m. US 101*

Along the route of US 101, due west from Sequim, cultivated fields and substantial farmsteads alternate with wooded plots. On the left are rugged peaks, the northern outposts of the Olympic Mountains.

At 11 *m.,* opposite the entrance to the PORT ANGELES GUN CLUB, is a junction with a dirt road.

Left here 18 *m.* to DEER PARK (5,411 alt.), a picturesque area on Blue Mountain (6,007 alt.), which is being developed for winter sports, particularly skiing. The Deer Park Lodge provides regular meals, but overnight guests must furnish their own bedding. From near-by Blue Mountain Lookout the skier can descend the rolling slopes to OBSTRUCTION POINT, 7 *m.* Within the radius of a mile from the lodge are more than 15 excellent skiing slopes. The Olympicans of Bremerton stage an annual ski festival at Deer Park.

West of the junction the highway follows rolling terrain. At 15 *m.* is a junction with a graveled road.

Left here 6.5 *m.* to HEART O' THE HILLS, a popular recreational center on placid Lake Dawn, at the foot of triple-peaked MOUNT ANGELES (6,039 alt.), with its many snowfields and glaciers. KLAHANE GARDENS has nearly 3,000 blooming flowers and shrubs, including 300 varieties of lilies and 100 kinds of heather. Snowbirds, partridges, peacocks, and swans are found in the zoological gardens.

A trail leads to the top of Mount Angeles, from which a panorama of bays, inlets, islands, mountains, and the Strait can be seen. To the west is the main divide of the Olympic Mountains. Peak after peak, many yet unnamed, thrusts up lofty pinnacles, deeply cut by cascading streams. The surrounding region is characterized by canyons, deep-cut glaciers, and turbulent streams, whose crystal-clear waters are the home of the gamy rainbow trout. Trails lead to high mountain meadows and close to glaciers.

In PORT ANGELES, 16 *m.* (50 alt., 9,409 pop.), seat of Clallam County, the business section slopes gently to the harbor front, while the residential section lies on bluffs above. Behind these hillside homes rise the snowcapped ridges of the Olympic Mountains. Directly across the Strait, approximately 17 miles in width at this point, is Victoria, British Columbia, on Vancouver Island.

A narrow spit of sand, EDIZ HOOK, a curving finger extending into Juan de Fuca Strait, protects the harbor. Industrial plants line the water's edge; coastwise and ocean freighters load and unload at electrically equipped docks. The harbor is the first American port of entry for ships coming into Puget Sound from the Pacific. On Ediz Hook are a COAST GUARD AIR BASE and EDIZ HOOK LIGHTHOUSE, built in 1908 to replace an earlier tower dating from 1865.

Three pulp and paper mills, a large export lumber mill, and a concrete-products plant contribute to the commercial importance of Port Angeles. Dairying in the district about the city supports three creameries. Clallam County claims the highest record for butter-fat production per cow of any county in the State.

Recorded history of the city goes back to 1791, when Captain Francisco Eliza, exploring for the Viceroy of Mexico, sailed into the harbor behind the sandy claw and found an Indian village. He christened it, eloquently, *Porto de Nuestra Senora de Los Angeles* (Sp. Port of Our Lady of the Angels).

In Port Angeles is a junction with State 9-A, a bituminous-surfaced road.

Right 4 *m.* on State 9-A to a junction with a graveled road; right here 3 *m.* to ANGELES POINT, a rounded promontory pushing out into the sea. On the west side of the point the broad mouth of the Elwha River empties into the JUAN DE FUCA STRAIT. The origin of the name of this famous inlet of the Pacific has long been a puzzle. Among early explorers, geographers, and mapmakers there existed a belief in the "Strait of Anian," a waterway that was thought to stretch between the Atlantic and the Pacific. In a geographical treatise, *Hakluytus Posthumus, or Purchas—his Pilgrimages,* Michael Lok wrote that an entrance had been discovered by a Greek sailor, Juan de Fuca, whose real name was Apostolos Valerianos. Juan de Fuca told Lok that he had been on a voyage with some Spaniards and had entered this waterway "between 47° and 48° latitude." Captain Charles William Barkley, sailing by in the *Imperial Eagle* in 1787, records seeing and naming the great opening in the coast after Juan de Fuca. The following year Captain John Meares of the *Felice* cruised about the entrance. Recalling Michael Lok's story, he also inscribed the

Greek's name on his charts. There is some evidence that Meares had talked with Barkley during the year's interval.

West of the junction State 9-A traverses a scrubby, cutover area. TWIN, 17 *m.* (25 pop.), is a small settlement huddled about the mouth of Twin Rivers. West of Twin the road follows along the Strait. (This road may be taken as an alternate route to the Cape Flattery district). At PYSHT, 34 *m.* (120 pop.), the main side road connects with another side road leading from US 101.

West of Port Angeles US 101 swings southward along the ELWHA RIVER, broadened by a power dam at the north end of its storage basin to the proportions of a lake. At 23.8 *m.* is a junction with a dirt road.

Left on this road along the east bank of the Elwha River. Heavily timbered mountains rise on either side of the swiftly flowing stream. Right are the green ridges of the ELWHA RANGE. The river plunges noisily in white cataracts through a canyon, whirling here and there in quiet green eddies. ELWHA FOREST CAMP, 3 *m.,* is an improved camping ground. At the ELWHA RANGER STATION, 4 *m.,* is a junction with a graveled road: Right here 11 *m.* on a winding course above steep-walled canyons to OLYMPIC HOT SPRING: (2,100 alt.), where 21 hot springs gush from the mountains. A hotel and a group of cabins surround a concrete swimming pool. Both mud and mineral baths are available.

At 6 *m.* on the main side road is LAKE MILLS, created by a second dam across the Elwha. The road winds high above the blue-green lake through dank forests festooned with moss.

At 13 *m.* is a junction with a trail: R. on this trail 1.5 *m. to* HUMES RANCH (*guides and horses available*), the last settlement encountered on the trip up the Elwha Valley, except for an occasional Forest Service station. In a forest of young Douglas fir is LILLIAN SHELTER, 5 *m.,* on the LILLIAN RIVER. At 9 *m.* on the trail is the northern boundary of the MOUNT OLYMPUS NATIONAL MONUMENT.

Here, mountains shoulder up from forested river valleys, like a great staircase carved from rock and ice, to the pinnacles of MOUNT OLYMPUS (8,150 alt.). Fifty-three glaciers inch their way down the slopes of the Olympic Range, and from these glacial heights course many rivers. Between the snow fields and sub-alpine forest lie expanses of meadowland, bright with wild columbine, dog-tooth violets, Indian pipes, and other flowers. The lower glens and hollows and the 350,000 acres enclosed within the monument form a veritable wilderness, where elk, deer, bear, cougar, and many smaller animals find sanctuary. Crossing two ridges, each more than 1,500 feet in elevation, the trail comes to ELKHORN GUARD STATION, 15 *m.,* an improved campground (*good fishing*). Westward is a magnificent view of the BAILEY RANGE.

Past the confluence of the Elwha and Lost Rivers, the trail leaves the Elwha Valley and enters PRESS VALLEY, named in commemoration of the Press Expedition of 1890, sent into this wilderness under the auspices of a pioneer Seattle newspaper. Through growths of small fir, mountain hemlock, larch, and spruce, with occasional patches of wild flowers, the trail ascends to its crossing of the Elwha River, at 25 *m.,* where it skirts the rim of the Elwha Basin (2,700 alt.). Dense forests extend nearly to the basin, then the change to sub-alpine growth is noticeable. The trail turns L. (25 *m.*), recrosses the narrowed waters of the Elwha, and begins a gradual ascent. Through sub-alpine timber and over barren slopes of rock, the route twists and winds, passing lakes Mary and Margaret (R), 28 *m.,* and Low Divide Chalet, 29 *m.* (3,662 alt.). Here the trail connects with another that comes up the North Fork of the Quinault River (*see Olympic National Park*).

West of the junction US 101 affords fleeting glimpses of LAKE SUTHERLAND (*fishing, cabins*), 28.9 *m.* (590 alt., 10 pop.), a slipper-shaped body of water in a narrow basin near the foot of

MOUNT STORM KING (4,534 alt.). West of Lake Sutherland the highway winds about precipitous bluffs.

At 30.5 *m.* is a junction with a dirt road.

Right on this road along the north shore of Lake Crescent to PIEDMONT, 3.2 *m.* (50 pop.), a beautiful district of summer homes and resorts.

Cutting into the side of a cliff, US 101 skirts the south shore of LAKE CRESCENT (*boats, fishing*), 31.5 *m.* (579 alt.). Cupped about by steep, forested mountain slopes, the lake's smooth surface reflects an alpine setting that has made it the leading resort center in the northern section of the Olympic Peninsula. Many inns, camps, and cottages border the route around its curving shores. The bottom of the lake, some 600 feet below the surface, is lower than sea level. It is the only known home of the Beardslee trout, noted for its fighting qualities; some of these fish weigh as much as 35 pounds.

The STORM KING GUARD STATION and a STATE FISH HATCHERY, 35.3 *m.*, are at the mouth of Barnes Creek; the huge bulk of Mount Storm King, center of a game refuge, rises darkly to the left. To the south and west of Storm King are the peaks of LIZARD HEAD (5,351 alt.), AURORA (4,708 alt.), and SOURDOUGH (4,250 alt.). At the guard station is a junction with a forest trail.

Left on this trail through a game refuge and up the slope of Mount Storm King. At 4 *m.* a promontory looks down on Lake Crescent, tinged in summer with sky-blue and the green of bordering mountain slopes, and silvered by snowy, overhanging peaks from late fall to early spring. Rising almost perpendicularly from its north shore is the sharp peak of PYRAMID MOUNTAIN (3,140 alt.). In the rugged region to the south, deer are plentiful.

US 101 skirts the base of Aurora Peak. Midway on the lake's south shore is the LA POEL FOREST CAMP AND GUARD STATION (*camping facilities*), 39.1 *m.*, an improved campground with individual camping spots. The highway passes the end of the lake, 41.2 *m.*, and traverses a narrow, flat valley bounded by abrupt ridges on either side. MOUNT MULLER (3,760 alt.) can be seen from here (R).

At 42.8 *m.* is a junction with a forest road.

Left here along the SOLEDUCK RIVER, one of the largest and longest streams on the peninsula, into the upper Soleduck area to EAGLE FOREST GUARD STATION, 12 *m.* The setting is one of rare beauty with many mountain tarns, cataracts, and large streams. Across the Soleduck River from Eagle Guard Station is the SOL DUC HOT SPRINGS, 0.3 *m.* (1,200 alt., 10 pop.), where a large swimming tank is filled with naturally hot mineralized water. A trail here leads south through the wilds of the Mount Olympus National Monument to the headwaters of the Soleduck River. A branch trail traverses the western slope of the Olympic National Forest along one of its largest streams.

An Indian legend relates that two dragons, *Sol Duc* and *Elwha,* engaged in bitter conflict. As neither could subdue the other, they crept back to their caverns, sealed the entrances, and wept tears of mortification. Their tears form the Sol Duc and Olympic hot springs.

West of the junction, a large area of burnt-over land reaches from the road to the crest of steep overhanging mountains. A sign along the way relates that 150,000 acres of virgin timber were burned here in four hours—an impressive fire warning. The SNIDER RANGER

STATION and a CCC Camp, 50.2 *m.,* lie along the highway within the SOL DUC PLANTATION, an area set aside for planting new forests. Two million trees were planted between the years 1909 and 1937.

SAPPHO (*tourist cabins*), 58.2 *m.* (115 alt., 130 pop.), is a Bloedel-Donovan logging camp. Nondescript cottages, lined one against the other in a vast expanse of logged-off lands, provide a startling contrast to the clean immensity of their mountain surroundings and to the swift rush of the Soleduck River, which flows at their doorsteps.

In SAPPHO is a junction with State 9A, a graveled road.

Right through a barren, logged-off area, State 9-A crosses a low pass and descends along the headwaters of Beaver Creek, traversing an amazingly broken country of small bluffs and deep, crooked gullies. Passing Beaver Lake, a small body of swamp-brown water set in a marshy valley, the road winds into the Pysht River Valley and along the river. Most of the timber has been logged off, but there are still some stands and considerable logging activity in the area.

At 9 *m.* is a junction with a graveled road: Left here to PYSHT (Ind. fish), 5 *m.* (sea level, 120 pop.), at the mouth of Pysht River. Large log rafts are made up here for shipment to Puget Sound ports. A group of 20 buildings at Pysht was built as headquarters of the Merrill-Ring Logging Company. The ground was laid out and work started on the buildings in 1918. It is believed to be the best-planned logging headquarters in the State. The buildings, built mainly to house single men, are heavy and sturdy. Dining hall, club and recreation hall, theater, school, shops, and a roundhouse are laid out along the curving banks of the Pysht River, where logging railroads converge.

On the main side road, which penetrates a logged-off area with a few patches of second-growth timber, is CLALLAM BAY, 15.2 *m.* (15 alt., 200 pop.), with a hotel, store, a few weathered buildings, and a long dock. West of Clallam Bay the road follows along the Strait. Across the Strait Vancouver Island appears, a blue mist in the distance.

At 16.5 *m.* is a junction with a dirt road: Right 0.2 *m.* to SEKIU, on the edge of a small, wide-mouthed bay. This village is a make-up point for Bloedel-Donovan log rafts. A dump pier extends far into the water to facilitate making up the log booms. At 18.7 *m.* is a junction with a graveled road. Bordered by dense timber, the road skirts the small and picturesque Hoko River on a steadily ascending grade; occasional openings cut into the forest are occupied by prosperous-looking farms.

At 18.3 *m.* is a junction with a dirt road: Right here to SWAN BAY, a small inlet on LAKE OZETTE, 19.5 *m.,* which stretches its length into the forest wilderness. Relatively undeveloped as a resort center, the lake retains most of its original wild beauty. OZETTE (*campgrounds*), 20 *m.,* is situated on a creek flowing out of the lake.

North of the junction the main side road traverses the north side of a valley marked by pastures and dairy farms. The route affords a sweeping view of the broad Strait, where huge waves driven by westerly winds from the Pacific Ocean roll through the passage. The highway crosses the boundary of the MAKAH INDIAN RESERVATION, 30.7 *m.*

The WAADAH POINT COAST GUARD STATION, 32.5 *m.,* stands on the shore of the Strait. During the spring, summer, and autumn the personnel is kept busy watching out for fishing boats and vessels in Neah Bay.

NEAH BAY, 33.7 *m.* (10 alt., 550 pop.), headquarters of the reservation, was known to early settlers as Poverty Cove. It occupies a crescent-shaped flat at the foot of wooded and logged-off ridges in a sheltered bay in the lee of Cape Flattery. Extending into the bay are two long slips, to which are tied dozens of fish boats and houseboats.

On May 29, 1791, the Spanish frigate *Princesa* landed here, with the first settlers to touch the soil of what is now the State of Washington. The colonists, coming from San Blas, Mexico, headed by Lieutenant Fidalgo, were ordered by the expedition leader, Bodega y Quadra, to "establish a small battery on the mainland, respectable fortifications, provisional barracks for the sick, a bakery and oven, and a blacksmith shop, and to cut down all trees within musket shot." The place was called *Bahia Nunez Gaona* in honor of an archbishop of Mexico. In five months, the establishment was abandoned. Documents, including letters to the Viceroy of Spain, the diary of the second mate of the *Princesa,* and a model of the ship are preserved in the collection of J. S. Whiting and A. J. Petite, of Seattle. Brick and tile used by these Spanish builders are occasionally found in the vicinity. Some are on display at the Washington State Historical Society's museum in Tacoma.

The early settlement at Neah Bay was fostered by Samuel Hancock, a wagon maker who was engaged to come West with a pioneer wagon train, in or about 1845. He arrived at Newmarket, now Tumwater (*see Tour 8d*), about 1847 and moved north to Neah Bay about 1851. Here he built the first trading post and a warehouse for storing and shipping whale oil brought to him by the natives.

Neah Bay is the headquarters of the MAKAH INDIAN RESERVATION. The Makah (Ind. cape people) are the last of a warlike tribe, a branch of the Nootka, whose chief abode is on the outer side of Vancouver Island, and more closely connected with the culture of southeastern Alaska than with that of other Washington Indians. The Makah once excelled in the art of canoe making, their finished canoes ranging from the shovel-nose dugout, used in ascending shallow streams and capable of carrying one or two persons, to the ocean-going whaling canoe. In great canoes, the Makah once braved the dangers of crashing surf and ocean. A harpoon or spear with detachable head was thrown at the whale. Attached to each harpoon was a stout rope about 20 feet in length (made from cedar bark chewed by Indian women) with a float attached, usually an inflated seal bladder. When close enough for the first thrust, the harpooner threw his barbed weapon, aiming just above the huge flipper of the exposed side. The float was thrown overboard, as the oarsman back-watered to avoid the lashing tail and pounding fins of the whale.

Floats prevented the whale from diving too deep and assisted the canoeman in tracing his course. When the animal came up to breathe, another spear was thrown. In this manner several floats were attached; the whale, unable to dive, was killed and towed ashore. Often as many as eight days were consumed in beaching the carcass. Chunks of blubber were cut from the carcass until the tenderloin lay exposed, and on this flesh the Indians feasted. Much meat was smoked and salted for future use.

From Neah Bay a trail leads L. to CAPE FLATTERY, 5 *m.,* where diminutive, rockbound TATOOSH ISLAND lies one-half mile off the Washington Coast, at the entrance to the Strait. A lighthouse and meteorological station here have served navigators of surrounding waters for many years. Captain John Meares named the island in 1788. In 1857, a lighthouse was built on the island to warn vessels from the dangerous rocks that menaced the entrance to the Strait.

Today, 12 families are stationed on the island. There are no wharves, and rock cliffs drop perpendicularly into the sea. The weekly mail and supplies are lifted from the boat by an overhanging crane. Besides a naval station on the island there is also a school and post office. The impossibility of landing or delivering supplies during heavy weather makes it advisable to carry six-months' supplies on this insular dot. During the fall, the sea in the vicinity is alive with fishing vessels. In October 1939, the light keeper counted 436 trolling boats within a radius of five miles.

South of the junction US 101 follows the Soleduck River through an area of burned-over lands.

BEAVER, 61.2 *m.* (400 alt., 50 pop.), a remnant of a former logging camp, is the site of the LAKE TYEE FOREST CAMP (R). In Beaver is a junction with a dirt road.

Right here 0.2 *m.,* to LAKE TYEE (*fishing*).

At 67.5 *m.* is a junction with State 9-B, a graveled road.

Right on this road through stump lands and a heavily forested region of large cedars and firs. Supplemented by "gyppo" outfits (small crews of men subcontracting certain portions of the job), the work of cutting this great timber goes forward under the direction of the contractor. Logging with a "sky-line" outfit entails expensive preparations, warranted only in large tracts of timber. First, two "spar trees" are selected, one at the pole deck (point of loading), and the other near the far side of the tract. A "high-rigger" climbs to the top of the tree to be felled, by looping his belt around the trunk and driving his spurs into the heavy bark, and then descends, stripping the tall, straight trunk of its branches as he goes.

At a point 120 to 150 feet from the ground, he chops or saws away until the top slowly leans over, falls away, and tumbles to the ground, leaving the bare pole swaying. The rigger clings to it as it whips about. Great care must be exercised in the use of the ax as a miss would sever the safety belt. The great cable is then suspended between the two spar trees, near the tops. Upon this aerial, or highline, is a huge block that acts as a trolley for the several cables suspended from it and the logs, or trees, being hauled to the pole deck. When the donkey engine begins to wind up the main line, the log is raised until it is suspended in mid-air, then drawn on to the pole deck. Tractors are coming more and more into use in modern logging.

At 2.8 *m.* on the main side road is a junction with a graveled road. Left here the dirt road winds through dank forests, where giant firs and cedars in heavy underbrush narrow the road until it seems a shadowed ditch, walled in by high green banks. At 7 *m.* is a junction with another graveled road: Right here 0.2 *m.* is the SOLEDUCK RIVER BRIDGE. A few hundred feet left of the bridge, the Soleduck and the Bogachiel Rivers converge to form a great pool 50 feet deep and perhaps 200 feet in diameter. From this confluence is formd "The river without a head"—the Quillayute (Ind.), only six miles long. At 4 *m.* on this graveled road is MORA (sea level, 50 pop.), a fishing village at the mouth of the river. The main side road crosses the QUILLAYUTE RIVER, 8.2 *m.*, and enters the QUILLAYUTE INDIAN RESERVATION, 11.8 *m.* At LA PUSH, 13 *m.* (sea level, 270 pop.), on the sea coast, a COAST GUARD STATION overlooks the village and the mouth of the river. In the town, cottages range raggedly about the old Shaker Church, built in 1880 and still in good repair. For a small sum the Indians will take a visitor for a canoe ride through the surf. This port, the only shelter between Cape Flattery and Grays Harbor, is noted along the coast for fishing activities. During the season, tenders come into the Quillayute estuary two and three times a week.

Where the long beach at La Push slopes down to the Pacific, surf breaks against giant rocks. One of these, JAMES ISLAND (183 alt.), with several acres of brush and trees on its summit, stands at the mouth of the Quillayute River and may be reached over the sand beach at low tide. Numerous smaller, wooded islands lie immediately north of it, on the edge of the heavily forested Quillayute River Valley. THE NEEDLES, a series of jagged rocks, extend for more than a mile out into the ocean (L).

A few picnic tables on the beach at La Push are most in use during the annual first of July celebration, when the Quillayute join with the Queet, Quinault, and Hoh tribes to commemorate the signing of their treaty with the United States in 1885. Besides the water sports in which these Indians excel, native games and dances are performed.

Basket weaving, to supply the tourist trade, has reached a high degree of craftsmanship among the women of the village. Baskets range in size and shape from those no bigger than a dollar to models shaped like cedar chests. The men of the village build their houses, carve seaworthy canoes with attractively hand-carved prows, make and mend their fish-nets, and do the fishing.

The legends of the Quillayute, filled with the exploits of the Thunderbird and other mythical characters, still live in La Push. Around the home fires old warriors tell how the oldest of five brothers helped the Great Man of the

West to get his wife back, so that the tribe could have salmonberries all the year around. They tell of the adventures of the brother, who was a great whale hunter, and of his girl-bride, Thrush.

At 69 *m.* US 101 enters FORKS (375 alt., 600 pop.), a thriving little logging town near the forks of three rivers, the Calawah, the Bogachiel, and the Soleduck. In marked contrast to the surrounding wilderness and the generally ramshackle air of many small logging settlements, the town is well planned and presents a neat appearance. Modern stores border the main street, where mackinaw-shirted loggers scrape their calked boots along the concrete walks. The town has a weekly paper. A creamery and sawmill supplement logging, its major industry.

Section c. FORKS to ABERDEEN, 117.5 m. US 101

South of FORKS, 0 *m.,* US 101 again enters the deep forest. At a bridge spanning the BOGACHIEL RIVER, 5.7 *m.,* is a junction with a graveled road.

Left here 1 *m.* to BOGACHIEL STATE PARK, a 110-acre tract of woodland with a picnicking and camping area along the river. A trail here follows the stream to its headwaters.

South of the junction the highway swings westward and descends through a heavily wooded area. At 12.2 *m.* is a junction with a graveled road.

Left here through a vast area that drains the western slopes of Mount Olympus. Roughly paralleling the winding course of the Hoh River, the graveled side road enters sections of the Olympic National Forest. Numerous swift-running streams offer good fishing along the route, which ends at a Forest Guard Station, 17 *m.*

The main road swings westerly along the course of the broad Hoh River, frequently following closely upon its wooded banks. At 22.2 *m.* is a junction with a graveled road.

Right here over a 400-foot suspension bridge spanning the Hoh River. The side road continues over frequent small bridges through the low country that borders the now smoothly flowing stream. In the HOH INDIAN RESERVATION, 3 *m.,* the road ends at the river's mouth on the ocean beach. Offshore, on either side of the river channel, are two huge rocks, subjects of an Indian legend. It is said that before human beings came into the world the Great Changer asked Raven and Crow, two animal people, if they would like to have human people come on earth. "No," they said, "human people would make so much smoke we could not see." Thereupon the Great Changer told them a race of human beings would come anyway, and asked what animals they would like to be turned into in order to meet the new conditions. "Then we would not like to be any animals at all," they answered: "neither bear, elk, or deer; let us be turned into rocks." So there they stand today, the north and south rocks at the mouth of the river.

West of the junction, US 101 skirts the shoreline of the Pacific. A rhythmical sweep of water rolls up the broad beach, breaking into foaming crests and spuming into small, rocky inlets.

At RUBY BEACH, 34.5 *m.* a store, service station, and cabin camp are perched on cliffs above the rumbling surf. Here and there a break in the trees affords a glimpse of white foam flying against the rocky embankment. A trail leads down the bluff 300 yards to the beach. Here huge rocks stand like stone pillars against the sea. Drifting logs and broken trees are ground to bits in the surge of breakers.

OCEAN VIEW STATE PARK (*picnic facilities*), 41 *m.*, is situated on a bluff, where a turnout affords a wide view of the Pacific. To the north a succession of bold promontories reaches into the sea. Westward is DESTRUCTION ISLAND, about four and a half miles offshore, grim and forbidding as a fortress. In 1775, the Spanish explorer Bruno Heceta, having suffered the loss of a small boat's crew in an Indian attack at Point Grenville to the south (*see below*), named the island Isla de Dolores (Sp. Island of Sorrows). In 1787 Captain Charles W. Barkley commanding the East Indian Company's ship *Imperial Eagle,* had a similar experience at the Hoh River, which he named Destruction River. Later the name Destruction was transferred to the Island, and the river was given the name of the Indians who lived along it.

Destruction Island is the nesting ground of some 10,000 horn-billed auklets, small migratory cousins of the celebrated great auk. Not unlike the penguin, they wear dress clothes of formal black or brownish black with a "boiled front" of smoke gray, which extends down the flank. These birds, whose range is the entire Pacific coast, arrive during April and either use their old nest or dig into a hillside to make a new one. Their arrival is marked by a noisy shrieking. They are considered very good eating by the Indians, who occasionally brave the surf to snatch an auklet for dinner during the nesting season. The beach, about 100 feet below the bluff, is easily reached by trail from this point.

KALALOCH, 42.3 *m.* (60 alt., 76 pop.), is a cabin-camp point on Kalaloch Creek, with a store, filling station, post office, and two hotels. The village is noted for the trout, starfish, mussels, sea anemones, and other salt-water specimens found along the shore. Ducks, hell-divers, and loons dive in pursuit of their prey; gulls plunge in spirals upon any fish or bit of food appearing on the surface. Clams especially appeal to the gulls. Picking one up from the beach, the hungry gull ascends, drops the clam unerringly upon a rock, then dives to eat the contents. Agates, moonstones, and oddly shaped bits of driftwood attract souvenir hunters.

A short distance by trail (R) along the beach from Kalaloch is BROWN'S POINT. Here a series of jagged rocks is habitat of the piddock, or boring clam, which has a rare and delicate flavor, easily detectable in soup. When the surf is favorable and the tide reasonably low, seekers for this unusual sea food chop away at the rock with miners' picks.

At 46 *m.* US 101 crosses a boundary of the QUINAULT INDIAN RESERVATION.

QUEETS, 47.6 *m.* (18 alt., 60 pop.), on a tiny inlet at the mouth of the Queets River, is the home of a handful of Indians, remnant of a once powerful Quiatso tribe. They live by fishing and the fashioning of souvenirs. An interesting collection of Indian artifacts may be seen at the village service station. Near the cabin camp is a hewn-log schoolhouse, built about 1914.

At 52.8 *m.* is a junction with a graveled road.

Left here 3 *m.* along the Clearwater River to CLEARWATER STATE PARK (*picnic and camping facilities*) (135 alt.). Right from the park a rough, unimproved road follows the river to the Olympic National Forest. Elk herds are often seen in this region.

At 55.2 *m.* is a junction with a graveled road.

Left here 11 *m.* to KELLY'S DUDE RANCH (*horses for trail trips; expert guides*), in a setting of forest and mountains on the Queets River.

Southeast of the junction, US 101 skirts the northern boundary of the Quinault Indian Reservation and penetrates one of the largest known stands of western red cedar. The trees rise to great heights in a forest darkened by old spruce and hemlock, festooned with hanging moss.

At 71.7 *m.* is a junction with a graveled road.

Left here 3.5 *m.* along the north shore of Lake Quinault to MUNCASTER FOREST CAMP (*camping facilities*), on the lake shore. JULY CREEK CAMP, at 3.5 *m.*, is a shady grove overlooking the lake and mouth of July Creek.

The Quinault River, which flows into the lake, at its northern end, forms a delta with sloughs on either side. Leaving the lake, the road follows the course of the Quinault River north fork through the wild, uninhabited recesses of the Olympic National Forest.

At the NORTH FORK GUARD STATION, 25 *m.*, a Forest Service camp marks the end of the road.

Left by trail here 2 *m.* along the north fork of the Quinault, past its confluence with Rustler Creek to Halfway House (*hotel accommodations by reservation*). Left here 5 *m.* by trail over broken, heavily forested hills to FRANCIS CREEK SHELTER. At 10 *m.* KURTZ LAKE is glimpsed remotely through the forest. THREE PRUNE CAMP, 11 *m.*, commemorates the experience of a party of mountaineers who, after failing to connect with their supply pack train, had three dried prunes each for dinner. The trail crosses a boundary of OLYMPIC NATIONAL FOREST at 15 *m.* and follows the mile-high SKYLINE—QUEETS TRAIL over the ridges toward MOUNT KIMTA, 18 *m.* (5,200 alt.). Precipitous slopes drop from the trail into the Queets Valley. Here MOUNT OLYMPUS, with its array of jagged peaks, stands in full view. Eastward (R) is spread the Quinault River Valley, with snow-clad summits beyond. The trail plunges down 1,000 feet to COLD SPRINGS CAMP, 19 *m.*, and follows Promise Creek (L) to its confluence with the Quinault River. On the bank of the river is SIXTEEN MILE SHELTER, 26.5 *m.* The trail continues through ELK PARK, 27 *m.*, and with steep ascent parallels the Quinault River; rounding MOUNT CHRISTIE (R), 29 *m.*, it passes LOW DIVIDE CHALET (*hotel accommodations by reservation*), at 30.5 *m.*

East of the junction US 101 skirts the south end of Quinault Lake.

AMANDA PARK, 72.4 *m.*, is a small settlement a few hundred yards from the lake, which is blocked from view here by a dense forest.

QUINAULT LAKE, 73.1 *m.* (300 alt.), is Indian property, situated in a recreational area of great beauty. (*Fishing permits obtained from Indian Agent at Hoquiam, or from Quinault Mercantile Company at Quinault Lake. Season from May 15 to July 15*). The Quinault

Indians have lived for centuries at Taholah, at the mouth of the river.

At 73.8 *m.* is a junction with a gravel-surfaced road.

Left here along the south shore of Lake Quinault past resorts and summer homes built among great spruce trees. (*Hotel, cabins, horses, boats, guides*). At 1.4 *m.* a long brown and white three-story hotel overlooks the lake, from the southern end of which the Quinault River flows westward to Taholah, on the ocean beach. Indian canoemen take passengers down the river to Taholah, a thrilling seven-hour journey through black and white water. On the return trip up river, outboard motors are used. An annual trout derby is conducted here by the local Poggie Club on Memorial Day, when Indians stage a water carnival.

A post office, several stores, garages, restaurants, comfortable cabin camps, and resorts dot the lake's shores. From here, guides lead hikers along wilderness trails to glacial peaks, waterfalls, elk country, and hunting areas and fishing spots.

At 1.6 *m.* on the graveled road is FALLS CREEK NATIONAL FOREST CAMP, where the United States Department of Fisheries operates a hatchery (*visitors welcome*). A forest ranger station and forest camp are situated near the mouth of the creek. A trail leads R. through tall timber, dense undergrowth, and a profusion of wild flowers and shrubs. Luxuriant mosses, lichens, and sword-ferns spread on every hand. A fir tree by the trail, more than 30 feet in circumference at the base and more than 500 years old, is a typical specimen of many trees found in this region. Continuing the climb the trail passes through a tunnel cut in a large fallen Douglas fir tree. Waterfalls are heard at many points along the trail; a few are seen. Following the canyon of Willaby Creek, which it crosses over a rustic bridge, the trail continues through jungles of forest growths and along steep rock walls. Dropping to the side of the stream, it breaks out into the sunlight near WILLABY CAMP, 4 *m.* Northeast of the camp the trail continues to GRAVES CREEK, 18 *m.*, and ends at 20 *m.*

From Lake Quinault the highway swings southward through a sparsely settled area of forest land and enters the QUINAULT NATURAL AREA, 73.7 *m.* A few small logging outfits operate here, and vigilance must be maintained for loaded trucks turning into the highway from obscure roads.

At HUMPTULIPS (Ind. hard to pole,) 90.1 *m.* (130 alt., 100 pop.), center of a small farming community, a few unpainted frame buildings stand on a bench above the Humptulips River. Humptulips was the logging outlet for the famous "21-9" (township 21, range 9) stand of Douglas fir, the greatest in the Northwest. Towering timber stood so dense that trees had to be felled in the same direction for lack of space. In one of the Humptulips saloons of that time, a garrulous foreman boasted: "Give me enough snoose and Swedes and I'll log 21-9 like it was a hayfield, dump the toothpicks into the south fork and ride 'em to tidewater like they was rocking horses."

At 108.5 *m.* is a junction with State 9-C, a gravel-surfaced road.

Right here on a loop route along the ocean front. At COPALIS CROSSING, 9.5 *m.* (73 alt., 160 pop.), State 9C divides into two branches. Left (west) here to COPALIS, 15.3 *m.* (15 alt., 400 pop.), a resort on the ocean beach (*swimming, surf-board riding, hiking*). Clams are present in abundance along the beach, and digging them is a favorite sport for both residents and visitors. The Copalis River flows through the town into the Pacific at this point.

Left from Copalis Beach on an unnamed graveled road along the ocean front to OCEAN CITY, 3 *m.* Crab catching is a popular sport here. Shallow lagoons are left in the sand by the retreating tide, and the crab hunters, armed with rakes, wade about in the shallows, poking about prospectively and peering anxiously for some sign of the crab, who is usually hidden just under the sand.

North of Copalis, the west branch of State 9-C follows the shoreline through several small oceanside resorts to PACIFIC BEACH (*modern hotel, cabin camps, garages, service station, cafés, and stores*), 22.8 *m.* In Pacific Beach is a junction with a graveled road. Right on this road, which hugs the coastline to SUNSET BEACH, 1 *m.*, the home of workers employed in the shingle mill at Moclips. Summer cottages and cabins line the shore.

MOCLIPS, 1.8 *m.* (sea level, 300 pop.), is a busy little settlement, supported largely by its shingle mill. The Moclips High School serves the oceanside region north of Grays Harbor, and its gymnasium is used for community gatherings. On the northern outskirts is the MOCLIPS FIRE OBSERVATORY (*open*), atop a 175-foot fir tree.

North along the beach from Moclips is POINT GRENVILLE, 7.8 *m.*, a high promontory jutting out into the Pacific and offering an excellent view. It was here that Bruno Heceta, in command of the *Santiago,* and Bodega y Quadra, commander of the *Sonora,* landed in 1775. Here, also, several of their seamen were ambushed by Indians and massacred. The hulk of the French barque *Ernest Reyer,* cast upon the beach near the turn of the century, is visible at extreme low tide near the mouth of the Quinault River.

TAHOLAH, 10.3 *m.* (sea level, 450 pop.), an Indian village, is agency headquarters for the QUINAULT INDIAN RESERVATION. The tribe is a branch of the Salishan, as are all coastal tribes except the Makah. The reservation comprises nearly 110,000 acres of virgin timber, providing grants of 80 acres to each tribesman, including those with as little as one-eighth Indian blood. Treaty negotiations with the Quinault required many years, and, although the pact was signed on July 1, 1855, the reservation was not established until November 4, 1873, when the treaty was signed by President Grant. In Pacific Beach, State 9-C loops southeast through a logged-off area that is slowly being converted into a district of small farms. Some of the prospective farmers, while they laboriously clear the stumps from the fields, live in weather-beaten frame houses built during the days when the area boomed with the activity of logging camps.

ALOHA, 24 *m.* (50 alt., 200 pop.), recalls some of the robustness of the intensive logging days. A small shingle mill employs most of the population. In CARLISLE, 28 *m.* (76 alt., 75 pop.), a ghost logging town, forlorn cottages line both sides of the road, mingling with weather-beaten business buildings and mill structures that hang on in anticipation of a lumbering revival.

At 37 *m.* the route returns to the junction of State 9-C and US 101.

South of the junction US 101 traverses a rolling region, logged-off, burned-over, and desolate. New growth is beginning to cover the logged-off areas. At POLSON STATE PARK, 110.5 *m.*, the State is converting a 310-acre stand of timber into a recreation area.

HOQUIAM, 113 *m.* (300 alt., 10,835 pop.), ABERDEEN, 117.5 *m.* (365 alt., 18,846 pop.) (*see Aberdeen-Hoquiam*).

Hoquiam and Aberdeen are at a junction with US 410 (*see Tour 2d*).

Section d. ABERDEEN *to* MEGLER, *US 101, 84 m.*

South of Aberdeen, US 101 cuts through a forested area to the meandering shore lines of Willapa Bay, home of the Pacific Oyster industry, a region of quiet lagoons and great oyster flats, redolent at low tide with pungent marsh grass and drying seaweed. Entering a wooded section, the highway comes out upon a long stretch of ocean beach, where a side road leads through a scattering of gay seaside resorts, and graying hamlets, remnants of Washington's earliest pioneering. Continuing southward, US 101 emerges at the mouth of the broad Columbia, where a ferry connects with Astoria, Oregon.

In ABERDEEN-HOQUIAM, 0 *m.,* US 101 swings southward across the steel and concrete Chehalis River bridge to a junction with State 13-A, an oiled gravel-surfaced road.

Right on State 13-A, which parallels the south shore of Grays Harbor, one of the world's greatest lumber-shipping ports. On the broad surface of the bay, lumber schooners, fish boats, and log booms move slowly against the background of the Aberdeen-Hoquiam industrial water front. On CHARLIE CREEK, 3.8 *m.,* is the BEACHWAY RIDING CLUB, where saddle horses may be rented for jaunts down the shore or through the country. Close-cropped meadow lands, dropping occasionally to marshes, border the ever-widening water boundaries of the harbor.

MARKHAM, 12 *m.* (10 alt., 260 pop.), long dependent upon a small shingle mill, has benefited in recent years from development of a large oyster bed. An oyster cannery now furnishes seasonal employment to residents of the community. At OCOSTA, 15 *m.* (6 alt., 157 pop.), an attractive group of modern school buildings serves a scattered community. In the nineties the Northern Pacific Railway boomed the site as its railway terminus on Grays Harbor. Lots were sold and buildings were erected, but shortly afterward, the railroad switched its terminal to Aberdeen, and the town lapsed into obscurity. On a bare, uninhabited flat near the beach, State 13-A passes between two leaning old buildings, the last remnants of the old town.

BAY CITY, 17 *m.* (sea level, 30 pop.), a scattered little community on South Bay, was for many years the site of a whaling station, where the rendering of whale oil and blubber, and sundry dissections of the world's largest mammal, treated passing motorists to an unforgettable olfactory experience. West of Bay City, the highway crosses a long, curving wooden bridge over the flats of the Elk River Slough, beginning of the midsection of a canal that will extend south from Puget Sound at Olympia, on Budd's Inlet, to connect with the Columbia River by an inland water route. Commencing at Olympia, the first section will run westward to Grays Harbor; thence south from South Bay to the north side of Willapa Bay near Tokeland (*see below*).

At COHASSET, 20 *m.* (sea level, 30 pop.), a summer oceanside resort (*beach cottages and cabins*), is a junction of State 13-A and another oiled gravel-surfaced road. Right on this road to WESTPORT, 2 *m.* (sea level, 272 pop.), on a sandy arm tipped by Point Chehalis, which bounds Grays Harbor on the southwest. Its wide, wind-swept street is bordered on one side by small store buildings. Modest cottages and summer homes are shaded by great fir and pine trees. The town looks down upon a sheltered cove, the harbor for a crab and salmon-fishing fleet of 200 boats. Ducks and geese are numerous along the saltwater marshes.

A gravel-surfaced road leads north from the end of Westport's main street to the port entrance and COAST GUARD BASE. The site was named Peterson's Point for Glenn Peterson, first settler in 1858, but with the growth of the settlement the name was changed to Westport. Established here in 1860 for the protection of white settlers was Old Fort Chehalis, long since in ruins. A tablet erected on the site commemorates the services of Company A, 4th United States infantry, occupants of the fort in early days. The first school in the county was established here in the late fifties. At Damon's Point, Government engineers are pushing a jetty into the ocean, to prevent the blocking of the harbor channel. Wastes of powdery sand stretch away on every side, sloping down to a smooth, hard floor that disappears under a thundering surf. A low white lighthouse looms dimly, and the intermittent wail of a fog horn comes through the mist that seems ever present. South of Cohasset the road, concrete-paved from this point, borders the ocean. Deep clumps of heavy fir grow close to the ground, their tops blown flat by ocean gales.

GRAYLAND, 24 *m.* (sea level, 250 pop.), is a village of Finnish cranberry growers. In the neighborhood are more than 100 cranberry bogs. One block (L) from the highway is a long street bordered with neat, well-painted houses, each set trimly at the edge of its own rectangular cranberry field. Narrow-gauge tracks run down the center of the field, carrying spraying apparatus and fertilizer. The plants, tiny green and pink rosettes, are wedged tightly together; in the autumn they take on a crimson tint. Cranberry plants require four years to mature and must be sprayed at least ten times each year; as no part of the field may be trod on during cultivation, spraying becomes a rather arduous task. In picking the berries, a pronged scoop is used, which strips the little plants clean without injuring them. Each planter handles his crop without hired help. The Finns, marketing the berries through a co-operative, have little difficulty in disposing of their entire crop.

Unlike the stump-ranching communities, nothing is ramshackle or rambling in Grayland; there are no broken fences, hanging gates, straying cattle, or other irregularities; fresh paint and shining windows are the rule in the village. The Finns credit their good health to the Finnish steam bath; some supplement the bath by beating their bodies with cedar boughs to aid blood circulation. Midsummer Day, the twenty-fourth of June, is celebrated with bonfires, folk dancing, and other outdoor exercises. Native costumes are worn at the festivities, which usually last all night.

South of Grayland, the road closely borders the ocean beach. Dunes of fine gray sand shift continually along the flat shoreline, restrained only by the rambling sand verbena, whose vining stalks, rubbery leaves, and small yellow blossoms stubbornly resist the wind. Here and there a fresh drift engulfs the brushy growth along the shore. Occasional clumps of stubby, gale-bent trees, gray with lichen, cling tenaciously to the land's edge, as though conscious that this is their last grip on the North American Continent—westward there is no soil for 5,000 miles. From the outer rim of the beach the traveler's gaze into space is interrupted only by the funnels of an occasional ship, reminding him in passing that the earth is a globe.

At NORTH COVE, 31 *m.* (sea level, 75 pop.), are Coast Guard and Life Saving stations and the Willapa Bay Lighthouse. During the summer, vacationists enjoy the Cove's sandy beach and sheltered waters. Adjoining is the SHOALWATER INDIAN RESERVATION, known locally as the Georgetown Reservation, after the George family of Indians. It skirts an indentation on the north shore of Willapa Bay and is a popular summer fishing ground for the Shoalwater and Quinault Indians.

Leaving North Cove, the gravel road continues to TOKELAND, 36 *m.* (sea level, 89 pop.), named for Chief Toke. Today it is the headquarters of a crab-fishing fleet and, because of its broad sandy beach and protected waters, a favored summer resort.

South of the junction US 101 bears away from the harbor toward COSMOPOLIS, 2.3 *m.* (9 alt., 1,207 pop.). Here a collection of old frame dwellings, many of them vacant, shows the harsh effects of the decline of lumbering in the region. Fittingly enough, the inhabitants of Cosmopolis are mostly millworkers of many nationalites. The town was one of the first sawmill centers established in the Grays Harbor district.

At 7.3 *m.* is a junction with State 9, which leads to Montesano (*see Tour 2d*). ARTIC, 8.5 *m.* (104 alt., 267 pop.), is a small settlement represented on the highway by a store and service station. The story of its naming may serve as a lesson to scrawly writers and hasty readers. Its founder named the settlement for his wife, Arta, but, when application for a post office reached Washington, the carelessly written final "a" was read as "ic". Hence Artic, a simplified form of "arctic," became the name of the town, and Arta, the wife, is not memorialized.

The highway bridges the NORTH RIVER, 9 *m.,* a tumultuous stream that flows with many twists and turns through a wild, unsettled country. RAYMOND, at 24.5 *m.* (11 alt., 4,045 pop.), is a lively and independent little town on the estuary of the Willapa River. It derives its prosperity from lumber manufacture, oyster culture, and shipping; and the ups and downs of the lumber industry are markedly reflected in Raymond.

In 1861, the schooner *Willamette* with its master and owner, Captain John Vail, was wrecked at the harbor entrance. Bearing no grudge for so costly an introduction to these shores, Vail homesteaded a claim on the present townsite. After his death his widow married John Adams, builder of the first sawmill in the Willapa Harbor. In 1895 the Northern Pacific Railway extended lines through the little settlement, but not until 1904 was a plat filed. The town was named for L. V. Raymond, the first postmaster.

The original business district straddled the odorous tide flats on "sea legs." Its narrow wooden sidewalks and roughly planked streets swarmed with reveling loggers on Saturday nights. The town grew rapidly with the expanding lumber industry, and in 1912 an enlarged city was planned, and dredging and filling were started. Then came one of the periodic slumps; lumber and shingle exports fell away, and Raymond's bubble burst. The depressed conditions resulted also in unemployment and economic distress. During this troubled time, members of the I.W.W. were driven from the city by a vigilante "pick-handle brigade." By 1915, however, prosperity returned, and the expansion of the lumber market resulted in the enlargement of the lumber plants; at the same time a branch of the Chicago, Milwaukee, St. Paul and Pacific Railroad was completed, making new markets accessible to the wood-products industry. Many new logging camps were opened up; and during the First World War ten wooden freighters were launched from a hastily built shipyard. Controversy between lumber operators and workers over hours, wages, and conditions threatened to curtail production at a time when lumber was acutely needed. After several companies of the United States Army's Spruce Division had been stationed in Raymond, the crisis passed. Working conditions were considerably improved, and several sawmills began to operate. The town's population soared to nearly 7,000.

During the twenties, disastrous fires reduced the number of sawmills, and population again dwindled; but new impetus was given the town by the dredging of the Willapa River channel and reclamation of the tideflat area. Ocean-borne trade was thus made possible, and the town itself had space for expansion of business and residential districts. The Weyerhaeuser Timber Company made available great areas of virgin timber, on which the mills could feed. Today the majority of the loggers and sawmill workers are organized in the A. F. of L. and C. I. O. Approximately 120,000,000 board feet of lumber are manufactured in Raymond annually; and an estimated 30,000,000,000 feet of timber remain in the region.

Raymond's PUBLIC LIBRARY (*open 1-6; 7-9 weekdays*), 6th and Duryea Sts., an attractive two-story frame building of gray shakes, houses a collection of 12,000 volumes. Windows in the adult reading room are fitted with art-glass panes reproducing old English bookplates, and in the children's room similar panes depict old nursery rhymes. The west-wing basement has a 200-seat auditorium, with stage lighting system and independent entrances to facilitate dramatic presentations.

The red buildings of the WILLAPA HARBOR LUMBER MILLS (*open by arrangement*), foot of Ellis St., sprawl under great belching smokestacks. Behind them a healthy forest of second-growth fir spreads over a hillside.

In Raymond, on 3rd Street, is a junction with State 12 (*see Tour 8d*).

Leaving Raymond, US 101 parallels the deeply dredged Willapa. At the southern outskirts, on a sheltered portion of the river, is the PORT OF WILLAPA HARBOR, where are numerous warehouses, docks, derricks, and other shipping facilities. Ocean-bound freighters may be seen loading lumber at the port. Here the Willapa flows through a channel at the foot of a great hill. The channel is not visible from the highway, and it is a startling sight to behold an incoming ocean freighter riding high and apparently pushing its way on dry land around the base of a small mountain.

SOUTH BEND, 28.8 *m.* (11 alt., 1,771 pop.), entered from the east on Water St., is the seat of Pacific County and a lumber and shingle-manufacturing center. Proximity to the great oyster-growing beds of Willapa Harbor has made oyster canning an important industry. The stores and dwellings of the town, built on a narrow shelf between the hills and the river, are crowded close to the principal street and highway for a distance of nearly two miles. An annual event is the Water Carnival, held on the Willapa River each Labor Day.

In the sixties and seventies, South Bend was the metropolis of the County and a key point in the water and stagecoach transportation system of Washington Territory. Many quaint buildings, ornamented with scrollwork and filigree and crowned with cupolas, reflect this early-day glory. The old-fashioned, silver-domed COURTHOUSE on Vine Street, in a carefully landscaped park overlooking the city, recalls the days when the streets echoed the soft clop-clop of horses' hoofs and the quiet rattle of buggy wheels.

South Bend's first school (1875) is remembered for the novel method of instruction employed by the first teacher, John Dodge, an elderly man with long gray hair and flowing beard. Dodge insisted on teaching his pupils the alphabet by singing it to them. Lewis R. Williams in *Our Pacific County* states that "it took beginners about two years to learn it under his system, and although many of his pupils were sixteen and seventeen years old, he made it plain they were not old enough, nor sufficiently advanced, to take up the study of English grammar!"

The pastoral calm of the little settlement was greatly disturbed in 1892, when the town won the county seat from Oysterville, a rival across the bay. After a heated argument over the elections, during which the opposing town refused to give up the county records, a body of South Bend citizens appeared suddenly in Oysterville, one Sunday morning in February 1893, and departed unceremoniously with books and records.

In 1895, the Northern Pacific Railroad tapped the rich timberland adjacent to South Bend, and a period of swift expansion began. Promoters built a turreted 400-room hotel on the crest of the highest hill; opened it with a grand ball and riotous celebration; but closed it immediately afterward, without its ever having sheltered a paying guest. The real-estate schemes of the period were similarly deflated, but they did succeed in attracting many settlers. Lumber, shellfish, and improved transportation facilities aided in stabilizing the town, which became the political center of the region.

US 101 leaves South Bend to swing around the palisades of Willapa Harbor on a picturesque route. Flats alternate with winding inclines over timbered headlands, where the road runs through gaps of red earth lined with varicolored strata. On the flats between headlands are marshy meadows, some diked and converted into lush fields where cattle graze.

At 39.2 *m.* is a junction with an improved road.

Right on this road is the village of BAY CENTER, 2 *m.* (sea level, 200 pop.), with its large oyster cannery and shell-crushing plant. The first discovery of oysters on the Pacific Coast was made between 1849 and 1851 at Shoalwater Bay, now known as Willapa Harbor, widely known for its oyster culture.

Midway across the bay (R) stand the ruins of WILLAPACIFIC, most shameless of the "land" ventures promoted about 1900. A platform, the size of a city block, was erected on piles driven into the tideflats—here was to rise the "Venice of the Northwest"—and adjacent lots were sold to remote investors. The planking has rotted away, but a cluster of piling remains.

South of the junction, US 101 borders the bay and crosses the north and middle forks of the Nemah River. At low tide the flats of Willapa Bay extend almost as far as the eye can see. Here, in the shallows, the long-legged crane is a common sight, standing motionless for long periods, resting gravely on one foot. At a crossroad known as JOHNSON'S LANDING, 55.8 *m.*, is a junction with US 830 (*see Tour 3b*). US 101 bears right from this junction, crossing the slough of the Naselle River. LONG ISLAND, seven miles long, sprawls lazily across the river mouth at the south end of Willapa Bay.

At 70.3 *m.* is a junction with two side roads, entrances to a popular playground, the NORTH PENINSULA, a slim finger of land extending parallel to the mainland for more than 25 miles along the coast. Little more than a mile wide, it forms the barrier between Willapa Bay and the ocean.

1. Right from the junction a gravel-surfaced road follows the bay shore along a slightly crested upland, a region of dairy farms, patches of woodland,

cultivated cranberry land, and several small lakes, the joy of bass fishers. Signs along the route offer fresh oysters for sale, and at intervals the traveler arrives at an oyster farm, its pastures the pungent mud flats of Willapa Bay. The warm, shallow tide creeps twice daily over the flats, bringing the oysters their food and furnishing the peninsula its leading industry.

At 12.6 *m.* on the graveled road is a junction with a side road. Left on this road 1.3 *m.* to OCEAN PARK (sea level, 250 pop.), which began as a camp-meeting resort. Along the main street is the WRECKAGE, a house built of material cast up on the beach: logs, planks, and shingle bolts. Furniture is constructed of curious bits of bleached driftwood and grotesquely shaped fragments of flotsam. Near by is the MARINE STUDIO (*open*) of Charles L. Fitzpatrick, a marine photographer known for his pictures of wrecks and other scenes along the ocean front.

NAHCOTTA, 13 *m.* (sea level, 50 pop.), near numerous oyster beds, is the site of a large oyster cannery. In 1889 Nahcotta became the northern terminal of a narrow-gauge railroad now abandoned, which once constituted the transportation system of the peninsula. OYSTERVILLE, 17 *m.* (sea level, 38 pop.), the most northerly settlement on the peninsula, was founded in 1854, and became the seat of Pacific County in 1861. For a while oystering prospered, but the town declined when parasites and pollution of the waters caused severe losses. The rival town of South Bend, pointing to promised railroad connections, won the county seat in 1892 (*see above*). In the long dispute that followed, Oysterville protested that railroad workers had been illegally allowed ballots in order to swing the vote. The Oysterville courthouse, from which determined South Bend citizens carried off the records, was used later as a schoolhouse but is now a dairy barn. Left from Oysterville, the main side road cuts across the narrow peninsula to the ocean beach and ends at 17.5 *m.*

2. Left (*straight ahead*) from the junction is SEAVIEW, 0.3 *m.* (sea level, 300 pop.), entrance to the seaside resorts of the North Peninsula. Along the ocean front are a number of beach colonies offering excellent opportunities for sea- and sun-bathing, clam digging, crab catching, deep-sea fishing, horseback riding, and bicycling over the hard beach sands. (*Resorts have life guards, but swimming is advisable only at flood tide, because of the strong undertow at the ebb*). The KNOWLES STUDIO (*open*) is maintained by Joe Knowles, an artist and exponent of woodcraft. Knowles, who is one-eighth Chippewa, was a guide in the Maine woods when a magazine publisher saw some of his drawings on birch bark and purchased a hunting subject for a cover design. Later Knowles became a portrait painter. In 1913 he entered the wilds of northern Maine, to prove that civilized man, having knowledge of woodcraft, could survive in the wilderness without clothing, weapons, or implements of any kind. After two months he came out of the forest, fully dressed in skins, and in better physical condition than when he went in. The Maine woods experience is related in his *Alone in the Wilderness*. In 1917 Knowles came to live at Seaview. The murals in the lobby of the Monticello Hotel, in Longview (*see Tour 3b*), are his work. Many of the etchings on display in the studio are imprinted on sheets of pulp paper that was washed ashore in the wreck of the *Iowa* in 1936.

Right from Seaview on State 12-A is LONG BEACH (*accommodations of all kinds*), 1 *m.* (sea level, 620 pop.), on what is claimed to be the longest hard beach in the world, approximately 300 feet wide at low tide and more than 28 miles long. There are no speed limits here, and auto racing is a favorite sport. The varicolored stones in the LEWIS AND CLARK MONUMENT at Long Beach were contributed by various communities along the route followed by the Lewis and Clark Expedition. To the monument is attached a marble plaque marking the end of the north coastal exploration. Near by is an attractive log building almost covered with vines, with a log observation tower. North of Long Beach, the highway passes a number of small beach colonies, their population varying with the seasons. At 8 *m.* is a COAST GUARD AND NAVAL RADIO COMPASS STATION.

South of the junction US 101 turns left, bordering marshy TAR-

LETT SLOUGH. On Baker Bay, just inside the mouth of the Columbia River, is ILWACO, 71.6 *m.* (sea level, 656 pop.), named for Elowahka Jim, son-in-law of the powerful Chief Comcomly, who was the leader of many Indian tribes in this region. Captain James Johnson visited the harbor in 1848, took up a donation claim and built a house, but left shortly afterward. Actual settlement was begun by Henry Feister in 1851, when he opened an ox-team transportation system for hauling supplies to settlers on Shoalwater Bay (Willapa Harbor). By the late sixties the town was a stopping point on the expanding stagecoach and ferry route between Astoria, Oregon, and the Puget Sound country. Stagecoaches were displaced in 1889 by a narrow-gauge railroad, variously called the Ilwaco and Shoalwater Bay Railroad and the Ilwaco Railway and Navigation Company. The road came under the control of the Oregon-Washington Railroad and Navigation Company in 1889 and served the North Peninsula until abandoned in 1930. Connecting with a ferry to Astoria, trains ran on a schedule that varied with the tides—it was only certain that no train would appear at the same hour two days in succession. Along the brief main thoroughfare, the trackage of the old railroad may still be seen.

Tall headlands on the west protect Ilwaco from blasts that seasonally rake the Pacific. The harbor, a haven for fishing vessels, has several salmon canneries; most of these have been closed since 1935, however, as a consequence of the removal of fixed gear, popularly known as fish traps, from Columbia River waters.

Right from Ilwaco on Fort Canby Road, 1.5 *m.,* to a junction with two roads. Right (north) to OCEANVIEW (*summer hotels*), 0.5 *m.,* from which the noted FISHING ROCKS can be seen along the cliff-lined beach. From these rocks fishermen cast lines into the surf below, catching sea bass, perch, flounder, skate, and occasionally halibut. (*No license is required except for cutthroat fishing*).

Left (south) 1.8 *m.* to BEARD'S HOLLOW, a rocky indentation at the base of a precipice. The hollow was named for Captain E. N. Beard, commander of the bark *Vandelia,* which foundered off the mouth of the Columbia in 1853. All hands were lost, and the ship was found floating bottom side up near McKenzie Head. Captain Beard's body was found on the beach below present Beard's Hollow.

The road swings R., 2 *m.,* on a short jog of a few hundred yards to the high promontory of NORTH HEAD, where a LIGHTHOUSE stands above the sea that roars against the rocks of DEAD MAN'S HOLLOW (L). This hollow also was named for the lost sailors of the *Vandelia.* At the U. S. WEATHER BUREAU OBSERVATORY a large telescope enables visitors to look to the south across the wide mouth of the Columbia. From this vantage point it is easy to understand why sailors feared this entrance; before the construction of jetties to control its bar, it was known as the "Graveyard of the Pacific." On Peacock Spit immediately below may be seen a few remnants of wrecked ships. On fair days Tillamook Rock, 22 miles distant down the Oregon Coast, is clearly visible.

FORT CANBY (*open by permission*), 4 *m.,* built in 1864, one of the earliest forts in Washington, was named for Major General Edward Richard Canby. An important base in pioneer days, overlooking the Columbia River entrance, it has been on the inactive list for some time. CAPE DISAPPOINTMENT LIGHT HOUSE, on the military reservation, stands on the tall headland named by Captain John Meares, who rounded the cape in 1788. Captain Meares, failing to perceive that he was at the outlet of a great river, named the cape in chagrin. The sheltered water behind the cape, now known as Baker Bay, he named Deception Bay.

East of Ilwaco, the paved road follows the shore line of Baker Bay, the prospective terminus of the proposed canal to link Puget Sound with the Columbia River by an inland water route (*see Tour 2d*) through Grays and Willapa harbors.

CHINOOK, 78 *m.,* (sea level, 500 pop.), is a weathered fishing village. Although antedated by the neighboring settlement of Chinookville, long since disintegrated, Chinook glories in its historic past. Captain Robert Gray's visit to this section in 1792 constituted a strong claim of the United States to possession of all the country drained by the Columbia River. Despite Chinook's somewhat storm-worn appearance, it boasted for many years the highest per capita wealth of any settlement of its size in the country. A fish conservation act in 1934, outlawing the use of fixed gear in Washington waters, nearly ruined the townsfolk, who were dependent for their income on this method of fishing.

South of Chinook, US 101 rims the north bank of the Columbia, nearly four miles wide at this point. The highway enters a tunnel under a steep promontory, 78 *m.,* on the top of which is FORT COLUMBIA, one of the many guardians of the river entrance, unobservable from the road. When Captain Robert Gray landed near here May 12, 1792, thousands of Indians from near-by villages flocked to the river to see his great winged ship, the *Columbia,* enter the mouth of the Columbia River—the first entry of which there is record. At 79.5 *m.,* a flagpole and weather-stained wooden tablet mark the SITE OF THE LANDING OF CAPTAIN ROBERT GRAY.

In McGOWAN, 81.2 *m.* (sea level, 20 pop.), are the remains of a former ferry dock, wrecked by a storm and abandoned many years ago. The old piling and deserted fish traps raise desolate gray forms above the surface of the river. A roadside post office is practically all that is left of McGowan. The Washington section of US 101 ends at MEGLER, 84 *m.* (sea level, 10 pop.), a ferry slip. Auto ferries (*fee $1; car and driver*) connect here with Astoria, Oregon. Across the broad, restless waters of the Columbia, the soft outlines of Onion Peak, Saddle Mountain, and Green Mountain headland rise mistily from the Oregon shore.

Tour 9A

Junction with US 101—Union—Port Orchard—Purdy—Gig Harbor; 52.7 *m.* State 14.

Bituminous-surfaced roadbed throughout.
Limited hotel accommodations in larger towns; numerous resorts and cabin camps.

State 14 follows the wooded eastern shore of upper Hood Canal, cuts through logged-off land to Sinclair Inlet, and skirts the numerous bays and coves of the west shore of Puget Sound. The highway twists and turns through wooded areas alternating with truck farms, berry fields, and grazing land.

The earliest thorough exploration of the waters adjacent to this route was made in 1841 by the expedition under the command of Lieutenant Charles Wilkes, and many of the place names in the region originated with that survey. The heavy stands of timber attracted lumbermen, and several mill towns were soon flourishing along the water front—Seabeck, Sidney, Port Gamble, and Poulsbo; in the fifties and sixties, these settlements were far more important trading centers than were Seattle and Tacoma on the eastern side of Puget Sound.

Logging, beginning along the waterways, rapidly advanced inland, and within a quarter of a century most of the virgin timber had been removed. Camps closed down and sawmills were dismantled. Farmers came in increasing numbers and settled near towns and along the water front; soon they were moving into the cutover areas, where they cleared small patches of land and seeded them to grain and garden truck or utilized them as pasture for herds of dairy cattle.

Fishing also increased in importance. Shrimp, clams, oysters, and crabs were found in abundance, and many a sheltered cove was converted into an outfitting point for the seining and halibut boats that operated in the sounds and straits and along fishing banks of the open ocean. Today, catches have diminished and the industry has become less important, but many of the villages are still marked by fishermen's docks, drying nets, and fleets of small craft at the moorings. An added source of income is the resort and recreation business. Thousands of city dwellers spend week-ends or entire summers in camps and cabins on the Canal or Sound, and additional thousands are attracted by the excellent hunting and fishing which Kitsap Peninsula offers.

Until recent years, communication with the east shore of Puget Sound was largely by water; a few rough roads and trails led from the water's edge to farms and camps in the interior. Ferries and small steamers, offering regular service, linked the larger towns with Seattle, and small tramp boats made their way into the secluded bays and inlets with mail, general cargo, and passengers. Today, a network of roads connects all parts of the peninsula and joins it with Sound points. This connection is still by the circuitous route leading westward through the bottleneck at the head of Hood Canal, and thence southward around the head of Puget Sound; but a more direct route will be established with the reconstruction of the fallen Narrows bridge to connect the peninsula with Tacoma.

State 14 starts at the junction with US 101, 0 *m.,* three miles south of Potlatch and runs eastward across the Skokomish River delta, a thinly wooded and swamp tideland. The highway swings across the SKOKOMISH RIVER, 1.4 *m.,* and around the upper end of Hood Canal (L), which bends northeast at this point. Placid tides ebb and flow over the flats below the steeply pitched foothills; beyond, the snow-crests of the Olympic range may be glimpsed occasionally. The panoramas of water, sandy beaches, massed banks of pink rhododendrons, and tall timber are ever-changing in the morning fog, afternoon sun, and long twilight shadows.

UNION, 5.1 *m.* (10 alt., 165 pop.), started in 1858 with the establishment of the Wilson and Anderson trading post. In the same year the Rush House, a two-story building with a bar and six bedrooms, was built. Guests were required to furnish their own bedding, and a cow's horn was used to summon them to eat. Anderson shortly sold his interest to F. C. Purdy, and a few years later John McReavy, a lumberman, assumed ownership and management of the store. By 1876 the logging camps on the Canal had increased to about 50; and most of these camps obtained provisions from the trading post. In 1889 the site was platted and named Union City. Then came the big boom of 1890-2 with the rumor that the Union Pacific was to make the town its salt water terminus. Tents were pitched everywhere, a half dozen stores and at least as many saloons sprang up. A sawmill, hastily built, was soon trying to meet the demand for lumber. Additions to the original townsite were platted for miles in all directions, and lots changed hands for $1,000 an acre. With the landing of construction gangs, horses, and equipment by the Union Pacific and the actual beginning of work, the dream seemed on the verge of realization. But on the very day the graders arrived, the Baring Brothers Bank of London failed, precipitating the panic of 1893, and when the news reached Union City a few days later, work was suspended. The boom was over.

In 1904 the postal department dropped the word "city." Today, the town is a popular summer resort, and lots along the water front are again bringing a good price.

The CAPTAIN WARREN GOVE HOUSE (*private*), a white frame dwelling, was constructed in the early seventies. It is a good example of sturdy frontier building, with a New England simplicity of design.

The JOHN MCREAVY HOUSE (*private*) is a large, three-story, yellow frame building. The interior is paneled with cedar boards cut in the Gove sawmill. It was completed in the late eighties for John

McReavy, son-in-law of Captain Gove. In spite of its age, it is still well preserved.

The highway continues eastward, hugging the shoreline along which are summer homes, interspersed with occasional taverns and roadhouses. Moored at small wharves or plying the smooth waters are boats of sportsmen and pleasure seekers. An occasional shrimp boat, the arms of its drags extended, cruises off shore.

TWANOH STATE PARK, 12.6 *m.* (*camping, picnicking facilities*), a pleasant woodland beside the water front, extends for nearly one-half mile between the beach and the highway. The name of the park derives from the word "twana" (Ind. portage).

This area is sparsely populated and still retains much of its wilderness character. Startled pheasant and quail frequently whir across the highway. Deer are often seen browsing in the open forest glades. In their frantic flight, they sometimes plunge recklessly in front of passing automobiles; markers caution the motorist to "Watch for Deer."

At 20.5 *m.* is a junction with State 14-A, a graveled road.

Right here past DEBORAH LAKE (R), 3.8 *m.,* to a junction with State 14-B:

(1) R. on State 14-A to ALLYN, 4.1 *m.* (sea level, 125 pop.), once a logging town but today a center for large berry farms in the environs. Scattered shops and dwellings, a small white church, and the unoccupied shell of what was once a resort hotel constitute the town.

At 10.8 *m.* is a junction with a graveled road: L. on this road to GRAPEVIEW, 1 *m.* (sea level, 100 pop.), a village with a post office called Detroit. About half a mile to the east is STRETCH ISLAND, often called the Isle of Grapes. A bridge connects the island with the mainland. In 1878 Walter Echert began viticulture here. Years of experimentation and selection by Echert and others have produced a variety of grape, the Island Belle, suited to the soil and the climate. Three wineries and two juice plants operate on the island.

State 14-A continues southward through logged-off land and second-growth timber to Shelton, 29 *m.* (*see Tour 9a*), and a junction with US 101.

(2) L. from the junction, on State 14-B along the winding east shore of Case Inlet. Bordering the road are old orchards (L), the trees gnarled and blighted, and a few berry fields. In the tidewater flats (R) are rows of stakes which mark extensive oyster beds. Sea fowl circle downward over the calm surface of the water, dip for an instant to seize some bit of floating debris, and then, white wings flashing, soar again. Occasionally, a crane stands motionless on the sands, awaiting some unwary fish.

At 9.2 *m.* is a junction with a dirt road; R. here to VAUGHN, 1 *m.* (sea level, 300 pop.), a cluster of houses around a miniature business district on the tree-lined shore of Vaughn Bay.

At 10.4 *m.* on State 14-B is a junction with an unnamed graveled road: R. here through second-growth alder, big leaf maple, fir, and cedar to HOME, 7 *m.* (sea level, 200 pop.), on Von Geldren Cove. Originally called Home Colony, the town was organized in 1909 by the Mutual Home Association, comprising a group of Socialists and political dissenters. Land was apportioned in two-acre plots, but other assets were administered collectively. A co-operative store flourished, and a newspaper was started by Jay Fox. The first jarring note in this modern Utopia was a controversy originating in a division of opinion over nude bathing. The conflict reached the local press, then the Pierce County courts, and, finally, the press of the Nation. The issue of freedom of the press became interwoven with the original disagreements. Hardly had this dissension worked itself out, when the colony was caught in the backwash of suspicion engendered by the First World War. A visit by Emma Goldman and other radicals led to renewed resentment, criticism, and investigations. Home Colony survives as Home, a neat agricultural village, with cottages surrounded by berry patches, gardens, and poultry runs. Huckleberry harvesting and the cutting of ferns and foliage of Oregon grape, cedar, and huckleberry bushes for florists are also sources of local income.

LONGBRANCH, 11.2 *m.* (sea level, 300 pop.), is a colony of country estates and summer homes screened by dense evergreen woods bordering Filuce Bay, whose shallow waters offer good crab fishing.

State 14-B swings in a northeasterly direction away from Carr Inlet through WAUNA, 15 *m.* (sea level, 50 pop.), and across Burley Lagoon. The STATE POLLUTION LABORATORY (L), 15.7 *m.*, a frame building beside large piles of oyster shells, maintains a staff of chemists and biologists who study stream and tidewater pollution and methods of prevention and control, in order to protect the fishing industry, particularly oyster culture.

At 15.8 *m.* is the junction of State 14-B with State 14.

State 14, the main highway, clings to the graveled east shore of Hood Canal. Evergreen trees line the road; huckleberry bushes, salal, and Oregon grapes form a dense green undergrowth. On the sandy flats just above the tide line marsh grass grows, and here thousands of migratory fowl find food and shelter during winter months (*hunting prohibited*).

BELFAIR, 21 *m.* (21 alt., 250 pop.), formerly called Clifton, is a supply point for summer colonists and for fishing and hunting trips in season. It is also the center of dairy farms and poultry ranches. The highway strikes overland east of Belfair through stands of alder and second-growth timber. Here and there, a gnarled tree left by loggers rises over the tops of the second growth.

At 31.7 *m.*, near the southern end of Sinclair Inlet on Puget Sound, is a junction with State 21, a concrete-paved road.

(1) Left on State 21 along the western shore of Sinclair Inlet to Bremerton, 3 *m.* (15 alt., 10,170 pop.), (*see Cross Sound Tour 2*).

North of Bremerton the road skirts the west shore of Dye's Inlet.

At 7 *m.* is a junction with a bituminous-surfaced road: L. on this road, is the CAMP WESLEY HARRIS RIFLE RANGE, 2.4 *m.*, its several ranges flanking the highway. Enlisted men are sent here from Bremerton in detachments to practice marksmanship.

The side road continues through stands of second-growth timber and small farms to SEABECK, 10.1 *m.* (10 alt., 150 pop.), on Hood Canal. In the seventies, the town grew up around a large sawmill. Except for brief shutdowns, it operated continuously for over a quarter of a century. Boats loaded lumber at the wharves—ties for railroads in California, boards for homes in New Jersey, or shingles for barns in Iowa. Each year roads ran deeper into the forests as lumberjacks sought logs to feed the saws. One of the early settlers was Jacob Hauptly, who ran a butcher shop in the thriving mill town. He bought his cattle in the Chehalis country, and drove them overland along narrow Indian trails to Union City, where he loaded them on scows to be towed to Seabeck by the steamer *St. Patrick*. Seabeck's prosperity fell into decline when a fire left the mill a mass of ruins and wiped out the means of livelihood for most of the town's inhabitants. Today, it is a supply point for the camps and summer homes that fringe the quiet warm waters of Hood Canal. A passenger and automobile ferry runs regularly across the canal to Brinnon (*see Tour 9a*).

At 11.6 *m.* the road is a junction with a forest road: L. here 0.2 *m.* to the PIONEER CEMETERY, surrounded by towering evergreens and partially overgrown by young trees. Cedar markers and skilfully carved marble headstones are fenced with hand-turned pickets which are fitted to hand-squared rails, doweled with wooden pins into the corner posts. The epitaphs tell briefly the story of the pioneer community.

The main side road, State 21, continues northward. The KITSAP GOLF AND COUNTRY CLUB (R), 7.1 *m.* (*18 holes; greens fee,* 79c), has a tree-dotted course, on which golf may be played throughout the year, within sight of the sheltered waters of Dye's Inlet.

CHICO, 8.4 *m.* (sea level, 589 pop.), consists of expensive country homes grouped around a large general store and a school. The town derived its name from Chief Chico, who at the time of his death in 1909 was said to be 105 years old.

At 10.9 *m.* is a junction with a dirt road: R. here 0.3 *m.* to SILVERDALE (15 alt., 300 pop.), at the head of Dye's Inlet. A large rambling building, once a hotel, a number of abandoned stores, and several weathered houses date back to the late nineteenth century, when transportation on the peninsula was still almost entirely by water. Today, Silverdale is an important receiving station for the Washington Co-operative Egg and Poultry Association.

State 21 cuts northward across the neck of Manette Peninsula. Occasionally, the shimmer of Puget Sound may be glimpsed through the screen of small fir, cedar, and madrona trees, as the road dips and curves through the low rolling hills.

At 15.8 *m.* State 21 forks: (1) R. here on one branch to KEYPORT, 2.8 *m.* (25 alt., 190 pop.), a village centering around the NAVAL TORPEDO STATION (*open 8-5 July 4 and Oct. 27* (*Navy Day*) *only; apply at guardhouse*), where torpedoes are serviced. A force of about 140 officers, marines, and sailors is stationed here. The brick barracks and shops are surrounded by a spacious lawn that slopes to the water's edge. On a hill are the steel towers of the radio station. Mounted on concrete bases are powerful searchlights. Surrounding the station is a strong metal-net fence.

(2) L. 3.2 *m.* from the fork of State 21 to a junction with State 21-A: R. here to POULSBO, 1.4 *m.* (sea level, 639 pop.), a picturesque fishing village which stretches along the sinuous shoreline of Liberty Bay. Substantial frame and brick buildings line the main street. Farms crowd into the town from the hillsides. Trawlers, seine boats, and other small fishing craft line the long wharves and docks or sway at anchor a short distance offshore. Before the fishing season begins, the water front is intensely active; nets and boats are mended and the air is heavy with the smell of tar and oakum. Many of the boats fish for salmon in the Sound and Straits; others work on the halibut banks; some operate in distant Alaskan waters. The bulk of the fish caught is cod, found in sufficient quantities in local waters to keep the Pacific Coast Codfish plant, a short distance southeast of town, in operation for several months of the year. The fish are cleaned, mild-cured (lightly salted), dried in the open air, and wrapped and packed for shipment to eastern markets. Sixty or seventy persons find employment in this plant.

The first settler on the site of Poulsbo was a Norwegian named Eliason, who arrived in 1882. Approximately 90 per cent of the people at present living along the bayshore are Norwegians. Annually, on May 17, the Norwegian Independence Day is celebrated with a bazaar, speeches, dances, and singing. Participants dress in old-country provincial costumes. Since 1905 the Kitsap Co-operative Association, with a membership of 400 farmers and fishermen, has successfully operated a general store. The Washington Egg and Poultry Co-operative Association also has a strong unit here.

State 21, the main side road, continues northward through young evergreen forests. Salal and huckleberry mingle with brake and sword ferns in the rank undergrowth. In spring masses of delicately pink rhododendrons are bright against the dark green of the open forests. At scattered points along the road are small farms and chicken ranches.

PORT GAMBLE, 27.2 *m.* (sea level, 500 pop.), dates back to 1853. In July of that year the 50-ton schooner *Julius Pringle* put out from San Francisco on a voyage of exploration to Puget Sound. The captain, one of the Talbots of Maine, whose shipping and lumbering interests reached across the continent, was seeking a mill site. Associated with him were two passengers, Cyrus Walker and A. J. Pope of East Machias, Maine. Talbot skirted the shores of Admiralty Inlet and Hood Canal and finally settled upon a deep bay backed by heavy forests. Port Gamble, as the bay had been named by the Wilkes expedition in 1841, satisfied all of Captain Talbot's demands. Without delay, he sent a crew of ten men ashore with the necessary tools and provisions to construct a bunkhouse, cookshed, and store, and to fell and dress lumber for the projected sawmill. Thus the firm of Pope and Talbot sired its company town in the Far West; and today the stamp of Pope and Talbot is still on the community as well as on the logs coming to the mill. For 50 years, it was a lucky brand, for the town flourished with the company's growing lumber trade. In recent years, the interests of the firm have spread beyond the area, and include holdings in the Puget Mill Company and the McCormick Steamship Company; but Port Gamble is no longer the bustling town where three- and four-masters used to stop almost daily to load lumber at its docks.

No absentee owners were the Popes and Talbots who came around Cape Horn to build an industry. Long lines of shade trees grown from Maine elm slips still mark the original main street, and bright flower gardens set off the severe houses, in New England style. For their employees the owners built rows of box houses with steep-pitched roofs; then they added a company store, a community hall, and a church; finally, they topped off this program with a large hotel. The more recently built barracks and cottages are a drab brown, the color of baked beans, and their yards are treeless and flowerless. A school, a hospital, apartment houses, a men's boarding house, a store, and a service station complete the business structures of the present-day town.

The Puget Hotel, built in 1903, but furnished with carved oak, mahogany, and rosewood shipped out much earlier, rears three stories above cropped lawns and gorgeous flower beds among magnificent maples, giant cherry trees, and other eastern shade trees. The mill, on the water front (R), is a mass of large gray buildings surrounded by piles of lumber. Five hundred fifty men, white and Indian, are employed in the mill when it is operating at maximum capacity (*visiting hours 8-5 work days; apply at mill superintendent's office*). On the streets of the town, Indians watch the small happenings of Port Gamble's day-by-day life. They are for the most part Clallams, descendants of the natives whom Captain Talbot found living in their village Teekalet (Ind. brightness of the noonday sun), called Boston by the white settlers, across from the site he had chosen for his mill. In early days, these natives used to sell fish oil to the mill store at 50c a gallon for greasing logging skids.

State 21 ends at KINGSTON, 31.2 *m.* (sea level, 175 pop.), a few business buildings surrounded by a score of beach cabins and summer cottages. Ferries run to EDMONDS on regular schedules (*see Tour 8b*).

State 14 continues due east to PORT ORCHARD, 35.7 *m.* (sea level, 1,566 pop.), seat of Kitsap County and one of the oldest settlements on Kitsap Peninsula. In 1854 William Renton and Daniel Howard landed near the towering forests along the protected waters of the bay named Port Orchard by Captain George Vancouver, in honor of H. M. Orchard of the ship *Discovery*. Here they erected a sawmill. The success of this venture soon attracted shipbuilders, and the sound of hammers mingled with the hum of the sawmill. The first vessel built in Kitsap County, the *I. I. Stevens,* was launched here in 1855. The village which grew up around the mill was named Sidney for Sidney Stevens, who platted the townsite. Early in the nineties, the Port Orchard Naval Station post office was established in Sidney, and in succeeding years the navy yard across the inlet assumed an important part in the town's economy. In 1903, by an act of the State legislature, the name was officially changed to Port Orchard, and shortly thereafter the town was made the county seat.

Present-day Port Orchard stretches along the rim of the bay, many of the buildings being built on pilings over the tide flats. East of the business district, the residential section climbs the steep hill, where terraced lawns, rock gardens, and bright flowers and shrubs make a colorful picture in midsummer. The courthouse crowns the hill. With the depletion of the forests on the peninsula, Port Orchard has come to depend primarily upon construction work in the Navy Yard at Bremerton and upon the agricultural development of the surrounding country. It is also an important shipping point for ferns and huckleberry greens for the florist trade.

At **36.2** *m.* is a junction with a bituminous-surfaced road.

Left here to ANNAPOLIS, 1.2 *m.* (10 alt., 500 pop.), a cluster of shops and houses around a dock from which a small ferry runs to Bremerton. At 1.4 *m.* is a junction with a concrete-paved road; R. here 0.1 *m.* to RETSIL and the WASHINGTON VETERANS' HOME (*open*). The plant consists of a modern hospital, a large auditorium, a number of frame and stucco-finished dormitories, and several cottages. Weeping willows, dark green holly trees, red-trunked madronas, and dogwood trees frame a superb view of Sinclair Inlet and the jagged Olympics beyond. In this institution about 500 veterans live with their families.

At **37.2** *m.* is a two-way fork of State 14.

Left on one branch of State 14 through COLBY, 5.5 *m.* (sea level, 55 pop.), to HARPER, 5.8 *m.* (sea level, 250 pop.), a summer colony clustered around a slip, from which ferries operate to Vashon Island (*see Island Tour* 1) and to Seattle (*see Seattle*).

The main section of State 14 continues southward through rolling, sparsely settled country, once covered by a heavy forest. Small gardens, poultry ranches, and dairy farms alternate with stands of second-growth timber and cutover land.

BURLEY, **45.5** *m.* (sea level, 150 pop.), a broken circle of frame buildings along a lagoon at the head of Carr Inlet, was started as a co-operative colony called Circle City—its buildings being laid out on the periphery of a wide circle reaching from the hills down to the bay shore where the sawmill stood. The board of directors of the co-operative selected colonists to join the settlement on the basis of their crafts and skills. A hotel, a store, a schoolhouse, and a number of dwellings were laid out along the water's edge, and a long sluiceway was constructed from a creek in the hills to bring water to the town and the mill. Land was cleared, and those who understood agricultural practices turned to farming. For a number of years, the affairs of the colony ran smoothly. The exhaustion of merchantable timber, however, and the consequent closing of the mill raised acute economic problems. This difficulty, together with differences over policies, resulted in the disintegration of the town's organization and the changing of the name to Burley. Only the community hall and a few dignified old houses remain.

PURDY, **47.8** *m.* (sea level, 80 pop.), is a scattering of buildings on the site of an old Indian camping ground. The culture of Japanese oysters along the sand bars and in the shallows of the lagoon has been developed recently. In Purdy is the junction of State 14 and State 14-B (*see above*).

At 51.1 *m.* is a junction with a concrete-paved road.

Left on this road to the OLD TOWN section of GIG HARBOR, 0.8 *m.* (sea level, 1,095 pop.). The first settlers, Dr. Burnham and his family, arrived in the early eighties. In the succeeding quarter of a century the town flourished around a sawmill and the wharves, where schooners and, later, steam freighters loaded the cut lumber. Within a score of years, however, the forests were gone, the mill was closed and dismantled, and the freighters sought cargoes in other ports. Only the substantial brick post office, the high school, a few stores, and a newspaper, the *Peninsula Gateway,* divert traffic to Old Town today.

Straight ahead, State 14 leads to the NEW TOWN section of GIG HARBOR, 51.6 *m.* The main flow of traffic passes a fringe of one- and two-story brick and frame buildings on both sides of Front Street. Black forests cover the hillside west of the highway, and on the east the tranquil haven of Gig Harbor keeps its craft safe from the rough waters of the open Sound. Scattered between woods and water are the prosperous modern homes of fishermen, whose tarred nets are spread to dry on well-kept lawns. Business is largely concentrated in New Town.

The Gig Harbor shipyard, owned by the Washington Navigation Company, shelters under a spreading sheet-iron roof its piers and ways, machinery, and benches. At its drydocks the company's five ferries, as well as sundry fishing boats, are maintained and serviced. Mitchell Skansie, organizer and part owner of this enterprise, began by building fishing boats, mostly purse seiners, of 65 to 85 feet, more than 100 of which have slipped down the Gig Harbor ways to a roving life on the waters off Western America. Formerly, Pierce County operated the ferries built with the hammers and caulking irons of Gig Harbor craftsmen; but, in 1921, the shipbuilding company took over the lines.

The lake-like haven of Gig Harbor is shut off by a narrow entrance from the open Sound; surrounding hills protect it from gales from any quarter, as the crew of the ship's gig from the Wilkes expedition gratefully found when it took refuge here from a storm in 1841. Gig Harbor is the home port for some 35 large purse seiners which follow the various fishing runs from Mexican waters to the Arctic seas. They are manned mostly by Croatians, Slovaks, and Austrians, who maintain a Catholic Church and its several societies, and a Croatian Fraternal Union, and form a strong unit of the Fishermen's Union.

Agriculture is also a source of income for Gig Harbor. The Washington Berry Growers Association and the Washington Co-operative Egg and Poultry Association both have depots here. Produce, flowers, and poultry are displayed at the community fair held each September in the high school gymnasium.

Gig Harbor presents an unusual sport in the rooster races held at the C. E. Shaw residence each Saturday and Sunday throughout the summer. The trained white leghorn racers, bred for speed, roost in the little houses of a miniature village laid out beside the track.

The COMMUNITY PARK, (L) at the north end of Crescent Valley Creek bridge, has picnic facilities on the landscaped grounds, developed by WPA labor.

At 52.5 *m.* is a junction with State 14-C, a concrete-paved road.

Right here, 0.9 *m.* to a junction with a graveled road: L. here to HOLLYCROFT GARDENS, 0.2 *m.*, a large holly farm, owned by P. H. Peyran. At 2.6 *m.* on 14-C is a junction with a graveled road. L. here 2.1 *m.* to the west end of the NARROWS BRIDGE, now (1941) being reconstructed. This suspension bridge will be 5,939 feet in length; its longest span will be 2,800 feet. Peninsula residents expect that suburban home developments and an influx of tourist traffic will follow, from which Gig Harbor, the nearest town to this portal of the Olympic Peninsula, will profit.

State 14 ends at the ferry slip, 52.7 *m.*, from which boats run regularly to Tacoma (*see Tacoma*).

Mount Rainier National Park

Season: Nisqually (SW.) Entrance open year-round; others closed in winter. Summer season of park approximately June 1 to Oct. 15. Ski season Dec. 1 to May 15.
Administrative Offices: National Park Service for Mount Rainier National Park, Longmire; branch office, Federal Office Bldg., Seattle. Public utility operators under contract with Department of the Interior for providing transportation and other accommodations are: Rainier National Park Co., Tacoma; branch offices, 418 University St., Seattle; and AAA Club, Commercial Hotel, Yakima; Dr. A. W. Bridge, 744 Market St., Tacoma.
Admission: Yearly automobile permits issued at Nisqually and White River entrances; fee $1. No permit required at Ohanapecosh or Carbon River entrances, but visitors should register.
Transportation: Entrance: Nisqually (*see Tour 8D*); Carbon River (*see Tour 1D*); Ohanapecosh (*see Tour 8E*); White River (*see Tour 2c*). No airplanes serve the park. Rainier National Park Co. operates stages through Nisqually Entrance to Longmire and Paradise Valley throughout year from Seattle and Tacoma; to Yakima (Sunrise) Park in summer from Tacoma, Seattle, and Yakima. Morton-Ashford stages every Saturday from Tacoma to Packwood, thence by private bus to Ohanapecosh Hot Springs. From Narada Falls, end of winter road, to Paradise Valley, 1.5 *m.* snow trail negotiated afoot or on skis; also accessible by shuttle stage (*50c one way; 75c round trip*).
Highways within park total 69 miles, all hard-surfaced, oiled, or graveled. Maximum speed limit 33 m.p.h. Marked trails total 241 miles. Summit, Pinnacle Peak, Nisqually, Paradise, and other glacier climbs require guides (*ask a ranger*). Foot, saddle, and pack-horse guide service available until Labor Day at Paradise Valley and Yakima Park.

Accommodations—Summer: Longmire—Public campgrounds; comfort stations, stores, wood, tables, water; trailers permitted. National Park Inn offers rooms on European plan; rooms also in Cottage Annex. Housekeeping cabins (three rooms, equipped) available. Cafeteria meal service available at National Park Inn.

Paradise Valley—Public campgrounds (same as Longmire). Paradise Inn offers rooms on American plan; Paradise Lodge offers rooms on European plan; table d'hote, cafeteria, and a la carte meal service to midseason; cafeteria throughout summer. Housekeeping cabins, one-room and three-room, available.

Yakima Park—215 one-room and three-room housekeeping cabins available; cafeteria service at Sunrise Lodge; camp supplies also available.

Ohanapecosh Park—Ohanapecosh Lodge offers rooms American and European plan; housekeeping cabins (two rooms), and housekeeping tents also available.

Accommodations—Winter: Longmire—Public campground closed. Rooms in National Park Inn and Cottage Annex; housekeeping cabins and cafeteria meal service also available.

Paradise Valley—Public campgrounds closed. Paradise Lodge offers rooms on American and European plan; cafeteria meal service week-ends and holidays only. Paradise Inn offers rooms on both American and European plan. Table d'hote meal service week-ends and holidays; a la carte during midweek. Dormitory facilities also available.

Clothing and Equipment: Winter sports visitors should bring winter clothing, preferably ski suits and boots. Hikers and trail riders may rent clothing and sports equipment at Paradise guide house; some may be purchased. Guides provide calked shoes, clothing, alpenstocks, colored glasses, and face paints, necessary for trips over snow and ice fields, at reasonable fees. Limited supplies of fishing tackle and bait available. Food supplies can be purchased at Longmire and Paradise Valley all year, and in summer at Yakima Park and Ohanapecosh.

Medical Service: Physician available at town of National, 7 m. from Nisqually entrance, all year. Trained nurses at Paradise Inn and Yakima Park in summer. Physician available at Paradise Valley every day of week in winter.

Post Offices: Longmire, all year; Paradise Inn and Sunrise Lodge, July 1 to Labor Day.

Communications and Express Service: Telephone and telegraph service available at inns and lodges in the park and at National Park Service Administration Bldg., Longmire.

Special Regulations: Permit required for building fires, in other than established auto camps; fires should be extinguished completely before leaving camp. All garbage must be deposited in receptacles. No smoking while on trails; no picking of flowers or shrubs. Feeding of bears is prohibited. (Since bears often break into automobiles in which they smell food, provisions should be suspended in box from the limb of a tree, well out of reach.) Penalty for violation of park regulations: Maximum of 180 days in jail or $500 fine, or both. (Complete regulations displayed at park superintendent's office and at ranger stations.)

Summary of Attractions: Most popular areas of the park are Longmire, Paradise Valley, Yakima Park, and Ohanapecosh (mineral baths here). Lakes and streams offer trout fishing (no license required); lakes open from June 15 to Sept. 30, streams from May 1 to Oct. 31, unless otherwise posted. Swimming in Reflection Lake. Excellent skiing over unobstructed terrain at Paradise Valley; ski runs for beginners at Longmire.

Scenic Points: Narada Falls, Reflection Lake, Indian Henry's Hunting Ground, Eagle Peak, Gobler's Knob Lookout Station, Tatoosh Range, Rampart Ridge, Spray Park, Klapatche Park, Paradise Park, Yakima Park, Ohanapecosh Park, Van Trump Park (where mountain goat may be seen), Summerland, Mowich Lake; numerous glaciers.

MOUNT RAINIER NATIONAL PARK, about 55 miles from Tacoma (*see Tour 8D*), comprises 337 square miles of rugged mountains, forested valleys beneath towering crags, moving glaciers melting

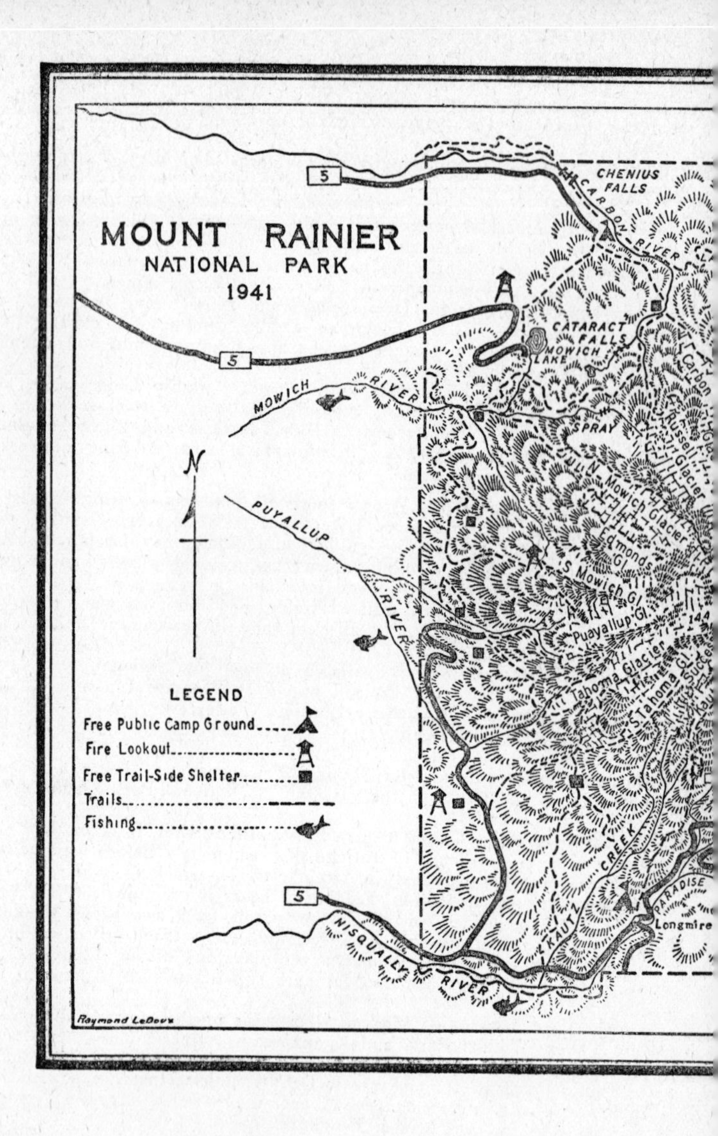
MOUNT RAINIER
NATIONAL PARK
1941
LEGEND
Free Public Camp Ground
Fire Lookout
Free Trail-Side Shelter
Trails
Fishing
N
5
MOWICH RIVER
PUYALLUP RIVER
NISQUALLY RIVER
CHENIUS FALLS
CARBON RIVER
CATARACT FALLS
MOWICH LAKE
SPRAY
Russell Glacier
Carbon
N. Mowich Glacier
Edmonds Gl.
S. Mowich Gl.
Puyallup Gl.
Tahoma Glacier
S. Tahoma Gl.
KAUTZ CREEK
PARADISE
Longmire
Raymond LeDoux

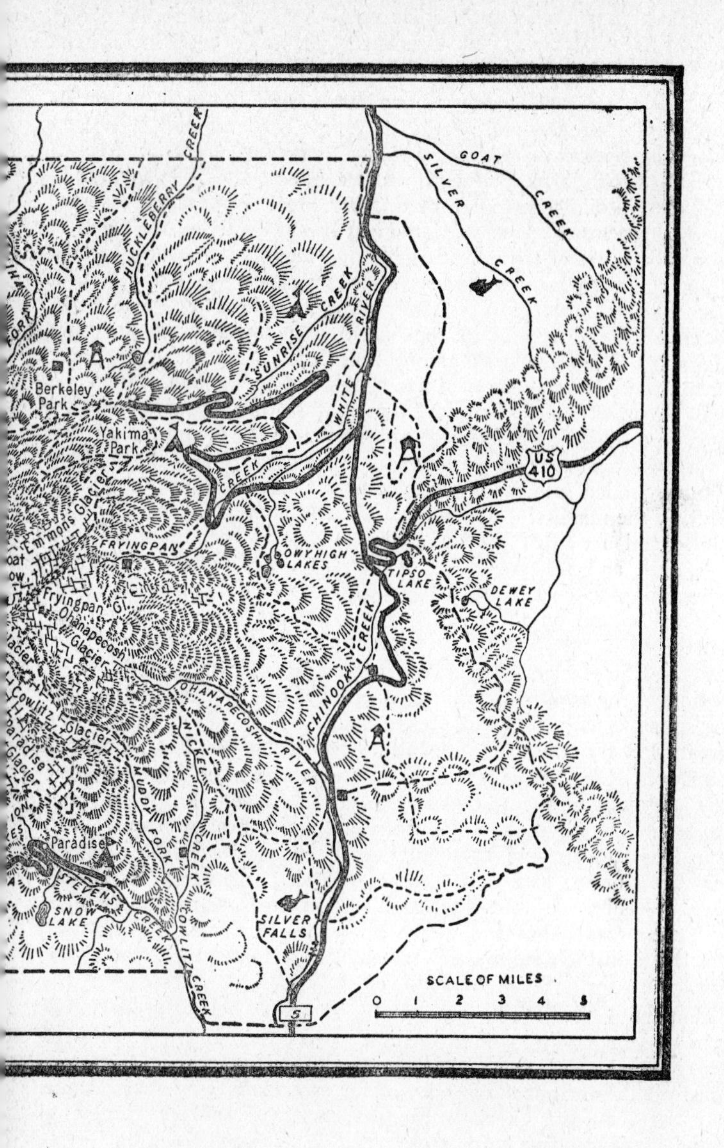
GOAT
SILVER
CREEK
CREEK
HUCKLEBERRY
CREEK
SUNRISE
CREEK
WHITE
RIVER
Berkeley
Park
Yakima
Park
CREEK
US
410
Emmons Glacier
FRYINGPAN
OWYHIGH
LAKES
TIPSO
LAKE
DEWEY
LAKE
Fryingpan Gl.
Ohanapecosh
Glacier
Cowlitz Glacier
Paradise
Glacier
CHINOOK
CREEK
OHANAPECOSH
RIVER
NICKEL
CREEK
MUDDY
FORK
Paradise
STEVENS
CREEK
SNOW
LAKE
COWLITZ
CREEK
SILVER
FALLS
SCALE OF MILES
0 1 2 3 4 5
5

into turbulent streams; of broad ice fields and flowered mountain meadows, great cirques, and crevasses; refuge for abundant wild life. Marking the approximate center is the glistening dome of Mount Rainier, third highest peak in continental United States (14,408 alt.); its base covers almost one-fourth of the park area. Seen from a distance the mountain seems to be isolated, its great height dwarfing the Cascade Range on the east and the other neighboring mountains; although these peaks and mountain ranges themselves average 6,000 to 8,000 feet in altitude. The mountain, unlike Mount Fujiyama, is a truncated cone, approximately 2,000 feet of its top having been lost through an eruption ages ago. That the peak at one time reached almost 16,000 feet is evident from the inclination of the slopes and lava strata. When the top was blown off, a vast cauldron more than three square miles in area was formed—one of the great attractions of the mountain. In this cauldron two cinder cones developed, gradually grew together, and eventually rounded into the dome known as Columbia Crest, the highest point on the mountain, which rises 285 feet above the jagged rim of the snow and ice-filled crater. Next in height are Point Success (14,150 alt.) and Liberty Cap (14,112 alt.). Feeble volcanic action was reported as late as 1843, 1858, and 1870; relatively weak steam jets are still found on the heights, and there are various hot springs around the base.

Twenty-eight glaciers—16 of which have a downward flow—cling to the sides of the mountain, forming one of the country's most extensive glacier systems, with a spread of approximately 48 square miles. The six great primary glaciers, Nisqually, Ingraham, Cowlitz, Emmons, Tahoma, and Kautz, originate in the summit *névé;* the five secondary glaciers are born in snow-filled cirques at levels between 12,000 and 10,000 feet. Between these major ice flows, which average from 4 to 6 miles in length, are found 17 smaller ice fields or interglaciers. As the glaciers have melted back—the average recession is 70 feet per year—weathering has broken down the harsh canyon walls, so that the valleys below them broaden out and merge with the tablelands of the lower wedges. Here in high valleys and tablelands are found the great alpine meadows with their riot of wild flowers.

Within the park the Transition Zone, characterized by heavy forest growths of Douglas fir, western hemlock, red cedar, and scatterings of maple, alder, western yew, and black cottonwood, reaches to elevations found at all the entrances and even as far as Longmire Springs, White River camp, and Ipsut Creek on the Carbon River road. Ferns, devil's-club, and skunk cabbage form rank growths; dogwood, trillium, white clintonia, and twinflower grow in abundance. The great forests provide a haven for black bear and many other animals. The band-tailed pigeon, northern spotted owl, western winter wren, and the Cooper chipmunk are frequently seen.

The Canadian Zone, merging into the Hudsonian above and the Transition below, is the least distinct of all the park zones; yet certain points, such as Narada Falls on the Nisqually Road, Yakima Park on the east, Mowich Lake on the northwest, and the glacier termini may be taken as arbitrarily marking its upper limits. The forests here, though dense, have smaller trees, of which the western white pine is the most common, with Noble fir, spruce, Alaska yellow cedar, and western hemlock. One of the picturesque plants is the goatsbeard moss, which forms great festoons on the trees. Undergrowth is thinner, and such plants as red and blue huckleberries, rhododendron, kinnikinnick, everlasting, and minulus flourish. The whistling marmot, Pacific beaver, varying hare, mantled ground squirrel, water ouzel, American black bear, Columbian black-tailed deer, and mountain beaver (*aplodontia*) are relatively common in both Transition and Canadian zones.

At the upper edge of the forest belt and extending to the timber line, is the Hudsonian Zone, supporting such hardy trees as the mountain hemlock, alpine fir, and white-barked pine under favorable conditions. Pre-eminently the zone of flowered alpine meadows, which carry right up around the glaciers, this area is one of the most scenic in the park, generally most colorful during July and August. Some 300 species of flowers occur in this zone alone, of which the more noteworthy are the heathers, the glacier and avalanche lilies, valerian, Indian basket grass, Indian paintbrush, western anemone, speedwells, asters, lupines, and buttercup. In this zone the Clark's nutcracker is the most common bird, but the sooty grouse, the pine siskin, rufous hummingbird, and bluebird are also numerous. The cony, pack rat, marmot, jumping mouse, weasel, and pine marten are encountered frequently.

The Arctic-Alpine Zone extends from the timber line toward the summit. In this region of wind-swept wastes and pumice fields, plant and animal life is limited to the most hardy, but the region presents a broad and interesting variety of herbaceous plants, among which are lupine and phlox and various saxifrages and grasses. A few junipers and arctic willow are found in sheltered locations. This zone is the habitat of the white mountain goat, the Rainier white-tailed ptarmigan, the pipit, rosy finch, and the pine siskin. Among occasional visitors are the Cascade fox, coyote, marmot, weasel, and marten; the juncos, hawks and eagles.

In all, nearly 700 species of flowering plants, more than 100 species of birds, and 60 species of mammals are native to the park zones. The lakes and streams offer rainbow, Eastern brook, and cutthroat trout; there have been some plantings of Dolly Varden and Montana black-spotted trout.

No attempt was made to explore the mountain until 1833, when Doctor William Fraser Tolmie of the Hudson's Bay post at Nisqually made "a botanizing excursion" to the northwest corner of the park, reaching the base of the small peak, which, with the stream that issues from it, bears his name today. In 1857, 24 years later, Lieutenant A. V. Kautz, stationed at Fort Steilacoom, with two soldiers, the post doctor, and Wah-pow-e-ty, Nisqually Indian guide, made the first attempted ascent; they reached an elevation of 12,000 feet but were turned back by bad weather and lack of food. General Hazard Stevens and P. B.

Van Trump made the first successful summit climb on August 17, 1870. On October 17 of the same year Samuel F. Emmons and Doctor A. D. Wilson of the United States Geologic Survey made the second successful climb. Annually, since the park was opened, many climbers reach the summit.

In 1884, James Longmire, pioneer, blazed a trail to Longmire Springs at the base of the mountain. This trail became a rough wagon road and over it came numerous other climbers in 1890 and 1891. Congress on March 2, 1899, created Mount Rainier National Park. Since the National Park Service was established as the administrative body in 1916, every effort has been made to preserve the natural beauty of the area, and to this end are dedicated the efforts of the park rangers, naturalists, and guides.

PARK TOUR 1

Nisqually Entrance to Paradise Valley. 20 m.

The Nisqually entrance to the park is marked by a huge log arch. Just beyond is the log checking station where park rangers issue automobile permits (*fee $1*) for the calendar year; near by are rest rooms.

Paralleling the Nisqually River, milk-white with rock flour eroded by Nisqually Glacier, the oil-macadam road winds through firs and cedars along the route of the old toll road constructed by James Longmire in 1890-1.

At 1 *m.* is a junction with the oiled West Side Highway (*see Park Tour 1a*).

TAHOMA CREEK (2,120 alt.), turbulent when flooded with melting snows, is crossed on a six-foot cedar-log bridge at 1.2 *m.* The highway serpentines through the timber, offering now and then a glimpse of wooded hills beyond the river. Frowning darkly above the highway is FALLEN ROCK (approx. 2,270 alt.), 2 *m.,* once a part of Tumtum Peak.

At 3.4 *m.* is a giant Douglas fir, eight feet in diameter, called the COLUMBUS TREE. Now more than 700 years old, this was a large tree when Columbus sighted the New World. KAUTZ CREEK (2,378 alt.), tumbling down from Kautz Glacier, swirls under a rustic bridge. Creek and glacier were named for Lieutenant Kautz, who, in 1857, first attempted the summit climb.

At BEAR PRAIRIE POINT, 4.8 *m.,* is parking space with a view of timbered Nisqually Canyon (L) and beyond a glimpse of Mount Rainier; right in the distance the TATOOSH (Ind. nourishing breast) RANGE sends up rugged crags around dominant Unicorn Peak (6,939 alt.). Bear Prairie near by was the starting point of the summit expedition led by General Hazard Stevens and P. B. Trump in 1870.

At LONGMIRE, 6.6 *m.* (2,750 alt.), is the rustic administration building of the National Park Service. Beside the highway (R) are housekeeping cabins operated in connection with the NATIONAL PARK

INN, and across the Nisqually River is a free public campground operated by the National Park Service.

At the fork of the road is the NATIONAL PARK MUSEUM (*open 8-9 summer months; 9-5 winter months; no charge*), where are displayed specimens of the park's flora and fauna. Maps show trails marked in color, and small models illustrate the formation of Mount Rainier.

The museum is the office of the park naturalist and his staff. Campfire programs and free lectures are offered nightly (*except Sunday*) at eight o'clock in the community house at the campgrounds. Hikes are outlined, and free hikes of from one to twelve hours' duration, to points of unusual interest, are scheduled weekly.

Numerous trails radiate from Longmire.

1. EAGLE PEAK TRAIL, 3.5 *m.*, E., leads through heavy forests to the Tatoosh Range. At two miles, the trail emerges into flower-strewn parks through which it winds toward the summit. From Eagle Peak, achieved by a rough trail, excellent views may be had of Mount Rainier, Paradise Valley, and the great domes of Mount Adams and Mount St. Helens far to the south.
2. RAMPART RIDGE TRAIL, 4 *m.*, leads to the heights of the ridge but bears left to the highest point, the RAMPARTS (4,080 alt.). Up the mountain appears VAN TRUMP GLACIER, a pendant from an interglacier between the Kautz and Nisqually. This glacier feeds Van Trump Creek, which flows down through the flowered park of the same name. The region of the Ramparts is noted for its cirques, moraines, rugged canyons, and waterfalls.
3. TRAIL OF THE SHADOWS, 0.5 *m.* S., is a popular short trip. Through the trees (identified by tags) the trail leads past Soda Springs and Iron Springs to the LONGMIRE CABIN, sole remaining structure of the group erected in 1888 by Elcain Longmire, son of James Longmire, who founded the settlement in 1883. The trail continues on to the interesting beaver flats.
4. The RIVER TRAIL, 1 *m.* N., another popular short trip from Longmire, follows the west side of the Nisqually River, crosses by a foot bridge, which gives an unusual view of the river's course, and returns to Longmire.

North of Longmire the mountain road, winding, curving, and switching back along the valley of the Nisqually, reaches farther and farther into the clouds.

At 7 *m.* is a junction with a trail.

Left here 6.5 *m.* to INDIAN HENRY'S HUNTING GROUND (*see Wonderland Trail, below.*)

COUGAR ROCK (3,000 alt.), 8 *m.* (L), is a great boulder at the base of Rampart Ridge.

At 10.9 *m.* the road bends, and lovely CHRISTINE FALLS comes into view. The falls was named for the daughter of P. B. Van Trump, who with Hazard Stevens, made the first successful ascent of the mountain in 1870.

Left from Christine Falls a trail leads up Van Trump Creek, past COMET FALLS—which drops 320 feet—and BLOCHER FALLS, to VAN TRUMP PARK, 1.2 *m.*, noted for its wealth of flowers. The trail continues left through increasingly timbered terrain along the crest of Rampart Ridge, then bears again left to drop down the side of the ridge to Longmire.

Near the upper reaches of the valley the road, which has followed the west side of the river beneath timbered mountain flanks, crosses the boulder-strewn Nisqually River over a picturesque bridge at 11.9

m. To the left is the mighty NISQUALLY GLACIER, its blunt end marked by piles of gray and brown ice and debris around a huge ice cave, from which issues the river. (*A turnout provides parking at this point; rest rooms are available*).

Left, a half-mile trail leads to the glacier's end, where the cave from which the river emerges can be more clearly seen: a great hole first carved out by the rush of the water. Originating in pure white snows 10,000 feet above on the mountain summit, the glacier undergoes many changes in color on its way down the gorge. Along its middle course snows, solidified into contorted masses through ages of melting and replenishment, are a rich indigo, lined with darker streaks—moraines that merge at the sides with marginal moraines of embanked debris, which in turn converge at the lower end. One of the greater glaciers of the peak, Nisqually is believed to have extended 1,500 feet farther down in its canyon as late as 1885. The Nisqually River emerges here, milky with its heavy load of eroded rock silt.

From the bridge the road climbs steeply along the east side of the valley. Hills stand out against distant crags and peaks, and the view is a tumbled sea of mountain ramparts.

RICKSECKER POINT (4,214 alt.), 13.4 *m.,* looks out over the surrounding heights and valleys: the view of the Nisqually Glacier and the southern flare of the mountain is noteworthy.

From CANYON RIM, 14.9 *m.* (4,400 alt.), is a panorama of the Nisqually Canyon (L) below sheer cliffs.

The SILVER FOREST, 15 *m.,* is a stand of fire-withered, gray tree trunks, a mournful reminder of the violation of fire regulations. However, over the area tiny pine, fir, and Alaska cedar again are taking root.

NARADA (E. Ind. pure) FALLS (4,572 alt.) at 16 *m.* (R), plunging 168 feet into the Paradise River, is one of the most attractive cataracts on the mountain. Here is a junction with a cross-trail.

Left to PARADISE VALLEY, 1.2 *m.;* R. to LONGMIRE, 3.7 *m.* (*see above*).

WASHINGTON CASCADES, 16.6 *m.,* in the Paradise River, bubble down over red and gray andesite rock, contrasting vividly with the green meadowland stretching through Paradise Valley.

From INSPIRATION POINT, at 17.3 *m.,* is obtained one of the finest impressions of the soaring peak—its flanks mottled with glaciers and icefields between dark pinnacles—above a broad valley, carpeted with flowered meadows and fringed with trees.

The road now climbs the opposite foothills into PARADISE VALLEY (5,400 alt.), 20 *m.,* at the very foot of the mountain, and Paradise Inn, with its steep roof, looking like a tiny chalet, beneath the vast peak and the surrounding crags. At the inn the road branches left, and at the bend are the ranger station, rest rooms, and the guide house. Beyond the ranger station is the Trail Hub, from which the main trails radiate.

The inn and the Sluiskin and Tatoosh winter dormitories around it form the center of the Paradise Valley winter-sports area. Here the snows lie as deep as 20 feet during the winter season, affording some of the finest ski terrain in the country. From Camp Muir, at an elevation of 10,000 feet, the skier may descend along hazardless courses to the valley. Ski schools are maintained, and each Sunday and holiday during the snow season, downhill and slalom races are held. On the higher levels, the snows hold throughout the spring and summer; winter sports are possible during the hottest part of the year.

The road leads on to the COMMUNITY HOUSE, public campgrounds, Paradise Lodge, and housekeeping cabins. The community house is the headquarters of Paradise naturalists, and lectures on the park are given nightly (*including Sunday, 8 p.m.*); hikes and trail trips are discussed. During spring and summer, short foot trips and saddle trail trips are popular. Daily (*9-2*) guides supervise short trips from the valley; longer trips, of a day's duration, are made twice weekly.

Following are a few of the possible trail trips from Paradise:

1. ALTA VISTA TRAIL, 0.6 *m.*, N., leads through fields of flowers to the eminence near the snow line, and almost directly in front of the inn. From Alta Vista, the entire valley and the peaks, each of which is indicated by a marker, are clearly visible. It is perhaps the best spot in the park to overlook the whole area.

2. MAZAMA (Ind. mountain goat) RIDGE TRAIL, 1 *m.*, SE., is another short trail trip that displays the floral splendor of the mountain meadows to advantage.

3. SLUISKIN FALLS TRAIL, 1.2 *m.*, NE., reaches the falls named by Stevens and Van Trump for their Indian guide, who aided them in making the first successful ascent of the summit in 1870. It was here that Sluiskin made his camp while waiting for the white men to enter levels he believed sacred. The falls plunge 300 feet to the river bed below—a diaphanous scarf of frosted blue and white between the basalt crags.

4. PARADISE GLACIER TRAIL, 1.5 *m.*, NE., leads to the end of the glacier itself. This glacier originates, not at the summit as does the Nisqually, but in the snows on the lower slope at an elevation of about 9,000 feet. It is a typical interglacier, lying between Cowlitz on the east and Nisqually on the west. Relatively unshielded, the Paradise receives the full heat of the sun and melts at a perceptible rate. In early summer it is a white blaze in the sun, but as the hot season lengthens, grayish patches—old ice of past seasons—are exposed. Small streams tumble down crevasses in the glacier's sides and drop to the glacier bed below. Uniting beneath the ice these streams, aided by warm air currents, yearly carve new and fantastic caverns and grottoes in the glacier's end. Here the Paradise River has its source.

5. REFLECTION LAKES TRAIL, 1.5 *m.*, SE. (*also reached by driving down the road two miles to parking area at junction with trail*), leads through timber to a stretch of meadow surrounding the lake. The sweeping meadowland is broken by scattered clumps of green pine; ragged spurs ascend toward the flanks of the central mountain, the white summit at times but a vague outline through enveloping mists. (*The lakes are the only ones in the park where boating and swimming are available. Fishing is also good.*)

6. The SKYLINE TRAIL (by saddle horse), 4 *m.*, a loop trail, is the most popular saddle trip in this park. From the inn the trail leads around Alta Vista and the rim of the canyon at Glacier Vista (from which is obtained a superb view of Nisqually Glacier) upward by bends and switchbacks to Panorama Point (6,800 alt.). From this point the panorama of the Nisqually watershed and Paradise Valley unfolds. Crossing the ice along Timberline Ridge, one reaches and fords the Paradise River. Here the trail turns down Mazama Ridge, passes Sluiskin Falls, and returns to the valley and Paradise Inn.

Other trail trips are:

Nisqually Glacier, 1.2 *m.* W.; Glacier Vista, 1.2 *m.* N.; Sluiskin Monument, 1.5 *m.* NE.; Panorama Point, 1.8 *m.* N.; Faraway Rock, 2.5 *m.* SE.; Lake

Louise, 2.5 *m.* SE.; Pinnacle Peak, 3 *m.* SE.; Summit Climb (*see Summit Climb below*).

PARK TOUR 1A

Nisqually Road to the North Puyallup River, 15.1 m.

One mile from the Nisqually entrance, the West Side Highway branches left and extends in a generally northern direction. MOUNT WOW (5,622 alt.), often called Goat Mountain, was a favorite hunting ground for Indian tribes years ago. The highway follows the course of tumbling Tahoma Creek, alder thickets giving way to stands of giant cedar and Noble fir. (*Caution is needed on the sharp turns*).

At 2.7 *m.* looms the bald face of a gigantic cliff, its base heaped with the debris of rock slides. The course of FISH CREEK (*moderately good fishing*) (3,000 alt.), crossed at 3.9 *m.,* is marked by numerous beaver dams. Mountain goats frequently are seen on the cliffs above.

TAHOMA CAMP (3,100 alt.), at 4.2 *m.,* is equipped with tables and fireplaces.

Right here 3.5 *m.* on a trail to INDIAN HENRY'S HUNTING GROUND (*see Wonderland Trail, below*).

Rising steadily the highway reaches TAHOMA VISTA (3,458 alt.), 5.4 *m.,* which offers a fine view of the surrounding country. Here are comfort stations and a large parking area. Far to the right TAHOMA and SOUTH TAHOMA GLACIERS cling to the side of the mountain. Tahoma Glacier, originating on the summit, sends its frozen flow almost in a straight line for five miles, only a comb of pinnacles separating it from the smaller South Tahoma Glacier, which rises in a cirque below Success Cleaver. At an elevation of 7,651 feet GLACIER ISLAND, a towering cliff-footed rock with dome worn smooth by centuries of ice action, divides the two; below the island the two streams again unite. South Tahoma, on its upper reaches, has formed ICE TERRACES resembling huge marble stairs.

The first glimpse of the northwest slopes and ice fields of Mount Rainier on this route is at ROUND PASS (3,879 alt.), 6.9 *m.* Stone steps lead to a LOOKOUT STATION with a superb view of Puyallup Glacier.

Here is a junction with a trail:

Left to LAKE GEORGE, 1.2 *m.,* and GOAT LAKE, 3.7 *m.* on the eastern slopes of Mount Wow. Fishing is good at both places and camping spots plentiful.

From Round Pass the highway winds downward to cross the south fork of the PUYALLUP RIVER (3,479 alt.), 8.3 *m.,* named for a tribe known as Puyallupnamish, who lived along its course.

At ST. ANDREWS CREEK (3,800 alt.), 11.2 *m.,* are two trails:

Left to two beautiful waterfalls; and right to KLAPATCHE PARK, 8 *m.,* and ST. ANDREWS PARK, 4.5 *m.* (*see Wonderland Trail, below*).

KLAPATCHE POINT (4,117 alt.), on Klapatche Ridge, is reached at 12.4 *m.* Here cliffs reach skyward, and gray snags, vestiges of a fireswept forest, mar the verdant foothills, beyond which rise Tahoma Glacier and the cleaver dividing it from Puyallup Glacier on the north. On the left spreads a broad basin, with the Olympic Mountains in the distance; occasionally Puget Sound also may be seen from here.

The road winds downward between great volcanic pillars to the NORTH PUYALLUP RIVER (3,707 alt.), 15.1 *m.,* which heads from the base of the PUYALLUP GLACIER in a sculptured canyon with almost sheer basalt walls. Above the canyon at an elevation of 12,000 feet, the glacier rises in a great cirque in the Sunset Amphitheater, whose perpendicular walls form the south base of Liberty Cap on the summit. From this volcanic bowl the glacier descends the mountain in a narrow gorge, is split by a rock wedge near its base, and spreads out to a mile in width, forming two joined ice lobes. On these great lobes are bizarre HANGING ICE CASCADES.

The parking area here marks the end of the road, although eventually it may be extended from this point to the Carbon River entrance to the park (*see State Tour 3C*). Here is a junction with a cross-trail.

Right 3 *m.* to KLAPATCHE PARK; and left 4.5 *m.* to SUNSET PARK (*see Wonderland Trail, below*).

PARK TOUR 2

White River Entrance to Yakima (Sunrise) Park. 16.9 m.

The rugged country leading to Yakima Park is enthralling, with its endless array of jagged peaks and wooded foothills spreading upward into a sea of clouds that billow around the summits.

From the junction of the park road with US 410, the highway descends gently for a mile through heavy timber to KLICKITAT CREEK (3,460 alt.), a tributary of White River. At 1.4 *m.* is the CHECKING STATION, where it is necessary to purchase park permits (*fee $1*) for automobiles. At 3.8 *m.* is a junction with the EAST SIDE TRAIL (*see Park Tour 4*).

Gradually ascending, the road crosses FRYINGPAN CREEK, an icy stream originating at the base of the eastern lobe of Fryingpan Glacier at an elevation of 6,000 feet. The road continues on practically level grade through timbered land.

The WHITE RIVER, crossed at 5.4 *m.,* is in the bed of a great valley gouged out by glaciers in the past; the steep V-shaped flanks of the ridges, deeply forested, reach from 1,000 to 2,000 feet to the barren serrated summits, which mark the valley like the edges of a great trough.

Here is a junction with a side road.

Left 0.7 *m.* to OLD WHITE RIVER CAMPGROUND, a public camping spot near a fork in the river. Two trails radiate from the camp, one to Emmons Glacier, the other to Yakima Park.

From White River the highway climbs along an ever-deepening canyon, with walls that drop sharply away from the road. (*Caution is advised*). At various levels the sinuous route that has been traveled may be seen far below, often veiled by clouds, as the road bears northeast, then north along mountain flanks to cross YAKIMA CREEK, at

8.2 *m.,* where water is available for overheated radiators. Here the road breaks out into scattered timber and flower fields.

At SUNRISE POINT (6,120 alt.), 12.9 *m.,* the most spectacular lookout point reached by road in the park, are rest rooms and parking space. Among the many peaks seen from here are Glacier Peak, Mount Adams, Mount Baker, and Mount Stuart. Several park trails converge at the point.

Straight ahead to SUNRISE LAKE, 0.6 *m.* and CLOVER LAKE, 1.5 *m.*

Rapidly gaining altitude, the highway leaves the zone of heavy forests and enters a sub-alpine area where the trees are more scattered and stunted and twisted by the winds. Beyond and to the left of Sunrise Lodge (*cabin camp, rest rooms, service station, free camp and picnic grounds*), at 15.4 *m.,* is the BLOCKHOUSE, comprising park museum and ranger station. The lodge is in the center of Yakima Park, where broad flower-dotted meadows spread toward the foothills; dark blotches here and there indicate clumps of Alpine fir and pine.

EMMONS GLACIER, largest in the United States, blankets the eastern slope of the mountain with formidable ice cascades five and one-half miles long and almost two miles wide. Its tremendous pressure has broken down part of the summit crater rim. This ice field was named for Samuel F. Emmons, geologist and mountaineer, who made the second ascent of the peak in 1870.

To the left and separated from Emmons by sharp crags is the FRYINGPAN GLACIER, which, with its interglaciers—Whitman and Ohanapecosh—unseen beyond, originates at a height of nearly 11,000 feet on the great triangular wedge extending down from Little Tahoma, the highest pinnacle on the eastern side of the peak. The Fryingpan, largest of the three, covers the eastern side of the flank and joins the Emmons at its apex. On the right of Emmons is WINTHROP GLACIER, extending toward the north.

As at Paradise, the park naturalist gives nightly lectures (*except Sunday; 8 p.m.*) on flora and fauna and scenic points of interest at the Blockhouse. Supervised saddle trips are available, and short hikes (*free*) are given daily; trips of a day's duration are taken twice weekly.

Many trail trips may be made from Yakima Park:

1. SOURDOUGH TRAIL, 2.5 *m.,* NW., is an easy trail leading into the Sourdough Range toward the north where the terrain becomes steadily more barren, yet which offers worthwhile views of the mountain toward the southwest. At 1.3 *m.,* in an almost barren region, is FROZEN LAKE (6,700 alt.), which serves as a reservoir for the Yakima Park water supply. A large bank of snow, the nearest perpetual snow to Yakima Park, lingers on the bank throughout the year. From the Lake the trail branches in three directions: one continues up to Burroughs Mountain; one to Mount Fremont, fire lookout station; and the other down the canyon to Mystic Lake and the Northern Loop trail (*see Park Tour* 3).

2. The DEGE PEAK TRAIL, 1.8 *m.,* NW., leads through some of the most rugged terrain in the region. Almost as high as the Cascade Mountains, which average approximately 8,000 feet, the peak offers a superlative view of the range, the surrounding peaks, and Mount Rainier itself.

3. BERKELEY PARK TRAIL, 2.8 *m.,* W., leads into flowering park lands

between Skyscraper Mountain, near which Huckleberry Creek heads, and the Burroughs Mountains, named after John Burroughs.

4. ST. ELMO'S PASS TRAIL, 6 *m.,* SW., leads over Burroughs Mountain to a high level at the timber line (7,415 alt.), from which both Emmons and Winthrop glaciers are visible. The view of the Winthrop from this point is spectacular. A stream of ice descending from the summit snows is split by a great wedge of rock, Steamboat Prow, around which it breaks in great icy waves. The unevenness of the glacier's course has resulted in many cascades and domes, formed of resistant rock coated and re-coated with ice.

Other trails include: Mount Fremont, 2.5 *m.,* NW.; Clover Lake, 3 *m.,* NE.; Glacier Basin, 5.8 *m.,* SW.; Camp Curtis, 6.5 *m.,* SW.; Summit Climb (*see Summit Climb, below*); the Wonderland Trail (*see Wonderland Trail, below*); Northern Loop Trail (*see Park Tour* 3).

PARK TOUR 3

Carbon River Entrance to Junction with the Wonderland Trail, 6 m.

One of the least frequented of the park entrances, nevertheless the Carbon River Entrance offers much in primitive beauty. There are few accommodations beyond rude cabin shelters along the trails; trails and road have been but slightly touched by man; there are no concessions—not even a filling station.

At the entrance (1,800 alt.), no automobile permit is required, but visitors are requested to register at the RANGER STATION. Here fire permits, necessary if trail tours are contemplated, are obtainable.

The road, winding among stately firs and cedars, is a tranquil, shaded land; mosses hang in veil-like folds from limbs and trunks of ancient trees and over wind-felled logs like a carpet.

A rustic bridge spans RANGER CREEK (2,026 alt.), 3.1 *m.,* which continues northward to join the Carbon River. From the bridge the road follows the right bank of the Carbon, climbing steadily. During the summer, when the glaciers melt most, the stream is a rushing torrent.

IPSUT (Ind. bear) CREEK (2,500 alt.), 5 *m.,* is spanned by a wooden bridge, at the south side of which is a junction with several trails.

Right to EUNICE LAKE, TOLMIE PEAK, AND MOWICH LAKE (*see Wonderland Trail, below*). At 5.5 *m.* is a junction with the Northern Loop Trail to Yakima Park.

The NORTHERN LOOP TRAIL leads left up Spukwush Creek, rounding TYEE (Ind. chief) PEAK (6,030 alt.) into the Chenuis Mountains, source of the creek. Skirting the drab benchlands of the YELLOWSTONE CLIFFS on the southern fringe of the mountains, the trail reaches WINDY GAP, 5 *m.,* between the Chenuis and Crescent Mountains. Here is a junction with a trail leading left for one mile to the NATURAL BRIDGE, a 200-foot stone arch spanning the gorge along the western border of Mosquito Flat.

The main trail continues down Van Horn Creek to the shelter cabin and ranger patrol station on the southern tip of LAKE JAMES, 8 *m.* The lake, almost round in shape, affords good fishing. To the north of Lake James, separated only by a narrow neck of land, is the slightly larger LAKE ETHEL, which has an outlet in the West Fork of the White River, where fishing, often better than in the lakes, may be found.

The trail leads east from the lake down a heavily forested ridge to

WHITE RIVER, 10 *m.,* then crossing the river, ascends the slopes, zigzagging back and forth through ever thinning conifers. Swinging south, away from rocky pinnacles, it enters the broad expanse of GRAND PARK (5,700 alt.), 14.5 *m.* This, the largest natural park area on the north side of the mountain, is a high plateau of relatively level land strewn with flowers and decked with groves of alpine fir and hemlock. From this elevation may be seen the Chenuis Mountains to the west; Mount Rainier to the south; and the Sourdough Mountains to the southeast. Many deer are found in this region.

The trail drops down to GOLD BASIN, then starts climbing up LODI CREEK, a tributary of White River named by early prospectors in the vicinity. At the junction of trail and creek is AFFI FALLS, one of the prettiest cascades on this side of the park. South of the falls the trail follows the creek into BERKELEY PARK, 17 *m.,* a region where trees are stunted but where daisies, columbine, larkspur, avalanche lilies, and anemones grow in profusion. The region south of the park grows more and more barren around FROZEN LAKE, 18.7 *m.* Here is a junction with a side trail, which parallels the narrow ridge of the Burroughs Mountains to the Wonderland Trail (*see Wonderland Trail below*). Southeast of Frozen Lake the trail descends through the barrens to YAKIMA PARK, 20 *m.* (*see Park Tour 2*).

Heading southeast the road narrows, winding among trees that almost graze the fenders of intruding cars. At 5.9 *m.* is a RUSTIC CAMPGROUND, where crudely fashioned logs provide rough tables; the clearing is suitable for an overnight stop. Near the camp is the SLIDE, hidden by a fringe of trees, where a great mass of rock has fallen from a crag.

SIX-MILE CREEK, 6 *m.,* is the end of the road. Here signs indicate the way to Mystic Lake, Spray Park, and the Wonderland Trail (*see Wonderland Trail below*).

PARK TOUR 4

Ohanapecosh Entrance to (US 410) Cayuse Pass. 13 m.

The Ohanapecosh Entrance, with numerous trails to scenic points, lakes and streams abounding with fish, and hot mineral springs, is popular with hiker, fisherman, and health seeker. The road leads from the park boundary to the RANGER STATION, 1 *m.,* where visitors must register. Here are public campgrounds amid scenery neither rugged nor charming.

The HOT SPRINGS (2,004 alt.), at 1.7 *m.,* offer mineral baths, Lodge, bathhouse, and cabins are clustered between the road and the Ohanapecosh (Ind. deep blue water) River. The temperature of the hot springs, which have their source in the heated heart of Mount Rainier, ranges from 110 ° to 125° F. Several trails lead from the hot springs to lakes and scenic points.

1. COWLITZ DIVIDE TRAIL, 4.5 *m.,* NE., leads upward from the hot springs along the rough ridge of the Cowlitz Divide, which separates the valleys of the Ohanapecosh and the Muddy Fork of the Cowlitz River. In the upper levels the trail emerges from timber into a broad open park on the

southern summit of the divide (4,770 alt.). Here is a junction with the Wonderland Trail (*see Wonderland Trail, below*).

2. TWIN LAKES TRAIL, 6.5 *m.*, NE., cutting through heavy stands of aged timber where game is abundant, rises steadily toward the rim of the Cascade Range. From an elevation of 5,000 feet, the lakes resemble twin emeralds resting in a deep nap of forest.

The road continues northward for three miles along the west bank of the Ohanapecosh River to its confluence with LAUGHINGWATER CREEK and on to SILVER FALLS, 3.5 *m.,* a beautiful cataract on the Ohanapecosh River. The deep green of the forest is reflected in the flying spray. A little beyond is CEDAR FLAT (2,300 alt.), one of the few remaining areas where tall red cedars stand untouched by man, scenting the air with their balsam.

At 6.5 *m.* is a junction with a trail.

Left here a short distance to OLALLIE (Ind. berries) CREEK, noted for its good fishing. The name was derived from the Indian tribes that, years ago, made camp in the vicinity to gather the plentiful blue huckleberries.

WHITTIER CREEK is crossed at 7.9 *m.,* and at 9 *m.* is STAFFORD FALLS. In a broad timbered basin at 10.3 *m.* is a fork in the river marking the confluence of the Ohanapecosh and its tributary CHINOOK CREEK (3,124 alt.), which rises miles toward the northeast in Tipsoo Lake and flows southward through timbered ridges, merging with Kotsuck and Deer creeks in its course. The road crosses DEER CREEK BRIDGE at 11.4 *m.,* near the junction of Kotsuck and Deer creeks.

A PARK SERVICE CABIN, 11.6 *m.,* affords temporary shelter. Here is a junction with the East Side Trail.

Swinging left along Kotsuck Creek, the trail reaches the picturesque cascades of HORSESHOE FALLS (5,000 alt.), where the waters plunge from their upper course near the southern base of Fryingpan Glacier. Constantly rising, the route enters GOATS PASS (5,300 alt.), at 2.1 *m.,* between the glacier ridges and pinnacles and the tumbled foothills of the Cascades. From the pass the trail dips down into a small bowl in the mountain ridges to OWYHIGH LAKE (5,150 alt.), 2.5 *m.,* named for the warrior chief of the Yakima. The trail continues below Tamanos Mountain through heavy timber to a junction with the White River Road at 6 *m.* (*see Park Tour 2*).

At 12 *m.* the road enters a tunnel through the mountainside; beyond the tunnel it winds along the upper course of Chinook Creek to a junction with US 410 at Cayuse Pass, 13 *m.* (*see State Tour 3c*).

SUMMIT CLIMB

Paradise Inn to Summit of Mount Rainier, 8,908 ft.

The climb requires approximately two days, with five to seven hours stop at Camp Muir. Parties usually leave between 1 and 2 p.m. and arrive at Camp Muir about 6 p.m. Guides are essential. Trip begun on clear day may end in storms at higher levels where 40-mile-an-hour gales are frequent. Equipment and guides are available at Paradise Inn. *Equipment*: Alpenstock or ice axe, amber glasses, calks, hobnails, crampons, leather and wool gloves, grease paint for protection against sun glare, and ropes. *Important*: Eat only light vegetables, raw or boiled, and lean meats or beef tea prior to climb. Follow guide's advice on eating en route; experienced climbers use sugar for building energy.

All climbers are required to register with a district ranger before starting and make a report of their success before leaving. As a matter of safety, climbers must be physically fit, more or less experienced, and have proper equipment and supplies. Qualified mountaineers are given permission to attempt the ascent without park guides.

The ascent begins easily from Paradise Valley (5,557 alt.), and the pace is brisk through the grassland but slower on the climbs. As the grassy slopes of the trail recede, rough basaltic rocks of odd shapes and sizes appear. The route follows a winding course but holds steadily toward McCLURE ROCK (7,384 alt.), from which Paradise Valley and the great forests of the park appear spread out below. The rock was named to honor Professor Edgar McClure, University of Oregon, who took barometric measurements at the summit in 1897 and met death in the descent.

Light refreshment is permitted at ANVIL ROCK (9,584 alt.), where a fire lookout station stands a short distance from the main trail. From the lookout it is possible to see points 100 miles distant, but the view to the northwest is blocked by the mountain. The sun's rays beat down unmercifully, and hikers are reluctant to leave the shade of the rock. From here the trail leads over the rubble between NISQUALLY and COWLITZ GLACIERS, which have begun to change from white to light brown, as snow slowly mixes with eroded rock and soil. The ascent continues for about two hours to the next major stop.

CAMP MUIR (10,000 alt.), in a saddle beneath Cowlitz Cleaver, about 4,000 feet above timberline, is reached about dusk. A heavier meal is eaten here before the hikers retire for the night. Provisions and fuel must be carried up from Paradise, and water is obtained by melting snow. Accommodations are simple but adequate. The ascent is resumed at one or two o'clock in the morning. There remains a climb of approximately 4,400 feet to the crest—11 hours of continuous effort.

At Camp Muir the route diverges from that pursued by General Stevens and Van Trump in 1870, which, until blocked by a 60-foot slide at Gibraltar Rock in the spring of 1937, had been the popular summit route. The new route crosses the ice fields of the upper Cowlitz Glacier and passes through Kadaver Gap in the CATHEDRAL ROCKS (8,262 alt.), an angular pinnacle of rough lava separating the upper Cowlitz and Ingraham glaciers. The course is difficult—a challenge to any mountaineer—more so than the old route, and much longer.

The INGRAHAM GLACIER, named for Major E. S. Ingraham, one of the mountain pioneers, originates at the summit and follows a deep trough down the mountain flank, its rough course resulting in numerous spectacular ice falls and cascades. Cathedral Rocks separates the Ingraham from the Cowlitz Glacier; at its base the two unite again.

The route swings upward, once the pinnacles of the great wedge separating the Ingraham Glacier from the Emmons on the north are reached. These tooth-like crags extend down the mountainside a distance of five miles to end in the Cowlitz Chimney—a castellated formation of rock that dominates the eastern slopes of the lower mountain. North of the line of crags the vast wedge carries three large interglaciers upon its back: Whitman, Ohanapecosh, and the Fryingpan. After hours of stiff climbing, the eminence of LITTLE TAHOMA (11,117 alt.) is attained,, the highest point on the eastern flank of the peak and the apex of the wedge spreading below. The steep, lava walls of the peak, in places 2,000 feet thick, point upward at an angle probably indicating the former crest of the mountain, about a half-mile higher than the present summit. Almost continuous ice and snow fields make climbing difficult; high winds that sweep the rocky heights clean of snow are frequently encountered. Hidden crevasses are an ever-present danger; alpenstocks must dig in and crampons grip solidly for holds in the snow. As the summit is approached the scenery achieves a bewildering grandeur. On clear days the surrounding country, softened by distance, spreads out far below; on cloudy days only the higher peaks and pinnacles project above the cloud mass that fills the valleys.

REGISTER ROCK (14,161 alt.), near the crown of the peak, offers a shelter against the whipping winds; here are metal cases where the successful climber may register his achievement. From the lee of the rock the snow-filled crater at the summit spreads out its mile and a half of drifts, mounds, and caverns. Little risk accompanies exploration of the crater, but care should be taken near the rim where slides may be precipitated.

At three-eighths of a mile beyond Register Rock, COLUMBIA CREST (14,409 alt.), the highest tip of the summit rim, rounds 247 feet above the crater proper. In favorable weather the view from the tip of Columbia Crest or Peak Success is magnificent: the massive glacier tentacles extending downward appear truncated at their ends, where rivers burst forth and descend through the dark crags and green forest. In the middle distance appear the peaks of the lower Cascades, the serrated Olympics, and the Canadian Coast Range.

The return to Paradise can be made in from four to eight hours from the summit.

WONDERLAND TRAIL

Circuit of Mount Rainier from Longmire, Approx. 100.5 m.

Without side trips tour can be made in 7 days, but 10 days can be well spent to allow trips to outstanding points of interest. *Equipment*: Full outfit of hiking clothes—high-top boots, breeches, and heavy shirts—first aid kit, snowglasses, mosquito and sunburn lotion, light hand ax, sleeping bag, and food.

Of all trails within the Rainier National Park the Wonderland Trail affords the greatest diversity of scenic grandeur; winding trails, dense forest, snow and ice fields, flowered alpine meadows, glacial streams, soaring peaks, and ghost forest—all between elevations of 2,500 and 7,200 feet.

From Longmire the trail gradually ascends through dense forest of fir and lodgepole pine. After crossing the silt-laden Nisqually River the trail ascends the crystal-clear Paradise River, passing CARTER FALLS and MAD-CAP FALLS at the base of Eagle Peak, northern end of the Tatoosh Range. Paradise River is crossed a few hundred yards above Narada Falls in a setting of huge fir and small hemlock. Along the banks of the river rockfern grows in profusion. The trail swings east into the forested hills that mark the southern extremity of Mazama Ridge, then enters the STEVENS CANYON.

At 12 *m.* the trail joins an incomplete road and skirts the south shore of REFLECTION LAKE, lying amid rank growths of wild flowers and fringed by clusters of blue huckleberry, with bright red and white blossoms. In many spots mountain polypody forms small brakes. (*No license is required for fishing in the lake, which is well stocked with Eastern brook trout*).

The trail swings east from the lake and approaches LAKE LOUISE, (4,890 alt.), a mile beyond, in a high saddle between Mazama Ridge and the Tatoosh Range. Here, too, the blue huckleberry is prolific, the tall bushes drooping with their fruit in late summer. The huckleberry was a favorite fruit of the Indians in days past, and many of the fires that occurred on the mountain are attributed to their efforts to clear a way for a greater spread of the bushes. In its course to the great U-shaped bottom of Stevens Canyon, the trail offers a view of the tumbling waters of MARTHA FALLS, 14.5 *m.* (3,110 alt.). Deer and black bear are met occasionally in the forest. Continuing its descent of the canyon, the trail turns directly toward Sylvia Falls. In quick succession MAPLE CREEK and STEVENS CREEK (2,730 alt.), 17 *m.,* are crossed.

Arching 100 feet above the turbid waters of the Muddy Fork of the Cowlitz River, in places but 20 feet wide, a horse and foot bridge spans the COWLITZ BOX CANYON, (3,040 alt.), 18 *m.* Tips of fir trees are level with the rail on either side of the bridge. A forest fire once laid waste 20 square miles of timber in this area, but in this moist level reforestation has been rapid.

At NICKEL CREEK (3,300 alt.), 19 *m.,* where shelter and patrol cabins are available, begins a difficult two-mile climb to the COWLITZ DIVIDE (4,770 alt.). Provision should be made for drinking water, as there are no springs for approximately four miles. The trail winds by switchbacks through heavy timber to open parkland. At the crest of the divide the trail bears left.

Straight ahead (R) a side trail descends the slope into OHANAPECOSH PARK and to the HOT SPRINGS, 2.5 *m.* (*see Park Tour* 4). Pursuing the spine of the divide through fragrant alpine meadows, affording splendid views of Rainier, the Cascades, and Mount Adams, the trail reaches INDIAN BAR, (4,150 alt.) 25.5 *m.,* a great gravel bank near the head of the Ohanapecosh River, surrounded by cliffs and glaciers. A three-sided shelter, overlooking

WAUHAUKAUPAUKEN FALLS in a basin of flowers, is an ideal camping site.

A corner of OHANAPECOSH PARK (5,500 alt.), is crossed at 26.5 *m.* This park is hedged by three glaciers: OHANAPECOSH on the south, FRYINGPAN on the west, and the SARVENT GLACIERS spreading their tentacles across the whole northern boundary. The trail is arduous along the higher ridges between Ohanapecosh Glacier and Ohanapecosh Park. It gains altitude and crosses the valley head beyond the timberland to pass through PANHANDLE GAP (6,900 alt.), which offers an unobstructed view in all directions. Toward the north the road winding up Sunrise Ridge into Yakima Park is visible.

From Panhandle Gap the trail drops down over large ice fields of Fryingpan Glacier (*watch closely for trail markers during foggy weather*) into SUMMERLAND (5,900 alt.), 29.5 *m.* This is a natural floral park, rugged and rocky, with dottings of alpine trees. An overnight stay at the shelter cabin is recommended, although mosquitos will keep the visitor company. The trail, almost continually above the timberline, is rugged but allows sweeping panoramas of mountain ranges and views of Little Tahoma on the mountain rim above. As the trail drops along the course of the Fryingpan Creek, which rounds Goat Island Mountain, the scenery changes from alpine meadow to deep cedar and hemlock forest. The trail crosses a bridge over the Fryingpan and continues to White River Road. The White River Road is followed to another bridge, across which is the former site of the OLD WHITE RIVER CAMP (4,600 alt.), 36.1 *m.* Left is a trail to the snout of EMMONS GLACIER, GLACIER BASIN, and BURROUGHS MOUNTAIN.

The Wonderland route winds upward 2,200 feet, for a distance of three miles through timber, arriving at YAKIMA PARK, 39 *m.* (*see Park Tour 2*). This is the last place on the trail where supplies can be replenished. An overnight rest is usually taken here. From Yakima Park the trail ascends to a junction of trails near FROZEN LAKE, 41.1 *m.*

Left a trail forks and climbs round the barren cliffs of BURROUGHS MOUNTAIN, where it swings left to GLACIER BASIN (5,900 alt.), a meadow on the mountain flank and, until a few years ago, the site of mining activity.

Continuing (R) between two tablelike buttes, the Wonderland Trail descends 2,000 feet through open country, crosses a ridge through heavy timber, and approaches the crevasses of WINTHROP GLACIER, 44.8 *m.*, second largest in the park. The cold breath of the ice mass chills the air. Rounding the discolored snout the route turns left, crosses the river bar, and ascends the west fork of the White River to MYSTIC LAKE (5,750 alt.), 47 *m.*, lying in a high park between Old Desolate and Mineral Mountains. The starkness of the domes seems to accentuate the blended colors of wild flowers. A shelter cabin and camp overlook the lake.

A side trail leads up the ridge between the lake and Moraine Park to points where great avalanches of snow are seen tumbling from WILLIS WALL (*see below*) during warm summer days.

The main trail leaves Mystic Lake and ascends a low divide that offers a rare view of Willis Wall; it crosses the small upper stream of the West Fork of the White River to the base of Old Desolate and skirts it along the lower levels of flowered MORAINE PARK. Beyond Moraine Creek, which the trail follows, is the rock-strewn ice of Carbon Glacier.

At 49 *m.* is a shelter. Almost facing it is the rocky formation of GOAT ISLAND high above, which splits the lower flow of the glacier. Descending from the uplands of the park, the trail enters heavy woods and skirts bald cliffs, along the border of CARBON GLACIER (3,355 alt.), to its terminus at 50 *m.* The lowest perpetual ice field in the United States, Carbon Glacier rises in an amphitheater-like cirque high on the mountain flank, gouged out and enlarged by the glacier itself beneath the dome of Liberty Cap. The upper wall of the cirque—Willis Wall—towers 3,600 feet above the great bowl, one and one-half miles across. From this wall, snows often 300 feet deep plunge down into this largest of the mountain cirques; it is a rare sight—magnificent and terrifying. The wall was named for Professor Bailey Willis, who explored the northern side of the mountain in 1881. In its lower reaches the glacier narrows to a mere snout a few yards wide but approximately a mile in length. It ends in a great canyon and gives birth to the Carbon River in a sculptured ice cave.

Crossing the rocky bed of the Carbon River the trail joins the CARBON RIVER ROAD at 54 *m.* (*see Park Tour 3*), where there is a shelter cabin. From the junction, the trail continues straight ahead, then dips down and crosses CATARACT CREEK; bearing right below the walls of the ECHO CLIFFS, it follows the wooded gorge between the foothills of Mount Rainier and MOTHER MOUNTAIN (6,840 alt.), through which the creek flows.

At 55.5 *m.* the trail crosses MARMOT CREEK, so named for the abundance of whistling marmot in the vicinity, to CATARACT FALLS, veiling the surrounding woods with its mist. The trail continues along Marmot Creek, zigzagging back and forth through heavy forest. Near three tiny bodies of water it veers right and enters the upper section of MIST PARK, a meadow of flowers that extends from the trail toward the slopes of Mother Mountain.

Rocky uplands, dotted with occasional ice fields, are encountered at 56 *m.* Foggy weather is not unusual here, and stone cairns, the only markers of the route, should be closely followed. On reaching an elevation of 6,700 feet the trail swings right and down the slopes to SPRAY PARK, 62 *m.,* famous for its flower fields and magnificent views. Here, beside a small lake, is a choice camping spot. Two excellent side trips by unmarked trails are possible from the camp:

Left 4 *m.* over rock and snow to OBSERVATION ROCK for good views;

3 *m.* by a shortcut through Knapsack Pass to Mowich Lake. From Spray Park the trail passes HESSONG ROCK (6,149 alt.). Another trail leads left to the thundering waters of SPRAY FALLS, 0.3 *m.* Below the falls to the point where Spray Creek joins the Mowich River, fishing is excellent.

Bearing right the trail leads on to the benches of EAGLE CLIFF (5,300 alt.), 63 *m.,* where the western ramparts of the mountain, the varicolored slopes of the park, and the timbered heights of Ptarmigan Ridge stand out clearly. Below the cliffs are the abandoned shacks and workings of a former mining camp. Timber becomes heavier, largely cedar, fir, and hemlock, as the trail continues downward to cross Lee Creek and lead northward to a ranger cabin (*telephone service*) and campsite at the southern tip of MOWICH (Ind. deer) LAKE (4,950 alt.), 65.5 *m.* Rude tables of split logs and a camp stove are the only facilities. The lake affords good fishing. The trail winds southward through the high, heavily timbered levels east of Paul Peak, then drops down by easy grades to the NORTH MOWICH RIVER, 69.5 *m.* Here is a junction with a trail.

Right 3 *m.* to MEADOW CREEK and the western boundary of the park at the MOWICH ENTRANCE (*see State Tour 3c*), dedicated September 2, 1933.

At 70 *m.,* midway between the North and South Mowich Rivers, in a delta formed by their confluence, is a shelter cabin that may be used as a base from which to take fishing expeditions to both rivers. At 70.5 *m.* the SOUTH MOWICH RIVER is crossed, the course continuing through wooded ridges to descend into the region of the GOLDEN LAKES, 74.8 *m.,* the heart of SUNSET PARK, a richly flowered area. A ranger patrol cabin (*telephone service*) and a shelter cabin stand on the shore of the group of lakes. Campsites on the lakes offer spectacular views.

Leaving Sunset Park, a mile of flowered meadowland is crossed before the trail descends through timber to the NORTH PUYALLUP RIVER, 80.5 *m.,* at the end of the West Side Highway (*see Park Tour 1A*). From the camp HANGING GLACIER, a great pendant of Tahoma Glacier, is visible.

After crossing the bridge, the trail climbs through heavy timber along Klapatche Ridge to another alpine flower bed, KLAPATCHE PARK (5,500 alt.), 83.5 *m.* A shelter cabin offers limited overnight accommodations. The park affords views considered among the best in the park, not only of the peak itself, but far to the west the great mass of the Olympic Mountains.

Keeping to the higher levels the trail attains ST. ANDREWS CREEK, where there is a patrol cabin; then follows along its course to the SOUTH PUYALLUP RIVER, 87.5 *m.,* and the West Side Highway. It springs upward from the highway over Emerald Ridge and through ROUND PASS (3,879 alt.), with a notable view of the canyon and the river rushing through the wild gorge. Beyond, sweeping toward the westward horizon, is a wild sea of green hills. At Tahoma Creek (*good fishing*), the trail bears left and follows the creek to its source at the lower tip of South Tahoma Glacier. Swinging across the stream by a bridge, bench lands are followed into INDIAN HENRY'S HUNTING GROUND (5,300 alt.), 93 *m.,* one of the prettiest alpine gardens in the park, set amid the studding peaks of Iron Mountain, Crystal Mountain, and Pyramid Peak, where mountain goats are numerous. A shelter cabin and ranger patrol cabin are set in the midst of the flowered meadows. Several trails of interest radiate from this point.

Left a half-mile to the MIRROR LAKES, where photographers find the most nearly perfect mountain reflections in the park. Right here one mile to the meadows of Pyramid Park. Right about a half-mile to MOUNT ARARAT (5,300 alt.), a great knoll, easily accessible.

From Indian Henry's the trail bears around the south side of Iron Mountain, through fields of avalanche lilies and heather, to the shore of SQUAW LAKE (5,000 alt.), 84 *m.,* dips down through timber line and crosses DEVIL'S DREAM CREEK, a veritable inferno on hot days. Continuing downward, the trail crosses Pyramid and Kautz creeks, less than a mile apart, at 97.5 *m.* Abruptly the trail rises and climbs Rampart Ridge (3,800 alt.). At the summit is a junction with two side trails.

Left 3.5 *m.* to VAN TRUMP PARK. Right 0.7 *m.* to the RAMPARTS, highest point on the ridge. On this ridge for four miles stretches an unbroken "field" of "deliciosum" (sweet bilberry), finest of all the huckleberries, as the black bears all know; for they climb to its essential high altitude to feast on the delicious purple harvest.

From the crest of the ridge the trail descends through two miles of timber and thickets to LONGMIRE, 100.5 *m.* (*see Park Tour 1*).

Olympic National Park

Season: Open year round but climatic conditions in winter often make the trails impassable. Officials at headquarters advise of conditions at all times.
Administrative Offices: National Park Service Headquarters for Olympic National Park, Port Angeles. Visitors are advised to secure detailed information when planning trips.
Registration: At first ranger station in Olympic National Park to secure fire permit or register destination.
Transportation: Olympic Peninsula is easily reached from Seattle, Tacoma, Hoquiam, Olympia, and Victoria and Vancouver, British Columbia, and other Northwestern cities. Ferry service on regular schedules is available from Seattle and Edmonds across Puget Sound to Port Townsend and Port Ludlow and from Victoria, British Columbia, to Port Angeles. Loop tour encircles peninsula, be-

ginning five miles west of Olympia; here US 101 swings north from junction with US 410, passes through Hoodsport and Port Angeles and skirts the south shore of Lake Crescent (only place where highway touches park). (*See Tour* 9).
Trails: Trails lead into and through park from ends of stub approach roads; the trails are narrow but safe and passable for both saddle and foot parties; trailside shelters are found at many camp sites.
Guide Service and Horses: Guide services and saddle and pack horses may be obtained from resorts or ranchers at the end of stub roads at Olympic Hot Springs, Whiskey Bend, Sol Duc Hot Springs, Hoh River, North Fork and East Fork of Quinault River, Skokomish and Dosewallips Rivers.

Accommodations: Excellent hotel accommodations and housekeeping cabins, under Government supervision, are available at Olympic Hot Springs on Boulder Creek; and housekeeping cabins at Sol Duc Hot Springs. Swimming pools with water from springs are available at both places.

Two chalets, accessible only by foot or horseback, are operated within park under Government supervision; one at Low Divide in the central part of park and the other at Enchanted Valley on East Fork Quinault River; chalets offer good accommodations and are excellent base camps.

Good hotels, inns, and camps, within the park include several on Lake Crescent, Lake Quinault, and one at Graves Creek, overlooking East Fork Quinault River, all privately owned and operated, but under Government supervision. Numerous resorts, hotels, and camping facilities along US 101 and on stub roads outside of park. National Park Service operates free auto campground, with simple accommodations, at Jackson Ranger Station, and Sol Duc Hot Springs. There are camps at La Poel Resort, Elwha River, Olympic Hot Springs, Graves Creek, Staircase on Lake Cushman; Altair and Elwha camps on Elwha River, and Muncaster and July Creek camps on Lake Quinault.

Climate, Clothing, and Equipment: Evenings are cool, and there is considerable snow on trails as well as frequent rain in winter. Clothing should be warm and loosely fitting, tweed preferably for all-round use; hobnailed or calked shoes are advised, and alpenstocks, colored glasses, and face paints for the snowfields.
Medical Service: Available at Port Angeles, Forks, Hoodsport.
Communication Service: Post offices at Quinault, Port Angeles, Forks, Hoodsport, and Ovington on Lake Crescent. Telephone communication to all sections of park is available from inns, ranger stations, and from park headquarters in Port Angeles.

Special Regulations: Hunting is prohibited. For fishing, County or State license is required; State license for residents, $3, nonresidents, $5; County license for nonresidents, $3. Permits are required for building fires in other than established auto camps; garbage should be deposited in receptacles and fires be completely extinguished before leaving camp. No smoking is allowed on trails. Firearms are not allowed on Government lands; dogs and cats are allowed when on leash or otherwise confined. It is unlawful to pick flowers or shrubs, or to carve initials or otherwise deface anything in park.

Feeding bears is prohibited. (Because bears search out food ruthlessly, provisions should be suspended from trees in covered receptacles, well out of reach). Complete regulations are posted in superintendent's office and at ranger stations. Fire guards and park rangers in various sections are always glad to assist campers.

OLYMPIC NATIONAL PARK, an area of more than 800,000 acres in the center of the Olympic Peninsula, is a wilderness of virgin forests, precipitous canyons, and alpine meadows, from which emerge lofty mountain peaks with shining glaciers and vast snow fields. With the surrounding Olympic National Forest, the region is one of the few great areas of primeval beauty left in the United States, and its unique rain forests are as spectacular as the inchoate mass of its mountains.

In 1774, Juan Perez, a roving Spanish sea captain sailing up the coast, sighted the snowy pinnacles of the Olympics against a blazing blue summer sky. He named them Cerro de la Santa Rosalia, but this euphonious name was not destined to last; 14 years later Captain John Meares, in command of a British barkentine off the Washington coast, declared the mountains a fit home for the gods and named the highest peak Mount Olympus.

There seems to be no exact record of the first ascent of Mount Olympus. A report made in *Steel Points,* published at Portland, Oregon, in July 1907, states that Henry D. Cook and B. F. Shaw, members of a private exploring expedition, accompanied by two Indians, climbed the peak in July 1854. In the park superintendent's files is a sketch of one of the earliest expeditions into the park area; in 1890 a company of picked men, headed by young Lieutenant Joseph P. O'Neil, blazed their way from Hoodsport up past Lake Cushman and on up the North Fork of Skokomish River to the East Fork of the Quinault, enduring severe hardships as they forged through great forests where no trails existed.

The park was created June 29, 1938, when the Wallgren Bill established a national park of 643,000 acres and empowered the President to increase the area to 892,000 acres. By order of President Roosevelt, 187,411 acres were added on January 3, 1940, making a total of 837,411 acres or approximately 1,308 square miles. Additional land, with an outlet on the Pacific, is being acquired. The policy of keeping this park in a primitive state is being strictly maintained; mountain trails, no more than 18 inches wide except in dangerous places, log bridges spanning mountain rivers, and shelter cabins with split-spruce bunks and stone fireplaces will be the only marks of man.

But the dense vegetation and rugged terrain make it easy to keep the park a wilderness. The finest example of the magnificent rain forests are found in the lower valleys of the western slopes, where great stands of Douglas fir, western hemlock, western red cedar, and silver fir grow to gigantic size and height. Temperate climate, winter rainfall, and other conditions favor a tropic luxuriance in both trees and undergrowth. The fallen trunks of enormous trees become nourishment for seedlings that take root upon them, and thus new trees continually replace the old. Great festoons of moss hang from the towering trees, and the ground in some places is an almost impenetrable tangle of fern, vine maple, and other jungle-like growth.

The Olympic Mountains arise in their splendid confusion about the center of the park, encircled by a belt of evergreen forest 50 miles wide and more than 200 miles in circumference. Here are no ordered ranges, but instead a vast pile of rugged rock and snow-covered knife-like peaks, varying in elevation from 3,000 to 8,000 feet, the height of Mount Olympus. Numerous mountains that have been explored are nearly as high as Olympus, and there are others yet to be climbed and named. In places the mountainsides drop almost vertically for more than 3,000 feet, and from the tops of these sheer stone cliffs flow hundreds of filmy waterfalls fed by melting snows.

More than 50 glaciers, with approximately 36 square miles of ice and snow fields, drape the peaks, among them some of the largest and best-formed glaciers in the United States. Those on Olympus are particularly remarkable, one of the most interesting and beautiful being the Blue Glacier, which is really a clear blue. Here the climber, making his way over the rugged terminal moraine, may observe, wherever the bedrock is exposed, deep grooves in the striated surface, the marks of the glacier when it filled the valley to a lower altitude. On the upper glacier where the slope becomes steep, the ascent is made over fields of ice and snow and ledges of glaciated rock to vantage points alongside and above the rugged and picturesque ice-fall. From these points may be viewed the broadly sweeping curves of the medial and lateral moraines and lines of flow in the ice, the curves of the glacier high in the cirques or ice-pockets near the summit; and crowning all, too steep to retain a mantle of ice and snow, the cliffs, the knife-edge crests, and jagged pinnacles of rock that rise between and above the ice-pockets.

Upon nearly every high peak several glaciers are slowly grinding down the rugged sides; at the same time they are receding and forming rivers of ice, the headwaters for the principal streams in the park. Within this glacial field are yawning crevasses and great boulders shielding columns of ice from the summer sun; there are smaller rock fragments sunk in deep wells and pits beyond reach of sunlight; silvery streams of melted ice and snow, plunging from shallow channels into the deep roaring moulins or devil's cauldrons; and above are the lonely pinnacles of rock and ice.

WILD LIFE ZONES

Because elevations in the park rise from about 300 feet in the river valleys, four climatic zones are represented. Great variation in rainfall also helps to produce diversity in the vegetation. In sharp contrast to the excessive rainfall on the western slopes of the peninsula, the average annual rainfall at Port Angeles is 27 inches, at Sequim, 16 miles east, but 17 inches, and farmers in the Dungeness Valley have to irrigate. Thus within a radius of 50 miles is found one of the heaviest rainfalls in the United States and the driest area on the Pacific Coast, exclusive of southern California.

In the transition zone, extending up to 1,500 feet, the profusely flowering plants are at their best, and along the shaded trails are magnificent Douglas firs, the dominant trees in this zone. Associated species are also found here—the western hemlock, western red cedar, western white pine, and white fir. Wild flowering plants include the Oregon grape, red huckleberry, salmonberry, salal, vine maple, wild strawberry, buttercup, Solomon's seal, trillium, and dainty yellow violets. The most noticeable ferns are of the western sword, bracken, and deer

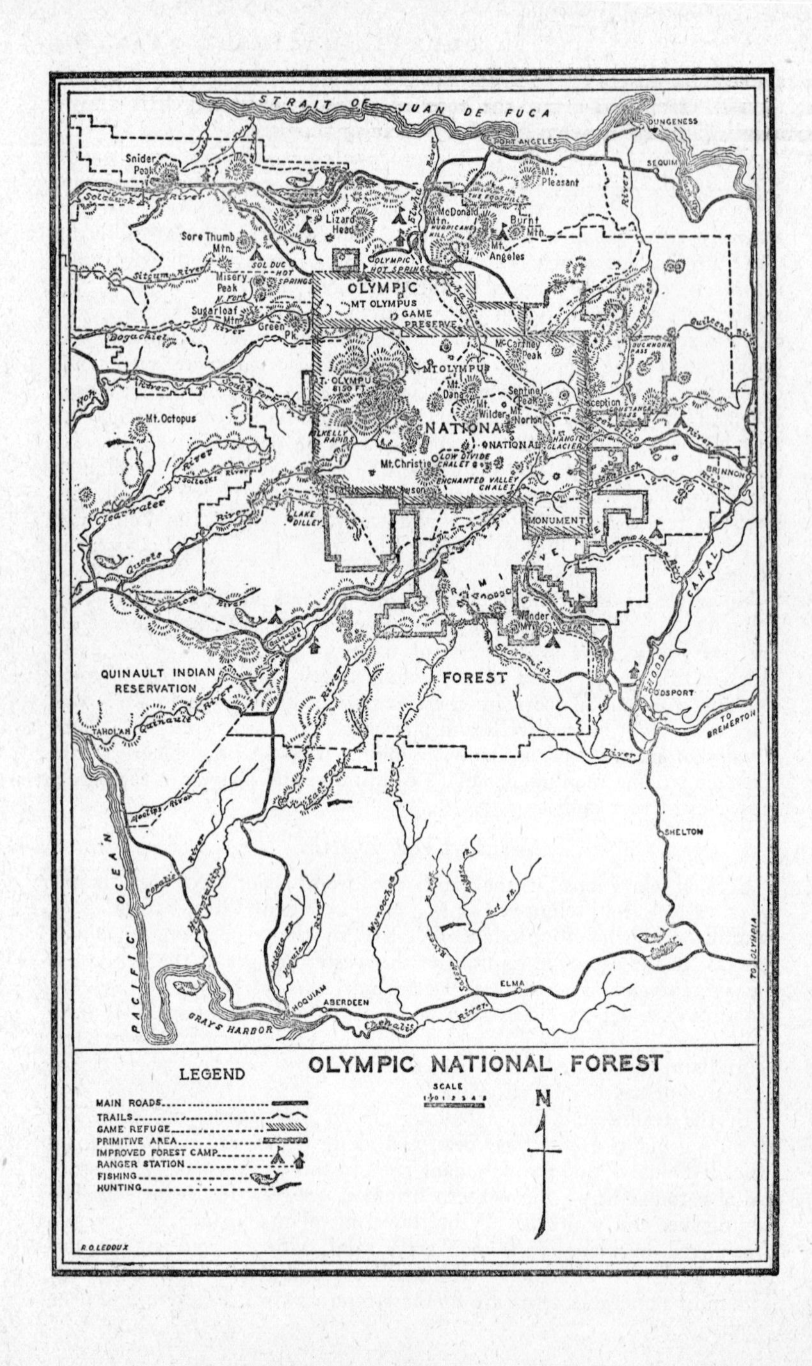
STRAIT OF JUAN DE FUCA
DUNGENESS
PORT ANGELES
SEQUIM
Mt. Pleasant
Snider Peak
Lizard Head
McDonald Mtn.
Burnt Mtn.
Mt. Angeles
Sore Thumb Mtn.
SOL DUC HOT SPRINGS
OLYMPIC HOT SPRINGS
Misery Peak
Sugarloaf Mtn.
Green Pk.
OLYMPIC
MT OLYMPUS
GAME
PRESERVE
McCartney Peak
BUCKHORN PASS
MT. OLYMPUS
MT. OLYMPUS 8150 FT.
Mt. Dana
Mt. Wilder
Mt. Norton
Sentinel Peak
Mt. Octopus
NATIONAL
LOW DIVIDE CHALET
Mt. Christie
ENCHANTED VALLEY CHALET
LAKE DILLEY
MONUMENT
BRINNON
QUINAULT INDIAN
RESERVATION
Quinault Lake
FOREST
HOODSPORT
TO BREMERTON
TAHOLAH
SHELTON
PACIFIC OCEAN
ELMA
HOQUIAM
ABERDEEN
GRAYS HARBOR
TO OLYMPIA
OLYMPIC NATIONAL FOREST
LEGEND
MAIN ROADS
TRAILS
GAME REFUGE
PRIMITIVE AREA
IMPROVED FOREST CAMP
RANGER STATION
FISHING
HUNTING
SCALE
N
R.O.LEDOUX

species. This zone is favorable to the growth of the rain forests, particularly in the Hoh and Bogachiel valleys. Here warm air currents from the Pacific strike against the colder reaches of the Olympics, and the precipitation is unusually heavy; most of the annual 144 inches falls as snow and during the winter rainy season. Douglas and silver firs, western hemlock and red cedar grow to remarkable size and height. The towering trees, heavy with hanging moss, and the lush undergrowth give the impression of a tropical forest. In the summer the valleys are very beautiful, with sunlight and shadow falling in fascinating patterns through the green, moss-draped trees.

In the Canadian zone, where elevations range from 1,500 to 3,500 feet, the silver fir is noticeable, with a sprinkling of western white pine, Douglas fir, and western cedar. Beside the trail or in a little meadow one finds species of bunchberry or Canadian dogwood, alpine beauty, twinflower, tway blade, and tiarella. As the elevation increases, the groups of trees diminish in both number and size.

The Hudsonian zone is the ending of the heavily timbered area, but here, at elevations from 3,500 to 5,000 feet, are found the most delightful mountain meadows. The conifers include mountain hemlock, Alaskan cedar, alpine fir, and some scattered mountain juniper. Shrubs vary from mountain ash to white heather, pink heather, false huckleberry, and spiraea. Sprinkled in the mountain grass and sedge meadows are the avalanche lily, buttercup, blue violet, shooting star, western anemone, valerian, languid lady, arctic lupine, monkey flower, elephant's trunk, aster, larkspur, and the lovely blue gentian. Wild flowering plants are at their best during late July and early August.

In the Arctic-Alpine zone the elevation begins at 5,000 and continues to nearly 8,000 feet. Those who follow switchback trails to these altitudes are rewarded by the sight of the plants and sedges above the upper limit of tree growth. Outstanding plants are the Alaska spiraea, mountain phlox, bluebell, goldenrod, sedge, and lady fern.

One of the principal reasons for establishing the Mount Olympus National Monument in 1909—now part of the Olympic National Park—was to insure protection for the largest remaining herd of Roosevelt elk, native to the Olympic Peninsula. There are more than 3,000 of these magnificent animals within the boundaries of the park. In the winter they browse and forage in the lower valleys and along the watersheds; in the summer they follow the melting snow line into high country. Park rangers and numerous visitors report that scattered bands of elk are often seen cooling themselves on the vast snow fields on hot summer days, and bands of elk, sometimes numbering 15 to 60, are commonly seen watering at some river bottom or crossing the alpine meadow.

The cougar, Columbia black-tailed and Rocky Mountain mule deer, the mountain goat, black bear, Olympic mountain lion, and northwestern wildcat also live in the park. The deer, related to the elk family, move, like the elk, from the valleys and river bottoms to high country in the summer months, following the melting snow line. Black bears are seen most often in late fall in the high country where they feed on patches of blueberry, a major part of the bear's diet at this season of the year; they also feed on fish, roots, herbs, and bark.

Among the smaller animals are the Pacific fisher, mink, raccoon, beaver, skunk, marmot, varying hare, chipmunk, squirrel, and the so-called mountain beaver, which is not a beaver. A most exciting experience for the hiker in the wilderness is to see the big brown eyes of a fawn or doe, watching motionless from behind some undergrowth. At certain times of the year, and especially in the early morning or at dusk, the hiker or horseback rider will see deer, numbering from 5 to 75, standing knee-deep in a quiet pool or stream, drinking.

Many birds, ranging in color from drab brown to the brightest hues, and in song from mysterious hoots and whirs to lilting melodies, are found throughout this primitive land. Most often seen are the sooty grouse, Oregon ruffed grouse, great blue heron, western red-tailed hawk, bald eagle, belted kingfisher, red-shafted flicker, Stellar's jay, Canadian jay, raven, crow, chickadee, water ouzel, towhee, robin, wren, varied thrush, pine siskin, rufous hummingbird, Clarke's nutcracker, American sparrow hawk, great horned owl, goshawk, Cooper's hawk, pine grosbeak, slate-colored Junco, and golden-crowned kinglet.

The fishing is excellent. Splendid catches of cutthroat, rainbow, and Eastern brook trout and Montana black spots are made in the icy mountain streams and lakes. In Lake Crescent, a 14-mile-long body of water deep blue in color (*see Tour 9c*), are found the famous Beardslee trout, native to the lake, defined by ichthyologists as land-locked steelhead. These fish sometimes weigh from 12 to 14 pounds. The steelhead, gamest of fish, is also found in several of the rivers.

TRAILS

Consistent with the National Park Service policy of maintaining this area as a primitive wilderness, the trails are rustic and meandering. The Master Plan for the long-time development of the area shows that one day there will be a network of trails which the hiker or horseback rider may follow to almost every section of the park. Certain areas, however, will be kept free from any work of man. The main approaches to the park are along stub roads following the larger watersheds.

The hiker enters the ELWHA TRAIL at the guard station. Around him are towering trees, making a soft murmur much like that of the near-by river. There is a sweeping bend in the trail, and suddenly far below is the rushing ice-cold water of the Elwha River, which has its source in the central part of the park. The trail winds along an easy grade and bears away from the river down into the rich green flat where the Lillian River flows toward the Elwha. Here is found a cedar-shake shelter cabin with table, benches, and fireplace. Crossing the bridge the hiker climbs steadily for several miles, with a view of the forested slopes of Bailey Range to the right, across the valley. Then the trail suddenly falls into a refreshing green meadow, and the log-framed

Elkhorn Guard Station comes into view. The trail follows along the river through grass-covered Press Valley, an expanse almost level for more than a mile. Five miles past Elkhorn, Hayes River Ranger Station and public shelter stand near the bank of the river. From this point, a trail branches off to the left, leading up over Hayden Pass and down to Dose Meadow, Camp Marion, and the Dose Forks at the eastern boundary of the park.

At Chicago Camp, 25 miles from the end of the road at Whiskey Bend, the trail branches right into the Queets country, through the Elwha Basin and to the source of the Elwha River in Dodwell-Rixon Pass, and left or south toward Low Divide. It is but a short distance south into Martin's Park, with its lovely Lakes Mary and Margaret, and to the chalet at Low Divide in the central portion of the park, an excellent base camp for hikes into the Mount Olympus section. It is possible to ascend in a one-day trip from here to Mount Seattle, Christy, or Meany. At the divide the lush valleys and flowers and snow-capped pinnacles are reflected with mirror-like clearness in numerous little lakes. From Low Divide to the end of the trail at the North Fork Quinault Guard Station is a 15-mile hike downhill, most of the distance through majestic stands of virgin timber.

The DUCKABUSH TRAIL is a route to test the mettle of the seasoned hiker. Leaving the end of the Duckabush road, the trail begins almost immediately to climb over Little Hump and then into a broad valley, bounded on the north by Mount Jupiter. Crossing rock ledges, one moment near the turbulent river, then high over the waters racing through canyons, the traveler nears the Big Hump, with its 89 switchbacks. Half-way up the Big Hump an excellent view may be had of St. Peter's dome. While the trail is generally upgrade for the remainder of the distance to the 17-mile shelter, it follows a gradual slope. Some of the finest trees to be found in the park are here, including the spreading yew and the lovely amabalis fir. At the 17-mile shelter is the junction of the Duckabush Trail with one coming up from the North Fork of the Skokomish, the two trails merging for the route to Marmot, Heart, and La Crosse lakes, one of the most beautiful regions in the park. Side trips may be taken to ridges above Marmot Lake to O'Neil Pass, thence around the basin of O'Neil Creek and along a ridge high above Enchanted Valley (where Lake Quinault and the distant ocean shore may be seen on clear days) to the junction of the trail with the East Fork Quinault and Anderson Pass trails.

DOSEWALLIPS TRAIL begins at the end of the Dosewallips road, 18 miles from Brinnon, and leads through forests of tall Douglas fir along the river to Dose Forks shelter. From here the North Fork takes an easy climb up past Camp Marion and Dose Meadows shelter to snow-covered Hayden Pass, thence down into the Elwha Valley at Hayes River; while the West Fork leads to Honeymoon Meadows shelter, Diamond Meadows, and Anderson Glacier, before going down Anderson Pass to Enchanted Valley.

SOLEDUCK TRAIL begins at the end of the road one and one-half miles beyond Sol Duc Hot Springs. Probably the finest high-country view in the Olympics is offered from points along this trail. It winds through forests and across little streams for three-quarters of a mile to Soleduck Falls, thence six and one-half miles to Bogachiel Peak Lookout Station, from which point is an unsurpassed view of the Olympics. Here, within a short distance, is the source of the Bogachiel River. Off to the north may be seen the blue waters of the Juan de Fuca Strait and westward the Hoh River Valley and the ground swells of the Pacific. It is two miles by trail down to Hoh Lake, and five miles over a switchback into the beautiful Hoh Valley and to the Olympus Guard Station.

HOH VALLEY TRAIL is enchanting, winding for nine miles through dense rain forest. The watershed of the Hoh River, a glacial stream, receives fully 85 per cent of the Mount Olympus drainage; consequently, it is not only the largest river in the Olympic Peninsula, but it maintains a more even flow of water throughout the year. From US 101, the Olympic Loop Highway (*see Tour 9*), a stub road leads 18 miles to the Jackson Ranger Station, where the trail begins.

In places off the trail the moss is easily six inches deep, soft as the richest rug. The path, under great trees festooned with moss, is flecked with mingled shadow and sunlight. Below, on the right, the winding Hoh River shimmers with countless diamond points of light. The gay notes of birds are the only sounds heard above the soft southwesterly wind riffling the tops of Douglas firs, old when William conquered England.

Beyond the rustic silhouette of Olympus Guard Station, the winding trail leads to Canyon Creek bridge three and one-half miles beyond, where the glacier-fed waters of the Hoh roar more than 200 feet below in the deep, narrow gorge. Three miles farther on is Glacier Meadows, base camp for those who wish to climb Mount Olympus. From the edge of these spreading alpine meadows the trail winds up toward Blue Glacier. Care should be taken to rub on sunburn grease, adjust crampons, and don colored glasses for protection against the glare of the ice and snow. When the ascent of the moraine to the glacier's edge is being made, climbing ropes are necessary. The trail follows a zigzag course to the snow dome, then an abrupt right turn is made through large, scattered rocks and on up over continuous fields of ice and snow. Mountaineers should be alert at all times for hidden crevasses. As the climb becomes steeper, alpenstocks come into valuable use and crampons search for solid footing. A steady breeze is almost invariably present at this altitude. The top is approached along a semicircular route, coming up from under the base of the final pinnacle to its opposite side and up steep rock for the last few hundred feet to the crest of West Peak. Here is the superlative lookout over the peninsula. On a clear day the mountain climber can see in the distance the waters of the Pacific, the Juan de Fuca Strait, and the shores of Vancouver Island; Mount Rainier to the southeast, and the vast panorama of the Olympics all around him.

From the end of the road one and one-half miles beyond the public campground on Graves Creek, East Fork Quinault, the ENCHANTED VALLEY TRAIL follows steep hillsides down into a deep, green gorge, where the Quinault River flows toward the ocean. The gorge is spanned by a log bridge and, after a short climb through heavy growths of Douglas fir, drops into a meadow shaded by thick growths of vine maple and fir. The trail follows the meandering river for 13 miles, over numerous small creeks, to Enchanted Valley Chalet and shelter. The Enchanted Valley, lying at the foot of a cliff that drops almost vertically for 3,000 feet, is often referred to as the Valley of a Thousand Waterfalls. The trail continues for approximately four miles up easy switchbacks—though steep in places—to the vast snow fields at Anderson Pass. Here one may look down to the headwaters of both the Dosewallips and the East Fork Quinault Rivers.

Puget Sound Tours

Puget Sound, an inlet connected with the Pacific Ocean by Juan de Fuca Strait, is a blue-green placid sea, 2,000 square miles in extent, guarded east and west by snow-capped mountains. Its sinuous arms embrace wooded peninsulas and isles and penetrate more than 100 miles into the heart of the State, to form a hundred navigable waterways and as many natural harbors. Its shores, directly on the Great Circle route to the Orient, are dotted with world ports. On local wharves, Japanese silk and soy beans are exchanged for fruit, grain, and forest products; in secluded coves, straining winches of ocean tramp ships whine within sound of axes ringing in the forests.

More than a score of islands, varying in size from Whidbey Island (*see Tour 8C*), second largest in the United States, to spots of land a few acres in area, lie in Puget Sound. Northward are the San Juan Islands, an archipelago of 172 islands on the edge of the Sound, and often considered a part of it. A few of the isles dotting the Sound have commercial importance; others, much smaller, are suitable only for limited agriculture, private residences, or resorts. Some have transportation facilities or bridges connecting with the mainland. Extending southwesterly from lower-Sound, in the shadow of the Olympic Mountains, is long, fjord-like Hood Canal (*see Tour 9a*).

Ages before adventuring prows broke the waters of the Sound and axes cleared portions of its shores, this section of the earth's crust had undergone many changes. The Cascade Mountains were slowly raised out of the ocean, forming between themselves and the Rockies broad half-tropical swamps, in which huge saurians crawled. The Coast Range rose to the westward, creating the Olympic Mountains and the San Juan Archipelago. Much later, volcanoes, the largest of which was Mount Rainier, built their cones along the Cascade Range. The Indians called the waters of the Sound Whulge (Ind. salt water). Nekhani, the great spirit, said they, created this land as an expression of love for La-wis-wis, queen of all beauty.

Ignorance of those unexplored water courses led to their being considered haunted. Early navigators told of the weird silence of the inner reaches, "only now and then interrupted by the croaking of the raven, the breathing of the seal or the scream of the eagle."

Disregarding the legendary figure of Juan de Fuca, the actual discoverer is said to be Captain Charles William Barkley, who sailed into Juan de Fuca Strait in 1787. Captain George Vancouver explored Puget Sound in 1792 and named most of its islands and landmarks. The Hudson's Bay Company steamer, *Beaver,* which entered these waters in 1836, was the first steamer in the Pacific.

As the American settlers began to arrive at Tumwater in 1845 and at Olympia in 1847, settlements gradually sprang up along the Sound on the more favorable bays and harbors. The booming days in California and, shortly thereafter, the northerly gold rushes toward the Fraser River called attention to the potential wealth of this timbered region. Piling, timbers, and shingles found an ever-increasing market. Premiums brought hundreds of ships to the Sound for cargo. The rapid development of sawmill towns, lumber ports, shipyards and docks followed. Puget Sound entered its most glamorous and strenuous period; years which saw a constant stream of vessels crossing its waters; a time of smuggling Chinese and opium; hi-jacking lumber cargoes; grog-shop brawls and shanghaiing; murder, shipwrecks, and mutiny. There were 100 vessels plying the waters of the Sound in 1877; by 1884 as many as 1,869 entered its bounds within the year, including ships, steamers, brigs, schooners, barks, and sloops. The names of some of these ships—*Frowning Beauty, Quickstep, Minnie May, Tesser, Phantom, Coquimbo, Colish, Vidette, Topgallant, Wailele*—and their traffic with the South Sea islands, the Malay States, Australia, Africa, Europe, China, and the north seas, spread a patina of romance over the ports of the Sound.

With the coming of the railroads and the increased use of coal, the square-riggers, the barks, and the brigs gave way to steam carriers. Timber, cut back into the hills, was now much less accessible—and this, too, helped to push the days of "wooden ships and iron men" into the past. Towns and villages along the Sound which had based their future on lumber alone now rose to become centers of diversified manufacturing. Seattle, Tacoma, Everett, Bellingham, and Olympia, connected with the rest of the Nation by fast railroads, demanded ocean lines to compete with the merchant marine of the world.

The east shore of the Sound is the most densely populated section of the State. Bellingham, a few miles south of the Canadian boundary and facing the San Juan Islands, is the most northerly city on Puget Sound; Olympia, the State capital, is the most southerly. Seattle, largest city west of the Missouri and north of San Francisco, spreads with its suburbs from spacious Elliott Bay over hills and lakes half way down the Sound's eastern shore. Southward is Tacoma, "Lumber Capital of the World," on a point jutting into a maze of passages. North of Seattle and opposite the southern tip of Whidbey Island is Everett, a bustling lumber-mill town and first seaport terminal of a transcontinental railroad. Bremerton, built around the Puget Sound Navy Yard, is ensconced within the narrow channels of Kitsap Peninsula, half way down the west shore of the Sound.

Though the day of the sailing ship is past, each cove and inlet, harbor, and decadent town on the Sound retains some of the flavor of vessels arriving from far-off ports; of the melancholy ringing of the ship's bell, and the odor of pitch pots, varnish, and freshly cut ships' timbers. Small fleets of fishing boats scatter over the waters, and aging houseboats huddle under wooded bluffs; while in the distance, long ribbons of smoke string out across the horizon from the giant smoke stacks of mills.

CROSS-SOUND TOUR 1

Seattle—Suquamish, 14 m. by ferry, 45 min.

Ferry: Black Ball Line. *Kehloken* leaves Colman Ferry Terminal, ft. of Marion St., approximately every 2½ hrs. (Schedules vary with the seasons).
Fares: 40c each way; car and driver, $1.10. Dining service.

The route offers many fine views of the inland waterway against the background of Bainbridge Island, which merges with the green foothills of the snowy mountain summits to the west. It also affords a visit to the birthplace and grave of Chief Seattle.

Upon leaving Elliott Bay, Seattle Harbor, the ferry passes WEST POINT LIGHTHOUSE to the right, above which, on a high bluff, is FORT LAWTON, an active military post (*see Seattle*). The main channel of Puget Sound is five miles wide at this point.

About 14 miles out, the ferry bears between MONROE POINT, left, and JEFFERSON POINT, right, to enter PORT MADISON BAY; these were named in 1841 by the Wilkes Expedition in honor of United States Presidents. Left from the bay is Agate Pass, a narrow channel between the mainland and BAINBRIDGE ISLAND (*see Island Tour 1*).

SUQUAMISH (sea level, 584 pop.), was first named Bartow after an early Indian agent in charge of the Port Madison Indian Reservation, which the village adjoins. After its development as a summer-home site about 1910 by Ole Hansen, later Seattle mayor, the name was changed to Suquamish. Fishing and boating equipment are available.

On a hill at the west end of the main street, a small white-steepled church overlooks an Indian burial ground containing CHIEF SEATTLE'S

GRAVE. A stone monument marks the last resting place of the Indian chief who gave much valuable service to the white settlers. On scout anniversary day, in late February, a ceremony is conducted by Boy Scouts beside the grave. A granite shaft bears the inscription: "Seattle, Chief of the Suquamish and Allied Tribes, died June 7, 1866, the firm friend of the Whites and for him the City of Seattle was named by its Founders."

Seattle was a man of unusual vision, the elected chief of six tribes, who won his place by personal worth. He saw the futility of resisting the whites and used his power to aid them, particularly befriending the early settlers who founded Seattle. Physically a large man, over six feet tall, broad-shouldered and deep-chested, he was an impressive and able orator.

Left from SUQUAMISH, 0.5 *m.,* down the beach is the SITE OF OLD-MAN-HOUSE, where Chief Seattle was born. One of the most unusual of Indian structures found in the region, this great communal dwelling has long ago rotted and fallen, but many of the large posts which supported it may be seen embedded in the earth. Historians disagree as to the original size of the abode; it is believed to have covered an area of one and a quarter acres. The house, as reported by George Gibbs to the American Bureau of Ethnology in 1877, was 520 feet long, 60 feet wide, 15 feet high at the front and 10 feet at the rear. The shed roof was covered with cedar shakes and supported by 74 split timbers from 2 to 3 feet wide and from 5 to 8 inches thick, and carved with grotesque figures. The cross beams were round logs 65 feet long and from 12 to 22 inches in diameter. The outside walls were split cedar planks. Inside were 40 apartments separated by partitions of split logs. The apartments of Chief Seattle and of the first sub-chief, Kitsap, were heavily reinforced. On the corner posts at the front of each was carved the omnipotent Thunderbird. Carlson, another authority, maintained that the house had a length of 900 feet. The structure faced the beach overlooking Agate Pass directly opposite, and was slightly curved, to follow the outline of the shore.

CROSS-SOUND TOUR 2

Seattle—Bremerton, 15 *m.* by ferry, 60 min.

Ferry: Black Ball Line. M.S. *Kalakala* and M.S. *Chippewa* leave Colman Ferry Terminal, ft. of Marion St., approximately every hr., between 6:30 A.M. and 12:30 A.M.
Fares: 45c each way; car and driver, $1.10 each way. Dining service.

One of the two ferries on this route is the silver-winged M.S. *Kalakala* (Kah-lock'-ah-lah; Ind. flying bird), advertised as the first streamlined ferry in the world. With a superstructure fashioned of welded aluminum-painted steel, molded in graceful streamline, and a bridge shaped to modified wings, its movement over the water suggests the gliding of a huge seaplane. Three large observation rooms, faced with broad plate-glass windows, afford a maximum view. On the upper deck aft is an open lounge.

Leaving Colman Dock, the ferry swings across Elliott Bay, revealing Seattle in an ever-widening panorama; long lines of wharves and warehouses, with the city marching back over long hills; the East and West Waterways, giving access to the Duwamish River around man-made HARBOR ISLAND to the left.

On the left also is green-crowned DUWAMISH HEAD, the southwesterly border of Elliott Bay, and a stretch of sandy beach which reaches in a gentle two-mile curve to ALKI POINT (*see Seattle*), where the founders of the city landed in 1851. A low sea wall guards many beach homes. The residential district of West Seattle perches on the bluffs above.

West of ALKI POINT LIGHTHOUSE, the main channel of Puget Sound, some six miles wide here, is entered. Extending from BAINBRIDGE ISLAND on the right, is the wooded tip of RESTORATION POINT (*see Island Tour 1*). To the left rises uninhabited BLAKE ISLAND, a mile in diameter, owned in its entirety by William Pitt Trimble, Seattle capitalist. Beyond it and farther to the south is VASHON ISLAND (*see Island Tour 2*), the largest in this part of the Sound.

Visible on Bainbridge Island are summer homes and small settlements. A dock juts into view, with faded green buildings in the background. Still farther back, a slanting roof, discernible above serried trees, bears in yellow letters the name "Fort Ward," a post long inactive but taken over by the Navy Department in 1938, for new development (*see Island Tour 1*).

Swinging northward, the ferry enters twisting RICH PASS, beset by strong currents and narrowed by submerged rock. Small whirlpools in the deep water mark the struggle of the tides. At times the left shore is very close. To the right, in a protected cove on Bainbridge Island, is PLEASANT BEACH. During the early 1900's it served as terminus of many roistering steamboat excursions.

Turning to the west again, the ferry crosses PORT ORCHARD BAY, named by Vancouver for H. M. Orchard, a clerk on the *Discovery,* who commanded a small boat expedition that explored this waterway. A giant crane in the navy yard ahead looms impressively. On the right is East Bremerton (Manette), separated from Bremerton by a concrete-piered bridge across Port Washington Narrows. Yellow buildings seem to crowd the bluff in a tight-packed huddle left of the bridge.

Left of the ferry are the cranes and red and gray buildings of the PUGET SOUND NAVY YARD. A gray battleship or two, several cruisers and destroyers, perhaps an airplane carrier, are usually to be seen at anchor.

Dark-brown gulls, perched atop clusters of old piling, watch undisturbed as the ferry berths at the BREMERTON MUNICIPAL DOCK.

BREMERTON

Accommodations: Cabin and auto camps; trailer facilities, governed by special city ordinance (for highway directions into Bremerton *see Tour 3a*); one hotel.

Information: Chamber of Commerce, basement Elks' Temple, Pacific Ave., Olympicans, Inc., Harrison Bldg., 4th St.

Transportation: Ferries—Black Ball Line, to Puget Sound points, auto and passengers; Greyhound, Union Pacific, and Washington Motor Coach stages serve suburban and State points from Municipal Dock. Taxi service: all hours. Special seaplane service to Seattle, from N. of Municipal Dock.
Recreation: Swimming pool, YMCA, 1st St. and Washington Ave.
Golf: Kitsap Country and Golf Club, 6 m. W. on State 21.
Tennis: Seven public and four private courts.
Baseball, Football: Warren Ave. Field, 15th St. and Warren Ave.

Annual Events: Olympican Caravan tour Olympic loop, summer season, nfd; Dahlia show, Kitsap Co. Dahlia Society, Aug. or Sept.; Navy Day celebration, Oct. 27.

Twice a day the streets of BREMERTON (12 alt., 15,134 pop.), teem with jostling, boisterous life—in the early morning and when the 4:45 p.m. whistle has blown and thousands of men pour in or out of the main gate of the PUGET SOUND NAVY YARD.

Almost everything in Bremerton owes its presence there to "the Yard," which is the ruling factor in the economic life of Kitsap County, one of the State's great industrial centers.

The city of Bremerton is spread over a shield-shaped arm of land, surrounded on three sides by water. The city may be reached by highway (*see Tour 3A*), but the land route from other large Puget Sound cities is extremely circuitous. There is no rail transportation; it is said that Bremerton is the largest city in the Nation not served by a railroad.

From the municipal dock the civic center is reached by turning left on 1st Street and right into Pacific Avenue, a wide, sloping thoroughfare. Old and new buildings crowd one another; and there are no tall commercial structures. Recent civic improvements (1937-8) include an $80,000 brick post office and a $65,000 library, the latter partly financed by the Work Projects Administration.

Eating places and beer taverns are numerous. The influence of the yard is evident in such names as "The Ship," "The Crow's Nest," and "Lou's Lockers." An enterprising Seattle hotel advertises at the municipal dock that "sailors may cast anchor at $1 a night—no extra charge for two." Local hotels are scarce, because of the proximity to Seattle.

One of the younger cities of a young State, Bremerton grew out of the communities of Charleston, Bremerton, and Manette. William Bremer, a native of Germany, who came to Washington in 1888 to engage in the real estate business, platted the townsite in 1891. He aided in securing the Navy Yard for the town by selling land to the Government at low price. Bremerton was a wild town in its early days. A. L. Croxton, the first mayor, says of the period: "There were 17 saloons in Bremerton when I took office. . . . The country was overrun by gamblers . . ." With the aid of the Secretary of the Navy, however, who ordered that these resorts be cleaned out, the town was finally put in order.

East Bremerton, until incorporated with Bremerton, was known as

Manette, and its post office still bears that name. It sprang up in the nineties as a small lumbering village around Bender's mill, which was located near the end of the bridge connecting the present town with Bremerton. Some of the piling which supported the mill may still be seen at this point. Oxen were used in logging in those days; and along the trails in the woods lay many skeletons of the work animals and the remains of those that had been turned loose in the woods when too old to be useful. It was necessary to row across the Narrows to get mail, and the one who went to get it would ask for the "String Town" mail, meaning the settlement strung out along the road. When a dock was finally built, the village took the name of the first boat that stopped there, the *Decatur,* but changed it to Manette when it had achieved the proportions of a town. Today, a new bridge connects East Bremerton and Bremerton.

In EVERGREEN PARK, Park Ave. and 14th St., facing the Narrows, trees have been planted memorializing World War veterans and yeomanettes. Here tourists may camp and trailers park. Larger FOREST RIDGE PARK, right from 1st St. and Lafayette Ave., has a Boy Scout camp and is being improved.

A new recreational development, aided by WPA funds, is the WARREN AVENUE FIELD, 15th St. and Warren Ave., on which $40,000 has been expended. The field is lighted for baseball and football and has stands to seat 5,000.

PUGET SOUND NAVY YARD. (*Guides furnished, visitors apply at main gate; open daily* 9-4; *Sun.,* 1-5. *Private automobiles admitted on pass. No cameras or firearms; no smoking*).

The main gate to the yard is at the foot of 1st St., a few feet right from Pacific Avenue. An ordinance passed in 1902 made it a misdemeanor to sell or roast peanuts, loaf, tell stories, whittle, or scatter litter near this entrance. Persons convicted of these offenses were subject to a fine ranging from $5 to $25.

The Navy Yard was established September 16, 1891, Lieutenant Wycoff in command. The first vessel to call at the yard was the Japanese ship *Yamagucha Maru;* the second was the old flagship U.S.S. *Oregon.* Land originally purchased comprised 190 acres; since then it has been expanded to 285 acres. Buildings and improvements today represent a valuation of $65,000,000. In addition to enlisted men of the naval and marine corps, from 3,000 to 4,000 civilians are normally employed. The civil pay roll amounts to more than $9,000,000 annually, and the Navy spends approximately $2,000,000 each year in local markets.

The area is policed by the marine corps, and sailors from warships berthed in the Yard are detailed to act as guides. The usual tour route leads straight ahead from the entrance along Farragut Avenue. Visitors are not customarily taken inside the buildings en route.

Operations of the yard include the repairing, overhauling, or building of battleships, destroyers, and submarines. Administration is in the hands of ninety United States Naval officers, headed by a rear admiral as commandant. Three drydocks are in the Yard: No. 1 accommodates cruisers, destroyers, and smaller craft; No. 2 cares for large airplane carriers; and No. 3, completed in 1919, is a ship-building dock, the largest of its type in the world. With a length of 926 feet, a width of 130 feet and a depth of 24 feet, it will hold 21,800,000 gallons of water, and has space for the construction of two cruisers or four destroyers at the same time.

In the yard, too, is one of the world's largest machine and electric shops, completed in 1935 at a cost of $1,300,000; it is 805 feet long by 251 feet wide, of heavy steel and concrete construction, with brick facing and of modern design. The walls are fabricated almost entirely of special glass, admitting a maximum of light. It will accommodate up to 1,000 men per shift.

The yard has its own railway system; it also provides in CRAVEN CENTER, right from Farragut Avenue, a recreational building for enlisted personnel. A modern hospital and officers' quarters are on a high bluff back of Farragut Avenue where it bears left to the water front.

CROSS-SOUND TOUR 3

Edmonds—Port Ludlow, 17 *m.* by ferry, 80 min.

Ferries: M.S. *Chetzemoka* and M.S. *Elwha* leave Edmonds about six times daily (schedules vary with the seasons).
Fares: One way 80c; round trip $1.35; car and driver, $2.25, round trip $3.80. Dining Service.

From the landing at Edmonds, the ferry moves in a diagonal, northwesterly course across the Sound. Midway, the route passes a long stretch of forested shore notched by inlets. To the northwest, the long bulk of Whidbey Island curves between Admiralty Inlet and Saratoga Passage; the entrance to the latter is seen to the right through the wide mouth of Possession Sound.

SCATCHET HEAD, on the right, is a high tan bluff on the southwestern corner of Whidbey Island. The name is derived from that of an Indian tribe commonly called the Skagit. Northwest of Scatchet Head is DOUBLE BLUFF, the western cape of Useless Bay.

POINT NO POINT, on the left, noted for its salmon fishing, is at the northeastern extremity of Kitsap County. A LIGHTHOUSE, one of the first established on Puget Sound, has given added importance to the point. Governor Isaac Stevens met the natives here and concluded the "Point No Point Treaty." The document was signed by 56 Indians, the principal ones being Chetzemoka, chief of the Clallams (*see Tour 9a*), Doh-whil-cuk of the Snohomish; and Kul-a-hon, chief of the Chimacums.

HANSVILLE, west of the point, consists of a few houses and poultry yards straggling along the beach beneath a bluff just south of Norwegian Point, where a number of Norwegians have settled. The bay north of Hansville is called Skunk Bay because many skunks formerly frequented the beach at low tide. Also on the left, FOULWEATHER BLUFF, on the north end of the Kitsap Peninsula at the entrance to

Hood Canal (*see Tour 9a*), overlooks a pointed beach strewn with large rocks. The Indian name for the place was Pitch Pol. The sight of deer licking the salt from wet rocks on the beach is not uncommon. The steamer *Traveler,* first vessel to navigate rivers emptying into the Sound, was wrecked here March 1858. At that time the area was under charter to the Indian Department.

The chain of snow sentinels which surround Puget Sound is best observed in mid-Sound. Mount Baker is a dazzling white cone far to the northeast; rising gradually from the ridges of the Cascades is Glacier Peak almost due east from Admiralty Inlet; Mount Rainier towers high in the southeast. Often Mount St. Helens is visible more than 100 miles to the south. As the ferry heads due west, a view is unfolded of the eastern slope of the Olympic Mountains and of Mount Olympus, a cluster of rock pinnacles. Fields of snow gleam in crevices along its shoulders. Brown, red, and gray abutments rise from a dark green mantle of forest.

SNAKE ROCK and COLVOS ROCK rise above the waves a few hundred yards off Basalt Point, to the right. Seal herds that formerly inhabited these rocks have disappeared. An Indian village once sprawled along a little cove back of the rocks. Passing Tala Point, on the left, the ferry heads into Port Ludlow Bay, shaped like a bird's head. The dark forest creeps down the slopes of low hills to the shoreline.

PORT LUDLOW (30 alt., 200 pop.), on a tiny peninsula forming the throat of the bay, presents a patchwork of green lawns, venerable maple trees, and a half-dozen well-painted houses on a bank sloping upward from the beach and ferry landing. To the left is a large abandoned MILL with a tall brick smokestack. This mill, the first in Jefferson County, was built around the original plant, erected in 1858 by Captain William F. Sayward and J. F. Thorndyke. Cutting more than 3,000 feet daily, its output was used for the construction of settlers' homes along the shores of Puget Sound. The mill was rebuilt and improved with new machinery in 1883. High-grade lumber was shipped to all corners of the world. Depletion of the region's timber caused curtailment of operations. The McCormick Lumber Company, a subsidiary of the McCormick Steamship Company, is the present owner. Together with a number of boarded-up houses, the mill is mute evidence of the decline into which a formerly flourishing lumber center has fallen.

Overlooking the harbor on the single main street extending from the ferry dock, is the old ADMIRALTY HOTEL (*closed: see caretaker*). Originally built as a home in 1883 by Cyrus Walker, a pioneer lumberman, the building was converted into a hotel in 1911. The long, vine-covered structure was designed along nautical lines by Walker, who came from Maine in the 1850's. The great center hall resembles a ship's interior and is paneled with native fir.

Massive pieces of furniture for the house were freighted thousands of miles from the Atlantic Coast around Cape Horn. The highboards of carved bedsteads reach almost to the ceiling. In each room is a marble-topped dresser. The dining room has a sideboard of carved walnut, fashioned in Germany more than 200 years ago. Antique spindle-legged chairs grace the red-carpeted hallway. The bathrooms are larger than modern kitchens, and some of the rooms are equipped with fireplaces. A broad veranda overlooks Port Ludlow Bay. Trees shading the sloping lawn were in many instances grown from slips brought from distant ports by old sailing masters.

A shipyard was one of the early-day industries of Port Ludlow. Many sturdy ships were constructed here of stout Douglas fir. The three-masted schooner *Courser,* the barkentine *Katherine Sudden,* the *Moses Turner,* the schooners *Waiehue, Lihuluho* and *Luke,* built for Hawaii, and the steamers *Augusta* and *Hyack,* were among a long list of craft launched from Port Ludlow ways.

Well-surfaced roads lead from Port Ludlow to US 101 (*see Tour 9b*), the Olympic Loop Highway.

Island Tours

ISLAND TOUR 1

Seattle—Vashon Island and around the island, 17 *m.;* by ferry 3 m., 20 min.; by auto, Vashon Heights to Tallequah, 14 *m.*

Ferry: Black Ball Line. ***Vashon*** leaves dock at the end of Fauntleroy Ave., approximately every 1½ hours, between 6:30 a.m. and 12:30 a.m. (schedules vary with the seasons).
Fares: 20c one way, 35c round trip; car and driver 70c one way, $1.30 round trip. Dining service.
Vashon Stages leave 308 Virginia St. in the morning and afternoon. Fare: 45c each way including ferry. The stage crosses with the ferry and makes stops at the principal settlements on Vashon.
Summer boarding places and cabin camps. Concrete-paved, bituminous-surfaced, and graveled roads.

Section a. SEATTLE *to* VASHON ISLAND, *3 m.*

Leaving Seattle from Fauntleroy Cove, the ferry *Vashon* heads southwest into Puget Sound. On either bow the gently rolling sea is enclosed by dark wooded shores and the occasional tawny face of a sheer bluff.

At three miles is the north head of VASHON ISLAND, rising some 300 feet above the water. Like the verdant crest of a young mountain, Vashon Island stretches for 14 miles along the west shore of the Sound, midway between Seattle and Tacoma, its fertile heights, above the timbered slopes, dotted with orchards and fields. George Vancouver named the island in 1792 for his friend, Captain James Vashon of the English Navy. Although it was surveyed in 1856, permanent settlement did not begin until 1877. In the next 25 years, it became one of the leading berry, fruit, and poultry-raising districts on Puget Sound.

The ferry docks at VASHON HEIGHTS.

Section b. VASHON HEIGHTS *to* TALLEQUAH, *14 m.*

From the ferry landing the paved highway ascends on a winding grade to the crest of the island. Far below (L), Puget Sound glints in the sun. To the east are the tumbled Cascades, broken by peaks and punctuated by the white crowns of Mount Rainier and Mount Baker. On the west is the Olympic Range.

Continuing south, the highway rolls past berry fields, orchards and poultry farms. Patches of woodland border the route.

VASHON, 4 *m.* (220 alt., 200 pop.), is the "metropolis" of the island, and its brief main street is lined on either side with modern store buildings. Near by are several greenhouses; one, perhaps the most noted in the Northwest, is housed under 350,000 square feet of glass. A truckload of flowers leaves here for Seattle markets every morning. On the island more than 500,000 feet of greenhouse space is given to flowers, tomatoes, and cucumbers.

An unusual enterprise at Vashon is a TRAVELING BARBER SHOP, mounted on a truck chassis. When trade is dull along the village street, the barber tours the country roads and the smaller settlements distributing his truckload of shaves and haircuts.

At 7 *m.* is a junction with an improved road.

Left here 1 *m.* to ELLISPORT (sea level, 135 pop.), a colorful summer village on the east shore, founded in 1879 by three Methodist clergymen, Ellis, Green, and Harrison, who took up homesteads.

At Ellisport is POINT HEYER, where Station KVI, a Tacoma broadcasting company, has erected its TRANSMISSION TOWER, a steel structure rising from the beach to a height of 444 feet.

PORTAGE, 2 *m.* (50 alt., 75 pop.), is situated at a narrow sand spit which connects Vashon with Maury Island, actually a mile-wide peninsula that parallels Vashon Island for five miles along its southeastern border. Lying between the two insular bodies is the picturesque bay of Quartermaster Harbor, a long, slim, twisting body of water. Portage received its name from the early settlers who carried their small boats from Quartermaster Harbor across the low strip of land at this point to Tramp Harbor on East Passage.

East of Portage, a causeway carries the road across to Maury Island, where it follows the east shore of Quartermaster Harbor (R). The long beaches and the sheltered waters offer camping and recreational opportunities.

VASHON STATE PARK, 3 *m.,* is a 21-acre recreational area along the beach, with camping facilities, community kitchens, and a diving float. Bordering the road (L) are the greens of the VASHON GOLF CLUB (*greens fee 25c*), a 9-hole community course. On the harbor, Vashon's first settlement was established in November 1877, when John Gilman, Daniel Price, and Captain S. D. Sherman landed with their families.

DOCKTON, 3.5 *m.* (sea level, 200 pop.), a weathered settlement on the east shore of Quartermaster Harbor, was named by the Puget Sound Dry Dock Company about 1891. In 1892 it became the scene of great activity when a drydock 182 feet wide by 325 feet long was put into operation. Ocean-going transports and an occasional four-master with furled canvas lay at anchor in its tiny port awaiting repairs; codfishers delivered their catch to a large curing plant here; boxcars were towed on barges into the harbor where they were loaded with dried codfish and returned to the railroad in Tacoma; brickyards about the bay added to its commerce. At the turn of the century, however, competition from larger industrial centers on the mainland reversed the tide of commerce, and today Dockton is a pale ghost, with graying remnants of wharves and ships along its water front. A developing berry culture, however, promises to sustain the town.

Left from Dockton, about two miles along the beach, near the present settlement of Manzanita, a Chinese village known as Hongking flourished in the early 1880's. It was reputed to have a population of 3,000, but this figure is doubted. Most of the Chinese were engaged in fishing. During the Chinese riots in many Puget Sound cities, the Orientals disappeared, abandoning most of their belongings, including a large number of pigs. These found warm welcome in some of the kitchens of the white settlers who followed.

At 8.2 *m.* the main route crosses JUDD CREEK. Somewhere along its banks is said to be a cache of buried treasure. Lars Hanson, logging here in 1877, married an Indian girl to whom he gave his savings, $800 in gold, with instructions to bury it for him in some secret place. She became ill shortly thereafter and died before he could learn the hiding-place. The gold has never been found, and it is believed to be somewhere near the mouth of the stream.

BURTON, 9 *m.* (100 alt., 250 pop.), on the eastern shore of Vashon Island, fronts on Quartermaster Harbor and is the southern terminal of the island stage route. The local population is scattered along the countryside and beaches, and the town seems scarcely to exist. Burton was named in 1892 by Mrs. M. E. Match for a town in Illinois in which she formerly lived. Vashon College, founded here in 1892, became a co-educational preparatory school; destroyed by fire in 1912, it has never been rebuilt. Near by, in a large park-like section, Baptists convene for the annual summer assembly of their Young People's Society. Ferry service between Burton and Tacoma links the town with the mainland.

South of Burton, the highway follows the winding shore, ascending high sand bluffs with an ever-widening panorama of small bays. Here, the country becomes rougher in character, broken by huge thinly timbered ravines.

At 14 *m.,* is TALLEQUAH, the southernmost point on Vashon Island, where a ferry connects with Point Defiance in Tacoma (*see Tacoma*), less than two miles across Dalco Passage.

ISLAND TOUR 2

Seattle—Bainbridge Island and around the island, 34.2 *m.,* by ferry, 9.5 *m.,* 45 min.; by auto around Bainbridge Island, 24.7 *m.*

Ferry: Black Ball Line. *Klahanie* leaves Colman Ferry Terminal, ft. of Marion St., approximately every 2 hrs., between 6:30 a.m. and 11:30 p.m.; fewer trips Sunday (schedules vary with the seasons). Fares: 35c one way, 60c round trip; car and driver, $1 one way, $1.70 round trip. Dining service.
Stage service to main points on island, 10c. Numerous cabin camps and cottages. Graveled roads encircle the island.

Section a. SEATTLE *to* BAINBRIDGE ISLAND, *9.5 m.*

From its slip at the foot of Marion Street in Seattle, the broad-beamed ferry swings west across the Sound to BAINBRIDGE ISLAND. Home and vacation-place of well-to-do business and professional people, university instructors, and artists, Bainbridge Island might be called the aristocrat among the islands of Puget Sound. Many beautiful residences are scattered about the island; summer camps are strung along the beaches. At the height of the vacation season, its normal population of 3,000 expands to 6,000.

On a spring morning in 1792, Kitsap, chief of many tribes, stood with his people on the south shore of Bainbridge Island, observing the approach of what must have appeared to be a visitation of the "Great Spirit": the first white man's ship to enter Puget Sound. Captain George Vancouver, its commander, did not know that the land he saw was an island. It remained unidentified until 1841, when Charles N. Wilkes, in command of an exploring expedition for the United States Navy, found Agate Pass, entrance to the west shoreline, and named the island Bainbridge for Captain William Bainbridge, hero of the U.S.S. *Constitution* (Old Ironsides). Twelve years later one of the first mills on Puget Sound was built here, and by the sixties, Bainbridge's ports were among the most important on the Sound. For many years the island was a leading lumber-manufacturing center. Today, the once bustling ports are gone, and in their place are quiet summer and country homes bordered by berry fields and small farms.

Nine miles from its starting point, the ferry slips behind the protecting arm of WING POINT, to the right, and enters EAGLE HARBOR, a wedge-shaped inlet less than half a mile wide at its mouth. Tipped with feathery green trees and dotted with country homes, the slender point thrusts out into the sea to form the north boundary of the harbor. On the left, a high bluff protects the inlet from the gusty "southwesters" that blow off the Sound. Small boats ride at anchor in the quiet water, or rest on the beach near the cottages along the shore. Eagle Harbor was named by the Wilkes Expedition of 1841 for Henry Eagle, a Navy lieutenant.

The ferry docks at WINSLOW (20 alt., 669 pop.), largest population center of the island and home of its largest industry, a shipbuilding plant covering 15 acres. Ocean steamers anchored in the harbor seem to dwarf the cove. Many boats of the halibut fleet moor here in slack season; a weathered old windjammer rides the tide in peaceful retirement. The shipbuilding plant is constructing twelve mine sweepers for the United States Navy.

Section b. WINSLOW-PORT BLAKELEY-PLEASANT BEACH-PORT MADISON-WINSLOW, *24.7 m.*

A graveled road runs west from Winslow, skirts the end of Eagle Harbor, and swings back along the crest of the south shore.

At 3.3 *m.* is a junction with a graveled crossroad.

Left here 1 *m.* to CREOSOTE (20 alt., 250 pop.), site of a wood-preserving plant for which the town was named.

South of the junction, the highway comes out upon the north shore of Blakely Harbor, site of old PORT BLAKELY, 5 *m.* (sea level; 100 pop.), a settlement which came to life in 1863 and was soon one of the leading lumber centers on Puget Sound. During the last quarter of the nineteenth century, the masts and spars of lumber schooners loading for world ports gave the harbor the appearance of a bleached forest. A shipyard was built, in which the S. S. *Julia,* largest stern-wheeler in the Northwest of that day, was constructed. During this period the Port Blakely mill, said to have been the largest in the world, at that time, employed 1,200 men and daily cut 400,000 feet of lumber. When the United States acquired Alaska, the old Russian gunboat *Politokofsky* was included in the purchase. The ship was bought by the Port Blakely Mill Company, its guns were dismounted, and for many years the boat was a familiar sight on Puget Sound. Shortly after the close of the World War, the mill was shut down and dismantled. Today, nothing remains but a few moldy bricks to mark its foundations.

The road turns westward along the north shore of the harbor.

At 5.4 *m.* is a junction with a graveled road:

Left here 2 *m.* along the south shore of Blakely Harbor to RESTORATION POINT, where Vancouver anchored in 1792. He first called the place Village Point, but since he here celebrated Restoration Day, anniversary of the Stuarts' return to the English throne, the name was changed to Restoration Point. On the reef off the point, the famed sloop-of-war, *Decatur,* first revenue cutter on Puget Sound, went aground in 1856, and the crew was barely able to make repairs in time to help rout the Indians in the Battle of Seattle (*see Seattle*).

The greater part of the point is occupied by the grounds of the exclusive BAINBRIDGE COUNTRY CLUB, many of whose members have built homes here and maintain stables and a nine-hole golf course.

At 6.4 *m.* is a junction with a graveled road skirting the beach along Rich Passage, a channel named for botanist William Rich of the Wilkes Expedition, 1841.

Left here to FORT WARD, 1.6 *m.,* a 330-acre military reservation and barracks established 1910-11, with 20 buildings which extend up the hill (L) from the water front. It is now under control of the Navy. From Fort Ward the road follows the shore to SOUTH BEACH, 3.0 *m.,* marked by a group of comfortable summer homes.

PLEASANT BEACH, 7 *m.* (10 alt., 450 pop.), is a summer resort spread around a picturesque semicircular bay. In a brick block are stores and a rakish theater building.

Left from Pleasant Beach a graveled road winds around WHITE POINT, 0.8 *m.,* a protecting peninsula between Pleasant Beach and Port Orchard Bay.

At 3.4 *m.,* are CRYSTAL SPRINGS, a suburban resort, and GAZZAM LAKE, a small body of water hidden in the forest a few hundred feet (R) from the highway. The lake is noted for its bass fishing. Bainbridge Island is a game preserve, with abundant wild life, including chinese pheasant, quail, and deer.

The road's end, at 3.9 *m.,* affords a view of Port Orchard Bay, known for its excellent salmon fishing. Butter clams are plentiful.

North of the junction, the highway passes through a timbered area, with occasional views of the bay and distant mountains.

At 10.5*m.* is a junction with a graveled road:

Left on this road to FLETCHER BAY, 0.6 *m.* (10 alt., 152 pop.), (*picnicking facilities*), a slender cove running inland for a half-mile with an average width of a few hundred feet. Along its banks are attractive homes; a dance pavilion provides a social center.

North of the junction the highway traverses a countryside dotted with strawberry fields, mainly cultivated by Japanese who operate lands under lease. BAINBRIDGE GARDENS, 10.9 *m.,* is one of the largest greenhouses on the island; many thousands of Easter lilies are shipped annually from here.

At 11.9 *m.* is a junction with a graveled road.

Left here to VENICE, 2.0 *m.* (20 alt., 60 pop.), a beach resort on ARROW POINT, whose protecting arm reaches out to form MANZANITA BAY.

At 12.4 *m.,* the route swings left, roughly paralleling the shore of Port Orchard Bay, and skirts the beach of an arm of Manzanita Bay and the small settlement of MANZANITA, 13.1 *m.* (sea level, 125 pop.), center of summer homes and camps.

At 14 *m.* are the forks of two graveled roads.

1. Left here 0.2 *m.* to Seabold (95 alt., 125 pop.), the water front center of a community of small ranches. Its situation, which overlooks a tidal shore, inspired William Bull, in 1894, to give the settlement its name. The beach in this section is a favorite spot for digging the succulent, but elusive, geoduck (goey-duck), largest of the burrowing clams.

2. Left (straight ahead) 3 *m.,* to AGATE POINT, the northwest tip of Bainbridge Island, which is separated from the mainland at this point by narrow Agate Passage (L), only 2 m. wide. On the crest of the point is AGATE PARK, seven acres of forest and beach set aside as a recreational area. The names, Agate Pass, Agate Point, and Agate Park, were bestowed in honor of Alfred T. Agate, an artist with the Wilkes Expedition of 1841.

Right from the junction, the main road bears northeasterly across the island through a pleasantly wooded country. Here and there, a small farm is leisurely cultivated.

PORT MADISON, 16.5 *m.* (25 alt., 576 pop.), once a leading industrial center on Puget Sound, is now a quiet little shore village sprawling along both sides of its almost toy harbor. Named by Wilkes for a former President of the United States, Port Madison stirred to life in 1853, when G. W. Meigs came from San Francisco and set up a sawmill. The great demand for lumber in early days, with prices reaching from $200 to $500 per 1,000 board feet, led to a continued expansion of the plant and the addition of a foundry, machine shop, and shipyard. For decades Port Madison thrived, and in 1861 it was voted the seat of Kitsap County, a distinction it later lost in one of the hottest political fights in county annals. Port Madison today shelters the country homes of a few city dwellers, and a scattering of faded old houses.

West from Port Madison on the main highway is an OLD BRITISH CEMETERY, (L), 17.4 *m.*, the burial place of several British sailors. Some of the headstones date back to 1854.

The highway turns south at 17.7*m.*, paralleling the shore along a high bluff. Second-growth timber and scrubby woodland border the road. The route continues towards the midsection of the island, its most cultivated area. ROLLING BAY, 20.7 *m.* (20 alt., 530 pop.), a few hundred yards off the highway (L), is one of the oldest summer colonies on Bainbridge Island.

SKIFF POINT, 21.7 *m.*, was so named to direct attention to its resemblance to an overturned skiff at low tide and for the number of skiffs stranded on its shallow bar. On the crest of the point are the buildings and grounds of the PUGET SOUND NAVAL ACADEMY, a private preparatory school which trains students for the United States Naval Academy at Annapolis and the United States Coast Guard Academy at New London, Connecticut. This was formerly the Moran School, founded in 1914 as a private boarding school for boys. After its sale in 1938 to Eastern interests, it was reorganized and renamed. New barracks were constructed and new equipment installed, including boats and other facilities.

South of Skiff Point the route follows around the shore, where small roads branch inland.

The Bainbridge Island Boy Scouts assemble at MAJOR HOPKINS BOY SCOUT CAMP, 23.7 *m.*, for their annual affair, during a weekend about the middle of June. Adjoining is a camp maintained by the Seattle YWCA; also in the neighborhood is a riding academy.

WING POINT, 24.2 *m.*, pushes its slim length into the Sound. At its base is the spreading green blanket of the WING POINT GOLF CLUB nine-hole golf course (*fees 50c*), a community course. Offshore here, the Seattle Yacht Club holds its annual regatta from May 28 to June 2.

At 24.7 *m.*, the route re-enters Winslow.

ISLAND TOUR 3

Chuckanut (mainland)—Orcas Island—San Juan Island—Anacortes (mainland)—Mount Vernon. County roads and State 1. Ferry crossings between mainland and Islands; for costs see section headings.
Chuckanut to Mount Vernon, 108.7 *m.* (48.2 *m.* by ferry; 60.5 *m.* by car).

Ferries: Puget Sound Navigation Co. and Inter-Island Transportation Co. Mail and passenger boats to smaller islands (schedules vary with the seasons). No regular bus lines. Summer resort and cabin-camp accommodations; hotels in larger towns; scattered general stores and garages. Graveled and dirt roads on larger islands; State 1 concrete-paved.

The San Juan Islands include 172 habitable islands and several hundred tide-washed rocks clustered in the northern waters of Puget

Sound and the southern extremity of Georgia Strait. The International Boundary Line, zigzagging through a maze of waterways, leaves a hundred or more islands to Canada; all are a part of the same submerged mountain chain that rises above sea level to a maximum of 2,454 feet in Mount Constitution.

Along the jagged shores of the islands, sinewy red-trunked madronas and wind-stunted green conifers stand above tawny rocks, white sand, and gravelly beaches. From the water, the woods present a leafy tangle, brightened in summer with gleaming white dogwood and rose-red flowering currant, each shaded sanctuary adorned with delicate green ferns, honeysuckle, trilliums, and other wild flowers.

Some of the islands in the "dry belt," which has only about 20 inches of rainfall annually, are so arid that a species of prickly cactus (*Opuntia polycantha*) flourishes. However, most of the islands are heavily wooded, and a temperate climate, together with a favorable average rainfall, has encouraged cultivation of the larger bodies of land.

The breeze-swept adjacent waters contain an extraordinary variety of marine life, and no less plentiful is the fauna of the islands. Deer are common; it is not unusual to see them swimming the narrow channels between the islands in search of fresh pastures. Rabbits overrun some of the islands, while on others wild goats, descended from domestic varieties abandoned by settlers, make their home. Eagles are frequently visible, soaring above rocky cliffs; water fowl abound, ranging from migratory ducks to the gull and the white-breasted black mudhen.

While the names of some of the islands embody the long record of successive explorations, from the Spaniards in 1790-2 and the English in 1792, to the American Wilkes and others of the 1840's, physical peculiarities are responsible for many homespun names such as Peapod, Goose, Dot, Ripple, Flattop, Saddle Bag, and Hat Islands.

Each of the two sections of this two-day, land-water tour is a day's journey, which represents perhaps the shortest time in which the traveler may acquaint himself with the intriguing maze of waterways and beckoning isles of the San Juan Archipelago, known as one of the most picturesque regions of the Pacific Coast.

Section a. CHUCKANUT-ORCAS ISLAND (*Obstruction Pass Landing*), *15 m. by ferry, 2 hrs.;* OBSTRUCTION PASS LANDING-ORCAS, *18.1 m. by auto;* ORCAS ISLAND-SAN JUAN ISLAND (*Friday Harbor*), *10.2 m. by ferry, 40 min.*

Fares: Chuckanut to Orcas Island: passenger, one way, 50c; car and driver, $1.50. Orcas Island to San Juan Island: passenger, one way, 35c; car and driver, $1.10.

West of the landing on Chuckanut Bay, six miles south of Bellingham, the ferry glides past miniature CHUCKANUT ISLAND, to the right, and enters Bellingham Bay.

On the right, too, about four miles farther, is thinly wooded ELIZA ISLAND, named by Wilkes in 1841 for the Spanish explorer, Fran-

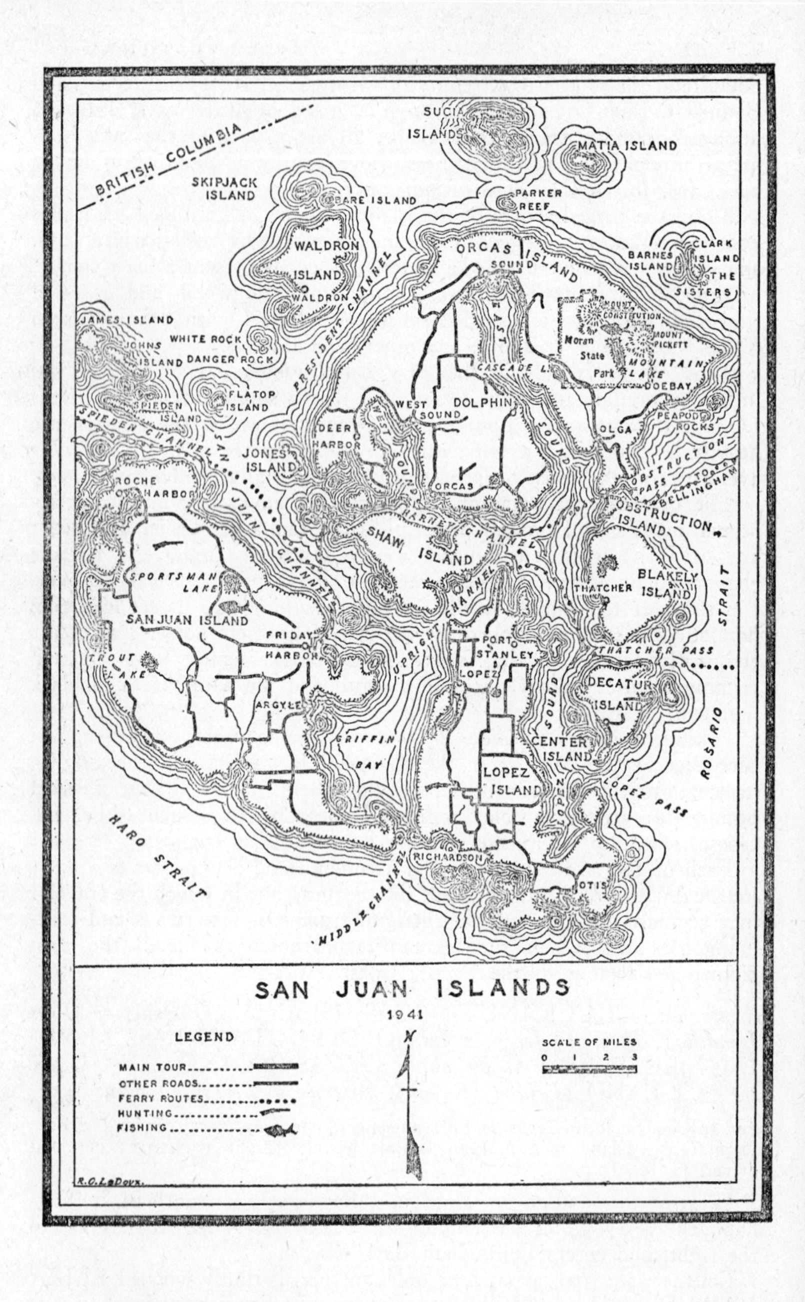
BRITISH COLUMBIA
SKIPJACK ISLAND
SUCIA ISLANDS
MATIA ISLAND
BARE ISLAND
PARKER REEF
WALDRON ISLAND
WALDRON
PRESIDENT CHANNEL
ORCAS ISLAND
SOUND
EAST
BARNES ISLAND
CLARK ISLAND
THE SISTERS
MOUNT CONSTITUTION
MOUNT PICKETT
Moran State Park
MOUNTAIN LAKE
DOEBAY
JAMES ISLAND
WHITE ROCK
DANGER ROCK
JOHNS ISLAND
FLATOP ISLAND
SPIEDEN ISLAND
SPIEDEN CHANNEL
CASCADE L.
WEST SOUND
DOLPHIN
DEER HARBOR
WEST SOUND
SOUND
OLGA
PEAPOD ROCKS
JONES ISLAND
ORCAS
OBSTRUCTION PASS
TO BELLINGHAM
ROCHE HARBOR
SAN JUAN CHANNEL
HARNEY CHANNEL
SHAW ISLAND
OBSTRUCTION ISLAND
SPORTSMAN LAKE
BLAKELY ISLAND
THATCHER
SAN JUAN ISLAND
UPRIGHT CHANNEL
STRAIT
FRIDAY HARBOR
PORT STANLEY
THATCHER PASS
TROUT LAKE
LOPEZ
DECATUR ISLAND
ARGYLE
SOUND
CENTER ISLAND
GRIFFIN BAY
ROSARIO
LOPEZ ISLAND
LOPEZ PASS
LOPEZ
HARO STRAIT
RICHARDSON
OTIS
MIDDLE CHANNEL
SAN JUAN ISLANDS
1941
LEGEND
MAIN TOUR
OTHER ROADS
FERRY ROUTES
HUNTING
FISHING
N
SCALE OF MILES
0 1 2 3
R.O. LeDoux.

cisco Eliza. The low, nearly flat island is owned by the Pacific American Fisheries, which at one time maintained a web-house and ship repair yards here.

To the west, the mountainous southern end of Lummi Island rises to LUMMI PEAK, 1,740 ft. in height. Here was the ancestral home of the Lummi Indians, who now live in the reservation on the mainland opposite (*see Tour 8a*). Westward, a beacon marks VITI ROCKS, inhabited by swarms of seagulls.

On VENDOVI ISLAND, less than a mile farther, on the left, a rockbound cove below a wooded hill opens into the channel. The Wilkes Expedition named the island after a native who was taken from the Fiji Islands and brought to the Northwest on one of its survey ships. The north shore was once the site of a Father Divine colony that attracted many members from New York and California during the summer.

SINCLAIR ISLAND, on the right, rises to flat-topped wooded hills from long sandy beaches surrounded by shoalwater. It was supposedly named for Arthur Sinclair, commander of the *Argus* during the War of 1812. Here was the home port of Larry Kelly, notorious smuggler, who evaded all efforts of revenue officers to stop the illegal importation of Chinese from Canada during the nineties. Under cover of darkness the Chinese were landed near Everett or Seattle for a fee of $500 each, cash in advance; it was said that when hard pressed, Kelly would throw the immigrants overboard to save himself from arrest.

The boat channel narrows between CYPRESS ISLAND, on the left, named in 1792 by Captain George Vancouver for what he took to be cypress trees, and little TOWHEAD ISLAND, on the right, a tiny dome-shaped isle with a scrawny thatch of scrub-growth where two eagles have made their home for many years. Right to the northwest looms the group of reefs grimly named THE DEVIL'S PLAYGROUND, because of its menace to mariners.

ROSARIO STRAIT, which links Georgia Strait with Juan de Fuca Strait, is much traveled by ships bound for the "inside passage" to Alaska. The current here often reaches a velocity of eight miles an hour, so that the waters are beset with boiling tide rips and whirling eddies. Sleek porpoises frequently bound in graceful arcs through the strait, and huge blackfish known as pilot whale, occasionally rear above the surface, flirting enormous black tails.

Discovered by the Spaniard, Quimper, who called it Boca de Fidalgo, the strait was renamed Canal de Fidalgo by Lieutenant Eliza, Ringgold's Pass by Wilkes, and finally Rosario Strait, by the British Admiralty in 1847.

Narrow PEAVINE PASS, on the left, lies between BLAKELEY ISLAND and diminutive OBSTRUCTION ISLAND, which is separated from ORCAS ISLAND by OBSTRUCTION PASS.

At Obstruction Pass Landing, the ferry docks at the end of a long wharf on Orcas Island, its terminus. The name "orcas" is of Spanish origin; Commander Wilkes (1841) renamed it "Hull's Island," for

Commander Isaac Hull of the U.S. frigate *Constitution,* but the original persisted.

North of OBSTRUCTION PASS LANDING, 0 *m.,* the road ascends a thinly forested grade.

At 2.2 *m.* is a junction with dirt road.

Right here through a cutover section to DOEBAY, 3 *m.* (sea level, 104 pop.), a small fishing resort in a wooded cove.

LAWRENCE POINT, 5 *m.,* is another fishing resort at the end of the road, where the rocky head of Lawrence Point overlooks Rosario Strait.

At 2.8 *m.* is a junction with a dirt road.

Left here to OLGA, 0.2 *m.,* at the head of Buck Bay, a resort center with a number of residences located on a bluff above the beach.

At 4.5 *m.* is a wooden bridge marking the southern entrance to MORAN STATE PARK, a 3,325-acre tract donated by the pioneer shipbuilder, Robert Moran. Across the bridge is a junction with a dirt road.

Right here through a deeply shaded woodland to CASCADE FALLS, 0.2 *m.,* where a 51-foot waterfall cascades down a mossy rock wall. Steps cut in the side of a huge fir log lead to the base of the falls at the bottom of the gorge, scented with overhanging fir, spruce, and flowering plants.

At 4.9 *m.* is a junction with a graveled road.

Right on this road 1.3 *m.* to a junction with a dirt road: Right here to MOUNTAIN LAKE, 0.2 *m.* (*camping, fishing, boating*), lying in a basin of evergreens and dammed to store the water supply for the community of Olga. To the east rises MOUNT PICKETT (alt. 1,889), whose name honors Captain George Pickett for his part in the boundary issue with Great Britain on San Juan Island in the summer of 1859. The graveled side road, flanked by log railings, continues northward, winding up the west slope of Mount Constitution. At 4 *m.* is a junction with Cold Spring Trail (L). At the junction is a camping ground and picnic area. Northward, the road rears more steeply upward on hairpin turns which yield glimpses of islands, channels, and straits.

At 5 *m.* is a junction (L) with the Twin Lakes and Mountain Lake Trails, which wind down the mountain through dense old-growth forest.

At 5.1 *m.* the road ends in a turn-around on the summit of MOUNT CONSTITUTION (alt. 2,454). From here a short incline leads steeply up a few hundred feet to the base of a 52-foot granite OBSERVATION TOWER set squarely upon the pinkish lava-rock dome of the peak.

Built in the style of the twelfth-century watchtowers which guarded Caucasian Mountain passes, the rectangular tower is topped by an open gallery and a log lookout shelter whose windows open upon a breath-taking panorama in every direction. Far below, the San Juan Islands stretch over the moving blue-green sea like a parade of prehistoric sea monsters. Some lie flat with sandy tails floating out behind, while dark bulky heights suggest the submerged shoulders of a creature feeding on the bottom. In the foreground the island-dotted tide flows through a 30-mile-wide channel between Canadian and American shores. On a clear day the outlines of Victoria and Bellingham and the crags of the mountain peaks beyond in the Cascade and Olympic ranges, stand out in clean-cut detail. Mount Constitution is a primary station in all geodetic surveys of this region, as indicated by a series of brass bench-markers. The International Boundary Line through this region was determined from this point.

At 5.1 *m.* on the main highway are the barracks of CAMP MORAN

(L), a large CCC camp, whose members have created most of the trails, campsites, roads, and other improvements in Moran State Park.

The highway, at 5.8 *m.,* skirts the brushy east shore (L) of CASCADE LAKE (*fishing, picnicking*), stocked with trout by the State Game Commission. Formerly, there were no fish in this lake, a fact attributed by an Indian legend to the anger of Raven, who destroyed them by hurling a thunderbolt into the lake from the top of Mount Constitution. Near the shore in a grove of Douglas firs are grassy picnic grounds with log shelter houses and outdoor cooking facilities.

A CONCRETE ARCH, 6.4 *m.,* over the highway marks the western entrance to Moran State Park.

At 6.6 *m.* is a junction (L) with a graveled road.

Left on this road, 1.5 *m.,* to ROSARIO, former estate of Robert Moran, donor of Moran State Park. Once a show-place of the islands, where visitors were welcomed, this 1,800-acre estate with its low, stone mansion was sold by its owner in 1938.

At CRESCENT BEACH, 10.2 *m.,* a few summer cottages face upon a beach that slopes gradually into the shallow water of SHIP BAY (L).

EASTSOUND, 10.5 *m.* (30 alt., 256 pop.), (*resorts, cabin camps, riding, tennis*), largest settlement on the island, is a crossroads trading center at the head of East Sound. Comfortable old houses with orchards are scattered behind the few frame business buildings along the bay shore. The W. R. GRIFFIN HOUSE MUSEUM (*open*) has a collection of fossils from Sucia Island.

Right from Eastsound on a graveled road to NORTH BEACH, 1.5 *m.,* a seaside resort district. Inn and cabin accommodations, riding horses, sand-beach bathing, salmon-trolling outfits, and boats ranging from powered skiffs to small yachts, are available here. Northward, in Georgia Strait, lie the rocky SUCIA ISLANDS, flanked on the northwest and southeast by PATOS and MATIA ISLANDS. (*Weekly summer service by motor launch; Wed. from Orcas Island; Thurs. from Lummi Island, 50c; Sun. from Bellingham, $1; launch also available for chartered trips*).

Sucia was named by Lieutenant Eliza from a Spanish word meaning "foul." Patos (Sp. ducks) was probably named for its wild fowl. The Sucia Islands have a peculiar formation, owing to alternating strata of rock, one resistant, the other yielding to erosion by sea water. FOSSIL BAY, at Sucia's southern end, is rich in paleontological specimens: a clay bank here once yielded the perfect foreleg and hoof of a tiny prehistoric horse; these specimens were sent to the Smithsonian Institution.

South of Eastsound the main road leaves the seaside and crosses to the western half of Orcas Island, skirting the foot of the TURTLEBACK RANGE (R). The route traverses the farming section of the island. Dairy herds and grazing sheep are seen along the way.

At 16.5 *m.* is a junction with a graveled road.

Right here to WESTSOUND, 0.9 *m.* 30 (alt., 75 pop.). A store and post office serve the community, represented by a row of attractive houses along the shore of White Beach Bay, an indentation of West Sound. Double Island, mainland-bound at low water, lies close to the sound's entrance; other small, green isles dot its surface.

1. Right from Westsound on a trail to TURTLEBACK MOUNTAINS (alt. 1,497), 1.5 *m.,* overlooking President Channel and Waldron Island. To the west lie Spieden and Stuart Islands, with the Canadian islands across Haro Strait huddled about the southeastern shore of Vancouver Island. On the southernmost summit of the Turtleback Range is an old MARKER, the origin of which has mystified the island's inhabitants since the earliest days. It consists of small boulders arranged on the ground in the shape of a large anchor, and is supposed to have been placed here by the survivors of some early shipwreck, more than 100 years ago. WALDRON ISLAND (*mailboat service from Orcas Island and Bellingham on regular schedule*), on the northwest, is seen to advantage from this point. Sheep-raising is the island's leading occupation. Quarries there once supplied sandstone for jetties at the mouth of the Columbia River. The ETHAN ALLEN HOUSE MUSEUM (*fee voluntary*) contains a large collection of artifacts, gathered over a lifetime by a descendant of the Revolutionary War hero, comprising more than 3,000 items, including arrowheads, spearheads, Indian baskets, pottery, stone dishes, grinding implements, paint pots, ornaments, and ceremonial pieces.

2. Right from Westsound, a graveled road rounds Haida Point, which divides White Beach Bay from Massacre Bay, at which a battle between Indian bands took place before 1860. Diminutive SKULL ISLAND (L), named for the number of skulls and bones excavated here, is thought to have been the common burial ground for fallen Indian braves. Many conflicts were provoked by the warlike Haidahs, Bella Bellas, and Bella Coolas of British Columbia, who preyed upon the more peaceful San Juan Islanders and frequently carried them off as slaves. The island Indians lived mainly on fish, clams, crabs, and other seafoods. Clams, dried before campfires, were preserved for winter food: and fresh venison was also obtainable, for the islands were overrun with deer. Remnants of willow-bark nets, bone fishhooks, stone sinkers, bone teeth from herring rakes, celts used for digging out canoes, and arrowheads and spear points have been found throughout the archipelago.

DEER HARBOR (*hotel, cabins, saddle horses*), 4.9 *m.* (20 alt., 99 pop.), is a resort district on a small bight of the same name. Along the western cliffs of the shady green cove are feldspar deposits which reach 60 feet in thickness and 300 in depth. Feldspar is used in glazing pottery and manufacturing glass, but the demand has not justified development at this point.

South from Deer Harbor, the road winds through thick glades along the western shore of the bay and breaks into the open at POLE PASS, 6.5 *m.* Although the narrow aperture seems only wide enough for a skiff, boats of considerable size negotiate the passage.

On CRANE ISLAND, directly opposite, the gnarled arms of windswept firs and junipers point the direction of prevailing winds.

South of the junction the main road leads into the forested middle lobe of Orcas Island and emerges on a small bay.

ORCAS, 19.1 *m.* (12 alt., 20 pop.), has a store and warehouse on the ferry dock. On the hill sloping back from the beach stands a white hotel converted from an old residence. A mile across the channel is Shaw Island (*flag ferry stop*).

Leaving Orcas, the ferry turns westward through a maze of waterways, studded with rocks and wooded islets. BROKEN POINT, a small cross-shaped peninsula, reaches out from the indented and stratified shoreline of SHAW ISLAND (*a flag stop*). The ferry enters narrow WASP PASSAGE, which separates Crane Island and heavily timbered CLIFF ISLAND, on the right, from Shaw Island, on the left. A cluster of small rocks, extending from NECK POINT (Shaw Island), marks the entrance to SAN JUAN CHANNEL, subject of controversy in 1859 when Britain claimed it to be the International Boundary Line (*see History*). On almost any summer day purse-seine boats with their elevated round sterns and swivel platforms are seen circling about. Purse-seining, which traps fish in an encircling net with a draw-string at the bottom, is said to have been introduced on Puget Sound by the Chinese in 1886. Occasionally, in this region are seen reminders of an easy but now illegal method of catching salmon—rows of piles, to which nets were attached, extending from the shore.

Slipping southward along San Juan Channel between SHAW ISLAND, on the left, and San Juan Island, on the right, the ferry reaches FRIDAY HARBOR (sea level, 658 pop.), on a crescent-shaped bay of the same name, almost completely land-locked by Brown Island at its entrance. Friday Harbor took its name from "Friday," an aged Kanaka brought here from the Hawaiian Islands by the Hudson's Bay Company to herd its sheep. Perched on the rocky shore (R) are the buildings of the University of Washington Oceanographic Laboratories. A large fish cannery (L) and a pea cannery (R) face the harbor from the water front.

From the ferry landing the main thoroughfare ascends a gradual incline, fronted by a variety of mercantile establishments, to the flat above the harbor where the residence district, school buildings, and courthouse spread out from the main street. Small-launch transportation between the islands has centralized insular business at Friday Harbor, the principal ferry point, and seat of San Juan County. It has the only bank, creamery, newspaper, automobile agency, motion picture theater, and drugstore in the San Juan Group.

Section b. FRIDAY HARBOR-FRIDAY HARBOR, *24.3 m.*

This section of the tour explores San Juan Island, with side trips to quaint old Roche Harbor and other points of interest.

Northwest of FRIDAY HARBOR, 0 *m.,* the main county road winds among garden plots and outlying homes.

At 0.8 *m.* is a junction with a graveled road.

Right on this road 0.7 *m.* to the UNIVERSITY OF WASHINGTON OCEANOGRAPHIC LABORATORIES (*open 2-5 weekdays; no visitors allowed in laboratories; firearms and pets not allowed; picking of flowers prohibited*). Seven concrete and tile buildings, on a 484-acre tract which fronts on two miles of water, include laboratories, a stockroom, dining and social hall, and the residences of the curator and director. During the summer months, tent houses spring up over the grounds to house visiting students. Field trips are made aboard the *Catalyst,* a 75-foot Diesel-powered research boat. The 50-foot vessel *Medea* is used for dredging and water sampling. The laboratories are in the center of a biological preserve which comprises all marine waters of San Juan County. The United States Coast and Geodetic Survey maintains a tidal station here, and the United States Weather Bureau has a meteorological station for observation of solar radiation.

The wide variety and abundance of the algae (seaweed) growing in the waters of San Juan archipelago is important both scientifically and economically. Brown, green, blue-green, and red specimens range in size from microscopic types to the giant kelp, or sea onion, with a 30 to 90-foot stem, usually attached to submerged rocks, and with wide ribbon-like streamers reaching to the surface.

Many varieties were cooked and eaten by Indians and early settlers. The Indians favored a green variety, called *slukkish,* with masses of narrow leaves. Research has recently found *slukkish* and other varieties exceedingly rich in vitamins, A, B, C, and G, and because of their high content of organic iodine they have been recommended for the prevention of goiter. The island waters also contain some unusual species of marine life.

North and west of the junction the main highway winds through a rolling country with sloping green fields.

Small SPORTSMAN LAKE (L), 4.1 *m.,* is bordered by rough, brush-lined shores to which anglers go down to catch the chubby bass.

At 8.4 *m.,* the entrance to the San Juan International Camp for Boys, is a junction with a graveled cross road.

Right on this road around the head of Westcott Bay (L), and down a hill through green junipers and madronas to Roche Harbor, enclosed by small islands.

ROCHE HARBOR, 1.6 *m.* (50 alt., 100 pop.), a picturesque little settlement at the northern tip of San Juan Island, is owned and controlled by the Roche Harbor Lime and Cement Company, but has none of the depressing aspects of the typical "company town." A pastoral air pervades the gardens and houses and the jagged rocks of the little cove. A small, white-steepled schoolhouse nestles snugly against a green-foliaged hillside. Roses and dahlias grow beneath tall, gay hollyhocks. Set between steep hillsides, the vine-covered and balconied Hotel De Haro (L), with its antique furniture, blends harmoniously with surroundings that re-create an atmosphere of the nineties. Arbored entrances lead to embowered and wistaria-hung gardens where immense outdoor fireplaces invite barbecues.

John S. McMillan opened lime quaries here in the eighties, and built the ROCHE HARBOR LIME PLANT (*visitors apply at office; guides furnished*). Snug Roche Harbor, virtually landlocked by little PEARL ISLAND in its northern entrance, is a favorite anchorage for yachts cruising among the San Juans.

Stripped of her sails and moored in the harbor is the famous clipper ship *La Escocesa* (Sp. The Scottish Lady). She was built in 1868 in Dundee, Scotland, and challenged *Young America,* a much larger vessel, to a race from San Francisco to Liverpool. *Young America* won, with a record cruising of 106 days; *La Escocesa* arrived 13 days later, losing her backers $40,000. In 1926 she was placed in service by the Roche Harbor Lime and Cement Company, but has not been used in recent years.

Right from Roche Harbor on a road marked "Private" to the COLUMBARIUM, 1.3 *m.,* a strange structure, built for a purpose known only to the designer, the late John S. McMillan. Seven Doric columns, one with a broken shaft, encircle the columbarium. Within the circle is a large round stone table with six stone chairs, each inscribed with the name of a member of his family. A space is left for a seventh chair.

West and south of the junction the main road turns south through rocky hills. At 9.8 *m.* is a junction with a dirt road.

Right here to the ENGLISH CAMP, 0.5 *m.,* the site of the British marines' camp between 1860 and 1872. It is entered through the Davis-Crook farm (*private, admission 10c*). The ENGLISH BLOCKHOUSE, a small log structure, with an overhanging upper story set diagonally across a lower room, stands at the border of Garrison Bay, which the grounds overlook. Two crumbling old buildings, reputedly the barracks and commissary occupied by the British, still mark the campsite (*see History*).

A path (L) leads up a hill to the BRITISH OCCUPATION MONUMENT, which marks the former site of the residence occupied by Captain Delacombe, British post commander.

On the grounds is the MARY C. DAVIS HOUSE MUSEUM, containing old photographs, relics, and a yellow time-worn map of the camp drawn by a British marine.

South of the junction, the main road passes alternating patches of woodland and cultivated farms. Looming ahead is MOUNT DALLAS (alt. 1,936), the highest point on San Juan Island, named after Alexander Dallas of the Hudson's Bay Company.

The road swings through rolling hills with the flat expanse of the San Juan Valley visible in the distance; well-tilled farms, many of them pea ranches, dot the valley. At planting time in the spring, each pea farmer is allotted a planting date: thus the crops ripen successively, assuring steady operation for the cannery at Friday Harbor.

At 21 *m.* is a junction with a graveled road.

Right here to AMERICAN CAMP, 5 *m.,* where, during a boundary dispute humorously referred to as the "Pig War," the Ninth United States Infantry, under command of Captain George Pickett, made camp in 1859, in opposition to the English camp. The British-American treaty of 1846 left the International Boundary through these islands so vague that both countries claimed them, and citizens of each settled here. Complications arose in 1858, when Whatcom County levied taxes on English sheep grazing on the island. The following year an English pig rooted up an American potato patch and was shot. The situation immediately became tense. Troops made camp at opposite ends of the island, and there was much international bristling. During the succeeding period of arbitration, however, the opposing camps vied with each other in an exchange of complimentary banquets. The matter was ended in 1872 when Emperor William I of Germany, as arbiter, selected the present boundary line (*see History*).

North of the junction the main road follows a ridge overlooking GRIFFIN BAY, named in honor of Charles John Griffin, overseer of the Hudson's Bay Farm on San Juan and one of the principals in the pig controversy. The bay is a crescent-shaped indentation formed by the southeast tip of San Juan Island.

Completing its circuit of the island, the main road ends at FRIDAY HARBOR, 24.3 *m.*

Section c. FRIDAY HARBOR-ANACORTES, *23 m. by ferry, 2½ hrs.;* ANACORTES-MOUNT VERNON, *17.1 m. by auto.*

Fares: Passenger, one way, 70c; car and driver, $2.15.

The ferry route from Friday Harbor follows an easterly winding course along deep green aisles between rock-bound, tree-covered islands, every turn presenting a new vista of tide-washed shore.

Leaving Friday Harbor, the ferry runs eastward for four miles across the San Juan Channel to Upright Channel. Soon, CANOE ISLAND, a rocky upthrust of about 50 acres surmounted by dark green conifers, narrows Upright Channel to river width. On the east looms the huge bulk of LOPEZ ISLAND. Twelve miles long and four miles wide, its deeply indented southern shore peppered with small islands and bare rocks, Lopez, with a population of 600, ranks third in size and agricultural importance among the San Juans. Its north coast is a salmon fishing center. The island was named in 1791 by Lieutenant Eliza for Lopez de Haro, thought to be the first to sight it. Several small settlements and a scattering of farming communities are connected by graveled roads to the ferry landing at UPRIGHT HEAD, where a large size sign offers water front property and individual islands for sale at an amazing variety of prices. One 20-acre island was sold in the 1930's for the bargain price of fifty dollars.

East of Upright Head, the passage emerges into Lopez Sound and swings through Thatcher Pass.

Not the least of this region's marvels is the skill of its navigators, who, during the fall and winter fogs, nimbly trace their way through treacherous passages in the blind mist. It is said that the late Captain Sam Barlow could thrust his head out of the wheelhouse window and with one sniff tell his exact location. Actually, local pilots can determine their ships' positions in fog-bound waters by the echoes of their whistles from the invisible shores.

Two miles farther, to the left, BLAKELY ISLAND, named for Johnston Blakely, an American naval hero of the war of 1812, rises with steep forested slopes from the sea to stony heights. Rocky DECATUR ISLAND, three miles beyond Blakely, on the right, was named for Stephen Decatur, distinguished American naval officer. Not quite four square miles in area, its heavily-forested slopes descend to a curving beach on the west; here crabs are found in abundance. Off-shore, a few hundred yards from the south headland of this half-moon bay, JAMES ISLAND, with a total area of 100 acres, closely resembles a half-submerged dumbbell, its high promontories on either end linked by a small central isthmus.

As the ferry crosses Rosaria Strait, BIRD ROCKS, to the right, thrust their three crags above the sea and serve as roosts for sea gulls and cormorants. Close by them, BELLE ROCK, marked by a bell buoy, is usually hidden under water.

Botanists say the trees Vancouver noted on CYPRESS ISLAND, two miles farther, on the left, were actually junipers. Virtually devoid of roads and scantily populated, the island has deposits of iron ore that have never been developed.

Midway across Rosario Strait, the open channel affords views of the Olympic Mountains to the south. GUEMES ISLAND is passed next, on the left, its southwest corner marked by a yellow bluff. It was named by Eliza for the Viceroy of Mexico. Triangular in shape, its eight square miles are heavily wooded. On the southeast, the shore land rises steeply to the highest point. A few farms are scattered about the island, and a tiny Indian village is on its northwest tip. Large deposits of plastic clay are found here.

The ferry heads into Guemes Channel between FIDALGO ISLAND, right, and Guemes Island.

ANACORTES, the ferry terminus (sea level, 5,875 pop.), is a fishing and lumbering center on the northwest point of Fidalgo Island, connected with the mainland over bridged sloughs. The town is a checkerboard of wide streets, where neat buildings of brick and concrete predominate over old frame structures. Parkways and skillful landscaping distinguish parts of the residential section.

CAP SANTE, a dominating headland, rises abruptly east of the flat occupied by the city, and forms a peninsula separating Guemes Channel and Fidalgo Bay, the town's north and east boundaries. Two deeply indented coves in Fidalgo Bay provide storage for the log booms that supply local mills, and safe anchorage for the fishing fleet that moors at the end of 13th Street.

Saw and shingle mills, box and plywood factories, a fish reduction factory, a pulp and paper mill, tuna, salmon, and codfish canneries, wharves and warehouses, are strung along the water front. The Fishermen's Packing Corporation, a co-operative, operates the biggest cannery on Puget Sound.

Whalers, seeking a place to careen their ships in order to rid them of barnacles, visited Fidalgo Island 100 years ago, finding what they called "Squaw Harbor." Later known as "Ship Harbor," and briefly as "Magic City," the settlement which took root in 1860 was finally named Anacortes for Anna Curtis, wife of Amos Bowman, an early settler. Surviving a somewhat exciting career of early booms and slumps, its basic industries periodically beset by fish pirates and "log slicers," Anacortes today has the air of a settled community, its thoroughfares reflecting a conscious civic pride.

East of Anacortes on State 1, the route traverses the Skagit Flats (*see Tour 8C*), to a junction with US 99 in Mount Vernon, 17.1 *m.* (*see Tour 8a*), which is 20.3 miles south of Chuckanut on US 99 Alt., where Island Tour 3 began.

PART IV
Appendices

Chronology

1579 Francis Drake sails to the Pacific Northwest coast, naming the region New Albion (New England).

1592 Apostolos Valerianos (Juan de Fuca) is alleged to have found a strait.

1774 Juan Perez sails along the coast; he sights a mountain (Olympus), which he names Sierra de Santa Rosalia.

1775 Bruno Heceta and Juan de Bodega y Quadra land on Washington coast (near the present Point Grenville) and take possession for Spain.

1778 Captain James Cook, on his last voyage, names Cape Flattery, misses discovery of the Strait near by, and makes survey from forty-fourth to seventieth parallel.

1787 Captain Charles W. Barkley finds strait northeast of Cape Flattery and "re-names" it Juan de Fuca, after its legendary discoverer.

1788 Captain John Meares explores Juan de Fuca Strait, re-names Mount Olympus, and, missing the River of the West, names Cape Disappointment.

1789 Estevan Martinez, Spaniard, confiscates British ships at Nootka Sound.

1790 Manuel Quimper, Spanish seaman, explores as far as San Juan Islands, and takes formal possession at Neah Bay.

1791 Francisco de Eliza, from a temporary base at Discovery Bay, sends small boats as far as Bellingham Bay.

Salvador Fidalgo sets up a provisional establishment at Neah Bay.

1792 Captain Robert Gray discovers and names Bulfinch (Grays) Harbor; he discovers and names the Columbia River, anchoring on the north side, trading for furs.

Captain George Vancouver, here to negotiate with Bodega y Quadra a settlement between England and Spain, explores Admiralty Inlet and Puget Sound; and, at a point near Everett, takes possession for George III of England, re-naming New Albion New Georgia. Lieutenant Broughton, under Vancouver's orders, ascends the Columbia River to Point Vancouver.

1794 Spain makes restitution for property seized by Martinez at Nootka Sound.

1803 United States purchases Louisiana Territory, increasing interest in the Oregon country.

1805 and 1806 Lewis and Clark reach mouth of Columbia River and return to St. Louis. This exploration gives the United States further claim to the Oregon country.

1810 North West Fur Company establishes Spokane House (nine miles northwest of present Spokane), the first white settlement within limits of the present State.

1811 Astoria, in present Oregon, is founded by John Jacob Astor's Pacific Fur Company.

David Thompson reaches mouth of Columbia River, after exploring from Kettle Falls to the mouth of the Snake River, and claims all land north of the Snake River for England.

Fort Okanogan is established by agents of the Pacific Fur Company.

1812 Fort Spokane is established by the Pacific Fur Company, near Spokane House, to compete with the North West Company.

1813 The North West Company, taking advantage of the War of 1812, purchases all of the property of the Pacific Fur Company in the valley of the Columbia.

1818 Fort Nez Percé (Fort Walla Walla) is built by the North West Company.

Joint occupancy of Oregon country by Americans and British is established by a convention to cover ten years.

1819 The Florida treaty with Spain gives the United States any and all rights claimed by Spain to the Oregon country.

1821 The North West Company and the Hudson's Bay Company amalgamate under the name of the latter.

1825 Hudson's Bay Company establishes Fort Vancouver on north bank of Columbia.

1826 Fort Colvile is built by Hudson's Bay Company; Spokane House is abandoned.

1827 A renewal of the convention with Great Britain continues joint occupancy indefinitely; one year's notice is required to modify the pact.

1832 Captain Bonneville arrives overland at Fort Vancouver, but is unable to purchase goods to compete with Hudson's Bay Company. Nathaniel Wyeth arrives at Fort Vancouver, but his business enterprises are temporarily halted by Dr. John McLoughlin of Hudson's Bay Company. First school at Fort Vancouver is taught by John Ball.

1833 Fort Nesqually, first trading post on Puget Sound, is established by Archibald McDonald.

1835 Lieutenant William Slacum of the United States Army arrives on the Columbia, to report on conditions of trade and population.

1836 Marcus Whitman and H. H. Spalding, missionaries, arrive with their wives, first American women in Oregon country. Whitman establishes a mission at Waiilatpu near Fort Walla Walla.

1838 The Walker-Eells Protestant mission to the Spokane is begun. Fathers Blanchet and Demers arrive at Fort Vancouver by way of the Columbia from Canada.

1839 A Roman Catholic mission is established at Cowlitz Landing. A Methodist mission is established at Fort Nesqually.

1840 A Catholic mission is established on Whidbey Island.

1841 The Wilkes Expedition arrives at Fort Nesqually. The main field of exploration is Puget Sound, but small parties go to Fort Okanogan, Fort Colvile, and Fort Walla Walla, also Fort Vancouver, Grays Harbor, and Shoalwater Bay (Willapa Harbor).

1843 Influx of immigrants assumes large proportions. Oregon Provisional Government forms at Champoeg.

1844 Boundary slogan, "Fifty-four-forty or fight," is prominent in the Presidential campaign.

1845 Lieutenants Warre and Vavasour of the British Army arrive incognito on the Columbia, to survey the territory, in view of a possible war with the United States.

1845 Michael T. Simmons and his party, first American settlers in the Puget Sound region, reach Tumwater.

1846 United States-Canadian boundary is fixed at 49° N.; Hudson's Bay Company plans to move headquarters to site of Victoria on Vancouver Island. Settlement begins at site of Olympia.

1847 A band of Cayuse Indians at Waiilatpu kill Dr. and Mrs. Whitman and eleven others at the mission. First American sawmill erected at Tumwater by Michael Simmons.

1848 Oregon Territory, including all of present Washington, is created.

1849 Fort Steilacoom is established by the United States Army, because Snoqualmie Indians have attacked Squally Indians at Fort Nesqually.

1850 The Donation Land Claim Law is passed by Congress.

1851 Schooner *Exact* brings members of Denny pioneer party to Alki Point (now in Seattle). The Cowlitz Convention memorializes Congress to create the region north of the Columbia a separate Territory to be named Columbia.

1852 Cowlitz convention meets and again petitions Congress for the Territory of Columbia. First settlers come to Bellingham Bay. Nicholas DeLin settles on Commencement Bay, at site of Tacoma. Claims are staked on Seattle metropolitan site by Denny, Boren, and Bell. First Washington newspaper, the *Columbian,* is printed in Olympia; it strongly advocates the new Territory.

1853 Washington Territory is created; white population number

3,965. First northern-route transcontinental-railroad survey is begun, under Isaac I. Stevens.

Isaac I. Stevens is appointed Territorial Governor and Supervisor of Indian Affairs. Olympia is named the temporary capital.

1854 First Federal Court session in Washington Territory convenes; first legislature meets and provides for University; Congress makes grant of two townships.

December 26, Medicine Creek Treaty is concluded, first with Indians of Puget Sound Basin. Treaties are negotiated with Puget Sound and Juan de Fuca Strait tribes.

1855 Indian war is waged both east and west of the Cascades; Klickitat Indians fail in an attack upon Seattle and later are severely defeated at Connell's Prairie. Eastern Washington is closed to settlers and miners.

1857 Governor Stevens is elected to represent the Territory in Congress.

Territorial charter is granted Northern Pacific Railroad.

1858 Lieutenant Colonel Steptoe is defeated near Rosalia. Colonel Wright defeats Indians at Spokane Plains and Four Lakes. Eastern Washington is opened to settlement.

1859 The Fraser River gold rush begins. San Juan Islands boundary controversy between England and United States becomes acute. The gold rush to eastern Washington Territory (especially the part now Idaho) begins.

Indian treaties negotiated by Governor Stevens are ratifiel by Congress.

1860 Population: 11,594.

Walla Walla becomes outfitting point for gold rush.

1861 The Territorial University is opened at Seattle, with Asa S. Mercer as teacher and president, and one student, Clarence Bagley, in the college department.

1863 Territory of Idaho is created from Washington Territory, establishing the present eastern boundary of the State.

1864 "Mercer girls"—Civil War orphans and widows—are brought to Seattle by Asa Mercer. They find husbands waiting.

Completion of first transcontinental telegraph lines.

1866 Some 95 more "Mercer girls" arrive.

1867 The legislature memorializes Congress to admit Washington to statehood.

Alaska, "the Great Country," is purchased from Russia.

1869 United States settles the Hudson's Bay Company's claim for property in the Territory.

1870 The first bank in the Territory is established at Walla Walla by Dorsey S. Baker.

Work is begun on the Northern Pacific Railroad, from Kalama on the Columbia northward to Puget Sound.

Population: 23,355.

1871 The San Juan Islands boundary dispute with Great Britain is submitted to arbitration.

1872 Settlement of Spokane Falls is begun.
The San Juan dispute is settled; the award, by Emperor William I of Germany, is in accord with the United States contention.
Dr. Dorsey S. Baker begins to build his railroad from Walla Walla to Wallula, on the Columbia.

1873 Northern Pacific Railroad from Kalama reaches Tacoma, which has won the coveted terminal.

1875 The railroad from Walla Walla to Wallula is completed.

1876 The Territory votes to hold a constitutional convention and again apply for admission as a State. The proposed State constitution is adopted, but Congress fails to respond.

1880 Population: 75,116.

1881 The transcontinental line of the Northern Pacific is completed to Spokane Falls.

1883 Railroad connections between Puget Sound and the East are established via the Columbia River route.

1885 Anti-Chinese riots occur in Issaquah, Coal Creek, Black Diamond, and Tacoma.

1886 Anti-Chinese riots occur in Seattle.

1887 The Northern Pacific reaches Tacoma, via switchbacks at the summit of the Cascades.

1888 The Stampede tunnel is opened, thus eliminating the switchbacks.

1889 The enabling act passes Congress and is signed on February 22.
The Constitution Convention assembles at Olympia on July 4.
The Constitution is adopted October 1. November 11, Washington is proclaimed a State by President Harrison.

1890 Population: 337,232.

1891 Puget Sound Navy Yard is voted by Congress and located at Bremerton.

1892 State College of Washington is opened at Pullman.

1893 Great Northern Railroad reaches Seattle, having passed up the new city of Everett as terminus.

1895 The University of Washington is moved to its present location.
The Barefoot Schoolboy Law is enacted, laying the basis for Washington's common-school system.

1896 Trans-Pacific steamship service is inaugurated by Nipon Yusen Kaisya.

1897 Gold rush to Klondike begins.

1898 Washington contributes 1,332 men for the Spanish-American War.

1899 March 2. Mount Rainier National Park is created.

1900 Population: 518,103.

1901 State Bureau of Labor is created.

1902 Federal Reclamation Act is passed by Congress; projects are begun in Okanogan and Yakima Counties.

1905 The State Railroad Commission, and the State Tax Commission are created.
1907 Direct primary law is passed.
1908 The North Bank railroad is built.
1909 Alaska-Yukon-Pacific Exposition opens in Seattle.
Chicago, Milwaukee, St. Paul Railroad reaches western terminus at Tacoma.
1910 Woman suffrage is voted for the State.
Population: 1,141,990.
1911 Workman's Compensation Act is passed.
1912 Initiative, referendum, and recall measures are enacted.
1914 State-wide prohibition law is approved by referendum vote, with one year to elapse before it becomes effective.
1916 First transcontinental telephone service is extended to Seattle.
The opening of the Panama Canal helps trade with East Coast.
1917 Washington sets many records in shipbuilding.
Pierce County donates land for Camp (Fort) Lewis.
Lake Washington Ship Canal is opened.
1918 Armistice. Washington has 67,694 men and 632 women in war service.
1919 Columbia Basin Survey Commission is appointed.
First State American Legion Post is established.
November 11. An armed clash, fatal to several, occurs at Centralia, between marchers in Armistice Day parade and I.W.W. members.
1920 Sand Point Naval Air Base is dedicated. Foreign air-mail service begins between Seattle and Victoria.
Population: 1,356,621.
1921 First airplane passenger service operates between Seattle and Vancouver, British Columbia.
The Anti-alien Land Ownership Law is passed.
1922 The Columbia Basin Irrigation League is organized at Pasco.
1924 United States Army's "round-the-world" flight begins at Sand Point Naval Air Base; the journey of six months ends at Sand Point in September.
1928 Capitol building at Olympia is completed.
1930 August. Olympic Loop highway is opened.
Population: 1,563,396.
1933 Work starts at Bonneville Dam.
Contracts are let on Grand Coulee Dam.
1934 State Liquor Law is passed, and control board is established.
General maritime strike centers in Seattle.
1936 Seattle *Post-Intelligencer* suspends publication because of Newspaper Guild strike.
November 30. Guild strike ends, and *Post-Intelligencer* resumes publication.
1937 State Department of Social Security is established.

1938 January 29. President Roosevelt signs bill to create Olympic National Park.

May 31. Boeing Pan-American Airways launches its 74-passenger clipper.

1939 The State celebrates Golden Jubilee, its fiftieth year of statehood.

1940 Population: 1,736,191.

1941 Grand Coulee Dam, on the Columbia, is completed.

Bibliography

GENERAL INFORMATION

Bauer, Eddie. *Fishing directory of western Washington and British Columbia.* Seattle, Bauer, 1937. 39 p., il.

Bauer, Eddie. *Ski Guide.* Seattle, Bauer, 1936.

Huse, Harry C. *Motor vehicle laws of the state of Washington.* Olympia, State Printing Office, 1937. 109 p.

Pollock, Dave. *Fishing guide of the Northwest.* Seattle, General Publishing Co., 1937. 190 p., il.

Smith, Charles Wesley. *Union list of manuscripts in the libraries of the Pacific Northwest.* Seattle, University of Washington, 1931. 57 p.

Washington biennial blue book and official record. Yelm, *Nisqually News,* 1936.

Washington State Bureau of Statistics and Immigration. *Washington: its people, products and resources; descriptive and statistical information of Washington, the "Evergreen State."* Olympia, Secretary of State, 1938, 288 p., tables.

Washington State Department of Game. *Game code of the state of Washington.* Seattle, 1937. 143 p.

DESCRIPTION AND TRAVEL

Fraser, Mary (Crawford), and Hugh C. *Seven years on the Pacific slopes.* New York, Dodd, Mead & Co., 1914. 391 p., il. pls.

Hunt, Herbert, and Kaylor F. C., *Washington west of the Cascades;* historical and descriptive . . . Chicago, S. J. Clarke Publishing Co., 1917. 3 v. front., plates, ports.

Meeker, Ezra. *Seventy years of progress in Washington.* Tacoma, Allstrom Printing Co., 1921. 381 p., il.

Whitaker, Robert. "Washington; dawn of tomorrow." (In Gruening, Ernest, ed., *These United States,* second series. New York, Boni & Liveright, 1924. v. 2; pp. 233-249).

Winthrop, Theodore. *The canoe and the saddle*: *or Klalam and Klickitat.* Tacoma, John E. Williams, 1913. 332 p., il. Travels in Washington in 1853.

NATURAL SETTING

Geography and climate

Fisher, L. C. *Climatological data, Washington (state) section.* Washington, Government Printing Office, 1937. tabs. (U.S. Department of Agriculture, Weather Bureau, v. 11, no. 13).

Landes, Henry. *A geographic dictionary of Washington.* Olympia, F. M. Lamborn, 1917. 346 p. (Washington Geographical Survey. Bulletin 17).

Meany, Edmond S. *Origin of Washington geographic names.* Seattle, University of Washington, 1923. 357 p.

Geology and paleontology

Bretz, J. Harlen. *Glaciation of the Puget Sound region.* Olympia, F. M. Lamborn, 1913. 224 p., il., tables, dgrms., charts. (Washington Geological Survey. Bulletin No. 8).

McLellan, Roy D. *Geology of the San Juan Islands.* Seattle, University of Washington, 1927. 185 p., il., maps. (University of Washington publications in geology, v. 2).

Plant and Animal Life

Abrams, Lorey. *Illustrated flora of the Pacific states.* Stanford University, Stanford University Press, 1923. 552 p., il.

Dawson, William Leon, and J. N. Bowles. *Birds of Washington.* Seattle, Occidental Publishing Co., 1909. 2v., il.

Piper, Charles V. *Flora of the State of Washington.* Washington, Government Printing Office, 1906. 637 p., il., pl., maps. (U.S. National Museum. Contributions from U. S. National Herbarium. v. 11).

Taylor, Walter P., and William T. Shaw. *Provisional list of land mammals of the state of Washington.* Pullman, State College Press, 1929. 32 p., il. Description of Roosevelt elk and other mammals of the Olympic Mountains.

Resources and conservation

Lewis, Howard T., and Stephen L. Miller. *The economic resources of the Pacific Northwest.* Seattle, Lowman & Hanford Co., 1923. 523 p., il., maps, tables.

Magnusson, Carl E. *Hydroelectric power in Washington.* Seattle, University of Washington, 1924-26-35. 3 v., tables, dgrms., maps. (University of Washington Engineering Experiment Station. Bulletins 26, 36, 78).

Patty, Ernest N., and Sheldon L. Glover. *Mineral resources of the state of Washington.* Olympia, F. M. Lamborn, 1921. 155 p., il., tables. (Washington Geographical Survey. Bulletin No. 21).

Washington State Planning Council. *Balance sheets of the state of Washington.* Secretary of State, Olympia, 1935. (Research publication No. 2). Concerned with food stuffs, fisheries, power, etc.

ARCHEOLOGY AND INDIANS

Bagley, Clarence B. *Indian myths of the Northwest.* Seattle, Lowman & Hanford Co., 1930. 145 p., il.

Carlson, Frank. *Chief Sealth.* Seattle, Pioneer Press, 1903. 35 p., ils. (Bulletins of the University of Washington, series 3, No. 2). The story of Chief Sealth (Seattle) and other Indians of King County.

Costello, J. A. *The Siwash; their life, legends, and tales.* Seattle, Calvert, 1895. 169 p., il.

Curtis, Edward S. *The North American Indian.* Seattle, E. S. Curtis, 1907-30. 20 v., il. (Washington Indians, v. 7-8-9).

Kip, Lawrence. *Army life on the Pacific.* New York, Redfield Publishing Co., 1859. 144 p. Journal of experience with the Indians of eastern Washington.

Krieger, Herbert W. A. "Prehistoric pit village site on the Columbia River at Wahluke, Grant County, Washington. (In U. S. National Museum, *Proceedings.* Washington, 1929. v. 73, art. 11; 1-29; il.)

Mourning Dove (Humishuma). *Coyote stories.* Caldwell, Idaho, Caxton Printers, 1933. 228 p., il.

Splawn, A. J. *Ka-mi-akin, the last hero of the Yakimas.* Portland, Oregon, Kilham Printing Co., 1917. 438 p., il.

Thomas, Edward H. *Chinook, a history and dictionary.* Portland, Oregon, Metropolitan Press, 1925. 179 p.

HISTORY AND GOVERNMENT

General

Allen, Paul. *History of the expedition of Lewis and Clark.* New York, Bradford and Inskeep, 1814. 500 p., il., maps.

Evans, Elwood, and others. *History of the Pacific Northwest: Oregon and Washington.* Portland, Oregon, North Pacific History Co., 1899. 2 v.

Fuller, George W. *A history of the Pacific Northwest.* New York, Knopf, 1931. 383 p., il., maps.

Fuller, George Washington. *The Inland Empire of the Pacific Northwest; a history.* Spokane, Linderman, 1928. 4 v. pl., ports., maps.

Pollard, Lancaster, and Lloyd Spencer. *A history of the state of Washington.* New York, American Historical Society, 1937. 4 v., il., maps, pl., ports.

Snowden, Clifton A. *History of Washington.* New York, Century History Co., 1906. 6 v., il., maps.

Taylor, Arthur Samuel. *Guide to the reading and study of the history of the Pacific Northwest.* Portland, Oregon, Metropolitan Press, 1935. 73 p., ils., maps.

Exploration and early settlement

Blankenship, George E. *Lights and shades of pioneer life on Puget Sound.* Olympia, 1923. 90 p.

Cannon, Miles. *Waiilatpu: its rise and fall,* 1836-1847. Boise, Capitol News Press, 1915. 171 p., il.

Cox, Ross. *Adventures on the Columbia River.* New York, J. J. Harper, 1932. 335 p. An historical narrative of the period 1811-1817.

Denny, Emily I. *Blazing the way.* Seattle, Rainier Printing Co., 1909. il. Tales of pioneer life on Puget Sound.

Federal Writers' Project, W.P.A. *The Oregon Trail; the Missouri River to the Pacific Ocean.* (American Guide Series). N.Y. Hastings House, 1939. Sponsored by Oregon Trail Association.

Lewis, Meriwether, and William Clark. *Original journals of the Lewis and Clark expedition,* 1804-1806; *printed from the original manuscripts . . . together with manuscript material of Lewis and Clark from other sources. . . .* Ed. with introduction, notes, and index by Reuben Gold Thwaites. N.Y. Dodd, Mead & Co., 1904-5. 8 v., il., map, facsm.

MacDonald, Ronald. *Ronald MacDonald, the narrative of his early life on the Columbia.* Spokane, Eastern Washington State Historical Society, 1923. 333 p., pl., ports., maps.

Montgomery, Richard Gill. *The White-Headed Eagle, John McLoughlin, builder of an empire.* N. Y. Macmillan, 1934. 358 p., pl., ports.

Ross, Alexander. *Adventures of the first settlers on the Oregon or Columbia River.* Smith, London, 1849. 352 p.

Ruffner, Wm. Henry. *Report on Washington Territory.* New York, Seattle, Lakeshore and Eastern Railway, 1889. 242 p., pl., tabs. Giving economic conditions in Washington Territory at time.

Tyrell,J. B. *Thompson's narrative.* Toronto, the Champlain Society, 1916. 582 p., il., maps, charts. An account of the explorations of David Thompson in the Northwest for Great Britain.

Vancouver, Captain George. *Voyage of discovery to the north Pacific Ocean and round the world.* London, Robinson, 1798, 3 v., il., maps. New ed. London, 1801. 6 v.

Vincent, W. D. *Spokane house.* Spokane, Cowles Publishing Co., 1930. 50 p., il., maps, charts. Story of early fur trading in Spokane County.

Wyeth, Nathaniel. *The correspondence and journals of Captain Nathaniel Wyeth,* 1831-6. Ed. by F. G. Young, Secretary, Oregon Historical Society. Eugene, Oregon, University of Oregon Press, 1899. Maps.

Statehood

Meany, Edmond S. *Governors of Washington.* Seattle, University of Washington, 1915. 114 p., il.

Meany, Edmond S. *History of the state of Washington.* New York, Macmillan, 1924. 325 p., il., maps.

Oliphant, Orin J. *A brief outline of the history of Washington.* Olympia, O. N. Olson, 1933. 46 p.

Sperlin, O. B. and Miles, Charles. *Building a State: Washington, 1889-1939.* Tacoma, Washington State Historical Society, 1940. 620 p.

Government

Chandler, George. *Civics of the state of Washington.* New York, American Book Co., 1915. 418 p., il.

Legislative manual of the state of Washington. Olympia, State Printing Plant, 1939.

Pierce, Frank. *Pierce's code: state of Washington.* Seattle, Frank Pierce, 1934. 1,981 p. Cyclopedic arrangement of the laws of Washington.

SOCIAL AND ECONOMIC DEVELOPMENT

Agriculture and farm life

Boening, Rose M. History of irrigation in the State of Washington. (*In Washington Historical Quarterly,* Oct. 1918, v. 9; 259; Jan. 1919, v. 10; 21.)

Johnson, Ernest Rueben. *Farming the logged-over uplands in western Washington.* Washington, Government Printing Office, 1924. 36 p., il., map, dgrm. (U.S. Department of Agriculture. Bulletin No. 1236).

Leedy, E. C. *Washington.* St. Paul, Great Northern Railway Co., 1934. 36 p., il., map, tabs. Statistics and general description of agricultural regions of Washington.

Martin, Edward Winslow. *History of the grange movement.* National Publishing Co. 1873.

Olin, Walter Herbert. *American irrigation farming: a systematical treatment of every phase of irrigation farming including its history.* Chicago, A. C. McClurg & Co., 1913. 364 p., il., tabs.

Industry, Commerce, and Labor

Bates, Edwin. *Commercial survey of the Pacific Northwest.* Washington, Government Printing Office, 356 p., il., tab., dgrms., maps. (U.S. Bureau of Foreign and Domestic Commerce. Domestic Commerce series No. 51).

Benson, Henry K. *Pulp and paper industry of the Pacific Northwest.* Seattle, University of Washington, 1929. 89 p., il., dgrms. (University of Washington Engineering Experiment Station. Report No. 1.)

Cobb, John Nathan. *Pacific cod fisheries.* Washington Government Printing Office, 1916. 111 p., pl., tables, maps. (Appendix No. 4 to report of the U. S. Commissioner of Fisheries, 1916).

Cobb, John Nathan. *Pacific salmon fisheries.* 4th ed. Washington, Government Printing Office, 1930. (U.S. Bureau of Fisheries. Document No. 1092).

Fischer, Arthur Holmes. *Summary of mining and metalliferous mineral resources in the state of Washington.* Seattle, University of Washington.

Hathway, Marion. *The migratory worker and family life.* Chicago, University of Chicago, 1934. 240 p., il., tables. Includes material dealing with the migratory workers in Washington.

Hopkins, William S. *Seasonal unemployment in the state of Washington*.....Seattle, University of Washington, 1936 (University of Washington publications in the social science, v. 8, No. 3). 161 p., diagrs., tables.

Neuberger, Richard. *Our promised land.* N.Y. Macmillan, 1938. 398 p., map.

Oakleaf, Howard B. *Lumber and lumbering.* Chicago, Commercial Journal Co., 1920. 182 p., il.

Parker, Carleton Hubbell. *The casual laborer; and other essays.* N.Y. Harcourt, 1920. 199 p.

Puter, Steven A. and Horace Stevens. *Looters of the public domain.* Portland, Oregon, Portland Printing House, 1908. 494 p. il., ports.

Smith, Walker C. *The Everett massacre.* Chicago, I.W.W. Pub. Bureau, 1917. 302 p., il.

Taylor, Paul Schuster. *The Sailors' Union of the Pacific.* New York, Ronald Press, 1923. 188 p.

Todes, Charlotte. *Labor and lumber.* New York, International Publishers, 1931. 208 p., plates.

United States Bureau of Foreign and Domestic Commerce. *American Douglas fir plywood and its uses.* Washington, Government Printing Office. 1937.

United States Bureau of Mines. *Analysis of Washington coals.* Washington, Government Printing Office, 1931. 203 p., maps, tables.

Washington Geological Survey. *The metal mines of Washington.* Olympia, 1921. (Bulletin No. 23).

Wright E. W. *Marine history of the Pacific Northwest* Portland, Oregon, Lewis and Dryden Publishing Co., 1895. 494 p., il.

Lumber lore

Shephard, Esther. *Paul Bunyan.* Seattle, The McNeil Press, 1924. 235 p. Same text. New York, Harcourt, 1924.

Stevens, James. *Paul Bunyan.* New York, Knopf, 1925. 245 p. il.

Transportation

Bryan, Enoch A. *Orient meets Occident.* Pullman, Students Book Corp., 1936. 296 p., il. Advent of the railroads to Pacific Northwest.

Coffee, Frank. *Forty years on the Pacific.* San Francisco, A. M. Robertson, 1920. 375 p., il., maps.

Estes, George. *The Rawhide Railroad.* Canby, Oregon, Clackamas County News Press, 1916. 54 p., il., ports. The story of Dr. D. S. Baker's line between Walla Walla and Wallula.

Lewis, Sol H. "A history of the railroads in Washington." (*In Washington Historical Quarterly,* July 1912, v. 3; 186-197).

O'Neil, Marion. "Maritime activity of the North West Company, 1813-21." (*In Washington Historical Quarterly,* Oct. 1930, v. 21, No. 4; 243-267). Trans-Pacific trade with China in the early days.

Purvis, Neil H. "History of the Lake Washington Ship Canal." (*In Washington Historical Quarterly,* April 1934, v. 25; 114-127).

Quiett, Glenn C. *They built the west: an epic of rails and cities.* New York, Appleton, 1934. 569 p., il.

Education and social institutions

Bolton, Frederick E., and Thomas W. Bibb. *History of education in Washington.* Washington, Government Printing Office, 1935. 448 p., tables. (U.S. Department of Interior. Office of Education. Bulletin No. 9).

Bowden, Angie Burt. *Early schools of Washington Territory.* Seattle, Lowman & Hanford Co., 1935. 631 p., il.

Washington State Department of Education. *State of Washington educational directory,* 1935-36. Olympia, State Printing Plant, 1936. 125 p.

Religion

Creegan, Charles C., and Josephine Goodnow. *Great missionaries of the church; Whitman and others.* N.Y. Crowell Publishing Co., 1895. 404 p., ports.

Drury, Clifford Merrill. *Marcus Whitman, M.D., pioneer and martyr.* Caldwell, Idaho, the Caxton Printers, 1937. 473 p., il., plates.

Eells, Myron. *History of Indian missions on Pacific coast.* Philadelphia, American Sunday School Union, 1882. 270 p., il.

Pearne, T. H. *Sixty-one years of itinerant Christian life in church and state.* New York, Easton and Mains, 1898. pp. 166-268. Includes Pearnes' travels and experiences in the Oregon country.

Smet, Pierre Jean de. *Life, letters and travels of Father Pierre Jean de Smet, S. J.,* 1801-1873. Collected by Hiram Martin Chittenden and Alfred Talbot Richardson. New York, F. P. Harper. 1905. 4 v., ports., maps.

Social Organizations

Buck, Mildred E. *Public welfare in Washington.* Olympia, Washington State Planning Council, 1934. 138 p., dgrms., tables. (Research publication No. 1).

Cadbury, Olive C., and others. *Social work in Seattle; an inventory and appraisal.....*Seattle, University of Washington, 1935. 137 p.

Rademaker, John A. Japanese in social organization of the Puget Sound region. (*In American Journal of Sociology,* Nov. 1934, pp. 338-343).

Newspapers

McMurtrie, Douglas C. "Newspapers of Washington, 1852-1890." (In *Washington Historical Quarterly,* April 1935, v. 26; 129-143. History, dates of founding, and politics of early newspapers.

Meany, Edmond S. "Newspapers of Washington Territory." (In *Washington Historical Quarterly*, 1922-23. v. 13-14).

THE ARTS

Literature

Hassell, Susan Whitcomb. *A hundred and sixty books by Washington authors.* Everett, Haskell Press, 1916. 40 p. A bibliography of scientific, historical, technical, juvenile, fiction, and travel books.

Pollard, Lancaster. "Check list of Washington authors." (In *Pacific Northwest Quarterly,* January 1940, vol. 31).

Powers, Alfred. *History of Oregon literature.* Portland, Oregon, Metropolitan Press, 1935. 809 p., il. Good study of literature of pioneer and middle periods.

Theater

Grant, Howard. *Story of Washington's early theatres.* Seattle, University Book Store, 1934. 47 p., il., mop.

Lincoln, Fred. "Vaudeville in the Northwest." (In *Washington Magazine,* Sept. 1906, v. 2: 29-30).

Painting and Sculpture

Ballard, Adele M. "Seattle artists—who are they?" (In *Town Chier,* Dec. 1914-17, v. 9-12).

Harney, W. D. *Art work of Seattle and western Washington.* Racine, Wisconsin,, Harney, 1910. 110 p., ils., 78 pls. A deluxe edition of photogravures.

Meany, Edmond S. *Art work of the state of Washington.* Oshkosh, Wisconsin, Art Photogravure Co., 1900. 122 p.

Seattle Art Museum. *Annual Report.* Seattle, Acme Press, 1936. 30 p.

Music

Griffin, Eldon. *Ralston Club handbook.* Seattle, Ralston Club, 1932.

Hanford, C. M. *Seattle and environs.* Seattle, Pioneer History Publishing Co., 1924, il., v. 1; 608-630. Chapter devoted to music in a four-volume history of Seattle.

Architecture

American Institute of Architects, Washington Chapter. *Monthly bulletin.* Valuable reference works on Washington architecture. April 1925, v. 1, no. 1; Sept. 1933, v. 13, no. 12.

Albertson, A. H. "Northern Life Tower: its theory of design." (In *Architect,* Oct. 1929, v. 13; 29-31; 39-49.

Alden, Charles H. "Architectural trends in the State of Washington." (In *Architect and engineer,* March 1938, v. 132, no. 3; 12-34).

Architecture of the Northwest. (In *Pacific Builder and Engineer,* Sept. 14, 1907, v. 5: 8-15).

Ballard, Adele M. "Pictorial Seattle: a study in homes and churches." (In *Town Crier,* Dec. 15, 1923, v. 18, no. 50: 17-32).

"City Light Building, Seattle." (In *Public Service Journal,* Aug. 27, 1937, v. 16, no. 8: 6-7).

Hadley, H. M. "Seattle Art Museum." (In *Architect and engineer,* Nov. 1935, v. 115: 10-24).

"Henry Art Gallery." (In *Architecture,* May 1930, v. 61: 289-290). Illustrations (only) of works in gallery at University of Washington.

Reamer, R. C. Edmond Meany Hotel at Seattle. (In *Architect and Engineer,* Feb. 1932, v. 108: 16-23).

Seattle Architectural Club. *Seattle architectural year book.* Seattle, 1910.

CITIES

Bagley, Clarence B. *History of Seattle.* Chicago, S. J. Clark Publishing Co., 1916. 3 v., il.

Carhart, Edith Beebe. "A history of Bellingham." (In *Washington Historical Quarterly,* April 1927. v. 18: 156).

Hunt, Herbert. *Tacoma, its history and its builders.* Chicago, S. J. Clark Publishing Co., 1917. 3 v., il.

Leighton, George R. "Seattle." (Ind. *Five Cities.* N. Y. Harper. 1939. il.). Excellent study of Seattle.

Lockley, Fred. *History of the Columbia River Valley from the Dalles to the sea.* Chicago, S. J. Clark Publishing Co., 1928. 3 v. v. 1: 317-331. Contains the history of Longview.

Sayre, James W. *This city of ours.* Seattle, 1936. 191 p., il.

Wilhelm, Honor L. "The artesian city." (In *The Coast,* Dec. 1917. v. 14, no. 6 401). Story of Pullman, Washington.

COUNTIES

Bagley, Clarence B. *King County.* Seattle, S. J. Clark Publishing Co. 1929. 3 v., il.

Blankenship, Mrs. George E. *Tillicum tales of Thurston County.* Olympia, 1914. 395 p. il.

Bonney, W. P. *Pierce County.* Chicago, Pioneer History Publishing Co., 1927. 3 v., il., ports.

Brown, William Carlos. *Early Okanogan History.* Okanogan, Okanogan Press. 1912, 27 p., ports. Account of the early settlement at the mouth of the Okanogan River in 1811.

Clark, William S. "Pioneer experience in Walla Walla." (In *Washington Historical Quarterly,* Jan. 1933, v. 24; 9-24).

Lingee, Ruby Lusher. *Pend Oreille County.* Newport, Wash., Miner Printing Co., 1930. 35 p.

Durham, N. W. *History of the city of Spokane and Spokane County.* Chicago, S. J. Clark Publishing Co., 1912. 3 v., il., maps, tables.

Farquhar, Frank S. "History and sketches of Yakima County." (In *The Washington Historian,* July 1901, v. 2; 190-194).

Fuller, George W. *The Inland Empire.* Spokane, Shaw & Borden Publishing Co., 1928. 4 v., il., maps, ports.

History of central Washington. Interstate Publishing Company, 1904. 941 p., il. The history of Klickitat, Yakima, and Kittitas counties.

Hull, Lindley M. *A history of central Washington: history of the Wenatchee, Entiat, Chelan, and Columbia river valleys.* Spokane Shaw & Borden Publishing Co., 1929. 824 p., il.

Lyman, Wm. D. *History of old Walla Walla County.* Chicago, S. J. Clark Publishing Co., 1918. 2 v., il.

Lyman, W. D. and others. *Skagit and Snohomish counties.* (n.p.), Interstate Publishing Co., 1906. 1,117 p., il.

Roth, Lottie R. *History of Whatcom County.* Chicago, Pioneer History Publishing Co., 1926. 2 v., il.

Steele, Richard F. *History of North Washington.* Spokane, Western Historical Publishing Co., 1904. 867 p., il. Illustrated history of Stevens, Okanogan, Ferry, and Chelan counties.

Steele, Richard F. *The story of Lincoln County.* Spokane, Hughes & Coates, 1909. 28 p., il.

Steele, Richard F. and others. *Illustrated history of the Big Bend country.* Spokane, Western Historical Publishing Co., 1904. 1,024 p., pl., ports. The story of Lincoln, Douglas, Adams, and Franklin counties.

Whitfield, Wm. *History of Snohomish County.* Chicago, Pioneer History Publishing Co., 1928. 2 v., il.

(Other county histories may be found in State Pamphlet Series).

POINTS OF INTEREST

Beck, George F. "Quest of the Gingko." (In *Washington Historical Quarterly,* Jan. 1935. v. 26: 3-9).

Grand Coulee Dam. Spokane, Shaw and Borden Publishing Co., 1935. 18 p., il., maps.

Kellogg, George A. *A history of Whidbey's Island.* Oak Harbor, 1934. 108 p., il.

Schmoe, F. W. *Our greatest mountain: a handbook for Mount Rainier National Park.* New York, G. P. Putnam's Sons, 1925. 366 p., il., map.

Index

B

E

F

I

J

N

S

T

Y

Z